R. Peter Burnham — AUG. 30, 99

WORDSWORTH'S LONDON, 1791-1795

1 Rev. Joseph Fawcett's Dissenting Chapel
2 The King's Head Tavern, #25 Poultry
3 The Bell Inn (Hogarth, *The Harlot's Progress*, #1)
4 Daniel Isaac Eaton's bookshop ("at the Sign of the Cock & Swine")
5 Joseph Johnson's bookshop
6 La Belle Sauvage Inn
7 Rackstraw's Museum (#197; later *The Albion*)
8 Mrs. Salmon's Waxworks (#17)

Aldersgate
Grub Street
St. Giles
Cripplegate Churchyard
London Wall
Bethlem Hospital
Broad Street
Street
Love Ln.
Wood Street
Maiden Ln.
Lad Lane
Guildhall
Excise Office
Milk St.
Cateaton St.
Lothbury
King St.
Mercer's Hall
Old Jewry
The Bank
South Sea House
Bishopsgate
Threadneedle St.
Cheapside
Royal Exchange
Leadenhall Street
Poultry
Cornhill
Watling Street
Bread Street
India House
Lombard Street
The Mansion House
Queen Street
Cannon Street
Thames Street
Fish Street
Monument
Lower Thames Street
London Bridge
RIVER

The HIDDEN WORDSWORTH

POET · LOVER · REBEL · SPY

The HIDDEN WORDSWORTH

POET · LOVER · REBEL · SPY

Kenneth R. Johnston

W. W. NORTON & COMPANY
New York • London

Printed in the United States of America
First Edition

Excerpts from *An Evening Walk* (James Averill, editor), *Descriptive Sketches* (Eric Birdsall, editor), *"The Ruined Cottage" and "The Pedlar"* (James Butler, editor), *Lyrical Ballads* (James Butler and Karen Green, editors), *Early Poems and Fragments* (Jared Curtis and Carol Landon, editors), *Home at Grasmere* (Beth Darlington, editor), *The Salisbury Plain Poems* (Stephen Gill, editor), *The Borderers* (Robert Osborn, editor), and *The Thirteen-Book "Prelude"* (Mark Reed, editor) are used by permission of the publisher, Cornell University Press. Excerpts from "The Prelude" by William Wordsworth are from *The Prelude* 1799, 1805, 1850: A Norton Critical Edition, edited by Jonathan Wordsworth, M. H. Abrams, and Stephen Gill. Copyright © 1979 by W. W. Norton & Company, Inc. Reprinted with the permission of the publisher. Some of the material in this book has been previously published in substantially different form in *Studies in Romanticism*, *The Age of William Wordsworth: Critical Essays on the Romantic Tradition* (Rutgers, 1987), and *Beyond Representation: Philosophy and Poetic Imagination* (Cambridge, 1996).

The text of this book is composed in Bembo with the display set in Weiss Titling.
Composition and manufacturing by Haddon Craftsmen Inc.
Book design by Charlotte Staub
Maps prepared by Suzanne Hull, Indiana University, Bloomington, Indiana.
Inset illustration on pg. 269 by Jim Hull, Indiana University.

Library of Congress Cataloging-in-Publication Data

Johnston, Kenneth R.
The hidden Wordsworth: poet, lover, rebel, spy / Kenneth R. Johnston.
p. cm.
Includes bibliographical references (p.) and index.
ISBN 0-393-04623-0
1. Wordsworth, Willian, 1770–1850—Childhood and youth.
2. Wordsworth, William, 1770–1850—Relations with women. 3. Poets. English—19th century—Biography. 4. Revolutionaries—Great Britain—Biography. 5. Spies—Great Britain—Biography. I. Title.
PR5882.J65 1998
821'.7—dc21
[B] 97-40317
CIP

W. W. Norton & Company, Inc., 500 Fifth Avenue, New York, N.Y. 10110
http://www.wwnorton.com

W.W. Norton & Company Ltd., 10 Coptic Street, London WC1A 1PU
3 4 5 6 7 8 9 0

for
ILINCA
and for
INDIANA

Contents

Illustrations ix
Maps xv
Acknowledgments xvii
A Note on Money xix
A Note on Texts xxi

Prologue: Images of Wordsworth 3

PART I

THE CHILD IS FATHER

1 *The Ministries of Fear and Beauty* 17
2 *The Vale of Esthwaite* 42
3 *"While We Were Schoolboys"* 69
4 *"Verses from the Impulse of My Own Mind"* 93
5 *Stranger, Lounger, Lover* 111
6 *Young Love-Liking* 135
7 *Weighing the Man in the Balance* 155
8 *Something of a Republic* 175
9 *Golden Hours* 188
10 *Golden Days and Giddy Prospects* 203

PART II

OF THE MAN

11 *The Mighty City* 235
12 *The Mighty Mind* 264
13 *Revolution and Romance* 284
14 *Castaway* 329
15 *A Return to France?* 358

16 *A Return to France:*
The Evidence of Speculation 378
17 *Legacy Hunting* 401
18 *Philanthropy or Treason?* 427
19 *Of Cabbages and Radicals* 468
20 *An Independent Intellect* 494
21 *The Spy and the Mariner* 516
22 *The Mariner and the Recluse* 550
23 *Triumphs of Failure* 565
24 *Wye Wandering* 588
25 *"Mr. Wordsworth"* 609
26 *Writing in Self-Defense* 630
27 *Destination Unknown* 654

PART III

WHAT IS A POET?

28 *"We Have Learnt to Know Its Value"* 673
29 *Home at Grasmere* 697
30 *A.k.a.* Lyrical Ballads 721
31 *Selling the Book, Creating the Poet* 751
32 *Peace, Marriage, Inheritance* 769
33 *Disciples and Partners* 792
34 *The End of* The Prelude 810
35 *Presenting the Poet* 821
Epilogue: Hiding the Man 834

Appendix A: Genealogical Chart 844
Appendix B: Was "Wordsworth" the "Name Not to Be Mentioned"? 847

Abbreviations 853
Notes 855
Bibliography 927
Index 935

ILLUSTRATIONS

Since Wordsworth is "seen" as well as read through a haze of later landscape imagery that his poetry helped stimulate, my aim has been rather to see his world as he saw it, looking forward through representations that did not bear his imprint, toward the culture on which he wished to stamp his image. Priority for illustrations has thus been given to faces over places, and to eighteenth-century images over nineteenth-century ones that look back at Wordsworth (and the Lake District) through post-Romantic spectacles. The young, "hidden" Wordsworth was the contemporary of caricaturists like Gillray and Rowlandson—both of whom delighted in exposing their society's hidden realities—more than of the great Romantic landscape painters like Constable and Turner, with whom his works have been subsequently (and appropriately) associated. Nevertheless, the "pre-Romantic" contemporaneity of even those images that have come to seem most indelibly "Wordsworthian" is indicated by the fact that four of Wordsworth's visionary scenes can be readily duplicated in the works of Francis Towne (1740–1816)—Mont Blanc, Mount Snowdon, Lake Como, and Grasmere—some taken a decade or more before Wordsworth, following the fashion set by Towne and others, went to see them for himself, and made them his own.

FIRST GATHERING *(between pages 8 and 9)*

Wordsworth, by William Shuter (1798). *Division of Rare and Manuscript Collections, Cornell University*

Wordsworth, by Robert Hancock (1798). *By courtesy of the National Portrait Gallery, London*

Wordsworth, by an unknown artist (ca. 1803–1810). *Maurice Dodd Booksellers, Carlisle*

Wordsworth, by Henry Edridge (1806). *The Wordsworth Trust, Dove Cottage*

Wordsworth, by Benjamin Robert Haydon (1818). *By courtesy of the National Portrait Gallery, London*

The Source of the Arviron with Part of Mont Blanc 1781, by Francis Towne. *© The Board of Trustees of the Victoria & Albert Museum, London*

"A View of Snowdon," by Francis Towne (1809). *Fitzwilliam Museum, Cambridge*

"Lake of Como, Light from the left hand, August 17th 1781," by Francis Towne. *Leeds City Art Gallery. Photograph Courtauld Institute of Art, London*

Grasmere, from the Rydal Road, by Francis Towne (1786). *Birmingham Museums & Art Gallery*

SECOND GATHERING *(between pages 104 and 105)*

Wordsworth's Birthplace, Cockermouth. *National Trust Photographic Library*

Sir James Lowther as a young man. *The Wordsworth Trust, Dove Cottage*

Satan In All His Glory, by James Gillray (May 8, 1792). *Copyright © The British Museum*

Lowther Castle in 1819. *Owen, Hugh, The Lowther Family (Phillimore & Co., 1990)*

John Robinson, by William Ward. *By courtesy of the National Portrait Gallery, London*

Penrith Beacon, from a nineteenth-century lithograph. *Penrith City Art Gallery & Museum*

Esthwaite Water, by James Bourne. *The Wordsworth Trust, Dove Cottage*

Hawkshead School. *E. T. W. Dennis & Sons, Ltd., Scarborough*

Ann Tyson's cottage, Colthouse. *Kenneth R. Johnston photograph*

Country Ferry, by W. H. Pyne. *Copyright © The British Museum*

Rural Road Scene, by W. H. Pyne. *Copyright © The British Museum*

To the Manes [ghost or remains] *of Gilbert Wakefield*, by Julius Ibbetson (1803). *© The Board of Trustees of the Victoria & Albert Museum, London/Art Resource, NY.*

Bucks of the First Head, by Thomas Rowlandson (ca. 1785). *Yale Center for British Art, Paul Mellon Collection.*

The Rookery, by Thomas Rowlandson. *Copyright © The British Museum*

A Master Parson with a Good Living. Copyright © The British Museum. George, Dorothy, Hogarth to Cruikshank

A Journeyman Parson with a Bare Existence. Copyright © The British Museum. George, Dorothy, Hogarth to Cruikshank

William Wilberforce, age 28 (June 1789), by John Rising. *Wilberforce House, Hull City Museums, Art Gallery & Archives*

William Frend, Fellow of Jesus College, Cambridge, by Sylvester Harding (1789). *By courtesy of the National Portrait Gallery, London*

Brougham Castle, by Joseph Powell. *The Wordsworth Trust, Dove Cottage*

THIRD GATHERING *(between pages 264 and 265)*

Dorothy Wordsworth, pencil drawing. *The Wordsworth Trust, Dove Cottage*

Cambridge coach setting off from La Belle Sauvage Inn, Ludgate Hill. *Borer, Mary C., An Illustrated Guide to London*

View of London over Blackfriars Bridge from the Albion Mills tower (1791). *Guildhall Library, Corporation of London*

A Bawd on Her Last Legs, by Thomas Rowlandson. *Copyright © The British Museum*

"Domestic Architecture: View of an old house lately standing in Grub Street." *Guildhall Library, Corporation of London*

The Quacks (Dr. Graham and Dr. Katterfello), 1783. *Copyright © The British Museum*

The Romp, featuring Mrs. Dorothea Jordan (1786). *Copyright © The British Museum*

Vauxhall Gardens, by Thomas Rowlandson. © *The Board of Trustees of the Victoria & Albert Museum, London / Art Resource, NY*

Such Things Are, or A Peep in to Kensington Gardens, by Thomas Rowlandson. *Copyright © The British Museum*

Bartholomew Fair, by Thomas Rowlandson. *Guildhall Library, Corporation of London*

Near Beddgelert, by Thomas Rowlandson. *Copyright © The British Museum*

Helen Maria Williams, by John Singleton. *Copyright © The British Museum*

Presumed miniature portrait of Annette Vallon. *The Wordsworth Trust, Dove Cottage*

Saint Mary Magdalene Renouncing Her Worldy Vanities, by Charles Le Brun (after 1650). *Giraudon/Art Resource, NY*

Jacques Pierre Brissot (1754–1793). *de Lamartine, Alphonse Marie Louis, Histoire des Girondins*

Antoine Joseph Gorsas (1751–1793). *de Lamartine, Alphonse Marie Louis, Histoire des Girondins*

Jean-Louis Carra (1742–1793). *de Lamartine, Alphonse Marie Louis, Histoire des Girondins*

Henri Grégoire (1750–1831), in detail from Jacques-Louis David's *Oath of the Tennis Court, June 20, 1789. Réunion des musées nationaux,* © *photo RMN*

Michel Beaupuy (1755–1796). *Permission granted by M. Henri de Beaupuy, photo courtesy of The Wordsworth Trust, Dove Cottage*

Fourth Gathering *(between pages 456 and 457)*

The Race for Doggett's Coat & Badge, by Thomas Rowlandson. *Copyright © The British Museum*

A Prize Fight, by Thomas Rowlandson. *Copyright © The British Museum*

Great News. Copyright © The British Museum

Thomas Holcroft and William Godwin at the 1794 Treason Trials, by Sir Thomas Lawrence. *Private collection*

Daniel Isaac Eaton, by W. Sharpe. *By courtesy of the National Portrait Gallery, London*

Joseph Johnson, by W. Sharpe. *By courtesy of the National Portrait Gallery, London*

Francis Wrangham. *By courtesy of the National Portrait Gallery, London*

The Republican Attack, by James Gillray (November 1, 1795). *The Lilly Library, Indiana University*

John Thelwall addressing crowds behind Copenhagen House, Islington (detail from James Gillray, *Copenhagen House*, November 16, 1795). *The Lilly Library, Indiana University*

Racedown Lodge, by S. L. May. *The Wordsworth Trust, Dove Cottage*

"Amid the gloom . . . appeared a roofless Hut," illustration for "The Ruined Cottage" by Foster Birkett. *The Wordsworth Trust, Dove Cottage*

Pedlar, by W. H. Pyne. *Copyright © The British Museum*

Gipsies, by W. H. Pyne. *Copyright © The British Museum*

Alfoxden Park, by C.W. Bampflyde. *The Wordsworth Trust, Dove Cottage*

Samuel Taylor Coleridge (1795) by Peter Vandyke. *By courtesy of the National Portrait Gallery, London*

Interior Scene, by John Harden. *Copyright © The British Museum*

Culbone Church, by S. Alken. *Courtauld Institute of Art, London*

Thomas Poole, by Thomas Stothard. *The Wordsworth Trust, Dove Cottage*

Basil Montagu, by George Dance. *Courtauld Institute of Art, London*

Robert Southey, by James Sharples. *City of Bristol Museums & Art Gallery*

Charles Lamb, by Robert Hancock. *The Wordsworth Trust, Dove Cottage*

William Hazlitt, by Thomas Bewick. *The Wordsworth Trust, Dove Cottage*

William Pitt, by James Gillray (1789) *By courtesy of the National Portrait Gallery, London*

William Wyndham, 1st Baron Grenville, by John Hoppner (1800). *By courtesy of the National Portrait Gallery, London*

George Canning, by John Hoppner. *Provost and Fellows of Eton College. Photograph Courtauld Institute of Art, London*

John Hookham Frere, by Henry Edridge (1800). *By courtesy of the National Portrait Gallery, London*

Richard Ford. *By permission of Sir Brinsley Ford, C. B. E. Photo: Eileen Tweedie*
William Henry Cavendish Bentinck, 3rd Duke of Portland, by J. Murphy. *By courtesy of the National Portrait Gallery, London*
Tintern Abbey, by J. M. W. Turner. *Bridgeman/Art Resource, NY*
The New Morality, by James Gillray (August 7, 1798). *The Newberry Library, Chicago*
"Coleridge & Co.," detail from *The New Morality*. *The Newberry Library, Chicago*

FIFTH GATHERING *(between pages 776 and 777)*

Town End, by T. M. Richardson. *The Wordsworth Trust, Dove Cottage*
Georgiana Cavendish, the Duchess of Devonshire, engraving by Bartolozzi. *By courtesy of the National Portrait Gallery, London*
Mary Robinson of Buttermere, by James Gillray (July 1800). *Copyright © The British Museum*
Samuel Taylor Coleridge, by James Northcote (1804). *Jesus College, Cambridge*
Thomas De Quincey, by John Watson Gordon. *The Wordsworth Trust, Dove Cottage*
Walter Scott, from portrait by Henry Raeburn. *Courtauld Institute of Art, London*
Mr. John Wordsworth (silhouette). *The Wordsworth Trust, Dove Cottage*
Sara Hutchinson (silhouette). *The Wordsworth Trust, Dove Cottage*
Mary Hutchinson Wordsworth (silhouette). *The Wordsworth Trust, Dove Cottage*

Maps

Cumberland, Westmorland, and Lancashire, with the English Lake District. 18

Wordsworth's and Jones's route across France, July, 1790. 193

Wordsworth's and Jones's route through Switzerland, July–August, 1790. 204

Wordsworth's Wales: North, 1791; South 1793 and 1798. 267

Climbing Snowdon, August, 1791. 269

The "Northern Vendée" (Northwest France), 1793. 380

Wordsworth's and Coleridge's West Country, showing their favorite coastal walk. 474

Wordsworth's and Coleridge's Germany, 1798–1799. 613

Grasmere, ca. 1800. 698

Acknowledgments

This book was begun with the support of a fellowship from the National Endowment for the Humanities, and ended with similar support from the John Simon Guggenheim Memorial Foundation, for both of which I am deeply grateful.

Throughout the time of its research and composition, I have received unflagging cooperation from Indiana University, especially successive chairs of its Department of English, Mary Burgan and Patrick Brantlinger, the dean of its College of Arts & Sciences, Morton Lowengrub, and Kenneth R.R. Gros Louis, the chancellor of its main, Bloomington, campus. My research was facilitated by the splendid resources and personnel of the Indiana University libraries, particularly the English collections under the supervision of Anthony Shipps and Perry Willett, as well as those in the Lilly Rare Book Library, directed by William Cagle when I started and by Lisa Browar when I finished.

No serious biographical study of Wordsworth can be attempted without the unique collections of the Wordsworth Library in Grasmere, to which I am also indebted personally for friendships with Robert and Pamela Woof, Jeff and Gill Cowton, Sally Woodhead, and others among the modern "Grasmere Volunteers." These debts have at times been inseparable from those I owe to the Wordsworth Summer Conference for invitations to lecture and other kindnesses, from Jonathan Wordsworth (critical inheritor), from Sylvia and the late Richard Wordsworth, and from its American representative, Marilyn Gaull.

Thanks as well to all those in other libraries and archives who made my work easier simply by doing theirs so well: the Public Records Office at Kew, as well as PROs at Carlisle (for Cumberland), Kendal (for Westmorland), Winchester (for Hampshire and the Wickham Papers), Halifax, and Norfolk (for Cookson records at Forncett); and to the Manuscripts and Prints collections of the British Museum, the Bristol University Rare Book Library (for the Pinney Papers), the Guildhall Libraries (Jeremy Smith), the Hawkshead School (John West), the Kendal Public Library, the Bibliothèque National, the Royal Post Office archives (for the Freeling Papers), and the Scottish PRO in Edinburgh.

Many friends and colleagues have helped make this book a reality. First mention must go to four who read and commented on the entire manuscript at various stages: Mark Reed, intrepid chronologist of Wordsworth's life from 1770 to 1815, Stephen Parrish, the Grasmere gourmet, Donald Lamm of W. W. Norton, who gave it the editorial attention it needed and (I hope) deserved, and Otto Sonntag, who caught, queried, and corrected more copy mistakes than I care to remember, knowing that those remaining are entirely my own. Others have read parts of the manuscript with insight and generous criticism: Linda Charnes, Jared Curtis, Morris Dickstein, Mary Favret, Marilyn Gaull (editor of the *Wordsworth Circle*), Bill Hamilton, Hilary Hinzmann, John Kerrigan, Christoph Lohmann, Richard Matlak, Jerry McGann, Stuart Proffitt, Nick Roe, Michael Rosenblum, Stuart Sperry, David Wagenknecht (editor of *Studies in Romanticism*), John Wright, Dean Young, and, last but always first, Ilinca Zarifopol-Johnston.

For other help and advice I am grateful to M. H. Abrams, J. V. Beckett, Ernest Bernhardt-Kabisch, Harold Bloom, Jim Chandler, Linda David, Richard Eldridge, Paul Elledge, Stephen Gill, Don Gray, Susan Gubar, Geoffrey Hartman, Suzie Hull (inventive cartographer), Michael Jaye, Herb Kaplan, Susan Nelson, James Riley, Gene Ruoff, Sharon Setzer, Michael and Mona Shea, Michael Shelden, David Simpson, Elizabeth Sparrow, Murray and Aneta Sperber, Orrin Wang, and Carl Woodring.

Special thanks to Mr. and Mrs. Russell Gore-Andrews for a tour and an excellent lunch at their home, Racedown Lodge, and to the present owners of Robert Jones's house at Plas-yn-Llan near Ruthin, in Wales, for letting a by-passing stranger have a look around.

My labors have been lightened by two tireless research assistants, Michele Thomas and Heather E. Frey, and final preparation of the manuscript would not have been possible without the dedication of my secretary, June Hacker.

A Note on Money

Wordsworth was a man getting and spending like other men, though he deplored the process more memorably than the rest of us. As a member of the new professional class slowly rising out of the old country aristocracy, he was keenly aware from childhood of the value of a pound. In the biography of his young manhood, three sums have special importance: the approximately £8,000 Sir James Lowther owed John Wordsworth Sr. at the time of his death, but refused to pay to his heirs; the £900 Raisley Calvert bequeathed to Wordsworth at the time of his death in 1795; and the £100 per year Wordsworth blithely said was all he would need to live an independent life.

Comparative historical economics is not an exact science, and there is no simple way to multiply the value of a late eighteenth-century pound to arrive at today's values. But the following comparisons give an idea of what these sums would have meant to young Wordsworth in terms of the kind of life they could buy.

A church "living" producing about £300 per year was considered sufficient for a young university graduate to get married and set up housekeeping. Henry Fielding's country parson in *The Deserted Village* (1770), "passing rich at forty pounds a year," provides a comparison from a generation earlier. Wordsworth's uncle William Cookson was engaged for almost ten years, waiting for such a post, before he gave up his university fellowship and finally married the Penrith vicar's daughter. A parson getting £400 a year could afford to keep five or six servants. A two-room country cottage in the north of England could be rented for £2 a year, and a whole house for £6; Sir Robert Walpole's London town house rented for £300 annually. In 1792 a man in Kendal could support a wife and three children on £30 a year, £20 of which went for food, and still live comfortably. But this was near the bottom of decent levels of existence.

Wordsworth lived within these ranges. His father started out with almost nothing, as a member of the "decayed" lesser gentry, worth £200–1,000 a year. But at his death his personal estate, independent of the Lowther debt, brought in more than £10,000 at forced-sale prices.

These comparisons are accurate until the mid-1790s, when the cost of living approximately doubled as a result of economic dislocations caused by the war with France—a special hardship for people trying to live on a fixed income. At the upper end of the scale, members of the English landowning aristocracy were better off than many European princes, with average annual *incomes* of £10,000.

A Note on Texts

Editions of *The Prelude* pose a special problem for a biography concentrating on Wordsworth's development, since different versions of this poem developed alongside his life. The Cornell University Press edition is definitive for the three major stages of the poem's growth: *The Prelude, 1798–1799,* ed. Stephen Parrish (1977); *The Thirteen-Book Prelude,* 2 vols., ed. Mark L. Reed (1991); *The Fourteen-Book Prelude,* ed. W. J. B. Owen (1985). I follow convention in referring to these versions by their dates of completion or (in the case of the fourteen-book version) publication: as *1799, 1805,* and *1850.* (*1805* signifies the AB-Stage MSS in Reed's edition: that is, MSS A and B of the poem, or Dove Cottage MSS 52 and 53.) However, when referring to editorial matter, I use a short form of the Cornell title (for example, *Thirteen,* for Reed's edition).

The 1805, thirteen-book version of *The Prelude* is the one closest to the time frame of this biography, and hence the one I cite most frequently; all otherwise unattributed citations to books and line numbers throughout (for instance, X.348–49) are to this version. For readers' ease of reference, I have used the Norton paperback edition combining all three versions, *The Prelude: 1799, 1805, 1850,* ed. Jonathan Wordsworth, M. H. Abrams, and Stephen Gill (New York: W. W. Norton, 1979). Variations between the Norton version of *1805* and Reed's scholarly edition are for most readers' purposes not important.

For Wordsworth's other poems, I have used the Cornell University Press editions as my basic reference text, occasionally referring to and quoting from the older edition of Ernest de Selincourt for additional information: *The Poetical Works of William Wordsworth,* 5 vols. (Oxford, 1940–49). I have also made use of John O. Hayden's two-volume edition, *William Wordsworth: The Poems* (New Haven: Yale University Press, 1981; first published 1977 in England by Penguin Books)

Bliss was it in that dawn to be alive,
But to be young was very heaven!

(*The Prelude* [1805], X.692-93)

I ask what is meant by the word Poet? What is a Poet? To whom does he address himself? And what language is to be expected of him? He is a man speaking to men . . . .

The obstacles which stand in the way of the fidelity of the Biographer and Historian . . . are incalculably greater than those which are to be encountered by the Poet who has an adequate notion of the dignity of his art . . . . there is no object standing between the Poet and the image of things; between this, and the Biographer and Historian, there are a thousand.

Emphatically may it be said of the Poet, as Shakespeare hath said of man, "that he looks before and after." He is the rock and defence of human nature; an upholder and preserver, carrying everywhere with him relationship and love.

(Preface to *Lyrical Ballads,* 1802)

. . . I could no more
Trust the elevation which had made me one
With the great family that here and there
Is scattered through the abyss of ages past,
Sage, patriot, lover, hero. . . .

(*The Prelude* [1805], XI.60-64)

The HIDDEN WORDSWORTH

POET · LOVER · REBEL · SPY

PROLOGUE

Images of Wordsworth

> Difference is especially desirable in the field of Wordsworth studies, which has tended to be extremely familiar with its object of study.[1]

Looking at Wordsworth's earliest portraits, one is forcibly reminded that he was not an immediately attractive man, especially compared with his great literary contemporaries, almost all of whom *look* Romantic. But Wordsworth, from first portrait to last, looks calm and resigned at best, sleepy or weary at worst. He often looks better with his eyes closed, and his life mask, though it looks like a death mask, is an improvement over some of his pictures. William Shuter's portrait, taken when Wordsworth was twenty-eight, has the liveliest expression of the more than eighty portraits, sketches, and busts produced during the poet's lifetime. The earliest portrait (1798), it was also the last to catch Wordsworth smiling, capturing that incongruous "convulsive inclination to laughter about the mouth," which William Hazlitt, then a young portrait painter himself, noted, adding that it was "a good deal at variance with the solemn, stately expression of the rest of his face."

Hazlitt, as it happens, is the only artist to have been suggested as the painter of that odd man out in the middle of our prologue gallery, which presents an image of Wordsworth very different from those we are used to. Weird, disturbing, "like a spy in a thriller" (my friends say), both the portrait's subject and its author are unknown. Yet its mysterious, unsettling quality tempts me to make it a pictorial emblem for *The Hidden Wordsworth: Poet, Lover, Rebel, Spy.*

It is plausibly Wordsworth. That at least was "the consensus of opinion of those who visited the poet's birthplace during the centenary celebration" of his death, the year (1950) in which it was discovered—perhaps too coincidentally—in a garage in the Lake District.[2] It has been claimed to be one of the two portraits, both now lost, that Hazlitt painted of Wordsworth and Coleridge in 1803.[3] According to other accounts, however, Hazlitt's "evidently lugubrious portrait appears to have been destroyed," and the most recent evidence indicates it was probably burned. But its destruction is not certain, and no other identification has been proposed for the picture we have, other than that it probably dates from ca. 1800–1820 and that it seems to be a north of England subject, perhaps (if not Wordsworth) an itinerant preacher.[4] The sitter's literary interest is indicated by the small book he holds: a Bible? Or a copy of *Lyrical Ballads,* which was printed in small format in its first editions?

The hair is still worn in the republican "crop" of the 1790s, as in Wordsworth's other youthful portraits, and the strong nose and large ears are prominent, as in all other pictures of the poet. The deep lines in the right cheek are the mark which help to "make" our man's ID, as the police say. The great majority of Wordsworth's portraits are taken from the left, his good side, because the skin on his right cheek, down to the corner of his mouth, was creased and pock-marked, almost scrofulous. What was a handsome cleft on his left side was an ugly scar on his right. Sometimes he covered it with sideburns, and almost all painters, including this one, flatteringly brushed it out.[5]

The chance that the picture *is* Hazlitt's portrait of Wordsworth, and that it thus pictures him just when he began to expand "the poem on the growth of my own mind" *(The Prelude)* into a time frame coterminous with this biography, makes it an appropriate symbol for a young man who in many ways hid himself from the gaze of posterity, covering over or destroying aspects of his life he did not want us to see. (That his word is the only authority for the picture's being burnt heightens the symbolism.)

How to describe the expression on that face? The rest of Hazlitt's first impression of Wordsworth fits it nicely: "There was a severe, worn pressure of thought about his temples, a fire in his eye (as if he saw something in objects more than the outward appearance), an intense high narrow forehead, a Roman nose, cheeks furrowed by strong purpose and feeling."[6] This in fact sounds more like the disputed portrait than like any of the others of young Wordsworth. The fire is gone from the eyes of all other Wordsworth portraits after Shuter's, even the melodramatic rendering by Benjamin Haydon (1818), aptly dubbed "The Brigand" by the family, after French revolutionary stage adaptations of Schiller's *The Robbers.*[7]

Robert Southey supplied a subtitle for the portrait Hazlitt painted of Wordsworth that also fits the disputed portrait well: "At the gallows—deeply affected by his deserved fate—yet determined to die like a man." Wordsworth himself studied Hazlitt's image carefully, and his description of it to Charles Lamb in 1816 fits the disputed picture better than it does any of his known portraits. He reported that his brother Richard "was literally *struck* with the strength of the signboard likeness; but never, till that moment, had he conceived that so much of the diabolical lurked under the innocent features of his quondam playmate, and respected Friend and dear Brother."

He pursued the implications of his devil metaphor into a comparison of his and Coleridge's characters for Lamb's amusement, based on Hazlitt's two portraits:

> Devils may be divided into two large classes, first, the malignant and mischievous,—those who are bent upon all of evil-doing that is prayed against in the Litany; and secondly those which have so thorough a sense of their own damnation, and the misery consequent upon it, as to be incapable of labouring a thought injurious to the tranquility of others. The pencil of W.H. is potent in delineating both kinds of physiognomy. My portrait was an example of the one; and a Picture of Coleridge, now in existence at Keswick (mine has been burnt) is of the other. This piece of art is not producable [*sic*] for fear of fatal consequences to married Ladies, but is kept in a private room, as a special treat to those who may wish to sup upon horrors.[8]

The "Wordsworthian" devil would seem to be the first one, malignant and mischievous, bent on the "evil-doing" that is prayed against in the Anglican Litany: i.e., "oppression, conspiracy, rebellion . . . violence, battle, and murder." Like Southey, Wordsworth associated Hazlitt's image of him with subversions of the body politic, a connection that the present book tends to confirm. Meanwhile, the second "devil" sounds very much like Coleridge's self-destructive character. Coleridge's portrait was evidently still in existence at this time (1816), and Wordsworth's close comparison of the two suggests that the image of his own portrait had lodged deeply in his mind—if indeed it had been burnt.

The Hidden Wordsworth: Poet, Lover, Rebel, Spy is a portrait in words that attempts to restore the fire to Wordsworth's eyes, to overcome his own strenuous efforts to damp his youthful passions down. With its urban revolutions and Alpine scenery, French mistresses and passionate sisters, secret agents and furious guardian uncles, Wordsworth's young life was a most exciting one: Byron might have envied it. I see Wordsworth's youthful face like the eyes in the unknown portrait: not calm but alert, the expression not pleasant but questioning, calculating, perhaps a bit startled—or a bit frightening.

By contrast, Wordsworth's uniformly calm gaze in all his other portraits matches the remarkable consistency with which he and his works have been perceived by the public. The young, unknown, unsettling Wordsworth has been replaced by the sedate, grave, and boring older poet. From twenty years before his death until a hundred years after it, he was, above all, *revered*. His youthful self has become to a large degree a prisoner of the later image that he himself created.

Wordsworth's name always provokes one immediate association: Nature. He is Our Nature Poet. But there are also contrary images of him, directly in reaction to this one. From the beginning, many people's reverence for him has stimulated others' irreverence; not infrequently, both attitudes are expressed by the same person. Robert Browning celebrated Wordsworth's "mild and magnificent eye" even as he lamented his "Lost Leader." From Byron and Shelley through Browning and Swinburne to Eliot and Pound, there have always been significant demurrals to Wordsworth's greatness. For some readers he is the poet they love to hate. Others try to divide him into two distinct poets, as Matthew Arnold did: the (bad) philosophical poet and the (good) lyrical one, or the reactionary and the radical, or the silly and the profound, or simply the Good and the Bad Wordsworth. Often these disparate Wordsworthian identities speak in very different voices, as a nineteenth-century parodist ventriloquized them: "one is of the deep," the other "of an old half-witted sheep."[9]

But there is one image, or story, that we have not seen fully—of *young* Wordsworth. Was Wordsworth ever young? On the evidence of his portraits, he seems to have looked old from a very early age, and his thoughts about death can almost be called precocious. But he was young once too, and this book tries to show him as he was then, even to suggest that his young life was his most important life. At the simplest level, it highlights the fact that Wordsworth's early years were more exciting, biographically, than any other part of his life. He was an extremely interesting young man who, even apart from his poetic re-creation of his early life in *The Prelude,* is worth seeing as an actual living person, not a secular saint in training. We know this in a general way, though we accept too easily Wordsworth's sweeping his whole young life under the carpet as "juvenile errors" to be forgiven and forgotten.

There is a good deal more to that young life than we have yet seen, certainly more than I expected to find when I set out writing this book: my research has outstripped my hypotheses. Almost more interesting than the new facts about his political life and his sex life—and his poetical life—is the Wordsworthian cover-up: the systematic and very successful efforts he made to bury his "juvenile errors" from the sight of his contemporaries and from posterity. But though he covered them up, they did not disappear: many of them stare us in the face from the pages of his greatest poetry, like purloined letters we have not seen, because they're so obvious—and because they were written by Wordsworth, that irreproachable name.

Repeatedly, when we can establish corroborated facts for an event in Wordsworth's life, his verse tends to confirm it, but silently or metaphorically, drawing our attention away from the facts, not toward them. What seem to be metaphors often turn out to be literalisms. A small example: in Book X of *The Prelude,* speaking about his disaffection from England in its war against revolutionary France, Wordsworth says he sat "like an uninvited guest" in a village church when "prayers were offered up . . . for our country's victories." The simile is a good one for expressing feelings of alienation, but its literal force is even stronger, for at that moment—when news of the allied victory at Valenciennes on July 28, 1793, reached England—Wordsworth (not normally a churchgoer in his young manhood) was precisely an *in*vited guest, at the home of his college friend Robert Jones, at Plas-yn-Llan in Wales, where Jones's father was the local vicar (a position to which his son succeeded in due course). So young Wordsworth felt estranged not only from his country and its national religion but even from the affections and hospitality of his closest friend.

A larger example of our sanitized reading of Wordsworth is the way in which we tend to interpret his statement about his involvement in the French Revolution: "Bliss was it in that dawn to be alive, / But to be young was very heaven!" These words, the second most famous in English about the Revolution (after Dickens's "It was the best of times, it was the worst of times . . ."), are quite regularly treated as a *generalization* about the attitudes of Wordsworth's generation, rather than his very particular expression of his own experience. Blissful youth has been a hard concept to attach to the Wordsworth of posterity, let alone his full hyperbole: *heavenly* bliss. That this kind of language matches exactly his expressions of sexual joy over his love affair with Annette Vallon ("pathways, walks, / Swarmed with enchantment, till his spirits sunk / Beneath the burden, overblessed for life" [IX.593–95]) should not surprise us; rather, it confirms the intensity of his early adult experiences. And that these emotions should be attributed in *The Prelude* to two characters named Vaudracour and Julia, rather than William and Annette, is only another species of metaphor.

These kinds of literal metaphors, or particular generalizations, have special importance for Wordsworth's biography. They imply that much of his poetry is more literally autobiographical than we realize, especially when we read it according to Modernist protocols of interpretation that insist on the separation between the artist and his art. Not that Wordsworth's poetry is literally "true." Great care must be exercised in interpreting the facts of his metaphors. But it is not surprising that the poet who often wrote as if "there were nothing else but him and the universe" (Hazlitt) should frequently take his metaphors from himself, from his own experience. As Shelley said, "He had as much imagination as a pint-pot" and "never could / Fancy another situation . . . than that wherein he stood" (*Peter Bell the Third,* IV.viii). Shelley, however, went on to say, "Yet his was individual mind, / And new created all he saw . . . and refined / Those new creations . . . by a master-spirit's law."

The Hidden Wordsworth: Poet, Lover, Rebel, Spy is an account of how Wordsworth transmuted the facts of his life into poetry—and also into an image of himself as "the Poet." It shows how deeply Wordsworth's poetry and metaphors are grounded in his life. He was a poet with remarkably low powers of invention and remarkably high powers of imagination. He almost could not make up a story on his own: he used literary sources, or he asked people (especially poor ones) about the facts of their experience. His poetry is a treasure trove of biographical resource, so long as we do not always take Wordsworth at his words' worth, or his literalisms too literally. His facts are not always facts: for example, when late in life he told his neighbor Isabella Fenwick about the circumstances of many of his poems' composition, he frequently neglected to mention clear literary sources, and even clearer facts about his own personal involvement with the persons or actions described. Nothing wrong here: it was all part of his continuing creation of "the Poet"; he was no more obligated than any writer to anatomize himself for posterity. Indeed, given his extreme literalism, he was more obligated than many to *cover* that anatomy. And he did.

Wordsworthian biography does not need more facts, though these are always welcome, so much as it needs more speculation. If I had an ax to grind when I started, it was from feeling that there's more here than meets the eye, or more than has yet met our eyes, as in that shifty portrait (whether lost or found) by Hazlitt. Anyone who studies Wordsworth's young life for long comes to agree with the feeling of the distinguished historian E. P. Thompson that there is something secretive about it. For a long time Wordsworth's supposed youthful "crisis" was thought to be a kind of nervous breakdown, but lately the finger of suspicion has turned back to his politics, as it did for his contemporaries.

Suspicion is a methodological necessity for writing about England in the 1790s, especially about someone who claimed that "to be young [then] was very heaven." The practice of sweeping youthful enthusiasms under the carpet reaches epidemic—and epic—proportions for these years. Much of England's domestic policy in the nineteenth century was predicated on a deep need to bury the specter of revolution which began stalking Europe in 1789 and continued to do so, with only brief interruptions, until 1917. The biographical correlative to this is that most people who wrote autobiographies drastically played down any involvement they might have had in the Jacobinism of the 1790s. The suppression, elision, or revisionary doctoring of one's radical republicanism in the 1790s was carried out as ruthlessly and with

Wordsworth, by William Shuter (1798)

Wordsworth, by Robert Hancock (1798)

Wordsworth? (disputed subject; artist unknown; ca. 1803–1810)

Wordsworth, by Henry Edridge (1806)

Wordsworth, by Benjamin Robert Haydon (1818)

The Source of the Arviron with Part of Mont Blanc 1781, by Francis Towne

"A View of Snowdon near Capel Cerig," by Francis Towne (1809)

"Lake of Como, Light from the left hand, August 27th 1781," by Francis Towne

Grasmere, from the Rydal Road, by Francis Towne (1786)

as utter seriousness of purpose in nineteenth-century biography as the suppression of youthful fascism or communism in the 1930s has been in twentieth century. And for much the same reason: equally ruthless and serious enemies were watching with eagle eyes, ready to pounce on and exploit "juvenile errors," to the ruination of lives and, especially, of *careers.* Tom Paine, William Godwin, and Mary Wollstonecraft were the most famous victims of this long cultural witch-hunt, as were Shelley and Byron in different ways. But Wordsworth is no exception; indeed, he helped establish the rule. He seems forthcoming about his years in France, but by admitting that "juvenile errors are my theme," he seems to excuse himself in the act of confession without confessing all. He suppressed even more completely his dangerous involvement in *English* radical reform politics, and still more about his clandestine, renegade actions *against* the Revolution, in Germany, which are here exposed for the first time. And of course posthumous publication of *The Prelude* guaranteed absolute immunity.

My "method" often consists of no more than raising questions. My rule of thumb has been: when there's a choice of possibilities, investigate the riskier one. I have tried to approach his life both as a lover of his poetry and as a modern investigative reporter. Since these two positions might define for many the apex and the nadir, respectively, of contemporary morality, I hope the result achieves something of a balance. It attempts to treat Wordsworth according to the standards—and with the same respect and gravity—he accorded his poetical subjects: (1) "I have at all times endeavoured to look steadily at my subject," (2) "I have wished to keep my Reader in the company of flesh and blood," and (3) "in a selection of language really used by men." Even without the new evidence I have found, there were many remarkable things about young Wordsworth's life that no one seems to have remarked, ordinary questions about everyday life that seem off-limits for him, as though he had been granted a diplomatic poetical immunity. Case in point: can it really be true, as the extant biographical record suggests, that he engaged in no sexual intercourse between leaving Annette Vallon pregnant, in October 1792, and marrying Mary Hutchinson, in October 1802? That is, between his ages of twenty-two and thirty-two, a young man's sexually most active time of life? This would be extraordinary if true, and would certainly go far to explain a pervasive sexlessness in much of his work. While I can't exactly disprove it, his writings of this period upon closer scrutiny evince a remarkable, if subterranean, sexuality that suggests his facts of life were different—and in this case, more normal—than we think.

When something seems to be going on, but there's no hard evidence for an answer, I will at least hazard an educated guess. For example, I take seriously the possibility that Wordsworth did return to France secretly in the fall of 1793. Repeatedly, I found myself chewing on facts that other biographers have recorded, or on the conclusions they have drawn—or refused to draw—and coming up with markedly different results. On such topics as Wordsworth's father's business arrangements with Sir James Lowther; or Wordsworth's connections with William Wilberforce, the rich Yorkshire playboy turned antislavery hero; or his familiarity with the prostitutes in Cambridge; or his participation in political journalism in London in 1795; or his role in the "Spy Nozy" incident in Somerset in 1797. My conclusions on these topics made it less surprising when I came across evidence pointing to Wordsworth's work for the Foreign Office's secret service in Germany in 1798–99.

Wordsworth's biographers have tended to be either exceedingly laudatory (Legouis, Meyer, Moorman) or bitterly disillusioned (Reed, Fausset, Elwin, Douglas), producing either hagiography or demonology, but I am indebted to them all.[10] George McLean Harper's once-standard study and Stephen Gill's recent one-volume account of the whole life present admirably balanced accounts.[11] They and Mary Moorman have been my constant points of reference, along with Mark Reed's indispensable *Chronology of the Early Years, 1770–1799*. I have also admired Wallace Douglas's shrewd dollars-and-cents, pounds-and-pence cost-accounting estimate of the Wordsworth self-construction project. Similarly, F. W. Bateson's and Richard Onorato's psychological savoir faire have been heartening when all seemed barren and sexless.[12]

With a succession of portraits like this, why attempt another? Because, except for the great French scholar Emile Legouis, a hundred years ago (1896), no one has attempted to draw the youthful poet's portrait since.[13] Legouis succumbed in homage almost immediately. His book, *The Early Life of William Wordsworth, 1770–1798*, groundbreaking as it was and important as it still is, is plainly subtitled "A Study of *The Prelude*," and what appears as biography is actually textual commentary. It instituted for nearly a century the common practice of interpreting Wordsworth by his own words, in which the biographer's work became essentially a matter of retroactive confirmation, reporting back on the gross details out of which Wordsworth revised and refined himself. For the biographer of Wordsworth's early years must confront his subject's own account of himself at every turn; and one's excitement at many an apparent discovery is immediately qualified by the realization that the biographical subject has been there before you, taking notes and writing poems on himself.

Every portrait is an interpretation. Mine stresses Wordsworth's self-creation, or what is now sometimes called "self-fashioning."[14] This is not the "natural," or inevitable, growth to greatness which Wordsworth laid down in *The Prelude*, where everything appears "all gratulant, if rightly understood." It is rather the sequence of actions and decisions, many far from "gratulant," that includes accidents, false starts, mistakes, and bad faith—and the adjustments, compromises, and changes of mind and life plan that they entailed. *The Prelude* includes a fair share of these, but by no means all of them. *The Hidden Wordsworth* shows that his young life was not so fortunate, but that it is the immediately recognizable story of a young man becoming an adult, with the usual measures of bad luck and bad decisions: an ordinary life, with ordinary decisions, temptations, and failures, out of which came extraordinary achievements.

During most of this book's composition, my working title was *Young Wordsworth: Creation of the Poet,* my intention being to show how Wordsworth created his mature self—or our received image of it—by creative handling of the exciting materials of his early life. On reflection, I have dropped the "Young," because my focus is on the process of self-creation rather than on youth as such, and because a biography that covers nearly half (1770–1807) of its subject's long life (1770–1850) is not dealing solely with youthful matters. By the same token, though, my chosen task guarantees that there is no sequel forthcoming, as "Young Wordsworth" might have implied. The last half of Wordsworth's life is not unimportant, but his self-creation project was largely finished after 1807. Instead, his self-creative energies were then devoted to maintaining and refining the image of himself established in the first complete version of *The Prelude,* principally through his repeated revisions of it, accompanied by his constant (so to speak) *non*publication of it.

Wordsworth's young life is not his whole life, but it is almost all of his Romantic life, and the one he created, crafted, revised, and preserved. We have Wordsworth's warrant for limiting our attention to his youth: 1770–1800 was the only portion of his life he found interesting enough for a poem; he recognized that the rest of his life would not make a good book. Romantic poets are supposed to live short, passionate, unhappy, and self-destructive lives, out of which they produce great poetry. So did Wordsworth, only he survived himself, preserving his Romantic life for future restoration. Like Goethe's, his Sturm und Drang period was transitional, falling between the eras of late eighteenth-century antirationalist Sentimentality and early nineteenth-century anti-Romantic social earnestness: between, say, 1789 and 1802, the fall of the Bastille and the phony Peace of Amiens. Wordsworth the Romantic poet "died" when he read the recently completed *Prelude* to Coleridge in January 1807. He was then thirty-six. The occasion marks his career like Byron's "On This Day I Complete My Thirty-sixth Year," except that Byron did not live to see thirty-seven. Coleridge's poem "To William Wordsworth," written in response, is at once a recognition of and an epitaph for the young poet whose growth is described in *The Prelude.*

When it comes to self-creation, Wordsworth wrote the book on it. The biggest obstacle to an account of Wordsworth's self-creation is his self-portrait in *The Prelude,* which hangs like a golden curtain in front of all other portraits of him. Over eight thousand lines long, it is one of the greatest long poems in modern English, and one of the great English originals in the literature of self-portraiture. It is not Wordsworth's biography, but neither is it his autobiography: his early life was both the same as, yet very different from, *The Prelude*'s account of it. It is a full-length portrait of the artist as a perennially young man, meticulously worked over for forty-five years by the aging master. Exactly the reverse of Dorian Grey's picture in his attic, which absorbs the horrid scars of his life of sin, the *Prelude* picture kept Wordsworth forever young while the man aged. It was endlessly retouched and revised, and published and reproduced for posterity in several different versions. The authorized 1850 version in fourteen books held sway until the 1805 version in thirteen books was edited and published by Ernest de Selincourt in 1926, out of the vast store of original manuscripts at the Dove Cottage Library, and the two dueled onstage together (*1805* steadily gaining adherents) until the 1799 version in two parts was published in 1977.[15] An 1804 version in five books has been hypothetically reconstructed,[16] and definitively corrected scholarly editions of both the 1805 and the 1850 versions have only very recently been published.[17] In the process, editorial specialists have come to speak seriously of an 1819 version and one of 1832. By his not publishing *The Prelude* in 1805, Wordsworth's subsequent life and writings themselves became in a way posthumous, like the publication of *The Prelude.*

But though we have *The Prelude,* we don't have all of the years it covers, either in detail or in interpretation. For example, *The Prelude* makes no mention of Wordsworth's privileged social position, of his many friends at Cambridge, of his mistress Annette Vallon and their daughter, Caroline, or of his clandestine political writings. Apparently a less biographical omission, but in its way even more striking, are the nearly eight thousand lines of poetry he wrote between 1784 and 1800—as many as in *The Prelude* itself—of which *The Prelude* mentions or alludes to barely a quarter. These lines, poems, and fragments represent a sort of proto-*Prelude,* for whatever their genre, quality, or state of completion, there is hardly one that does not have a strong autobiographical element. We must try to see what Wordsworth left *out* of his self-portrait, before we accept that it all turned out for the best.

The Prelude must be used in writing Wordsworth's biography, but it must also be suspected and disputed. The biographer must challenge it: "Who goes there?" And not necessarily accept the password that comes back: "It's only Me, the Poet." We cannot assume that we already know the Poet when we catch him in his acts of self-creation. *The Prelude* is a poem, not an autobiography, and we must respect the differences between poetry, biography, and criticism. It is like one of those Renaissance paintings with the artist himself represented down in a lower corner, gesturing toward his subject. Except that, in this case, the subject turns out to be . . . the subject himself.

And if with this I mix more lowly matter, if with the thing contemplated I describe my mind and myself contemplating, and who and what I am, be not this labor useless. These are not my words, but Wordsworth's, from his "Prospectus" to *The Recluse.* He intended them to indicate that "the first great philosophic poem in English" (as Coleridge touted *The Recluse*) could not exclude the perspectives and experience of its author. I use them to acknowledge that a biographer's subjectivity cannot be kept out of any biography, least of all Wordsworth's. Henry David Thoreau, Wordsworth's best American disciple, laconically remarks on the first page of his book ostensibly about Walden Pond (which he pointedly called "my lake district"), "In most books, the *I,* or first person, is omitted; in this book it will be retained; that, in respect to egotism, is the main difference. We commonly do not remember that it is, after all, always the first person that is speaking."

Wordsworth was one of the first poets, as Werner Heisenberg was one of the first physicists, to discover life's great Uncertainty Principle: that observation, no matter how scientific, subtly changes the nature of the object under observation. Mass cannot be held constant relative to velocity, any more than identity can be held constant to life. In this respect, science has at last caught up with poetry, as Wordsworth predicted: "the Poet will . . . be at the side [of the man of Science], carrying sensation into the midst of the objects of Science itself. The remotest discoveries of the Chemist, the Botanist, or Mineralogist, will be as proper objects of the Poet's art as any upon which it can be employed . . . *and the relations under which they are contemplated* by the followers of these respective Sciences shall be manifestly and palpably material to us as enjoying and suffering beings." There *is* an object standing even between the Poet and Things, and it is precisely his "image" of them. Ditto the biographer; ditto-ditto, a hundred times over, the Wordsworthian biographer.

My cautionary proviso about subjectivity is finally necessary because of the time between us and our subject. One can still go to most of the places Wordsworth went, as I have. Some of them have not changed much—the older buildings of Cambridge University, for example, may have changed less than the hills of Cumberland, where thousands—nay, millions—of hikers' footsteps, many of them trying to follow Wordsworth's, have created real erosion problems and altered the landscape. Wordsworth's Cambridge, London, and Paris are still monuments of culture, but so is Wordsworth, now. Not only is he a monument, as Coleridge predicted he would be—"the Giant Wordsworth, God love him"—but so is the *idea* of the Poet which he did so much, with Coleridge's great help (God love him for it), to erect. "Thy monument of glory will be raised," he said to Coleridge, and the monument is called "Wordsworth." Hence a biography of Wordsworth, charting the creation of the Poet, must acknowledge from time to time that such self-creating is something we all do, and feel free to comment or intrude upon the distance between him and us, which is yet another cause of the distorting discrepancies and weird looks we get when we try to stare that subject in the face.

PART ONE

THE CHILD IS FATHER

1770–1790

1 THE MINISTRIES OF FEAR AND BEAUTY

Cockermouth and Penrith, 1770–1779

> Fair seed-time had my soul, and I grew up
> Fostered alike by beauty and by fear . . . .
> (I.305–6)

The earliest picture we have of young Wordsworth is his snapshot of himself as a little noble savage, jumping into the river Derwent behind his home at Cockermouth, in the northwest corner of the English Lake District. He is naked, tan, and alone: the wild child of Cumberland. His only playmates are flowers, and they are violently beaten down. No parents are in sight.

> I, a four years' child,
> A naked boy, among the silent pools
> Made one long bathing of a summer's day,
> Basked in the sun, or plunged into thy streams,
> Alternate, all a summer's day, or coursed
> Over the sandy fields, and dashed the flowers
> Of yellow grunsel; or, when the crag and hill,
> The woods, and distant Skiddaw's lofty height,
> Were bronzed with a deep radiance, stood alone
> A naked savage in the thunder-shower . . . .
> (*1799* I.17–26)

The river Derwent was a companion who "loved / To blend his murmurs with my nurse's song," and Mount Skiddaw was a distant father figure, against whose "lofty height" this rambunctious boy dared to measure himself: at that time, Skiddaw was thought to be the highest mountain in England.

With this kind of writing, begun in 1798–99 and unmatched since,

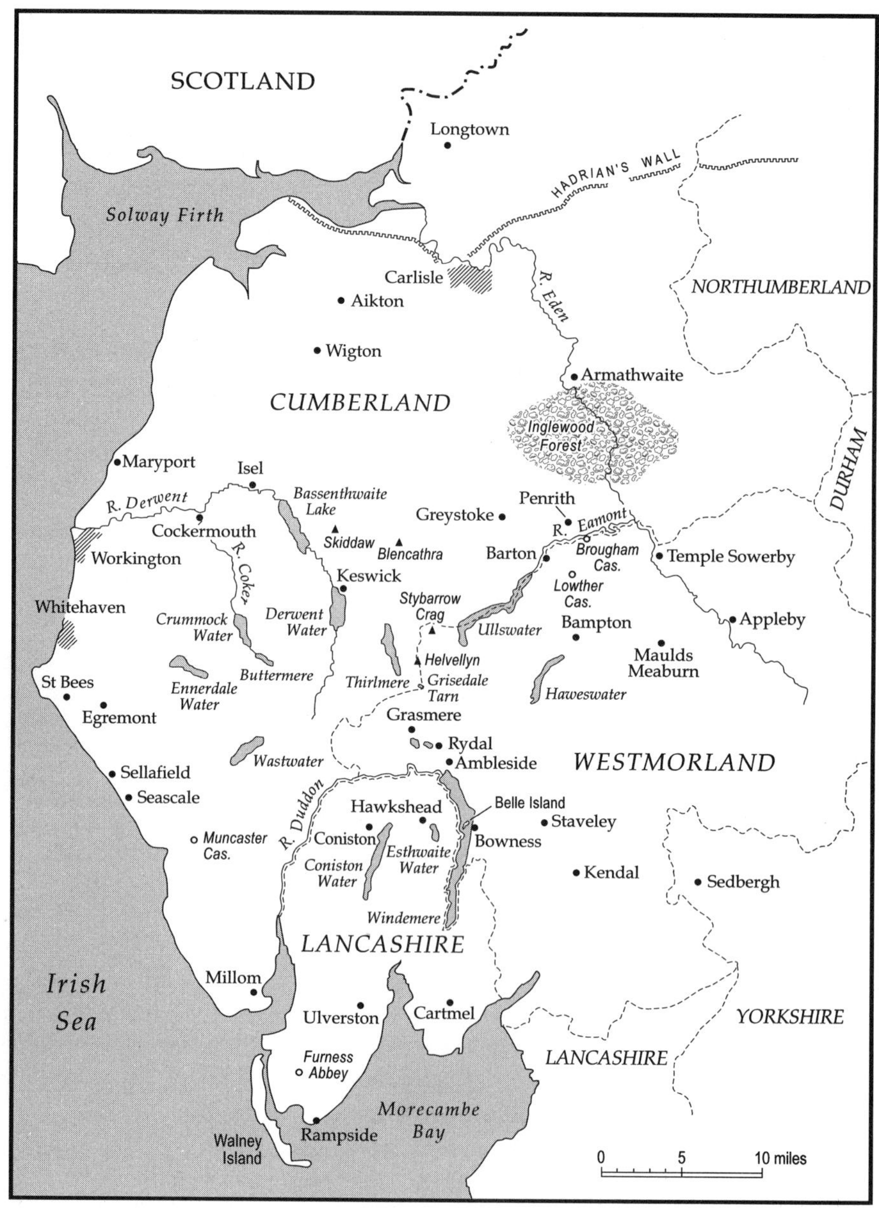

Cumberland, Westmorland, and Lancashire, with the English Lake District.

Wordsworth introduces himself as Nature's child in the poem "on the growth of my own mind." Another picture represents his childhood as a "fair seed-time," "fostered alike by beauty and by fear," making his growth seem more vegetable than human. In this view he was fostered not by John and Ann Wordsworth but by Fear and Beauty, the primary categories of aesthetic fashion in late eighteenth-century Europe. Fear (like Skiddaw) signified the threatening but thrilling experience of the Sublime; Beauty (like the Derwent), the pleasurable feminine feelings associated with home and the Picturesque. The child Wordsworth seems not only at home in nature but at one with it. In later versions he added more human points of reference, to "my father's house" and, metaphorically, to "my mother's hut." But still the dominant impression, as *The Prelude*'s narrative begins, is of a child beyond the pale of civilization—those "fretful dwellings of mankind" whose troubles, he suggests, the Derwent soothed him *not* to hear. He heard nature, not other people, not society.

But if we widen our camera's focus on that naked four-year-old in the river to what stands behind him, what comes gradually into view is the largest, newest (built 1745), and most splendid house in Cockermouth in 1774, so large and splendid that it remains unmatched in the town to this day: this was his "father's house." Wordsworth's birthplace was a spacious town mansion, with impressive drawing rooms on the first floor and plenty of bedrooms for a large family and servants on the second, plus a subterranean ground floor that opened out at the rear to an exquisite long garden running down to the river Derwent.

But it was not truly his "father's house." It was the designated residence for the Cockermouth agent of Sir James, the fifth baronet Lowther (1736–1802), the most powerful, feared, and hated aristocrat in all of Cumberland and Westmorland. Later known as "the bad Earl" or "gloomy Earl" of Lonsdale, James Lowther was a man so irascible in all his personal dealings, political and domestic, that Thomas Carlyle's brother believed only his wealth kept him from being committed to a madhouse: "more Detested than any man alive, a Shameless Political Sharper, a Domestick Bashaw, and an Intolerable Tyrant over his Tenants and Dependents."[1]

John Wordsworth, the poet's father, was one such tenant and dependent of Lord Lowther, and one of the key agents in a different ministry of fear by which Lowther sought to achieve his life's ambition: political control of Cumberland and Westmorland, where another local nickname for him was "Jimmy Grasp-all." It is ironic that the man whose name above all is associated with the English Lake District, William Wordsworth, should have been, as a child and young man, one of the many victims of the man above all in the eighteenth century who sought to stamp his name on Cumberland and Westmorland. But James Lowther's career is much more than mere background to Wordsworth's poetical life. The facts of his father's—and later his own—connections to the house of Lowther are often glossed over, or else the Wordsworths are presented as the innocent victims of Lowther's villainy. But their relations were much more complicated, so much so that we can leave the "infant babe" Wordsworth to "sleep upon his mother's breast" for a few years after his birth in 1770, to devote some attention to his father's career.

The Lowthers have been called the region's one indigenous aristocratic family, though this slights the claims of the le Flemings, Wordsworth's eventual landlords at Rydal Mount. But the Lowther-Lonsdales were grander than the Flemings in the late eighteenth century, and were not absentee landlords like their main opponents, the powerful young duke of Portland or the notoriously debauched Charles Howard, earl of Surrey and future duke of Norfolk, who owned Greystoke Castle near Penrith.* Lowthers had been leaders in the border wars against Scotland, and today almost every town in Cumberland and Westmorland (modern Cumbria) has its Lowther Street or Lonsdale Square, or both. There are very few named after Wordsworth.

James Lowther inherited his uncles' and grandfather's political acumen, commercial orientation, and puritanical thriftiness. He had "no opinion of anyone that is not punctual in business, a head not turned to it and that do not look strictly and principally into their own affairs."[2] "Fussing about in black smalls, silks, buckles, cocked hat, and always with a prodigious nosegay," Lowther could not conceivably have been a less romantic character.[3] He did, however, have what was then called his "sentimental" side. According to one tale, he as a young man developed a passion for the daughter of a local farmer and persuaded the father (one wonders how) to put the daughter under his protection. "Whilst yet young and beautiful, she died," the chronicler notes, and the young lord had her—or her head—embalmed and placed under glass, so that he could visit (one wonders where) "this sad memorial of his former happiness."[4] The story is probably exaggerated, but another one is true and almost as bizarre. When Betsey Lewes, his mistress of twenty-five years, died in 1797, he kept her body in an open coffin in his London town house for more than seven weeks before suffering her to be buried.[5] But for the most part this gothic cast of his character was submerged beneath an irascible and overbearing temper. He had no patience for the feelings of other people, especially underlings, and little enough for those of his peers or superiors, including his wife, Lady Mary Stuart, though he took care not to of-

*Howard had himself painted as Solomon with the Queen of Sheba because he said he "had had as many concubines as that salacious monarch."

fend her father, Lord Bute, prime minister from 1762 to 1763, and for fifteen years at midcentury the most powerful man in England.

He had hoped for a trade ministry in Lord Bute's government, to aid his shipping interests in Whitehaven, but he was too unpredictable to be trusted and too temperamental to work with: the king thought his support "scarce worth gaining."[6] Disappointed in this ambition, he set about establishing personal control over Cumberland and Westmorland, with occasional thrusts into Lancashire and Yorkshire as well.[7] In Westmorland the Lowther interest was returned to Parliament uncontested for over a hundred years, from 1775 to 1880, except for one year of disputed occupancy of one of the borough seats.[8]

Eighteenth-century English country lords, like those in nineteenth-century Russia, can be classified as those who neglected their lands and tenants, those who milked and oppressed them, and those who sought to improve them. Lowther was mainly in the last category, but his methods smacked of the second, for he was not motivated by any ideology beyond enlightened self-interest. As politicians, most landlords were little interested in public improvements except as they might spin off private advantages; providing for public welfare in the modern sense was held to be the business of religious institutions and private charity, and education for the poor, in the few places where it was provided, was considered dangerous. The Lowthers resented the public's envy of their wealth: " 'tis a grievous spirit there is in mankind, to be against anybody's laying things together though it is for the benefit of the public as well as the particular family." They were classic liberals in economic theory and practice, and were quite happy to support any profitable investments in "anything going forward in any part of the county to employ the poor and labouring people."[9] By diversifying his interests from agriculture to mining and trade, James Lowther was in global terms a man of the future.[10]

"It is probable that even the most reactionary man now living would be shocked, if he were to awake some morning in the last decade of the eighteenth century in England, by the oppressiveness of the social atmosphere," George Harper has written. "The law favored the owners of property, particularly landed property. It was still barbarously severe. The debtor, the poacher, the seditious person, were punished out of all proportion to their offenses, while political corruption and vice in the upper classes were winked at. . . . There was almost as much reason for a revolt in England as in pre-Revolutionary France."[11] This was not the light in which the principal actors at the time saw their reality, of course. Life depended on the pursuit of one's *interests* through one's *influence.* The pursuit of "interests" in politics may sound corrupt to naive modern ears, but in those franker times that was all there was. "All classes, except the lowest, asked or intrigued for places and promotions, for themselves, their relations, their protégés; and the most highly placed were the most ruthlessly insistent."[12]

The story of electoral politics in mid-eighteenth-century England is more diverting than much of its poetry; even the picaresque novels of Fielding and Smollett are hard-pressed to match it. Hogarth's comic painting *The Country Election* looks like no more than social realism to anyone who studies the period closely. A hundred years after the Glorious Revolution of 1688, representative democracy (so called) had settled down to a continuation of baronial warfare by other means, principally the buying and selling of votes, a process lubricated with vast amounts of free drinks. This was not quite as corrupt as it sounds, for freeholders who owned the requisite income-producing acreage for enfranchisement could drive hard bargains with large landowners to deliver their votes.

The main reason to seek control of a large number of parliamentary seats in eighteenth-century England was not party loyalty, still less national policy. Both of these more modern reasons entered in from time to time, but the real reason was simply to get enough local power to "make a great deal of [one's] affairs go on with great ease and quietness." So said another of Lowther's agents, when urging him to extend his influence by taking over the Cockermouth seat.[13] Lowther took over Cockermouth in 1756 by his characteristically direct method of buying up almost all (134, to be exact) the burgage rents in town—narrow strips of property whose title deeds carried ancient voting rights—at the astronomical cost of £58,000 (over £500,000, in modern terms), including Wordsworth's future birthplace.[14] Lowther's land buying was "not so much investing money . . . as buying up the perquisites of a social class, the undisturbed control of the life of a neighborhood." He very probably owned the Derwent's "sandy fields" with their "yellow grunsel" that Wordsworth played in, and many a neighboring "crag," "hill," and "wood" as well, if not Skiddaw's "lofty height" itself.

John Wordsworth's life was devoted to Lowther, and Lowther was the domineering presence on the Wordsworth family, filtered through their father. Lowther consumed people who could not stand up to him, and so he did his steward, John Wordsworth. When Wordsworth later participated in the French Revolution and the English radical reform movement, he had the hated features of James Lowther somewhere in his mind's eye, giving feudal tyranny a local habitation and a name.

John Wordsworth Sr. was Lowther's law or land agent. In the late twentieth century this sounds like the steward or overseer of an estate. But in the mid–eighteenth century it signified mainly a political business agent, or nonstop campaign manager, comprising the tasks of borough monger, ward heeler, vote canvasser, election rigger, briber, and payer-off of innkeepers—

none of which were regarded as reprehensible or, within reason, illegal activities. Such agents were not popular, since they tended to treat people as their master treated them. With an employer like this, and with enormous responsibilities in record keeping, rent collecting, and vote delivering, all involving large sums of money, Wordsworth's father's house was frequently one of the most "fretful dwellings of mankind." In this service John Wordsworth was expected to keep scrupulous accounts and give accurate advice and intelligence. In addition to dealing with innkeepers, he might also be expected to spread rumors, forge documents, manipulate opinion, and abuse the trust of his public offices to further the interests of his employer. All this would be considered "honest" behavior, where the standard of honesty was loyalty to one's employer, not necessarily public morality.* One of John Wordsworth's letters gives the gist of this field lieutenant's reports to his general:

> At Grey southern [an election district] Lord Egremont's people have not been able to stir a Jot. They could not even get a hand to the Petition for Leave to carry in the Bill; so that this matter is over for the present session. I have not yet received the article for the purchase of Mrs. Tiffin's Royalties in Grey southern but shall have it in a day or two and will then send the copy.
>
> I hope to hear from Mr. Garforth very soon in relation to Mr. Gilfred's rights at [another town], and am Sir your most obt & most hble servant.[15]

The freeholders of Westmorland and Cumberland fiercely resisted Lowther's efforts to acquire total command of the two counties,[16] especially during the three decades of William Wordsworth's birth and growth, and his estrangement from and return to his native country. Lowther's political ambitions were not an abstract historical process for him, but one in which his father was a principal actor who paid a high price for his actions in local unpopularity. By simultaneously associating young Wordsworth with the dominant social power in his home region, while alienating him from its popular base, James Lowther determined much of poet's wandering life during the formative years of his manhood. But young Wordsworth was not a natural rebel: both prior to and immediately following this twenty-year period, he and his family unhesitatingly allied themselves with the Lowther interest and worked actively for it. Thus Dorothy Wordsworth, who at nineteen called

*John Beckett, "Estate Management in Eighteenth-Century England: The Lowther-Spedding Relationship in Cumberland," in *English Rural Society,* ed. J. Charter & D. Hey (Cambridge: Cambridge Univ. Press, 1990), 62–67. Beckett's case study is that of John Spedding (1685–1758), agent for another Sir James Lowther (1673–1755), the uncle of Wordsworth's Lowther, but the parallels to Wordsworth's life situation are very close. The Spedding and Wordsworth families maintained very friendly relations, both fathers being in the same line of work for the same employers. A Spedding grandson was one of Wordsworth's best friends at Hawkshead, thanks to their earlier childhood associations at Cockermouth and Whitehaven. Eventually the two families were related by marriage.

Lord Lonsdale "the greatest of tyrants," would before she was fifty stoutly maintain, "For my Part I wish not success to any opposers of the House of Lonsdale; for the side that house takes is the good side."[17]

John Wordsworth was far from being Lowther's only agent, and the "estate" he oversaw was not Sir James's personal residence at Lowther Castle near Penrith. He held forth at Cockermouth, where his job was to gain control of as much land as he could buy, rent, steal, or lay claim to through non-stop lawsuits against Lowther's rival landowners; elections were simply another strategy in the game. Cockermouth was one of the three "urban" boroughs in the two counties, along with Carlisle and Appleby. Each had two seats in Parliament, which, along with the two county boroughs themselves, made a regional total of ten. Cockermouth and Appleby were both "pocket" and thoroughly "rotten" boroughs, much less populous than unrepresented urban centers like Kendal and Whitehaven.[18] Whitehaven's population was over 12,000, while Cockermouth consisted of one road enclosed between the Derwent and a wall, with access to the countryside through gates at either end of the street.[19] For the twenty years of his tenure at Cockermouth (1764–83), John Wordsworth was active in Lowther's successful campaign to extend his parliamentary interest to all ten seats. This was the period from Lowther's greatest debacle, the infamous election of 1768, to the time of his greatest triumph, the election of 1784, when his interest helped the younger Pitt to an ascendancy that lasted nearly twenty years. For his help, Lowther was rewarded by being created the first earl of Lonsdale. When Lowther initially took up the seat for Cumberland, in 1757, following the deaths of his father and two uncles in rapid succession that made him (in the prime minister's estimate to George III) "perhaps the richest subject that His Majesty has," the family held only one seat in Parliament.[20] But during the next twenty-odd years, thanks to the hard work of agents like John Wordsworth, he came to control as many as nine of the region's seats. Seven was his more usual number, which he supplemented by buying two seats in Surrey (at Haslemere) on speculation. In one combination or another, these nine seats were known as "Sir James's Ninepins."

John Wordsworth had difficulty in bending himself to Lowther's rod, and he was not nearly strong enough to stand up against it.* He worried that his

*James Boswell was more suited to dealing with Lowther than John Wordsworth was. He was closely associated with him for four years, 1786–90, the last two as his recorder for Carlisle. Their tempers clashed constantly, but when Boswell tried to resign his post—in order to finish his biography of Samuel Johnson—he was refused and "dragged away, wretched as a convict," to canvass for his master. On the trip north they quarreled so furiously there would have been a duel, except for the fact that they had but one pistol between them. See Hugh Owen, *The Lowther Family* (Chichester: Phillimore, 1990), 299–302.

terms of office—defined as agent and bailiff—had not been spelled out clearly enough regarding salary and expenses. He pleaded with his cousin Captain Hugh Robinson to intervene for him, because nothing had been settled though he had been in Cockermouth nine months. "I really hope Sir James will have no such thoughts as those of deferring the main business any longer."[21] His fears were well founded, but he did not have—being only nineteen at the time—the foresight or courage to make his employer sign a contract of obligations.

But John Wordsworth was not simply a naive victim of these hardball politics; he was a willing and expert player in the game. He was a practicing attorney "in the way of acquiring a fortune."[22] He "took into his keeping most of the estates Sir James Lowther purchased for his election purposes," and his own account book was titled "Rental of Lands and Schedule of Real and Personal Securities belonging to Mr. Wordsworth."[23] Its "General Index" charts the steady growth of what would have been the young Wordsworth's inheritance; it shows that John Wordsworth owned nearly twenty parcels of property throughout the district, from a seventy-acre farm at Sockbridge to individual crofts and barns dotted across the countryside, which produced more than £100 a year in rents. In addition, he had smaller investments like cattle gates, which controlled livestock's access to pasturage; these might return only a pound a year, or less, but they added up: on the High Moor, he and Lowther were the two biggest owners, holding more than a third of fifty-six such gates between them and thus effectively controlling the market there. He also held a 1/32 interest in the brigantine "Welcome" out of Maryport.[24]

Agents like John Wordsworth were less salaried employees than junior partners in an entrepreneurial business in which elections were only one of the variables to be monitored and controlled as best one could, like the weather and the price of labor. It was expected that agents would often lay out their own money for bribes, retainers, and other kinds of payments, in expectation of remuneration by their lord, but also in anticipation of other sorts of returns on such investments: offices, favors, rents, and other quid pro quo that they could hold as their own, with or without their employer's knowledge. The great lords both dispersed and disguised their power by investing it in the hands of their underlings through the distribution of "loaves and fishes," as the spoils or "harvests" of office were then genially known: a whole host of minor offices of little power or remuneration but of great usefulness whenever land or water rights were to be exercised for mining, fishing, and timbering ventures. There were sheriffs, coroners, distributorships, seigneuries, customs and port officers, and so on. Sometimes the fees charged by these offices were paltry sums, but they could be administered on an ad hoc basis according to what the official thought he could get away with. In the same year of 1774 when Wordsworth remembered himself as Nature's savage child, his father was made coroner of the seigneury of Millom, a little office for a large stretch of seacoast running from the mouth of the Duddon almost to the mouth of the Derwent,[25] and he also held the semi-official title of "Steward of Ennerdale."[26]

Active landlords like the Lowthers aided the independent business interests of trusted stewards by way of loans, partnerships, and political influence. John Spedding, whose son was one of William Wordsworth's best friends, rose from an impoverished orphan serving-boy to the lesser ranks of the Cumberland gentry.[27] John Wordsworth, starting out from a social position close to where Spedding ended, and with professional education and a small estate to boot, certainly expected to rise to a proportionately higher rank. Such professional inheritances had ample precedent: Wordsworths had long worked in the Lowther interest.[28] Wordsworth's paternal grandfather, Richard, had first come to Westmorland from South Yorkshire in 1700, to recoup his fortunes with the then baron Lonsdale, having been done out of his fortune by his own guardian's chicanery, which left him landless among a host of rich and influential Wordsworths.[29] He was agent for James Lowther's father's Westmorland estates from 1728 until his death, during which time he was clerk of the peace, mayor of Appleby, and receiver general of Westmorland.[30] He left the position of estate steward in 1738, but this was a mere technicality,[31] for loyalty and service to one's patron carried over into the government posts. This Richard Wordsworth particularly distinguished himself for loyalty in 1745, when he personally spirited away the county monies to Patterdale to protect them from the invading Jacobite armies of Bonnie Prince Charlie, while his wife, Wordsworth's grandmother, coolly entertained the rebel officers at their home in Penrith.[32] (Lord Lowther was less equal to the situation, dying of a heart attack shortly afterward, purportedly from the shock of seeing the rebel army march across his lands.) John Wordsworth took over some of his father's responsibilities immediately upon his death in 1760, when John was only nineteen years old. This is four years earlier than has usually been thought, and four years before his removal to Cockermouth, when he was already busily requesting "the goodness of your vote" for the Lowther interest.[33]

The poet's uncle Richard (1733–1794), who was disinherited from the family's small estate at Sockbridge in favor of John Wordsworth Sr. for marrying against his father's wishes,[34] was named collector of customs at Whitehaven, Cumberland's major seaport. Whitehaven was at the time second only to London in tonnage of materials that passed in and out of its harbor,[35] thanks largely to vast increases in profitable trade from North America, especially in Virginia tobacco. It was, with Kendal, the largest town in the Lake District, nearly the same size as Nottingham or Leeds. If James Lowther bought Cockermouth, it is not too much to say that he and his brothers and their agent Richard Wordsworth *made* Whitehaven, since they laid out its streets on a plan (apparently never paid for) prepared by the great architect and planner Robert Adam, and improved its harbor by way of improving their trading business, in one of the earliest examples of centralized town planning in England.[36]

But the most successful of all the Wordsworth-related clan was John ("Jack") Robinson, John Wordsworth's first cousin and son of another Appleby mayor, who also started out as a Lowther agent, and was "qualified" for Parliament in 1764 by Lowther's investing in him the money necessary to make him a man of £2,000 a year, the minimum financial requirement.[37] Though some aristocrats considered it degrading to send their agent or man of business to Parliament, Lowther did not show this kind of snobbery, and Robinson held the ultra-safe Appleby seat until 1774, when he broke with his patron on the issue of the rights of the American colonists. (Lowther was sympathetic to them, and made a motion in Parliament opposing the use of Hanoverian troops against them.)[38] Robinson then joined Lord North's administration, moved to the seat for Harwich, and soon became treasury secretary and the government's leading polltaker, political strategist, and paymaster.[39] Lowther never forgave him.*

Many elements of Lowther's policy and personality, and John Wordsworth's role in furthering the one and suffering the other, came out illuminatingly in the election of 1768, a Pyrrhic victory that made the names of Lowther and Wordsworth hated for years to come. Next to the Oxford election of the same year, the Carlisle and Cumberland elections of 1768 are reckoned the most sensational of the century by parliamentary historians. Wordsworth's father was very active in the Cumberland contest, and what Lowther's uncle said of his agent John Spedding could as well have been said of John Wordsworth: "it is notorious in the country that you are my agent in everything."[40]

Lowther had decided to run candidates for both of the Cumberland county seats, thereby upsetting the agreed-upon balance of power between his family and the Howards, that each should have one of the two seats.[41] Usually seats were disposed of by aristocrats casting lots, so as to avoid the tremendous cost in bribes and "entertainments" of a contested election.[42]

*Robinson's name and reputation were once put to good use by Richard Brinsley Sheridan, the playwright and last of the great Augustan Whigs. Having made an accusation in Parliament too close to the mark, Sheridan was challenged to name the accused. He demurred, claiming that the villain's identity changed "faster than you can say 'Jack Robinson.' "

("Contested" did not mean "disputed," but literally an election in which there was a choice between two or more candidates.) Contests were the exception rather than the rule, on a principle enunciated by James Lowther's great-grandfather: "The first thing that contributes to a national settlement must be unanimity in elections."[43] One item in John Wordsworth's hand from this election reads, "Lent freemen in notes £680 which after they were polled were ordered to be cancelled."[44] Did Wordsworth's father double-cross the freemen, or did the freemen vote otherwise than they were supposed to? And in 1772, four years after the election and two after Wordsworth's birth, some friends of Mrs. Perle, an innkeeper at Cockermouth, applied to Lowther for payment of "her Election Bills," the hefty sum of £500, of which only £181 had been paid since the election. Mrs. Perle had "applied to Mr. Wordsworth about two years ago for more money, and that she found from his answer that she had no expectation of any payment from him, and as he then told her that all the Cockermouth bills were then before [Lowther], she has waited since that time without giving any further trouble, in hopes of hearing from some of your agents." Her friends wouldn't have bothered Lowther "about a matter of this nature" if they hadn't been solicited by her friends from Lorton, who frequented her house, "and as they served you at the Election, notwithstanding they are Tenants to Lord Egremont." Lowther would get the point of this thinly veiled threat of political defection.[45]

Not everything was so venal in this operation, however. Sometimes votes were bought outright, but this was frowned on if the sums were too high: not because it was illegal and immoral, but because it inflated prices on the election markets. In addition to the deals made before elections for favors in exchange for votes, there was the much livelier business of the "canvass" of votes, a euphemism for the punch, pies, and tobacco provided free throughout the polling period, which could run as long as two weeks.[46] By far the largest item in all the money handled by John Wordsworth and other election agents was for paying publicans who kept their inns open for drinks on the house, it being well understood which inns stood open for the supporters of which candidate or party. Jack Robinson's account to Lowther for his first election in 1757 gives the flavor—or flavors—of these festivities:

> There are 7 houses fixed for the entertainment of your friends, viz. the Globe, Mr. Dixon's, *unlimited,* the House late John Lucock's, Ordinarys 130—Wine 10 Dozen. Punch and ale proportionable—Two others at 50 ordinarys each—one of them allowed 4 dozen of Wine, and punch and ale, and the other punch and ale proportionable. . . . It is proposed also to have 13 other houses, for taking off the lower class as much as may from the better houses . . . besides likewise some ale from the other houses for the mob. These means

> it is hoped may lessen the expense at the great houses where it used to run high by the rabble getting in and stealing and carrying off all the liquor they could . . . .[47]

And all this was for an uncontested by-election for one seat, which had been held successively during the three preceding years by the candidate's uncles!

"Punch and ale proportionable" was the working slogan, whatever the more serious issues might be, in these elections that would make a Chicago alderman blush. The election of 1768 has been reckoned to have cost nearly £100,000 pounds, mainly in this kind of expenditures. More cautious estimates put the figure at "only" £30,000,[48] but since John Wordsworth's records alone show £24,000 paid out between January 1767 and April 1769, chiefly for innkeepers' bills, they suggest that the higher estimates may not be excessive. All in all, approximately ten thousand votes were cast in the five boroughs, an exceptionally high number due to the artificial inflation of the voter rolls, which proved the proverbial wisdom of avoiding election contests to avoid costs.

But Lowther's victory was challenged in Parliament by the duke of Portland, who was able to prove that the Cockermouth sheriff, Giles Lawson, had improperly canceled votes for his opponent, Portland's man, Henry Curwen, one of Lowther's competitors in the coal-mining business. Lowther's defense was prepared by John Wordsworth, who set about a counterattack, claiming that Portland's other candidate, Henry Fletcher, had "paid the Bills of the Innkeepers after the Election" and bought votes in exchange for reduced tithes for some of his tenants—who readily acknowledged they would not have voted for him otherwise.[49] Many MPs had a hard time keeping a straight face when such normal practices were proffered as "charges," but they did not affect the verdict, which turned solely on Sheriff Lawson's inconsistently allowing some voters to participate in the poll while forbidding others.[50] Sometime during the proceedings, the Wordsworth house in Cockermouth was searched by officers, but they found nothing incriminating.[51] Nonetheless, Lowther lost his Cumberland seat, with no kind thoughts for the agent who had prepared his unsuccessful defense. Lowther himself was not greatly incommoded by losing his seat, for he served out the rest of the term simply by switching over to his safe Cockermouth seat. But this setback may have cost John Wordsworth his own parliamentary career, since in the election of 1780 Lowther put another of his agents, John Garforth, into the Cockermouth seat.[52]

There may have been costs—or perhaps benefits—for the Wordsworth family from the other side as well, as we shall see in 1799, when the secret accounts book of the duke of Portland—then home secretary, in charge of domestic security and espionage—records a payment of nearly £100 to "Mr. Wordsworth," the son of his old antagonist's chief agent in this cause célèbre.*

The land disputes and election of 1768 were the most notorious events in Cumberland for many a year, though the major participants in this skirmish of their "ten years war"[53] settled it amicably enough. An altogether typical compromise was worked out whereby the Lowther and Portland interests agreed again to divide the two Cumberland seats between them, so there would be no more contested elections. But for the population at large feelings were let loose that did not disappear for many years. A pamphlet war of squibs and cartoons ran for years, portraying Lowther as the great Satan incarnate (see illustration), and his minions as fools and traitors.

> Oh! where is gone that country's love,
> Which once our race inspir'd,
> That stoopt to tyrant L-w-——r's nod [*sic*],
> My honest soul hath fir'd.
>
> Villain repent, repent thy late,
> Thy black and partial deeds;
> Eternal shame hangs on thy brow,
> And all thy honour bleeds.[54]

*In fact, the 1768 election was but a skirmish in a much longer running war between Lowther and Portland, from 1765 to 1787, over rights to the vast Inglewood Forest, north of Penrith. Charges, judgments, and appeals went back and forth for years before the Court of Exchequer decided that Lowther's claims, though legally valid, were invalidated by the dukes of Portland's having been in "undisturbed possession" of the forest for over sixty years, giving them de facto ownership. Like the 1768 election, this was no mere local dispute, but one with national political implications. The new duke of Portland was a prime recruit of the Rockingham Whigs in 1765, which put him in settled opposition to Lord Bute, James Lowther's father-in-law. Legal activities were especially intense in 1767–71, throwing "the whole county of Cumberland . . . into a state of the greatest terror and confusion"; 400 ejectments against Portland's small landholders were served in one day, after Lowther's initial victory (*Annual Register,* 1771, p. 56). John Wordsworth would have served some of these writs of ejectment. Portland's counterattack was so ferocious, enlisting the aid of the author of the "Junius" letters, that for a time the duke himself was suspected of being Junius. When the exchequer finally decided for Portland nearly twenty years later, no less a figure than Edmund Burke congratulated him, very much in the ideological terms of the day: "the glorious Victory at Carlisle [is] the Triumph of Truth, Equity, and Reason, over obstinacy, malice, and arbitrary power. . . . These modern Whigs [Lowther had acted with the Whigs during Lord North's administration, 1770–82] are strange people . . . if their ancestors were such we should have had no Liberty, no ["Glorious"] Revolution, no Duke of Portland . . . ." By 1793–94 Burke, a regular correspondent of Portland's, was assuring him that the "Jacobin war abroad" was no "party squabble about place or patronage," but an ideological fight to the death. The equable Portland—still one year away from becoming home secretary—admitted that his "imagination . . . feelings . . . conclusions, do not, and cannot keep pace with yours." (See Arthur Strong, ed., *A Catalogue of the Letters and Other Historical Documents . . . in the Library at Welbeck* (London: Murray, 1903), ix, 119–20, 156–57, 161–64.

Giles Lawson was regarded as a well-meaning though incompetent fool, but if the sheriff of Cockermouth could be painted with this kind of ridicule, we can be sure that Lowther's main agent in the district, John Wordsworth—no fool—was regarded with less good-humored distaste. When his son at age twenty-five penned (but did not publish) a satire on the English aristocracy that asked, "Must honour then to Lonsdale's tail be bound?," he was remembering the shame he felt as a child for the violations of his father's honor that employment in Lowther's service brought with it.*

We can only guess at the effect all this power brokering and borough mongering had on Wordsworth as a small child, but he would have been conscious of it by the time he was four or five, given his preternatural ability to recall sensations from early childhood. The effects of a direct, personal, familial involvement in the Lowther "interest" did not simply stop with his father's death but continued for the nearly twenty years afterward, while the Wordsworth children's guardian uncles were suing Lowther to recover John Wordsworth's money.

Dorothy Wordsworth's recollections illustrate the psychological cost to the children of their father's exploitation by his employer. She reflected that it "it is indeed mortifying to my Brothers and me to find that amongst all those who visited at my father's house he had not one real friend."[55] By age fifteen, when she wrote this letter, she had come to the disillusioned realization that "all those who visited . . . my father's house" had done so only because of their father's identification with Lowther. On another occasion she speculated, "My uncle Kit . . . having always espoused the Cause of the Duke of Norfolk, has incensed him [Lowther] so much that I fear we shall feel through life the effects of his imprudence."[56] This, plus the defection of Wordsworth's cousin Jack Robinson to the opposition, did indeed work against the Wordsworth children's interest. And it suggests that John Wordsworth, by marrying Ann Cookson of Penrith, sister to Christopher Cookson, later Christopher Crackanthorpe of stately Newbiggin Hall, had entered into a star-crossed match that would eventually pit her husband's employer's interests against those of his in-laws, to the great detriment of their children when both mother and father died young. The Crackanthorpes of Newbiggin Hall, near Penrith, were another old gentry family on the way up, but their wagon was hitched to a different lord. They were not proud of their daughter's (Wordsworth's grandmother) marriage alliance with the Cookson family, who were "in trade," and they ignored the Wordsworth connection completely when they compiled their family tree.[57]

*Boswell worked for Lowther in another notorious election, as recorder of Carlisle, where another satiric song ran (to the tune of "A-voting we will go"), "My Lord shall guard you with his mob, / And Boswell with his law."

These family connections lead us back to Wordsworth's mother and her ministry of beauty, and require a change of scene. Wordsworth spent nearly half of his first eight years in his maternal grandparents' rooms above their linen shop in Penrith, not in his father's grace-and-favor mansion at Cockermouth.[58] He was at Penrith mainly in the winter, when he attended Dame Birkett's school, along with his sister, Dorothy, and Mary Hutchinson, the daughter of a local tobacco merchant and granddaughter of the postmaster,[59] to whom he was already related by marriage. When in Cockermouth, he attended the Reverend Mr. Gilbanks's school, but he said he "used to pass my summer holidays under the roof of my maternal Grandfather."[60] However, his fourth year was spent in Cockermouth, making his "naked savage" fantasy on the Derwent chronologically accurate.

It is not difficult to understand why the children spent so much time in Penrith. Ann Wordsworth had three younger children after Richard and William (Dorothy, born 1771; John, 1772; Christopher, 1774), and could certainly use the help of her parents' more established household. Her husband was not at home regularly, traveling the length and breadth of Cumberland for Lowther. The Cockermouth house, though large and well staffed, was an important political headquarters, not the most peaceful place to raise children, especially after the crisis of 1768. And this was exactly when the children began to arrive: Richard was born that year. The political issues made little impression on the children, but they picked up the tension in the atmosphere in the way that children do, especially sensitive ones like William and Dorothy and John. So frequent shifts to Penrith were desirable for family reasons, but politics couldn't be escaped so easily. In spending so much time with the Howard-supporting Cooksons in Penrith, Ann Wordsworth and her children were, in effect, consorting with the enemy.

These tensions were palpable in the rooms above their grandfather's neat white-and-red shop on Cornmarket Square, off Castlegate.[61] (Though the street has been sentimentally rechristened Poet's Walk, the house was occupied in 1992 by Jackie's Unisex haircutters, a nice illustration of the Lake District's insouciance toward its native poet.) As adults, the Wordsworth children registered blankly regretful feelings toward Cockermouth, a birthplace they rarely visited in later years. But their feelings toward their grandparents and their uncles in Penrith were actively negative. Their father was not there, and his job with Lowther was a source of irritation to the Cooksons. Even family memories were in political conflict. The Cooksons remembered with pride how they and their neighbors had provided for the needs of the Pretender's troops in "the '45," the same uprising in which Wordsworth's paternal grandfather was busy spiriting the Lowther valuables out of harm's way.[62]

The Cooksons were small-town tradespeople, linen drapers, and church wardens. Their lives, like their house, were altogether more pinched and conventional than the reflected glories of the Cockermouth manse. Every indication that has come down to us about them is of disapproval and nagging correction of the Wordsworth children's behavior. More than once they spoke those wonderfully unhelpful words "We told you so" to their daughter, who bore John Wordsworth five children between her twenty-first year and her twenty-seventh. It may seem hard, in terms of conventional clichés, that grandparents should be so cold. But there were good reasons of class and politics to motivate the Cooksons' disapproval of the Wordsworth children.

The Cooksons were upwardly mobile too, though on a different line. It has been claimed that their small-town snobbery held them aloof from the lower working classes, making Wordsworth "for the rest of his life . . . not entirely at ease with social inferiors."[63] William Cookson, the poet's maternal grandfather, had made a highly advantageous match in marrying Dorothy Crackanthorpe, heiress of Newbiggin Hall. When Uncle Kit (born 1745) inherited Newbiggin Hall on his mother's death in 1792, he quickly dropped his father's name and took his more prestigious middle name as his family name, becoming Christopher Crackanthorpe. This Uncle Kit, twenty-five when Wordsworth was born, kept up the line of complaint against the children as his parents aged, and intensified it with constant outspoken criticisms of their father's employer.

Wordsworth's memories of his mother are few and dim, as he regretfully admitted: "O lost too early for the frequent tear."[64] But they are more definite than his recollections of his father. He was seven when he last saw her, just before she died in March 1778, resting in a chair in her bedroom at Penrith. She died of a "decline" after catching a cold when she was put up in someone's uncomfortable "best room" in London, and it developed into pneumonia. The main image that emerges from his memories of her is one of unselfconscious good sense. She was the "parent hen" around whom the children trooped. But she was so much the "centre," so much "the heart / And hinge of all our learning and our loves," that when she died the center did not hold: "she left us destitute, and as we might / Trooping together" (V.246–60). Their father was unable to keep them together. Responsibility for the "destitution," emotional and financial, of the Wordsworth children's young adult life must be laid at John Wordsworth's feet and, ultimately, to James Lowther's harsh employment requirements.

When Wordsworth undertook to describe his mother's influence, he stopped himself, saying he did not wish to disturb her memory "with any thought that looks at others' blame." This plausibly refers to the harsh parenting of the Penrith Cooksons, but it also applies to John Wordsworth. It is a criticism of adults with too strong plans for the children in their care, either constantly "shaping novelties" and "false unnatural hopes" for their future success or else being full of "feverish dread of error and mishap" (V.260–80), very unlike Ann Wordsworth's easygoing ways. John Wordsworth had very definite plans for his sons' careers, for what they *should* be, while the Cooksons had very definite feelings of what they should *not* be—namely, dependent on them.

In the absence of clear physical images of Wordsworth's mother, we find numerous psychological ones, suggesting that his maternal experience was as strong in the inner realm of feelings as his paternal experience was in the external world of power politics. His image of himself as a "naked savage" is one of the few images he retained from his childhood's male-dominated ministry of fear. He recollected many more images of his mother's ministry of beauty, even though she died five years before his father. Not surprisingly, all these memories concern women, but almost all of them concentrate on women in jeopardy, in pain, or dead.

In a late sonnet titled "Catechizing," Wordsworth fondly recalled his mother pinning a nosegay to his "new-wrought vest" as he went off to say his catechism before Easter Sunday. Another recollection, also associated with Lent, arose from the heightened awareness that ritual church observances often stimulate in young children. One day he came home from school and proudly told his mother he had witnessed "a woman doing penance in the church in a white sheet," but complained that he had not been given a penny for his observance.[65] His mother commended him for having been present, and hoped that he "should remember the circumstance for the rest of [his] life," wisely adding that he was "very properly disappointed" of his venal penny.

But was this only a lesson against base motives for virtuous behavior? The circumstance was in fact a rather unusual one: a woman doing public penance, in a white sheet, in the Church of England, ca. 1775. Such public penances had all but disappeared from the watered-down liturgical practices of late eighteenth-century Anglicanism, except in remote provincial places. The woman was doing penance for sexual sin: incontinence, incest, adultery, or, most probably, for having borne a child out of wedlock. Her penance was part of the "Cleansing of women" rite, one of the five stated orders in the *Book of Common Prayer* of 1741. After safely giving birth, a woman came to church to give thanks to God, and was readmitted to the congregation, in what amounted to a sort of Christianized purification rite for her "uncleanness." But if she was unmarried, the ceremony had to be preceded by the public penance that Wordsworth saw and that his mother hoped he would always remember.

And he did. For though it is impossible to sort out the psychosexual reactions contained in such a memory, its recollection was not accidental. He also composed a sonnet on this "Thanksgiving after Childbirth" rite, and placed it close to his sweeter remembrance in "Catechizing." In the latter he said only that whenever he saw flowers like those in his catechism nosegay, his mother's "countenance, phantom-like," rose up before him. But in "Thanksgiving," his "imagined view" of the safely delivered young mother kneeling penitently is presented as a refuge of "safety" to her "Heir," who walks in "courses fit to make a mother rue / That he was ever born."[66] This is a very strange idea with which to end a poem about thanksgiving. Ann Wordsworth probably wished her son to remember only the shameful wages of sin, not those of fallen women particularly. Yet she did fear for, even if she did not live to "rue" (as her parents and brothers abundantly did), the future of her second child. William was the only one of her five children about whose future life she was anxious; she is reported to have said that he would be remarkable either for good or for evil.[67] This is how he fashioned himself in *The Prelude,* where Beauty is associated with goodness, and the Sublime, if not with downright evil, at least with strong disobedience. The insistent peacefulness of Wordsworth's later poetry should always be measured against the extreme violence of his thoughts and actions as a child.

"I was of a stiff, moody, and violent temper," Wordsworth told his nephew, and as an example of his character he brought up a memory of another threatened woman.

> Upon another occasion, while I was at my grandfather's house at Penrith, along with my brother Richard, we were whipping tops together in the large drawing-room, on which the carpet was only laid down upon particular occasions. The walls were hung round with family pictures, and I said to my brother, "Dare you strike your whip through that old lady's petticoat?" He replied, "No, I won't." "Then," said I, "here goes;" and I struck my lash through her hooped petticoat, for which, no doubt, though I have forgotten it, I was properly punished.

As with his recollection of the woman in white, his punishment faded in comparison with his transgression. He even questioned the punishment: "possibly, from some want of judgment in punishments inflicted, I had become perverse and obstinate in defying chastisement, and rather proud of it than otherwise."[68]

Was his violence cause or effect? He seems to be recalling perfectly the logic of children, who often perceive punishment as a wrong far greater than the act that provoked it. Yet the crime, not the punishment, fills his memory. The old lady's "hooped" petticoats seem almost three-dimensional in his memory; he seems almost to feel she was flaunting them presumptuously, or provocatively. Why should "that old lady" be picked out from the family portrait gallery for punishment, to get a whipping like the one Wordsworth then doubtless received, but totally forgot? One explanation is that her big skirts made her a better target; another is that skirts themselves seemed a more inviting target than the severe faces of the male portraits hanging there.

He liked to dare and disobey, even if he had to take his own dares. Throughout his early childhood, his violence toward nature contrasted with Dorothy's more tender feelings. His recollected images of violence or shame upon women are matched by images of his own violence exercised in the company of his sister's tenderness. It is but a small step to see this violence carrying over from the male world of social violence to the feminine world of natural love and beauty.

He had "a heart / That doubtless wanted not its tender moods," but he could not remember them. He "better recollect[s]" breathing

> Among wild appetites and blind desires,
> Motions of savage instinct my delight
> And exaltation. Nothing at that time
> So welcome, no temptation half so dear
> As that which urged me to a daring feat.
> Deep pools, tall trees, black chasms, and dizzy crags,
> And tottering towers; I loved to stand and read
> Their looks forbidding . . . .

This sounds promisingly humble, but it ends up wholly in Wordsworth's willfulness: "read *and disobey, /* Sometimes in act, and *evermore in thought.*"[69] He had his gentler side, but more often than not it was embodied in Dorothy *at* his side.

Dorothy Wordsworth's extreme susceptibility to emotion in scenes of natural beauty was as notable as William's more violent responses to such scenes. This is beautifully represented in his recollection of their first vision of the sea. They were on their way to visit their cousins in Whitehaven, and as they came up over the crest of the enormous hills that surround the town, they saw all at once the whitecaps that give the town its name, rushing into the crablike arms of the harbor breakwater on one of that coast's perpetually windy days. Dorothy, "when she first *heard* the voice of the sea from this point, and beheld the scene spread before her, burst into tears."[70] "The family at Cockermouth"—that is, their earliest family—often mentioned this incident, "as indicating the sensibility for which she was so remarkable."

Wordsworth, by contrast, remembered "being *struck*" by the panorama of town and harbor, and identified himself emphatically with the waves' striking motion—"the white waves breaking against its quays and piers." His reaction is an instance of "that mysterious awe" with which he "used to listen to anything said about storms or shipwrecks."[71] This sounds appropriately adventuresome for a boy, but storms and shipwrecks were not romantic matters for a boy whose uncle was chief of customs at Whitehaven, and whose relations were heavily invested in a "family bottom" of the East India Company, on a coast where storms and shipwrecks were very frequent disasters. We would not be wholly charmed to hear a modern boy confess a fascination with airplane crashes, however "natural" we take boys' attraction to violence to be.

One of the Whitehaven stories that fascinated him was his uncle's account of the raid of John Paul Jones on April 23, 1778, in the American frigate *Ranger.*[72] Jones, the naval hero of the American colonists' war for independence, was something of a local boy made good—or bad, from a strictly political English point of view, though the trading interests in Whitehaven tended to support the colonists' claims. Born in Kirkcudbright, Scotland, just across the Solway, Jones had been bred to the sea in a Whitehaven slaver, working in the infamous triangular trade of African slaves for Caribbean rum for American cotton. His raid, had it been successful, would have been one of the war's greatest blows to the British, given Whitehaven's importance to shipping. He landed in two boats, surprised the guard, spiked the cannons, and gave the order to burn the three hundred ships in the harbor. Only a confusion in relaying the order prevented its being carried out, and by then the alarm had been raised, alerting Wordsworth's uncle among others, and Jones had to flee in his boats.

Wordsworth did not love the sea, but he was fascinated by all massively destructive natural forces, and even "beauty, . . . as Milton sings / Hath terror in it" (XIII.225–26). This allusion to *Paradise Lost* is a revealing indicator of Wordsworth's relations with his mother and with Dorothy. It is usually taken to be simply a sign of his preference for the Sublime over the Beautiful, but it actually shows how inextricably the two were bound together in his mind. It is spoken by Satan as the serpent in Eden, rousing himself from being rendered "stupidly good" by Eve's beauty, and steeling himself against thoughts of love and pleasure, except "all pleasure to destroy, / Save what is *in* destroying" (*PL,* IX.477–78). The woman is "opportune for all attempts," her husband "not nigh," and she "Not terrible, though terror be in love / And beauty, not approached by stronger hate" (490–91).[73] That is to say, *beauty is dangerous if left undestroyed.* The sentiment is appropriate to Satan, but also surprisingly consistent with repeated incidents from Wordsworth's childhood involving both nature and women.

Poems like "The Sparrow's Nest," "To a Butterfly," and "To a Daisy" have high standing in many people's admiration of Wordsworth, but it might truly be said that the Wordsworth they love is Dorothy, not William, since sparrow, butterfly, and daisy all stood in as much danger from him as that old lady in petticoats. Dorothy recalled that William wanted to kill all white butterflies "because they were Frenchmen" (French soldiers wore white).[74] The butterfly was for him the "historian of my infancy": "Dead times revive in thee . . . A solemn image to my heart / My father's family." But it got no such respect from him as a boy. He chased after it ferociously:

A very hunter did I rush
Upon the prey; with leaps and springs
I followed on from brake to bush;

Not so Dorothy: "But she, God love her! feared to brush / The dust from off its wings."[75]

He chased one such butterfly through the "green courts" of Cockermouth Castle, a few hundred yards east along the Derwent from his home. There, in a poem originally titled "Castle to the Author," he received a lesson to his own violent temperament that he never forgot. Entering by chance the "soul-appalling darkness" of its dungeon, his "young thoughts" were suddenly made "acquainted with the grave."[76] The scene, with him and Dorothy playing in it, is in effect a miniature of the twin ministries of Beauty and Fear, for the castle was not then a picturesque medieval ruin, still less the renovated family home it is today. It was the seat of the old earls of Egremont and later of the Howard family, both traditional Lowther enemies, and the precise location of the polling place where Wordsworth's father helped fight latter-day versions of the old barons' wars.

It was the same with the eggs they discovered in a sparrow's nest in the privet hedge along the terrace walk above the Derwent at the foot of their garden. To him, "the chance-discovered sight / Gleamed like a vision of delight," but Dorothy "looked at it and seemed to fear it; / Dreading, tho' wishing to be near it." She gave him what he did not have, "humble cares" and "delicate fears" for nature—all imagined, in sparrow and butterfly and daisy, as feminine.[77] Though he could moralize at age thirty-two on daisies as symbols of universality, in his youth he was much less wise:

from rock to rock I went,
From hill to hill in discontent
Of pleasure high and turbulent,
Most pleased when most uneasy.[78]

The last line chimes perfectly with the minor chord of his description of reading nature in "Home at Grasmere": "read *and disobey.*"

His last clear recollection from his first eight years, before he, "fair seed," was transplanted to school at Hawkshead, brings this pattern of feminine Beauty and masculine Sublimity to a dramatic conclusion. He made it famous by identifying it as one of the two "spots of time" he said were central to the growth of his mind—the other being his imagined guilt for his father's death in 1783. Both, that is, are associated with his parents' deaths, and with their replacement by Nature's emotional foster parents, beauty and fear.

One day, when he was five or six, he rode out from Penrith with his father's servant, James. He was just learning to ride, just being initiated into men's activities. Somehow they became separated. It seems very inattentive of James, but perhaps the disobedient boy separated himself from the servant and rode down off the road (the present A686) toward an abandoned quarry, a rather steep declivity. He, with an ear attentive to "tragedies of former times," well knew the superstition of the place. Here, "in former times / A man, the murderer of his wife, was hung / In irons." His memory conflated two local stories,[79] adding to a recent (1767) Penrith homicide a much older (1672) Hawkshead superstition of matricide, or wife murder. All was gone, of gallows, chains, and bones associated with those public executions, except that "a long green ridge of turf remained / Whose shape was like a grave," in which "the murderer's name" in

> The monumental writing was engraven
> In times long past, and still from year to year
> By superstition of the neighbourhood
> The grass was cleared away; and to this hour
> The letters are all fresh and visible.
>
> (XI.293–98)[80]

Like the spirit of Cockermouth Castle, this scares even the little boy who liked nothing better than destruction and disobedience. It still scared the man in his early thirties who wrote about it, as the present tense of "and to this hour" suggests.

Certainly there are enough reasons of the usual sort to explain everything away, if we want to: he was lost, he was scared, and he may have been disobedient. But he remembered, or added, much more about the scene, elements having to do with a violated woman. Thoroughly frightened, he dismounted and struggled back up the slope to the road, where he found not James but a woman whose image never left him.

> . . . reascending the bare slope I saw
> A naked pool that lay beneath the hills,
> The beacon on the summit, and more near
> A girl who bore a pitcher on her head
> And seemed with difficult steps to force her way
> Against the blowing wind.
>
> (*1799*, I.313–19)

That's all. By way of further explanation, he offers only a repetition of the same three elements: beacon, pool, and woman:

> It was in truth
> An ordinary sight, but I should need
> Colours and words that are unknown to man
> To paint the visionary dreariness
> Which, while I looked all round for my lost guide,
> Did at that time invest the naked pool,
> The beacon on the lonely eminence,
> The woman and her garments vexed and tossed
> By the strong wind.
>
> (*1799*, I.319–27)

An ordinary sight, but extraordinary poetry, much odder than it appears at first glance. Is the wind masculine like the murderer? The girl, who firmly pursued an ordinary purpose in his first perception of her, has become a woman whose clothes are being violently disturbed in the second.

Penrith Beacon, "the beacon on the summit," was not an ancient monument, as many modern readers think, but a relatively new piece of military hardware, dating from 1719, when it was erected as part of an early-warning system for national rebellions like those of 1715.[81] It had most recently been activated in the Jacobite uprising of 1745, when the Scotch rebels marched down that same road. This was in fact the last time the beacon was ever used for its intended purpose, and the Wordsworths' role in "the '45" was proudly recounted at family gatherings.[82] Such gatherings almost always contain hidden contests, and dead Grandfather Wordsworth's loyal heroism to Lowther and the king was complicated by live Grandfather Cookson's sympathy for the rebel cause. Old Mr. Cookson was not one to resist improving the occasion by addressing moralistic maxims to the son-in-law he disapproved of, or to the headstrong grandson who was giving his daughter so much worry. At every level, from violence in the family to violence in the state, and ambivalence about which side—or which grandfather—was right, the Penrith Beacon focused the historical and personal forces brought to bear on the young Wordsworth.

And where, to return to the feelings of the boy in that scene, were one's father's servants when one needed them? My father is a servant too, he may well have thought, of a terrifying master who embalmed his paramour's head. They hang wife killers, don't they? What do they do to parricides? The literal scene can never be recovered, for it is all conflated by imagination. The "long green ridge" might as well have been the wife's grave as the husband's. It is the words, letters, and names that fixate the boy, not the iron cage and bones, which are no longer present—though such sights were still common all over England, where "the amount of punishment by death was awful," and executed criminals were left to hang and rot as a spectacle of royal power.[83] And whose name was kept "fresh" there, his or hers? The names Thomas Parker, Thomas Nicholson, and Thomas Lancaster have all been proposed, along with the letters "TPM" (for "Thomas Parker Murdered").[84] What was being remembered, a heinous murder or an unjust execution? It may in truth be an ordinary sight, of husbands killing wives (and sometimes vice versa), but Wordsworth felt that the "colours *and the words*" needed to speak the meaning of this violence were, like the letters on the grave, "unknown to man."

The child Wordsworth was violent, moody, and melancholy. He was a paragon only of extremes—whether for good or evil, even his mother was in doubt. He loved nature mainly to destroy it, or to feel the thrill of his destructive impulses in contrast to his sister's tender sympathies. When his mother was near death, his busy and efficient father was too busy and efficient for his children's good. Dorothy was packed off to relatives in anticipation of the coming sad event, right after Christmas 1777.[85] After Ann Wordsworth's death in March 1778, John Wordsworth kept his four boys, aged ten, eight, six, and four, with him at Cockermouth for a while. But he "never recovered his former cheerfulness," William recalled, and was kept as busy as ever by his harsh taskmaster, who faced another important election in 1780. Deprived of what little maternal presence seven-year-old Dorothy might have provided, they trooped around awkwardly, a reproach to their father. Toward the end of 1778 it was clear they could not make a home at Cockermouth, and they were sent back to Penrith, where they were not welcome. So, at the awkward school-beginning time of Whitsuntide (May) 1779, William, just turned nine, and his older brother, Richard, were packed off to Hawkshead school by their grandfather, who shortly thereafter presented their father with "a very big bill."[86] They returned home to Cockermouth rarely, and after Christmas 1783 not at all. Even before John Wordsworth's death, these were melancholy vacations; Wordsworth more poignantly recalled throwing himself into his father's library rather than into his arms on these vacations. The boys' vacations, however much longed for, were often less enjoyable than their school days. But perhaps I judge John Wordsworth too harshly. Perhaps he sought rather to remove the boys from the unpleasantness surrounding his own unpopular reputation, in the house rightly regarded as a field headquarters for the ministry of fear emanating from Lowther Castle. Or perhaps, caught up himself in remaking his family's fortunes in those unsavory campaigns, he did not care.

THE VALE OF ESTHWAITE 2

Hawkshead and Colthouse
1779–1787

> Beloved Hawkshead . . . thy paths, thy shores
> And brooks, were like a dream of novelty
> To my half-infant mind . . . .
>
> (*1799*, i.261–63)

The village of Hawkshead, in the little Lancashire valley of Esthwaite, can well claim to be the heart of that imaginary country called "Wordsworthshire."[1] By far the largest number of famous passages describing Wordsworth's sublime experiences in nature derive from his years spent at the grammar school there, from May 1779 until October 1787, when he departed for Cambridge. But sublimity is, even more than beauty, in the eye of the beholder, and before admiring Hawkshead's imaginative reconstruction by the twenty-eight-year-old poet who wrote those passages, we should try to enter into the frame of mind of the nine-year-old who arrived there at Whitsuntide 1779.[2]

The dominant impression of Wordsworth's Hawkshead memories is one of boisterous release: the explosion into a new psychic space of an emptied-out sensibility. Motherless, practically fatherless, separated from all his siblings except the somber Richard, and with disapproving grandparents and antipathetic uncles, Wordsworth burst into the region, desperately attaching himself to its places and persons. His sense of himself at Hawkshead was so keen because, with his emotional and intellectual precociousness, he was entering a second childhood with the awareness that this would be all the childhood he was likely to have, and that he must make the most of it. It would be a bit nonplussing to hear any nine-year-old in full gallop stop to exclaim, "Gosh, it's great being a kid!" But this sudden and by no means entirely happy consciousness of himself *as* a child bulked large in the emotional baggage Wordsworth brought with him. There is plenty of evidence that other boys also had a wonderful time at Hawkshead school, but coming when and as he did, Wordsworth exploded into the vale of Esthwaite as if shot from an emotional cannon. And he was, we have seen, already a highly volatile projectile.

His special consciousness of himself as a child was closely connected to an awareness of himself in that place, markedly different from his later feeling at Cambridge, "that I was not for that hour / Nor for that place." Here, he definitely *was* for that hour and that place, and for all the neighboring places which soon entered into his consciousness: Colthouse, Coniston, Windermere, Furness, Grasmere, and many points in between. Wordsworth's Hawkshead years appear in retrospect as one long, nonstop career of boyish jaunts, climbs, rides, and races. To judge from *The Prelude*'s account, "one would say that because they were boys and happy they were all more or less poets."[3] For eight and a half years, around the clock, day and night, summer and winter, "from week to week, from month to month . . . the year span round / With giddy motion" (*1799,* ii.46–47). The active focus of Wordsworth's life during these years was less the school than the vale of Esthwaite itself, and the valleys, hills, and lakes around it, as far off the coast of the Irish Sea, twenty-five miles away. These passages in *The Prelude* are everybody's favorites, and Wordsworth knew how good they were, for he scattered them judiciously throughout the poem as thematic flashbacks, not limiting them to the first two books on "Childhood and School-time." If they were excerpted and arranged sequentially, they would read like a dream childhood in the Valley of Happy Boys. They are a fast-paced, nonstop narration of boyish larks and sports, up hill and down dale, pell-mell in every direction, on foot, on horseback, or in boats, in which every person—all boys, of course—seems to be moving full speed ahead, and the devil take the hindmost. They may be too good to be literally true, but their truth is in their imaginative power, and the release of his imagination into these recollections of boyhood is a very large part of what made Wordsworth the poet he is—a large part, that is, of his self-creation.

The general sense of energy is intensified by the fact that it was a lot of motion in a relatively small area: one hundred schoolboys sprung loose at intervals like so many puppies to range up and down a little valley less than three-quarters of a mile wide, most of which is occupied by Esthwaite Water itself. Their free time was similarly compressed, since they were in school eight or nine hours a day, from six or seven in the morning till five at night, with two hours for lunch. Saturday was also a partial school day, and Sunday required church attendance, so most activities were confined to the dawn and dusk hours, weekend afternoons, and the occasional holiday. On the other hand, there was little or no homework, time being set aside for it during school hours since candles for nighttime study were a luxury, and no very stringent rules about bedtime, at least for the older boys, especially those like the Wordsworths who boarded with indulgent local families.

For the next eight years, the boys' lives were effectively divided into spring and winter half years. John joined them in 1782 and Christopher in 1785, just before Richard left.[4] School took up "three divisions of the quartered year," and they went home only twice a year, for a month at Christmas and for six to eight weeks in the summer, from late June to late August. There was a shorter break at Easter, but no record of their ever leaving Hawkshead then, for the time did not merit the grudged expense, and besides they would miss the Easter Monday fair.[5] "Home," moreover, varied both geographically and emotionally. At Christmas, it was Cockermouth until 1783, when John Wordsworth died. After that they went to Whitehaven with their paternal uncle Richard and his large family of nine children, happy fruits of the love marriage that had caused him to be disinherited in favor of William's father. Summers were divided between Cockermouth and Penrith, but again only through 1783, and sometimes they stayed longer at or returned earlier to Hawkshead.[6]

For more than three-quarters of every year, they lived with old Ann Tyson and her husband, Hugh, a carpenter. Until late 1783—a decisive year in many ways—they lived in a house at the end of Vicarage Lane in the center of Hawkshead. After that they moved out to Green End Cottage in the tiny hamlet of Colthouse, a small collection of houses about half a mile east of Hawkshead along Sweet Willy Lane—a traditional name, not a tribute to its famous adopted son, who did not stimulate this kind of affection.[7] In these residences, and in Ann Tyson, they were extremely fortunate. About sixty of the schoolboys stayed in the headmaster's large house in town, near the school, but the rest stayed with individual families like the Tysons, who could use the money and didn't mind the bother.[8] Married in 1749, the Tysons had no children of their own. Ann had sold groceries and dry goods in a small way since 1759, but by 1779 she and Hugh were old folks (sixty-six and sixty-five, respectively), ready to take up the more domestic work of boarding schoolboys.[9] She boarded a few other boys after 1785, but starting with Richard and William, the Wordsworth boys were her main source of income for the better part of thirteen years, until Christopher departed for Cambridge in 1792.[10] John Wordsworth erred in parting Dorothy from her brothers for so long, but by luck or design he did well to keep his boys together as a group during all their school years, and in a family setting. In Ann Tyson they got a surrogate mother for Ann Wordsworth, and simultaneously a loving stand-in grandmother for the censorious Dorothy Crackanthorpe

Cookson. Although she was a simple, uneducated woman, Ann Tyson's importance to the boys is unmistakable in Wordsworth's tribute to his "grey-haired dame":

> With thoughts unfelt till now I saw her read
> Her bible on the Sunday afternoons,
> And loved the book when she had dropped asleep
> And made of it a pillow for her head.
>
> (IV.218–21)

For the better part of these eight years, Wordsworth's life was one great round of seasonal activities. In good weather, he fished, flew kites, and set traplines to snare woodcocks; both fish and birds brought a good price at market, augmenting their "little weekly stipend." (In fact, Ann Tyson's accounts show a healthy outlay for large cuts of meat.)[11] There was an enormous amount of what would now be called hiking or fell walking, but then it was only basic transportation. Rock and cliff climbing were undertaken not just for the fun of it but to find and destroy ravens' nest and eggs, since these large birds often destroyed young lambs. The bounty was four pence a bird, and Wordsworth recalled "bunches of unfledged ravens suspended in the churchyard" as trophies of the "adventurous destroyers."[12] During one of these excursions, in 1783, one of the local boys, John Benson, lost his nerve and became "crag-fast": frozen with terror and unable to move in any direction.[13] The older boys hurried down to find some adult workmen to rescue him, but one, the youngest of the group, stayed behind to enjoy the sublime possibilities of the situation:

> Oh, when I have hung
> Above the raven's nest, by knots of grass
> And half-inch fissures in the slippery rock
> But ill sustained, and almost, as it seemed,
> Suspended by the blast . . .
> . . . oh, at that time
> While on the perilous ridge I hung alone,
> With what strange utterance did the loud dry wind
> Blow through my ears; the sky seemed not a sky
> Of earth, and with what motion moved the clouds!
>
> (I.341–50)

Later in the fall there were expeditions to gather hazelnuts, again with a small economic incentive, but violent excitement was clearly the prime motivating power for Wordsworth: "Then up I rose, / And dragged to earth both branch and bough, with crash / And merciless ravage" ("Nutting," 43–45).

The excitement of these exploits was heightened both by competition and, not infrequently, by disobedience: stealing woodcocks from someone else's traps, or "borrowing" a boat for a nighttime joyride. In great contrast to the censorious Cooksons in Penrith, no one seems to have disciplined Wordsworth very much at all in Hawkshead, but at these special moments he himself supplied the missing authority, larger and more grave than any father or schoolmaster. After snatching "the bird / Which was the captive of another's toils," he felt "Low breathings coming after me . . . steps almost as silent as the turf they trod" (I.326–27, 330–32). Over on more distant Ullswater, hidden cliffs rose above the shore's horizon as he stroked a stolen boat farther out into the lake, and "the huge cliff . . . / With measured motion, like a living thing / Strode after me" (I.409–12).

In the winter there was ice-skating on Esthwaite Water, furious games of chase up and down the narrow length of the lake, "ignoring the summons" of the six o'clock church bell and the lighted cottage windows until they were thoroughly exhausted and ready to eat. Inside, the contests continued after supper, with games of whist or loo, and "Strife too humble to be named in verse": noughts-and-crosses, ticktacktoe.

As they got older, the boys branched farther afield, packing picnics and renting boats or horses for the day. They raced boats from the ferry-landing narrows at the middle of Windermere out to the little islands scattered there, inviting targets for boyish daring: Lady Holme, Hen Holme, Crow Holme, Longholme, and Ramp Holme. "In such a race, / So ended, disappointment could be none . . . / We rested in the shade, all pleased alike, / Conquered and conqueror" (II.65–69). Or, over to the west on quieter Coniston Water, they trolled the shore, confidently stopping to borrow butter and a chafing dish from the caretakers of the le Flemings' dilapidated Coniston Hall, so after they caught their trout they could eat it too. Still older, when they could command attention as sons of worthy gentlemen of the region, they would saunter into the old White Horse Inn at Windermere and spend the afternoon bowling on the back lawn, ordering up strawberries and cream for refreshment.

These activities, mainly from Book II of *The Prelude* and after 1783, are more adult, less crossed by the excitement of danger or disobedience. But in the best of them, the rides down to Furness Abbey on the coast and back along Morecambe Bay, Wordsworth admits their "sly subterfuge" upon "the good old innkeeper," "for the intended bound / Of the day's journey was too distant far / For any cautious man" (II.106–8). The reckless boys did not tell the innkeeper just how hard they would have to push their rented steeds to get them back within the appointed time: "With whip and spur we . . . flew / In uncouth race . . . / . . . down the valley . . . / In wantonness of heart . . . / We scampered homeward. . . . / Lighted by gleams of moonlight from the sea, / We beat with thundering hoofs the level sand" (II.122–44, passim).

One wonders what rules, if any, Ann or the school had for these boys. Though the boys were of higher social standing than she and her main source of income besides—ample warrant for spoiling them—she seems to have inspired lifelong respect as well as affectionate remembrance among her charges. The effect of such indulgence on Wordsworth's development can hardly be overestimated, when, after 1783, he began staying out almost all night, with a special partiality to nights of "storm and tempest" in which he later said he heard "the ghostly language of the ancient earth."

But all this activity was frequently cut short or crossed for him by moments of silence, solitude, and fear. He often emphasizes the speed of his exploits by a sudden sharp contrast, as when ice-skating he "glanced sideway" into one of Esthwaite's small bays, and "stopped short . . . reclining back upon my heels," as only an expert skater can. His visual illusion—"yet still the solitary cliffs / Wheeled by me"—is entirely accurate, for the upper body, head, and eyes are still experiencing a movement of perhaps twenty miles an hour, while the feet stand still. On this perceptual basis he builds a huge metaphorical leap: "as if the earth had rolled / With visible motion her diurnal round" (*1799,* i.179–82). On the wild horseback rides to Furness Abbey, the sound of their "thundering hoofs" was cut so sweetly by the song of a "single wren" when they lay resting, "that there *I could have made / My dwelling-place, and lived forever there,* / To hear such music." This contrast is particularly hyperbolic, since the boys were at that moment lying among tombs of "the cross-legged knight / And the stone abbot" in the damp shade of the "roofless walls" of the ruined abbey (*1799,* ii.120–30). Yet here, as at other moments on Coniston and above Grasmere, Wordsworth's perception of a beautiful or peaceful moment seems to have sunk down unimpeded onto his naked psyche, imprinting for later decipherment the idea that these places might supply what he most desperately lacked, a home.

At other moments, these silences deepened further, to death. His first picture of himself at Hawkshead, "in the very week / When I was first transplanted to thy vale" (actually it was the first month), catches him in perfect psychological focus,

> when thy paths, thy shores
> And brooks, were like a dream of novelty
> To my half-infant mind . . . .
>
> (*1799,* i.259–63)

But as he crossed one of the two or three "ear-shaped" peninsulas that bulge out from Esthwaite Water's smooth shores, a nightmare gradually unfolded before his mind, dreaming on the scene. With dusk coming on, he saw "distinctly on the opposite shore . . . a heap of garments."

Long I watched,
But no one owned them; meanwhile the calm lake
Grew dark, with all the shadows on its breast,
And now and then a fish up-leaping snapped
The breathless stillness.

(V.462–66)

Here the contrast came in reverse, as death rose up next day when men went out in boats to investigate the "plain tale" of those "unclaimed garments."

At length, the dead man, 'mid that beauteous scene
Of trees and hills and water, bolt upright
Rose with his ghastly face, a spectre shape—
Of terror even.

(V.470–73)

Revising these lines in 1805, Wordsworth credited his reading of the *Arabian Nights* and other fairy tales for not being too terrified by this scene in 1779, of which he was ostensibly the first eyewitness. But the fact that the drowned man was a schoolmaster in the nearby hamlet of Sawrey seems a reason at least as significant as his familiarity with fantasy literature for the incident's impressing itself on the motherless nine-year-old's memory.

Death's strongest impress on him in Hawkshead came with his father's death in 1783. But it came also in imaginations of his own death, like his fantasy of entombment in Furness Abbey. And his description of the deceased "Boy of Winander" is, as its manuscripts make clear, a description of himself. He and his friend William Raincock loved to blow "mimic hootings to the silent owls" roosting in the woods across the lake, "And they would shout / Across the watery vale, and shout again, / Responsive to his call." But sometimes the boy was frustrated by the owls' refusal to take the bait.

Then, sometimes, in that silence, while he hung
  Listening, a gentle shock of mild surprise
  Has carried far into his heart the voice
  Of mountain-torrents; or the visible scene
  Would enter unawares into his mind
  With all its solemn imagery, its rocks,
  Its woods, and that uncertain heaven received
  Into the bosom of the steady lake.

(18–25)

Nature entered into him, not vice versa. The smooth, calm "bosom" or "breast" of the lake in both episodes is pierced by, or calmly rebukes, violent human actions. That Wordsworth should present this boy as one of two twelve-year-olds at the school who actually did die of disease in 1782—when he himself was twelve—is his way of underwriting the significance of the experience with a kind of metaphysical shorthand.[14]

For biographical purposes, we can add back the names of the boys who were with Wordsworth when he experienced these things, and subtract the names of the metaphysical abstractions with which he peopled these scenes when he wrote about them (for example, "Wisdom and Spirit of the Universe"). Not because the former are truer than the latter, but because the latter did not have names for young Wordsworth, ca. 1780, except as conventional religious pieties. We may also be curious to know why the names of his friends dropped out of most of his accounts of his formative boyhood experiences.

There is no indication in the poetry or in his prose recollections that Wordsworth was particularly the leader in these exploits, but every indication that he was very much one of the group,[15] as he is very rarely elsewhere in his poetry. Who were these wild boys of Esthwaite? Wordsworth's friends and friendships pose an interesting question. Neither his appearance nor his manners were conventionally attractive, yet he always had good, supportive, often long-suffering friends. He was a serious-looking boy (some said "horse-faced"), who developed rapidly into a large-boned, strongly built young man, with a heavy mouth and a prominent nose.[16] His face in repose could appear tough and forbidding; when he laughed he sometimes looked even worse. But he was strong and healthy; for all his eight years at Hawkshead, there is no record in the accounts of his ever requiring a doctor or medicine. One early rumor has him fighting an older boy to protect his brother Christopher.[17] He later compared himself to a craggy mountain eminence; this was not merely poetic license or regional propaganda, but the closest resemblance to himself he could find in his chosen landscape. In Hawkshead, which had to come to terms with his fame, he was compared to Wetherlam, the high ridge of the Furness Fells "which stretches its impressive bulk across the Colthouse sky . . . known by all from afar but rarely climbed for pleasure except by visitors."[18]

But unlike the mountain, he was restless. We see this in his outdoor activities, we see it in his conversation, and we see it affecting his friends. He was even restless in his sleep. Thomas Maude, one of a set of brothers who roomed with him at Colthouse, recalled "he was the uneasiest bedfellow I've ever had." If he couldn't sleep, he thought nothing of going out for a walk at one in the morning or even later.[19]

Wordsworth's friends were often very different from him, and this preference for difference began to emerge at Hawkshead. It suggests that Wordsworth's personality was neither as comforting nor as pompous as it is understood to be, or as it later became. He was, in a word, impressive. People were drawn to him, rarely he to them. He does not seem to have gone out of his way to appeal to anyone, unless he thought the person might do him some good. This is not to say that he did not care for other people's opinions, nor was he unfriendly. Indeed, he seems to have had a special genius, and need, for friendships, especially of men somewhat older than himself—understandable in a boy whose father died at the beginning of his crucial teenage years. But Wordsworth was a high-risk friend. One found oneself in impressive company, but it had its costs. During his young manhood, he had three close male friends, all of whom came to rue their association with him: John Raincock Fleming at Hawkshead, William Mathews at Cambridge, and Coleridge in Somerset. They all attached themselves (or were attached by Wordsworth) to his imaginative development, and they all fell afoul of it for one reason or another. There is no need to apportion blame: if Wordsworth disappointed them, perhaps they disappointed him too.

Our earliest glimpse of the boy Wordsworth, while he was still living in the village of Hawkshead, comes down to us with the veracity of eyewitness report. Philip Braithwaite (1764–1849) was a poor crippled boy who was thrown onto parish relief by the death of his father, a local hatter who had tried but failed to make his way in London, where Philip was born. A great-uncle took him into his blacksmithy, but soon cast him off again, and he was apprenticed to a farmer, where an accident made his deformed leg worse. In 1781, to help make him employable, he was allowed into the reading, writing, and arithmetic classes at the grammar school, even though they were for much younger boys, and he was boarded with Ann Tyson. He and Wordsworth shared a room and carved their names on the window seat:

PHIL^P BRAITHWAITE
1781
WM WORDSWORTH

Philip lived to eighty-five, and old people at the beginning of this century remembered talking to him when they were young. He said that while at the Tysons he never had much conversation with Richard Wordsworth, "but that William talked to him quite a lot, and was always asking him questions about one thing or another, anything in fact that he, Philip, happened to know something about because of his greater age and wider experience."[20] He added that though he saw little of John, he "thought perhaps he was the nicest of the Wordsworth boys he had known."

This picture of Wordsworth as a pesky questioner is preserved in a passage from *The Prelude* where Wordsworth recalls pumping Philip for particulars of his trip to London. He went there in 1780 or 1781 to establish his legal settlement so he would be entitled to parish relief at Hawkshead. Their exchange is typical of many other important instances of flawed communication in Wordsworth's poetry, where what is not said is more important than what is.

I well
Remember that among our flock of boys
Was one, a cripple from the birth, whom chance
Summoned from school to London—fortunate
And envied traveller—and when he returned,
After short absence, and I first set eyes
Upon his person, verily, though strange
The thing may seem, I was not wholly free
From disappointment to behold the same
Appearance, the same body, not to find
Some change, some beams of glory brought away
From that new region. Much I questioned him,
And every word he uttered, on my ears
Fell flatter than a cagèd parrot's note,
That answers unexpectedly awry,
And mocks the prompter's listening.

(VII.93–108)

So marvelous was Wordsworth's imaginative conception of London that he imagined a cripple might be cured just by going there. Philip Braithwaite was notably "queer" or touchy all his life about both his disability and his poverty, and he got irritated when eleven-year-old William went on very long in this vein. His irascibility fits the type and matches the edginess of some of Wordsworth's other boyfriends.

But this sense of an edge is notably missing in Wordsworth's best friend at school, John Fleming. Born John Raincock, he had his name changed by his parents in 1779 to honor his inheriting Rayrigg, a large estate on Windermere, from his mother's uncle. Two years older than Wordsworth, born and raised in Penrith, he left Hawkshead in 1785, proceeding duly to St. John's, Cambridge, where he graduated in 1789. He is memorialized in Wordsworth's first published volume, *An Evening Walk* (1793): "Friendship and Fleming are the same." He and William used to walk the five miles around the lake in the early morning, talking and memorizing school verses, especially from Thomson's *The Seasons* (1726), the most popular poem of the eighteenth century, whose subject was more or less the very action they were performing at such moments: enjoying the natural world as landscape scenery. Sometimes they worked up verse compositions of their own, quietly murmuring and musing together as they strolled along, a very intimate kind of communication. Wordsworth later made this strolling, outdoor method of composition his own, "booing and hawing" as he walked back and forth in his garden like a metrical shuttle, creating and memorizing his own verses for later dictation to his amanuenses at home. No one other than Coleridge or Dorothy—and Fleming—ever accompanied him in these exercises.

Fleming is also remembered, but not named, in *The Prelude*'s account of these walks:

> five miles
> Of pleasant wandering—happy time, more dear
> For this, that one was by my side, a friend
> Then passionately loved. With heart how full
> Will he peruse these lines, this page—perhaps
> A blank to other men—for many years
> Have since flowed in between us, and, our minds
> Both silent to each other, at this time
> We live as if those hours had never been.
> (*1799*, ii.380–88)

This is an odd message to send to an old, or former, friend, if contemplated for a published poem, but even odder if the friend is known to be dead (Fleming died in 1835). We can always wave off Wordsworth's oddities, in this case calling it merely a conventional detail of stylized regret for the lost joys of youth. We all have such long-lost friends. But how many do we remember for so long, *as* forgotten? Is Fleming only supposed to regret his own boyhood, or is he also to be reminded how long their minds have been "silent" to each other—that is, out of mental sympathy with each other? Not so many years had "flowed in between" them when these lines were written: ten, at most. Wordsworth and Fleming were subsequently at college together, yet their former school days are first recalled as being all the happier for Fleming's "passionately loved" presence, and then regretted as lost, like their friendship. "We live as if those hours had never been" is a powerful line. Set against "passionately loved," it suggest that something else is going on here, recrimination perhaps as much as regret. Mary Moorman rarely criticizes Wordsworth, but she does not disguise anomalies: Wordsworth and Fleming "formed a passionate friendship of which a mutual love of poetry was the basis, but, though in later life they were neighbours, Fleming living at Rayrigg and Wordsworth at Grasmere, intimacy did not continue."[21]

Though late in life Wordsworth recalled Fleming in a list of his former "*intimate* acquaintances" at college—all then dead[22]—Fleming probably became too conventional for Wordsworth's taste, stuck in the conventions of their youth (Thomson's landscape poetry), and was left behind. For they certainly did know each other all the rest of their lives. Fleming inherited the

Rayrigg estate from his maternal uncle—the last thing in the world Wordsworth could ever expect from his uncle Kit—returned to the Lakes after university, and married Jane Taylor, one of the heirs of the estates of William Braithwaite. From 1825 on, his son Fletcher was the Wordsworths' curate at Rydal Chapel, just a few steps down from Rydal Mount. Dorothy could be snide about his *"goody* sermons," which she thought mixed sincerity and obscurity in about equal parts.[23] Did Wordsworth hold a grudge, partly on principle and partly on personality, against his "passionately loved" school friend who lived the life that Wordsworth was supposed to have led, but didn't?

This view of the risks of a Wordsworth friendship is strengthened when we contrast Wordsworth's relations with John Fleming's brother, Fletcher Raincock (1769–1840), the "Fleck" of many a Hawkshead escapade, including the rescue of John Benson from the ravens' crags. Fletcher was the ringleader of Wordsworth's Hawkshead gang. He chatted up the Castlehow boys, the local semibandits, and delighted in school tricks against the masters, not being particularly afraid of punishments. He also went to Cambridge, distinguishing himself as second wrangler and fellow of Pembroke, and lived out an active legal and political career in the north, serving as the last recorder of Kendal (1818–40). He also acted as agent for the Lowther family at their Appleby elections.[24] He was remembered in Liverpool as "one of the most remarkable characters of his day" for his legal powers, his "gluttonous" reading, his habit of producing odd bits of information, his agreeably eccentric conversation, and his originality.[25] In short, he sounds about as different from his brother as can be—and very much the kind of person Wordsworth liked, though Wordsworth himself is never recalled in such affectionate detail. Fletcher Raincock even looked like Wordsworth, or worse: "He was a man with a very plain face and ungainly gait. On one occasion, in cross-examining a female witness who had used once or twice the then newly-coined word 'humbugging,' Mr. Raincock inquired what she meant by 'humbugging'? 'Whoi if oi war to ca' yer a handsome mon, that ud be humbugging.' "[26]

Another such eccentric high in Wordsworth's esteem was Robert Hodgson Greenwood (1768–1839), "the minstrel of our troop," in Wordsworth's phrase, or "t' lad wi' t' flute," in Ann Tyson's.[27] After an afternoon of bowling or boating, the boys sometimes put Greenwood on one of the small rocky islands near the Windermere ferry "and left him there, / And rowed off gently, while he blew his flute / Alone upon the rock" (II.174–76). This is another of those moments of precocious aestheticizing, like the walks with Fleming, which Charles Farish and his brother William, the school's star poets before Wordsworth, memorialized in *The Minstrels of Winandermere* (published 1811). Greenwood lived with Wordsworth at Ann Tyson's during his last year and a half there, and they both left for Cambridge from Hawkshead in October 1787. Like Fletcher Raincock, Greenwood as a man was known for his dry, eccentric humor. Wordsworth, writing to his new friend William Mathews in 1791, gives a picture of Greenwood's personality: "He is in Yorkshire with his Father, and writes in high spirits, his letter altogether irregular and fanciful. He seems to me to have much of Yorick in his disposition [i.e., the "Yorick" of Laurence Sterne, author of *Tristram Shandy*]; at least Yorick, if I am not mistaken, had a deal of the male mad-cap in him, but G. out-mad-caps him quite."[28] One would like to know what distinction Wordsworth was trying to make in calling him a "*male* mad-cap": it may be a collegiate code for homosexuality. The implications of such a suggestion are neither irresponsible nor implausible. Several young men attached themselves passionately to Wordsworth between 1787 and 1798, as did several young women, and some of both sexes had occasion to be disappointed by him.

Wordsworth first appeared in print in company with Greenwood. Both sent poems to the *European Magazine* which appeared in March 1787. Wordsworth's was a throbbing tribute to Helen Maria Williams, one of the most successful members of the popular school of Sensibility. It was signed "Axiologus," a Latin pun on his name (*axiom,* value or worth, + *logos,* word), and since their plan seems to have been to reveal themselves cleverly only to those in the know, Greenwood's submission was probably this one, thinly disguised for Hawkshead readers who knew his musical abilities.

"To a GENTLEMAN playing very ill on the FLUTE"
By Miss Kemble

To Israel's king when Jesse's son
Upon the harp did play,
With such a force he swept the strings
He drove the fiend away.

Tho' some may doubt, I hold it true,
Who thy discordance hear;
For if the Devil himself was nigh,
He'd run away for fear.[29]

Writing against himself in the persona of the famous actress Fanny Kemble was another instance of Greenwood's male madcappery.

More than a dozen other names can be associated with Wordsworth's years in Hawkshead and Colthouse, but these are the major significant ones. There was something a bit eccentric about his best friends, and we can infer that he had, or enjoyed, similar qualities himself. Wordsworth also knew and played with town boys in the neighborhood, like John Benson and "Tailor"

Tyson. In contrast to William's rough and ready bunch, Thomas Gawthorp was notably spoiled with large expenditures for coal, wine, and velvet. He dutifully followed the typical Hawkshead-Cambridge career of successive university fellowships and church rectorships which Wordsworth was supposed to follow but didn't.[30]

"Thee and thy grey huts, my darling vale"

The vale of Esthwaite was not as attractive in Wordsworth's time as it is today. People were then just beginning to look at nature like a picture, as "picturesque," and beginning to regard the Lakes as a place to enjoy their hard-earned leisure. Windermere, the region's largest and most accessible lake, had begun to develop a tourist and resort business, as had Grasmere, following Thomas Gray's discovery of "this little unsuspected Paradise" in 1757.[31] But they were both on the main north–south road, while Esthwaite was literally a backwater. We have learned to look at it with eyes made quiet by two centuries of applied Wordsworthianism, but the idyllic vista of the vale today was not the image it presented in 1780. This is especially true of the village, which today looks like a movie set for *Brigadoon,* with its well-preserved nooks and crannies, trim tearooms and souvenir shops. One half expects the residents to prance out singing and dancing in regional costumes. In fact, "a smart assembly room" was built for dances and other public assemblies in 1790, at the height of Hawkshead's prosperity, partly at the instigation of the "new people." Few realized that these signs of prosperity were among the last vestiges of its old resource market economy, and the first signs of a new economy based on touristic services and organized leisure.

But in 1779 life was different there, and much different from how it appears in *The Prelude.* "Nature" in Wordsworth's Hawkshead was mainly a resource for industry, especially the coal and armaments industries, not for tourism. Landowners around Hawkshead were felling and burning their trees on Furness Fells and in Grizedale Forest as fast as they could to make charcoal, for the huge Blackbarrow Foundry Company, established in 1711, or for its main competitor, the Newlands Mills Company, in Ulverston.[32] The main products of these companies were cannon and shot for the British navy, increasingly lucrative contracts as the eighteenth century wore on. The landowners, like James Lowther with his coal mines in West Cumberland, were themselves a new kind of entrepreneur, and often became shareholders in the foundries in exchange for the guaranteed sale of their coppice woods,[33] a controlled futures market.

Besides timbering, there was also slate quarrying, Coniston slate being one of the prime grades for this expanding construction market.[34] Wordsworth and some other Colthouse boarders once inflicted a strange revenge upon

"Old Slaty," a Quaker slate merchant who lived nearby and frequently complained about the boys' noisy antics. They would stand in a row and stare at him in total silence as he rode by, until one day they quite unnerved the old man. He stopped to talk, but they suddenly sprang to attention and saluted like soldiers, a clever if mean insult to the peaceable Quaker. He wheeled about and made as if to whip them, but then apologized for losing his friendly temper, and tried to recoup his shame by pointing out the moral differences in their situation, much to Wordsworth's disgust.[35]

Lumber, slate, and coal were, relatively speaking, new industries in the region, which had subsisted for centuries on wool. With the invention of the spinning jenny and other industrial improvements, the large wool factories in Kendal expanded rapidly, though no one foresaw how quickly a generation-long war with France and the simultaneous boom in American cotton would bring it all to an end. The war against the American colonists was very unpopular in Kendal because it interrupted the profitable trade in its specialty, the light woolen cloths, or frieze, known as Kendal cottons, which were much in demand in Virginia and Maryland.[36] Hawkshead was the main wool market in the southern part of the region, because the vale of Esthwaite, with easy access at its southern end to the ferry across Windermere, was the shortest and quickest route by which these raw materials could be extracted from the north, since there were no good ports on the coast near there: they went out to Kendal first, and then down to the Lancaster and Manchester mills. The ferry itself was no small rural curiosity, but a link as important to the region as any Suez or Panama Canal, and a profitable franchise worth a tidy thirty guineas a year.[37]

With all these labor-intensive industries and their many subsidiaries (cartage and hostelry, for example) came workers of all types and their families: miners, loggers, charcoal burners, saddlers, joiners, peddlers, and so on, in addition to the local sheepherders and stone and slate "wallers." Another kind of labor force was represented by the steady traffic of mostly sickly discharged veterans straggling down from Whitehaven and Workington, the walking wounded from the American war, and those ravaged by malaria and other tropical diseases in police actions against slave rebellions on British sugar plantations in the Caribbean.

Wordsworth and his friends talked to all these people working in or traveling through the valley. Wordsworth in particular entered into conversation with them, asking where they were from, what they did, and what had happened to them along the way. He is said to have made friends with people of all ages; he was a boy who "listened."[38] These experiences were the personal source of the most common situation or "plot" in Wordsworth's early poetry: a wayfaring observer, the poet figure, meets a traveling man or woman, usually poor, and asks how he or she came to be so. The Hawkshead boys were well placed for these kinds of encounters. They were boarders, away from home, and almost all sons of gentlemen or well-to-do tradesmen, who would feel no reserve, past a certain age, about accosting passing laborers and engaging them in conversation. Also, the number of local gentry in Esthwaite was very small, relative to the large number of boys at the school, so the boys were not often entertained by acquaintances of their parents' class. To use an American analogy, Wordsworth and his friends were Tom Sawyers playing at being Huck Finn, privileged even if—like Tom and William—orphaned. Most of Wordsworth's later accounts of this time, like Mark Twain's, concern the lower classes, in literature presented for the edification and entertainment of readers in the middle or gentry classes. Often he spoke in the persona of the frustrated or disappointed gentleman, a type he especially cultivated in Hawkshead.

He was in daily contact with old Hugh Tyson, who was a man of all work around the village. He went fishing at an early age with John Martin, a weaver, who took him on a five-mile jaunt over two ranges of fells to the river Duddon, and then carried him home piggyback much of the way, when a luckless day ended in a driving downpour.[39] He had a particularly wide acquaintance among the peddlers or packmen in the neighborhood. Most of them were Scots, and lived in Outgate, a collection of poor hovels a mile north of Hawkshead. But he knew at least two peddlers from the Ulverston end of their rounds, David Moore, "travelling merchant," and John Moor, "chapman" (both terms synonyms for peddler).[40] In various composites, they helped to model the character of "the venerable Armytage," the philosophical peddler in Wordsworth's first major narrative poem, "The Ruined Cottage" of 1797–98. The degree to which he was capable of identifying himself with such characters should not be underestimated. "Had I been born in a class which would have deprived me of what is called a liberal education, it is not unlikely that, being strong in body, I should have taken to a way of life such as that in which my Pedlar passed the greater part of his days. . . . I . . . freely acknowledge that the character I have represented in his person is chiefly an idea of what I fancied my own character might have become in his circumstances."[41] This may be wishful thinking, but it was a fantasy that gave strong motivation to his imagination.

The six or seven Hawkshead peddlers who contributed to the idealized portrait of Armytage were not so fortunate themselves, being known to posterity mainly through the disbursements made for their relief by the parish overseer of the poor. But others made it a point of lifetime pride that they "never once had a penny from the parish."[42] One of these was Thomas Wishert (or Ushart, or Usher), an ex-soldier, who did however lay several claims on behalf of the bastard children his unmarried daughter Sarah produced at intervals.[43] Such cases remind us that the rapid rise of the poor rate (the charge assigned to every parish by the Church of England for relief of indigent residents) was one of the decade's increasing alarms, until it burst out in riots in the mid-1790s. Wordsworth said Wishert singled him out "for my grave looks, too thoughtful for my years." What he seems to have wanted most from the peddlers was stories of their travels, Armytage's main stock in trade.

There is no record of Wordsworth's associating with the loggers and charcoal burners farther back in the hills. But among the "wallers" were two of the valley's day laborers, Tom and Frank Castlehow, "the Castlehow robbers," as they were melodramatized later in the nineteenth century.[44] These tough men were from a still-lower rung on the social ladder than peddlers. They did not plead for poor relief, but worked when they could and stole or otherwise helped themselves when they couldn't. They had hideouts of rude wattle construction scattered about the vale, as well as the hovels on Hawkshead Moor and Hawkshead High Cross where they lived with their extended families.[45] It was to one of the latter that a party of local authorities, including Mr. Varty, the grammar school writing master, came in August or September of 1784 to arrest Frank's son Jonathan—the very boy, though he was as big as a man, who had rescued "crag-fast" Johnny Benson. But as they approached he burst from the back door and took off toward the west, leading his pursuers on a magnificent chase for several miles. They finally caught up with him in Little Langdale, only to discover that "he" was his sister Ruth, "a strapping young woman two or three years younger than he was, and nearly as tall."[46] Jonathan had made good his escape while she decoyed his captors.

The schoolboys enjoyed the escapade out of loyalty to their onetime savior, and because it embarrassed their master. When the fall term began, they started an oral ballad-composing marathon on the incident, raising and lowering their voices with clever calculation so Mr. Varty would hear just the parts least complimentary to him. Bill Wordsworth started the verses out well, for he was just at that time beginning to show signs of becoming another one of the school's excellent verse writers, in a curriculum that regularly required it. But in this instance Fletcher Raincock and Ted Birkett outstripped him—to their grief, for they were the ones the Reverend Taylor caught and punished. Unfortunately no scrap remains of these verses, in which a typical incident of ballad tradition is instantly reproduced by "sophisticated" writers close to the characters, yet far enough removed by social standing to be able to treat it as entertainment. Something of William Taylor's wisdom as a teacher is indicated by the fact that part of his punishment was to make the boys write out their own verses in full. Something further is indicated about the school's social regimen and Taylor's authority by the fact that he forbade the boys ever to visit the Castlehows again, and that they apparently never did.[47]

The Castlehow boys remind us that the mountains of the Lake District still served in Wordsworth's youth the social function of mountains through all civilizations: as a refuge for bandits and other social outcasts. He knew some highwaymen named Weston and Gilbert who "used often to resort for concealment" to Old Brathay, near the head of Windermere, and recalled their knowledgeable talk with the Kendal saddlers about the best quality of leather for strong bridles and other "professional" riding needs.[48]

Out-of-the-way character types in Esthwaite more important to Wordsworth than outlaws were the men who had missed out on the eighteenth century's great leap onto the bandwagon of the rising middle class. These men had had good prospects but failed to realize them and retired to remote spots like Esthwaite to eke out the rest of their existence and rue their great expectations. They seem to have appealed to Wordsworth a good deal anyway, but after his father's death and his own subsequently disappointed expectations, they flowed back into his imagination with added force. Men like this usually have time on their hands and bitterness to spare. They are happy to find audiences of eager youngsters who are just rising onto the crest of their opportunities, the better to caution or cynically puncture their optimism. The most well known of these Esthwaite prototypes to survive in Wordsworth's poetry are the composite characters of "Matthew" in "The Two April Mornings" and "The Fountain," and the disappointed builder of the yew tree seat in one of the earliest-composed of the 1798 *Lyrical Ballads.* But there are others as well.

Three men melded into one for Wordsworth's Matthew poems: John Harrison (1709–1789?), a failed businessman turned local schoolmaster and tutor, Thomas Cowperthwaite (d. 1782), ironmonger, and John Gibson (1728–1800), a tipsy attorney. Each shared elements of Matthew's disappointed life story: rural retreat, an ironical, facetious temperament, expressed in song, doggerel verse, and exaggerated literary allusions—aided, in Gibson's case at least, by liquid high spirits.

Harrison, having "failed more than once in business," went off to Liverpool but came back to Hawkshead with three young children after his wife died, and "set up as a wool merchant, but the Kendal buyers were too smart for him, and soon had him out of business" again.[49] In 1746 his only daughter died, like Matthew's. He then set up a school and tutoring service, which, in a way that seems connected to the early deaths of his wife and daughter, specialized in women's education. First he took over the remnants of a school for village children that an ex–grammar school usher had run for thirty years, and kept it up, as "Mr. John," for the next thirty-four years, though he rarely earned enough to keep both himself and his pony comfortably.[50] The pony was important, not only for the fishing expeditions which were his chief recreation, and on which Wordsworth and other boys loved to accompany him (he let them ride the pony while he fished), but also for his tutoring. He held evening classes in different parts of the parish at different times of the year, from poor Outgate in the north to Far Sawrey in the south. His specialty was teaching young women and girls how to write, and "from about 1750 there was a notable increase in the proportion of Hawkshead brides who could sign their names."[51] Wordsworth wrote more poems (especially epitaphs) on his Matthew figure than he published, and one of these unpublished poems records this special aspect of "Mr. John's" tutelage:

> Ye little girls, ye loved his name,
> Come here and knit your gloves of yarn,
> Ye loved him better than your dame
> —The schoolmaster of Glencarn.*
>
> For though to many a wanton boy
> Did Matthew act a father's part,
> Ye tiny maids, *ye* were his joy,
> Ye were the favorites of his heart.
>
> Ye ruddy damsels past sixteen
> Weep now that Matthew's race is run
> He wrote your love-letters, I ween
> Ye kiss'd him when the work was done.
>
> Ye Brothers gone to towns remote,
> And ye upon the ocean tost,
> Ye many a good and pious thought
> And many a [*word lacking in MS*] have lost.
>
> (*PW,* 4:454)

The interweaving of details from John Harrison's life with those of the sons of John Wordsworth could hardly be tighter than in the last stanza: Richard was sent away to law clerking, first in Whitehaven and soon to London, and John apprenticed to the sea in his midteens. These biographical correspondences make me suspect that the "wanton boy" of line 5, who seems jealous of the schoolmaster's attention to girls, is young Wordsworth, in search as always of a father. If this is the case, we can hardly dismiss those "ruddy

*The Scotch place-name is one of Wordsworth's typical distancing devices; it associates the story with a location more renowned for legend and folklore, and also serves to deflect its autobiographical reference.

damsels past sixteen" as stock figures, for they are surely the same as the "frank-hearted maids of rocky Cumberland" (VI.13) with whom Wordsworth began dancing and flirting at about age sixteen, and among whom he cut a particular figure when he returned from Cambridge for his first summer vacation. If they kissed Matthew for writing their letters, one hopes they did at least as much for the letters' recipients. And who would the recipients be but the literate and literary boys from Hawkshead school? Ruddy shepherd boys and frank-hearted young wallers would not be very interested in billets-doux, even if they could read them, which was unlikely.

John Harrison was also noted for his democratical manners, his readiness to pass a pleasant word with anyone, of whatever social status. He and other less successful men associated with the village stimulated Wordsworth's imagination in the creation of Matthew, a complex creature of insight and irony, personal success and public failure, who utters one of the most revealingly self-critical lines in all of Wordsworth's romantic egotism: "My life has been approved, / And many love me; but by none / Am I enough beloved" ("The Fountain," 54–56).*

Thomas Cowperthwaite, the ironmonger, was one of the old men who on pleasant evenings sat on the benches in the Hawkshead churchyard, which rises steeply behind the grammar school, looking out across the valley. His gravestone, set against the same church wall, notes his "facetious" disposition. During his early years living in town, the boy Wordsworth often sat and talked with these men. Having fewer expectations for a career than Harrison or Gibson, Cowperthwaite had less obvious disappointments in life. But he was the actual rhyme maker of the three, and one quatrain attributed to him is about his failure to make his mark on life in that place.

> The last of my Name in this Conny Spot,
> That's what I'm destined to be;
> My Course it's near run, decided my Lot,
> And there's no one to rue it but me.[52]

This was a life lesson that Wordsworth took much to heart.

The third major Hawkshead ingredient in Wordsworth's Matthew character was "Little John" Gibson, an attorney well known to John Wordsworth

*Years later, in 1823, the Wordsworth and Harrison families were united when Wordsworth's niece Dorothy became the second wife of Benson Harrison, the son of Matthew Harrison, a relative of John Harrison's niece, who had been first her steward and later the major shareholder in a large conglomerate of timber and iron interests uniting her vast Grizedale Forest plantations with those of the Newlands foundries in Ulverston (T. W. Thompson, *Wordsworth's Hawkshead* (London: Oxford Univ. Press, 1970), 164–64, 216–17). Robert Woof notes that the Wordsworth and Harrison arms are impaled together from this marriage in the east window of the Ambleside parish church (ibid., 376).

from consultations about his customary rights and rents in the seigneury of Millom, fifteen miles down the road in Broughton-in-Furness. "Little John" was a lady's man like "Mr. John," but of another sort. His wife, the daughter of a Quaker preacher, was well along with child when they were married in 1758: "no uncommon thing in the district generally."[53] He had more "quips and pranks" than either Harrison or Cowperthwaite, and shared with them the sense of regret for the course of his life, expressed in the ambivalent terms of love and sorrow that fused these men together in Wordsworth's imagination. Both Harrison and Cowperthwaite disappeared from Wordsworth's life around the time his father died, which was also the time, at about age fourteen, that he began composing verses "from the impulse of my own mind."[54]

Gibson was an avid practical joker whose antics delighted generations of Hawkshead schoolboys. One of his best tricks was to prop a scarecrow up at a roadside gate on cloudy nights and then, being an excellent mimic, to greet passersby and hold them in conversation as long as he could, until they lost patience with what they took to be, variously, an old soldier, a wandering beggar, a drunk, or a village idiot. Thus Gibson's antics are comic anticipations of such well-known Wordsworth poems as the lines on the Discharged Veteran, "The Old Cumberland Beggar," "The Waggoner," and "The Idiot Boy."

A wandering soldier, Joseph Budworth, was once rescued from a quarry by the happy chance of Gibson's strolling by, roaring drunk. In his *Fortnight's Ramble to the Lakes* (1810), Budworth preserved specimens of Gibson's literary language which so tickled the schoolboys, mixing chivalric romances, the Bible, Shakespeare, and Spenser. Budworth hallooed up from the quarry and got this elaborate answer: "old Gibson will ever lend a hand to damsels in distress, or quarry-bound mortals. . . . beest thou a spirit of health, or goblin damn'd I will speak to thee." Then Gibson fell in the hole himself, protesting, "If I can't extricate you from durance vile, I'll share in it; . . . I am quite happy to meet you in regions of darkness; for, had it been day, drunken Gibson might have passed unnoticed; now he is the good Samaritan . . . ever happy to pour oil into other people's wounds, and wine into his own." Once they clambered out, Budworth invited Gibson for dinner, to which he replied, "As to that, Sir, I am at your service; and if I cannot eat with you, it will do your heart good to see me drink." So they staggered back to Hawkshead, where Gibson claimed his reward: " 'for grog is the liquor of life—the delight of a Hawkshead attorney.' "[55]

Budworth also captures the regret in Gibson's life in terms similar to those Wordsworth used for all these characters: "probably, had he lived in a city, where he would have met a reciprocity of intellectual communication, instead of an obscure village, such [drinking and pranking] might not have been his failing; he began his profession with fair prospects, and might have had as good practice as most in the country; but, as he said, 'I am buried in these mountains, and never wished to quit them, till I became too old and foolish to succeed any where.' "[56]

The most important to Wordsworth personally of the disappointed-gentleman types in his Esthwaite experience was William Braithwaite of Satterhow (no relation to Philip), one of many Hawkshead graduates who followed the preferred route to St. John's, Cambridge (B.A. 1776, M.A. 1780). He missed becoming a fellow by failing to take the mathematics tripos; he then took orders, but was not offered a living until he received two pluralities in the south in 1787, just as Wordsworth was preparing to leave for Cambridge. Braithwaite's frustrations can hardly *not* have been in Wordsworth's mind in the early 1790s when his uncles were urging him to take orders and promising to arrange church livings for him. Wordsworth considered him "a man of talent and learning." He is the original of the disaffected misanthrope of the "Lines, Left upon a Seat in a Yew-tree, which stands near the lake of Esthwaite, on a desolate part of the shore, commanding a beautiful prospect." Wordsworth probably met him around 1785, when he was thirty-two, in the deepest trough of his disappointments, and a well-known neighborhood melancholic. His yew tree seat looked out over the lake at Waterside, less than a mile south of Ann Tyson's cottage, close to the local poorhouse, along a bleak stretch of road supposed to be haunted by monstrous animals and the "Waterside Boggle," an old woman with glaring red lantern eyes. Braithwaite found this charming spot appropriate for brooding on the world's neglect of his talents, finding in its desolation "an emblem of his own unfruitful life." The spot was directly in the route of Wordsworth's and Fleming's favorite morning walk around the lake. Braithwaite was a man of the place, yet he was out of "place" because of expectations raised by his education, which had been disappointed: "descendant of a long line of local statesmen who was so untypical of his class, *at any rate at that time in his life.*"[57]

Braithwaite did not die of mournful melancholy, as the yew tree lines have it. He became quite active in local affairs after 1790, when he at last began receiving income from his two livings. He then dramatically rejected the bleak comforts of his vista on Esthwaite by renovating an elaborate two-story viewing tower on the hill between Esthwaite and Windermere, known as "the Station" (but he called it "Belle-View") overlooking the Windermere ferry—a shift from Gothic melancholy to Picturesque beauty we can also mark in Wordsworth's early poetry. Braithwaite also contributed more money to the construction of Hawkshead's "smart" new market house than anyone but the lords of the manor and two rich London merchants. But his bad luck finally caught up with him, and he died at forty-seven in 1800, just a year after taking possession of "the Station."*

Wordsworth never wrote a sequel to his "Lines on a Yew-tree seat" to tell the latter half of Braithwaite's story. But he was quite capable of capitalizing on the imaginative possibilities of "Belle-View," as in the smart-aleck trick he played on the Irish boy who assisted Bartholomew Purcel, the local gypsy conjuror and magician. He took the boy on a trek from Hawkshead over Claife Heights so as to come out exactly at the point where the view above the Ferry Inn would burst upon them with maximum impact—as it did, astonishing the boy. This "natural" surprise sprung on an agent of the commercial surprise trade suggests both intellectual precociousness and adolescent preciousness. But Braithwaite's two kinds of viewing stations remind us that a good deal of Wordsworth's preference for the "natural" was in fact a preference for one popular *style* of landscape over another.

William Braithwaite brings us near to the upper reaches of Esthwaite society, the local gentry who were Wordsworth's own social peers. He may have met Braithwaite at Belmount, the splendid new four-story country house resembling Wordsworth's Cockermouth town house, built in 1774 by the Reverend Reginald Brathwaite [*sic*], the vicar or stipendiary minister of Hawkshead from 1769 to 1809. This kind and jovial man, also of St. John's, Cambridge, exerted much good effort in the parish, "at a time when the ministration of the clergy was at its lowest ebb."[58] All over England, younger sons of gentry families were ordained simply so that they could collect church livings, as profitably as aristocrats pocketed boroughs. Reginald Brathwaite also held other livings, but unlike William Braithwaite he made his home and did his work in his principal one. One of his plurality livings was the post of prebendary of St. Cross in Llandaff Cathedral in Cardiff, which he had from his neighbor, Bishop Richard Watson of Calgarth Hall, about two miles due east of Belmount across Windermere Lake. This is one of several close associations between Watson, the leading Whig bishop in the House of Lords, and people Wordsworth knew well—John Fleming was another—that may have affected Wordsworth's decision to write his violently republican "Letter to the Bishop of Llandaff" in 1793.

Young William spent a good deal of time at Belmount, which he recalled fondly in later years.[59] Mrs. Brathwaite's daughter remembered Wordsworth as an "eager young boy," full of questions, just the impression we have of him in almost all his associations in the valley.[60] The Brathwaites' daughters and

*The mixture of melancholia and entrepreneurship in his disposition is given a last, poignant testimony in his purchase of a hearse for the parish in 1796. It was to be used free in all local funerals, but rented for five shillings "if the Corpse was carried outside the parish for burial."

their girlfriends had good reason to value presentable grammar school boys like the Wordsworth brothers, as we shall see.

At Belmount he often met and talked to Gilbert Crackenthorp [*sic*], not quite a relation but a member of the junior line of Grandmother Crackanthorpe's Newbiggin Hall family. This Crackenthorp was another, milder version of the disappointed talent that appealed to William. He had been headmaster of the Kendal grammar school until 1774, but retired early because his frank admiration of the Hawkshead school interfered with his own prospects. "There's no better school hereabouts, and no better Schoolmaster than James Peake," he cheerfully told friends who asked him about schools for their sons. Peake was the master in charge when Wordsworth arrived, and his high reputation was John Wordsworth's reason for choosing Hawkshead.[61] Gilbert Crackenthorp lacked ambition, but was a source of much conversation, and sometimes of small loans, to the Wordsworth boys, for he was well-off, being the owner (through his wife) of the White Hart Inn and Coffee House in Kendal, the regional center for newspapers and lending libraries. The high point of his life had come at age thirty, when he dared to preach before the assembled officers of the Young Pretender who attended his church during the invasion of 1745, when other Wordsworth kin were reacting in different ways.

In Gilbert Crackenthorp's leisured style of existence we enter into the class of "new" gentry who were beginning to populate the Lake District. To them the trees of the region were more a source of picturesque enjoyment than of profits from charcoal, though the two uses were by no means incompatible. Sometimes called "strangers" or "moderns," these folk were either local gentry or, increasingly from about 1780, summer people who found in the Lakes a more cultured form of leisure than the hunting, gaming, and drinking amusements of the average Squire Booby. Wordsworth by his age and class, and by the accident of his time and place of birth, was right on the edge of this social change. On the one hand, his father was the agent of one of the most ruthless of the land-exploiting aristocracy. Had he lived, John Wordsworth might have become a commercial success like Michael Knott, or a political one like John Garforth. Or, on the other hand, he might have employed his success in cultivating new leisure opportunities, like John Christian Curwen. In the event, his son the poet became a kind of ideological apologist for this newer sense of landscape, but in ways that associated it with the older socioeconomic organization of the region—that is, the communities of freeholding "statesmen," or "estatesmen." Wordsworth's treatment of them wavers unsteadily between penetrating insights into the human costs of economic displacement, and commodification of the locals for middle-class tourist consumption. These were the independent voters of Wordsworth's youth, but they were being increasingly forced off their holdings by the relentless enclosure movements of the eighteenth century. Enclosure favored larger holdings and more efficient land use, but it could also accommodate, as a sort of luxury by-product, the creation and maintenance of beautiful estates.

Often the visually most attractive land was the least economically useful. For example, the islands of Windermere were virtually useless for farming, grazing, or timbering, but made excellent locations for splendid vacation homes. The conflict between the old and new uses of the lake's resources is well captured in the description of a Windermere boating excursion in *An Excursion to the Lakes* (1774), a tourist guide that also served as a real estate prospectus:

> The vessel was provided with six brass cannon, mounted on swivels;—on the discharge of one of these pieces, the report was echoed from the opposite rocks, where by reverberation it seemed to roll from cliff to cliff, and return through every cave and valley; till the decreasing tumult died away upon the ear . . . . At intervals we were relieved from this entertainment . . . by the music of two French horns . . . . As we finished our repast, from a general discharge of the guns we were roused to new astonishment; for altho' we had heard with great surprise the former echoes, this exceeded them so much that it seemed incredible: for on every hand the sounds were reverberated and returned from side to side, so as to give us the semblance of that confusion and horrid uproar, which the falling of these stupendous rocks would occasion, if by some internal combustion they were rent to pieces, and hurled in to the Lake.[62]

This artificial re-creation of the apocalyptic Sublime, described like the destruction of the world, was paralleled at the milder Picturesque level by the introduction of elegant swans to the lake, in place of the hardier but less attractive native species. There is no record of the locals' reaction to such cannonades as Hutchinson records, but if we may judge from their reaction to the apparently innocuous swans, they didn't like it at all: the swans "were got rid of at the request of the farmers and proprietors [of fishing rights in the lake]."[63]

The high points of this new lifestyle were its "summer gaities": regattas, hunts, plays, elections of queens, and, above all, dances and balls. One summer renter active in them was William Wilberforce (b. 1759), MP from Hull and future opponent of slavery, who spent several summers from 1780 at Rayrigg,[64] the estate inherited by young John Fleming in 1779. He wrote to his mother, "Boating, riding, and continual parties at my own house and Sir Michael le Fleming's, fully occupied my time until I returned to London in the following autumn."[65] It is likely that Wordsworth met Wilberforce at many similar gatherings, for Wilberforce was the best friend of his kindlier Penrith uncle, William Cookson, and had helped Cookson to the living at Forncett, in Norfolk, that finally allowed him to marry.[66] Wordsworth later expected to get exactly this kind of help from Jack Robinson, and possibly from Wilberforce himself. Shared experiences of this sort helped form an immediate bond when they met again later as adults.

Wordsworth and the other Hawkshead boys eagerly joined in these regattas as keen competitors. But they were especially in demand for the dances. This resource of socially accomplished boys accounted for Hawkshead's "superiority" in young Maria Spedding's eyes, writing to the Reverend Brathwaite's stepdaughter Martha Irton at Belmount, because "so great a majority of Beaux can seldom be boasted of in this part of the world."[67] This was especially true outside the main summer season, when many more visitors flooded in from London and the south. The Wordsworth account books show sums being laid out from 1784 for dancing instruction for the boys from Mr. Mingay, who taught "the most fashionable Dances, now in Use at Court and the first Assemblies in Great Britain."[68]

Mingay covered the Lake District from Lancaster to Carlisle, but focused his activities around Hawkshead, where his wife was born. He was so much in demand that he opened a "Military Academy," a kind of finishing school for extracurricular accomplishments (dancing, music, and fencing, as well as French, accounting, and navigation) adjacent to the grammar school. If Wordsworth's memory is to be trusted, Mingay was his only instructor in French.[69] But he taught the boys to dance well, and Wordsworth was as skilled a dancer as he was a skater until late in life, thanks to his Hawkshead tuition. "Wordsworth dancing" sounds like an oxymoron, given his conventional image. But like skating it is a rhythmic activity well suited to a poet who developed a unique method of composing outdoors out loud, striding back and forth to the five-beat cadences of his own chanting. His account of these dances on his first summer home from Cambridge in 1788 shows that he had become one of Hawkshead's most accomplished "Beaux."

The ferry landing on Windermere was much frequented on dance nights, either to cross the lake to estates like Rayrigg or to get out to estates like the newly redone mansion of John Christian Curwen on Belle Isle, as Longholme had been renamed in the fashionable refurbishing of the region. Another old house of Curwen's on the shore of Windermere was similarly upgraded, from "Sandbeds" to "Belle Grange." Curwen was one of the area's leaders in timbering, charcoaling, and quarrying, and the moving force behind the enclosure of Claife Heights, the ridge above the ferry crossing, planting 30,000 larches there "by the desire of my respected friend Dr Watson Bishop of Llandaff,"[70] much to the dismay of William and Dorothy when they returned home to the Lake District.

This Christian Curwen connection can serve as an emblem to conclude our tour through Wordsworth's Hawkshead, for it connects back to his own family in ways that illuminate the complex texture of Lake District society out of which Wordsworth emerged and to which, with poetic and intellectual differentials, he returned. John Christian's father had been one of the most active political agents of the old duke of Somerset's struggles at Cockermouth against the encroachments of the Lowther interest.[71] The Curwen family was one of the new sources of opposition to Lowther's encroachments—which is to say they were competitors in business. Henry Curwen was the man who replaced Lowther as MP for Cumberland in the disputed election of 1768. John Christian (born 1756), following his father's footsteps, was the Curwens' agent and joined the family as an in-law when he married the heiress Isabella Curwen, taking her name as well as all her property, as his second wife in 1790—as Wordsworth's uncle Kit had opted for the more prestigious Crackanthorpe name over Cookson, and John Raincock for the name of Fleming when he inherited Rayrigg. Curwen was a staunch "Old" or "Country" Whig reformer, as Lowther had been originally, but he stayed with his party and principles after Lowther switched to Pitt and the proto-Tories in 1784.

John Christian's uncle was a Cockermouth attorney, and his two sons (that is, John Christian's cousins) played important roles in two late eighteenth-century legal actions, one small and petty, the other forever famous, against the injustices of entrenched established privilege. Edward Christian was the Wordsworth family's lawyer in their unsuccessful action against Lord Lowther. But his brother, Fletcher, Wordsworth's slightly older Cockermouth neighbor and Hawkshead schoolmate, became first mate of a ship called *Bounty,* under the infamous Captain Bligh.[72]

3

"WHILE WE WERE SCHOOLBOYS"

Hawkshead Education and Reading

> a scanty record is deduced
> Of what I owed to books in early life;
> *Their later influence yet remains untold* . . . .
> (V.630–32; italics added)

In Wordsworth's Hawkshead, the boys always seem to be running, never reading; it's hard to find the school in the midst of all this activity. The first two books of *The Prelude* both have "School-Time" in their titles, but there is not a line in them describing school activity: no masters, no subjects, no punishments, no tedium, nothing. As far as they tell it, Wordsworth's Hawkshead curriculum was entirely extracurricular. He was at an excellent school at the top of its form, but in *The Prelude* he had an interest in minimizing his debt to culture and society, relative to nature. But *The Prelude* is not literally his biography, and we have to hold ourselves at a distance from his romantic nature myth to recognize that most of his time in Hawkshead was in fact spent in school and that he was an excellent, very bookish student.

Scholars charmed by the energy of Books I and II of *The Prelude* have speculated that Hawkshead grammar school's educational philosophy was influenced by the theories of Rousseau, stressing children's natural innocence.[1] This we may very much doubt. Wordsworth's *description* of it was indeed influenced by his admiration for the more optimistic parts of Rousseau's pedagogical theory. But the academic discipline at Hawkshead grammar school was hard old-fashioned classicism, combined with hard new-fashioned mathematics, and the value of the boys' freedom out of class was more accidental than philosophically inspired. Much of the time the school had the appearance of a library: one hundred boys and four or five masters working in a building not much larger than a comfortable two-story house, with two large rooms on each floor. Reading and study took place in the library on the upper floor; lessons and recitations were done on the ground floor.

Founded in 1585 by Edwin Sandys, archbishop of York, who was born at Esthwaite Hall, the school was one of about four hundred grammar schools in Great Britain to which the gentry and well-to-do merchants could send their sons; sons of the very rich were still tutored at home.[2] It was also one of the best, both in its traditional, classical curriculum and in its modern, scientific one. The school's proximity to Scotland helped it participate in the "Northern Enlightenment," evident in its strong emphasis on mathematics. Then as now, schools that specialized in preparing students for admission to the most prestigious universities often provided a more rigorous education than the universities themselves. Hawkshead's success was prodigious, in placing students at Cambridge and helping them to succeed there. Sandys had gone to St. John's College, Cambridge, and so did many of the Hawkshead schoolboys, where they did very well indeed: four of the six senior wranglers at Cambridge between 1788 and 1793 came from Sandys's school.

There were great expectations behind John Wordsworth's expedient decision to send the Wordsworth boys to Hawkshead. Although founded as a charity school for local boys, it had by Wordsworth's time become a thriving establishment for the preparation of sons of the rising middle class. Only about 10 percent of its hundred students were still charity boys, and they were usually on one- or two-year rotating scholarships. The grammar school should not to be confused with the local village schools, which were start-and-stop, one-room affairs dealing in basic literacy and catering to children who were either too young (under ten), or not clever enough or rich enough to attend the grammar school.[3] It was a point of pride in the villagers' lives (such as Hugh Tyson's) to have been fortunate enough to spend a term or two in the privileged precincts of the grammar school. The school's endowment kept tuition down to a "cockpenny" per year, about a guinea and a half, derived from the ancient custom of awarding prize money to the student with the best fighting cock.[4] Room and board cost thirty to forty pounds per year on a national average, but charges for each of the Wordsworth boys' "Sabine fare" ran less, in the twenty-pound range.[5] Lawyers and estate agents like John Wordsworth, local squires, wool merchants from Kendal and slate traders from Coniston, and other gentry from as far away as Carlisle and even Edinburgh were happy to pay these charges for a school that could virtually assure their sons a place at Cambridge.[6]

This was the route Wordsworth was supposed to follow, and he had every intention of doing so. John Wordsworth's career plans for his sons continued to mold them even after his death: he succeeded with three of them, but William spoiled the family plan. Richard became a lawyer like his father, leaving school early to clerk with his Whitehaven uncles and cousins. John was slated for the sea, and dutifully left school at age fifteen for the East India Company, starting out in the Wordsworth "family bottom" sailing from Whitehaven. Christopher, the youngest, was the most successful of all, in a career that can be viewed as filial overcompensation along the path his older brother William was supposed to tread: B.A. Trinity in 1796 (tenth wrangler); fellow in 1798 until his marriage in 1804; then successive rectorships in Norfolk, Surrey, and Kent, with prestigious intervals as chaplain to the archbishop of Canterbury and the House of Commons; then back to Trinity as master in 1820 until his retirement in 1841, serving two elected terms as vice-chancellor of the university.[7] The social history of the Wordsworth family in the nineteenth century is a chapter in the story of the formation of England's intellectual aristocracy out of its educated middle class, and in this history it is Christopher and his sons and grandsons who are the success stories, not his rebellious older brother.

At Hawkshead, Wordsworth was supposed to begin his conventional success, and by all accounts he did so very well, in both the classical and the modern parts of the curriculum. One of his masters once left him alone in his office for a moment, looking at Newton's *Opticks;* he found him still poring over it an hour later, when he returned after a delay, and was astonished to hear the boy ask if he could take the book with him to read more.[8]

The literary curriculum was of course in Greek and Latin, included the standard authors (Anacreon, Homer, Ovid, Virgil), and moved smartly along from linguistic to literary training, as translating led to "imitating" the classics in both English and the original language, a popular genre throughout the eighteenth century. Wordsworth was quickly awakened from his dame-school slumbers by Mr. Shaw, one of the ushers, "who taught me more of Latin in a fortnight than I had learnt during two preceding years at the school of Cockermouth."[9] Translation was still a dominant literary genre; the mighty achievements of Dryden's Virgil (1697) and Pope's Homer (1715–25) remained unsurpassed for at least another century. The curriculum was arranged to take the boys up the ladder of genres from epigrams to lyrics to epistles and narratives, and finally to epics. Wordsworth expressed an early independence by preferring Ovid over Virgil. "Before I read Virgil I was so strongly attached to Ovid, whose Metamorphoses I read at school, that I was quite in a passion whenever I found him, in books of criticism, placed below Virgil [i.e., almost always]. As to Homer, I was never weary of travelling over the scenes through which he led me."[10] This was a mildly naughty predilection, for Ovid is the classical "nature poet" whose Just-So stories reveal natural forms as the result of men or women's attempt to escape from—or the consequences of their not escaping from—the lascivious embraces of the gods.

But he soon graduated to Virgil, and later in life began a project to translate the *Aeneid* which, had he completed it, might well have supplanted Dryden's.[11] Virgil marked the acme of the Latin curriculum, but his *Georgics* were more important than the *Aeneid* in eighteenth-century pedagogy and general culture.[12] These four long poems celebrating rural labor in the unsettled period following the Roman civil wars had an explicit ideological role in Neoclassical, Augustan England. They represented the classical ideal of rural republican virtue checking urban imperial excess, which Whig philosophers and pedagogues skillfully used to distance the country from the trauma of its own civil wars of 1642–60.

Thanks largely to his Hawkshead training, Wordsworth was a lifelong student and master of languages, in fact a formidable linguist. His knowledge of—and debts to—a variety of literary traditions is usually not appreciated, because it often suited his purposes to minimize such debts in the interest of promoting his views about "natural" imaginative creativity.

Wordsworth was not simply the beneficiary of large sociocultural educational trends, however. They had a human face in Hawkshead, and its name was William Taylor (1754–1786), schoolmaster from 1782 till his death, during Wordsworth's critically important twelfth through sixteenth year. There were three other masters during Wordsworth's years at the school, but none of them had anything like Taylor's impact on him. James Peake was master when he arrived, but had little responsibility for the younger boys. Edward Christian, though a family friend and legal defender, was master for less than a year (1781–82), and not much in residence. Thomas Bowman took over from Taylor in Wordsworth's final year. Bowman modestly admitted he taught Wordsworth more by the books he suggested to him than through lessons: "Tours and Travels . . . Histories and Biographies," George Sandys's *Travels in the East,* Ovid's *Metamorphoses,* Foxe's *Book of Martyrs,* Evelyn's *Forest Trees,* and many contemporary poets, such as Cowper and Burns "when they first came out" (1785 and 1786, respectively).[13]

The measure of Wordsworth's high esteem for Taylor is paradoxically indicated by his not saying a word about him in *The Prelude* until Book X, "Residence in France and the French Revolution." This chronological displacement juxtaposes his gentle, beloved schoolteacher to, of all people, the archfiend of revolutionary demonology, Maximilien Robespierre. Wordsworth first learned of Robespierre's death (July 28, 1794) in early August of 1794, when crossing Leven Sands during a summer visit to relatives on Morecambe Bay. A passing traveler told him the news, and Wordsworth in a flash associated the news with the fact that he had just come from visiting Taylor's grave at Cartmel Priory, directly behind him on the east side of the bay, with its inscription from Gray's "Elegy Written in a Country Church Yard." He also connected it with Hawkshead, which "lay, as I knew," slightly to the north, beneath some very impressively represented clouds:

> . . . clouds, and intermingled mountain-tops,
> In one inseparable glory clad—
> Creatures of one ethereal substance, met
> In consistory, like a diadem
> Or crown of burning seraphs, as they sit
> In the empyrean.
>
> (X.478–83)

In this elaborate Miltonic diction, the clouds are made to gather over Hawkshead like the crown of heaven over—in a word—God.[14] Wordsworth never backed away from representing his poetic calling in the highest rhetorical terms available to him: he means to suggest that his becoming a poet, thanks to Taylor, made his career a creative challenge to, and ultimately an imaginative victory over, the misplaced redemptive energies of Robespierre's Jacobins, who are duly represented as a consistory of fallen angels from Milton's Hell. The angels and devils comes from *Paradise Lost,* the landscape is Wordsworth's boyhood paradise, Taylor was his favorite teacher, and Gray was Taylor's favorite poet. By connecting Taylor to Robespierre, and Gray to Milton, and placing himself at the nexus of them all, Wordsworth suggests that Taylor helped him to be the next English Milton.

Taylor's influence on the young Wordsworth was underscored with the psychological authority of a deathbed commission. Before he died, in June 1786, Taylor called in some of the older boys to say a last good-bye: "He . . . said to me, 'My head will soon lie low.' " Wordsworth never forgot the encouragement Taylor gave him: "[he] Would have loved me, as one not destitute / Of promise, nor belying the kind hope / Which he had formed when I at his command / Began to spin, at first, my toilsome songs" (X.510–14). Taylor had chosen four modest lines from Gray's "Elegy" for his tombstone, praying for repose in "the bosom of his Father and his God." Wordsworth does not mention which lines of Gray *he* had in mind, but we can easily find them by cross-referencing the allusions in his *homage* to Taylor, for they are the heart of the lesson Gray teaches from "the short and simple annals of the poor": "Some mute inglorious Milton here may rest, / Some Cromwell guiltless of his country's blood."*

William Taylor was a Cambridge graduate, and like many eighteenth-century schoolmaster-vicars combined his duties with a cultured love of literature, construing his profession as essentially "literary," though he was also well trained in mathematics. He had excellent ideas about literary instruc-

*Curiously, Gray's "Elegy" was also the favorite poem of Wordsworth's nemesis James Lowther, who could quote from it at length and who appreciated it in terms not unlike Wordsworth's coming revolution in English poetics: "I love elevated thoughts, but I'd like 'em as well when plainly expressed" (Hugh Owen, *The Lowther Family* [Chichester: Phillimore, 1990], 300).

tion. He set his young charges to imitate not only the best classical models but also a wide range of contemporary literary ones: not just Homer, Ovid, and Virgil but also Gray, Collins, Goldsmith, and other midcentury poets of "Sensibility," who reacted sentimentally against the urbane, satiric verse of Dryden, Pope, and Swift. These poets, many of whom lived unhappy, reclusive lives and wrote poems to match, raised a self-consciously minor poetry to the status of a major genre, or at least a very popular one, in the half century between the deaths of Pope and Swift in 1744 and 1745 and the publication of *Lyrical Ballads* by Wordsworth and Coleridge in 1800. They were the poets of an age of prose. To be sure, the Hawkshead boys read Shakespeare, Spenser, Milton, Dryden, and Pope as well. But Taylor gave his best boys extraordinary opportunities to read poetry by living writers. He and other masters or ushers lent the boys their own books and encouraged them to join book clubs and lending libraries in Kendal and Penrith, where the boys read Gray, Goldsmith, Thomson, Collins, Cowper, Burns, Akenside, Williams, Shenstone, the Warton brothers (Joseph and Thomas), Percy, Smith, Beattie, Chatterton, Crabbe, Langhorne, Carter, and Aikin. Few twentieth-century readers who are not literary specialists will get very far in that list before starting to inquire, *"Who?"* It was as if students born in 1970 were, as they finished high school in the late 1980s, reading not only Eliot, Yeats, Pound, Stevens, and Frost but also Larkin, MacNeice, Hughes, Harrison, Muldoon, and Heaney—or, in the United States, Lowell, Sexton, Wright, Rich, Nemerov, and Levine.

These long roll calls give the lie to Wordsworth's disingenuous claim in 1791 to William Mathews, one of his best college friends, who had asked him for some contemporary reading suggestions: "God knows my incursions into the fields of modern literature, excepting in our own language three volumes of *Tristram Shandy,* and two or three papers of the *Spectator,* half subdued—are absolutely nothing."[15] The facts are far different.[16]

The range and energy of Wordsworth's early reading, both in and out of school, is revealed in two quite different accounts of it. In the *Memoirs,* his nephew reported that "the Poet's father set him very early to learn portions of the works of the best English poets by heart, so that at an early age he could repeat large portions of Shakespeare, Milton, and Spenser."[17] This sounds right; it fits with what we see elsewhere of Wordsworth's linguistic precocity. But in his "Autobiographical Memoranda," the poet himself says this: "Of my earliest days at school I have little to say, but that they were very happy ones, chiefly because I was left at liberty, then and in the vacations, to read whatever I liked. For example, I read all Fielding's works, Don Quixote, Gil Blas, and any part of Swift that I liked, Gulliver's Travels and the Tale of a Tub, being both much to my taste."[18] This also sounds true, but very different from the other statement.

The first comment shows Wordsworth's literary precociousness, how he was trained by his father from a very early age to succeed in a certain professional line—not that of meagerly self-supporting poet, but the general arena of "literary" accomplishments associated with university fellowships, lucrative positions in great men's houses (tutor, chaplain, or secretary), comfortable church livings, or, at the bottom of this professional line, schoolmastering. This is the kind of training William Taylor had had, that Christopher Wordsworth would have, and that many of the poets of Sensibility used as the basis for their amateur standing in the arts. A clear performance ethic was at work in the boy's being "set" to "learn portions" of the "best," and to "repeat large portions" from memory. This is not all bad, as we know from the nearly contemporaneous example of Mozart's father's severe regimen for his son.

But, set against this rigorous standard for high achievement, the feeling of release and enthusiasm in the second quotation is notable: "happy . . . at liberty . . . to read whatever books I liked." It sounds like the book-reading equivalent of his breakneck horseback rides. This description confirms the educational romanticism which Wordsworth celebrated in Book V ("Books") of *The Prelude* and exemplified with apparently innocuous fairy tales, *The Arabian Nights,* Jack the Giant Killer, Robin Hood, and "Sabra in the forest with St. George." But his enthusiasm for the raffish, amoral picaresque novels in his second list was based on his personal inclination toward their very similar heroes and plots. Like their fairy-tale counterparts, they are all underdogs who become rescuing heroes: precisely the deep-structure plot of *The Prelude.* They are all stories of young men at large, on the road, alone, seeking their fortune. They are orphans, foundlings, or other family castoffs—Tom Jones, Joseph Andrews, and Gil Blas—or inspired, half-crazed wanderers moving through worlds of imagined wonderment: Don Quixote, Lemuel Gulliver, and Sterne's "Yorick." They are all "road novels" in the way that much of Wordsworth's life from 1790 to 1800 will be a "road" experience, and like his poems of the same period. Some of them are tours that unravel, trailing off into quests for life directions. Their young hero is seeking his fortune but also seeking to "find himself," and trying to understand the people he meets along the way—who, by virtue of their also being out on the road, are frequently poor and lost themselves.

The story of Tom Jones the foundling, who is revealed to be a gentleman's son and thus eligible to claim the hand of the beautiful heiress, Sophia Western, played as lively in Wordsworth's youthful imagination as it did for many other hopeful, up-and-coming young Englishmen, making it one of the first best-sellers in the dawning age of the novel. But the influence of Alain-René Lesage's *Gil Blas of Santillane* has been entirely neglected by Wordsworth scholars. Lesage's rambling novel, beautifully translated by Smollett in 1749, delighted Wordsworth when his father purchased its four-volume edition on December 27, 1781.[19] It was an interesting gift to set before an eleven-year-old son. Gil Blas is sent off by his poor father to be educated by his clerical uncle, who turns out to be a fake, who turns Gil over to an increasingly dubious set of tutors, until he sets out to complete his education at Salamanca. He reaches it only after hundreds of pages of adventures, captures, escapes, and seductions, by the end of which he has become a practiced gigolo, go-between, and double agent. Like the works of Cervantes, Fielding, and Swift, *Gil Blas* has a much larger element of sexual adventure and misadventure than we are used to associating with Wordsworthian delight. (It also uses the word "madcap" in contexts suggesting homosexuality, reminding us of Wordsworth's fond reference to Robert Greenwood as a "male mad-cap.")[20]

All of these heroes are more seduced than seducing, but none is excessively moral. They all skirt deliciously close to total ruin, but they triumph by gaining the goal—financial independence—which made them so popular with their rapidly expanding audience of middle-class readers. As cautionary tales, they were the radical alternative, or therapeutic detour, to the route from respectable family to proper school to best university to quasi-independent profession which was so assiduously mapped out by Wordsworth's elders. They were precisely about what promising young men should *not* do, which is why they were so popular. Young Wordsworth's life until he was well past thirty must often have looked to his guardians like the self-indulgent acting out of a picaresque novel.

But Wordsworth's future course of development is best charted through his Hawkshead reading in contemporary poetry. Even if he did not read the complete works of all the poets listed above, it is still a remarkable range, and anticipates much of his later achievement. Hour for hour, book reading took up as much of his time as ice-skating, bird nesting, horseback riding, and boat racing. Just as he knew Philip Braithwaite, John Gibson, and the Castlehow boys, so too he knew and "conversed" with Helen Maria Williams, Joseph Warton, James Thomson, and many others, and the traces of *these* boyish acquaintances can be followed in the textures of his work with as much confidence as his references to boyhood games and sports in Hawkshead. Even when Wordsworth wandered at night, or when he and his friends played at minstrelsy, they were not "just being boys"; they were trying on ready-to-wear cultural fashions.

A common understanding of the influence of contemporary eighteenth-century poets on Wordsworth's youthful development simply takes him at his word in the preface to *Lyrical Ballads* and grants him high cultural status as a wholly original Romantic poet. A somewhat more sophisticated approach allows that he was indeed influenced in his youth by the "poetic diction" of his Sensibility predecessors, but asserts that he recognized the error of his ways and created the new poetry of ordinary language for which he is deservedly famous, "a man speaking to men." A still more comprehensive view recognizes not only that these poets influenced his immature juvenile verse but that their signatures can be traced even in the revolutionary work of Wordsworth's first maturity, *whose novelty is presented by Wordsworth as if it rejected the habits of thought, diction, and imagery characteristic of the poetry of Sensibility.* This "later influence" has indeed, for the most part, "yet remain[ed] untold," as Wordsworth plainly admitted in his discussion of his early reading. In his notes to his poems he was not forthcoming about these influences, usually associating the poems with their time and place of composition but saying little or nothing about their literary debts. There is nothing unusual or reprehensible about this: Wordsworth is not required to be the scholar of his own work. But when time and place and local inspiration are wholly substituted for other literary influences, we have not learned all we should about the process of Wordsworth's self-creation.

The poetry of Sensibility permeates the great work of Wordsworth's first maturity: that of the Poet of *Lyrical Ballads.* Just a few salient examples will show strong influences in the themes and subjects of his poetry, as well as in settings, imagery, and other aspects of his style. Equally noteworthy in the Poet's self-creation, and even more frequently overlooked, are the ways in which the careers and "lifestyles" of these men and women provided models for Wordsworth to follow—and ultimately to reject. Not only what they wrote and how they wrote it, but also the career conditions these poets established in order to give themselves time to write, were matters of keen estimation for the young Wordsworth, especially the degrees to which these writers depended on the old system of patronage or on the emerging new one of marketplace capitalism. For both options the mighty figure of Samuel Johnson (d. 1784) was highly symbolic, from his famous rejection of Lord Chesterfield's patronage to his heroic endeavors in producing the first great English *Dictionary* virtually single-handed.

In varying degrees, the two dozen or so poets that Wordsworth read and imitated at Hawkshead all wrote elaborate descriptions of rural scenes of natural beauty, with intermittent scenes of Sublime terror and apostrophes to mytho-religious "Powers!" that were vaguely orthodox or Deistic. Their descriptions were marked by a new realism, or attention to detail, and an interest in describing common rural sights and objects (such as sunsets and peasants' cottages) that had not appeared much in English poetry before. They often expressed a desire for simplicity in life and expression, in language that was anything but. These elements were frequently cast into the theme of returning, sadder but wiser, to one's "native vales," sometimes motivated by loss of youth, love, and success in the larger world, and sometimes in revolted reaction against the high degree of corruption in urban centers, particularly London. In this outline of elements, we can already see the main outlines of Wordsworth's poetical career image.

The desire to go back to simple places with simple manners and sincere language was often extended historically into a broad program for recovering older, more genuine ways of living and speaking. Sometimes this focused on the era just before the national trauma of the civil war, the reign of Elizabeth I, but more often it tried to go "all the way" back, not only to the antique Greek and Roman patterns of England's Neoclassical myth, but to ancient or fictitious traditions of Welsh, Scottish, and generally Celtic bards and minstrels, as in Percy's *Reliques of Ancient English Poetry* (1765) and Beattie's *The Minstrel* (1770). The semifictions of James Macpherson's *Fragments of Ancient Poetry Collected in the Highlands of Scotland* (1760), "translated" from fragments of oral tradition about third-century Gaelic warrior-bards named Fingal and Ossian, and the brilliant if fraudulent imitations of Thomas Chatterton's "Rowley Poems" (1770), which he claimed to have recovered from fifteenth-century manuscripts in Bristol, were another part of this enthusiasm for native origins. So too were the recurring fads for more or less authentic "primitives" like Stephen Duck, called the Thresher Poet, Mary Collier, the Poetical Washerwoman, Ann Yearsley, the Bristol Milkmaid (a.k.a. Lactilla), and other farmer or plowboy poets from Robert Burns to John Clare.[21] It is not hard to associate much of Wordsworth's oeuvre with this broad program.

Sophisticated theorists of the simple life diffused it into fashionable intellectual life. Hugh Blair's *Critical Dissertation on the Poems of Ossian* (1763) and *Lectures on Rhetoric and Belles Lettres* (1783) are one source for the literary impact of these ideas on Wordsworth, as are the various literary essays and dissertations of Blair's fellow Scot James Beattie.[22] Thomas Warton's history of English literature (1774–81) is generally acknowledged to be the first systematic attempt to establish a *history* of English cultural artifacts—that is, poems—that had heretofore been taken for granted. By the time Wordsworth arrived at Hawkshead, despite ferocious rearguard actions by Johnson and his London circle against what they regarded as "the dangerous prevalence of imagination," such views were nearly official culture: Thomas Warton was named poet laureate in 1775.

The philosophical basis for the liberating value of emotion, against the rigidifying claims of reason, had long been reasserted, most notably by Anthony Ashley Cooper, the third earl of Shaftesbury (1671–1713). But a poet was wanting to make them good. Calls for original new bards went out regularly, but in poems whose melancholy tone undercut their effectiveness. They simply re-expressed the problem, and faded away from the challenge of a solution. Manifestos of imaginative freedom were written in the most regretful ways imaginable, enlivened with merely histrionic exclamation marks. Joseph Warton—for the movement was most often called "the school of Warton"—said forthrightly in the "Advertisement" to his *Odes on Various Subjects* (1746) that "the fashion of moralizing in verse has been carried too far" and that his poems were "an attempt to bring Poetry back into its right channel": more imaginative and descriptive, and less didactic. His first ode, "To Fancy," calls for "some chosen swain" who sounds very like Wordsworth's later estimation of himself as "a chosen Son": "Like light'ning, let his mighty verse / The bosom's inmost foldings pierce; / With native beauties win applause, / Beyond cold critic's studied laws." But Warton could not do it himself: he kept up his spirits with some odes on Liberty, on Health, and against Superstition, but gradually he turned away from his intellectual message toward his melancholy medium, with odes on Despair, Evening, Solitude, and "To a Lady Who Hates the Country." Similarly, William Collin's "Ode on the Poetical Character" (1746) starts strong but ends weak: England's poets were once inspired by godlike power, but "Heav'n, and *Fancy,* kindred Pow'rs, / Have now o'erturned th'inspiring Bow'rs."

Since Wordsworth is the poet of origins and originality par excellence, he has stimulated, from the beginning, a search for the Ur-point of his imagination, despite his sensible disclaimer:

> Who knows the individual hour in which
> His habits were first sown even as a seed,
> Who . . . shall point as with a wand, and say
> "This portion of the river of my mind
> Came from yon fountain"?
>
> (II.210–15)

But readers have never wearied of seeking that fountain, either in a place (Hawkshead?), a person (Ann Wordsworth?), or a poem—many poems. The search is appropriate, given the subject, but it is also endless, or rather beginning-less. As Wordsworth went on to say, in his self-protective advice to himself, it is a "Hard task to analyse a soul, in which . . . each most obvious and particular thought— . . . in the words of reason deeply weighed— / Hath no beginning" (II.232–37).

Hence it is fitting that "the first poem from which he remembered to have received great pleasure," an "Ode to Spring" attributed to Elizabeth Carter, should turn out not to be by her but by Lucy Aikin, known to contemporaries as Mrs. Anna Barbauld (1743–1825), a consistently successful author of poems for children who also enjoyed a wide adult readership.[23] Elizabeth Carter (1717–1806) owed her literary reputation to Samuel Johnson, based primarily on her translations of Epictetus. But her *Poems on Several Occasions*

(4th ed., 1789) contained many elegies and odes in the new Sentimental style, including several that anticipate its Romantic revival, such as her "Ode to Melancholy."

Carter and Barbauld were not typical of the poets who influenced Wordsworth at Hawkshead. Their combination of emotion with natural metaphors was still strongly framed by didactic abstractions, just the sort of thing Joseph Warton wanted to get away from. They were entirely appropriate for William Taylor to introduce into the Hawkshead schoolroom, but different from what he offered his older, more intelligent boys outside of class.

Yet Carter and Barbauld were typical of Wordsworth's earliest influences in another way: they were women. Wordsworth's share in the sector of the literary market sometimes called "women's writing" is notable, because his first productions were so conversant in this mode and because his poetic revolution depended in part on distinguishing what he was doing from its characteristic and highly successful productions: novels and poems of sentiment and romance. Though Wordsworth is, as Coleridge said, one of the most "masculine" of poets (referring to his ability to distance himself emotionally from his subjects), he like the other major Romantic writers sought to retain a "feminine" valuation of emotion that was supposed to be part of women writers' natural stock-in-trade.[24]

Much stronger feminine influences on the young Wordsworth's reading and writing were Charlotte Smith and Helen Maria Williams. Wordsworth's first published poem was addressed to Williams, and he went to France in 1791 with a letter of introduction to her from Smith, to whom he was distantly related by marriage: she was John Robinson's sister-in-law. From Helen Williams, Wordsworth got emotion and lots of it. "She wept" is the opening phrase of his "Sonnet on Seeing Miss Helen Maria Williams Weep at a Tale of Distress." Tears are shed on virtually every page of her *Poems* of 1786; one of her special effects was to represent tears as if falling on the very page we are reading. But Williams's locales and situations were of more lasting interest to Wordsworth than her language. Her "Edwin and Eltruda: A Legendary Tale" opens "where the pure Derwent's waters glide . . . [and] A castle rear'd its head"—that is, Cockermouth Castle, a neighborly setting for a fantastic love story of immediate adolescent interest to Wordsworth.

Extensive borrowings from Helen Williams's friend Charlotte Smith (1749–1806) have been found in many of Wordsworth's poems, especially from her *Elegiac Sonnets,* first published in 1784.[25] Wordsworth's own copy is inscribed, "St. John's Cambridge '89."[26] In 1833 he backhandedly acknowledged his debt to her in a note to his "Stanzas Suggested in a Steamboat off St. Bees' Head": "The form of the stanza in this poem, and something in the style of versification, are adopted from the 'St. Monica,' a poem of much beauty upon a monastic subject, by Charlotte Smith: a lady to whom English verse is under greater obligations than are likely to be either acknowledged or remembered. She wrote little, and that little unambitiously, but with true feeling for rural nature, at a time when nature was not much regarded by English poets; for in point of time her earlier writings preceded, I believe, those of Cowper and Burns."[27] This is really quite disingenuous, especially the vague "I believe," from the poet who had, by 1833, established in perpetuity the priority of *his* claims on true feelings for rural nature. For Smith's "earlier writings" also "preceded" those of Wordsworth, whose verse is therefore also "under greater obligation" to hers than he has "either acknowledged or remembered."

The dominant theme of her poems is the loss of youth and happiness, in contrast to the constant beauty of her beloved home district. She celebrates the river Aurun in much the same way that Wordsworth does the river Derwent, and the difference in quality between her expressions of this theme and his is moot. Smith: "Ah! hills beloved!—where once, a happy child, / Your beechen shades, 'your turf, your flowers among.' / I wove your bluebells into garlands wild, / And woke your echoes with my artless song" ("To the South Downs," ll.1–4). Wordsworth: "Fair scenes! with other eyes, than once, I gaze, / The ever-varying charm your round displays, / Than when, erewhile, I taught, 'a happy child,' / The echoes of your rocks my carols wild" (*An Evening Walk,* ll.17–20). Smith identifies her internal quotation (from Gray) in a note; but Wordsworth's quotation—of Smith (he removed the quotation marks in his final, 1849 edition)—was not attributed until 1982, with the deadpan scholarly comment "It seems clear that the . . . passage contains Wordsworth's first acknowledgment of his obligations to Charlotte Smith's poetry."[28] If this be acknowledgment, what constitutes neglect?

The male poets of Sensibility were stronger influences on Wordsworth, not because they were better poets, but because they enjoyed by right of cultural tradition precisely what the women poets lacked: careers whose patterns could be studied and imitated by young admirers.

James Thomson's "Winter" (1726) and *The Seasons* (1730) anticipated Joseph Warton's call to return poetry "into its right [descriptive] channel" by nearly a generation, and became one of the most popular poems in Europe. Thomson described the appearances of the seasons elaborately but not naturally. Or rather—since the question of what constitutes a "natural" description of natural phenomena is logically undecidable—he used very ornate diction to describe many ordinary natural occurrences. Samuel Johnson was still admiring *The Seasons* in the 1770s, though he criticized its "lack of method." But Wordsworth as a fourteen- to seventeen-year-old boy was more interested in images and actions than abstract ideas, and his debt to *The Seasons* was first incurred by adapting Thomson's descriptions directly to his Hawkshead activities.[29] For example, ice-skating: "they sweep / On sounding skates a thousand different ways / In circling poise swift as the wind along . . . / Their vigorous youth in bold contention wheel / The long resounding course" ("Winter," ll.768–70, 774–75). "I wheeled about / Proud and exulting, like an untired horse / That cares not for its home. All shod with steel / We hissed along the polished ice in games / Confederate, imitative of the chace" (*Prelude* I.458–62). Or nutting, where Wordsworth picked up Thomson's romantic, idyllic swains and virgins—

> Ye swains, now hasten to the hazel bank . . .
> In close array
> Fit for the thickets and the tangling shrub,
> Ye virgins, come . . .
> . . . the clustering nuts for you
> The lover finds amid the secret shade;
> And, where they burnish on the topmost bough,
> With active vigour crashes down the tree . . . .
> ("Autumn," ll.611ff.)

—and transferred their emotions to his own sexual intercourse with the natural scene:

> . . . the hazels rose
> Tall and erect, with tempting clusters hung,
> A virgin scene!—A little while I stood,
> Breathing with such suppression of the heart
> As joy delights in; and, with wise restraint
> Voluptuous, fearless of a rival, eyed
> The banquet . . . .
> Then up I rose,
> And dragged to earth both branch and bough, with crash
> And merciless ravage . . . .
> ("Nutting," 19–25, 43–45)

Where Thomson's "shepherd stalks gigantic" through the fog ("Autumn," 727), Wordsworth's follows him, "In size a giant, stalking through the fog" (VIII.401).[30] When Thomson's "western sun withdraws the darkened day" ("Autumn," 1082), Wordsworth's "western clouds a deepening gloom display."[31]

At this point we may simply feel we have reached the limits of what sixty years of stylized descriptive language can do with sunsets. But Thomson's introduction to "Autumn" is so like Wordsworth's in "The Ruined Cottage" that it's clear his early reading of Thomson went far beyond sharing common literary conventions. " 'Tis raging noon; and, vertical, the Sun / Darts on the head direct his forceful rays. / O'er heaven and earth, far as the ranging eye / Can sweep, a dazzling deluge reigns; and all / From pole to pole is undistinguished blaze" ("Autumn," 432–36). Here is Wordsworth's similar scene: " 'Twas Summer, and the sun was mounted high, / Along the south the uplands feebly glared / Through a pale steam, and all the northern downs / In clearer air ascending shewed far off / Their surfaces on which the shadows lay / Of many clouds far as the sight could reach" ("The Ruined Cottage," 1–6). These close verbal parallels continue for nearly fifty lines. The story that Wordsworth proceeds to tell in this setting shows great advances upon Thomson, but the close similarity of the two passages indicates that Wordsworth's advance depends upon Thomson's text as much as—if not more than—the observations of landscapes and poverty in Dorset to which Wordsworth attributed his descriptions: "All that relates to Margaret and the ruined cottage, etc., was taken from observations made in the South West of England."[32]

Thomson was a precursor of the new school, and, as a Scotsman who succeeded in London (thanks to Pope's patronage), he also anticipated the frequency with which practitioners of the new descriptive poetry hailed from the north. Thomas Percy, James Beattie, and Robert Burns were other authors in this northern constellation whom Wordsworth read toward the end of his Hawkshead years. Each in his own way called for a national cultural revival to rise from approximately the region where Wordsworth lived, and each located the source of a new imaginative power in a romantically historicized "north countrie" setting, peopled by simple folk following rural pursuits far from urban corruption, and speaking a native dialect.

Thomas Percy (1729–1811) changed his name from Piercy when he took up his first parish, in Northampton, after his M.A. from Oxford. Although born a grocer's son in Shropshire, he associated himself with the Percys of the north for both cultural and practical reasons; he eventually became chaplain and secretary to the duke of Northumberland.[33] He dedicated his famous *Reliques of Ancient English Poetry* (1765) to the countess of Northumberland, a well-known "romantic" diarist, who lived near his parish. His career as a literary priest, like many of these authors' lives, was another influence on Wordsworth, who was intended for the same profession and who knew these writers' lives well from the biographical notices and memoirs which prefaced their works.

Percy's essay "The Ancient English Minstrels" stimulated young Wordsworth's developing sense of himself as a poet. It stresses the northern associations of minstrelsy—signifying Scotland and all of England north of the Humber. "There is hardly an ancient Ballad or Romance, wherein a Minstrel or Harper appears, but he is characterized by way of eminence to have been 'of the North Countrie': and indeed the prevalence of the Northern dialect in such kind of poems, shews that this representation is real."[34] Whatever the Welsh or the Irish may have thought of this, such a nearby geographical identification enthused the self-conscious "Minstrels of Winandermere," Charles and John Farish, Robert Greenwood, and William Wordsworth. Many of the ballads have local settings, like "The Nut-Brown Maid," a popular favorite, who is sorely tested by her lover, "a squyer of low degre," but finally taken home in triumph "to Westmarlande, / Which is myne herytage."

As in *Lyrical Ballads,* there is a series of Mad Songs in the *Reliques,* though Percy notes this was more of a southern specialty: "the English have more songs and ballads on the subject than any of their neighbors." One of these, "The Frantic Lady," has very close parallels to Wordsworth's "The Mad Mother."[35] Wordsworth's poem is also indebted to Percy's "Lady Bothwell's Lament" for its question-and-answer dialogue between mother and her baby. Percy's Frantic Lady was mad for love, but not evidently a mother, whereas his Lady Bothwell is not mad but has a baby, her husband having divorced her to marry Mary, Queen of Scots: "Balow, my babe, ly stil and sleipe! / It grieves me fair to see thee weipe: / If thou be silent, Ise be glad, / Thy maining maks my heart ful sad." Wordsworth: "Sweet babe! they say that I am mad, / But nay, my heart is far too glad; / And I am happy when I sing / Full many a sad and doleful thing." Wordsworth brilliantly combined the two themes of motherhood and madness, creating a dangerous instability in his speaker that his two models individually lack. But his only note to the poem shifts the debt for its inspiration from literature to life: "Alfoxden, 1798. The subject was reported to me by a Lady of Bristol who had seen the poor creature." Percy's two Ladies, Frantic and Bothwell, must share in the credit given to this Bristol Lady, if indeed she existed.

Within five years Percy's call for a modern revival of old minstrelsy was taken up by his countryman James Beattie. The first version of *The Minstrel* (1770) was so successful that a second installment was called for; Books I and II were published together in 1774. Like Percy, Langhorne, Crabbe, and others in this group—including Wordsworth—Beattie came of poor but respectable professional gentry background. But without benefit of a university education and contacts, he achieved his independence by stitching together schoolmastering jobs and low-level church appointments. He had made a stout defense of Scotland's honor against Charles Churchill's hilarious attack, in *The Progress of Famine* (1763), which put its finger exactly on the way these "rude" bards were condescendingly adopted by London:

Thence simple bards, by simple prudence taught,
To this *wise* town by simple patrons brought,
In simple manner utter simple lays,
And take, with simple pensions, simple praise.

Beattie's *Minstrel* was well received by the conservative old literary lions in London, as well as by the young literary cubs in Hawkshead. Wordsworth and his friends adopted the style and manners of this ersatz chivalric minstrelsy, in Charles Farish's *The Minstrels of Winandermere* and in the boys' picturesque placing of Greenwood, "the minstrel of our group," on the Windermere "holmes" for relaxing, pseudo-sophisticated sunset concerts. The Hawkshead boys aped the mannerisms of Beattie's poem with a devotion akin to that of late twentieth-century teenagers adopting the dress, style, speech, and mannerisms of contemporary rock stars, and their youthful minstrelsy on the lakes echoes in the sound of amateur rock-and-roll groups practicing in garages and basements around the world.

Remarkable similarities of tone, theme, and attitude between Beattie's minstrel persona, Edwin, and Wordsworth's developing poetical role have been noted.[36] The minstrel was a prototype of Wordsworth's juvenile poet figure, and Beattie's subtitle, "The Progress of Genius," parallels Wordsworth's working title for *The Prelude,* "the poem on the growth of my own mind," but on a national rather than an individual level. Such was Beattie's plan for Edwin: educated by a wise old hermit, "He meditates new arts on Nature's plan," and is tutored in the history of poetry to a new level of achievement. Exactly how he does this, Beattie "fain would sing:—but ah! I strive in vain," and so he too dwindles into the characteristic melancholy of Sensibility.

The earliest commentator to recognize Beattie's influence on Wordsworth was his sister, Dorothy. In her charming letters of 1787 to her friend Jane Pollard, recording her rediscovery and exploration of her long-lost brothers, she presents "my dear William" as a version of Beattie's model: " 'In truth he was a strange and wayward wight fond of each gentle &c. &c.' That verse of Beattie's Minstrel always reminds me of him, and indeed the whole character of Edwin resembles much what William was when I first knew him after my leaving Halifax—'and oft he traced the uplands &c, &c, &c.' "[37] Doubtless she was prompted in this identification by the favorite parts of Beattie that William read or recited to her, which are reflected in various ways throughout his works. When he represented himself as "singled out . . . from a swarm of rosy boys . . . For my grave looks, too thoughtful for my years" (*The Excursion,* I.56–59), he was adapting Beattie's words for Edwin: "no vulgar boy, / Deep thought oft seem'd to fix his infant eye" (I.16).

Robert Burns (1759–1796) took the innovations of Thomson and Beattie a big step further by writing many of his poems in the regional dialect of southern Scotland, and on contemporary topics. Wordsworth purchased Burns's most important volume, *Poems, Chiefly in the Scottish Dialect* (1786), from the Penrith book club as a present for Dorothy before he went to Cambridge in 1787, having read it enthusiastically during his last year at Hawkshead.[38] Burns's use of Scottish (though a third of the poems are in standard English) marks a shift in theme and focus not present in the tamer innovations of Beattie and Thomson. Like all the writers of Sensibility, they were mild rebels, proffering their works from the margins of contemporary literature as self-consciously minor productions hopeful of acceptance by mainline culture, symbolized by the "Great Cham," Samuel Johnson.

But Robert Burns was not such a co-optable rebel. He interwove poems about the proper language and subjects for poetry with poems about country manners and problems. On the first manuscript page of "The Ruined Cottage," Wordsworth penned an epigraph from Burns, the first two and last two lines of this stanza from "Epistle to J.L. L★★★★★k [John Lapraik], an Old Scots Bard. April 1st, 1785":

> Gie me ae spark o' Nature's fire,
> That's a' the learning I desire;
> Then tho' I drudge thro' dub an' mire
> At pleugh or cart,
> My Muse, tho' hamely in attire,
> May touch the heart.

These are the same sentiments that Burns had prefixed to his own volume, in English:

> The Simple Bard, unbroke by rules of Art,
> He pours the wild effusions of the heart:
> And if inspir'd, 'tis Nature's pow'rs inspire;
> Her's all the melting thrill, and her's the kindling fire.

Burns's volume ends with "A Bard's Epitaph," which uses the same sequence of challenges delivered to other, supposedly more useful vocations (soldier, priest, merchant) that Wordsworth later adopted in "A Poet's Epitaph" to arrive at a remarkably similar conclusion: "Is there a Bard of rustic song / Who, noteless, steals the crouds among . . . / . . . Here pause—and thro' the starting tear, / Survey this grave" (7–8, 17–18). Wordsworth: "But who is He, with modest looks, / And clad in homely russet brown? . . . / . . . Here stretch thy body at full length; / Or build thy house upon his grave" (37–38, 59–60). Both poems are indebted to the pastoral tradition of one shepherd piping a lament at the grave of another. But Burns invoked this tradition mainly to distinguish his poems from it: "The following trifles are not the production of the Poet, who, with all the advantages of learned art, and perhaps amid the elegancies and idlenesses of upper life, looks down for a rural theme, with an eye to Theocritus or Virgil." This, the lead sentence of Burns's preface, helped prepare the way for Wordsworth's great preface of 1800.

The Scottish or Northern Revival was not the only kind of poetry that interested William Taylor and his best students. The contemporary English poets George Crabbe, John Langhorne, and William Shenstone were also high on their lists of extracurricular reading. These were some of the first poets who took it upon themselves to describe the plight of the poor as a fit subject for serious poetry. The literature of Sensibility, with its large funds of pathos, expended much emotion on the poor, but predominantly in sentimental pastoral rhetoric like Thomson's and Beattie's. The one great poem that transcends this level before the 1780s is Gray's "Elegy Written in a Country Church Yard" (1751), which purports to read "the short and simple annals of the poor." But we do not look to Gray to learn what poverty is like, still less what to do about it, unless we are disposed to accept his view that its greatest claim on our attention is to "implore the passing tribute of a sigh."

Crabbe's *The Village* (1783) was written against these fashions of affected pastoral representations of poverty, but it was not a protest poem in the modern radical sense. Crabbe, another of the many literary divines on Wordsworth's extracurricular reading list, was surely "against" poverty, but his best hope was for an enlightened aristocracy to take better paternal care of the peasants in their parishes, following the example of his patron the duke of Rutland. Wordsworth read Crabbe as early as 1783, when the best parts of *The Village* were excerpted in the *Annual Register,* available at Hawkshead.[39] These were Crabbe's set pieces of naturalistic description, the worn-out laborer, the parish poorhouse, the cheating apothecary, the jovial hunting parson, and the pauper's funeral.

Crabbe knew the world of parish politics that Wordsworth also knew from Cockermouth, where many social issues were resolved by "the yearly dinner, the septennial bribe" (I.114). His exhausted old laborer anticipates Wordsworth's Simon Lee, the Old Huntsman: "He once was chief in all the rustic trade; / His steady hand the straitest furrow made; / Full many a prize he won, and still is proud / To find the triumphs of his youth allow'd; / A transient pleasure sparkles in his eyes, / He hears and smiles, then thinks again and sighs" ("The Village," 188–93).

The situation of Crabbe's laborer is the same as that of Wordsworth's "Old Cumberland Beggar." Both authors describe the same social phenomena: "roundsmen," paupers sent around the parish from house to house by the overseer of the poor to get work (for about sixpence a day) and food.[40] But what Crabbe simply reports with pity, Wordsworth finds a way to celebrate as the occasion for virtuous philanthropy: "the villagers in him / Behold a record which together binds / Past deeds and offices of charity." Whether his view or Crabbe's description of villagers' "ruthless taunts of lazy poor" is more accurate depends a lot on the parish in question. Both men deplored the alternative, the poorhouse, which was in many parishes purposely left in a terrible state to discourage applicants. But though Crabbe represented the condition of the poor more realistically than the fashionable conventions of picturesque description, he did not have a theory of language and its relations to culture and politics such as Wordsworth proposed in 1800.

In 1837, when he was nearly seventy, Wordsworth compared Crabbe to John Langhorne (1735–1779), "our Westmorland Poet," on the question of poverty as a subject for poetry, with a side glance at Shenstone:

> ["The Country Justice"] is the first Poem, unless perhaps Shenstone's Schoolmistress be excepted, that fairly brought the Muse into the Company of common life, to which it comes nearer than Goldsmith, and upon which it looks with a tender and enlightened humanity—and with a charitable, (and being so) philosophical and poetical construction that is too rarely found in the works of Crabbe. It is not without many faults in style from which Crabbe's more austere judgment preserved him—but these to me are trifles in a work so original and touching.[41]

Wordsworth made this subtle discrimination for an admirer who accepted the new opinion that the great poet of the poor was now Wordsworth. He apportions value to Langhorne for content and to Crabbe for style, and modestly leaves unspoken the name of the poet who might be said to have united the two. He unfairly links Crabbe's "austere" style to his ostensibly less charitable views of common life, for Crabbe was nothing if not a social critic. Today Crabbe remains an important minor poet, but Langhorne is almost completely forgotten, except for his associations with Wordsworth, which are worth remembering because Langhorne also combined Lake District origins with poetical attentions to social suffering.

Possibly Wordsworth did not actually read Langhorne until he was at Cambridge,[42] but Langhorne's influence on him is close to Crabbe's, as his proprietary phrase "our Westmorland Poet" indicates. For their differences, we have only to imagine Wordsworth's reaction if he were called "our Cumberland Poet"! Langhorne, born in Kirkby Stephen and schooled in Appleby, offers another instance of a local boy struggling through difficulties to make good. He did not have Wordsworth's social advantages, for his formal education, like Beattie's, ended with grammar school. But by dint of tutoring and schoolmastering he was able to register for an extramural B.D. degree from Cambridge at age twenty-five, the same age at which Beattie achieved the same shaky start, and the age at which Wordsworth would depart for London to throw himself into political journalism. Langhorne's path also led him toward London, "the metropolis, that mart for genius and learning"[43] (Wordsworth would call it "that mighty gulph . . . of talents" when he made the same move),[44] where he became a reviewer and writer for the *Monthly Review* from 1764 until his death in 1779.

His "Ode to the Genius of Westmorland" was one of many contemporary stimuli to Wordsworth to praise the Muse in the Lakes. It runs over all the usual picturesque keys—"wild groves," "mountains grey," "dark woods," the poet claiming that he has caught from them "the sacred fire, / That glow'd within my youthful breast," and that he will eventually return to repay his debt to them. But Langhorne's "Ode to the River Eden" (1759), on the Lake District river that flows just east of Penrith into Solway Firth, points to even more specific similarities between these two poets' recognition of their muse in the features of their childhood landscape.

> Delightful Eden! parent stream,
>   Yet shall the maids of Memory say,
> (When, led by Fancy's fairy dream,
>   My young steps trac'd thy winding way)
> How oft along thy mazy shore,
> That many a gloomy alder bore,
>   In pensive thought their Poet stray'd;
> Or, careless thrown thy banks beside,
> Beheld thy dimply waters glide,
> Bright thro' the trembling shade.

These opening lines prepare the way for perhaps the most famous of all Wordsworth's beginnings:

> Was it for this
> That one, the fairest of all rivers, loved
> To blend his murmurs with my nurse's song,
> And from his alder shades and shallows, sent a voice
> That flowed along my dreams? For this didst thou,
> O Derwent, travelling over the green plains
> Near my "sweet birthplace," didst thou, beauteous stream,
> Make ceaseless music through the night and day . . . .
>
> (*1799*, i.1–9)

Wordsworth's lines read almost like a translation of Langhorne into another language. But Wordsworth's memory—which must include his memory of

Langhorne—shares many elements of setting and attitude with Langhorne: the river as parent/nurse, the shady alders (Langhorne has "the poplar tall"), the flowers, the boyish play, the passage's movement toward sunset, and the question if imagination can respond adequately to childhood memories. Wordsworth's lines are of course remarkable for their clear, modern simplicity, though written only forty years later. But perhaps most telling, as his response to a remembered text, is the subtle symbolism by which he transmutes Langhorne's allegorical and abstract personifications into organic metaphors. Langhorne pleasantly imagines old Father Time skipping like a boy, but Wordsworth much more impressively, yet without sacrificing the charm of the situation, manages to suggest that Skiddaw is something like a "bronzed" primitive deity and he a little "naked savage" worshiping before it.

The stylized, artificial quality of nature in these and other contemporary poems owes more to William Shenstone (1714–1763), who was criticized during his lifetime for the excessive prettiness of his poetry. Shenstone's favorite topics are a veritable roll call of Sensibility, featuring elegies on retirement, simplicity, death, friendship, domesticity, disinterestedness, humility, solitude, and benevolence. Shenstone's "Schoolmistress" is another prototype for Wordsworth's idyllic portrait of Ann Tyson (above), in parallels of tone rather than diction.

Here oft the dame, on Sabbath's decent eve,
Hymned such psalms as Sternhold forth did mete;
If winter 'twere, she to her hearth did cleave,
But in her garden found a summer-seat:
Sweet melody!

(118–22)

Wordsworth's idyllic descriptions of his Hawkshead "School-Time" also owe a debt to the idealized school in Shenstone's popular poem. The single longest section of Shenstone's poem describes the punishment of a wild, wayward boy, but ends with a caution against too severe punishments that might cramp future great spirits:

E'en now sagacious foresight points to show
A little bench of heedless bishops here,
And here a chancellor in embryo,
Or bard sublime, if bard may e'er be so,
As Milton, Shakespeare, names that ne'er shall die!

(245–49)

The immediate source of such sentiments is Gray's "mute inglorious Miltons," but the theme of a hoped-for new poetic savior echoed through the works of almost all these poets, and it resonated loudly with Wordsworth at Hawkshead, stimulating thoughts about the creation of the Poet that became his master theme.

Wordsworth's sense of the power of his imagination is often expressed in the contrary terms of how great his loss would be if imagination should fail him. Hence it is not surprising that one of Shenstone's clearest influences on him should be in the Lucy poems, those privately coded meditations on the imagined death of his sister, Dorothy, or, what amounted to the nearly same thing, a loss of his confidence in his developing genius. Many of Lucy's characteristics are borrowed from Shenstone's "Nancy of the Vale." The rivers Dove and Avona are far apart, but the maids the poets place on their banks are virtually twin sisters—one generation removed: " 'Twas from Avona's banks the maid / Diffus'd her lovely beams, / And ev'ry shining glance display'd / The Naiad of the streams" (Shenstone, 18–21). "She dwelt among the untrodden ways / Besides the banks of Dove . . . Fair as a star, when only one / Is shining in the sky" ("She dwelt among the untrodden ways," 1–2). Wordsworth's terse late note, "1799. Composed in the Hartz Forest," again identifies only the physical time and space of his poems' composition: their roots in creative memory very evidently go to "hiding places" at least ten years further back, in Hawkshead.

William Cowper's *Poems* (1782) and *The Task* (1785) were both critical and popular successes when they appeared in the middle of Wordsworth's Hawkshead years, but Cowper's influence on Wordsworth, though long felt, has only recently begun to get its due.[45] Lines like "I gaz'd, myself creating what I saw" (*Task,* IV.290) touch very closely on "Tintern Abbey's" "mighty world / Of eye and ear, both what they half create, / And what perceive." This influence was first set in motion when Wordsworth, like all the other Hawkshead schoolboys, was set to write celebratory verses on the Bishop Sandys's school's bicentenary in 1785. They had immediately before them Cowper's new poem "Tirocinium; or, A Review of the Schools" (1785), which they were expected to refute, since it argued against public school education like theirs in favor of the older aristocratic idea of private education at home by tutors.

But Cowper's influence is as broadly cultural as it is specifically literary. The cool, sensible blank verse of *The Task* is only a step or two from the limpid clarity of *The Prelude* at its best, but those two steps are the stride from talent to genius. Cowper's unassuming voice of personal meditation encouraged Wordsworth's self-examination, though Cowper stopped far short of Wordsworth's claims for his imagination: "no prophetic fires to me belong; / I play with syllables, and sport in song" ("Table Talk," 504–5). The similar motives but different outcomes of these two long poems make all the difference between a major Romantic poem and an amusing, intelligent, but finally unchallenging poem like *The Task*. Many of its episodes start out like those in *The Prelude,* but they never develop into visionary "spots of time." Cowper presciently imagined the fall of the Bastille: "There's not an English heart that would not leap / To hear that ye were fall'n at last" (V.389–90). But his lines "leap" nowhere near the height Wordsworth's heart did when the event actually occurred: "Bliss was it in that dawn to be alive, / But to be young was very heaven!"

These moments of poetic influence are very close, but worlds apart. Cowper's best-loved, most poignant poem, "The Castaway," was written in 1799, the same year that Wordsworth began *The Prelude.* Both *The Task* and *The Prelude* are preparatory, therapeutic poems. But one was written from the last stages of mental debility, while the other took its first steps toward recovery by imagining the creation of a new kind of mind. Cowper's "warfare [was] within" (VI.935), as was Wordsworth's, but Wordsworth raised the stakes of mental struggle much higher. Yet there is no point using Wordsworth as a stick to beat Cowper. The point, rather, is to see how close Cowper, like all these poets of Sensibility, came to Wordsworth, and how far Wordsworth went beyond them.

The time, the place, the occasion, and the mastership of William Taylor combined to make Wordsworth's response to Cowper, his first extended verse production, an unexceptionally positive celebration of his school. What might not have been expected was that the assignment led Wordsworth into a course from which he never thereafter was fundamentally diverted: "This exercise . . . put it into my head to compose verses from the impulse of my own mind."[46]

4

"VERSES FROM THE IMPULSE OF MY OWN MIND"

Wordsworth's Earliest Poetry

> Thirteen years,
> Or haply less, I might have seen when first
> My ears began to open to the charm
> Of words in tuneful order, found them sweet
> For *their own sakes*—a passion and a power—
> And phrases pleased me, chosen for delight,
> For pomp, or love.
>
> (V.575–81)

On December 13, 1783, William walked out, "feverish, and tired, and restless," to the road junction at Borwick Lodge, a mile and a half north of Hawkshead, to wait for the horses coming to take him and Richard and John home for Christmas. It was a cold, misty, windy day, not a good one for mounting a lookout. But he was impatient, and so he went, alone. The horses finally came, but the boys were home barely ten days before their father died. John Wordsworth, like his wife, caught a cold and died of it, or from a "dropsy" which it aggravated—the same immediate cause as that of Wordsworth's death sixty-seven years later. He had spent a night without shelter on ill-omened Cold Fell, having lost his way back to Cockermouth after finishing up some coroner's duties at Millom.[1] Millom is even farther from Cockermouth than Hawkshead, so he must have been as eager as his sons to return home, if he was willing to travel by night.

The occasion of his father's death lodged deeply in Wordsworth's mind at—or *as*—the beginning of his writing career. His recollection of waiting for the horses stuck in his imagination a long time—at least twenty years, when it joined his other childhood "spot of time" at Penrith Beacon to form the visionary diptych by which he symbolized the final resolution of *The Prelude*'s crisis: "Imagination, How Impaired and Restored."* Both "spots of

*In the version of 1799, the diptych was a triptych, including the Drowned Man of Esthwaite, another dead authority figure (*1799*, i.263–374).

time" are thus powerfully about the death of parents: his father in one and a murdered wife in the other. He wrote his first version of this episode in 1787, four years after the event. He tries to intensify the feeling of loss by imagining his own death as well, and the cultural signature he put on it underscores its deep significance for him: "In church-yard such at death of day / As heard the pensive sighs of Gray."[2] Thus his 1787 fantasy about the loss he suffered in 1783 is framed in terms from William Taylor's death in June 1786 and his tombstone's epitaph from Gray's "Elegy." Such palimpsests of memory, composition, and revision are fundamental to the operation of Wordsworth's self-creating imagination.

His life changed dramatically with his father's death, and other events conspired to intensify its disruptive impact. In that same autumn of 1783 the Wordsworth boys had moved with the Tysons out of Hawkshead village into the little enclave of Colthouse, leaving the school-home they had enjoyed since 1779. Shortly after they returned from that sad Christmas, Hugh Tyson made another sad parallel in Wordsworth's life: he died, aged seventy, on February 28, 1784, and the boys had to attend another fatherly funeral.[3]

John Wordsworth's estate was sold off quickly in two spring sales. The first disposed of personal items like his watch and rings that would normally have been reserved for his sons, had the executor been less efficient and more generous than Christopher Crackanthorpe. A second sale, in May, disposed of the rest of the household goods, netting £260.[4] The two uncles (Richard Wordsworth of Whitehaven was the other executor) were determined to raise as much cash as they could for the five children who now fell onto their care. They did quite well, even before confronting the question of James Lowther's debt to his deceased agent: by the time John Wordsworth's land holdings were liquidated, they had raised a total of about £10,500, or more than £2,000 per child. Dorothy overoptimistically estimated that this would give them each £200 per year at interest: a modest lower-middle-class income, but not enough to provide the cost of a college education. For that—and for William and Christopher only—the uncles would have to advance money in anticipation of Lowther's eventual payment of the expenses he owed his late steward.

Other painful events of the sort that local gossip delights in soon reached the boys' ears. On May 24, 1784, the new Lowther agent, Michael Satterthwaite, arrived to demand the keys to the Cockermouth house. By cruel coincidence this was the very date on which James Lowther came into his full harvest of honors for the success of his protégé William Pitt in the parliamentary elections of 1783. Pitt, defeated in 1780 in his first run for Parliament, had held Lowther's Appleby seat (formerly Jack Robinson's) as a courtesy in 1781–83, while he positioned himself for the next election, which came very soon, given the unpopularity of the government's unholy alliance between the liberal Fox and his conservative former opponent Lord North. Lowther now officially abandoned the country Whigs to join a new version of the court Whigs (Pitt's followers were not yet called Tories), and was rewarded for his help by being created Viscount Lonsdale, Viscount Lowther, and Earl of Lonsdale, on top of his former ranks, Baron Lowther of Lowther, Baron of Kendal, Baron of Burgh.[5] Perhaps it was just a coincidence, or else a calculated whim, but he had his new agent, Satterthwaite, move into the Cockermouth house on that same May 24. Satterthwaite soon set up a regime very different from John Wordsworth's, gaining infamy as the "Rum Justice" for his expertise in liquor and ineptitude in law.[6]

Another cruel coincidence of the election that brought Pitt and Lowther into power was that the Wordsworths' other political refuge, Jack Robinson, was thrown out of it. He retained his seat at Harwich, but was no longer in the government, where his influence as secretary of the treasury and his established position as Lowther's enemy could have done the Wordsworth children untold good. The balance of life was tipping against the Wordsworths, though the full force of the change didn't appear immediately. Wordsworth's verses on his father's death show that he came to realize only gradually how much he had lost:

> I mourn [now] because I mourn'd no more [then].
> For ah! the storm was soon at rest,
> . . . .
> Nor did my little heart foresee
> —She lost a home in losing thee . . . .
>
> (441–42, 445–46)

When he returned to school in the fall of 1784, the boys were assigned verses on a topic as old as school itself: the summer vacation. After all that had happened during the year, the assignment must have seemed a cruel joke to Wordsworth. His lines have not survived, but they might have given us a record of his first summer as an orphan, living not at home in comfortable Cockermouth but in despised Penrith. It had been, after his mother's death in 1778, the worst summer of his young life.

During the following Christmas vacation, December–January 1784–85, Wordsworth wrote what he called his "first *voluntary* verses . . . after walking six miles to attend a dance at Egremont" (from Whitehaven, where he was staying with his cousins).[7] These verses also have not survived, but they were written during the first anniversary of his father's death. They were about returning to school after the winter holidays, and Wordsworth implies that he added them to his earlier verses on the summer vacation. To either or both of these compositions he gave the title "The Pleasures of Change," which fits all the topical possibilities and was very much in the contemporary style: "Pleasures of Imagination" (Akenside), "Pleasures of Memory" (Samuel Rogers), and "Pleasures of Hope" (Thomas Campbell). A slight oddity of Wordsworth's title is that *change* did not usually give much pleasure to the poets of Sensibility. But then, neither did it to Wordsworth, in the majority of his verses surviving from this period, which turn compulsively on changes in his life occasioned by John Wordsworth's death. If, in the oversimplifications of psychobiography, his mother's death made him turn to Mother Nature for a substitute, the loss of his father, the family provider, turned him toward poetry for restoration, but with a host of attendant guilt feelings. In the *Prelude* version of Waiting for the Horses, he drew a trite moral from the experience, though perhaps appropriate for a thirteen-year-old: he interpreted his impatience as a sin for which God punished him by taking his father. But his earlier versions of the event seem more mature: they betray his guilt for enjoying poetry so much, now that his father's death had rendered it a suspect, unprofitable pastime—to say nothing of a career.

When he returned to school for the spring term, the boys were assigned to write verses for the school's bicentenary, with Cowper's "Tirocinium: or, A Review of the Schools" (1785) as their polemical foil. Praise of public education was the theme, against Cowper's strictures, but Wordsworth managed to work into his contribution fathers and their hopes for their sons. These "Lines Written as a School Exercise" are the earliest surviving lines of his poetry. Most of the poem is, as he said, "but a tame imitation of Pope's versification, and a little in his style," although at 112 lines it is a considerable teenage production in any style.[8] It gives an unexceptionably Anglican vision of Britain's progress since the Reformation: Religion and Science join together to drive out Superstition and advance the arts of this "cheerful isle," which heretofore had "deemed all merit centered in the sword." After paying his respects to religion and science, Wordsworth turns to the moral dimension of the school's curriculum: it quenches "the passions kindling into flame," shames Pleasure's "blushing beauties," and teaches "the tender tear to flow." Among the few evidences we have of Pleasure's "blushing beauties" at Hawkshead are those "ruddy damsels past sixteen" (in Wordsworth's unpublished verses on Matthew the Schoolmaster) who commissioned John Harrison to write their love letters to the grammar school boys.

Why this moralistic section of the goddess of Education's speech should come as the conclusion of the poem is revealed by its next-to-last words:

> "*So* shall thy sire, whilst Hope his Breast inspires,
> And wakes anew life's glimmering, trembling fires,
> Hear Britain's Sons rehearse thy praise with joy,
> Look up to Heav'n, and bless his darling Boy."
>
> (99–102; italics added)

This sounds as bland as the rest of the poem: work hard, avoid temptation, and you'll be successful and your father will be proud of you. But it was a brave quatrain for a boy whose father had just died to recite publicly in front of all the other boys and their parents at the ceremony. As far as Wordsworth personally was concerned, the proper locution for the last line would be "Look *down* from Heaven, and bless his darling Boy."

A considerable amount of other poetry survives from Wordsworth's Hawkshead days, most of it written between 1785 and 1787. It would of course be possible to pass over all of it as derivative from available models, and no more interesting than what we would expect from a boy of his class and training at that time and in that place.[9] But they cannot be wholly dismissed as generic late eighteenth-century verse. He was somewhat exceptional in being considered "rather the poet of the school," though not more so than Robert Greenwood or the Farish brothers.[10] We can hear the actual voice of his schoolmates' admiration in a marginal comment recorded over a hundred years ago: "One day after he had gained some credit from his Master for some English Verses—a bigger boy took him by the arm and led him off into the fields, & when he had got him quite apart, gravely said to him, 'I say, Bill, when thoo writes verse dost thoo invoke t'Muse?' "[11] It's like a moment from Joyce's *Portrait of the Artist as a Young Man.* It recaptures our school memories of awe at peers who do easily what we can't do at all, whether it be math, drawing, sports, or singing. One wonders why the bigger boy took him so far off. Was he embarrassed? Threatening? Probably the reason for distance, and confidentiality, was pragmatic: if poetry required invoking the Muse, could Bill show him how, so he could gain some much needed credit with the master?

On the basis of his summer vacation and school exercise lines, Taylor encouraged him to write more. This was more than a recognition of talent; it was a wise teacher's way of helping a favorite pupil deal with his grief. Taylor's personal literary tastes ran to the melancholy-sentimental, and his pedagogical methods were flexible enough to use verse writing as a reward, punishment, or encouragement, as he did in the Castlehow incident of September 1783.

But the strongest reason for not passing over Wordsworth's earliest verses is that they have been preserved by a very reputable authority—Wordsworth himself. In several notebooks never thrown away during many shifts of residence and travels between 1787 and 1799—not to mention the ensuing fifty-one years at Grasmere and Rydal Mount—he kept by him many juvenile poems and fragments, amounting to well over a thousand lines of verse. This is exceptional: no comparable body of juvenile poetry in English exists for any major poet before him. These notebooks were some of his few easily transported possessions, and they helped develop his lifelong habit of reading himself when no other books were available—or even if they were. It seems perfectly natural in retrospect that Wordsworth, the poet of childhood, should save them, but his doing so was by no means automatic. Facetiously, he said that he kept on composing after his "School Exercise" because he'd been given a new notebook for it and it seemed a shame not to make use of the remaining pages.

He continued to write Greek, Latin, and English verses in school, but the poems in the Hawkshead notebook were his own. They reflect the kind of verses he was writing in school, but they are markedly different from the style of the "School Exercise" lines, clearly representing his *voluntary* selection of models among the many that William Taylor exposed him to. As such, they have a remarkable consistency: with very few exceptions they are all about love and death. They are either lyrics translated from Greek and Latin or written in imitation of contemporary Sensibility poems, or narratives of his own adventures, emotions, and fantasies.[12] Most often, his themes of love and death appear in conventional contexts—for example, the aftermath of disappointed love affairs—and do not support very much psychological interpretation. Less often, Wordsworth presents love more broadly, as toward a parent or a place. Death is likewise generalized broadly to include the loss of a friend, an impending departure, or a generalized mood of melancholy. There are no satires or topical, occasional poems, and few narratives involving characters other than himself. The longest of them by far, "The Vale of Esthwaite," appears to be a narrative poem, but it is actually a desperate effort to *control* his wildly free-floating emotions by forcing them into narrative line.

His translations of Anacreon and Catullus are suitably frank and sexy like their originals, and not the kind of poems he was assigned in school, if the "School Exercise" is any indication. His imitation of Anacreon updates the Greek poet's instructions to a painter of ancient Rhodes by addressing instructions for a portrait of his lover to Sir Joshua Reynolds. Wordsworth cleverly substitutes local nature metaphors to describe the mistress's arching eyebrows (the moon's "silver crescent") and her eye's "lunar beams." But when his description drops below her neck—everything that Anacreon dismisses with a sly glance—Wordsworth extends the original by several lines, to produce one of the sexiest—if most awkward—descriptions of Grasmere on record. Anacreon simply says, "the rest / Be in a chastened purple drest, / But let her flesh peep here and there / The lines of beauty to declare."[13] But Wordsworth pursues his innovative nature imagery to describe how the robe draped over the beloved's body like a mist on Grasmere lake, which "Hides half the landskip from the sight." So far, so good. But then the metaphor takes over from the message, and he begins wandering through a thoroughly anthropomorphized landscape to some spots revealed with considerably more frankness than the peeping flesh Anacreon alluded to.

While Fancy paints beneath the Veil
The pathway winding through the dale,
The cot, the seat of Peace and Love,
Peeping through the tufted grove.
(43–46)

If the landscape is the beloved's body and the mist is her robe, the identification of that "seat" of Love behind the "tufted grove" that Fancy imagines beneath the robe can be found in only one place. Wordsworth here achieves a transformation of landscape into sensual terms that parallels the more "spiritual" transformations of his greatest poetry. In choice and execution, the translation reflects the preoccupations of any healthy sixteen-year-old, and participates in a centuries-old schoolboy tradition of finding a stimulus to classical translation in the promise of illicit erotic rewards.

Wordsworth's translations and imitations of Catullus are closer to the original than his Anacreontics, but equally erotic.[14] His Septimius and Acme (Catullus XLV) are sensually lost in each other. If anything, Wordsworth's translation is more passionate than the standard English version: "Then Acme, slightly bending back her head, kissed with that rosy mouth her sweet love's swimming eyes, and said, 'So, my life, my darling Septimius, so may we ever serve this one master as (I swear) more strongly and fiercely burns in me the flame deep in my melting marrow.' "[15] Here is Wordsworth's version:

But Acme lightly turning back her head
Kissed with that rosy mouth th'inebriate eyes
Of the sweet youth, and kissed again and said:
"My life, and what far more than life I prize,
So may we to the end of time obey
Love our sole master, as my bosom owns
A flame that with far more resistless sway
Thrills through the very marrow of my bones."
(13–20)

So too his Lesbia (Catullus V), where he adds contemporary details of lovelorn melancholy that are no part of his original. Catullus's poem is a hyperbole of kisses, mounting up to "many thousands," the better to befuddle any "malicious person" who might give him and his lover the evil eye, "when he knows that our kisses are so many." For this aggressive policy of erotic economy, the teenage Wordsworth substituted intimations of loss. He raises the stakes to "a million" kisses, but his conclusion is abrupt, original with him, and adolescently apocalyptic: "That I for joys may never pine / That never can again be mine." Why so pale and wan, young lover?

The title of "Beauty and Moonlight" promises more of the same love-and-death clichés, but it was good enough for Coleridge to pick up years later and revise, as "Lewti," for the *Morning Post,* and it almost got into *Lyrical Ballads.*[16] It is a cinematic version of Wordsworth's Anacreon translation, with a Hawkshead lover wandering "high o'er the silver rocks" trying to forget his Mary. But he keeps seeing her in anthropomorphic imagery of land, sky, and sea. A waterfall seen through the trees reminds him, "So shines her forehead smooth and fair / Gleaming through her sable hair." But if the God of Love would let him really see her, then the metaphors of the poem might be returned to their right relation to human life, which is the main technical problem in all these poems.

> *Then* might her bosom soft and white
> Heave upon my swimming sight
> *As* these two Swans together ride [MS: heave]
> Upon the gently swelling tide. [MS: soft heaving wave]
> (31–34; italics added)

That is, better to see her breasts as swans than swans as her breasts: the former is ecstasy; the latter, fantasy. The imagery of swans for breasts is a Renaissance figure, or *blason,* that Wordsworth took from Spenser and Milton, but it curiously always caused him trouble whenever he tried to use it, as he frequently did throughout the 1790s.

The speaker of this poem could be the hero, or the villain, of the only ballad Wordsworth composed at Hawkshead, since the girl in both poems is named Mary. The date of this poem ("And will you leave me thus alone?") can be fixed with extraordinary accuracy at March 23–24, 1787, by Wordsworth's date on the manuscript.[17] The real-life biographies of its characters are well established in Hawkshead records, but his treatment of them is a surprising variation on the theme of love and death which dominates his juvenilia. It looks like a curse poem to start with, as Mary tells William, who has jilted her, "Be sure her Ghost will haunt thy bed / When Mary shall lie low." The revenge of wronged lovers is a dominant feature of folk ballads, but Wordsworth's poem reverses this tried-and-true formula. Instead of seeing William haunted by Mary's curse, we observe her dawning realization that she has been abandoned, in a series of natural signs which the narrator interprets in lugubrious detail. Instead of haunting William, her ghost haunts *her:* "oft her waft [ghost] was seen / With wan light standing at the door"—a sure folk sign of imminent death. Mary dies of love by stages, which the natural scene prefigures:

Oft has she seen sweet Esthwaite's lake
Reflect the morning sheen;
When lo! the sullen clouds arise
And dim the smiling scene.

The last touch is the most melodramatic one. To warm her up as she lies chilled in bed, her friends bring her some gloves, but it was "the glove her William gave; / She saw, she wept, and sighed the sigh / That sent her to her grave."

It is tempting to imagine that this William and Mary are teenage fantasy prototypes of William Wordsworth and Mary Hutchinson, the Penrith playmate who would become his wife. But whatever the state of his feelings for her at age sixteen, the identities of the lovers in this ballad are too well known to allow such an identification. However, the poem's empathy for the young woman instead of the man is not in doubt. When Wordsworth gave her the words "My head would soon lie low," we can be sure his identification with the poem's emotions is very deep, since these are, once again, his oft-repeated words from William Taylor's deathbed less than a year earlier.

The Mary of the poem is actually Mary Rigge (d. 1760), who had been a friend and confidante of Ann Tyson's and whose parents still lived in the Green End house next to hers.[18] The Wordsworth boys stayed with the Rigges for two or three weeks in early 1784, during Hugh Tyson's final illness, when Ann was too busy to care for them—a time of critical emotional susceptibility for them in many ways. Mary's mother took such good care of them, and they were so quiet and well behaved that her husband—the stern father of the ballad—softened his initial opposition to having noisy boys in the house. From Mrs. Rigge and Ann Tyson, reinforced by neighborhood gossip, the boys heard a lot about Mary Rigge's sad story, for it was one of the neighborhood's scandals, and its actors were, with one exception, still very much alive. Mary had been seduced by David Kirkby, of Kirkby Quay on Coniston Water. She bore his child, baptized David Benoni on June 17, 1759, a year before her own death. Kirkby did not marry her, reserving his choice for one Agatha Sawrey, whom he married in 1762. His father, another William, was, like William Rigge, a considerable man in parish affairs. Wordsworth made a note of the affair in a comment on *Peter Bell* (where he used the biblical name Benoni) that conceals as much as it reveals: "Benoni, or the child of sorrow, I knew when I was a school-boy. His mother had been deserted by a gentleman in the neighborhood, she herself being a gentlewoman by birth. The circumstances of her story were told me by my dear old dame, Ann Tyson, who was her confidante. The lady died brokenhearted." William Kirkby was "commonly styled 'Mr.' in parochial records," but was not of quite the same gentlemanly status as William Rigge, who owned "ancient customary estates."[19] Kirkby was a successful slate trader and shipper, just a cut below the professional gentry rank that Rigge, like John Wordsworth, occupied in the carefully calibrated social scales of the time. David Benoni was not a Sandys schoolboy, but he was very much alive when the Wordsworth boys lived with his grandparents, and had received the hefty sum of £700 in June 1786, when his grandfather died—two weeks after William Taylor.[20] Without drawing causal connections, we can hardly be surprised, given this tissue of associations, that the Mary in the ballad should utter William Taylor's dying words.

The poem's reversal of the usual terms of the curse ballad and Wordsworth's sophisticated manipulation of its natural symbols make it more than a "feeble" imitation of a standard model.[21] He was able to accomplish so much with it because of the proximity of the persons involved to his residence—and to the facts of his own life. David Benoni, unrecognized by the natural father whose surname he bore, lost the grandfather who had raised him in June of 1786, the same month in which the recently orphaned William Wordsworth, now also a "child of sorrow," lost the schoolmaster who was his most important father substitute. David's inheritance was not as large as William's, but at least it was uncontested and paid immediately. Meanwhile, David and Agatha Kirkby, blessed and not cursed, became pillars of the parish at Coniston, parents of ten children, the last christened in 1784: the same year that the Wordsworth boys stayed with the Rigges and their David, all of whom kept close tabs on the life and doings of that other David who had ruined their daughter's life and their grandson's prospects.

William in the ballad is something of a sadist. His emotional insensitivity makes him the anti-type of another poetical character Wordsworth adopted at this same time, February–March 1787, for his sonnet "On Seeing Miss Helen Maria Williams Weep at a Tale of Distress," which was good enough for the *European Magazine,* a leading London journal which favored her verse, to publish.[22] Thus by 1787 Wordsworth was a writer fully capable of imagining himself persuasively into states of mind diametrically different from his own. The well-known tears of Helen Williams, sprinkled liberally throughout her poetry, are the catalyst to the speaker's own: "She wept.—Life's purple tide began to flow / In languid streams through every thrilling vein." The strange idea of a "languid thrill" captures much of Sensibility's appeal. The swoon in this sonnet swoops near to death-by-poetry, until "a sigh recall'd the wanderer [Life] to my breast." Yet the speaker is in doubt which was most valuable in his experience, the dying tear or the saving sigh. His tears, like Williams's, are a sign of virtue: the strongest moral guarantee in the world of Sensibility.

He wrote two other sonnets in the same mood, upon losses closer to his own experience: the coming departure from Hawkshead for Cambridge. These two sonnets also indicate some of the difference between what Wordsworth felt or wrote in 1787, and what he later *represented* himself as feeling then. "Extract from the Conclusion of a Poem, Composed in Anticipation of Leaving School," dated from 1786 by Wordsworth in 1843, is a published poem, included in his first collected works (1815), the earliest of his poems to be so retained. Because of later reworking, its polish sets it apart from the rest of the juvenilia, especially "The Vale of Esthwaite," which it was supposed to conclude.[23] The hysteria of that wild narrative could scarcely be further from this accomplished example of Wordsworthian mythmaking, as comparison with its original conclusion shows.

1787:
As Phoebus, when he sinks to rest
Far on the mountains in the west,
While all the vale is dark between
Ungilded by his golden sheen,
A lingering lustre softly throws
On the dear hills where first he rose.

1815:
Thus, while the Sun sinks down to rest
Far in the regions of the west,
Though to the vale no parting gleam
Be given, not one memorial gleam,
A lingering light he softly throws
On the dear hills where first he rose.

The latter version's subtle management of the connection between the speaker's memory and the setting sun is exactly the kind of relation the young Wordsworth failed to establish successfully in most of his other early poems, where his metaphors become so intricate we lose their point. The earlier version expresses a teenager's fear of dying, not the reflective views of a forty-five-year-old man. The published version is an example of primitive *style* rather than of juvenile poetry strictly speaking. Appearing in print in 1815, when Wordsworth was well established as the bard of the Lakes, the poem gained the additional effect of a self-fulfilling prophecy, since the speaker seems to regret that he will never return to such places, but almost all readers would have known perfectly well that he had, and very successfully so.

Quite different is the other "farewell" sonnet, dated ca. October 23, 1787, perhaps the very day he departed Hawkshead for Cambridge.[24] Not revised for later publication, it is a poem much more like his other early creations.

What is it that tells my soul the Sun is setting?
For not a straggling ray tell[s] her he is in the
Eas[t] or west[;] 'tis the brown mist which
descends slowly into the valley to [shed?] [?]
that burden of [ghosts?]. See where a
son of other worlds is sailing [s]lowly or the
lake—no! 'tis the taper that twinkling in the
cottage casts a long wan shadow over the [lake?].
Lo[ud] howls the village dog. Spirit of these
Mountains I see thee throned on Helvellyn, but
thy feet and head are wrapped in mist.
Spirit of these mountains if thou can [?Speak]
bid the mist break from thy forehead, and nod
me thrice farewell. farewell [,] farewell.—
For [no?] more shall the ghosts leaning from
The rocks or look[ing] from the parting of the cloud
listen while thou instructed me in the lore
of Nature. Bid the mist break from thy brow
an[d] thrice nod me a Farewell.

Though an incomplete fragment, it needs only a little technical help to become a perfectly adequate sonnet. As a farewell poem, it is saying good-bye not to the region but rather to the Gothic modes the poet has used to represent it. Its message is "No more ghosts." Its plea is simply for a more naturalistic way of interpreting meaning in landscape—the same issue, though with different content, that Wordsworth explored in the Mary Rigge ballad and "Beauty and Moonlight."

If this sonnet, like most of Wordsworth's earliest poems, claims that Nature chastened his overheated imagination, then "The Vale of Esthwaite" is the text that the sonnet was written *against.* Very little of what we have seen of Wordsworth's life, reading, and writing at Hawkshead prepares us for the unrestrained Gothicism of this extraordinary poem. Its innocuous title is the first of many surprises; it might better have been called "Revenge of the Phantom Minstrel." As a personal narrative poem summing up his eight years at Hawkshead, "The Vale of Esthwaite" sounds a cautionary note for any estimate of the range of Wordsworth's youthful imagination: not because it is so bad but because it is at once so powerful and so powerfully out of control. His later characterization of it as "a long poem running upon my own adventures, and the scenery of the country in which I was brought up" is laughably inaccurate, unless we reflect that his sense of "adventure" (and equally of "scenery") could be as strongly mental as it was physical. It reads

Wordsworth's birthplace, Cockermouth

Sir James Lowther as a young man, in Vandyke costume, by Thomas Hudson

Satan In All His Glory, by James Gillray (May 8, 1792)

The satirist "Peter Pindar" [John Wolcott] is pleading for mercy in Lowther's suit against him for libel. Several of the "glories" in his halo were familiar to the Wordsworth family: ruining creditors by non-stop lawsuits, undermining the town of Whitehaven, bribing witnesses to perjure themselves, bringing sham trials to ruin the country, and making hell-hounds of his clerks and attorneys.

Lowther Castle in 1819, by J. P. Neale

John Robinson, by William Ward

Penrith Beacon, from a nineteenth-century lithograph

The structure is approximately thirty feet high. It stands on the top of Beaconhill (937 feet), on the east edge of Penrith. The hill is covered by forest: the Beacon Plantation, property of the Lowther Trust.

Esthwaite Water, by James Bourne

Hawkshead School

Ann Tyson's cottage, Colthouse (photo by Kenneth Johnston)

A Country Ferry, by W. H. Pyne (published 1802)

Rural Road Scene, by W. H. Pyne (published 1824)

To the Manes [ghost or remains] *of Gilbert Wakefield*, by Julius Ibbetson (December, 1803)

Drawing of Bishop Richard Watson (with wand). Wakefield was imprisoned in Dorchester jail in 1798 for two years for libeling Watson; he did not long survive his sentence.

Bucks of the First Head, by Thomas Rowlandson (ca. 1785)

The Rookery, by Thomas Rowlandson

Not necessarily the rookery near Cambridge, at Barnwell, since any house of prostitution could be so designated. But the rural setting fits the Cambridge locale, and the costume of the young man matches those of Rowlandson's Cambridge "bucks."

A Master Parson with a Good Living, after Dighton (1782)

A Journeyman Parson with a Bare Existance, after Dighton (1782)

William Wilberforce, age 28,
by John Rising (1789)

William Frend, Fellow of Jesus College,
Cambridge, by Sylvester Harding (1789)

Brougham Castle, by Joseph Powell

like the nightmare underside of the splendid boyhood adventures recounted in *Prelude* I and II. It is Hawkshead by Night, or what ran through Wordsworth's mind on those nighttime rambles he loved. Of course, it can be pigeonholed as "conventional" Gothicism, but that only explains away what surely wants explaining, when a convention is allowed to run loose at such length. Published texts of its fragmentary manuscripts run to nearly six hundred lines, by far the longest of Wordsworth's juvenilia, but the condition of the manuscripts suggest that almost twice that number of lines have been torn out at various points in the notebooks to supply the "thoughts and images . . . which have been dispersed through my other writings."[25]

The uncertain and probably unhappy future course of his life was becoming pretty apparent by 1787 when Wordsworth came to write it. In May of that year Richard Wordsworth and Christopher Crackanthorpe finally faced up to the fact that they would have to bring suit against Lowther to get the more than £4600 still outstanding in his accounts with John Wordsworth.[26] No one knew, though some perhaps dreaded, how long Lowther would hold out: he stalled for five more years before they got him into court, and even when the judgment came in their favor it produced no action. Suing James Lowther was not simply a personal lawsuit; it was an action against a vast, powerful sociopolitical institution, a kind of international corporation.

The conventional landscape narrative that we might have expected Wordsworth to write was in fact mapped out (but never written) over many pages by the dutiful, industrious, and conventional Christopher Wordsworth in a notebook they shared.

> Outline of a Poem descriptive of the lakes etc. Febry 1792
>
> I sing lakes, woods & mountains, & the charms of a delightful country. O Muse assist my weak endeavours lest my unfledged wing be unequal to the attempt. I confess myself unequal to the attempt . . . but . . . I haste to conduct you, & be your guide to these lakes the glory of rugged Westmorland, of Cumberland distinguished for the vigour and courage of its men, & Lancashire for the beauty and charms of its women.[27]

Christopher rambles on for fifteen pages, past all the standard touristic points of reference, ending in the approved emotional state of melancholy:

> But alas! I must leave you, time with swift wing approaches, I shall not see another spring, but oh fields still be you blest, may science ever flourish & you my companions pursue with ardour the course of science, & may not Phoebus refuse coronas for your brows, & you little ones let no vice stain your present innocence. For me, whithersoever the stream of life may carry me, wheresoever or whatsoever I be, I will still remember you . . . even till death's cold hand chills my vital faculties . . . .

"The Vale of Esthwaite," though still in Wordsworth's earliest stages of self-mining, is much more concerned with what the mind imagines than with what the eye sees, let alone with Christopher's conventional moralisms. Its sprawling shapelessness indicates "automatic" writing of the most therapeutic kind, and suggests that his saying they were "verses composed on the impulse of my own mind" may be a statement of subject rather than of motive—that is, *about* the impulses of his mind, about what was "on his mind." He used the materials of landscape description, the machinery of Gothic horror, and the motives of his own mind—especially his impending vocational choices—to produce a psychosexual monodrama of a Lake District minstrel's quest for meaning in life.

There can be no complete or unified version of such a fragmentary poem; its published versions are all the result of many editorial interpretations.[28] This does not make much difference, since for all its weird grotesquerie "The Vale of Esthwaite" is very much of a piece, holographically. No matter where you slice into it, you find yourself reading the same poem, not merely in style and subject but, much more important, in theme and plot. This is exactly what we should expect of such a compulsive text: reading it is like hearing someone recount a dream or a nightmare, and interpreting it requires some minimal skill in the interpretation of dreams. Like a dream, it is highly repetitive. What it mainly repeats is, as in many anxiety dreams, the speaker's fear of being destroyed: in this case by a malevolent agent represented as a harp, a lyre, a bard, or a minstrel—the nightmare agents or secret police of poetry. But since it is not a dream but a consciously produced poem, its forward movement is marked by its speaker's determined effort to stay *on* his subject, which is basically poetical landscape description. What could be more "Wordsworthian"? But on the evidence of "The Vale of Esthwaite," we would have to say that for Wordsworth at age seventeen there was no more life-threatening, scarifying topic than that one. It is impossible for modern readers not to smile at its Gothic excesses, but we should not ignore the pathos of its situation, which is something like a young boy's exploring the very real sadness of his life in—for a modern equivalent—the plot, imagery, and language of a comic book. No fancy critical skill is needed to reach this conclusion; the poem deconstructs itself over and over again before our very eyes. By its end—wherever we locate it—the poet seems to have lost the battle.

Generically, "The Vale of Esthwaite" is yet another eighteenth-century imitation of Milton along lines first laid down by James Thomson: a walk through the landscape and the seasons, alternating between moods of L'Allegro and Il Pensoroso. But this convenient arrangement is continually knocked askew by the interruption of a third term, the Gothic-Sublime, with life-threatening thrills of horror that make it impossible to maintain the usual balance between charming beauty and pleasant melancholy. The demonic bard figures are always associated with these Gothic interruptions. Statistically, less than 10 percent of the extant text is in the L'Allegro mood, and while Il Pensoroso gets almost 30 percent of the total, the Gothic passages take up fully 40 percent of the whole. In his melancholy passages Wordsworth tried to be serious and mature; these are the parts of the poem containing benevolent "social" references to village poverty. The Gothic parts are intensely personal and, not surprisingly, are the best parts of the whole, if you like that sort of thing, which Wordsworth clearly did. Yet they also repulsed him; such was his double bind. The remaining 20 percent of the lines are autobiographical: self-pitying thoughts about his coming change of scene, and the hard life awaiting him: "full soon must I resign [the cheering joys of Fancy] / To delve in Mammon's joyless mine" (Text 1.V.13–14). The only human agents able to offer him any support are John Fleming's friendship and Dorothy's confidence.

Wordsworth was saying farewell to the dearest spot he knew on earth, and he dreads the thought so much that it returns *as* dread to haunt the beloved landscape: the return of the repressed. He goes to face "the real world," as high school and college graduates are fond of saying, but his vision is complicated not only by "Mammon" but by his realization that his growing attachment to poetical Fancy is going to complicate his work in Mammon's "joyless mine." No minstrels need apply. In light of the family plan that he should achieve honors at Cambridge, proceed thence to a fellowship, possibly a professorship, or at least ordination, the attractions of a life of poetry appeared to this serious teenager like nightmarish delusions of his own badly conflicted motives.

What happens at the beginning of the poem happens repeatedly throughout it. It starts with a command—"avaunt!"—and that is its password throughout, as the speaker tries to ward off the various specters that try to kill him. Even the opening couplet is fragmentary, but it's fairly easy to fill in the blanks:

> [?] avaunt! with tenfold pleasure
> I ga[ze] the landskip's various treasure.
>
> (1–2)

That is to say: "avaunt!" . . . "Ye shades of night," or "Ye thoughts of death," or some such specter, for "I" . . . "will now gaze on the landscape for relief." Forcing down these nightmare thoughts, he starts out with the morning lark for his usual walk around the beautiful "lake's lovely bosom." Then, "at noon I hied to gloomy glades." This is the standard next move for L'Allegro to become a bit more *pensoroso,* but things quickly get out of hand. In three lines Wordsworth accelerates himself from "gloom" to religion to superstition to horror, a woman in a black dress ("She wove a stole of sable thread"), and then all hell breaks loose, or rather the precisely articulated hell of this poem:

> And hark[!] the ringing harp I hear
> And [lo!] her druid sons appear.
> Why roll on me your glaring eyes[?]
> Why fix on me for sacrifice[?]

That these lines are imitated straight out of Helen Maria Williams is less important than the special use Wordsworth puts them to.[29] There are many demons in eighteenth-century Gothic poems and novels, and plenty of ancient bards, druids, and harps, but few in which the harps are identical to demonic instruments of destruction. The trademark—or psychic scar—of "The Vale of Esthwaite" is that the demons represented *in* the text have taken over control *of* the text.

Wordsworth desperately tries to save himself by getting back to the landscape,

> But Lo, the stream's loud genius seen
> The *black* arched boughs and rocks *between*
> That brood o'er one eternal night
> Shoot from the cliff in robe of *white.*
>
> (35–38; italics added)

Such sharp contrasts in the landscape, Wordsworth said of a particular oak leaf he once saw at twilight between Hawkshead and Ambleside, were the natural appearance he claimed no poet had yet captured (though Thomson is full of them), and supplying this deficiency occurred to him as an excellent motivation toward a career in poetry. But here the contrast is only a metaphoric vehicle that returns him to the horror that is the burden of the passage, which continues to spin out of control.

> *So* oft in castle moated round
> In black damp dungeon underground
> Strange forms are seen that white and tall
> Stand straight against the coal black wall.

And then . . . he wakes up. This transparent device of primitive or naive writing ("I woke up and realized it was all a dream") is actually managed quite nicely, in terms of Wordsworth's ostensible subject and immediate surroundings:

> Then fancy, like the light'ning gleam
> Shot from wondrous dream to dream

Till roused; perhaps the flickering dove
Broke from the rustling boughs above
Or straggled sheep with white fleece seen
Between the Boughs of sombrous green[,]
Starting wildly from its sleep
Shook the pebble from the steep
That gingling downward shrill and slow
[ ] in the Rill below.—

(65–74)

Here he made a paragraph break, but all he could do was start over: "Lone wandering oft by Esthwaite's [stream] / My soul has felt the mystic dr[eam]." And so the pattern continues, with repeated efforts to keep his "mystic" or "twilight" moods from deepening into something worse, but with repeated failures, which he hideously elaborates and obviously enjoys.

All this is made more poignant and realistic in the latter portions of the text, where he refers to his father's death and to Dorothy and John Fleming. But the poem can only be "the shipwreck of the thought" it means to be conveying, so long as "fancy in a daemon's form / Rides through the clouds and swells the storm, / To . . . sweet Melancholy blind, / The moonlight of the Poet's mind" (Text 1.V.2–6). At the very end of the poem he asserts bravely that he'll still be able to think of the beauties of Nature and Art even while toiling in Mammon's mine. That may be so, but it was not the main problem of "The Vale of Esthwaite," which has been, rather, that Fancy all too regularly takes on a demonic form that throws him into a terror and a darkness far worse than Mammon's gloom, and that paralyzes his mind from working at all. Poetry, his own career dream, not Mammon, his uncles' plan, is the enemy, and the source of the contradictions between his projected life plan and his personal desires that "The Vale of Esthwaite" tries but fails to overcome.

Wordsworth returned to Penrith after graduating in June 1787. Christopher Crackanthorpe knew that school was out and the boys ready to come home, but did not send horses for the boys, because they had not specifically requested them—nor had any family member attended the closing ceremonies. The homecoming tragedy of 1783 was now replayed as farce. William finally hired a horse himself to ride to Penrith to see what was the matter; he thought somebody must be ill. Dorothy related the incident to her friend Jane Pollard in Halifax with shrewd insight into Crackanthorpe's mean punctilio. Their guardian's treatment of them affected the servants, who did not miss an opportunity to make snide comments about the children's lowered expectations. Because of William's strongly independent bearing, they particularly delighted in thwarting his requests with variations on the theme of "Who does he think he is, a gentleman?"

The situation that summer was all the more painful because it was the boys' first reunion with Dorothy since their mother's death nine years earlier. The happiness of the occasion was deeply scarred by their sense of what they had lost: parents, prospects, a whole world of possibilities. They frequently wept together. Yet they were also happy together: William and Dorothy and Mary Hutchinson had some fine rambles about the countryside, including a return visit to Penrith Beacon, reinforcing its earlier emotional associations with new intensities from this time of school ending and family reunion, and laying powerful depth charges in Wordsworth's young imagination.

William returned to Hawkshead and Ann Tyson many weeks before he departed for Cambridge: further evidence of the mutual distaste with which he and Crackanthorpe now regarded each other. Crackanthorpe's only claim to merit was that he had received an inheritance, whereas Wordsworth's only "shame" was that he hadn't received his, and thus had no status as an independent person and a very dubious one as an heir prospective.

Dorothy returned not to Halifax and her aunt Threlkeld but to Forncett (near Norwich), to live with her kindlier uncle, the Reverend William Cookson, whose personality was not so distorted as his brother's by a fixation on social advancement. As a younger son, Cookson had lesser expectations in this direction anyway. But he was working his mild, stolid, yet expertly calculating way up the social ladder via influential friends like William Wilberforce, MP for York and one of Pitt's closest friends. The Forncett vicarage was the prime stock in Cookson's portfolio of nonresident "livings" and preferred ecclesiastical appointments, which had allowed him at last to marry the daughter of the Penrith vicar after a courtship of seven passion-deadening years.* Such arrangements, which were also characteristic of several of the poets of Sensibility who influenced young Wordsworth, marked out the late eighteenth-century path of advancement that he expected to follow, and Cookson's hard experience in this road eventually made him a severer, more knowledgeable critic of his young nephew than Christopher Crackanthorpe, who mainly resented the money.

*The unpublished Cookson-Cowper correspondence in the Wordsworth Library makes for painful reading, like the raw material of a Jane Austen novel. The careerism and financial calculation of both parties—another William and Dorothy—is shaded by her increasingly mysterious physical ailments and his temporizing excuses, a mixture of hollow gallantry and condescension.

5 STRANGER, LOUNGER, LOVER

Residence at Cambridge

> . . . I had . . . a strangeness in my mind,
> A feeling that I was not for that hour
> Nor for that place. But . . .
>
> We sauntered, played, we rioted, we talked
> Unprofitable talk at morning hours,
> Drifted about along the streets and walks,
> Read lazily in lazy books . . . .
>
> (III.79–81, 251–54)

Wordsworth set out for Cambridge with his maternal uncle William Cookson and paternal cousin John Myers in late October of 1787. The boys were full of enthusiasm for the opportunities and challenges of university life; William in particular "had raised a pile upon the basis of the coming time" of fantastical proportions. But the two boys would need help making their way in the world: Wordsworth was an orphan, and Myers's mother had died earlier that year. William Cookson was just the man to help them.

Cookson was much more than an uncle at this moment: he was a fellow of St. John's College, one of two fellowships the college reserved for men from Cumberland, at least one of which was usually held by a Hawkshead graduate.[1] This meant he was one of fifty-five fellows of the autonomous corporate body which legally owned and administered the college and the forty-six church livings in its gift, each paying about £300 per year. A similar parity existed between the number of fellows in each Cambridge college and the number of benefices it owned, for though Cambridge and Oxford were educational institutions, neither was truly a national university.[2] They were still Anglican foundations whose primary social function was to supply parishes with priests. By the late eighteenth century the priests-to-be were much more interested in the process than most parishes, and it was said that "the emoluments of Cambridge have been its ruin, as a place of genuine education."[3] In the normal course of events, students elected to fellowships stayed on at college after their B.A., advanced to their M.A. by payment of a fee, and then drew an annual stipend of about £200 until a living became vacant. About two per year opened up, on the average, in the larger colleges.[4] Upon being awarded a living, a fellow left the college, was released from his vows of celibacy, and, if he had cultivated his marriage prospects well—as Cookson had—retired to a country parish to begin his adult life of religious leisure and good works.[5] Cookson knew a fellowship would be waiting for William on graduation because he would soon vacate his own fellowship to get married: both King George and Pitt had assured Wilberforce that his "fat little Canon's" long wait for a living was almost over.[6]

Besides his fellowship, William Cookson had other important connections with which to ease his nephews' transition into adult life via the university. Now thirty-three, he had spent nearly five years (1781–86) as preceptor to George III's sons, particularly the fifth, Ernest Augustus, duke of Cumberland (1771–1851), in the palace at Kew.[7] He regularly held long conversations with the concerned monarch about his sons' progress—those unimpressive, when not actively infamous, boys who grew up causing great concern for the crown's succession during the regency period. George, the Prince of Wales (b. 1762), was already beyond paternal control, as the first "Regency Crisis" (1788–89) made abundantly clear, when King George suffered the first of his fits of "madness." It was sometimes suggested that the pious regimen enforced by the princes' tutors contributed to their later licentiousness—or, in the case of Ernest, who became king of Hanover in 1837 on Victoria's ascension to the English throne, his extreme conservatism. Tutors of royalty and nobility often became figures of considerable social importance in their own right. George III was "completely devoted" to his tutor, John Stuart, eventually making him first lord of the treasury (that is, prime minister) in 1762, as Lord Bute: Sir James Lowther's father-in-law and the elder Pitt's schoolmate.[8] Cookson was on familiar enough terms with the king to be teased by him about his weight, and this intimacy, plus George's entire satisfaction with Cookson's tutoring, made his appointment as a canon of the chapel royal at Windsor an easy matter.[9] William Cookson was one of "the round pegs for whom the round holes of preferment are intended,"[10] and there was no reason at this time to suppose that his nephew William was not equally malleable.

Still more important for his young charges was Cookson's intimate friendship with Wilberforce, who was just emerging as the parliamentary champion of the fight against slavery. Their friendship dated from their college days at St. John's ten years earlier. Wilberforce was, in turn, one of Pitt's closest friends. For several years beginning in 1788, Wilberforce spent weeks or months at a time at Cookson's house in Forncett, reading up to nine hours a day and using Cookson as a tutor to make up for his wasted time at Cambridge.[11] Cookson had recently helped Wilberforce (who was very rich) obtain a property in the Lake District, where he loved to holiday. He had leased Rayrigg, the Windermere estate of Wordsworth's friend John Fleming, from as early as 1782.[12]

Wordsworth was very fortunate to have an uncle with William Cookson's connections, which were sure routes to preferment and independence if his university career ended with even a modicum of success. In this respect, Cookson was a younger complement to John Robinson, who, though now sixty, was still active in court and government politics. He had by this time moved from his service in Lord North's prime ministership, when he was "at the centre of governmental jobbery and corruption,"[13] to being the trusted political agent for no less a client than George III himself. Using the electioneering skills he had learned in Cumberland, especially the ability to predict votes on crucial divisions, he was now the king's chief go-between in his relations with Parliament, and had already demonstrated his usefulness to Pitt.[14] For young Wordsworth's prospects, Robinson's shrewd dealings were all to the good; it would be hard to name a man in England at the time more experienced in securing and dispensing places, especially the comparatively trifling matter of finding a place for a needy, deserving nephew after graduation. Robinson was certainly alert to all these possibilities. He kept a keen eye on his nephew during this first year at college: "my earnest recommendation to you is to stick close to College for the first two or three years .... It will give me great pleasure to hear you go out high in your year, and I cannot by words alone express to you the satisfaction I shall feel in hearing you go out Senior Wrangler, strive for that, and establish a reputation at College which will go with you, and serve you thro' Life."[15]

With two such uncles, young Wordsworth was, speaking in modern terms, never more than two phone calls away from the king or the prime minister of England throughout his years at Cambridge. One of the best measures of his independence is that he never placed those calls, or let others make them for him; and when he finally did make them, out of personal desperation, it was much too late and his credit along those lines long since expended.

En route to Cambridge the three Cumberland travelers spent their first night at the home of John Robinson's brother, Captain (later Admiral) Hugh Robinson, in York. The fifty-two-year-old captain had just married John Myers's sister Mary, aged twenty-two; she would bear him thirteen children in the remaining fifteen years of his life.[16] At dinner that night the family's expectations and interests were on everyone's mind when the captain pointedly commented, "I hope, William, you mean to take a good degree." William answered with a sweeping challenge to himself: "I will be either Senior Wrangler or nothing!"[17] The boast was not idle. He was the most favored student in his year at Hawkshead, and one of the best in the past several years. The school had a steady record of high-ranking wranglers for many years, most of them at St. John's, where several of the fellows were always sure to be Hawkshead alumni: Cookson's friend Edward Christian, Hawkshead master in 1781, was now a Johnian fellow and professor of law.[18]

That Wordsworth more nearly achieved the other alternative in his ultimatum is the real story of his Cambridge years. But, backed by this stern family's support and buoyed by his own confidence, he rolled into Cambridge three or four days later, along the northwest road from Huntingdon, over the Cam at Magdalene Bridge, into Bridge Street, "and at the Hoop we landed, famous inn." This is one of those awkward lines that even Wordsworth's admirers like to smile at, but the Hoop Inn, or Hotel, an old coaching inn, was indeed very much at the center of Cambridge life, being the unofficial headquarters of the Whig party until well past the middle of the nineteenth century.[19] Located near the three-way intersection of the main northwest–southeast road (Bridge Street and Sidney Street) with Jesus Lane, the east–west road to Newmarket, and High Street (now St. John's Street), the north–south road to Trumpington, it was physically at the center of Cambridge as well. It was the main hotel for families of students at St. John's College, which stood right across the street.

Just as the world of personal social connections that Wordsworth now entered was by modern standards extremely small, so too was its university outpost. From St. John's College at the top of High Street to Peterhouse at the bottom was less than a thousand yards, and all but five of the colleges were strung along that axis. The town center was not much different in its physical layout from what it is today. The same three major streets still intersect each other at the same angles near St. John's, forming a rough trident pointing southeast. Thomas Gray likened it to "a Spider, with a nasty lump [the university] in the middle of it, & half a dozen scrambling long legs."

But in other respects it differed greatly. The sixteen oldest colleges were there in all their Gothic splendor, one of the largest and most coherent groupings of well-preserved Gothic-Renaissance buildings in Europe. But the town, with fewer than ten thousand inhabitants living in fourteen different parishes, was small and miserable, a far cry from today's upscale urban milieu. On fine days it presented a vision of rural simplicity surrounding Gothic magnificence. But on bad days it was all mud and flowing gutters, and every night the streets nearest the university were filled with drunken roistering students, making passage dangerous.[20] Town-and-gown fights or riots went on constantly, for despite the town's dependence on the university, relations between the two were extremely hostile, producing "a state at times comparable to petty warfare."[21] There were stocks and pillories in public places, a spinning house for female vagrants and prostitutes, and a treadmill for male criminals. The streets were unpaved and almost completely dark at night; the first citywide illuminations were not installed until 1796. One of the arguments against streetlighting was that the students and the "snobs" (as students called all townspeople) would recognize each other more easily and fight even more. During Wordsworth's time, illuminations were reserved for special occasions, such as the celebration in March of his second year (1789) for King George's recovery from the "madness" (porphyria) which would eventually handicap him permanently.[22] But at least the traffic was not bad; only three people in town kept carriages, one of them Richard Watson, professor of chemistry and bishop of Llandaff, the Lake District boy whose successful ascent up the ladder of place and preferment was legendary, and often held up to young Wordsworth as a model—or a reproach.

"The Evangelist St. John My Patron Was"

The massive entrance to St. John's three "gloomy courts" (constructed 1511, 1598, and 1671) was on High Street, just off the main Cambridge intersection. Wordsworth's "nook obscure" was Room 23 in the southwest corner of First Court, up Pump staircase, above the busy kitchens with their "shrill notes of sharp command and scolding intermixed."[23] Its courts are not "gloomy" today (East Anglian weather permitting), in their manicured beauty, but in Wordsworth's time the courts and cellars were all work areas, piled up with coal and wood deliveries, and bustling with porters and shoeblacks, laundresses and cooks, "gyps" (menservants assigned to each entryway) and bed makers—more like a small village than today's privileged park for paying tourists to wander in. The kitchens were huge subterraneous places, with fireplaces as big as rooms, and "cooks, sub-cooks, and scullions in abundance, as black and greasy as so many devils."[24] Wordsworth's small, cheap room looked out on the dark squalor of Back Lane toward the splendid chapel of Trinity College, designed by Christopher Wren. His bedroom was but a closet, and he used to pull the bed out into his "keeping room" at night to have a view of the chapel spires through his little window.[25]

St. John's was one of the two largest Cambridge colleges, along with Trinity, its next-door neighbor and constant rival. In various college publications one detects a slight note of restive inferiority with regard to Trinity, which has more often attained a reputation for academic excellence, as measured in famous names, like Newton. A similar paradox afflicts the relationship between St. John's and Wordsworth, in that the man "almost universally regarded as the greatest of the Johnians"[26] was one of its least distinguished students. Yet university records and chronologies must frequently use him as a reference point ("Wordsworth's year," "friend of Wordsworth," etc.). Some of St. John's lagging reputation came from its long association with conservative positions and professors, especially in religious matters; it is directly across the street from the university divinity school.[27] In its present chapel, completed in 1869, Wordsworth, Wilberforce, Trinity's Newton, and Pascal are the only secular figures represented among eighty illustrating the history of Christianity. But the latter three were much more renowned for piety than Wordsworth even in his maturity, and his younger self was altogether another subject.[28]

In the civil war, St. John's was a Royalist college in a parliamentary town, used as a prison by Cromwell's troops. High Church orthodoxy returned in 1661, but for the next hundred years St. John's went into a steady decline that leaves its own historians puzzled.[29] At the time Wordsworth arrived, its reputation was reviving, thanks to the energetic reforms of Samuel Powell, master from 1765 to 1775, mostly involving more rigorous examinations—which had a direct effect on Wordsworth. But with about two hundred students and fifty fellows, and generally low enrollments throughout the eighteenth century, living conditions were fairly spacious through its three courtyards. Its Williams Library was considered by many to be one of the finest in the university, second only (as in so many things) "to Trinity in splendour, though far less well known to the public at large."[30]

Wordsworth was one of the forty-four students who entered St. John's as freshmen in 1787. The number was low, but up significantly from the doldrums of the 1760s and 1770s. Among the students who started with him, or already there, were many known to him from Hawkshead and others with whom he soon became acquainted on the basis of other northern family connections. Far different from the solitary existence portrayed in *The Prelude* and rehearsed in his standard biographies, the full range of Wordsworth's friendships and acquaintances included more than two dozen names.[31]

Also entering with Wordsworth and Myers were Thomas Gawthorp, who had roomed with Wordsworth at Ann Tyson's the previous year.[32] Other Hawkshead boys entering other colleges in 1787 included Robert Greenwood, the minstrel of Windermere, next door at Trinity and John Millar at Jesus. Many of William's best friends were already at nearby colleges: John Fleming and William Penny at Christ's; Fleming's brother Fletcher Raincock at Pembroke; Charles Farish, another of the "minstrels," at Queen's (Farish's brother William was a tutor at Magdalene), as was James Losh from Carlisle, whose younger brother William had been with Wordsworth at Hawkshead.[33] This gallery of familiar faces lengthened in subsequent years: Thomas Maude, also a boarder at Ann Tyson's with the Wordsworths, came up to St. John's the next year (he, not Wordsworth, would succeed William Cookson as rector at Forncett), and Reginald Brathwaite, son of the Hawkshead vicar at whose Belmount country house Wordsworth had been so well received, came in 1790.[34] At least thirteen other Hawkshead boys arrived at other colleges between 1787 and 1790. When Wordsworth says he felt "a strangeness in his mind," that he was "not for that place," the reference must be understood as strictly subjective, for there was no place in England that could have been less strange and more familiar to him in personal terms than St. John's College. In fact, there was no place on earth, in default of a family home, that stood more ready to give the young Wordsworth a warm, comfortable reception than Cambridge University.

College friendships are always important, but in eighteenth-century England, with a much smaller population and far fewer participants in public life, college associates were central to one's mature life. The inner circle of Pitt's government—and of his Foxite opponents—was peopled to an extraordinary degree by Cambridge men (such as Wilberforce). Not only Wordsworth's friends but also the people he knew *of* (and vice versa) at college are significant data for charting his development, as persons who might be expected to remain more or less aware of him as "someone I knew at university."* For example, among students already at St. John's in 1787 was a young man named Robert Stewart, later Viscount Castlereagh, the Pitt protégé who helped put down the Irish rebellion of 1798 and who as foreign minister would put together the coalition which finally brought Napoleon down. We don't know if he and Wordsworth knew each other well, but they can hardly have been unaware of each other's existence.

At other colleges Wordsworth also knew men who became later friends, especially Francis Wrangham and John Tweddell of Trinity, members of the brilliant class of 1790. Other noteworthy names that come close to Wordsworth's orbit are Thomas Malthus of Jesus, ninth wrangler in 1788, author of the famous *Essay on Population* (1798). (He was one of the fellows who ordered Coleridge to return to college and pay his bills in 1794. His father had been one of Rousseau's executors and his tutors were Gilbert Wakefield and William Frend, important Cambridge radicals known to Wordsworth in London in the early 1790s.)[35] On the other side of the political coin were future enemies: John Hookham Frere, another Cambridge contemporary (Caius, 1792), became, like Castlereagh, a member of Pitt's coterie of brilliant young protégés: he was one of the main contributors, along with George Canning, future prime minister, to the *Anti-Jacobin* of 1797–98, which savagely attacked Coleridge, Southey, and Lamb by name, and alluded knowingly to Wordsworth. Frere could have been the means by which Wordsworth was recruited, or blackmailed, by the secret service in 1798—if he was (Chapter 24).

Despite his later statement that he "was not . . . for that place," he catches

*A university "acquaintance" of a different sort was Sir James Lowther, who spent his sixteenth and seventeenth years at Peterhouse in 1752–53, living in rooms directly below Thomas Gray (Hugh Owen, *The Lowther Family* [Chichester: Phillimore, 1990], 281, 300).

very well the dizzy pleasure of first college days spent among so many old friends and new acquaintances: "In a world / Of welcome faces up and down I roved" (III.19–20).

Freshmen entering St. John's were assigned randomly to either Edward Frewen or William Pearce as tutors, a position of counsel and discipline, more than instruction. William Cookson saw to it that Wordsworth was assigned to his friend Frewen, who had just been elected one of the college's eight senior fellows. The chain of influence began to work immediately. There were over a hundred scholarships and "exhibitions" available at St. John's for financial aid, and Frewen secured Wordsworth a Foundress's scholarship and two small exhibitions worth about £10 each annually, from those designated specifically for students from Hawkshead or Cumberland.[36] Wordsworth's preparatory school record entitled him to some of these, but his connections helped, for Cambridge was far from a pure meritocracy. These awards, and the cheap room he was assigned (£7 a year),[37] should have covered his university expenses nicely, which were officially estimated at about £15 per year, not including tuition.[38] Thomas Malthus's father thought £50 per year, for everything, was plenty.* But Wordsworth's actual expenses for his first two years ran over £100 per year, and in 1794 Mrs. Richard Wordsworth, his guardian's widow, claimed £400 of Chris topher Crackanthorpe, almost all of it laid out in payment for William's education; Wordsworth still owed his college tutor £10 in 1803.[39] Considering his scholarship, cheap room, and "exhibition" awards, such a high rate of expense shows that he had not yet adopted his policy of "plain living and high thinking," and his college lifestyle shows where the money went.

He signed up for the normal academic schedule, one classics and one mathematics lecture or tutorial each morning between nine and noon, in preparation for the first examination in December. This was a leisurely schedule, and an eminently fair one, as the exams were keyed directly to the readings set for each subject. In classics that fall the subject was the last book of Xenophon's *Anabasis* (in Greek), and in mathematics, basic algebra. Normally the boys in groups of four or five would construe their way through Xenophon and work out equations on demand. Wordsworth, who had already read the first six books of Euclid's *Elements* (the second-year math text) and knew both simple and quadratic equations, was so well prepared in

*It is difficult to establish an average cost for college expenses. Fellow commoners could easily spend more than £200 per year; students of any rank were capable of ruining themselves (and their families) by running up unpayable debts. On the other hand, some notable sizars got by for much less than £50 per year (Christopher Wordsworth, *Social Life at the English Universities in the Eighteenth Century* [1877], 412–15).

mathematics that he did not need to attend many of his math classes. "Accordingly," he said, "I got into a rather idle way, reading nothing but classic authors according to my fancy, and Italian poetry."[40]

Although Cookson had brought his young nephews up nearly two weeks after the official start of the term (ca. October 10), neither of the boys had any trouble with the first exam. Both finished in the first class, as did nearly half of the other freshmen, including Robert Jones from Wales and William Terrot from Scotland, who were becoming two of William's new friends. Two other friends, both from Pembroke, were Thomas Middleton (fourth senior optime in 1792), Coleridge's school friend and future liberal bishop of Calcutta, and William Mathews, the unhappy son of a London bookseller and Methodist preacher, Wordsworth's "most intimate friend."[41]

After the Christmas break (which Wordsworth, having no other place to go, spent at college) the distinction between "reading" and "nonreading" men began to emerge. Most students were "nonreading" men, or gradually became so as the years went by: they would not compete for honors degrees, but do only the undemanding minimum necessary to pass the university final exams in January of their fourth year. In this respect Wordsworth's university career, and his account of it, is very typical; well over half of the students in his year did not compete for honors. But he actually read quite a lot, both in required and in nonrequired texts: he could technically be classed as a "reading nonreading" man.

In the Lent (winter) and Michaelmas (spring) terms, the texts were Tacitus *(De Moribus Germanorum)* and some books of Euclid. In this exam, Wordsworth slipped to second class, though Myers stayed in first, while Jones tumbled to third. This was not very serious. The college exams had little bearing on the degree one would finally receive. When William Cookson resigned his fellowship in that spring of 1788 to get married, he felt confident that his nephews had started out well and gave every indication of continuing to do so. In the event, neither did.

As a gentleman's orphan, dependent on educational loans from his guardians which he was expected to pay back, Wordsworth was entered at St. John's as a sizar, the lowest category, one of seven in his year. The other ranks were nobleman (one in his year), fellow commoners (four), and pensioners, the largest category (thirty-two). Sizar was a reduced-fee status, traditionally requiring such duties as waiting on tables in commons, but luckily for Wordsworth's pride this requirement had been discontinued in 1786. Sizars and pensioners could be stared out of countenance by fellow commoners or noblemen, and dismissed as irretrievably "low" persons, who "ought not to exist."[42] Sizars were looked down on, but they were also elected to fellowships proportionately more than any other class of students.[43] They were expected to distinguish themselves by hard work and success: Newton had been a sizar, as had Paley, and Richard Watson, that indefatigable Lakeland success story. So had William Cookson. If the designation of sizar caused Wordsworth any pain, he had plenty of friendly company in which to assuage it, for Myers, Gawthorp, Greenwood, Farish, and John Millar were all sizars. (Interestingly, Christopher Wordsworth was entered in 1792 as a pensioner.) Wordsworth's comments about Cambridge's "republican" spirit may be special pleading, but almost every account of Cambridge life stresses the ease of acquaintance between boys from different social backgrounds, though it is probably too much to claim that "no differences of rank or wealth or university status affected the social intercourse of the students."[44] The *Gradus ad Cantabrigiam,* a contemporary handbook of student advice and slang, claims that the gap between sizars and pensioners at Cambridge was much smaller than that between Oxford's servitors and its pensioners, noting that their gowns were identical at St. John's and that some sizars "endeavor to vie [with pensioners] in fashionable frivolity."* Wordsworth's self-descriptions and the family accounts show that he was one of these. He neither lived nor looked like a sizar: he went "to tutor or to tailors" with equal frequency, got himself "attired in splendid clothes," and purchased a "lordly dressing gown"—that is, as good as any of the young lords' who were his classmates, such as Lord Bute's grandson, James Lowther's nephew.[45]

Dress was very important at Cambridge, both for condescending discriminations between insecure, fashion-conscious young men, and because it immediately distinguished members of the university, as a class, from all other members of the surrounding community. Rowlandson's picture *Bucks of the First Head* (see illustration) gives a good idea of what Cambridge students looked like, and how they spent their time. The two "bucks" are probably fellow commoners, their elaborately disheveled costumes, long curly hair, and girlish good looks very much part of the "effeminate" manners and appearance which writers of the time criticized,† along with the violence and rampant sexual license which went arm in arm with it, as they are with the market girl. She would be one of the "lady snobbesses" of the town who were a focus of constant interest, harassment, and satisfaction to those nonreading men whose subspecialty was to be "gay-men" or "varmint-men."

Cambridge students wore a sleeveless gown, or "curtain," at all times, fel-

***Gradus ad Cantabrigiam* (London, 1824), 122–23. I will cite the *Gradus* throughout this chapter for specialized Cambridge terms.

†*Remarks on the Enormous Expense in the Education of Young Men* (1788) says that "the Dress of the Undergraduates [should] be taken into most serious Consideration: Being in its present State, Indecent, Expensive, and Effeminate" (cited in Christopher Wordsworth, *Social Life at the English Universities in the Eighteenth Century* [1877], 476.)

lows wore cocked hats, and the students, as Dorothy noted on her visit during Wordsworth's second year, had "smart powdered heads with black caps like helmets," which they were expected to touch in deference to senior college and university officials.[46] Hair could be curled in the "Apollo" style, as well as powdered; the republican "crop" did not come into fashion until a couple of years later. "Gay silks, ruffles, and embroidery" were additional fashion accents,[47] which Wordsworth's account gives us to understand he did not stint. Quite the contrary. He later spoke of himself as "a simple rustic," but this was editing himself for poetical effect: his family had laid out 11*s.* 5*d.* for silk hose and velvet coats before he left Hawkshead,[48] and he powdered his hair till it "glitter[ed] like rimy tree when frost is keen"—a description that strains to give a naturalistic twist to his wholly artificial, fashionable appearance. When he speaks of "the surfaces of artificial life / And manners finely spun, the delicate race / Of colours, lurking, gleaming up and down . . . woven with silk and gold . . . wily interchange of snaky hues" (III.590–94), the very intricacy of his description (which owes something to Milton's Satan) and his family's accounts belie his claims that he was "content with the more homely produce rudely piled / In this our coarser warehouse." He had his own silks and satins and velvets, if not the splendid colored robes of the young noblemen—bright purple for Trinity, white silk for conservative St. John's[49]—and his description matches very well the *Gradus*'s definition of fellow commoners: "their gowns are richly trimmed with gold, or silver, lace—their caps are crowned with velvet, the tassels to which are of gold, or silver."

He had "smooth housekeeping within, and all without / Liberal and suiting a gentleman's array," just like any other young gentleman. His housekeeping was "smooth" because, although he had a small room, he had the services, along with the other students in his stairwell, of a "gyp," who brought coal and meals and wake-up calls and fended off tradesmen bearing bills, and a female bed maker who made up the boys' beds in the morning and turned them down at night. Gyps and bed makers were also available for services and favors beyond their normal duties.

Academic work was not the highest priority for most men at Cambridge. In Wordsworth's descriptions of what he did there, nonacademic pursuits outnumber academic ones by three to one. On the one hand, he shopped, went to parties, sauntered, played, "rioted," rode horseback, sailed on the Cam, drank, laughed at the college fellows, walked out in the countryside, and dreamed of becoming a writer; on the other, he attended lectures and compulsory chapel, read both required and nonrequired books, dabbled in geometry, dealt in "classic niceties" on themes and declamations, and worried about his future maintenance. This was the normal ratio for most students, and Wordsworth's account of it in *Prelude* III, one of the few extended descriptions of eighteenth-century university life in a major work of serious literature, is in fact quite unremarkable as to content. Almost everyone reminiscing about Cambridge in the eighteenth century mentions what Wordsworth does, and with roughly the same attitudes: awe at Roubillac's statue of Newton in Trinity Chapel, complaints about compulsory chapel attendance, abhorrence of the dissipated social life of the idle students, and fear of and loathing for the dreaded final examinations. Book III opens with Wordsworth's first sight of "the long-backed chapel of King's College," a focus so common that the *Gradus* defines it simply as "Freshman Landmark": "This stupendous edifice may be seen for several miles." Byron's "Thoughts Suggested by a College Examination" (1806) match Wordsworth's very well, though Byron was more explicit about the connection between performance and preferment, "When Self and Church demand a bigot zeal."

Students were considered to be adults. (*Gradus:* "every stripling is accounted a *Man* from the moment of putting on his gown and cap.") Masters and tutors rarely inquired into their domestic arrangements as long as they showed up often enough at chapel. Attendance at lectures and tutorials, while not technically optional, quickly dwindled down to the "reading men." The proportions in Wordsworth's description of "the lecturer's room" are just about right:

> All studded round, as thick as chairs could stand,
> With loyal students faithful to their books,
> Half-and-half idlers, hardy recusants,
> And honest dunces . . . .
>
> (III.60–64)

Here again, the ratio is three to one between frivolous and serious students, and this vignette is likely to have been based on a vivid first impression of an eagerly anticipated early class meeting. His own progress went steadily downward through the first three types he mentions, from faithful study, to increasing idleness, ending in hardy "recusancy"—refusal to do the required work on the basis of principle. What that principle could have been for him at the time requires some speculation. In *The Prelude* he says it was to preserve himself as a poet, but it can hardly have appeared so then. If it did, it was a very desperately invoked principle.

The morning's lead-up to dinner at one, the most important official event of each day, was leisurely. Chapel was at seven, and attendance was required: meaning that if one missed too often one might be called on the tutor's carpet. There was a lively trade in bribes, conveyed via gyps, to the "marker" who pricked pinholes after the names of absentees in the college lists. Breakfast was at eight, served in one's room, and then came the two classes in classics and mathematics, between nine and noon. A good hour was allowed for dressing for dinner, donning white waistcoats and white silk stockings, visiting the hairdresser, and so on, following the recommendations in *Ten Minutes Advice to Freshmen* (1785).[50]

At dinner the fellows sat at the high table across one end of the hall, where they were joined by their noble students and fellow commoners. Pensioners and sizars sat crowded together at the tables running perpendicularly down the length of the hall. Sizars' meals were still sometimes made up from the leftovers of the high table, but so full, rich, and varied was the menu of these well-endowed establishments that one hardly ever hears, in all the university histories and reminiscences, a single complaint about the food, that staple gripe of modern-day college life. Descriptions of college meals fairly burst with calories and cholesterol: meat pies, pidgeon pies, sirloins of beef, hams, tarts, and plum puddings. One of the main perquisites the celibate fellows could enjoy, legitimately, as they waited for their benefices, was good food, and the amounts they were willing to spend on it spilled over to the benefit of their students.

After dinner organized academic work was done for the day. Afternoons could be spent riding in the fields or rowing on the Cam in good weather, both of which Wordsworth did enthusiastically, going forth "to gallop through the country in blind zeal / Of senseless horsemanship, or on the breast / Of Cam sail . . . boisterously." This was exactly what he had done regularly at Hawkshead, and many his fellow horsemen and boatsmen there were with him here. In *The Prelude*'s image of a better, simpler university where he might have done better, Wordsworth seems to be describing an imaginary Hawkshead University, for the majority of student activities he includes were but a continuation of his grammar school pursuits, with a few "mature" additions.

In cold and inclement weather, not infrequent in marshy Cambridgeshire, there was much " 'good-natured lounging' " in friends' rooms[51] or "reading lazily in lazy books." "Lazy" and "lounging" are not vague general words here; these books designated a specific class of collegiate leisure reading. The *Gradus* glosses as, "to lounge," all the verbs from an epigram of Martial's—"Prandeo, poto, cano, endo, lego, caeno," which Wordsworth adapted to summarize his activities ("sauntered, played . . . rioted . . . talked . . . Read lazily"). The "most choice collection that the genius of Indolence could desire" was that of John ("Maps") Nicholson, who in addition to his bookshop hawked his wares aloud through all the college courts. Its most popular authors and titles were "Rabelais in English; several copies of the Reverend Mr. Sterne's *Tristram Shandy;* Wycherley and Congreve's plays; *Joe Miller's Jest Book* [a.k.a. *The Wit's Vade-Mecum*], Mrs. Behn's novels ["the English Sappho"], and Lord Rochester's Poems, which are very *moving!*"[52] Wordsworth ruefully admits his attraction to this kind of reading: he turned with "sickly appetite" to the "daily fare [of books] prescribed," but even when reading on his own,

> I chaced not steadily the manly deer,
> But laid me down to any casual feast
> Of wild wood-honey; or, with truant eyes
> Unruly, peeped about for vagrant fruit.
>
> (III.524–30)

This is one of many naturalized allusions to *Paradise Lost* which he used to dignify his report of his Cambridge experiences. Eve ate the "vagrant fruit" when she was tempted with godlike knowledge, but the "truant" or "vagrant" element in Nicholson's Lounging Library was obviously semisophisticated sexual stimulation at best, dirty books at worst, exactly of the sort we could expect to appeal to young men on their own as adults for the first time in their lives.

At the end of the afternoon, one took tea or went out to coffeehouses to read the newspapers. Evening chapel followed, and then the bed maker made her appearance and the gyp came in with the "sizing" bill of fare, for ordering hot food to be brought up to one's rooms from the busy college kitchens: part of a fowl or duck, roasted pigeon, a piece of apple pie or cake, or "any little luxury that might tempt you, in addition to commons fare." Most often these "invitations, suppers, wine, and fruit" (III.41) were clubbed together in the rooms of a member of a group of friends; Wordsworth, Myers, Jones, Terrot, and Gawthorp formed one at St. John's. The host would furnish bread, butter, cheese, and beer, and all would share the snacks they had ordered, sometimes roasting meat and sausages in the fireplace. These "sizing parties" were the most enjoyable event of the day and the focus of students' social life. Wordsworth indulged in them at least as regularly as his more proper brother Christopher a few years later, and Christopher's diary shows they were very regular indeed. The idea was to collect the best bunch of "good fellows" that one could, and to "endeavor to make each other drunk, [with] a pride in being able to resist the effects of the wine [oneself]. If any one wished to go to chapel he was pressed to return afterwards."[53]

"Buzzing" was a favorite strategy in these college parlor games. The decanter of wine was passed round, and a man receiving a nearly empty flagon could demand that the person passing it drink off the dregs in a single glass. But if the amount left exceeded the glass, the challenger had to finish what remained, and toss off a bumper of the newly filled decanter as well. Naturally, inexperienced boys got drunk fast. Toasts were proposed, first to a lady, then to a gentleman, and then to a friend. In these toasts, puns were very much in order, especially at St. John's. Johnians were called Hogs or Pigs (Trinity students were Bulldogs; Clare, Greyhounds), and had presumptive rights to wretched punning, in a community where Latin and English wordplay was a favorite mode of enlivening conversation.

This fed into the perennial adolescent penchant for humorous nicknames: an ugly student named Castley was quickly dubbed Ghastly. It would be interesting to know what Wordsworth's nickname was, but it is not hard to guess. People who are named Wordsworth, not a very uncommon name then or now, have heard about their "words' worth" ad nauseam. Since Wordsworth was known to be a prodigious reader and talented writer, and known *not* to be competing for the university's prestigious literary prizes, he must have been taunted on more than one occasion to give the supper group some of his words' worth. He delivers himself of a typical Johnian pun when he speaks of "Examinations, when the man was weighed / As in the balance" (III.65–66): *examen* being Latin for "a balance."[54] A snapshot of one of these parties may show us an image, dim and obscure, of him at the time:

> A party of Johnians were one day assembled in order to moisten the inward man with a bumper of wine, when the conversation turned upon a discussion of the different festivals and days. Amongst others, sidereal and solar days were mentioned. A dry fish, who looked anything but a punster, putting a bumper to his lips, observed, "I think we should have *jovial days* as well."[55]

The description fits Wordsworth's appearance and manner, and the pun is certainly bad enough. But what makes it more probably our young man is the fact that Wordsworth considered Jupiter (Jove) "my own beloved star" (IV.239), because he was born under its sign. Hence the purely linguistic aptness of the pun to the situation was matched by an internal, egotistical satisfaction that he was in effect proposing a feast day for himself.

The longest single episode Wordsworth recalls from his account of his Cambridge life occurred at just such a party, and has similar egotistical undertones. It was in the rooms of his friend Edward Birkett, who had the honor of living in the rooms in Christ's College reputed to have been Milton's. Heavily invoking the great man ("O temperate bard!"), Wordsworth sat down with the "others in a festive ring of commonplace convention"—that is to say, it was the usual routine. Wordsworth proposed the toast to Milton, "I to thee poured out libations," but (like the "jovial" punster) he also kept a mental reserve: "to thy memory drank / Within my private thoughts." They weren't drinking to Milton all the time, and soon his brain "reeled," "Never so clouded by the fumes of wine / Before that hour, or since." Wordsworth became a connoisseur of fine wines, and left a valuable cellar at his death, but we can take his claim straightforwardly, since no one ever records him as drinking too much. Yet when he ends the episode by asking Milton's forgiveness for his "empty thoughts" in "the weakness of that hour," he also clearly indicates that he continued to join regularly in such practices: "In some of its unworthy vanities / Brother of many more" (III.326–28).

Suddenly hearing the chapel bell, he ran desperately to put in his appearance. He humorously sketches his "ostrich-like" appearance, with white surplice thrown up over his shoulder for greater speed: easy to do, for the sleeveless gowns were short, being also known as "cover-arse-gowns" *(Gradus)*. But this surplice, "gloried in and yet despised," gave him the right to cleave "in pride through the inferior throng / Of the plain burghers," townspeople standing at the back of the church. Curiously, this moment of shame combined with privilege also contains a slight Miltonic echo, of Satan's entrance into Pandemonium through the crowds of expectant demons after his successful mission to seduce Adam and Eve in Paradise:

> . . . he through the midst unmarked,
> In show plebeian angel militant
> Of lowest order, passed; and from the door
> Of that Plutonian hall, invisible
> Ascended his high throne . . . .
> (*PL,* X.441–44)

The sense of special status, as distinct from an "inferior" or "plebeian" one, shows Wordsworth in the compositional moment (about 1803) still recalling his "reeling" sense of identification with the great Cambridge rebel—or with his great villain—some fifteen years earlier at college, when he bought his first personal copy of *Paradise Lost* and began to annotate it heavily.[56]

Very commonly these supper parties spilled out into the streets, where, as Wordsworth says with technical accuracy, "we rioted": street fights. These occurred virtually every night during term time. Students met, boasted, argued, and quarreled in the taverns with each other or with the town "snobs." Between students, these fights sometimes led to sword duels; Wilberforce was greatly relieved that he never felt called upon to defend his honor in such a way. But between the students and the town boys, the fights were very frequent and very violent. In March of Wordsworth's first year, a drayman was killed in a fight with two students, who were let off on grounds of insufficient evidence.[57] One of the two, the notorious "Turk" Taylor of Trinity, also assaulted Wordsworth's second tutor, the brilliant mathematician James Wood, outside the Union Coffee-House.[58] Drinking was universal, and in successive years (1783–85) special contests were set up for the best English declamation against gaming, dueling, and suicide, with Bishop Richard Watson as one of the judges.[59]

These "disgraceful tumults" broke out everywhere,[60] but especially outside Trinity Church in Sidney Street, exactly where Wordsworth passed on his run back to St. John's from Birkett's room at Christ's. Indeed, he may have been going to church *at* Trinity, or at King's next door. The day was therefore likely Sunday, since townspeople could also attend college chapel services, and did so especially on Sundays, when the favored place was "The long-backed chapel of King's College." Here the "Cambridge Beauties" or lady snobbesses flocked, "emphatically be it understood, to see and be seen," for "King's cool shades" along the college backs were a notorious trysting place: "But ah how fatal oft these Walks do prove / To injur'd Innocence, and constant Love."[65]

The most frequent cause of the street fights, and the most frequent topic at the drinking parties which preceded them, was women, not surprising in such an male environment, especially given their scarcity in a technically celibate society. Toasts were drunk much more frequently to "virgin snobbesses" than to Milton: to the three "Miss Go-to-beds," friendly daughters of the master of the *Bull,* the "Brown St. Venus," daughter of a cigar vendor, or to "the Trinity Venus, one of the few . . . pretty virtuous bed-makers of the time."[66] The writer means pretty *and* virtuous, not relatively virtuous, but on the subject of bed makers the ambiguity is appropriate. The bed makers and other female servants employed by the colleges were the members of the opposite sex nearest the students, and thus the immediate focus of attention in a situation which was, soberly put, "the greatest drawback of college-life . . . this lack of the society of virtuous females."[63] The only other women in the colleges were the masters' wives and daughters, since only masters could marry, and only about half of them did.[64] Sometimes virtue preserved the women servants from affront, or their looks did, as in the case of the "wry-nosed beauty" and "noseless Jenny," or their age, for some were elderly and more given to getting tipsy on students' wine than to seducing them. But often they were less interested in preserving their virtue than in catching one of these highly eligible and relatively rich young men, either in matrimony or in some other profitably compromising situation. Some "matriculated tradesmen" (butlers, barbers, cooks, and others permanently attached to a college) were called "petticoat-professors" because they trained their daughters almost from infancy to be "ladies" in this trade.[65] Gyps' daughters were also very useful in such entrapments, especially with freshmen whose experiences with wine, women, and mathematics were all about equally new.

Of course, many of the boys were willing victims and equally unscrupulous players in the game. When a Caius varmint man proposed a toast to the "virgin snobbesses," he was met with the derisive cry "Aye, where are these maidens?"—whereupon he whipped out armfuls of love letters he had received and regaled his friends by reading them aloud.[66] J. M. Wright, our

Trinity correspondent, tells how he came to "understand" his bed maker while studying Greek tragedy at three in morning:

> Whilst musing over the choruses, the strophes and the anti-strophes, analyzing caesuras and quasi-caesuras, I myself was being scanned by a fair household goddess, who tripping into my presence, in the most celestial accents, breathed apprehension lest I should ruin my health by such midnight meditations, and *looking* unutterable things, a language I then understood less than Greek (and of this I was ignorant enough), hastily withdrew, covered with confusion. Joseph-like, I retired to my solitary pillow, dozing away the few hours that intervened before the hour of chapel.[67]

With typical student archness, he casts himself as virtuous Joseph to the bed maker as Potiphar's wife. Wright, like Wordsworth, was a northern sizar, from Kendal, and also began his college days holed up in a high little room. But everyone was entitled to a bed maker's services. The *Gradus* took a longer, more sophisticated view of what these might be:

> They are not only adept at making beds *(secundum Artem),* but when they have had a mind to it, have shewn themselves very alert in helping to *UN*-make the bed they have made, *secundum Naturam!* Indeed, these their *natural* parts and endowments were at one time so notorious . . . that, by a most merciless and *unmanly* decree of the Senate, the whole sex was rusticated! . . . [But] O tempora! O Mulieres! there is no *scruple* in the present *Saturnian* age, respecting the admission of *"young maids"* into "the students' chambers." (*Gradus,* 7, 18)

Most fellows were considered "men of gallantry." The longer they stayed waiting for a living, the more restive they became under their celibate status, and the more exposed to the dangers of venereal disease, like the "most violent flame [syphilis] that carried off poor Dr. H. some years agone."[68] Getting married was the Catch-22 of fellowship life, for it solved one problem at the cost of another. "The scheme therefore is—a wife and Fellowship."[69] "Graces" or petitions were offered in the university senate in the 1760s and 1770s for abolition of the celibacy requirement almost as frequently as petitions against the Test Acts in the 1770s and 1780s. Some fellows lived with their housekeepers—and their housekeepers' daughters—"in a very equivocal capacity,"[70] and almost every Cambridge reminiscence has its anecdote about women coming to call for fellows under cover of night and running afoul of a gate porter who has not been tipped off. It was said of William Chevallier, the master of St. John's when Wordsworth arrived, who was nearly blind, that his "dark hours" were "cheered by Day"—that is, Mrs. Day, the wife of the town clerk, who lived more in the master's lodge at St. John's than she did at home.[71]

Some women of the town did as well by their charms as college fellows did by their gallantry. Jemima Watson (no relation to Bishop Richard Watson) "lived in expensive lodgings, where she was in the habit of receiving some of the most fashionable men of the University."[72] These might be fellows or wealthy noblemen or fellow commoners, but most pensioners and sizars could not, by age and by pocket, keep company with such courtesans. For them, if they were not successful with their bed maker or local girls, there was the "rookery" at Barnwell, the theater and brothel district out past Jesus College along the Newmarket Road: "a notorious place of amorous resort in ancient times," *Gradus* notes, tongue historically in cheek. The section of road connecting Jesus Lane to Newmarket Road is still called Maids Causeway, suggesting the rarity of any true maids crossing it, or of returning with their maidenhood intact.[73] Plays were put on at Barnwell, the ancient site of an Augustinian nunnery, at the beginning of each academic year, and regularly featured "rows between Cyprians and Gownsmen." "Cyprians" was the universal code word among educated eighteenth-century males for prostitutes (from Cyprus, birthplace of Venus), and the "Barnwell Ague" is defined by the *Gradus,* in a rare moment of restraint, as "French ★★★."

Prostitutes were as common in Cambridge as nightly drinking, and presented an attractive threat to the college boys. Playhouses and taverns were subject to regulations against keeping any "daughter or other women in [houses to which] there shall resort any scholars of the University of what condition soever."[74] Such establishments were subject to arbitrary search and arrest by the two proctors and their two subproctors who patrolled the streets every night

> to prevent rioting in the streets, knocking down snobs, too great a familiarity with a certain class of the fair sex, tandemizing [reckless coach driving], and other unsightly exhibitions. . . . Their powers are more particularly directed against the Cyprians, over whom they have unlimited control; being permitted by the statutes to enter by force any house in the town, suspected of concealing them, and afterwards to lodge them in the Spinning-House. . . . It would be easy enough for the University by means of the Spinning-House, to exterminate the whole race of these unfortunates, but they know human nature too well to act so madly. Whatever the saints may say to it, the Philosophers of Mathematical Cambridge know and feel them to be necessary evils . . . .[75]

As with expressions of dissenting political and religious views in Cambridge, so too with sexual behavior: almost anything was tolerated as long as it was kept quiet and private; only public indecorum was punished.

Neither the collegians nor the fellows regarded the Cyprians in such an unfavorable light. They used them in a variety of ways, such as dressing them up in academic gowns and bringing them to church—a great inside joke among some Emmanuel students until an accident discovered the identity of one of these fair "boys." Sometimes the insults ran in the other direction. "Agreeable" (that is, attractive) respectable women were exposed, even in church, "to the same insults as in a bawdy house," so widespread was licentious behavior in the 1780s.[76] A young man from St. John's coming out of church with his visiting sisters heard their virtue derided by two snobs lounging in the street and knocked each one down with a single blow.[77] When Dorothy visited William briefly in the fall of 1788, his tall, rugged appearance, not his stature as a student, was her best protection against such insult.

Not all boys were licentious or promiscuous, of course. Many recoiled in the face of such widespread public vice to become "Simeonites," followers of the evangelical preacher Charles Simeon at Holy Trinity Church, or even Methodists. Wilberforce is said to have held himself off from sexual adventures in his otherwise typical "gay-man's" career, though he took tea in a well-known London brothel.[78] But every boy's experience was colored in some way by this onslaught of sexuality, especially to the degree that he had not been exposed to anything like it before. It was in no way dissimilar from anything else we know about the sexual aspect of class relations in the eighteenth century, as a glance at Boswell's journals will confirm. But at Cambridge and Oxford the "Beauties" and their go-betweens had a particularly intimate "interface" with the ruling class, through its vulnerable youth.

Where is Wordsworth in all this? We have seen a few tantalizing glimpses or possible identifications of him, but he apparently deliberately canceled these out in the final item of a list of "deeper passions" from which, he says, he held himself off:

> . . . envy, jealousy, pride, shame,
> Ambition, emulation, fear, or hope,
> Or those of dissolute pleasure—were by me
> Unshared, and only now and then observed . . . .
> (III.532–36)

All of these could be called academic vices except the last, which was more likely to be extracurricular than intramural. "Dissolute pleasure" is certainly not reflected in Wordsworth's later life and reputation, yet the question is not impertinent. Sex is biologically relevant to his biography not only in normative terms but also in relation to its more unusual features, such as his fathering a daughter at age twenty-one with a French woman four years his senior, his strange passionate relations with his sister, Dorothy, and his marriage to his childhood playmate at age thirty-two. It may be that Wordsworth's first sexual experience occurred in March of 1792, when he was twenty-one and living in a foreign country, his lover twenty-five, and relatively free of parental control. But we want to know how he came to that moment prepared or unprepared for it. The facts of his life show him to have been a sexually attractive and active man, and his love letters to his wife are written in moving, passionate language.[79] His poetry makes this abundantly clear too, though its sexual element is frequently displaced onto a strongly feminized Nature, making it easy to ignore any overtones of actual human sexuality. But his best contemporary readers, like Shelley and James Hogg, did not miss it.* Given the facts of life between ages seventeen and twenty-one, and the realities of Cambridge between 1787 and 1791, the reputedly asexual quality of Wordsworth's poetry becomes an issue that asks for interpretation.

Wordsworth was not of course obliged to write about sex, and to look for a sexual component in his oeuvre is indeed to labor in a barren field. But he does write about it, to an extraordinary degree and in extraordinary ways, in the compositions of his first thirty years. Sleuthing for evidence of writers' sexual experience can seem prurient, but just as there are writers like Byron and Wollstonecraft where it is obviously relevant, so too there are writers like Wordsworth and Dickinson where its large absence, coupled with certain rhetorical excesses and biographical hints, makes it equally relevant, if not more so.

Given the extensive evidence of an atmosphere of sex and violence in Cambridge while Wordsworth was there, he could not have avoided its prostitutes and provocative "snobbesses." But how the sexuality they boldly offered filtered into his work requires careful reading of scattered evidence in *The Prelude.* The overall impression he gives of his Cambridge life is of hearty engagement in extracurricular social pursuits. True, there were solitary midnight walks, as at Hawkshead. But "if a throng was near / That way I leaned by nature, for my heart / Was social and loved idleness and joy" (III.234–36). The words bear repeating, in light of Wordsworth's later image, because they are his own youthful self-description: *"My heart was social and loved idleness and joy."* And a "throng" was nearly always "near." Speaking in merely statistical terms of the facts of Cambridge life and the burden of his own commentary, it would be more likely than not that he had some experience with these women. But the issue, complicated for any teenager, was

*"But from the first 'twas Peter's drift / To be a kind of moral eunuch, / He touched the hem of Nature's shift, / Felt faint—and never dared uplift / The closest, all-concealing tunic. / She laughed the while, with an arch smile, / And kissed him with a sister's kiss, / And said—'My best Diogenes, / I love you well—but, if you please, / Tempt not again my deepest bliss" (Shelley, *Peter Bell the Third,* 313–22). Hogg's parodies are less serious, but equally insightful: Nature is the "great wet-nurse of the human race," and on her "similitude / In dissimilitude, man's sole delight, / And all the sexual intercourse of things, / Do most supremely hang" ("James Rigg" and "The Stranger," in *The Poetic Mirror; or, The Living Bards of Britain,* 1816).

especially so for Wordsworth. There are many references to sexuality in *The Prelude* referring to the period between his seventeenth year and his twenty-first, but they are not found in the Cambridge books. Instead, they are dispersed to other parts of the poem and must be transposed in order to be brought to bear on the subject.

When he says he "laughed with Chaucer . . . beside the pleasant mills of Trompington" [*sic*], the next town down the river from Cambridge, he is directing us to more of his "lazy," "lounging" reading. But to characterize Chaucer's gritty "Reeve's Tale," set in Trumpington, as a tale of "amorous passion" is to sanitize it ridiculously. This Cantabrigian riposte to the Oxford-based bawdy of the "Miller's Tale" was loyally included in every collection of Cambridge "facetiae" (bawdy, satirical collegiate writings). It is a seamy tale of sexual revenge, wholly consonant with everything we can learn about daily town-gown relations in Cambridge, and since it was written four hundred years earlier, an indication of the marked consistency of university life in this respect. Wordsworth's pleasure in the story was heightened by the fact that Allen and John, the two students who cuckold the thieving miller, are "both northern men, both in one town were born," like Wordsworth and his Hawkshead mates. The whole thrust of the story turns on the boys' sneaking into the beds of the miller's wife and daughter and pleasuring them mightily while he snores away.

Wordsworth recalled that it was on his trip down to Cambridge with John Myers and William Cookson that he "for the first time in my life did hear"

> The voice of woman utter blasphemy,
> Saw woman as she is to open shame
> Abandoned, and the pride of public vice.
> (VII.417–20)

He locates the spot with some care, "southward two hundred miles . . . from our pastoral hills," as if to establish a moral quarantine in the distance. The scene has been located in Stamford or Grantham on the Great North Road, with the explanation that the shock was all the greater because "love children" who appeared in Lakeland were not banished or degraded into lives of raucous ugliness.[80] One hopes not, though the incident of the woman in white at Cockermouth and the tale of Mary Rigge at Colthouse suggest that all was not quite so idyllic in those pastoral hills. In any case, such "blasphemy" would have been repeated many times in Wordsworth's hearing when he got to Cambridge—which may be why he does not mention it there, but instead associates it with his later experiences in London. Several of his recollections of seeing dissolute women in public are from London, but their placement in Book VII ("Residence in London") makes them appear chronologically later, whereas the specific details are from his Cambridge years when, as early as 1788, he first visited the city.

Student trips to London, it is not surprising to learn, were often undertaken for more refined or extreme versions of the fleshly pleasures of Cambridge. A satirical examination question addressed the subject in mock-botanic manner: "Where is Covent Garden situate, and what flowers thrive best there? Upon what principle is it that the productions reared in the neighborhood of this celebrated garden delight in hot beds, and yet come to maturity without being forced?"[81] Coleridge knew the Cambridge-London circuit well: "I formed a Party, dashed to London at eleven o'clock at night, and for three days lived in all the tempest of Pleasure . . . . I again returned to Cambridge—staid a week—such a week! Where Vice has not annihilated Sensibility, there is little need of a Hell!"[82]

Wordsworth loved London, but he also feared its temptations, and many of these are cast in feminine roles. The whole of Book VII in *The Prelude* turns upon the story of Mary Robinson, the Maid of Buttermere, "the artless daughter of the hills," whose story of seduction and abandonment was a hit play in 1803. But he says it was "at least two years before" Book VII's account of his first (1791) residence in London that he first began to visit there—that is, in December 1788 or January 1789, while he was still at Cambridge. Many of the images he recalls are feminine: the "gorgeous ladies" of Vauxhall and Ranelagh gardens, or "some female vendor's scream—belike / The very shrillest of all London cries." He especially loved playhouses, "whether some beauteous dame" appeared, "or *romping girl* / Bounced, leapt, and pawed the air" (446, 454–55; italics added). These two ostensibly generic descriptions probably attach specifically to Sarah Siddons and Dora Jordan, the reigning Muses of Tragedy and Comedy, respectively, on the London stage throughout Wordsworth's young manhood.* He retained the novelty of these experiences with a strange kind of gender-reversing osmosis: they stayed fresh in his mind "with something of a girlish childlike gloss" (479). The playhouse managers in London, as at Barnwell, "were but a higher sort of brothel-keepers; pimps to the public," and their establishments so indecent that one could not take a woman there, for "sights scarcely to be imagined, much less described."[83] Wordsworth's story of Mary of Buttermere is crossed by a recollection very much of this kind: his sight

*The identification of Dora Jordan as the "romping girl" is virtually certain, since one of her most famous roles was that of Priscilla Tomboy in the operatic farce *The Romp*. Her beautiful legs and sensual athleticism featured prominently in both her stage reputation and the gross caricatures which greeted her liaison with William, duke of Clarence, the future William IV. See Claire Tomalin, *Mrs. Jordan's Profession: The Actress and the Prince* (New York: Alfred A. Knopf, 1995), 70–71, 121–23.

of a prostitute's child amid "chance spectators, chiefly dissolute men / And shameless women"—and including Wordsworth too, of course. He wonders with amazement how such innocence can appear there, "A sort of alien scattered from the clouds," when "on the mother's cheeks the tints were false, / A painted bloom." It is the *contrast* that boggles his mind. The whole episode is full of strange, overdetermined, loaded language, making us feel that Wordsworth's early experiences with sexuality provoked an almost destructive sense of contrast: whatever was not pure must be terribly contaminated.

But we see most of the fallout from his Cambridge experiences not in London but in the Lake District, during his first summer vacation. As with his poetic energies and his reputation, he displaced his sexual energies back into Cumberland and released them there.

YOUNG LOVE-LIKING 6

Summer Vacation, 1788

> Spirits upon the stretch, and here and there
> Slight shocks of young love-liking interspersed
> That mounted up like joy into the head,
> And tingled through the veins.
>
> (IV.324–27)

He set out alone from Cambridge in early June, heading back to Hawkshead and Ann Tyson, not to Penrith and Dorothy. Eager as he was to see her, he was even more eager not to see his uncle Crackanthorpe, and the feeling was mutual. The coach stopped at Ashbourne (beyond Derby) on a Sunday evening, and he took advantage of the break to rent a horse and ride over to Dovedale, which already had a reputation as one of England's prime picturesque locations. He described it in a unique notebook entry: not an excerpt from an ongoing diary, for he rarely had the patience to keep one, but a one-off trial run at the literary fashion of landscape painting with words. The passage is worth listening to as the earliest nonpoetic words we have from Wordsworth, unaffected by any presumptions of audience.

> Cambridge to Hawkshead. June 8th. Saw nothing particularly striking till I came to Ashburn. Arrived there on Sunday evening and rode over to Dovedale. Dovedale is a very narrow valley, somewhat better than a mile in length, broken into five or six distinct parts, so that the views it affords are necessarily upon a small scale. The first thing that strikes you on descending into the valley is the River Dove fringed with sedge and spotted with a variety of small tufts of grass hurrying between two hills, one of which about 6 years ago was clothed with wood; the wood is again getting forward; the other had a number of cattle grazing upon it—the scene was pleasing—the sun was just sinking behind the hill on the left—which was dark—while his beams cast a faint golden haze upon the side of the other. The River in that part which was

> streamy had a glittering splendour which was pleasingly chastized by the blue tint of intervening pieces of calm water; the fringe of the sedge and the number of small islands, with which it is variegated. The view is terminated by a number of rocks scattered upon the side of one of the hills of a form perfectly spiral.[1]

The description is generally accurate, but accuracy is not the main point of its quasi-technical idiom of the picturesque. His attention to the woods and grass is a bit too agricultural to be purely picturesque, while his frank evaluation, "the scene was pleasing," is too blunt.

What is potentially "Wordsworthian" about the passage is its fixation on the contrasts in the scene. The phenomenon of hills in the east being brighter than those in the west because of the angle of the setting sun strikes anyone walking in mountainous country, but Wordsworth never tired of recording it, or of its varied thematic possibilities (life in death, promise in despair, and the like). But the sentence about the "streamy" river being "chastized" by its own intervening sections of calm is pure proto-Wordsworth, anticipating such important later formulations as "emotion recollected in tranquillity." Both words are almost neologisms, especially his usage for "chastized." It can be reduced to a commonsense meaning, but its direct suggestion is that "glittering splendour" is—and perhaps well should be—chastised by "blue calm." Of course, chiaroscuro effects were a staple of picturesque landscape painting and description, often with specific emotional equivalents (for example, "glittering" signifies emotional delight; "calm" signifies mental repose) intended to produce an overall sensation of landscape unity and mental affirmation.[2] The moment had much more than a passing interest for Wordsworth. The Dove would return to his mind ten years later in the Lucy poem about a mysterious maiden he loved, where he drew out the contrasts between love and beauty, and loss and death, with maximum force and mystery: "She dwelt . . . beside the streams of Dove, / A Maid whom there were none to praise / And very few to love . . . But she is in her grave, and, oh, / The difference to me!"

There is a similarly strong sense of the *difference,* or contrast, between himself as a "glittering" Cambridge personage wearing "gay attire" and the calm, chastising effect on him of persons and places around Hawkshead in Book IV of *The Prelude,* "Summer Vacation." He returned to a community of "frank-hearted" country girls who behaved according to traditional rural standards of morality that, though far from unsexual, were worlds apart from the extraordinarily immoral sexual milieu of Cambridge. In *The Prelude*'s account of his summer vacation of 1788, Wordsworth highlights his experiences with women, in strong contrast to the relative absence of such evidence from his description of his Cambridge years. The commonsense explanation, that things naturally look different after a year away at college, was intensified for him by a more important contrast, between the erotic energy of sex and that of art. His very first statement about the changes that had occurred at home while he was gone concludes in terms of feminine beauty, very oddly expressed:

> 'Twas not indifferent to a youthful mind
> To note . . .
> . . . growing girls, whose beauty, filched away
> With all its pleasant promises, was gone
> To deck some slighted playmate's homely cheek.
> (IV.191–92, 197–99)

Promised to whom, and slighted by whom, one might wonder? At the end of this summer, he bade farewell not only to Cumberland's mountains, as we expect, but also to its girls, as we tend to forget:

> . . . and you,
> Frank-hearted maids of rocky Cumberland,
> You and your not unwelcome days of mirth
> I quitted, and your nights of revelry . . . .
> (VI.12–15)

These "nights of revelry" are the focus of the two main incidents Wordsworth remembered from his vacation: his self-dedication to poetry at dawn after one dancing party, and his encounter with a discharged army veteran after another.

For nine weeks, until the round of obligatory family visits to Whitehaven and Penrith just before he returned to college, Wordsworth stayed with Ann Tyson, the only mother he knew, at Colthouse, the only home he had. Christopher was there too, but Richard was clerking near Whitehaven, and John, not yet sixteen, had set sail for Barbados at the beginning of the year as a cabin boy.[3] So William received all of Ann's attention and had full leisure to measure the effects of change in himself and in his beloved neighborhood.

His sense of difference was heightened by his new status as a young gentleman, much in demand at both local parties and the grander ones in high society resorts like John Fleming's Rayrigg estate, in the last summer it was leased by Wilberforce. Wilberforce had spent the month of May in residence at St. John's, recuperating from the "corrupt imaginations" and other side effects of his opium medication. It would have very been odd if he had not spoken to Wordsworth in college, the favored ward of his best friend, though he would hardly have broached the moral crisis he was experiencing at the time. The quiet of Windermere, along with prayer and Bible reading, provided his cure that summer, though the "dissipation" of the parties continued.[4] Wordsworth was undergoing a similar regimen, but in different directions and with different results.

Ann was very proud of her charge, and trotted him around to show off his "fancy habilments." But Wordsworth also felt a sense of inner change, which he associated with his increasing desire to write poetry, which he frequently experienced as an erotic sensation, a common writerly emotion, not limited to Romantic poets. Taking Ann's old "rough terrier of the hills" as his companion, he resumed his poetry-composing walks around Esthwaite. He "affect[ed] private shades like a sick lover," and "some fair enchanting image" would rise up in his mind, "full-formed like Venus from the sea." He would discharge the erotic emotions raised by these full-bodied female images onto the dog: "let loose / My hand upon his back with stormy joy, / Caressing him again and yet again." The dog, though pleased, must have wondered what the occasion was, and so can we. Wordsworth's summary statement of the value of these poetry-composing walks continues the same strong language of physical exposure and sexual vulnerability:

> Gently did my soul
> Put off her veil, and, self-transmuted, stood
> Naked as in the presence of her God.
>
> (IV.140–42)

Poetry, and especially his feelings about it, took on the erotic charge of his age and experience. The image can be explained as a reference to Moses' interviews with God,[5] but if this is what Wordsworth had in mind, he has made a striking change in gender. The relationship between his soul or consciousness and its "God" (which is nothing more or less than his conception of his own identity) is that of a willingly submissive woman, perhaps a slave girl, giving herself up to her master's pleasure.

As he contrasted his new splendor with his homely old neighbors, he began to feel a new "human-heartedness" about his love for them, which previously he had felt only "as a blessèd spirit / Or angel, if he were to dwell on earth, / Might love in individual [i.e., private] happiness" (IV.228–30). That is, he had felt, before this, like Raphael or Michael in *Paradise Lost,* observing the human life of Adam and Eve without revealing himself as God's messenger—or perhaps (an even stronger contrast) he felt more like Satan, who looks long and lasciviously on Eve in just this way. But now Wordsworth actually began to feel like a human being himself, and sexual awakening contributed mightily—as it does for all of us—to de-etherealizing his sense of what love meant.

His new sense of both contrasts and connections between himself and other human beings came to him most strikingly as he returned to Colthouse after two dances in that busy social summer. These dances were as glittering as the "streamy" river Dove:

> . . . a swarm
> Of heady thoughts jostling each other, gawds
> And feast and dance and public revelry
> And sports and games—less pleasing in themselves
> Than as they were a badge, glossy and fresh,
> Of manliness and freedom . . . .
>
> (IV.272–77)

Like the "vagrant fruit" of his "lounge" reading, all these activities "seduce[d] [him] from the firm habitual quest of feeding [i.e., nutritious] pleasures," yet there is a relish in his description of them that suggests either the thrill of seduction or the agonies of puberty, or both. The language could certainly suggest sexual initiation, though what a "glossy and fresh" badge of manhood might be is hard to say. As it happens, no commentator has tried to say what it means. The clear sense of the lines is that he didn't actually like all the partying and the thoughts it stimulated, but he felt at least that he had "earned his badge" of manhood there: he was a man. The only other time Wordsworth used such language was to describe his pleasure at remembering actresses in London playhouses during visits from Cambridge and later: "something of a girlish childlike gloss / Of novelty survived for scenes like these" (VII.479–80). Here the "gloss" is "girlish," not manly, but in both cases his sense of pleasure is strongly gendered. Probably one should not push the sense further than to imagine a *new* badge, and yet the two contexts, put together, are very sensual, suggestive of fresh, glowing, postcoital skin.

He contrasts himself to these experiences as "a wild, unworldly-minded youth, given / To Nature and to books," but that image does not sit at all well with his first year's behavior at Cambridge. He is obviously wrestling with something contradictory in his experience: "it would demand / Some skill . . . to paint even to myself these vanities, / And how they wrought." The conflict arises because the "vanities" were not felt to be bad at the time, but are the product of the time of *The Prelude*'s composition, whose mythic structure demands that the boy Wordsworth be presented as "wild" and "unworldly-minded" as possible.

Yet a very important aspect of Wordsworth's greatness is the way he lets his poetry reveal conflicts that he cannot wholly resolve. Rather than admit that this new "human-heartedness" involved—not unusually—sexual awakening, he instead goes on for over a hundred lines, worrying the idea this way and that. In weary *"chastisement* of these regrets," he recalls the moment of dedication at dawn he experienced after one of these dances. So pious has

Wordsworth's afterimage become that most readers ignore that his Dawn Dedication came not in chastisement of his "heartless chace of trivial pleasures" but of his *regretting* them. The dance had been a "promiscuous rout," signifying not so much people's behavior as the fact that all classes and ages were in attendance, as was still widely the case in rural England. But of the nature of Wordsworth's behavior there is no doubt:

> I had passed
> The night in dancing, gaiety and mirth—
> With din of instruments, and shuffling feet,
> And glancing forms, and tapers glittering,
> And unaimed prattle flying up and down,
> Spirits upon the stretch, and here and there
> Slight shocks of young love-liking interspersed
> That mounted up like joy into the head,
> And tingled through the veins.
>
> (IV.319–27)

This is a physiological description of sexual stimulation as convincing as "Tintern Abbey's" description of the chaster pleasures of landscape viewing: "sensations sweet, / Felt in the blood, and felt along the heart; / And passing even into my purer mind, / With tranquil restoration." But he goes no further here: the lines continue, "Ere we retired . . . the sky was bright with day." It is clear he mildly disapproves of the dance, but we can also see that he knows what he's talking about, despite his Miltonic diction. The metaphors push the passage beyond its evident intention, in a clear example of the "deconstructive" force of figurative language. Wordsworth doth protest too much his dancing feet and glancing eyes, but his language of sensual indulgence also exposes what he seeks to disapprove in his youthful character. The girls' forms are not only "glancing" in the light but glancing *at him,* causing those "slight shocks" of glandular reaction, from head to veins.

Leaving the party, he walked the two or three miles home over Claife Heights and beheld a sunrise of "memorable pomp . . . more glorious than I ever had beheld."* Compared with the sharp contrasts of his Dovedale notes, or the provocative "glittering/glancing" nature of his dance flirtations, this is a comprehensively unified landscape, where the maximum number of contrasts are allowed in, the better to be hierarchically arranged and ordered:

*Moorman suggests some other locales where Wordsworth might have seen this dawn (MM1, 109). They all require a hilltop from which the sea could be seen "at a distance"—probably Morecambe Bay. Also, since Wordsworth sees things as illuminated *by* the sun, rather than the rising sun itself, he was probably walking from east to west, with the sun behind him, as he would have been, returning from Windermere to Colthouse.

> The sea was laughing at a distance; all
> The solid mountains were as bright as clouds,
> Grain-tinctured, drenched in empyrean light;
> And in the meadows and the lower grounds
> Was all the sweetness of a common dawn—
> Dews, vapours, and the melody of birds,
> And labourers going forth into the fields.
>
> (IV.333–39)

The easy modulation from heavenly brightness to earthly calm shows how much Wordsworth became master of the landscape idiom he first essayed at Dovedale. But the dawn's direct *connection* with the dance's "promiscuous rout," not simply its chastising contrast, is also pointedly suggested. The laughing sea echoes the girls' "gaiety and mirth" at a more comfortable distance, and "empyrean light" heightens, not darkens, the ballroom's glittering tapers. The relation between the two scenes is cumulative, not contrastive. The moment of dedication came to him because he was in a very stimulated and alert state of mind, fulfilling him, not frustrating him, very much as his childhood "spots of time" came to him in moments when he was already feeling some guilt, for having robbed a bird trap or stolen a rowboat. Certainly sin is on his mind when he says that "vows were then made for me . . . that I should be—else sinning greatly— / A dedicated spirit" (IV.341–44). But these are vows different from the ill-kept pledges of celibacy made by the fellows of Cambridge. He was beginning to imagine that he too might go forth to labor in a field, of poetry. But that labor is charged up and stimulated by those "shocks of young love-liking . . . that mounted up like joy into the head," which are in turn akin to the "stormy joy" with which he caressed his terrier, "again and yet again," when "Some fair enchanting image . . . rose up, full-formed like Venus from the sea."

The sexual "feel" of these dance descriptions in *Prelude* IV is strongly confirmed when we read back to the passages from *Paradise Lost* to which they allude. They were not composed until about 1804, but they are written *about* a time when he was thoroughly and self-consciously steeped in Milton, and much given to refracting his own experience through Milton's poetry, as we saw at his Cambridge "sizing" parties. Some key terms in Wordsworth's vocabulary do not achieve their full force and meaning until *Paradise Lost* is brought to bear on them as a defining context.[6] In the Dawn Dedication "grain-tinctured" (that is, red) comes from "sky-tinctured grain" in Milton's description of Raphael descending to Paradise to warn Adam and Eve that their enemy is in the garden (*PL,* V.285). The little phrase "and the melody of birds" comes from Book VIII, when Adam describes to Raphael "the sum of earthly bliss" he felt in Nature—"I mean of taste, sight, smell, herbs, fruits, and flow'rs, / Walks, *and the melody of birds."* But all of this bliss was surpassed when Adam discovered Eve:

> . . . here
> Far otherwise, transported I behold,
> Transported touch; here passion first I felt,
> Commotion strange, in all enjoyments else
> Superior and unmoved, here only weak
> Against the charm of beauty's powerful glance.
> (*PL*, 522–33)[7]

It is impossible to dismiss these echoes as adventitious, given the similarity in subject matter. Wordsworth's "slight shocks" parallel Milton's "commotion strange," and "glancing forms" is close to "beauty's powerful glance." But no echo of Milton by Wordsworth is ever innocent, even if unconscious—and probably even less innocent then.

Wordsworth invoked his youthful sexuality to help define the transforming power of artistic creativity he first felt that summer. We can see this when we set his small verbal echoes of Milton in tandem with an entire scene in Book XI, Adam's discussion with the archangel Michael about the future course of human history.[8] Michael shows Adam a vision of the sons of Seth, walking *to* a dance.

> . . . they on the plain
> Long had not walked, when from the tents behold
> A bevy of fair women, richly gay
> In gems and wanton dress; to the harp they sung
> Soft amorous ditties, and in dance came on:
> The men though grave, eyed them, and let their eyes
> Rove without rein, till in the amorous net
> Fast caught, they liked, and each his liking chose;
> And now of love they treat till th'evening star
> Love's harbinger appeared; then all in heat
> They light the nuptial torch, and bid invoke
> Hymen, then first to marriage rites invoked;
> With feast and music all the tents resound.
> Such happy interview and fair event
> Of love and youth not lost, songs, garlands, flow'rs,
> And charming symphonies attached the heart
> Of Adam, soon inclined to admit delight,
> The bent of nature . . . .
> (*PL*, *XI.580–97*)

The whole situation is parallel to Wordsworth's. Wordsworth coins his innocuous-sounding phrase "young love-liking" from Milton's scattered uses of "liking," "love," and "youth." His "spirits upon the stretch" repeat the motion of the sons of Seth's eyes roving "without rein," and both scenes end with a heavenly portent (evening star or morning sun). Milton, however, is at once more straightforwardly sexual and more moralistic about the meaning of his dance scene than Wordsworth. Adam, poor fellow, is delighted with it. Following on his enthusiasm for the sexual delights of "transported touch," he thinks it shows some promise of better times to come for mankind, compared with the dreary scenes "of hate and death" that Michael had been showing him. Not so, says Michael: "For that fair female troop thou saw'st, that seemed / Of goddesses, so blithe, so smooth, so gay," is "empty of all good wherein consists / Woman's domestic honour and chief praise," and "the smiles / Of these fair atheists" shall delude "that sober race of men, whose lives / Religious titled them Sons of God" (*PL,* XI.614–26). Wordsworth's context plays down, relative to Milton's, the sexual aspect of the life of a "dedicated spirit." But his linking of the two has more continuity and less destructive contrast than Milton's, and is therefore more appropriate to describe an eighteen-year-old's altogether normal simultaneous awakening to sexual achievement and vocational choice. He goes from a dance on Windermere to artistic dedication, whereas Adam must reject utterly the attractions of the scene Michael showed him. Furthermore, to suppose that the young women at these Windermere dancing parties were merely "frank-hearted maids of rocky Cumberland" is as much a retroactive naturalizing of the facts as imagining Wordsworth to be entirely "a wild, unworldly minded youth." Maria Spedding, sister of Wordsworth's friend John, might gush innocently to Martha Irton of Belmount about Hawkshead's "great majority of Beaux," but many other of Wordsworth's partners, even at Wilberforce's Rayrigg, were gentry and upper-class girls on vacation, whose Christianity, to say nothing of their morality, was so nominal that Milton would without hesitation have labeled them "fair atheists."

These links between sex and art were confirmed at a second dance that summer, which ended in a much sterner confrontation, between young Wordsworth and a sickly veteran recently discharged from terrible service in the Caribbean. Wordsworth now imagined his whole mind as a dance party:

> Strange rendezvous my mind was at that time,
> A party-coloured shew of grave and gay,
> Solid and light, short-sighted and profound,
> Of inconsiderate habits and sedate,
> Consorting in one mansion unreproved.
>
> (IV.346–50)

This mixture of grave and gay, shortsighted and profound, is like a vacation version of Cambridge's "hard reading" and "gay men," or silly students and serious fellows. And when are "consortings" in "mansions" subject to "reproof"? One can almost hear the Cambridge proctors' reproofs for the illicit behavior in the Barnwell "mansions" that their search powers gave them access to, and when Wordsworth goes on to characterize his thoughts that summer as "transient and loose" (IV.354), we can hear, further, the proctors' formal language of complaint against those "lewd women," the Cambridge Cyprians.

Wordsworth said his encounter with the veteran proved that,

> when—by these hindrances
> Unthwarted—I experienced in myself
> *Conformity as just as that of old*
> *To the end and written spirit of God's works,*
> Whether held forth in Nature or in man
> (IV.355–60; italics added)

This is because he is directly following Michael's warning to Adam about the danger of chasing after loose dancing women:

> Judge not what is best
> By pleasure, though to nature seeming meet,
> *Created, as thou art, to nobler end*
> *Holy and pure, conformity divine.*
> (*PL,* XI.603–6; italics added)

Wordsworth's lead-up to his encounter with the discharged veteran, like the dance before the Dawn Dedication, is highly sensual. It was another one of that summer's "primitive hours" that was not canceled by, but somehow confirmed by, what followed. Again, he establishes a sense of vocation via sexually charged language, mediated through Milton.

He was walking along the familiar road up from the Windermere Ferry toward Colthouse, in a dreamy mood of physical well-being that sounds like nothing so much as adolescent fantasizing. He speaks of himself as filled with

> the listless sense,
> Quiescent and disposed to sympathy,
> With an exhausted mind worn out by toil
> And all unworthy of the deeper joy
> Which waits on distant prospect—cliff or sea,
> The dark blue vault and universe of stars.
> (IV.379–84)

This indicates that no dawn dedication from the landscape is forthcoming here: he was "unworthy" of it. His *"body* from the stillness drink[s] in / A restoration like the calm of sleep, / But sweeter far. Above, before, behind, / Around me, all was peace and solitude." Here the echo confirming the sexual subtext comes not from Milton but from the seduction lyrics of his less pious contemporary John Donne, whose works Wordsworth also knew: "License my roving hands, and let them go / Before, behind, between, above, below. / O my America! my new found land!"[9] But if Wordsworth could naturalize Milton in one direction, he was certainly capable of spiritualizing Donne in another, and given his age, situation, and the whole context of sexual alertness he sketches, it does not seem too much to say that more than a few of the pictures running through his mind on this night must have been sexual ones:

> O happy state! what beauteous pictures now
> Rose in harmonious imagery; they rose
> As from some distant region of my soul
> And came along like dreams—yet such as left
> Obscurely mingled with their passing forms
> A consciousness of *animal delight,*
> A self-possession felt in every pause
> And every gentle movement of my frame.
> (IV.392–99; italics added)

It could sound like a young man reflecting on recent sexual fulfillment, or anticipating it, or simply musing enjoyably upon it, if the man were not the "Wordsworth" we have come to presume we know in advance from the cultural history he constructed for himself.

Suddenly he saw a gaunt man leaning on a milestone, quietly groaning. Alarmed, he slipped "back into the shade of a thick hawthorn" where he could observe him, "myself unseen." The man looked like the Cockermouth beggars and Hawkshead peddlers Wordsworth had known all his life, but his work had consisted mainly of courting malarial infection while keeping the West Indian native and slave populations at their backbreaking labor on the lucrative British sugar plantations.[10] By 1796 this service would be estimated to have cost the lives of forty thousand soldiers since the plantations were first established. Overcoming his initial fear, Wordsworth stepped out and saluted the man. Even at that time and that place, his behavior reflects the most basic impulse of his creative method: "I asked his history." He learned the man had been discharged ten days before, probably at Whitehaven: that it had taken him ten days to walk from Whitehaven to Far Sawrey suggests he was a very "meagre" man indeed. Wordsworth could conceivably have taken him home to Ann Tyson's house, but instead he lodged him safely with a laborer in the woods, whom, he knew, "will not murmur should we break his rest."

Wordsworth does not say directly that his preceding "consciousness of animal delight" was canceled out by playing Good Samaritan to the veteran, but that is the general impression one gets from the juxtaposition of these two passages. Certainly there is no carryover of sensual well-being, transferred from a dancing party to a beautiful landscape at dawn. Instead, we go from "a consciousness of animal delight . . . felt in . . . every gentle movement of my frame" to an encounter with a man who, far from wearing any "badge, glossy and fresh, of manliness and freedom," seems to have been *un*manned, or wounded in and by his very manliness, especially in Wordsworth's first draft of the incident.

> He was in stature tall,
> A foot above man's common measure tall,
> And lank, and upright. There was in his form
> A meagre stiffness. You might almost think
> That his bones wounded him. His legs were long,
> So long and shapeless that I looked at them
> Forgetful of the body they sustained.
> His arms were long & lean; his hands were bare;
> His visage, wasted though it seem'd, was large
> In feature; his cheeks sunken; and his mouth
> Shew'd ghastly in the moonlight.[11]

Wordsworth does not explain the relevance of this encounter to his sensual feelings before it, still less to his other postdance experience. Book IV ends abruptly at this point, in its first version, after Wordsworth has seen the veteran safely to rest, "Then [I] sought with quiet heart my distant home." (Calling his home "distant," even though it was only a mile or so up the road, helps remove from our minds the question of why he didn't take the veteran home with him.) But in his final manuscript of *The Prelude,* Wordsworth added three lines which challenge his readers to try to interpret these contrasts, these "obscure minglings" of spiritual dedication and sexual awakening he felt that summer, though few editors have seen fit to include them in printed texts of the poem:

> This passed, and he who deigns to mark with care
> By what rules governed, with what end in view,
> This Work proceeds, *he* will not wish for more.
>
> (1850 IV.469–71)[12]

One connection between these scenes of delight and terror is that in the first Wordsworth dedicates himself to poetry, while in the second he is dedicated to, or forcibly reminded of, the great subject of his poetry: the extreme suffering of individual human beings at the mercy of economic and political powers far beyond their control. Another connection, not inconsistent with the first, is that in the discharged veteran Wordsworth recognized a version of himself: from a quick reading of his first draft describing the man's appearance one might surmise that he looked like Wordsworth on a bad night. I don't doubt that young Wordsworth saw the veteran very much as he reports him. But he too was tall and lank and often ghastly and meager looking, and it is the very signature of Wordsworth's greatest poetry that the force of his descriptions of suffering poor people comes very often from his powerful projection onto them of that person whose sufferings he knew best: himself.

The date, place, and persons of Wordsworth's first sexual experiences, if there were any before March 1792, remain matters of speculation and opinion. I am inclined to place them somewhere in Cambridge, London, or with the "frank-hearted maids of rocky Cumberland" between 1787 and 1790. But the probability is almost equally strong that he held himself off from indulgence, if not from initiation, and displaced his erotic energies not into Methodism or Evangelism but into poetry, or an *idea* of poetry and of himself as the Poet. Some readers of poetry may insist that they are not clinical psychologists, and therefore not interested in Wordsworth's early sexual experiences. But since imaginative *development* is his master topic, especially in *The Prelude,* we cannot help being interested in suggestions that his imaginative awakening was tied to his sexual awakening. And, since nothing is more common in general human experience than this connection, we must be all the more interested because we find it apparently so markedly *absent* from Wordsworth's account of his imaginative growth, and from most critical interpretations of his account. There can be no doubt that sexual images, situations, and feelings are present in his account of his first being alone with his sense of himself as a poet. An interpretation correlating exactly with biographical reality is impossible: the possibilities are polymorphous. The content of Wordsworth's poetry is rarely sexual, and no one will ever call him sexy. But in the larger sense of imbuing his readers' poetic pleasure with deeply erotic feeling, Wordsworth is one of the most sexual poets in the language.

After spending the first part of the summer at Hawkshead, he went to Whitehaven to visit Richard and his cousins, and then to Penrith to be with Dorothy and Mary Hutchinson. He placed some of these visits in Book VI of *The Prelude,* thus creating the impression that they occurred in the summer of 1789. But this is impossible on factual grounds, and we recognize in his descriptions of these visits the same intermingling of self-consciousness, social difference, sexual awakening, and poetical stirring that are characteristic of the summer of 1788.[13] In August he roamed again with Dorothy through their early childhood haunts around Penrith, renewing the delightful novelty of their first reacquaintance the previous summer. His descriptions are suffused with a spirit of first love and brotherly love that connect them to other parts of his account of this vacation. To Dorothy he appeared doubly changed: the successful schoolboy she first saw in 1787 was now an impressive college gentleman. As in his descriptions of the Windermere dances, Wordsworth again used Milton to give a sense of the excitement he felt at the time. Dorothy appeared to him "with a joy / Above all joys, that seemed another morn / Risen on mid-noon" (VI.211–13). The last phrase repeats Milton word for word, from the same passage in *Paradise Lost* Wordsworth used in Book IV, describing Adam's amazement at Raphael's splendor descending into the Garden at noon.

With Dorothy he visited the ruins of Brougham Castle, on the south edge of Penrith, and he stressed his "fraternal love" for her by linking the castle to poetical composition. He recalled the legend that Sir Philip Sidney had composed part of his *Arcadia* there for *his* sister, the countess of Pembroke, "in sight of our Helvellyn," on the banks of the river Eamont, "hitherto unnamed in song"—unnamed, that is, until this moment of its being named in *The Prelude.* That Sidney did not compose his poem there is not important; Wordsworth is linking the two because of his newly reawakened love for his sister. Equally important poetically is his reference to the "sight of our Helvellyn," a sight difficult if not impossible to catch from Brougham Castle, where the two immediate vistas are the grounds of Lowther Castle to the south and the town of Penrith and its beacon immediately to the north.

He describes his and Dorothy's adventures there with light suggestions of danger and eroticism. They climbed up "in danger through some window's open space" to look abroad from the castle's walls. Or they would climb even higher, to "the turret's head," and "lay listening to the wild-flowers and the grass / As they gave out their whispers to the wind." His slight personification of the weeds gives a queer sense of something being overheard, as if the flowers and grass were whispering to each other, like the listening brother and sister. Lying down outdoors somewhere with Dorothy is something he seems to have done almost every time he visited her, weather permitting, a practice they continued once they started living together in 1795. More than just neutral relaxation and sensory enjoyment, the habit seems occasionally to have overtones of sexual sublimation or therapy, overtones that become stronger in the later 1790s, reaching their climax after William's engagement in spring 1802.

Just at this intimate moment in Brougham Castle comes the necessary, chastising addition: "Another maid there was." This was Mary Hutchinson, now "first endeared" to him "By her exulting outside look of youth / And placid under-countenance": she is virtually a personification of the river Dove's combination of "streamy" and "glittering" chastised by calm blue tints.[14] Both Mary and Annette Vallon, Wordsworth's only two known sexual loves, were mediated to him through Dorothy's presence. Just how Dorothy mediated these loves, or even what, precisely, she was mediating, is too complicated to say. But it is quite clear that she was the tutelary spirit at the crux in Wordsworth's creative psychology where sexual and poetic inspiration come close together.

With Mary, and probably with Dorothy too, he visited another poetically charged childhood spot, Penrith Beacon, on the northeast edge of town, where he had had the terrifying experience of seeing the murderer's grave at age five or six. Wordsworth recounted sights such as we expect from a young lovers' idyll: they walked "through narrow lanes of eglantine, and through shady woods." But his effort to link his feelings of awakening love (the Beautiful) with his earlier feeling of terror (the Sublime) at the place results in a contrast so strong that the passage almost breaks in two, marked by a desperate dash:

> And o'er the Border Beacon and the waste
> Of naked pools and common crags that lay
> Exposed on the bare fell, was scattered love—
> A spirit of pleasure, and youth's golden gleam.
> (VI.242–45)

Mary's presence is not recorded in the *1799* version, which deals solely with his childhood. But we may remember, as Wordsworth certainly did, that there had been another woman in that scene: "The woman and her garments vexed and tossed / By the strong wind" (*1799*, i.326–27), a living surrogate for the murdered wife whose husband was hanged there. Given the terrible associations of the place for Wordsworth, his wish to revisit it as a grown-up and rechristen it with healthy romantic and fraternal emotions is understandable. But the strain of the effort shows through.

On August 27 there was a wedding in the family. Uncle Christopher Crackanthorpe, aged forty-three, married Charlotte Cust of Penrith. Both Cookson uncles married in this year (William in October), having been freed to do so, financially, by the death of their father, Wordsworth's maternal grandfather, the previous December. William and Dorothy attended the

Crackanthorpe-Cust nuptials, but they did not include the newlyweds in the "golden gleams" of love they had been scattering over the countryside. Dorothy fairly spat out her contempt of Charlotte Cust and her sisters: "a mixture of Ignorance, Pride, affectation, self-conceit, and affected notability . . . so ill-natured too."[15] The Custs' affectation of nobility had a material effect on the Wordsworth children, no doubt influencing Dorothy's contempt, since the Custs, not content with marrying the heir to Newbiggin Hall, induced Crackanthorpe to extract an additional £500 from old Dorothy Cookson (d. 1792), an amount William considered to belong by right to her grandchildren. He felt so strongly about it that when Uncle Kit died eleven years later, he refused to attend the funeral or pay his respects to the family.[16]

Old William Cookson's death also stimulated a flurry of activity on the Lowther case. In January a bill and a summons were delivered to the earl, but in the Easter court term he obtained an injunction against the Wordsworth executors, maintaining that John Wordsworth had agreed to do all his business for £100 a year. Recalling John's confused and uncertain letter in 1764 to Captain Robinson, we cannot say that Lowther was actually lying, though we can be sure he was always calculating. In May, Crackanthorpe and Richard Wordsworth obtained an order nisi dissolving this injunction, but Lowther then embarked on various delaying tactics which kept matters in limbo for three more years.[17] The sequence of events shows again how financial obligations governed action in this stringently middle-class merchant family striving for gentry status, and reminds us that these assumptions and habits were also at work in Wordsworth's character.

With these unpleasant reminders of the obstructions that lay in the course of his young life, Wordsworth returned to Hawkshead to get himself ready to return to Cambridge. He may have gone back briefly to Penrith for the happier occasion of William Cookson and Dorothy Cowper's wedding on October 17, departing for Cambridge the next day, while Dorothy accompanied the newlyweds to their new home in Norfolk.[18]

William tried to capitalize on his recent associations of love and poetry by starting to compose *An Evening Walk,* addressed "To a Young Lady from the Lakes of the North of England." The poem is, in part, an aesthetic reclaiming of the Lake District in Dorothy's name. He published it in 1793, partly as a recompense for having failed to succeed at college as his family expected him to. He continued working on it the following summer, as well as during term time at Cambridge, but its inspiration and subject matter place its genesis in the summer vacation of 1788.

Biographically *An Evening Walk* was another version of "The Vale of Esthwaite," composed the previous summer, but with the Gothic ghosts removed in favor of Sentimental emotions, by virtue of Dorothy's replacing

Wordsworth's dead father as the family spirit in the poem. Whereas "The Vale of Esthwaite" turned on Wordsworth's fear that his attraction to poetry would unsuit him for labor in "Mammon's mine," his 1788 redaction of the same material is based on an *assumption* of worldly failure and disappointment, modified only by wishful thinking about spending his life together with Dorothy in these delightfully melancholy scenes. Otherwise, it is much the same poem, only in a different genre: loco-descriptive idyll rather than Gothic horror story. The former poem's nightmare walks around Esthwaite Water are expanded to a larger itinerary through the Lake District, though most of its scenes are still drawn from the Hawkshead neighborhood.

An Evening Walk is nearly unreadable to twentieth-century tastes, especially in its first, 1793 version, which is full of horrendous examples of the "poetic diction" Wordsworth made much of his reputation by attacking: he knew whereof he spoke. But it is a creditable piece of description and meditation in the mode of Sensibility. It aims at little more than a sequence of verbal picture postcards, though its participial cinema is closer to amateur video than anything as definite as a snapshot: gerunds predominate over verbs to keep the action moving, but they also render it inconclusive. Dorothy had, as yet, seen very little of the Lake District, and this collection of landscape vistas is intended to reassure her "that some joys to me remain," despite the poem's conventional pose of disillusionment. Its "history of a poet's evening" is offered as proof.

The speaker is a young man who was happy as a child, but now is older and sadder, if not wiser. He has wandered "far from my dearest friend"; the wanderer's itinerary is approximately that of Wordsworth's life, from Cockermouth to Hawkshead. Following the course of the Derwent, out onto Derwent Water and past the falls of "high Lodore" near its southern tip, the speaker climbs over the Borrowdale Fells, down into Grasmere, past Rydal, to Winander and Esthwaite. Thus the poem, autobiographical like virtually everything the young Wordsworth wrote, is a stylized record of his freshman despondency, stimulated not only by the recollections of his and Dorothy's happier childhood but also by the recent joys of their few brief weeks together, and complicated by fresh reminders that they were not much loved by the adults who held their lives and futures in trust. *An Evening Walk* gives us the external actions of Wordsworth's 1788 vacation, whereas *The Prelude* version of 1804 gives us his internal thoughts and emotions; but neither poem, of course, is a literal record of facts.

But all this is apparent only in the poem's framework. The bulk of it consists of more and less successful attempts to capture landscape in language, as Wordsworth had tried to do at the summer's beginning, at Dovedale. It moves from a noontide idyll at Lower Rydal Falls to an evening walk around Esthwaite, with some sights and sounds transferred from Windermere. It recapitulates his poetry-chanting walks with John Fleming three years earlier, and also "those walks, well worthy to be prized and loved," when his companion was Ann Tyson's terrier. Even at this early stage, the chronological layers one uncovers in the palimpsest of a Wordsworth poem are numerous: Dorothy in *An Evening Walk* substitutes for father, Fleming, and terrier all at once, and her role is adjusted to perform the diverse functions of each: family romance and tragedy, social friendship, and sexual surrogate.

With Memory at his side, the speaker finds that "th'unbidden tear . . . starts at the simplest sight / A form discover'd at the well-known seat" (43–44).[19] This is the yew tree seat of the melancholy Reverend Braithwaite, sadly waiting all those years for his benefice. Wordsworth had now seen many more Cambridge fellows doing the same thing, and he was beginning to comprehend the kind of life he was expected to lead.

All scenes in the poem are constantly darkening, and then rebrightening, as infinitely extendable variations on a "plot" of time that moves from noon to full dark—whereupon the moon rises as yet another source of Hope. The hope the moon illumines, that the poem hopes for—the point of its story—is stated directly as the speaker's wish for the day when he and his friend will be together:

> —E'vn now she [the moon] decks for me a distant scene,
> (For dark and broad the gulf of time between)
> Gilding that cottage with her fondest ray,
> (Sole bourn, sole wish, sole object of my way;
> How fair it's [*sic*] lawns and silvery woods appear!
> How sweet it's [*sic*] streamlet murmurs in mine ear!)
> Where we, my friend, to golden days shall rise,
> 'Till our small share of hardly-paining sighs
> (For sighs will ever trouble human breath)
> Creep hush'd into the tranquil breast of Death.
>
> (413–22)

It's hard to say which is more longed for, the cottage or the grave. As wish fulfillment, the poem invokes those mingled scenes of love and death which William and Dorothy regularly acted out together. To suggest that Dorothy appears here only because Wordsworth's financial situation made it impossible for him to entertain thoughts of marriage is to underestimate the depth of the siblings' passion.[20]

As a fraternal domestic fantasy, however, it is censored by two cautionary scenes: one of a happy pair of swans caring for their young (191–240), the other of a female beggar whose two babes die in her arms as she staggers along the lakeshore (241–300). Together they account for nearly a quarter of the poem and were among its earliest-composed parts.[21] The swans are

Wordsworth's first description of the pair on Grasmere whose absence he will strive to account for with bizarre energy in "Home at Grasmere," the extraordinary poem he wrote in 1800 when he first went to live there. So too, the unfortunate beggar woman and her dead children, whatever they may have signified to Dorothy Wordsworth, now make the first of their many varied appearances throughout Wordsworth's poetry of the next decade. These suffering women and children take on many values, the most general one being Wordsworth's sense of social responsibility and what poetry might have to do with it, if anything. In *An Evening Walk* the woman realizes with horror that her children have died while clinging to her back: "No tears can chill them, and no bosom warms, / Thy breast their death-bed, coffin'd in thine arms." Then, without a break, the poem continues blithely on to a new subject—"Sweet are the sounds that mingle from afar"—sounds which, we learn, have "compos'd" the breast of the observer agitated by such horrors: that is, the abrupt transition is not accidental. But this way of handling mind-boggling contrasts was conventional in the genre, and several reviewers in 1793 singled out the lines on the female beggar as among the poem's best.

Psychological interpretation of the poem must be checked by the recognition that its personal elements are pressed into utterly conventional material that Wordsworth borrowed wholesale, with or without acknowledgment, from other poets. The borrowings do not negate the personal elements, but they do illustrate clearly how young Wordsworth managed his emotional life in terms of poetic vocation. Such borrowings were themselves conventional, in the eighteenth-century "poetics of allusion." Wordsworth's notes to the 1793 edition acknowledge ten borrowings from other poets; the definitive scholarly edition (1984) adds twenty-three more, sometimes aided by Wordsworth's use of unattributed quotation marks (another convention), sometimes not. Besides poets, Wordsworth also quoted from James Clarke's *Survey of the Lakes* (1787) and consulted West's (1778) and Gilpin's (1789) *Guides to the Lakes.*[22] This rate of borrowing from one's predecessors is not unusual in eighteenth-century poetry, but Wordsworth strains credulity in his claim to Isabella Fenwick in 1843, "There is not an image in it which I have not observed; and now, even in my seventy third year, I recollect the time & place where most of them were noticed," even though he covers himself by asserting his "unwillingness to submit the poetic spirit to the chain of fact and real circumstance." By 1843 he had himself fallen under the sway of the poetic myth of originality, which in the summer of 1788 he had little thought of creating.

He was insistent about two lines in particular: "fronting the bright west in stronger lines, / The oak its dark'ning boughs and foliage twines" (192–93). He told Miss Fenwick, "I recollect distinctly the very spot where this first struck me. It was in the way between Hawkshead and Ambleside, and gave me extreme pleasure. The moment is important in my poetical history; for I date from it my consciousness of the infinite variety of natural appearances which had been unnoticed by the poets of any age or country, so far as I was acquainted with them: and I made a resolution to supply in some degree the deficiency. I could not have been at that time above 14 years of age."[23] The very large number of his borrowings elsewhere in the poem shows that many poets of his own "age and country" had in fact already made a quite good start at describing "the infinite variety of natural appearances." This particular couplet does not have exact parallels in the many instances cited by scholars, but in that respect they are exceptions proving the contrary fact: that very many images in the poem *do* have earlier parallels.

It is the *literariness* of *An Evening Walk,* not its naturalness, that is most relevant to Wordsworth's self-creation. Its self-consciously poetical quality underscores a more important fact in his biography than its lack of originality as a nature poem: namely, the increased extent to which he was beginning to consider becoming an author of some sort. "The poet's soul was with me at that time . . . . A thousand hopes were mine . . . a daring thought, that I might leave some monument behind me" (VI.55–68, passim). The literary borrowings in the poem are themselves proof of a new kind of confidence, apparently modest, natural and "feminine," but ungirded by an aggressiveness toward previous literary history unmatched by any English poet since Milton.

The *instinctive humbleness,*
Upheld even by the very name and thought
Of printed books and authorship, began
To *melt away;* and further, the dread awe
Of mighty names was *softened down,* and seemed
Approachable, admitting fellowship
Of modest sympathy.

(VI.69–76; italics added)

The first sign of this "fellowship" of sympathy was *An Evening Walk* itself, into which he modestly admitted so many "mighty names."

It was in this frame of mind that he returned to Cambridge and began unraveling his public, university career in earnest.

7 WEIGHING THE MAN IN THE BALANCE

> . . . of important days,
> Examinations, when the man was weighed
> As in the balance; of excessive hopes,
> Tremblings withal and commendable fears,
> Small jealousies and triumphs good or bad—
> I make short mention.
>
> (III.64–69)

When Wordsworth got back to college in October, he decided to turn over a new leaf, the excellent decision of many a junior soph, as second-year men were known at Cambridge:

> the bonds
> Of indolent and vague society
> Relaxing in their hold, I lived henceforth
> More to myself, read more, reflected more,
> Felt more, and settled daily into habits
> More promising.
>
> (VI.20–25)

But more promising to whom, and for what? In that "indolent and vague society" he had placed in the first and second classes in his two 1787–88 exams. But now, reading, reflecting, and *feeling* more, he set off on an ambivalent course, taking only parts of his college exams during the next two years. He kept more to himself, reading and working on his drafts. He began frequenting the "Wilderness" in St. John's Backs, and often wandered out into the adjacent countryside. Most students and fellows roamed and rode through the fields around Cambridge, but though solitary promenades were a literary fashion, cultivated in poems like *An Evening Walk,* they did not have much currency at Cambridge.

It is usually understood that Wordsworth spoiled his academic career and chances for future advancement by failing to take his exams. This is only partly true. In fact, he took more exams than many other undergraduates, especially those in the "nonreading" category. He did not take the mathematical part of his 1788–89 and 1789–90 college exams; this was a bad omen at rationalistic Cambridge, but not taking the whole exam did not, in and of itself, spoil his chances for the honors degree which would lead to a fellowship and church preferment. William Terrot, one of Wordsworth's new friends, followed a course of reading and nonreading very similar to Wordsworth's, but by hard cramming during the summer of 1790 was able to graduate as eighth senior optime (the second-highest category for honors degrees), and duly proceeded to a career of upwardly mobile church livings. William Paley, the influential moral theologian, said he spent his first two college years "happily, but unprofitably . . . constantly in society, where we were not immoral, but idle and rather expensive." A friendly fellow commoner shocked him out of it by cutting his company because, as he said to Paley, "you could do everything and cannot afford the life [you are] leading."[1] It would have been good advice for Wordsworth as well.

Honors degrees, signifying placement in one of the three classes in the Tripos listing (wranglers, and senior and junior optimes), required some excellent performance in the universitywide examinations held in the Senate House in January of a student's final year. But the college exams—if one's college had any—were intended only to prepare students for the final exams, and to establish a preliminary estimate of the class in which they might be placed there. Students at St. John's had to take more examinations than any other students at Cambridge: two a year. Trinity, the other large college, had one annual exam, but some of the smaller colleges had none, relying instead on tutors' reports of students' progress. St. John's twice-yearly examination system had only recently been instituted, to halt the college's alarming slide into mediocrity. By the time Wordsworth arrived, St. John's was again one of the "preeminent" colleges in quality, as it always had been in size. Parents could again be assured that "a steady course of reading was obligatory on undergraduates," and as a result it was "increasingly resorted to by the sons of the nobility and old country families"[2]—just the kind of social milieu that Wordsworth's father had intended for his sons and that his uncles aspired to.

Hence Wordsworth had to sit for six examinations before his final year. He had done very well in his first two exams, and in the next two years he consistently distinguished himself in the classical literature and history sections. The only exam he apparently did not take at all was in December of his third year. In December of 1788 he was listed first among those "who did not go thro' the whole of the examination and yet had considerable merit."[3] Every placement on any list at competitive Cambridge signified an important value judgment. He was "in excellent spirits" when Dorothy saw him during a one-day visit with the Cooksons in November, and he felt even better after this exam.[4] The texts set for it were *Oedipus at Colonus,* the first six books of Euclid, and Thomas Rutherford's *Institutes of Natural Law* (1756), which alternated with Paley's *Moral Philosophy* (1785) as the standard philosophy text. Since he had already read Euclid at Hawkshead, he could at least have taken a stab at the mathematical section of the exam: his cousin John Myers did, and achieved a first.

There is no evidence that Wordsworth, as a literary person, did not like mathematics. Quite the contrary. He goes out of his way in *The Prelude* to deliver a tribute to "the pleasure gathered from the *elements* of geometric science": that is, Euclid's *Elements,* as the first six books were collectively known. In Book V, he pairs geometry with poetry as the two human creations most worth saving from an apocalyptic deluge. His praise of geometry used the same ecstatic rhetoric of "Indian awe and wonder" which he reserved elsewhere in *The Prelude* for celebrating the powers of Imagination itself. But in subsequent school terms, his failure to keep up his reading of the required subjects (calculus, hydrostatics, conic sections) did indeed make it impossible for him to take those portions of the exam.

As for natural philosophy, he was as conversant in its contemporary styles of argument as any other intelligent young man, if not more so. In 1793–94 he would propose to William Mathews to start a journal by drafting a whole series of essays in this vein, and his fragmentary "Essay on Morals" (1798) shows him finally turning away, in revulsion, from its mechanical modes of argument. Not only could he have, with no very large expenditure of effort, done better on his college examinations than he did; he could easily have placed himself along with most of his friends at the top of his class—as his family knew very well. No wonder he makes "short mention" of the Cambridge exams and his performance on them.

Even if a student didn't like math, however, or didn't want to be tested on it, there were prestigious literary prizes to be won, which could be used as leverage to gain fellowships by other means than an honors degree. These were the Greek ode and the Latin ode, the Greek and Latin epigrams, the two chancellor's medals and the two Smith prizes. Tweddell won four of these prizes in three different years, and a brilliant freshman named Coleridge carried off the Greek prize in 1792. College officials coveted these awards nearly as much as wranglerships for their students. None were won by St. John's in 1791 or 1790, though normally it got one or two, and with desire so keen, a strong candidate who refused to compete was persona non grata. St. John's winning ways resumed in 1792, the year after Wordsworth graduated.[5]

Wordsworth gave early evidence that he would snub this route to preferment. In March of his second year William Chevallier, the master of St. John's, died. According to custom, undergraduates wrote elegiac verses in Latin or English and pinned them to the coffin. The funeral was a grand event, costing over £100.[6] Wordsworth did not contribute any verses, to the mortification of his uncle Cookson—not because it showed insufficient grief but " 'because,' he said, 'it would have been a fair opportunity for distinguishing yourself.' "[7] This was true. Wordsworth was an excellent young poet, with a marked predilection for the elegiac mode, especially for dead schoolmasters. But William Chevallier was a far cry from William Taylor, though Wordsworth pled ignorance of the deceased rather than disapproval of his morals as his excuse. "I did not regret, however, that I had been silent on this occasion, as I felt no interest in the deceased person, with whom I had had no intercourse, and whom I had never seen but during his walks in the college grounds."[8]

Both views were right, but from totally different perspectives: Cookson's, from the vantage of collegiate advancement; Wordsworth's, from the vantage of Sentimental sincerity, and also from his growing distaste for collegiate competition. The low quality of the poetry may also have influenced his decision. Tom Butler of Trinity, a friend of Francis Wrangham and Basil Montagu, regaled a supper party on the night after the funeral with some terrible verses he claimed to have snatched off the pall as it passed through the chapel doors. He was having fun at the Johnians' expense: he had composed them all himself. But, recalling Chevallier's reputation for "gallantry," Butler's jokes show that the occasion was not one of very deep grief for anyone, except perhaps Mrs. Day, the master's mistress. "No buck was he, no Don Diego queer, / No gallant youth, and yet a Chevallier!"[9] But Wordsworth stubbornly held himself off from both the opportunistic cynicism of his adult mentors and the moral cynicism of his fellow students.

In the May exam two months later, Wordsworth and Jones "distinguished themselves in the classic." Myers and Terrot, still taking the whole exam, dropped into the third class. The set texts now were the final book of Livy's *History of Rome,* elementary mechanics, and selections from Locke's *Essay on Human Understanding.* Livy's account of Hannibal's march on Rome struck a deep chord in Wordsworth, which resonates throughout his early development. Young Hannibal vows to avenge his father's defeat by the Romans, rises through difficulties to a position of leadership, where his own provocative policies make war inevitable. His amazing feats of crossing Spain and the Alps with his elephants and Numidian cavalry give the book a glorious feeling of high adventure, and the initial defeats Hannibal inflicts on the Romans in northern Italy add a satisfying sense of psychological justice.[10] These kinds of stories—avenging defeats wreaked upon the worldly powers that be by an orphan or some other outcast—appealed terrifically to Wordsworth's imagination. At the beginning of *The Prelude* he gives a list of possible epic topics he might have written about if he hadn't been writing about himself; almost all of them correspond to this pattern.[11] His own Alp crossing in *Prelude* VI is described with a military rhetoric reminiscent of Livy's descriptions of Hannibal—reinforced, by the time of its composition, with overtones from contemporary accounts of Napoleon's equally astounding feats of generalship.[12] He eventually cast his early life as a version of the same story: the orphan boy from a remote district single-mindedly overcoming the entrenched intellectual, political, and poetical powers of eighteenth-century Europe.

But this was not what St. John's examiners were looking for, not at all. Their expectations were much lower, especially for a student of Wordsworth's mental power. The substantive questions they asked were these: "1) Give a short account of the style and character of Livy, from ancient authors; 2) Mention the real and pretended origin of each of the Punic Wars, with their consequences; 3) What was the established form of government at Carthage during the Punic Wars?"[13] There were about twenty questions like this, plus ten grammatical or vocabulary questions, and five short passages of translation. Not a pushover exam, but it is not surprising that Wordsworth and Jones distinguished themselves on it.

The questions on Livy, like virtually all classical texts set at Cambridge during the eighteenth century, reflected a classical curriculum whose ideological bias was thoroughly republican and anti-imperial. Whether from Xenophon, Thucydides, and Demosthenes in Greek, or from Livy, Tacitus, and Juvenal in Latin, there was a consistent focus on texts and questions that stressed individual, republican virtues, either directly or by contrast to accounts of foreign or domestic imperial corruption. Despite its Tory traditions, St. John's did not differ from its Whiggish sisters in this respect.[14]

Though Wordsworth did not take the exam on Locke, he certainly read the *Essay on Human Understanding,* one of the great books of the age and, along with Newton's *Principia,* one of the two foundational books of eighteenth-century Cambridge.[15] A contemporaneous question on Locke from Trinity College shows how his theory of association of ideas helped frame Wordsworth's variations on the theme in "Tintern Abbey" and *The Prelude:* "The ideas as well as the children of our youth often die before us, and *our minds represent to us those tombs to which we are approaching,* where, though the brass and marble remain, yet *the inscriptions are effaced by time and the imagery moulders away."* This powerful passage, from Book II of Locke's *Essay,* lies immediately behind Wordsworth's desperate realization of the need to record everything that he could about the foundations of his mental growth while he still recalled them—or before he hid them even from himself:

> Oh mystery of man, from what a depth
> Proceed thy honours! I am lost, but see
> In simple childhood something of the base
> On which thy greatness stands . . . .
> The days gone by
> Come back upon me from the dawn almost
> Of life; the hiding-places of my power
> Seem open, I *approach,* and then they *close;*
> I see *by glimpses* now, when age comes on
> May *scarcely see at all* . . . .
> (XI.328–31, 333–38; italics added)

Some examiners' questions actively encouraged students to pursue such dilemmas: "Distinguish between the retentive power of Memory, and the other powers of that faculty." (A harder question than it appears at first glance.) Or they were asked to comment on verses like these from Edward Young, one of the eighteenth century's verse propagandists for the faith that the new worlds of rational splendor discovered by Locke and Newton were still inherently divine:

> In the Soul, while Memory prevails,
> The solid power of Understanding fails;
> Where beams of bright imagination play
> The Memory's soft figures melt away.[16]

The only disagreement that Wordsworth would later have with such a formulation, under Coleridge's tuition, was the exclusivist hierarchy of its faculty psychology. Their Romantic psychology of creativity would strive for a unified field theory of all three powers, Understanding and Memory yoked or fused together by Imagination. But any such formulation (supposing he had had one) written on his second junior sophs' exam would have been marked a failure.

After his June 1789 exams Wordsworth went north via Forncett to visit Dorothy. There, hidden away in the rolling flats of East Anglia south of Norwich, she was busy with a Sunday school she had started and other useful projects around the Cooksons' three parishes (St. Peter, St. Mary, and St. Edmund), exercising her strong nervous energy with a scope never before possible in her life. The rambling yellow brick parsonage where she lived with her uncle and aunt still stands, very much in use, and it is pleasant to imagine the Church of England primary school facing the road beside the church's graveyard as a descendant of Dorothy's school. William accompanied her on her rounds through Cookson's parishes, and drafted a sonnet which began as an English idyll along these remote Norfolk country lanes:

> Sweet was the walk along the narrow lane
> At noon, the bank and Hedge-rows all the way
> Shagged with wild pale green Tufts of fragrant Hay,
> Caught by the Hawthorns from the loaded wain . . . .[17]

But he ended it in the conventional manner of *An Evening Walk,* going from noon to night, happiness to sadness, ending in "melancholy's idle dreams," and straying "through tall, green, silent woods and Ruins grey." These were the cedars in the churchyard, now immensely tall indeed, with black crows cawing in their branches and swooping down to light on the crooked headstones, a melancholy dead space between the charming big parsonage and its industrious little school.

But such conventional melancholy may also have been Wordsworth's actual emotion when he got back to Hawkshead, for 1789 was a much lonelier summer than the previous one. Ann Tyson was giving up her boarding establishment, Dorothy was gone, and Mary Hutchinson left early in the summer to live with her brother in Durham.[18] He wandered about alone, probing down into the Pennines between Lancashire and Yorkshire. But the events in *The Prelude* he gives us to understand as occurring this summer date mostly from the previous year. He worked some more on *An Evening Walk,* and again paid family visits to Whitehaven and Penrith. He was becoming more and more of a family problem, and had to fend off increasingly pointed inquiries about what he was going to do. Two of his brothers and his sister were settled in new walks of life; young Christopher was doing well at school—and William wasn't. He was well received by his paternal cousin Mary Wordsworth Smith at Broughton-in-Furness, but his visit at Penrith was so short—a couple of hours—as to be rude.[19] Christopher Crackanthorpe and his unpleasant new wife were the only family members left there, besides old Mrs. Cookson. Wordsworth was in an impossible dilemma with this uncle. On the one hand, Crackanthorpe complained that William did not spend enough time with them: "I should have been happy if he had favoured me with more of his company, but I'm afraid I'm out of his good graces." This was plain snideness, for the fact was that William was out of *his* good graces. On the other hand, Crackanthorpe complained that William was shamefully extravagant at Cambridge, "considering his expectations,"[20] and this charge was unanswerable. The unavoidable sticking point was that *any* expense provided grounds for chiding disapproval, given his apparent intention to flout family expectations by not taking his math exams.

He was going nowhere fast in this summer of 1789, when the world suddenly began speeding up to modern velocity. One would like to know just where William Wordsworth was standing when he heard the news of the fall of the Bastille. Not simply because it was one of those world-shaking events that tend to isolate spots in time for everyone, but because we have just such a detailed account of what he was doing when he heard the news of Robespierre's death five years later, in July 1794: the end of the Terror, and effectively the end of the Revolution as such. Probably his reaction to the news of the Bastille was much milder than his ecstatic response to the death of Robespierre; it was certainly favorable, as the news was generally received in England at the time. People felt it was a good thing, and high time too: a basically internal affair that might move corrupt old France a bit closer to England's vaunted self-image of representative parliamentary democracy. No one foresaw a whole generation of war coming; indeed, the fall of the Bastille was seen at first not as the beginning of a sequence at all but as a single event containing the whole Revolution in itself. But for Wordsworth personally, the summer of 1789 was silent, solitary, and sour: the kind of going-nowhere, doing-nothing period that sometimes provokes adolescents into compensatory overreactions.

He faced his last set of college exams in 1789–90. The December 1789 exam is the only one for which there is no record of Wordsworth's participation, although his two friends Jones and Myers continued to "distinguish themselves in the classic." The classical texts were Demosthenes' *Olynthiacs,* I–II, and his first *Philippic,* all urging Athens to take a stronger stand against the provocations of Philip of Macedon, the *Philippic* being Demosthenes' maiden "parliamentary" oration. The other two topics were optics and Bishop Butler's *Analogy of Religion, Natural and Revealed, to the Constitution and Course of Nature.* The latter was one of the century's standard rationalist defenses of Christianity, and Wordsworth had to know it for his final exams a year later. Optics and color theory were two of the most popular scientific subjects of the eighteenth century; writers from Newton to Blake to Goethe were deeply engaged by them, and Wordsworth had read Newton's *Opticks* with great interest on his own during his last year at Hawkshead. His interest in the anatomy of visual perception was stimulated by reading Young's popularizations of Newton, as we recognize from the line in "Tintern Abbey" about "the mighty world / Of eye, and ear,—both what they half create, / And what perceive," adapted from Young. Again, the distance between what the exam required and what Wordsworth already knew about or was interested in is not very great, making the question of why he didn't take it all the more puzzling.

But almost half of Wordsworth's class failed to sit for this exam, so again his behavior followed that of the majority,[21] though Terrot roused himself enough to vault to a high second-class result. One might guess that the news of revolution from France and its ripple effect in university life distracted Wordsworth and many others. But the examiners were quite ready to give their questions a contemporary application, for example, by suggesting parallels between the Athenian context of Demosthenes' orations and a very widespread view of the condition of England at this time: "its ancient liberties in a state of decay, with a government full of placement and pensioners and a legislature that no longer represented the citizens," all under the sway of an absolute monarch: Philip of Macedon, or Louis XVI (as he had been until just six months earlier), or George III as he seemed to want, increasingly, to become.[22]

The French Revolution immediately became a favorite illustration for freshening up the standard theme of Liberty in classical declamations. The brilliant John Tweddell's "Address to Liberty" in the spring of 1790 set a new standard for outspokenness: "[he] took every opportunity of speaking his sentiments most freely, and, to those who watched the signs of the times, most indiscreetly."[23] But within a few years this theme decayed into another hackneyed academic topic, less popular as the Revolution became more violent and English enthusiasm for it cooled. By 1796 Charles Le Grice, a close friend of Coleridge and Lamb, was parodying the fervent declamations of the early 1790s in "A General Theorem for a College Declamation":

> Three or four Sidneys, and Hampdens, and Lockes,
> And on the present times at least three or four knocks . . .
> Three or four tears with Sympathy's sigh,
> Three or four sweet things of I myself I,
> Three or four hurricanes, three or four ravages,
> Three or four Monarchs who are three or four savages . . .
> Three or four Statesmen the three or four guides
> Of three or four ships through political tides,
> Three or four marks of interrogation,
> Three or four Os! of dire exclamation,
> With pause, start, and stare, and vociferation,
> Whatsoe'er be the theme, make a fair Declamation.[24]

Two of Wordsworth's longest poems of the 1790s, *Descriptive Sketches* and the Salisbury Plains poems of 1793–95, contain this same odd mix of introspective sentiment ("Sympathy's sigh," and "I myself I") with vociferous political outbursts. The point is not that he was influenced by Le Grice but that he was totally familiar with this rhetorical manner from college exercises.[25]

In his sixth and final college exam, in June 1790, Wordsworth's name appears, again coupled with Jones, Myers, and Thomas Gawthorp, his old Hawkshead housemate, as having "considerable merit in the subjects which they undertook."[26] By now barely a third of the class of '91 was taking the whole exam, and Wordsworth and his friends were part of a small group of eight students who did very well, but not enough. His family's question would have been, Why take it at all, at this late date? The subjects were plane and physical astronomy, the Gospel of Matthew, and three satires of Juvenal: Satire III, on country virtue versus city vice; X, the basis for Johnson's "Vanity of Human Wishes," on the heroism of the virtuous life; and XV, dedicated to the proposition that all men are capable of high moral feeling. Wordsworth again did the classical part, which inevitably heightened his awareness of social ills, of simple country life as one sort of answer to them, and of satire as a common intellectual way of addressing them. His own Juvenal imitation, of Satire VIII, still five years off, would attack the nobility for failing to exercise the virtue incumbent upon their elevated status, citing as one particularly debased example the house of Lowther. Nor would the astronomy topic have been so terribly forbidding, aside from the required demonstrations in celestial geometry. For it is the spiritual heart of Newton's *Principia,* attempting to demonstrate God's power by quantifying the astronomical forces He must wield, and hence more susceptible than other parts of Newton to quasi-scientific rhapsodizing, if one was so inclined—as Wordsworth says he was: "there . . . did I meditate / Upon the alliance of those simple, pure / Proportions and relations, with the frame / And laws of Nature" (VI.143–46). Wordsworth owned a copy of John Bonnycastle's *Introduction to Astronomy* (1786), a typical Cambridge textbook illustrating Newton with quotations from Milton, Thomson, and Young.[27] This is another instance among several where he had the required text, and read it well enough for certain parts to stick with him for years, but did not take the exam given on it at the time.

As a nonreading man, he participated but minimally in the oral Latin "Acts & Opponencies" of the third and fourth years.[28] These oral disputations, whence the term "wrangler" derives, can be made to sound horrendous, but they were mostly excruciatingly boring, especially for students of Wordsworth's gifts, not to mention for the faculty who had to administer them. They allowed a very broad, not to say laughable, range of achievement, and Wordsworth's strong command of Latin would have made him a formidable opponent. In each of the last two years, one was expected to defend a set (an "Act") of three propositions, one moral and two mathematical, while on two different occasions each student opposed someone else's "Act." For example, one could defend or oppose Paley's thesis that virtue consists in "doing good to mankind, in obedience to the will of God, and for the sake of everlasting happiness."[29] These "huddlings"—college slang for the way most students prepared and performed their materials—were spoken before a faculty moderator in the Senate House, one student standing on each side of the moderator's raised dais, like a miniature Parliament. One chose the propositions one wished to defend, usually lifted from a standard text like *Johnson's Questiones Philosophicae,* which efficient students used to bone up for weeks or months in advance. You knew who your opponents would be, they also got their arguments from *Johnson's,* and by custom you invited them to tea before the disputation to talk over subjects and strategies. There was a good deal of self-interest on the part of everyone involved not to produce any untoward surprises, since every opposer knew he would have to be a proposer in his turn. On the other hand, there was also a great deal of self-interest in showing up brilliantly, if one aspired to a wranglership, so the ordeal placed students in a dilemma of mutual dependence and deceit, because of the temptation to keep one's best arguments secret until the event.

These mock debates epitomized the pressures of the Cambridge exam system, with its emphasis on performance over substance. Left over from the age of religious disputation in which the university was chartered, they rewarded, in an age of supine religious energy, memorization and verbal facility over independent thinking. For the most part, they were acts of embarrassment to be got over; an efficient "huddler" could dispose of eight disputations in ten minutes.[30] They were nightmares for dull students who were actually trying to get a good degree, and occasions of high drama for brilliant students who tried to succeed with displays of wit and erudition. For Wordsworth and his friends, smart enough to do well and intelligent enough to recognize the abuses of the university examination system, they were an artificial exercise that was not worth the effort if one "set the pains against the prize" (III.632). Byron's conclusion would be surprisingly similar: "The premium can't exceed the price they pay."[31]

This extenuating view of Wordsworth's performance in Acts & Opponencies often appears alongside other "romantic" justifications for his university failures, but it was not one he could afford to take at the time. For him the pains were not all that great, more demeaning than difficult, and the prize—a church living—was for him a life necessity. Competent Latinists, or hard-reading memorizers, or intelligent young men actually interested in the moral question they had proposed (which could be quite timely: "Does Scripture argue in favor of deposing unjust kings?") could make things awfully uncomfortable for their colleagues. Wordsworth was all of the above, except that his hard reading and memorizing was done in classical and modern literature, not in moral philosophy or mathematics.

By not taking the math sections of his college math exams in 1788–89 and 1789–90, Wordsworth came to his Senate House exams in January 1791 already in one of the two lowest categories, the seventh or eighth class: the hoi polloi who would be matched against each other in oral and written exams only to determine their relative merit and to be sure they did not deserve "plucking"—given no degree at all. The minimal standard was so low that in all probability Wordsworth could have passed much of this exam in his freshman year. All that was required was some demonstrations from the first two books of Euclid's *Elements,* some ability to solve simple and quadratic equations, and familiarity with the arguments in the early parts of Paley's *Moral Philosophy* and Butler's *Analogy.*[32] The first two classes fought it out for the wranglerships, the third and fourth for senior optimes, and the fifth and sixth for junior optimes—forty to fifty honors degrees in all.[33] Few or none fell out of the honors classes into the hoi polloi, and lower-classed candidates could challenge those above them to raise their rank, or even their classification. The worst a reading man could do was to be given the "wooden spoon" for the year: last of the junior optimes.

The experience of the university exams was, however, much more traumatic than college exams, or the Acts & Opponencies. They brought mathematics rather than moral philosophy to the fore. The morning of the first day of the week was the worst. Examiners read mathematical problems aloud, in Latin, and proceeded to the next problem as soon as the fastest student finished the first one, creating a nightmarish atmosphere of falling ever further behind. There was some temporary relief in the "window problems," where each student was given a sheet of problems to solve by himself, standing by the light of the windows, as examiners proceeded to other classes. But following this, students were called upstairs in pairs and rigorously set against each other in head-to-head competitions aimed at discovering the smallest degrees of superiority or inferiority between them. It was not uncommon for students to faint or fall into fits before or during this ordeal, sometimes not recovering their mental composure or consciousness for hours or days afterwards. John Tweddell, "the English Marcellus" and the star of 1790, almost lost his mind when he found he had placed only as a senior optime, not a wrangler.[34] The young men who survived these yearly ordeals deserve respect as well as sympathy.[35] One cheers for some students' acts of semi-rebellion, such as that of Blackburn of Trinity in 1790, who refused for two days to answer any question, but who, when threatened with "plucking," contemptuously rattled off answers to the hardest questions posed, and finished as fourteenth senior optime.[36] These exams were at once the acme and the nadir of the eighteenth-century educational system at Cambridge. "It ought to be considered not as a school, where anything is to be learned, but as an arena, where skill and practice are to be displayed. Contests of one kind or another are continually going on; and the student ambititious of honour, is always kept in a feverish state extremely unfavorable to the acquisition of knowledge. . . . [I]f the studies were the art of making watches and shoes . . . the same enthusiastic application would be displayed upon wheels and lasts which is now expended on Euclid and Newton."[37] The emphasis was almost entirely on performance, at a nerve-racking level of exactitude, and of hackneyed material that allowed very little room for individual creativity or intellectual nuance.

Furthermore, the whole system was notoriously corrupt, and Wordsworth's not taking an honors degree also means that he chose not to avail himself of a wide range of perfectly acceptable alternate routes to preferment. The least objectional of these was the *aegrotat* degree, awarded to students who claimed to be ill at examination times, "though commonly the real complaint is much more serious; *viz. indisposition of the mind" (Gradus).* This kept one in the category to which one had been preliminarily assigned, albeit at the bottom of it. Given the states of high anxiety which some students reached, it was a merciful option, and one that Wordsworth could easily have exercised—had he been competing—for little or no shame was attached to it. One or two of these were awarded every year, and three in 1791—Wordsworth's year—one to a Johnian.[38] There were also four honorary senior optime degrees every year which moderators awarded at their discretion, often to deserving students who, like Wordsworth, didn't study mathematics.[39] Even fellowships could be awarded without completion of the exams.[40] Wordsworth's Hawkshead friend Thomas Gawthorp was elected Lupton Fellow at St. John's without taking the Senate House exams, and Robert Jones was given one of the automatic Welsh fellowships without an examination.[41] But such arrangements required a little negotiating, a little politic use of one's connections, and some seemly subservience, none of which Wordsworth would bend himself to. He was also in an awkward position to seek favors because he was in disfavor at college for refusing to write for any of the university's seven major literary prizes, despite his demonstrated classical and poetical talents.

Then there was outright jobbing or exam fixing: "men of commanding talents and great acquirements scrupled not, as Examiners, for the sake of making money, to assign the highest honours in the power of the University to bestow, not on the most deserving, but upon those who had been fortunate enough to avail themselves of their instruction as Private Tutors!"[42] Sometimes this took the "higher" form of deciding that a student's moral excellence outweighed his mathematical deficiencies, and promoting him over others who had better test results. A Clare Fellow claimed to owe his election to his "never absenting himself from chapel, night or morning, during the whole period of his residence."[43] Given some colleges' grim fixation on these observances, and some students' (like Wordsworth's) extreme detestation of them, the claim is not unlikely. Wordsworth's complaint against compulsory chapel attendance is the single longest item (III.407–59) in his extensive bill of complaints against Cambridge, and is all the more interesting because his brother Christopher was noted, as master of Trinity, for rigorously enforcing this requirement.*

At the lowest level of test jobbing were "pupil-mongering" fellows who simply gave precedence to students who had paid them well as private tutors, independent of their exam performance. If artificially competitive exams were the outward sign of Cambridge's intellectual debility, private tuition and its corruptions were the internal motors that kept the system going. Given the exams' emphasis on rapid recall, students were glad to pay for the services of fellows who had recently done well on the same exams; indeed, it was commonly assumed to be almost the only way to prepare successfully for the exams.[44] Some fellows supplemented their college incomes by more than £1,000 a year by such pupil mongering: in 1786 a former fellow commoner left his tutor a bequest of £20,000.[45] Such a system of tuition, intended to overcome deficiencies in the regularly assigned teachers, drastically undercut them instead, and created ever-higher levels of competition among the students who were determined to succeed. In 1833 Wordsworth warned a new Cambridge graduate against taking on pupils in this way, calling it "an absolute blight" on "the blossoms of the mind . . . setting to take fruit." He meant the mind of the young tutor, not his students'.

On balance, Wordsworth's collegiate examination career was considerably better than most of his biographers have allowed, from their being too much under the sway of his dramatized self-presentation in *The Prelude.* In his college, he placed in the first class once and second once, received three honorable mentions, and failed to sit for only one exam. These supposed failures are often extenuated on the basis of (1) his love of nature and poetry, (2) his lower social status, and (3) his provincial origins and northern accent or "burr." The second of these, as we saw in Chapter 5, was much less determining than modern assumptions might suppose, while the first is based on a misunderstanding of Cambridge's intellectual context. (As to northern accents, they were doubtless occasionally laughed at, but there were so many boys and faculty from the north that such condescension would have run its own risks. If being a regional outsider was a disability, three of Wordsworth's

*Christopher Wordsworth earned a reputation as a strict, dour master at Trinity, strong on chapel and firmly against drinking, as a description of 1820 indicates: "Apropos to masters, W——d begged pardon of the Trinitarians, but could not help d——g the whole race of 'Milk & Waters.' Hereupon, the Wordsworthians looked milk-and-watery" (*Facetiae, Cantabrigienses* [1825] 187). When he added a second compulsory chapel service on Sundays to the daily requirement, the Society for the Prevention of Cruelty to Undergraduates was formed (C. R. Benstead, *Portrait of Cambridge* [London: Robert Hale, 1968], 157).

best friends, Myers from Cumberland, Jones from Wales, and Terrot from Scotland, all shared it with him, yet all did as well as he or better.)

Poetry and literature were oft-lamented casualties of the mathematical tripos system, and Wordsworth was not the first to bemoan their loss. The mathematics tripos had been fully instituted only in 1748, and a classical literary exam was reinstituted early in the nineteenth century. So Wordsworth was at Cambridge during the half century it was most inimical to literature, when students were "Wean'd from the sweets of poetry / To scraps of dry philosophy . . . [and] tedious philosophic chapters / Quite stifled [their] poetic raptures."[46] Traditionally it had not been so; Cambridge's list of poetical lights is longer and brighter than Oxford's: Spenser, Marlowe, Jonson, Herbert, Crashaw, Marvell, Milton, Cowley, Dryden, Otway, Prior, Collins, Smart, and Gray, to mention only the standard anthology names; Chaucer, Butler, and Donne can be added by association; Coleridge and Byron and Tennyson of course came afterwards. (Tennyson's father was a Johnian of Wordsworth's year who also took a pass degree from dislike of mathematics.)[47] Such stifling of the literary was particularly associated with St. John's because of its strong emphasis on mathematics, rigorously enforced by its new twice-yearly exams, so much so that one writer implied that only a huge transformation could return the Muse to its precincts:

> Now, in the name of dullness and small beer,
> Ye *Northern* wits of fam'd St. John's appear,
> That scarce taste wine or wit throughout the year.
> Had she, who by the pow'rful charms of wine,
> Transform'd *Ulysses'* men to grunting swine;
> Had she and you [Johnian "Pigs"] the experiment tried again,
> By contrary effects you'd poets been.
> . . . .
> When *Whig* religious, Trimmer loyal turns;
> When *Cambridge* wives, and *Barnwell* wh——s turn nuns;
> When am'rous fops leave hunting handsome faces,
> When craving beadle begs no more for places . . .[48]

then, when all these unlikely millennial events occur, Johnian swine might write again. This writer is from Trinity, and thus biased against St. John's, but the young Byron, a later Trinity Bulldog, was in close agreement with Wordsworth on the costs to literature of this examination system.[49] But Byron as a nobleman could afford to walk his pet bear down the streets and scorn the exams; Wordsworth as a sizar could not.

Yet his beloved William Taylor had managed to combine excellence in mathematics with sensitivity to poetry, and had given him strong competence in both in grammar school. Gilbert Wakefield, a man whose career (like Tweddell's) bears close comparison to Wordsworth's, found mathematics "odious beyond conception," but submitted to the discipline and graduated as second wrangler and chancellor's medalist before embarking on a career as a classical editor, translator, and liberal political writer.[50] Most of Wordsworth's close friends with literary interests did likewise: Losh, Farish, Fleming, Raincock, Wrangham, Montagu, Tweddell, and Greenwood. In sum, being a poet and getting honors were not at all incompatible in Wordsworth's set.

Hence we come to the question that every student of Wordsworth has asked, just as every member of his family must have: Why, given his superior intellectual powers, his excellent family connections for future preferment, and the strong necessity of providing for himself and repaying the guardians who had invested their money in him, did he not do better? Far from being "senior wrangler or nothing!" it took considerably more effort, though of a negative kind, for him to end up with "nothing" on the honors list than it would have taken to place himself among the twenty-one wranglers of 1791 (the largest number in years).[51] As the master of his college said, with an extreme of donnish understatement, on the bicentenary of Wordsworth's birth, "for a Hawkshead boy of his ability, Wordsworth's Cambridge career was an exceptional one."[52] Other students in similar circumstances worked harder and did better: T. G. Bonney's father died during his first summer vacation, "which made sticking to work more than ever imperative, for I was the eldest of ten and my mother's means were very limited."[53] Given Wordsworth's college exam record, the question that arose from his family was not why he had done so poorly but why, having done so well in what he did do, he could not have improved his prospects by doing a bit more.

The course he followed seems ridiculously, not sublimely, egotistical, and one explanation fits it very well: that he did not want to take examinations in which he would not show up well—that is, *best*—and which he would have to subject his mind to others' materials for an intensely competitive performance. Merely by sitting for the mathematical and moral/religious sections of the college exams, he would inevitably have landed in the second or third collegiate categories, since classifications were based on overall performance, and outstanding classics work pulled up mediocre mathematical work. Even the smallest calculation of his interests could have earned him a junior optime degree. This was not normally sufficient for election to a fellowship (three were elected at St. John's in 1791), but there were all sorts of loopholes and special exceptions that could be made, if a student was prepared to demonstrate his willingness to follow merely the letter, not the spirit, of the requirements. This was especially true of mathematical weakness when combined with literary strengths: Trinity fellowship candidates needed only to " 'clear' it, or even nearly so," to qualify.[54]

Wordsworth was in the most comfortable collegiate group: bright students who elected not to try for honors. Reading for honors was considered "a slow sort of suicide"; Christopher Wordsworth, who was tenth wrangler in 1796, estimated he read nearly ten hours a day in the four months before his Senate House exams.[55] But when Wordsworth parts himself from this company—"Willingly did I part from these"—his explanation is dubious:

> I turn[ed]
> Out of their track to travel with the shoal
> Of more unthinking natures, easy minds
> And pillowy, and not wanting love that makes
> The day pass lightly on . . . .
>
> (III.516–21)

Such "easy" and "pillowy" minds might have included Jones and Myers, though their exam performances were on a par with Wordsworth's. But there is almost no one among all the men Wordsworth knew at Cambridge who did not achieve some academic or intellectual distinction. Wordsworth's friends were just as smart as he was, as we would expect them to have been, unless we imagine a wholly unknown group of "easy" and "pillowy" persons who loved him in a way that made "the day pass lightly on." No, as a later St. John's master shrewdly noted, Wordsworth constantly saw his friends and acquaintances receiving honors of one sort or another, and he chose not to enter into competition with them, even though most of them were his intellectual inferiors.[56]

The Prelude would lead us to believe that his confidence in his future greatness made him reject Cambridge requirements, but this was not true when he wrote it (1803–4), and would have been a mere fantasy when he lived it. To have acted upon such a reason in 1790 would have been "crazed" in mind—or selfishness—indeed, however well it fits ex post facto with the later Romantic idealization of great writers' keeping faith with their art. Not that Wordsworth had no poems to point to by 1787 as evidence of a future vocation; he had many. But none of them, on any calculation, would have permitted him to say (except perhaps to Dorothy), "I renounce all of this for these."

What he did have, what formed the basis of his foolhardy turn against Cambridge, was enormous, if almost desperate, pride and egotism, neither of which quite constitute self-confidence. Few things in the young Wordsworth's life are more "romantic" in the colloquial (and usually pejorative) sense than his rejection of Cambridge's opportunities, such as they were. But we should be wary of *romanticizing* it: it cost him opportunities for church livings that were by no means incompatible with poetry, it cost his family dearly, it was not easy, it was not very successful, it was risky and dangerous. He could not know what the result would be, but eventually it was crucial to the creation of the Poet. He was a late bloomer whose psychological profile fits very closely the model for genius developed by Erik Erikson in *Young Man Luther,* particularly its elements of fatherlessness and a difficult, unforthcoming personality that nonetheless craved affection. It is clear from *The Prelude* that what he rejected was the Cambridge *system:* not the exams per se, but the personally humiliating subservience to a course of social advancement of which they were the prime instruments. He could clearly see—as who could not?—"that here in dwarf proportions were expressed / The limbs of the great world."[57] Though the examination contests were a "mock fight," the blows were "hardly dealt," and it was "no mimic show [but] itself a *living* part of a *live* whole, / A creek of the vast sea": the stream up which these young men struggled to gain the *livings* that gave them position in eighteenth-century English society.

One of the best, least temporizing parts of Book III of *The Prelude,* "Residence at Cambridge," is also one of its least romantic. Its concluding peroration shows Wordsworth's mastery of the tradition of allegorical social satire of which he is supposed to be the enemy, but which writing about his Cambridge experiences brought forcefully into his mind. We can imagine the real names he saw behind each allegorical personification in this powerful passage, which harks back to bludgeoning denunciations of both Bunyan's Puritan *Pilgrim's Progress* and Samuel Butler's Royalist *Hudibras:*

> And here was Labour, his own Bond-slave; Hope
> That never set the pains against the prize;
> Idleness, halting with his weary clog;
> And poor misguided Shame, and witless Fear,
> And simple Pleasure, foraging for Death;
> Honour misplaced, and Dignity astray;
> Feuds, factions, flatteries, Enmity and Guile,
> Murmuring Submission and bald Government
> (The idol weak as the idolator)
> And Decency and Custom starving Truth,
> And blind Authority beating with his staff
> The child that might have led him; Emptiness
> Followed as of good omen, and meek *Worth*
> Left to itself *unheard of and unknown.*
>
> (III.630–43; italics added)

If we look for Words*worth* in this catalog, rhetorical inevitability and his rights as a Johnian punster put him in the climactic position, which is verified by its echo of his self-presentation earlier in the book: "So was it with me in my solitude . . . *Unknown, unthought of*" (139–41; italics added). And if we look for what he considered to be the worst abuse, to which he assigned the worst punishment, we find it in his attitude toward the immorality described in Chapter 5, dismissed with the chilling overkill of "simple Pleasure, foraging for Death."

But his university failure was still worse than this, for he was not even true to himself. Book III of *The Prelude,* if recast as a letter home from college, would be enough to make any parent weep, with its tissue of weak excuses and temporizing admissions, self-blame and institutional critique, shoulder-shrugging insouciance and chin-out arrogance. In the propriety of his later public life Wordsworth expressed conventional regrets for not having studied harder at Cambridge, but in the *Prelude* account he criticizes himself for having given in as much as he did to the exam-and-preferment system.[58] Some excellent students followed more independent courses of action and were often rewarded for their hardy perseverance. The young Pitt, for example, spent an extra two years reading history, politics, and government with famous results, and Wilberforce put himself under the tutelage of William Cookson to recover his wasted time at college. To a considerable degree, Wordsworth did do this. He read classical literature, much more than was required, and also modern literature and modern European languages. He hired an Italian tutor, Agostino Isola, a friend of Gray's, who was beloved as one of the best teachers in the university (he had tutored young Pitt), and who had just published in 1787 a scholarly edition of Tasso's *Gerusalemme Liberata*.[59] He also taught himself Spanish, and his French was already quite good, thanks to Mr. Mingay at Hawkshead. It was almost unheard of for sizars to study modern languages, as this instruction was offered mainly for noblemen and fellow commoners in preparation for their grand tour of the Continent.[60] In a sense, this is what Wordsworth was doing too, only his grand tour would be made on foot. But members of his family were not slow to see a presumptive arrogance in his study of modern languages and his desire to go abroad.[61]

But he did not have the courage to break off college work and follow his own bent single-mindedly. He continued to post "distinguished" exam performances on parts of the exam, results that inevitably drew even more attention to the parts he was omitting. His failures toward himself were very much like his failures toward the system, revealing the neither-this-nor-that, "amphibious," "spungy texture" of his mind which he compared to the floating island of weeds and aquatic flowers that drifted about Derwent Water.[62] He sampled all the options of Cambridge: its "deep quiet and majestic thoughts," its "empty noise and superficial pastimes," its "forced labour, and more frequently forced hopes." But none of it added up; instead, it produced only "a treasonable growth of indecisive judgements that impaired / And shook the mind's simplicity" (III.210–16).

To wish that Wordsworth had followed his own lights more faithfully is to remind ourselves that he was still an adolescent, not a romantic epic hero, and to recognize the fundamental honesty of his self-presentation in *The Prelude.* It is the most typical adolescent behavior to rebel *partially* against authority, to refuse to do exactly what is required of it, and yet not to do what the young person says he most desires to do, because he does not know himself exactly what he wants. When such behavior finally does make itself manifest, it frequently does something that is at once cowardly, like running off to France without telling anyone, and irreparably self-destructive—such as returning to college so late there was no possibility of preparing for the honors questions. Like that of Stephen Daedalus, who also leaves for the Continent rather than take his university degree, Wordsworth's refusal to complete his university exams was a romantic "Non serviam," delivered with the same Miltonic overtones—and subject to the same charges of adolescent posturing—as its refracted image in Joyce's later portrait of the artist as a young man.

8 SOMETHING OF A REPUBLIC

Politics at Cambridge

> Nor was it least
> Of many debts which afterwards I owed
> To Cambridge and the academic life,
> That something there was holden up to view
> Of a republic, where all stood thus far
> Upon equal ground, that they were brothers all . . . .
> (IX.226–31)

William's return to Cambridge in the fall of 1789 had dramatically raised his consciousness of events in France. The Revolution was being avidly discussed, especially by popular and influential young fellows who were not only favorable to the events in France but also outspoken partisans of reform at home, and hoping to begin with the university itself. "Long before 1789 the republican ideal had had extensive circulation at Cambridge; with the French Revolution to give it support, it must have been well-nigh irresistible."[1] If we connect the Cambridge ideal of exact mathematical understanding of natural forms and processes to the broader faith of an Age of Reason that social forms and practices might be grasped with similar exactitude, we see why Cambridge produced so many "friends of liberty" in the generation of the 1790s.

Chief among the university's revolutionary enthusiasts was William Frend, a brilliant, popular and controversial fellow of Jesus College ("Frend of Jesus," inevitably), who had been in Europe during the summer and felt the aftershocks radiating out from the epicenter at Paris. He narrowly missed the sudden attack of the populace of Ghent on the imperial garrison there, heard news of other short-lived "revolutions" breaking out in Germany, and got firsthand reports on the events in France from William Priestley, son of the famous Unitarian scientist, preacher, and reform politician Joseph Priestley, who was in Paris during those July days.[2] Frend's accounts of these events generated great interest among the students because he was a dedicated clergyman as well as a very popular teacher. He had been publicly involved in university reform issues since October 1787, the very month that Wordsworth first arrived at Cambridge.

The political life of "unreformed" Cambridge was far more active than that of somnolent, orthodox Oxford. Throughout the 1770s and 1780s it was a simmering caldron of mixed political issues that came to a boil in 1789–90, Wordsworth's third year at college. It was real politics now, going beyond the preferment politics which governed so much of student and faculty behavior, though the two were intimately connected, as Frend's career shows. He had renounced his Anglican faith in the spring of 1787, following a close study of the church's Thirty-nine Articles; other fellows like John Jebb of Peterhouse had earlier come to similar conclusions. There was a continuous line of such "dissentience" in eighteenth-century Cambridge, going back to Edward Law of St. John's and Francis Blackburne of St. Catherine's, northern men (Blackburne attended Hawkshead) who both died in 1787.[3] All these men were in various ways theorists of perfectibility: committed Protestants who based their theological and scriptural researches on Newtonian logic and Lockean psychology, and followed wherever they led, in full confidence that reason and revelation could not be ultimately irreconcilable. (Jebb's brother, one of the king's physicians, told his master that his brother would be a reformer even in heaven.)[4] Their decisions were not taken lightly. They usually began with the Test Acts, the requirement that anybody wishing to receive a university degree must subscribe to the Thirty-nine Articles of the Anglican creed. This of course excluded Catholics and Dissenters from degrees, though not from a university education. Nobody was much worried about the Catholics, still under the cloud of international conspiracy theories from the Jacobite risings forty years earlier. But many intelligent Dissenters were being denied their intellectual rights by the Test Acts, and rational research into the articles often led to the conclusion not only that the test requirement was unfair but that the articles themselves were untenable, especially the doctrine of the Trinity, which not even differential calculus could prove. The great classicist Richard Porson was almost equal to the task, however. A friend once pointed out to him a buggy carrying three men, saying, "There is an illustration of the Trinity." "No," said Porson, "you must show me one man in *three* buggies, if you can."[5]

The intellectual route from opposition to the Test Acts, through doubts about the Trinity, to Unitarianism, and thence into republicanism, was the intellectual fast track of the era. Cambridge in the late 1780s was a hotbed of Unitarianism, which amounted to a sort of eighteenth-century "green" radicalism: its practitioners were more fervent in pursuit of good works, without faith in an afterlife, than most Anglicans, whose faith in revelation had settled down to a mere convention of theological good manners. Frend's mentor was Theophilus Lindsey (1723–1808), formerly a fellow of St. John's, one of the founders (along with Jebb) of the first Unitarian church in England, the Essex Street chapel in London, and a close associate of Priestley and Richard Price, the Dissenter whose 1791 sermon in praise of the Revolution provoked Burke's *Reflections.* Lindsey's letters to Frend about the rapid spread of Unitarianism in the north and west, "and in Lancashire particularly," have all the urgency of a political campaign, and were of course regarded by the authorities in that light.[6] To combat this virulent new strain of protestantism, the king promulgated a statute reinforcing an older one of William III, making it blasphemy to deny the Trinity, and excluding persons who did so from the Acts of Toleration. The most celebrated martyr of this guilt by association between Unitarianism and republicanism was Thomas Fyshe Palmer (1747–1802), a former fellow of Queens, who would be exiled to Botany Bay in the notorious Edinburgh treason trials of 1794, and who died in the Pacific trying to return home after serving his term. The university's charters, written in times of a different Reformation zeal, were very strict against public expressions which tended to "teach, or treat of, or defend any thing against the religion . . . received and established by public authority."[7] Some fellows gave up their Anglicanism but kept their opinions to themselves and were allowed to remain in college. Those who made their opinions public suffered the consequences, and William Frend was the most famous example.

Wordsworth's religious opinions at the time were so mild as to be nonexistent; he had no trouble subscribing to the Test Acts for his degree. But as he contemplated the life in orders he was supposed to follow, the successive acts of the drama of conscience that William Frend enacted during his college years made him feel more keenly the exactions of the Cambridge system on the individual will.

Frend published his *Thoughts on Subscription* in the spring of 1788.[8] In the fall of 1788 he widened both his audience and his target, publishing an *Address to the Inhabitants of Cambridge,* explicitly against Trinitarianism. This cost him his £150 tutorship, but he retained his fellowship. The dismissal threw him out of his university circle of "dissentients" (oppositional thinking) into a larger group of political dissidents and Dissenters (oppositional actions) in both the university and the town. One of the respected leaders of the latter group was Robert Robinson, minister of a Baptist church (though he too slid into Unitarianism) and mentor of George Dyer, a close friend of Wordsworth's revered schoolteacher William Taylor. In 1789 Dyer was living in Robinson's house when he published his own *Inquiry into the Nature of Subscription to the Thirty-nine Articles.*[9] Given Wordsworth's deep feelings for Taylor, we can assume he had some contact with Dyer in Cambridge, as he did later in London. He would call Dyer's biography of Robinson "the best in the language":[10] such hyperbolic praise for a merely workmanlike job signals a feeling of solidarity for these men and what they represented, rather than impartial literary judgment. Robinson had been one of the founders of the Society for Constitutional Information in 1780, and hosted a dinner on November 5, 1788, honoring the Glorious Revolution. The town mayor and several aldermen were present, Robinson preached a sermon, and the evening wound up with several choruses of "good revolutional songs,"[11] the veritable spirit of 1688.

Frend, buoyed by his new support, strengthened his convictions and revised his Cambridge address in the fall of 1789, publishing it as an *Address to the Members of the Church of England.* For this he was kicked out of the Society for the Promotion of Christian Knowledge, which Wilberforce had helped to found. Frend's writings over the next four years would be increasingly associated by his enemies with the rising specter of Jacobinism, until he was finally dismissed from all university positions for the publication of his *Peace and Union Recommended to the Associated Bodies of Republicans and Anti-Republicans* (1793), a tract whose clear purpose was to *avoid* the increasingly intense polarization of opinions to which it fell victim. Many other writers urging academic or religious reform at this period suffered the same imputation of guilt by association, and not all of them were cautious about dissociating themselves from "French principles." Henry Gunning was a Whig who suffered slights for sticking to his party during Pitt's ascendancy, but his analysis of the situation is precise on the ways in which university politics were now hooked up with national politics: "To those who studied the signs of the times it was very evident that Whiggism would be an unpopular profession, and that a good opportunity now presented itself [in the Frend case] for abandoning their [Whig] principles; thus their apostasy assumed the garb of patriotism, and a regard for the established religion."[12]

When Frend's university hearings finally came to an end, he had won all the moral and rhetorical points, to the great delight of crowds of student spectators (including Coleridge). But he lost all the technical and substantive ones. The vice-chancellor, Isaac Milner, who had personally converted Wilberforce to Evangelical Christianity, assured Wilberforce that the trial was "the end of the Jacobinical party as a *University* thing." Milner wrote to Wilberforce as the surest way of reaching Pitt's ear, the better to increase Pitt's appreciation—which he felt was insufficient—for Milner's role in putting down the threat.[13] This sequence describes perfectly the circles through which public politics were recycled as preferment politics, and reminds us that Wordsworth's connections along this circuit were of exactly the same order and magnitude as Frend's: Cookson to Wilberforce to Pitt.

Cambridge could appear very conservative or very radical, depending on which corners one looked into, but its atmosphere of political agitation was pervasive. As at American and European universities in the 1960s, there was no single issue until *the* single issue, supporting or opposing war with France (declared in 1793), preempted all the others. There were university reformers and parliamentary reformers, but since the university itself was Pitt's rotten borough, the two were often indistinguishable. There was religious reform and political reform, from Dissenters through Unitarians to republicans. There were philosophical reformers who would find their great text in William Godwin's *Political Justice* (1793) and "philanthropists" whose hero was Tom Paine ("philanthropy" signified a love of mankind beyond the confines of one's own country, and was often used in opposition to "patriot").[14] There were practical politicians, Foxite Whigs, and other Whigs who increasingly supported Pitt, becoming the leading edge of the great wave of "apostasy" which would roll back like a treacherous moral undertow through the 1790s, pulling almost everyone of liberal persuasion with it. Through it all, like a moral beacon, shone the agitation against slavery and the slave trade, initiated with all the force of religious conversion in Thomas Clarkson's student disputation of 1784, and now taken up in Parliament by Wilberforce, but still twenty discouraging years away from victory. For the promise of liberal reform, it was the best of times; for liberalism's actual achievements, it was the worst of times. Oxford gained a reputation as "the home of lost causes" in the nineteenth century, but in late eighteenth-century Cambridge, the cause of liberal reform was one long string of near-misses. The Test Act requirement was not abolished until 1870.

In all this, what tended to impress itself on undergraduates' minds was the sight of popular tutors and fellows, young, intelligent, and well meaning, proposing changes in university regulations that affected the students themselves, and being punished, even deprived of their livelihood, for their actions. One "grace" or petition after another was offered to the university senate, calling for greater or lesser reforms, written in the best Latin and argued with scrupulous rationality, but almost all of them lost out, sometimes by the slimmest of margins. Some changes did get through, particularly with regard to the content of examinations, but on the big questions, of which the Test Acts were the cornerstone, there was no victory. Jebb and William Tyrwhitt had petitioned for their repeal in 1771, and Thomas Edwards, who helped Coleridge with the *Watchman* in 1796, offered another grace against them in December of 1787.[15] Charles James Fox offered his last bill against the Test Acts in Parliament in March 1790, but it lost, 294 to 105, with Wilberforce active against it.[16] The ideological issue was clear in the debate. Fox argued not only "for General Toleration, but for that system [which ensures] the Universal Rights of Human Nature." Pitt responded that such principles would "throw open a door for the entrance of some individuals who might consider it a point of *conscience* to shake our Establishment to its foundations."[17] Had any of these academic initiatives won out, the political atmosphere in Cambridge would have been much less lively. But by constantly losing, the reformers effectively if unhappily kept politics constantly in the forefront of everyone's mind.

Wordsworth's Christmas vacation in 1789 had its own political overtones. The three older brothers had a brief reunion in London; William's desire to be with them probably explains his missing the December college exams, the only ones he did not take. Richard was just finishing his first year with the firm of Parkin & Lambert, legal associates of Jack Robinson. He had been sent off to London by Christopher Crackanthorpe with very particular instructions, which repeated the advice given earlier to William: "I would recommend it to you to pay attention to Mr Robinson as much as you conveniently can, as he has it much in his power to be of service to you in future."[18] John, for his part, had recently returned from the East Indies; he was to sail for India in January, aboard the *Earl of Abergavenny,* captained by his cousin John of Whitehaven, owned in part by Robinson, and named for Robinson's son-in-law, Henry Nevill, the second earl of Abergavenny.[19] Wordsworth's cousin Thomas Myers married the earl's daughter; his sister was already married to Robinson's brother the admiral. So young Wordsworth that Christmas was very much at the crossroads of several successful family ventures in law, trade, and matrimony.

What he recalled of the time, however, was that he purchased William Bowles's *Fourteen Sonnets, Elegiac and Descriptive* and annoyed his brother John by stopping to read them "in a niche of London Bridge."[20] Bowles's influence on the first Romantics has been overrated, largely because of Coleridge's excessive praise in *Biographia Literaria.*[21] What brought Wordsworth up short on London Bridge was not great poetry, still less English literature's first combination of "natural thought with natural diction" that Coleridge claimed to find in Bowles. It was, rather, the shock of recognition: the realization that he himself was already writing poetry like this, and writing it as well or better. Not that Wordsworth's poetry was at this moment more original than Bowles's; both owed large debts to the tradition of Sensibility, especially the Wartons and the sonnets of Charlotte Smith and Helen Maria Williams. But one look at Bowles's slim volume convinced Wordsworth that he could do as well, and also energized him with the unpleasant realization that he was being anticipated by a lesser talent.

Bowles's collegiate, church, and literary career was an epitome of the kind Wordsworth was supposed to follow (B.A. Oxon. 1787, with many prizes), and he was one of the small conduits by which "feminine" poetic attitudes and subjects were diverted into streams that eventually produced a new Romantic poetry.[22] Like Charlotte Smith's *Elegiac Sonnets,* Bowles's are dominated by the emotion of regret for childhood joys in the country. Directly to Wordsworth's taste, Bowles's are often set, lamely, in the north: "O North! as thy romantick vales I leave, / And bid farewell to each retiring hill . . . I shall return, your varied views to mark." Here was the same idea of poetic subject matter that was just forming in the young Wordsworth's mind, but stillborn at the moment of invention. Moreover, Bowles's sonnets were presented as if found in a traveler's memorandum book, and are loosely grouped as reflections arising from a tour through ruined northern castles and abbeys, and along some northern rivers. (His "Monody" of 1791 is set along "the dark Derwent's wand'ring way.") Wordsworth's mini-tour in *An Evening Walk* came immediately to his mind, as did his recent emotional walks with Dorothy and Mary around Brougham Castle and Penrith Beacon. If he dreamed of being a professional poet, here was proof that such themes could find a publisher, and a warning that the market might soon be glutted with inferior productions.

Dorothy's 1789 Christmas was equally eventful, well connected, and forward looking. Wilberforce spent the holidays with the Cooksons at Forncett, staying more than a month, and paid her much attention—so much that her friend Jane Pollard teased her with being distracted by an eligible suitor. Wilberforce was much impressed with the school for parish children Dorothy had started, and gave her ten guineas to distribute to the poor "in what manner [she thought] best."[23] He also gave her *A Practical Treatise on Regeneration* and the tireless Mrs. Trimmer's *Economy of Charity,* a book about Sunday schools with "some desultory hints towards improving the condition of the poor." The Sunday school movement was just beginning in these years (William Frend had started one in his parish near Cambridge), and Dorothy's model and Wilberforce's advice show that it was as much a movement responding to social crisis as one of religious education. All in all, Dorothy found Wilberforce "to be one of the best of men." This led to Jane's tease, which Dorothy laughingly denied, but Jane had struck a tender spot. Besides protesting too much against her own romantic interest in him, Dorothy modestly insisted, "Mr. W. would, were he ever to marry, look for a Lady possessed of many more accomplishments than I can boast, and besides he is as unlikely a man ever to marry at all as any I know." Her first reason is false modesty, but the latter is a frank assessment of Wilberforce's decidedly unhandsome face, with its large snub nose, a gift to all future caricaturists. In fact, Wilberforce had just been jilted, and might have been in a receptive mood at the time, though he soon made a resolve never to marry—which lasted for seven years. A marriage between Dorothy Wordsworth and William Wilberforce was not implausible, for though Wilberforce's eventual wife, Barbara Ann Spooner, was both beautiful and rich (and Evangelical), he was rich enough for them both, and Dorothy, as the niece of his bosom friend Cookson and an heir-dependent of Lord Lowther, a Wilberforce ally, needed no social apology. She had been introduced to the royal family at Windsor during one of Cookson's visits there as a canon of the Chapel Royal (a permanent stall would be his next appointment),[24] and the king was very pleased to meet a young cousin of his children's trusted tutor who was also the cousin of his chief political agent, Jack Robinson. Wilberforce's nervous, vivacious temperament and talk would have made him, in one respect, an ideal match for Dorothy. But he came to feel that he needed a calmer spirit than his own for a spouse, and Dorothy was beginning to come to the same conclusion. Indeed, she had already made her choice, of the best of men, "my Dear William," though she may not yet have put it to herself, consciously, that she would always have a brother, but never a husband.

She was more ready than William to act in the family's political interest, telling Jane, "Tell your Father I hope he will give [Wilberforce] his vote at the next general election," which was held in June. Wilberforce seemed to be in need of help, for his dramatic change in principles since 1784 (the year of his conversion), and his exhaustive parliamentary efforts against the slave trade which had been its result, had given his Foxite opponents grounds to accuse him of neglecting his constituency.

As with the facts of prostitution in Cambridge and the rigors of the university exam system, the question regarding its political atmosphere must be, How far did all this agitation affect Wordsworth, granting that he could not have been unaware of it? He used the word "republican" twice in talking about his university experience, and that word, eminently respectable today, was potentially treasonous in Wordsworth's Cambridge. Imagining a better university that "should have bent me down to instantaneous service," he describes a place whose "majestic edifices" had a "corresponding dignity within": "a healthy sound simplicity, / A seemly plainness—name it as you will, / Republican or pious" (III.380–407). His offer of a "pious" alternative —that is, a simple religious community—shows how dangerous the "republican" one—Roman, Swiss, or French—was construed to be.[25] His language here is close to that of Samuel Parr, the "Whig Dr. Johnson" and a nonresident fellow of St. John's, in his Latin preface to a new edition (1787) of Bellenden's *De Statu,* which was regularly used as a text in the college for themes and declamations. This preface, titled "Tria Lumina Anglorum," is a highly partisan celebration of Fox, North, and Burke—the three English luminaries—who are sharply contrasted with Pitt, to urge the role of the university in training young men to republican virtue. Parr sets up the same connections between impressive buildings and moral fiber that Wordsworth later employed: "the goodly effects that are wrought on the temper as well as the taste, by the daily and hourly view of edifices, agreeable from convenience, or striking from magnificence, or venerable from antiquity."[26] Parr was one of several Cambridge Whigs whose political "dissentience" was coupled with an interest in the structure of language, based on its original or "natural" forms. All such inquiries were heavily indebted to Rousseau's *Discourse on Inequality,* with its cheeky demonstrations that as civilization has increased, so has human inequality. Other investigators in this line were Porson of Trinity, his liberal classicist opponent Gilbert Wakefield, and, most radically, John Horne Tooke (1736–1812), yet another Johnian, founder of the Constitution Society and author, in 1786, of *The Diversions of Purley.* This famous text developed a nominalist theory of language and thought, anticipating the modern linguistic view that right and wrong, like right and left, are arbitrary constructs always dependent on context.[27] In each of these works we find anticipations of Wordsworth's arguments in the 1800 preface to *Lyrical Ballads* for a correlation between agricultural labor, unaffected sincerity of feelings, and "the language really spoken by men." They all shared elements of classical republican theory, based on landowning, conservative elites, as distinct from the newer theories other Whig philosophers were developing, based on commerce, capital, profit, and individual talent and enterprise.[28]

Wordsworth also used his Cambridge experience to describe his receptiveness to the democratic impulses of the French Revolution:

> Nor was it least
> Of many debts which afterwards I owed
> To Cambridge and an academic life,
> That something there was holden up to view
> Of a republic, where all stood thus far
> Upon equal ground, that they were brothers all
> In honour, as of one community—
> Scholars and gentlemen—where, furthermore,
> Distinction lay open to all that came,
> And wealth and titles were in less esteem
> Than talents and successful industry.
>
> (IX.226–36)

This idealized view of Cambridge sits very ill with his account of it in Book III, and even less well with his actual performance there: who was he to invoke "talents and successful industry"? But the more relevant point is that he recalled it as being "something . . . of a republic" at a very pertinent point in time: the summer of 1792, when he was in France and when, on August 10, the National Assembly first declared France a republic.

These two sympathetic references do not make young Wordsworth a republican in 1787–91. Though he sympathized with the direction of liberal reform and republican sentiment, he also contained within himself tendencies of a sharply opposite nature. His own personal, family politics, his *interests,* were Pittite all the way. Pitt was certainly not a republican, but then neither was any other politician of any standing at the time, including Fox, the florid, generous, flawed leader of the liberal Whigs during all of Wordsworth's young manhood. Applying Keats's romantic "test act" for judging the intensity—and sincerity—of experience, we can be sure that Wordsworth felt all these conflicts on his pulses.

This is much more than mere political background, for these same persons and issues held center stage in British public life without significant interruption throughout Wordsworth's early development. The enormous change in the English political system in the half century between 1783 and 1832 was very much centered on Pitt's career and his Cambridge power base. Pitt was one of the two MPs for Cambridge: that is, for the university, not the town borough.

St. John's College retained its conservative profile during Wordsworth's time. Traditionally, it "had the character of *the* Tory college in the Whig University."[29] But Henry Gunning, Cambridge's leading memoirist and himself an outspoken Whig, declared that ca. 1789 "St. John's was decidedly a Whig College," though the "true Johnian feeling" was anti-Pitt.[30] At the time of Wordsworth's arrival at college, Pitt owed his seat to 351 of the 554 university fellows who voted in the election of 1784, an actual victory margin of only 73.[31] In strictly numerical terms, Cambridge University was one of the rottenest boroughs. Wordsworth was personally familiar with these events—"I had so often seen Mr. Pitt *upon his own ground* at Cambridge"—and, later in life, with their significance—"upon whose counsels and public conduct, during a most momentous period, depended the fate of this great Empire and perhaps of all Europe."[32] It was nothing less than the creation of the modern Conservative party, to which the mighty events of the French Revolution were, for practical domestic purposes, frequently only a dramatic and sometimes useful propaganda backdrop. For not only was Pitt not a republican; it was an increasingly open question, by the time Wordsworth arrived in Cambridge in 1787, whether he was a Whig or even a liberal. This is an overstatement, but it highlights the actual political situation, which changed with lightning rapidity during the decade; its future outlines were revealed in their eventual form by the end of Wordsworth's third year at Cambridge, June 1790.

In 1780 Pitt, aged twenty-two, had finished last in a field of five in the university's parliamentary election, with 142 votes. In the election in 1784 Pitt stood again for Cambridge, having spent the intervening three years in James

Lowther's seat for Appleby, and was elected, ratifying the king's controversial appointment of him as prime minister in 1783. Pitt and his friend George Henry Fitzroy (1760–1844), earl of Euston and fourth duke of Grafton, unseated the two "old Whigs," Pitt running first in the field. In 1785 Pitt, who along with Burke and Fox had been a supporter of the cause of the American colonists, and who was by definition a liberal reform politician, offered a mild bill for parliamentary reform. It lost, and he never offered another. In August of 1786 Fox and Sheridan and other Whig leaders were made "freemen" of Cambridge. In the election of June 1790, at the beginning of Wordsworth's last long vacation—the same election for which Dorothy had been stumping for votes for Wilberforce—Pitt increased his university vote total to 510, fewer than 100 fellows failing to vote for him, and was elected high steward of the university. In December of 1792 the innkeepers of Cambridge formed a local chapter of John Reeves's reactionary Association for the Protection of Liberty and Property against Republicans and Levellers, and on that New Year's Eve, shortly after Wordsworth's return from his second trip to France, Tom Paine, a local boy from nearby Thetford, was burned in effigy.[33]

In Wordsworth's Cambridge there was a constant political contention between the university Whigs who supported Pitt and those who felt betrayed by him. By the end of the decade Whiggism "was at a considerable discount,"[34] not only because of growing concern over what was happening in France, but because the kind of liberal reform politics originally associated with Pitt was no longer associated with him, and because the university fellows, like all political constituencies at the time, quickly switched their allegiances to match those of the person in power. Pitt was their source of preferment, master of the only market on which they could sell their vote. Byron had it exactly right: "With eager haste they court the lord of power, / Whether 'tis Pitt or Petty rules the hour; / . . . / But should a storm o'erwhelm him with disgrace, / They'd fly to seek the next who fill'd his place."[35] Those who refused to give in to this natural opportunism looked to Fox as their leader. By doing so, they too helped create something new on the political scene: a permanent political opposition, a party and a coherent leadership which, though out of power, could hold its members together long enough to form an institutional focus for alternative policies.[36] Fox and his chief lieutenant, Charles Grey, who in old age would be prime minister when the Reform Bill finally passed, were formed in the cradle of Cambridge just as surely as Pitt and Wilberforce and young Wordsworth.

Pitt came up to Cambridge about twice a year when the university was in session, "usually with a Deanery or some preferment in his pocket."[37] These were painful occasions, for Pitt was both arrogant and shy, the very antithesis of Fox personally, and most of the fellows could not disguise their squirming lust for place, preferment, or a pension. Sometimes they would stupefy their benefactor with irrelevant displays of erudition, or alternatively confuse him with bizarre donnish humor. A fellow like Richard Farmer of Emmanuel was invaluable on such occasions for his ability to smooth down his colleagues' desire for favors, while at the same time aiding Pitt's calculating design: to keep his constituents both continually hungry and occasionally satisfied. William Paley was a philosopher whose insights into moral behavior were greater than his ability to act on them: asked to sign a petition for repeal of the Test Acts (which he favored), he replied, "I cannot afford to keep a conscience": it might hurt his chances for future preferments. His "shuffling" chapter in *Moral Philosophy* showed how to get round the Test Acts without overtaxing one's moral sense. But even Paley preached a pointed sermon during one of Pitt's visits, taking his text from the parable of the loaves and fishes: "But what are they among so many?"[38] The system was certainly corrupt from a modern point of view, but it was normal and natural to those enmeshed in its contradictions, and within these limits it worked very well. The Cambridge preferment system was not tied to politics by public issues, for one might have almost any opinion, within reason, on such volatile issues as parliamentary reform, the slave trade, or the East India Company. Rather, its connection to the political system was directly based on votes given to a candidate, from whom favors flowed down as a matter of course.

Given his superior abilities and need, his family's great expectations and powerful connections, Wordsworth's failure to take an honors degree at Cambridge was a spectacular flouting of them all, and one of the decisively determining events of his youth. It turned him out of the mainstream of eighteenth-century genteel life into the by-waters of literary and political journalism inhabited by unsuccessful university students—particularly, in his generation, those who tried to buck the practices of this cozy establishment with notions of Whiggish reform or, far worse, of fundamental change on the model of the American and French Revolutions. His university career was never intended to be primarily an intellectual affair. Rather, he was supposed to become a fellow and join Pitt's majority, standing ready to deliver his vote whenever the next election was called, for his career interests lay, as we have seen, decidedly on the conservative, Pittite side. Hence his failure to prepare himself even minimally for the mathematical honors examinations was not only a personal failure, or simply a family matter; it had, in a manner of speaking, national ramifications. Lacking an inheritance, he did not have the land necessary to make him a "freeman" or "freeholder" eligible to vote in the Cumberland elections. But with an honors degree and a college fellowship he could have earned these same rights in Cambridge by his own intellectual exertions. He could have gone on reading and studying and writing whatever he liked, including poetry, as Gray and Smart and many others before had done. With his connections, frayed though they were by two years of unfocused—but not undistinguished—study, a concerted effort from June 1790 to the following January could at least have landed him somewhere among the optimes. Terrot did it, as did Fleming, and Raincock, and Greenwood, and Farish, and Gawthorp, and Losh, and many of his other friends and acquaintances.

To journey to Europe instead at this crucial time not only threw him out of the system of preferment politics for which he was well groomed; it also drew him into systems of thought, and among people, opposed not only to that comfortable system of benefices and emoluments but to the entire sociopolitical ideology of hierarchy and constitutional monarchy on which it was based.

GOLDEN HOURS

The 1790 Walking Tour: France and Switzerland

France standing on the top of golden hours,
And human nature seeming born again.
(VI.353–54)

In the summer of 1790 Wordsworth would have been well advised—and surely was advised—to join a Lakeland reading party to study for his university exams. But he decided to take a walking tour of Europe instead. With this act of disobedience, his career as a Romantic poet may be said to have begun.

"William . . . lost the chance, indeed the certainty of a fellowship, by not combating his inclinations," Dorothy ruefully admitted.[1] It is almost impossible to overestimate the importance of this summer's tour in Wordsworth's development. In a life thus far marked by only small acts of disobedience, like slashing family portraits with a whip, this was a decisive act of rebellion, his personal "French" revolution, and the culmination of his minor college lapses. It was a public flouting of his family's expectations for his adult career, confirming their worst suspicions about his college life. Like his stealing the rowboat on Ullswater, which produced one of his visionary "spots of time," this initially clandestine tour became a three-month-long spot of time, opening an entire decade when Wordsworth's senses were always preternaturally heightened, because almost everything he did could be construed by his elders as an extension of this one act of rebellion.

He took his last college exam in June, and again did well in the parts he attempted. But if he was trying to placate his relatives by taking it, he could hardly have done more to infuriate them by what he did next. Seducing his good friend Robert Jones to his cause (easy to do, since Jones was guaranteed a Welsh fellowship no matter what his exam results), he spent the month after his exams preparing for a tour of the Alps that all their friends agreed was "mad and impracticable." Drawing a draft of twenty pounds on his brother Richard—ostensibly for current college expenses—Wordsworth ordered special greatcoats for each of them, "made light on purpose," from a local tailor. Closeting themselves in the now deserted college, he and Jones sat down to plan a detailed itinerary while the tailor worked.[2]

The idea was very much a Cambridge fashion, within the larger context of Picturesque ramblings Wordsworth had tried out in the two previous summers. William Frend's 1789 tour had been all the rage in college talk, and though the French Revolution was still the main item of international news, beautiful landscapes were Wordsworth's primary motivation: "Nature then was sovereign in my heart, / And mighty forms seizing a youthful fancy / Had given a charter to irregular hopes" (VI.346–48). But his political diction ("sovereign," "seizing," "charter") suggests similarities between his own declaration of independence and the larger public sphere which encouraged it: " 'twas a time when Europe was rejoiced, / France standing on the top of golden hours, / And human nature seeming born again." En route once more for the Picturesque Sublime, he was swept up in the world history of his times and was himself "born again" . . . as *Wordsworth.* His success at pulling off such a "mad and impracticable" scheme, "far beyond my most sanguine expectations," gave an enormous boost to his confidence for pursuing other impracticalities, on almost a year-by-year basis, throughout the 1790s.

Wordsworth and Jones were making a new version of the grand tour. This had been a standard item in the education of wealthy young men for over a century, but they were going to Switzerland rather than to Italy, and on foot for three months instead of in a carriage for two years, as Thomas Gray and Horace Walpole had done fifty years earlier (1739–41), when they too were Cambridge undergraduates. Gray's precedent was very much in Wordsworth's mind, since Gray's account of his tour was "a favorite volume" with him, containing as it did the *Journal of a Tour in the Lakes.*[3] In his poetical rendering of this tour, *Descriptive Sketches* (1793), Wordsworth remarked the "great difference between two companions lolling in a post chaise, and two travellers plodding slowly along the road, side by side, each with his little knapsack of necessaries upon his shoulders." Gray and Walpole did indeed "loll" in their post chaise, a large vehicle drawn by three horses, suited to the wealth and prestige of the youngest son of England's prime minister, but this was a model of tourism which Wordsworth tried at every turn to subvert. Gray had been called "Miss Gray" at college: his contemporary Christopher Smart said his mincing walk made him look like a man who had just soiled his underclothes. Wordsworth was known to be both a poet and a walker, and he now brought these two talents together with an athletic energy that put Gray's delicate image of the poet to shame.

If his imaginative inspiration came from Gray, his practical information came from another Cambridge fellow, William Coxe of King's, whose *Sketches on the Natural, Civil, and Political State of Switzerland,* first published in 1776, had been republished with additions in 1779 and 1789 as *Travels in Switzerland.* Coxe emphasized economic and political matters more than landscape description, but he included enough of the latter, in the current idiom of the Sublime, for Wordsworth to respond to: "What a chaos of mountains are here heaped upon one another! a dreary, desolate but sublime appearance: it looks like the ruins and wreck of a world."[4] Coxe's book was well known in Wordsworth's circle: it had been donated to the Hawkshead school library by his friends the Raincock brothers and Edward Birkett, along with John Moore's *A View of Society and Manners in France, Switzerland, and Germany,* which contained much discussion of localities associated with Rousseau.[5] Wordsworth and Jones adapted their itinerary from Coxe, reducing it considerably, and for the most part running it in reverse, from southern to northern Switzerland.

They studied these sources much harder than the required math texts they should have been reading. This point must be stressed: the distance they covered and the pace they maintained could not have been accomplished without very detailed planning in advance, as a glance at any contemporary map of France and Switzerland makes clear. Europe was not signposted, paved, and hosteled for pedestrian tourists, though other middle-class young men like Wordsworth and Jones were beginning to create the more modern fashion. Well-off persons traveling by coach, on roads, between inns, could expect to advance reasonably well in settled regions, but not young men of uncertain class and dubious appearance, on foot in the mountains in unsettled times. Wordsworth noted this lightheartedly to Dorothy: "Our appearance is singular, and we have often . . . excited a general smile . . . and our manner of bearing our bundles, which is upon our heads, with each an oak stick in our hands, contributes not a little to that general curiosity which we seem to excite."[6] But they knew exactly where they were going, almost every day of the way. And they knew it was going to take a long time, because they planned it that way, arriving back in Cambridge at the last possible minute for the residency requirement, and leaving the smallest possible amount of cramming time for the January exams. This tour has become one of the archetypes of Romantic wandering, in our cultural memory, but it was far from a lighthearted summer's *Wanderjahr,* following wherever their fancy led. Rather, they were following Wordsworth's fancy, and that they lost their way only two or three times during the whole summer indicates how well he supplied his fancy with facts. There can have been hardly a day that started with a leisurely café au lait, a stretch, and the lazy inquiry "Right, then: where shall we go today?" The huge impression made on Wordsworth by the few times they did get lost indicates, further, how much emotional energy he invested in his preparation for the trip.

In a sketch of their final preparations, a word on Jones is in order. His main qualification was his unflappable good humor. In practical terms this meant he could put up with Wordsworth. Jones was "the best-tempered creature imaginable—an inestimable quality," especially to "me, who am apt to be irritable," said Wordsworth, grateful for Jones's "calm and even temper so enviable compared with mine."[7] Well-matched emotionally (at least from Wordsworth's point of view), they were an odd couple physically, as Dorothy later noted: Wordsworth, "active, lively, and almost as strong as ever on a mountain top; Jones, fat and round-about and rosy, and puffing, and panting while he climbs the little hill from the road" to Rydal Mount. "Never was there a more remarkable contrast."[8] Jones recalled the trip in warm terms all his life, and the two remained lifelong friends. Yet a deeper sense of what Jones had to put up with is suggested by Wordsworth's condescending caricature of him in "A Character," published in the *Lyrical Ballads* of 1800. It starts innocuously enough: "I marvel how Nature could ever find space / For so many contrasts in one human face." But some of the contrasts go beyond the limits of friendly teasing, even for a comic poem: "There's thought and no thought," "There's weakness, and strength both redundant and vain," "[There's] a temper that's soft to disease." Especially wounding, since Jones was a clergyman, "There's virtue, the title it surely may claim, / Yet wants heaven knows what to be worthy the name."[9] The poem seems to have strained even Jones's forbearance, for it was omitted from all subsequent editions between 1802 and 1832. Yet it says something about Wordsworth's sense of the worth of even his lightest words that he reprinted it in the very next edition (1835) after Jones's death and did not hesitate to inform Isabella Fenwick that "the principal features are taken from that of my friend Robert Jones."

On July 10 they set out, without Wordsworth's informing any of his relatives that he was leaving the country.[10] They went first to London, where William drew more money on his account, but did not contact Richard. In their haste to get out of reach, they spent the first night barely beyond Greenwich, at Shooter's Hill. Proceeding through Canterbury to Dover, they crossed to Calais on July 13, and immediately fell into the first of many surprises that awaited them on this trip. Awaking on the morning of July 14, they found themselves foreign observers of the world's first great celebration of modern state democracy. The Fête de la Fédération was of course scheduled to coincide with the first anniversary of the fall of the Bastille, but it was not a celebration of the Revolution as it is today. Rather, its main purpose was to dramatize Louis XVI's oath of loyalty to the new constitution, sworn like a marriage vow upon an "altar of the country" in a huge amphitheater in the Champ de Mars, erected by the volunteer labor of thousands of joyous Parisians. Wordsworth and Jones could hardly have been unaware that such an event was coming, but they could never have anticipated the effect it would have, by rapid degrees, on them.

All France was mad with joy at the prospect of freedom that lay before it, and liberal spirits everywhere were rushing to join its celebration. Helen Maria Williams, crossing the Channel from Brighton to Dieppe on the same day as Wordsworth, took a fast coach to get to Paris in time for the festivities, and the spectacle did not disappoint her: "it required but the common feelings of humanity to become in that moment a citizen of the world."[11] A year later Wordsworth would cross again, bearing a letter of introduction to Williams, but in 1790 her boundless political enthusiasm was not yet his. Still, he and Jones were enough struck by the joy they saw in Calais to do what few tourists ever do: spend the day there, observing the festivities. "How bright a face is worn when joy of one / Is joy of tens of millions!" Gradually, their own faces came to wear a similar expression, for the first *quatorze juillet* was much more than a one-day affair. For the next two weeks, all through the French part of their trip, Wordsworth and Jones were in constant presence of this public ecstasy, passing by the "gaudy reliques of that festival" festooned in each town, or observing local continuations of *la grande fête* in Paris.

But they were not distracted from their itinerary, which called for a beeline southeast to the Seine, thence down to the Saône, and thence into the Rhône at Lyons. They were heading for the Grande Chartreuse, and the deep cultural shift from Enlightenment Europe to early Romantic Europe is clearly marked by the fact that this severe monastery, which had been for Gray and Walpole a fascinating distraction from their goal, Rome, was for Wordsworth and Jones the first object of interest on the way toward theirs, the Alps.

To get there as fast as possible, they enforced "a march . . . of military speed." Wordsworth's language is both literally and metaphorically apt, for their pace was indeed extraordinary. Through the summer, covering 2,000 miles on foot, they averaged nearly 30 miles a day, mostly on foot, including many days in difficult mountainous terrain.* There are no histories of hiking, but if there were, the entry for "Wordsworth and Jones, 1790" would

*They traveled another 820 miles on the continent by boat. Their total mileage, London and return, was over 3,000 miles (Donald E. Hayden, *Wordsworth's Walking Tour of 1790* [Tulsa: Univ. of Tulsa, 1983], 119).

"A march it was of military speed": Wordsworth's and Jones's route across France, July, 1790.

rank very high in the amateur standings. Figuring four miles per hour as a good pace, and even allowing full twelve-hour days in summer weather, they still must have been walking almost all of the time. They did not take much time to stop and look at the sights. In a tour of ninety days there were only four occasions when they spent two nights at the same place, suggesting an almost obsessive determination to crowd as many sensations as possible into the time available.

Neither old nor new cultural monuments distracted them. They ignored Amiens and Rheims and their famous cathedrals (where Gray and Walpole had spent several days), and they were not tempted by revolutionary Paris, though it lay within fifty miles of their route. Instead, hurrying through the green fields of Picardy like any modern tourist racing along the autoroute to Paris, they kept to the Calais–Paris public roads as far as Peronne. There, hewing to their southeasterly course, they branched off, and for "three days successively [walked] through paths / By which our toilsome journey was abridged— / Among sequestered villages." They came out at Château-Thierry, and a day and a half later, just a week after they set out from Calais, were walking alongside the Seine at Troyes.

This part of their trip was hard work, and Wordsworth recalled it without fondness. In 1838 he wrote that "the only part of the journey . . . to me uninviting is the space between Paris and [Chalon-sur-Saône]." What he wanted to do then, as an old man, is exactly what he did as a young one: "my wishes are bounded to getting to Chalon-sur-Saône and floating down that river to Lyons, and downward by the Rhône."[12]

They saw joy spread round them everywhere, but they were lonely and a bit homesick, making it easy to indulge in the fashionable melancholy which was considered the necessary emotional complement to picturesque experiences. " 'Twas sweet at such a time—with such delights / On every side, in prime of youthful strength— / To feed a poet's tender melancholy" (VI.375–77). Jones was too round and fat, and Wordsworth too tall and severe, to *look* very tender or melancholy, but they wore their mental fashion as best they could, even if it looked as awkward as their greatcoats bundled up on their heads.

Reaching the Seine on July 22, they followed it through "the vine-clad hills of Burgundy," and finally gained some welcome shade in the sheltered village of St.-Seine-l'Abbaye, which Wordsworth called a "Town in a hole," on July 25.[13] Here both their mode and their mood of conveyance changed dramatically.

On the 27th, at Chalon-sur-Saône, they boarded a boat bound for Lyons, crowded with *fédérés* returning from the Fête de la Fédération. Over 100,000 provincial delegates, armed with symbolic swords, had attended the fete, and they were still streaming homeward two weeks later.[14] Confined with this "merry crowd" in the narrow bounds of a river boat, Wordsworth and Jones soon found themselves in a new community—even, one might say, a new *kind* of community. Before this, they only *"saw* dances of liberty, and, in late hours / Of darkness, dances in the open air." Now, although they were just "a lonely pair of Englishmen" when they boarded the boat, by the end of the first day they found that they "bore a name / Honoured in France, the name of Englishmen," and were invited into the dance of freedom themselves. They chatted, they ate, they drank, and, above all, they danced—Wordsworth's favorite physical activity after walking, and now once again crucial to his developing sense of himself, as it had been in the summer of 1788.

> In this blithe company
> We landed, took with them our evening meal . . .
> . . . The supper done,
> With flowing cups elate and happy thoughts
> We rose at signal given, and formed a ring,
> And hand in hand danced round and round the board;
> All hearts were open, every tongue was loud
> With amity and glee. . . .
> And hospitably did they give us hail
> As their forerunners in a glorious course . . . .
>
> (VI.401–12)

These were glorious moments for two very fortunate young men. They joined in "dances of liberty" that were repetitions—overflowings—of those in Paris. Wordsworth's phrase "dances in the open air" repeats the formal designation of *salle de bal en plein air* for the dances in Paris, held outside not only for greater comfort but also to honor the Revolution's openness to Nature, with its doctrines of "natural rights."[15] Wordsworth and Jones were caught up in the effervescence of a national political event that represented the hopes and dreams of the best spirits of the age. Their academic republicanism disposed them to endorse it, and their accidental tourism allowed them to enjoy it to the full. The very repetition of "round and round" in the passage makes it a kind of round dance and conveys the dizziness of the experience for Wordsworth. It swept him away.

Wordsworth sets out their welcome in no uncertain terms: they were "Guests welcome almost as angels were / To Abraham of old" (VI.391–404). That is to say, in Wordsworth's retrospective editorializing, the Englishmen *(les anglais)* were received like the angels *(les anges)* who announced to Abraham the birth of a new nation. Never underestimate the power of a Wordsworthian figure of speech: he means to say that they, not the French delegates, carried the new annunciation. In the context of *The Prelude,* this was not a national miracle but a spiritual one, manifested in the growing self-consciousness of its young hero.

Wordsworth and Jones drifted downriver with the *fédérés* for three or four days to Lyons, where many disembarked. Then they continued down farther in a smaller boat on a swifter river, the Rhône, which joins the Saône in Lyons and becomes the name for both.[16] Since the *fédérés* who continued south of Lyons were heading directly to the mouth of the Rhône, "it is easy to recognize [among them] the delegates sent from Marseilles to the Federation."[17] And, since Wordsworth finished his poem describing all this in 1792, when he was in Orléans and Blois, it is also easy for us to realize—as he must have by then—that some of the disgruntled *citoyens* who came back to Paris from Marseilles that summer, dragging their cannon, their grievances, and their radically new demands with them, would have included some of the very *fédérés* with whom he danced and drank in the happier days of 1790. But by 1792 they were singing a new song, having appropriated Rouget de Lisle's "War Song of the Army of the Rhine" (composed at Strasbourg, April 24, 1792) and made it their own: "La Marseillaise." These lyrics and tune were very different from the 1790 Liberty dances, but the circumstantial coincidence is worth restating: young Wordsworth danced with the people who brought "La Marseillaise" to Paris, and with it the republic and the Terror.

More important for him and Jones at the time was the fact that they were no longer lonely. They were young, they were strong, they could speak the language well enough, and if they were not very handsome, they were something even more attractive at the moment: they were English. The sense of being recognized and welcomed as an interesting person outside of one's own country, simply by virtue of being *of* that country, is one of the delights of foreign travel for young people, and such recognition could hardly have come at a higher pitch than it did for Wordsworth on the Saône at the end of July 1790. It was on this boat trip, in this company, that Wordsworth's personal attachment to the ideals of the French Revolution began, and the attachment had as much to do with the lift it gave to his sense of himself as it did with those political ideals, abstractly considered. No longer bypassing observers of "gaudy reliques," he and Jones were now participants in a joyous community of fellow travelers.

They got off the boat at St.-Vallier and started hiking across country. In two days they reached the neighborhood of the Chartreuse, not far from the modern winter resorts of Albertville and Val d'Isère. On their third night (August 3) they stayed in a village near the monastery, and for the next two nights they were guests of the Carthusians themselves.

Thomas Gray's visit to the "awful solitude" of the Chartreuse was Wordsworth's immediate motive for visiting it. Gray's response is still the most famous in English: "In our little journey up to the Grande Chartreuse, I do not remember to have gone ten paces without an exclamation, that there was no restraining: Not a precipice, not a torrent, not a cliff, but is pregnant with religion and poetry. There are certain scenes that would awe an atheist into belief, without the help of other argument. One need not have a very fantastic imagination to see spirits there at noon-day."[18]*

Curiously, Gray's response was more "romantic" than Wordsworth's. All these young Englishmen were predisposed to regard the monastery as a living relic of Catholic superstition. Its motto, "Never deformed, never reformed," seemed the vestige of a corrupt past to these heirs of Enlightenment. Gray emphasized the spirituality that appeared inherent in the monastery's natural surroundings, but Wordsworth gave as much attention to the religious institution itself.[19] He did so partly because he was seeing a working monastery for the first time, reawakening his interest in England's ruined abbeys, such as Furness near Hawkshead.[20] His sympathy for the place was stimulated even more by the fact that he came to it at the very moment when it was about to pass out of existence, because of "the gleam of arms" which now threatened it. The first goal of his tour was already under attack by the new social order of revolution; the Grande Chartreuse thus became the first item in a growing catalog of reversals that gradually became the basis for all Wordsworth's interpretations of the meaning of his tour.

The Chartreuse was one of only two man-made sights that Wordsworth had included in his plan for the tour.[21] The other one was similar: the monastery of Einsiedeln in Switzerland, home of the Black Madonna. His deepest emotions were touched by these two places, according to Dorothy's estimate thirty years later: "I do not think that any one spot which he visited . . . made so great an impression on his mind."[22] Around 1816–19 he added a long passage on the Chartreuse to *The Prelude,* giving full vent to his already *post*-Romantic feeling for the spiritual loss humanity incurred there, when eight hundred years of Christian observances were blasted away by the "rage of one State-whirlwind" (*1850,* VI.488).[23] The monastery was still in full operation in 1790, though monastic vows had been forbidden by the National Assembly in February. The final vote on the Civil Constitution of the Clergy had just been passed on July 12, and the bad news must have reached the monastery just about the time Wordsworth arrived. Some of its treasures had already been appropriated, but it was not officially disestab-

*Even Gray's frivolous companion Walpole was moved: "the road! winding round a prodigious mountain, and surrounded with others all shagged with hanging woods, obscured with pines or lost in clouds! Below, a torrent breaking through cliffs, and tumbling through fragments of rocks! . . . Now and then an old footbridge, with a broken rail, a leaning cross, a cottage, or the ruin of a hermitage! This sounds too bombastic and too romantic to one that has not seen it, too cold for one that has" (to Richard West, Sept. 28–Oct. 2, 1739; in R. W. Ketton-Cremer, *Horace Walpole* [London: Faber and Faber, 1946], 54).

lished, and its inmates routed, until the summer of 1792, when for five months it was subjected to a "dragonade" by troops.[24]

During the two days they spent there—their first rest after three weeks of haste—they walked through the St. Bruno's woods, "contemplating, with encreased pleasure its wonderful scenery," and sampled the famous Chartreuse liqueurs.[25] In Vallombre, the Valley of the Shadow, they watched monks sworn to silence digging their own graves. For Wordsworth, the overwhelming impression was one of *solitude,* a special sense of place that eventually became his dominant frame of mind. He later tried to imagine a sort of mutual protection treaty between Nature and Religion: " 'Stay your sacrilegious hands!' " cries Nature, "from her Alpine throne," to the soldiers. But this is post-Romantic wishful thinking. His youthful reaction to it is better caught in *Descriptive Sketches'* allusion to the "parting Genius" of Milton's Nativity Ode, for this fits exactly with his earlier image of himself and Jones being welcomed by the *fédérés* as angels. For Milton, the "parting Genius" was the mythological spirit of the classical world, sadly departing before the new spiritual reality of Jesus Christ. But for Wordsworth, who accurately guessed that they might well be "the last, perchance the very last, of men / Who shall be welcom'd here," the "parting Genius" was now Christianity itself, and he the last among men who could appreciate its spiritual value even as its institutional forms disappeared. He imagined himself saving the spirit of religion as one might save an endangered species:

who,
If the ability were his, would dare
To kill a species of insensate life,
Or to the bird of meanest wing would say,
Thou and thy kind must perish? Even so,
So consecrated, almost, might he deem
That power, that organ, that transcendent frame
Of social being.[26]

This new Sublime is not religious, nor even in nature as it was for Gray, but in the mind of man—perhaps, as he entertained the thought, this one man alone.

Wordsworth and Jones left the Grande Chartreuse on August 6, making for their next destination, Mont Blanc, the ultimate symbol of European sublimity. They went via Geneva because it was the easiest way to get there, but also because of its associations with that strangely enlightened mind whose ideas lay behind many of their beliefs about connections between nature and virtue: Jean-Jacques Rousseau, the "Citizen of Geneva." One of Wordsworth's primary wishes on the tour was to track the great philosopher of republican virtue and personal egoism. They visited Rousseau's lake district at the end of the tour, but from Geneva they passed into the provinces of Vaud and Vallais, which he had glorified in *La Nouvelle Héloïse* (1761), already regarded as one of the books responsible for seducing the European mind into revolution.[27]

Staying at a French village outside Geneva, they walked along the north shore of the lake for two days. Wordsworth recorded his observations to show Dorothy that he was "a perfect Enthusiast for Nature in all her various forms":

> The lower part of the lake [near Geneva] did not afford us a pleasure equal to what might have been expected from its celebrity. This was owing partly to its width, and partly to the weather, which was one of those hot glaring days in which all distant objects are veiled in a species of bright obscurity. But the higher part of the lake made us ample amends, 'tis true we had the same disagreeable weather but the banks of the water are infinitely more picturesque, and as it is much narrower, the landscape suffered proportionally less from that pale steam which before almost entirely hid the opposite shore.[28]

These conventional, quasi-mathematical measures of the Picturesque, with their bookkeeping language of emotional profit and loss, are the axis along which Wordsworth's later estimates of the 1790 tour's significance are plotted, from the "rich amends" which the vale of Chamonix made for their disappointment with Mont Blanc, to the "dislodging" of the heavy sadness they would soon feel in the Simplon Pass.

At the "higher part" of the lake, they passed through Montreux and by the Castle of Chillon, which would captivate Byron a generation later. But Wordsworth made no mention of it; castles, like cities, were simply not on his mental map: he was already thinking himself into his role of "mountain youth."

The attention of the landscape-wandering public had been concentrated on Mont Blanc for over ten years, since the first modern attempts to scale it began in 1776. Its first ascent, in 1786, by Dr. Michel Paccard was followed in 1787 by the more scientific Horace-Bénédict de Saussure, whose success in commercially marketing his achievement made it more than ever a popular item of touristic cultural consumption.[29]

When Wordsworth and Jones reached Martigny, they checked their knapsacks and headed up the Col de Balme toward the great white mountain. They must have had Saussure's feat much in mind, for the days they spent there, August 12–14, coincide almost exactly with the third anniversary of his renowned success (August 13–15, 1787). Wordsworth and Jones did not expect to climb the mountain themselves: that remained a business for professionals. But getting to it involved them in their first mountain *crossing,* since the Col de Balme reaches 5,006 feet above Martigny before descending down to the region of the Chamonix glacier (3,402 feet). Coxe made high claims for it which raised Wordsworth's hopes: "an extensive prospect, which many travellers consider as equal to the most sublime prospects in Switzerland."[30] But again they encountered difference and disappointment.

> That day we first
> Beheld the summit of Mount Blanc, and grieved
> To have a soulless image on the eye
> Which had usurped upon a living thought
> That never more could be.
>
> (VI.452–56)

This is a common experience. For though Mont Blanc is the highest point in Europe (15,770 feet), and was still thought by many experts to be the highest point on earth,[31] it does not always look impressive. William Coxe, Wordsworth's tour authority, had a similar letdown. He and his companions had set off from the same place as Wordsworth and Jones, "with the expectation of seeing the sun rise on the summit of Mt. Blanc, but were disappointed . . . it did not impress me with that astonishment which might be expected." It is too broad and round. Its three peaks are "compressed hemispheres" called *domes,* the highest being called, more ridiculously than sublimely, La Bosse du Dromadaire. It is too remote and spread out: "it ends abruptly, and loses itself amid the mountains that bound from the vale of Chamouny." And it is far too often obscured by clouds and snowy mist to really live up to its reputation, the very whiteness of its glare rendering it "in many situations . . . less lofty in appearance than it is in reality," in contrast to the Matterhorn and the Schreckhorn, which match almost everybody's idea of what a real mountain should look like.[32]

Wordsworth's expectations of a "sublime" experience were far beyond reality—how far beyond, he now began to suspect. Although Mont Blanc came relatively early in their trip, he planned in his published account of the tour to place it as the climax of the whole, as the superlative of the Sublime.[33] This was the position of honor it held in Coxe's *Sketches.* But Wordsworth did not follow his plan, though in *Descriptive Sketches* he did describe Mont Blanc with some of the apocalyptic imagery that, in *The Prelude,* he reserved for his next mountaintop experience, in the Simplon Pass.

> Alone ascends that mountain nam'd of white,
> That dallies with the Sun the summer night.
> Six thousand years amid his lonely bounds
> The voice of Ruin, day and night, resounds.

Where Horror-led his sea of ice assails,
Havoc and Chaos blast a thousand vales.
(*DS*, 690–95)

Which is to say that Mont Blanc combined the sublimity of Creation and Apocalypse all at once; it was the Alpha and Omega of earthly meanings, from primeval Chaos to ultimate Ruin.

They needed a night's rest before they could really enjoy the vale of Chamonix, for they had been walking a very long time, over thirty-five miles by the time they reached the village on the night of August 12, and they could indulge the comforts of an inn since they had left their bedrolls in Martigny. They also had the recompense of seeing the mountain from one of its most impressive perspectives, almost straight upward from the little village lying some 13,000 feet below it. All the next day, and part of the following day as well, they explored "the wondrous Vale of Chamouny." Wordsworth in *The Prelude* painted a set piece of typical touristic amazement at the five brutal ice rivers of the glacier cohabiting with the green fields and human activities between them.

There small birds warble from the leafy trees,
The eagle soareth in the element,
There doth the reaper bind the yellow sheaf,
The maiden spread the haycock in the sun,
While Winter like a tamèd lion walks,
Descending from the mountain to make sport
Among the cottages by beds of flowers.
(VI.462–68)

This typological allegory follows Coxe very closely: he also noted that the five glaciers are "separated from each other by forests, corn-fields, and meadows": a sequence exactly repeated in Wordsworth's "leafy trees . . . yellow sheaf . . . haycock in the sun."[34] But this *Prelude* picture sits rather uneasily next to *Descriptive Sketches'* earlier version of what Wordsworth saw there:

At such an hour I heav'd the human sigh,
When roar'd the sullen Arve in anger by,
That not for thee, delicious vale! unfold
Thy reddening orchards, and thy fields of gold;
That thou, the slave of slaves, art doom'd to pine,
While no Italian arts their charms combine
To teach the skirt of thy dark cloud to shine;
For thy poor babes that, hurrying from the door,
With pale-blue hands, and eyes that fix'd implore

Dead muttering lips, and hair of hungry white,
Besiege the traveller whom they half affright.
(702–12)

This earlier version, though poetically awkward, is keenly observed human reality, its last four lines stunningly *sur*real, from an obviously frightened young poet. "Dead muttering lips, and hair of hungry white" is a line to conjure with, not explain. The poetic diction of the loco-descriptive mode profits by its artificiality, projecting landscape sights that the "affrighted traveller" feels *should not be* in the landscape: this was not the kind of *blanc* he had come so far to see. No doubt the little girl of 1793 is better off when transmuted into the maiden of 1805 spreading her haycock in the sun. But the focus of Wordsworth's grief has shifted entirely in the interim, from "a human sigh" for poverty to a disappointed expectation of sublime scenery.

Of course, these are different poems with different purposes written at different times, and both disappointments, the human and the natural, were Wordsworth's. But the Arve was "sullen" in 1790–92 because the people living beside it were; Wordsworth appended a note to his phrase "slave of slaves," explaining, "It is scarce necessary to observe that these lines were written before the emancipation of Savoy." By 1805 the personified river's complaints would in effect be silenced, "With its *dumb* cataracts" (458).

GOLDEN DAYS AND GIDDY PROSPECTS

The 1790 Walking Tour: Switzerland and Italy

> . . . and such a summer night
> Did to that pair of golden days succeed,
> With now and then a doze and snatch of sleep . . . .
> (VI.654–56)

Lost in Sublimity

Their second touristic mission completed, Wordsworth and Jones returned to Martigny and reclaimed their knapsacks. Resuming their course up the Rhône next morning, they passed through Sion and came to Brig on August 16. "At Brig we quitted the Valais and passed the Alps at the Semplon [*sic*] *in order to visit part of Italy.*"[1] Wordsworth's contemporary words are important, especially their matter-of-factness, because he and so many readers have subsequently built so much on—and beyond—the facts of what happened on August 17, 1790. *The Prelude* records a visionary experience of imaginative power, evidently stimulated by Wordsworth's sudden—though very much delayed—realization "that we had crossed the Alps" without realizing it. One of the very highest points of their tour had apparently been missed by an act of consciousness which failed to register a fact of physical perception. His account of crossing the Simplon Pass has achieved in many readers' minds a nearly iconic status, almost completely separated from its surrounding textual and historical environments. But an account of the creation of the Poet requires that we restore as much as possible its enabling contexts. This is not to say that the crossing and the verse it inspired are not important. Wordsworth's crossing the Alps unawares is as important in the development of European Romantic culture as Goethe's trip to Italy in 1786, as Byron and the Shelleys' summer on Lake Geneva in 1816, or, for that

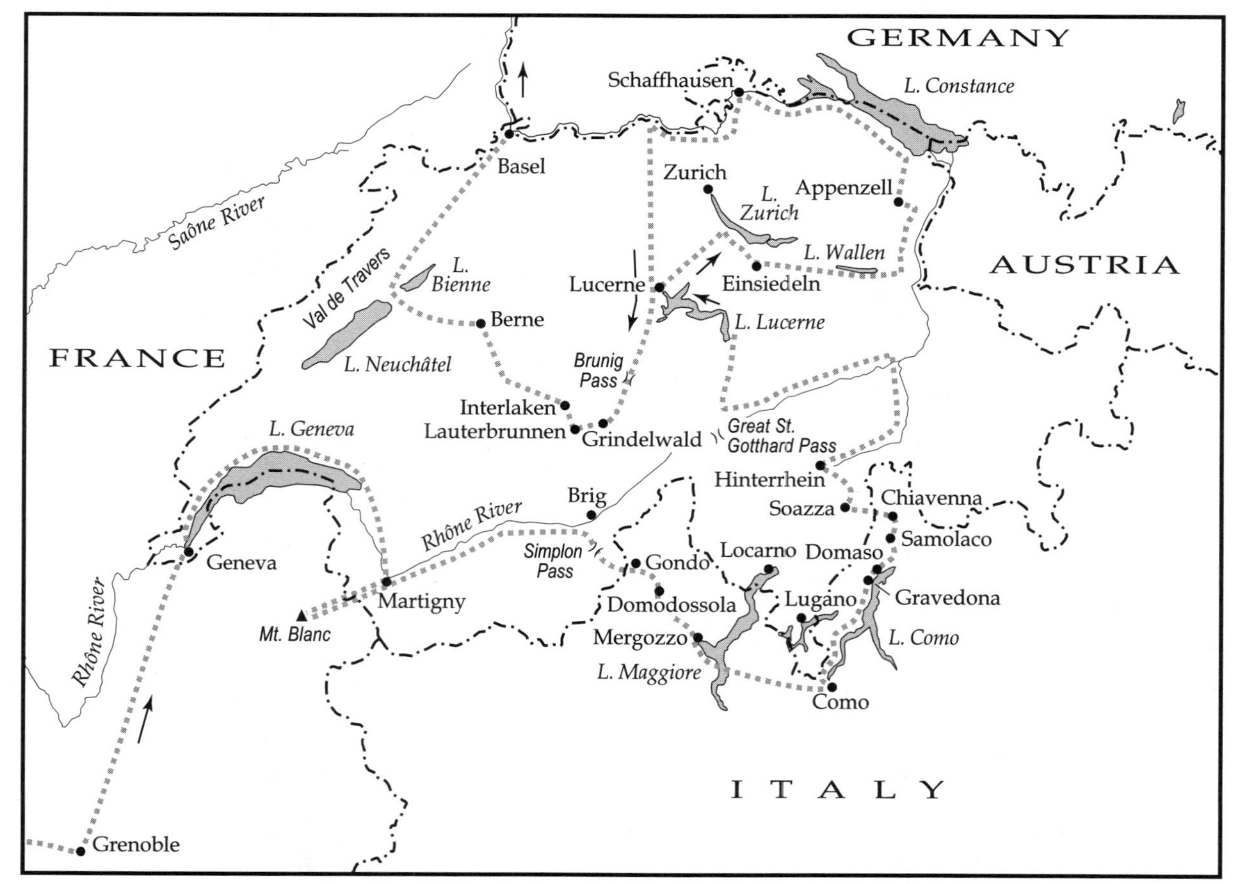

"Thence onward to the country of the Swiss": Wordsworth's and Jones's route through Switzerland, July–August, 1790.

matter—since Wordsworth employs the same kind of rhetoric to describe it—as Paul's vision on the road to Damascus.

Year by year, text by text, revision by revision, Wordsworth steadily raised the level of the tour's meaning for him, from his letter to Dorothy in 1790, through his 1792 composition of *Descriptive Sketches* (published 1793), through his extensive (but unpublished) revisions of that poem in 1794, into his rewriting and recasting of the whole tour in 1804 for the 1805 *Prelude,* and beyond, to his 1808 drafting of the Grande Chartreuse passage and his 1816–19 incorporation of it into *The Prelude,* to his preparations for a return pilgrimage with Dorothy and Mary in 1820, and finally into his composition of *Memorials of a Tour on the Continent, 1820,* published in 1822. Later revisions and letters take the process still further, to very near the end of his life. We have more texts and sources for Wordsworth's three-month tour in 1790 than for his three years at Cambridge. These revisions are a paradigm of the way Wordsworth's imagination worked, and the 1790 tour is a paradigm for the kinds of experiences—including writing experiences—it worked on.

But his contemporary letter to Dorothy makes clear that they were not crossing the Simplon primarily to have an Alpine experience; the thought foremost in his mind was simply to cross over into Italy. Their rigid itinerary demanded it. They were heading for their third main touristic goal, the Italian lake district. Their source-authority, Coxe, had added an extensive segment on the Italian lakes to his revised edition of his *Sketches* (he came via Milan and never crossed the Simplon), and Wordsworth naturally wanted to include it. As he and Jones toiled up the road from Brig, they were, given Wordsworth's emphasis on speed, probably less concerned with an Alpine crossing than with how close they might get to Lake Maggiore by nightfall. This was one of their longest daily jaunts and may have been the basis for Wordsworth's boast to Dorothy "We have several times performed a journey of thirteen leagues [approximately thirty-nine miles] over the most mountainous parts of Swisserland, without any more weariness, than if we had been walking an hour in the groves of Cambridge." But nearly a quarter of their time and distance on this day was taken up with wandering around, lost, near the top of the pass.

To climb from Brig to the top of the Simplon Pass, a distance of sixteen linear miles (and 4,265 vertical feet), is a matter of a morning's walk. Baedeker recommends five to five and a half hours for modern all-purpose touring hikers, but young men "in prime of youthful strength" could do it faster, after a month of on-road conditioning. Wordsworth and Jones joined in with a troop of muleteers who were traveling "along the road that leads to Italy," as he says in 1805, revising it for the 1850 version to "the Simplon's steep and rugged road." This is one of a number of subsequent revisions in which the 1805 text is altered to dramatize the mountainous quality of the experience, blurring the fact that in 1790 it was not conceived as such a *meta*physical crossing. They had little communication with the muleteers because the local dialects of French, German-Swiss, and Italian were terribly mixed up at such border-crossing junctions; Wordsworth's phrase "making of them our guide" suggests the boys just tagged along behind. Tough mule drivers were unconcerned about being gracious to young men who were evidently very much at leisure.

After "a length of hours," sometime around noon, they stopped for lunch, "having reached an inn among the mountains" (498–99). Just where Wordsworth had lunch on August 17, 1790, is a matter of some critical importance, for all the available evidence, as well as common sense and empirical observation, suggests that they were already at the top, or well past it—"that [we] had crossed the Alps"—by the time they stopped for lunch. A small but significant difference would have been created in the history of European Romanticism if one of the muleteers had happened to say, "Okay, boys, we're just now coming to the top of the pass." Again Wordsworth's revisions are revealing, for he does not mention an inn in 1850, but says only, "We reached a halting-place."[2] Inns and halting places in mountain passes tend to be at the top, unless the way is very long—as it is not, here. There are two possible places where they might have stopped for lunch, either the spital erected by Kaspar Stockalper a hundred years earlier to control this important trade route, or the inn in Simplon Village. Wordsworth says "inn," though the hospice seems also to have still been in use in 1790.[3] But both of these places are well past the top of the pass: the spital two miles, the inn another four miles farther on—and 1,640 feet lower down. Even if Wordsworth and Jones could not communicate with the churlish muleteers, they were both mountain boys and could hardly have misinterpreted the meaning of the relief they felt in their muscles as they eased their legs under "the board" at noon. Their very eagerness for sensation may have led them to doubt, or ignore, the evidence of their senses, and the Simplon, like the other great Alpine passes, does not look very dramatic at the top, being "a fairly wide, level glacial terrace."[4] But these passes were chosen for ease of crossing, not for touristic good looks. These different motives for crossing accounts for the muleteers' apparent rudeness, which Wordsworth's revision italicizes: "Hastily rose our guide, / Leaving *us* at the board."[5] In addition, Wordsworth's language in both versions makes perfectly clear that they were already on the downhill slope. Taking their time over their leisurely lunch, they got up to pursue their erstwhile guides: "we followed, / *Descending* by the beaten road" (1850: "the beaten downward way"). It is true that the road up has some dips, and the road down has some rises, but by the time one approaches the old spital, to say nothing of the inn in Simplon Village, it is quite clear that one has crossed the Alps.

Here their real mountaintop experience began, and it had to do not simply with *crossing* but with being lost, or with losing control of their carefully charted itinerary. This loss quickly ramified in Wordsworth's mind into thoughts of losing one's way more generally, losing one's way in life, or even losing one's mind. Where Wordsworth and Jones got lost, exactly, is still in dispute, but how they managed to do it is not hard to see. The road, though "beaten," was nothing like a highway. (That improvement awaited Napoleon's engineers between 1800 and 1805: a celebrated feat that may well have filtered into Wordsworth's contemporaneous composition [1804] of his experience.)[6]

> . . . the beaten road . . . led
> Right to a rivulet's edge, and there broke off;
> The only track now visible was one
> Upon the further side, right opposite
> And up a lofty mountain.
>
> (VI.503–6)[7]

The road *down* the mountain ran in the streambed for a while, which at this height and this season was usable as a roadbed, particularly since its usual passengers were surefooted mules and muleteers, not touring foreign gentlemen. The two Englishmen, not grasping this bit of local economy, crossed the stream and followed the upward path to a nearby mountain village: Freerberg, in one interpretation of the error of their ways; an unnamed hamlet, in another.[8] Their misstep is easy to understand because the correct downward path swerved sharply left below Freerberg into the Gondo Gorge, while another path ran straight up a hill directly opposite the point at which the downward path entered the streambed.

In either case, they crossed the stream and continued upward—or rather, since they had clearly already been "descending . . . downward," they changed course upward. What they climbed was "a lofty mountain" only by the courtesy that anything at this height might be called "lofty"; it was steep, but it did not prevent them from "climb[ing] with eagerness." They continued on for three or four miles, the better part of an hour, and "at length" their eagerness gave way to "surprize and some anxiety / On finding that we did not overtake / Our comrades gone before." The muleteers had not been very friendly before, but now, traveling without them, they suddenly seemed like lost "comrades."

Eventually, coming in sight of some huts, they met a peasant, and after the double difficulty of discovering in a foreign language that they were lost in a foreign place, they figured out that the right road lay back down in the streambed and, coincidentally, "that we had crossed the Alps" (524).[9] Modern scholarship has made clear that the apostrophe to "Imagination!" which interrupts *The Prelude*'s narrative at this point (VI.525–48) is the product of emotion recollected in tranquillity fourteen years later. And this apostrophe was itself a second thought; his first lines attempting to describe the mental effect of the experience were relocated into Book VIII (711–40), where crossing the Alps is curiously compared to visiting caves in the Aegean and in Yorkshire. Both passages tend in the same direction (VI: "something evermore about to be"; VIII: "A spectacle to which there is no end"). The final version imagines all of human imaginative life as an endlessly rewarding mountain climb to infinity ("our home is with infinitude—and only there"). But the first version suggests that imagination often has to do the best it can, when visionary "flashes" fail us ("Till . . . the scene before him lies . . . lifeless as a written book"; VIII.725–28). Most pertinent to what went through Wordsworth's mind on August 17 is the fact that the originally drafted passage states clearly what he had to do repeatedly on his 1790 tour: force his imagination to work on its own, in the face of disappointments with external nature: "But let him pause awhile and look again, / And a new quickening shall succeed, / Beginning timidly, then . . . embodying everywhere some pressure / or image, recognised or new, some type / Or picture of the world."[10]

His confusion was real enough in 1790, though not yet formulated in such high language. To Dorothy, in his journal letter of the trip, he said simply, "The impressions *of three hours of* our walk among the Alps will never be effaced" (italics added). These three hours, so central to the definition of Romanticism as a faith in the transcendental powers of the human imagination, can pretty accurately be pinpointed as the three hours after lunch on August 17, 1790. If they walked four miles before meeting the peasant, one hour was lost in each direction, and the third hour in confusions before and after—or in the Gondo Gorge, for which Baedeker allows one and a quarter hours, though Wordsworth says it took them "several hours at a slow step." Thirty years later the force of this intensely meaningful experience remained, when he found, again somewhat accidentally, the place where he had got lost thirty years before. Dorothy said it was "impossible" for her to say how much seeing that little "upright path . . . on the green precipice" moved her brother, "when he discovered it was the very same which had tempted him in his youth . . . [disappointing] the ambition of youth."[11]

Back on track, they now entered the Gondo Gorge, for which Wordsworth produced one of the best descriptions of Alpine landscape ever recorded, a description heightened line by line with metaphors in which the imagination finally outstrips altogether its mountain passage:

The immeasurable height
Of woods decaying, never to be decayed,
The stationary blasts of waterfalls,
And everywhere along the hollow rent
Winds thwarting winds, bewildered and forlorn,
The torrents shooting from the clear blue sky,
The rocks that muttered close upon our ears—
Black drizzling crags that spake by the wayside
As if a voice were in them—the sick sight
And giddy prospect of the raving stream,
The unfettered clouds and region of the heavens,
Tumult and peace, the darkness and the light,
Were all like workings of one mind, the features
Of the same face, blossoms upon one tree,
Characters of the great apocalypse,
The types and symbols of eternity,
Of first, and last, and midst, and without end.
(VI.556–72)

His comment to Dorothy about this time was more orthodox: "Among the more awful scenes of the Alps, I had not a thought of man, or a single created being; my whole soul was turned to him who produced the terrible majesty before me."[12] His note on this raving stream in *Descriptive Sketches* is still more diffident: "The river along whose banks you descend in crossing the Alps by the Sempion [*sic*] pass [is the Tusa]. From the striking contrast of its features, this pass I should imagine to be the most interesting among the Alps."[13] It took several years of creative incubation before he was able to transform the weak subjunctive of "I should imagine" into the strong imperatives of the *Prelude* passage. For Wordsworth's description is far from merely referential. His allusion to Milton's description of God in the concluding lines means that he saw—or projected—the face of God on this trip. "Him first, him last, him midst, and without end" (*PL,* V.165).[14]

Besides being sublime, the Gondo Gorge was also very dangerous, so their "slow step" had physical as well as metaphysical justification. The path was barely wide enough to walk on, and so close to the raging stream—really one long waterfall—that it was frequently rendered impassable or, in the case of sudden thaws or rainstorms, instantly fatal. It was constantly in need of repair. A friend of Gray's almost persuaded him to visit it, and later (1777) left this record: "You go across pastures and over rocks, over unstable, swaying bridges, past the ruins of older and better bridges [unnerving observation!] . . . the rock face towers high above you and down below seems gnawed away by the pounding waves of the wild Toggia. The pass leads over colossal threatening ruins. The river beside us was sometimes almost hidden by mountains, and sometimes it tumbled like smoke into hideous depths below."[15]

This was the sort of thing Wordsworth had come expecting to see; the Gondo Gorge is the only place in the Simplon Pass that merits a "must see" star in modern touring guides. Hence the immensity of his imaginative reaction to the blandness of the top of the pass and to the quotidian circumstance of getting lost there is all the more noteworthy. His imagination, already prepared for disappointment by his experiences at the Grande Chartreuse, Mont Blanc, and Lake Geneva, was not satisfied quickly enough by the Gondo Gorge. In the interim, only three hours by the clock but an instantaneous mental "flash" that revealed "the invisible world," he found by personal experience that the Sublime was located exactly where Kant had already logically deduced that it must be, without ever leaving the University of Königsberg: in the mind of man.

Coming out of the gorge at last, they spent the night at another one of Stockalper's old spitals, in Gondo Village. Here the trauma Wordsworth experienced began to sweep over him.

> That night our lodging was an alpine house,
> An inn, or hospital (as they are named),
> Standing in that same valley by itself,
> And close upon the confluence of two streams—
> A dreary mansion, large beyond all need,
> With high and spacious rooms, deafened and stunned
> By noise of waters, making innocent sleep
> Lie melancholy among weary bones.
>
> (VI.573–80)

The building was large because it was a warehouse for goods transported over the dangerous pass in small, mule-size loads, Gondo being exactly on the Swiss-Italian border. Here the Doveria dashing down the gorge joins the Tusa in full force, producing the echo effect in the empty spital.

Wordsworth's last two lines—"making innocent sleep / Lie melancholy among weary bones"—are extraordinarily good, and biographically significant. The image is finally one of a charnel house. Sleep is disembodied from their "weary bones": the cliché is recast with ghastly literalness, so that the two travelers are personified as that which they cannot do: sleep. They are represented as lying down among the bones of their own bodies. Dorothy participated in her brother's horror of this experience with all the power of her vicarious imagination. Returning to the spot thirty years later, Wordsworth flatly refused to enter the spital, and even Dorothy could not persuade him to do so. "I now regret not having the courage to pass the threshold alone. I had a strong desire to see what was going on within doors for the sake of *tales of thirty years gone by;* but could not persuade W. to accompany me."[16] If he would not enter, neither would she. Wordsworth's biographers have been a little naive in their puzzlement about Dorothy's report that her brother and Jones were "unable to sleep *from other causes"* than just the noise of the water.[17] We are clearly in the presence of some kind of trauma when a fifty-year-old man in the broad light of day and in the company of his family and friends, amid all the luxuries of a more modern, well-heeled tourism, refuses even to enter a house where he had waking nightmares thirty years earlier, even though his dearly beloved sister pleads with him to do so. Clearly Dorothy wanted to go in, to find some concrete image on which to hang those oft-repeated "tales of thirty years gone by," and nobody was proposing that they *sleep* there again.

Wordsworth's reluctance in 1820, like his morbid melancholy in 1790, had something to do with the whole sequence of his experiences on August 17: muleteers–Simplon–path–peasant–Imagination–Gondo. Relaxing after the exertions of the day, the real meaning of what had happened to him began to break in upon him. In later years he would describe this process as one of the primary ways in which his imagination worked: access of imaginative vision following close upon the *relaxation* of *disappointed* attention.[18]

"Making innocent sleep / Lie melancholy among weary bones." Of what were they "innocent," and why? The lines contain an allusion, which does not, however, provide any simple clarification. They are from *Macbeth,* when Macbeth is trying to recoup his courage for the murder of Duncan, after funking his first attempt.

> Methought I heard a voice cry "Sleep no more,
> Macbeth doth murder sleep"—the innocent sleep,
> Sleep that knits up the ravelled sleeve of care,
> The death of each day's life, sore labour's bath,
> Balm of hurt minds, great nature's second course,
> Chief nourisher in life's feast . . . .
>
> (II.ii.33–38)

Lady Macbeth brusquely interrupts him to ask, "What do you mean?" No allusion is innocent in Wordsworth, and especially not this one. It will come to his mind again in writing about the September massacres of 1792, when he imagined he heard a voice crying out "Sleep no more!" over bloody Paris (X.77).

More than "innocent sleep" was murdered that night in Gondo Village. Wordsworth's youthful innocence had been done in, by the disappointment of his own misplaced hopes. Everything that Macbeth laments he (Wordsworth) also needed: "sore labour's bath," "balm of hurt minds," "great nature's second course." His *mind* was hurt: what else is trauma? Macbeth had failed in an attempt to do something he had agreed to do, because he knew it was a bad thing. Similarly, though in ways as yet unclear to him, the whole motivation of Wordsworth's trip was being superseded, and he had invested—or squandered—a lot in following that motive. The tour was turning out to be disappointing, not in his uncles' terms, but in his own: not mountains, not "mighty forms," not the highest point in the natural world would give a "charter" to his hopes. Somehow, his own mind would have to do so.

Although mountain climbing was becoming an enjoyable leisure fashion and a legitimate vacation activity, there was no public fashion, as yet, for Romantic egotism. If Wordsworth's consciousness could get lost beyond recognition on the top of the Alps, then no *place* was safe for human consciousness, no place on earth. This meant that his mind or consciousness was lost, or alienated, from the earth on which it dwelt. Yet at this moment, his whole life was invested in the idea that Nature *could* underwrite his hopes, that "great nature's second course" was always forthcoming, that there was always a way or a path or a course one could follow. If not, where will the mind go, or dwell, then? "Apocalypse is not habitable," Wordsworth would eventually see.[19] Our imaginations must make the best habitations they can, but his failed him in the Gondo spital, finding nothing but a charnel house in which to rest his weary bones, the death of his "innocent" youthful ambitions.

The next day they passed Domodossola, the first big town across the Italian border. They spent the night of the 18th at Mergozzo, on its own little lake connected to Lake Maggiore. Their motives are clear: "we proceeded to the lake of Locarno [Maggiore], to visit the Boromaean [*sic*] islands."[20]

After Gondo Gorge, the Borromean Islands are the next "must see" sight for anyone following this route. They were highly artificial beauties, especially Isola Bella—a partner for Windermere's Belle Isle—which had been developed by Count Borromeo in the seventeenth century to approximate a Renaissance earthly paradise. On Isola Bella the count had constructed ten terraces, accentuating the island's natural terraced effect. A hundred years later Wordsworth was seeing it at its natural best, for though the buildings were run-down, the plantings had grown to magnificent effect, frequently compared to the Garden of Eden and the Hanging Gardens of Babylon.[21] Earthly paradises began to run much in Wordsworth's mind over the next two or three days. His descriptions of his entire tour, with their deep Miltonic substratum, veer back and forth between presenting it as a trip through Paradise, or one through Hell; soon this fundamental ambivalence began to show up in his actions, and rose to trouble the surface of his verse.

Rather than go north or south around Maggiore to get to Como, either route prodigiously long and circuitous, Wordsworth and Jones continued right across the lake to reach the other side on August 19: "Village beyond Lake Maggiore."[22] Wordsworth was always ready to get out onto any of the lakes he visited that summer, for they were his top priority, even more than mountains. Years later he twitted some fatuous aristocrats in the Lake District for overpraising Windermere relative to Maggiore, Como, Geneva, and Zurich—all points on his 1790 itinerary. He fired off some good comic rhymes aimed at what he calls "Folly's own hyperbole" in such comparisons, based on his own experience: "And [I've] seen the Simplon's forehead hoary / Reclined on the Lago Maggiore."[23] It's always heartening to see Wordsworth able to laugh at himself, but the next two lines are not required for the joke, and were not meant to be funny at all: "At breathless eventide at rest / On the broad water's placid breast—." This position is perfectly appropriate not only to his itinerary but to his state of mind, drifting out across Maggiore on the 19th to look back up at Simplon's "forehead hoary," another "feature of the same face" that had scared him so badly two days earlier—all the more so as he was beginning to realize that the face he saw in the picture was not God's but his own.

Lost in Beauty

Coming to Lake Como the next day, Wordsworth and Jones had "a pair of golden days" and two terrible nights. Or maybe not so terrible. Their visit to Como was specifically intended to provide them with a real-life experience of ideal Beauty, to complement the Sublime of the Alps. About the latter Wordsworth could as yet say little, because he had not found it where he expected to. But he wrote at length to Dorothy about the beautiful effects of light and shade they saw on Como's shores as they passed along its "pathways roofed with vines," heading back up toward Switzerland. "The lake is narrow and the shadows of the mountains were early thrown across it. It was beautiful to watch them travelling up the sides of the hill for several hours, to remark one half of a village covered with shade, and the other bright with the strongest sunshine." In *Descriptive Sketches* Wordsworth spoke of it with blasé connoisseurial authority: "if any of my readers should ever visit the lake of Como, I recommend it to him to take a stroll along this charming little pathway; he must chuse the evening, as it is on the western side of the Lake."[24] Wordsworth's experiences seemed at last to match perfectly the expectations raised by Coxe: "Como is indeed most pleasantly situated, in a narrow vale, enclosed by hills, upon the southern extremity of a beautiful lake."[25] But where Coxe digressed into the region's military history, Wordsworth skirts close to his own sexual history.

The beauties he enjoyed at Como were not only those of the mountains and the lake but also of the "dark-ey'd maids" he saw there. That single phrase is all *The Prelude* says on the subject of women; indeed it is the only indication that there was anybody else on the lake at all but Wordsworth and Jones, unless we press a bit on the Miltonic allusion in Wordsworth's metaphor for it: "a darling bosomed up / In Abyssinian privacy" (591–92). Milton's line "where Abassin kings their issue guard" (*PL,* IV.280) is about the Garden of Eden, which had come into Wordsworth's mind at Lake Maggiore, but any thoughts about bosoms and darlings were entirely his own. However, Milton is speaking of Satan's secret, leering with "delight" at all he saw in Eden, especially the two creatures he spied on in their "naked majesty" there, and Wordsworth's account of himself in *Descriptive Sketches* gives us many indications that his experience at Lake Como had more to do with Satan's voyeurism in Eden than with the depopulated garden spot he presents in *The Prelude.* Only in the earlier poem does he make clear that *he* was looking at the "dark-ey'd maids," and the position from which he viewed them was "invisible" like Satan's. He is "a viewless lingerer" (*DS,* 92), and questions of seduction, fall, and ruin were very much on his mind as it ran through the various texts and subtexts which this adventure produced over the next thirty years. These thoughts were not fueled by guilt for sexual immorality in any simple sense, but sexuality as a snare and a distraction from resolutions he was beginning to form for his future. What happened to him at Lake Como was not, as at Mont Blanc or the Simplon Pass, a disappointment of his expectations but a superseding of them in a direction very different from what his guidebook had led him to expect.

Writing to Dorothy, he said nothing about dark-eyed maidens, but much about his mind's running "thro a thousand dreams of happiness which might be enjoyed upon its banks, if heightened by conversation and the exercise of the social affections."[26] This was yet another expression of their dream of living together someday on a lake somewhere, but it was not only that, nor did the thought arise merely from landscape. Jones was right there next to him for "conversation" and "social affection," but was evidently not relevant to Wordsworth's thoughts at the time. As to any girls he saw, his Cambridge Italian would have been good enough for some communication, but their poverty and ignorance would have made conversation frustrating and unsatisfactory.* Nevertheless, passing along the lakeshore on August 21 and 22, Wordsworth found himself increasingly attracted by the girls he saw, until, sometime between the mornings of the 22d and 23d, he parted company with Jones and went to seek one out. What happened then is a matter of conjecture, though Wordsworth seems to have been dis-

*Coxe compares the virtual slavery of the inhabitants on the Italian shores to the freedom and prosperity across the lake in Switzerland.

appointed, or shamed, in his quest. But we can follow his long paper trail with some confidence to place him in some such spot at that time. The following account could be presented as a straightforward narrative ("he went there, he did this"), but to really appreciate the complex, self-revealing, self-concealing processes of Wordsworth's self-creation it is better to track his manuscript revisions and erasures, not just the paths he took alongside Lake Como.

In *Descriptive Sketches,* his account of the Como sequence of his tour (ll.80–175) swerves erratically between two topics, attractive landscapes and attractive dancing girls. The ratio of lines devoted to each is about two to one, with the landscapes repeatedly coming back into the narrative to correct the sensual lines of fantasy the girls stimulate in his mind. Again we see the importance of dancing in Wordsworth's poetical development, relative to his sexual growth, as the dancers on Como link up with the "frank-hearted maids" on Windermere in 1788.

The very first snapshot in *Descriptive Sketches,* characterizing its lonesome wandering narrator, establishes this focus:

> His humble looks no shy restraint impart,
> Around him plays at will the virgin heart.
> While unsuspended wheels the village dance,
> The maidens eye him with inquiring glance,
> Much wondering what sad stroke of crazing Care
> Or desperate Love could lead a wanderer there.
> (39–44)

Other scholars take a chaster view of all this.[27] In fact, Wordsworth dropped nearly half of the lines from the 1793 version describing these girls, and drastically toned down those that remained when he first reprinted excerpts from the poem in his collected *Poems* of 1815. He further truncated these passages when he republished the entire poem in 1836 as a specimen of his juvenile work. And in *The Prelude,* as we have seen, they are reduced to a single phrase and a Miltonic allusion.

Not only does the negative evidence of later revisions suggest what is going on in these lines; we find it also in the proposed additions Wordsworth made in the margins and between the lines of his published poem in late 1793 and early 1794.[28] These revisions—never printed by him—give much more detailed physical descriptions of the girls, and stress the loss of willpower experienced by the narrator who watches them.

> The viewless lingerer hence, at evening, sees
> From rock-hewn steps the sail between the trees;
> Or marks, mid opening cliffs, fair dark-ey'd maids

Tend the small harvest of their garden glades,
Or, led by distant warbling notes, surveys,
With hollow ringing ears and darkening gaze,
Binding the charmed soul in powerless trance,
Lip-dewing Song and ringlet-tossing Dance,
Where sparkling eyes and breaking smiles illume
The bosom'd cabin's lyre-enliven'd gloom.
(92–101)

The last six lines, describing a pulsating voyeuristic lust, disappear entirely in 1815. But in 1794 Wordsworth added to the passage at various points, "the panting dance's neck revealing maze," "dewy lips prolong the magic strain / That locks in powerless [trance] the swimming brain," concluding,

Yes, sweet languor here the failing soul involves
That from the best might steal their best resolves
While breathe soft amorous wishes[29]

The most direct line in the 1793 version—"With hollow ringing ears and darkening gaze"—is an expression of glowering desire so strong that it hurts, and the hurt might be taken as equally threatening to the viewer or the viewed.

The next description is explicit enough as it stands:

Soft bosoms breathe around contagious sighs,
And amorous music on the water dies.
Heedless how Pliny, musing here, survey'd
Old Roman boats and figures thro' the shade,
Pale Passion, overpower'd, retires and woos
The thicket, where th'unlisten'd stock-dove coos.
(114–19)

Wordsworth evidently thought it was too explicit, because he cut all but the first two lines in 1815 and 1836, since they retain the appropriately censorious notion of *"contagious* sighs." Coxe speaks of the unhealthy air which was thought to cause malaria in the upper reaches of the lake, but Wordsworth has clearly transferred the danger to a different disease.[30] Pliny the Younger appears here not simply because he was born on Como but to represent a stern figure of Roman stoic virtue to shame, by contrast, "Pale Passion, overpower'd." And what *is* that "heedless" personified figure retiring to do in that thicket, ostentatiously *not* listening to the stock dove? Hard not to listen to a bird; harder still to "woo" a thicket. The artificiality of the verse allows several interpretations, from pure lust or sheer fantasy, through flirtation or casual dancing, to masturbation or an actual sexual encounter, successful or otherwise.

Finally, we come to the climax:

> Farewell! those forms that, in thy noon-tide shade,
> Rest, near their little plots of wheaten glade;

[Clearly these are the same girls he saw earlier.]

> Those stedfast eyes, that beating breasts inspire
> To throw the "sultry ray" of young Desire;
> Those lips, whose tides of fragrance come, and go,
> Accordant to the cheek's unquiet glow;
> Those shadowy breasts in love's soft light array'd,
> And rising, by the moon of passion sway'd.

[The passage and perhaps the principals in it have moved from noon to moonlight.]

> —Thy fragrant gales and lute-resounding streams,
> Breathe o'er the failing soul voluptuous dreams;
> While Slavery, forcing the sunk mind to dwell
> On joys that might disgrace the captive's cell,
> Her shameless timbrel shakes along thy marge,
> And winds between thine isles the vocal barge.
> (148–61)

Sultry rays, young desires, lips, and breasts—all these are gone from this passage in 1815, but the last four lines remain because, like "contagious sighs" earlier, they contain their own moral censor, being a personification of the exploited social condition of the northern Italians under Austrian domination.

This "sunk mind" is an attribute of the "failing soul" musing on these girls. He feels tempted by their slavery, their easy availability, and is ashamed of himself as a result. The 1794 additions make the 1793 text's allusion to the casual prostitution of oppressed women more particular, and draw the "sunk mind" much closer to its objects of desire: "those eyes" become "dark eyes," and the lips' "tides of fragrance" are, additionally, "soft." The 1794 additions also intensify the earlier statement about the threat of disaster for "the best" that lurks in all this reckless beauty: "Charms which in powerless trance the *wisest* view / Robb'd of their resolves all adieu."[31] Farewell, that is, to all the high resolves I have begun to form for my life. And if there is any doubt as to what "the failing soul's voluptuous dreams" are, 1794 makes it explicit: "amorous wishes and voluptuous dreams."

If we arrange these alternating sequences of descriptions of the girls' charms and their watcher's reactions into a narrative sequence, we come close to what might have happened to Wordsworth on Lake Como sometime between August 20 and August 23, 1790. Discrepancies in the various accounts of these days have exercised specialists considerably, for it is indeed "difficult, if not impossible, to reconcile" all the statements he made about it.[32] On their second or third night along the lake, Wordsworth and Jones were separated, by a thunderstorm (they said), and spent the night in two different towns, the only time they were apart during the entire tour. "Interestingly enough, Wordsworth did not describe the mishap at the head of Lake Como in his letter to his sister Dorothy, just as he did not detail the mistaken path at the Simplon Pass."[33] His omissions of these two incidents, one the apex of the frustrated Sublime, the other the nadir of frustrating Beauty, is indeed interesting, and for reasons beyond William's brotherly concern not to alarm Dorothy.

The usual account is that on the night of August 21, their second night along the lake, in the town of Gravedona, Wordsworth and Jones got up by mistake at 1:45 A.M. (that is, early morning of the 22d) and set off, aiming to "behold the scene in its most deep repose" (VI.628–29). They wanted to see the sunrise on the lake; this is entirely characteristic of their touring habits. They heard four chimes and thought it was 4 A.M., not realizing that the local church bells rang once for the hour and once for each quarter. "Coasting the water's edge as hitherto," they "soon were lost, bewildered among woods immense," and had to sit on a rock overlooking the lake to wait for daybreak, a night whose terror Wordsworth described in Miltonic cadences and images of conflict that approach the power of his Gondo Gorge description:

> On the rock we lay
> And wished to sleep, but could not for the stings
> Of insects, which with noise like that of noon
> Filled all the woods. The cry of unknown birds,
> The mountains—more by darkness visible
> And their own size, than any outward light—
> The breathless wilderness of clouds, the clock
> That told with unintelligible voice
> The widely parted hours, the noise of streams,
> And sometimes rustling motions nigh at hand
> Which did not leave us free from personal fear,
> And lastly, the withdrawing moon that set
> Before us while she still was high in heaven . . . .
>
> (641–53)

These, he concludes, amazed at the contrast, "were our food" that succeeded the "pair of golden days" they had just had on that "same delicious lake." But was it only the clocks that confused them, or were they, as in the Gondo spital, "unable to sleep from other causes"?

One notices immediately his convincing specificity, and his refusal to assign a pat meaning to this experience. Milton's seducing archangel was again on his mind when he composed these lines in 1804, not only in the well-known tag phrase "darkness visible" but also in his archaic diction for their progress, "coasting the water's edge," which echoes Satan's nefarious approach to Paradise: "Coasting the wall of heav'n on this side Night" (*PL,* III.71). One thing seems to be clear: unpleasant as the experience was, it was not raining.[34] Therefore, if they were separated in a rainstorm, it must have been during the coming day or night, August 22.

On the 22d Wordsworth stayed behind at Samolaco, the last town on the lake, while Jones went on ahead to Chiavenna, some ten miles farther up, the first large town up the river Mera, past the little tributary lake of Mezzola. The explanation usually supplied is that they were separated by a thunderstorm and spent the night wandering in the woods between Gravedona and Chiavenna, a distance of more than twenty miles. But Dorothy's journal of 1820 gives three slightly different accounts of the misadventure, and it is not clear whether she refers to this incident outside Gravedona or to a subsequent one—or if they are both part of the same incident.

First she says she was interested in Gravedona "for the sake of an adventure of our youthful Travellers recorded by my brother in the poem on his own life. They were parted in a thunder storm, and wandered all night in the forest between Gravedona and Chiavenna."[35] The first sentence fits with the *Prelude* account, but the second doesn't: there, it is not raining, and they stay put. Dorothy's second account says, "My Brother, when parted by mischance from his companion, had seen the moon hanging over the highest point of that same mountain [Colico], while bewildered in the forest on the opposite [i.e., west] side of the Lake."[36] In this account they are separated and lost, and the appearance of the moon matches the *Prelude*'s account, but it does not seem to be raining—though of course thunderstorms move fast on mountain lakes, obscuring or revealing the moon as they go. Finally, she speaks of a location closer to "the upper small reach . . . called Chiavenna. The path my Brother had travelled, when bewildered in the night thirty years ago, was traceable through some parts of the forest on the opposite [west] side of the lake—then most dismal with thunder, lightning, and rain."[37] Now it seems to have been raining very hard, and they are at a location near to, if not beyond, Samolaco, where Wordsworth is said to have spent the night.

Scholars have assumed that Dorothy made a mistake when she said that the incident of being separated in a thunderstorm appeared in "the poem on his own life," and it is easy to see how she might have conflated two incidents that may have occurred so close together. But barring the discovery of a manuscript which records such an incident, and given Dorothy's thrice-repeated emphasis on an event outside of Gravedona,[38] Wordsworth's account of their too-early rising and Dorothy's account of their being separated seem to refer to one and the same incident, or to two parts of an essentially single experience, running from 1:45 A.M. on August 22 to whatever time on the morning of the 23d Wordsworth and Jones were reunited and continued on their way. Though it is not raining in the *Prelude* account, the weather does not seem good ("the breathless wilderness of clouds"), and it could well have rained before dawn or sometime the next day. If they stayed together till dawn, they were separated sometime before late afternoon, when they would have sought out lodgings. On the other hand, the only authority for its being a *rainstorm* that separated them is William's word to Dorothy, though a rainstorm and some other reason—such as a return visit to a "bosom'd cabin"—are not mutually exclusive.

What with one thing and another, these were two very disorienting days. If the storm started toward evening, they had plenty of time to reach Chiavenna before that.[39] Twenty miles in a day was nothing for these striders, and on this day of all days they had a *very* early start. It is possible that they lingered at the head of Lake Como before pushing on, but why should they linger there, and if the storm came on during the day, how could they get separated by it? Granted, it's possible. But then how could they get so easily reunited the next day and continue on their way back into Switzerland without a pause? They could hardly have had the foresight to arrange a meeting before they got separated, and even if they did, would it not have been for the same rendezvous? Again, an explanation is possible: they may have said, "If this storm separates us, let's meet in Chiavenna," and Jones sensibly held tight there the next day until Wordsworth turned up. Nor is it entirely out of the question that those same Italian paths could rapidly carry news—up and down their grapevines—of two outlandishly dressed young Englishmen who were evidently lost and looking for each other. News about foreigners travels fast in the country, but it is nearly miraculous that they could have got lost, been reunited by word of mouth, and still left Chiavenna together in good time to cross back over the river (Chiavenna is on the opposite, eastern shore) and up the Forcola Pass to spend the next night (August 23) in the mountains at Soazza.

In *Descriptive Sketches,* these nights—if they *are* two nights—are in essence treated as one (201–42). But they are removed from their Como context, and attributed to the experience of the "Grison gypsey" who appears next on their itinerary. The poem cannot be held to geographical accuracy or consistency, but the night outside Gravedona is unmistakable in this passage: "Heavy, and dull, and cloudy is the night . . . Glimmer the dim-lit Alps, dilated, round . . . insect buzz, that stuns the sultry woods . . . On viewless fingers counts the valley-clock," and so on. Wordsworth introduces this passage with an equally unmistakable thunderstorm, the details of which are taken from later parts of his tour. But their placement here tends to associate "thunderstorm" with images that are clearly from the night, or nights, outside Gravedona, August 21 or 22. He speaks of something—the coming storm? bypassing wanderers?—disturbing the birds: "and chattering breaks the night's respose" (230). Compare "the cry of unknown birds" from *The Prelude* (VI.644). "The bushes rustle near . . . with strange tinglings" (237–38), exactly as in *The Prelude:* "sometimes rustling motions nigh at hand / Which did not leave us free from personal fear" (650–51). What—and where—are those "strange tinglings"? Rhetorically, they are transferred epithets, describing a human reaction to a natural sound, a transference not unlike "wooing" a thicket. This is one of only two occurrences of the verb "to tingle" in Wordsworth's poetry, and the other comes in precisely the same kind of context: the "slight shocks of young love-liking" he felt at the summer dances on Windermere, which "mounted up like joy into the head / And tingled through the veins" (IV.325–27).[40] The wind is blowing—or somebody is walking—with sinister sound effects: "the dry leaves stir as with the serpent's walk" (233).

Is Wordsworth again imagining the Garden of Eden, where one serpent actually could "walk"? A quick check with Milton provides another uncanny confirmation that not only Milton but also Milton's subject matter is on Wordsworth's mind. For, turning to the place in *Paradise Lost* where Satan approaches Eve in serpent guise, we find: "she busied heard the sound / Of rustling leaves but minded not" (*PL,* IX.518–19). There too, a smooth-talking seducer in outlandish guise is approaching, and a woman is in danger. Wordsworth puts a sinister spin on his every perception; voices are heard and attributed to "Banditti." His fear, in *The Prelude,* is made the gypsy's fear, in *Descriptive Sketches.* But the gypsy most likely is a stand-in for another woman Wordsworth both lusted after and, as a result, feared or *feared for* at Lake Como, as he watched her "with hollow ringing ears and darkening gaze," and as he returned to approach her now. All this is lost in *The Prelude,* and displaced and disjointed in *Descriptive Sketches,* but it is recoverable. In *Descriptive Sketches* he projects all these fears outward onto bears, bandits, and famished wolves coming to devour their prey. The complicated but intriguing textual evidence suggests that a spying, seducing Satanic figure is more in his mind than those poor dumb creatures of picturesque melodrama.

Hence it is worth considering, even if we cannot finally decide, in light of all Wordsworth's emotional and guilt-ridden language about Como's "dark-ey'd maids," that some kind of internal storm, corollary to—or substituting for—an external thunderstorm, led him to spend a night by himself (or at least not with Jones) and join up with Jones by appointment next day. The final passage in *Descriptive Sketches* does place him, alone, in the woods, visiting—or spying on—a "far-off peasant's day-deserted home." What he sees is a charming domestic scene that finally lays to rest all the preceding eroticism.

> Once did I pierce to where a cabin stood,
> The red-breast peace had bury'd it in wood,
> There, by the door a hoary-headed sire
> Touch'd with his wither'd hand an aged lyre;
> Beneath an old-grey oak as violets lie,
> Stretch'd at his feet with stedfast, upward eye,
> His children's children join'd the holy sound,
> A hermit—with his family all around.
>
> (168–75)[41]

This is the first time, but not the last, that a well-placed hermit enters a Wordsworth poem to restore moral order, the hermit in "Tintern Abbey" being the most famous instance. Here as there the hermit's sudden appearance seems a bit forced, since true hermits normally do not have children, let alone grandchildren. In these young faces we see again "stedfast" eyes, but now they belong not to dark-eyed maids but to children listening to a "holy sound." A musical detail from the sexy dances—"Where sparkling eyes and breaking smiles illume / *The bosom'd cabin's lyre-enliven'd gloom*" (100–101)—is repeated with a deadening difference: "a hoary-headed sire / Touch'd with his wither'd hand an aged lyre." The former cabin was "bosom'd"; the latter, "bury'd": two very different ways of being hidden. Order thus restored, the poem's narrator can finally leave Como, as he does in the very next line: "Hence shall we seek where fair Locarno smiles."

Having come to the nadir of his sexual fantasies, where "the sunk mind . . . dwell[s] on joys that might disgrace the captive's cell," after hearing the "shameless timbrel" of sexual slavery, he shakes these joys off for other images to restore his poem's moral equilibrium:

> I lov'd, mid thy most desert woods astray,
> With pensive steps to measure my slow way,[42]
> By lonely, silent cottage-doors to roam,
> The far-off peasant's day-deserted home;
> Once did I pierce to where a cabin stood . . . .
>
> (164–68)

Taken literally, these lines indicate that he went—perhaps by accident ("astray"), perhaps by design ("I lov'd")—to a peasant's cottage during the day, when he knew the man of the house would be away—and found a grandfather and his grandchildren instead. That this incident occurred on a Sunday—and the day he and Jones were parted was Sunday, August 22—is suggested by lines preceding it, as well as by the "holy sound" of the grandfather's lyre. The speaker is watching the lake very early in the morning, when it is "still hid from morning's ray," and hears "the matin-bell / Calling the woodman from his desert-cell." Wordsworth and Jones were certainly awake before dawn on that sleepless night. The woodman goes to church by boat, evidently passing near an observer who can hear him, but not see him, from the shore: "the sound of oars, that pass, / Spotting the steaming deeps, to early mass." The word "desert-cell" links up with what seems like a repetitive tic in the following report, that "mid thy most *desert* woods astray . . . The far-off peasant's day-*deserted* home." That is to say, deserted *for the day.* Or, to put all bluntly, has Wordsworth watched his chance to go back to a cottage near a "little plot of wheaten glade" to say good-bye—or something—to one particular girl who caught his eye on the 21st?[43] And did he find instead, perhaps not without some relief, that she and the other adults were gone, leaving only the grandfather and grandchildren at home? Or was she one of the grandchildren?

Not surprisingly, there is little mention of these possibilities in the records of the family's re-tour in 1820. Dorothy and Mary, no beauties themselves, do record that "the women on the banks of the lake of Como are often handsome—the girls graceful,"[44] but their journals are mainly taken up with old paths lost and found—and with the sleepless night outside Gravedona. But Wordsworth wrote a poem for his memorial volume on the 1820 tour which taps into some different memories of the time. Titled "The Three Cottage Girls," it compares an Italian, a Swiss, and a Highland cottage girl on the theme of youthful innocence, virginity, and the desirability of remaining unspoiled by "Love's uneasy sovereignity."[45] The Swiss girl is valued for her mountain independence, the Highland girl for having already appeared in a Wordsworth poem ("To a Highland Girl," 1803), and only the Italian, who comes first, for her beauty. Mary Wordsworth's journal indicates that they saw this "smart looking girl" by Lake Lugano, as her mother arranged her hair before "she entered the village, where also was a festival."[46] But Wordsworth's poem introduces her with an awkward, self-interrupting stutter that suggests, or enacts, some other untoward thoughts:

> Such (but O lavish Nature! why
> That dark unfathomable eye,

Where lurks a Spirit that replies
To stillest mood of softest skies,
Yet hints at peace to be o'erthrown
Another's first, and then her own?)
Such, haply, yon ITALIAN Maid . . . .
(14–20)

He then goes on to describe the scene Mary reported. But his parenthetical question, worthy of Blake's naive virgin in *The Book of Thel,* is about "dark" attractions that somehow correlate with "soft" moods and scenes, yet disrupt emotional "peace." Granting the immense power of Wordsworth's memory over his own texts and past experiences, did that girl's "dark unfathomable eye" bring back to his mind's eye those "dark-ey'd maids" of 1790, whose "sparkling," "stedfast," "sultry" looks met—or caused—that "darkening gaze" in the "viewless lingerer" who stood watching them, and "o'erthrew" his peace of mind with lustful thoughts? And did his recollections of his uncontrollable feelings then—"Pale Passion, overpower'd"—prompt his moralizing threat about "peace to be o'erthrown" now?

When they returned to this neighborhood in 1820, Wordsworth set off for a day's walk by himself, or rather he set off with Henry Crabb Robinson but returned alone: "and at 7 o'clock W. arrived enchanted with *his* rambles. He had found, high up on the hills, cottages within pastoral hollows, among groves of chestnut trees and olives—every cottage with its garden and vineyard. From those sequestered places he had descended by a direct road to the palace."[47] This could be interpreted as the behavior of a man well pleased with himself, who had "lov'd," thirty years before, "mid thy most desert woods astray . . . by lonely, silent cottage-doors to roam," and whose special enjoyment on his return tour was to search out places where he had got lost before. They certainly sound like the same kinds of places, and the way in which he found them, and returned from them ("descended . . . direct"), sounds as if he knew his way around the area. A return visit to a scene of sexual initiation would be hard to resist, given the time and opportunity, and especially given Wordsworth's fascination with his own development as the master subject of his poetry.

In *The Prelude* all this is generalized out onto the "impassioned . . . beauty" of the landscape, quite in contrast to the specificity of *Descriptive Sketches* and the Gravedona passage. Fair enough: different poem, different time, different purposes. But to the extent that these biographical issues lie behind any account of his experiences on Lake Como, his apology in *The Prelude* for the "undisciplined verse" he wrote about it in *Descriptive Sketches*—as contrasted with his present mature morality—sounds even more pompous than it already does, lacking any life context:

. . . [Como:] ye have left
Your beauty with me, an impassioned sight
Of colours and of forms, whose power is sweet
And gracious, almost, might I dare to say,
As virtue is, or goodness—sweet as love,
Or the remembrance of a noble deed,
Or gentlest visitations of pure thought
When God, the giver of all joy, is thanked
Religiously in silent blessedness . . . .

(VI.607–15)

We almost want Lady Macbeth to enter and demand, "What do you mean?" There's too much pious mumbling here, trying to link up beauty, passion, and love with nobility, purity, and God. Not because the two groups of subjects are incompatible, but because the speaker seems to feel they are, with his awkward "almost, might I dare to say." It may not be simply guilt or bad faith that causes Wordsworth to stammer so; it might equally well be a feeling of thankful relief that he did not give into temptations he felt so strongly there.

In *The Prelude* he simply stops here, but with language about where his poem is heading that we can now interpret as referring to the nature of the events he is recording as much as to the formal proportions of his poem:

But here I must break off, and quit at once,
Though loth, the record of these wanderings,
A theme which may *seduce* me else beyond
All reasonable bounds.

(658–61; italics added)

In *The Prelude* this statement refers to the proportions of his poem, the "circuitous" path that led him to "tender thoughts" about Lake Como. But in *Descriptive Sketches* and its various revisions and corollary texts, seduction is a temptation threatening the proper—"reasonable"—course of his life.

Any real-life scenario constructed from these texts is of course subject to challenge as an overly literal reading of scenes and figures that are wholly conventional, especially in a poem as artificial as *Descriptive Sketches.* Yet Wordsworth is also the most literal and matter-of-fact of all major English poets. Like Gray, he wove the conventions of his genres into his own experience, but, being Wordsworth, and invention not his forte, the possibility that he is using literal representations of his own personal experiences is proportionately much higher. Given the various strands of evidence, the burden of disproving the scenario sketched here would seem to fall on those who want to insist upon either the young Wordsworth's moral chastity or his strict allegiance to the conventions of his genres.

A major shift occurs after Lake Como in both poems Wordsworth wrote about the 1790 tour, which further suggests that there was something critical about his experiences there. He and Jones were at this point precisely halfway through their itinerary: one month and eight days had passed, and one month and eight days remained, before their last-recorded stopping place, at Aix-la-Chapelle, on the German-Belgian border. In *The Prelude* the account of the tour finishes at this point, except for a brief reference to their final dash across Belgium, skipping all of Switzerland in between. In *Descriptive Sketches,* though only a quarter of the poem has passed, he shifts from the particularity of his first two sketches (Chartreuse and Como) to geographical and moral generalizations: from this point on, there are only half a dozen place-names, but much more moral allegory, drawn from the everyday lives of Swiss peasants, who are usually viewed from a considerable distance up on the mountains. Thus the two poems give different accounts of two separate parts of the tour. *The Prelude* concentrates almost entirely on the first, southern half of it, while *Descriptive Sketches,* after a detailed opening look at Chartreuse and Como, moves into Switzerland and spends most of its time on the second, northern half of the tour. But its remaining "sketches" are less fully realized and detailed, and more clearly indebted to Wordsworth's sources.

In the latter half of the tour, Wordsworth and Jones followed Coxe's itinerary very closely, in reverse, and in segments cropped out from Coxe's longer, more leisurely coverage. The Swiss lakes were the pivot points of his adaptation of Coxe's itinerary,[48] for the obvious purpose of comparing them with his home district, even though this required some circuitous loops and backtracking, to include Lake Constance in the north and Neuchâtel far to the west. But the Swiss lakes finally made less difference to the meaning of his tour than the people he met on their shores or the mountains he saw from below.

They crossed up over the Forcola Pass on August 23. Going from Lake Como to Lake Lucerne, there was only one way to go, dictated by the rivers and passes through the mountains. Crossing the San Bernardino Pass at 6,775 feet, they came down into Hinterrhein, cradle of "th'indignant waters of the infant Rhine." For four days they followed first one, then the other of the Rhine's source streams (Hinter and Vorder), up through the Via Mala, whose name stimulated Wordsworth to a heavy allegory about "life's long deserts with its charge of woe," in which their collegiate summer walking tour suddenly becomes part of "a mighty caravan of pain," representing all of human life.

Coming down along the Vorderrhein on August 26, they crossed without comment the taxing Oberalp Pass, arriving at the base of the Great St. Gotthard on August 27. Alpine mountain crossings were becoming routine. But Dorothy's journal of 1820 shows how the effect of the Simplon disappointment persisted in family memory. Her party climbed to the top of the St. Gotthard to enjoy the view toward Italy, but she turned aside for reflection: "At the top of the ascent of St. Gotthard a wide basin—a dreary valley of rocky ground—lies before us . . . . Unwilling to turn down the mountain, I sate down upon a rock . . . . Entering into my Brother's youthful feelings of sadness and disappointment when he was told unexpectedly that the Alps were crossed—the effort accomplished."[49]

Wordsworth and Jones reached Lake Lucerne on August 28, a week after leaving Lake Como. Moving out into the "open vale serene" of Urseren (a name combining the canton, Uri, with its habitual adjective), Wordsworth paints an Alpine scene of almost complete generality: "On as we move, a softer prospect opes, / Calm huts, and lawns between, and sylvan slopes." But it was on "Uri's lake" (Lucerne) that Wordsworth painted the sunset that is the poem's best descriptive sketch, and that was immediately recognized as such when it was read by Samuel Coleridge in an undergraduate discussion group at Cambridge that included the poet's brother.

> . . . the Sun walking on his western field
> Shakes from behind the clouds his flashing shield.
> Triumphant on the bosom of the storm,
> Glances the fire-clad eagle's wheeling form;
> Eastward, in long perspective glittering, shine
> The wood-crown'd cliffs that o'er the lake recline;
> Wide o'er the Alps a hundred streams unfold,
> At once to pillars turn'd that flame with gold;
> Behind his sail the peasant strives to shun
> The west that burns like one dilated sun,
> Where in a mighty crucible expire,
> The mountains, glowing hot, like coals of fire.
>
> (336–47)

Coleridge, writing years later with the undimmed enthusiasm of hindsight, declared that "seldom, if ever, was the emergence of an original poetic genius above the literary horizon more evidently announced."[50] But though this apocalyptic passage is indeed the best thing in the poem, Coleridge also noted that it "demanded a greater closeness of attention, than poetry, (at all events, than descriptive poetry) has a right to claim." Many admirers of Wordsworth's "nature poetry" have consistently ignored this apt observation. Coleridge had recognized what Wordsworth was only beginning to sense in

1790, that his poetry described not landscapes but the mind at work on them.

The canton of Uri was home to memories of William Tell, exactly the kind of simple mountain hero fighting alone against overwhelming odds who appealed most strongly to Wordsworth's egotistical imagination. Like his republican reading assignments at Cambridge and *The Prelude*'s catalog of possible epic heroes, Wordsworth generalizes from the immediate instance to other examples of "honour'd men of ancient days" who fell in the very moment of their greatest triumph. He fleshes out a Swiss peasant's "confused" recollections of the legendary Tell with an epitome of the last three centuries of *English* history, from "the bleeding Sidney," who fell at Zutphen in 1586, to "the plaided chief," Graham of Claverhouse, who died in victory at Killiecrankie in 1689, to Wolfe, expiring with his "happiest sigh" on the Plains of Abraham above Quebec in 1763.

From Lake Lucerne they crossed over to Zurich to visit the convent of Einsiedeln. This was only the second cultural monument they sought out on the tour, and Wordsworth's empathy with the credulous pilgrims coming to the Black Madonna is similar to his plea that the Chartreuse might be spared from revolutionary violence: "Oh give me not that eye of hard disdain / That views undimm'd Einsiedlen's [*sic*] wretched fane." But it is the pilgrims' hope, not their faith, that Wordsworth celebrated and wished to preserve in otherwise hopeless human breasts: "If the sad grave of human ignorance bear / One flower of hope—Oh pass and leave it there." When he says that "there are [those] who love to stray" out at evening to watch the pilgrims, he's referring to himself, as a proposed revision from 1794 makes explicit: "I forlorn dejected weary slow / A pilgrim wandering round this world of woe / Oft as I meet a brother . . . ."[51] His note on the little outdoor sheds provided for the pilgrims combines, in effect, two versions of himself: "Under these sheds the sentimental traveller and the philosopher may find interesting sources of meditation."

The pilgrims were neither sentimental nor philosophical, but he was both, and very much in progress from the first role to the second at precisely this moment. His conclusion directly anticipates his coming Romanticism: "My heart, alive to transports long unknown, / Half wishes your delusions were its own." This is the same role he had adopted at Chartreuse: a secular preserver of religious mysteries that are apparently about to pass forever from the world. His only complaint about the credulity of the pilgrims was a provincial one: "I cannot help remarking, that the superstitions of the Alps appear to be far from possessing that poetical character which so eminently distinguishes those of Scotland and the other mountainous northern countries. The Devil with his horns, &c. seems to be in their idea, the principal agent that brings about the sublime natural revolutions that take place daily before their eyes."[52] Religion and superstition are, in this view, simply other kinds of poetry, and "sublime natural revolutions that take place daily" are more dependable and therefore less threatening than human revolutions.

Leaving Einsiedeln on September 1, they spent a day and two nights "visiting the romantic valley of Glarus,"[53] only their fourth two-night stay in fifty days. From Glarus they skirted Lake Wallen (Walensee) and turned north again along the Rhine to reach Lake Constance on September 6, where Wordsworth began a long journal letter to Dorothy. It brought her up to date with everything that had happened since the Grande Chartreuse, rambling back and forth between the two poles of his interest. First, he began listing their itinerary, then realized that "this Catalougue must be shockingly tedious." (It wasn't: Dorothy repeated it almost verbatim, including the apology for being tedious, in her next letter to Jane Pollard.) Second, he detailed his thoughts and impressions, but in the midst of it he finds he has "again lapsed into Egotism." On both topics he realized he was "too particular for the limits of my paper," and indeed, it turned out that a lifetime was not too much for expanding upon the limits of either topic from this trip.

The sight to see at Lake Constance was the Rhine Falls, near Schaffhausen, west of Konstanz, to which they dutifully proceeded. In what had become by now a regular pattern, they were again disappointed: "Magnificent as this fall certainly is I must confess I was disappointed in it." And for the usual reason: "I had raised my ideas too high."[54] The falls are more wide than high, with a drop of only sixty feet, but that was not the problem. By now he could recognize what was happening: anything he hoped for (Mont Blanc, the Simplon Pass) would be less grand in reality than in imagination. Conversely, those places where he had not expected much often surprised him, not because of the scenery but because of the *people* there—the French *fédérés,* the Como dancers.

They dropped back south into the heart of Switzerland, returning to Lucerne on September 10. Then they undertook a westward circuit, past Interlaken's twin lakes to Neuchâtel and Bienne, Rousseau country. Moving south on the 11th, they reentered "the very heart of the high Alps" at Grindelwald and Lauterbrunnen.[55] The next four days were the center of their purest *Alpine* experience, as they passed in sight of the splendid mountains whose names Wordsworth explained by using Cumbrian equivalents: "As Schreck-horn, the pike of terror. Wetter-horn the pike of storms, &c. &c."[56] They also saw the Eiger, the Jungfrau, and the Engelberg (Angelmount), from which in 1820 Dorothy recognized her brother's still-youthful spirit: "in view of the flashing silver-topped Mount Titlis, and its grey crags, a sight that rouzed W's youthful desires; and in spite of weak eyes *and the weight of fifty winters,* he could not repress a longing to ascend that mountain."[57] She knew him very well; her phrasing echoes the family's premier artwork, which they always referred to by its definite article, as *"the* Tintern Abbey": "the length of five long winters!" The smaller lakes they passed, Sarnen and Lungern, put him in mind of home: "Those two lakes have always interested me especially, from bearing, in their size and other features, a resemblance to the North of England."[58]

On September 12 they passed over the Brünig Pass into Unterwalden, a crossing, Dorothy wrote, "well remembered by my brother; he and his companion, owing to the jealousies and disorders of the French Revolution [were] rudely treated by persons stationed there."[59] As foreigners, and obviously not aristocrats, they were taken as fellow travelers in the modern sense. Wordsworth drew an invidious contrast between the beauty of the country and its people, "with regard to manners." He had come to Switzerland nurturing a Rousseauistic fantasy about direct correlations between man and nature: "My partiality to Swisserland excited by its natural charms induces me to hope that the manners of it's inhabitants are amiable." But now a different kind of correlation has been suggested to his mind: "I cannot help frequently contrasting them with those of the French," whose absence of class feeling had so impressed him a month earlier: "that politeness diffused thro the lower ranks had an air so engaging, that you could scarce attribute it to any other cause than real benevolence." But he realized that this new class *un*consciousness came from a deeper cause than nationality: "I must remind you that we crossed it at the time when the whole nation was mad with joy, in consequence of the revolution."[60]

On the way into Lauterbrunnen from Grindelwald, Wordsworth's physical fitness saved him when his quest for ever more picturesque viewing stations put his life in danger.

> At the head of the valley of Lauterbrunnen, in order to have a more perfect view of a magnificent waterfall [Staubbach Falls], I crossed over a broad and rapid mountain torrent by the aid of fragments of rock which strewed its bed. I did not stay above a few minutes; but on my return I found the difficulty of recrossing the stream much increased [by the rapid melting of the snow in the morning sun]; and, being detained among the large stones in its channel, I perceived the water swell every moment, which, with the dizziness of sight produced by the furious dashing of the foam, placed me in a situation of considerable personal danger.

He jumped to safety, and as they descended back down the valley they saw that a place under a bridge where they had stopped on the way up had "such a quantity of water rolling over our late resting place as would have swept us away before it."[61]

Posting his journal letter from Bern on the 16th, he and Jones headed for their final goal, the Lakes of Neuchâtel and Bienne, Rousseau's visionary haunts. They rowed out to the Isle of St. Pierre in the Lake of Bienne, where Rousseau sought refuge in 1765 from a mob whipped up against him by the local priest, and which he lovingly memorialized both in his *Confessions* and *The Reveries of a Solitary Walker.*[62] The island becomes, in Rousseau's representation of it, the very symbol of his imaginative project—which is to say, of himself:

> . . . the ardent desire I had to end my days in that island, was inseparable from the apprehension of being obliged to leave it. I felt a singular pleasure in seeing the waves break at my feet. I formed of them in my imagination the image of the tumult of the world contrasted with the peace of my habitation, and this pleasing idea sometimes softened me even to tears. . . . Permitting me to live on the island is but a trifling favour, I could wish to be condemned to it, and constrained to remain here that I may not be obliged to go elsewhere.[63]

Here at last—and perhaps saved for last—was a cultural monument that was simultaneously a natural beauty, and one that piqued a more than merely historical interest in Wordsworth's mind, recalling all the islands in Windermere he had so often rowed out to with his "minstrel" friends, and of the melancholy Reverend Braithwaite watching the little waves of Esthwaite break at the foot of his yew tree seat.

Reaching Basel early on the morning of September 21, they bought a boat and set out down the Rhine the next day. Their aim was to travel north until they were due east of the Channel ports and then strike out cross-country again. They spent a week on the river, selling their boat at Cologne and spending their last-recorded itinerary night at Aix-la-Chapelle on September 29. Wordsworth's sonnets from his 1820 tour recalled the young sailors' fears, as they, expert lakesmen, now trusted themselves to river sailing for the first time: "Jesus! bless our slender Boat, / By the current swept along."[64]

More danger awaited them when they disembarked, but now again from culture, not nature. As luck would have it, on this incredible trip for coincidences, they walked right through another country torn by revolution and counterrevolution. A Belgian revolution had risen up in imitation of the French, and the République des Etats-Unis Belgiques had been declared in January of 1790, the first independent Belgian republic.

Wordsworth saw only the Belgian, optimistic half of this, and his account of it, *Prelude* VI's last words on the 1790 tour, stresses that he knew little about the details of politics, which was true enough at the time:

> We crossed the Brabant armies on the fret
> For battle in the cause of Liberty.
> A stripling, scarcely of the household then

Of social life, I looked upon these things
As from a distance—heard, and saw, and felt,
Was touched but with no intimate concern . . . .
(684–96)

Wordsworth exaggerated this enthusiasm in order to distance himself from it—"I needed not that joy"—because by 1804 he was attuning himself to a deeper joy in nature. But vague references to "the cause of Liberty" were his wisest course here, anyway, since the reasons for the Brabançonne (Brabant) revolution of December 1789 were very murky, politically. It was in large part an aristocratic and clerical *conservative* reaction against the relatively enlightened religious policies of the Austrians, and the constitution adopted on July 11 included no declaration of the rights of man or provisions for religious freedom. The high-handed ways of the Holy Roman emperor, Joseph II, had provoked it, but when he died, in February, his brother succeeded him as Leopold II and soon decided to restore law and order. He retook some provinces in the summer, and early in October, just as Wordsworth and Jones were crossing the territory, he was marshaling his forces for a decisive assault on the capital. Leopold was "perhaps the only Hapsburg ruler who was a genuine constitutionalist and a believer in Montesquieu's doctrine of the separation of powers";[65] on the other hand, he was the brother of Marie Antoinette and no republican, so Wordsworth's pose of distant naïveté was a shrewd one, since the particulars of this small event were soon swallowed up and forgotten in the maelstrom of world revolution and counterrevolution.

Having entered France on the very day of her feast of federation, Wordsworth left Belgium just in the days that its brief feast of *apparent* republican enthusiasm was about to be spoiled. Between July and October of 1790 the fortunes of republican revolutions began to shift in less optimistic directions, and William Wordsworth and Robert Jones walked through or around much of it. By the time Wordsworth visited Dorothy at Forncett at Christmas to tell her in person all about the tour, the Belgian republicans had been defeated and empire restored by the Peace of the Hague (December 10). One thing, above all, the tour left in Wordsworth's heart: the desire to get back to France as soon as possible, though in the event it took a year's doing—and undoing—to bring it about.

PART TWO

OF THE MAN

1790–1799

THE MIGHTY CITY 11

London, 1791

> O, blank confusion, and a type not false
> Of what the mighty city is itself . . . !
> (VII.696–97)

Disembarking at Dover, Wordsworth had originally planned to unwind for a few weeks with Dorothy at Forncett. In a letter posted from Basel about September 21, he said he would be home in two or three weeks, with "no necessity for me to be in Cambridge before the 10th of Novbr." This was the last possible date at which he, now a thorough "term trotter," could still meet the residency requirement. Disingenuously, he hoped that his uncle Cookson might be glad to see him because, knowing that he had "given up all thoughts of a fellowship, he may perhaps not be so much displeased at this journey."[1]

Who was he kidding? Had he forgotten that he and Jones had left the country three months earlier without telling a soul, knowing full well how "mad" their adventure seemed to anyone who cared for them? His optimistic self-presentation was diverging more and more from the perspective of his elders. If the Cooksons had welcomed him for a visit while the university was filling, they would have appeared to condone the madcap jaunt which had put the final tap to their ward's fellowship hopes, the very fellowship that Cookson had vacated—and connived to keep open for two years—so that his nephew could get it. There would be no friendly homecoming at Forncett.

So, after stopping briefly in London to present Richard with his next request for funds (£30), he returned to Cambridge around October 20.[2] He had nowhere else to go, really. As "Questionists," fourth-year men had to be in residence only for the term before their final exam in January. Instead of delicately conveying the raptures of his European experience to Dorothy, Wordsworth spent most of the next six weeks "exulting" over his friends—as he had eagerly looked forward to doing, triumphing in the success of the scheme they had scoffed at. His bragging was not attractive, and he did not enjoy the popular success that William Frend had won the previous year for his "revolution" tour. But Jones's good humor helped soften Wordsworth's hard edges, and the occasion was an excellent excuse for parties with their lively social group, whose members had plenty of time on their hands since most of them were not reading for honors either. And at least he paid for many of the toasts, for he settled a wine bill of over £5 with Messrs. Wilkinson & Crossthwaite on November 6: a substantial part of his latest allowance.[3]

Wordsworth cost his uncles £110 in advances between October 1790 and May of 1791. All the money he spent was accruing debt, at interest, against the share he could reasonably expect (about £1,000) if Lowther settled with the five Wordsworth children. Wordsworth's life during most of this year seems irresponsible on any accounting principles, but a settlement with Lowther did seem to be in the offing. It was quite normal for young heirs presumptive to run up huge bills on expectations no greater than Wordsworth's. Still, William's share, uniquely among his siblings, was already heavily encumbered with several hundred pounds of educational—and recreational—expenses.

After six weeks of nonstop celebrations, he traveled fifty miles north through Newmarket and Thetford to Forncett for the Christmas holidays. The Cooksons' displeasure had cooled enough to make the visit acceptable. It was after all vacation time, he had nowhere else to go, and Dorothy longed to see her favorite brother. He spent most of his time with her, and as little as possible in strained conversation with his uncle. Brother and sister had not seen each other for more than a year, and she was in an ecstasy of anxiousness to hear the details of his great tour. There was no question of "relapsing into Egotism" now; it was all egotism: anything he said was interesting simply because he was saying it. They walked outside in the garden behind the parsonage for nearly four hours every day, two hours in the morning after breakfast and two in the afternoon after tea.[4] Even allowing for "uncommonly mild" winter weather, this indicates a hardy determination to be alone together, away from disapproving ears. Years later Dorothy recollected "the tales brought to me the following Christmas holidays at Forncett; and often repeated while we paced together on the gravel walk in the parsonage garden, by moon or star light."[5] These tales began to form "the shapeless wishes of [her] youth" into the image of the brother of whom she was becoming "particularly fond."

The "tales" that Dorothy heard were the first versions of the dramatic turning points in *The Prelude*'s narrative of the growth of the young poet's mind: the dancing *fédérés,* the disappointment of Mont Blanc, the aftershock of Simplon, the thunderstorm on Como (did he mention the dancing girls?), and the catalog of Alpine high points. In these conversational descriptive sketches, she was given emotional shadings which William had omitted in the rowdier company of his Cambridge friends.

He was beginning to work his notebook jottings into the verses that became *Descriptive Sketches,* though there is little record of any extended composition during this unsettled year. One draft from the tour, "Septimi Gades," proposes to a friend named "Mary" that they might live together in "Grasmere's quiet vale" even if they cannot reach "that humble shed / Which sheltered once my pilgrim head . . . below . . . the solemn Rhône."[6] This pleasant conceit, modeled on Horace's ode to his friend Septimius, adapted Wordsworth's recent experiences neatly into Dorothy's fantasies about "my little Parsonage," where she would shift her busy life of doing good from the Cooksons' parsonage to one occupied by her and her brother. Horace had sworn to Septimius that if they couldn't travel around Rome's Mediterranean empire (Gades = Cádiz), and if they couldn't stay in Rome, they could at least return home to southern Italy: "that part of the world has a welcome for me beyond all others."[7] Such sentiments always appealed to Wordsworth, as a poet weaned on Sensibility, and he cleverly adjusted Horace's regretful catalog of all the places he couldn't visit to fit the places he (Wordsworth) had just visited, but that Dorothy couldn't, in order to reassure her that home is best after all. But he retained one significant detail from Horace, correcting Dorothy's hope that she might be the mistress of a parsonage: he will be to her, as Horace was to Septimius, "thy *poet* and thy friend," not the local parson in "Grasmere's quiet vale."

The strongest part of the poem is the passionate friendship it expresses, especially in Wordsworth's image of his distraught sister's face when they parted in 1787, and his determination to blot it from his memory:

Oh thou, whose fixed bewildered eye
In strange and dreary vacancy
Of tenderness severe,
With fear unnamed my bosom chilled
While thus my farewell accents thrilled,
Or seemed to thrill mine ear;

Think not from me, my friend, to roam,
Thy arms shall be my only home
My only bed thy breast;
No separate path our lives shall know,

But where thou goest I will go,
And there my bones shall rest.

(1–12)

As brotherly care, this is very strongly expressed, even allowing for sentimental conventions, especially the allusion to the Book of Ruth in line 11, and the close contact between breasts and bosoms throughout.

In her letters to Jane Pollard, Dorothy transcribed verbatim not only her brother's descriptions of Switzerland but also his loving expressions of regard for her. The question of what William was going to do with his life was closely entwined with Dorothy's similar concerns for herself. She was preoccupied with questions of marriageability—natural in a young woman of nineteen or twenty. Her growing conviction that she would not marry, even if she received a proposal, was another version of the family problems being created by William's refusal to take up a paying profession. Her dependent financial position made her less eligible for marriage, but not marrying also meant that she would continue to be a drain on family finances. Unlike Richard, John, and Christopher, neither she nor William was producing income, or seemed likely to start doing so. They were entirely a liability in the family's scrupulous account books.

In her letters to Jane, Dorothy repeatedly asked for details about her former playmates in Halifax. She had left them only three years earlier, but the difference between sixteen and nineteen is enormous where marriage is concerned. Dorothy wanted to know how her friends were faring on the marriage market, and her own estimates indicate her shrewd expertise in such matters.

> I often figure to myself my old companions whom I left mere girls become women. You, I fancy tall and rather slender; Ellen, I suppose, is not much altered, but Harriot, I think must [be?], I fancy her a smart looking girl with a light, slender person. Harriot Brachen I suppose, is a tall fine-looking woman, and Mary Grimshaw rather fat and I should suppose about my height; I think I must be *nearly* as tall as Patty Ferguson, certainly not quite so tall, I believe, however I am much grown since my aunt saw me; if Mr. Griffith comes to Forncett he shall have my weight and measure; you can then form an idea of me, and if he goes to Halifax before he visits Forncett pray send me yours, but indeed, by letter you may tell your weight.[8]

A lot is being left to the imagination here. At the end of the letter, she runs through all these names again, under the heading of beauty and fashion, particularly pudgy Mary Grimshaw, who was "about [her] height": "You never mention Mary Grimshaw, is she handsome? is she lively or grave? or talkative, or silent?" Dorothy is making sure there is at least one old acquaintance less eligible than she, for though she would never be tall or handsome or rich, she knew she was not fat, grave, or silent.

She both invites and rejects Jane's teasing about her own prospects. She asks her not to mention the subject of Wilberforce again, but then inquires if she should extend her compliments to one Edward Swaine of Halifax: "Ought *I* to *rejoice* at his marriage, for do I know what might have been my chance for him?" She gives Jane the measure of her brothers, confessing, "You are right in supposing me partial to William," although allowing, "When I next see Kitt I shall love him as well . . . his disposition is of the same cast as William's, and his inclinations have taken the same turn, but he is much more likely to make his fortune; he is not so warm as William but has a most affectionate heart, his abilities though not so great perhaps as his brothers may be of more use to him as he has not fixed his mind upon any particular species of reading, or conceived an aversion to any." Christopher's malleability was the making of his fortune, for he overcame his aversion to mathematics long enough to study for the examinations. But William's "warmth" won her affections, even more than his poetry, which she well knew was "not the most likely thing to produce his advancement in the world."[9] One way and another, Dorothy was casting William as her lifetime companion, the hope of her life.

He, amid all this speculation about future prospects, lounged about reading Richardson's *Clarissa Harlowe,* that eight-volume masterpiece of the epistolary novel. This doubly annoyed the frowning Cooksons because it openly exhibited his disdain for the kind of serious reading that his brother Kit was bending himself down to. Wordsworth's choice of vacation reading could be regarded as insignificant: he was "just reading." Yet the choice of *Clarissa* is not incidental to this milieu of marriages and prospects. Richardson's detailed exposure of the vices of seduction, prostitution, and calculated rape in eighteenth-century England, though nearly half a century old, had not lost any of its currency. Thoughts of how young women could be given—or taken—away were not only a diversion but also cause for reflection in young Wordsworth, as he contemplated his own slim prospects and saw how Dorothy projected hers upon him. In default of his failed university career, he might better have concentrated his energies on any eligible young ladies in the neighborhood, rather than his ineligible and penniless sister or the rich but fictitious Clarissa Harlowe.

Taking this Clarissa with him, Wordsworth returned to Cambridge in mid-January to endure the rigors of the Senate House final university examinations, which commenced at eight o'clock on Monday morning, January 17, 1791, and lasted for three days. This combination oral and written exam was finely calculated to drive weaker natures to distraction, but for

Wordsworth and his friends these terrors were remote, and hence all the more contemptible. They would not get honors, but they could hardly fail, and they didn't. He stayed calm by reading *Clarissa,* and participated in the spirit of the exams only to cheer on the members of his set who actually were seeking honors.

They were few enough. In comparison with many of his friends from the brilliant class of '90 who had gained honors (Wrangham, Tweddell, and five others), only two of his close friends did so in 1791: Robert Greenwood was sixteenth wrangler, and William Terrot came eighth senior optime. Wordsworth might have felt a twinge of envy, if not remorse, for Greenwood's success, his old fellow "minstrel" from Hawkshead, and a literary man with no greater love of mathematics than his own. Another statistic—the kind an insider like William Cookson would brood over—was that 25 percent of the graduating Johnians accounted for approximately 25 percent of the entire university's honors degrees in 1791, but his brilliant nephew was not among them.[10] Given the high hopes and good connections with which Wordsworth had entered St. John's in 1787, his was a bitter harvest indeed.

After being formally admitted to his B.A. degree on Friday, January 21, William did not stay around long for celebration parties that, unlike his triumphal "exulting" in October, held little praise for him. He went off at the earliest possible opportunity—that very weekend or the following Monday, January 24—to bury himself, and the world's current valuation of him, in the "blank confusion" of London.

He took a seat on the roof of the London coach to save money and get a better view. He never forgot the moment at the end of the day's ride when, "having thridded the labyrinth of suburban villages," he passed over the "threshold" into the city itself and was swept away by it: "great God! / That ought *external* to the living mind / Should have such mighty sway, yet so it was" (VIII.700–702). The spot was most likely the turnpike gate where Mile End Road becomes Whitechapel, near Bethnal Green. This was the main route from Cambridge, continuing on directly into Leadenhall, Cornhill, and Cheapside: the City, where Wordsworth resided for the next four months.[11] Cambridge coaches usually deposited their passengers on Ludgate Hill, in front of St. Paul's at La Belle Sauvage inn.[12] The name suited its owners, Messrs. Bell and Savage, who accentuated their pun with a sign featuring the exotic Pocahontas, symbolizing the delights of tobacco; it also fit young Wordsworth, much of whose London experience revolved around the various ways in which beauty was treated, savagely or otherwise, in the city.

People rarely ask where Wordsworth lived in London. The question seems irrelevant to our nature poet, or perhaps his disclaimer *Prelude* VII ("Residence in London") has successfully put us off his trail:

> To have a house,
> It was enough—what matter for a home?—
> That owned me, living chearfully abroad
> With fancy on the stir from day to day,
> And all my young affections out of doors.
> (VII.76–80)

This diffusing of himself into his ambience works very well in his evocations of natural scenery. But Nature has no addresses, and though we cannot find Wordsworth's actual address in London in 1791, we can, by tracing his references to places in the city, establish pretty accurately where and how he lived. His London is not a generic amalgam of city sights, nor was it the London he cast as Imagination's enemy in *Prelude* VII. Rather, it was very specifically the political and cultural London of spring 1791 that affected his development with a vigor that shines through—"deconstructively"—his own efforts to control it for different purposes in the poem on the growth of his mind.

Not surprisingly, he stayed where almost everybody else stayed, in the old central hub of the City, where Cheapside splits into Threadneedle, Cornhill, and Lombard streets, and the Lord Mayor's Mansion House, the Royal Exchange, and the Bank of England face each other across the intersection (see illustration). By far the greatest number of Wordsworth's urban references fall within the compass of less than a square mile around this central point. In *The Prelude* we read of "the renowned Lord Mayor," "the river proudly bridged" (Blackfriars), "the giddy top and Whispering Gallery of St. Paul's," "the Giants of Guildhall" (Gog and Magog), "Bedlam and the two figures at its gates . . . Maniacs carved in stone,"[13] and "the Monument" (Wren's memorial of the Great Fire of 1666, at the top of Fish Street Hill). It was still very much the heart of everyday London life, not the stark financial district it is today, built on the ruins of the Battle of Britain. When he says, "Obscurely did I live, / Not courting the society of men / By literature, or elegance, or rank, / Distinguished" (IX.20–24), he means that he did not live in Westminster or in the fashionable new squares being constructed in the West End. It also meant he lived alone, not with his brother Richard, nor seeking out people of rank who might still—barely—have been disposed to help him, such as John Robinson or William Wilberforce. He was being irresponsible, but at least he was doing it on his own, in a kind of internal self-exile: "a transient visitant . . . single in the wide waste."

His first contact in the city was Dorothy's adored "aunt" Elizabeth Threlkeld, an enterprising woman in the woolen trade, who at forty-six had recently married a widower four years her junior (much to Dorothy's fascination)[14] and who frequently came to London on business.[15] She introduced

William to Samuel Nicholson, a wholesale mercer who supplied her shop in Halifax as well as that of the Wordsworths' Newcastle cousins, the Griffiths. Nicholson lived in Cateaton Street (originally "Cat Eaten," now Gresham Street), one street north of Cheapside; Wordsworth often dined with him on Sunday evenings. After dinner, they would go around the corner to the Dissenting chapel in Old Jewry to hear the sermons of Joseph Fawcett, the future author of *The Art of War* (1795) and other political satires. Fawcett was at this time capitalizing on the spectacular revival of the old meeting house's reputation by the radical Dissenter Richard Price, especially his sermon the previous November in praise of the French Revolution. This had provoked Burke's *Reflections on the Revolution in France* (1790), which in turn provoked the "pamphlet wars" of 1791–95: two dozen responses were published during the four months of Wordsworth's residence in London.[16] Price died in 1791, and Fawcett took his place, attracting "the largest and most genteel London audience that ever assembled in a dissenting place of worship"; even the actors Mrs. Siddons and John Kemble attended, to admire Fawcett's projective technique.[17] He would later become Wordsworth's model for the disaffected Solitary in *The Excursion:* "And there with popular talents [he] preach'd the cause / Of Christ and of the new-born Liberty."[18] Both Fawcett and Nicholson were members of the Society for Constitutional Information, and their religious faith in 1791 was newly inspired by the hope that the fires of France might be fanned into reform in England, to remove the political restrictions of the Test and Corporation Acts.

A likely address for Wordsworth would be Wood Street at its intersection with Maiden Lane and Lad Lane, just below Love Lane.[19] These punningly named streets were close to his reality, for Lad Lane connected Cateaton Street, where he met his aunt Threlkeld and visited Samuel Nicholson, to Wood Street and Lothbury, two well-known urban reference points which establish the location, and the occupation, of his "Poor Susan":

> At the corner of Wood Street, when daylight appears,
> Hangs a Thrush that sings loud, it has sung for three years:
> Poor Susan has passed by the spot, and has heard
> In the silence of morning the song of the Bird.
>
> 'Tis a note of enchantment; what ails her? She sees
> A mountain ascending, a vision of trees;
> Bright volumes of vapour through Lothbury glide,
> And a river flows on through the vale of Cheapside.
>
> (1–8)

There were rooks (not thrushes) at the corner of Wood Street and Cheapside in a large plane tree there, a natural landmark which still stands, though it is now a ten-story-high sycamore tree visited only by starlings and pigeons. Wordsworth's Susan is ailing not simply because she misses her home in the country but in all likelihood because she has been cast out from it by her father for sexual misbehavior. This has led her where such transgression led most young girls in the late eighteenth century, into a life of prostitution in the streets. Love Lane was a euphemistically renamed version of the notorious Gropecunt Lane of Elizabethan times. The first plate of Hogarth's *Harlot's Progress* is set outside the Bell Inn in Wood Street, and shows a young girl fresh from York being met by the infamous bawd Mother Needham. Naive country girls arriving unaccompanied in the morning could, if not met by friends, sometimes be trapped and debauched into prostitution by noon of the same day. Procurers would board coaches at the last stop before London to sniff out likely prospects, to be met by "infernal hirelings who . . . put on the demure shew of modesty and sanctity for their deception."[20]

Wordsworth's original last stanza in the poem makes this connection:

> Poor Outcast! return—to receive thee once more
> The house of thy Father will open its door,
> And thou once again, in thy plain russet gown,
> May'st hear the thrush sing from a tree of its own.[21]

This was cut out in response to Lamb's objection ("the last verse of Susan is to be got rid of at all events"), because it made perfectly clear that Susan "was no better than she should be": not a serving maid going to work but a prostitute returning *from* work, wearing a more colorful, provocative gown than her "plain russet" homespun. Wordsworth's late note to the poem throws us even further off the scent of this working girl: "This arose out of my observation of the affecting music of these birds hanging in this way in the London streets during the freshness and stillness of the Spring morning." What it really arose out of, as much of his best poetry always did, was the contrast between a fresh spring morning when he set out lightheartedly for his day's walk, and a tired prostitute he met returning home: a country thrush turned city rook.[22]

Among the many ancient guilds thriving in the City, prostitution was one of the busiest. The "chartered streets" of Blake's "London" were right here, where commercial charters were drawn up, and where "thro' midnight streets" he heard "How the youthful Harlot's curse / Blasts the newborn Infant's tear / And blights with plagues the Marriage hearse." By the estimate of the police magistrate Patrick Colquhoun, one of the first reformers trying to come to grips with the exploding dimensions of human misery in London, nearly 5 percent of the *total* population of the city at this time—about 50,000 women—was composed of prostitutes, in addition to another 5 percent who made up the rest of the criminal classes.[23] This would mean (assuming that women constitute about half of any population) that every tenth woman Wordsworth saw was likely to be a prostitute. But their frequency was in actuality even greater, since many respectable women never ventured out into the public street for fear of insult or assault. The Wood Street and Poultry "compters," verminous little holding jails intended for debtors and felons, were used particularly for prostitutes who tried to rob their patrons; cases charging women with assault and battery against customers were far more common than any directed against prostitution itself.[24] Wordsworth was familiar with the Poultry, the little street connecting Cheapside and the Mansion House; he mentions the famous turtles of its King's Head Tavern (no. 25, exactly at Mansion House corner) in his imitation of Juvenal.[25] A large percentage of the women and girls in Bedlam, two blocks north, were said to have lost their reason through aborted or forbidden or swindled marriage plans, the victims of faithless lovers or harsh parents. Clarissa was still alive, and still threatened, in London in 1791.*

We can just make out one of these women, close to Wordsworth's residence, in a blurred snapshot from *The Prelude:*

> When the great tide of human life stands still,
> The business of the day to come unborn,
> Of that gone by locked up as in the grave;
> . . . empty streets, and sounds
> Unfrequent as in desarts; at late hours
> Of winter evenings when unwholesome rains
> Are falling hard, with people yet astir,
> The feeble salutation from the voice
> Of some unhappy woman now and then
> Heard as we pass, when no one looks about,
> Nothing is listened to.
>
> (VII.631–42)

This reads like a strong first impression. "The business of the day" was at the Royal Exchange, where, as Addison and Steele noted eighty years before, pimps and their prostitutes came out in the evening to traffic among the shops and stalls as the stock traders and commodity buyers left. Wordsworth's "winter evening" is sometime in February 1791. The "we" would be

*Magdalen Hospital in Southwark was for girls who had been literally seduced and abandoned. The Foundling Hospital in Lamb's Conduit Fields had been established fifty years earlier to help stop the widespread practice of murdering unwanted babies, but it was soon swamped with more abandoned infants than it could care for (5,000 out of 15,000 died during one five-year period: that is, it was taking in about 10 a day). By the early 1790s it would only accept babies for a fee of £100, no questions asked: that is, a service limited to rich girls, or their rich lovers. See Mary Cathcart Borer, *An Illustrated Guide to London, 1800* (New York: St. Martin's Press, 1988), 177–78.

Wordsworth and Nicholson returning home, Wordsworth wondering about his pious companion—and himself—neither of whom looks at or says anything to the unhappy woman. In his peculiarly chilling abstraction, they not only ignore her; they listen to "nothing." She is standing in a doorway, as we learn from Wordsworth's wrestling with the lines in manuscript, which might read, "From door or arch a word [?hesi] [?pollu] tant breathed."[26] With this addition earlier words in the passage—"human life," "unborn," and "the grave"—suddenly stand out not as metaphors but as living responses to something actually seen in these mean streets.

Besides challenging his sense of what it meant to be a man in the city, Wordsworth's neighborhood also contributed to his sense of what it meant to be a writer in this society. He was well aware that his hero Milton, in whose Cambridge rooms he had got drunk, had been born in Bread Street, directly across Cheapside from Wood Street.* Though Milton's birthplace was destroyed in the Great Fire, Milton had also lived in St. Giles, Cripplegate, just at the other end of Wood Street, near the turning to Grub Street, the hack writers' slum. A newspaper scandal had arisen around the disinterment of Milton's body in 1790, when St. Giles was being repaired and a memorial to the poet proposed.[27] Some enterprising parish clerks with inside knowledge saw a chance for big profits and dug up the body the night before the official disinterment was scheduled. Before they were caught, they had sold off one rib, ten teeth, and several handfuls of hair. The ensuing recriminations produced a *Narrative of the Disinterment of Milton's Coffin*, plus some strong doubts expressed in the *St. James Chronicle* and other papers as to whether the violated corpse was really Milton's. The dispute continued a lively public life until 1793, when Samuel Whitbread, the Whig brewer and friend of Sheridan, placed a memorial to the poet inside the church. The ironies for poetic reputation in the incident were not lost on Wordsworth, nor the symbolism of Milton's residence's proximity to Grub Street, the degraded antipodes of literary sublimity.

His thoughts were further stimulated in this direction by the enormous publicity leading up to the publication of Boswell's *Life of Johnson* in early May, and the huge success it immediately enjoyed.[28]† The competition to

*The early market character of the City was retained in street names like—besides Love Lane—Milk Street, Beer Lane, Water Lane, Fish Street, Garlick Hill, Pudding Lane, and Grub Street.

†Boswell had been blocked from completing the *Life* for two or three years because of demands on his time from his patron, "the Northern Tyrant," Sir James Lowther, whom he belatedly recognized as "the worst man in the world for a patron" (Hugh Owen, *The Lowther Family* [Chichester: Phillimore, 1990], 301–2). Hence Lowther's bad influence had an impact on the first great modern biography in English—of the last great Neoclassical writer—in a way that parallels his impact on the first great autobiographical poem in the language—of the first great Romantic writer—Wordsworth's *Prelude*.

write the first, or best, biography of—as it then seemed—England's last great literary figure had been intense since Johnson's death in 1784, and Boswell was preceded by two successful competitors, John Hawkins and Hester Thrale Piozzi. The literary press had been whipping up the competition between the rival biographers (aided of course by the rivals themselves) ever since Hawkins's biography appeared in 1787. Although Boswell's brilliant work carried the field with posterity, one side effect it had was a spate of gloomy reflections that there no longer seemed to be any writers of Johnson's stature, especially in poetry. Hogarth's image of "The Poet" as a Grub Street *garreteer* was the popular one, and though Johnson's own career had spanned the immense gap between Grub Street and George III's library, no single author had emerged since his death to occupy his vacated eminence.[29] Boswell's success drew more attention to the vacuum, and we can easily imagine young Wordsworth meditating on it as he turned past Milton's old church on the corner of Wood Street on his way home.

What should he do in London with no obligations and no commitments? What direction did he take, directionless as he was? There is no plot to Wordsworth's first residence in London, but there was plenty of movement: "Free as a colt at pasture on the hills / I *ranged* at large through the metropolis / Month after month" (IX.18–20; italics added). A "ranger" in London slang was a man of the town on the prowl, as in the contemporaneous *Ranger's Magazine,* an illustrated guide to the prostitutes of Covent Garden, listing names, addresses, prices, and specialities.[30] Is that "colt" ranging at pasture another one of Wordsworth's naturalizing metaphors? Wordsworth could sound the note of the insouciant man-about-town when he wanted to: "Think not however that I had not many very pleasant hours; a man must be unfortunate indeed who resides four months in Town without some of his time being disposed of in such a manner, as he would forget with reluctance."[31]

For the most part, he walked, a four-month urban tour to complement his recent three-month mountain tour of the Picturesque-Sublime. He lived "chearfully abroad / With fancy on the stir from day to day, / And all my young affections out of doors." Wordsworth entered into his majority, his twenty-first birthday, in London, not in Grasmere. Especially noteworthy, in light of his later reputation, is Wordsworth's fascination with dramatic spectacle. He went to shows of all kinds, especially at the lower end of the price scale. One still goes to London to see as many shows as possible, and Wordsworth took in the whole city as a show, from jugglers and prostitutes and beggars in the streets, through legitimate and illegitimate theater, to popular Anglican and Dissenting preachers and the stirring debates in Parliament. Later, in *The Prelude,* he remembered all this as a "domination of the eye" from which he had to recover, but at the time, on the spot, he experienced it as a passion. Book VII of *The Prelude* is one of the most exciting representations of the energy of urban life in English literature; it compares favorably to the achievement of London's later presiding literary genius, Charles Dickens.[32]

Thinking of modern London, one may not deem it excessive to roam about the city for four months. But London in 1791 was far smaller than it is now, and since Wordsworth spent most of his time outdoors his coverage was very thorough indeed. The city, including Westminster and Southwark, had barely a million inhabitants—though this made it, to be sure, the largest city in Europe. Neighborhoods like Islington, Bethnal Green, and Hammersmith were of course just where they are today, but they were villages separated from the main body of the metropolis by open fields and extensive market gardens. Most of the city was comprehended within a very compact compass, from Park Lane on the west to the Tower on the east, and from the river north to Oxford Street. The British Museum was there—as Montague House—but there were very few buildings behind it. A new thoroughfare was emerging along Oxford Street, but it was the northern limit of the town, while the present Euston Road, part of the "New Road" from Paddington to Islington, was a kind of suburban bypass. On a diagonal, the built-up area of the city ran from Tyburn or Cumberland Gate (Marble Arch) in the northwest to the Tower in the southeast, and from Westminster Abbey and Hall in the southwest to Spitalfields in the northeast. The entire metropolis was only about four miles across in any direction, no challenge for a walker like Wordsworth. He could easily on any day go from his lodgings in the City to one edge of the city, then back across to the opposite edge, and still return to his rooms in good time for dinner at nine o'clock.

Despite its dirt, Georgian London was really quite beautiful, with over three hundred churches (fifty of them Wren reconstructions), whose slender spires were almost the only structures over fifty feet high, two new bridges, and a markedly rural aspect. Wordsworth was seeing the last of the best of eighteenth-century London, before a generation-long war broke out in 1793, which, by the rapid industrialization it stimulated, helped create the much more hellish city of Dickens's youth. The eighteenth century saw "the birth of the consumer society," and by 1791 the birth was safely accomplished, and London was its name.[33] There was plenty of poverty and degradation in the London of the early 1790s, but little of the grinding, systemic hopelessness of early Victorian times. To a considerable degree the poor were still able to help themselves, not least by means of the very shows, quackeries, prostitutions, and other amusements which caught Wordsworth's eye. Every tenth woman might be a prostitute, but she had plenty of space to work in: there was one tavern for every two hundred inhabitants.[34] Small wonder that the whole city appeared to Wordsworth as one huge advertisement:

> Shop after shop, with symbols, blazoned names,
> And all the tradesman's honours overhead:
> Here, fronts of houses, like a title-page
> With letters huge inscribed from top to toe;
> Stationed above the door like guardian saints . . . .
>
> (VII.174–78)

His movements in the first four months of 1791 can be charted along two axes. One, running from east to west, was the great thoroughfare formed by Cheapside, Ludgate Hill, Fleet Street, and the Strand, to Charing Cross, thence curving down to Whitehall. No less an authority than M. de Saussure, the conqueror of Mont Blanc, considered this the finest street in all Europe. It was in effect London's High Street: most of the city lay within half a mile, mostly to the north, of this long arc. Wordsworth arranged his description of London roughly along this line, conducting us on a walking day tour that we can still follow. His other, less traveled route went from south to north, from the City out to "half-rural Sadler's Wells" and the open fields beyond.

Stepping westward on his favorite walk from Cheapside, he came immediately into St. Paul's Churchyard, the center for bookshops and printers. He entered the lively shop of his future publisher, Joseph Johnson, at no. 72, where he might see on any given day the rising stars of the exploding radical publishing universe, William Godwin, Mary Wollstonecraft, even Tom Paine himself—and perhaps glimpse Johnson's strange engraver, William Blake. All of them were arming for the polemical wars provoked by Burke's *Reflections,* which Wordsworth himself would enter two years later. At no. 65 was the shop of John Newbery, first serious publisher of children's books in England, whose productions influenced both Blake and Wordsworth. One street north, in Paternoster Row, was the shop of his future longtime publisher, Longmans-Owen-Rees. At the time, however, he had more regard "for the humble Bookstalls in the streets."[35] These specialized in pathetic ballads, sensational accounts of robberies and murders, and ghost and monster stories, frequently illustrated with engravings "of the altogether most horrible contents."[36] This was the kind of literature that Wordsworth would later take it as his life's mission to counteract ("idle and extravagant stories in verse"), but he loved it as a child, and its appeal was not lost on him yet: "Wild produce, hedgerow fruit, on all sides hung / To lure the sauntering traveller from his track" (IX.33–34).

Pushing through the massive congestion of Ludgate Hill, Wordsworth crossed Old Bailey, the street that led up to Ludgate and Newgate prisons, the latter recently rebuilt after its destruction in the Gordon Riots of 1780. He heard "the brawls of lawyers in their courts," and saw the Quaker Elizabeth Fry carrying on the heroic work of John Howard (who had died the year before) to improve prison conditions. At the bottom of the hill, he came to the Fleet debtors' prison and the relics of its "marrying inns." These sleazy dives, thriving on loopholes in the debt laws which made marriage a way to escape imprisonment, had been largely put out of business by Lord Hardwicke's act of 1753, but many still carried provocative signs of grotesquely coupled men and women, which Wordsworth's description sanitizes into "allegoric shapes, female or male"; they were anything but allegorical.[37] To enter Fleet Street, he crossed New Bridge Road, which led to "the river proudly bridged": Blackfriars Bridge, barely twenty years old and considered the most beautiful bridge in the country. It was one of only three bridges in London at the time, along with the also new Westminster Bridge (1750) to its west, and the old and oft-rebuilt London Bridge, which led into the City on the east. Crossing what is now Farringdon Road, Wordsworth glimpsed the little Fleet River, or ditch, soon to be entirely covered by pavements. London's first covered sewer, constructed along one side of the Strand, ran into this, but it was still ten years in the future, so he picked his way carefully.[38]

Entering Fleet Street, he found more bookshops and printers, the beginnings of the modern newspaper industry. The *Morning Advertiser* was in the first block, at no. 127. The liberal *Morning Post* (founded 1772) was regaining ground against its new rival, the *Times* (1785), and would soon, under the editorship of Daniel Stuart, return to a fully competitive position, partly by employing brilliant young university men like Coleridge, Southey, and Wordsworth. However, the fledgling newspaper offices were less evident than the inns, which from the Fleet to Charing Cross set up shows in their yards to pull customers out of the passing tide of humanity. Here Wordsworth observed, "with basket at his waist, / The Jew; the stately and slow-moving Turk, / With freight of slippers piled beneath his arm." There was indeed an old Turk who for years plied the area between Cornhill and the Strand, "well known for the soundness of his wares," but, by the end of decade, outdone by Jewish competitors.[39]

He frequently paused at Chancery Lane, a busy corner then as now, for his observations here are particularly exact. Isaac Newton's head was one of the "physiognomies of real men" (VII.180–82) over the door of Rackstraw's Museum of dead monstrosities near the corner at no. 197; it soon became the *Albion,* where Charles Lamb joked that it was "our occupation . . . to write treason"[40]—another example of a Romantic writer facetiously distancing himself from his Jacobin youth. At no. 193 was a popular Whig tavern, the Green Man, covered with carvings. Across the street at no. 17 was Mrs. Salmon's waxwork, featuring effigies of England's kings and queens. This was "the waxwork" Wordsworth saw in 1791, conflated by the time he came to write *The Prelude* with Mme Tussaud's collection, brought over to London in 1802, and offering, as competition for Mrs. Salmon, effigies of the dead bodies of France's royal victims of the Terror.[41] Dead and disgraced royalty were coming to be more marketable than live ones, as the modern era dawned.

From Chancery Lane, Wordsworth takes us forward with a darting skill that cannot be matched by paraphrase. He gives "the look and aspect of the place,"

> The broad highway appearance, as it strikes
> On strangers of all ages, the quick dance
> Of colours, lights and forms, the Babel din,
> The endless stream of men and moving things,
> From hour to hour the illimitable walk
> Still among streets, with clouds and sky above,
> The wealth, the bustle and the eagerness,
> The glittering chariots with their pampered steeds,
> Stalls, barrows, porters, midway in the street
> The scavenger that begs with hat in hand,
> The labouring hackney-coaches, the rash speed
> Of coaches travelling far, whirled on with horn
> Loud blowing, and the sturdy drayman's team
> Ascending from some alley of the Thames
> And striking right across the crowded Strand
> Till the fore-horse veer round with punctual skill . . . .
>
> (VII.154–70)

The breathless sequence ends with the kind of arresting detail that we might call Dickensian, but it is indubitably Wordsworthian. It brings us exactly to the neighborhood of the Savoy, where the Fleet took on a "broad highway appearance" as it passed out of the City at Temple Bar and flowed around St. Clements Church to become the Strand.

For relief from all the noise, Wordsworth on his first walks turned aside and followed the side streets: "Conducted through those labyrinths unawares / To privileged regions and inviolate, / Where from their aery lodges studious lawyers / Look out on waters, walks, and gardens green" (VII.201–4). These are the Middle and Inner Temples near St. Clements at the old Temple Bar, for only they of all the Inns of Court "look out on waters." But all had "walks, and gardens green," and Wordsworth had acquaintances at many of the lawyers' inns who gained him admission, such as John Myers at Grey's Inn, and John Tweddell and Felix Vaughan.

Moving "thence back into the throng" of the Strand, Wordsworth came into the heart of his urban delights. First, directly opposite Somerset House and the Savoy, he saw Exeter 'Change, the location of the menagerie he describes in VII.246–47, and of Philippe de Loutherbourg's Eidophusikon ("moving-image machine"): "the painter—fashioning a work / To Nature's circumambient scenery." It also housed Robert Barker's "Panorama."[42] When Wordsworth cites "The Firth of Forth, and Edinburgh, throned / On crags," he is exactly contemporary and accurate, for Barker's panorama featuring these views was the only one in London in 1791. Such detailed coincidences increase our confidence that much of the rest of *Prelude* VII is equally contemporaneous. When he says that the diorama's perspectives "Plant us on some lofty pinnacle" like "angels or commissioned spirits" (VII.260–61), he is simultaneously alluding to the angels in *Paradise Lost* eyeing Eden and referring to the fact that Barker's Edinburgh perspective was soon replaced by one of London itself, painted by Barker and his brother from the top of the huge Albion Sugar Mills at the south end of Blackfriars Bridge (see illustration)—a unique view, as it turned out, since the mills burned down in March 1791.[43] Besides large-scale views the Exeter 'Change entertainment complex also offered vast miniature replicas of famous sights of Italy and Greece, done with an exactitude—"All that the traveller sees when he is there" (280)—that Wordsworth could appreciate, having been a minute observer in the Alps just six months earlier.

A few steps up from Exeter 'Change brought him to the Drury Lane theater, where Sarah Siddons and her brother John Kemble were the stars, under the brilliant, erratic direction of Richard Brinsley Sheridan, leading playwright of the preceding generation and a politician very much of this one. The spring season of 1791 was Drury Lane's last for nearly three years; it closed down in June for rebuilding. Its finances were in confusion and it was unsafe structurally, not to mention the riots and protests that frequently broke out when the crowds did not get what they liked, or disliked what they got.[44] Mrs. Dorothea ("Dora" or "Dolly") Jordan, "the Muse of Comedy" to Siddons's Tragic Muse, contributed to the debacle of 1791 by leaving the theater and her lover of five years, Richard Ford (son of Sheridan's partner), to set up housekeeping with George III's son William, the duke of Clarence.[45] Both she and Ford would touch significantly on Wordsworth's life before the decade was out. It was here, "within the walls of Drury's splendid house,"[46] that Wordsworth saw one of his most startling urban sights, a prostitute's child seated on the bar during the interval of a play.

Upon a board,
Whence an attendant of the theatre
Served out refreshments, had this child been placed,
And there he sate environed with a ring
Of chance spectators, chiefly dissolute men
And shameless women—treated and caressed—
Ate, drank, and with the fruit and glasses played,
While oaths, indecent speech, and ribaldry
Were rife about him as are songs of birds
In springtime after showers.

(VII.383–92)

As with his sight of Poor Susan, it is the starkness of contrast that stimulates the visionary moment that follows, where the child is compared to the children of Israel in Nebuchadnezzar's fiery furnace. The image was part of his complicated reaction to what "the daring brotherhood" of London hack playwrights had dared to do with the story of Mary Robinson's bigamous seduction and abandonment in the Lake District, an event of 1799 recounted in a play of 1803, *The Beauty of Buttermere.* But the image itself is from 1791, when Wordsworth himself was among the "chance spectators" at the bar. Many actresses were prostitutes, and some prostitutes were actresses; the area around Drury Lane and Covent Garden was rife with them and their pimps and children. The coffeehouses in this area were considered little better than brothels, but they were so well established that they were not considered "disorderly" houses in contemporary usage.[47] Preeminent among them were the Rose, featured in Hogarth's *Rake's Progress,* and the Shakespeare's Head, mentioned in Wordsworth's London progress poem (VII.182).

Coming back down into the Strand from this detour, he passed genteelly dressed streetwalkers who in groups of five or six importuned passersby to "Come and have a drink, dearie." (The going rate here was two or three shillings—for a woman, not a drink, which cost twopence.)[48] Wordsworth found himself opposite the Beaufort Buildings, soon the residence of the radical orator John Thelwall, fast rising to public prominence, who sometimes held meetings in his rooms here to frustrate infiltration by Pitt's informers. Wordsworth knew of Thelwall in 1791; Thelwall gradually learned about Coleridge from his political speeches and essays during the 1790s; by the end of the decade he would seek out Coleridge and Wordsworth in their West Country retreat as almost his last friends in the country.

Continuing west, Wordsworth came to the Royal Adelphi Terrace, one of the most expensive of the new town house developments, abutting the Adelphi Wharves, and dominated from the Strand by a huge sign of "the attractive head / Of some quack-doctor, famous in his day" (VII.183).[49] This was James Graham (1745–1794), an enterprising Scotsman whose "Temple of Health and Hymen" was notorious for its "Celestial Bed," a supposed cure for sterility and impotence, aimed at the idle rich and noted for its fantastic advertising (see cartoon). Here, for the staggering price of £50, a couple could lie on a nine-by-twelve-foot mattress, "filled with the strongest, most springy hair, produced at vast expense from the tails of English stallions which are elastic to the highest degree," beneath a mirrored dome supported by forty glass pillars, serenaded by live birds and mechanical musical instruments.[50] Circulating magnets added their potency to the "elastic" powers of stallions' hair. The contraption was calculated to produce "both pleasure and results, for the bed could be tilted after coition, presumably to aid conception."[51] The scientific aura of the place was meretricious; if a patron didn't have a partner, he could select one from the teenage Goddesses of Youth and Health assisting the good doctor, one of whom was the beautiful Emma who later became Lady Hamilton. The price for this early sex clinic was of course far too high for any but the very rich; it was a marketing ploy that we would now call a "loss leader," since for the (comparatively) trifling sum of two guineas one could gain admission to see the amazing device and hear a lecture on sex and health. This reduced rate did not return Graham a sufficient profit, but the advertising he gained by the business helped him succeed in his next venture, cosmetic mud baths.

Even two guineas would have been beyond Wordsworth's means, supposing he wanted any lectures on sex or health. But it is noteworthy that he singles out this one of London's sights for emphatic mention, because it quite likely *was not there* in 1791. Graham had sold out in 1783, when he was satirized as the Emperor of the Quacks in George Colman's play *The Genius of Nonsense*.[52] But his immense sign was still there, and Wordsworth seems to have been very interested in Graham's notorious sex machine, for he returned to it in his Juvenal satire of 1795. By then he was scoffing at Graham's mud bath business, but he concludes with a particularly detailed sarcasm recollecting Graham's earlier sensation:

> For them [the rich] though all the portals open stand
> Of Health's own temple at her Graham's command
> And the great high-priest baffling Death and Sin
> Earth [i.e., bury] each immortal idiot to the chin,
> Ask of these wretched beings worse than dead
> If on the couch celestial gold can shed
> The coarser blessings of a Peasant's bed.[53]

The concluding rhetorical question seems to want a negative response, but its reference is ambiguous, as to whether it means producing children or gaining sexual pleasure, or both. That the question was important to

Wordsworth beyond the level of a mere joke is indicated by his Miltonic allusion to Graham as Satan, in his encounter with the most perversely incestuous couple in English literature, his daughter Sin, whom he conceived and then raped, and her offspring Death, who continually rapes and gets children upon his own mother. No allusion to Milton is innocent in Wordsworth's poetry, but those with sexual overtones usually indicate heavily loaded psychological material. Such historical and literary details are recondite, but they match perfectly with other more obvious points of reference in Wordsworth's particular, but by no means abnormal, fascination with the spectacles of sexuality in London.

Immediately after the Adelphi Terrace, Wordsworth crossed Buckingham Street and in all likelihood stopped at the bookshop of William Mathews's father, at no. 18 Strand. Mathews himself was at this time struggling unhappily to harness himself in the profession of schoolmaster in Leicester, but Wordsworth would have been very rude not to have introduced himself, for Mathews was one of his best friends, and he knew that Mathews's father was a kind man, despite the Methodist zealots who infested his shop, making young Mathews's life a misery.[54]

Just before reaching Charing Cross, Wordsworth passed another important political landmark, the Crown & Anchor inn, site of dinners celebrating each anniversary of the fall of the Bastille. It soon became one of the hotly contested civic symbols in this era of rapid political change. In 1791 "Crown & Anchor men" became an epithet for disaffected radicals, thanks to the belittling rhetoric of Burke's *Reflections.* But scarcely more than a year afterward the phrase came to stand for rabid reactionism, when John Reeves's Association for the Preservation of Property from Republicans and Levellers began meeting there.

At Charing Cross, Wordsworth turned down Whitehall to Westminster, passing "from entertainments that are such / Professedly, to others titled higher . . . Where senators, tongue-favoured men, perform, / Admired and envied" (VII.517–24). Wordsworth was not "tongue-favoured" for speech making, though he often held forth at length in private conversation. But he envied those who were, particularly the three great speakers who dominated Parliament at this time: William Pitt the Younger, Edmund Burke, and Charles James Fox. Their oratory has rarely been matched in parliamentary annals, and in the spring of 1791 they clashed on issue after issue provoked by the French Revolution. Pitt and Fox performed a virtual duet throughout the session, rising about forty times each to speak; Burke spoke twenty times, but his speeches were very long: he earned the nickname Dinner Bell because members often fled for the exits whenever he rose. At the beginning of the session he and Fox were still speaking to each other and giving at least the appearance of friendly cooperation, but for the last time.

From early February to early June, almost exactly the period of Wordsworth's London residence, Parliament was in one of its most dramatic sessions in history, reaching a climax on May 6, when Burke and Fox had their final falling-out. Their rupture signaled that men of good will could no longer agree to disagree on the significance of the French Revolution, but would have to take stands that broke old patterns of proper behavior and, indeed, old conceptions of human nature itself. British enthusiasm for the French Revolution had just crested, but it soon began to recede rapidly. (The fashion for republican-style cropped hair began in 1791, and Wordsworth adopted it instead of the "rimey" powder he had used at Cambridge.)[55] Burke's *Reflections,* which had appeared the preceding November, was the breakwater which eventually stemmed the tide of revolutionary zeal, but it was being badly battered in early 1791; Burke lamented that it "stood an object of odium."[56] Mary Wollstonecraft's *Vindication of the Rights of Man* had been first into the lists against it; of the two dozen counterattacks published during Wordsworth's London residence, Tom Paine's *Rights of Man* was the first, from Johnson in late February, and James Mackintosh's *Vindiciae Gallicae* on May 7 was the last.[57]

The first attraction was Pitt, whose brilliant orations had already achieved the emerging standard of modern mass politics: they sounded impressive even though it was hard to say exactly what he meant. Wordsworth attested that he had "often seen Mr. Pitt upon . . . the floor of the House of Commons,"[58] and he makes a pun on the prime minister when he describes "the beating heart / When one among the *prime* of these rose up" (VII.524–25; italics added). But Wordsworth's apparent praise is only a setup for a satiric undercutting, as Pitt's manner soon outstrips his matter: "Words follow words, sense seems to follow sense— / What memory and what logic!—till the strain / Transcendent, superhuman as it is, / Grows tedious even in a young man's ear" (VII.540–43).

But Fox and Burke made the more lasting impression. Wordsworth said that one "always went from Burke with your mind filled; from Fox with your feelings excited; and from Pitt with wonder at his having the power to make the worse appear the better reason."[59] Wordsworth added his praise to the "Genius of Burke!" to Book VII in 1832, but in the first drafts of the addition he gives almost equal homage to Fox. His details suggest that he saw them as they sat and talked, for they were close enough to overhear each other's whispers: Westminster Hall was a much smaller room than the present parliamentary chambers. Wordsworth pictures Fox as one of the "younger brethren" who sat "Listening beside thee—no longer near / Yet still in heart thy friend. Illustrious Fox / Thy grateful Pupil. In the power of words / Thundering & Lightening when *his* turn shall come / A British Pericles."[60]

It is quite likely that Wordsworth was in attendance for the confrontations between Fox and Burke, for he was there "night by night,"[61] and sessions often ran into the early morning hours. We could expect him to have been present on April 18–19, when Wilberforce made his motion against the slave trade. Pitt, Fox, and Burke all supported him, but to no avail; the motion lost, 163 to 88. After temporarily uniting on this lost liberal cause, Fox and Burke immediately resumed their sparring. Public attention to their conflict was intense; their speeches were reported in detail in the newspapers, and it was clear at the adjournment on April 29 that the two men must confront each other directly when debate resumed after a week's recess. On May 6 Burke began laboriously by casting himself as an old man, very much put upon, but Fox waited patiently through his speech, not calling him to order as other MPs tried to do. When Fox did rise to answer, his first words deprecated his own "feeble powers . . . compared to those of his right honorable friend, whom he must call his master, for he had taught him everything he knew in politics."[62] Wordsworth's manuscript lines seem to catch this moment exactly, like a contemporary newspaper cartoon, "The Scholar lamenting the departure of his Master," which featured Fox as sniveling urchin schoolboy and Burke as a stern old pedagogue. Indeed, Wordsworth may have been prompted by a similar image used by Burke at the time, recalling the young Fox being brought to him at age fourteen, full of promise, in a scene marked with biblical overtones of the young Samuel or Jesus being brought before their elders. But Burke's rhetorical thrust was far different, when he concluded that this man, whom he had encouraged from his youth into "the most able, eloquent, and powerful [adversary] that was ever encountered," now dared to accuse him of deserting his principles![63]

Wordsworth's lines in *The Prelude* praising Burke are not simply evidence of his elderly conservatism. They actually give a fuller view of his earlier self, and of the excitement that these mighty antagonists made on "a youth . . . in ancient story versed, whose breast had heaved / Under the weight of classic eloquence," and who could not but "sit, see, and hear," thankful and inspired.[64] Both Fox and Burke loaded their speeches with classical and literary allusions, and Wordsworth's later predilection for alluding to *Paradise Lost* and *Macbeth* when writing about the French Revolution was certainly stimulated by Burke's rhetoric.[65] On the fateful sixth of May, Burke satirically cast the revolutionaries and their English sympathizers as the witches in *Macbeth,* full of "Hubble bubble / Toil and trouble," when they stirred the pot of social ferment—leaving the hint, for those who wished to take it, that Fox was the Macbeth of the moment.

The actual topics of this debate, contrary to what we might think, were not the French Revolution or domestic dissent but the war between Russia and Turkey, the regulation of the Corn Laws, and the new constitution for the government of Quebec. However, there was hardly a topic on which the question of revolution versus reform did not obtrude itself, and it was on the Quebec question that Burke and Fox finally broke. This is not so surprising, for in talking about framing a constitution, even for a faraway province, they inevitably entered into the nature of constitutions per se and of the legal or illegal conventions that might establish them. It was on the technical question of whether Burke or Fox were out of order in going into these larger constitutional issues that they reached an impasse. They attained chilling heights of ironical deference to each other, seeking to avoid a direct confrontation while coming ever nearer to one. Burke, who went increasingly over the top when anything approaching fundamental questions of government arose, was the one most frequently called to order, especially when he said that adopting the proposed Quebec constitution would be like shipping a cargo of *The Rights of Man* to the colonies, which he compared to shipping them a bale of infected cotton from Marseilles. And besides (he could not resist adding), what had this vaunted French Revolution accomplished after two years, anyway? Everyone was well aware that another constitutional debate was going on simultaneously across the Channel, where the National Convention was thrashing out the document that would make France—for one more year—a constitutional monarchy. (Louis was forced to swear allegiance to the new document after he was brought back from his disastrous flight to Varennes in late June.)

Fox, apparently rising to defend Burke, delivered instead the cutting retort that Burke could hardly be called out of order when the order of the day seemed to be that any man could rise and abuse any government he chose. Burke, amid conflicting cries of "Order! Go on! Order! Go on!," sardonically replied that there was such an enthusiasm for order that it was hard to go on, but he thanked God the English government was as yet "untainted with the French malady." This sly thrust drew smiles, but Fox's Whigs immediately demanded that if Burke knew of any actual design afoot to overturn the English constitution he should make a direct charge. Fox put his finger on Burke's main rhetorical tactic when he observed that much was being claimed about "the danger of theory" versus "the safety of practice." But he in turn could not resist repeating his earlier provocative claim (on April 15) that the French Revolution was "on the whole, one of the most glorious events in the history of mankind." Burke, in a "grave and governed tone of voice," said he had patiently sat through "the most disorderly speech that perhaps was ever delivered in the House." Over Fox's whispered protest, he said he must put his duty to the constitution above friendship, and declared their friendship at an end. Fox rose to reply, but was unable to for several minutes, standing alone with tears running down his cheeks.

Leaving these heated scenes of national passion, Wordsworth walked through fashionable Westminster, passing "processions, equipages, lords and dukes" until he came to "the King's palace" (VII.110–11). This was the new town mansion built by the duke of Buckingham in 1762, recently bought by George III as a residence for his large family. Ever the devoted husband, he wanted to call it the Queen's Palace, but the name never caught on, and through many expansions that have dwarfed the original structure it is still associated with the name of Buckingham.

More frequently, Wordsworth headed in the other direction from Parliament, visiting the nearby pleasure park of Ranelagh, across the market gardens of Chelsea, or, crossing over Westminster Bridge, Vauxhall Gardens:

> Vauxhall and Ranelagh, I then had heard
> Of your green groves and wilderness of lamps,
> Your gorgeous ladies, fairy cataracts,
> And pageant fireworks.
>
> (VII.123–26)

He visited Ranelagh first, for, besides being the more fashionable of the two,[66] it was an all-weather facility, and he arrived in February. It featured a huge open fireplace several stories high in its central rotunda, around which long dining tables were deployed, where hundreds of diners could be accommodated at a single sitting, looked down on by wealthier patrons seated in galleries. Crowds of strollers revolved around this vast circle, for the main entertainment at both places, beyond what the management offered, was to see and be seen, to ogle and to preen. Later in the spring Vauxhall reopened across the river in Lambeth, a fresh-air rural fantasia that appealed more to Wordsworth. It declined steadily in gentility through the 1790s, attracting increasing numbers of London "cits," and a good many of its "gorgeous ladies" were prostitutes, who were encountered at these pleasure gardens as reliably as at Covent Garden, though here they cultivated a more elegant appearance: "Where each spruce nymph from city compters free / Sips the froth'd syllabub or fragrant tea."[67]

From here, at the end of a long day, Wordsworth turned toward home, retracing his steps back through Westminster and along the Strand and Fleet to his lodging in the City. He took this long east–west walk, with countless variations and detours, many times during his four months in London.

His other favorite walking route was more northerly, past Smithfield and Gray's Inn to Sadler's Wells at New River Head, and into the fields between Clerkenwell Green and the hamlet of Pentonville. Sadler's Wells was only a mile and a half away from Wordsworth's lodgings near the Exchange, and not far removed in time from when it had been a watering hole for horse saddlers. It was a quarter of a mile beyond any urban buildings, and almost that far south of Pentonville—hence very literally, *"half*-rural Sadler's Wells." In this rural amusement arcade, among the "lowest" and "humblest" the city had to offer, Wordsworth "more than once" took his seat to see "singers, rope-dancers, giants and dwarfs, / Clowns, conjurors, posture-masters, harlequins, / Amid the uproar of the rabblement, / Perform their feats" (VII.291–97). When he later scorned those who talked about "a *taste* for Poetry . . . as if it were a thing as indifferent as a taste for Rope-dancing," he knew whereof he spoke, on both amusements. The literal accuracy of his description—which might otherwise be read as only a vague impressionistic catalog—is noteworthy. A young German lady visiting Sadler's Wells five years earlier, gives details of a very similar program: "In three hours we witnessed nine kinds of stage craft. First, a comedy, then a ballet, followed by a rope-walker, after this a pantomime, next some balancing tricks, an operette, and the most miraculous feats by a strong man, another comedy, and finally a second operette."[68] She also comments on the mixture of classes at such entertainments, though less favorably than Wordsworth, who, by the time he wrote his lines in 1803–4, was at pains to excuse his presence among the "the rabblement" by claiming it as a kind of research trip into the lower reaches of Imagination: "Nor was it mean delight / To watch crude Nature work in untaught minds, / To note the laws and progress of belief" (VII.297–99).

Past Lincoln's and Gray's inns, the streets were newer, hence "wider" (VII.207), allowing "straggling breezes of suburban air." The "files of ballads" he saw "dangle from dead walls" may have been exactly at Cumberland Gate (Marble Arch), where special permission was granted for this kind of display, since ballads were often represented to be the final lament or confessions of criminals hanged here on Tyburn's triple gallows.[69] But public executions had been moved to Newgate in 1783, putting an end to the eight-times-yearly "execution fairs" at Tyburn, and this manner of displaying ballads for sale was more widely spread around the town by 1791.

"As on the broadening causeway we advance" (VII.215)—City Road or Gray's Inn Road—Wordsworth saw a beggar whose very name, neighborhood, and mode of operation have been identified:

> Behold a face turned up towards us, strong
> In lineaments, and red with over-toil:
> 'Tis one perhaps already met elsewhere,
> A travelling cripple, by the trunk cut short,
> And stumping with his arms.
>
> (VII.216–21)

This was Samuel Horsey, a.k.a. the King of the Beggars, later recalled in Lamb's essay "The Decay of Beggars in the Metropolis" for his "sailor-like complexion."[70] Wordsworth's next vignette, of a sidewalk artist, begins, "In sailor's garb": perhaps a detail transferred from Horsey. Lamb grew up in the same area of London that Wordsworth was now living in, and was there in 1791, having just completed his schooling with Coleridge at Christ's Hospital, three streets above Cheapside. Horsey's main beat was very much in Wordsworth's neighborhood, running from Bow Church in Cheapside north along Wood Street, and then back down Aldgate to St. Paul's. Hence he was more than likely "one perhaps already met elsewhere," with no "perhaps" about it. There were two stories of how Horsey lost his legs: either in the Gordon Riots of 1780 or in a cannonade at sea. But there was general agreement that, though "half a Hercules," he was twice a man, for he openly kept two wives, satisfying them both with his vigor and, perhaps more impressively, his wealth, for he was able to give them each enough money to keep them from fighting. We often skip over such pictures of urban energy in Wordsworth's London, in our haste to fasten on his supposedly more characteristic pathetic solitaries, such as the Blind Beggar. But the facts of Horsey's frank, successful bigamy surely resonated at some level of Wordsworth's mind when he wrote Book VII's lines about Mary of Buttermere's bigamous seducer.

On his other route out to Sadler's Wells, Wordsworth passed by Lamb's "old blind Tobits that used to line the wall of Lincoln's Inn Garden . . . casting up their ruined orbs to catch a ray of pity, and (if possible) of light." One of these could very well have been Wordsworth's Blind Beggar:

> . . . who, with upright face,
> Stood propped against a wall, upon his chest
> Wearing a written paper, to explain
> The story of the man, and who he was.
> My mind did at this spectacle turn round
> As with the might of waters, and it seemed
> To me that in this label was a type
> Or emblem of the utmost that we know
> Both of ourselves and of the universe . . . .
> (VII.612–20)

His conclusion, though rhetorically impressive, is a bit histrionic for the twenty-one-year-old urban tourist who saw the beggar, though not for the transcendentalist thirty-four-year-old poet who made him into a symbol. Wordsworth's amazement that so many people could live so close to each other without knowing each other is certainly a reaction of 1791; the generalizations he built upon it are a later growth.

After a day in the country or an afternoon at Sadler's Wells, he returned "homeward through the thickening hubbub" (VII.227), to his quarters in the City. More foreigners lived in this mercantile section than anywhere else, with its India House, South Sea House, and Post Office, and Wordsworth drew upon the fact to conclude his perambulatory catalog with a stylized representation of the four points of the world's compass in his own London neighborhood:

> . . . all specimens of man
> Through all the colours which the sun bestows,
> And every character of form and face:
> The Swede, the Russian; from the genial south,
> The Frenchman and the Spaniard; from remote
> America, the hunter Indian; Moors,
> Malays, Lascars, the Tartar and Chinese,
> And Negro ladies in white muslin gowns.
> (VII.236–44)*

The strong contrast in the last detail had, as contrasts always did for him, a strangely conclusive effect. Though later a good friend of Thomas Clarkson and already well acquainted with William Wilberforce, the moral and political heroes of the fight against the slave trade, Wordsworth was always struck by the sight of black people in England, as in another of his London snapshots, "the silver-collared negro with his timbrel" (VII.677). He remarked a similar contrast in a black woman on the boat to Hamburg in 1798, and in later years he and Dorothy assayed a small joke about Toussaint L'Ouverture that did not go down well with the Clarksons. That Wordsworth participated in the cultural racism of his time is not surprising; the specifically biographical point here is that this strong, black-and-white sense of difference graphically illustrates the contrasts of London which set his mind in motion at almost every turn. The last and most dramatic of these came at Bartholomew Fair.

His fullest experience of Bartholomew Fair dates from 1802, when he and Dorothy were escorted there by Charles and Mary Lamb. But he was very familiar with its location, Smithfield, from all of his visits to London, and especially from his residence in 1791, for the Smithfield markets began at the head of Wood Street, just west of the Barbican.[71] Saint Bartholomew's Day is September 3; the fair dates were technically September 3–7, but in fact it

*Wordsworth's description owes something to Addison's essay on the Royal Exchange: "Sometimes I am jostled among a Body of *Armenians:* Sometimes I am lost in a Crowd of *Jews;* and sometimes make one in a Groupe of *Dutch-men.* I am a *Dane, Swede,* or *French-man* at different times" (May 19, 1711). Wordsworth was reading the *Spectator* that summer (*LEY,* 56).

ran for a good two weeks, by far the largest of London's many fairs.

He presents the fair's wild hodgepodge of novelties as ostensibly destructive of "the whole creative powers of man" (VII.655), but the verbal energy of his description belies his thesis, matching that of Rowlandson's print (see illustration), and wonderfully summing up the visual attractions that drew him on throughout his "Residence in London."

> . . . the open space, through every nook
> Of the wide area, twinkles, is alive
> With heads; the midway region and above
> Is thronged with staring pictures and huge scrolls,
> Dumb proclamations of the prodigies;
> And chattering monkeys dangling from their poles,
> And children whirling in their roundabouts;
> . . . buffoons against buffoons
> Grimacing, writhing, screaming; him who grinds
> The hurdy-gurdy, at the fiddle weaves,
> Rattles the salt-box, thumps the kettle-drum,
> And him who at the trumpet puffs his cheeks,
> The silver-collared negro with his timbrel,
> Equestrians, tumblers, women, girls, and boys,
> Blue-breeched, pink-vested, and with towering plumes.
> All moveables of wonder from all parts
> Are here, albinos, painted Indians, dwarfs,
> The horse of knowledge, and the learned pig,
> The stone-eater, the man that swallows fire,
> Giants, ventriloquists, the invisible girl,
> The bust that speaks and moves its goggling eyes,
> The waxwork, clockwork, all the marvellous craft
> Of modern Merlins, wild beasts, puppet-shows,
> All out-o'-th'-way, far-fetched, perverted things,
> All freaks of Nature, all Promethean thoughts
> Of man—his dulness, madness, and their feats,
> All jumbled up together to make up
> This parliament of monsters. Tents and booths
> Meanwhile—as if the whole were one vast mill—
> Are vomiting, receiving, on all sides,
> Men, women, three-years' children, babes in arms.
> (VII.663–95)

It requires a very special perspective to call a city crowd enjoying itself a "parliament of monsters"—which is not to say that Bartholomew Fair was at all innocent. But the detail that makes this an impression from 1791, that fits best with other urban details in Wordsworth's synoptic account in Book VII, is the final sequence, running backwards from men to women to children to babies, like the nauseating produce of a human regurgitation machine. Such perverted connections stimulated his earliest experiences of the City where, amid all its shows, his attention was always most forcefully arrested by the sight of "woman as she is to open shame / Abandoned, and the pride of public vice." At such moments, "a barrier seemed at once / Thrown in, that from humanity divorced / The human form, splitting the race of man / In twain, yet leaving the same outward shape" (VII.419–27). The "barrier" was not simply that between men and women, but that between human beings lost to shame (mostly women, in Wordsworth's judgment) and those who managed to retain their self-respect. In Wordsworth's London of 1791 this demarcation ran along gender lines more often than not.

12 THE MIGHTY MIND

Wales, 1791

> Upon the lonely mountain when the scene
> Had passed away . . . it appeared to me
> The perfect image of a mighty mind . . . .
> (XIII.67–69)

Toward the end of May, with the season coming to an end, Parliament about to rise, and his funds running low, Wordsworth decided to accept Robert Jones's standing invitation to visit him in Wales. By leaving London, he missed some of the wildest demonstrations of public enthusiasm for reform, but they would reach out to touch him, oddly, in deepest Wales.

He took the coach for Liverpool as far north as Chester, then hopped a local wagon to Ruthin and walked the remaining five miles to the Jones family rectory, in the vale of Clwyd between Ruthin and Denbigh.[1] It was called Plas-yn-Llan, meaning hall (or mansion) in the churchyard (or village), and it was—and still is—a very accommodating residence, the best part of the living which the Jones family enjoyed through several generations. A Jones family plot, protected by tall iron railings, still holds pride of place next to the churchyard's main entrance, announcing to all who enter, "This vault belongs to the family of JONES who resided many years at *Plas-yn-Llan* in this Parish, and contains the bodies of the Rev'd. John Jones A.M., the Rev'd. Robert Jones B.D., and Anne Jones."

Once again young Wordsworth found himself ensconced in a spacious country house. As the rectory for St. Cynhafal's Church in Llangynhafal, it was almost as big as the church itself, a rambling Tudor house with a courtyard the size of a country inn's, and a separate kitchen as large as a modern town house. In the nineteenth century a new rectory was erected in front of the church, and Plas-yn-Llan passed into private hands. The Victorian rec-

Dorothy Wordsworth, pencil drawing
(The bottom of the sheet has been torn away.)

Cambridge coach setting off from La Belle Sauvage Inn on Ludgate Hill
(By the costumes, an illustration from the 1830s or 1840s.)

View of London over Blackfriars Bridge, from Albion Mills Tower (1791)
(The view taken for Barker's Panorama in Exeter Change.)

Opposite:

"... all the portals open stand
Of Health's own temple at her Graham's command"
(*Imitation of Juvenal*, lines 168–69)

(*The Quacks* [Dr. Graham and Dr. Katterfello], 1783)

Illustrating Graham's Temple of Health & of Hymen, with its "Prime Conductor and Gentle Restorer, the Largest in the World." The thistle marks Graham as that "Scotch Doctor, famous in his day" (*Prelude*, VII.183, MS. variant [*Thirteen*]). He holds a "medicated tube" and extolls "that renewed Vigour! that full-toned juvenile virility which speaks so cordially and so Effectually home to the Female Heart, Conciliating its Favour & Friendship, and rivetting its Intensest Affections."

"To have a house, it was enough—
what matter for a home?"
(*The Prelude,* VII.76–77)

("Domestic Architecture: View of an old house lately standing in Grub Street. Drawn in July 1791.")

A Bawd on Her Last Legs, by Thomas Rowlandson (October 1, 1792)

The pox is far advanced. The doctor's grimace combines human and medical disgust. The younger prostitute looks on with naive concern that does not seem to register her own coming fate.

". . . or romping girl
Bounced, leapt, and pawed the air"
(*The Prelude,* VI.454–55)

(*The Romp,* featuring
Mrs. Dorothea Jordan, 1786)

"Vauxhall and Ranelagh, I then had heard
Of your green groves and wilderness of lamps,
Your gorgeous ladies, fairy cataracts,
And pageant fireworks."
(*The Prelude,* VII.123–26)

(*Vauxhall Gardens,* by Thomas Rowlandson)

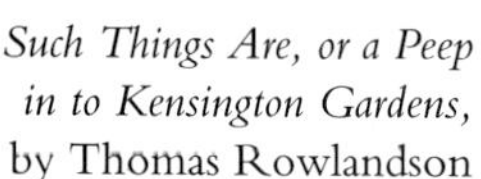

Such Things Are, or a Peep in to Kensington Gardens, by Thomas Rowlandson

Another view of London's pleasure grounds. Rowlandson's drawings of the "hidden" life of his times rarely rise to this level of symbolic grotesquerie.

"What a hell
For eyes and ears, what anarchy and din
Barbarian and infernal" (*The Prelude,* VII.659–61)

(*Bartholomew Fair,* by Thomas Rowlandson)

Near Beddgelert, by Thomas Rowlandson

Imagine, left to right: Jones, Wordsworth, guide, and cur

Helen Maria Williams, by John Singleton

Presumed miniature portrait of Annette Vallon, artist unknown

Saint Mary Magdalene Renouncing Her Wordly Vanities, by Charles Le Brun (after 1650)

Jacques Pierre Brissot (1754–1793)

Antoine Joseph Gorsas (1751–1793)

Jean-Louis Carra (1742–1793)

"—Carra, Gorsas—add
A hundred other names, forgotten now,
Nor to be heard of more; yet were they powers,
Like earthquakes, shocks repeated day by day
And felt through every nook of town and field."
(*The Prelude,* IX.179–183)

Henri Grégoire (1750–1831)
(Detail from Jacques-Louis David, *Oath of the Tennis Court, June 20, 1789.*)

Grégoire stands in the middle of the central group symbolizing the union of the clergy and the aristocracy. The other priest was not actually present, but Grégoire was, representing the regular parish clergy.

Michel Beaupuy (1755–1796), artist unknown

"Beaupuis—let the name
Stand near the worthiest of antiquity—"
(*The Prelude,* IX.426–27)

tory stands there stiffly with redbrick rectitude, but Plas-yn-Llan stands out, glowing like a color feature in *Country Life,* by far the most impressive house in the neighborhood. It is beautifully situated, just a few hundred yards below the ridge at the top of the Clwydian Range, looking out over the five-mile-wide vale of Clwyd, a highly satisfactory prospect of just what a *valley* should look like: long and broad and green. One feels here very much master of all one surveys, a feeling that William conveyed to Dorothy as the "Vale of Meditation."[2]

The Reverend Edward Jones, Robert's father, was glad to have a large house, for he had a large family. Besides his son, there were five daughters, now between the ages of twelve and twenty-three, three of whom were still living at home in 1791. Dorothy asked Jane Pollard with slightly uneasy humor, "Who would not be happy enjoying the company of three young ladies . . . without a rival?"[3] And Robert Jones hinted many years later that William had not been insensible to the eldest sister's charms: "Surely you remember my sister Mary?"[4]

The young men soon decided to repeat their wonderful adventure of the previous summer, this time through the popular picturesque sights of Wales. They took three weeks preparing for their ramble, but there was no need for the detailed research of the preceding year, for Jones was now on home ground, ready to function as Wordsworth's guide and personally acquainted with the current experts on all matters pertaining to Welsh topography and history.

Someone else who very much wanted to accompany them was William Mathews, living not far away near Loughborough, but his letters to Wordsworth were delayed, as were Wordsworth's responses, and they did not quite make connections. Wordsworth may have been trying to keep Mathews out of the Welsh tour. The contrast between their positions, five months after graduation, was notable. Mathews was trying to make his way in the world, serving as English master at a clergyman's school, and deeply depressed about his position and his prospects. Wordsworth, by contrast, seemed to be doing everything in his power *not* to make his way in the world, frittering away his time and his relatives' money. But he was in the best of spirits, laughing at his lack of resolution, and dispensing lordly advice to Mathews on how to avoid depression: he recommended reading the Cave of Spleen episode in *The Rape of the Lock,* though he acknowledged that a tour "would have contributed greatly to exhilirate [Mathews's] spirits."*

*He was unforthcoming to Mathews on other subjects as well, responding to his request for observations on modern literature by saying he had read only *Tristram Shandy* and "two or three papers of the *Spectator":* "you might as well have solicited me to send you an account of the tribes inhabiting the central regions of the African Continent." But Wordsworth's knowledge of contemporary English literature went far beyond Steele and Sterne, encompassing almost all the con-

He and Jones began their tour by striking briefly eastward, back over the top of the Clwydian Range and down to Holywell, where they visited Thomas Pennant, a noted travel writer, amateur geologist, and leader in the burgeoning Welsh national revival. He was the author of *A Tour in Wales* (1778–84), dedicated to John Jones, Robert's grandfather, from which the two young men derived their itinerary: its special feature was an elaborate description of a sunrise ascent of Snowdon. Pennant's *Tour* set their course, but in reverse: a roughly counterclockwise oval, west along the North Wales coast to the Menai Strait, then southerly past Caernarfon, Snowdon, Harlech Castle, and Cadair Idris, down as far as Aberystwyth, then eastward past Devil's Bridge and thence back northeasterly via the river Dee and Betwys-y-coed to the Jones family manse.[5] It was a good three hundred miles, but with six weeks to devote to it, Wordsworth and Jones explored North Wales in much greater detail than any part of their European tour the previous summer.

Wordsworth never wrote a separate poem describing this tour, but in his dedication of *Descriptive Sketches* to Jones (1793) he listed the places he remembered best:

> With still greater propriety I might have inscribed to you a description of some of the features of your native mountains, through which we have wandered together, in the same manner, with so much pleasure. But the sea-sunsets, which give such splendour to the vale of Clwyd, Snowdon, the chair of Idris, the quiet village of Bethgelert, Menai and her Druids, the Alpine steeps of Conway [*sic*], and the still more interesting windings of the wizard stream of Dee, remain yet untouched.[6]

There are only two places in this catalog from which one *cannot* see the sun set over the sea: the village of Beddgelert and the river Dee. And these were the only two places on the tour where Wordsworth found things "still more interesting" than he had expected.

When they came to Snowdon, Wordsworth, following Pennant, wanted to see the sunrise. The most famous mountain climb in his entire oeuvre, the ascent of Snowdon which concludes *The Prelude,* derives from this trip. As in crossing the Simplon Pass, his expectation of landscape sublimity, formed by cultural models—Gray's "The Bard" (1757) is set there—was again disappointed, and his mind surprised into poetry by the difference.

Matched against the mountain itself, Wordsworth's description of ascending Snowdon is a masterpiece of his ability to wed literal details to visionary interpretation, the two polar opposites of his creative genius. Large

---

temporary poets of Sensibility with a familiarity that was vast, expert, and highly interested: he knew those "tribes" very well. For some reason, Wordsworth did not want to give Mathews access to his intensive course of poetical self-education.

Wordsworth's Wales: North, 1791; South, 1793 and 1798.

quantities of critical ink have flowed into explaining his explanation of his vision (XIII.66–119), written in his transcendental idiom of 1804, but little or no indication has been given of how exact his description of the climb itself is (XIII.1–65). They were following Pennant very closely, for his "Journey to Snowdon," complete with a separate title page, takes up the first half of the second volume of his *Tour of Wales.* The ascent that Pennant describes proceeds from north to south, beginning at the town of Llanberis and closely following the path of the present Snowdon Mountain Railway, completed in 1897 (see map). Wordsworth's and Jones's route was almost certainly from south to north, beginning near the hamlet of Rhyd-Ddu to the west of Snowdown, about seven miles north of Beddgelert. They started out "westward" only in the sense that the road from Beddgelert to Rhyd-Ddu runs slightly northwesterly at the beginning, but it soon turns almost straight north. They took the Rhyd-Ddu path because only by this route would they be able to see the sun rise in front of them as they reached the top. Easier routes from the east and north had the drawback that the sun creeps up behind one by degrees, whereas they were aiming for the maximum dramatic impact of seeing the sun rise up in front of them.[7] They would not have started climbing from Beddgelert, for such a route, if there were one (there isn't), would have taken them up and down many intervening foothills, and both were from mountainous districts and could read the lay of the land better than that. Wordsworth says they left at "couching-time," a country phrase for sheep's bedtime, about midnight, and this is about right: Pennant refers to another climb that started from this direction, saying he "sat up at a farm on the west till about twelve."[8] If they wanted "to see the sun rise from the top of Snowdon," they would, in July, have had to be on the top between 4 and 5 A.M. Even modestly accomplished walkers can get to the top in three hours or less along this path, weather permitting, which means they would have had to set off from the bottom about 1 A.M. Covering the seven miles from Beddgelert to Rhyd-Ddu on a dark and foggy night would probably require another two hours. So we can imagine them setting off from their lodgings at about 11 P.M. If anything, they were too eager, for they arrived too early.

Reaching "the cottage at the mountain's foot," they "rouzed up the shepherd who by ancient right / Of office is the stranger's usual guide"; Pennant recommended him by name, Hugh Shone.[9] This confirms that they went to a well-known starting point, and did not just ramble up on their own. Hugh gave them some "short refreshment," probably a stiff drink, because they'd already been walking for two hours. They needed a guide to find the best path, not yet marked out by thousands of tourists, because "It was a summer's night, a close warm night, / Wan, dull, and glaring, with a dripping mist / Low-hung and thick that covered all the sky, / Half threatening storm and

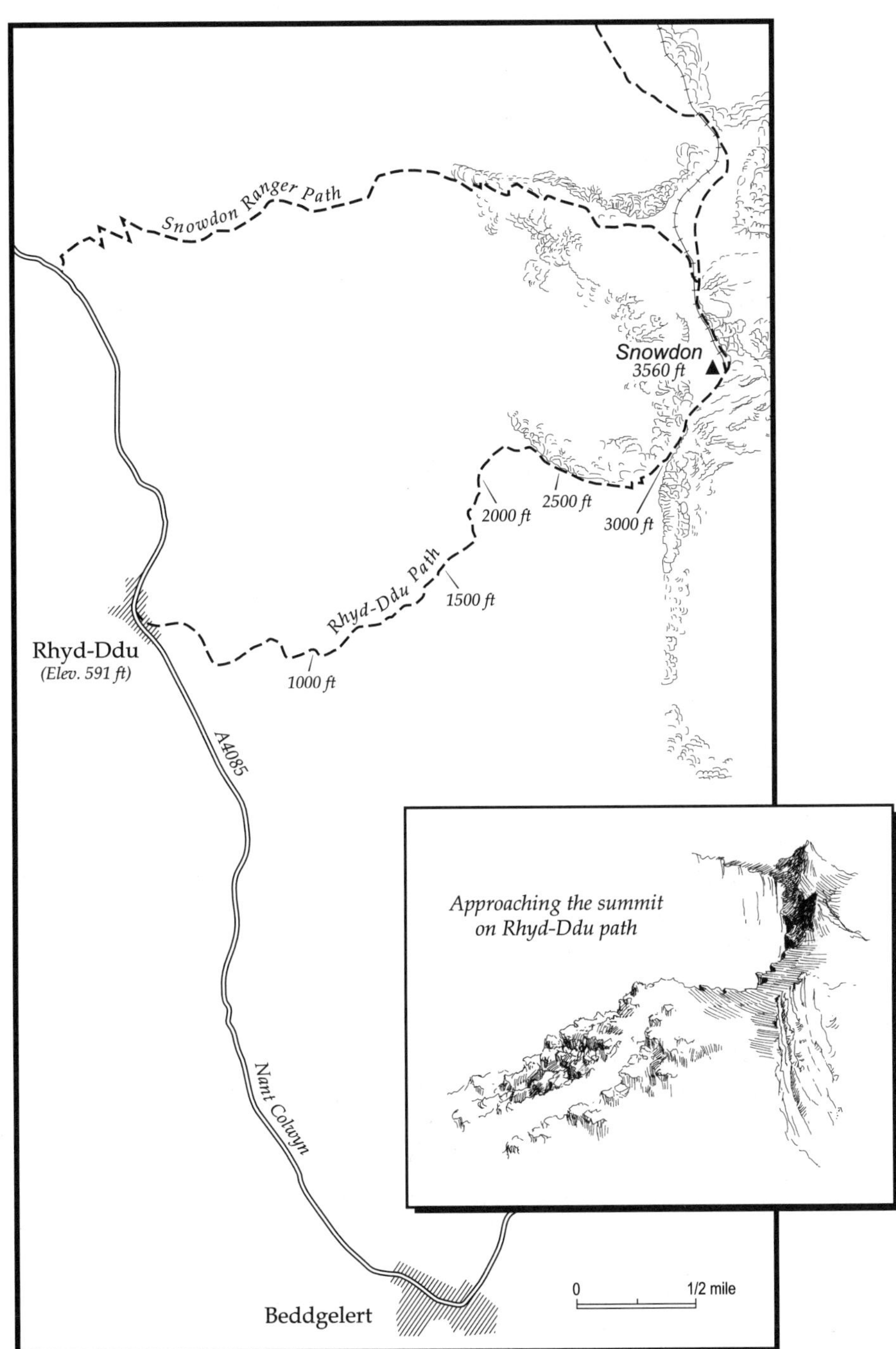

Climbing Snowdon, August, 1791.

rain" (XIII.10–13). They also needed the shepherd because only their "faith in our tried pilot" assured them that such an unlikely night would result in a morning on which one could actually see the sun rise. (This suggests they had contacted Hugh the day before, since he could only predict, not control, weather conditions.) As Pennant said, "It is very rare that the traveller gets a proper day to ascend the hill; for . . . by the evident attraction of the clouds for this lofty mountain, it becomes suddenly and unexpectedly enveloped in mist."[10] Wordsworth's shepherd, however, knew his weather signs well, for they eventually emerged out of the mist into the clear well before sunrise.*

Wordsworth's description fits a Rhyd-Ddu ascent precisely; it is not just a generic account of a mountain climb, though it can be read that way. Though it is true that Wordsworth "hardly needed to go near a mountain, let alone have a specific occasion in mind," to compose his first version of the event, the *Prelude* account is extremely circumstantial.[11] Like the Rhyd-Ddu route itself, Wordsworth's description is broken roughly into thirds. First, there is a gradually ascending base plateau ("thus did we breast the ascent") across sheep-grazing land marked by holding pens, in which "the shepherd's cur" might well "unearth a hedgehog . . . to his own great joy" (XIII.23), and the hikers might comfortably engage in "ordinary travellers' chat" (17). Second, there is a much steeper middle section, through huge boulders and so covered with rocks of all sizes that it is difficult to find anything resembling a path, still less a hedgehog. Here one no longer "breasts" the ascent, but, more accurately, "with forehead bent / Earthward, as if in opposition set / Against an enemy, I panted up . . . thus might we wear perhaps an hour away" (29–33).[12] This section does take about an hour, and one is too busy keeping one's balance and breath, especially if it's dark and foggy, to engage in much conversation. Third, there is a wide plateau of about two miles to the summit as one surmounts this rocky steep, from which, "At distance not the third part of a mile," is the edge of a very steep precipice of horseshoe cliffs, falling away from the western summit of Snowdon, hundreds of feet straight down, "a blue chasm, a fracture in the vapour, / A

*Such predictions are by no means easy in the mountains of North Wales, close to the sea, where any day, even in midsummer, can produce thick mist and rain that obliterates everything. I arrived there one splendidly sunny afternoon, and the park ranger recommended I ascend immediately to take advantage of the weather, since even a day like that was no guarantee for the morrow. He was right. The next morning was misty and overcast, and at 2 or 3 A.M. looked unlikely to produce any visible sunrise. Being lazier and less fit than Wordsworth, I finally arrived "at the mountain's foot" about 5 A.M. and saw what little sunrise there was to see from the bottom, not the top, of Snowdon. And that was the best view I got, for by the time I reached the top, about 7:30, it was swathed in a mist that thickened so quickly that I had to hurry back down immediately before I lost all visibility—having climbed the mountain twice in the space of eight hours with no romantic vision for my pains.

deep and gloomy breathing-place, through which / Mounted the roar of waters, torrents, streams / Innumerable, roaring with one voice" (55–59). Here, where the mountain falls sharply downward, the mists resume, but with a gap in midair, because they do not lap as smoothly on the cliff face as they do on more gradual slopes. This is the "dark deep thoroughfare" where Wordsworth said "Nature lodged the soul, the imagination of the whole." The sound of falling waters is audible, especially when there has been rain, but its source is mysterious and invisible because the streams come out of crevices in the cliffs: they are apparently "homeless" (63). The cliff is so literally *precip*itous that it seems concave, as if cut back in beneath the observer. Nor can one hear these waters from any place but the top of the mountain. Sometimes readers think Wordsworth heard the sound of "the sea, the real sea," but that is too "far, far beyond" to be heard from the top of Snowdon. It was here that Wordsworth had his visionary sight, for only here could "a light upon the turf / [fall] like a flash," since there is little or no turf to speak of until one reaches this plateau.

But the light Wordsworth saw was the moon, not the sun. (Actual or metaphorical confusion of heavenly bodies seems endemic on Snowdon: Pennant saw the sun on one of his ascents "with the rotundity of the moon.") It was all the more startling because they didn't become aware of its light in advance, as they would have with the sun, which would have brightened the mist around them by degrees. The moon, being much less bright than the sun, just hung there, "naked in the heavens at height / Immense above my head," invisible until Wordsworth suddenly emerged from the sea of mist as if emerging from under water, "and on the shore / I found myself of a huge sea of mist" (XIII.41–43). They were still well in advance of the dawn for the light/dark contrast to be so sharp: their shepherd guide had underestimated the climbing prowess of his two young tourists. In fact, Wordsworth never does say whether he saw the sun rise, so much did this unexpected, contrary vision move him. Well might he here invoke Milton's account of the creation of the world—"A hundred hills their dusky backs upheaved / All over this still ocean"[13]—for it is exactly here that one begins to see again all of the neighboring summits, after a hard climb with one's forehead bent "earthward."

The "meditation" that "rose in [him] that night" was not written down until thirteen years later, but though its idiom is Wordsworth's transcendental language of 1804, the process of imaginative transformation that it explains must have begun very soon. In a general way, Wordsworth's experience was similar to Pennant's: "A vast mist enveloped the whole circuit of the mountain. The prospect down was horrible. It gave the idea of numbers of abysses, concealed by a thick smoke, furiously circulating around us. Very often a gust of wind formed an opening in the clouds, which gave a fine and distinct visto [*sic*] of lake and valley. Sometimes they opened only in one place; at others, in many at once, exhibiting a most strange and perplexing sight of water, fields, rocks, or chasms, in fifty different places."[14] But as in the Simplon Pass, Wordsworth's mind was affected by the sight of something quite different from what he had expected. The language of his first version of this experience, transferred to Switzerland for *Descriptive Sketches,* borrows heavily from his favorite youthful model, Beattie's *Minstrel* (1771). The Minstrel too "oft traced the uplands, to survey, / When o'er the sky advanced the kindling dawn," and

> . . . oft the craggy cliff he loved to climb,
> *When all in mist the world below was lost,*
> *What dreadful pleasure! there to stand sublime,*
> *Like shipwreck'd mariner on desert coast,*
> And view th'enormous waste of vapour, tost
> In billows, lengthening to th'horizon round,
> Now scoop'd in gulfs, with mountains now emboss'd!
> *And hear the voice of mirth and song rebound,*
> *Flocks, herds, and waterfalls, along the hoar profound!*
>
> (*The Minstrel,* I.xxiii)

Wordsworth's recollected his experience in very similar terms:

> Far stretch'd beneath the many-tinted hills,
> *A mighty waste of mist the valley fills,*
> *A solemn sea!* whose vales and mountains round
> *Stand motionless,* to awful silence bound.
> A gulf of gloomy blue, that opens wide
> And bottomless, divides the midway tide.
> *Like leaning masts of stranded ships appear*
> The pines that near the coast their summits rear.
> Of cabins, woods, and lawns a pleasant shore
> Bounds calm and clear *the chaos still and hoar:*
> Loud thro' that midway gulf ascending, sound
> Unnumber'd streams *with hollow roar profound.*
> *Mounts thro' the nearer mists the chaunt of birds,*
> *And talking voices, and the low of herds,*
> *The bark of dogs, the drowsy tinkling bell,*
> And wild-wood mountains lutes of saddest swell.
>
> (*Descriptive Sketches,* 492–509)

Wordsworth's description in *The Prelude* draws from both sources, particularly the image of a mariner shipwrecked on a coast. But Beattie and his own earlier version are mainly frameworks that he invests with his own experience: they have no shepherd's cur, no forehead bent against an enemy, no chasm so precisely "the third part of a mile" away from the exact spot where he was standing: no unique details at all. Beattie's Minstrel and the narrator of *Descriptive Sketches* are generic figures; but Wordsworth is himself, nowhere more so than in his vast generalization to something far beyond Beattie's range: "the perfect image of a mighty mind."[15] He needed no source for mountain mists; he had seen them innumerable times in his life. What he had to account for was the surprise of *different* sights and sounds. This, as in London and Switzerland, is what released his mind from its planned itineraries and helped him to create himself as the poet of the unexpected. His "perfect image of a mighty mind" refers not only to the constituent parts of the vision he perceived—mist/moon/mountain/sea—but also to the image *he* created there, of

> . . . the glorious faculty
> Which higher minds bear with them as their own.
> This is the very spirit in which they deal
> With all the objects of the universe:
> They from their native selves can send abroad
> Like transformation, for themselves create
> A like existence . . .
> . . . They build up greatest things
> From least suggestions . . . .
>
> (XIII.84–99, passim)

Few greater passages of poetry have been built up from lesser suggestions—cur, hedgehog, and guide—than Wordsworth's redaction of his midnight ascent of Snowdon's Rhyd-Ddu path in July 1791. But the spirit of his "native self" depended equally on his cultural reading, in this case from James Beattie and Thomas Pennant.

Here, however, his narrative stops short. His eye was blanked out by his mind, and the physical itinerary became completely unimportant. We hear no more of Wales in *The Prelude* or in Wordsworth's poetry generally until, significantly, he recorded a similar reassessment of imaginative power above Tintern Abbey on the Wye in South Wales seven years later. But the 1791 tour went on after Snowdon without recorded incident, which is to say that he and Jones saw the sights pretty much as anyone might see them.

This lasted until they came to the summer country house of Thomas Pennant's neighbor Thomas Thomas, at Pennant Melangell, in the midst of the barren Berwyn Range, near nothing at all in Montgomeryshire, fifteen miles west of Oswestry on the Welsh-English border. Thomas's house, Llechweddgarth, was the principal house in the district, and the Thomases had long been one of the most distinguished families in the parish.[16] Here, in another border country, not far from "the wizard stream of Dee," Wordsworth had another liminal experience, "still more interesting" than that on Snowdon. Again it had something to do with his misperception of the countryside, but this time the confusion arose in political, not aesthetic, terms.

Since Wordsworth's recollection (written in 1829) is the only account we have of the incident, we can let him tell it, as he says it was "so characteristic of the Cambro Britons that I will venture upon a recital of it."

> I was introduced to Mr Thomas by my old friend and fellow Pedestrian among the Alps, Robert Jones, fellow of St. John's Cambridge. One day we sat down une partie quarrée at the Squire's Table, himself at the head; the Parson of the Parish, a bulky broad-faced man between 50 and 60 at the foot and Jones and I opposite each other. I must observe that "the Man of God" had not unprofessionally been employed most part of the morning in bottling of the Squire's "Cwrrw" anglisé strong Ale, this had redden'd his visage (we will suppose by the fumes) but I sat at table not apprehending mischief.

Having set up his protagonist for a coming fall, Wordsworth continues,

> The conversation proceeded with the cheerfulness good appetite, and good cheer, naturally inspire—the Topic—the powers of the Welsh Language. "They are marvelous," said the rev[d] Taffy. "Your English is not to be compared especially in conciseness, we can often express in one word what you can scarcely do in a long sentence." "That," said I, "is indeed wonderful be so kind as to favor me with an instance?" "That I will" he answered. "You know perhaps the word Tad?" "Yes." "What does it mean?" "Father" I replied. "Well," stammer'd the Priest in triumph, "Tad and Father there you have it"—on hearing this odd illustration of his confused notions I could not help smiling on my friend opposite; whereupon, the incensed Welshman rose from his chair and brandished over me a huge sharp pointed carving knife. I held up my arm in a defensive attitude; judge of the consternation of the Squire, the dismay of my friend, and my own astonishment not unmixed with fear whilst he stood threat[e]ning me in this manner and heaping on my poor English head every reproachful epithet which his scanty knowledge of our language could supply to lungs almost stifled with rage. "You vile Saxon!" I recollect was one of his terms, "To come here and insult me an ancient Briton on my own territory!" At last his wrath subsided "et me servavit Apollo."[17]

Wordsworth's account would still not please Welsh readers, with its pattern of archly condescending linguistic puns in English, Welsh, French, and Latin; it shows his parochial conservatism hardening into reactionary prejudice. But his accurate recollection of the Welsh word for beer or ale *(cwrw* or *cwrf),* not to speak of the carving knife, shows that the incident had a deep impact on him.

Wordsworth here was the outlander smiling at the natives, and he had touched a nerve of political nationalism that in 1791 was coming close to the surface of everyday life. Jacobitism was still a vital memory in Wales and Ireland as well as Scotland, especially for people (like the parson) fifty or sixty years of age. Welshmen were well represented in the various liberal groups then forming to use the occasion of Jacobin constitutional reform to press for similar reforms in England: the Reverend Richard Price, whose sermon touched off Burke's *Reflections,* was a Welshman. Pennant's second edition of his *Account of London* had just appeared in the spring, and might be called a Welsh tour of the city. It drew heavily on sources among the radical "London Welsh" of the period, men from Denbighshire and Flintshire particularly, whose antiquarian nationalism was rapidly turning into political agitation for "Liberty in Church and State."[18]

Welsh does strike the native English speaker as a "long" rather than a "short" language, especially its proper names, though a place-name like Plas-yn-Llan, for example, is nominally more concise than "the mansion in the church-village." The priest chose to take insult in territorial terms, but Wordsworth might have reflected, before he smiled, that beneath the surface of good manners among social equals, he was the only foreigner present, a guest, and a much younger one at that. The "characteristic" of the Welsh was, in his view, that they take offense when they think their language is being laughed at by outsiders, but this is hardly a "Cambro Briton" peculiarity. It may even be that the parson was having Wordsworth on in a complex set of cultural association jokes involving "long knives," exaggerated boast curses, and strategically coded uses of Welsh (*Sais yw ef syn* = "He is a Saxon, beware").[19] The shock of the situation was not its foreignness (the parson's "scanty knowledge of our language" is belied by Wordsworth's own report), but rather finding *himself* regarded as foreign. It was as surprising in its way as coming to the top of Snowdon and finding not the sun but the moon standing naked in the heavens, and as on Snowdon, he explains his surprise in terms not unlike those of "the glorious faculty" of his own "higher mind" he used there: "et me servavit Apollo" (and Apollo preserved me).

Pennant Melangell ("where Melangell rules or is chief") was a place of proud tradition, with Christian associations reaching back to the early seventh century. The virgin Melangell (Saint Monacella), a daughter of the king of Ireland, established a nunnery there after her miraculous escape from the hunting dogs of the earl of Chester, who surprised her at prayer. The dogs' miraculous retreat from a hare that had taken refuge in her lap may be a monkish metaphor for the massacre of Cambro Britons by Roman Christians at Bangor in 603. This story, the founding legend of the place, would have been related to Wordsworth as an English visitor, and may have led to the discussion of the characteristics of the Welsh language. The parson, who was probably the vicar, Ezekiel Hamer, may have been touchy about any apparent condescension from Wordsworth, since the absentee rector who held the living as a sinecure was, like Wordsworth's uncle Cookson, a chaplain to George III, and resided at Winchester as a prebendary at the cathedral. "Jacobitism" among Protestants meant mainly local control of churches, and much of its contemporary revival as British "Jacobinism" did not go far beyond this, consisting mainly of agitation for reform of rotten boroughs and removal of restraints on Nonconformists. The fact that the major income of his parish flowed out to an English priest in comfortable circumstances like the young visitor's uncle may have made the priest, who was evidently in a dependent status at Thomas's house, particularly resentful, and ill disposed to suffer smirks from a young, unemployed bachelor of arts. Welsh parsons were traditionally the poorest of the poor among clergy, receiving about £35 per annum for the care of up to four parishes.[20] One hopes Wordsworth did not call him Reverend Taffy to his face, even as a joke. But if ethnic slurs were on anyone's mind (for example, "Taffy was a Welshman, Taffy was a thief"), the parson had good reason to think of nonresident English priests—those in possession and those in prospect—as the real culprits.[21]

The incident reminded Wordsworth of the precarious position of curates who cared for a parish while the substantial "living" went to an absentee who might hold several of them. Hence when the tour was over, and he was back at Plas-yn-Llan contemplating the return to Cumberland that he and Dorothy supposed to be his only remaining course of action, he read with mixed emotions a letter that awaited him. It was from John Robinson, informing him that Robinson was prepared to make him curate of a parish in Harwich (Robinson's parliamentary district for nearly twenty years), with a good possibility that the living itself would soon be his. The position was already in the family, the present occupant being none other than Aunt Cookson's brother, William Cowper (not the poet of that name), who had fallen into debt and fled to Holland to avoid imprisonment.[22] If one branch of the family was in trouble, it made good sense to protect a steady source of income by lending it out to help another branch. It made particularly good sense if the other branch was also heavily in debt, especially when his creditors were other members of the family itself.

Wordsworth soon bade farewell to Jones and his sisters and traveled back to London in early September. His purpose, however, was not to take up the living that at the last possible moment seemed to rescue him from aimlessness. He went instead to thank John Robinson—and explain that, as he was not yet twenty-three, he could not technically take up orders yet! As if Robinson and Cookson, who had collaborated on the deal, did not know how old Wordsworth was and—equally well—how easily this regulation could be temporized and bent ("anticipated" was the technical term)[23] for the intervening nineteen months.

Arriving to pay his compliments and give his excuses, Wordsworth came once more into contact with the powerful tangent in his family universe which, had he been willing to follow it, could easily have been the making of his independence, an independence by no means incompatible with a certain kind of poet's life. Some part of the difference that marks Wordsworth off from a Crabbe, a Cowper, or a Beattie, a difference that we now call Romantic, has to do with the refusals he made in the next two months to offers that would have rescued him from his feckless university career and set him on a proper way after all. The difference between what he was giving up and what he was choosing (essentially, nothing at all) began to focus his mind as he rode back to London.

John Robinson resided at Wyke House in Isleworth, just west of London, not far from Heathrow, on a manor he had purchased in 1778 after switching his allegiance from Sir James Lowther to the king, which also allied him with Lowther's main northern antagonists, the dukes of Norfolk and Northumberland. The manor was nearly a mile long and half a mile wide, and Robinson had modernized Wyke House into a very handsome villa.[24] The neighborhood was a sort of suburban fiefdom of Lowther's new friend, the duke of Northumberland, Hugh Percy, whose seat, Syon House, "one of the most conspicuous ornaments of the county of Middlesex," was directly across the Great Western Road from Robinson's. Syon House was in effect a castle, one of three that the duke, a newcomer to the name and title, restored magnificently during his lifetime.[25] Robinson's Wyke House was only half a castle, but it was the next biggest villa in the neighborhood, reflecting Robinson's success in his lifelong ambition of raising his social status. Living with him, when not at their town house in Hanover Square, were his daughter, Mary, and her husband of ten years, Henry Nevill, soon to become earl of Abergavenny: that is, Wordsworth's second cousin by marriage. Brother John was now an officer of, and would later become captain of, the *Earl of Abergavenny,* which had just returned on August 19 from another successful voyage; John had his position through Robinson's influence and soon stopped by to pay his respects as well.[26] Mary Robinson Nevill had borne five children by 1791; Wordsworth's first cousin Thomas Myers (brother of John) married one of them.[27] Her sixth and last, christened William, was born the following August,[28] and we can be sure that the one William in the family he was *not* named after was his mother's second cousin.

Wordsworth entered into this splendid milieu to thank his uncle for his interest and beg off on a technicality. Robinson's initial perplexity soon changed to anger. Here was the nephew who, almost exactly four years earlier, had sworn to his brother, Admiral Hugh Robinson, to apply himself at university and be "Senior Wrangler or nothing!" Four years later he had achieved—if that is the word—the second alternative. Robinson had no special obligation to help William: there were fifteen other Wordsworth second cousins of his generation to be helped, not to mention the thirteen nieces and nephews that Mary Myers was producing for his old but virile brother, Hugh. One wonders just how Wordsworth expressed his reservations. To Mathews, referring to "a gentleman you most likely have heard me speak of" (Robinson), he said only, "I thought it was best to pay my respects to him [in] person, to inform him that I was not of age."[29] It took a certain amount of courage to confront Robinson directly at Wyke House, but it also looked like effrontery to turn down such a favor for such a reason. The Harwich living was securely in Robinson's pocket; the current incumbent was embarrassed and abroad. It is extremely unlikely that anybody would have raised the question of Wordsworth's ineligibility by reason of age, and wholly likely that the position could have been held open under temporary authority until he was.

But Wordsworth may have been bluffing his uncle, refusing a small but certain income against the possibility of a much larger independence. In late February the courts had dissolved the earl of Lonsdale's nuisance injunction against the Wordsworth claimants, and by late spring Dorothy's letters were full of hope that she and her brothers might at last be coming into their independence: "We shall either be very well off in regard to money matters or be left without a farthing."[30] In late August her hopes seemed realized, for the Carlisle Sessions found in favor of the claimants and referred the case to an arbitrator to determine the actual amount due. Robinson would surely have talked to William about the results from Carlisle, where he had, at long last, appeared as a witness against Lonsdale.[31] The court ordered Lonsdale to pay the administrators of the Wordsworth estate an amount to be determined by arbitration in London. The prospect of a successful termination of the case after all these years was in Wordsworth's mind as he temporized about the Harwich curacy. But in the event, Dorothy's fears, not her hopes, came true, for Lowther contrived to get some of his own lawyers appointed to the board establishing the amount of restitution. One was the powerful surveyor general of London Customs; another held John Wordsworth Sr.'s old post and had recently been rewarded for his loyalty with the Cockermouth seat in Parliament: probably the man least likely in the kingdom, after Lonsdale himself, to look sympathetically on the claims of the Wordsworth children. This kind of chicanery, plus the fabled incompetence of Edward Christian, allowed the process to drag on into the next year and peter out in the deadlock of endless rounds of meetings and negotiations for which rich men retain lawyers. William's share of the settlement was always subject to deductions for his education and travels, but the idea that he might soon come into something approaching £1,000 may have emboldened him to decline Robinson's offer.

The wonder is that Robinson did not wash his hands of this troublesome nephew once and for all. But, in concert with William Cookson, he kept up an interest in him for at least another year. Wordsworth did not stay long as a guest at Wyke House after the reason for his visit had become clear, and as soon as Cookson heard the outcome of his interview with Robinson, he peremptorily ordered Wordsworth to Cambridge. But William first spent some weeks in London in September, staying near his old lodgings in the City. This was the time of his first exposure to the frantic excitements of Bartholomew Fair. He could have stayed with Richard, but under the circumstances such a visit would have been very uncomfortable, since Richard would only have remonstrated about his folly in turning down such an agreeable living.

When he got back to Cambridge, he found some vacant rooms at St. John's before the bulk of the students arrived. He had first to deal with another deeply depressive letter from William Mathews, who sounded near breakdown, if not suicide. Mathews seemed to have picked up some hints of coolness in their correspondence about the Wales tour. Wordsworth's response was kind and supportive, assuring Mathews of his interest in his welfare. He urged Mathews to look at things more positively, basing his advice on his own recent experience. "It is an observation to whose truth I have long since consented that small certainties are the bane of great talents." He and Mathews, like most of their Cambridge friends, were convinced of their talents. The question of how talent could survive and prosper by itself, free of the entanglements of influence and toadying, was a cultural-political topic of great importance throughout the eighteenth century; many of the men who made the French Revolution were middle-class lawyers and writers who despised the system of advancement they faced and despaired of succeeding in it. To Mathews's desperate proposal that they should throw up all efforts at conventional social advancement and adopt the wandering life, Wordsworth says he would prefer it "to vegetating on a paltry curacy"—his estimate of Robinson's offer—"were I [not?] so situated, as to be with relations to whom I were accountable for my actions." He had strange notions of accountability, if he was turning down offers from relatives for alternatives that to them looked little better than Mathews's fantasy of the wandering life.

Even as he tried to help his old friend Mathews, his future friend Samuel Taylor Coleridge came into residence at neighboring Jesus College, on October 16, with a considerable reputation for brilliance preceding him. But Wordsworth was too preoccupied with sorting out the failures of his own college career to be much interested in the arrival of the rising star of the class of '95. Cookson demanded an accounting of his reasons for turning down Robinson's offer. The refusal was especially galling to Cookson, who not only had firsthand information about William's university failures but who also had painful memories of the nearly ten years through which he and his fiancée had waited and schemed for an offer like the one which had now dropped into their nephew's lap, only to be thrown away.

But Cookson was more forbearing than Robinson; he had another idea. William should undertake the study of Oriental languages—that is, Hebrew and Aramaic, plus more Greek and Latin—with a view toward becoming either a more learned clergyman or a university tutor. Cookson thought this field "the best field for a person to distinguish himself in as a man of Letters."[32] It appears that Cookson talked seriously and sympathetically to his nephew about what he wanted to do with his life, and understood that it was something in the field of letters. Whether Wordsworth would have had the temerity to propose poetry writing as a career at this date is very doubtful. Although poetry was altogether acceptable as a polite accomplishment of a clergyman, full-time writing for profit was not a respectable vocation, and was not what Wordsworth had in mind, yet. What he *did* have in mind was hard to say, even for him—hard for anybody who did not have the visionary power to foresee that something now called Romanticism would, over the next two decades, make of *creativity* a virtual way of life. William Cookson was no such seer. Yet he reasoned, not unsympathetically, that William was good at languages, had taken considerable French and Italian instruction already, and was teaching himself Spanish, so why not study languages?

Wordsworth's reaction to this decent compromise was extreme: "What must I do amongst that immense wilderness, who have no resolution, and who have not prepared myself for the enterprise by any sort of discipline amongst the Western languages? who know little of Latin, and scarce anything of Greek. A pretty confession for a young gentleman whose whole life ought to have been devoted to study." The last sentence sounds as it were taken straight from the mouth of William Cookson. The preceding sentences were not true with respect to his knowledge and aptitude for languages, but all too true with respect to his lack of resolution and discipline. And the sentence about little Latin and less Greek was an allusion—as he and Mathews knew very well—to Ben Jonson's praise for the supposedly minimal language skills of another young English poet in hard family circumstances: William Shakespeare.*

Cookson's plan also had the advantage of keeping William occupied for the next two academic years, at which point it might still be possible to install him in the Harwich curacy with no pettifogging excuses about ineligi-

*Jonson's line was "though thou hadst small Latin, and less Greek" ("To the Memory of My Beloved . . . Mr William Shakespeare" [1623], line 31).

bility. At first, in early October, Wordsworth apparently agreed to this plan, so far as Dorothy knew: "He is going, by the advice of Uncle Wm, to study the Oriental languages."[33] But then, to disengage himself from this plan, Wordsworth came up with the idea of improving his French so as to become a tutor for young noblemen on the grand tour. For this, the best method would be to go to France: "in some retired Place in France which will be less expensive and more improving than in England."[34] This was how he proposed "to pass the Time previous to the Time of his Taking Orders," pledging himself to take up Cookson's plan after a year in France, if no employment was forthcoming.

One must admire Cookson's forbearance, or smile at his naïveté, in accepting William's alternative, which was much less good, sure, and plausible than the ones he and Robinson had offered. By trying to help their irresponsible nephew in the fall of 1791, Cookson and Robinson contributed a good deal to the creation of the Poet Wordsworth. Pressing his opportunities and duties on him, they forced him to dream up other alternatives. Had they left him alone, he might have returned to Cumberland, to do God knows what, very possibly never to be heard of again: only in early October did Dorothy drop her year-long expectation that William must now return to their home district in default of all other options. By giving him options that he could refuse only with difficulty, Robinson and Cookson forced him, like a cornered animal, to find a way of escape. He did know French, and his time in France the previous year had been the high point of his life so far. But even on its surface the French option looked dubious; there was still the small matter of finding the requisite young nobleman to tutor, and going to France in the fall of 1791, just as the crestfallen Louis XVI was being forced to accept the new constitution, cannot have seemed the wisest course of action, even if at the time it appeared only that France was at last becoming a constitutional monarchy like England. It would have been like going to Moscow in 1917 to improve one's Russian.

This French trip would alter the course of Wordsworth's life irrevocably. Until now it resembles the plot of a Jane Austen novel, like *Sense and Sensibility,* he and Dorothy playing Sensibility to their more commonsensical siblings and cousins. Wordsworth's second trip to France breaks the frame of this tale of manners in which he had so far been acting the role of the wayward provincial dependent. Ironically, its upshot—a child by his French mistress—would make him very eager, a year hence, to rejoin that comfortable if rigid world of privileged connections, and to accept the offers he now refused.

He went back to London to outfit himself for the trip, making yet another draft on his putative inheritance and establishing an address where money could be sent him in France: Les Trois Empereurs at Orléans, the best hotel in the city.[35] His home address was equally impressive, and still depended on the line of powerful family associations he would soon break: Richard Wordsworth, c/o their father's cousin Anthony Parkin (1745–1827), head partner in Richard's law firm, solicitor to the General Post Office, and long-time associate of John Robinson.

Even Robinson relented a little at the last minute. Despite William's ungrateful foot-dragging, Robinson suggested that he visit his sister-in-law, the best-selling poet and novelist Charlotte Smith, at Brighton before his departure. Finding himself delayed by unfavorable weather and remembering his pleasure in her *Elegiac Sonnets,* William did call and was very kindly received by her. Smith's kindliness is all the more notable because she was no longer on good terms with John Robinson. He and Anthony Parkin were the trustees of her suit to recover her husband's estate, another runaway debtor like Mrs. Cookson's brother. But she had become disenchanted with their desultory handling of the case and was contemplating filing suit against them, which she finally did in 1793; in the prefaces of successive editions of her sonnets, she did not hesitate to refer sarcastically to certain "Honorable Men" whose actions were anything but. In her just-published novel, *Ethelinde; or, The Recluse of the Lake* (1790), she had satirized Robinson in the thinly disguised figure of Mr. Royston, an unprincipled place-buying politician. (By 1798, in *The Young Philosopher,* he had become Sir Appulby Gorges, reminding those who knew that his rapacious political career had begun in the Lowther interest at Appleby.) But none of this affected Smith's welcome to young Wordsworth; perhaps she sympathized with him for having such hard relatives. And Charlotte Smith's need to write for profit was a motive Wordsworth would soon come to feel on his pulses.

Wordsworth seems to have visited her several times during the week he was waiting for his ship, and copied down some of her poems.[36] If they discussed her latest novel, he would have been surprised to recognize a virtual allegory of parts of his own life. *Ethelinde* is set in a renovated (but fictitious) Grasmere Abbey, the pleasure retreat of a set of jaded London aristocrats, and concerns the efforts of an impoverished but sensitive and well-educated young Scotsman in the neighborhood to make his way in life, partly through the patronage of operators like Royston. His options include the East India service or "some place under Government, for which . . . my knowledge of languages qualifies me," options virtually identical with those taken by the other Wordsworth boys, John, Richard, and Christopher. Smith was already hard at work on her fourth novel, *Desmond,* in which she would openly declare her sympathies for the French Revolution, and she now provided Wordsworth with letters of introduction to several important people she knew in France, principally Helen Maria Williams and Jacques-Pierre Brissot, that would materially influence his experiences there.

He sailed for France on the evening of November 26, fourteen months after his return from his European walking tour, ending a year of aimless wandering in which he had ten different addresses. He would never enjoy such a randomly free year again during his early life, for much of what he did henceforth was motivated and determined by the fallout from events set in motion by his residence in France.

13

REVOLUTION AND ROMANCE

Residence in France 1791–1792

"Oh, happy time of youthful lovers!"
(IX.556)

Wordsworth crossed from Brighton to Dieppe on the night of November 26, proceeding next day to Rouen, where he spent two days waiting for the diligence to Paris.[1] Wandering among the churches and towers associated with Joan of Arc, he learned that Helen Maria Williams had been there just before him. Throughout the coming year, their paths kept approaching each other but never quite crossed.[2] Williams had been visiting her friends Thomas and Monique du Fosse, whose happy story of true love triumphing over *ancien* privilege formed the opening episode in her immensely successful *Letters from France* (eight printings in 1790 alone). It told how Thomas, a young aristocrat, wooed a local merchant's daughter, despite furious opposition from his father, the old count, including imprisonment by lettre de cachet; the young man escaped by scaling a fifty-foot wall, fled clandestinely to England with his beloved (where Helen Williams became her tutor), and returned after the privileges of the nobility were dissolved to dance with his bride around a Liberty Tree newly planted on his ancestral estate, the very image of the world well lost for love. Three thousand copies of Williams's letter of thanks to the Rouenais for their enthusiastic reception of her work had been printed up and distributed. Some were still in circulation when Wordsworth arrived and would have been drawn to the attention of a visiting Englishman. Williams's account of the du Fosses had made it famous in England, but it already had a wide currency in Rouen as evidence of the Revolution's promises coming true. Spending his first two days in France in the city which had provided the inspiration for England's best-selling book about the positive aspects of the French Revolution, Wordsworth could not have dreamed how useful the story would be to him as a way of framing, and disguising, the events of his exciting, frustrating year in France. It would eventually provide the base—or the cover—for his extremely *un*happy story of Vaudracour and Julia, his literary representation of his love affair with Annette Vallon in Orléans and Blois.*

Helen Williams had gone on to Orléans, but Wordsworth, who carried a letter of introduction to her, would also miss her there, because he went first to Paris. We already remark a change in his motives from 1790. Then, though he and Jones had come closer to Paris than he was at Rouen, they kept straight on their way toward the Alps. Now the places and events of the Revolution had a greater claim on his imagination, and he allowed himself a brief detour to see them: "each spot of old and recent fame—the latter chiefly" (IX.42–43).

Paris

Arriving in Paris on Wednesday night, November 30, he exchanged half his money the next day, at the excellent rate of 643 livres for £20.[3] He then spent five efficient days touring, crisscrossing the city (see map) visiting the ruins of the Bastille and the Faubourg St. Antoine in the east, the Panthéon and the Carmelite convent in the south, the National Assembly (since October 1, the Legislative Assembly), the Jacobin Club, and the Champ de Mars in the west, and Montmarte in the north. This was still pre-Terror Paris, jubilant in the throes of liberation despite internecine political struggles and war clouds gathering on France's northern borders. Wordsworth stayed in the exact center, near the Palais Royal, in the neighborhood of the present Bibliothèque Nationale and the Bourse. Possibly he took a room at White's Hotel, facing Notre-Dame des Victoires in the place des Petits-Pères, just off the rue de la Banque, where most polite English visitors congregated. Or if this was too expensive, he may have walked two or three streets east to the Hôtel d'Angleterre, which still stands, abandoned and dilapidated, at no. 56 rue Montmarte. The British who stayed at the d'Angleterre tended to be

*Two other Englishmen in Rouen at the time were Richard Ford and his father. The elder Ford had come to France to avoid entanglement in Sheridan's financial disasters at Drury Lane; his son arrived at very nearly the same time as Wordsworth, seeking relief from the public embarrassments that accompanied his separation from Dora Jordan, who had published his letters attesting to her good character in the *Morning Post* (Claire Tomalin, *Mrs. Jordan's Profession: The Actress and the Prince* [New York: Alfred A. Knopf, 1995], 125–26). There is no evidence of his meeting Wordsworth at this time, but less than six years later Ford was in charge of the secret service, and a Home Office agent spying on Wordsworth and Coleridge in Somerset would report that the "name *Wordsworth* [is] a name I think known to Mr. Ford" (Chapter 21).

more actively engaged in French affairs and included many Scotch and Irish, among them the extremely radical Colonel John Oswald, one of those unbelievable characters rendered all too plausible by the intense pressures of the time. Once a hack journalist in London, Oswald had traveled to India, become a vegetarian and nature mystic, walked back to Europe overland, thrown himself into the French Revolution with the direct intention of carrying it back to England, and been given command of a company of *piquiers* for his zeal. Wordsworth undoubtedly saw and heard about this extremist, who lodged in his imagination as the haunting figure of revolutionary excess that he would later try to purge from his psyche in the character of Oswald in *The Borderers.*[4]

Paris was a small, crowded, and very dirty city. Each day Wordsworth sallied out from his room and "coasted round and round the line / Of tavern, brothel, gaming-house, and shop" in the arcades of the Palais Royal: "Great rendezvous of worst and best, the walk / Of all who had a purpose, or had not" (IX.51–54). He of course was in the latter category, and he, like many young men on their first visit to Paris, was both shopping and perhaps sampling its pleasures. The arcades and cafés of the Palais Royal, owned by the Anglophile duc d'Orléans, were "the center in Paris not just of high politics and high ideals, but also of low pleasure," and the three-to-one ratio in Wordsworth's description in favor of haunts of dissipation is perfectly accurate.[5] Even the apparently innocent "shop" he mentions could have been very seductive, if it was the bookstore of Orléans's secretary, Choderlos de Laclos, author of *Les Liaisons dangereuses,* which stocked an extensive erotic inventory. Much of the area was below street level, full of dark cafés offering "sexual and narcotic delectations" in an atmosphere of "playful irreverence and utopian speculation" favoring witty scatological language. Louis-Sebastien Mercier, scandalmonger turned Jacobin hack, celebrated the Palais as "a temple of vice, the brilliance of whose votaries has banished shame," adding that "a young man can get a very fair education just by frequenting it," but warned that it was fatal to genius.[6] Its gardens had long been the resort of prostitutes; since the outbreak of the Revolution their number had increased dramatically, especially of very young girls.[7] To coast "round and round the line" of such temptations indicates extensive reconnoitering: just looking? Or does his use of Milton's verb ("coasted") for Satan's approach to Paradise suggest a determination to taste temptation? His parting letter to Mathews had suggested, with the studied savoir faire of a Cambridge bon vivant, that he intended to do more than that: "I expect I assure you considerable pleasure from my sojourn on the other side of the water, and some little improvement, which God knows I stand in sufficient need of."[8]

He "stared and listened with a stranger's ears to hawkers and haranguers, hubbub wild," another Miltonic allusion for this modern Pandemonium, but he was far from being a complete stranger.[9] On the contrary, among his letters from Charlotte Smith was one addressed to Jacques-Pierre Brissot, whom Smith knew from his work with antislavery groups in England, and who was just at this moment rising to the crest of his brief fame as the next ill-fated leader of the Revolution.[10] Going to Paris in 1791 carrying an introduction to Brissot would have been approximately like going to Moscow in 1919 with a letter for, say, Trotsky. "The stage beginning with the Legislative Assembly in October 1791 and ending with the September Massacres in 1792 belonged to Brissot": just about exactly the time frame of Wordsworth's residence in France.[11] Brissot, a lawyer-journalist-*publiciste* like so many of the Revolution's leaders, had narrowly gained election to the new Legislative Assembly in late September, but was now rapidly advancing his influence as a speaker for the most radical views of the Jacobin Club, favoring immediate war against the German princes and the émigrés.[12] Although Wordsworth did not actually stay at Brissot's house in this neighborhood as was later rumored,[13] he was introduced into the Assembly by him, and on December 2 attended a lively meeting of the Society of the Friends of the Constitution, or Jacobin Club, so called in Paris because it met in rented rooms at a former Jacobin convent off the rue Saint Honoré (see map). There he heard a sharp exchange of accusations between a Jacobite Englishman, James Rutledge (another *publiciste* and convicted speculator),[14] and other persons claiming to be official representatives of the Society of the Rights of Man and of the Citizen. Wordsworth also heard the *publiciste* Jean-Louis Carra, whom he mentions in *The Prelude,* speak out in favor of Brissot's war policy.[15]

Brissot took some interest in his young English visitor because he, a Protestant, had lived and worked (and been imprisoned for debt) in England in the early 1780s, and was well known to people in Wordsworth's orbit, such as Charlotte Smith, and especially Wilberforce, for lobbying against the slave trade through his humanitarian organization, Les Amis des Noirs. Wilberforce had recently had French citizenship conferred upon him, to his embarrassment, in company with radicals like Tom Paine and the Unitarian scientist Joseph Priestley. Wordsworth confidently reported to his brother Richard, "I shall profit [by this acquaintance] on my return to Paris."[16]

Wordsworth's association with Brissot is usually interpreted as a sign of his fundamental "Girondism," signifying a liberal rather than a radical view of the Revolution. But this is truer after Wordsworth's return to Paris in October 1792 than at the time of his arrival in December 1791. In late 1791 Brissot, like Carra and Antoine-Joseph Gorsas (another journalist known to Wordsworth), was still a leading member of the Jacobin Club, indeed of the radically militant Jacobin minority that remained after more than half the members broke away to form the more moderate Feuillants Club following the Champ de Mars "massacre" in July: the anniversary celebration of the Fête de la Fédération had turned violent under provocation by radicals who wanted to depose Louis immediately for his "treason" in attempting to flee the country in June.[17] Radicals and democrats had been thrown into disarray by Lafayette's tough dealing with the mob in reaction. Danton and Robespierre, finding their positions temporarily overexposed and unpopular, took evasive action, Danton fleeing to England and Robespierre prudently retiring home to Arras, from which he had returned—for those who like coincidences—the day before Wordsworth arrived in Paris.[18] Brissot was at this moment more radical than Robespierre, who distrusted Brissot's war policy because he suspected (rightly, in many cases) the loyalty of the officer corps. And Jean-Baptiste Louvet, another Jacobin whom Wordsworth would praise as the one man brave enough to stand up against Robespierre, was at this time breathing fire in the same vein: "with the swiftness of lightning let thousands of our citizen soldiers precipitate themselves upon the domains of feudalism. Let them stop only where servitude ends; let the palace be surrounded by bayonets, let the declaration of rights be deposited in the cottage."[19]

The domestic political story of France in 1792 is largely the story of the creation of a Girondin "party" out of the "Brissotins" in the internecine warfare of the Jacobin Club, around a core of delegates from the Gironde (the Bordeaux region). But in Paris in December, as in most of the following year in Blois, Wordsworth was associated with radical leaders of the Jacobin Club. Of course, these shifting groups, like the proletarian Cordeliers Club, the unstable *enragés,* and innumerable societies devoted to Truth, Liberty, the Constitution, and the People in the various *sections,* were not political parties in the modern sense. Party politics as such was uniformly scorned throughout the Revolution, in keeping with the classical republican bias against factionalism: each politician took pains to appear independent, "loyal only to the national interest."[20] Wordsworth's comment on the difficulty of doing justice to the political complications of these months could stand as an admonition to all writing on the French Revolution: "Oh, laughter for the page that would reflect / To future time the face of what now is!" (IX.176–77). Or as he said more prosaically to Richard in his first letter home, "I have said nothing of Paris and its splendors; it is too copious a theme."[21]

Brissot welcomed his tall, quiet young visitor not only because of the letter from his good friend Charlotte Smith but also because young English men and women were much in demand during the year of Wordsworth's residence in France. Drawn by the excitement of the Revolution, they ranged in their politics from sympathetic "Friends of Liberty" to activists hoping to export revolution to England. Some were government spies or commercial double agents, adding zest to the mixture. Besides Helen Williams young people well known to Wordsworth (then or later) who were in and around Paris between late 1790 and late 1792 included James Losh, brother of his Hawkshead schoolmate; Felix Vaughan, the fellow of Jesus; Tom Wedgwood, the ceramicist's son; Francis Tweddell, brother of Wordsworth's friendly rival at Cambridge; and James Watt Jr., son of the great scientist and inventor, who was there as a traveling salesman for a Manchester carpet company.[22]

Only for Watt do we have hard evidence that Wordsworth knew him there and then, but it is quite emphatic: "I went over to Paris at the time of the revolution in 1792 or 1793, and so was *pretty hot in it;* but I found Mr. James Watt there before me, and *quite* as warm in the same cause."* It is in fact doubtful that Watt was there when Wordsworth arrived, and he had departed by the time Wordsworth returned to Paris the next fall.[23] But the significance of the statement is that Wordsworth said it at all, and in tones of such sympathetic identification. Even if he was not physically present with Watt, he clearly knew what Watt was doing, and just as clearly allied himself with the same actions and opinions.

The French were doing all they could to influence young Englishmen who might write things, or carry messages, that would favorably affect British opinion of the Revolution. Parisians were generally "devenus fous des Anglois," as Helen Maria Williams reported, and people in power in the Assembly like Brissot were extremely receptive to delegations and messages from individuals and from representatives of London and provincial corresponding societies.[24] (Watt and his friend Thomas Cooper came over as representatives of the Manchester Constitutional Society.) Two weeks after Wordsworth's introduction to the Assembly, "Citizen" Philip Stanhope, the cousin of Lord Grenville and brother-in-law of Pitt, was introduced.[25]

Wordsworth began to take instruction in the new politics immediately, from one of the hottest items being sold by the "hawkers" outside the Palais Royal, *L'Almanach du Père Gérard,* by Jean-Marie Collot d'Herbois. This was a simple catechism explaining the new (and still monarchical) constitution by means of conversations between virtuous peasants and Michel Gérard (1737–1815), a respected old delegate from Brittany to the first Na-

*Wordsworth's italics jocularly convey his avuncular disapproval for the error of his youthful ways: "We thus both began life as ardent and thoughtless radicals, but we have both become, in the course of our lives, *as all sensible men, I think, have done, good soberminded Conservatives*" (James Patrick Muirhead, *The Life of James Watt, with Selections from His Correspondence,* 2d ed. [London: John Murray, 1859], 480; italics added).

tional Assembly of 1789. This little volume was the great-granddaddy of Mao Tse-tung's "Little Red Books" and thousands of other simplified revolutionary tracts. It had recently won the prize offered by the Jacobin Club for the best means of educating people in the new political realities. It was part of a successful Jacobin effort to counteract their recent setbacks by creating a propaganda center from which their affiliated clubs in the provinces could become "apostolic missions for liberty."[26] The volume appeared on the streets in great quantities late in November, and on December 2, at the meeting of the Jacobin Club Wordsworth attended, the newly appointed procurer of the commune, Pierre Manuel, promised to carry a copy with him always, the better to stay true to revolutionary principles. Members were invited to come to a special morning meeting on December 5 to witness Collot, Robespierre, and the "schoolmaster Jacobin," Léonard Bourdon (future petty dictator of Orléans and mortal enemy of Annette Vallon's brother), instructing a group of children in this new catechism. An English translation by John Oswald, called *The Almanack of Goodman Gerard,* appeared almost simultaneously.[27]

Wordsworth refers honorifically to Père Gérard in his 1793 "Letter to the Bishop of Llandaff," and the form of Collot's work, a series of twelve conversations in which sturdy peasants are educated by a kindly but bluff interlocutor—who is enlightened in turn by their outspoken bluntness—played its part in anticipating the dialogue poems of *Lyrical Ballads.* The genre, which already existed in children's books and the growing British Sunday school movement, was soon adapted in England for opposite political purposes. *Dialogues on the Rights of Britons* appeared in 1792, and in 1793 came Hannah More's immensely popular *Village Politics,* featuring the philosopher Jack Anvil's account (as reported by Will Chip) of how good old Sir John refused to remodel his manor house according to the newfangled French ideas of his fashion-crazed wife.[28]

Another publication involving Oswald appeared at this same time, and its influence can also be traced in Wordsworth's subsequent development. This was the *Chronique du mois,* a monthly journal of sophisticated essays on politics, philosophy, and the arts, for intellectuals who wanted deeper analyses of events than they got from the daily newspapers, or the stream of partisan pamphlets which flooded the streets.[29] The *Chronique* is ranked "among the most important and enduring journals of the Revolution," and its existence (November 1791–July 1793) neatly brackets—like the period of Brissot's ascendancy—Wordsworth's time in France.[30] It was the kind of journal Wordsworth had in mind—quite literally, I believe—when he explained his ignorance of politics at the time by saying he had "read, and eagerly . . . the master pamphlets of the day,"[31] but couldn't grasp the big picture because he had

never chanced
To see a regular *chronicle* which might shew—
If any such indeed existed then—
Whence the main organs of the public power
Had sprung, their transmigrations, when and how
Accomplished (giving thus unto events
A form and body) . . . .

(IX.100–106; italics added)

This is exactly what the *Chronique du mois* did, and to believe that Wordsworth "never chanced" to see it is to believe he wasn't much interested in reading, for it was exactly the kind of journal he was most likely to pick up. His disingenuous disclaimer, "if any such existed then," gives him away, just as his honesty makes him include it (though he excised it in *1850*).

Oswald was on the *Chronique*'s board of editors as British correspondent, listed as the friend of Tom Paine, James Mackintosh, and John Horne Tooke, and charged with "destroying the popular prejudices which have so long sown discord and rivalry between two nations truly distinguished for their love of justice."[32] The other editors were the crème de la crème of the political moment, headed by Brissot, the philosophe Condorcet, and Collot d'Herbois (later replaced by Paine). Modeled on the *London Chronicle* (where Oswald had also worked), the *Chronique du mois* was published by the Cercle Social, a sort of liberal-Masonic think tank devoted to worldwide liberation and regeneration, which has been called "the prototype of a modern revolutionary organization."[33] The Cercle Social absorbed Brissot's Amis des Noirs, and the *Chronique* became the primary organ of French abolitionists. The *Chronique*'s mixture of political and literary reviews, coupled with general essays on geography, philosophy, history, science, and reprints of Enlightenment classics (Montesquieu, Rousseau, Hume),[34] provided a strong precedent for the "monthly miscellany" to be called the *Philanthropist,* which would shortly become Wordsworth's main literary project, for personal as well as political reasons.[35]

From fellow travelers like Helen Williams and John Oswald to journalist-politicians like Brissot, Louvet, and Gorsas, Wordsworth was exposed throughout his year in France not simply to politics but to politics mediated by actively interventionist writers who sought to shape the reality they simultaneously described. Over five hundred new journals were started up in France between 1789 and 1792, "an unprecedented number that reflected a separate revolution in the history of journalism."[36] Brissot exclaimed on August 2, 1791, in his *Patriote français,* that "the great tribune of humanity has been found: it is the press." Publishers and writers—and politicians—were not such different roles as they usually are today; the repeated designation of *publiciste* in many revolutionary biographies indicates how often they were one and the same person. Brissot's *Patriote* made him a fortune, its income at its height being estimated at 30,000 livres per year; the skills he had learned in his former jobs as lobbyist and police spy paid off well.[37] Staying in power had a profit motive as well as a political one. Brissot, Carra, Gorsas, and all the others reported and defended their own actions as deputies in the pages of their journals: the line between politics, print, and profit described a complete and satisfactory circle.

None of this was lost on Wordsworth when, a year later, he had to return to London to raise money fast by his own publishing exertions. But in the first week of December 1791 he was not yet very "hot in it." He was still primarily a tourist, and revolutionary Paris did not long deter him from his plans. He went to the Bastille, "and from the rubbish gathered up a stone, / And pocketed the relick in the guise / Of an enthusiast" (IX.65–67). He claimed he was not much moved by it, because he did not yet fully understand what it meant. In *The Prelude* Wordsworth presents himself at this moment as still the Man of Feeling, not a man of action. Of all the things he saw, the only one he "hunted out" was Charles le Brun's painting *The Repentant Magdalene* (1657), in the Carmelite convent in the Faubourg St. Jacques: "A beauty exquisitely wrought—fair face / And rueful, with its ever-flowing tears" (IX.79–80). Hung with special lighting, featuring recommended viewing stations for different perspectives, and accompanied by organ music, its baroque sensuality was so voluptuous that the Magdalene looked like a woman in the throes as much of passion as of repentance—or, with her imploring eyes, in the passion of being abandoned (see illustration). The picture was a popular tourist attraction, though by the following summer the convent, along with the Grande Chartreuse and most other religious houses, was shut down as part of the increasingly severe drive against priests who refused to swear allegiance to the Civil Constitution of the Clergy.[38]

Orléans

Sticking to his plan, Wordsworth left Paris on December 5—the day Mozart died in Vienna—and traveled seventy-five miles southwest to Orléans. Leaving Paris for Orléans, he was leaving the future for the past. Orléans was still a royal city, as the entire Loire valley had been the playground retreat of French aristocracy for centuries, away from the crowds, dirt, and dangers of Paris. Lord Gower, the British ambassador, considered the Loire to be the dividing line between monarchical and antimonarchical France. The Orléans Jacobin Club was much more conservative than the one in Paris.[39] Several national administrative and financial bureaus still had their headquarters in

Orléans, including La Haute Cour Nationale, the venue for state treason trials until August of 1792, when the Revolutionary Tribunal was created in Paris with infamous results.[40] These qualities made Orléans a favorite resort throughout the eighteenth century for English visitors eager to cultivate French fashions and manners, and sons of prosperous middle-class families were regularly sent there to learn the language and get some Continental polish.[41]

Orléans in late 1791 was falling out of step with the times. Helen Williams, arriving shortly before Wordsworth, had quickly sized it up as "confined, illiberal, and disagreeable," and departed almost on the day he arrived, heading for Paris, where the action was and where she soon became the leading hostess of the most advanced English salon. Felix Vaughan had had the same reaction a year earlier.[42] But Williams and Vaughan were already committed political reformers, and Wordsworth was not. The established, conservative nature of Wordsworth's sense of himself at this time, for all his rebelliousness against his family's wishes, is illustrated by the fact that his activities were virtually identical with those of young Joseph Jekyll, son of a prosperous Whig merchant, who visited Orléans and Blois in 1775–76, when he also was twenty-one. Almost everything Jekyll did, Wordsworth did too: came to learn French, spent a week in Paris (where he too "lounged [*sic*] to see . . . that wonderful portrait of Madame de la Vallière in the character of Magdalen"), stayed in the rue Royal in Orléans, danced and flirted and gamed there, visited the parks and villas at La Source near Orléans, proceeded to Blois, thought Blois provincial but interesting, found the company of women the most agreeable way of learning the language, noted the frequency of poor girls winding distaffs while they led cows to graze, visited the famous châteaux of the Loire, and was finally called home by his father for spending too much per the money bills of the banker Sir Robert Herries, which Wordsworth also used.[43]

But the times were changing: Wordsworth found almost no Englishmen in Orléans, whereas Jekyll had found so many he had to leave "that stupid town of Orléans, where an Englishman never got into French society," in order to be able to speak French.[44] The conservatism of the city suited Wordsworth quite well at the outset, and he told Richard he looked forward to meeting "the best society this place affords."

> I loitered, and frequented night by night
> Routs, card-tables, the formal haunts of men
> Whom in the city privilege of birth
> Sequestered from the rest . . . .
>
> (IX.115–18)

In the way that foreign travel often takes us above our usual social strata, Wordsworth was now moving in better circles than he had in either London or Paris, and more elegant than the company of fellows at Cambridge. It was very much the kind of society frequented by those young gentlemen whom he was ostensibly training himself to accompany on their grand tours.

He stayed first at Les Trois Empereurs, the best hotel in the city, where he had knowledgeably made advance reservations.[45] When he learned he had just missed Helen Williams, the news was "a considerable disappointment" to him. But meeting her might have been a shock, since her ideas of "best society" were already very different from his. "However I have in some respects remedied it by introducing myself to a Mr. Foxlow an Englishman who has set up a Cotton manufactory here. . . . I shall I flatter myself by their means be introduced to the best society this place affords."[46] Thomas Foxlow's half brother Francis (1771–1841) had been a classmate at St. John's for the last two years, and Wordsworth was not shy about using slight acquaintance to social advantage.[47] Foxlow himself was an early sympathizer with the Revolution, a liberal Whiggish entrepreneur secretly backed by the duc d'Orléans, soon to become "duc d'Egalité." Foxlow entertained Helen Williams's lover, the radical intriguer and businessman John Hurford Stone, the following September, and had already performed services for the new government.[48] Helen Williams unhesitatingly called him "a friend of liberty," but either Wordsworth didn't know of Foxlow's sympathies or Foxlow didn't find Wordsworth a likely confidant, for on December 19 William wrote Richard that he had found "almost all of the people of any opulence are aristocrates [*sic*] and all the others democrates [*sic*]. I had imagined there were some people of wealth and circumstances favorers of the revolution, but here there is not one to be found."[49] At first, "the chief of [Wordsworth's] associates . . . were men well-born . . . the chivalry of France" (IX.130–33), military officers who were royalist sympathizers. They were eager to get to the frontier, in order—as Robespierre shrewdly saw, with his genius for suspicion—to turn their coats and join their friends in an émigré army that would march back upon Paris to rescue it from the republican rabble. These officers tried to convince Wordsworth of the justice of their cause, while making allowance for his youth, his awkward language, and his nationality—"born in a land the name of which appeared / To license some unruliness of mind," as he suavely put it.

Eager to demonstrate his frugality to Richard, he soon moved out of Les Trois Empereurs and found lodging and board above the shop of M. Jean Gellet-Duvivier in the rue Royale, Orléans's main street, for 80 livres a month. These fine Neoclassical buildings are still standing on both sides of the rue Royale, running south from the central city plaza to a bridge over the Loire. The buildings are as impressive as those in Paris's rue Royale, on which they are modeled, and provided an address well suited to a young English gentleman abroad. Living there with two or three royalist cavalry officers, and with his initial capital of 643 livres and his native frugality, Wordsworth seemed well set for months to come.

During his hunt for cheaper lodgings, he came across a "very agreeable" family whose rooms were too expensive, but they struck up an acquaintance, and by December 19 he was already telling Richard, "I have passed some of my evenings there." This was the home of André-Augustin Dufour, a magistrate's clerk living in the rue de Poirier, near the rue Royale. One of Dufour's tenants was Paul Vallon, a lawyer's clerk working nearby, who was being visited that holiday season by his youngest sister, Marie-Anne, aged twenty-five, called Annette.[50] This was the woman who changed the course of Wordsworth's young life.

Annette Vallon was not a great beauty, though her presumed miniature is certainly attractive (see illustration). But everyone who met her soon commented, or complained, about her vivacity. "Vivacious" was not a lively enough word for most, who called her, depending on their political perspective, either an "active intriguer" of "unscrupulous astuteness," a woman combining "great sensibility with a very vivid and impassioned imagination [and] rare firmness in her designs," or "a sort of Scarlet Pimpernel."[51] Annette was as full of outgoing energy as Wordsworth was of power held in reserve, "gifted with that natural intrepidity which was to make her a model conspirator."[52] She took initiatives in hundreds of matters in dozens of different ways, from braving the secret police (of, successively, the Terror, the Directory, and Napoleon) to arranging the marriage of her dissolute brother to a neurasthenic semi-invalid, a stroke of matchmaking genius which cured them both. No doubt she often went too far. But she was a dynamo of action, a Théroigne de Méricourt or Olympe de Gouges of the right, and, if not as stunning as those revolutionary beauties, far more politically astute and successful than they. Olympe ended up on the scaffold and Théroigne in a madhouse, but Annette, an underground fighter against the Revolution, was ultimately pensioned as a heroine of the royalist resistance to Napoleon: "the valiant Chouanne of Blois," a young woman as devoutly attached to king and country as her region's dominant historical figure, the Maid of Orléans.[53]

The contrast between this first love of Wordsworth's life and his second, mild Mary Hutchinson, could hardly be greater, but Annette's intensity was not very different from Dorothy's, and Annette eventually found in Dorothy a true soul mate. That Annette swept William off his feet with her energy, as a relatively independent woman four years his senior, is doubtful. But if she seduced him, he was overdue for seduction, if (as seems unlikely) none of his experiences among the "frank-hearted maids" of Cumberland, the Cyprians and snobbesses of Cambridge, or the dancing girls on Lake Como had gone that far. Though he was reserved, he was not shy. Dorothy spoke of his "violence of Affection," and the judgment that he was "a dangerous young man . . . if there were unattached feminine hearts in the vicinity" seems just.[54] Their passion seems to have been gratifyingly mutual.[55]

Whatever else she may have been, Annette was one of the best things that ever happened to Wordsworth. Commentators on this love affair take sides even more than is usual with other people's affairs, but both he and she seem to have acted with exemplary tact, sensitivity, and understanding through it all—never perfect, but far above what might be considered the norm in such a tangled affair. One is glad to know that young Wordsworth had enough liveliness to attract a woman of Annette's spirit, just as one admires Annette's loyalty in never marrying, and calling herself Mrs. or Widow (Veuve) William, or Williams, for the rest of her life. To put their affair in perspective, we have only to consider how many love affairs there were between foreigners and French men and women in these times of "perturbing promiscuity," "extraordinary laxity of morals," and "mad thirst for pleasure,"[56] how many might have resulted in illegitimate births, and how few of the principals stayed in touch with each other as long as William and Annette did. They wrote letters throughout the first stage of the war between France and England, hurried to Calais to make contact at their first opportunity (the Peace of Amiens, 1802), kept up relations as best they could throughout the Napoleonic Wars, even though Wordsworth was married, then reestablished connections—and financial arrangements—as soon as possible after Waterloo. They finally met, all families together, in Paris in 1820 on the great Wordsworthian pilgrimage back to the scenes of his youth. On this view, William Wordsworth and Annette Vallon have few equals for constancy as lovers in the French Revolution, even though, as is always the case, each was true to the other in her fashion, in his way.

The Vallons, whose family home was in Blois, were of only slightly lower social class than Wordsworth. Like William, Annette had uncles who were clerics; both had duly taken the oath of the Civil Constitution, and one of them was at this time vicar to the great bishop Grégoire, who had taken office in Blois in March 1791. One of her brothers was, like one of William's, a lawyer, while the other two had followed their recently deceased (1788) father's footsteps as surgeon-barbers at the main hospital in Blois.

Her two uncles (actually older first cousins) were sometimes called the "Welsh uncles," not because they were Welsh but because the entire family had Jacobite connections, dating back to the Scotch and Irish who had come over to France with James II in 1688. At that time the family was called

Léonard, which was still the middle name of Annette's father and her younger uncle, corrupted to Léonnar.*

There were thousands of descendants of the Jacobites in France by this time, some of whom saw their own opportunities for a return to British power in the Revolution, even though the Young Pretender had died, with his family's usual bad timing, in 1788. (The body of James II was on display in Paris at the English Benedictine monastery near the Carmelite convent, his brain encased in a gilt urn nearby. The coffin was opened and the body stolen during the Terror.)[57] Far from being mere historical curiosities, these displaced persons gave real meaning to the contemporary epithet "old Jacobite turned new Jacobin." These British family connections were one of those nice coincidences that gave the two young people something to talk about at first, things they already had in common to help explain their uncommon interest in each other. Annette may have been, initially, only an item in Wordsworth's frugal budget. "I do not intend to take a [language] master," he reported to Richard; "I think I can do nearly as well without one." This must have startled Richard, since the whole point of William's elaborately arranged trip was to learn the language to a *professional* standard. But William was employing another method, well known to young men abroad, learning the language by falling in love—or falling in love while learning. Annette, along with her tremendous physical energy, loved to talk,[58] and Wordsworth was for once disposed to listen.

Few expressions better capture the first enthusiasm that greeted the French Revolution than Wordsworth's "Bliss was it in that dawn to be alive, / But to be young was very heaven!" But we must appreciate Annette's part in creating Wordsworth's bliss, for there are also not many expressions that better capture the transfiguring effect of young love at first sight than Wordsworth's description of Vaudracour's vision of Julia:

> Oh, happy time of youthful lovers—
> . . . oh, balmy time
> In which a love-knot on a lady's brow
> Is fairer than the fairest star in heaven!
> . . . .
> —he beheld
> A vision, and he loved the thing he saw.
> Arabian fiction never filled the world
> With half the wonders that were wrought for him:
> Earth lived in one great presence of the spring,

*Leonard is the name of the sailor in Wordsworth's "The Brothers" (1800), who comes home to the Lake District only to find his brother dead and himself unrecognized, one of Wordsworth's most intricate tales in the romantic mode of "you can't go home again."

Life turned the meanest of her implements
Before his eyes to price above all gold,
The house she dwelt in was a sainted shrine,
Her chamber-window did surpass in glory
The portals of the east, all paradise
Could by the simple opening of a door
Let itself in upon him . . . .

(IX.556–59, 582–93)

Whenever Wordsworth uses "Oriental" diction like this, invoking Arabia, India, or Babylon, his imaginative commitment is at its highest emotional pitch. It has been plausibly argued, albeit with Freudian hindsight, that we can read, in those portals and other opening apertures, and in the lines immediately following, Wordsworth's sublimated expressions of the first dizzying, then grateful, quality of happy sexual experience: "pathways, walks, / Swarmed with enchantment, till his spirits sunk / Beneath the burden, overblessed for life" (IX.593–95).[59]

Annette's language matched Wordsworth's passionate expressions, though no one has seen fit to translate her accurately in print. At the end of her letter of March 20, 1793, after symbolically embracing Caroline in his stead and expressing her concern at worrying Dorothy, she turns at last to state directly, though discreetly, her feelings for him: "Aime toujours ta petite fille et ton Annette qui t'embrasse mil fois *sur la bouche, sur les yeux et mon petit que j'aime toujours, que je recomande bien à tes soins.*"[60] This is a series of increasingly intimate kisses, "on the lips, on the eyes and [on] my little [one] that I still love, and that I warmly commend to your care." "Mon petit" is not Caroline; it is lovers' code for something masculine, and in his keeping.

Wordsworth gives two different accounts of how Vaudracour and Julia began the physical part of their intimacy, which for him and Annette must have occurred in the protective intimacy of the Dufours' house. One option is merely generic: "some delirious hour." But the other is so complicated that it can only be Wordsworth:

the youth,
Seeing so many bars betwixt himself
And the dear haven where he wished to be
In honorable wedlock with his love,
Without a certain knowledge of his own
Was inwardly prepared to turn aside
From law and custom and entrust himself
To Nature for the happy end of all,
And thus abated of that pure reserve
Congenial to his loyal heart, with which

> It would have pleased him to attend the steps
> Of maiden so divinely beautiful . . . .
> (IX.597–608)

As the ex post facto rationalization of a married man, aged thirty-four, this does not wash very well. But as the confused rationalization of a twenty-two-year-old, it is fittingly inconsistent. What does it mean to be "inwardly prepared" to do something "without a certain knowledge of [one's] own"? It does not signify unconscious intent, or emotional inclination without a conscious decision; either would fall under the heading of "some delirious hour." Rather, it seems to mean, Well, let's go ahead, and if she gets pregnant, that will show that Nature intended her to, "for a happy end of all." Thus did Rousseau come in aid of the feelings of many young lovers in the late eighteenth century. But, as to the question of who seduced whom, the lines, for all their charming confusion, center directly on "the youth." It is only in conclusion, describing the outcome of this line of reasoning, that the woman's part returns: "[I] reluctantly must add / That Julia, yet without the name of wife, / Carried about her for a secret grief / The promise of a mother" (IX.609–12).

By allying himself with Annette, Wordsworth put himself and his interests directly athwart one of the two most important political issues threatening to rend France apart at that time: the treatment of nonjuring priests. The other was the treatment of émigrés. Fierce laws against both groups had been adopted on November 29, exactly as Wordsworth arrived in Paris; Louis soon gave notice of his intention to veto them, thus stirring up another constitutional crisis. The two issues were closely connected in the popular patriot mind, because conservative priests were seen as—and in some cases were—fanatical fifth columnists whipping up dissent and plotting sabotage at home, while providing a network of information and supply for the feared invasion of émigré armies from the frontiers.[61] At the same time, in conservative areas like Orléans, renegade actions against constitutional priests also increased. The Vallons were the kind of family that was driven out of an initial sympathy with the Revolution by its harsh policies toward *réfractaires.* That Annette's two priestly uncles had taken the civil oath immediately, and were important local council officials in Blois both during and after the Terror, shows how these issues could simultaneously divide and protect members of the same family: her uncles were surely the source of some of her extraordinary escapes from punishment in some of her riskier escapades on behalf of priests and aristocrats during the Directory and under Napoleon.

Wordsworth said he left Orléans because he tired of royalist proselytizing, but he covers his motive for leaving town in double-edged language:

But 'twas not long ere this
Proved tedious, and I gradually withdrew
Into a noisier world, and thus did soon
Become a patriot—and my heart was all
Given to the people, and my love was theirs.
(IX.122–25)

This sounds like a political decision, but it was not purely so. The "noisier world" was Blois, the "not long" was less than two months after he arrived in Orléans, and the person among those people to whom he had given his "heart" and "love" was of course Annette—who was hardly "a patriot," in current usage.[62]

Blois

Wordsworth followed Annette home to Blois sometime between early February and mid-April 1792. He was following as an ardent lover, but by the later date he would already have been a prospective father, since they conceived a child in mid-March. The affair must have been first consummated in Orléans for him to make such a precipitate move, for Blois figured nowhere in his plans, and changing his planned course of action was not characteristic of him. Annette had been visiting her brother Paul for the Christmas holidays, and by February she had stayed long enough, even though she was a very independent young woman.

In his next communication home, Wordsworth's sense of time is clearly that of a man in love: "Since my arrival day after day and week after week has stolen insensibly over my head with inconceivable rapidity."[63] A huge difference lay between his last letter to Mathews the previous November, when he had yawned, "I am doomed to be an idler throughout my whole life," and his new spirit of "confidence and resolution" about finding "some method of obtaining an Independence." He now directed Mathews to scout about in "the field of Letters" for "some little corner, which with a little tillage will produce us enough for the necessities, nay even the comforts, of life."[64] Obviously, something had happened in the interim to motivate him: something beyond his control. If Mathews does not find something in the literary line, Wordsworth says, he will take orders, accepting the intervention of the Reverend Cookson despite the personal humiliation: "My Uncle the Clergyman will furnish me with a title. Had it been in my power I certainly should have wished to defer the moment." But events were no longer in his power, nor could he easily "entrust himself to Nature for a happy end of all."

A February arrival in Blois is more likely on political grounds as well. On February 3 two Englishmen were given permission to attend meetings of Les

Amis de la Constitution, which met in the desacralized church of St. Laumer (now St. Nicolas) directly below the imperial château.[65] These are the only Englishmen ever referred to in the records of the Blois Amis.[66] This was the local chapter of the Jacobin Club, known everywhere outside Paris by its proper name, Society of the Friends of the Constitution. Since Wordsworth had been introduced at the Paris headquarters, it is not unlikely that he was furnished with a letter or ticket of entry for use in the provinces. The Blois chapter was particularly associated with the Brissotins at this time[67]—as was Wordsworth—and Brissot's name continued to gain luster. On March 15 he became in effect the prime minister of France, when Louis asked him to form a new ministry.

In coming to Blois, a mere thirty-five miles west of Orléans along the Loire, Wordsworth was entering a more attractive town, but a more vexed political climate. It was smaller (population 12,000), more provincial, less royalist than Orléans, and much more divided. It was a mustering center for a battalion of volunteers being raised in the new department of Loire-et-Cher, of which it was the new capital. Its chapter of the Friends of the Constitution was more radical than the one in Orléans, especially under its new leader, the constitutional bishop Henri Grégoire, who had been elected its president in November. Grégoire was one of the admirable idealists of the time, a Jansenist Catholic who sought to reform past ecclesiastical abuses with republican virtues while at the same time softening the excesses of revolution with Christian charity. Sitting in the chair, he was a sympathetic auditor to appeals on the need for moderation and tolerance. Under his leadership the Blois Amis de la Constitution formed a much more open debating society than its mother club in Paris, which Grégoire regarded as a "factious hell."[68] His time as bishop of Blois (October 1791–September 1792) overlaps the period of Wordsworth's residence there. His chief aide was Annette's uncle Claude, and he would have been particularly receptive to Wordsworth if he came recommended by Brissot, since he was also a member of Brissot's Les Amis des Noirs, and the fight against slavery (and anti-Semitism) remained his chief cause long after the Revolution had lost its original claims to virtue.[69]

But at the same time Blois was becoming a center of zealous counterrevolution, rife with agents from the Vendée, farther west. "Vendée" was a term used loosely to signify royalist insurrections all over the west of France, including not only the Vendée proper, south of Nantes, but also Normandy and Brittany. Many of these royalist Catholic agents were later tracked by the police to the residence of "the demoiselles Vallon, one of whom is married to an Englishman named Williaume."[70] The priestly class was proportionately larger and wealthier in Blois than in Orléans. Before the Revolution broke out, there had been seven monasteries and five nunneries there, and the properties and personnel of these old religious enclosures cast a somber air over whole sections of the city.[71] Annette's other uncle, Charles, was the priest at St. Saturnin, which served the Hôpital-Général, south of the river, where her two brothers were surgeon-barbers.[72]

Yet, for all its divisions, Blois was (and is) a cozier town than Orléans. Young Joseph Jekyll had found it so in 1775, when, as "Monsieur Anglais," he had been included in the fall wine making and country dances, "and the girls smeared his face with the lees [and] he was obliged to dance in wooden shoes, and was as gay and as dirty as possible."[73] Similarly, the comte de Cheverny, no republican but no émigré either, found it equally charming, much preferable to Orléans for its lack of class distinctions, friendly family-like gatherings, and elegantly dressed women and pretty, marriageable girls.[74] Annette was one of these, and it was her hometown; all her family were there except Paul, and she was better known and "better looked after."[75] These were mixed blessings for the two lovers, who had had more freedom in the relative anonymity of Orléans. But in the heady days of first love in springtime—"One great presence of the spring"—they were free to walk about, down the rue du Pont, the busy shopping street where she lived, to the river, and up into the old medieval section by the convent where she had been educated.

But Annette needed more care as the months went by and became more dependent on family and friends, who were not pleased by her connection to an unemployed and evidently not rich young Englishman, who was at best a Protestant and at worst a republican—and a poet. Wordsworth was in no position to provide practical help and, as a result, was left more on his own, far less disposed than before to devote himself to the charade of learning French to become a traveling tutor; that career option was now completely out of the question. He was slowly determining himself to marry and provide for Annette. It was in this mixed state, of deep passion, desperate responsibility, and wandering loneliness, that his acquaintance with Michel Beaupuy ripened quickly into deep friendship—indeed, as *The Prelude* freely acknowledges, the most important male friendship of his life before Coleridge.

Michel-Arnaud Bacharetie de Beaupuy (1755–1796) is known in English, if at all, as a character in one part of Wordsworth's long poem on "the growth of my own mind." But he is honored in France as one of the heroic generals who died protecting the Revolution in its vulnerable infancy. In 1798 he was celebrated posthumously as "le Nestor et l'Achille de notre armée," and his fame has endured, as one detail will suffice to illustrate. A monument was erected in 1802 at the order of General Moreau, Beaupuy's commanding officer, at Biesheim, on the French side of the Rhine (near Colmar), to commemorate Beaupuy's death at the battle of Emmendingen, on the German side (near Freiburg), in 1796. This monument was destroyed by the invading Germans in 1940, but a new one was erected in 1979, by public subscription in Biesheim, in the nearby towns of Vogelsheim and Neu-Breisach, and in Beaupuy's distant hometown of Mussidan in the Limoges/Périgueux area of Périgord.[76] Napoleon's marshals are the famous military men we remember from this period, but in the early 1790s France's fate hung upon the skill and bravery—and loyalty—of other generals, several of them foreign freedom fighters, who gave their lives for the Revolution or were destroyed by it, men like Charles-François Dumouriez, Theobald Dillon, Francisco Miranda, Adam Philippe de Custine, and Louis-Lazare Hoche. One of these lesser military officers finally did what was clearly becoming more necessary with each succeeding year, and returned to Paris to restore order by force. His name also began with a *B*, but it might have been far better for the course of European history had it been Beaupuy, not Bonaparte.

Beaupuy's father, like Wordsworth's, had been a steward of aristocratic estates, and by the time of Michel's birth had attained to the minor nobility.[77] On his mother's side, he was descended from Montaigne; the family stressed education and public service for its sons: a complete edition of Diderot's massive *Encyclopédie* dominated the family library. Beaupuy had been one of the first to speak out in Mussidan in favor of the changes which led up to the Revolution. He supported the call issued in October 1790 by the leaders of the Limoges Amis de la Constitution for a deputation to be sent to London to meet with English sympathizers. Hence he was happy to meet an Englishman in Blois, especially one so ripe for the final stages of conversion to the good new cause. That Wordsworth was of roughly his same class and educational background made him all the more attractive to the busy young captain.

At the time they met, in February 1792, Beaupuy was rising fast in rank as mobilization, war, and desertions multiplied opportunities. Under the new Legislative Assembly, he had been named to the national military committee headed by the engineer Lazare Carnot.[78] It is unlikely that Wordsworth would have become well enough acquainted with him by February 3 to have been introduced to the Amis by him, but it is very likely that Wordsworth met him there, since Beaupuy was a regular member, and on the two previous Sundays had repeated, by popular demand, his speech on the dangers of excessive mistrust in politics.[79] His regiment, the Thirty-second Bassigny, was in Blois to raise itself to full strength before leaving for service on the Rhine. By his friendship with Beaupuy, Wordsworth became personally involved in the other great political issue racking France at this time, the proper attitude and policy toward aristocrats, particularly those in the military, and most especially those who might become dangerous émigrés if given command of troops near the volatile frontier. Beaupuy's speeches on January 22 and 29 against excessive political mistrust were thus very timely, and he was much in advance of the rest of his class in moving rapidly beyond support of limited constitutional monarchy toward full-blown republicanism.[80]

Wordsworth was attracted to Beaupuy's literary tastes as well as his political views, going so far as to consider his friend a special kind of literary hero: "He through the events / Of that great change wandered in perfect faith, / As through a book, an old romance, or tale / Of Fairy" (IX.305–8). This may be more Wordsworth's self-projection than a realistic description of Beaupuy, but he was something of a ladies' man—"somewhat vain he was, or seemed so"—though this could safely be affirmed of almost the entire officer class. Yet he had effected a personal transformation in the ethos of his class, so that the gallantry which "in his idler days [he] had payed to woman," he now "unto the poor / Among mankind . . . was in service bound / As by some tie invisible." Instead of questing in the service of his Lady, Beaupuy, like a paradoxical Chevalier de la Révolution, sallies forth to meet the Enemies of the People. Doubtless Wordsworth over-idealized his friend, and when he added, "man he loved as man," we can see that Beaupuy is being cast as a military version of the "man speaking to men" of Wordsworth's ideal Poet in 1802.

Wordsworth claimed that Beaupuy was "with an oriental loathing spurned as of a different cast[e]" by his fellow officers (IX.297–98). But this is an imaginative transference of the attitudes of the officers with whom Wordsworth had mixed in Orléans, the better to set off Beaupuy's republican virtues. It is one of several ways in which Wordsworth makes a coherent story out of his "residence in France" by treating it as though it all happened in *one* unnamed "city on the borders of the Loire." Beaupuy was so active and admired at the Amis that he cannot have been as lonely and scorned as Wordsworth paints him, especially since the "brothers" of the Thirty-second Bassigny took the oath of allegiance to the Legislative Assembly there on February 3 (the same day the two Englishmen were given attendance privileges), and on March 14 the regiment was invited to assist at meetings.[81] Royalists among Beaupuy's fellow officers might have sneered at him, but they would have kept their opinions to themselves, especially since their regimental colonel had been stripped of his rank for refusing to sign the oath of obedience to the Assembly. But if his aristocratic fellows did scorn his friendship, Beaupuy was all the more receptive to a young, open-minded Englishman. Wordsworth, listening to Beaupuy speak before the local Jacobins, improved his French in a register different from the one he used with Annette. His political education now began to accelerate rapidly, for here as throughout France the most basic questions of citizens' rights and responsibilities were thrashed out night after night, often with immediate consequences in action the next day. The "stale matter" of the classical republican texts Wordsworth had read at Cambridge was now each day's lively order of business, in meetings whose secular liberalism shocked Annette's sister when she visited them in the dechristianized cathedral.

After meetings, Beaupuy elaborated on the questions of the day for his new friend.

> Oft in solitude
> With him did I discourse about the end
> Of civil government, and its wisest forms,
> Of ancient prejudice and chartered rights,
> Allegiance, faith, and laws by time matured,
> Custom and habit, novelty and change . . . .
> (IX.328–33)

These topics marked the range of contemporary debate, from Burke ("custom and habit") to Paine ("novelty and change") in English terms, though the passage as a whole leans toward conservative views. If these lines reflect Beaupuy's interests and not simply Wordsworth's change of heart by 1804, they indicate that Beaupuy took longer views in conversation than he could in debate, though his speeches show he was capable of resisting popular hysteria.

But they were still young men of their class, in the process of transition to new political allegiances, and they both took "more delight," when they were alone, Wordsworth confesses "freely,"

> In painting to ourselves the miseries
> Of royal courts, and that voluptuous life
> Unfeeling where the man who is of soul
> The meanest thrives the most, where dignity,
> True personal dignity, abideth not . . . .
> (352–56)

There is a touching realism in this detail of two young men discussing such a topic at such a time and place, when "royal courts" themselves were so soon to pass out of existence, amid far worse "miseries." One of Beaupuy's first political acts had in fact been to present a *cahier de doléances* against royal excesses in his home region.[82] But in Blois he and Wordsworth were talking about the difficulty of advancing in the kinds of careers their families and training had set before them—based on influence and connections—just as the arena for this particular historical form of institutionalized meanness was disappearing. New career models were being created, in which both Wordsworth and Beaupuy would succeed in ways they could as yet barely conceive of.

On weekends they ranged farther afield, walking out into the profound silences of the great oak and beech forests of the châteaux south and east of Blois. Wordsworth mentions Chambord and Romorantin by name, in addition to "the imperial edifice of Blois" itself, and alludes to others, such as Beauregard and, north of the Loire, Vendôme.[83] The châteaux themselves, then as now, give grand testimony to both the power and the price of passion, since the story behind many of them is one of beautiful mistresses demanding of their "royal knight" some magnificent demonstration of his love—Diane de Poitiers's Chenonceaux being only the most stunning example. Grégoire was not one to miss these associations, singling out Menars, "built in honor of the impure La Pompadour," and regularly referring to their "bloody shades" in his puritanical sermons.[84] In fact, from Joan of Arc through Diane de Poitiers to—for young Wordsworth—Annette Vallon, the power of women controlling politics through passion is a sensation one can still feel strongly all along the Loire valley.

In the deep woods of these immense pleasure palaces, Wordsworth and Beaupuy talked of two topics especially: individual heroism and, as a dramatic example of it, rescuing damsels in distress. Wordsworth mentions Ariosto's Angelica and Tasso's Erminia, but his own Annette was the real case in point. No one ever asks if Wordsworth mentioned Annette to Beaupuy, but he must have, given the older man's reputation as a gallant. In the rich confusions of life and literature which Wordsworth concocted out of this period of his life, one can almost wish his Julia had met Beaupuy instead of Vaudracour. And the topic of solo heroics, though apparently far afield, was not inapt for either man's situation. The debates in Blois and in Paris gave daily evidence of what could happen when "single spirits . . . catch the flame of heaven . . . and how the multitude of men will feed / And fan each other" (IX.376–78). The rapid rise and fall of individuals who tried to harness this process dramatized its costs. Their abstract models were "philosophic wars led by philosophers," from ancient Greek examples, which were also standard Jacobin points of reference, but Wordsworth's account shows a marked predeliction for successful assassins whose actions spoke more eloquently than their words (IX.415–24, X.161–67). Assassination was already in everybody's thoughts in Paris, though technically an unspeakable subject; bodyguards were becoming common, though Charlotte Corday's shocking murder of Marat in his bathtub was still a year away.

Beaupuy brought Wordsworth's romanticizing up short. One day they came upon "a hunger-bitten girl" following her heifer, to which she was looped by a cord, "busy knitting in a heartless mood of solitude." " 'Tis against *that* which we are fighting," said Beaupuy, startling Wordsworth from his romantic daydreams (*1850*, 517–18). Such sights were common in the region,[85] but Beaupuy touched here on the deepest and most elusive promise of this and all future democratic revolutions, that after liberty and fraternity would come equality, or something nearer to it:

> that poverty,
> At least like this, would in a little time
> Be found no more, that we should see the earth
> Unthwarted in her wish to recompense
> The industrious, and the lowly child of toil . . . .
> (IX.522–26)

This was the issue that successively more radical leaders in Paris could never get ahead of, either by means of a maximum imposed on the price of bread, or by a reign of terror instituted against those who were supposedly hoarding bread or speculating on its scarcity. The cowherd girl was "bitten" by hunger because of the high price of grain and flour in Blois in the spring of 1792, which led to riots of varying intensity all the way down the river from Orléans to Tours.[86]

Beaupuy departed from Blois and from Wordsworth's life on July 27, 1792. He died at Emmendingen in 1796, but Wordsworth in *The Prelude* says he died fighting on "the unhappy borders of the Loire," in action against the Vendean counterrevolution of 1793. If Wordsworth ever learned the truth, he never corrected it in the poem on the growth of his mind, and it is more fitting dramatically that *his* Beaupuy should have died there rather than in Germany. In a sense, Beaupuy's "death" on the Loire may be said to represent the death that Wordsworth courted by returning to France in 1793—or escaped by not returning—a poetical "sacrifice" of his heroic friend, representing the heroism he wished he could achieve.

After Beaupuy left, Wordsworth remained in Blois until early September, tending to Annette as much as he could, and attending Grégoire's meetings even more than he had. His "Letter to the Bishop of Llandaff," composed the following March, quotes directly from one of Grégoire's sermons he attended and snidely contrasts Bishop Richard Watson to Grégoire as "a man of philosophy and humanity as distinguished as your Lordship."[87] He wrote the final drafts of *Descriptive Sketches* in late spring and summer of 1792, and the influence of Grégoire's millennial republicanism is clearly evident in the sections of the poem devoted to Switzerland. In a sermon in March, Grégoire referred to places Wordsworth had actually visited, to make a conventional point about natural republicanism: "On the brow of the mountains of Appenzell and the Alps one often still finds man in all his dignity, gifted with exquisite reason, manly virtue, and even crowned with broad understanding;

but it is also there that at the head or the rear of his flocks he marches carrying a sword, a crook, and some books."[88] Wordsworth virtually sets the images in this passage to verse, with the added license of poetic diction:

> here
> The traces of primaeval Man appear.
> The native dignity no forms debase,
> The eye sublime, and surly lion-grace.
> The slave of none, of beasts alone the lord,
> He marches with his flute, his book, his sword.
> (IX.528–33)

His motives for going to Switzerland in 1790 had been formed by traditional idealizations of the Swiss cantons as bedrocks of mountain republicanism. But, drafting the final version of the poem in 1792, this ideal republicanism was infused with his daily experience of the debates and actions that were creating a modern republic in the largest country in Europe. Grégoire's religious interpretation of the process fit well with Wordsworth's secular motives of 1790. But when the monarchy was dissolved, two weeks after Beaupuy's departure, the new state was bathed in blood. The first republic was declared on September 21—on a motion by Grégoire[89]—and these political pieties became harder to sustain.

Wordsworth could hardly have found two more congenial mentors for his conversion to republicanism than Beaupuy and Grégoire. Each was a convert himself, from the old Estates of the nobility and the church, and each tried to preserve the best of the old while seeking to realize the best in the new. But his change of opinions was both quickened and complicated by Annette's ambivalent attitude toward the course of events. He met her at almost the last moment when she and her immediate family regarded the Revolution with sympathy; by the time he left her, they were dead set against it. Hence the contrary motions of love and politics at work on Wordsworth in 1792 had an extremely strong torque: a bishop and a nobleman, natural enemies of revolution and republic, persuaded him to accept it; a daughter of the Third Estate, the bourgeois professional class which created the Revolution, increasingly urged him against it. Paris was too far to the left for him, Orléans too far to the right; only in Blois did the combination fall fortuitously into place. To say that Annette and Beaupuy existed on "two separate planes of being" for Wordsworth is to miss the rich point of his experience in France.[90] He was "radicalized" in love and politics simultaneously, and it is moot to say which came first, though it is true that one would not have occurred without the other. But who could have predicted the odd ways in which they came to him? It is not unlikely that Annette's social conservatism helped make her attractive to him. But it is equally clear that conservative nobles and clergymen had earned his contempt in both France and England, whereas his respect for *constitutionnels* like Grégoire—and Annette's uncles—stayed with him to the end: "he had known many of the abbés and other ecclesiastics, and thought highly of them as a class; they were earnest, faithful men."[91]

Political events soon began to outstrip personal affairs for Wordsworth, as they did for everyone else in France. In May he had written disingenuously to Mathews about his lack of information on the progress of the Revolution: "You will naturally expect that writing from a country agitated by the storms of a revolution, my Letter should not be confined merely to us and our friends. But the truth is that in London you have perhaps a better opportunity of being informed of the general concerns of France, than in a petty provincial town in the heart of the kingdom itself. The *annals of the department* are all with which I have a better opportunity of being acquainted than you, provided you feel a sufficient interest in informing yourself."[92] But he immediately went on to give a very specific account of the murder of the French-Irish general Theobald Dillon by his troops at Lille on April 2. By the end of the summer, Wordsworth was very much better informed on current affairs, thanks to his talks with Beaupuy. Nor were the "annals" or journals he refers to inadequate sources of information. Quite the contrary; if they were "all" he had, they were plenty. Jean-Louis Carra's *Annales patriotiques et littéraires* and Antoine-Joseph Gorsas's *Courrier des LXXXIII départements* were two of the most influential of these, particularly among the provincial Jacobin Clubs; in Blois they were the only two papers subscribed to by the Amis.[93] At times it seemed that each one of the 749 delegates to the Legislative Assembly had his own journal or newspaper, which he not only sent home to his constituents but distributed broadcast across the land. These journals are the "locusts" and "passions" in the following passage.

> The land all swarmed with passion, like a plain
> Devoured by locusts—Carra, Gorsas—add
> A hundred other names, forgotten now,
> Nor to be heard of more; yet they were powers,
> Like earthquakes, shocks repeated day by day,
> And felt through every nook of town or field.
> (IX.178–83)

The annals covered the land like a plague of locusts, their effects repeated "day by day" as different issues of different journals appeared in each day's mail, to fill "the walls of peaceful houses [like Annette's] with unquiet sounds." Both Carra's and Gorsas's were tours de force of individual energy and invention, Gorsas's especially, being written largely by himself almost daily for the better part of four years (Carra co-edited his journal with

Mercier). Carra and Gorsas were also alike in being the two Girondins who held out longest in trying to reach a compromise with the more moderate Montagnards.[94] This very much describes the arc of Wordsworth's political opinions during his time in France.

Between Beaupuy's departure and Wordsworth's next letter to Richard, on September 3, events moved so fast that "the soil of common life" soon became "too hot to tread upon" (IX.169–70), especially for a young man trying to arrange complicated personal affairs in a very unstable foreign country. On July 25 the German duke of Brunswick issued his infamous manifesto, threatening an "exemplary vengeance" on the city of Paris and its inhabitants if they did not submit to the rule of their king. Two days later Beaupuy's regiment and many others were hastily called up to the front.

Then, on August 10, came the successful assault on the Tuileries by the aroused Paris *sections,* raised by strategies of provocation that Hébert and Robespierre and their colleagues were rapidly perfecting. Six hundred of the king's Swiss guards were massacred, prelude to worse to come. The Legislative Assembly immediately suspended the monarchy and imprisoned the king, dissolved itself into the National Convention, and on August 11 appointed its own ministers: the audacious Danton at justice, the earnest Roland for the interior. Lafayette fled and defected to the Austrians within the week. The new ministry, with the extraordinary powers of the July 11 decree—"la patrie en danger!"—began ordering the arrest of hundreds of prisoners, notably religious houses full of priests and nuns (many of British descent), who were easy to catch and easy to accuse of complicity in the much feared invasion of émigré and foreign armies. French families like the Vallons were turned irretrievably against the Jacobin version of revolution by these measures. With the news on August 23 of the fall of the border fortress of Longwy to the émigré princes and their Austrian allies, followed a week later by the siege and subsequent loss of Verdun, fear grew to panic and suspicion to paranoia, because both losses were widely believed to be the result of internal subversion and betrayal. Spines were stiffened by incredible feats of rhetoric, none more magnificent than Danton's "L'audace, l'audace, et encore l'audace!" Refractory priests were attacked by a new decree on August 26 and rounded up in Paris and in the nearby department of Loire-et-Cher. For two weeks the jails filled, and the stage was set for the signal to be given—though everyone except Danton and Marat denied having given it[95]—for the horrible massacres of September 2–5. Half the prison population of Paris, over a thousand persons, most of them nonpolitical, were butchered in their cells and courtyards by the infamous *septembriseurs,* freelance murderers drunk on blood, and the Revolution was set on its course toward the Terror. The head of Princess Lamballe on one pike and her torn genitalia on another are all the symbolism one needs to trouble thoughts of the "inevitability" of democracy's progress. James Watt, an eyewitness to both August and September massacres, tried: "I am filled with involuntary horror at the scenes which pass before me and wish they could be avoided, but at the same time I allow the absolute necessity of them." He fled within the month, when his sympathy for victims led Robespierre to accuse him of being an agent for Pitt.* Wordsworth and Mary Wollstonecraft would make the same argument, but the further one gets from the experience, the more trite and fastidious the metaphors sound. Wordsworth: "The animal just released from its stall will exhaust the overflow of its spirits in a round of wanton vagaries, but it will soon return to itself and enjoy its freedom in moderate and regular delight." Wollstonecraft: "Let me beg you not to . . . throw an odium on immutable principles, because some of the mere instruments of the revolution were too sharp—children of any growth will do mischief when they meddle with edged tools."[96]

Orléans Again

In the midst of these fever-pitched days, somewhere between the *journées* of August 10 and September 2–5, Annette's family spirited her away, possibly without telling Wordsworth. She was now in her sixth month, and her appearance had begun to raise comment, so she was removed to Orléans. The circumstance is recorded in *The Prelude,* and has no parallel in Helen Williams's account of the du Fosses.

To conceal
The threatened shame the parents of the maid
Found means to hurry her away, by night
And unforewarned, that in a distant town
She might remain shrouded in privacy
Until the babe was born.

(IX.612–17)

*Muirhead, *Watt,* 479–80; DVE, 155, 163, n. 22. On August 14 Watt and three other Englishmen presented a message of sympathy and some money to the Assembly for the victims of August 10. The others were James Gamble, an engraver and part owner of White's Hotel; Robert Rayment, an economist who had recently presented a study of Britain's economy to the Assembly; and one "Amvifide (William), Anglais" (*Archives parlementaires,* 1st ser. [Paris, 1868–92], vol. 51). David Erdman plausibly suggests that this may have been a brother of Thomas Armfield, a member of the Paris "British Club." But Erdman also speculates that, as "Ambifide" or "Amphifide," the name might have been Wordsworth's code name or cover ("double-faith" or "double-worth") for himself, given his fondness for punning on his name (cf. "Axiologus") (DVE, 164–65). I like the possibility, which certainly captures Wordsworth's ambivalent situation, but it seems too far-fetched. Beaupuy's brother Nicholas made a similar donation on August 21, Beaupuy may still have been in Paris himself, and Wordsworth may have gone up to see him one more time. But he was probably too preoccupied with his own affairs to get involved in such public gestures.

Vaudracour's desperation at this moment—he "chafed like a wild beast in the toils"—is similar to Wordsworth's, judging by his letter to Richard of September 3, demanding more money. He is obsessively particular in giving Richard instructions on how to remit an additional £20 by means of Sir Robert Herries's bank bills, though these were as common as traveler's checks are now.[97] His last words, added after his French *adieux,* are "You will send me the money immediately."[98] Given his initial capital of £40, his proposed budget of expenses, and the continuing decline in the value of the livre, he should not have been in such bad straits. Richard sent the money, enough for several more months, but some word of why William needed it must have reached the two uncles who had to approve these disbursements, for they refused a subsequent request, forcing Wordsworth home within four months, "compelled by nothing less than absolute want / Of funds for my support" (X.190–91).[99] What he really needed, of course, were funds adequate to support a wife and child.

He posted his letter from Blois on September 3, but he left town in a hurry, because he was in Orléans at the time of the September massacres, which continued to the 5th, with further outrages reported in the provinces until the 9th. He volunteered this information in the last year of his life to an American visitor, turning to Mary to remark self-ironically, "I wonder how I came to stay there so long, and at a period so exciting?" The remark has been variously interpreted, the most congenial view being an appreciation of Wordsworth's ability to smile at his constitutional aversion to immediate excitement. However, though there were enough atrocities in Orléans between late August and mid-September to make this interpretation plausible, he could as well have been quizzing himself for staying in the provinces when most of the "excitement" was in Paris. But neither interpretation gets at the shared understanding between Mary and William—which the American visitor was certainly not let in on—that they both knew perfectly well how he came to be and stay there at a period so exciting: because Annette was soon to have her baby.

Annette may have stayed at the town house of her friends the Dufours, near Wordsworth's old quarters in the rue Royale, since Mme Dufour attended at Caroline's birth in mid-December.[100] But it is also possible, on the evidence of *Descriptive Sketches,* that she stayed outside of town in a cottage near the little river Loiret, just south of the city. Wordsworth places the conclusion of *Descriptive Sketches* on the Loiret, and the last seventy lines of that poem are some of the most immediate, contemporaneous lines he ever wrote, where his emotion is least "recollected in tranquillity." They are set under the mild light of "October clouds," which can only be October of 1792. Since he departed Orléans at the end of that month, for a six-week stay in Paris that would not have been conducive to the composition of loco-descriptive poetry, and since *Descriptive Sketches* was published in London before the end of January, these lines must have been composed virtually on the spot.[101]

If we bring together the conclusions of *Descriptive Sketches* and the story of Vaudracour and Julia, the difference between them opens up a space in which we can compare Wordsworth as he was in 1792 and as he chose to represent himself in 1804. In *Descriptive Sketches* he says nothing directly about a birth, though it was very much on his mind as he wrote. Conversely, in his tale of Vaudracour and Julia he says little about the French Revolution, though we know that his attitudes toward it and participation in it were very much affected by his affair with Annette. "The voice of freedom" could not rouse Vaudracour from "personal memory of his own deep wrongs." In *Descriptive Sketches,* by contrast, the voice of Freedom is very loud ("on ten thousands hearths his shouts rebound"), and seems to promise everything, but the details of the speaker's "personal memory" are almost completely covered over by generalized poetic diction.

In the same interview in which Wordsworth said he had been in Orléans at the time of the September massacres, his American visitor, Ellis Yarnall, noted that the subject of France "seemed very near his heart." The interview ended with the old poet—still in the presence of his wife—offering a kind of final testament: "I should like to spend another month in France before I close my eyes."[102] This is an extraordinary testimony to the emotional debt Wordsworth knew he owed to France, the Revolution, and to Annette—all of which came together for him in Orléans in September and October 1792. Wordsworth, one of the most quintessentially *English* of all British poets, became so in no small part because of his experiences in France. His late expression of desire to Yarnall matches his sudden apostrophe to the Loire at the beginning of the conclusion to *Descriptive Sketches:*

> —And thou! fair favoured region! which my soul
> Shall love, 'till Life has broke her golden bowl,
> Till Death's cold touch her cistern-wheel assail,
> And vain regret and vain desire shall fail . . . .
>
> (740–43)

The depth of personal emotion expressed here is profound, its extent revealed not only by the biblical images and cadences but also by the fact Wordsworth cut these lines from all subsequent printings of the poem. In his words to Ellis Yarnall we can hear the aged poet fulfilling the pledge, made here, that his "vain regret and vain desire" for Annette—clearly not simply for the Loire valley—would be with him all his life. The allusion to Ecclesiastes' "golden bowl" and cistern reveal a still-deeper chord of emotional resonance, since this particular passage had a talismanic quality for him.[103] He used it in *An Evening Walk* and repeated it five years later in "The Ruined Cottage" to give a similar biblical quality to the sufferings of Margaret, also caused by a husband's abandoning her in the midst of social upheavals.

All this arises confusingly on a first-time reader of *Descriptive Sketches,* who would think until this moment that he is still in the Alps, as announced on the poem's title-page, which promises sketches "In the Italian, Grison, Swiss, and Savoyard ALPS." But the poem's conclusion swerves several hundred miles west with no explanation.[104] Its closing scenes on the banks of the Loiret are ruminations in the mind of a speaker who can hear "the rumbling drum's alarm" and see "the red banner" of martial law being raised.[105] Orléans was close to civil insurrection at the time Annette and Wordsworth returned to it, hardly an ideal place for having a baby, making Annette's removal to a suburban cottage all the more plausible. The city's outspoken royalists were being made to pay for their former arrogance, and they now lamented "notre triste et malheureuse ville."[106] The street in which Wordsworth had stayed, the rue Royale, was now dubbed the rue d'Egalité, following the lead of the duc d'Orléans. The "marseillaise" was heard in town for the first time on August 23, and there were food riots in which a flour merchant was murdered.

But there were also furious reactions *against* local democrats for the massacres in Paris.[107] On September 9 fifty state prisoners sent in a wagon from the old high court in Orléans to the new one in Paris were slaughtered before they got there.[108] Léonard Bourdon, the "schoolmaster" Jacobin and a native Orléanais, had been sent down by the Convention to supervise the transfer of these prisoners to the new venue (presided over by the implacable Fouquier-Tinville), and he was heavily implicated in the massacre. On September 1 he had become *conseiller général de la commune* and begun a series of vengeful provocations against local aristocrats. These culminated in a trumped-up charge the following March that they had tried to assassinate him; two of the accused were Paul Vallon and Gellet-Duvivier, Wordsworth's former landlord.

Wordsworth in *Descriptive Sketches* hopes for universal freedom in every cottage in every valley, but acknowledges that at this moment of crisis such hopes are hard to entertain: "no more thy maids their voices suit / To the low-warbled breath of twilight lute" (748–49). His own domestic cottage fantasies, already shared with Dorothy in "a thousand dreams of happiness," are here interwoven with a commonplace of revolutionary rhetoric, the contrast between court and cottage. Thomas Christie of the London Corresponding Society, soon to join Williams and Stone in composing further editions of the *Letters from France,* wrote at this time to General Miranda, the Venezuelan commander of the Revolutionary Army of the North, vowing "Guerre aux châteaux, paix au chaumières [cottages]!" Wordsworth has mixed in his idealized recollections of Swiss cottages with the cottage where Annette, his own sad maid, was lodged, so that apparently innocuous phrases like "the little cottage of domestic Joy" (601) and "the central point of all his joys" (571) become loaded with personal significance, upon examination.

Rousseau's cottage ideology of a universal republic seemed to find concrete form with the declaration of the new French republic on September 21, which was reinforced locally by a public festival in Orléans the next day, presided over by Bishop Grégoire.[109] This day, September 22, 1792, the fall equinox, was a millennial date indeed, for it would become Day One of Year One of the new republican calendar. The speaker in *Descriptive Sketches* is in the countryside beside the Loiret, and though he can hear the rooster (the Gallic cock of republican liberty) "crow . . . with ear-piercing power 'till then unheard," in his own mind "the falling leaf" chases these "delightful dreams" of freedom away, awaking "a fainter pang of moral grief" (769). There is no explanation in the context of the poem for this minor note of "moral grief," and it is inconsistent with the emotions and images immediately surrounding it.[110] What seemed publicly so promising—if dangerous—was privately distressing. This is Vaudracour's situation as well, bringing these two solitary characters (Vaudracour and the speaker of *Descriptive Sketches*) into a proximate identity:

> Nor could the voice of freedom, which through France
> Soon afterwards resounded, public hope,
> Or personal memory of his own deep wrongs,
> Rouze him, but in those solitary shades
> His days he wasted, an imbecile mind.
>
> (IX.931–35)

By the time he wrote these lines, Wordsworth knew very well the further excesses to which the Revolution descended in order to defend itself. But in the earlier poem he, unlike Vaudracour, is able to imagine a new birth because he personally is very near to one about to occur, and he can, unlike Vaudracour, combine them symbolically, and sympathetically:

> Lo! from th'innocuous flames, a lovely birth!
> With it's [*sic*] own Virtues springs another earth:
> Nature, as in her prime, her virgin reign
> Begins, and Love and Truth compose her train . . . .
>
> (782–85)

As Wordsworth walked alone at night along the Loiret, near the cottage where Annette was lodged, he tried to imagine how the Revolution, so hellishly ferocious at the moment, might eventually overthrow "every sceptred child of clay" and restore peace and quiet to all villages and village maids with *its* newborn child. This hope for a coincidence between his own personal situation, disguised here, and the terrible events of the Revolution threatening to engulf him and Annette is indeed the only thing that enabled Wordsworth to bring *Descriptive Sketches* to a close. It is of course exactly the failure of this coincidence between private and public hopes that led Wordsworth twelve years later in *The Prelude* to represent that *un*worthy heart, Vaudra-cour, as the most tragic figure appearing anywhere in the poem "on the growth of my own mind": "His days he wasted, an imbecile mind."

Paris Again

Wordsworth left Orléans for Paris on October 28, 1792. He did not intend to return soon, for he authorized M. Dufour, Paul Vallon's landlord, to represent him as father when the child was baptized.[111] His paternity clearly and legally acknowledged, he turned homeward to seek some means to support his new family. He intended to marry Annette as soon as he was sure he could provide for her responsibly, but this would require considerable funds. He could hardly apply for the sizable amounts he now needed to be sent through the uncertain mails, and in any case his uncles had decided, like Joseph Jekyll's father and many another parent with children abroad, that enough was enough. He was determined to take church orders, the position he had so long avoided but now so desperately needed, or to exercise his second option, an advance in anticipation of the payment of the Lowther debt. This seemed more plausible at the time than it does now, and is clearly alluded to in *The Prelude,* for no one imagined how long Lowther's technical objections would be strung out:

> The lovers came
> To this resolve—with which they parted, pleased
> And confident—that Vaudracour should hie
> Back to his father's house, and there employ
> Means aptest to obtain a sum of gold,
> A final portion even, if that might be . . . .
>
> (IX.645–50)

There were difficulties in the way of marriage in France as well. Wordsworth's religious opinions were not so strong that he would have caviled much at a Catholic ceremony for Annette's sake, but a Catholic wife would have scandalized the Reverend Cookson and his arch-Evangelical friends like Wilberforce. However, Annette's family would have been equally unhappy with a constitutional marriage to a liberal, freethinking English Protestant, and a secret marriage before a nonjuring priest would have been, strictly speaking, illegal.[112] Here too there were fateful double binds. Just at this time, on September 20 to be exact, the Convention completed the legislation which made the recording of marriages entirely a civil affair. But this new law, which would have suited Wordsworth well, made marriage more difficult for the Vallons, although Annette's two uncles were constitutional priests who could have performed the ceremony in a manner acceptable to their family's feelings and loyalties. This issue, like all others, was very much up in the air at the time. The new republic might be defeated or fall apart at any minute. Indeed, this added ambiguity may have determined Wordsworth to go home to see what he could accomplish at his end.

Annette, in her letter of the coming March, speaks without hesitation about her desire to get married as soon as possible. One detail in particular made it urgent: she was not allowed to keep her baby at home, because of her unmarried state. This closely parallels the situation of Julia and Vaudracour and is not present in Helen Williams's account of the du Fosses. Nor does Annette try to disguise how much this circumstance hurt her. But the baby had a father even if Annette did not have a husband, and so the two lovers made their farewells, and Wordsworth set off. Now indeed was he like a hero in romance, setting out to seek his fortune, and as a land of adventure Paris in October of 1792 could hardly be improved on.

With his gift for being at the right place at the right time, he arrived back in Paris on October 29 and awoke next morning to the cries of street vendors hawking Louvet's *Denunciation of the Crimes of Maximilien Robespierre,* potentially one of the most decisive publications of this incredibly literate revolution. Louvet had daringly taken up Robespierre's challenge to Brissot's attack on him two days before in the Convention: that anyone who suspected him of aiming at supreme power—dictatorship—should say so. Crypto-royalism was the more damning, contemporary form of the charge: the French title of Louvet's pamphlet is *A Maximilien Robespierre et ses royalistes.* After a terrific pause Louvet rose from his seat and walked to the rostrum, declaring, "Moi, Robespierre, je t'accuse!" The moment had great theatrical effect, but like many such moments at the time, its apparent spontaneity was carefully orchestrated. Louvet's pamphlet was closely modeled on Brissot's *A tous les républicains de France sur la Société des Jacobins de Paris,* written after his expulsion from the Jacobins on October 10, and published immediately both as a pamphlet and in the *Chronique du mois.*[113]

Brissot, Louvet, and other erstwhile Jacobins were finally starting to realize that Robespierre and the more radical delegates were isolating them for blame in the massacres and the unsuccessful prosecution of the war. Louvet's speech and pamphlet had instant popularity, for Robespierre was always more feared than admired among his fellow delegates, though the galleries loved him, especially the women. But Louvet and the other Girondins (whom Brissot and the other Paris liberals joined only now) were publicists more than politicians. They—like young Wordsworth—expected that words alone could accomplish their desires, perhaps turning a tidy profit as well. Secretly, they were being massively subsidized by the Bureau de l'Esprit Public within Roland's Ministry of the Interior, a well-endowed little ministry with a budget of 100,000 livres and a mission for manipulating public opinion that even Robespierre approved: "all writing appropriate for enlightening minds on the criminal plots of the enemies of the state." Instead of following Louvet's accusation with a motion of no confidence against Robespierre, these new converts to moderation rewarded Louvet with the editorship of a new tabloid, *Bulletin des amis de la vérité,* the Girondins' belated attempt to begin influencing sansculottes opinion: their "Friend of Truth" was to oppose Marat's "Friend of the People." Hence it is a mistake to attribute too much personal heroism to Louvet's "hardihood" and the weakness of his "irresolute friends," as Wordsworth does, though in retrospect they certainly appeared so. Until the September massacres, Louvet, Brissot, Gorsas, and others had all been speaking and writing fiery Jacobin rhetoric; Louvet's *Sentinelle* had warmly endorsed Robespierre's election to the National Convention in late August. They were fighting with all the weapons they had, but these were mostly words, and as journalistic intellectuals they overestimated the persuasive power of language, especially in print.

Left surprisingly alone, Robespierre, though he had been utterly confused and incoherent in the uproar produced by Louvet's accusations, prepared an effective defense of himself, which Wordsworth would certainly have read. It was characteristic of all Robespierre's responses to criticism and based on a principle which might also be said to inform *The Prelude.* He identified himself personally with the Revolution, but avoided what might appear to be gross egotism by essaying "a presentation of general principles as an account of his own personal life and standing," brilliantly adapting Rousseau's confessional manner to the purposes of political oratory.[114]

For Wordsworth, walking out from his lodgings to see the new revolutionary sights, this pamphlet war was but one of several concrete signs of the immense change that had come over the city in the year he had spent in the provinces. If Orléans had gone bad, Paris was much worse. Brissot's *A tous les républicains de France* warned that the country was passing beyond participatory democracy into manipulated anarchy, a charge that Wordsworth echoes. A year earlier, to be the friend of a friend of Brissot's had been enough to gain one entrance to the Jacobin Club, but now Brissot was no longer a member, and Louvet and Roland were ejected on November 26. Similarly, the revolutionary sites that Wordsworth visited in late 1791 had been places of honorific mass demonstrations or celebrations: the National Assembly, the Champ de Mars, the Panthéon, and the ruins of the Bastille.

Now they were sites of murder and imprisonment: the place du Carrousel, where the king's Swiss guards had been killed and their bodies burned on August 10, and the Temple, "the prison where the unhappy monarch lay . . . with his children and his wife" (X.42–43). (Ironically, just as royalty was being destroyed in Paris, Dorothy was being introduced to George III and the royal family at Windsor, when the Reverend Cookson arrived there with his household to take up duties as canon of the chapel royal.) The change was evident even in the way people looked and moved.[115] People kept close to the walls, avoided eye contact, were more guarded in conversation, and adopted a studied uniformity of dress and demeanor, in contrast to their earlier zany costumes and harmless outlandish behavior. Strange people began turning up in public whom nobody seemed to know. They were variously identified as rabble from the *sections,* "scum of all nations, Genoese, Corsicans, Greeks," or "a convocation from hell," as François Buzot, a Girondin delegate, characterized the mob organized by Marat to pack the galleries at the Convention. The people whom Wordsworth knew in 1791 had been "standing on the top of golden hours," but now they were fighting for their lives.

Wordsworth was scared by the new atmosphere: "The fear gone by / Pressed on me almost like a fear to come" (X.62–63). Thinking about the massacres, he could not sleep at night and seemed to hear, like Macbeth, a voice crying "to the whole city, 'Sleep no more!' " (77). "It seemed a place of fear . . . Defenceless as a wood where tigers roam." This was no metaphor, or not Wordsworth's metaphor alone, for "tigers" was consistently the word most commonly applied to the *septembriseurs* and the tough-looking thugs now swaggering on the boulevards. Within a year it became the epithet for virtually one man alone, Robespierre.*

Why, then, did Wordsworth stay in Paris, "at a time so exciting," for nearly six weeks? Few questions have exercised his biographers more. Their apparent assumption is that, with all his personal problems, he should have hurried home to try to make arrangements for a new life with Annette. But this is an excessively antiromantic judgment. If he had gone straight home, with such mighty changes working all around him, we would probably fault him for that. He now saw clearly the *causes* of what he had registered only as effects in Orléans and Blois:

*Mme Roland, on the massacres: "Women brutally raped before being mauled to bits by these tigers!" (Peter Vansittart, *Voices of the Revolution* [London: Collins, 1968], 183); the spy "Hesdin," on the Committee of Public Safety: "the tigers who sit in this seat of judgement" (*The Journal of a Spy in Paris during the Reign of Terror, January–July 1794* [New York: Harper, 1895], 115); Sir Samuel Romilly, giving up his revolutionary faith after the massacres: "one might as well think of establishing a republic of tigers in some forest of Africa as of maintaining a free government among such monsters" (*Memoirs,* 1:351, cited in Phillip A. Brown, *The French Revolution in English History* [London: Allen & Unwin, 1923], 89).

now
In some sort seeing with my proper eyes
That liberty, and life, and death, would soon
To the remotest corners of the land
Lie in the arbitrement of those who ruled
The capital city . . . .

(X.106–11)

He was "in some sort seeing with my proper eyes" because, among other reasons, he was using them to read Brissot, for Brissot's main point was that Robespierre was trying to elevate the Paris Commune above all the other departments, and that Robespierre's insistence on the unity of the republic masked his determination to consolidate his control of it.[116] Wordsworth might have deduced this without reading Brissot, but he follows his new insight with an apparently stray bit of Pentecostalism that has a close parallel in Brissot's writings:

Yea, I could almost
Have prayed that throughout the earth upon all souls
Worthy of liberty, upon every soul
Matured to live in plainness and in truth,
The gift of tongues might fall . . . .

(X.117–21)

Brissot, in his celebration of the power of the press in his *Patriote français,* had maintained on August 2 that "if all we did was to convince all men to speak the same language, the press would soon spread the French Revolution everywhere."[117]

Wordsworth's possible reasons for delaying his departure to the Channel ports range from the mundane to the portentous. He might have had trouble securing a passport, no small matter at the time, when a desire to go to the frontier could be interpreted as the first step toward treason. The undersecretaries of the British embassy had passport troubles themselves after the ambassador, Lord Gower, was recalled following the coup of August 10. The military attaché, Captain Munro, used these hassles as his cover story for staying in town—the better to relay reports on the identities and activities of the English community back to Whitehall.

Wordsworth might simply have been sticking to his original plan, as he had explained to his brother, "I shall return that way [via Paris] and examine it much more minutely." This, however, besides being inappropriate to his new situation, had referred to the "splendours" of the city, and it no longer seemed so splendid. But now a new type of splendor, or fantasy, was available, and Wordsworth indulged it to the full, as he had with Beaupuy: imagining oneself as the heroic savior of the Revolution:

> Inly I revolved
> How much the destiny of man had still
> Hung upon single persons . . . .
> . . . not doubting at that time—
> Creed which ten shameful years have not annulled—
> But that the virtue of one paramount mind
> Would have abashed those impious crests . . . .
> (X.136–38, 177–80)

This was not Wordsworthian egotism; it was the thought of almost anyone involved in public affairs in Paris at the time, when fantasies about turning private thoughts into world-shaking actions were rife, and not at all unrealistic. It describes the actions of Louvet, Brissot, and Robespierre, as well as the "one paramount mind" Wordsworth alludes to at the end, Bonaparte's.

As events moved to an ever-higher pitch of intensity, public life entered that state of gigantic humanity which Wallace Stevens characterized as the condition of imagination in time of war. The spaces between thought, word, and deed became smaller and smaller. The great French Romantic anatomist of the Revolution, Victor Hugo, perfectly captured this aspect of its dialectical simultaneity of voice, text, and action when he noted that in the convention

> were uttered those mysterious words which sometimes possess unconsciously to those who pronounce them the prophetic accent of revolutions, and in whose wake material facts appear suddenly to assume an inexplicable discontent and passion, as if they had taken umbrage at the things just heard; events seem angered by words; catastrophes follow furious, and as if exasperated by the speech of men.[118]

Talking, writing, and reading became nonstop activities, as daytime debates in the Convention were followed by nighttime meetings in the clubs, which usually adjourned about ten. Each night was capped with visits to the theaters, where new plays were rapidly composed, or old ones adapted, to reflect—and influence—the events of each day, and were then keenly reviewed for whiffs of treason. (One of the most celebrated actresses was Louvet's wife, the beautiful Lodoiska.)[119] To fill up any remaining time, there were the dives and cafés of the Palais Royal and, for people of Wordsworth's class and associations, the salons. Helen Maria Williams's in the rue du Bac was the leading English one, half a dozen streets away from its French sister, that of Manon Roland in the rue Guénégaud, both near the river on the Left

Bank, with clear views across to the Louvre, the Carrousel, and the Tuileries. They interchanged visitors regularly. Here informal commentary and conversation were honed and polished into rhetoric for the next day's public appearances. The great Girondin orator Vergniaud improvised and rehearsed his speeches in both ladies' apartments.[120]

Though we cannot place Wordsworth definitely at either of these salons, he clearly spent time at the theater, perhaps unusually much for a man in his straits, but very much in line with his theater-going habits from London in 1791. An adaptation of Schiller's *Die Räuber* (The Robbers), the base text for Wordsworth *The Borderers* (1796), was one of the most popular propaganda plays of 1792. As *Robert, chef de brigands,* it played at Beaumarchais's Théâtre du Marais five or six times during Wordsworth's stay in Paris in November and December.[121] Schiller's play, like Wordsworth's, was a psychological study of remorse for assassination. But the version at Beaumarchais's theater, as adapted by Jean-Henri Lamartelière, was more like a justification of it. Its hero, according to a Girondin reviewer, is "a tyrannicide, an avenger of oppression, a new successor to Hercules. He has set up his assassinations as acts of republican virtue, his principles of destruction into laws." This closely approximated the Jacobin interpretation of the September massacres as a manifestation of the people's justice, in contrast to the Girondins, who saw it as an attack on the republic.[122] *Robert* gained even more political relevance once the idea of putting Louis XVI on trial for his life was broached at the Convention by Saint-Just on November 13. But no text was unequivocably safe. Lamartelière, whose play had been attacked in March by royalists as "a school for brigandage" when it opened, was now denounced by sansculottes for unfavorable depictions of republicans in his sequel, *Le Tribunal redoutable,* which alternated with *Robert, chef de brigands*—and which he retitled *Robert républicain* after an instructive visit from the Committee of Surveillance.

Wordsworth, attending the plays, listening to the gossip, and reading the scandal sheets, absorbed powerful lessons about the range and limits of literature's ability to influence public events. For a copy of the play, he was less likely to have read Lamartelière's script than the more accurate translation of Schiller's play by Nicolas de Bonneville (now co-editor with Oswald of the *Chronique*), *Les Voleurs* (1785).[123] Here he found a drama of thought recoiling from action, rather than one recommending violent actions. His subsequent close attention to the relations between "the revolutions not of literature alone but likewise of society itself" (preface to *Lyrical Ballads*) was first cast in this crucible. His development throughout the 1790s is marked first by an attempt to bring his writing much closer into contact with politics and then by an effort to distance it from immediate public reference while maintaining a symbolic topicality.

This was exactly the opposite direction that the revolutionary publicists were following. Louvet and Mercier and others, like writers in Eastern Europe after the fall of communism in 1989, found that reality was outstripping fiction, that the news was becoming more sensational than the novel, and that if they wanted to survive in the market they would have to change their product, which they did accordingly. But they soon got beyond their depth. As Mme Roland said, "the talent of writing is only one small part of being a legislator. It is easy to moralize about men in ingenious fictional works. It is difficult to change them by wise laws."[124] They could use the power of their pens to get elected, but once in the convention they were almost useless. Mme Roland considered Mercier more likable than most men of letters, but a zero in the Convention. Those few of Le Cercle Social who survived the Terror recoiled completely from politics. They were then called, in one of the first upper-case, consciously favorable usages of the term, "Romantics."[125]

Hence it is not surprising that Wordsworth imagined putting himself at the service of the Revolution: "Yet would I willingly have taken up / A service at this time for a cause so great, / However dangerous." But his modesty about his situation is overstated: "An insignificant stranger and obscure." He had more than adequate connections for a twenty-two-year-old Englishman. He knew Brissot, he was a friend of Beaupuy, he had probably talked with Grégoire on more than one occasion. And he must by this time have made the acquaintance of Gorsas, if his later statement "I knew this man" has any meaning at all.[126] His connections in the English community were equally good. He still carried—but apparently never delivered—a letter of introduction to Helen Williams; he knew Thomas Foxlow, James Watt Jr., Francis Tweddell, and others, all "active partisans." But he was also known to be closely associated with a prominent royalist and clerical family in Orléans and Blois. Nor were his English credentials of the best sort for this company, if the subject ever came up: nephew of George III's notorious old paymaster John Robinson, and of his chaplain William Cookson, and dependent heir—however disaffected—of one of the hated Pitt's most enthusiastic supporters, James Lowther, Lord Lonsdale.

But granting that to imagine serving the Revolution was the most natural thing in the world at the time for a young man of active imagination, what kind of "service" did he have in mind, and for which country? Writer or orator, messenger or spy, agitator or assassin? Wordsworth was not given to indulging passing fancies, and when he said he "doubtless should have made a common cause / With some who perished" (X.194–95), he doubtless meant it, for he had "great self-control, tenacity, courage, enthusiasm, and depth of conviction."[127] He had the advantage now of being fluent in French, which was more than some important figures like Tom Paine could say. The flood of English sympathizers rose to a crest between September and

November, and the Convention redoubled its efforts to disseminate favorable views of the Revolution to England.[128] Some of it involved concrete matters like raising money, or soliciting and shipping quantities of shoes, pikes, and even cannon for the patriot armies, to which service men as diverse as Francis Place, the radical London tailor, John Hurford Stone, businessman and lover of Helen Williams, and Robert Burns lent, or tried to lend, their aid.[129] Others, like John Oswald and many Irishmen, were rumored to be involved in plots to assassinate George III, in synchronization with the widely expected execution of Louis XVI. Although Wordsworth said, truthfully, that he was "all unfit for tumult and intrigue," it is worth noting that the thought he said now came to him "with a revelation's liveliness" was "that tyrannic power was weak"—because dedicated idealistic assassins like Harmodius and Brutus could kill it (X.158–67).

The reports of Captain Munro to Whitehall concentrate on the *writing* being done by Paine, Oswald, and Priestley (who was not even there), and some eight or ten "others" around them, of whom he mentions only young Watt (who had left October 7), Thomas Wilson (of Manchester), Stone, and Mackintosh, "who wrote against Burke." They are said to be "writing a justification of democracy and an invective against monarchy," a description that fits very well the "Letter to the Bishop of Llandaff," which Wordsworth would begin writing as soon as he had seen *An Evening Walk* and *Descriptive Sketches* through the press a month later. Every scene in Paris at this time is crowded, and the backgrounds of the crowd are necessarily indistinct. We cannot clearly see a tall, awkward-looking young Englishman in any of these groups, but we can say without hesitation that his actions when he got back to England were highly congruent with theirs.

The increasing concentration of English sympathizers culminated in the creation of the "British Club" in October, officially called The Friends of the Rights of Man Associated at Paris, building on the organization Wordsworth had heard James Rutledge arguing about the previous December at the Jacobin Club. They met at White's Hotel, in Wordsworth's neighborhood, if he was not actually staying at the hotel himself. Two of its leaders were flatteringly referred to by the French as "the two best poets in England": William Hayley, Blake's patron, and Robert Merry, the "Della Cruscan" poet of the English colony in Florence. The high valuation would have piqued Wordsworth's interest, if not his assent; Hayley was also a close friend of Charlotte Smith and William Cowper.[130] The British Club's meetings were devoted to discussing how the spirit of revolution and reform might best be exported back to England. Great extremes of opinion and commitment coexisted there, ranging from those who simply wanted to keep open channels of sympathetic communication between the two countries to those who wanted to provoke a revolutionary uprising in England. The latter was a serious option, not just the fantasy of a lunatic fringe. It had the considerable precedent of William III's Glorious Revolution, when a few hundred troops took over the country without serious resistance. It also had the negative precedent of the failed Jacobite returns in 1715 and 1745, but the French republican government was now more committed to supporting such an invasion than Louis's father or grandfather had been, and the Directory and Napoleon finally would do it, in Wales in 1797 and in Ireland in 1798, though still insufficiently.

On November 18 about a hundred of these British sympathizers gathered at White's to draw up a manifesto of solidarity with the National Convention, celebrating "the brilliant successes of your arms" on the occasion of General Dumouriez's triumphant entry into Brussels. "It doubtless appertained," the address continued, "to the French nation to enfranchise Europe, and we rejoice to see it fulfilling its great destinies." The document is dated November 24, but because of delays in final preparation, it was not presented to the Convention until November 28, after the Edict of Fraternity had been passed, offering aid to all peoples wishing to overthrow tyrants and "recover" their natural liberty. Hence a cheerful message of congratulations sent by visiting Britons to the armies of the new republic was turned by the rapid movement of events into an endorsement of exporting revolution and a direct challenge to the British constitution, signed, for all the French knew, by fifty leading British citizens.

Wordsworth's name is not among the fifty signatories, who were chosen by vote from the more than one hundred English there that night. But Francis Tweddell, son of a Northumbrian squire, signed, and given Wordsworth's associations, it is not hard to believe that he was in the company, standing preoccupied in the background. Helen Maria Williams was there: as unofficial hostess of the event, she sang a composition of her own to the tune of the "Marseillaise."[131] She was toasted along with Charlotte Smith and Anna Barbauld as representatives of the women of England who had distinguished themselves by writing in favor of the Revolution. Years later, fondly reminiscing about the early days of the Revolution, Wordsworth linked Williams and Smith in his recollections, and spontaneously began reciting one of the latter's sonnets.[132] Many of the signatories were of Wordsworth's age and class. Half of them were middle-class, university-educated professionals, and a quarter were young men in their twenties.[133] Some who were chosen to sign chose not to (like John Hurford Stone) for various expedient reasons, and though one hardly would expect young Wordsworth to have been chosen, he too had good reasons for demurring. He was not afraid for himself, but he now had others to think of. For the sake of Annette and their child, he could not afford to get into trouble, either in France or in England.

This was hardly the time or the place to approach Helen Williams with his letter of introduction. And although Wordsworth was by then a committed republican, the sophisticated crowd at White's Hotel was for the most part beyond him in age, reputation, experience, and political savvy. Some of them were the top celebrities of the moment, not easily approached by a young man with deep problems of his own. But fame could bring wealth, as the careers of Brissot and other writer-politicians demonstrated, so we can imagine Wordsworth watching events with an eye to duplicating them in England—if not by revolution, then through publications that improved the climate of political opinion, and might make their author rich in the bargain. Like Annette, who would shortly be saying, "Je vouderois voir les deux nations [réconciliées]," Wordsworth's personal interests were very much caught up in maintaining friendly relations between France and England.[134]

Events rapidly went beyond the depth of most of the British sympathizers, and the club, formed in October, fell apart in less than three months. Bishop Grégoire made a formal reply to the November 18 resolution, hoping that he might soon address "the National Convention of England," to which nonexistent body he conveyed the greeting of its French sister.[135] In doing so, he was merely responding to the resolution's claim that "the great majority of our countrymen" would share their sentiments "if public opinion were consulted as it ought to be, in a national convention." Whether by mistake or design, the Convention appeared to be addressing the British government. This was alarming to more than a few of the British Club, for it implied the calling of a constitutional convention, the dearest hope of the burgeoning working-class correspondence societies in England, and the worst-case scenario, short of open rebellion in the streets, of not only Pitt and his ministers but of most of the English property-owning class. The preliminary "national" convention held in Edinburgh in December immediately provoked arrests, trials for sedition and treason, and transportation to "the fatal shore" of Botany Bay for the convicted leaders.[136]

This implicit constitutional challenge to George III was underscored by the debates on the trial of Louis XVI, already under way. The vexed questions of whether he could or should be tried, by whom, and with what punishment if found guilty utterly consumed the Convention's energies for the next two months, and ruined the Girondins in the process. Only the most radical British sympathizers were prepared to associate themselves with a republicanism that entailed regicide; the English Revolution gave no comforting precedent here, and the French did not give them any cause for optimism. On December 8 the Provisional Executive Council (soon to become the Committee of Public Safety) voted 2,000 livres to "le poète célèbre," Lebrun-Pindare (1729–1807), for the publication of his "Patriotic Ode" on events between August 10 and November 13, which drew explicit parallels between Louis XVI and Charles I.[137]

On November 29 the Convention forced Louis to send a double-edged message of peace and warning to the other European powers, saying that France wished them no ill, but that if they continued to plot against her they would approach not with the olive branch but with the sword.[138] By the kind of coincidence that one comes to expect in these heated days, this was the same day on which the Convention received England's response to Grégoire's message of November 19: a formal note of protest against its language as tantamount to meddling in England's internal affairs and fomenting rebellion. England's next action was no coincidence: on December 13 it put Paine on trial in absentia for treason, the same charge Louis faced. Popular opinion, expertly manipulated in both countries, kept pace nicely: the homes of young Watts's friends, Thomas Cooper and Thomas Walker, were burnt to the ground on the same day in Manchester.[139]

And on December 15, in the Orléans cathedral, Father Perrin, the episcopal vicar, certified that he had "baptized a girl, born the same day in this parish to Williams Wordwodsth [*sic*] an Englishman, and Marie-Anne Vallon, her father and mother; named Anne-Caroline by Paul Vallon and Marie-Victoire-Adelaide Peigne, wife of André-Augustin Dufour. Williams Wordsodsth [*sic*], being absent, was represented as the child's father by the aforesaid citizen André-Augustin Dufour, recorder of the court of the district of Orléans, by virtue of a power of attorney *ad hoc* presented to us and signed 'Williams Wordsworsth' [*sic*]."[140] The official certificate managed to get his name wrong three different ways in as many attempts, stumbling on those consonantal combinations of "th" and "rdsw" so taxing to the French tongue. "Vaudracour" would have been much easier, and Annette opted for "Williams" as her new family name, but there was no doubt as to who the child's father was.*

It was perhaps very nearly on this day that Wordsworth finally decamped from Paris to return to London, for on December 22 Dorothy is reporting that he "is in London [and] writes to me regularly." On December 21 Captain Munro informed Lord Grenville that "young Mr. Woodfall" would be the bearer of his latest report to the Foreign Ministry.[141] This was William Woodfall Jr., son of the proprietor and editor of *The Diary; or, Woodfall's Register,* and Munro got his British names right unless he wanted to disguise them. But one can also wonder if a "young Mr. Wordsworth" might not have been deputized to carry, as Erdman suggests, the text of a placard to be printed in England, from the "Friends of the Rights of Man associated at Paris, December 4." This was a frankly republican but carefully noninflam-

*Wordsworth's name is misspelled on every French document relating to his parentage of his daughter. On the baptism certificate: Wordwodsth, Wordsodsth, and Wordsworsth; on the marriage certificate: Wortsworth. Only Caroline, signing the latter with the name of the father she loved and admired, got it right, confidently signing "A. C. Wordsworth" (*WFD,* 29–30, 38).

matory statement, in which the signatories (though no signed copies survive) expressed their happiness for three things: "that our temporary residence in this enlightened and regenerated capital enables us [1] to become the organ of communicating knowledge on the most interesting subjects, [2] of administering to the moral improvement and social happiness of a considerable portion of our fellow-men, and [3] of undeceiving the minds of our countrymen, abused by the wretched calumnies of a wicked Administration . . . [about] the glorious exertions of the French."[142] The placard's first claim to happiness fits Wordsworth's experience and his political conversion during 1792, the second describes the newly conscious aim of his writings from 1793 to 1800, and the last accurately characterizes the short-term polemic of his "Letter to Llandaff" and the long-term ideals of his proposed *Philanthropist.* On either side of the political fence, innocuous young men like Woodfall or Wordsworth were entrusted with dangerous information or errands: they did not raise much suspicion and were, in any case, expendable—"poor mistaken and bewildered offerings"—if they got caught.[143]

Leaving Paris in mid-December 1792, Wordsworth was leaving at almost the last possible moment. The British Club was falling apart, wrecked on the rocks of regicide. Munro reported on December 27 that, "from being levellers and enemies of our constitution, many are now become friends of Royalty," and considered the few remaining English sympathizers to be persons of no consequence, "really much beneath the notice of anyone." He observed "the greatest confusion imaginable in all the coffee houses," and he firmly expected either a massacre of the Convention or a civil war,[144] both of which came soon enough, in the purge of Girondins and on the killing grounds of the Vendée.

CASTAWAY 14

> . . . more like a man
> Flying from something that he dreads, than one
> Who sought the thing he loved.
>
> ("Tintern Abbey," 71–73)

If Wordsworth was dilatory in staying so long in Paris, he made up for it by the dispatch with which he attended to his affairs as soon as he returned to London. In little over a month, he prepared and saw through the press not one but two quarto volumes, *An Evening Walk* and *Descriptive Sketches,* over twelve hundred lines of poetry, which were printed and sold by the most distinguished liberal publisher of the time, Joseph Johnson, at his shop in St. Paul's Churchyard.

He accomplished this in an atmosphere almost as hysterical as that in Paris. He arrived in the midst of a journalistic outcry against the government's disinformation campaign concerning "an infernal plot, planned by some foreigners." French agents were rumored to be assassinating pedestrians in the City, poisoning the Thames, and occupying the Tower.[1] This was the infamous "insurrection that wasn't," the climax of the "heresy hunt" of 1792 against the reform societies.[2] The charges (a plot to subvert the capital) and the danger (foreign invasion) were similar to those Wordsworth had witnessed ricocheting between Robespierre, Louvet, and Brissot. So were the means employed to substantiate them. The government exploited the stockjobbing capabilities of newspapers, in an early instance of news management.[3] Suborned journalists manufactured facts in government-subsidized newspapers, particularly the *Sun* and the *True-Briton.*[4] Other literary men rallied to the government's support in other ways: James Boswell was probably the spy who infiltrated the Edinburgh "national convention," which opened on December 11, and reported on the extent to which its agenda for creating a British constitution seemed likely to gain popularity.[5] Henry Pye, the poet laureate, contributed a New Year's ode contrasting British peace and prosperity with French anarchy and violence: the official ideological line during the year.[6] Opposition writers were intimidated by slanted interpretations of their words according to the new theory of close reading called "constructive treason."[7]

It took about a week for even opposition newspapers to notice that none of these dire events were happening, but the panic permitted George III to call out the county militias, a legal technicality making it possible to call Parliament on short notice and put the country on a war footing. The evidence that Grenville presented in the House consisted of little more than copies of the congratulatory addresses bouncing back and forth between Paris and England, accented with a rich mixture of lurid details of plots for insurrection and sabotage—which certainly were being bruited about freely, in Paris. But he could produce none from England, though cries of "No King!" and "Damn Pitt!" could be heard on the streets and read on the walls all the way from London to Edinburgh.[8] Burke crossed over to join Pitt on the treasury bench for the first time on December 15, and soon thereafter gave his amazing "dagger" speech, dramatically throwing a concealed knife onto the floor of the Commons and threatening that thousands more were being manufactured for "domestic consumption." Like many of his histrionic gestures, this one was immediately exploded by satire, as Whig members demanded he reveal his hidden spoons and forks as well.

William moved into his brother Richard's new rooms at Staple Inn, at the junction of Holborn and High Holborn, not far from his haunts of two years earlier. His London spring of 1793 was in some ways a reprise of 1791, in a more anxious key. His previous freedom and irresponsibility were now changed to heavy duties and unpleasant confrontations. As he worked feverishly to get *An Evening Walk* and *Descriptive Sketches* ready for the printer, he dissuaded Richard's roommate, Joshua Wilkinson, from writing a sensational "Jacobin" novel based on the du Fosse episode from Helen Williams's *Letters from France.* He laid claim to this literary option on the moral grounds that his need to raise money for Annette and Caroline was greater than Wilkinson's profit motive, and on the artistic grounds that his own recent experiences could very easily be adapted to Williams's tale. He was so upset generally that Wilkinson and other friends spent much time simply playing cards with him over the next six months, to keep him from dwelling too much on his troubles.[9]

Wordsworth is very reticent in all his later reminiscences about the names of his London associates in the 1790s.[10] In his autobiographical memorandum the next three years are dismissed in a single sentence: "I came home before the execution of the King [21 January], and passed the subsequent time among my friends in London and elsewhere, till I settled with my only sister at Racedown in Dorsetshire, in the year 1796."[11] The reason for such circumspection was the usual one for liberal young gentlemen of his generation: covering up their Jacobin youth. His success in securing Joseph Johnson as his publisher shows that his radical credentials were in good order at this time. He had no known prior acquaintance with Johnson, the friend, encourager, and guide of the most brilliant writers of the day: Tom Paine, Mary Wollstonecraft, and William Godwin. Very possibly he came with a recommendation from his new acquaintances in the English Club of Paris.[12] Having so narrowly missed Helen Maria Williams on his way into France, he now just missed meeting Mary Wollstonecraft, who entered Paris as he left it, and on the same slender pretext as he, to improve her French, the better to fulfill Johnson's daunting journalistic assignment, a short history of the Revolution—which she eventually did. With Johnson's assistance, she immediately established contact with Helen Williams, so far the leading English commentator on the Revolution. Wordsworth completed this circuit in the other direction, making straight for Johnson's shop in St. Paul's Churchyard on his return, and had no trouble getting not one but two large, difficult, and expensive books accepted immediately. Johnson was an astute businessman as well as a cautious liberal, and one might suppose he would have needed some additional recommendation to add the sentimental *Evening Walk* and the picturesque tourism of *Descriptive Sketches* to his list. Perhaps it was the latter's revolutionary peroration that persuaded him to see more politics than meets the eye on its title page, where the author's pedigree was circumspectly announced as "William Wordsworth, B.A., of St. John's College, Cambridge":

> Oh give, great God, to Freedom's waves to ride
> Sublime o'er Conquest, Avarice, and Pride,
> To break, the vales where Death with Famine scow'rs,
> And dark Oppression builds her thick-ribb'd tow'rs . . . .
> (792–95)

The books were quite well received, especially *An Evening Walk,* the more innocuous (and shorter) of the two. Though the pressruns were small, some major reviews (among the two dozen or so that controlled published opinion), the *Critical* and the *Analytical* (Johnson's house organ), commented approvingly on the accuracy of the poet's landscape descriptions and on the novelty of his firsthand views of the Alps, though they criticized the obscurity of his hackneyed poetical diction, especially in *Descriptive Sketches.*[13] At a time when journalistic wisdom ranked the insipid Catherine Manners as the best poet of the day and Mary ("Perdita") Robinson as the best of modern times (though as much for her notoriety as ex-mistress of the Prince of Wales as for her poetry), such notice and praise was not inconsiderable, especially when political news was rapidly pushing poetry toward a more marginal status.[14]

But in October, Thomas Holcroft, an important radical man of letters (his *Road to Ruin* played to enthusiastic audiences all during this year), tore into Wordsworth with a reformer's zeal: "More descriptive poetry! Have we not enough! Must eternal changes be rung on uplands and lowlands, and nodding forests, and brooding clouds, and cells, and dells, and dingles?" He proceeded to explode a quantity of Wordsworth's images by the simple (and unfair) device of taking their metaphors literally. Some seeds of the preface to *Lyrical Ballads* were planted in Wordsworth's mind by this attack, and so, perhaps, were some for *The Prelude,* in Holcroft's closing advice to this cliché persona: "He is the happiest of mortals, and plods, and is forlorn, and has a wounded heart. How often shall we in vain advise those, who are so delighted with their own thoughts that they cannot forbear from putting them into rhyme, to examine those thoughts until they understand them? No man will ever be a poet, till his mind be sufficiently powerful to sustain this labour."[15]

The last contemporary review, by an anonymous writer who had known Wordsworth at Cambridge, saw in him the longed-for inheritor of the loco-descriptive tradition: "I trust he will restore to us that laurel to which, since Gray laid down 'his head upon the lap of earth,' and Mason 'declined into the vale of years,' we have had so slight pretensions."[16] By the end of the year, the poems were well enough regarded to be discussed at avant-garde student literary groups at Cambridge, where young Christopher Wordsworth and Coleridge were members, and in provincial literary societies at Exeter and Derby, along with the works of such other leading contemporary poets as Anna Seward ("the Swan of Lichfield"), Charlotte Smith, William Bowles, and Erasmus Darwin (grandfather of Charles).[17]

Dorothy and Christopher were harder on their brother's poems than the press was, sending "a very bulky criticism" to him, pointing out the excessive liberties he had taken with readers' patience in constructing his complicated images.[18] Wordsworth hated criticism more than most, especially from people he loved, though he frequently adopted their suggestions after initially rejecting them. But his siblings underestimated his needy motive for getting something published as soon as possible.

Good reviews were extremely important to Wordsworth at this juncture. When he told Mathews a year later that he had "huddled up" these two poems for publication, his use of the university slang term for exam cramming accentuated his motive: "as I had done nothing by which to distinguish myself at the university, I thought these little things might shew that I could do something."[19] Whom, in particular, did he intend to "shew"? Preeminently, William Cookson, an intention underscored by his title page identification with Cambridge University. Though he had pointedly *not* "huddled" for his university exams, he was now, exactly two years later, trying to show that he could "do something." There is an endearing earnestness in Wordsworth's hope that his poems would please his elders. Having spurned or deflected both Cookson's and Robinson's last best offers for his future in the fall of 1791, he was now working very hard to show himself worthy of the formerly despised Harwich curacy. He now had a real, pressing need for it, and as he was only three months away from his twenty-third birthday, his former legalistic excuse could be waved aside.

But his long-suffering benefactors turned him down flat. His very reason for wanting the curacy became their reason for refusing it: Freud himself could hardly have imagined a clearer instance of the double binds characteristic of the "family romance." Wordsworth had to make his reasons clear, but with each one he put the curacy farther and farther out of reach: a mistress, a Frenchwoman, a Catholic, and an illegitimate child. "Anything more?" one can imagine the weary Cookson inquiring. Annette's royalism might have been one forlorn hope in her favor, to the chaplain and the paymaster, respectively, of George III. But the illegitimate child was literally a scandal, and the Cooksons' shocked reaction to it was heightened by their close friendship with Wilberforce.[20] It is hard to say which of the objections was the decisive one, though a Catholic wife (if acknowledged) was a technical disqualification. Years later Cookson cited Wordsworth's "French principles" as the straw that broke the back of his patience, though by then he was referring to several more years' worth of his nephew's near-treasonous advocacy of Paineite republicanism, and his passing infatuation with Godwinian philosophical anarchism.[21]

We do not know exactly when Wordsworth was hit with the news that his strenuous effort to get his two volumes published was all for naught, but we can trace its fallout. In Annette's letters of March, she still pleaded with him not to say anything about their situation to his uncle. But she was out of touch with the pace of events. The news, and the break with Cookson it soon occasioned, probably came sooner rather than later, for this shocking refusal propelled Wordsworth into another fast and furious effort of composition. This was his "Letter to the Bishop of Llandaff," whose great difference from *Descriptive Sketches*—as regards showing his uncles what he could do—is marked, not to say flaunted, on *its* title page by a much more provocative sign of authorship: "By a Republican." He might never have written this, the most outspokenly radical statement of his life, if his uncles had not turned down his bona fide effort to gain their favor by publishing *An Evening Walk* and *Descriptive Sketches;* holding a curacy and publishing such an attack on an Anglican bishop were mutually exclusive acts. Having shown what he could do in one direction, he proceeded almost immediately to do something in an entirely opposite direction. Just as the uncles' well-intentioned plans to fit him with a place in the established church had forced him to come up with his French language scheme, now their self-righteous retraction of the same plan helped push him over the brink of notional liberalism into declaring himself an enemy of that establishment and just about everything that it stood for. Or rather, almost over the brink—since he did not publish the "Letter to Llandaff," a career-saving decision which he probably owed to the cautions of Joseph Johnson. But in written word if not in published deed, he now became an "active partisan" in the pamphlet wars for Liberty which had been raging in London since the publication of Burke's *Reflections on the Revolution in France.*[22]

His two poems appeared in Johnson's shop in St. Paul's Churchyard on January 29. The very next day, Richard Watson, the bishop of Llandaff, fellow of Trinity College (Cambridge), Windermere estate owner, and Lake District success story, republished an old sermon, with an appendix recanting his former support of the Revolution (the appendix was dated January 25). Two days later France declared war on Britain, and Pitt's government shortly returned the favor. Given this concatenation of events, it is no wonder that Wordsworth's reaction was so strong. The moment was, in fact, Wordsworth's revolution:

> No shock
> Given to my moral nature had I known
> Down to that very moment—neither lapse
> Nor turn of sentiment—that might be named
> A revolution, save at this one time . . . .
>
> (X.233–37)

The wonder is, rather, that scholars have tended to see Wordsworth's shock primarily in political terms. True, he generalizes it to his whole generation: "Not in my single self alone . . . / But in the minds of all ingenuous youth, / Change and subversion from this hour" (231–33). But he also admits that the coming of war was perfectly obvious to everybody: "Nor had I doubted that this day would come." The full reason for his great shock was his immense personal involvement in the stakes:

> Now had I other business, for I felt
> The ravage of this most unnatural strife
> In my own heart; there lay it like a weight,

> At enmity with the tenderest springs
> Of my enjoyments.
>
> (X.249–53)

This, cut from all later versions, could hardly be clearer. The war was "an unnatural strife in [his] own heart" because it separated him from Annette and Caroline, "the tenderest springs" of his enjoyments. The appearance of Watson's appendix at this moment, matched with his uncles' refusal of the curacy, gave Wordsworth a target on which to vent his frustrations, as the childhood helplessness to which his father's early death had reduced him now began to have adult consequences.

The arguments in the trial of Louis XVI were well represented in the London press, with substantial excerpts from persons known to Wordsworth: Paine, Carra, and Léonard Bourdon. During the trial, almost every delegate had dutifully spoken against the monarch, but after his conviction there was a lengthy debate about sentencing in which his accusers' unanimity broke apart on various extemporizing measures that might avoid the death penalty: exile, house arrest, probation on good behavior, confiscatory fines, and so on. Richard Watson had inserted himself directly into this process—an important point, lest we see him entirely in Wordsworth's perspective as a reactionary renegade. For Watson was one of the most liberal Anglican churchmen in his attitude toward the Revolution, and by far England's most outspoken bishop on liberal issues.[23] The so-called leveling prelate, he complained all his life that he suffered in his preferments for his outspoken support of liberal causes, though it is hard to see how he could have done much better in collecting profitable benefices. A year earlier he had promulgated through his diocese a sermon on "the advantages which would probably result to human society from the French Revolution."[24] He had dined with Talleyrand and several members of the National Assembly at Earl Stanhope's in late 1792, and he subsequently sent to Stanhope, for him to convey to the Assembly, his suggestion that Louis be confined to one of his palaces on a pension of £4,000 per year, subject to forfeit on any sign of treasonous behavior.[25] "I had no great expectation of success attending the application of an individual, buried in the wilds of Westmorland," he said, sounding uncannily like the Wordsworth to come, "yet knowing that the greatest events had often sprung from the slightest causes," he tried to save the royal family.[26]

When Louis was guillotined on January 21, Watson's recoil was the leading edge of a massive tide of reaction, horrified as much by the method as the fact of the execution. As frequently happens in politics, those closest to a controversial issue are often the first and most vehement in distancing themselves from its consequences once they see that the cause is lost. Watson, an astute politician, must have had his fallback position ready, considering the date and timing of his sermon's publication. The vehicle he chose for his recantation was a sermon of 1785 extolling God's almighty wisdom in creating both rich and poor, which he reissued to help "in calming the perturbation . . . in the minds of the lower classes of the community," and the "strong spirit of insubordination and discontent" which he observed among the common people. With the kind of self-satisfied calculation that gives conservatism a bad name, he estimated that the provision for the poor in England was already so liberal as to discourage industriousness, whereas the expense of the monarchy, if calculated on a per capita basis, would come to only sixpence a year—neglecting to note that much of the population could not even afford that.

Wordsworth was infuriated by the smug self-righteousness of Watson's tactic, though he would not have written so vehemently against it without his uncles' refusal to goad him. Watson's appendix was not, however, quite so hysterical as Wordsworth's "Letter" might lead us to believe. It is a liberal defense of the established order, on essentially the same grounds as Burke's *Reflections.* To a degree, it gave fresh life to Burke's polemic, since Burke was by this time being attacked on every possible ground for his hysteria, ignored by the ministerial papers, and attacked as "the Minister from Beelzebub, B[eaconsfield]" in the opposition press.[27] Watson said he had wished the French well at first, hoping they would soon have a constitution to replace their former absolutism. But now they had gone too far, staining the altar of Liberty with the blood "of the aged, of the innocent, of the defenceless sex, of the ministers of religion." All true enough, and worse was yet to come. Watson was writing with the memory of the September massacres still fresh in his mind, and they seemed to have been capped by Louis's execution: Liberty's altar was now "streaming with the blood of the monarch himself." This was Watson's most emotional paragraph, and it well expressed the widespread revulsion in England against the turn of events in France. But the main thrust of his appendix is to defend the English constitution's guarantee of property rights against the threat of republican theorists: "the wild fancies and turbulent tempers of discontented or ill-informed individuals . . . the licentious principles of such petulant outcasts of society," who address themselves not to the "opulent" middle classes or to "honest" laborers, but to "the flagitious dregs of a modern nation . . . always ripe for revolutions." Like Burke, he feared that the disaffected might lead the disenfranchised toward fundamental change in the status quo.

Wordsworth, as "A Republican," set himself directly against Watson's premises. As a man now explicitly "discontented" in his expectations, he made a dramatic shift in social roles from that of the author of *Descriptive Sketches.* His "Letter to Llandaff" is written in the white heat of anger, an anger seen nowhere in his writings up to this time. He lets loose the violence of his passionate nature, which Dorothy had noted with half-proud, half-worried concern: "a sort of violence," where objects of his affection are concerned, as Annette certainly was in the implications of changing English public opinion toward France.[28]

Wordsworth wrote with Watson's volume open on the desk before him, refuting it point by point. This accounts in part for his letter's labored structure and obscure references: one can hardly understand it without Watson's appendix ready to hand. But he also raised objections to many points that are nowhere mentioned by Watson. The letter is basically a defense of republicanism, followed by an attack on the institutions of British monarchy and aristocracy, and on Watson's excessive confidence in them. But these two long addresses are framed within a virulently ad hominem introduction and conclusion. One would think Wordsworth knew Watson personally, and it is not unlikely that he did, having seen him frequently at Cambridge and at social events like the summer dances on Windermere. The promise and now the disappointment of Watson's *career* particularly drew Wordsworth's scorn, reminding us how often Watson must have been held up before him, by the likes of Cookson and Wilberforce, as the epitome of what a Lake District boy of intelligence but limited means could make of himself. Watson was the son of a headmaster of Heversham grammar school, twelve miles southeast of Hawkshead, one of Hawkshead's main rivals in preparing boys for Cambridge.[29] Hence Wordsworth takes considerable satisfaction, at the beginning of the letter, in imagining Watson falling off the "immense bridge" of reputation, tumbling through one of its many "trap-doors, into the tide of contempt to be swept down to the ocean of oblivion."[30] At the end, to satirize Watson's hypocrisy, he adopts a homelier figure of speech that he could expect Watson to recognize from their common home in "the wilds of Westmorland": "In some parts of England it is quaintly said, when a drunken man is seen reeling towards his home, that he has business on both sides of the road."[31]

So much for Watson's principles and his progress: "the friends of liberty" are glad to lose such a renegade.[32] "Besides the names which I" . . . but at this exact point the manuscript ends, any further pages were torn off, just when the writer is about to name names. Probably Wordsworth was going to cite some more names like those he has already mentioned, Lafayette and Mirabeau, for their "insidious mask of patriotism." But possibly he would have named others who remained true to Liberty, among whom we could certainly include the author himself, a republican who vows not to shrink from stating "any truths, however severe, which I may think beneficial to the cause which I have undertaken to defend."

The "Letter" stated some very "severe" truths indeed, in the polemical context of 1793. Far from crediting Watson's shock at the sight of the altars of Liberty "streaming with the blood of the monarch," Wordsworth insouciantly comments, "At a period big with the fate of the human race, I am sorry you attach so much importance to the personal sufferings of the late royal martyr [and have joined] in the idle cry of modish lamentation which has resounded from the court to the cottage." This is a very bold statement, beyond even what Paine ventured (he was against the death penalty for Louis). But Wordsworth backs it up with the authority of his own experience. He cites another bishop, Grégoire, whom he knew personally at Blois, and who spoke on the fateful 10th of August the words that Wordsworth quotes: that any French citizen could have dragged before Louis "the corse [*sic*] of one of his murdered brothers [and] exclaimed to him, Tyran, voilà ton ouvrage."

There is another pattern of images in Wordsworth's "Letter" which is as noteworthy biographically as his outspoken political position: a leitmotif of references to the naturalness of passion in a time of the pregnancy, labor, and birth pangs of a new social order. These are partly conventional metaphors, but Wordsworth could not have employed them without thinking of their personal reference to Annette's recent labor and delivery of their child. These positive metaphors are counterpointed with negative ones of a similar provenance, including the unnatural (that is, illicit) sexual practices to which the poor are driven by economic hardship. Picking up on Watson's bluff confidence that Englishmen will not "deluge their land with blood," Wordsworth turns the question away from French revolutions toward English social problems: "does your lordship shudder at the prostitution which miserably deluges our streets?" This recalls his recoil from the prostitutes of London two years earlier. Reflecting his and Beaupuy's hope that the Revolution might ultimately put an end to the poverty which leads to prostitution, his main point is "that the miseries entailed upon the marriage of those who are not rich will no longer tempt the bulk of mankind to fly to that promiscuous intercourse to which they are impelled by the instincts of nature, and the dreadful satisfaction of escaping the prospect of infants, sad fruits of such intercourse, whom they are unable to support." He could not write such a sentence without having his own experience in mind: he who, not being rich, had just felt the full force of such miseries entailed (literally) on his own wish to marry. His "dreadful satisfaction" clause is obscure, but it seems to signify, not avoiding conception, but fleeing from the *sight* of infants who are sad because they are poor—because they are unsupported by their fathers. This is what he had just done to Caroline, an act he had returned to England to find a means of rectifying. In this context his references to the times as "big with the fate of the human race," and to "a time of revolution" as "a convulsion from which is to spring a fairer order of things," make us see, behind his feminine personification of the lady Liberty, the mother of his own child, Annette Vallon. Unlike Watson, Wordsworth *can* accept the convulsions of revolution because he can link them to his own—Annette's own—experience, all the more so as he feels guilty for not being with her.

If published, the "Letter to Llandaff" would have been one of the most radical of all responses to Burke, Watson, or any other conservative writer on events in France. Though congested, its prose is often eloquently passionate—a combination characteristic of Wordsworth's prose all his life. Its author, if identified, would have been subject to a prosecution as severe as that of Paine, who had been convicted of sedition in December and condemned to death and who never returned to England but died forgotten and rejected in America. As a vulnerable and increasingly unprotected young man, Wordsworth would have faced punishments at least as severe as those meted out—the pillory, prison, and transportation to Australia—to Thomas Muir, Thomas Fyshe Palmer, and William Skirving, "the Scottish martyrs," later in the year for their role in organizing the Edinburgh constitutional convention. (Burns composed "Scots wha hae" in September, upon hearing of Muir's conviction.[33]) All of these men were members of properly constituted societies seeking nonviolent reform.[34] Wordsworth was not, so far as we know, a dues-paying member of any society, but the implications of his "Letter to Llandaff" can hardly be called nonviolent. The Traitorous Correspondence Bill and Seditious Practices Act had just been introduced; though technically aimed at commercial transactions, it had the intended practical effect of fanning public fears about revolutionary fellow travelers. It was aimed specifically at persons who had recently come from France, who were known to have associated with revolutionaries or their English sympathizers, and who now maintained a correspondence with France—all conditions that applied to Wordsworth.

The wise advice of Joseph Johnson seems the most plausible reason for Wordsworth's not publishing the "Letter" in such a repressive climate. Johnson's behavior was generally careful; he could see that the "Letter" was simply a ticket to jail. He was recommending exactly the same course of restraint at exactly the same time to another of his authors, Mary Wollstonecraft. Early in the year she had sent him her "Letter on the Present Character of the French Nation," intended as the first in a series of letters commenting on French affairs, a more intellectual version of her friend Helen Williams's successful *Letters from France.* Wollstonecraft's letter is, surprisingly, closer to Watson's recantation than to Wordsworth's attack. She found herself losing her "theory of a more perfect state" and fearing "that vice, or, if you will, evil, is the grand mobile of action" in Paris.[35] Johnson knew that she, like Wordsworth, was affected by both personal and political troubles, and he did not publish her "Letter" either. A circumspect liberal, he could keep Wordsworth from reacting too far toward the left while at the same time preventing Wollstonecraft from reacting too far toward the right. He thus saved Wollstonecraft from a recantation in language that would later (when her confidence in rational reform returned) have sounded embarrassingly like Burke's: "little is to be expected from the narrow principle of commerce which seems to be everywhere shoving aside *the point of honour* of the *noblesse.*"[36] And he saved Wordsworth from extremes of expression that not only were near treason but were soon to be very badly outstripped by events.

If Wordsworth had published the "Letter to Llandaff," he would, even if he had escaped prosecution and conviction, have set his life on a course very different from the one he took. He would have become a marked man in political discussions throughout the rest of the decade. He would have been noticed in the newspapers far more notoriously than he was as the author of *An Evening Walk* and *Descriptive Sketches.* He would have been damned shrilly by the ministerial press, and hardly praised at all by the opposition papers, since his views were far too radical for establishment Whigs. The name Wordsworth, like those of Burke, Paine, Wollstonecraft, Godwin, Mackintosh, Watson, Thelwall, and others, would have been indelibly fixed (or sunk) in public memory as one of the participants in the great, failed "Revolution Debate" of 1790–95. Many of these men and women were never heard from again; even if they lived, they passed into an obscurity almost as deep as death. About ten years older than Wordsworth, they formed a generation without a political future. From being the history makers of their era, they found themselves bypassed by history, and have only very recently been rehabilitated. Wordsworth could not have known this would happen, but by not publishing the "Letter to Llandaff" he saved himself for the future as the history of the 1790s receded into his obscure youthful past. By the end of the decade he had transformed himself into a man of a different era. Much of the language of the "Letter to Llandaff" is consistent with that of the preface to *Lyrical Ballads,* but the subject under discussion has changed dramatically, from politics to poetry, and from the immorality of nobles to the nobility of the poor.

Instead of publishing the "Letter to Llandaff," Wordsworth did what he had done at earlier crisis moments in his life: he took a vacation. Sometime during the spring, he became reacquainted with William Calvert, an old Lake District friend, whose father had held the same position for the duke of Norfolk at Greystoke Castle (near Penrith) that Wordsworth's father held for Lord Lonsdale at Cockermouth. Calvert's father had died two years earlier, and William as eldest son had inherited the substantial estate of a father who had prospered in a rich man's service. He was now a man of very independent means (Dorothy called him "a man of fortune"), who did not need to bother going to university to become a gentlemen. The thought "there but for the grace of God go I" can hardly not have crossed Wordsworth's mind when they met.[37]

Most Wordsworth biographers, working backward from the fact that a bequest of £900 from Calvert's younger brother, Raisley, two years later was the beginning of Wordsworth's independence, take William Calvert's appearance in Wordsworth's life at this time as part of the providence that genius is heir to. It was not a very unusual coincidence, for there was a northern network of mutual friends and acquaintances in London at the time. (Joshua Wilkinson, for example, was from Cockermouth: his grandfather had built the house Wordsworth was born in.)[38] But there is no record that Wordsworth and Calvert were particularly close friends at Hawkshead, they probably had not seen each other for at least five years, and Wordsworth did not even know young Raisley Calvert at this time. (Raisley entered Magdalen College, Cambridge, in February.) That their fathers had identical posts with rich noblemen gave them a certain common ground, one they shared with several other Hawkshead boys.

Wordsworth and William Calvert could have met at any one of several public meetings held at the Crown & Anchor tavern in London early in the year, sponsored by the Friends of the Liberty of the Press, a liberal umbrella organization. Public invitations to these meetings were published on the front page of the *Morning Post,* signed by (among others) James Losh of Newcastle and Henry Howard, MP. Losh, one of the stewards of the organization, was well known to Wordsworth by name and face, though not yet the close friend he later became; Howard was the scion of the duke of Norfolk, and thus very well known to William Calvert. These were exactly the sorts of meetings, drawing four to five hundred persons, that liberal young men might attend (John Christian Curwen, the Westmorland MP, was a member), rather than the more radical and activist gatherings of the London Corresponding Society.

Calvert soon proposed to underwrite the expense of a leisurely tour of the west of England during the summer. In June his brother Raisley passed through town bound on an adventure familiar to Wordsworth: he was off to the Continent, proposing to educate himself by traveling for a few years, having decided Cambridge was too lax and licentious. William Calvert's money, his lack of the finish of a university education, and his desire to improve himself were motives for his generosity to Wordsworth. But generosity, philanthropy, and benevolence were very much in the air at the time among liberal young intellectuals, and Calvert may have proposed the tour with Wordsworth just out of the goodness of his heart.

By degrees, first Calvert and then his brother Raisley came to play the role of that "young gentleman" on whom Wordsworth's supposed career plan (traveling tutor) focused at this time. In the late spring Wordsworth's last prospect in this line fell through, when someone else got the position as tutor to Lord Belmore's son in Ireland, the grandson of the earl of Buckinghamshire.[39] As often happens in life, plans projected with high aims were realized in more limited, proximate terms: instead of the grandson of the earl of Buckinghamshire, Wordsworth would "tutor" the son of the duke of Norfolk's steward. Wordsworth had a university degree, was more disposed toward a teaching or tutoring career than anything else, and had substantial credentials as a connoisseur-practitioner of the popular arts of the Picturesque, both as an Alpine traveler and as the author of a well-reviewed book of descriptive sketches. In Book XI of *The Prelude* Wordsworth alludes to this period as the time when he was most engrossed by the finicky principles of landscape discrimination characteristic of Picturesque fashion: he may have been preoccupied with them because he was teaching them to Calvert.

They left London in late June or early July, amid wildly conflicting press reports as to whether the forces of the French republic were about to be finally overwhelmed by the royalist forces massed against them, or might yet snatch recovery from the jaws of imminent defeat which were closing down on them everywhere. The Girondins' effort to purge Marat had backfired, leading instead to a general order for *their* arrest. The London newspapers gave several accounts of the escapes of Girondins into the provinces, some of them—Brissot, Gorsas, and Louvet—well known to Wordsworth.

This was the third summer in four years that Wordsworth had set off on an ambitious tour: this one was planned to last until October. He and Calvert began by going to the Isle of Wight, a seaside diversion before tackling their intended object, the west of England. Thanks to successive editions of William Gilpin's *Tour . . . of the Wye* (1782), and its proximity to the fashionable resort center of Bath, the West Country was the most popular and accessible of all picturesque touring routes. Its popularity is reflected in such London shows as *The London Hermit; or, Rambles in Dorsetshire,* which opened the 1793 summer season, starring Mrs. Kemble.[40]

The Isle of Wight was not yet the cozy miniature country it became following the Napoleonic Wars, though its touristic potential was emerging. At the time Wordsworth visited it, its ambience was still mainly military, like its history. A modern tourist brochure mentions only one cultural association before Wordsworth's sojourn there: William Davenant's imprisonment in West Cowes Castle in 1649.[41] The center of the island is dominated by Carisbrooke Castle, where Charles I was imprisoned before his execution. These literary-political associations were known to Wordsworth, since Davenant, successor to Ben Jonson as poet laureate, was saved from execution by Milton—and was in turn among those who, like Dryden and Marvell, secured Milton's life following the Restoration. But in 1793 a more familiar recommendation came from John Wordsworth, whose favorite anchorage was Cowes Roads, at the northern tip of the island, directly across the Solent from Southampton. John had just sailed in May for China on the *Earl of Abergavenny,* under the captaincy of his cousin John Wordsworth, using the £100 legacy Dorothy had recently received from her grandmother's estate as part of his investment in the profits of the voyage.[42]

Watching the shoals of pleasure craft scudding along the Solent today, one must multiply and enlarge them many times in the mind's eye to imagine what the region looked like in the early summer of 1793. Between Southampton and Portsmouth, and all along the island from Spithead on the east to The Needles on the west, the British naval and merchant fleets were busily arming themselves for worldwide action against the French in the war declared just five months earlier. The naval arm of the British empire, the most powerful armed force in the world, was flexing itself as it had not done since the American war, for action against a much more dangerous and despised enemy. Most energy was being expended on behalf of Lord Hood and the Mediterranean fleet, which was going to blockade the French republic on its southern flank, with Hood in the flagship, *Victory.* This strategy came near to success—the population of Toulon having revolted against the directives of Paris—except for the brilliant tactics of a Corsican artillery officer named Buonaparte. Wordsworth recalled spending July "in view of the fleet which was then preparing for sea off Portsmouth," and he "left the place with melancholy forebodings. The American war was still fresh in memory."[43] But his mood was provoked far less by the ten-years-past American Revolution than by his personally unhappy situation vis-à-vis the French Revolution.

Under the cover of conducting a rich young gentleman's tour, Wordsworth could have reconnoitered possibilities for slipping back over to France. Along with its strategic military value, the Isle of Wight was also a headquarters for smugglers, who were currently enjoying a very lucrative business in transporting goods, letters, and passengers across the Channel to Cherbourg and Dieppe. Their usefulness to the government was like that of criminals to police at all times: communications could be opened, encouraged, compromised, or confiscated for a wide variety of purposes.[44] The south coast of the island is generally too precipitous or exposed for good smuggling operations, but Freshwater Bay at its southwest corner (the farthest remove from official Portsmouth) was an excellent spot, complete with rocky caves that might—depending on one's interest—be described either as picturesque or as well hidden.

Spending a month on the island, Wordsworth and Calvert covered it pretty thoroughly. We have only one written record of Wordsworth's time on the island in 1793, from Book X of *The Prelude* ("Ere yet the fleet of Britain had gone forth," 290–305). He is watching a beautiful sunset, and accenting for Calvert the best ways to see and feel it. He may have been looking across at the island from Portsmouth, opposite the village of Ryde (where the mainland ferries alight), but a more plausible vista is from the west of the island, near the "steeps" above Freshwater Bay now known as Tennyson Downs (from another laureate's affection for the place), which give a much better picturesque station for watching the sun set over water.[45] It was the frustration of this "normal" expectation that started, then blocked, Wordsworth's original version of the passage, which gives us a further glimpse into the "revolution" that was working in his mind that summer.

The lines begin with all the tranquillity of a quiet summer sunset, "How sweet the walk along the woody steep / When all the summer seas are charmed to sleep," and continue through ten unexceptionable lines, reminiscent of Wordsworth's imitations of Bowles,[46] until the setting sun's light hits the warships, and literally breaks the poem apart, as the manuscript shows:

> Now lessened half his glancing disc de[scends]
> The watry sands athwart the forest [ ]
> Flush [ ] radiance not [ ]
> While anchored Vessels scattered fa[r] [ ]
> Darken with shadowy hulks [ ]
> O'er earth o'er air and oce[an] [ ]
> Tranquillity extends her [ ]
> But hark from yon proud fleet in peal profound
> Thunders the sunset cannon; at the sound
> The star of life appears to set in blood
> Old ocean shudders in offended mood
> Deepening with moral gloom his angry flood.
>
> (8–19)[47]

The poem's problem, like the "Letter to Llandaff," is the speaker's inability to negotiate between his distress over social crises and his love of natural beauty. War fleets spoil a beautiful sunset here, as a ruined economy and rigid marriage laws cause promiscuous intercourse and illegitimate children in the "Letter to Llandaff." Nature has been violated by Culture: history, politics, and war. Wordsworth literally cannot establish any interaction between the natural scene and the shadow of the human institutions which lay cross it: the British navy. The "tranquillity" conventionally associated with a picturesque sunset is canceled out by the "sunset cannon." But after stuttering through this crisis point, his descriptive powers suddenly revive, and he ends up with a poem different from the one he started. The fragment seems to be a sonnet whose structure has been blown apart by an afterthought, exposing the author's determination to be true to actual experience. Instead of ending at the fourteenth line ("Tranquillity extends her . . ." [peaceful reign?]), he continues on with a forced editorial comment, which appears to be coming from Nature itself, and for the first time in the poem. Of course, the last three lines are all projections of the human observer's emotions: Wordsworth's is the shuddering offense, his the deepening anger and gloom, and for deeply personal reasons as well as strongly felt political ones. It would take him almost five years to complete the process of healing the break in the fabric of his imagination which we can first mark, textually, here. Then he will be able to say, "I have learned / To look on nature, not as in the hour / Of thoughtless youth, but hearing oftentimes / The still, sad music of humanity."[48]

In early August, Wordsworth and Calvert left the island and began their tour of the West Country. Almost immediately, however, their route and plans were changed by an accident. Somewhere near Salisbury, Calvert's horse "began to caper . . . in a most terrible manner, dragged them and their vehicle into a Ditch and broke it to shivers. Happily neither Mr C. nor William were the worse but they were sufficiently cautious not to venture again in the same way."[49] Calvert mounted his horse and rode off "into the North," while Wordsworth was left with his only "firm Friends, a pair of stout legs," and strode off, not to the West Country but in a different direction, to Robert Jones's house in North Wales, more than two hundred miles away.

Whether this accident occurred at all, or in quite the way Dorothy reported it, will be considered in the next chapter. For the moment we can take Dorothy's word for it and accept that Wordsworth and Calvert split up and went their separate ways. Whether Jones was expecting him or not, Wordsworth knew he could always count on a welcome there, and may have posted a letter announcing himself.[50]

Like his mountaintop experiences in the Alps and Wales in 1790 and 1791, Wordsworth's walking "tour" across Salisbury Plain—if that is the right word for a long trudge by the survivor of a dangerous road accident—produced some of the most intense emotional experiences contributing to his poetic self-creation. But the literary results of his experience were—also like those in the Simplon Pass and on Snowdon—barely visible to his contemporaries. In 1793–94 he wrote a poem called "A Night on Salisbury Plain," which he revised heavily between 1795 and 1799 into another version, called "Adventures on Salisbury Plain."[51] But that poem not appear in print until 1842, as a specimen of his juvenilia (though so much reworked as to be anything but that), and retitled *Guilt and Sorrow.*

Our knowledge of what actually happened to Wordsworth on Salisbury Plain in August 1793 is buried between the lines and revisions of these poems.[52] Our warrant for searching through them is provided by a stylized excerpt from them which he attributes to his own experience at the end of Book XII of *The Prelude* (312–53), where we see him "wandering on from day to day," "a youthful traveller," meeting "the wanderers of the earth." This is a complex vision of the wisdom of the ancient druids (traditionally associated with Stonehenge), which he says gave him confidence that he "seemed about this period to have sight / Of a new world . . . / . . . in life's everyday appearances." The Salisbury Plain poems are the first significant sign, along with his "Letter to the Bishop of Llandaff," of something new and different in Wordsworth's life and work: an empathy with the poor people who, from this moment onward, began to suffer immensely from the hardships caused by England's new war against France, which would last for an entire generation.

Wordsworth late in life spoke of "a couple of days rambling about Salisbury Plain," including a noontime nap at Stonehenge, overcome with heat and fatigue;[53] in *The Prelude* he says, "three summer days I roamed." The events in the Salisbury Plain poems cover two days, and their opening description clearly reflects Wordsworth's firsthand experience. His nap at Stonehenge would have been on his first day out from Salisbury. The narrator looks back regretfully at "the distant spire" of Salisbury cathedral as he measures each "painful step"—a hint that even "a pair of stout legs" were sore after an accident that broke a carriage into "shivers." He is advancing "o'er Sarum's plain," specifically Old Sarum, the ancient castle ruins a couple of miles outside Salisbury: "an antique castle spreading wide. / Hoary and naked are its walls" (*NSP,* 78–79). He had practical reasons for concern, as he notes "the troubled west . . . red with stormy fire." Salisbury Plain is not a place to be caught outside, alone, on a stormy night: all conditions that obtain in the poem. A terrific storm on the plain on August 7 was reported in the London newspapers.[54] An even worse scenario would be to be poor, unprotected, and female, like the Female Vagrant the narrator stumbles onto in "the dead house of the plain," a ruined traveler's spital which—the final Gothic twist—is supposed to be haunted, and in which each of the characters at first mistakes the other for a ghost.

Salisbury Plain is not a good place for a leisurely walk. It is one of the most desolate open spaces in England, with little or no shade, hardly a stream, and few human habitations of any kind. The villages of the farmers who cultivate it are scattered around the perimeter: "wastes of corn . . . but where the sower dwelt was nowhere to be found" (*NSP,* 45). In his headnote to the 1842 version, Wordsworth noted that "though cultivation was then (1793) more widely spread through parts of it, [it] had upon the whole a still more impressive appearance than it now retains." It has not lost that quality. It is not hard to walk across except where crops are thickly planted, but there are few marked footpaths. Even today, two hundred years later, only three roads cross its twenty-five-mile length and breadth, and half of its area has been put permanently off-limits as a firing range and field for war games by the Ministry of Defence. Gilpin's *Observations of Western England* called it "one vast cemetery," full of "mansions of the dead."[55]*

It is not exactly a *plain,* but rather a vast expanse of swales, swelling ridges, and slopes, in which the walker is paradoxically more often out of sight of the horizon and his general whereabouts than he would be in climbing a mountain. Both Wordsworth's traveler and his Female Vagrant comment on this aspect of the plain. "Long had each slope he mounted seemed to hide / Some cottage," but there are none, hence place-names like Breakheart Bottom. The woman mentions seeing an old man "beckoning from the naked steep . . . tottering sidelong down to ask the hour; / There never clock was heard from steeple tower" (*NSP,* 165–67). These details are irrelevant to the narrative, but they establish the reality of the experience and suggest how close Wordsworth was to the events he narrates. Why an old man might expect such a poor woman to have a watch is inexplicable, but it is true that one sees other human beings with mixed emotions on Salisbury Plain: it's the sort of place one goes to in order to get away from people.

The Female Vagrant's life story is a wide-ranging account that starts in the Lake District and crosses to America, whence she has returned, widowed and childless.[56] But her account of her departure and return has several details which correlate well with the Southampton-Portsmouth area, from which she seems to have recently departed, since both she and the narrator are traveling west. Wordsworth's own situation in early August 1793 and his subsequent revisions of the poem tend to increase his surrogate narrator's implication in her plight. He was now, for the first time in his life, nearly as "vagrant" as the woman. This was no long-vacation walking tour, triumphantly conducted. Still less was it the 1791 tour of Wales under Jones's protection, and far less the all-expenses-paid jaunt in William Calvert's whiskey. To put it bluntly, Wordsworth suddenly found himself between meal tickets. His only money was whatever he had left from the five guineas

*A modern version of what Wordsworth calls the "dead house of the plain" is a new purpose-built village near Tilshead for practice in house-to-house fighting, circled around a central "church," which is actually a military observation tower. I found myself dodging the sightlines of the watchman in this tower because I didn't relish trying to persuade an authority of the legitimacy of what I was doing there—tracing the footsteps of a poetic refugee from the French Revolution. Three tanks clanked up a ridge in front of me, and the leader swiveled its turret toward me for one heart-stopping moment before they filed off in a different direction.

Richard advanced for pocket money when he set off with Calvert. Moreover, his indigent condition was painfully symbolic of his life situation at the moment, with no "prospects" to speak of and, like the Female Vagrant, with a spouse and child abandoned in a foreign land torn by civil war, whom he could not get to, and could not help much even if he did.

Like the woman in the poem, he too had lost property and comfortable family circumstances in the Lake District. The first words of her "artless story" are "By Derwent's side my father's cottage stood." Her family has been driven off its land by the machinations of a rich neighboring landlord, machinations that Wordsworth was very familiar with, not only from Lowther's treatment of him and his siblings but also from some of John Wordsworth's more unsavory duties in Lowther's service. The woman's story has been shown to derive from legends of the Philipson family of Calgarth Hall on Windermere,[57] and this detail further connects the story to Wordsworth's experience. For the present tenant of Calgarth Hall, he well knew, was none other than Richard Watson.

In *An Evening Walk* and *Descriptive Sketches,* the unfortunate creatures he describes (such as the vagrant mother of Esthwaite and the Grison gypsy) were genre figures painted into the landscape, not actual persons with unique histories. But the Salisbury Plain poems zoom in on the conventional beggars and peasants of loco-descriptive poetry, breaking the frame of the convention and opening the way toward a new poetry of social realism. Yet, as is often the case with Wordsworth's notes to his poems, he seems to want to establish several degrees of separation between himself and the actual experience. His very insistence on the authenticity of the woman's report raises questions about his knowledge of it. He said it was "faithfully taken from the report made to me of her own case by a friend who had been subjected to the same trials and affected in the same way." This is a remarkable series of coincidences: why rely on the friend's report of "the same trials" which affected her "in the same way"? Why not just tell her story directly? And what down-and-out, long-suffering "friend" of this class did Wordsworth have in 1793?

A year later, writing to Mathews about the poem, Wordsworth adopted his facetious sophisticated tone, but with a choice of diction that reveals his personal investment in the poem. "You inquired after the name of one of my poetical bantlings, children of this species ought to be named after their characters, and here I am at a loss, as my offspring seems to have no character at all. I have however christened it by the appellation of Salisbury Plain, though, A night on Salisbury plain, were it not so insufferably awkward would better suit the thing itself."[58] What "species" of children did he have in mind? To have a "character" meant also to have a good, reputable name, something that Wordsworth's eight-month-old "bantling," Caroline, barely had, though she was christened with the name of Wordsworth. Thus another difficulty of *naming this poem after its characters* might be that one of its character's names was Wordsworth, or someone very closely resembling him.

Personal experience and imaginative projections, real children and poetical bantlings, were richly mixed together in Wordsworth's adventures on Salisbury Plain. The narrator's interest in the Female Vagrant is stimulated by something that neither of Wordsworth's supposed informants would have told him. As the storm abates and the moon comes out, the traveler begins to see her in a new light:

> Gently the Woman gan [*sic*] her wounds unbind.
> Might Beauty charm the canker worm of pain
> The rose on her sweet cheek had ne'er declined:
> Moved she not once the prime of Keswick's plain
> While Hope and Love and Joy composed her smiling train?
>
> 24
>
> Like swans, twin swans, that when on the sweet brink
> Of Derwent's stream the south winds hardly blow,
> 'Mid Derwent's water-lillies swell and sink
> In union, rose her sister breasts of snow,
> (Fair emblem of two lovers' hearts that know
> No separate impulse) or like infants played,
> Like infant strangers yet to pain and woe.
> Unwearied Hope to tend their motions made
> Long Vigils, and Delight her cheek between them laid.
>
> 25
>
> And are ye sped ye glittering dews of youth
> For this—that Frost may gall the tender flower
> In Joy's fair breast with more untimely tooth?
> Unhappy man! thy sole delightful hour
> Flies first; it is thy miserable dower
> Only to taste of joy that thou may'st pine
> A loss, which rolling suns may ne'er restore.
>
> (*NSP,* 203–23)

These highly overdetermined breasts have a literary source: they are a Renaissance *blason,* appropriate to a poem written in Spenserian stanzas.[59] However, Wordsworth loads them with some personally suggestive weight, developing their symbolic capabilities to include memories of past happiness in the Lake District, his love for both Annette and Dorothy (he often compared himself and Dorothy to a pair of Grasmere swans), his infant Caroline ("stranger yet to pain and woe"), the "glittering dews of youth" that he has enjoyed, only to see his "sole delightful hour [fly] first," leaving him (and Annette) with a "miserable dower" from his uncles, which brings only bitterness, since "rolling suns" seem unlikely to restore her to him. In addition to all this, they may also describe an attractive destitute woman with whom he sheltered from a storm one night in 1793.

But the poem written out of these experiences was anything but personal. It is a determindedly *im*personal reflection on human suffering. The Female Vagrant's story and the narrator's stumbling upon her are framed in a philosophical perspective that holds them, not simply at arm's length, but at the length of the whole distance of human social evolution. The first stanzas, paraphrasing Rousseau's *Discourse on Inequality,* ask whether men in developed societies do not suffer more from hardship than primitive men who know nothing else. The only conclusion one can draw from such a hypothesis is Rousseau's unsettling paradox, that increased civilization leads to increased human inequality and mental suffering.

The poem's conclusion comes not from Rousseau but from Tom Paine. Between the two of them, the narrator and the woman are but a "friendless hope-forsaken pair," and "life is like this desart broad, / Where all the happiest find is but a shed / And a green spot 'mid wastes interminably spread." This confirms the woman's estimate of the "dreadful price of being" she and her children have paid, following their father through the horrors of the American Revolution: "dog-like wading at the heels of War . . . a cursed existence with the brood / That lap, their very nourishment, their brother's blood." Her thoughts stimulate the narrator's historical reflection on Stonehenge, which Wordsworth in *The Prelude* attributed to himself. Though one no longer hears the "horrid shrieks and dying cries" of human sacrifice, the only progress that enlightened reason shows us is "How many [are] by inhuman toil debased, / Abject, obscure, and brute to earth incline[d] / Unrespited, forlorn of every spark divine." Against this depressing reflection, Wordsworth opposes the hope that some unspecified "Heroes of Truth" will "uptear / Th'Oppressor's dungeon from its deepest base"—an obvious allusion to the Bastille—and "rear / Resistless in [their] might the herculean mace / Of Reason," an allusion to the young French republic, which Wordsworth like everyone else frequently compared to the young Hercules.[60] In contemporary English terms, such a hero was preeminently Tom Paine, the intellectual godfather of Wordsworth's "Letter to Llandaff," "Who fierce on kingly crowns hurled his own lightning blaze" both in *The Rights of Man* and by his participation in the trial of Louis XVI.

Anyone who thinks he can resist such "Heroes of Truth" is "insenate"—stupid—like Pitt's administration, which imagines that it is wise policy

That Exile, Terror, Bonds, and Force may stand:
That Truth with human blood can feed her torch,
And Justice balance with her gory hand
Scales whose dire weights of human heads demand
A Nero's arm.

(515–19)

These are clear if melodramatic references to the government's sequence of actions against its vulnerable opponents throughout the spring and summer of 1793, culminating in the transportation sentences of Muir, Palmer, Maurice Margarot, and Skirving handed down by the severe Scottish courts. Wordsworth's linking of Stonehenge and the Bastille as symbols of oppression is sincere and impressive, but histrionic. The poem's framework is as recklessly confident about the future as his "Letter to Llandaff," but Wordsworth's faithfulness to the particulars of his characters' stories works to contradict it.

Once off the plain, he resorted to public transport or cadged what rides he could. "From that district," he recalled, "I proceeded to Bath, Bristol, and so on to the banks of the Wye, where I took again to travelling on foot. In remembrance of that part of my journey . . . I began the verses—'Five years have passed.' "[61] Before he got to Tintern Abbey, however, we can track him near the mouth of the Wye, in two poems he wrote at Chepstow Castle, just above Bristol, the first obligatory sight for any picturesque walking tour up the Wye valley.[62] Like the Isle of Wight fragment, and like the Salisbury Plain poems in all their versions, these fragments also show Wordsworth's landscape vision being complicated, not to say ruined, by reflections on the inhumanity of human history.

The first one is a sonnet, partly torn away in manuscript, but its missing lines can be hypothetically reconstructed by extrapolating from its meter and imagery:

In vain did Time and Nature toil to throw
Wild weeds and earth upon these crumbled towers;
Again they rear the feudal head that lowers
Stern the wretched huts that crouch below.
[*Here w*]here the cornfield waved and varied sound
[*Of rural*] pleasure charmed the Cottage shade,
[*Along the*] path the careless infant stray'd,
[*Now the*] [?w]ild deer calls his mates around.
[*But soon a new breeze*] and a form divine
[*O'er all the*] [?earth] shall stretch her equal reign
[*To every humble*] [?home] on every plain,

> [*E'en to a rude*] [Hy]mettus low as thine—
> [*Among the poor she*] dwelt, and loved to shed
> [*Her equal blessings round*] thy honor'd head.[63]

As a three-part Shakespearean sonnet, moving from the unhappy present to an idyllic past and then pivoting toward an ideal projected future, the poem is over almost before it begins, given its strong opening statement that all is "in vain." Chepstow Castle, like Tintern Abbey and many other ruins from Henry VIII's dissolution of the monasteries 250 years earlier, was at this time inhabited by vagrants, gypsies, beggars, and outlaws. Their number would swell dramatically during the next five years as the "Minister's War" spread its ruinous economic consequences.*

What Wordsworth imagines completing the inadequate efforts of Time and Nature to cover over unhappy feudal remnants (now seen to be reviving) is not an "equal reign" of agrarian reform—the radical idea of land redistribution which Wordsworth took pains in the "Letter to Llandaff" to say he opposed—but a hierarchy of mutual respect in which higher and lower classes still exist, but without the need for any "lowering" or "crouching." In this respect, the fragment can be viewed as a liberal young intellectual's effort to breathe a new spirit into inherited forms, for the sonnet is otherwise an uninspired reprise of those by the extremely conservative Reverend William Bowles which had fired Wordsworth's enthusiasm a few years earlier (for instance, in "Netley Abbey" or "Bamborough Castle"). Bowles's melancholy emotions are entirely personal, but Wordsworth's poem has a kind of sociopolitical resolution, with its egalitarian female personification ("a form divine") returning like a messiah of Liberty to distribute equal justice in an "equal reign" of natural plenty: Hymettus being the mountain near Athens famous in ancient pastorals for wild flowers and honey. One reason this poem about "wretched huts" remained in manuscript, unlike "Tintern Abbey" with its similar "vagrant dwellers," is that in the intervening five years Wordsworth learned—created—a way of hearing such "still, sad music of humanity" without feeling that it was in contradiction to the beauty of nature. But in "Tintern Abbey" he achieves his resolution almost entirely in personal terms, with equally vague social overtones.

*Chepstow Castle was also historically famous as the prison for thirty years of the Puritan regicide Henry Marten, another reason Wordsworth might have been drawn to reflect poetically on it, as Robert Southey did four years later, to the joy of the *Anti-Jacobin* satirists. In its first issue, November 20, 1797, the *Anti-Jacobin* printed Southey's "Inscription for the Apartment in Chepstow Castle, where Henry Marten, the Regicide, was imprisoned thirty years" next to an imitation, "Inscription for the Door of the Cell in Newgate, where Mrs. Brownrigg, the Prentice-cide, was confined previous to her Execution." His crime: "He had REBELL'D AGAINST THE KING, AND SAT / IN JUDGMENT ON HIM"; hers: "SHE WHIPP'D TWO FEMALE PRENTICES TO DEATH, / AND HID THEM IN THE COAL-HOLE."

A second fragment, thirty-two lines beginning, "The western clouds a deepening gloom display," places Wordsworth at Chepstow Castle even more precisely, with mention of a "traveller" standing before its high "central bridge," and references to torture and executions that recall the castle's role as a prison after the civil war. It repeats the problem of the Isle of Wight and "In vain" sonnets, as well as the Salisbury Plain poems. Again Wordsworth sees a beautiful sunset through or across the ruins of a repressive human institution. He wants to draw a comfortable moral about human progress but can't. He comes to a kind of conclusion:

> 'Tis past and in this wreck of barbarous pride
> Now mortal weakness only views the tomb
> Of years though savage still to man allied
> And o'er their terrors breathes a softening gloom.
> (17–20)[64]

This is not much, but at least it is something: a vaguely forgiving sympathy for the bad old days of yore. Yet his "mortal weakness" will not leave well enough alone, and he pushes on into the present tense: "Now." The result is that, as in the Isle of Wight sonnet, the poem disintegrates before our very eyes. His eyes "draw from the streams . . . below [the Wye] / New tints of tender sadness *not their own*" (italics added). What these melancholy tints might be is not specified. He knows that "the moonlight beams" should lie "still" on the flowing waters, but at "midnight hours" the meditating mind "starts" at what it thinks.[65] A standard recipe of picturesque ingredients has failed to provide an antidote, and the poem suddenly reverts to scenes of Gothic horror. At this point the manuscript, like the poem itself, degenerates into a tissue of conjectures, and a purely escapist conclusion:

> When fragrant Morn forth issues glistering bright
> With heedless music and unaltered smile,
> [No] fond regret the ravage shall excite
> In musing sage or thoughtless [son] of toil.
> (29–32)

This comes close to saying, Don't worry, be happy. All we can say is that the "ravage" the poem describes has shifted from that of Time upon the towers of Chepstow Castle to include the ravage of the meditating mind upon itself, as it explores its "new tints of tender sadness" more closely.

But we know very well what those tints of sadness were for Wordsworth: almost any thoughts about his life in general, and in particular his thoughts about Annette and his inability to provide for her. In his famous lines in "Tintern Abbey" about his mood when first he "came among these hills," he introduces his twenty-three-year-old self with a strange reverse hyperbole: he was "more like a man / Flying from something that he dreads, than one / Who sought the thing he loved" (71–73). He was *not* a man seeking the thing he loved (Annette); he was rather a man flying from something he dreaded—which may also have been Annette, or the whole collection of circumstances that was keeping him from her (the war, his uncles, and his own growing desperation about what being with her might entail for his life). The 1793 fragments break down because the observer cannot bring his negotiations between Nature and History to a successful conclusion. The 1798 poem succeeds because he has incorporated *both* into terms of his own emotions: he is sadder but wiser. His scope is more general and may thus seem more mature, but some painful particulars have dropped out of mind when he says, "I have learned / To look on nature, *not* as in the hour / Of thoughtless youth, but hearing oftentimes / The still, sad music of humanity."

The differences of Wordsworth's 1793 reflections on Chepstow Castle and those of 1798 on Tintern Abbey, compared with other contemporary models, are clear in a "Sonnet on the River Wye" (by "M."), which appeared in the *Morning Post* for July 29, 1793, just about the time young Wordsworth was passing by it:

O Wye, romantic stream! Thy winding way
Invites my lonely steps, what time the night
Smiles on the radiance of the moon's pale light,
That love upon thy quivering flood to play.
O'er thy steep banks the rocks fantastic tower,
And fling their deepening shadow cross the stream;
To Fancy's eye worn battlements they seem,
Which on some beetling cliff tremendous lower.
Hark! Echo speaks, and from her mazy cave
Sportive returns the sailor's frequent cry,
Ah! how unlike thy old Bard's minstrelsy
Warbled in wild notes to the haunted wave!
Unlike as seems the hurricane's rude sweep,
To the light breeze that lulls thy placid sleep.[66]

In its use of natural contrasts to mark historical change, this is more or less identical to Wordsworth's lines on Chepstow Castle. The main difference is his attempt to work his own private emotional states into it, though his conclusion is no less vapid. His effort to be true to his own experience, in poems written mainly to produce pat moral generalizations, ruined his poems of 1793. But this effort is the point of origin of his immense advance beyond mere landscape poetry into a comprehensive vision which could contain, if only uneasily, both history and the individual consciousness.

The next day's walk brought him to Goodrich Castle, where he records meeting the little girl of "We Are Seven," who insisted that the number of her siblings was undiminished, though "two are in the church-yard laid." Wordsworth gave her a slight Welsh identification with her information that "two of us at Conway [Conwy] dwell," but we must hope that the obtuse narrator of the poem, who insists that dead children are dead, buried, and in heaven, is not identical with the young man whose own infant child was much on his mind at the time.

Continuing north along the river, he came to Builth Wells, where he met the "wild rover" who became Peter Bell: "He told me strange stories. It has always been a pleasure to me through life to catch at every opportunity that has occurred in my rambles of becoming acquainted with this class of people." This "class" consisted of those "wanderers of the earth" who had for Wordsworth the same "grandeur which invests / The mariner who sails the roaring sea" (XII.153–54): a pointed comparison, since *Peter Bell* became his land-locked companion to Coleridge's "Rime of the Ancient Mariner." Such itinerant vagrants always interested Wordsworth as long as they were not in groups, like gypsies: "From many other uncouth vagrants, passed / In fear, [I] have walked with quicker step" (XII.159–60). Sometimes the feeling was mutual, if we may credit some canceled lines from one of the many manuscripts of *Peter Bell:*

Now Peter do I call to mind
That eventide when thou and I
Over ditch and over stile
Were fellow travellers many a mile
Near Builth on the banks of Wye.

Oh Peter who could now forget
That both hung back in murderer's guize?
'Twas thou that was afraid of me.
And I that wast afraid of thee,
We'd each of us a hundred eyes.[67]

After more than a week on the road on foot, Wordsworth the wanderer evidently looked not much less "wild" than Peter the rover. One would give a lot to know what Peter's "strange stories" were, and whether Wordsworth told him some of his own. They were not, apparently, accounts of Peter's bigamy (he had six wives) and subsequent redemption, for Wordsworth attributed this behavior to "a lawless creature who lived in the county of Durham . . . attended by many women, sometimes not less than half a dozen, as disorderly as himself."[68] Like the "King of the Beggars" who fascinated him in London, the Durham bigamist stuck in Wordsworth's mind for his ability to control so many women: "he had been heard to say while they were quarrelling, 'Why can't you be quiet? there's none so many of you.' " Wordsworth was particularly receptive to stories of bigamy as he labored up the Wye valley toward Jones's sanctuary, "more like a man / Flying from something that he dreads, than one / Who sought the thing he loved."

Peter has trekked all over England and Scotland. One of his early points of reference is close to Wordsworth's recent experience—"well he knew the spire of Sarum"—and the main action of the poem includes one location that seems to indicate Salisbury Plain: "Where, shining like the smoothest sea, / In undisturbed immensity / A level plain extends."[69] The facetious narrator of *Peter Bell* presents his story as a frankly escapist relief from troubling public events that fit 1793 better than 1798 (its time of composition), though applicable enough to both years: "what care we / For treasons, tumults, and for wars?" The name of the stillborn child in the poem, Benoni, Wordsworth attributes to his own knowledge—not of Caroline Wordsworth but of the illegitimate (not stillborn) son of Ann Tyson's neighbor, Mary Rigge, who, like Peter's Scottish wife, "died broken-hearted" and who was the subject of his very early ballad of William and Mary of Esthwaite.

But the closest connection to 1793 is *Peter Bell*'s plot, which is in many respects a reprise of the Salisbury Plain poems. Peter, heartless bigamist that he is, finds an untethered ass staring down into a stream where his master lies drowned. Unnerved, and unable to control the stubborn ass, Peter follows him home, where the owner's daughter at first mistakes him for her lost father ("My father! here's my father!"), but the wife rushes out, "And saw it was another!" As Peter tells the distraught widow what has happened, her grief works upon him like the Female Vagrant's on the Salisbury traveler: "He longs to press her to his heart, / From love that cannot find relief." But, as in that poem, a denouement that might bring the two sufferers together is precisely the one the author rejects, and it is the ass, not Peter, who subsequently "Help[ed] by his labour to maintain / The Widow and her family." Peter, instead, becomes a land-rover prototype of the Ancient Mariner: "And, after ten months' melancholy, / Became a good and honest man."

Other traces of Wordsworth's 1793 experiences flicker throughout the poem.[70] However, it is a much smaller detail, or inconsistency, that leads me to think that young Wordsworth's thoughts of Annette and Caroline contributed or attached themselves to this wild rover's strange stories. Wordsworth said he walked with Peter "from Builth, on the river Wye, *downwards* nearly as far as the town of Hay." But if he met him on the itinerary we are following, he should have being going *upward* from Hay-on-Wye toward Builth Wells. Scholars have tried to account for this apparently small inconsistency, ruling out the easy solution, that Wordsworth simply misspoke himself, on the basis of the poet's usual clarity and accuracy about such matters.[71] One proposes an alternative itinerary to get our hero moving in the right direction for this account, across the Black Mountains from Ross-on-Wye to the Brecon Beacons.[72] But this entails twenty miles of backtracking down from Builth, and such circuitous tourism on Wordsworth's part in 1793 can be ruled out, because of the condition of both his mind and his purse, to say nothing of his legs. Peter's stories would have had to be awfully strange for Wordsworth to turn about-face and go a total of forty miles out of his way just to listen to them.

But Wordsworth's movements can be aligned with Peter's if we assume that he met Peter not on his way north to Plas-yn-Llan but on his way *back* down south some weeks later, as the news from France and his growing uneasiness of mind about Annette and Caroline finally determined him to slip back across the Channel to France to see what he could do for them. This small detail about which direction Wordsworth was heading when he met the "wild rover" gives us a fulcrum on which to pivot our hero around and head him back to France on his own, a wilder rover than Peter ever was, who confined his romantic adventures to the British mainland. The one element in *Peter Bell* that Wordsworth got from no source but his own imagination (or experience) is the hero's remorse for having abandoned his wives and children. Here again we can entertain the thought that what seems strangest in the saga of Wordsworth's heroes may be what is closest to his own literal experience.

To explore this possibility we must backtrack a little and try to put ourselves into Wordsworth's mind from the time of his return from France the preceding December, and to imagine what he might have been thinking as he heard about what was happening in France, and how he might have imagined these terrible events affecting his mistress and child.

15 A RETURN TO FRANCE?

"A season dangerous and wild"
(X.286)

"that terrible moment, '93"
(Victor Hugo, *Ninety-three*)

Wordsworth's life in the late summer and early fall of 1793 presents two very different scenarios, like a "Choose Your Own Adventure" book for adolescents, where one chapter choice lands you with monsters, while another gets you home free; or like the famous alternative endings of novels such as *Great Expectations* or *Caleb Williams.* From late August until about Christmas there exists no firm contemporary evidence as to his whereabouts. Such a stretch of empty months is notable in itself, since the biographical record for his life is relatively full by this time. One option is to think of him "quietly sitting down in the Vale of Clwyd," a long-term house guest of the indulgent Robert Jones, biding his time until he could travel ninety miles east to see Dorothy at Halifax.

The other choice is to imagine Wordsworth embarked on an adventure of astonishing danger: going back to France sometime in September to see, marry, or rescue Annette, passing through intense counterrevolutionary actions in Normandy, entering Paris just as the trial of his former acquaintances among the Girondins begins, and witnessing the execution of Gorsas on October 7. He pushes on toward Blois to try to see Annette and then, in the greatest possible danger, escapes north through frozen fields, hiding in caves and forests along the route of the desperate Vendean army as it skirmishes its way toward vainly expected British aid on the Normandy coast. This view has Wordsworth crossing back to England in late October or early November.

The two different accounts return to a single narrative line at Christmastime, with Wordsworth as guest of his guardian uncle, Richard Wordsworth, at Whitehaven. The first alternative seems eminently more likely, except that there is not a shred of evidence to support it, other than what we can infer from letters written before August 31, 1793, and after February 17, 1794. The second alternative seems more like an excerpt from Victor Hugo's *Quatre-vingt treize*—an English love episode rejected, one might imagine, even by the great Romantic novelist as too implausible. Yet there are two accounts by trustworthy reporters which place Wordsworth in Paris in 1793, to which we can connect a pattern of associations from Wordsworth's poetry and contemporary records that give this wild surmise more substance than its tame alternative. None of Wordsworth's recent biographers is prepared to reject the evidence for a clandestine return; instead, after carefully turning over the evidence, all make the considered judgment that it is the more likely possibility.[1] What remains to be done, since none of these authorities ventures beyond the positive evidence, is by a finer sifting of the evidence to construct a scenario for each possibility.

The first alternative is easily sketched, a still life without action. If Wordsworth stayed "quietly sitting down" in Wales until about Christmastime, we can imagine him passing his time as Dorothy said, following his cross-country hike from Salisbury Plain, "as happily as he could desire; exactly according to his Taste, except alas! (ah here I sigh) that he is separated from those he loves."[2] Dorothy appropriately took herself as the "separated" object of her brother's love, but she knew Wordsworth's loves also included Annette and Caroline, because both she and William had been describing in detail in their letters to Annette a ménage where they might all live together, and Annette had been replying in the same vein.

But along with her desires, Dorothy stressed to Jane Pollard to an inordinate degree the need for secrecy. Above all, she insists that Jane not betray her knowledge that Dorothy knows that William may soon be there. Thus her letter of July 10 opens with the peremptory caution *"None of this is to be read aloud, so be upon your guard!"* It then continues blithely in the most banal vein of the provincial young lady: "My Aunt is gone to take an airing with my Uncle and Mary. The evening is a lovely one."[3] This reiterated secrecy is explainable because of William Cookson's increasing distaste for his nephew, now that Wordsworth's reasons for seeking a curacy had become clear. Dorothy did not want to appear as conniving in a plan to meet with a relative who is so much in disgrace with her aunt and uncle. Nor did she relish explaining the grounds of the Cooksons' disapproval to Jane. "The subject is an unpleasant one for a letter, it will employ us more agreeably in conversation, . . . though I must confess that he has been somewhat to blame, yet I think I shall prove to you that the Excuse might have been found in his natural disposition." To explain his "natural disposition," she offers Beattie's description of his Minstrel: "In truth he was a strange and wayward wight fond of each gentle &c. &c . . . and oft he traced the uplands &c, &c, &c."[4]

But all this insistence on secrecy, all those unmentionable etceteras, have another dimension, which draws our two options for Wordsworth's movements closer together. William and Dorothy were certainly involved in at least one family plot this fall: their plot to meet at Halifax "accidentally," so that no blame would fall on Dorothy for seeing him. This plot was unsuccessful, since they did not meet there at Christmas. But it may be that all these promised movements and adjurations to strictest secrecy were intended to give William an alibi, placing him firmly in Wales until such time as Dorothy got to Halifax, while he was actually going elsewhere, somewhere that truly could not be communicated to anyone in the family. Moorman, commenting on the unusual obscurity of this period in Wordsworth's life, and allowing the possibility of a French trip, says, "At least there is no *alibi* for the period in question."[5] Constructing one may have been the function of all the talk about Halifax. It seems a far-fetched plot, but if it was a cover for a clandestine trip to France it would have had to provide very deep cover indeed. Dorothy was certainly capable of the insouciant deception necessary for such things: she casually mentions to Jane, "I should like to talk a little broken French with you; seriously, however, I should like to *read* French with you."[6] The emphasis here is all hers, and has to do—as she does not inform Jane—with her new role in the William-Annette correspondence. Annette wrote longer letters to Dorothy than to William, and trying to reply in French taxed Dorothy's linguistic capabilities. In any case, Jane Pollard was being given information that she was not to communicate to anyone else—"*You* are the only person to whom it has been mentioned." If anyone should allude to William's coming, Jane is not to let on that she knows anything about it. "My secret still remains a secret notwithstanding you fancy it was disclosed to you by Mr. G[riffith]. Do not speak of it I entreat you."[7] This is all explicable on ordinary grounds, though there are certain inconsistencies in Dorothy's presentation of the plan. But Jane was being given so much information, and being so strongly pledged to secrecy about it, that one could almost think she was being provoked to let the cat out of the bag—in which case the desired alibi would fall neatly into place.

Other details from the summer increase the likelihood of such a secret plan. William's sojourn on the Isle of Wight provided an opportunity for reconnoitering the possibilities for slipping out of some small bay like Freshwater for a safe landing spot on the Normandy coast. We might question his entire trip with Calvert, and wonder why he undertook it at this time, and at such length. Dorothy already knew in July, very shortly after the idea of the tour had been broached, that it would not be finished until October; that is, a clear time frame has been established. Traveling with Calvert afforded William not only financial independence but also freedom of movement: "he is perfectly at liberty to quit his companion as soon as anything more advantageous shall offer." Such an "offer" throughout the spring and summer of 1793 was supposed to mean a traveling tutor's job, the old fallback position, but Wordsworth never sought one very seriously and had very different notions of where his "advantage" lay.

Then there is the question of the accident to Calvert's carriage and the oddity—which other commentators have remarked on[8]—that Wordsworth and Calvert separated following it, in two different directions: Calvert to the north and Wordsworth to the west. Did this accident actually occur, or was there some other reason for a parting of the ways? For a whiskey and its occupants to be "dragged . . . into a Ditch and broke . . . to shivers" is a very serious accident, unless Dorothy was exaggerating for Jane's amusment. A whiskey was a light two-wheeled vehicle, essentially a seat on leather straps attached to springs, that could easily break into "shivers" if dragged into a ditch. Newspapers carried almost daily accounts of similar accidents, usually accompanied by grave injuries or death, like highway accidents today. So it is a little hard to believe that the two young men got out, unharmed, that one of them mounted that same dangerously capering horse and rode off to the north of England, while the other, with conspicuously noted "firm . . . stout legs," headed off toward Wales. Of course this account is possible, but it does raise questions. Why was the tour to the west of England now abandoned? Why did Calvert leave Wordsworth so abruptly? Had their separation been planned? Presumably the whiskey was irreparable, but why didn't Calvert, rich as he was, buy or rent another, or rent a horse for Wordsworth? He might have quailed a bit if Wordsworth had suddenly proposed a *walking* tour, feeling his own legs to be not quite so firm and stout as all that. But he was an active soldier, an ensign in the duke of Norfolk's regiment at the time, and an eminently practical man, who later became a well-known inventor and mechanical experimentalist: very much the sort of man one would like to have on board in case of an accident. Their separation is strange, though to be sure a road accident can damp holiday spirits, even if there are no serious injuries. But it could also be an excuse to cover the fact that the proposed sightseeing tour had other motives. Wales was a plausible destination for either plot, for if anyone could be trusted to keep the details secret, it was Robert Jones, European companion par excellence.

Wordsworth in Wales is one option for the fall of 1793, but it is not without connections to its dramatic alter ego, Wordsworth in the Terror, or Wordsworth in the Vendée. It is not necessary to link up the Halifax "plot" with a French one, but it is the essence of good plotting to cover one's movements with other plausible accounts for "deniability." With the Wales–Halifax connection firmly established, an England–France connection might be pursued more freely. "William in France? Good heavens, no! He's with Calvert on the Isle of Wight, he's in the west of England, he's with Jones in Wales, he's just waiting to come over to Halifax . . . anywhere but France!"

The Life Record

It starts with Thomas Carlyle. The year is about 1840. Carlyle had met and talked with Wordsworth on several occasions, at breakfasts and dinner parties. On literary topics he found Wordsworth quite unsatisfactory, and the feeling was mutual. Carlyle admired Wordsworth's "fine wholesome rusticity," but found his literary opinions exceptionally narrow: "Gradually it became apparent to me that of transcendent unlimited [genius] there was, to this critic, probably but one specimen known, Wordsworth himself!" Still, Wordsworth was willing to talk with Carlyle "in a corner" at these large London social gatherings which neither of them liked very much, and in "another and better corner dialogue . . . which raised him intellectually some real degrees higher in my estimation than any of his deliverances, written or oral, had ever done," Carlyle decided to drop literature and to try to get from Wordsworth "an account of the notable practicalities he had seen in life, especially of the notable men."[9]

This is what he got:

> He went into all this with a certain alacrity, and was willing to speak whenever able on the terms. He had been in France in the earlier or secondary stage of the Revolution; had witnessed the struggle of Girondins and Mountain, in particular the execution of Gorsas, "the first deputy sent to the scaffold;" and testified strongly to the ominous feeling which that event produced in everybody, and of which he himself still seemed to retain something: "Where will it end, when you have set an example in this kind?" I knew well about Gorsas, but had found in my reading no trace of the public emotion his death excited; and perceived now that Wordsworth might be taken as a true supplement to my book, on this small point. He did not otherwise add to or alter my ideas on the Revolution, nor did we dwell long there; but hastened over to England, and to the noteworthy, or at least noted men of that and the subsequent time. "Noted" and named, I ought perhaps to say, rather than "noteworthy;" for in general I forget what men they were, and now remember only only the excellent sagacity, distinctness and credibility of Wordsworth's little biographical portraitures of them.[10]

They went on to speak about Wilberforce, "the famous Nigger-philanthropist." Carlyle was enchanted with the dry way in which Wordsworth cut this "drawing-room Christian" down to size. The fact is noteworthy, because it is about Wilberforce that Wordsworth begins speaking as he opens his *Prelude* account of returning from France in late 1792: "I found the air yet busy with the stir . . . against the traffickers in Negro blood." That is, his thoughts when speaking to Carlyle about being in France follow the same sequence of subjects as in *The Prelude.*

Antoine Joseph Gorsas was executed on October 7, 1793, in Paris. And Thomas Carlyle, the reigning British expert on the French Revolution, was deeply enough impressed with the "distinctness" and "credibility" of Wordsworth's recollections to wish he could add it as "a true supplement" on this one point. "No man could have been more alert for such information."[11] Carlyle was markedly *un*interested in correcting his *French Revolution* once it was published, hence his extensive analysis of this conversation is all the more noteworthy. Authors, especially famous ones, are not eager to admit publicly that there are additional facts they wish they could add to their best-known works, especially if they have been pointed out by no very friendly authority. Yet Carlyle's credibility is as firm as Wordsworth's, for he readily admits he could no longer remember what other men they talked of, besides Gorsas and Wilberforce, making it that much more likely that his remembrance of what Wordsworth said about these two is clear. Nor does he exaggerate the importance of Wordsworth's information: it is a "small point," and Wordsworth "did not otherwise add to or alter" Carlyle's voluminous store of revolutionary facts. Finally, he appreciates "the incomparable historical tone" of Wordsworth's recollections, his "luminous and veracious power of insight, directed upon such a survey of fellow-men and their contemporary journey through the world . . . you perceived it to be faithful, accurate, and altogether life-like, though Wordsworthian."

There are two stages in Carlyle's recollection of Wordsworth's recollection: first, his being in Paris to "witness . . . in particular the execution of Gorsas" and then, afterward, when he "hastened over to England" (though this could refer to their shift in subject matter as well as to an actual trip). Some aspects of Wordsworth's testimony apply to 1792 almost as well as to 1793, but not the execution of Gorsas. Especially notable are the two internal quotations where Carlyle seems to be recalling Wordsworth's actual words. "Where will it end?" is very much in the spirit of Wordsworth's nightmare vision that "all things have second birth" on his return to Paris in October 1792.

The struggle between the Gironde and the Mountain broke into the open in the fall of 1792 and ended a year later with the execution of the leading Girondins on October 31. Wordsworth had indeed "witnessed" it all, if, having been in Paris in October 1792, he returned there a year later. His "hastening" back over to England could apply to either year. In 1793 his reasons for haste would have been his own safety, whereas in 1792 they had to do with his need to raise money for Annette. "The ominous feeling" Gorsas's execution produced was not generally public. Like most guillotine victims at the outset of the Terror, he was jeered by the crowd around the scaffold, so great was the fear and hatred whipped up against this newest group of "traitors." The ominous feeling, rather, would have been among "everybody" whom Wordsworth knew in Paris, to some of whom he would have turned for aid on his dangerous return, and who were wondering, like him, "Where will it end?"—a feeling Wordsworth "still seemed to retain." It is possible that Wordsworth shifted in the course of his conversation with Carlyle from what he had actually witnessed to reflections on the meaning of Gorsas's execution, in which case the "everybody" would refer to public opinion in England. But the reference to "hastening" over to England follows his mention of the execution, and the "subsequent time" would therefore seem to be after 1793. After a sifting of alternative explanations, the firmness and accuracy of both Carlyle and Wordsworth stands up very well.*

A second thread of evidence is the marginal notation opposite Gorsas's name in Wordsworth's edition of the collected works of Edmund Burke: "I knew this man. W.W." This surely indicates personal acquaintance and some level of conversational familiarity. It would be pointless to take it to mean, "I knew *of* him," since many people still retained some knowledge of Gorsas at whatever time after 1827 (the volume's publication date) Wordsworth jotted the note. In fact, Wordsworth specifically picks Gorsas out of a lineup of suspects that Burke has purposefully assembled to contrast the dubious

*The external evidence of Carlyle's text also supports this conclusion. The *Reminiscences* were put together by J. A. Froude, a conscientious scholar and historian, with Carlyle's consent, "to protect him from biographers" by giving a measure against which their inevitable "degrees of falsity" might be measured (vi). Froude stresses Carlyle's methodical habits of preserving letters and recording his inmost thoughts. His recollections of Southey and Wordsworth come at the end of the book, as an appendix, "being merely detached notes of a few personal recollections." They were written down between January 28 and March 8, 1867, for Carlyle's own self-satisfaction, "with austere candour, and avoidance of anything which I can suspect to be untrue." He was not writing with an eye to publication or reputation; "even in regard to myself the one possible profit of such a thing is that it be not false or incorrect in any point, but correspond to the fact in all." He expected to find the two renegade Romantics antagonistic to the topic of the French Revolution, but to his surprise he found them both interested in his view of things. The last words of the book are on Wordsworth, and indicate the low likelihood of any exaggeration in Carlyle's account: "Why should I continue these melancholy jottings, in which I have no interest . . . ? I will cease." His contemporaneous journal entry seconds the same thought: "Finished the rag on Wordsworth to the last tatter; won't begin another: *Cui bono,* it is wearisome and naught even to myself" (from the 1887 London edition, edited by C. E. Norton, 309–10). It would be hard to imagine a more disinterested account, and Carlyle's memory and perceptions seem remarkably sharp, for a seventy-two-year-old man, recalling an incident from twenty-seven years earlier, of an event witnessed by another man forty-seven years before that. Even his revision of his manuscript supports this view of the matter: it is carefully revised, and his revisions do not change the substance of what he said Wordsworth said, only make it more precise.

characters associated with the Revolution with the higher-quality persons who were in charge of France before the Revolution. It is the only mention of Gorsas in Burke's entire oeuvre, occurring in his *Letter to a Noble Lord* (1796), defending himself against attacks on his government pension by the duke of Bedford. Burke means to frighten Bedford with the danger posed to him, his class, and his estates by "the Frenchified faction" in British politics. He asks whether Bedford can imagine that the Turennes, the Luxembourgs, the Colberts—all the illustrious governing families of old France—

> that these should be given up to the cruel sport of the Pichegru's, the Jourdans, the Santerres, under the Rollands, and Brissets [*sic*], and Gorsas, and Robespierres, the Reubels, the Carnots, and Talliens, and Dantons, and the whole tribe of Regicides, robbers, and revolutionary judges, that, from the rotten carcase of their own murdered country, have poured out innumerable swarms of the lowest, and at once the most destructive of the classes of animated nature, which like columns of locusts, have laid waste the fairest part of the world?[12]

In this tally of low-class locusts, assembled by the leading British opponent of the French Revolution, we find Wordsworth's notation referring not to Brissot, who is immediately adjacent, and where we might better expect to find it, but to Gorsas. Moreover, Wordsworth was indebted to Burke as early as 1804 for exactly this imagery, and in precisely this context, in *The Prelude*'s description of France, as a "land all swarmed with passion, like a plain / Devoured by locusts—Carra, Gorsas" (IX.178–79).

To *sign* one's marginal note, in a volume that already has one's name or bookplate inside the front cover, suggests a certain amount of wished-for identification, namely, "among all the many French revolutionaries named here, I, William Wordsworth, *knew this man.*" It is, moreover, the only written comment in the whole of Wordsworth's sixteen-volume set of Burke's works. When he knew him is another question. That he knew or conversed with Gorsas in early October 1793 is not very likely, though not impossible. It is more likely that he knew Gorsas in the fall of 1792, during his six-week sojourn in Paris, when he was closest to the journalistic milieu of the Revolution.

The third line of evidence placing Wordsworth in Paris in 1793 is equally serendipitous, but goes in the same direction. It is from a biography of the minor writer and publicist Alaric Watts (1797–1864), published by his son in 1884, recounting his father's visits to the London salon of John ("Walking") Stewart, ca. 1812–14. Stewart was an eccentric Scots vegetarian and revolutionary like John Oswald, but much less dangerous; his eloquent harangues on living according to nature much impressed Wordsworth (according to De Quincey) "when he had met him at Paris between the years 1790 and 1792, during the early storms of the French Revolution."[13] This again places young Wordsworth close to the journalistic front of the Revolution, for Stewart was one of the English writers in Paris whom the British spy Captain Munro reported to London. Two frequent visitors at Stewart's London open houses (he returned to London after 1792) were the socialist Robert Owen and "an old Republican named Bailey, who had been confined in the Temple at Paris with Pichegru [in 1804]. He had met Wordsworth in Paris, and having warned him that his connection to the 'Mountain' rendered his situation there at that time perilous, the poet, he said, decamped with great precipitation."[14] There are problems with this account, but also plausibilities. Like parts of the two earlier lines of evidence, it can be attributed almost as well to 1792 as to 1793. Wordsworth was not associated with the Mountain, although in 1792, when the Mountain and the Gironde were in the process of separating definitively, the distinction between persons belonging to either group was not so clear. Wordsworth, we know, was clearly associated with the Jacobins and with the radical Brissot for most of his 1791–92 sojourn, and Gorsas was one of the Girondins who tried "to the last minute" to achieve a compromise with the more moderate Montagnards.[15] British sympathizers were rapidly dispersing from Paris in late 1792, but more from demoralization than from any sense of peril. But Wordsworth's decamping "with great precipitation" coincides nicely with Carlyle's note of his *hastening* over to England. His "connection" with the Mountain may, in Alaric Watts's recollection of Bailey's recollection, have signified his *wrong* connection with the Mountain, insofar as it harked back to Brissot and Gorsas, since neither in 1792 nor in 1793 would a direct connection with the Mountain have been a danger—quite the contrary. Finally, there is the fact that this recollection is attributed to Bailey, whom Wordsworth clearly knew in Paris, rather than to Stewart, who had left in 1792. That is, knowing an Englishman in Paris in 1792 was not a particularly remarkable thing, but in 1793 it most certainly was.*

The record, such as it is, is in good order. Alaric Watts is quoting from his father's own notes, particularly those "more perfected than others," which he reserved for the conclusion of his memoir of his father.[16] Walking Stewart may seem an untrustworthy source, but De Quincey stresses that Stewart's

*Thomas Bailey was an Irish republican who fled back to France in 1798 after the arrest of the Irish leader O'Connor in the abortive revolutionary uprising there, and seems to have been connected with Lafayette's brand of republicanism, a dangerous enough affiliation in itself in 1793; but there is no other record than his recollection of Wordsworth of what *he* was doing in Paris in 1793 (Piper, 67). In this connection it is interesting that the original *Blackwood's Magazine* article, "A Day with Wordsworth" (January 1927), reports Wordsworth saying "he went over to Paris at the time of the Revolution in 1792 *and* 1793, and so was 'pretty hot in it' " (italics added), not "1792 or 1793," as stated in James Patrick Muirhead, *The Life of James Watt, with Selections from His Correspondence,* 2d ed. [London: John Murray, 1859], 480).

reputation for marvelous adventures (he had indeed perambulated much of the globe, from Asia to North and South America) made him chary of relating "any part of his adventures which approached the marvellous," since people naturally suspected him of "using the traveller's immemorial privilege of embellishing." Hence "one foremost feature" in his character "was his noble reverence for truth . . . to have won a universal interest with the public, he would not have deviated, by one hair's breadth, from the severe facts of the case."[17]

There is a fourth strand of textual evidence pulling Wordsworth toward France in 1793. Its existence must be inferred from other texts, but these come from a very authoritative source: Annette Vallon. In her letter of March 20, 1793, confiscated by the French police, suspicious of correspondence with England in general and of the Vallon family in particular, this was her train of thought:

> I would feel more comforted if we were married, but at the same time I consider it almost impossible that you risk the voyage if we have war. You could be taken prisoner. But where do my desires lead me? I speak as if this minute I touched my happiness. Write to me what you think on this subject, and do everything you can to hurry the happiness of your daughter and mine, but only if there is not the least risk, but I think that the war will not be too long. I would like to see the two nations reconciled. It's one of my most sincere wishes.[18]

What a pushing and pulling is here, what a provocative "almost"! You might . . . but no . . . and yet . . . . Is she responding to a possibility Wordsworth has already broached or introducing it herself? Her last words in the letter, added after her potent farewell—"Good-bye, I love you for life"—return to the same subject: "Tell me about the war, and what you think of it, because this preoccupies me much." By March 20 the declaration of war was nearly two months old, so her phrase "if we have war" must mean something like, "if we have war *here,* in Blois, the destination of your risky voyage."

Annette's come-hither rhetoric was even stronger in her letter to Dorothy, where she subtly associated her situation vis-à-vis William with Dorothy's, and gracefully co-opted Dorothy into her own desires. She reproaches William for not adequately conveying to her how charming his sister was:

> I would like to reproach him one day when we will be reunited, but when will he come? Oh, how far off I believe he still is! I must still buy him with many sighs. But when we will be reunited, oh, my sister, how happy we shall be! . . . You like me are deprived of the happiness of seeing him. How unhappy you are, if his absence is as painful to you as it is to me. Only that you are not as far apart as we are. You receive news about him more often than Annette, you exchange thoughts . . . . But I assure you that I could be comforted if I

> were lucky enough that my dear Williams could make the voyage to France to come to give me the title of his wife. First of all, my daughter would have a father, and her poor mother would enjoy the happiness of having him always with her. . . . I would no longer make my family blush when I call my daughter, my Caroline . . . .

This is indeed buying with sighs, a pleading impossible to ignore. Only by marriage could she gain possession of Caroline. Wordsworth has owned his daughter, why not now legitimize her, even if he cannot—yet—provide for her?[19] Just the other day (Annette says), the woman caring for Caroline passed right by her house without even stopping! If they will not come to her, she suggests wildly, she will go to them, and Dorothy's identification with her will be as complete and as intimate as possible:

> Call your father, my little one, soon I will take you in my arms, I will go to meet this father who costs your mother so many tears. [Vaudracour says, "Julia, how much thine eyes / Have cost me!"] You will hold him in your little arms, your little lips will give him a tender kiss, he will hold these innocent caresses very dear. Yes, my dear sister, I will go to take him his child. I already showed Caroline the road. I'll go again tomorrow. We shall call him but he will not hear us. . . . I think that she will respond to the goodness and care that you will want to give her, for dear sister, you shall be her second mother . . . .
>
> We all four are just one, dear friend; a day will come when, reunited, our union will be unbreakable. . . . You wouldn't believe it, but at least *I can assure your truthfully that if it is possible that my friend should come back to give me the glorious title of his wife, despite the cruel necessity which would force him to abandon his wife and child right away, I would suffer a painful absence with more ease.* But I would find in his daughter a recompense which at this moment is forbidden to me.[20]

This clearly supplies both the motive and the plan for Wordsworth's trip.

Other parts of Annette's letter show that she was fully apprised of the unhappy situation with Uncle Cookson, and also with Dorothy's desperate desire to see William in Halifax, which she identifies and preempts for her own situation. To be pleaded with and pulled by two different women at the same time, both of whom he loved dearly, both of whom construe his absence as a nearly life-threatening situation for themselves, and from both of whom he is also separated by very strong (though very different) prohibitions, was an incredible burden for the twenty-three-year-old Wordsworth. How long could he hold out against such persuasions? Annette allied herself with Dorothy, and Dorothy allied herself with Annette. The Halifax and French "plots" come to seem plausible halves of the same overarching goal: to be with William. Annette, as inventive, daring, and energetic here as in her later *chouannerie,* even provides the plan, acceptable to her, that would allow him to do both: come over here, marry me, and then return to Dorothy until such time as we can all four live together.

How many such appeals did William receive from Annette in 1793? He never received these two letters, of course, which came to light only in the twentieth century.* But Annette refers to at least five other letters, either sent by her or received from William and Dorothy, all within the space of the last eight days. If we extrapolate this rate of correspondence over the next six months, we come to more than two hundred letters: clearly too high a figure. But it was obviously "a copious correspondence," and even if we reduce it to one exchange per week in this kind, and remember that both governments were winking at mail packets crossing the Channel (though routinely intercepting them for inspection), we can estimate, at a minimum, at least two dozen such letters received by William through this spring and summer.[21] And we must also contemplate his making a nearly equal number of replies—or efforts to reply—to these strong appeals. After a while, trying to go there, despite the danger, might well have seemed easier than sitting down to write yet another answer to Annette.

The Public Record

To return with Wordsworth to France in 1793, we should put ourselves in his mind as well as in his shoes. He was suffering a personal crisis intimately connected to a national one. But though he could not for the moment bring Annette to England, he could still marry her in France. She referred to them as husband and wife in her letters, and was urging actual marriage on him in the strongest possible terms, for only if she was properly a *wife* would her family allow her to assume publicly the role of a *mother.* By not marrying his mistress, Wordsworth was keeping her from her one source of consolation in distress, her daughter: the double bind Annette presented to him was as bad as his uncles', or worse. Wordsworth was capable of loving very few people strongly, but his moral commitment to those he did love was rock solid. This and his proven willingness to take foolhardy trips to France in his own interest create a powerful impetus to send him on his way.

But where, when, and how? Wordsworth watched and calculated his chances, mainly on the basis of newspaper reports, fleshed out by rumors, and interpreted by Annette's occasional and voluminous letters. He was always an avid newspaper reader, but never more so than in 1793. In review-

*These and other documents relating to Annette were uncovered in French and English archives by George McLean Harper and Emile Legouis between 1915 and 1922.

ing the news for 1793, there is little danger of our underinterpreting what Wordsworth might have made of this or that item of information; he would have made the very most of everything.[22] He was not interested in an accurate account of the French Revolution except as it affected his life and happiness. He was not writing a book about it; he was not a historian, a journalist, or even a poet in these feverish news-reading sessions; he was a young man in love, and with enormous responsibilities and difficulties on his shoulders.

For most of the spring and much of the summer, events seemed to favor the lovers' plight. As Hugo says, " '93 was the war of Europe against France, and of France against Paris," and it looked as if the war would soon be over, as Annette hoped. Although counterrevolutionary activity ebbed in the winter of 1792–93, following Louis's execution, it began again in March, fueled in Paris by demands for food and in the provinces by reactions against the *levée* for 300,000 men voted on February 24.[23] There were riots throughout Normandy and Brittany, and in the Vendée proper, south of the Loire. The central government had regained control north of the Loire by early April, but its authority south of the river virtually collapsed, and the Vendean war began in earnest. By the end of March the Vendeans had raised an army of 40,000 men, led by experienced generals of the old nobility, and egged on by fanatical recalcitrant priests. The Grande Armée Catholique et Royale, with the imprisoned Louis XVII as its child commander in chief and the Sacred Heart as its emblem (also chosen by Annette for her seal), was established in early April, and it immediately sent emissaries to England seeking assistance. " 'Long live the English!' is the cry of the rebels."*

Blois, whence Annette had returned after Caroline's birth, was only thirty miles east of Tours, the rebels' prime target along the critical Loire line. Lying just outside the area of conflict, it was an important staging area both for republican thrusts into the Vendée and for relief efforts secretly channeled to the royalists through families like the Vallons.

The spread of counterrevolution was so rapid into June that the allied governments began to feel that the French republic's collapse was imminent.

*Hugo, *Quatre-vingt treize* (pt. 2, bk. 4, chap. 5), quoting Mellinel's report of March 31. Hugo's novel was based on solid research, as well as close personal experience: "In that war my father fought, and I can speak advisedly thereof." This expert knowledge, reinforced by Hugo's own political exile on Jersey off the Normandy coast, encourages me to adopt him as a sort of foreign correspondent of the imagination, in trying to reconstruct Wordsworth's possible experiences, a narrative which combines history and imagination in measures similar to Hugo's novel. One of Hugo's two main characters is a ci-devant noble republican general, idealized very much like Wordsworth's Beaupuy, and the entire action of his plot turns on an effort to rescue children separated from their mother by the civil war, a plot fueled with an emotional intensity that is expressed no less melodramatically than Annette's letters in a very similar situation: "To have been a mother, and to be one no longer! To have been a nurse, and to be so no more!" (pt. 3, bk. 1, chap. 6).

To Helen Williams "it seemed doubtful of which party [royalist or republican] France was destined to be the prey," for, she thought, the Vendeans controlled the Loire "almost as far as Paris."[24] This was an exaggeration, but an expansion as far as Tours—or Blois—was not. Wordsworth's decision not to publish his "Letter to Llandaff" may have been affected by this turn of events in March as much as by concern for his reputation and career.

The sansculottes *journées* of March 9–10 failed to purge the Convention of the Girondins, but they did plant the suggestion in the public consciousness that the Gironde, the Bordeaux coastal region immediately south of the Vendée, was not unsympathetic to the royalist rebels' cause. An anticipation of worse things to come, which would certainly have caught Wordsworth's eye, was the mob's smashing the presses of both Brissot's and Gorsas's newspapers.[25] These March "days" also established the Revolutionary Tribunal, whose original purpose was to intern foreigners and "suspects" without passports. "Foreigner" and "suspect" were becoming virtually interchangeable terms, so from Wordsworth's perspective at this time, there was every reason to wait and see what would happen before venturing dangerously into France. Even so, we should not imagine that going to France from England in 1793 was anything remotely like, say, parachuting behind Nazi lines in World War II. For all the repression and hysteria in both countries, there was, by modern standards, an extraordinary openness between belligerents in late eighteenth-century Europe. While thousands of noble émigrés flooded into England, many hundreds if not thousands of English traveled to, or continued to reside in, France.

However, in early March, Annette's brother Paul was implicated in a trumped-up assassination charge made by Léonard Bourdon, the Convention's representative in Orléans.[26] Bourdon was shoved about and slightly wounded on the street in a drunken altercation between celebrating Jacobins and the National Guards at the town hall, where Paul was working late. There were already tensions between Bourdon and the conservative Orléans establishment because of his enthusiastic enforcement of the Paris government's measures, and he revenged himself on his assailants by calling them assassins. (Paul Vallon seems in fact to have been trying to disengage the fighters.) Bourdon formally made the charges in a letter sent to the Convention on March 19, the day before Annette sent her two (confiscated) letters to William and Dorothy. Knowing that Paul was in trouble added urgency to her tone. By coincidence Bourdon's letter reached the Convention in the same post that first reported the full seriousness of the new Vendean uprising, and the two were immediately linked as internal and external parts of a monarchist plot, and martial law was reinstituted in Orléans. Forty members of "notable" families that Bourdon accused were indicted, many were arrested, including Wordsworth's former landlord of the rue Royale,

M. Gellet-Duvivier, while some, like Paul Vallon, went into hiding. Annette would not have included many of these details in her letters, if she expected them to pass the censors, as they evidently did. But the affair of "the forty notables of Orléans" was used by the English press as a frequent point of reference during the next six months to document the rise of French horrors.

Wordsworth may thus have known as early as March that Paul Vallon, and perhaps his sister and mother, had run afoul of one of the harshest of the Jacobins, frequently associated with the *enragés*.[27] Bourdon, the "Schoolmaster Jacobin" (1754–1807), was one of the leading educational reformers of the new republic. He makes one blush for teachers, but he was—like many academics—a shrewd survivor: he became president of the Jacobin Club after Robespierre's fall. He was named *greffier au tribunal* (clerk of court) for his role in the August 10 rising, and sent to Orléans the following March. His first antagonists were the local *greffiers,* one of whom was André-Augustin Dufour, the landlord and close friend of Paul, whose wife helped Annette deliver Caroline. Though the Convention gradually began to get a clearer picture of the assault on Bourdon, he managed to push aside all the documents incriminating him and get nine of his assailants (M. Gellet-Duvivier among them) indicted, arrested, and—on July 13—executed.

The agreeable prospect that the Revolution might soon be defeated began to change with the second of the three great *journées* of '93, those of May 31–June 2, which succeeded where those of March 9–10 had failed. A mob of twenty thousand sansculottes invaded the Convention and forced the arrest of twenty-nine deputies—all the main Girondins, including Louvet, who sat for Loiret. It was Marat's greatest moment, and Hugo accurately "quotes" his reasons for urgency: "If we lose an hour, tomorrow the Vendeans may be at Orléans."[28] However, every successful revolutionary action had its immediate counterrevolutionary reaction, and though the *journées* of early June succeeded in consolidating the Jacobins' control of Paris, they had exactly the opposite result in the provinces. The Vendean revolt now suddenly spread north of the Loire. Five departments in Brittany and three in Normandy leagued together at Caen against the Convention, soon drawing to them a number of the proscribed Girondins: "the journalists Gorsas and Louvet" among them.[29] This was the beginning of the short-lived "federalist" revolt. Now "the Vendée had the Gironde for accomplice" (Hugo).

The Girondins in Normandy immediately began acting like a government in exile. It gained an important convert when General Wimpfen, commander of the Army of the Coasts of Cherbourg, defected from the republic and joined their new coalition, with the majority of his troops. Wimpfen was known to have English connections, but that was a plus for the Girondins, as it would have been for any young Englishman contemplating a crossing to the coasts of Cherbourg. By June 30, battalions from Brittany were reported on their way to Paris under Wimpfen to deliver the city from the commune and the Jacobins.[30] These battalions got to within fifty miles of the capital before they were routed, also on July 13, at Pacy-sur-Eure.

But on the day after they decamped, there set out from the rebel headquarters at Caen a single person who ultimately did more damage to their cause than any defeat their army suffered. Her name was Charlotte Corday. A young woman of noble family, descended from Corneille and steeped in Plutarch's *Lives,* she had decided to become the Brutus of France. But her assassination of Marat—on July 13—was the event that began to tip the balance decisively against all counterrevolutionaries, since it demonstrated the reality of the radicals' constant warnings of spies, traitors, and assassins in their midst. By making Marat a martyr, Corday galvanized the majority of the Convention behind the Jacobins' energetic revolutionary measures, and guaranteed almost the opposite of what she claimed as her justification: "J'ai tué un homme pour en sauver cent mille." It was apparently newspaper reading that pushed her into action: she had read a tract that said Marat's "head must fall to save two hundred thousand others," and when she arrived in Paris she bought a paper that contained Bourdon's renewed demands for a death sentence against her friends the Girondins.[31]

Corday's assassination of Marat in July was insistently linked in British newspapers with the attempt on Bourdon in March. This was easy to do, because of the coincidence that the executions in the Bourdon case were carried out on the very day of Marat's murder: July 13, 1793. There are several reasons that the long title of "Tintern Abbey" ends with the date "July 13, 1798," and the connection between these two dates is one of them, especially in a poem whose opening lines repeatedly invite us to subtract five years from the date we have just read: "Five years have passed; five summers, with the length / Of five long winters!" Hereafter, accusations against counterrevolutionaries were routinely made in terms of the Marat and Bourdon assassinations, the one more famous publicly, the other far more important to Wordsworth privately.[32] During the trial of the Bourdon case in late June, parents *and sisters* of the accused were reported pleading for their relatives, a group which in Wordsworth's mind's eye could well have included Annette, since the one item she would certainly *not* have put in her letters was the reassuring news that Paul was safe in hiding and not among those on trial. Among the women crying out "Grâce! grâce!" there was one surely known to Wordsworth, M. Gellet-Duvivier's daughter, who pleaded her father's mental instability, to no avail. The judge rejected these pleas in the severe terms of the prevailing ideology: "Point de grâce pour les assassins des patriotes!" When the verdict was announced, "plus nombreuses" of these women fell fainting at the foot of the tribunal, "et de ce tableau sortaient par intervalle *des cris déchirants et des invocations qui arrochaient l'âme*" (heart-rending cries and pleas which break one's soul).[33] If descriptions like these reached Wordsworth's eyes or ears, they contributed their share of pathos to his nightmare image of himself pleading before "unjust tribunals" in *Prelude* X.373–80.

When the *Times* for August 10 reached Wales, its front page would have startled Wordsworth. A column headed "Mad. Marie Ann Char. Corday" gave an account of her dignified bearing during her trial, ending with the shocking detail of the executioner impertinently slapping the cheeks of her severed head. Though known as Charlotte, her first name was Marie-Anne, and a letter signed with her full name was printed the day before. Wordsworth knew a Marie-Anne who went by a different form of that common name. Yet another was the focus of even more news coverage at this time: Marie-Antoinette, and the renewed agitation for bringing her to trial. All these Marie-Annes were on the wrong side (unlike "Marianne," the popular female representation of French Liberty) and were suffering heinously as a result. In addition to his own thoughts and Annette's letters, public discourse was provoking Wordsworth to desperate thoughts of France. He felt especially close to these events when he read how Corday was assisted by "Mr. Stone, an Englishman," well known to him as Helen Williams's lover, who held her hand throughout the trial and received her "tears of sweet sensibility" in gratitude. The smallest details of Corday's trial brought his Paris haunts home to him: her lodgings were in the rue des Victoires, which begins at the corner where White's English Hotel was located.

About this time "les hommes des Londres" became a new bogey for the Terror, following Fabre d'Eglantine's August 3 account—exaggerated but true—of English efforts to destabilize the French economy by circulating false assignats. England's secret agents—"la Correspondence," "les Amis de Paris," and "le Manufacture" were their code names—were just getting organized under the direction of first Evan Nepean and later William Wickham, undersecretaries in the Home Office. They were never very effective,[34] but in the late summer they were actively recruiting young men who could speak French and were willing, for high pay (£100–200 per mission), to take the risk of carrying messages to England's agents among the various counterrevolutionary groups and make observations on their troop strength compared with that of the republicans.[35] There were the usual code names ("Mr. Martin" was the Home Office contact in Paris), assumed identities ("the character of a dealer in Merchandise," "the character of a Smuggler in Tobacco"), and a good deal of amateurism along with a high degree of risk, since the disappearance or detainment of couriers kept the demand for replacements high.[36] Most of these agents were French royalists from Jersey and

Guernsey, but some came from England as well. The British government used them to communicate with the Vendean army, but Pitt and his ministers (on excessively fastidious constitutional grounds, in light of their actions in the north and at Toulon) held publicly that they could not involve themselves in subverting the French constitution, all the while trying privately to ascertain the chances of such a venture's success. All this activity reached a fever pitch of confidential and secret letters, reports, pleadings, and urgings in late August and early September.[37]

Toulon fell to Admiral Hood on August 27–28, betrayed internally according to Jacobin reports, and in the first week of September the Vendeans won a great victory—their high-water mark, as it turned out—at Chantonnay. The republican forces fled all the way back to Saumur, a day's march from Blois. Take-no-prisoners became the Vendeans' response to the republicans' scorched-earth policy; it was now total war on both sides, with unspeakable reprisals: no mercy, no quarter.

Into this new atmosphere of increased viciousness came the news of the *journées* of September 4–5, which I believe prompted Wordsworth to push off for France within the week for his own Normandy landing. These *journées* were the most successful of the entire Revolution, surpassed only by August 10, 1792. They were provoked by the fall of Toulon and the defeat at Chantonnay, and by the subsequent need for scapegoats; the as-yet-untried Girondins and Marie-Antoinette were ready to hand. Reverses or defeats were ideologically unacceptable to the republic, since republican virtue was held to be naturally, inevitably triumphant: any other outcome could be the result only of treason or subversion. Few believed this doctrine literally, but on September 4 it produced three major results: (1) the creation of the revolutionary army, (2) new steps toward identification and arrest of suspects, and (3) the declaration that "terror was the order of the day."[38] All three of these, Wordsworth could see, would directly affect Annette.

The revolutionary army was a corps of roving vigilante troops, each equipped with its own portable red guillotine, sent out across the countryside in search of suspected hoarders and rebels, who were summarily executed. The aim of the Terror was precisely that: to terrorize people into submission, to discourage potential traitors and profiteers. It is no good lamenting for very long the abuses of fair judicial practice allowed by the Revolutionary Tribunals, for it was their main intention to impress upon people the idea that if they opposed the republic in any way, they didn't stand a chance of a fair trial. After September 5 the number of courts in Paris was quadrupled, each sitting concurrently with equal powers, in addition to the large number of guillotines now traveling about the country with the new revolutionary army.[39] There were more executions in Paris than anywhere else, except for one region: the Vendée and the parts of Brittany and Normandy which joined its revolt.[40]

On September 4 the *Times* printed the following account of the Revolutionary Tribunal, which seems to anticipate Wordsworth's "unjust tribunals" passage: "One word compasses the great part of the history of the three [French national] Assemblies, and that word is FEAR! . . . A dreadful picture is presented of the Revolutionary Tribunal, a Tribunal adapted, indeed, to make us regret Monarchy and her Bastilles. A Tribunal *in which two directors of the massacres of the 2d of September sit as judges!!"*

As its first example of "those execrable Commissioners [who] have deluged France," the story introduces "Léonard Bourdon, one of them, produces a tumult in Orléans, which, until his arrival, had, during the whole revolution, been tranquil." Wordsworth knows this is an exaggeration, but reads on: "He fills the prisons of that unfortunate city with his victims, and when the wives and children of the prisoners come to him to expostulate, he compels them, at the point of a bayonet, to dance and drink, as if displaying a savage triumph at the miseries of their husbands and fathers. A few are provoked to give this Bourdon a drubbing. This is called the assassination of a Deputy, and they have expiated their offense on the scaffold." To the extent that Wordsworth knew anything about Paul Vallon's involvement in this affair, such an account would have made his hair stand on end and finally have determined him to act.

Soon there came news—which we know reached Wordsworth—that the ferocity of the revolutionary state against its internal enemies was paying off in success against its external ones. Although Valenciennes (on the Belgian border) had fallen to the besieging allies on July 28, the duke of York, in a colossal strategic misconception, separated his forces from those of the prince of Coburg and set off to liberate Dunkirk on the Channel. If the combined allied forces had continued down the main road toward Paris, the first French republic would likely have soon collapsed, squeezed as it now was between five pressure points: Belgium, the Rhine, Lyons, Marseilles-Toulon, and the Vendée.[41] York's move was not simple stupidity but dictated by Pitt's narrow-minded wish to placate British commercial interests who wanted access to their continental trading markets reopened.

This shift in tactics soon impinged upon Wordsworth. York took up an unfavorable position near Dunkirk, and on September 6, at the nearby village of Hondschoote, the English army was routed. This victory gave the morale of the French an enormous lift. It was their first victory after a string of defeats stretching all the way back to March—that is, the period of event watching and decision making we have been reconstructing in Wordsworth's mind. This defeat received Wordsworth's full attention; it is the one he refers to in *Prelude* X, at precisely this point in his narrative's chronology, when he "exulted in the triumph of my soul / When Englishmen by thousands were o'erthrown, / Left without glory on the field, or driven, / Brave hearts, to shameful flight" (X.260–63).

16

A RETURN TO FRANCE

The Evidence of Speculation

> Such ghastly visions had I of despair,
> And tyranny, and implements of death,
> And long orations which in dreams I pleaded
> Before unjust tribunals . . . .
>
> (X.374–77)

Sometime between September 6 and 17 Wordsworth's perception of increased Terror in France and a turn in the tide of the war led him to steel his resolve to cross the Channel, possibly from a smuggler's haven at Freshwater.[1] The latter date seems more likely because it was the day on which the Law of Suspects (sometimes called the charter of the Terror) was passed, though perhaps he might not have left until the 20th or 21st, after the new law had been fully reported in the English papers.[2] The first provision of this law was that any citizen of a country with which France was at war should be arrested. Much of its effectiveness lay in its vagueness, as Helen Williams recalled: *"suspected!* that indefinite word, which was tortured into every meaning of injustice and oppression."[3] In fact, though arrests of Englishmen were called for at various times throughout the year, and though the measure passed on the 17th contained detailed regulations for enforcing the arrests authorized on the 5th, this law was still not executed rigorously for another month, and even longer in the provinces.[4] Wordsworth could not have known this, reading about it in England. Yet for him to have departed for France *after* its promulgation seems unlikely, for then his trip would have appeared not only dangerous but inefficient, if he was going to be subject to immediate arrest, and he was ever of a practical turn of mind. Still, even such a possibility cannot be ruled out, for he could well have recognized that the main danger of the law, so far as his own life and prospects were concerned, was not for him but for Annette, since its main application was against counterrevolutionaries, partisans of monarchy, federalism, Girondism, and other enemies of liberty.[5]

A crossing from the Isle of Wight promised the greatest safety. Dover was out of the question; a departure from there would have landed him nearly on the front lines. Brighton boats generally went to Dieppe, north of Rouen, which was firmly in republican control: seven Girondin sympathizers and journalists were executed there in early August. But from Portsmouth-Southampton one crossed to Le Havre or Cherbourg or, more to Wordsworth's liking, to smaller villages along the coast, either east of the Cherbourg (Cotentin) peninsula, in the neighborhood of Deauville, or to the west, near St. Malo. Counterrevolutionaries on the Normandy coast around Caen were actively soliciting Englishmen in the fall of 1793—and the Foreign Office was actively encouraging volunteers to meet this demand. The royalist Vendean generals and their strange new bedfellows, the republican Girondins, had begun to draw up elaborate plans for an English invasion, to be aimed either at Rouen to the east, the provincial capital, or at Rennes in the west, the key to Brittany. Their goal, according to Victor Hugo (whom we may now take on board as foreign correspondent for Wordsworth's trip), was "to get possession of some point on the coast and deliver it up to Pitt." Hugo re-creates the specialized propaganda of that time and place, which linked old national enemies against the new ideological one: "The English invasion is preparing; Vendeans and English—it is Briton with Breton."[6]

Once in Normandy, Wordsworth would likely have gone to Caen to make contact with his former acquaintances among the Girondins who were still there: Gorsas and Louvet, to name the most obvious. But we should not forget that for every name that history remembers, there were dozens of others, friends and relatives, hangers-on and spear-carriers, who might have been the young Wordsworth's actual contacts. It may seem unlikely that they would have had much time for him in their current plight, but unknown young Englishmen, interesting enough to all revolutionaries in Paris in 1792, assumed a disproportionately greater importance to the isolated Girondins in late 1793. And Wordsworth's potential contacts in 1792 (Helen Williams) and his actual friends (Michel Beaupuy) and acquaintances then (Grégoire, Gorsas) had, after all, moved at a significant level of public visibility.

With some help from the Girondins—and perhaps carrying their messages—Wordsworth would have advanced fairly rapidly to Paris, more probably on foot than in public transport, where he would have been more apt to be challenged. Here Wordsworth's physique and walking experience stand our scenario in good stead, for it is hard to imagine many young Englishmen better conditioned to walk across country at a rapid rate, and fluent in

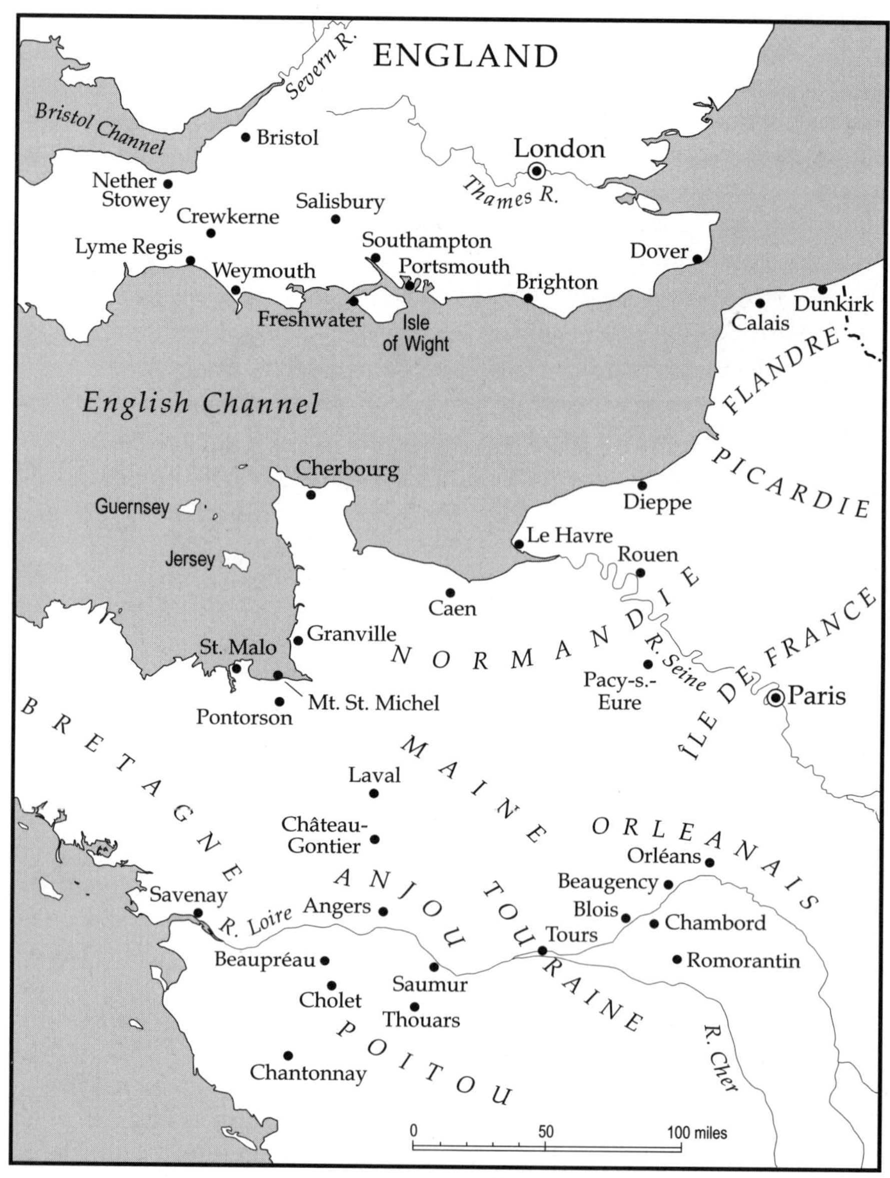

The "Northern Vendée" (Northwest France), 1793.

French besides. He was bold to foolhardiness and resourceful "as an Indian scout," in the circumstances.[7] The challenge to his bravery and presence of mind was immense. He was fairly secure in the Normandy countryside as an Englishman, as long as he could be construed as an enemy of radical Jacobinism. But the closer he got to Paris, the more he would have had to be ready to change his stripes, because the Vendeans and the republicans had exactly opposite views of who the real "foreigners" were.[8] From a royalist fifth columnist, Wordsworth would have had to transmute himself into a fellow-traveling international revolutionary sympathizer, of which there were of course many in the National Convention and the armed forces, from the famous (Tom Paine) to the bizarre (Jean-Baptiste ["Anarchasis"] Cloots, the Dutch representative for humankind) and the ubiquitous John Oswald. Since the situation was very much one of shooting first and asking questions later, he would have had to be finely attuned to signs and signals, code words both literal and figurative, and a wide range of discursive attitudes, not excluding body language. A royalist white cockade in one pocket and a revolutionary tricolor in the other would have been handy travel aids (providing one could avoid being searched). Even the weather conditions were in his favor. The summer of '92 had been wet, but '93 was very dry. The war had rendered most roads impassable in other ways; "still it was possible to get about, thanks to the beauty of the season. Dry fields make an easy route" (Hugo)—a fact Wordsworth knew well, setting off to hike across French fields for the fourth time in as many years. We might wonder, with more reason than for 1791, why he did not make directly for his destination in the Loire valley, where he now had much more urgent business than he had had two years earlier. But that route headed directly toward the fiercest fighting, and if he had any other cover or mission, it would most likely have involved Paris. In any case, one of our firmest points of reference for this whole scenario is October 7, when Wordsworth said he was in Paris to witness the execution of Gorsas.

Wild as it seems, it is not wholly outside the realm of possibility that Gorsas and Wordsworth traveled to Paris together, especially if they already knew each other. They were both desperate men in their different ways, and Wordsworth was taking a route from Normandy similar to Gorsas's for an identically romantic reason: to visit his mistress. Moreover, they were both making for the same neighborhood near the Palais Royal, where Gorsas's mistress, Brigitte Mathey, had her bookshop.[9] Gorsas's residence was in the rue Tictonne (or Tiquetonne), three streets east of White's Hotel, very much in Wordsworth's old neighborhood. The English community was still there, largely unmolested despite the Law of Suspects. Helen Maria Williams and her family were not interned until after the middle of October, and Mary Wollstonecraft moved back *into* Paris from the suburb of Neuilly in September, but took the precaution of registering at the American embassy as the wife of her lover, Gilbert Imlay. This gave her protection as a friendly foreign national in a situation not unlike Wordsworth's: by then she knew she was pregnant with Imlay's child. As late as October 10 a group of four Englishmen successfully petitioned the Convention against their internment.[10]

Gorsas was arrested on October 6, at Mme Mathey's bookstore, where he was recognized by a passerby. He was executed the next day.[11] It is difficult to find a report of the effect of his execution that matches exactly what Carlyle said Wordsworth told him. The crowd jeered him, and later hagiographers said he showed courage, which is likely, and ended his life by declaring his religious sentiments, which is not. The one group of people who would have been asking themselves, "Where will it end, when you have set an example in this kind?"—as Carlyle reported Wordsworth to have said—is of course whatever collection of English and Girondin sympathizers he was associating with around White's Hotel.

Gorsas's execution was a decisive event, and would have forced Wordsworth to get a move on. The concentration of public attention on foreigners, particularly English, was intense for the next three or four days, because the trial of the Girondins was about to begin, and these English residents were seen—correctly—as persons who might help the Girondins escape, or give them safe hiding.[12] The Convention was readying itself for a decisive purge of its enemies, and it wanted everything under maximum control. On October 9 Robespierre himself for the first time proposed the arrest of all Englishmen remaining in France. Bertrand Barère went so far as to propose that all English goods be confiscated and all English-language signs destroyed. He had strong motives for such fervor, since it is now clear that he was one of the principal secret protectors of some English agents, including John Hurford Stone, and he needed to appear as anti-English as possible. But the only known victim of this fit of chauvinism was an English-language teacher, who suffered the indignity of having to re-advertise herself as a teacher of "American."[13]

More seriously, Louis de Saint Just, Robespierre's acolyte and hatchet man on the Committee of Public Safety, gave on October 10 one of his severest speeches, demanding the government remain "revolutionary" until a peace was won: that is, revolutionary laws must be enforced with revolutionary fervor. Robespierre had for weeks been perfecting a speech in which avid gallery audiences were adjured to be ready to "strike" against "enemies," and on October 11 he delivered a hysterical version of it, promising that many such enemies would be "revealed" on the morrow, with great "victories" resulting. Many were arrested, including the Englishman named Rutledge, whom Wordsworth heard speak in the Jacobin Club in November 1791. Marie-Antoinette's trial began on October 14, and the preliminary examination of Brissot on the 15th, the ever-present Bourdon serving as one of ten prosecution witnesses. The revolt at Lyons had finally been crushed on October 8, with terrible reprisals, and calls went out from the Convention to destroy the Vendean revolt before the end of the month, when the roads would become impassable. On October 18 the move against English residents became draconian, and included all Scotch, Irish, and even Hanoverians; only children under twelve in French schools and factory workers were excepted—though even the exception reveals how common it was for Englishmen to be resident in France.[14] If there was any time that could be called favorable for decamping precipitately from Paris, as old Bailey reported Wordsworth doing, it was the week of October 7–14. Wordsworth the literalist confided to Carlyle that he had seen the execution of Gorsas on October 7; we can be sure that if he had been present in Paris at the time of Marie-Antoinette's trial, he would have said so. Gorsas's death was duly noted in the English press, but details from the queen's trial and execution were printed for weeks and months afterward, and have remained one of the primary sources of antirevolutionary imagery ever since.

We could of course put Wordsworth en route directly back to England from Paris, on the assumption that things were becoming just too hot. But having come so far, would he not try to go farther, to complete his own mission? The provinces were always less dangerous than Paris, but as he moved out shortly after October 7, he went again from the frying pan into the fire, just as he had in coming from Caen to Paris. A *représentant en mission* named Laplanche had created a sensation in the Convention less than a month earlier with his revelation of a plot in the departments of Loiret and Cher involving an "anglaise" (that is, a woman) named Brown and her protégé, a French priest named Charles, the main evidence being a mass of letters, "moitié anglaises, moitié françaises."[15] Terrible retributions had been exacted, especially against priests, which caused riots and other disturbances in their turn. Coming into this maelstrom, Wordsworth would have had to be ready to reverse his procedure of calculating turncoatism, but this time from rabid republicanism to relative royalism, as he moved cautiously down along the Loire.

Hugo's cavalier, the marquis de Lantenac, was also a fugitive seeking his way in the maelstrom of the Vendée, and his exchange with an innkeeper uncannily echoes such a one as we might imagine Wordsworth having.

> The traveller listened, and said, "In fact, I think I hear cannon."
>
> The host listened. "Yes, citizen, and the musketry. They have opened the ball. You would do well to pass the night here. There will be nothing good to catch over there."
>
> "I cannot stop. I must keep on my road."
>
> "You are wrong. I do not know your business; but the risk is great, and unless it concerns what you hold dearest in the world—"

"In truth it is that which is concerned," said the cavalier.
"Something like your son—"
"Very nearly that," said the cavalier.[16]

Then, on October 17–18, the fire got even hotter. The Vendeans suffered their strategically decisive defeat at Cholet, twenty-five miles south of the Loire. The revolt could well have ended there, if the republican forces had given pursuit, but the next day the Vendeans began their tragic long march to the sea: eighty thousand men, women, and children forded the shallow Loire and headed for the Channel ports, desperately hoping for an English rescue. This move north caught the Convention completely by surprise, for it was thought "impossible for the Véndee to cross the Loire" (Hugo). Robespierre and the other Jacobin leaders were dumbfounded when they heard that a large rebel army had crossed the Loire and actually had republican forces on the run again.

This sudden turn of events brings another Wordsworthian figure back into the picture: Michel Beaupuy. He had returned to the Loire valley in late July, commanding part of the Légion du Nord, the fierce garrison forces from Mayence (Mainz), which had been released when the city fell on condition that they would no longer fight against the allies. They immediately became the republic's shock troops against the counterrevolution. Coincidentally, John Oswald, another of Wordsworth's symbolic alter egos in France, was killed a month earlier twenty miles away from Cholet, at Thouars, also "upon the borders of the unhappy Loire," in the particularly intense fighting for the Ponts-de-Cé which led to the deployment of Beaupuy's troops in the neighborhood.[17]

If Wordsworth had reached Blois before October 17 or 18, we could entertain the idea of a secret marriage with Annette, or some other permanent arrangement. A marriage ceremony of some sort might have been performed to legitimize Annette's status, and we could presumably have a record of it, as we do of Caroline's baptism. But priests were scarce, and a civil wedding might have been unsatisfactory to the Vallons, to say nothing of its danger in exposing Wordsworth to the local authorities. It is not completely outside the realm of possibility that such a ceremony actually occurred, and was kept quiet by all concerned, since at some point between 1793 and 1802 Annette did regain custody of Caroline, her first priority in any case. But this would be a conspiracy too deep for words, and we have words enough to support another possibility: Wordsworth tried heroically to reach Blois, but failed because in mid-October some of the fiercest fighting in the entire counterrevolutionary war broke very nearly upon his head. He was now so close to the theater of operations that he would have received daily reports of what was happening, or exaggerated rumors of what was not happening, or might have happened, or was soon to happen. It seems almost certain that one such rumor came to his ears.

Beaupuy was active in the victory at Cholet, his cavalry cutting down fleeing peasants ruthlessly. Still, he had a high estimate of the Vendeans: "As soldiers they lacked nothing but the uniform. Troops who have succeeded in defeating such Frenchmen as these can flatter themselves that they can defeat the united armies of the Coalition in the service of Kings."[18] He was the first republican general to report that the Vendeans had crossed the Loire en masse and to note how small an opposing force might have prevented them from doing so. The republican armies set off in pursuit and decided to attack the royalists again at Laval on October 25. In a confused action over two days, François-Joseph Westermann, the "butcher of the Vendée,"[19] with Beaupuy as his second-in-command leading the cavalry, moved back and forth between Laval and Château-Gontier, constantly being ambushed because a member of their general staff was a traitor who passed all their plans on to the enemy. On the 27th, at Entrammes, between the two towns, Beaupuy was ordered to attack well-entrenched rebels, who were at this moment under the leadership of their most charismatic leader, the twenty-one-year-old Henri La Rochejaquelein. Thus the best of the royalists and one of the best of the republicans, the ci-devant nobleman Beaupuy, faced off against each other in a confrontation worthy of Hugo's *Quatre-vingt treize.* But the raw republican recruits, no match for the sharp-shooting Vendeans, soon fled in panic back to Château-Gonthier, twenty miles north of the Loire, their general Bloss killed and "Beaupuy himself mortally wounded" as they attempted to defend the town.[20] News of their deaths spread like wildfire through both camps and the surrounding region, for this was still the kind of warfare in which the death of a charismatic leader counted as much for victory as the loss of any number of troops in the field.[21] Hugo's fiction confirms the fact, when his cavalier is captured: "with his extinction, civil war would be extinct. . . . Vendée is dead." The effect on the republicans of the apparent loss of Beaupuy was similar, for he was much loved and admired and had been very active and popular in Tours and Blois and the surrounding countryside just the year before, sometimes in company with his tall young English friend. His supposed last words were reported to good effect in the *Moniteur* two months later: "Je n'ai pu vaincre pour la république, je mourrai pour elle!"[22]

One measure of a theory's persuasiveness is what mathematicians call its elegance, that is, its ability to account efficiently for other pieces of data in the problem under consideration. Just such an important piece in the puzzle of Wordsworth's life in late 1793 falls into place if we account for his erroneous reporting in *The Prelude* of Beaupuy's death "upon the borders of the unhappy Loire" (IX.432) by the simple fact that he was thereabouts at the time. Beaupuy's biographers report, "(His wound was so grave that they despaired at first of saving him and the news of his death spread among the Vendeans)."[23] This is hardly a report which would have reached Wordsworth in Wales, and though the *Moniteur* of December refers to Beaupuy's severe wound, this account (supposing Wordsworth saw the French paper) makes it clear that Beaupuy has survived ("blessé à mort . . . n'a cessé, malgré ses blessures").

Furthermore, the victory at Laval was as decisive—temporarily—for the Vendeans as it would have been for Wordsworth. It opened up a path to the sea for both of them. The republicans, having lost over ten thousand men to death, wounds, and desertions, fell back to Angers. The Vendeans, fatally led on by their aristocratic leaders' promises of British aid, advanced into Normandy without much hindrance. And Wordsworth, trying desperately to stay ahead of the action, would have had small leisure to inquire into the accuracy of the rumors about Beaupuy's death, even supposing he doubted them. The distance he had to cover, from the Loire to the Channel, ninety miles, was just about the same he would have crossed in going from Wales to visit Dorothy at Halifax in his other "plot"—or, as it now must have seemed, his other life. This was three days walking for him in ideal conditions, probably more than a week in these wholly un-ideal conditions. Another Englishman, Thomas Eldred, estimated sixteen days walking time from Paris to Brest in January of 1794, because of bad roads, lack of horses, outrageous prices, and the presence of fifty thousand armed men running across the countryside.[24] Wordsworth would have had to push on to the coast as rapidly as he could, finding cover as he might, since any persons aiding the escape of "brigands," "insurgents," or "foreigners" (all lumped together now) faced an instant death penalty. Perhaps he found shelter "in an empty barn; civil wars leave many such . . . four walls, an open door, a little straw beneath the ruins of a roof" (Hugo). If we imagine him having missed connections with Annette and hearing of Beaupuy's death more or less at the same time and in the same place, we can begin to grasp the traumatizing effect of this trip, and find strong internal reasons for his repressing it, in addition to many good external reasons for keeping it quiet.

By November 13 the Vendean army reached the coast and laid siege to Granville, near Mont-Saint-Michel. But the promised English ships did not appear, even though Lord Moira's fleet lay just offshore in the Channel Islands, almost within sight, ready to land if Grenville gave permission. He delayed his decision so long that by the time it came, in December, it was useless. The large contingent of rebels from Poitou, finding themselves with their back to an apparently unfriendly sea, decided to return home. The dashing La Rochejacquelein was recalled from his push toward Rouen, and on November 14 all the Vendeans began their demoralized flight back south to final defeat. Their Royal and Catholic Army was finally destroyed at Savenay, at the mouth of the Loire estuary, on December 23. By then Wordsworth had probably been back in England for a month or more. "He had accomplished that masterpiece—the most difficult of all in such a war—flight" (Hugo). He spent the Christmas holidays with his kindly uncle Richard Wordsworth and their large family at Whitehaven. The contrast to where he had just been was almost too great to bear thinking of, let alone expressing; as Coleridge would later say of *The Prelude,* it was matter for "Thoughts all too deep for words!"[25]

The Textual Record

Along with the general incredibility of such an adventure, there is the glaring oddity that we should have so little evidence of it in Wordsworth's own writing. True, we have even less record of any time spent in Wales between August and December, but somehow we don't expect any, given Wordsworth's benign reputation. But if he had such an adventure, wouldn't he have written something about it, as he did about his adventures on Salisbury Plain? Perhaps he did, more than has been recognized.

Nearly two hundred lines of Book X in *The Prelude* (201–380) are devoted to this period. They are oblique, but they do give hints of a French adventure, for their chronology of events and those of Wordsworth's life fit together closely, once we supply the necessary details. His account of his return to England in late 1792 begins with the lines about Wilberforce's antislavery agitation. Wordsworth, we recall, followed his comments on Gorsas to Carlyle with some unflattering observations about Wilberforce, suggesting that the two men inhabited roughly the same time frame in his memory of his experiences of that time, and for opposite sides of the same reason: "For me that strife [against slavery] had ne'er / Fastened on my affections." Because, if old feudal tyranny would fall, it would take slavery along with it: "this most rotten branch of human shame . . . Would fall together with its parent tree" (X.218–25).

Hence, it was relative to liberals' disappointment at the defeat of Wilberforce's antislavery legislation that Wordsworth took up his own disillusionment at the much greater shock he experienced: the "revolution" that occurred in his "moral nature" when France and England declared war on each other. This passage is usually given a strictly political interpretation: that is, his idealization of the French Revolution was betrayed, first by those in power in England, who would tear "the best youth in England [from] their dear pride," and second by France's own Reign of Terror. The political reference of "a season dangerous and wild" at this point (286) is to the perversion of English patriotic values under Pitt's artificially stimulated war policy.[26] But it may also, given Wordsworth's powerful literalism, refer simply to the weather in France that fall. A narrowly political interpretation of the lines overlooks the fact that Wordsworth says he actually *did not doubt* that war would eventually break out between the two countries. What shocked his general expectation was his own personal interest in the event. Why was there such a "revolution" in his "moral nature"? Because, as we noted in Chapter 14, "Now had I other business, for I felt / The ravage of this most unnatural strife / In my own heart" (X.249–51). Indeed, he did have "other business" which the war interrupted: Annette and Caroline. It was an "unnatural strife" for him especially, since he experienced it as a civil war dividing his own family.[27]

His recollections of the Isle of Wight fall right into place here (290–305). The fleet was "gone forth" from late July to join Hood in the Mediterranean. His thoughts at the sound of the sunset cannon were, like his reaction to the declaration of war, a fine mixture of the personal and the political: "seldom heard *by me* / Without a spirit overcast . . . And sorrow for mankind, and pain of heart." "Pain of heart" closely parallels his feeling "the ravage of this most unnatural strife / In my own heart." When he goes on to say that "afterwards" he rejoiced in English defeats and French victories, the chronological indicator for a reader in 1805 or 1850, to say nothing of a twentieth-century reader, is very generalized: after what? It could be almost anytime between February 1793 and the fall of Robespierre in July 1794. But in the immediate context, the battle in which "Englishmen by thousands were o'erthrown" could only be the Battle of Hondschoote (September 6). By contrast, his feeling "like an uninvited guest" in a village congregation (266–74) where prayers are offered up for English *victories* refers either to the taking of Valenciennes on July 28 by Anglo-Dutch armies or to the fall of Toulon to Admiral Hood on August 28. But the salient point is that he himself was an *in*vited guest, attending services in Jones's parish at Plas-yn-Llan out of politeness, for Wordsworth was not otherwise a churchgoer at this time. When he says he felt "a conflict of sensation without name" (265) it is not only a political dilemma he refers to but one impossibly conflicted *for him*.

Immediately following his lines of the Isle of Wight, there is a verse paragraph beginning, "In France" (X.306–45). Normally, this is read as his *report* of what was happening there. But the lines could as well be a *record* of what happened there then, when he went over, from (say) the first week in September to the second or third week in October. Placement may not mean much in a poem as heavily revised as *The Prelude,* but this is exactly where such lines would occur, if Wordsworth were giving a sequential but disguised account of his adventures in France.

Speaking of these "devilish pleas" of the new French tyrants, he provides a series of nine different kinds of motives driving the speakers in the Convention at this time (315–26). This is an extraordinarily detailed and nuanced set of thumbnail portraits, much more particular and knowledgeable than anything appearing in English newspaper accounts, where the revolutionary leaders were caricatured indiscriminately as devils from hell. In "the sternness of the just" at the beginning of the catalog, it is easy to read a reference to Saint Just, who was typically very stern and who had been described standing just so, at the tribunal which condemned Wordsworth's Orléans landlord to death on July 13. Similarly, "the steady purposes of the suspicious" near the end (323) is almost indubitably Robespierre. "The blind rage of insolent tempers" (321) would fit Hébert and other *enragés,* though "the light vanity of intermeddlers" and "slips of the indiscreet" have too many plausible referents to be pinned down exactly. Wordsworth was given to catalogs of this type, complete with private internal puns, as in the allegory of Folly at the end of his account of his Cambridge residence. Hence his reference to "the faith of those / Who doubted not that Providence had times / Of anger and vengeance" (315–17) would refer to Bishop Grégoire, who bravely stood his ground during these months when the dechristianization frenzy was at its height, and did not suffer for it, so high was his reputation for integrity. Wordsworth's immediate contrast, to those "who throned the human understanding paramount / And made of that their god" (315–17), would refer to Pierre ("Anaxagoras") Chaumette, who finally got his Festival of Reason celebrated at Notre-Dame on November 10. It had been under debate earlier, in October, when Wordsworth was in Paris. Finally, "the hopes of those / Who were content to barter short-lived pangs / For a paradise of ages" (319–21), would be those weak members of the Plain—the "shoals" or the "marsh" of the Convention (Hugo), and the majority at any time—who had sacrificed the Girondins to the prevailing millenarian ideology. Wordsworth's description of the various devilish debaters and their silent auditors could be applied to several eras of the pre-Terror Convention, but the one that it fits best on all counts is the final trial of the Girondins, beginning with their general indictment on October 3, 1793.

When he goes on in the very next line to say, "Domestic carnage now filled all the year" (329), his chronology is as exact as his generalization is accurate. That "now," the execution of the Girondins, was the operative beginning of the Reign of Terror: late October 1793, "season dangerous and wild," when the number of executions began to rise steeply, doubling, tripling, and quadrupling by the month.[28] Similarly, such victims as Wordsworth records, or imagines, though usually understood as random vignettes, had close personal parallels for him:

> Domestic carnage now filled all the year
> With feast-days: the old man from the chimney nook, [Gellet-Duvivier?]
> The maiden from the bosom of her love, [Annette from William?]
> The mother from the cradle of her babe, [Annette from Caroline?]
> The warrior from the field [Beaupuy?]—all perished, all—
> Friends, enemies, of all parties, ranks,
> Head after head, and never heads enough
> For those who bade them fall.
>
> (329–36)

Even the imagery of free-falling heads, made so surreal when he compares the motion of the guillotine to that of a child's "windmill," was contemporaneously French, as in the newspaper editorial that spurred on Charlotte Corday, or in similar rhetoric used against the Vendean and other rebels: "Still more heads and every day more heads fall!"[29]

The *Prelude* passage continues with the execution of Manon Roland (345–60), which occurred on November 8. This is too late a date to imagine Wordsworth in Paris, but if his chronology is correct, it would indicate that everything *preceding* this one datable event in his narrative line also preceded it in his autobiographical experience—that is, the executions, the cowardly "Senate . . . heart-stricken . . . none to oppose" the arguments against the Girondins, and so on.

Then comes a temporal indicator—"meanwhile" (361)—that we can make sense of by a generalized interpretation: namely, *while* all these executions were going on, "the invaders fared as they deserved," referring to the sequence of victories which saved the republic in late 1793. But this "meanwhile" also includes one of Wordsworth's most powerful passages describing the Revolution, the "unjust tribunals" sequence, which closes this entire sequence:

> Most melancholy at that time, O friend,
> Were my day-thoughts, my dreams were miserable;
> Through months, through years, long after the last beat
> Of those atrocities (I speak bare truth,
> As if to thee alone in private talk)
> I scarcely had one night of quiet sleep,
> Such ghastly visions had I of despair,
> And tyranny, and implements of death,

And long orations which in dreams I pleaded
Before unjust tribunals, with a voice
Labouring, a brain confounded, and a sense
Of treachery and desertion in the place
The holiest that I knew of—my own soul.
(368–80)

Are these the bad dreams of a man who has vividly imagined the horrors of the Reign of Terror, which had been plentifully detailed in English publications by 1804? Or are these the recollections of a man who has seen the terror whereof he speaks? We must not underestimate the terrific power of Wordsworth's imagination, but we should also never forget his strong tendency to base even his wildest imaginative flights on actual facts and extremely literal details.

At first, it seems that he is pleading for himself before the "unjust tribunals," though very few foreign nationals were actually guillotined. If he saw Gorsas executed, he saw more than one scene like this, and could have feared for others, in Blois. But why does he feel betrayed, not before the Revolutionary Tribunal, but in an even sterner court, "the place the holiest that I knew of—my own soul"? Why should he feel "a sense of treachery and desertion" there? Has *he* been betrayed and deserted? Or does he feel "a sense" that he has betrayed and deserted *someone else?* If there has been treachery and desertion in his own soul, does this not mean he feels that he has betrayed and deserted someone else, who could only be Annette? The reference to his soul takes us back to the beginning of these post-1792 passages, when he said the war made him feel "the ravage of this most unnatural strife / In my own heart . . . / At enmity with all the tenderest springs / Of my enjoyments" (250–53). The tribunals were certainly unjust, but the real nightmare in this passage is that the advocate feels untrue to himself.

Closer attention to these lines brings us still closer to Annette and to France in late 1793. His testimony that this is "bare truth"—written in utter sincerity for Coleridge in 1805—seems unnecessarily strong to attest to the reality of a dream, but not so for a fact. Along with many other indications of his personal involvements in the Revolution, it disappears from the 1850 published version. But five or six additional lines were cut before Coleridge saw the early version, from between his "ghastly visions of despair" and the "implements of death":

Such ghastly visions [clung to me of strife
And persecution—strugglings of false mirth
And levity in dungeons where the dust

Was laid with tears, such hauntings of distress
And anguish fugitive in woods, in caves
Concealed, of scaffolds,] implements of death . . . .[30]

Where are we here? Accounts of the pathetic mixtures of levity and tears in the prisons of the Terror were a standard feature of newspaper accounts, and by 1804 the genre of *lettres des condamnés* was already initiated, though it did not fully blossom until after the Restoration. But in the second line from the end, we are clearly not in Paris but in the countryside, most likely the Vendée. Was Wordsworth there? The "tribunals" were not confined to Paris or the towns; they included traveling detachments of the revolutionary army, each with its own portable "implements of death"—scaffold and guillotine—combing the countryside, as suggested in Wordsworth's "woods [and] caves." Anyone traveling alone near the region of the Vendée uprising had to consider himself a "fugitive" if he was not known in the neighborhood, and had to advance by brief furtive sprints from woods to caves, lest he fall afoul of vindictive troops from either side. Although "woods" and "caves" are generic words signifying the countryside, they were also of quite specific importance in the Vendée. Hugo speaks of "the seven Black Forests of Brittany" by name, almost as though they were characters in the action of *Quatre-vingt treize,* for the spiritual and physical comfort they gave the Vendeans, especially any fugitive: "this forest of Bocage was the fugitive's auxiliary. He did not flee—he vanished."[31] Similarly, the caves of the region were often round, narrow wells leading to underground chambers that could hold large numbers of men, as Hugo's Westermann discovered: "the caves of Egypt held dead men, the caves of Brittany were filled with the living" (II.4.1).

The committees of surveillance were charged to ask, at a minimum, name, age, place of birth, profession, and means of support; the last two items would have stumped Wordsworth in either France or England.[32] What kind of account would he have given of himself? "C'est bien, citoyens: I'm sympathetic to the Revolution in principle, but just now I'm trying to get to Blois to marry my royalist mistress—whose brother, by the way, is in hiding for his part in the assassination attempt on *représentant* Bourdon." No, if he had been stopped by republican units, the smartest thing—almost the only account he could have given—would have been not to say a word about anyone connected with the Vallon family, even though this might well have engendered "a sense of treachery and desertion" in that other court, "the holiest that I knew of—my own soul." Small wonder he imagined himself pleading "with a voice labouring, a brain confounded."

When treachery and betrayal come so close to home, it is altogether characteristic of Wordsworth that, having skirted close to revelation, he swerves away widely from present-tense narration into vast generalization, as he does immediately after the "unjust tribunals" passage: "When I began at first, in early youth, / To yield myself to Nature . . ." (381–82). We can still parse a continuous general sense here, by saying that Wordsworth shifts from these horrible visions of the Revolutionary Tribunal to his understandable difficulty at this juncture in moving from love of Nature to love of Mankind. But this is not inconsistent with a reading that says that such a movement was particularly hard for *him* (a) because he was there and (b) because he had deeply personal reasons, which involved *"a sense* of treachery and desertion"—even if not the actual fact of them—in his own soul, for having gone to rescue Annette and having failed. Or for not having gone. For whether he actually went back to France or not, we must imagine him always thinking about going back and planning such a journey many times over in his mind. An echo of his Vaudracour role attaches even to this transitional line: *"To yield myself to Nature"*—Vaudracour too was a romantic hero prepared to "entrust himself to Nature for a happy end of all" (IX.604–5).

We saw such a textual pattern of near-revelation, followed by immediate concealment or self-censorship, on Lake Como in 1790 and on Lake Windermere in 1788, and we see it again here. And here, as there, we can recognize it by its deep conjunctions of autobiographical narrative, Wordsworth's sexual experience, and his use of Milton.

In "Vaudracour and Julia," published in 1820 without any reference to his own life, and therefore allowing him to be somewhat freer about the story's associations, Wordsworth included seasonal and geographical details that are not in the *Prelude* account. The mental perturbation of the young lovers is represented as their being "driven by the autumnal whirlwind to and fro," a line which fits Wordsworth's autumn journey of 1793 very well. It also fits his oblique account of this period in *The Prelude,* where he represented himself as "a green leaf on the blessed tree / Of my beloved country . . . / Now from my pleasant station . . . cut off / And tossed about in *whirlwinds"* (X.254–58; italics added). "Whirlwind" is a naturalistic word weighted with political significance for Wordsworth; more than half the times it occurs in his oeuvre (seventeen) have a political connotation, as in "the rage of one State-whirlwind" that threatened the Grande Chartreuse.

His metaphor for the two young lovers' feelings of sympathy with each other when they were apart foreshadows their coming separation, and also his own experience of it in 1793:

> . . . in their happiest moments, not content,
> If more divided than a sportive pair
> Of sea-fowl, conscious both that they are hovering
> Within the eddy of a common blast,

> Or hidden only by the concave depth
> Of neighbouring billows from each other's sight.
> ("V. & J.," 24–29)

This could well express a feeling of so near yet so far that afflicted Annette and William as they realized, in her or his own way, that he was not coming, or was not going to make it, to Blois because of the fury of the *"common blast"*—an apt metaphor for *civil war* as well. Images of "sea-fowl" and "neighbouring billows" might also have been called up by recollections of a Channel crossing in a small boat in stormy autumn weather.

These seasonal references in "Vaudracour and Julia" link up with others in the *Prelude* account, including the woods and caves of the canceled manuscript lines, that suggest firsthand experience. Wordsworth added the "autumnal whirlwind" and "common blast" to his published version of the tale of Vaudracour and Julia, but the *Prelude* version contains other images that match his experience of living in France in 1792. The description of how Vaudracour came to be arrested is best suited to our biographical purposes. His father had a warrant out for him, but he stayed with Julia as long as he dared:

> he lingered still
> To the last moment of his time, and then,
> At dead of night, with snow upon the ground,
> He left the city, and in villages,
> The most sequestered of the neighbourhood,
> Lay hidden for the space of several days,
> Until, the horseman bringing back report
> That he was nowhere to be found, the search
> Was ended. Back returned the ill-fated youth . . . .
> (IX.729–37)

None of this has any parallel in Helen Williams's story, but insofar as the passage refers to Wordsworth's experience in 1793, the return of the "ill-fated youth" back would be to England, in very cold weather that is consistent with the "autumnal whirlwinds" and "common blast" of "Vaudracour and Julia." His lying "hidden for the space of several days" is consistent with the "anguish fugitive in woods, in caves concealed" of the lines from the *Prelude* manuscript, despite the fact that Vaudracour stays in villages. Of course, we must make many adjustments for character and action to reconcile these various accounts: the fictional Vaudracour, the real M. du Fosse, many victims of the Terror and of the Vendean war, and Wordsworth's own thoughts about possibilities of action are all represented here, as well as what he and Annette may actually have done. But all these variations were written by him, and they all are consistent with the climate, both natural and political, of late October 1793. The *Gentleman's Magazine* recorded "temperature below freezing for several days at the end of October," just what is needed for "autumnal whirlwinds" to produce an early "snow upon the ground."[33]

The Evidence of Imagination

Even if all these coincidences of imagery derive only from Wordsworth's imagination and not from his experience, they show how powerful that imagination was. For the "unjust tribunals" themselves are imaginary—literary—*as well as* historical, and in this double aspect we may find a last confirmation, either of the fact of Wordsworth's return to France in 1793 or of the deep emotional impact of his desire to return, and his strong "sense of treachery and desertion" for not doing so.

As at many of the *The Prelude*'s most powerfully entwined biographical and literary moments, we are again dealing with an allusion from Milton, from *Samson Agonistes,* where the Chorus laments how God deals harshly with those who are "solemnly elected . . . To some great work, thy glory" (678–80). This was certainly how Wordsworth was beginning to see himself by the time he came to write *The Prelude:* "thy monument of glory will be raised" (XIV.430). He, like Samson, was a "chosen Son," not one of "the common rout," not one of those "Heads without name no more remembered" (674, 677). Yet it is precisely these predestined heroes whom God seems to throw down farthest, to the dogs,

> Or to th'unjust tribunals, under change of times,
> And condemnation of th'ungrateful multitude.
> (695–96)

It is not surprising that Wordsworth would call this image to mind, reflecting Milton's experience of civil war in the English Revolution, as he wrote about his experience of civil war in the French Revolution. But what makes the recollection especially potent and revealing at this moment, like so many of the Miltonic depth charges in Wordsworth's poetry, is what happens next in Milton's text, and our confidence that Wordsworth knew it. After a weak plea to God not to deal so unfairly with Samson, the Chorus suddenly sees someone else coming:

> But who is this, what thing of sea or land?
> Female of sex it seems,
> That so bedecked, ornate and gay,
> Comes this way sailing
> Like a stately ship

Of Tarsus, bound for the isles
Of Javan or Gadier,
With all her bravery on, and tackle trim,
Sails filled, and streamers waving,
Courted by all the winds that hold them play;
An amber scent of odorous perfume
Her harbinger, a damsel train behind?

(710–21)

They don't recognize Delilah, but Samson does, blind as he is, and in no uncertain terms: "My wife, my traitress, let her not come near me." She is the woman who brought Samson low, and we must wonder if some of Wordsworth's "sense of treachery and desertion" in his soul applied not simply to his going back to France but also to his sense of having been foiled in his own career resolves by falling for Annette. Vaudracour was capable of voicing such thoughts about Julia, even to her face: "He would exclaim, 'Julia, how much thine eyes / Have cost me!' " Delilah, like Annette in her letters, at first weeps profusely for the pain she has brought her foreign husband: "Like a fair flower surcharged with dew, she weeps, / And words addressed seem into tears dissolved" (*SA,* 728–29). This would not be an unjust representation of some parts of Annette's letter to Dorothy, where tears are metaphorically distilled into words. But Samson is totally unforgiving: "Out, out hyena!" Gradually, the effects of their different countries and religions come into the argument. Delilah pleads with the arguments the Philistine officials used on her, and blames Samson for entrusting his secret to her in the first place. It is fitting that the English, Protestant, republican Wordsworth should think of this passage as he remembered the contemporaneous "unjust tribunals" that threatened his attempted reconciliation with the French, Catholic, royalist Annette. And by the time he composed this passage in 1804, he knew that Annette had a reputation for political resistance that Delilah, spurning Samson, would also lay claim to, becoming a heroine in her own country: "among the famousest / Of women . . . who to save / Her country from a fierce destroyer, chose / Above the faith of wedlock bands" (*SA,* 982–86).

No exact correlations are possible here, where text, context, and intertext lie so closely together, and where Wordsworth's personal experience of love and revolution is so deeply underwritten by Milton's. We cannot simply say, for example, that Wordsworth felt betrayed by Annette as Samson was by Delilah. But more to the point is the realization that we have even less warrant to *deny* that his feelings for Annette were somehow bound up with Milton's representation of Samson's experience. We cannot separate these kinds of evidence neatly into the biographical and the literary: for Wordsworth, the "literary," especially if it was Miltonic, *was* biographical. The "unjust tribunals" were French, they were Miltonic, and they were dream fragments; the sense of betrayal Wordsworth felt there was personal, imaginary, and historical—and real in all of these senses.*

In the end, the summary of Wordsworth's life in the fall of 1793 is not a simple choice between a passive hero and an active one. If he stayed in Wales, we have not a jot of evidence for it, though such evidence is easy to supply conjecturally (he wrote some poems, he went for walks, he visited Jones's church, and so on). But if Wordsworth went back to France, it's not simply a new and different fact that we can now entertain in thinking about him. If he did all these things, or anything remotely like them, such hair-raising adventures would have had permanent consequences of incalculable magnitude for his future development, at least as great as his 1790 walking tour and his affair with Annette itself. An exploit like this would clearly mark one for life. Do we find any telltale scars of it in the body of Wordsworth's work? Or rather, since the effects of such a trip must *already* have manifested themselves, without being recognized, what are the signs of it, which we have heretofore taken as "natural" birthmarks?

We have already seen some from *The Prelude* and "Vaudracour and Julia," and we will see others as we follow Wordsworth's life through the 1790s. But there is one body of evidence that clearly refers to 1793: the language of passion in the "Lines Composed a Few Miles above Tintern Abbey." This is the poem, more than any other, which announces the creation of the subject we call William Wordsworth. It is his decisively self-creating text and is strongly marked by a sense of recovery from traumatic losses. It is set a few miles above the abbey in 1798, and harks back insistently to the time in 1793 when he passed by it en route to Jones's home in Wales. The main point of the poem, very simply put, is to say that his return to this same landscape five years later, in company with Dorothy, reassures him of its value for his present sense of mental recovery. In 1793 he badly needed such reassurance to convince himself that his life had not come to a dead end. It would take him the next five years to complete the cure.

We recognize the poem's language of erotic passion underlying its pas-

*In Wordsworth's account in *The Excursion* of the Solitary's disillusionment with the French Revolution, there are other points of coincidence with his experience with Annette. In one MS, the Solitary's wife is called Anna, and in the poem her salient characteristic is brightness: "bright form," "silver voice" (II.481–82). Julia was similarly "a bright maid," and her dominant impression on Vaudracour is one of shining brilliance. During Anna's pregnancies the Solitary meditates on his past life with a phrase that sounds like Wordsworth's 1793 trip: "like a weary voyage escaped / From risk and hardship" (558–59). More generally, there is the similarity of a man who has lost both wife and children, and who seeks relief from despair and guilt by throwing himself desperately into the French Revolution.

sionate love for Nature more easily if we reflect that (a) he did not talk about Nature in this way in any of his extant texts from 1793 or earlier, but that (b) he did use such language in writing to Annette, insofar as we can take her letters to him, and his descriptions of Vaudracour and Julia, as indicators of his own love language.

We have remarked the curiously self-incriminating rhetoric in Wordsworth's presentation of himself as "more like a man / Flying from something that he dreads, than one / Who sought the thing he loved," and its aptness to his situation vis-à-vis Annette at the time. He then goes on to present *himself* as a landscape painting, of which he says, "I cannot paint / What then I was"—but then proceeds to do just that, in highly charged erotic language:

> The sounding cataract
> *Haunted me like a passion:* the tall rock,
> The mountain, and the deep and gloomy wood,
> Their colours and their forms, were then to me
> *An appetite: a feeling and a love,*
> That had *no need of a remoter charm,*
> By thought supplied, *or any interest*
> *Unborrowed from the eye.*—That time is past,
> And *all its aching joys* are now no more,
> And *all its dizzy raptures.*
>
> (77–86; italics added)

The metaphoric language of passion in these lines is more clear and explicit than the words actually referring to the landscape: it is very much the language of attraction and infatuation, appropriate to first love affairs. It is also language very similar to that which Wordsworth used in describing the passion of Vaudracour and Julia: "the raptures of the pair," "swarmed with enchantment," "some delirious hour." Vaudracour's regard for Julia is also preeminently an affair of the *eye,* as Wordsworth here says of his first, immature, adolescent attitude toward nature: "He beheld / A vision, and he loved the thing he saw"; Julia turned everything he saw "before his eyes to price above all gold" (IX.582–83, 588). Her "presence" was to him in 1793 exactly as great as Nature's presence was to Wordsworth in 1798: "Earth lived in one great presence of the spring" (1793); "A presence that disturbs me with the joy / Of elevated thoughts" (1798). The later poem is an explanation of why he is still "a lover"—but of meadows, woods, and mountains, rather than of a person. It also gives a reason for his new constancy that is connected to that "sense of treachery and desertion" he felt before the "unjust tribunals" of his soul: "Nature *never did betray* the heart that loved her." Does this mean he feels he has been betrayed in love before? Or does it reflect his feeling of having betrayed Annette?

But there is another person present in "Tintern Abbey": Dorothy Wordsworth. To say that Wordsworth is transferring his former passions to her is, on one level, simply to paraphrase the obvious sense of the poem. But to say that he is transferring his former passions *for Annette* to her as well is not inconsistent with a simple, accurate reading of the poem, and furthermore makes sense in the most rudimentary terms of psychological biography. Moorman asks how it was possible for William and Dorothy, "feeling for one another what and as they did," to imagine sharing their cottage with Annette, as her letters show them freely doing.[34] But the question carries its own answer: feeling for each other what and as they did, they *needed* some other woman there, lest their passions be tempted in forbidden, taboo directions. Something of the same situation developed with Mary Hutchinson at Racedown in 1797, and eventually in their married life together. Wordsworth's feelings for Annette, as later for Mary, could be accommodated (literally: domiciled) with his feelings for Dorothy. Indeed, they had to be. He sees in Dorothy what he was then, but he also makes her the object of what his passion was then:

> thou, my dearest Friend,
> My dear, dear Friend, and in thy voice I catch
> The language of *my former heart,* and read
> *My former pleasures in the shooting lights*
> *Of thy wild eyes.*
>
> (116–120; italics added)

This reads one way if we suppose he is talking about his attachment to Nature, and another way if we imagine he is talking about his attachment to Annette. But the two readings are not mutually exclusive, for both are positive effects of the influence of nature: "one great presence of the spring" or "a presence that disturbs . . . with the joy of elevated thoughts."

By the time he comes to his peroration in "Tintern Abbey," escalating from "warmer love" to "deeper zeal" to "holier love," it is easy to feel that a process of sublimating human sexual passion into a passion for nature is complete. It is only a small step further to suggest that a transference of passion from Annette to Dorothy has also been effected, and that it has been accomplished by means of a projection outward onto the body of nature, necessary to avoid the prohibitions of the incest taboo. He is proposing a new and different kind of love to Dorothy in July 1798, but if we take the arithmetic of "Tintern Abbey" as seriously as its passion, we are being strongly urged to identify those agonizing times of "former pleasures" with July 1793.

In psychoanalytic terms, Wordsworth has *sublimated* and *cathected* (introjected) his love for Annette by a process of *projection* onto Dorothy, accompanied by a *transference* to Nature.[35] But the process is plausible even without this technical language. Wordsworth's heavily loaded language points to the enormous force of the emotions which made him feel that such a journey was at once his strongest desire and his deepest responsibility. On this view, we should look at the language of all Wordsworth's texts between 1793 and 1798 for evidence of deeply held fantasies about what might have been, as much as for evidence of deeply hidden facts of what was.

Finally, Wordsworth's options for late 1793 are not simply a matter of choosing our own personal preference for the adventures we want to imagine him having (or not), but more properly one of decisively different alternative endings for this chapter in the novel of his life. Hence the option I proposed from Dickens at the outset of the last chapter is apt, if we could merge the plot of *Great Expectations* with that of *A Tale of Two Cities.* Having used Victor Hugo as a foreign correspondent in one part of this chapter, I refer in conclusion—with cheerful anachronism—to Charles Dickens, Hugo's friend and contemporary, to propose that the choices facing Wordsworth in late summer of 1793 were on a par with those facing both Charles Darnay and Sidney Carton. Carton's last words, so trite-sounding from constant repetition, were nothing more than the simple truth of the situation facing Wordsworth: "It is a far, far better thing that I do, than I have ever done." As a tonic to the thick sentiment with which this statement has become coated, we can add Dickens's little-known prefatory words from this novel, which also apply very well to Wordsworth:

> When I was acting . . . I first conceived the main idea of this story. A strong desire was upon me then, to embody it in my own person; and I traced out in my fancy, *the state of mind of which it would necessitate the presentation to an observant spectator,* with particular care and interest . . . . Throughout its execution, it has had complete possession of me; I have so far verified what is done and suffered in these pages, as that I have certainly done and suffered it all myself.[36]

Dickens was not the last English writer to wish to represent his own life in terms of the French Revolution, a fantasy identification which he encoded in his hero's initials. But Wordsworth was one of the first, and he also had Dickens's awkwardly stated but accurate desire "to embody it in [his] own person": presenting an individual's "state of mind" through the medium of a national state. Yet what for Dickens could only be fiction, verified to the greatest possible extent by fact, could for Wordsworth only be fact, modified to the greatest possible extent by fiction—that is, by language, by rhetoric, by displacement, by imagery, by all the considerable means available not to his historical researches but to his imagination.

17 LEGACY HUNTING

Windy Brow, 1794

A youth—he bore
The name of Calvert; it shall live, if words
Of mine can give it life . . . .
(XIII.349–51)

Almost everything Wordsworth did in the next year was dictated by his overriding need for money: for himself, for Annette, for Caroline, and, increasingly, for Dorothy, as she threw her lot in with his. Throughout 1794 he moved from one temporary residence or guesthouse to another, circulating between Halifax, Keswick, Whitehaven, Rampside, and Penrith. He spent two idyllic months with Dorothy at William Calvert's house, Windy Brow, above Keswick in the spring, and three grim months there in the fall, caring for Raisley Calvert, William's younger brother. It looks like a *Wanderjahr* without a plan, but beneath the surface he was pursuing a strategy for gaining his independence. On the one hand, he and Dorothy tried to settle their small inheritances from recent family deaths; on the other, he cultivated his new friendship with Raisley Calvert and nursed him through his last illness: he died on January 9, 1795, at Penrith. At the beginning of the year Wordsworth had quite possibly just returned from an incredibly dangerous trip to France. At the end of it, following Calvert's death, he embarked for London to throw himself into the "mighty gulf" of political journalism in London. At the beginning he had no money and no prospects; at the end he had the inheritance of £900 from Calvert's estate, enough to produce income sufficient to maintain himself independently.

Wordsworth and Dorothy did not have their long-anticipated reunion in Halifax until January or February of 1794, and it is hard to say what—if not France—kept them apart so long. Dorothy was waiting at Forncett all through the summer and fall for her cousin Robert Griffith to pass through toward Newcastle and escort her to Halifax. He never did come, and her anxiety, on top of her heavy load of domestic duties, began to affect her health. She described her condition to Jane Pollard as *"pallid"* and *"wishy washy"*; she could not go upstairs without throwing herself on her bed to rest.[1] Finally, early in February, she set off by herself, with five guineas from kindly Aunt Cookson, via London.

Our next verified sighting of William is at Christmastime in Whitehaven, whence he had come either from Jones's house, after an unconscionably long "stand" upon Jones's hospitality, or from his trip to France, when, returning to Jones in late October or early November, he found he was no longer welcome there. So he headed home. But where was that?

William and Dorothy's visits to family and friends in Cumberland in the spring and summer of 1794 seem so "natural" that nobody questions them. But there was little to call home there any more; in 1794 William had not been in the region for five years, and Dorothy was returning for the first time in fifteen. Family visits need not be scrutinized too closely for motives, but the only sense in which William and Dorothy's return to Cumberland was inevitable was that they had nowhere else to go. A visit to the Cooksons was unthinkable; William was persona non grata there. And Dorothy definitely did not want to return to Cumberland just to visit relatives, especially those in Penrith: "Perhaps my Uncle Crackanthorpe will invite me into Cumberland . . . but . . . I am not *very* desirous of an Invitation, and shall make my stay as short as possible."[2] But going with William, to Cumberland or anywhere else, was a different matter altogether. In his effort to establish an income, Wordsworth was shifting his theater of family operations. He was retreating from his influential uncles in the south—who had done all they could to help him, only to have their favors rejected—to his poorer ones in the north, the ones legally responsible for him. Like it or not, they were to a certain extent obliged to take him in.

Seventeen ninety-four was a good year anyway for retiring into the country and the bosom of one's family, if one was known to have French connections and divisive political opinions. In January, Maurice Margarot and William Skirving were unfairly convicted of sedition by the notoriously corrupt Judge Braxfield in Edinburgh; in February, Thomas Muir and Thomas Fyshe Palmer were led on board the prison ship bound for Botany Bay, having exhausted the appeals of their convictions the previous summer; in March, Joseph Gerrald received the same fourteen-year sentence in a London court. These were all middle-class young men, Whigs, Cambridge graduates, and, variously, lawyers, classical scholars, or high-thinking Unitarians.[3] In May, Parliament gave Pitt the right to suspend habeas corpus, and King's Messengers began arresting members of the Constitutional and Corresponding societies in a series of early morning raids. Artisans and shopkeepers were in the majority of the thirteen persons arraigned for the famous treason trials held in November, but the group also included lawyers and parsons, as well as John Horne Tooke, Thomas Holcroft, and John Thelwall. They were arraigned for treason, not for seditious utterance, a charge which all authorities agree would have been sustained. The penalty for conviction was death (technically with drawing and quartering) or, if leniency was granted, fourteen years' transportation. Horne Tooke, showman though he was, was not beyond the mark when he wrote from prison, "They want our blood—blood—blood!"[4]

Between the Edinburgh convictions in January, and November, when the treason trial acquittals were announced in London, the national political climate made lying low a very prudent posture. Wordsworth continued to be imprudent in expressing his political opinions, but the January–November time frame neatly encloses the time from his heading north for family visits to his beginning to wish to be back in London.

First he and Dorothy enjoyed their reunion in Halifax, where they were the guests of the amiable Mrs. (Threlkeld) Rawson. Dorothy had the pleasure of introducing her beloved brother to Jane Pollard and all the other girls of her Halifax childhood. Some of them were getting married, and though she had no prospects that way, she had what (she said) she considered better: her best male friend, in company with her best female friend. Her happiness was complete. It was also comfortable, because the Rawsons, Threlkelds, Pollards, and their friends were members of the prosperous mill-owning class who were beginning to transform Halifax from a picturesque market town to an ugly industrial center. Some of them had already begun to move out of the city to nearby country estates, but Mrs. Rawson's house and shop were in town.[5] These families do not appear in Wordsworth's accounts of his development, but they contributed something to his self-creation, in the generosity they extended to the two dependent Wordsworth children. They, along with the Griffiths of Newcastle, were the only branch of Wordsworth's relations in trade at the time, and they had more leisure time and money than the straitened professional circumstances his uncle Cookson and brother Richard provided, or the uncertain cash flows of his seagoing venture capitalist cousin, John Wordsworth of Whitehaven and his apprentice sons and nephews.

As soon as spring weather was well established in early April, William and Dorothy left these distant Halifax relatives to visit their closer relations in Cumberland. Their six-week stay at Windy Brow may well have been a detour, a small declaration of independence to act out the cottage fantasy which had filled their imaginations for the last five years. Dorothy wrote back to Jane, "We set forward by coach towards Whitehaven, and thence to

Kendal."[6] Kendal is only about seventy miles northwest of Halifax, but Whitehaven is nearly that much farther beyond Kendal, so one doesn't go "towards Whitehaven, and thence to Kendal" unless one backtracks half the distance of one's trip—or unless one gets off the Whitehaven coach at Kendal. They were both adults and could do what they wanted within the tight limits of their budget. But the Windy Brow visit involved a considerable change in plans, since it expanded almost immediately from "a few days" to "a few weeks."

At Kendal, Dorothy fell into step with her brother's wayfaring style, and walked thirty-three miles to Keswick at his side, breaking for an overnight stay in Grasmere. Leaving Kendal in the morning, they advanced to Windermere by noon, passing through Staveley, which got from Dorothy the best touristic notice it has ever enjoyed, by virtue of being "the first mountain village that I came to with William, when we first began our pilgrimage together."[7]

They stopped beside Windermere for lunch, just before Ambleside at Low Wood, where a "little unpretending Rill" trickles—still—into the lake. "Eating a traveller's meal in shady bower," they shared a basin of milk from the inn house on the road, and William gave Dorothy some expert hiking tips, suggesting she slip on her silk stockings to prevent chafing.[8] Dorothy was not used to such long walks, and was justly proud of her "wonderful prowess in the walking way." The first stop for refreshment on the first day of a holiday always makes a big impression, and their lunch at this little rill was still strong in Wordsworth's mind when he came to write a sonnet on it in 1802, from the heightened emotional perspective of his wedding trip. "The immaculate Spirit of one happy day / Lingers beside that Rill, in vision clear": this refers not to his wedding day but to the day of their lunch in April of 1794. The rill symbolized *them,* "furrowing its dubious way with shallow will." His original draft contains still more intimate thoughts of the time; the conventional "Emma," for Dorothy, was first written as "O faithful Anna!" This "Anna" is asked to say why the stream is so dear to them—unlike the published "Emma," who already knows—and his relation to "Anna" is more particularly specified: "My Love and I." This is not quite to say that Dorothy was a safe substitute for Annette, a virginal "immaculate Spirit," but it shows that Dorothy was inextricably bound up in his feelings for Annette. He and Dorothy came there bound together not only by their long-standing desire to rejoin each other but also by their secretly shared knowledge of Annette and their determination to remain true to her in spirit.

They stopped for the night at Grasmere. This was the first time Dorothy saw it, and she took in the full impact of the valley's vista from its lower entrance at Rydal, extending up to its high terminus over Dunmail Raise.

After a night at the old village inn at the center of Grasmere (not the Dove & Olive Branch on the high road that would become their Dove Cottage five years later),[9] they walked the remaining fifteen miles to Keswick next day, and took up their lodging at Windy Brow, a small house perched halfway up the first hills rising toward Skiddaw behind the town. William had a standing invitation from William Calvert to use the house.*

Here he met again Calvert's brother Raisley, who was staying at Ormathwaite, a farm over the hill behind Windy Brow, directly below Skiddaw, one of the several properties he stood to inherit when he came of age in September. Raisley had returned home from his own impetuous jaunt to the Continent in the spring of 1793, and was now trying to recover from the ill effects of strenuous travel on a consumptive constitution. The two young men's rebellious attitude toward Cambridge soon ripened into closer friendship. Wordsworth's dire situation was soon made clear to Calvert in the natural opening gambits of youthful conversation: what are you doing? what are your plans? your hopes and dreams? what will you do next?

Their friendship was also based on the fact that their fathers had known each other, being employed in identical positions by two of the most powerful landowners in the county, James Lowther, Lord Lonsdale, and Henry Howard, the duke of Norfolk. Raisley saw more sympathetically than his brother that Wordsworth represented an unhappy instance of what might have been for them. Their father had succeeded where Wordsworth's had not, but the Calverts were also powerfully connected in their own right. The duke of Norfolk was the most important Catholic peer in the land, and other members of the Calvert family had strong histories in aristocratic service, being allied to the Lords Baltimore who established the only Catholic colony in America, and to the Lords Calvert whose new aristocratic title would in time lend its prestige to a popular American whiskey. Raisley, like Wordsworth, was a scion apparently not destined to add luster to these family connections, and was at present living on an allowance of £100 per year, from a trust fund set up by his late father (d. 1791) and administered by the duke of Norfolk, who resided occasionally at nearby Greystoke Castle. But he would inherit thousands of pounds when he turned twenty-one in September.

Dorothy's first letters from Windy Brow are like all-points bulletins of newly perceived intentions for her life, revolving around two interrelated topics, the beauty of the country and the possibility of living cheaply in it, both based on the emotional bedrock of "so full an enjoyment of my

*Generosity might be attributed to the Calvert family's genes. Besides Raisley's gift to poetical posterity, the family's philanthropic tradition continues to this day in the Calvert Charitable Trust. It sponsors outdoor holidays in the Lake District for handicapped persons and is centered at this same Windy Brow farmhouse.

brother's company."[10] She tells Jane, "You cannot conceive any thing more delightful than the situation of this house . . . . [I]t is impossible to describe [the] grandeur" of the view. But she herself was equal to the challenge:

> . . . we command a view of the whole vale of Keswick (the vale of Elysium, as Mr. Grey [*sic*] calls it). This vale is terminated at one end by a huge pile of grand mountains in whose lap the lovely lake of Derwent is placed, at the other end by the lake of Bassenthwaite, on one side Skiddaw towers sublime and on the other a range of mountains not of equal size but of much grandeur, and the middle part of the vale is of beautiful cultivated grounds interspersed with cottages and watered by the winding stream which runs between the lakes of Derwent and Bassenthwaite.

The people were as fine as the place, as she described Windy Brow's caretakers:

> I have never been more delighted with the manners of any people than the family under whose roof I am at present. They are the most honest cleanly sensible people I ever saw in their rank of life—and I think I may safely affirm *happier* than any body I know. They are contented with a supply of the bare necessaries of life . . . and declare with simple frankness unmixed with ostentation that they prefer their cottage at Windy Brow to any of the showy edifices in the neighbourhood, and that they believe there is not to be found in the whole vale a happier family than they are. They are fond of reading, and reason not indifferently upon what they read.

She too reasoned not indifferently on what she observed in the life of this family, the Iansons: "We please ourselves in calculating, from our present expences for how very small a sum we could live." She and William worked on this equation of natural plus economic simplicity throughout the summer, but at present they had not even the "very small" sum necessary to begin solving it.

The Iansons also commented on them: my landlady "more than once exclaimed in my hearing, 'Bless me! folk are always talking about prospects. When I was young there never was sic a thing neamed.' "[11] William's expertise in landscape viewing had contributed to his renewed friendship with William Calvert the year before, but Calvert's younger brother proved more susceptible to the charms of Wordsworth's picturesque fluency.

They renewed their friendship with the Speddings of Armathwaite, a few miles up the shore of Bassenthwaite behind Windy Brow. Here was another steward's family whose fortunes had been made, not lost, in the interest of the Lowthers.[12] John Spedding was a classmate from Hawkshead, and his unmarried sisters were of Dorothy's age. Mary (twenty-five) and Margaret (twenty) were "in every respect charming women . . . [who] have read much" and "whose acquaintance [she was] very desirous of cultivating."[13]

The Spedding family, like the Calverts, seemed immediately attractive because they lived "in the most beautiful place that ever was beheld," and because they could afford to. With less native talent than the Wordsworths, they were less crossed by personal worries and family pressures, but these same pressures helped William and Dorothy sharpen their own talents.

Dorothy's unbounded enthusiasm was repeated in a defensive key when her aunt Crackanthorpe from Penrith wrote a most unwelcoming letter, aimed precisely at the desires Dorothy was trying to connect in her new life: "rambling about the country on foot," when she could ill afford to do so, either financially or morally. Dorothy answered with her first declaration of independence from her long-suffering dependent status. "I am much obliged to you," she wrote, "for the frankness [in expressing] your sentiments upon my conduct and am at the same time extremely sorry that you should think it so severely to be condemned." Christopher Crackanthorpe's wife had written with the full authority of eighteenth-century domestic tyranny, telling her niece exactly what was wrong with her behavior and ordering her in no uncertain terms to change it. Dorothy defended herself on three grounds, all of which involved William; what was reprehensible in her behavior became acceptable, even admirable, in his, as a man. (This point should be kept in mind by modern readers disposed to criticize Dorothy Wordsworth for being so dependent on her brother: she knew degrees of humiliating dependency compared with which her life with William was an extreme of freedom.) As to the expense, "I drink no tea . . . my supper and breakfast are of bread and milk and my dinner chiefly of potatoes from choice." Second, as to her being in "an unprotected situation": "I affirm that I consider the character and virtues of my brother as a sufficient protection." Finally, against the charge of "rambling," Dorothy defended herself in terms of the new cultural fashion, extending it from young gentlemen riding in whiskeys or post chaises to young women rambling on foot, with the benefit shifted from aesthetics to health: "I rather thought it would have given my friends pleasure to hear that I had courage to make use of the strength with which nature has endowed me, when it not only procured me infinitely more pleasure than I should have received from sitting in a post-chaise—but was also the means of saving me at least thirty shillings."[14] But she rests her case on her brother, from whom she will not be moved without, Mrs. Crackanthorpe is warned, a considerable domestic crisis: she had "only for a *very few* months" of her entire life enjoyed the society of her brother, and to be forced to give it up now would cause her "unspeakable pain."

Their aunt's reproach and Dorothy's response to it sprang to Wordsworth's memory eight years later when he contemplated bringing his real bride back home to Grasmere. "To a Young Lady Who Had Been Reproached for

Taking Long Walks in the Country" and "Louisa, After Accompanying Her on a Mountain Excursion" are addressed to an amalgam of Dorothy, Mary, and Joanna Hutchinson, but the first in force of memory was Dorothy.[15] He recommends ignoring such reproaches not only because the exercise is healthy but because such walks lay the ground for a kind of immortality of "joy." The alternative, which rebounds on hidebound reproachers like Aunt Crackanthorpe, is to find oneself in old age "a melancholy slave." The young woman in the second poem walks more like Dorothy than either of the Hutchinson sisters—"nymph-like, she . . . can leap along"—and her willingness to go out with him "in weather rough and bleak" is no small part of his love for her, which he expressed in sensual terms that closely identify him with the forces of nature: "And, when against the wind she strains, / Oh! might I kiss the mountain rains / That sparkle on her cheek."

During these six weeks Wordsworth told Mathews he was "quite at leisure," with more uninterrupted time for concentrated writing than he had had for several years. He began regulating the routines of housekeeping to accommodate those of a professional writer, with Dorothy's full cooperation. He asked Richard to send him his Italian grammar and his copies of Ariosto's *Orlando Furioso* and Tasso's *Gerusalemme Liberata,* which he and Dorothy were translating.[16] This was not mere language training, for these stories of heroes rescuing their damsels resonated both with his thoughts of Annette and with his main work, a revision of "A Night on Salisbury Plain" and extensive additions to *An Evening Walk* and *Descriptive Sketches.* He told Mathews the former was now "ready for the press," but as with almost every aspect of their life this year, he can think of it only in commercial terms: "I certainly should not publish it unless I hoped to derive from it some pecuniary recompence."[17] He also plaintively asked Mathews to stop by Johnson's bookshop to "ask him if he ever sells any of those poems" which he had published with such high hopes eighteen months earlier, but which had so far failed to return any significant profit.

Two ultimately contradictory thoughts were growing in his mind. On the one hand, he seemed in his writing to be committing himself to radical social thought and action. On the other, his progressive revisions of "A Night on Salisbury Plain" show that he was beginning to identify personally with human suffering, but in ways that led to no necessary action and that disarm almost all attempts at ideological explanation. Wordsworth's political tendencies led toward agitation for reform, but his compositional drift was toward empirical psychology or quietism. The extreme rationalism of William Godwin's *Enquiry concerning Political Justice* (1793) promised a way between these extremes, and Wordsworth soon began to fall under Godwin's sway.

An Evening Walk and *Descriptive Sketches* had been failures both in terms of profit and in showing his family "that he could do something" to make up for his university failures. So he now undertook to revise them along the lines of his own developing interests.[18] To *An Evening Walk,* primarily a landscape poem of private emotions, he added many lines of sociopolitical commentary; to *Descriptive Sketches,* a generalized view of the Alps with passing social observations and an apocalyptic political conclusion, he added a good deal of physically erotic imagery and intimate personal reactions to it. One might almost think he got his additions mixed up, making *An Evening Walk* more social and *Descriptive Sketches* more private, when the reverse combination would seem more likely, given the underlying subject matter of each poem. But this is so only if we expect Wordsworth's imagination to work in a linear fashion, which at its best it rarely did. Instead, the apparent contradictoriness of his additions can better be seen as a stubborn effort to force his *Evening Walk* landscapes to yield up more by way of moral insight and, conversely, to make the wide social vision of *Descriptive Sketches* more personally satisfying.

His additions of 1794 thus stand as further advances upon his failed poems of the previous spring and summer, where human history and its institutions (naval fleets, state prisons) fell across the landscapes of England in a way upsetting to their hopeful, naive viewer. But now his narrator, no longer so naive, expects less by way of congruence between Nature and Society, and can suggest more by way of their revealing contrasts. Or, conversely, when these two poles come close together, and threaten to stand out from each other in sharp contrast, he blurs the point of their contact (both its visual point and its moral one) in a way that suggests significant meaning without actually saying what that meaning is. For example, these new lines from *An Evening Walk* at first sound very much like a poetical counterpoint to Dorothy's description of the view over Derwent Water:

> How pleasant, as the sun declines, to view
> The total landscape change in form and hue!
> Here, vanish, as in mist before a flood
> Of bright obscurity, hill, lawn, and wood . . . .
> (155–58)[19]

But the description gradually moves toward a pure impressionism of light. Skiffs, cottages, "the industrious oar [of] the charcoal barge," and other human objects and actions only occasionally peep out from the increasing brilliance of a "thousand thousand twinkling points of light." The conclusion adds what is implicit in Dorothy's letter, the virtue of *having* such views: "Blest are those spirits tremblingly awake / To Nature's impulse like this living lake." Their spirits are unlike those of others—such as the Crackanthorpes—"whose languid powers unite / No interest to each rural sound or sight." But William and Dorothy are "different . . . favoured souls." Their visionary powers comprehend social divisions as well, because it is the vision of

> . . . a soul by Truth refined [who feels]
> Entire affection for all human kind;
> A heart that vibrates evermore, awake
> To feeling for all forms that Life can take,
> That wider still its sympathy extends,
> And sees not any line where being ends;
> Sees sense, through Nature's rudest forms betrayed,
> Tremble obscure in fountain, rock, and shade;
> And while a secret power those forms endears
> Their social accents never vainly hears.
>
> (123–32)

Many things are happening in these excellent passages, not least a rapid advance in the craft of composing fluent imagery. Much of "Tintern Abbey" and *The Prelude* is here in embryo, lacking only the autobiographical emphasis. But foremost among his advances was Wordsworth's new way of accommodating a sense of social responsibility into his landscape viewing. The identity of that "secret power" capable of inflecting the landscape's "social accents" is not clear, except when it is baldly asserted: "From love of Nature love of Virtue flows, / And hand in hand with Virtue Pleasure goes." But such assertions lose in persuasiveness what they gain in clarity, exposing the hand-me-down Rousseauism behind such wishful feeling. In fact, the "secret power" is the subjective authority of the poet.

Other additions to *An Evening Walk* give its "social accents" a more specific identity. The shadowy horsemen suggested by mountain mists are almost purely legendary in the original version, though linked to the border wars by a passing reference to "the lonely beacon" above Penrith. But in his additions Wordsworth tried to work up a political situation behind them, asking, "Why, shepherds, tremble thus with new alarms / As if ye heard the din of civil arms?"[20] This was a good, if dangerous, question in 1794, when the government was doing everything in its power to keep popular mass meetings from spilling out into insurrectionary protests. He allows that Penrith Beacon is now lit only by "the thunder-tempest's splendid fire," and asserts that Scottish shepherds in "Romantic Tiviot" are now as calm as those in Cumberland. But his imagination keeps playing with the current forms of Britain's warlike past, and he can't avoid the revolutionary tendency of his thoughts, except by swerving abruptly back into beautiful landscape visions:

> Mute Havoc smiling grimly backward slunk.
> Low-muttering o'er the earth that gasped beneath,

Hung the dim shapes of Solitude and Death,
And all was theirs save that the plover passed
With screams and bittern blew his hollow blast.

Now while the solemn evening shadows sail,
On red slow-waving pinions down the vale . . . .
(405–11)

The white space between these stanzas covers a multitude of, not sins, but probable crimes, including seditious utterance. Once we have been shifted back into landscape mode, we forget that those "red pinions" might easily, if Wordsworth had stuck with his military metaphors and meditations, have symbolized the red flags of revolution, civil disturbance, and martial law.

The main reason he could not publish a revised *Evening Walk* is the fact that its landscape's "social accents" were not translated into a consistent meaning, however suggestively they could be conveyed in misty imagery. But he could easily imagine one of the "favoured beings" who *could* embody this nature-society linkage. For he and Dorothy, "meek lover[s] of the shade," have a heroic precursor: "In dangerous night so Milton worked alone, / Cheared [*sic*] by a secret lustre all his own, / That with the deepening darkness clearer shone." This is the first explicit mention of Milton in Wordsworth's writing, though there are many echoes and allusions to him before this; "it is understandable that in 1794, an English republican would cite the lonely example of a republican of an earlier age."[21] But republicanism is not the only issue here, and his image of Milton is not simply a political one. Coming near the end of a set of revisions which turn *An Evening Walk* into a significantly different poem, Milton's appearance is highly symbolic. It identifies one name of the "secret power" that *can* read the "social accents" of both the landscape and the times. "The deepening darkness" is the sun setting across Derwent Water and also England sliding into its own reign of terror, as the mid-1790s increasingly recalled the mid-seventeenth century to thoughtful minds. Milton is an example of the kind of "favoured being" who could arise, amid post-revolutionary despair of Restoration, and begin dictating his masterpiece, *Paradise Lost,* with comprehensive views of the causes and effects of human failure.

But actual republicanism also is at stake here. Richard wrote in late May warning William to be "cautious in writing or expressing your political opinions. By the suspension of the Habeas Corpus Acts [on May 16] the Ministers have great powers." Richard knew very well how political tyranny maintains itself, so he refused to go into detail about his glum view of their chances for success against Lord Lonsdale: "I have always avoided writing and speaking upon this subject, because His Lordship has so many Spies in every part of the country."[22] Dorothy replied stoutly, "I can answer for William's caution about expressing his political opinions. He is very cautious and seems well aware of the dangers of a contrary conduct."[23] But at exactly this time William was writing a letter to Mathews about their journal-publishing project that opened with a very "explicit avowal" of his "political sentiments": "I am not amongst the admirers of the British constitution," which is being perverted by "the infatuation profligacy and extravagance of men in power."[24] And this was just part of the first paragraph of a letter that went on for pages with detailed plans for a journal that would promulgate such opinions and that certainly could have been brought to trial as "seditious utterance."

These "social accents" are clear and unmistakable, but the journal they anticipate was never published, at least not with Wordsworth's name on it (Chapter 18). Nor was the revised *Evening Walk;* it ended in a darkening landscape which saw in present-day Lakeland shadows the memories of other freedoms lost centuries ago in the same place, and which calls out, faintly, to the brother poets who mourned them then:

> What bards, in strains more faint at every close,
> Pour griefs which once the troubled winds scarce bore
> To meet the languid battle's dying roar,
> When Freedom here beheld the bird of Rome
> O'er her last barrier shake his deepest gloom;
> And sighs, from every fountain, shade, and cave,
> Wept the last remnant of the great and brave?
>
> (730–36)

With these thoughts we are very close to William himself, returning home from a midnight vigil above Windy Brow. He had watched the setting sun gild "that cottage with her fondest ray, / Sole bourn, sole wish, sole object of my way." His cottage fantasy had been there from his very first drafts of the poem (1788), but he now added some lines which draw from the humble lives of their new friends the Iansons:

> Who now . . .
> Can pass without a pause the silent door,
> Where sweet Oblivion clasps the cottage poor?
> Here, while I bend o'er this half useless gate,
> And muse on human being's various state;
> This path, that door, those peaceful precincts own
> A charm at any other hour unknown.
> Now subtle thought a moral interest sheds
> On the cool simples of these garden beds . . . .
>
> (771–80)

But this merely repeats the problem of this completely revised, though incompletely resolved, poem. For the "moral interest" that "subtle thought" draws from the Iansons' vegetable garden is only another version of the "social accents" that some "secret power . . . never vainly hears," accents that he has been unable to articulate in the context of his evening walk.

Toward the end of May, William and Dorothy left Windy Brow and set out for Whitehaven, the ostensible first destination of their trip north, to visit with their aunt Elizabeth and uncle Richard Wordsworth and the several cousins of this large, friendly family. They passed along the east shore of Bassenthwaite to say good-bye to the Speddings at Armathwaite, for Dorothy did not know when, if ever, she might see these good new friends again. Crossing the Ouse Bridge over the Derwent at the top of the lake, they soon came to Cockermouth, their birthplace. Dorothy had not seen the grand house by the river since she was six; it was now deserted and marked by neglect: "all was in ruin, the terrace-walk buried and choked up with the old privot hedge which had formerly been beautiful, roses and privots intermingled—the same hedge where the sparrows were used to build their nests."[25] The ruin of their prospects could hardly have found a more objective symbol as they walked along, moving from playing at adult independence at Windy Brow toward the reality of their dependent status among their Whitehaven cousins.

The sight had a similar resonance for William, though he did not write it down for another year or two. When he did, the impact of seeing his decayed family home is apparent in the cadences of these soon-to-be-famous lines:

> Yet once again do I behold the forms
> Of these huge mountains, and yet once again,
> Standing beneath these elms, I hear thy voice,
> Beloved Derwent, that peculiar voice
> Heard in the stillness of the evening air,
> Half-heard and half-created.[26]

It is as though we are hearing simultaneously the beginning of "Tintern Abbey" and *The Prelude,* as the memory of time in the former and that of place in the latter come together in a literal point of origin for both Wordsworth's life and his poetry. He is looking at natural objects and listening to natural sounds while standing near a decayed but unmentioned building, as he also will do above Tintern Abbey. The situation shows how deeply Wordsworth's creative imagination was stimulated by feelings of loss or absence *at the very point from which* it speaks its deepest affirmations. The difference between his imagination and Dorothy's—yet also his dependence on hers—is noticeable in the contrast between her realistic focus on the shabby building before shifting to *her* childhood memory: of the sparrows' nests that she used to worry over when young William threatened them. By contrast, he skips the present decay of the house in order to shift his memory forward into a uniquely Wordsworthian verb tense, a present future of hope: "Yet once again . . . yet once again." Adapting these lines to the Wye valley four years later, he changed the name of the river, and the "huge mountains" (Skiddaw) and northern elms become the cliffs and sycamores of South Wales. By 1798 this memory would be thoroughly mixed with his recollections of his first trip past Tintern, in 1793, a trip whose motives were in turn very much bound up with his reasons for being with Dorothy at Cockermouth in 1794. Uniting them all was an overwhelming sense of his life returning to its origins, and now beginning to play itself back to him in an adult—and decidedly minor—key. In the perspective of their young adult lives, the neglected mansion of their former hopes gave very little promise for the future. His memory is stimulated by being back in the same place at a different time, but he marks the difference in nature's continuity rather than in the ruinous human structure.

Passing rapidly on from this solemn moment, William and Dorothy arrived before nightfall in the little village of Branthwaite between Cockermouth and Whitehaven. There they stayed with their uncle Richard, now retired and ailing. Dorothy could see immediately that their uncle would "never enjoy a *good* state of health." She spoke truer than she knew, for he died less than a month later. The death of this uncle, the kindliest of the four who were the overseers of their destiny, had immediate repercussions on their lives that summer. As soon as they arrived in Whitehaven, Dorothy wrote a letter to Richard, urging him to do everything he could, and as quickly as he could, to put their financial affairs on a settled basis. "These things make me very uneasy." Principally, she was concerned that their uncle Crackanthorpe be brought "to an immediate settlement" of the accounts which he coadministered with Richard Wordsworth of Whitehaven, for that very small part of their father's estate which was not contained in the evidently hopeless claim against Lord Lonsdale. Such a "settlement" might have resulted not in a sum of money coming to William and Dorothy but only in a final statement of their debts to their uncles. As administrators of their nephews' and niece's trust, Richard Wordsworth and Christopher Crackanthorpe had for years been engaged mainly in making advances beyond the present balance of the estate, in anticipation of future repayment. William and Dorothy had received less than £200 in bequests from their recently dead grandparents, some of which Dorothy had immediately lent to John for his East India investments. Her pressing question was how much of that money they could count as their own, and how much they owed to their executors.

She had no hopes for anything on the Lowther front: "at present it cannot be advancing one step . . . it is said that nothing can be done without applying to the House of Lords." This was the common view around Whitehaven because, two days before she wrote, Henry Littledale, a local mercer, had finally won a settlement of £4,000 against Lowther in the House of Lords, for damages incurred when his house at St. Bees sank into a shaft which Lowther's mining company had burrowed beneath it. It had taken three years, but the victory, a very popular one, showed that Lowther could be beaten with perseverance. But after ten years of waiting, Dorothy could only opine regretfully, "I wish our [cause] had been pursued with equal vigour"—precisely the quality that everybody agreed was lacking in their principal lawyer, Edward Christian.

In their summer visits along the coast, William and Dorothy were passing through the more settled, populous part of Cumberland, which is not identical with the Lake District, though the two terms are often used synonymously by outsiders. The "Lake District" was not then, as it has since become, the profit-making center of the region. None of William and Dorothy's relations lived there. Places like Windy Brow and other gentry houses in the region of mountains and lakes were picturesque retreats where money was spent, not earned. Far more money and many more people were to be found outside the region of the lakes, along the coast from Maryport, Workington, and Whitehaven, down to Barrow, Ulverston, and on to Lancaster, working in the coal mines that had swallowed up Mr. Littledale's house, or in the renewed, profitable shipping trades with the former American colonies, now independent and united states. Their cousins all dwelt on this periphery, either in trading towns like Penrith or in the shipping ports of the coast, where, as ship captains, lawyers, and innkeepers, they earned their livings by working hard.

One shouldn't overdo this connecting of people with places, but these were nevertheless the kind of people William and Dorothy's Whitehaven cousins were, no more given to enjoying the "prospect" of the gray Irish Sea from their town's huge hills than the Iansons were with Derwent Water. William and his sister stayed with the wife of their cousin John, captain of the ship on which their brother John was serving. These eight living cousins (Favel Wordsworth had died in 1783, aged twenty-three) were warm and welcoming for a three-week summer visit. But the question of their cousins' debts was the deep family issue that was on everyone's mind even as they all tried to avoid it in conversation. It could not be wished away, and it was nobody's fault that John Wordsworth had died leaving five young orphans. It came to over £400, the great bulk of it for William's college education—and for his frequent touring expenses. The question of fault, or deserts, especially crossed the mind of Aunt Elizabeth Wordsworth, as she contemplated paying off the debts of her dying husband's estate, and the looming educational expenses of her youngest child, the promisingly named Robinson Wordsworth (1775–1856). He had just turned nineteen, and was beginning to seek his place in life. (He found it a year and a half later, when his name paid off, and John Robinson awarded him the lucrative collectorship of customs at Harwich.) Mrs. Wordsworth could not avoid comparing her son's prospects to those of his visiting cousin William, the most gifted of her late brother-in-law's children, but the only one who, so far, had shown no sign of getting himself forward in the world in a way to repay the debts that had been contracted on his behalf. The money that had put Cousin William through college would now be very convenient for Robinson. It is no bad reflection on Mrs. Richard Wordsworth, but quite the contrary as a devoted mother, that she seems to have been the one who began pressing, after a couple more years' lenience, for her own children's due. Her justified claims also remind us of what everybody in the family remembered, that her husband had been disinherited for marrying her by his father, Wordsworth's grandfather, in favor of Wordsworth's father.

Even before leaving Windy Brow, William had accepted an offer from Raisley Calvert to share in his allowance in anticipation of the inheritance that would come to him in mid-September. This was a polite formulation of the fact that Raisley was already helping to defray some of the Wordsworths' expenses, as his brother William had the summer before. Dorothy does not mention this fact in her letters to Richard, and one feels quite sure that William did not bring it up in conversation at Whitehaven. But his letters to Mathews at this time make a small but significant shift reflecting this news, regarding his ability to contribute financially to their proposed journal. On May 23 he said, "I am so poor that I could not advance any thing," though he did not think "being in the country would have any tendency to diminish the number or deduct from the value of my communications."[27] But on June 8 Wordsworth concluded a long letter of detailed suggestions for the magazine by saying he must still decline coming to town, but now for nearly the opposite reasons he had given two weeks earlier: "I have a friend in the country [Raisley] who has offered me a share of his income. It would be using him very ill to run the risque of destroying my usefulness by precipitating myself into distress and poverty at the time when he is so ready to support me in a situation wherein I feel I can be of some little service to my fellowmen, hereafter, if our exertions are sufficient to support us by residing in London, perhaps I may be enabled to prosecute my share of the exertions with greater vigour." He continues, maddeningly, "Will it not be necessary to free [yourself] from some of those occupations to which your time is at present devoted? . . . As to money I have not a single sixpence of my own to advance . . . ."[28] If Wordsworth suffered cruel double binds at the hands of his uncles, he seems to have fallen into the habit of creating them for others: I have no money, only a free allowance from a new friend. You are gainfully employed, but shouldn't you give up some of your salary in order to give more time to our journal project—the one I dare not invest in?

Richard Wordsworth's heirs finally put their claim forward in legal form in 1797. But it was not paid until 1812, and then by William's brother Richard, in the amount of £412, very close to the amount due in 1794: little or no interest was computed in the payment. Eighteen years elapsed between the time the debt could first be said to have come due, and fifteen years after a claim for it was filed in court. In a strict comparison to this situation, the poet's family could not complain overly much of their treatment by the Lowther family, which finally paid off James Lowther's debt of £5,000, with interest of £3,000, in 1802, nineteen years after John Wordsworth's death, and fifteen years after his brother and brother-in-law filed suit to recover it. But until Wordsworth got the Calvert bequest and the Lowther settlement, the Whitehaven Wordsworths had no reason to expect anything at all from him, and even so they had to wait another ten years for it.

Aside from these financial tensions, the visit passed enjoyably enough. Wordsworth's image of the "children sporting on the shore" in the Intimations Ode may date from this summer, the only one he spent by a seaside before he wrote it.[29] But their visit closed on a somber note with the funeral of their uncle Richard on June 20 in Branthwaite, less than a month after their overnight stay with him.

From Whitehaven, Dorothy went to visit another of her cousins from this family, Elizabeth, who in 1790 had married Francis Barker and now lived in comfortable circumstances in Rampside, a tiny fishing village directly across Morecambe Bay from the Morecambe-Lancaster region. The Barkers' house is still standing, large enough to serve as a hotel.[30] William accompanied Dorothy as far as Broughton-in-Furness, where they visited with another cousin, Mary, who in 1789 had married a tavern keeper, John Smith. Francis Barker came to escort Dorothy on to Rampside, while William turned north to ride back to Keswick. Of these shadowy cousins in his youthful biography Wordsworth only recorded later a "whisper from the heart," for "friends and kindred tenderly beloved."[31]

He spent most of July in Keswick, writing and caring for Calvert, whose health was beginning to deteriorate rapidly. In August, William returned to Rampside to spend the month with Dorothy and the Barkers. Rampside is merely a small collection of buildings by the side of the ramp where the ferry from Morecambe puts in. It is also the port, so to speak, for tourist excursions to the closest and smallest of the raggedy little collection islands at the end of the North Lancashire coast, the promontory occupied by the ancient fortress called Peele (or Piel) Castle, originally built to ward off marauding pirates from the Isle of Man.*

Short though it was, Wordsworth's summer by the sea at Rampside was marked by two events connected and terrifically amplified in his memory. One was his recollection of this calm time eleven years later, when his brother John drowned off Weymouth and Portland Bill, which hooks out into the sea in much the same way the Isle of Walney does at Piel Island. The other was his recollection of hearing the news of Robespierre's execution. Both moments exploded in his imagination because of his strong reaction to the sense of difference between a peaceful, naive "then" and a violent, tragic "now." In this respect, his quiet time at Rampside was a seedbed for memory, very much as his reaction to seeing his childhood home at Cockermouth anticipated further imaginative growth upon his return to Tintern Abbey.

"Elegiac Stanzas, Suggested by a Picture of Peele Castle, in a Storm, Painted by Sir George Beaumont" (1805) stresses the dreamy inactivity of that summer, as contrasted with a dramatic picture by Beaumont, his new patron, almost to the point of a paralysis:

> I was thy neighbour once, thou rugged Pile!
> Four summer weeks I dwelt in sight of thee:
> I saw thee every day; and all the while
> Thy Form was sleeping on a glassy sea.
> So pure the sky, so quiet was the air!
> So like, so very like, was day to day!
>
> (1–6)

If he could have painted what he saw and felt then, it would have been a picture very different from Beaumont's stormy picture, which he now feels is more realistically suited to life's tragic losses. But in 1794 he would have set the stolid "Pile" in a "light that never was, on sea or land . . . Amid a world how different from this!" Though the contrast he felt then was caused by John's death, some of the very practical issues from that summer peep out beneath his idyllic representation of himself: "A Picture had it been of lasting ease, / Elysian quiet, without toil or strife." His lack of a position, his financial relations with his cousins, and even his financial arrangement with Raisley Calvert involved a considerable amount of both "toil" and "strife."

Wordsworth's reaction to the news of Robespierre's death also had strong personal dimensions. He had ridden around to the east side of Morecambe Bay on an errand, and he returned by way of Cartmel Priory, where there

*Like that of the *pele* towers in Scotland's Borders region, its proper name originates from a redundant common noun, signifying "fortress castle," deriving from the same root as "pile."

accompany Raisley, and that William should give his brother "as much pecuniary assistance as would enable me to accompany him thither, and stay with him till his health is re-established."

He then goes further, pressing the idea with a bit of moral arm-twisting: "This I think, if possible, you ought to do. You see I speak to you as a friend. But then perhaps your present expenses may render it difficult." This might well have struck William Calvert as presumptious. But, having intimated that Calvert might not be willing or able to help his dying brother, Wordsworth then increased the moral pressure: "Would it not exalt you in your own esteem to retrench a little for so excellent a purpose?" That is, can't you cut back a little on your extravagant lifestyle as a dashing ensign in the duke of Norfolk's regiment to help your poor sick brother?

Having pushed Calvert to the limit, Wordsworth revealed the ground of his importunity. Raisley had been helping out with some of Wordsworth's expenses since June, but this help was now in a fair way to becoming considerably more substantial:

> Reflecting that his return is uncertain your brother requests me to inform you that he has drawn out his will, which he means to get executed in London. The purport of his will is to leave you all his property real and personal chargeable [i.e., all his debts as well] with a legacy of £600 to me, in case that on enquiry into the state of our affairs in London he should think it advisable to do so. It is at my request that this information is communicated to you [i.e., I am telling you this now because I asked permission of Raisley to do so], and I have no doubt but that you will do both him and myself the justice to hear this mark of his approbation of me without your good opinion of either of us being at all diminished by it. If you could come over [from Newcastle] yourself it would be much the best. At all events fail not to write by return of post, as the sooner your brother gets off the better. He will depart immediately after hearing from you.
>
> I am dear Calvert,
>
> Your very affectionate friend,
>
> W. Wordsworth.[36]

This is a very careful, very bold, and very lawyerly letter. It shows the influence of Wordsworth's having had a father, a brother, and some cousins in the legal profession. He is breaking to William Calvert the news that the large amount of ready cash in Raisley Calvert's estate, which William Calvert stood to inherit, was now going to Wordsworth. He is saying, Surely you will not take this news badly, or in the wrong way—any more than you would take badly my earnest argument that you support my expenses while I accompany Raisley to Portugal. And you should still pay my travel expenses, even though if your brother dies I will inherit the cash balance of his estate.

They did in fact set off for Portugal on October 9—and got as far as Penrith. They returned to Keswick the very next day because Raisley "found himself worse." It was the shortest, but by far the most profitable, of Wordsworth's several trips "abroad" in the 1790s. If William Calvert had taken Wordsworth's letter in the wrong way, it would have meant that he suspected Wordsworth of legacy hunting, in one of the most usual situations where such suspicions arise: toward the caregiver of a terminally ill person who is isolated, without family or dependents or any other close friend nearby, in the last months of his life. Though some element of legacy hunting certainly informs Wordsworth's relations with Raisley Calvert from spring to fall of 1794, it is important that we see his actions in their cultural context. Given his and Dorothy's dependent family financial situation when they came north in April, complicated by the claims arising from their uncle Richard's death in June, his positioning himself to inherit something was only common sense, and need not be taken as evidence of morbid plotting.[37]

To a later patron, George Beaumont, Wordsworth was at once franker and more innocent sounding: "though I call him [Raisley] Friend, I had had but little connection; and the act was done entirely from a confidence on his part that I had powers and attainments which might be of use to mankind."[38] Wordsworth brings *The Prelude* to a close by giving Calvert his due in similar terms:

The name of Calvert; it shall live, if words
Of mine can give it life—without respect
To prejudice or custom, having hope
That I had some endowments by which good
Might be promoted, in his last decay
From his own family withdrawing part
Of no redundant patrimony, did
By a bequest sufficient for my needs
Enable me to pause for choice, and walk
At large and unrestrained . . . .

(XIII.350–61)[39]

This is surely part of the truth. Raisley Calvert did admire Wordsworth, and Wordsworth was apparently at the beginning of a poetical career—insofar as he could be said to be at the beginning of any career. But as Wordsworth pointed out to his brother Richard, literature was not the only goal in sight: "He would leave me this sum to set me above want and to enable me to pursue my literary views *or any other views* with greater success or with a consciousness that if these should fail me I would have something at last to turn to."[40]

Far from being underhanded, such behavior at the imminent death of a friend or relative was perfectly normal for the times, as it still is wherever inheritance is a major way of acquiring wealth. The hope to inherit was a normal kind of "interest" one had in the dead and dying, perfectly consistent with the constant cultivation of "interest" among one's influential superiors that was the basis of almost every kind of advancement in eighteenth-century England. Almost all marriages of persons in Wordsworth's class were still arranged on precisely this basis. Indeed, it might be argued that courting the dying had fewer unfortunate long-term consequences than courtships which produced the many loveless and cruel marriages that women were forced into. Jane Austen's *Sense and Sensibility,* which was being drafted at exactly this time (though not published until 1811), is based squarely on this reality, and neither of her heroines, neither the sensible Elinor nor the sentimental Marianne, would think of marrying without adequate financial provision. In 1794 Wordsworth's situation approximated that of both sisters' suitors. Like Colonel Brandon, he had a secret illegitimate ward; like Henry Willoughby, he had seduced an unprotected woman; like both of them, he had relatives living in France and had been "refined" in his morals and behavior by long residence there.

Dorothy's attachment to her brother shared this same economic motivation. Her lack of marriage prospects was directly proportional to her lack of an estate and her very small "provision." These very considerations led William to remind Raisley Calvert of his sister's dependence on him, with the result that Calvert soon increased the amount of his bequest by £300, to £900: that is, the full amount of the cash portion of his inheritance, the most liquid, and most useful, part of his estate.[41] In its effect, this additional amount became something like a marriage portion settled on Dorothy.

It would have been ridiculously circumspect, given Wordsworth's circumstances and prevailing social practices, to have behaved in any other way. However, only an excessively sentimental view of the situation could imagine that Wordsworth did nothing to encourage or manipulate Raisley's generosity. The only person who stood to lose anything by Raisley's generosity was his brother William, since their sister Ann had also recently died. There are suggestions in Wordsworth's letter to William Calvert that he knew the elder brother did not share his younger brother's enthusiasm for Wordsworth's future: "He deemed that my pursuits and labors lay / Apart from all that leads to wealth, or even / Perhaps to necessary maintenance, / Without some hazard to the finer sense" (XIII.362–65). Raisley Calvert "deemed," that is, what Wordsworth's relatives were also beginning to deem was the case with him in 1794: that he did not seem likely to be able to earn a living. But the Richard Wordsworth family of Whitehaven were much less worried about any "hazard to the finer sense" William might risk by trying to find a job.

Wordsworth's language at the time was a good deal less lofty than his tribute composed ten years later. In two letters fired off to Richard on October 10 and 17, Wordsworth was in agony of anxiety lest Raisley die before his intended will could be properly executed and witnessed, and lest his Whitehaven relatives lay claim to this new inheritance for payment of the £400 he owed to his late uncle's estate. He had to satisfy Raisley on the latter count, for Raisley did not want to leave a bequest that could be seized immediately to pay prior debts. This was a possibility that had really emerged only *after* he began sharing his income with Wordsworth, that is, with the death of Uncle Richard Wordsworth. In the first of these letters, Wordsworth stumbles all over himself, repeating the interrelated matters of Richard's standing bond to protect him from any claims originating from Whitehaven, the chances of independence the bequest offers him, and his solemn vow that he will repay the debt to his cousins if ever he is "worth more than this six hundred pounds."[42] (It was not paid until 1812.) He asks Richard to reply by return post, and then goes further, urging him to leave his London business and travel north to make sure all the legalities are being properly observed. He pushed his case so far that he insulted Richard by hinting that Richard might not be willing to be bonded to protect him. This was similar to the provocative moralizing with which he had wheedled William Calvert about paying his travel expenses to Lisbon. We do not have Calvert's replies to such importunings, but we do have Richard Wordsworth's, and it suggests that neither older brother was pleased by such high-handed treatment: "You will allow me to assure you that I have always had my Sisters yours and my younger Brothers Interest at Hearth [*sic*] although I have not been fond of making professions which It could not be my intention to carry into effect .... It has been and I hope will always be my [MS torn] to say little upon such heads whate'er my secret intentions may be."[43] In short: I act, not talk.

After agreeing to enter into the bond that would indemnify William against claims from their uncle Richard's family, Richard continued more pointedly,

> There is one Circumstance which I will mention to you at this time. I might have retired into the Country and I had almost said enjoyed the sweets of retirement and Domestick life if I had only considered my own Interest. However as I have ent[ere]d into the Busy scenes of a Town life I shall I hope pursue them with comfort and credit. I am happy to inform you that my Bus[ines]s encreases daily and that altho' our affairs have been peculiarly distressing I hope that from the Industry of ourselves at one time we will enjoy more ease and independence than we have yet experienced.

In other words, Not all of us can retire so blithely to the country. I am working hard so you may enjoy the "sweets of retirement and Domestic life," and I hope you will soon start doing the same. He closes with a caution that we may be sure William Calvert, his opposite number in the role of elder brother in this family drama, shared: "I suppose [Raisley] has maturely weighed the matter and taken into consideration the claims of his Brother to keep any provision he may make for you alone. I cannot get to Cumberland this vacation."[44]

Wordsworth's reply of October 17 is feverishly fearful that Raisley will die before the will is drawn up. "It is his wish that the will should be made immediately and yet he is naturally of a dilatory disposition; and one does not wonder that he seizes any opportunity to defer it, though at the same time it is his wish to have it done immediately." Wordsworth was hardly the one to speak of dilatory dispositions, but the accumulation of excuses and delays drove him nearly frantic: Raisley didn't like his Keswick lawyer (wonderfully named Lightfoot), but the Penrith lawyer wanted a guinea and a half for the trip over, so Raisley thought he'd draw it up himself, but William wasn't sure he knew how to do it correctly. "At all events no time is to be lost as he is so much reduced as to make it probable he cannot be on earth long." Finally Raisley convinced William he could draw up a legal document by himself, so William told Richard, in an ongoing journal-letter which proceeds almost like a minute-by-minute record of events, "I retract then what I have said about your coming down and think there can be no occasion for it."[45]

The will was signed at last on October 23, 1794, less than a month after Wordsworth returned from his seaside vacation to find Calvert "much worse" than he had left him. It provided "one or more annuities for his use and benefit" and "full power to invest any portion for the use and benefit of his Sister Dorothy Wordsworth." The nervousness was over, but it had been real and justified. Despite Richard Wordsworth's concern about William Calvert's attitude toward the legacy, and despite Wordsworth's reassurances, it was clearly no part of anyone's thinking that William Calvert might make a bequest to him anyway, out of the goodness of his heart, should his brother die intestate, or with his stated intentions not legally documented. William Calvert may have been Wordsworth's friend, but he was not *that* friendly. £900 was nine years' maintenance, at the allowance rate on which Raisley Calvert had been living: exactly the rate (£100 per year) that Wordsworth told William Mathews he would need before he could consider Mathews's plan of throwing up all their worldly aspirations to adopt the wandering life.

Wordsworth's efforts to settle his affairs at this critical juncture in his self-creation were not without costs in friendship and ruffled personal feelings. It may be more than coincidental that there are no further references to William Calvert in any of the Wordsworth correspondence until 1802. His younger brother's impetuous decision to sink the family's assets in poetry futures cannot have seemed like the best of investments of money that he stood immediately to gain. In the course of little over a year, Wordsworth's reacquaintance with William Calvert had moved from being his expenses-paid traveling companion, to the free use of his house at Windy Brow, to sharing his brother's maintenance income, to proposing to be his brother's expenses-paid traveling companion, to becoming Raisley's cash heir in place of William, and finally to beginning to collect the inheritance money within three months of first broaching the news to William.

Another silent but ruffled observer of all this was Cousin Robinson Wordsworth and his family. Wordsworth, in getting Richard to stand a bond of £400, the amount of his debt to his cousins, was effectively hindering, or at least mortgaging, another young man's efforts to move forward in life. There is a clear and cruel symmetry in the fact that the bequest that set Wordsworth on the road to financial independence should have been legally prohibited from performing the same function for Robinson Wordsworth. True, the Whitehaven Wordsworths were in more comfortable circumstances than their orphaned cousins, but the nonpayment of this debt nearly compromised Robinson's marriage plans three years later, causing William and Dorothy acute embarrassment when their brother Richard, as their banker, delayed payment of it.[46]

Raisley Calvert lingered on for three more months, during which William removed him to Penrith for better care. He stayed faithfully at his younger friend's side till the end, and had "a most melancholy office of it," as he wrote restively to Mathews. "I begin to wish to be much in town; cataracts and mountains, are good occasional society, but they will not do for constant companions; besides I have not even much of their conversation, and still less of that of my books as I am so much with my sick friend, and he cannot bear the fatigue of being read to. Nothing indeed but a sense of duty could detain me here under the present circumstances. This is a country for poetry it is true; but the muse is not to be won but by the sacrifice of time, and time I have not to spare."[47] He conveys more of a sense of duty than of grieving affection toward Calvert, and he is almost equally reserved about the lakes and mountains of Cumberland.

Raisley Calvert died shortly after this letter was written. He had lived just long enough to gain personal control of the money left him by his father.[48] William "probably" supervised his burial at Greystoke on January 12 and left the north almost immediately, stopping at Newcastle to see Dorothy at the Griffiths'. One wonders, but doubts, whether he also called on William Calvert, who was stationed at the Tynemouth barracks.

18

PHILANTHROPY OR TREASON?

London, 1795

> . . . demanding proof,
> And seeking it in every thing, I lost
> All feeling of conviction, and, in fine,
> Sick, wearied out with contrarieties,
> Yielded up moral questions in despair . . . .
> (X.896–900)

In two long letters to Mathews written from Whitehaven in May and June 1794—just when his family financial predicament was intensifying—Wordsworth had set forth in great detail his plans for a political and moral publication, to be called the *Philanthropist,* which he and Mathews would initiate as soon as they could coordinate their time, money, and energy. His proposed editorial policy was firmly republican. Following Godwin's example, he would not begin the project without a full, mutual disclosure of their political views,[1] which he initiated with legalistic formality: "here at the very threshold I solemnly affirm that in no writings of mine will I ever admit to any sentiment which can have the least tendency to induce my readers to suppose that the doctrines which are now enforced by banishment, imprisonment, &c, &c, are other than pregnant with every species of misery. You know perhaps already that I am of that odious class of men called democrats, and of that class I shall for ever continue."[2]

Penned ten days after the first arrests for the treason trials, and after the general promulgation of the suspension of habeas corpus, such heightened language seems less pompous than brave—or foolhardy, when sent through a post that was now being systematically opened by government agents. He was reading the political signs of the times very carefully, and his comments on the treason trial acquittals turn shrewdly upon his own situation: "The late occurences in every point of view are interesting to humanity. They will abate the insolence and presumption of the aristocracy, by shewing it that neither the violence, nor the art, of power can crush even an unfriended individual, though engaged in the propagation of doctrines confessedly unpalatable to privilege." He himself was now "an unfriended individual" in terms of influence and patronage.

Receiving Mathew's "explicit avowal of . . . political sentiments with great pleasure," Wordsworth launched into "a similar declaration of my own opinions." He proceeds with a deductive logic that leads him directly to statements that, in the current climate of law, constituted seditious utterance and could have been called treasonous in any court willing to accept the government's legal doctrine of "constructive treason": "I disapprove of monarchical and aristocratical governments, however modified. Hereditary distinctions and privileged orders of every species I think must necessarily counteract the progress of human improvement."[3] Coleridge, more astute politically than Wordsworth, would shortly lecture in Bristol about the risk of such communications: "If any man, even in a private letter or social conversation, should say a Republic is the best form of government, he is guilty of high treason."[4]

But Wordsworth feared radical excesses more than government repression: "The destruction of those institutions which I condemn appears to me to be hastening on too rapidly. I recoil from the bare idea of a revolution."[5] He was thus opposed to "all inflammatory addresses to the passions of men," favoring instead a "gradual and constant reform" of ministerial extravagance and profligacy in public administration, as the best way of avoiding the "execrable measures" into which the French had been led. This prudence reflects Wordsworth's new familiarity with Godwin's *Political Justice,* which he read very carefully in the winter of 1793–94. Mankind's gradual but inevitable progress toward political justice by the unstoppable force of truth in open discussion was the key element in Godwin's thought. Its necessary corollary was strict avoidance of any kind of writing or public speech that would raise the passions of men to violent actions which might prove counterproductive to progress.

By mid-February of 1795 Wordsworth was back in London, eagerly checking out the journalism opportunities he had asked Mathews to look into. Although their plans for the *Philanthropist* had apparently fallen through, he was still persuaded by Mathew's arguments in favor of journalism. In November he had intimated he might even abandon Raisley in favor of his prospects for employment on a London newspaper:

> If he should not recover, indeed whatever turn his complaint takes, I am so emboldened by your encouragement that I am determined to throw myself into that mighty gulph which has swallowed up so many, of talents and attainments infinitely superior to my own. . . . Pray let me have accurate information from you on the subject of your newspaper connection. What is the

> nature of the service performed by you, and how much of your time does it engross? &c &c. You say a newspaper would be glad of me; do you think you could ensure me employment in that way in terms similar to your own? I mean also in an opposition paper, for really I cannot in conscience and in principle, abet in the smallest degree the measures pursued by the present ministry.[6]

Mathews had replied by the end of December, and Wordsworth immediately fit himself to the jobs available. The only thing he ruled out was parliamentary reporting (Mathews's specialty), because he had "neither strength of memory, quickness of penmanship, nor rapidity of composition . . . [and because of] a further circumstance which disqualifies me . . . viz. my being subject to nervous headaches, which inevitably attack me when exposed to a heated atmosphere or to loud noises . . . with such an excess of pain as to deprive me of all recollection."[7] But he was sure he would be able to translate excerpts from the French and Italian gazettes, confidently adding, "With two or three weeks reading I think I could engage for the Spanish." He thought he might also furnish the odd paragraph on current events, "and now and then an essay on general politics," but this was just a show of confidence. He really preferred translating—a substantial job, since most newspapers devoted one full page out of four to war reports from the *Moniteur* and other foreign sources.

He had not yet seen Mathews's newspaper, the *Telegraph,* which commenced publication on December 30, 1794, but had heard "that it is democratical, and full of advertisments!" Mathews may have told him about other young men who were just then signing up for the new paper's staff. In mid-January, Coleridge was in London negotiating for a position on it; by mid-February, Southey was its regular Bristol correspondent.[8] Mathews was probably one of the first connections through which knowledge of these future friends came to Wordsworth. Significantly, Wordsworth's tone with Mathews begins to cool just as his acquaintance with Coleridge starts to ripen.

Wordsworth was very insistent that Mathews do something definite for him: "I cannot be detained long by my present occupation [nursing Calvert], so that you are not likely to give yourself trouble to no purpose." This was in response to Mathews's annoyed reminder of how much he had done to try to get the *Philanthropist* started, only to have Wordsworth hold back his time and money throughout the summer of '94. Now he had money, but he was not about to sink his capital into a speculative venture like a new journal. His independence was not yet secured: he got only about a third of the Calvert bequest to start with, the rest being paid out in segments over the next five years. If he could find consol funds that would pay 4 to 7 percent of the whole £900, he would never have to do more than occasional reviewing to maintain himself. Ironically, the removal of the condition that kept him out of the *Philanthropist* project, lack of money, became his prime motive for launching himself into newspaper work, to protect his nest egg. The Calvert bequest, far from relieving Wordsworth from money pressures, determined him to go to work.

He arrived in the city in early February, staying with Mathews at the Middle Temple. On March 16 there appeared the first issue of the small liberal paper called the *Philanthropist.* It ran for eleven months, through January 25, 1796.[9] The *Philanthropist* discussed by Wordsworth and Mathews corresponds very well to the one that actually appeared in London in March 1795. Wordsworth had first broached the idea of "some literary scheme, a project which I have much at heart," in 1792, writing from Blois when he learned that Annette was pregnant. Though he was then sure that he would have to accept a church living (and that his uncles would provide it), he was still interested in possibilities of obtaining "an Independence" from the system of preferments in which he and Mathews and all their college friends were enmeshed.

> The field of Letters is very extensive, and it is astonishing if we cannot find some little corner, which with a little tillage will produce us enough for the necessities, nay even the comforts, of life. . . . [T]ho' I may not be resident in London, I need not therefore be prevented from engaging in any literary plan, which may have the appearance of producing a decent harvest. . . . [N]othing but confidence and resolution is necessary. Fluency in writing will tread fast upon the heels of practice, and elegance and strength will not be far behind. . . . Would it not be possible for you to form an acquaintance with some of the publishing booksellers of London, from whom you might get some hints of what sort of works would be the most likely to answer?[10]

Nothing had happened for two years, but when their correspondence resumed in 1794, it quickly reverted to the topics of politics and journalism. As soon as Mathews brought up again "the possibility of setting on foot a monthly miscellany from which some emolument might be drawn," Wordsworth assured him "most heartily [that he wished] to be engaged in something of that kind."[11] But his motives had changed since 1793 when he penned the "Letter to the Bishop of Llandaff": now he sought political journalism that would *make money.* It does not appear that he ever told Raisley Calvert about the negotiations he was carrying on with William Mathews while he nursed Calvert and his legacy.

Wordsworth and Mathews's *Philanthropist* would be opposed to the "minister's war" with France, and to Pitt's methods of silencing opposition by regulation and intimidation, imprisonment, and banishment. It was obviously to be an opposition paper, but fundamentally a loyal one, and was thus devoted to freedom of the press—which, rather than limit at all, Wordsworth was ready, in the purest Godwinian confidence, to "suffer the most atrocious doctrines to be broached." Wordsworth coolly estimated the small size of their likely audience, dashing Mathews's high hopes of attracting "as great a variety [of readers] as possible." "We must . . . look for protection entirely amongst the dispassionate advocates of liberty and discussion; these whether male or female, we must either amuse or instruct."[12] This included the young men at the universities, the Dissenters "in every town of any size," and those working for independence or reform in Ireland: "I entirely approve of what you say on the subject of Ireland, and think it very proper that an agent should be appointed in Dublin to disseminate the impression." In sum, the *Philanthropist* of Wordsworth and Mathews was to be a reformist, antiwar, nonrevolutionary, and pro-British journal, devoted to improving social justice by increasing political justice, and propagating to a mainly middle-class, educated audience "those doctrines which long and severe meditation [had] taught them are essential for the welfare of mankind."

The proposed *Philanthropist* would have been considered radical in the hysterical climate of political opinion in England in 1795, more so than the one that actually appeared, at least in its initial numbers. For example, the published *Philanthropist* accepted the existence of the king and the aristocracy as being, along with the clergy, "admirably adapted to the genius of the English people." But Wordsworth and Mathews's journal would have been, like Godwin's, philosophically radical, and need not have troubled the powers that be. "A vehicle of sound and exalted Morality," it was devoted to diffusing "by every method a knowledge of [the] rules of political justice" and to expounding principles of "social order applicable to all times and places." Wordsworth's allegiance to Godwin is clear, as is the bias of the actual *Philanthropist* in its early numbers, in such statements as "All improvements [in society] are necessarily slow and progressive."

The name of both the proposed journal and the actual journal was one of the code words of Godwinism, the personified abstraction of his key concept—benevolence. (The actual journal has contributions from two even more literal forms of Godwinian personification, "Benevolus" and "Weldonious.") "Philanthropy" was a fashionable liberal term in the early 1790s, dialectically related to the more unstable term "patriot" (which could be co-opted by all parties at need), and signified a more-than-nationalistic patriotism, "a loyalty to the welfare of mankind."[13] Wordsworth preferred his title to one that Mathews had proposed, which seemed to him "too common to attract attention." It is hard to think of a more common word than "philanthropy" in 1795, but Wordsworth was confident that "this title . . .

would be noticed; it includes everything that can instruct and amuse mankind, and, if we exert ourselves, I doubt not that we shall be able to satisfy the expectations it will raise."[14]

Almost all the differences between their proposed journal and the actually published *Philanthropist* can be accounted for by the inevitable contraction of aims that often occurs when youthful publishing plans encounter the banal realities of printing, finance, and editorial decision making. Wordsworth proposed a monthly miscellany, whereas the published *Philanthropist* was an eight-page penny weekly. But many of the kinds of material Wordsworth proposed for his monthly do appear in the published version. Theirs would "open with the topic of general politics . . . accompanied with such remarks as may forcibly illustrate the tendency of particular doctrines of government; next should follow essays upon morals and manners, and institutions whether social or political."[15] Following these "instructional" essays, Wordsworth proposed a long list of "essays partly for instruction and partly for amusement": biographical papers (arranged in "a series exhibiting the advancement of the human mind in moral knowledge"), reviews of other philanthropical publications, some poetry (but no "original communications" [i.e., unsolicited contributions], to avoid "the trash which infests the magazines"), essays of taste and criticism, works of imagination and fiction, parliamentary debates, and selected state papers. He also mentions essays on painting and gardening, translations from the French and Italian gazettes, and foreign correspondence from Poland and Portugal.

Each number of the published *Philanthropist* had many fewer essays than Wordsworth proposed, but the same kind of essays do appear sequentially in it, and in roughly the same order and proportion as those at the top of Wordsworth's list. Besides essays on general politics, it had several analytical essays illustrating the tendency of particular doctrines of government, and others on social and political institutions generally. Some of these were original essays; others were reprinted from the standard works in the Whig tradition of parliamentary reform (for instance, John Trenchard's *History of Standing Armies in England* and Montesquieu's "On Liberty"). These essays were neither radical nor scurrilous. The early ones especially are clearly written and squarely situated within the Enlightenment tradition of intellectual rhetoric (for example, first principles derived from assumed "facts" about primitive or ancient societies). Their main fault, from a literary point of view, is that they are dull. The *Philanthropist* also published a few essays on morals and manners, and though it has few "biographical papers" other than tributes to victims of Pitt's policies—such as Joseph Gerrald and the other recent transportees—it does contain in its pages honorific references to three of the same figures Wordsworth proposed for his series of biographical sketches: Algernon Sydney, Milton, and Machiavelli.

More than "some" verse, the actual *Philanthropist* contained about 25 percent verse over its life span, most of which would doubtless have been considered "trash" by a horrified Wordsworth—thus contributing much to his later complex arguments about the relationship between a nation's poetry and its moral character. A good deal of the verse *is* scurrilous, and some of it is funny, but little of it is poetry, strictly speaking, being rather parodic satires upon contemporary personages such as "your affectionate fellow-swine, Wm. Pitt," forced into the meter of traditional tunes like "Oh, Dear, What Can the Matter Be?" (Like all liberal journals at the time, the *Philanthropist* never tired of ringing satiric changes upon Burke's sneering reference to "the swinish multitude" of disaffected reformers and their followers.) However, some of its poetry is close in both spirit and language to poems Wordsworth was writing at the same time, particularly his imitation of Juvenal, and more generally his attempts since 1793 to link descriptions of natural beauty to interpretive comments about human suffering.

These parallels indicate that the congruences between Wordsworth's proposed *Philanthropist* and the one that actually appeared are coincidences "too large to pass off in a little cough in a footnote [as] scholars have generally done."[16] And there is more evidence, both external and internal, that corroborates in detail the case for Wordsworth's involvement.

For Mathews and Wordsworth to revive their plans for the *Philanthropist* and get it into print within about six weeks of Wordsworth's arrival in London, there had to be an economic and political climate favorable to such publication, and they would have had to have help. Both of these conditions existed, and the way in which they manifested themselves strengthens the likelihood that Wordsworth did participate in such a project.

He and Mathews still had their enthusiasm, their ideas, and their draft essays. Wordsworth's preference all along had been for the more leisurely measures of periodical publication, rather than the hurly-burly of daily production. There was an unusual window of opportunity in the publishing business as a result of the reformers' apparent victory in the treason trials; a liberalized climate of public opinion prevailed through much of 1795. In actuality the government's scare tactics in the treason trials proved largely successful, and the more knowledgeable reformers began withdrawing from action—wisely, as events showed.* John Thelwall and Thomas Hardy gave

*Home Office records show that the duke of Portland, with his undersecretary John King, William Wickham, head of the new Alien Office, and the Bow Street magistrate Richard Ford, began in January to put into operation an elaborate new system of payrolls and payoffs designed to consolidate Westminster's control over the heretofore loose system of unpaid magistrates, honorary local officials, Bow Street "runners," and informers of all stripes. Wickham's brief as superintendent of aliens was tracking French spies, to which he soon added the innovation of using French spies to find suspicious Englishmen: this strategy would lead the Home Office to Words-

up their membership in the London Corresponding Society and, like Horne Tooke, Holcroft, and Godwin, stopped attending the meetings of any public political society.[17] Thelwall turned his energies to his own lecturing and publishing enterprise, the *Tribune,* but he closed it down in April. The LCS's eight-page weekly, the *Politician,* ceased publishing in January after only a month's run. Thomas Spence's more eccentrically radical *Pig's Meat* also closed down in 1795.

However, all these defections from the cause of reform opened the field for more naive and less experienced writers, especially of a more palatable liberal cast: exactly the profile of the *Philanthropist.* Most fortunately for Wordsworth's and Mathew's plans, Daniel Isaac Eaton's *Politics for the People* ceased appearing in March 1795, and Eaton was the publisher of the *Philanthropist,* which began appearing that same month and which eventually followed the same format as *Politics for the People:* reprinted extracts used to fill up issues when miscellaneous original contributions were insufficient.[18] Eaton's shop, at the jaunty sign of the Cock & Swine, dedicated to "the Supreme Majesty of the People," was at the end of Newgate Street, just before it gave into Cheapside, right round the corner from Wordsworth's publisher, Johnson, and only two streets away from Wood Street, Cateaton Street, and Lad, Love, and Maiden Lanes, Wordsworth's haunts four years earlier. (Coleridge had spent much of January drinking, smoking, and talking with Charles Lamb about similar projects in the snug of the Cat & Salutation in Newgate Street.)[19] These various public groups and private citizens were linked by many personal ties nearly invisible to the historian's eye. Thus, Eaton's son Henry was Thelwall's assistant; Thomas Best, one of the two identifiable writers for the *Philanthropist,* worked with Thelwall on the *Imperial and Biographical Magazine;* and William Mathews first met Godwin at Thelwall's chambers in December.[20]

The greatest obstacle in the way of Wordsworth and Mathews's plans had been money, but an enterprising and fearless publisher like Eaton had the necessary capital investment, and was ready to take on a new organ. At a penny an issue the *Philanthropist* was half the price of *Politics for the People,* but it had the advantage, in a nervous publishing climate, of being by unknown writers who, in its early numbers, held safe opinions about standard liberal issues. The largest single piece of evidence tying Wordsworth and

---

worth and Coleridge in 1797. The complicated budget and payment arrangements needed for "the establishment of your office" present a picture of a government extremely worried about internal subversion and possible overthrow. See PRO HO/65/1, *Police Entry Books, Series I: 1795–1921,* vol. 1 *(1795–1811);* Bernard Porter, *Plots and Paranoia: A History of Political Espionage in Britain, 1790–1988* (London: Unwin Hyman, 1989), 29–31. The year 1795 was a very busy one for the new intelligence system; its entries take up eighty pages in this volume, while the years 1796–99 altogether take up only seventy-five pages.

Mathews's *Philanthropist* to the one published by Eaton is not a stylistic or verbal parallel, but the fact that Wordsworth had proposed to Mathews that they "communicate to each other a sufficient portion of matter to compose at least two numbers . . . of general not temporary nature." The first four issues of the *Philanthropist* are exactly that: single-essay issues on the uses of talent (no. 1), the freedom of the press (no. 2), and the Glorious Revolution of 1688 (no. 4). The exception is no. 3, which turns away (with a great show of annoyance) from inculcating "truths of a very pressing and important nature" to "the political concerns of the day": the defeat of Fox's recent motion against continuing the war. The first two of these topics are strongly represented in Wordsworth's letters: he mentions freedom of speech directly in relation to the *Philanthropist,* and the uses of talent was a leitmotif throughout all his letters to Mathews about what they should do with their lives.

Even with their enthusiasm and ready copy, however, Wordsworth and Mathews could hardly have run such an enterprise on their own. Since the reopening of Parliament on December 30, Mathews was much engaged in covering the session, and had little time to make contacts. They needed help. Mathews's father was a bookseller, but he dealt mainly in religious books and was too pious for such an undertaking. Wordsworth could write, though his prose would have needed heavy editing for the *Philanthropist*'s direct approach, and his business skills were negligible. In the earlier stages of their planning, a young Irishman named Henry Burleigh (b. 1772) had been assisting Mathews. Wordsworth had read Burleigh's declaration of political principles with pleasure and looked forward to meeting him, but we hear no more of him in London, though he probably lived with his brother in Lincoln's Inn, where most of Wordsworth's London friends also resided.*

Our first definite piece of evidence for Wordsworth's whereabouts in London in 1795 points directly to a source for the help he and Mathews needed. It was a gathering of some of the most radical intellectual writers of the day, quite the most famous company he had yet entered, if we exclude his acquaintance with Brissot, Grégoire, Beaupuy, and Gorsas in France. It

*Burleigh was one of several intriguing Irish connections in the project. Mathews's editor at the *Telegraph,* James Joseph McDonnell, admitted to the Middle Temple in 1793 along with Mathews, was another (*LEY,* 135, n. 1). Wordsworth included the Irish in his estimate of the *Philanthropist*'s necessarily small audience, and he was ready—like Shelley a generation later—to make a voyage to Dublin, "which may be done at any time from this place [Whitehaven]," if Mathews thought it would do any good. The epigraph to the *Philanthropist*'s first essay was addressed to Earl Fitzwilliam, the liberal lord lieutenant of Ireland who had been recalled at the end of February. The condition of Ireland represented, for young intellectual liberals in England, the closest thing to an absolutist tyranny in their own backyard, with real potential for violent revolution on the French model. Hence it became a test of their political commitment, somewhat as the condition of blacks in the southern United States was a rallying point for young white liberal northerners in the 1960s.

took place on February 27, at the Buckingham Street lodgings (off the Strand) of William Frend, the popular former Cambridge don whose 1793 trial for heresy had ended with his dismissal from the university. This tea party, as recorded in Godwin's diary, has all the marks of a meeting for some kind of political publishing venture. Except for Thelwall, who was not present, it is hard to imagine a more radical group of intellectuals than those present that night: "the center of political disaffection was to be found somewhere within this circle."[21]

All the younger men at Frend's gathering were from Cambridge, slightly older than Wordsworth, but still at university when he arrived, and several of them had won university honors or medals: James Losh, John Tweddell, Jonathan Raine, Thomas Edwards, Godfrey Higgins, and William French.[22] Most were now reading for the law, and all had a lively interest in periodical publications. Tweddell had published his brilliant classical *Prolusiones Juveniles* in 1793, and was an outspoken admirer of the French experiment. He was the member of their Cambridge set whom Wordsworth most often inquired after in his correspondence with Mathews. Losh was an older brother of Wordsworth's Hawkshead classmate and was probably known to Wordsworth from Paris, where a crowd had nearly executed him because his fine head of hair made him look like an aristocrat. (He was saved by the personal intervention of Marat, who knew Losh's family from the years he had spent as a medical lecturer in Newcastle, Penrith, and Carlisle in the early 1770s.)[23] There is evidence that Losh and Wordsworth shared a rough Channel crossing back to England in late 1792.[24] At the moment, Losh was busy raising money to pay for the expenses of the treason trial's defendants. After returning north in 1797, he briefly published a cautiously liberal farmer's almanac called the *OEconomist.* Raine was another northerner, from Northumberland (like Tweddell), had been one of Frend's lawyers, and was the son of Tweddell's old schoolmaster. Edwards was a fellow of Jesus College, where he had befriended Coleridge; in the next year he would help Coleridge in the production and circulation of his short-lived *Watchman.* Higgins was a Yorkshireman who had come to Cambridge in Wordsworth's last year there; he would shortly inherit his family's estates and devote himself to writings on religion, lunatic asylums, and the reform of the Corn Laws. French was the only one in orders, but was currently a teacher in his father's school at Bow.

More important for our scenario were the four older men at the gathering: Frend, Godwin, Thomas Holcroft, and George Dyer, all highly experienced and successful polemicists in the pamphlet wars of the day. Godwin (b. 1758) was then at "the very zenith" of his "temporary fame" (as he later saw it), blazing "as a sun in the firmament of reputation," "in a degree that has seldom been exceeded."[25] The intellectual success of *Political Justice* had been followed in 1794 by the popular success of his novel, *Things as They Are; or, Caleb Williams,* an attack on England's legal and penal system that was at the same time one of the earliest and most compelling English novels of psychological disintegration. This had been followed later in the year by the polemical success of his *Cursory Strictures,* on the government's conduct of the treason trials, which Horne Tooke credited equally with Thomas Erskine's courtroom brilliance for securing acquittal. By the end of 1795 Godwin's star would begin to dip, when he published a pamphlet in November daring to suggest that radicals must bear some responsibility for provoking the government into passing the repressive "gagging acts." But in February he was still the most famous intellectual in London, and the most admired by all friends of liberty.

Thomas Holcroft (1745–1809), whom Godwin considered one of his best composition teachers—along with Coleridge, Dyer, and Joseph Fawcett—had become a defendant in the treason trials by the headline-grabbing strategy of turning himself in and demanding to be arrested. An early example of what we now call a publicist, with very much the same profile as many of the underworld hacks who became leaders in the French Revolution, he had for twenty years turned his hand profitably to every kind of literary journeyman work: adapting *Les Liaisons dangereuses* for the London stage (*Seduction,* 1787), translating Beaumarchais's *The Marriage of Figaro* by memorizing successive performances in Paris, writing the most popular play of the times (*The Road to Ruin,* 1792), and, inter alia, tossing off a sharp review of Wordsworth's *An Evening Walk* and *Descriptive Sketches* in 1793. In 1780 he coauthored a novel with Wordsworth's London friend and host Samuel Nicholson.[26] Translation was his bread and butter, especially from French. When the introductions were made, Holcroft looked sharply at this young William from Cockermouth. He was thinking of his own dead son, William, also born there, three years after Wordsworth, during a period of three years when Holcroft lived in Cockermouth as a singer and player in an itinerant theater company, and well aware of the powerful establishment position held by Wordsworth's father.[27]

Dyer (1755–1841) was a close friend of Wordsworth's revered schoolmaster William Taylor. He averaged nearly a book a year through the 1790s on all the most timely liberal topics: the price of bread, the treatment of convicts, the theory and practice of benevolence, the Test Acts, the British doctrine of libel, plus assorted odes, elegies, and dialogues. He was also the author of a biography (published 1796) of another Cambridge liberal, Robert Robinson (d. 1790), which Wordsworth exaggeratedly declared "the best biography in the English language";[28] extracts from Robinson's earnestly satirical *Political Catechism* (1784) are reprinted several times in the *Philanthropist.*

A gathering such as this inevitably turned its conversation to writing for publication, and Wordsworth's ready-formed plans and opinions for his *Philanthropist* would have been eagerly seized upon for their flattering congruence with Godwin's rationalist ideology. But this tea party was not an isolated occasion. Both before and after the publication of *Political Justice,* Godwin was an ardent member of a small debating club called the Philomathean Society ("lovers of learning"); he and Holcroft had to be timed with a small hourglass to keep them within the fifteen-minute time limit for speeches.[29] Given Godwin's passion for "colloquial discussion," which turned any social encounter into a kind of seminar (Lamb called him "the Professor"), the February 27 tea party can plausibly be regarded as a version of a meeting of this group.[30] A publication called the *Philanthropist* can with equal plausibility be considered one of its likely activities, of the sort that Wordsworth had in mind when he proposed to Mathews that they circulate their essays and look for financial and editorial support "entirely amongst the dispassionate advocates of liberty and discussion," and "by no means neglect to stir up our friends to favour us with any papers which a wish to add to the stock of general knowledge may induce them to write."[31]

The likelihood of some such group effort is increased when we hear Wordsworth asking Mathews, when he wrote back to London from the tranquillity of Racedown in 1796, about the proceedings of "the society": "Pray write to me at length and give me an account of your proceedings in the society.... Are your members much encreased? and what is of more consequence have you improved I do not ask in the [art] of speaking, but in the more important one of thinking?"[32] His phrasing implies a group of which he was a member (as *"the* proceedings in *your* society" would not), or at least an occasional attender, and the substance of his question implies a relatively small group, not a large one like the London Corresponding Society. His last crack shows bluntly how taxing the young Wordsworth's friendship could be on its recipients.

Alternatively, the society may have been the Cannonian club, named after its founder, an elderly Irishman of bohemian habits, which was attended by Samuel Nicholson, a good friend of Godwin's and Holcroft's, who had taken Wordsworth under his wing when he first came to London in 1791 and who continued to invite him for dinners in 1795.[33] Nicholson had been a member, as had George Dyer, of the Society for Constitutional Information, the polite precursor of the London Corresponding Society, whose "Address to the Public" was extensively reprinted in the *Philanthropist*'s pages in May and June. The ubiquitous Holcroft also attended the Cannonian club, and Nicholson's brother William, who was business agent for Coleridge's benefactors the Wedgwoods, edited a small publication called the *Philosophical Journal*.[34]

In sum, a wide variety of support groups were available for young men like Wordsworth seeking help for liberal publishing ventures in 1795, "the last, and the greatest, period of popular agitation" in the eighteenth century.[35] Hazlitt remembered it as the time when "the doctrine of Universal Benevolence, the belief in the Omnipotence of Truth and in the Perfectibility of Human Nature . . . were whispered in secret, were published in quarto and duodecimo, in political treatises, in plays, poems, songs, and romances." In short, when Godwinism was triumphant, and Wordsworth was in the thick of it.[36]

Among the four senior figures present on February 27, Dyer and Frend were the most likely aiders and abettors of the younger men, though we should not rule out tough practical lessons in street journalism from Holcroft. Dyer was a particularly generous encourager of liberal young writers. Coleridge wrote letters to him at this time that sound like verbatim copies of Wordsworth's eager letters to Mathews, particularly one postmarked March 10, six days before the appearance of the first issue of the *Philanthropist,* in which Coleridge asks, "Is it possible that I could gain an employment in this new work, the Citizen?"[37] This proposed *Citizen* never appeared, but the *Philanthropist* could have been substituted as safer title for the "new work," based on Wordsworth's and Mathews's suggestion. There are more than enough parallels between the style and content of Dyer's voluminous writings and the *Philanthropist* to suggest that he could have been a kindly supervisory master of the work. Any help from Holcroft would have been harder to take, and he was not shy of offering it. When Coleridge was asked if he was not much struck with Holcroft, he replied that "he thought himself in more danger of being struck *by* him," complaining that Holcroft "barricadoed the road to truth . . . setting up a turnpike-gate at every step" by requiring you to define even the commonest words: " 'What do you mean by a *sensation,* Sir? What do you mean by an *idea?'* "[38] Wordsworth, outwardly taciturn but inwardly volatile, could not have endured such treatment for long and might have left the room to avoid striking Holcroft himself. These men favored a much simpler, more direct and overtly polemical style of periodical prose than is represented in Wordsworth's contemporaneous writing. Given Holcroft's published opinions, apt though harsh, on Wordsworth's poetry of 1793, any advice from him would have cut very close to the bone if applied to Wordsworth's prose in 1795.

When Wordsworth wrote back to Mathews from Racedown in early 1796 about two of their London associates, he did so in terms of their *style* and his Olympian disapproval of it: "I have received . . . Godwyn's [*sic*] second edition. I expect to find the work much improved. I cannot say that I have been encouraged in this hope by the perusal of the second preface. . . . Such a piece of barbarous writing I have not often seen. It contains scarce one sentence decently written. I am surprized to find such gross faults in a writer who has had so much practise in composition. . . . I have attempted to read Holcroft's *Man of Ten Thousand,* but such stuff! Demme hey, humph!"[39] The last exclamation quotes the blustering speech mannerism of the play's comic lead, Major Rampart, which Holcroft had specifically defended in the play's preface. The "Humphs?" and "Heys?" had been omitted in performance "because they offended" (they were a well-known feature of George III's conversation), but were restored in print "and left to the consideration of the reader." In Wordsworth's consideration, this attempt to represent natural speech patterns did not succeed, and Holcroft's play was, besides, a very unstable mixture of social satire and social conscience.[40] But Wordsworth's damning of Godwin's preface to the second edition of *Political Justice* by calling its style "barbarous" is quite gratuitous; Godwin could say outrageous things, but he almost always said them with extreme clarity.[41] No, something other than dispassionate literary judgment motivated Wordsworth's remark about the man whom, a year earlier, he had gladly called his mentor, and whose style and intellectual manner of proceeding he followed scrupulously in setting forth his plans for the *Philanthropist.*

The circumstances of the published *Philanthropist*'s production suggest a good deal of instability in editorial control. It was a reckless vehicle, obviously in flux politically, a battleground on which liberals and radicals fought for ascendancy, first one, then the other, winning control for the space of a few issues. This would have terrific ramifications for Wordsworth, who initiated the idea, only to suffer the indignity of seeing it wrested out of his control.

Five distinct phases of editorial policy can be identified during its short existence. The first two phases are the most Godwinian, unexceptionally liberal: this was its period of high-minded moral journalism, from the first issue through the fourth (April 6). After its fourth number, the *Philanthropist* interrupted its regular publication schedule for three weeks, suggesting a sudden lack of available copy. When it resumed again, on April 27, it began printing smaller pieces sent in by contributors, just the sort of "reliance on any accidental assistance" which Wordsworth said they should avoid. Contributors had been asked to send their "favours (post paid) to the Editors," but now this call, printed at the end of each issue, was changed to the singular "Editor."[42] This may suggest that Eaton had resumed command, his amateur enthusiasts having spent themselves. After another three issues, it fell back on Eaton's practice in *Politics for the People* of filling whole issues with reprints from older works, a sure sign of flagging contributions. The next three months are an unstable period, from April 27 (no. 5) through July 13 (no. 16), in which some provocative antiwar and anticlerical satires in nos. 5–7 are counterbalanced, as if correctively, by nine numbers given over almost entirely to reprints from the Society for Constitutional Information's "Address to the People" and from Trenchard's *History of Standing Armies.*

The third period, from late July to late October, is the *Philanthropist*'s radical phase, containing scurrilous attacks on government policies and personages, defenses of convicted traitors like Gerrald, and, most dangerously, celebrations of French victories. Pertinent to our story here is the fact that Wordsworth abruptly left London in mid-August, probably by the 18th, and that the editor's call for contributions ceased being printed after August 24. The fourth period, like the second, is a mixed one, and also begins after a temporary hiatus in publication (on October 26) and runs into early December. These numbers are marked by contributions which refer to, and disagree with, each other, suggesting that contributors' wrangling had supplanted any firm editorial policy. The journal's endgame begins on December 14 (no. 37), with an issue given over to an essay by "W." Alas for confirmatory evidence, this is not Wordsworth but the code initial of a contributor to the Norwich *Cabinet,* one Dr. Rigby, "a thorough-going Democrat of the French type."[43] But Rigby's essay, "On the Influence of Some Human Institutions on Human Happiness," confirms the direction of the *Philanthropist*'s development, for it is implicitly a rejection of the journal's original attraction to Godwinian necessarianism. This essay was followed until the last two issues by a turgid, anonymous, serial essay titled "REASONS Why the People Are the Best Keepers of Their Own LIBERTIES," which though republican is relatively innocuous, being a historical analysis of the Roman model. (The title was a conventional formula in republican arguments, employed by Kant among others, and Wordsworth's "Letter to Llandaff" shows he was also conversant in its use: "I shall be told that the people are not the proper judges of their own welfare.") These late numbers obviously betray an attempt to keep the journal outside the scope of Pitt's recently passed "gagging acts." But the end was clearly in sight. The *Philanthropist* finishes at no. 43, with an index which scrupulously records all its contributions, though it is still six weeks away from its first anniversary.

Wordsworth's movements in London correlate suggestively with this account of the *Philanthropist*'s development. He visited Godwin at weekly or biweekly intervals during the spring and summer of these "puzzling lost months," a highly relevant circumstance when connected to the appearance of so Godwinian a publication as the *Philanthropist.*[44] Godwin's scrupulous diary shows that Wordsworth called on him six times between late February and late April, twice with Mathews alone, and once with Joseph Fawcett accompanying them. The first of these visits was on the day after the February 27 gathering at Frend's rooms. The next five were in March (10, 25, 31) and April (9, 22). By then it had become very easy for Wordsworth to call on Godwin: he had moved into rooms at 15 Charlton Street in

Somers Town (near the present St. Pancras Station), just a few doors away from Godwin, who lived at no. 25.[45] Of these five March–April visits, four are on Tuesday or Wednesday: that is, a day or two after the *Philanthropist*'s normal publication day, which was Monday. The first Tuesday, March 10, was the one before the *Philanthropist* commenced appearing, and probably saw a meeting of the Philomathean Society, which met fortnightly on Tuesdays. On that day, when Wordsworth breakfasted with him, Godwin recorded the Philomathean Society's discussion topic as "soldier vs. priest." Wordsworth's interest in the topic, which he may have proposed, derived from his close association and friendship in France with General Beaupuy and Bishop Grégoire.[46]

After late April there is a long hiatus in Wordsworth's visits to Godwin. Godwin left London after April 22, not to return until July. If he was in any way lending his advice or authority to the journal, his absence may well have made possible the brief spurt of polemical satires that burst into it in April–May. Such satires smacked of inflammatory addresses to the passions of the people, which both Godwin and Wordsworth wished to avoid. After he returned to London, Godwin recorded four attempted meetings with Wordsworth in July (14, 29) and August (15, 18), all but the third *his* calling on Wordsworth. Only the first of these was successful; for the rest, Godwin wrote "nah" (not at home) in his diary. But that one visit may be significant, for it was the day after the *Philanthropist*'s last safely liberal appearance: its radical phase began with no. 17, on July 20. By August 18 Wordsworth had left London for Bristol. The cooling of relations between Godwin and Wordsworth at this time could be explained by the *Philanthropist*'s leftward lurch and misunderstandings as to who was responsible for it.

In the *Philanthropist*'s early essays there are several resemblances and parallels to Wordsworth's other writings and experiences—though we should keep in mind that little of his prose would have been published without considerable editing.[47] The four essays that filled the first four issues, each issue consisting of a single essay, are the most likely to have been contributed by Wordsworth and Mathews. These essays are wholly Godwinian in temper and tendency, commiserating the state of the poor, deploring the frustrations of talent dependent upon patronage, and generally manifesting the Whig interpretation of English history. But it is in the third number, where the *Philanthropist* turns with an almost comically literal tone of regret "from his original plan and intention" to current events, that we discern language close to Wordsworth's policies for his proposed journal. "It was the intention of the Philanthropist to have proceeded in a regular discussion of *those subjects,* which involve in their consideration the rights, and happiness, of man, and not to have engaged the attention of the public with the political concerns of the day, till he had *enforced,* and inculcated some truths of a very pressing, and important nature" (3.1). This, stating the reverse of what the writer would really prefer to do, uses the same language for the "duty" of such a journal that Wordsworth had used with Mathews the previous summer: "There is a further duty incumbent upon every enlightened friend of mankind; he should let slip no opportunity of explaining and *enforcing those general principles* of the social order which are applicable to all times and to all places."[48] Wordsworth's statement comes in the middle of his critique of the ministry's lack of "oeconomy in the administration of the public purse . . . abuses which, if left to themselves, may grow to such a height as to render, even a revolution desirable." The next issue of the *Philanthropist* returns to exactly that point, telling the king's ministers that if they do not merit the public trust by keeping "the administration of public affairs just, pure, and uncontaminated," they had better warn their royal master about his throne's security: "AS IT WAS WON TO HIM BY ONE REVOLUTION, HE MAY LOSE IT BY ANOTHER" (4.7).

The *Philanthropist*'s first essay, on talent, deserves closest scrutiny, for it is the use and nature of talent, and its differentiation from the greater quality of genius, that forms the leitmotif of Wordsworth's writings throughout the 1790s. Points of contact and congruence between this essay and Wordsworth are abundant, though Mathews, a stickler for smooth, clear prose, may have been its final polisher. It turns on the rhetorical pivot that the world's neglect of talent is paralleled by society's neglect of suffering humanity. It asks why God gave man talent, and answers: "to inspire him with a sense of the dignity which he sustained in the creation, to teach him the duties which were due to him from his God, to himself, and to his species, and thus, by awakening within him all those benevolent sympathies . . . which animate to [*sic*] philanthropy . . . to bind him to his fellow-creatures in social charities, and in endearing intercourse" (1.1–2). This perfectly Godwinian thesis is launched from the antithesis that talent should not be coerced or impeded, or "its radiance . . . obscured in darkness." Such motives are not attributed to anyone in particular but are likely to have been perceived as a general condition by liberal young gentlemen in 1795, especially that one who had enthusiastically thrown himself into London's "mighty gulph which has swallowed up so many, of talents and attainments infinitely superior to my own." The implicit subtext of the *Philanthropist*'s first essay is, If only I could be great, humanity could be too. It is no disservice to *The Prelude* to say that its subtext is the same.

Wordsworth was a keen connoisseur of talent, his own and others', and, like the author of the first *Philanthropist* essay, of their operational effectiveness: "It is an observation to whose truth I have long since consented that small certainties are the bane of great talents." This lordly Johnsonian sentence was written to Mathews in 1791; four years of enforced consent to it had forced Wordsworth to extend its application. There are few topics to which he adverts more frequently in the mid-1790s. We hear him saying to Mathews, obviously projecting his own self-image, "You . . . are furnished with talents and acquirements which if properly made use of will enable you to get your bread. . . . You have the happiness of being born in a free country, where every road is open, where talents and industry are . . . liberally rewarded" (May 19, 1792); "if you could depend on the talents, and above all the industry of the young man [Burleigh] you speak of, I think we three would be quite sufficient with our best exertions to keep alive such a publication" (May 23, 1794); "Coleridge was at Bristol . . . his talent appears to me very great" (October 24, 1795). The free exertion of one's talents was a highly political issue throughout the late eighteenth century, as an old order based on patronage was breaking up in favor of—to use Napoleon's exemplary formula for it—"the career open to talent." Like the *Philanthropist*'s lament over the impediments to talent, Wordsworth's prefatory essay to *The Borderers* (1796) indicates that he had come by then to consider less optimistic viewpoints, and in the same dialectics of philanthropy versus misanthropy: "Let us suppose a young man of great intellectual powers yet without any solid principles of *genuine benevolence.* His master passions are pride and the love of distinction. . . . His talents are robbed of their weight, his exertions are unavailing, and he quits the world in disgust, *with strong misanthropic feelings"* (italics added).

In this context the *Philanthropist* tries to establish a connection between natural beauty and moral beauty, which Wordsworth pursued in almost all his poetry between 1793 and 1798. But the *Philanthropist* is no more successful than Wordsworth, except to assert the talented individual's *wish* to do good. Like Wordsworth, the *Philanthropist* locates the real tragedy of poverty in its subjective mental effects, "the tyrannies which have been exercised over the human mind itself."

> What a gloomy picture . . . is presented to us of the human mind! —We behold the understanding, the genius and the intellect of man prostrated, as it were, before the shrine of the most abominable idols! We behold every faculty of the soul enchained, its best powers either totally annihilated, or perverted to promote the most despicable views of power, rapacity, and ambition! (1.2)

Reading this gloomy history, the writer knows not whether he "ought the more to commiserate the fortune of a people depressed and enslaved . . . or to execrate the remorseless authors of their afflictions, their sufferings, and their persecutions!" On the basis of what he wrote to Mathews before coming to London, Wordsworth in early 1795 was still disposed toward execrating persecutors, but he very soon turned to his more lasting vein of commiseration with victims. In his lines on the Female Vagrant he had already begun exploring the mental perversions caused by poverty. She, "robb'd of [her] perfect mind," says her tale "would thy brain unsettle even to hear." Her worst suffering is the same as that envisioned in the first *Philanthropist* essay: "what afflicts my peace with keenest ruth / Is, that I have my inner self abused, / Forgone the home delight of constant truth / And clear and open soul, so prized in fearless youth" (258–61).

A connection between the *Philanthropist*'s attack on the profligate luxury of the upper classes and Wordsworth's later attack on the gaudy splendor of poetic diction is plausible in light of the very special reasons the first essay gives for the failure of the English rich to appreciate the condition of the English poor: "They read of the afflictions of their fellow-creatures, as they would amuse themselves with a tale or a romance, and they pity the unfriended child of want, perishing for a morsel of bread, as they would pity the desponding and lovelorn hero of the piece, or the unfortunate virgin confined by necromancy in some enchanted castle" (1.6). This is incisive literary criticism in the service of strong social criticism. The larger point, peculiar to what Wordsworth will argue later, is not merely that the rich regard the sufferings of the poor like something in a book but that they do not understand its significance because they "read" it like a *bad* book: steeped in vapid tales of Sensibility or escapist Gothic novels, they fail to see the reality around them. It is but a small step in content, though a large one in sophisticated context, from this argument to Wordsworth's lament in the 1800 preface that "the invaluable works" of Shakespeare and Milton "are driven into neglect by frantic novels, sickly and stupid German tragedies, and deluges of idle and extravagant stories in verse," and thence to his suggestive assertion that a "healthy or depraved . . . public taste" affects "the revolutions not of literature alone but likewise of society itself" because of the manner in which "language and the human mind act and react on each other."

In contrast to those who read about poverty as an item in romance, the *Philanthropist,* like Wordsworth more or less continuously since 1791, has gone out to see for himself: "The children of fortune and of affluence, have seldom leisure or inclination *to contemplate so melancholy a picture* . . . . But there are some hearts made to sympathize with those that suffer. To some minds it is a *pleasing, though melancholy office,* to leave the sunshine of prosperity, to view awhile amid the gloom of hard necessity and want, the scene of wretchedness in which thousands of their race are engaged" (1.6–7; italics added). This is very close to Wordsworth's statement "The sorrow I feel from *the contemplation of this melancholy picture is not unconsoled by a comfortable hope* that the class of wretches called mendicants will not much longer shock the feelings of humanity" ("Llandaff," 460–63; italics added).

Finally, coming full circle on its central theme, the link between the terrible mental pains of poverty and the suffering endured by talented minds who would justify their gifts by service to mankind, the *Philanthropist*'s first essay concludes with a poem, "Address to Poverty." In no other issue are prose text and poetic text so integrated. Though we may strain to hear a Wordsworthian note in its rhymed couplets, the quality of the verse is not much below that of the "Address to the Ocean" and the "Address to Silence," which he wrote in the coming year, and is somewhat above that of the framing narratives in the Salisbury Plain poem of 1793–95, which also concentrate on the mental effect of unwarranted suffering, in ways and words that have close parallels in the *Philanthropist.*

This "Address" is structured, like the Neoclassical odes of Gray and Collins, around a long introductory afflatus telling a personified figure of Poverty what " 'tis not" in its reign that causes the speaker to mourn: not looks of anguish, famished limbs, or even "that voice, whose melancholy tale / Might turn the purple cheek of grandeur pale." Halfway through, it comes to the point of Poverty's real evil: "But chief, relentless Power, thy hard controul, / *That to the earth bends low* the aspiring soul, / Thine iron grasp, thy fetters drear, which bind / *Each generous effort of the struggling mind!*" This is close in theme, image, and rhyme to one of Wordsworth's perorations in the "Salisbury Plain" lines of 1793–94, similarly addressed to a personified abstraction, "Oppression": "How many by inhuman toil debased, / Abject, obscure, *and brute to earth incline* / Unrespited, forlorn of *every spark divine*?" (*SP,* 439–41; italics added.) As these excerpts make clear, there is little if anything to distinguish between Wordsworth's poem and the *Philanthropist*'s on the basis of artistic quality.*

It may be objected that most of this, prose and poetry alike, does not sound much like Wordsworth's style, however close it may be to his literary and political concerns. Indeed it does not: compared to the turgid "Letter to Llandaff," the *Philanthropist*'s first essays are much clearer and more to the point, though their strident exclamations sometimes are less effective than Wordsworth's sardonic brooding. However, the difficulty of proving Words-

*A similar poem on the evils of poetry, signed "Philanthropos," without the special focus on its mental damages, appeared in the *Oracle* on December 25, 1794. The *Oracle* was the paper Mathews worked on until he jumped to the *Telegraph* on December 30. Also in late 1794, Eaton's *Politics for the People* published a long blank verse poem titled "The Effects of War" by a "Philanthropos." This poem, focusing on "the wretched hovel" of a starving laborer's family, has been compared to Wordsworth's "The Ruined Cottage," but it lacks Wordsworth's concentration on his heroine's mental disintegration (Michael Saivener, *Poetry and Reform* [Detroit: Wayne State Univ. Press, 1992], 86). However, in making a transition from its pathetically exaggerated description of the dying mother to some hopes of improvement, this poem invokes the name of "HOWARD . . . -Heaven's messenger / To poverty distrest," the same prison reformer Wordsworth alludes to in "The Convict." It could be that "Philanthropos" was Mathews and that the *Philanthropist*'s "Address to Poverty" is his work, intensified by the newly arrived Wordsworth's increasing interest in the effects of suffering on the mind.

worth's authorship, or partial authorship, of these and other parts of the *Philanthropist* is part and parcel of the hypothesis which makes his involvement in the enterprise plausible. Proving it requires that we abandon the convenient fiction of single, or even unitary, authorship. Wordsworth was certainly not a consistent sum of political opinions and literary options in 1795 (if he ever was), and neither was the *Philanthropist.*

Besides Godwinian overtones, there are other echoes between the *Philanthropist* and Wordsworth's known writings of this period, not only in subject matter, vocabulary, and imagery but also in special turns of argument that are characteristic of him. They are too numerous to present in detail, but their general outline and particular resonances can quickly be suggested. Parallels in mere subject matter are legion, as we would expect, given the common discourse of so many journals of the day on these topics. Wordsworth and the *Philanthropist* expressed essentially identical views on the wages of the poor, the freedom of the press, the length of legislative terms, the value of enlightenment (especially as provided by the educated classes to the uneducated), the malignancy of frustrated talent, and the expectable boisterousness of the French people after their sudden release from tyranny. On more particular subjects, we find them both similarly interested in fluctuations in the price of bread; the situation of discharged veterans and of widows left destitute by husbands gone to seek work or pressed into military service, including one in "a sea-port town in the north of England" who was denied an annuity promised by her husband's murderer (13.1–2); and deep ambivalence toward the victories of the French general Pichegru in the Low Countries (23.4–5)—an important stage in Wordsworth's growing disillusionment with the Revolution.[49]

The *Philanthropist*'s first, high-minded period is where we find the greatest number of verbal parallels to Wordsworth's known writings, all with about the same order of similarity as between these sardonic belittlements of Burke: "the futile, and danger-brooding imagination of Mr. Burke may draw . . . many pathetic and many frightful descriptions" (*Philanthropist,* 4:5); "Mr. Burke, in a philosophic lamentation over the extinction of Chivalry . . . rouzed the indignation of all ranks of men" ("Llandaff," 629–31). Burke was of course a standard target for liberal and radical journals, but some of the other verbal and topical parallels are even closer, as "The tawdry lustre which shines around Kings" (*Philanthropist,* 5:2) and "[The nobility] have presumed that lustre which they suppose thrown about them" ("Llandaff," 505–11); or "I reverence Kings only . . . when they are virtuous" and "The office of king is trial to which human virtue is not equal."

Other topics discussed in similar language include lack of admiration for the "fabric" of the British constitution (2.6–7; *LEY,* 123–24); freedom of the press as a bulwark in battle (2.2–4; *LEY,* 125); demagogic bishops compared to Peter the Hermit in analogies between the French Revolution and the Crusades (6.2–3; "Llandaff," 666–70); state ministers chosen for sycophancy as in the decadent Orient (7.6; "Llandaff," 363–79); and the parallel decline of both rich and poor as a result of the war with France: "How many honest, and flourishing families in the course of the last two years have been plunged into the most dreadful abyss of bankruptcy, want, and penury? How many unfriended wretches have been turned loose on the mercy of mankind? (3.3). Compare Wordsworth's "The Ruined Cottage": ". . . many rich / Sunk down as in a dream among the poor, / And of the poor did many cease to be, / And their place knew them not."[50]

When it resumed publication on April 27, the *Philanthropist* introduced verse, the sort of "trash" that Wordsworth hoped to avoid in his venture with Mathews by allowing no "original communications," only reprints. Did they abandon this decidedly conservative editorial policy and try to control the journal's productions in this department by using their own compositions? The sonnet from "Sylvanus Amicus" in no. 7 suggests as much. Its pseudonym, some of its lines, and even its verb tenses point toward the Wordsworth of later reputation:

> Who but must feel his indignation strong,
> On Nature's honest, broad, and gen'ral plan,
> Against that head, that heart, that hand, that tongue,
> Which makes mankind a foe to fellow-man?
>
> (7.8; lines 5–8)

Compare:

> If I these thoughts may not prevent,
> If such be of my creed the plan,
> Have I not reason to lament
> What man has made of man?
>
> ("Lines Written in Early Spring,"
> lines 21–24)[51]

The connection between apparent design in nature and its obvious frustration in society was a commonplace in eighteenth-century sentimental morality. Thelwall has been suggested as a more likely author for these lines, another incarnation of the "Sylvanus Theophrastus" of his own earlier journal, the *Peripatetic.* The resonant last line, with a sentiment as old as human history, had also recently appeared in the epigraph to Godwin's best-selling 1794 novel, *Things as They Are:* "Amidst the woods the leopard knows his kind; / The tyger preys not on the tyger brood: / Man only is the common foe of man." But any combination of these possibilities links Wordsworth closer to these writers and their politics than many of his admirers would like to have him, and one of them puts him squarely among those trying to publish—and maintain control of—the *Philanthropist.*

Wordsworth departed from Godwin's neighborhood in Charlton Street at the end of April; the move also marked a change in his friendship with Mathews. He did not move back in with Mathews at the Middle Temple, but returned to the Inns of Court and began moving in other directions with other friends. Mathews served as his entrée to this group, but soon found himself excluded from it. Wordsworth took up lodgings at Lincoln's Inn with Basil Montagu, another outstanding Cambridge contemporary, of exactly Wordsworth's age. They were drawn together by their shared opposition to the war and the government; Montagu was also now regularly exchanging visits with Godwin.[52] He was the acknowledged illegitimate son of the fourth earl of Sandwich, whose country house near Cambridge had been a favorite place of resort for undergraduate parties from the university. His mother was the polite society singer Martha Ray, who had been shot to death outside Covent Garden in 1779 by an estranged lover, the Reverend James Hackman, a friend of Boswell's.[53] It was one of the great scandals of the era, given a second life in a transparent "novelization" titled *Love and Madness* (1786) by the Reverend Herbert Croft, an aristocratic clergyman hard up for money.[54] Wordsworth rather tactlessly used her name for the distraught mother in "The Thorn" who has murdered her child, but much of his early association with Montagu did involve questions about the right and wrong way to raise children. Montagu had married against his father's wishes and found himself disinherited on his father's death in 1792, his young wife died from childbirth complications in early 1793, and he was at this time beginning with difficulty what would become an outstanding career as a lawyer while taking care of his son, Basil Caroline, named after his parents. Wordsworth's interest was piqued by a man-child named Caroline whose birthdate was December 27, 1792, approximately two weeks after "Caroline Williams" (the surname adopted by Annette), and his sympathy naturally went out to a young father whose elders had, like Wordsworth's, been willing to ruin his prospects because they disapproved of his marriage. That he should give Montagu's natural mother's name to the unwed infanticide mother of "The Thorn" strongly suggests a deep psychological empathy with Montagu's situation.

Montagu's own habits were those of a dissolute and irregular young aristocrat, and in his unpublished autobiography he gave credit to Wordsworth's slow steadiness and apparent maturity for saving him from ruin. "He saw me . . . perplexed and misled by passions wild and strong. In the wreck of my happiness he saw the probable ruin of my infant. He unremittingly . . . endeavoured to eradicate my faults and encourage my good dispositions."[55] Montagu was also chronically in need of money. In 1793 he had been the beneficiary of a bequest of £700 from his former college tutor.[56] But he had run through it all, and was now in the habit of borrowing money from the wealthy pupils he tutored. Wordsworth was prepared to help him here as well, with interest. In a gesture at once calculated, generous, and ill considered, Wordsworth agreed to lend £500 from the Calvert bequest, as soon as he received it, to Montagu at 10 percent interest, and later another £200 to Montagu's "opulent" friend Charles Douglas at the same rate. This was far above the 3 to 5 percent rate prevailing in bank interest and the consol funds, so Wordsworth hoped to do very well by doing good. Two years later, when the arrangement began to go bad, one of his first concerns was that he might be liable to prosecution for usury for charging such rates.[57] But his desire for larger gain led him into error, for Montagu was soon in arrears in his payments. Eventually the whole schedule was disrupted for several years, no interest being paid until about 1800, and Montagu did not repay the principal until 1814. Thus Wordsworth's precious capital was tied up in ways that again prevented his independence and freedom of movement, and forced him again to borrow advances from his brother Richard.[58]

Through Montagu, Wordsworth became friends with Francis Wrangham, whom he also knew from the university, where Wrangham had been third wrangler and won two prestigious all-university literary prizes.[59] For three years after graduation, Wrangham and Montagu had taken in students cramming for the university exams, specializing in the sons of West Indian planters. But in 1793 Wrangham lost an expected fellowship at Trinity Hall because of his sympathy with the French Revolution, and his protests to the vice-chancellor were to no avail.[60] At the time he was introduced to Wordsworth, he had just taken a curacy in Surrey, another victim, like William Frend, of the establishment's crackdown on its intellectual opponents. Wrangham had been forced into parish ministry because his French sympathies derailed his plans for a university career; this was similar to Wordsworth's unsteady career path: first avoiding the ministry, then seeking it out, only to be refused when he most needed it, because of his French sympathies. So he and Wrangham met as kindred spirits and fellow sufferers.

One of the closests verbal echoes between the *Philanthropist* and Wordsworth's writings may owe something to his new association with Wrangham. It occurred on August 31, in no. 23, the first issue after the journal stopped requesting contributions, and about two weeks after Wordsworth had left town, in the "Lines, Addressed to the Editor of the *Philanthropist,* on contrasting it with the general History of this Country, and the

Writers of the present Day in particular." This highly self-conscious piece of literary reflection is by "Clericus," who may well have been the Reverend Francis Wrangham. It scorns the government's policies of warfare abroad and repression at home:

> But, Ah! such scenes [of bloody history] delight the men alone,
> Who void of love to man, and fond of war,
> Made dupes by Princes to support the throne,
> That rules by rapine and continual jar,
> *For what can War but endless War still breed,*
> Till truth and right from violence be freed.

The sentiments, and the last two lines, match those from a concluding stanza of Wordsworth's "Salisbury Plain," the poem he had brought with him to London, ready to publish if he could realize a sufficient profit from it:

> How weak the solace such fond thoughts afford,
> When with untimely stroke the virtuous bleed.
> Say, rulers of the nations, from the sword
> Can ought but murder, pain, and tears proceed?
> *Oh! what can war but endless war still breed!*
>
> (505–9)

The identical lines have a common source, Milton's sonnet "On the Lord. Gen. Fairfax at the Siege of Colchester" (line 10).[61] But this does not rule out a connection, for Wordsworth had read his Salisbury Plain poem to Wrangham while in London, and when writing back to Wrangham in November he assumed Wrangham remembered it well.[62] None of the other republican reformers had as deep a familiarity with Milton's poetry as Wordsworth. The epigrammatic quality of the line (not unlike the alliterative bounce of "what man has made of man") may have been the reason it stuck in Wrangham's mind—presuming that he was "Clericus." Milton's sonnet's last lines ("In vain both Valour bleed / While Avarice, and Rapine share the land") also anticipate Wordsworth's indictment of Pitt's policies: "Insensate they who think at Wisdom's porch / That Exile, Terror, Bonds, and Force may stand: / That Truth with human blood can feed her torch" (514–16). And the passage from the *Philanthropist* develops Milton's idea in the same way: "Till truth and right from violence be freed. / The philanthropic mind forbears to tell / The carnage, death and slaughter that attend / Contending armies."

Wordsworth and Wrangham launched almost immediately into a joint project, updating Juvenal's eighth satire, on corrupt noblemen. (Wrangham was already exchanging contemporary satires in Latin with Coleridge, and exploring with him ideas for other writing projects.)[63] Like Wordsworth's plans with Mathews for the *Philanthropist,* the Juvenal project shows again how well disposed he was toward cooperative ventures on politically volatile subjects. They continued to work on the project over the next two years, but it was a brainchild of the year 1795, and closely related to Wordsworth's involvement with the *Philanthropist.* A complete, continuous version of Wordsworth's and Wrangham's imitation of Juvenal has only now appeared, some two hundred years after they began it, strong testimony to Wordsworth's success at erasing unwanted items from the curriculum vitae of his radical youth.[64]

The light this text shines on Wordsworth's biography is narrow but intense. It is a scathing criticism of the morals of the upper classes, not excluding the royal princes and the king and queen themselves. If published, and its authors identified, it would not have improved the precarious position of either man. Wordsworth's nervousness lest Wrangham publish it (in 1806, when he had considerably more to lose) shows that he feared it would be seen as more than a classical exercise.

Their choice of Satire VIII was unusual, and noteworthy. Satire VII, on poets, teachers, and poverty, or IX, on the griefs of career men, would have been much closer to their own interests and situations at the time. (Satire III, on Rome, and X, on the vanity of human wishes, had been successfully imitated by Samuel Johnson half a century earlier, triumphs of the Augustan mode which the young men knew better than to compete with.) By choosing VIII, which is addressed to a young Roman nobleman setting out to govern a remote province of the empire, Wordsworth and Wrangham suggest that their satire has an addressee, who is sometimes treated as a target, or at least as someone who should know better, but who on other occasions is regarded almost as a potential patron. This nobleman was Charles Howard, the eleventh duke of Norfolk (1746–1815), who was William Calvert's patron and a trustee of Raisley Calvert's estate. Norfolk is addressed in company with the other leading northern peer, Hugh Percy, the second duke of Northumberland (1742–1817), who was John Robinson's patron and neighbor at Syon House outside London, close to Wrangham's rectory at Cobham. In short, they picked as their putative heroes two men closely connected with persons who had actively sought to help Wordsworth in his confused movements toward a vocation since leaving university. A motive of revenge might be understandable in criticizing Percy (namely, to embarrass Robinson),[65] but an attack on Norfolk was a bit like biting the hand that fed him, if he had thought of Calvert. Charles Howard was no saint, but an aristocratic libertine of more than ordinary decadence. But his politics were liberal, and dead set against those of the other northern lord in the poem, James

Lowther, earl of Lonsdale, whose bad influence in Carlisle he alone was capable of checking. Toward Lowther, as we might expect, the poem shows no mercy, nor any hope of his return to virtue:

> Must honour still to Lonsdale's tail be bound?
> Then execration is an empty sound.[66]

The lines can be read two ways: that the "Honor" tag is inappropriate to corrupt persons like the earl of Lonsdale; or that honorable persons should not have to remain "bound" to (dependent on) dishonorable creditors like him, as Wordsworth was. Wordsworth's habit of attacking authority figures who were in a position to help him suggest a young man who was harder on his friends—or symbolic father figures—than on his natural enemies.

A secondary theme in their argument against unworthy nobles, also present in Juvenal, is the neglect of lowborn worth, which Wrangham and Wordsworth took up with alacrity, like the author of the first essay in the *Philanthropist,* who had pointedly contrasted the neglect of honest talent with the vices of the great. The truly noble are the truly virtuous: Juvenal's words are "nobilitas sola est atque unica virtus"; Wordsworth's are (punctuated as a quotation) " 'The virtuous only are of noble kind' "; the Howards' motto is "Sola virtus invicta."[67] These lines are probably by Wrangham, but they seem to be addressed to someone *else* from the north of England, other than Howard or Percy. Wordsworth's segment of the translation pursues this implication into a direct comparison between the speaker's virtues and Percy's, without consideration of rank:

> Were such your servant, Percy! (be it tried
> Between ourselves! the noble laid aside)
> Now would you be content with bare release
> From such a desperate breaker of the peace?
> Your friend the country Justice scarce would fail
> To give a hint of whips and the cart's tail.

The "breaker of the peace" might refer to the duke of York or to an unidentified "stripling" who has faults to atone for that resemble the young Wordsworth's: the punishments described—being tied to the rear of a cart and whipped as it drove through town—are those parish authorities could mete out for adultery or for refusing to acknowledge and support illegitimate children. And John Robinson, Percy's friend and neighbor, had been a country justice in Westmorland.

The eighth issue of the *Philanthropist* includes a piece, "Satire on Modern Clergymen," that is so close in spirit, form, and content to Wordsworth's imitations of Juvenal (especially the common attack on corrupt bishops like

Richard Watson) that only the most knowledgeable specialists are likely to be able to say which of the following excerpts is from the *Philanthropist* and which from Wordsworth:

> Is Common-sense asleep? has she no wand
> From this curst Pharaoh-plague to rid the land?
> Then to our bishops *reverent* let us fall,
> *Worship* Mayors, Tipstaffs, Aldermen and all.
> Let Ignorance o'er monstrous swarms preside
> Till Egypt see her ancient fame outvied.
> The thundering Thurlow, Apis! shall rejoice
> In rites once offered to thy bellowing voice.
> Insatiate Charlotte's tears and Charlotte's smile
> Shall ape the scaly regent of the Nile.
> Bishops, of milder Spaniel breed, shall boast
> The reverencc by the fierce Anubis lost.

> So sing the Bishops, when they fast and pray;
> That is, in language each may understand,
> When Fast-Day Sermons darken all the land.
> Unnumbered glories shine around the Bench,
> Where sleep the Bishops, fearless of the French;
> Ten thousand sylphs and gnomes around them stay,
> And—wanton, in their wigs and cassocks play;
> The guards of those who sweet Religion guard
> Against her countless foes, who press so hard
> Upon her life; such are the noble band;
> Such men, Church-Militant, the times demand.
> In Egypt once, 'this said in holy writ,
> A crowd of locusts came; and there, (to wit),
> Destroy'd some corn which flourish'd on the soil . . . .

In fact, the first excerpt is Wordsworth's, but the secret agents of the duke of Portland would not have made nice discriminations between them; both are equally suspicious. Wordsworth's passage might be read as calling for a Paineite revolution (that is, "Common-sense"); the *Philanthropist* lines could be read as sneering at the monarchy, since fast days, long in abeyance, were being reinstituted at the orders of George III to celebrate military victories. If Wordsworth's Juvenal imitations had been published, it would have given ample warrant for keeping an eye on him, and the *Philanthropist* satire is by "Clericus," who once again may be Wrangham. Wordsworth and Montagu left London for a few days on July 14 (the day after the *Philanthropist*'s last moderate issue appeared), to visit Wrangham at his rectory in Surrey.[68] The satire of "Clericus" is modeled on Pope's Neoclassical *Rape of the Lock,* a piece of literary sophistication very much on the order of Wordsworth's and Wrangham's adaptation of a classical model for their joint project. The metaphor from Exodus of a plague of locusts to describe contemporary ecclesiastical and political abuses is present in neither Pope nor Juvenal, but is common to both "Clericus" and Wordsworth.

Wordsworth contributed mostly elaborations of contemporary London scenes he had seen that spring and summer. He sketched vignettes of noblemen's regattas on the Thames, extraordinarily expensive events which the public loved to watch and wager on: "The cry is six to one upon the Duke" (of Manchester)! He also pointed out, like a society gossip columnist, the Prince of Wales "wedged in with blacklegs at a boxer's show / To shout with transport o'er a knock-down blow." Nobles are consistently shown to be encouraging public vice, rather than behaving nobly.

But the two or three most specific glimpses of Wordsworth, or of a persona in the poem very like him, are outside the main lines of satiric crossfire, and all are new additions to or significant variations of Juvenal's text. Most of Wordsworth's work on the imitation begins just past the halfway point of the Latin text, where, in an apparent transition from unrelieved invective, an older voice responds to the broad-brush attacks of the first half by counseling sympathetic moderation. "An apologist will say to me, 'We too did the same as boys.' "[69] But whereas Juvenal cites drinking and whoring, Wordsworth's lines turn strangely inward to other kinds of sin, or shame:

> But whence this gall, this lengthened face of woe?
> We were no saints at twenty,—be it so;
> Yet happy they who in life's [later] scene
> Need only blush for what they once have been,
> Who pushed by thoughtless youth to deeds of shame
> 'Mid such bad daring sought a coward's name.
>
> (146–51)

This order of remorse is entirely different from Juvenal's crude attack on grog shops and male prostitutes. It goes beyond the Latin text to think, obscurely, about those who are *not* so "happy," fixing on youthful indiscretions that will *always* be a cause for shame. The unfinished state of the manuscript permits two interpretations of the passage. "Thoughtless youth" may be the generic condition of being young, used as special pleading to explain what "pushed" someone in his early twenties to "deeds of shame"—deeds which he dared to do, but then turned cowardly toward. Or "thoughtless youth" may be some specific young men who pushed someone (who is now "happy" because he has to blush only for "what [he] once [had] been") to "deeds of shame" that he refused, preferring to be called a coward rather than accept such "bad daring." This could refer to his work on the *Philanthropist* or, in light of its editorial history, to some escalation of its provocations that he refused to participate in. Or it could refer to something much worse: "deeds of shame" is a strong phrase, in Wordsworth's mouth. But whatever the precise reference, since Wordsworth is adding his own language to Juvenal's here, the chances are great that he was writing about something he knew personally.

Among contemporary aristocratic vices that Wordsworth cataloged were illegal faro tables, most notoriously those run by the earl and countess of Buckingham at their town house. But Wordsworth shunts his attack aside toward something else, which is nowhere in Juvenal. He asks why the police and magistrates do not sniff out this kind of corruption instead of expending their efforts on much smaller fry:

> . . . is no informer there [among the rich],
> Or is the painted staff's avenging host
> By sixpenny sedition shops engrossed
> Or rather skulking for the common weal
> Round fire-side treason parties en famille[?]
> (179–83)*

Cheap seditious publications and intimate conversations that might be deemed treasonous are precisely the two kinds of activities with which we can most closely associate Wordsworth at the time, and from the government's point of view such shops and meetings were much more dangerous than the high stakes aristocrats wagered and lost at faro. Daniel Eaton's shop at the Cock & Swine was one such "sixpenny sedition shop," where the *Philanthropist* was published, and a meeting of radical writers could certainly be construed as a "fire-side treason party," especially one in February, if it was the one at William Frend's, when a circle drawn up "round [the] fire-side" would have been comfortable. A further implication of the lines, in light of his earlier reference to "bad daring" and "a coward's name," is the suggestion that he *knew* of an "informer . . . skulking" round such gatherings. An entry in Portland's private account book records a payment of £200 on May 9 to George Dyer; Dyer's legendary naïveté may have made him an unwitting pawn—or a highly effective operative—in such machinations.[70]

Agents working on newspapers or in the theater were one of the government's best sources of information, and the newly organized secret service at the Home Office rapidly recruited a special cadre in this area,

*The "painted staff" was the mace of office carried by the night-watch patrol in each parish of the city.

"The cry is six to one upon the Duke" [of Manchester]
(*Imitation of Juvenal,* line 90)

(*The Race for Doggett's Coat & Badge; River Thames at Chelsea,* by Thomas Rowlandson)

"Are these the studies that beseem a prince?
Wedged in with blacklegs at a boxer's show
To shout with transport o'er a knock-down blow"
(*Imitation of Juvenal,* lines 122-24)

(*A Prize Fight,* by Thomas Rowlandson)

"the street-disturbing Newsman's horn"
(*The Prelude,* VII, MS. 52, 271v
[*Thirteen*])

Thomas Holcroft and William Godwin at the 1794 Treason Trials, by Sir Thomas Lawrence

Daniel Isaac Eaton
(published May 14, 1794), by W. Sharpe
(Motto: Frangas non Flectes:
"Break, Don't Bend")

Joseph Johnson, by W. Sharpe

Francis Wrangham, artist unknown

The Republican Attack, by James Gillray (published November 1, 1795)

George III is in carriage at left, Lords Westmorland and Onslow with him. Pitt is the coachman; the four postillions behind are Pepper Arden, Dundas (with plaid and whiskey bottle), Grenville, and Loughborough, the Lord Chancellor. The assailants are (l. to r.) Sheridan, Fox, and Lansdowne (with blunderbuss); trying to stop the coach at rear are (l. to r.) the Duke of Grafton and Lords Stanhope and Lauderdale. Britannia is run over.

John Thelwall addressing crowd behind Copenhagen House, Islington (detail from *Copenhagen House,* by James Gillray, published November 16, 1795)

(in foreground: Charles Lamb (l.) and Robert Southey (r.) as urchins playing a roulette game, "Equality and No Sedition Bill")

Racedown Lodge, by S.L. May

"Amid the gloom . . . appeared a roofless Hut"

(Illustration for "The Ruined Cottage" by Foster Birkett)

Pedlar, by W. H. Pyne (published 1824)

Gipsies, by W. H. Pyne (published 1802)

Alfoxden Park, by C.W. Bampflyde

Samuel Taylor Coleridge, by Peter Vandyke (1795)

Interior Scene, by John Harden

Imagine, left to right: Dorothy Wordsworth, Charles Lloyd, Wordsworth, Coleridge, and Thelwall

Culbone Church, ca. 1800, by S. Alken

Thomas Poole,
by Thomas Stothard

Basil Montagu,
by George Dance

Robert Southey, by James Sharples

Charles Lamb, by Robert Hancock

William Hazlitt, by Thomas Bewick

William Pitt, by James Gillray (1789)

William Wyndham, 1st Baron Grenville, by John Hoppner (1800)

George Canning, by John Hoppner

Richard Ford
"His name is *Wordsworth* a name I think known to Mr. Ford." (James Walsh to John King, August 15, 1797)

John Hookham Frere, by Henry Edridge (1800)

William Henry Cavendish Bentinck, 3rd Duke of Portland (1738–1809), engraving by J. Murphy after Sir Joshua Reynolds

Tintern Abbey, by J. M. W. Turner (1793)

The New Morality, by James Gillray (published August 7, 1798)

"Coleridge & Co." (detail from *The New Morality*)

Showing, left to right, John Thelwall (reaching out with book), Joseph Priestly, Gilbert Wakefield, Charles Lamb, Charles Lloyd, Wordsworth? (hand beneath cornucopia), Southey, and Coleridge. In rear, *bonnets rouges* roses, from Erasmus Darwin's *The Loves of the Plants,* and Lord Moira, Francis Rawdon-Hastings (1754–1826), Irish peer and hero of British actions in America, France, and (later) India.

frequently blackmailing sentimental liberals into service by threatening them with dire consequences. One of these "literary agents" later had a direct connection with Wordsworth: John Taylor, editor of the *Morning Post,* 1788–90, who continued spying after he moved to other papers (Chapter 31). Another of these literary spies was a minor dramatist named James Powell, who had by 1798 become the government's leading infiltrator of the United Irishmen. He was in Hamburg at the same time Wordsworth and Coleridge were, and is mentioned in dispatches by the British chargé d'affaires, which also mention persons known to have associated with the two poets and which possibly allude to them as well (Chapter 25).[71]

There is one last tantalizing glimpse of these shadowy London scenes in a nearly illegible text brilliantly recovered by Carol Landon and Jared Curtis from one of Wordsworth's manuscript jottings on the Juvenal project:

> These equal liberties [?] [??] [?]ing
> One s[?] one gin glass and one broken ring
> Mid beggars   specious [?packs]
> And bowstreet runners [?powerless] on their back
> It[72]

Like a smudged fingerprint on a murder weapon, this little piece of imagism teases us to reconstruct the scene, the crime, and the victim. We can see for sure only a political topic, a pub in a poor neighborhood, and police officers or undercover agents. Is it about the government's infiltration of "fireside treason parties"? The convivial scene and the police are common to the two passages. Or is it about the easy recruiting, or suborning, of informers? "One broken ring" seems to refer to a secret cadre or cell meeting broken up. If the two last conjectural readings are correct, then we have beggars with false wares—or false beggars—and Bow Street runners either on the backs of their victims or perhaps flipped over on their own backs and rendered powerless like noxious insects. It all smacks of sordid betrayals: not the stirring, broad vision of Liberty which Wordsworth sketched out in his letters to Mathews, but one he evidently saw, in dangerous company and dark circumstances, in London in 1795.

Yet Wordsworth's scorn for the secret police's misplaced energy is nearly matched by his rhetorical belittling of "sixpenny sedition shops" and "treason parties en famille." As with his references to the great Whig and Tory lords, the total rhetorical effect is one of casting a plague on both parties, from a perspective which would rather be disengaged from the conflict altogether.

Finally, this "Pharoah plague" of corruption spreads over the whole land, and the poem falls into fawningly sarcastic cynicism: "Then to our bishops *reverent* let us fall / *Worship* Mayors, Tipstaffs, Aldermen and all."* Wordsworth's bitter disillusionment is extended by implication to an entire country flooded with corruption. Placed at the end of the poem, they sound like exit lines. Their penultimate thrust is a sneer at tractable "Bishops, of milder Spaniel breed," who for Wordsworth would include the bishop of Llandaff.

The final couplet is exactly contemporaneous. Corruption has gone on so long it has become general, "things as they are":

> . . . devotion has been paid
> These seven long years to Grenville's onion head.

Wordsworth was not sure how long William Wyndham, Baron Grenville, Pitt's cousin and foreign secretary, had "enjoyed the honour of the peerage . . . five six or seven, I do not know."[73] In fact it was five years since Wyndham had been given the title in 1790. But Wordsworth knew exactly why he closed the poem on this reference. The king's coach was mobbed in Hyde Park on its way to the opening of Parliament on October 29, to cries of "No War! No Pitt! No King! Peace! Bread!" Sticks and stones were thrown at the carriage, breaking two of its large glass panels; the king thought he had been shot at. A man in a green coat leapt on the carriage and tried to drag the king out, before troops galloped up.[74] One of the men leading the carriage back to the stable was trampled to death, and the carriage badly damaged (see illustration). When the king attended Covent Garden next night there was a riot, with much hooting at the duke of Portland, the well-known head of the Home Office's secret police. This all looked very near to insurrection, and the government no longer hesitated to implement the plans it had been preparing all year. On November 6 Grenville introduced the Treasonable Practices Bill; his cousin the prime minister proposed the Seditious Meetings Bill four days later. These were the two acts which, known as the Gagging Acts, were pushed through Parliament by large majorities despite huge public protest gatherings estimated at 150,000 persons. They made it possible for written and spoken *language,* as well as overt actions, to be defined as treason. Wordsworth sent these explicit and graphic lines (none of them in Juvenal) to Wrangham ten days later. By this time he had already left London, but his sudden departure in mid-August was taken with a keen awareness of what might be in store for those who exerted themselves too energetically "on an opposition newspaper."

Basil Montagu was also the occasion of Wordsworth's meeting John and Azariah Pinney.[75] He steered Wordsworth their way as a source of income

*A tipstaff was the constable or bailiff in court, or the head officer carrying the night watch's painted staff.

that might substitute for the debts he himself was failing to pay them. John, the elder, was studying law at Lincoln's Inn, and Azariah had been Wrangham's pupil at Cobham and was now back living in London.[76] They were the sons of John Pinney Sr., one of the Caribbean "sugar kings," who owned the largest plantation on the island of Nevis; he was known as the King of Nevis. In that spirit of the times which Hazlitt, thinking in part of this very transaction, characterized as "not a time when *nothing was given for nothing* [but] the mind opened, and a softness [came] over the heart of individuals," the Pinney brothers offered Wordsworth their country house, Racedown in Dorset, rent free, as soon as they learned of his situation.

Things had begun to go badly wrong with the *Philanthropist* in mid-July, and Wordsworth became as eager to leave London as he had been ready to "throw" himself into it six months earlier. A house in the country began to seem a desirable option to many other radical writers at this time. As the government's intentions with regard to internal surveillance and provocation became clearer, the leadership of the radical reform movement looked to the provinces for safety. Wordsworth was ready to reestablish the housekeeping relationship he had had with Dorothy at Windy Brow the year before, and here was another rent-free situation which provided it. Dorothy did not want to return to Forncett; the Cooksons' fifth child was due in December,[77] and she knew she would soon be drawn back into the increasingly onerous child care and household duties she had so long performed for them. Her skill at child rearing and Montagu's obvious need in this area came naturally together: William and Dorothy would provide room, board, and tutelage for Basil junior at the Pinneys' house—for an additional £50 pounds per year. This, along with the expected repayments from Montagu and the freedom from rent, made an attractive package. But the general political situation in London rendered it all the more compelling, and Wordsworth's involvement with the *Philanthropist* was all that was needed to mother the invention of such a scheme.

The summer saw several public events which suggested that a sharp change in the political climate was in the offing. Richard Brothers, the apocalyptic prophet who was at the height of his notoriety in 1795, predicted an earthquake that would end the world on June 4, the king's birthday. Thousands left town, and a great storm that night caused hysterical panic—the sort that leaves an emotional residue easily attachable to other events.[78] At the end of June, on the 29th, a huge public gathering was called by the London Corresponding Society for St. George's Fields in Southwark. The occasion passed without any major incident, but the Home Office records show that the government was fully informed about every particular of the meeting, and fully prepared to treat it as an insurrection to be put down by force.[79] The ominousness of the occasion and the sense of disaster barely averted was widespread on all sides. Throughout July and August the newspapers carried headline reports of "Riots" and "More Riots!" in London and throughout the country, usually directed against impressment gangs or farmers and bakers who were held responsible for the scarcity and high price of bread.

Mary Moorman says that "the alacrity with which Wordsworth accepted the offer of Racedown shows the he had not found it possible to live permanently in London," but does not offer to say why, except to imply the usual mythology that as a nature lover he could not stand the city, and to conjecture that "nothing apparently had come of the plan of joining the staff of a newspaper."[80] But the *Philanthropist* hypothesis provides us with reasons that are real reasons: concretely demonstrating how the newspaper plan had not worked out, why it was impossible to do his own writing, and what some of the confusion and disorder in Montagu's lodgings consisted of. These reasons were, from Wordsworth's point of view, very compelling. He had certainly not arrived in London as a nature lover and city hater, but quite the opposite ("cataracts and mountains, are good occasional society, but they will not do for constant companions"). The experience of London in 1795 marks his first, and fundamental, revisal of this estimate.

One obvious course for a defense of Wordsworth against this construction of his London life in 1795 would be to say that all these ideas and expressions were simply "in the air," and that Wordsworth no more need be connected with the *Philanthropist* than any other young liberal intellectual of the time. True, but the number of likely candidates is finite, and with so many lines of connection and overlap existing between all these people and texts, it requires too much suspension of disbelief to think that Wordsworth did not trip or tread on some of them.

But how can all of this have gone undetected so long, if it really is true? For one thing, we should recall Wordsworth's success in keeping secret all knowledge of his other youthful indiscretion, with Annette Vallon, until long after all the principals were dead. And William Mathews died early, of malaria in the West Indies in 1801, "a disappointed man." Though his family would later recall that he was "remembered by a numerous list of his early associates, men of first-rate talent; amongst who may be mentioned Mr. Wordsworth, who was his most intimate friend and correspondent," this, published in 1838, was harmless.[81] They probably knew no more of the contents of his correspondence with Wordsworth than Dorothy and Richard did, which was clearly very little. If we ask whether Wordsworth would not have made some mention of their *Philanthropist* experience in his subsequent letters back to Mathews, the answer is, Decidedly not. Given what we know of his activities and associates in London, there is plenty of reason to regard his removal to Racedown as something on the order of a fugitive flight to a safe house.

But such secrets, if they are secrets, are never really hidden. Rather, like Poe's purloined letter, they are already in front of our eyes, could we but recognize them. If we look to *The Prelude* for information about this or any other aspect of Wordsworth's months in London, we do not find much that is definite. This is not surprising, since we are dealing with events which, like his imitation of Juvenal, he was eager to cover over. However, there are places in *The Prelude* which connect to the *Philanthropist* scenario.

The place to look is in Book X: between Wordsworth's account of hearing the news of Robespierre's death as he crossed Leven Sands in early August 1794 and his departure from London in mid-August, 1795 (567–904). His attachment to Godwinism is not hard to document, as "the philosophy / That promised to extract the hopes of man / Out of his feelings" (806–8). His reference to France's changing "a war of self-defence / For one of conquest" (792–93) can confidently be taken to refer to General Pichegru's conquest of the Netherlands in late 1794. But when "events" could no longer be trusted to provide "the immediate proof of principles," he did what most liberals tried to do in 1795:

> . . . rouzed up, I stuck
> More firmly to old tenets, and, to prove
> Their temper, strained them more; *and thus, in heat*
> *Of contest, did opinions every day*
> *Grow into consequence,* till round my mind
> They clung as if they were the life of it.
>
> (X.799–804; italics added)

If we refuse these lines' invitation to keep us wholly in the mental theater of Wordsworth's life, and try to get out into the fervid atmosphere and feverish debates of London in summer 1795, a phrase like "heat of contest" provides an exit: it gives a glimpse of Wordsworth arguing with someone other than himself, the kind of situation obtaining for his participation in the *Philanthropist.* He is clearly talking about London, and about not being alone, when he recalls how "the street-disturbing Newsman's horn" gave hopes to those who wished to hear of French defeats. But, "with my ardent Comrades," he laughed at the foolishness of "men clinging to delusions so insane."[82] The two particular details of the newsman's horn and the company of his comrades are dropped from the finished manuscript of the 1805 *Prelude,* though both return in the posthumously published version of 1850—which is to say that Wordsworth was willing to have it known only in posthumous publication that he was a member of an "ardent" group at this time. But this indicates that his later statement "I was an active partisan" (736) means that he was a partisan active among others of the same persuasion.

Were he and his friends doing anything other than thinking and talking, the main activities of groups like the Philomathean Society? He speaks with a retrospective sarcasm about his infatuation with Godwin's necessarianism, but when he says he "pursued / A higher nature," he suggests activities that seem more than merely mental exertions:

for I was perplexed and sought
To accomplish the transition by such means
As did not lie in nature, sacrificed
The exactness of a comprehensive mind
To scrupulous and microscopic views
That furnished out materials for a work
Of false imagination . . . .

(X.841–47)

This "furnishing" of materials could be a reference to the group discussions and compositions—and the dull task of selecting standard reprints when they failed to produce any ready copy—which produced that "work of false imagination," the *Philanthropist*. A "comprehensive mind" running up against the barricades of "scrupulous" rationalistic minds like Holcroft's and Godwin's, demanding proofs and "microscopic" views at every step, might well feel itself "sacrificed" in such an effort.

This leads him to his summary of moral crisis at the heart of *The Prelude* (X.878–904), which may well have occurred at about the same time the *Philanthropist* was undergoing its crisis of identity in July and August. He says he "was betrayed / By present objects, and by reasonings false / From the beginning." But it was a mutual process, not one that he suffered alone, for as he was "confounded more and more," he was *both* "misguid*ing*" and "misguid*ed*" (883–88, passim). He was leading others astray even as he was being led astray. The depth of this crisis, by its placement in *The Prelude,* becomes the fulcrum on which the entire plot and eventual happy ending of the poem turn.

Time may come
When some dramatic story may afford
Shapes livelier to convey to thee, my friend,
What then I learned—or think I learned—of truth,
And the errors into which I was betrayed
By present objects, and by reasonings false . . .
. . . .
Misguiding and misguided. Thus I fared,
Dragging all passions, notions, shapes of faith,
Like culprits to the bar, suspiciously
Calling the mind to establish in plain day

Her titles and her honours, now believing,
Now disbelieving, endlessly perplexed
With impulse, motive, right and wrong, the ground
Of moral obligation—what the rule,
And what the sanction—till, demanding proof,
And seeking it in every thing, I lost
All feeling of conviction, and, in fine,
Sick, wearied out with contrarities,
Yielded up moral questions in despair . . . .
. . . .

Ah, then it was
That thou, most precious friend, about this time
First known to me, didst lend a living help
To regulate my soul. And then it was
That the beloved woman in whose sight
Those days were passed . . .
. . . .
Maintained for me a saving intercourse
With my true self . . . . (X.878–915)

Formally, *The Prelude* breaks down at this point: it cannot continue by developing further the terms it has been using up to this point, and it swerves without explanation to an entirely different set of terms, places, and persons—from excessive rationality to overflowing love, from a debating hall (or a magistrate's court) to the countryside, from London to Dorset, and from his own mind to the hearts of Coleridge and Dorothy. The text itself opens up the gap it must leap over, in the break between the paragraphs. But what it describes, referentially, is what actually happened: Wordsworth left town. The crisis of London, 1795, is thus the crisis that initiates the drama of *The Prelude,* providing the plot it must resolve in order to reach its conclusion.

The trial metaphor is Godwinian mental theater, notoriously first staged in Godwin's example of disinterested rational choice in *Political Justice:* in a fire, should one save the philosopher Fénelon or his by-standing valet? Godwin's faith in the "bar" or "tribunal" of Reason is also evident throughout *Caleb Williams,* as the one place in an otherwise repressive society where a man could still hope to speak the truth and be justified—though Caleb learns it is a vain hope. "Sanction" was also a word with Godwinian overtones.[83] And the stuttering demand of "what the rule, / And what the sanction," sounds close to Coleridge's caricature of Holcroft's barricades on "the road to truth": " 'What do you mean by a *sensation,* Sir? What do you mean by an *idea*?' " Rational moral argument could no longer provide Wordsworth with a personally persuasive motive for action; instead, he fell back on something spontaneously given, not as the solution to his problem, but as his escape from it: Nature. Here it means gratitude for his sister's unquestioning love. This is not simply a sentimental generalization but specifically pointed advice: she gave him a "sudden admonition," warning him to avoid certain social definitions of his "true self" to "preserve me still / A poet, made me seek beneath that name / *My office* upon earth, and nowhere else": not, as he had tried to be in London, a journalist, an essayist, a political activist, or a moral philosopher.

The passage begins with a hint that fuller revelations might be forthcoming: "Time may come / When some dramatic story may afford / Shapes livelier to convey . . . what then I learned—or think I learned." Did this time ever come? The reference is usually taken to mean Books III and IV of *The Excursion,* the "dramatic" segment of Wordsworth's ongoing, lifelong master project, *The Recluse.*[84] In the character of the Solitary in *The Excursion,* ostensibly based on Dissenting preachers like Joseph Fawcett, Wordsworth gives details of emotions so intimate that they must arise from something very close to direct personal experience:

> . . . he forfeited
> All joy in human nature; was consumed
> And vexed, and chafed, by levity and scorn,
> And fruitless indignation; galled by pride;
> *Made desperate by contempt of men who throve*
> *Before his sight in power or fame, and won,*
> *Without desert, what he desired* . . . .
>
> (II.296–302; italics added)
>
> *Among men*
> *So charactered did I maintain a strife*
> *Hopeless,* and still more hopeless every hour . . .
> —In Britain, ruled a panic dread of change;
> The weak were praised, rewarded, and advanced;
> And, from *an impulse of a just disdain,*
> *Once more did I retire into myself.*
>
> (III.770–74, 787–89, 827–30; italics added)[85]

Academic readers have often failed, when studying Wordsworth's statements of disaffection with city life and politics in the mid-1790s, to note how heavily they are loaded with the language of wounded self-esteem and personal affront, of frustrated ambition, and a feeling of having been beaten, perhaps unfairly, in some kind of intensely competitive effort. But these are just the kinds of emotions he would have had as a young writer, launched percipitately into the "mighty gulph... of talents and attainments infinitely superior to my own," and forced to work along with other highly promising young men in an enterprise of his own devising but soon taken beyond his control.

Several of his London friends also suffered near-breakdowns at this time, further suggesting that these young men had got involved in something in 1795 that they could not control, with traumatic results. If the gagging acts tolled the death knell of the popular reform movement in Britain in the 1790s, their effect on many individuals associated with Wordsworth was psychologically traumatic. James Losh, a very hardy character, suffered in 1795 either "a serious nervous breakdown" or an attack of pulmonary tuberculosis (or one disguised as the other) which forced him to leave London and retreat to the Bath-Bristol region to recover, exactly as Wordsworth did.[86] Whatever his ailment, he soon recovered and immediately became active in Bristol's intellectual and political life.

John Tweddell also suffered the effects of a mysterious "event" which he described as the wreck of hopes "madly conceived and cruelly frustrated." This led him to quit London abruptly on September 24, for Hamburg, just a month after Wordsworth's departure for Racedown. No one knows what this event was. It could have been a romantic disappointment, but it has also been associated with Tweddell's infatuation with Godwin. Samuel Parr, "the Whig Dr. Johnson," lamented Godwin's influence on three of his especially esteemed students; the only three of Parr's students who also knew Godwin were Joseph Gerrald (the transportee), Robert Merry, the Della Cruscan poet and revolution groupie, and Tweddell.[87] Tweddell also recovered soon, traveling through Germany to Russia and eventually to Greece, where he died suddenly of a fever in 1799. (His archaeological papers and collections had a posthumous notoriety when it was revealed in 1815 that they had been given to Lord Elgin in Athens—he of the famous marbles—but mysteriously lost.) At the time of his death, Tweddell was looking forward to returning to England, refreshed and restored, and his anticipation of his return sounds very Wordsworthian, as we would now say. He longed to leave the world and its crowd, and "in the midst of the fields, in the heart of some retreat . . . confine myself to the sweet joys of nature, to the innocent pleasures of the study, and to the exercise of the domestic affections." His analysis of his malady also parallels Wordsworth's rejection of Godwinism: he would no longer be one of those "duped men" who "the slaves of systems which they want to have always uniform and connected in all parts, . . . that affect maxims which are too universal and too absolute."[88] This is precisely the condition that Coleridge in 1798 would urge Wordsworth to write *The Recluse* as an antidote for: "I wish you would write a poem [reviving the spirits of those who], in consequence of the complete failure of the French Revolution have thrown up all hopes of amelioration and given themselves over to [solitude] and the cultivation of the domestic affections." That is, *The Recluse* should address the condition of their entire generation.

Nor, in this rash of nervous disorders that broke out in Wordsworth's London circle at this time, should we forget William Mathews, who soon found himself dropped from Wordsworth's acquaintance. Always a melancholy, despondent character, Mathews described himself as having been "for several years . . . a disappointed man," when he set out in 1801 to make his fortune in the West Indies.[89] He died of fever within months of his arrival, yet another victim (like John Wordsworth) of the dreams of empire that were the fallback position of this liberal generation. We know Mathews's disappointments were connected with the failure of his various vocational choices; how much they were linked to Wordsworth and the fate of their *Philanthropist* plans we do not know, but we can now see in considerable detail the background for such a context.

Wordsworth's letters to Mathews after his departure from London become increasingly cool and peremptory. Their relationship seems to have slid backwards, from close friendship to mere acquaintance. Participation in a failed enterprise can have this effect. As to politics, there is nary a word; compared with their detailed and enthusiastic discussions before Wordsworth's arrival in London, it is now difficult to believe that these young men ever talked about anything but their friends, the weather, and poetry—and this, with reference to spying authorities, was very much the point. More to our point is the changed nature of their relationship: what they thought of each other.

One particularly clear indication of the terms of their separation fits neatly with Wordsworth's political retrenchment after 1795. Among the various London errands with which he charged Mathews as his factotum after leaving town (picking up some new shoes he'd ordered and so on), he asked for Mathews's copy of the volume in John Bell's *Classical Arrangement of Fugitive Poetry* which contained "Poems in the Stanza of Spenser," including Beattie's *The Minstrel.* In an awkward but revealing gesture, he proposed that they exchange books, Mathews accepting Wordsworth's copy of *Cato's Letters* for his volume of Bell. To make the switch seem more worthwhile to Mathews, he proposed the following very concrete mechanism for carrying it out:

> You will write your name in it as presented to me. If you chuse to take the trouble of inserting my name in the Cato's Letters, here it is: you may cut it out and paste it in.
>
> From W. Wordsworth
>
> to
>
> W. Mathews[90]

Unlike his letters to Mathews from Penrith in late 1794, where he brushed aside all stylistic difficulties in his enthusiasm to connect his writing with the kind Mathews was doing, these letters show Wordsworth migrating from one textual universe to another. If he was bidding farewell not only to Mathews but also to London and the dangerous world of committed journalism they had shared there, he could hardly have hit upon a more symbolic exchange. For "Cato" is none other than that John Trenchard whose work figures so prominently in the *Philanthropist,* especially when the going got rough and some acceptably traditional liberal material was needed to fill up issues which might otherwise have been filled by uncontrollably radical volunteer contributions.

Not everything was politics, however. Or rather, nothing—and especially not politics—happens in complete isolation from anything else in life. On August 21, about three days after Wordsworth left town, his translation of a French poem called "L'Education de l'Amour" was published in the *Morning Chronicle* as "The Birth of Love," with an introductory note by Wrangham. Both the French and the English titles are curiously askew, since what the poem records is a bizarre *death* of love: Cupid is so precociously aroused by the sight of his mother's breasts ("malgré son jeune âge") that he cannot nurse: "by the beauty of the vase beguil'd, / Forgot the beverage—and pin'd away." Venus asks for help from "the most discreet" of the personified abstractions who are her attendant goddesses. Hope is chosen, but Enjoyment is jealous, and, disguised as Innocence, fills her laps with sweetmeats, "and gave, in handfuls gave, the treach'rous store. / A wild delirium first the Infant thrill'd; / But soon upon her breast he sunk—to wake no more."[91] It seems a strange poem to be translating in London in August of 1795, but not so strange in Wordsworth's case. He probably first drafted his translation sometime in 1792 or 1793. But a French poem about love, disappointed hope, innocence betrayed, and destructive enjoyment still had many angles of interest for him, all the sharper as his distance from Annette seemed to increase. And his writings of the 1790s both before and after 1795 show that the attraction of women's breasts and wild deliriums in their sweet laps were not merely abstract or metaphorical aspects of his writing, but very much part of his lived experience.

19 OF CABBAGES AND RADICALS

Racedown Lodge, 1795–1797

Let us suppose a young Man of great intellectual powers, yet without any solid principles of genuine benevolence. His master passions are pride and the love of distinction. He has deeply imbibed the spirit of enterprize in a tumultuous age. He goes into the world and is betrayed into a great crime.

The influence on which all his happiness is built immediately deserts him. His talents are robbed of their weight; his exertions are unavailing, and he quits the world in disgust, with strong misanthropic feelings. In his retirement, he is impelled to examine the reasonableness of established opinions and the force of his mind exhausts itself in constant efforts to separate the elements of virtue and vice.

(preface to *The Borderers,* 1797)

Wordsworth left London so hastily that Godwin was not aware of it; he called on August 18, but Wordsworth was already gone. The prospect of exciting remunerative work had brought him rushing to town in February, but a much more leisured prospect now beckoned him out of it, made all the more attractive by the dangers and anxieties he was leaving behind.

There had been a vague plan that Dorothy would join him in London, to help earn money by writing and translating. But now, rather than wait for her, Wordsworth departed immediately for Bristol as the houseguest of the Pinneys' father. John Pretor Pinney was delighted to entertain a tenant who (he thought) was finally going to start producing some return on the considerable investment he had made in his country seat, Racedown Lodge. The town house that Wordsworth arrived at in Bristol was built on an equally grand scale. It still stands in Great George Street, in the elegant Clifton section of town, commodious enough to house the city's museum of furniture from this era of mercantile opulence. It was a symbol of John Pinney's advancing fortunes, built in 1788 following his return from Nevis in 1784. His success as a sugar trader was even greater than the success he had enjoyed as a plantation owner.[1] He now ran the Bristol West Indies Trading Company in partnership with John Tobin, "one of the most prominent and intelligent adversaries of the abolition movement" and father of two sons, John and James, who both became close friends of Wordsworth.[2]

To the senior Pinney, Wordsworth appeared a gentlemen of some means, if he could afford Racedown. Pinney, a complete arriviste himself, was ready to do the genteel thing by entertaining Wordsworth until his sister arrived with young Basil Montagu. That the boy's father was connected to the earl of Sandwich was not lost on Pinney; though disinherited by his father, Montagu was on good terms with his half brother, the fifth earl.

John Pinney had just completed an extensive four-year renovation of his country house; he elegantly renamed it Racedown, rather than Pylemarsh Lodge, the homely local designation.[3] He had originally intended to use it as a safe haven from Nevis, if slave uprisings or a French invasion made it expedient to do so.[4] (He also had secret passages and money caches in his Bristol house for the latter purpose.) He was looking for tenants for the newly renovated house but, not finding any takers, had put it at the disposal of his sons, naturally assuming that the tenant they had found for it was paying rent, since he was charging them £50 a year for the use of it.[5]

John Pinney Sr. did not participate in the generous feeling of giving things for nothing that Hazlitt later recalled as "the spirit of the age." Like Richard Wordsworth and Christopher Crackanthorpe, he made a religion of his accounts and spoke in self-help copybook maxims like Benjamin Franklin's.[6] Nervous, irritable, and energetic, he was a mercantile version of Sir James Lowther. He had not been born rich, but he had been lucky, and he knew how to capitalize on his luck. In 1764 he had been named heir to the Pinney fortune by two aging, childless cousins. He was the son of one of their female cousins; his father, Michael Pretor, was reported to be "worse than a footman," a reference to his way of gaining access to his lady's favors. When they made him their heir, he promptly changed his name to John Pretor Pinney, just as Christopher Cookson had changed his to Crackanthorpe. He "danced attendance" so assiduously on his old cousins that they finally complained that "a continual repetition of expressions rather bordering on flattery are by no means agreeable."[7] He went out to Nevis in 1764 and returned in 1784, with a profit of £35,000. He never intended to stay longer than was necessary to raise a fortune that would allow him to set up independently in England. "My greatest pride is to be considered as a private country gentleman . . . . [I] shall avoid even the name of a West-Indian."

He wanted to avoid the name of West Indian because fortunes gained there were, as everyone knew, built on the backs of slaves. When Wordsworth stayed at Pinney's house, Pinney was the owner of over two hundred slaves, working three different plantations in Nevis: the largest single holding on the smallest of Britain's West Indian possessions. For liberal young men like the Pinney brothers, tutored by even more liberal Cambridge graduates like Montagu and Wrangham, at a time of fundamental social upheaval and nonstop talk about revolutionary virtue and the rights of man, this background was an unspeakable embarrassment. Matthew ("Monk") Lewis was another young man in the same bind, as was Charles Douglas, Montagu's friend.[8] John Frederick Pinney, "a rabid Whig," wanted to get rid of their plantations as soon as possible.[9] (They finally did so in 1807: conveniently, the year before Wilberforce's bill against the slave trade finally passed through Parliament, after a fifteen-year struggle.) Pinney had been shocked by the sight of slavery when he first went out to Nevis, but quickly made his peace with it: "surely God ordained 'em for the use and benefit of us: otherwise his Divine Will would have been made manifest by some particular sign or token." No sign or token appearing, he undertook to care for his human stock in the best way he knew how, providing them the same fodder he gave his animals. Unusual among his neighbors, he always laid in enough corn to keep them fed, because the idea of any slave's being without the usual day's allowance made him, he said, "unhappy."

He was also a shrewd manipulator of other people's perceptions of how West Indians earned their fortunes. When young Tom Wedgwood, heir to the pottery fortune, went out to Nevis in 1801 for his health, Pinney gave the following instructions to his overseer:

> Do not suffer a negro to be corrected in his presence, or so near for him to hear the whip—and if you could allowance the gang at the lower work, during his residence in the house, it would be advisable—point out the comforts the negroes enjoy beyond the poor in this country, drawing a comparison between the climates—show him the property they possess in goats, hogs, and poultry, and their negro-ground. By this means he will leave the island possessed of favorable sentiments.[10]

Pinney did not put any worse face on the source of his fortune if he was asked about it by the young Wordsworth—who was, however, in no position to inquire very closely into the largesse he was about to receive from a landlord who was unaware he was giving it. Wordsworth was something of an honored guest, but he certainly understood the Pinney boys' subterfuge on their father, and knew better than to thank John Pinney for letting him have Racedown for nothing.

Wordsworth's visit lasted five weeks, during which time he observed the active Bristol political scene as well as its bustling commercial aspect. It was England's second-largest city, though at sixty thousand souls a far distant second. With its broad channel estuary, it was more obviously a seaport than London, and opposition to the war with France was more openly and widely expressed, not only because political opinion was more liberal there but because the costs of the ill-advised war bore more heavily, proportionately, on Bristol's import-export economy. Wordsworth was particularly eager to see two young men frequently mentioned by Mathews, Dyer, and Godwin and others in his London set: Samuel Taylor Coleridge and Robert Southey. Wordsworth reported back to Mathews, "Coleridge was at Bristol part of the time I was there. I saw but little of him. I wished indeed to have seen more—his talent appears to me very great. I met with Southey also, his manners pleased me exceedingly and I have every reason to think very highly of his powers of mind."[11] Wordsworth speaks of both men as persons he and Mathews already know about: there was no miraculous first vision of his future soul mate and collaborator. Coleridge anticipated the chance to meet Wordsworth with almost equal enthusiasm. He had been a friend of Christopher Wordsworth during his time at Cambridge, and had defended his admiration of *Descriptive Sketches* in their little literary group there; he alludes to *An Evening Walk* in his manuscripts and magazine poems from as early as October 1793.[12] They might have met at Pinney's house, for though the elder Pinney himself would not entertain anyone as "democratical" as Coleridge, he could have gained entrée as an acquaintance of Pinney's indulged sons.[13]

Coleridge was already "a noticeable man," as was Southey, a well-connected local boy who had published a volume of poetry, following a promising career at Oxford.[14] Coleridge, it is not too much to say, was to Bristol what Thelwall was to London, and that, in late 1795, was very much indeed.[15] He and Southey and their friends (Charles Lloyd, Robert Lovell, and the Fricker sisters, Edith and Sara) were notorious in the region for their plans to found a utopian community, "Pantisocracy," on the banks of the Susquehanna River in Pennsylvania. The location was near where Joseph Priestley, the famous scientist and radical, had fled in 1794, when events subsequent to the destruction of his laboratory by a Birmingham mob in 1791 made it clear that he could no longer live and work in England. The Pantisocracy plan (government by all) had involved strenuous local efforts to recruit like-minded communalists, but it had just fallen through, to bitter recriminations among its principals—not unlike the cooling of relations between Wordsworth and Mathews following the wreck of their "philanthropic" work in London. This occasioned great glee and wise I-told-you-so's among their Bristol elders, and became a permanent point of satiric reference throughout Coleridge's and Southey's career. Wordsworth was frequently drawn into these satiric pictures by virtue of their later association in the Lake District, which had similar communal overtones of "plain living and high thinking." George Dyer, for example, linked them all together in a footnote in *The Poet's Fate* (1797), advising young poets to "join Pantisocracy's harmonious train . . . [where] freedom digs, and ploughs, and laughs, and sings." The note singles out Southey and Coleridge, but adds the names of "three young men, who have given early proofs, that they can strike the true chords of poesy": Wordsworth, Charles Lloyd, and Charles Lamb.[16]

Dorothy arrived in mid-September, and she and William set out almost immediately for Racedown, fifty miles to the south. They arrived at midnight on September 26, rousing up Joseph Gill, a "ruined and unhappy" cousin of John Pinney's who served as Racedown's family caretaker and custodian, broken down from years of drink and dissipation on Nevis.[17] The house they entered was splendid, three stories high, glistening with the new improvements detailed in Pinney's advertisement for it:

> To be let furnished or unfurnished. Race-down lodge consisting of two Parlors, a Kitchen with a scullery and pantry. Servant's hall and Butler's pantry on the ground floor. Four excellent Bed-chambers with Closets and a large light Closet on the Chamber floor. Four excellent Bed-chambers with a long wide Passage out of which a small Chamber may be taken, if wanted, on the Attic floor: also two exceeding good arched Cellars. Milkhouse and Coal Cellar, with a place, at the foot of the Cellar stairs, for a Larder. A complete wash and brewhouse with a Coach-house adjoining and Rooms over for a Laundry etc. Stabling for four Horses with a Harness-room and a woodhouse the whole length formerly used as a Cart-house Stables, in which there remains a good hay rack and therefore may be easily converted into a Stable again if wanted. Two Necessaries and the following Lands and Cottages . . . . Garden and pleasure ground before the house plus two meadows = *c.* 14 acres. Rent £ 42 p.a.[18]

Dorothy, ever the keen estimator of domestic arrangements, wrote to Jane Pollard Marshall, "We found every thing at Racedown much more complete with respect to household conveniences than I could have expected. You may judge of this when I tell you we have not had to lay out ten shillings for the use of the house."[19]

Racedown is now twice as big as it was then, from a nineteenth-century addition, but it was a very spacious house in 1795, as Coleridge rightly pegged it after his first visit: "the mansion of our friend Wordsworth."[20] It had a beautiful long parlor running from front to back on the left as one entered, with a pretty view of the croquet ground on the south side and of the formal pleasure garden to the rear (west), decorated with gilded busts on stone columns—the "images," as Joseph Gill queerly called them. It boasted a pianoforte, mahagony furniture, two glass-front bookcases on either side of the fireplace, and a library of over four hundred books.[21]

It may have been the model for Sir Walter Elliot's Kellynch Hall in Jane Austen's *Persuasion* (1818), set just over the border in Somerset. The region is dotted with places and houses named Pinney, Pinhay, or Pinny, the name of the village Austen's characters visit near Lyme Regis, eight miles away on the coast: "Pinny, with its green chasms between romantic rocks, where the scattered forest trees and orchards of luxuriant growth declare that many a generation must have passed away [here]."[22] Much of Wordsworth's life in the 1790s reads as if he were an errant son or brother in an Austen novel, whose goings-on are heard of, but not seen, in her books' narrowly domestic focus. *Sense and Sensibility* has seemed the closest parallel till now (and it too is set in the same region), but his move to Racedown brings *Persuasion* into the picture. The initial motive for its action is Sir Walter's realization that he must rent Kellynch Hall in order to economize, and like John Pinney he is concerned that it might be taken by unworthy tenants. The Pinneys were certainly well enough known in the region to make their misadventures with the strange radical poet legendary (Wordsworth's nocturnal wanderings and mutterings were still local gossip in the early twentieth century),[23] and Austen may have been drawing on more recent memories of John Pinney's outlandish tenant.

Racedown lies nestled in a region of burly hills crowded together in a remote corner of Dorset that thrusts out between Devon and Somerset: "a secluded no man's land" that even today seems as well suited to hobbits as to humans.[24] The roads are narrow and unimproved, twisting and turning around the base of the hills, the inhabitants more intent on their privacy than on providing rapid transit for strangers. Forde Abbey, eerily untouched by time, lies a few miles to the west, and the Devonshire border lay only a wide field and a narrow stream away from the Wordsworths' new home. Coleridge's birthplace at Ottery St. Mary is twenty-four miles farther west.

The house is only eight miles from the sea, but it is hard to imagine that anything as wide open as a sea is nearby; even sea "haar," a fog which descends frequently, only deepens its atmosphere of obscurity. But a short walk up any hill gives a brilliant sight of the ocean on a clear day, when the countryside shines like an emerald. William and Dorothy could see the Channel from their upper floors in winter, through openings between the hills.

Directly across the road, Pilsdon Pen rises steeply nine hundred feet above the vale of Marshwood, the highest hill in Dorset. A mile east is Lewesdon Hill, upon which William Crowe wrote a hill-by-hill Whiggish survey poem in 1788 that Azariah Pinney presented to the Wordsworths for the pleasure of placing themselves in their literary landscape.[25] Crowe's vista of English beauty-cum-prosperity celebrates the unbroken views on all sides, "save only where the head / Of Pillesdon rises, Pillesdon's lofty Pen." Crowe held the common contemporary idea of nature's visionary possibilities ("on this height I feel the mind / Expand itself in wider liberty"), but had no radical courage about his convictions: "our better mind / Is as a Sunday's garment, then put on / When we have nought to do . . . To-morrow for severer thought; but now / To breakfast, and keep festival today."[26] Wordsworth's convictions when he arrived in 1795 were not much stronger; his main interest was Crowe's starting point: to be "sequester'd from the noisy world."

On November 15 William saw from the top of Pilsdon the West India

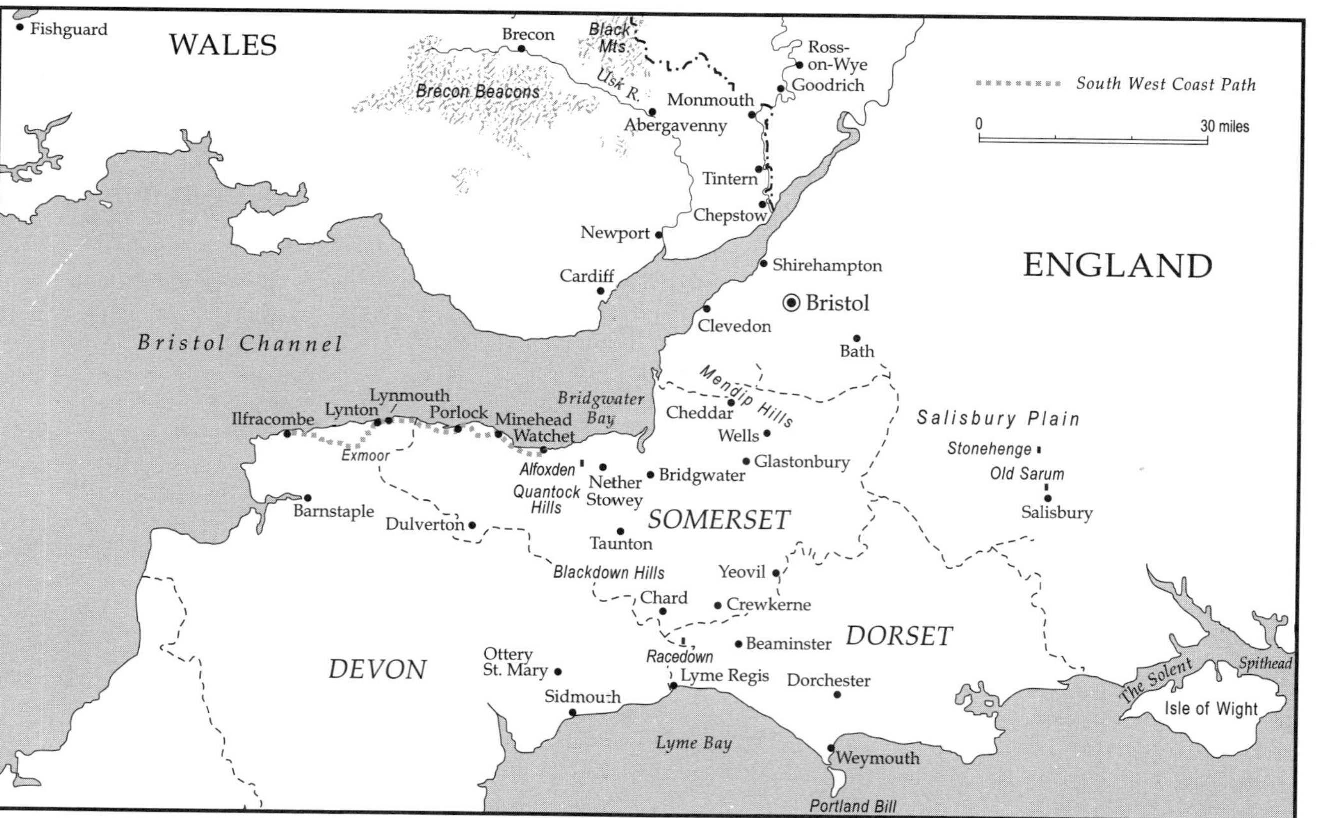

Wordsworth's and Coleridge's West Country, showing their favorite coastal walk.

fleet setting out "in all its glory." Two days later he and Dorothy learned that it had run into a hurricane; many ships had gone down, and for two weeks thereafter the coast was littered with corpses.[27] Crowe's survey poem had included these risks of empire, referring to another famous local loss, of the *Halfwell* off Portland Bill. Ten years later these moments flashed through William's and Dorothy's minds when they learned that John's first command, the *Earl of Abergavenny,* had gone down along the same stretch of coast.

Their first days and weeks were taken up with arrangements for delivery of eggs and butter from the little farms associated with Racedown, and with paying courtesy visits to the local gentry. They called first on the Pinneys of Blackdown, just up the road, relatives of their landlords whom they found polite but uninteresting. Farther up the road, past Crewkerne, they visited Hinton House, the seat of Earl Poulett, and admired its "very fine view."[28] Their domestic arrangements required care because their original plans soon fell through, leaving them considerably worse off than they had expected to be, house rich but cash poor. Dorothy had calculated that their annual income would be a tidy £180 per year, from the yield of Wordsworth's loans to Montagu and Douglas, plus £50 a year for young Montagu and a similar amount for taking care of the illegitimate daughter their cousin Tom Myers had recently sent back from India.* On top of Dorothy's estimate was the possibility that they would be given the care of John Pinney's latest and rather unexpected child, Charles, born in 1793. If the elder Pinney paid for him at the rate he paid Montagu and Wrangham for tutoring his older sons, they might expect another £200 a year. Dorothy imagined that she and William would be as comfortably situated as their childhood friends the Hutchinsons, whom she had visited near Durham in April. These brothers and sisters, also orphans, had recently inherited £1,800 from their uncle and were now "quite independent and have not a wish ungratified, . . . situated exactly as [their] imaginations and wishes used to represent" their hopes for their adult lives. Wistfully, she added in another letter to Jane Pollard, "You know the pleasure which I have always attached to the idea of home."[29]

But the last two of these rosy prospects never materialized, and the first two, Montagu's and Douglas's repayments, soon fell in arrears, so they were left with only the £50 per year for Basil Jr. Even that lasted only two years; by the time they moved to Somerset in mid-1797, they were maintaining lit-

*Tom knew better than William how to avoid mistakes with illegitimate children in the high-stakes marriage game. When he returned from the colonies, he married a distant cousin, Lady Mary Nevill, John Robinson's granddaughter and daughter of the earl of Abergavenny, twenty years his junior. He was awarded Robinson's Harwich seat when the old politico died in 1802. This was another life story Wordsworth could have had, if he'd accepted Robinson's offer of the Harwich curacy four years earlier and made other arrangements for Caroline.

tle Basil at their own expense.[30] It turned out to be a very good thing they didn't have to pay rent. Far from living a leisured country life as master and mistress of an elegant preschool nursery for rich colonials and demi-aristocrats, at an income surpassing that of a decent church living, they found themselves instead eking out an existence with barely enough cash to cover their basic expenses. The "plain living and high thinking" that Wordsworth would later idealize was thrust upon them as a rude shock at Racedown.

Their "system" for educating young Basil was as Dorothy said "a very simple one," but not as unaffected by "this age of systems" as she claimed.[31] It followed the tenets of one of the century's archsystematizers, Rousseau: an apparently nondirective method that allowed the child to follow the evidence of his senses rather than book learning. Since he was not yet three years old, this was good common sense as well. Little Basil Caroline explored his new rural surroundings along with them, and they answered all his questions about "the sky, the fields, trees, shrubs, corn, the making of tools, carts, &c &c &c." Since their "grand study ha[d] been to make him *happy,*" they were not disappointed of success.[32] In discipline, however, they stressed consequences more than explanations. If he cried, he was sent to his room (his "apartment of tears") and not allowed to return until he had stopped. The methods were well adapted to the child, and he soon got the point. He had been very much in the way in Montagu's lodgings in London, "extremely petted from indulgence and weakness of body." Now, out of doors in fresh air, with no regimen but what struck his fancy, he became a much better-tempered boy. But he never lost his habit of lying.

They were soon forced to turn to gardening for their diet. By the beginning of the new year, Wordsworth was outside helping Joseph Gill, as Dorothy smilingly noted: "My brother handles the spade with great dexterity."[33] This was largely because of Gill's inability to get the regular gardener, John Hitchcock, to do anything: talking to him was "as useless as it would be to sing Psalms to a dead horse." Gill and the Wordsworths suffered a certain amount of insubordination from the rest of the Racedown staff, because though friends or relations of the Pinney family, they clearly had no money to spare and hence no basis for authority. Since they arrived late in the year, their own first crops would not be ready until the next spring, so they had a long, hard winter of it. The expense of coal was one of the first things Dorothy remarked: "You would be surprized to see what a small cart full we get for three or four and twenty shillings [about 10 percent of their tutoring income], but we have such a habit of attention and frugality with respect to the management of our coals that they last much longer than I could have supposed possible."[34] Wordsworth knew whereof he spoke when he cast back to Dorset for the setting of "Goody Blake and Harry Gill" two years later:

> This woman dwelt in Dorsetshire,
> Her hut was on a cold hill-side,
> And in that country coals are dear,
> For they come far by wind and tide.[35]

The poem's setting, Goody's actions, and Harry's surname all derive immediately from Racedown. Poverty was so widespread that desperate people had no compunction about stealing from gardens. Once Joseph Gill and Wordsworth had, with difficulty, got their garden in, they prevailed on Hitchcock to build a protective fence around it, only to discover that bypassing wanderers tore out the boards for firewood. Laws passed earlier in the decade restricting tenants' gleaning rights had made it much more difficult to gather fuel.[36] Thus William partly occupied the position of Harry Gill in the poem, and some of his attitudes toward the poor were not unlike Harry's, though he foisted Joseph Gill's surname on him. When Wordsworth joked to Wrangham in February of 1797, "I have lately been living upon air and the essence of carrots cabbages turnips and other esculent vegetables, not excluding parsley the produce of my garden," he was trying to put a witty face on the reality of their situation.[37]

William and Dorothy also had difficulties with Gill arising from the dependent status of both parties. He began presenting them with inventories to be signed, attesting that "Mr. Wordsworth has taken call over all the things in the house and certified it on the inventory—therefore, as he says, he is now answerable for the whole."[38] Gill was not about to take the blame for any Wordsworthian accidents. But Wordsworth was also an adept student of family accounts, after many years of being charged for every shirt his aunts washed for him. He went over Gill's inventories with a fine-tooth comb, noting which queen's ware dishes were cracked, where wine glasses were missing from the set, that two butter pots had been sent to Bristol, that the tin-tinderbox candlestick was not "compleat" but "want[ed] a steel," and the fact that one of the towels had been "brought by Miss Wordsworth from Bristol." If he was not sure, he wrote, "Not well understood. W.W." Gradually they worked out a working relationship, but anytime guests came and more dishes or silverware were needed, Gill had to be asked to unlock cabinets and dole out the carefully inventoried supplies.

Gill had done well as an overseer and shopkeeper on Nevis, but he failed dismally as Pinney's first manager in the 1770s and had to be sent home. Like Wordsworth (though one doubts they ever shared the fact), he had left a lover behind him in another country, a mulatto woman named Penny Markham whose freedom he bought for £100. He had no more money than the Wordsworths, and once had to resort to eating the flesh of a cow that had died in calving, noting in his diary that is was "cruel hard to be starved to death in a Christian country."[39]

Wordsworth soon felt the truth of this from the walks he took around the neighborhood. Prices were rising everywhere because of the war, soon doubling the average cost of living. Between 1790 and 1795 the price of oats rose 75 percent, that of a loaf of bread doubled in the country and tripled in London, and that of a pound of potatoes quadrupled.[40] Dorothy complained, "Every thing has been very dear for house-keeping this season; we can get no meat under 6d. and Tea and Sugar, our only luxuries, are rising."[41] These two luxuries, the main imports of the British East Indian and West Indian imperial trade, respectively—and of John Wordsworth and John Pinney in their immediate acquaintance—were increasing in price also because of the number of ships being commandeered for the war effort. One of these was the *Earl of Abergavenny* itself, but another, larger and more profitable, was soon built by the Robinson-Wordsworth shipping interest to replace it.

These economic factors bore hard on Joseph Gill and the Wordsworths, but they were catastrophic for the rural poor, as Wordsworth soon saw: "many rich / Sunk down as in a dream among the poor, / And of the poor did many cease to be, / And their place knew them not."[42] Poverty was bad all over England, but it was worst in the West Country, which suffered more from the war's impact on trade and shipping. Wordsworth's first letter back to Mathews in October conveyed the ambivalence of their situation: "We are now at Racedown and both as happy as people can be who live in perfect solitude. We do not see a soul. Now and then we meet a miserable peasant in the road or an accidental traveller. The country people here are wretchedly poor; ignorant and overwhelmed with every vice that usually attends ignorance in that class, viz—lying and picking and stealing &c &c."[43] Solitude and happiness, poverty and viciousness: the two extremes lay close together. To "not see a soul" technically meant they received no visitors, but at Racedown Wordsworth learned to see the "soul" in wretchedly poor country people like Goody Blake, who had to pick and steal to keep themselves alive. Dorothy too, amid details of their house's splendid furnishings and situation, allotted one sentence to the same contrast: "The peasants are miserably poor; their cottages are shapeless structures (I may almost say) of wood and clay—indeed they are not at all beyond what might be expected in savage life."[44] Reactions to these realities could differ widely: plantation owners and sugar factors like Pinney and Tobin used them to justify owning slaves, maintaining not inaccurately that they sometimes got better care than the poor in England.

Wordsworth was in an anomalous position to observe all this. On the one hand, he was to all appearances the lord of the manor, living in a splendor based on the profits of slave labor. Like the Pedlar in his soon-to-be-composed "Ruined Cottage," he "could afford to suffer with those whom he saw suffer." The point is not simply that Wordsworth was privileged and the poor were not, or that he was somehow hypocritical in his way-wandering walks on "lonely roads [which] were schools to me."[45] On the contrary, his precarious situation gave him a motive to empathize with "souls that appear to have no depth at all / To vulgar eyes." He was well aware that he stood blessedly but precariously outside their suffering. The uneasiness of their situation helped redefine his poetry in a fundamental way over the next two years: How does one write poetry about poverty? What is the perspective from which telling stories about it can be seen as part of a solution, rather than part of the problem? Wordsworth had low powers of invention, but at Racedown he began to develop a kind of human inventiveness, the ability to project himself into the minds and bodies of the poor, the old, the senile, and the sick.

During his two years at Racedown, Wordsworth wrote nearly a dozen poems or fragmentary pieces which show these issues working their way haltingly into his major works of this period, *The Borderers* and "The Ruined Cottage." Their focus is so narrow that the light they shed on his poetic development is particularly sharp. Their subjects, beggars, convicts, deserted mothers and children, are pencil sketches in the genre of Wordsworthian solitude, anticipating the great solitary set pieces of his mature period: the Discharged Veteran, the Blind Beggar, the Leech Gatherer, and the Solitary Reaper.

The fragments do not lack for verbal power—quite the contrary. What is missing is any explanatory framework in which the suffering they depict might be interpreted. When he made an effort to supply an explanation, it was manifestly inadequate to the emotional force with which he represented the suffering itself. Questions are raised and discomfort created, but no resolution is achieved. When he described these experiences in *Prelude* XII, he boldly concluded that such subjects were fit for prophetic poetry: "the genius of the poet hence / May boldly take his way among mankind / Wherever Nature leads." But no such confidence is discernible in the manuscripts of 1796–97. These vignettes, taken as a group, cry out for some larger understanding: What are you going to do about us? They represent human suffering, very specifically in terms of social conditions in England ca. 1796, stubbornly persisting independent of any attempt to explain it, or relieve it, or even sympathize with it.

"The Baker's Cart" is photo-realism from Dorset in the late 1790s. It is set on a road like the one in front of Racedown, where a baker's cart did make rural rounds.[46] Wordsworth overheard a woman mutter seven words, " 'that waggon does not care for us,' " and he swiftly sketched in an entire social world around them. The cart does not stop to make its usual delivery at the woman's house as expected by her children, who "had all come forth . . . at the rumbling of the distant wheels." The baker's horse, equally innocent, also halts expectantly. But the driver knows the woman has no money, smacks his whip, and moves on, followed by the woman's sullen curse:

> The words were simple, but her look and voice
> Made up their meaning, and bespoke a mind
> Which being long neglected and denied
> The common food of hope was now become
> Sick and extravagant—by strong access
> Of momentary pangs driv'n to that state
> In which all past experience melts away
> And the rebellious heart to its own will
> Fashions the laws of nature. (17–25)[47]

She is a revolutionary in the making, an anticipation of the amoral villain of *The Borderers,* who fashions "the laws of nature" to the will of his own heart. Worse than lacking bread, she has been denied "the common food of hope." Though Wordsworth implicitly disapproves the woman's words ("sick and extravagant"), he offers no judgment on her. The fragment simply says this is what will result if these things happen. Walking about the countryside, Wordsworth might have tried to relieve the needs of some people he met with an alms, but he had no ready cash himself and could do little more than talk with the people he met. And he heard what they said.

"The Convict" is probably the earliest of these fragments, and its framework reflects the wishful thinking of Wordsworth's London sojourn. It clearly exposes the difficulty Wordsworth was having in making some kind of satisfactory statement about such socially unpromising materials. It is ostensibly about penal reform, but it suggests instead the attractions of simply giving up hard moral questions in despair. The speaker turns from watching a beautiful sunset on a hill, to ask, " 'And must we then part from a dwelling so fair?' " This could be Wordsworth on Pilsdon Pen, turning back toward Racedown after watching the sun set over the Channel, at just about the time that John Pinney found out about the (non)-rental arrangement and wanted his new tenants out. The speaker "repairs" to a place where he has evidently just come from, "the cell where a convict is laid." How a dungeon came to be so close to a picturesque viewing station is not explained, though there were rural holding jails, or compters, as in London, and arrests were being made every day because of all the "thieving and picking" that hard times had produced. But the jail's proximity to the sunset is mainly a symbolic contrast, in which the "Nature" alternative is badly defeated. The poem's surface concern is why aristocratic criminals get better treatment than common ones, who may be more remorseful for their crimes and are certainly more fearful of their consequences. But the poem's *object,* the dejected convict with matted hair lying in the back of his cell, raises a quite different question, which very nearly ruins the whole composition. A tear runs out of his eye, and "the silence of sorrow it seems to supply, / And asks of me why I am here." Good question: why indeed? Wordsworth here puts to himself the question implicit in all these fragments, namely, what is the moral responsibility of a poet who observes the human suffering caused by the action of contemporary British institutions—aided and abetted by the actions of nature (disease, age, bad harvests), and often by the behavior of the sufferers themselves (jealousy, anger, lust)?

He tries to answer the question, but the weakness of his answer shows why most of the rest of his short pieces of 1796–97 are free-standing icons of pain without commentary:

> "At thy name though compassion her nature resign,
> Though in virtue's proud mouth thy report be a stain,
> My care, if the arm of the mighty were mine,
> Would plant thee where yet thou might'st blossom again."
> (49–52)

This is merely a wish for an enlightened policy of transportation for criminals, as advocated by John Howard and Elizabeth Fry, and most recently pleaded in theoretical terms by William Godwin.[48] The speaker would, if he could, transport ("transplant") the convict to Botany Bay—a good place for blossoming, from the sound of it, but horrifically not so, in reality. "The Convict" is modern in its emphasis on rehabilitation over punishment, and its sympathy is preferable to the conventional moral self-righteousness it rejects, but its moral is simple: don't despise criminals, try to reform them. This was better than urging more hangings as a solution to the nation's growing crime wave, but it exposes its own weakness when it says, "if the arm of the mighty were mine," since it obviously isn't.

Like the *Philanthropist*'s "Address to Poverty," "The Convict" is more concerned about mental than about physical suffering, and this is true of all the Racedown fragments. What Wordsworth really wants to get at are the prisoner's *self*-tortures: " 'Tis sorrow enough on that visage to gaze . . . Yet my fancy has pierced to his heart, and pourtrays / More terrible images there." This is what Wordsworth will be doing for the next four years at least: trying to see suffering from the inside—including, increasingly, the suffering of the person who observes it.

The "Argument for Suicide" sums up the moral conundrums of the entire group of 1796–97 fragments. The title is Wordsworth's, but does not make clear exactly whose argument this is:

> Send this man to the mine, this to the battle,
> Famish an aged beggar at your gates,
> And let him die by inches—but for worlds
> Lift not your hand against him—Live, live on,
> As if this earth owned neither steel nor arsenic,
> A rope, a river, or a standing pool.
> Live, if you dread the pains of hell, or think
> Your corpse would quarrel with a stake—alas
> Has misery then no friend?—if you would die
> By license, call the dropsy and the stone
> And let them end you—strange it is;
> And most fantastic are the magic circles
> Drawn round the thing called life—till we have learned
> To prize it less, we ne'er shall learn to prize
> The things worth living for.[49]

We see Wordsworth here in the very act of yielding up moral questions in despair. Is this an argument for or against suicide? And whose argument is it? Someone contemplating suicide? Or someone who is causing death without being charged for murder: the business and military establishments of the opening lines, who kill people legally "by inches"? Only in the fourth line is the potential suicide addressed directly and warned of eternal damnation, as if the deaths described had been his idea. The "resolution" of the suicide question proper (9–11) seems to recommend contracting a fatal disease.

But the statement of this macabre quasi-sonnet is complete, and its method is of a piece with Wordsworth's in all these poems: until we cut away the usual explanations for the sanctity of life (here presented as fantastic magical acts), "we ne'er shall learn to prize / The things worth living for." End of poem. What these prized things are is not specified, but they are clearly not economic prosperity, military glory, social charity, religious belief, or whatever other excuses society uses to rationalize its behavior to the suffering poor. The poem is negatively radical, saying that unless people recognize murder and suicide as viable alternatives to the terrible conditions people find themselves living in, we will never come to any truly positive ideas for life.

Efforts like these were clearly not going anywhere, in terms of poetic closure, so once he and Dorothy were well settled in at Racedown, Wordsworth began more concentrated writing in the same way he had at Windy Brow the previous summer, by revising an already completed work: this time, "A

Night on Salisbury Plain" (NSP). This occupied most of his writing time through the end of the year.[50] But his impulse was directly opposite to the one he followed with *An Evening Walk* in 1794. There he had taken a decidedly unpolitical poem and filled it with sociopolitical commentary. Now, following several hectic months in London at the nerve centers of agitation for reform, attending philosophical discussions and drafting compositions on justice and benevolence, he produced a poem in which explicit political argument is stripped away, by "alterations and additions so material as that it may be looked on almost as another work."[51] In revising *An Evening Walk,* he was still focused on the landscape; now his vision concentrated on the people in it. He gave the revised poem a new title, "Adventures on Salisbury Plain" (ASP). The change in titles accurately captures the essence of his changes, for the first version is a relatively static "night-piece," a fugue of suffering articulated by the Female Vagrant, whereas the second is a narrative with a beginning, middle, and end, and two developed characters whose interactions move the story forward. His main change was to lop off a philosophical and political framework from Rousseau and Paine around the Female Vagrant's story and recast the nameless narrator of the first poem into a new character, a homeward-bound sailor, whose story of suffering complements the vagrant woman's and resembles Wordsworth's.

The increased narrative realism makes ASP a better poem than NSP, but not a more reassuring one. Quite the contrary. The new direction of the poem, toward an unmediated examination of the human condition in England, ca. 1795, is characteristic of all Wordsworth's poems written at Racedown. They all display the starkest possible framing of the problem of human suffering, coupled with what we tend not to notice, because it is not there: a determined refusal to offer any kind of interpretation that might be taken as advancing toward a solution of the problem. This is a symptom of Wordsworth's giving up moral questions in despair, but it also indicates that giving up moral questions did not mean giving up poetry, only seeking answers in a more humble fashion. Rarely have the deprivations and injustice of the English social system been presented in such somber, unsparing colors.[52] Yet none of these poems were published in their original form at the time; they contributed more to Wordsworth's self-creation than to contemporary debates on the condition of England. But it was not for lack of trying, especially with ASP, which he actively sought to publish by subscription in early 1796, and which would be frequently mentioned in Wordsworth's negotiations with the publisher Joseph Cottle in Bristol in 1798.

This change in direction is usually interpreted as the sign of Wordsworth's rejection of politics, specifically his revulsion from Godwin's benign necessarianism. This is partly true, but not the whole truth. Retreat from politics became a general condition in 1796, the year in which Coleridge claimed to have "snapped the squeaking baby trumpet" of his "sedition" (a clever obfuscation which understates the impact of his radical activities while overstating their criminal status). Yet Wordsworth walked twice to Lyme Regis in the fall to make connections with Nicholas Philpot Leader, another Irish friend of Mathews's, once bringing him back for a brief visit to Racedown. Little is known about this young man at this time; like Wordsworth, he was the son of an aristocrat's law agent, and he published a pamphlet on the union with England in 1800. He was part of that Irish connection which the *Philanthropist* was to have developed, and one sign among several that Wordsworth's rethinking his political stance was a deep, gradual process, not a rapid one.

Far from being a rejection of Godwin, ASP can well be called Wordsworth's "most Godwinian" work.[53] But it is not Godwin the benevolent necessarian. Rather, it is the Godwin of *Political Justice,* unsparingly criticizing the failure and hypocrisy of social institutions; it resembles the Godwin of *Caleb Williams* even more. The sailor's wanderings and foiled attempts to return home, and the unjust treatment he suffers, are very like Caleb's wanderings (incidentally, across the same landscape in southwest England) to find a fair hearing for his complaints against his cruel, devious master. Both are stark illustrations of Godwin's central critical truth, that circumstances can lead good people into crime.[54]

Revising NSP into ASP, Wordsworth was attempting to see "men as they are men within themselves." He rejected all categories of explanation except those provided by his own observation, or else he tried to create new categories of explanation by inductive experiments with his own materials. "Nature" was the catchall category in which he began to cast for answers to these nearly impossible questions. But the nature he invokes is not the picturesque landscape associated with him from the Lake District, nor is it Nature with any supportive metaphysical principle or god term behind it. On the contrary, it is more like the grimly competitive nature of Malthus and later of Charles Darwin.[55] Aldous Huxley's sneer that Wordsworth would have had a different attitude toward nature if he'd visited the tropics falls flat on the hard surfaces of "Salisbury Plain." Nature here is bleak, barren, sublimely terrifying and morally unconcerned, more an objective correlative to the characters' bleak lives than a benign alternative reality. It is less an external reality to be described, beautifully or otherwise, than simply a given: whatever is just *there,* surrounding mankind, when all support systems of meaning or help are pulled away, and we seek "for good in the familiar face of life . . . among the natural abodes of men" (XII.67, 107). It is radically *other* than man and his institutions, but its otherness carries no comfortable moral charge; it is entirely open to interpretation.

Wordsworth's changes in the plot of NSP turn upon the relationship between the man and the woman, and lay down the lines of what could be an appalling family tragedy. Consciously or unconsciously, Wordsworth now identified with both characters. The woman's story is one of passive suffering and sorrow, commencing with her family's losing their freehold in the Lake District to rapacious estate builders, reflecting Wordsworth's own early life experience. The Sailor's story is one of unmerited suffering complicated by guilt (for involuntary manslaughter), reflecting Wordsworth's more recent adult experience in France. Together they stand for *Guilt and Sorrow,* the title under which Wordsworth published the poem many years later (1842). The Sailor had served two years aboard ship, and returned home "enflamed with long desire . . . while in thought he took his rich reward / From his wife's lips"; "pleasure fondly made / Her dwelling in his dreams." These frank expressions of sexual desire are otherwise "notably absent from Wordsworth's mature poetry,"[56] but were very much in his thoughts as memories of Annette faded into dreamlike fantasies.

In both versions, but much more so in the second, Wordsworth raised the possibility that the Sailor and the Female Vagrant might support each other in their misery. The Sailor meets an old soldier who might be his father-in-law (how he failed to recognize him is a problem that Wordsworth knew would require some rewriting), whereas the man he killed could have been the Female Vagrant's husband. As it is, the Female Vagrant discovers the Sailor's wife dying on a cart near the inn, somehow recognizes her, and rushes back to him to bring them together for an affecting deathbed scene. Wordsworth knew this piling up of coincidences was too much: "So much for the vulgar," he wryly commented.[57] This would have been a Gothic thriller worthy of Monk Lewis, since Wordsworth proposed to make the Female Vagrant into, variously, the widow, the daughter, or the sister of the very man the Sailor who befriends her has murdered. But such a plot would have left open one denouement which the revised ending dramatically rejects: the Sailor and the Female Vagrant could have stayed together and perhaps lived happily ever after. In NSP the mutual attraction between the two main characters was represented physically, in the Traveller's kindling interest in the Vagrant's snow-white breasts, rising and falling like swans among the lilies of Derwent Water. In ASP this strong physical attraction is replaced by a moral one: "And still the more he grieved, she loved him still the more." In one kind of moral reasoning, the Traveller, in becoming the Sailor, has moved to a more admirable position: not a man attracted by a woman's body, but a man whose griefs make him attractive to a woman's finer feelings. Similar love relations exist in all the major poems he wrote over the next three years, from *The Borderers* to "Tintern Abbey," where husbands and wives, or lovers, or brothers and sisters, come agonizingly close to being united or reunited. But this solution, close to Wordsworth's personal desires regarding both Annette and Dorothy, is for just that reason held back from being realized.

Wordsworth told Wrangham that the intention of the new poem was "partly to expose the vices of the penal law and the calamities of war as they affect individuals,"[58] but this is a very abstract synopsis. What motivates the changes and gives the new poem its greater power, despite its bleaker political views, is the fact Wordsworth developed the two characters into a greater proximity to his own life situation. Thoughts of human suffering as represented by abandoned women, already present in Wordsworth's work, now become the dominant motif of his narrative poems. Sociopolitical issues remain in the poem, but they are made more, not less, difficult by the addition of psychological elements which clearly derive from Wordsworth's personal situation, living with Dorothy and longing for—or feeling guilty about—Annette.

That Annette was still much on his mind is also clear from a French poem ("The hour-bell sounds") he translated in 1796, from Helen Maria Williams's *Letters from France.* She had published the poem with a translation, or imitation: it is the supposed address of a twenty-four-year-old French prisoner to his mistress before he goes to the guillotine.[59] Wordsworth's translation returns to the French original, reestablishing the fact that the speaker is a husband leaving his wife "dans le veuvage et la douleur," which Wordsworth correctly translates as "In widowhood and lonely pain," adding the notion of loneliness to that of sadness. When Wordsworth finally let Coleridge publish this poem in the *Morning Post* in May 1798, he had it signed "Mortimer," the name of the naive young hero of *The Borderers,* whose tragic predicament is clearly a symbolic representation of parts of Wordsworth's own.

During the winter months, he and Dorothy read extensively in Racedown's large library. They continued their study of Italian, reading Machiavelli and Boccaccio. There were also Whiggish books of political economy and a good representation of writing from the English republican tradition: John Frederick Pinney particularly recommended a copy of the works of Algernon Sydney.[60] Though Wordsworth's writings were becoming less overtly political, he had by no means lost interest in politics. Throughout their time at Racedown he requested from his friends in London and Bristol the latest works of political controversy, including the *Monthly Magazine* and the *Analytical Review.* These covered a wide spectrum, from Burke through Coleridge and his Unitarian friend John Estlin, to Thomas Erskine *(The Causes and Consequences of the Present War),* although their overall tendency was more conservative than radical. The *Monthly Magazine* was a new and highly successful production, whose editorial policy in the increasingly repressive publishing climate appealed to Wordsworth: liberal, but not aggressively so, and maintaining a wide interest in cultural topics beyond political news and argument.[61] The Pinney library also had a remarkably full collection of seventeenth- and eighteenth-century verse, including not only major authors like Milton, Dryden, and Swift but also many now obscure second- or third-rank authors: Sandys, Burnet, Glover, Buckingham, Aubrey, and Blackmore. Wordsworth's poetical education, already prodigious, began to approach the encyclopedic level. The common element linking all these diverse writers was the intricate, varied relation between politics and poetics in their art. Wordsworth was reading voraciously not merely to improve his stock of poetry but because these writers addressed the question that he personally was most troubled by, the social responsibility of the poet.

At the very end of 1795 they received three French books: the memoirs of Mme Roland, written as she awaited execution; those of Wordsworth's onetime hero Louvet, who had lived to tell about the Terror; and the latest installment of Helen Maria Williams's *Letters.* These were all people Wordsworth had seen close-up during his residence in France, and perhaps talked to. Their chastened accounts of the crimes committed in the name of liberty reinforced his growing disillusionment with direct political action. Other signs pointed in the same direction; the brother of Helen Williams's lover, John Hurford Stone, was tried for treason in early 1796, and got off only thanks to character testimonials from the leading parliamentary Whigs.[62] At the same time, Napoleon rejected feelers for the "regicide" peace that Burke denounced, while the success of his Italian campaign made it clear that the war was not simply a calculated exercise in cynical realpolitik by Pitt.[63]

The Pinney boys arrived in a bustle on January 2 for a week, returning again in February for a month which featured a "grand rout" of winter feast and party. Writing was "out of the question" when they were there, for the visits of these playboys of the west of England were always festive occasions, devoted to coursing for hares and foxes, in which both William and Dorothy joined enthusiastically.[64] The main use of Racedown to the younger Pinneys was as a hunting lodge; a main benefit of their visits to the young Wordsworths was to replenish the larder with supplies of fresh meat. Azariah noted, "While we were with him [Wordsworth] he relaxed the vigour of his philosophic nerves so much as to go a Coursing several times, & I assure you did not eat the unfortunate Hares with less relish because he heard them heave their death groans . . . for his usual appetite showed itself at the dining table."[65]

Azariah Pinney was the "active and shrewd" son, slated to enter the business, and he shows here a nice ability to take the measure of his man.[66] His keen eye may account for his being not "so great a favourite" with Dorothy as his brother was. The coolness was mutual: "Miss Wordsworth has undoubted claim to good humour, but does not possess that je ne sais quoi, so necessary to sweeten the draught of human misfortune." One wonders what drafts of misfortune this spoiled young man had quaffed, but the sweets he liked are obvious enough. He felt that if a man was a poet he should produce poetry, and asked William to "write a few lines panegyrical" on the object of John Frederick's affections, helpfully reminding him that her name had three syllables. Panegyric seems to have been called for by the fact that John was under treatment for veneral disease by a London doctor.[67]

John Frederick, as the elder son, enjoyed the privileged status of being "of no profession," though he had gone to the "great schools" and Oxford and developed a personality more pleasing to Dorothy: "a charming countenance and the sweetest temper I ever observed." This was not surprising, since he "had always plenty of money to spend and every indulgence: all these things instead of having spoiled him . . . have wrought the pleasantest and best effects, he is well-informed, has an uncommonly good heart, and is very agreeable in conversation."[68] The historian of the family takes quite a different view of John Frederick's qualities: "a showy, peevish nonentity, without any claim to distinction besides an early friendship with Wordsworth and Coleridge, which cannot have gone very deep," his studies "a mere show," and displaying "all the fretfulness of a weak man."[69] Basil Montagu's attitude toward both young men was condescending to the point of insult, especially when he was refusing to pay the money he owed them. He told them it was their duty "to assist in the progress of wisdom" by subsidizing him, often holding up his obligations to "that good man Wordsworth" as his excuse.[70] But the four young people got on well enough, despite these differences in temperament. The Pinneys were flattered to have such advanced intellectual guests, and the Wordsworths were glad to have such generous wealthy admirers.

Not that John Frederick or Azariah were uninterested in literature. They were the main conduit for information and works in progress between the Racedown solitaries and their new Bristol acquaintances—Coleridge, Southey, and the enterprising Dissenting publisher, picturesque poet, and moral reformer Joseph Cottle. They brought Southey's *Joan of Arc* with them, and Azariah took the new version of "Salisbury Plain" back with him in March to show to Coleridge. He reported Coleridge's "lively interest" in "so valuable a Poem (as he terms it)," and relayed Coleridge's suggestion that Wordsworth publish it in the *Watchman*.[71] Southey's poem, with its dedicatory sonnet to Mary Wollstonecraft, showed how historical subjects could be used to highlight contemporary issues, an example that Wordsworth imitated when he began *The Borderers* in the fall. But Southey's egotistical preface convinced him that Mathews had been right after all in declaring Southey a "coxcomb."

Coleridge made copious comments on "Adventure on Salisbury Plain" and wrote Wordsworth urging him to publish it separately as a book. This endorsement of his work was enormously heartening to Wordsworth, and he never forgot the imprimatur of originality which Coleridge's praise gave him: "That . . . I must then have exercised / Upon the vulgar forms of present things . . . / A higher power . . . / An image, and a character, by books / Not hitherto reflected" (XII.360–66). Mathews had also read the Salisbury Plain poem, but had failed to remark it with anything approaching Coleridge's enthusiasm. Unstinting praise like this is what Wordsworth needed, in the harsh economy of genius, not Mathews's finicky advice about the need for "incessant" revision. Coleridge probably did say something this extreme; it was part of his character to see immense possibilities in the work of his friends. Writing to John Thelwall in May, defending himself against Thelwall's charge of excessive metaphysics in "Religious Musings," Coleridge used Wordsworth's Salisbury Plain poem as an affidavit for his political credentials: "this man is a republican, and, at least, a *semi*-atheist." But he added something more important to Wordsworth than Coleridge's estimate of either his religion or his politics: "a very dear friend of mine, the best poet of the age." For Wordsworth this kind of praise coming at this time was crucial. It was the first time he had received such praise from a contemporary whose judgment he respected, and whose own level of achievement he frankly envied: Dorothy and Mathews had been very well in their way, but Wordsworth needed more. His career and sense of himself needed Coleridge far more than Coleridge needed him at this moment, and Wordsworth did all he could in the coming months to keep up his contacts with his new friend.

The day after he heard from Coleridge, he wrote to Wrangham, his current collaborator, full of heavy facetiousness, bluffly congratulating him on his induction to a lucrative living in Yorkshire worth £600 a year.[72] He made several heavy comparisons between Wrangham's new status ("You are now a rich man") and his own poverty ("I think it no bad employment to feel 'the penalty of Adam' "), which seem vaguely calculated to get Wrangham to take an interest in him. Wrangham is now "entirely above the necessity of engaging in any employment unsuited to your taste and pleasures," while Wordsworth has been "engaged an hour and a half this morning in hewing wood and rooting up hedges."[73]

There was a bad moment after the Pinneys returned to Bristol, when they had to tell their father about "the whole transaction relative to the deficiency of the Cash I rec'd for him at Racedown, as circumstances rendered it impracticable to conceal it effectually from him." John Pretor Pinney was only with difficulty kept from suing Wordsworth. This matter sounds less like a discovery that Wordsworth wasn't paying rent than that Wordsworth was borrowing, or otherwise making use of, the petty cash at Racedown.[74]

As soon as the Pinneys left on March 6, William and Dorothy resumed their busy domestic schedule, which again made new writing difficult. As spring approached, William was out cutting wood and digging up hedges to help Joseph Gill. Time was taken up with arrangements for fetching coal and walking the seven miles to Crewkerne, to see if Montagu or anyone else had responded to their desperate invitations for company. They planted cabbages, "and into cabbages we shall be transformed."[75]

But William managed to crank out a hundred more lines on the Juvenal project and sent them off to Wrangham with more labored punning. He assured Wrangham of his continued interest in their project: "I now feel a return of the literary appetite I mean to take a snack of satire by way of Sandwich," alluding to his intention to throw in a hit at the extramarital adventures of Montagu's father, inventor of the "sandwich."

Appetite whetted, he wrote a small new poem, "Address to the Ocean," which eventually appeared in the nearby Sherborne *Weekly Entertainer,* which also published contemporary works by Coleridge, Southey, and Charlotte Smith.[76] Partly an imitation of Coleridge's Ossianic "Complaint of Ninathoma," it has much less to do with the ocean than with lost love. Another variation on his new theme of lost or separated lovers, it is the lament of a woman who lives in a hut near the ocean's edge, crying for her drowned lover and horribly imagining what the action of the sea is doing to his beautiful body: "By monsters beset in its falling / The brood of the bottomless world." Though Wordsworth could see the Channel quite easily and frequently walked to it, this is not a "nature poem"; it has much more to do with his brooding thoughts about Annette across the Channel. It was an effort to do something in the manner of the admired Coleridge, using conventional materials that nonetheless had enough personal edge to spur his emotions to the effort of composition.

After his fallow spring, Wordsworth was eager for more stimulation. On June 1 he set off for a six-week visit in London. He had supper with Godwin on at least four occasions; his disapproval of the philosopher's style and thought did not affect his personal esteem for him. Wordsworth never dropped Godwin's acquaintance as so many later did, but he now began moving in less radical company than he had the previous summer. Godwin's diary makes no mention of William Mathews at any of their meetings, and there is no further record of Mathews in Wordsworth's life after a letter sent to him in March, inviting him to Racedown for a summer visit.[77] Montagu was in attendance at these gatherings, but the other young men were richer, less intellectual, and altogether less impressive than Wordsworth's 1795 circle: the Pinney brothers, the Tobin brothers, and John Stoddart, "a cold-hearted, well-bred conceited disciple of Godwin's" (according to Lamb). Stoddart like the others was engaged in literary pursuits (translating Schiller's *Fiesco*) while balancing his marriage prospects against chances for ecclesiastical preferment (he eventually became chief justice of Malta, and his sister Sarah married Hazlitt). It may have been the experience of listening to Godwin in these less stimulating circumstances that helped push Wordsworth into the sweeping indictment of Godwinism in *The Borderers,* the major work that he began in the fall. He noticed how Godwin had smoothed his radical edge to accommodate criticisms of *Political Justice* and protect himself in the new atmosphere of repression.

But this London visit also marked the beginning of Wordsworth's lifelong friendship with Charles Lamb, whom he now met, Coleridge having prepared the way by sending Lamb a copy of "Adventures on Salisbury Plain," which he read "not without delight."

After his return from London he took out life insurance policies on Basil Montagu's life to protect his ill-fated loan. At the end of August he and Dorothy picked their first crop of French beans from the garden.[78] A series of late summer and early autumn visits from John Frederick Pinney and Henry Moncrief (whose sister Stoddart would marry) kept him and Dorothy busy as host and hostess.

In late November, Mary Hutchinson arrived, escorted by her sailor brother Henry, who was on his way to join his ship at Plymouth.[79] She came directly from nursing her younger sister Margaret's in a fatal illness, and was in need of a rest. The visit lasted six months and contributed to William's growing happiness through the winter and into the next spring. Wordsworth attested to the happiness of this reacquaintance with the childhood friend who would become his wife in lines set down in the middle of his account of wandering the lonely roads of Dorset. His bleak walks were second in his enjoyment only to

> one dear state of bliss, vouchsafed
> Alas to few in this untoward world,
> The bliss of walking daily in life's prime
> Through field or forest with the maid we love
> While yet our hearts are young, while yet we breathe
> Nothing but happiness, *living in some place,*
> *Deep vale, or anywhere the home of both,*
> From which it would be misery to stir . . . .
>
> (XII.127–34; italics added)

The purposeful vagueness of the locale fits well the conditions of their residence at Racedown. Of course, he could be referring to Dorothy as well, and he probably was.

Yet is Annette not ruled out of this picture, as we see in another fragmentary text Wordsworth began at this time, a ballad called "The Three Graves," which he eventually abandoned as too "depressing" and turned over to Coleridge. The ballad's materials are not so depressing as they are psychologically loaded. It is not surprising that Wordsworth abandoned it—nor that he started it—when Mary's presence in the household inevitably stirred up thoughts and desires about his sexual life and his continuing obligations to Annette and their daughter. "The Three Graves" is only the second ballad that Wordsworth had so far composed in his life, and the first since 1787, when he wrote about Mary Rigge's seduction and betrayal by David Kirkby of Coniston. He produced about two hundred lines of this one, setting out the complications of a potentially incestuous love triangle, or quadrangle. No profound psychoanalytic insight is needed to recognize that the poem projects fantasy materials from his own situation that he could not resolve.

The poem concerns the love of Edward for Mary, and the intense jealousy of Mary's widowed mother, which leads her to offer herself to Edward instead. Edward, amazed and disgusted, repulses the mother and, worse, laughs at her, whereupon she casts a curse upon her terrified daughter. The two young lovers leave the house with the mother on her knees in the orchard, gesticulating after them. There Wordsworth's fragment ends. Throughout her trials, Mary is supported by her friend Ellen, who "though not akin in blood . . . did bear a sister's part" to her. This is exactly the kind of relationship Dorothy and Mary had begun to establish—as had Dorothy and Annette, in correspondence—and after 1802 it would be the pattern of the rest of their life together.[80] These three symbolic identifications are clear enough, but the identity of the "ruthless mother" is much more problematic.

At first the mother agrees to the marriage, though Mary feared she wouldn't, because, as she tells Edward, "you have little gear" (wealth), like William. But the mother's assent is given on quite different grounds: "In truth you are a comely man." The "course of wooing" goes on "beneath the mother's eye." Then, the night before the wedding, she suddenly sends her daughter upstairs—to the bridal chamber, it seems—with the cry "Would ye come here, ye maiden vile, / And rob me of my mate?" The girl flees and the mother offers herself to Edward on the grounds that Mary "is not fit / To be your paramour." Edward, of course, is looking for a wife, not a paramour, but a paramour was what, strictly speaking, Annette was to William—just as she was the only "mother" among the three women in his life at this moment, and the only one who herself had a mother alive at the time—a mother who was, furthermore, opposed to her daughter's marrying her English adventurer.

As they leave "this wicked house," the mother, with a weird irony, wishes them well ("let the night be given to bliss") and tells them not to worry about her: "What can an aged woman do, / And what have ye to dread?" The focus at the end of the fragment is very much on the mother—a mad mother, another version of the dominant character emerging in Wordsworth's poems, whose curse has rebounded upon herself. She is last seen baring her breast to show strangers "the milk which clinging imps of hell / And sucking daemons drew." Unless one arbitrarily decides the poem could have nothing to do with Wordsworth's life (exactly contrary to everything we have seen about every text he produced in the 1790s), it is easy to infer that he is imagining the anger or reproaches of Annette if he were to marry Mary Hutchinson, an idea which may now have first been seriously entertained by him, by Mary, and of course by Dorothy.

The whole story is told long after the fact by an old sexton in a churchyard where the three graves of the title are lined up beneath a thorn tree: "a ruthless mother," "a barren wife," and "a maid forlorn." The women are all dead, but where is Edward/William? Is he that blooming thorn near the graves? "It blossoms sweet," yet round "its roots / The dock and nettle meet," and hemlock too, adding a suggestion of suicide to this steamy mixture. The sexton's tale may be Wordsworth's fantasy of the death of all three of the women troubling his constricted life, and his longing for freedom. Such a possibility seems finally more ordinary than shocking or surprising.

20 AN INDEPENDENT INTELLECT

From *The Borderers* to "The Ruined Cottage," 1796–1797

> ... the only law that wisdom
> Can ever recognize: the immediate law
> Flashed from the light of circumstances
> Upon an independent intellect.
>
> (*The Borderers,* III.v.30–33)

From early October, Wordsworth was "ardent" in the composition of *The Borderers,* his only surviving drama. He worked on it steadily through a winter of heavy, isolating snows and brought it to its first complete form by the end of February: over two thousand lines of blank verse in less than six months. At the end of 1797 he tried to make it suitable for stage production, but after it was rejected by the manager of Covent Garden he put it aside for over forty years. It was published in revised form in 1842, when he was seventy-two, more as a matter of record for his oeuvre than as a living document of his career.

Though unsuccessful as a stage vehicle, *The Borderers* was a strong conception, taking risks that face down easy criticisms. Wordsworth was attempting, seven years after the fall of the Bastille, to dramatize a fundamental critique of the spirit of revolution. He was not alone in doing this, of course. Several works of English fiction had already taken up the implications of a radical application of reason to human institutions. Robert Bage (*Man as He Is,* 1792) and Wordsworth's old nemesis Holcroft (*Anna St. Yves,* 1792; *Hugh Trevor,* 1794–97) pursued the paradox that "arguments advanced by one [view of reason] to attack the hypocrisy of institutions were employed by another to sap the foundations of human nature."[1] Godwin's *Caleb Williams* and Burke's *Reflections* had probed the same paradox.

At its furthest stretch of implication, *The Borderers* asks why noble ideals of human liberation so often become tyrannical in their turn, and why the break with traditional, hierarchical—and often oppressive—moral categories, though based on the best deductions of the best minds about man's "natural" rights, leads to rationalized murder and heartless behavior. It confronts the central moral dilemma that has dogged efforts to decide whether the French Revolution was worth it after all: How much does it matter that acts of unspeakable brutality are committed in the name of admirable political ideals? *The Borderers* does not confront these questions directly, since its villain, Rivers, is no Robespierre, but at best a provincial caricature of him. But it anticipates questions which thoughtful revolutionaries asked themselves, often in crushed despair, over the next two hundred years.

Wordsworth's version of these questions is strongly skewed to produce a negative answer. His villain representing the dark side of revolution is a much stronger character than his naive liberal hero, Mortimer. Swinburne (who seems like a good authority on such matters) thought the play and its villain "unparalleled by any serious production of the human intellect for morbid and monstrous extravagance of horrible impossibility."[2] Mortimer is ready to break the law in order to help suffering poor people, but he cannot quite take the steps urged on him by Rivers, to go beyond all conventional moral considerations and act upon the right as he alone sees it.

Yet Wordsworth was not primarily writing a tract for his times in *The Borderers.* His motives arose from his personal history, dramatizing his emotional involvement in the Revolution, especially his love affair with Annette Vallon, now complicated by his responsibilities for Dorothy.[3] The play enacts his attempt to purge himself of both kinds of personal commitment he had made to revolutionary possibilities since 1792, the emotional and erotic as well as the intellectual and political. Given the scope of its public theme, and the intensity of its private one (which was deepened by Wordsworth's inability to *act on* his love), it is no wonder that the play fails dramatically; Stendhal, Dickens, and Tolstoy had great difficulties at the very height of their powers writing love stories set in the French Revolution. The effort of writing *The Borderers* brought Wordsworth closer to those heights, but did not achieve the goal; it has well been called "a failed play of successful repression," or a play that *"intends* to be a bad play."[4]

Intellectually, *The Borderers* is a critique of the enlightened moral expediency which Wordsworth learned from Godwin. Rivers's monologues are shot through with the language of *Political Justice,* and the remorse-driven plot and the hero tricked into seeking vengeance are virtually identical to the basic situation of Godwin's popular *Caleb Williams.* Yet the play rarely broaches social or political issues directly, though they are implied by its military ambience: the Crusades and the border wars between England and Scotland. Instead, it enacts the personal dimension of philosophical issues, which arise prior to social action, and in so doing exposes the consequences of an egotistical misappropriation of the entire range of "wild theories [then] afloat," Godwin's among others.

When placed in the contexts of its larger resonance, the actual plot of *The Borderers* seems more than a bit bizarre. It concerns Rivers's efforts, through five very talky acts, to persuade Mortimer that his beloved Matilda has been groomed all her life by a man who pretends to be her father, the old blind Baron Herbert, to be delivered as a concubine to the depraved Lord Clifford. Herbert, according to Rivers, purchased Matilda as an infant from a beggar woman (actually a woman in Rivers's pay) and has bound her to him—made her his moral slave, in effect—by telling her moving tales of how he saved her from the flames of Antioch in which her mother and brother died. Rivers goads Mortimer to kill Herbert for these heinous crimes, having beforehand poisoned Herbert's opinion of Mortimer as a lawless freebooter, thus separating the two lovers. He does all this because he resents owing gratitude to Mortimer for having once saved his life.

Rivers's deeper motive is a kind of philosophical seduction of Mortimer, to make him repeat a crime, and suffer its psychic aftershocks, that Rivers himself was tricked into en route to Palestine. Convinced by the ship's crew that its captain meant to lead them to destruction, and that he had spoken slightingly of the proud, ambitious Rivers, he agreed to lead their mutiny. They left the captain stranded on a piece of barren rock to die of starvation and exposure to the elements.* Later, when the crew members tell Rivers they have tricked him, he flees his troop in remorse. But after three days of self-torment in a biblical wilderness, he succumbs to his own temptation, rejecting remorse in favor of an ethic of personal expediency, raised to the level of an existentialist philosophy, which he subsequently tries to foist on Mortimer. In the end, Mortimer cannot quite bring himself to kill Herbert outright, but, in a duplication of Rivers's crime, abandons him on the barren heath.

The trouble with *The Borderers* is that everybody but Mortimer can see right away that Rivers is evil. It's the kind of play at which an audience wants to cry out, It's the guy in black, stupid! He's the villain! Mortimer's band of borderers virtually foam at the mouth every time they see Rivers, so spontaneously do they mistrust him. (They are named Wallace, Lacy, Lennox, and Norwood, ecumenically representing both sides of Wordsworth's border-

*The fate of Captain Bligh of the *Bounty* contributed directly to this detail. On October 23 Wordsworth wrote his only known letter to an editor, to the Sherborne *Weekly Entertainer,* protesting that a collection of letters it had reviewed, attributed to the mutiny's leader, Fletcher Christian, his old Cockermouth and Hawkshead schoolmate, was spurious. This was his contribution to a national letter-writing campaign that his uncle Cookson, the family lawyer Edward Christian (Fletcher's brother), his college tutor Edward Frewen, and his cousin Captain John Wordsworth mounted to defend their relative's behavior under Bligh's extremely authoritarian command. See *The Borderers,* ed. Robert Osborn (Ithaca: Cornell Univ. Press, 1982), 5.

land.) They gleefully dispatch him in a mass stabbing as soon as Mortimer gives them leave in the final scene.

Wordsworth could not easily have solved this problem of plausibility without diluting the philosophical problem that was his real concern. The play, as a psychological thriller, lacks what Alfred Hitchcock called a "maguffin," some concrete plot device the audience can keep its eye on as the horror grows. A leadership struggle between Rivers and Mortimer would be an obvious solution, or a rivalry for Matilda's love. But any motive that Wordsworth gave Rivers would blur his radical existential focus and weaken his Iago dimension: the powerful attraction of moral behavior based solely on a virtuous conviction of the rightness of one's own motives, bolstered by total confidence in the scrupulous accuracy of one's efforts to learn the truth:

> . . . the only law that wisdom
> Can ever recognize: the immediate law
> Flashed from the light of circumstances
> Upon an independent intellect.
> (III.v.30–33)[5]

These famous lines, a twisted paraphrase of passages in *Political Justice,* are virtually identical with the description in *The Prelude* of the radical faith in "the freedom of the individual mind," which ultimately led Wordsworth to yield up all moral questions in despair.[6]

Wordsworth's prefatory essay defends Rivers's Iago-like "motiveless malignity" in terms which also relate to his own experience: "to make the nonexistence of a common motive itself a motive to action is a practice which we are never so prone to attribute exclusively to madmen as when we forget ourselves . . . . In private life what is more common than when we hear of law-suits prosecuted to the utter ruin of the parties, and the most deadly feuds in families, to find them attributed to trifling and apparently inadequate sources?" There speaks the victim not only of James Lowther's unscrupulous manipulation of the legal system but also of its fallout among Wordsworth's guardian uncles who interpreted their responsibility to their wayward nephew in ways that he felt were ruining his life. This explanation of huge effects arising from petty causes underlines his consistent tendency—the hallmark of Romantic subjectivity—to understand his own personal experience in terms of the largest forces operative in his society, and vice versa.

The Borderers rose from deep psychological roots, but it has many literary sources as well: the books poets read are also part of their emotional life. First among these is Schiller's *Die Räuber,* published in England in 1792 as *The Robbers.* Wordsworth almost certainly saw this play during one of his two stays in Paris in 1791–92; an adaptation, titled *Robert, le brigand,* held the stage there regularly for the better part of two years.[7] The Norwich *Cabinet* printed two long essays on *The Robbers* during 1795, when the *Philanthropist*'s editors were rifling it for reprints. They emphasize "the principle of fatalism" which pervades it, praise its animated pictures of human nature and its representation of the finely spun threads of human guilt, and excuse its lack of dramatic unity by citing similar instances from Shakespeare.[8] Schiller's play breathes the quintessence of the so-called new morality, which Coleridge felt with fearful exhilaration when he read it at Cambridge in October of 1795, asking Southey in wonderment, "Did he [Schiller] write his tragedy amid the yelling of Fiends? . . . I tremble like as Aspen Leaf."[9]

The Robbers is one of the most influential texts of German Sturm und Drang Romanticism, and Wordsworth's handling of it is instructive. In effect, he ruined its *Affekt,* just as in adapting Helen Maria Williams's *Letters from France* for his cautionary tale of Vaudracour and Julia, he turned her thrilling tale of true love saved by revolution into a frustrating account of a young man's failure to rise to the opportunities of the moment. He had a talent for making antiheroes out of heroes, a process he repeated until he made himself his own hero, in *The Prelude.*

Schiller's hero, Charles de Moor (or Karl Moor), is a very commanding figure. Tricked out of his father's inheritance, he abandons himself to his fate and becomes the leader of a band of roving robbers, not Robin Hoods like Mortimer's band, but marauding highwaymen, totally outcast from society. Moor's external actions are bad, but his personal impulses have consistency and integrity. Wordsworth turned Schiller's hero into a better man but a weaker one, like Vaudracour, who causes evil where he should do good. Legitimizing Mortimer at the level of social value, Wordsworth undercut him at the level of character. He took a stirring melodrama of revolutionary moral nihilism and turned it on its head, producing a frustrating, nonstop monologue by a hero who repeatedly mouths the outrageous claims of the villain, a Satanic character with no counterpart in Schiller's play.[10]

Another fruitful source was Shakespeare. *The Borderers* reads at times as if Hamlet had stumbled into the plot of *Othello,* in a political situation out of *Macbeth*'s Scotland, all set down on the blasted heath from *King Lear.* These Shakesperean echoes and pastiches can be sneered at, but individually they are often very good. In Wordsworth's self-creation, his use of them marks a new access of literary energy, for it says a good deal about the confidence of a twenty-six-year-old, first-time playwright that he should combine elements of his country's greatest dramatist's four greatest tragedies into a single play. If Wordsworth yielded up moral questions in despair in late 1795, he undertook the literary representation of that despair a year later with a sublime artistic confidence: taking on the best of Shakespeare to write a history play that was simultaneously an intellectual history of the French Revolution and of his own emotional involvement in it.

Finally and most typically, he recast his experience in the light of Milton's *Paradise Lost.* Rivers's temptation of Mortimer—to repeat a fall into sin that he himself has made—is the template from *Paradise Lost* that Wordsworth used to organize all his other sources: Rivers is Satan to Mortimer's Eve. But if Rivers acts like Satan, Mortimer talks like him: "I am weak.—There is my hell." In the play's multiple ironies, such weakness—that is, common human sympathy—is in fact the heavenly virtue of spontaneous fellow feeling that would save Mortimer from a tragic mistake if only he could preserve his belief in it.

Wordsworth found one more source very ready to hand in Burke's *Letters on a Regicide Peace,* excerpted at length in the Sherborne *Weekly Entertainer* between October and December, the same time Wordsworth sent his letter to its editor about Fletcher Christian.[11] He knew Burke's arguments already, but this shrill intensification of them worked strongly on him. Some of Burke's passages sound like a direct refutation of Rivers's arguments: "As to the right of men to act any where according to their pleasure, without any moral tie, no such right exists. Men are never in a state of *total* independence from each other. It is not the condition of our nature: nor is it conceivable how any man can pursue a considerable course of action without its having some effect upon others; or, of course, without producing some degree of responsibility for his conduct."[12] This is just the advice that Mortimer needs, but he can only stumble toward it because of his uneducated emotions.

Burke also excoriated the influence of French theaters in producing this horrible new morality. When the old courts and churches were destroyed, Burke says, a new prominence was given to the Parisian theaters, in whose productions (among which *The Robbers* figured prominently) we get "a view of their social life." This view looks very much like the set of *The Borderers:* "Their society was more like that of a den of outlaws upon a doubtful frontier; of a lewd tavern for the revels and debauches of banditti, assassins, bravos, smugglers, and their more desperate paramours."[13]

With Burke to the right of him and Godwin to the left of him, Wordsworth was well equipped to give Rivers speeches that are dramatic paraphrases of the mental actions he attributed to himself at this time in *The Prelude:* when he "dragged all precepts, judgments, maxims, creeds, / Like culprits to the bar; calling the mind . . . to establish in plain day / Her titles and her honours . . . demanding formal *proof* / And seeking it in everything" until he "yielded up moral questions in despair." Rivers has undergone the same process, but emerged in triumph, not despair:

Methinks
It were a pleasant pastime to construct
A scale and table of belief—as thus—
Two columns, one for passion, one for proof;
Each rises as the other falls: and first,
Passion a unit and *against* us—proof—
Nay, we must travel in another path,
Or we're stuck fast for ever;—passion, then,
Shall be a unit *for* us; proof—no, passion!
We'll not insult thy majesty by time,
Person, and place—the where, the when, the how
All particulars that dull brains require
To constitute the spiritless shape of Fact,
They bow to, calling the idol, Demonstration.
A whipping to the Moralists who preach
That misery is a sacred thing: . . .
. . . We dissect
The senseless body, and why not the mind?—
These are strange sights—the mind of man, upturned,
Is in all natures a strange spectacle;
In some a hideous one—hem! shall I stop?
(*1842,* III.ii.1145–60, 1166–70)

This brilliant speech anticipates *The Prelude*'s mental trial scene, and is as close as Rivers ever comes to self-recognition. Wordsworth was beginning to plumb the "strange sights [of] the mind of man, upturned."

Wordsworth could hardly have stamped the play more strongly with his own imprimatur than he did by setting it in the border region between England and Scotland at the time of the barons' league against King Henry III, in the late thirteenth century. Mortimer and his gang are "rievers," or raiders, operating in the power vacuum created by the Crusades, at the beginning of the border wars that continued more or less without interruption until the accession of James VI of Scotland to the throne of England. Despite the play's apparently remote location in space and time, its locations are easily identifiable with Penrith and its Border Beacon,[14] the scene of one of his most traumatic early memories of male sexual violence. Other references in the play plot a line of coordinates just across the Scottish border above Carlisle: Kirkoswald, Liddesdale, Cheviot Beacon, the Esk, and the Tweed. Almost all the character names in the play have North Country analogues. Besides Mortimer and Rivers (Rivaulx), the Cliffords were the ancient lords of Brougham Castle, whose ruins lie directly between Penrith Beacon and

Lowther Castle, in clear sight of both.[15] The name Clifford was commonly associated in Cumberland with aristocratic excess.

That Wordsworth signed two newspaper poems "Mortimer" around this time clinches the fact, though not the degree, of his identification with the play's issues, as does the symbolism of his later calling himself "an outlaw and a borderer of his age." Finally, though the play's villain was not renamed Oswald until sometime between 1796 and its publication in 1842, it is now widely accepted that Wordsworth must have had Colonel John Oswald partly in mind when he used the name, from recollections of the bloodthirsty Scottish mercenary he had seen in Paris. Oswald had traveled in the East, where he adopted certain religious practices, including vegetarianism; Rivers is also represented as a superstitious worshiper of natural forces. But Wordsworth may additionally have had in mind Kirkoswald in Scotland, named for Saint Oswald, who is also the patron saint of the Grasmere village church, a heroic medieval soldier-priest. The mixture of such very different characters as namesakes perfectly embodies the ambivalent attractions of Wordsworth's border villain.

Wordsworth's essay analyzing the character of Rivers biographically draws his own experience further into the play. In the excerpt I used as epigraph to Chapter 19, connections with the immediately preceding years of his own life are remarkable: "great intellectual powers . . . pride and the love of distinction . . . talents robbed of their weight . . . quits the world in disgust, with strong misanthropic feelings . . . his mind exhausts itself in constant efforts to separate the elements of virtue and vice." The references do not fit Wordsworth exactly—or rather, different words are used to describe essentially the same actions. He felt his abandonment of Annette as a "great crime," specifically the crime of desertion, which both Rivers and Mortimer commit against their lovers' fathers, and which the sailor of "Adventures on Salisbury Plain" and Robert of "The Ruined Cottage" commit upon their wives. Wordsworth could view himself as "betrayed" into this crime by his uncles' refusal to give him the aid he expected, or by his getting Annette pregnant in the first place by "trusting" his passion "to Nature."[16] In any case, we have an oversupply of motives, just the sort of psychological overdetermination that can lead to intensely cathartic composition.*

Wordsworth's prefatory essay picks up his representative young man as he

*In a play where one inadvertent crime is about to devolve into another, the betrayal may also refer to some entrapment, or fear of one, by government agents that occurred during Wordsworth's six months in London in 1795. There is less evidence for such a possibility, but having mentioned it in a previous chapter, I cite it again, because it does carry the element of guilt for unwittingly putting others' lives at risk, which is the essence of Rivers's account of his crime: "casting as I thought a guilty Person / Upon Heaven's righteous judgment, did [I] become / An instrument of Fiends."

is about to make a new start, recovering from a first, nearly fatal error, very much as Wordsworth was at Racedown following the debacle of the *Philanthropist.* It is a biographical analysis of events and feelings that are hardly present in the play at all, not much represented in Rivers's past actions, and not very necessary to understanding what goes on in the play, except as what might be called biographical generalization. It is, rather, a deep-structure analysis of "the growth of [Rivers's] own mind," and it matches, paragraph by paragraph, quite well with what we know of Wordsworth's life to 1795. In historical hindsight, his later comment about "the hardening of the heart and the perversion of the understanding" which he witnessed in France sounds like an observation about political personages. But nothing prevents us from applying it to his own character as well.

To stress *The Borderer*'s biographical connections is not strictly to call it an autobiographical work, however. Instead, Wordsworth wrote it from one of the most powerful of all writing perspectives: exploring *tendencies* he recognized in himself, worked out in actions provided mainly by other sources. In recasting his sources, he produced a signally *un*dramatic recension of them: most of the action takes place in Mortimer's mind, as he decides whether or not to act on Rivers's claims. Both of the play's main characters, Rivers and Mortimer, are aspects of Wordsworth's personality, as their precisely matched fates suggest. Both options were attractive to him, making the composition of the play a deeply cathartic experience: both are promising quasi-military adventurers, and both are tricked into the same cruel criminal act. Both are guilty, furthermore, of causing the death of the father of the woman they love.[17]

Biographically, Matilda would seem to stand mainly for Annette Vallon. Her real father was dead, but as a royalist her "father" was Louis XVI (a metaphor Annette used), whose execution Wordsworth had defended in his letter to the bishop of Llandaff. But in her dependence on Mortimer, hero of the north, Matilda's character also partakes of Dorothy—and of Mary Hutchinson, now living with them and literally under Wordsworth's protection. Given Matilda's double "identity" in Wordsworth's biography, it is easy to see why *The Borderers* could never have reached a happy romantic ending. Wordsworth deeply wished, wanted, needed to live with both Annette and Dorothy, as Annette's letters suggest. But he was deeply prohibited from doing so, by distance and political calamity in the case of Annette and by proximity and psychosexual taboos in the case of Dorothy.[18]

Baron Herbert, Lord Clifford, and Rivers's captain partake variously of John Wordsworth, James Lowther, John Robinson, William Cookson, and Christopher Crackanthorpe. None of these correlations are exact, but they are all figuratively powerful: the father who abandoned him by dying young, the aristocrat who manipulated the law to deny him his inheritance, the uncles who would not provide him help when he needed it most. What is astonishing about these connections, however, is that instead of paying them back, Wordsworth shows that "authority is innocent."[19] All the play's authority figures appear to be fiendishly cruel monsters, but all are finally exonerated. Old blind Baron Herbert is just what he seems, Rivers's captain may have been harsh tempered but was no villain, and even Lord Clifford's fiendish reputation, though not restored, is not borne out by the action of the play. The only authority who is wrong is Mortimer, the hero of the story and the leader of the band.

Having taken great pains to suggest that established authority is as bad as can be imagined, the play reveals that *it is not so:* violent revolution is not justified, especially by an individual trying to convince himself that his personal motives serve a higher good. The play does not examine Wordsworth's personal failings so much as it filters his intense sense of creative individualism through his political and psychological motives, showing that his tendency to feel that his imaginative powers were godlike tended finally toward "destructive omnipotence," rather than toward social benevolence.[20] To put it another way, Wordsworth had identified his growing sense of his enormous creative individuality with the immense power for good represented by the French Revolution. After the Terror, after seeing—and participating in—the extremes to which both French and English ideologues were prepared to go to defend "the new morality" which produced it, Wordsworth's reaction was not merely one of disillusionment, though it was that too, as it was for thousands of other European intellectuals. He was forced, in addition, to recognize in his own individualism the same kind of demonic tendencies that goaded the Jacobins, with the result that he was left in an extreme crisis of self-confidence. In this sense, "Rivers is the furthest extrapolation of one of Wordsworth's self-explorations."[21]

Wordsworth was working out these biographical parallels in the context of political allegiances he had formed over the past four or five years, which he was now in the process of rejecting. At the end of the play, Rivers asks Mortimer how old he is. Mortimer replies, "Just three and twenty summers": Wordsworth's age in the summer of 1793, when he had composed (but not published) his regicide pamphlet, and when he went to France to try to rescue Annette—or didn't go, but deeply wished to—and in either case failed in the basic manly action of saving his lover. (Schiller composed his play at the age of twenty-three as well.) If ever there was a text in which the personal is the political, Wordsworth's *Borderers* is it. And yet, on the face of it, as on the face of so many Wordsworthian texts, we see none of this. It looks like a failed medieval adventure story, set long ago and far away, with a damsel in distress sorely in need of rescuing. But she couldn't be. Instead, she was writing very unhappy letters to the author, as he resided in manorial splendor amid wretched poverty, on a subsistence income thanks to unreliable friends, with his beloved sister and his childhood playmate.

In the play's bleak catharsis there is no redemption for Mortimer. Civil and domestic order are not restored but left in worse shape than when the play opens. Herbert's lands have been restored, but he is dead and his daughter heartbroken; the man who should have been the source of their lives' continuity has been the cause of its destruction. The paradoxes cannot be screwed down any tighter. *The Borderers* is of a piece with Wordsworth's Racedown fragments of unrequited pain: we see everything that's wrong, but nothing that's right. Everyone in the play who is right is weak and helpless, and finally Mortimer is too. But he could have made the difference, if he had followed his feelings rather than his intellect—an attractive doctrine, but easily as dangerous as Rivers's existential opportunism.

Mortimer is not simply a naive dupe, however.[22] Rivers's outrageous arguments work because Mortimer really is tempted by them. They promise not only justice against an apparent monster, and the satisfaction of saving his beloved from a fate worse than death, but also the idea of personally representing an absolute force for good in his world:

> Self-stationed here,
> Upon these savage confines we have seen you
> Stand like an isthmus 'twixt two stormy seas
> That checked their fury at your bidding—
> 'Mid the deep holds of Solway's mossy waste
> Your single virtue has transformed a band
> Of fierce barbarians into ministers
> Of beauty and of order.
>
> (II.i.60–67)
>
> Henceforth we are fellow-labourers—to enlarge
> The intellectual empire of mankind.
>
> (IV.ii.188–89)

"Self-stationed" thus, Mortimer sounds uncannily like Wordsworth addressing Coleridge at the end of *The Prelude:* "joint labourers in the work . . . Of [mankind's mental] redemption." This is a heady temptation, and Rivers recognizes in Mortimer's heroic impulses the chance to tempt him on higher ground. Rivers fell like Satan, a victim of his own pride, but Mortimer is susceptible to Eve's temptation, that breaking the moral prohibition will make him godlike—and incidentally more appealing to Matilda. But as he says, "I am weak—there is my hell." The play's paradox, driven home relentlessly with too much dramatic irony and not enough dramatic plausibility, is that his weakness—human weakness—is his only chance of heaven.

Hence the climax is pure tragedy. All that is left for Mortimer is a life of penitence. He wanders off across the heath where Herbert died, like a Hamlet who has discovered that the ghost was an evil spirit after all:

> I will go forth a wanderer on the earth,
> A shadowy thing, . . .
> Living by mere intensity of thought,
> A thing by pain and thought compelled to live,
> Yet loathing life, till heaven in mercy strike me
> With blank forgetfulness—that I may die.
> (V.iii.265–75)

Mortimer here anticipates the Old Cumberland Beggar, but cursed with a keen self-consciousness that does not trouble that old man in his "Animal Tranquillity and Decay." Mortimer at the end is—not unlike his penniless creator—a *young* Cumberland beggar.

The Borderers develops a situation that Wordsworth returned to constantly in the next few years, where a character perfectly placed to aid or save a suffering and vulnerable innocent person (usually a woman) is simultaneously poised or tempted to destroy that very person. This paradox, highly developed in the poetry of Helen Maria Williams, and implicit in Wordsworth's poetry of 1793–95, now becomes explicit. It relates not only to the play's paradox of arrogant individualism but also to Wordsworth's questioning of his role as the narrator of many of these poems. To what extent is writing poems about suffering an adequate human response to it?

Still, the play did accomplish something for Wordsworth, analogous to the benefits he derived from describing the free-standing sufferers he met around Racedown. It remorselessly stripped away his philosophical and moral pretensions, just as his verse fragments about the poor stripped away benevolent explanations for particular social evils. The philosophical arena has been left bare, but not before Wordsworth has enacted within it the defeat of that philosophical nihilism which says that no traditional or natural restraints should be allowed to drag down the actions of the enlightened, creative individual.

As soon as *The Borderers* was finished, William sent off another section of the Juvenal imitation to Wrangham. He thanked Wrangham for his offer to find some more pupils for him, but finally rejected that vocational option: "upon a review of my own attainments I think there is so little I am able to teach that this scheme may be suffered to fly quietly away to the paradise of fools."[23] He was still casting about for something to produce more income, and teaching always seemed to come up as the first possibility. His tone indicates high good humor, and Dorothy's letters at this time are full of the same report: "we are as happy as human beings can be; that is when William is at home . . . [he] is as chearful as any body can be; perhaps you may not think it but he is the life of the whole house."[24] Clearly the time of depression and despair was over.

At the same time, there came good news of John's safe return from nearly two years as fourth mate on the *Osterly.* He shipped out again in September, for Bengal, as second mate on the *Duke of Montrose,* having failed to get a berth on the family "bottom," the *Earl of Abergavenny.*[25] Family ties went only so far. But these voyages were highly profitable to the officer-investors on any ship that did not sink, and John's rapid rise in rank shows he was doing very well indeed. He regularly invested one or two hundred pounds of Dorothy's money along with his own; he and his sister managed their money much more profitably than William did by seeking higher returns among his aristocratic acquaintances.

In mid-March, Basil Montagu arrived, with more good humor. He and William soon departed for a two-week visit to Bristol, with side trips to fashionable Bath. In Bristol they paid calls on local society, notably the wealthy Wedgwoods (the pottery industrialists) at Cote House. They were frequently in company with James Losh, now fully recovered from the breakdown that had sent him packing from London in September of 1795.[26] When Wordsworth first saw him in London, Losh was raising money to help pay expenses for the treason trials defendants; now he was devoting his energies to the cause of Unitarian Sunday schools in Bath.[27] Both were worthy causes, but their difference in scope indicates the kinds of changes in social activism young men of Wordsworth's class and persuasion were making at the time.

Montagu returned to London, but Wordsworth, before returning to Racedown, went down to Nether Stowey to visit Coleridge for a couple of days. This is the first visit of either poet to the residence of the other. He met Sara Coleridge and observed the Coleridges ensconced in their little cottage at the end of Lime Street; he also got an earful from Coleridge about the difficulties of providing food for three mouths by the labor of one's pen. On this topic they gossiped enviously about Southey's irritating fluency in verse production. Coleridge delighted in Wordsworth's description of Southey producing writing *"too much at his ease*—that he seldom 'feels his burthened breast—Heaving beneath th'incumbent Deity.' "[28] This Miltonic allusion was the kind of thing Wordsworth often uttered normally in conversation with people he considered his equals.

In this same vein they talked—alone together for the first time—of their highest ambitions, the great epic poems they dreamed of producing. The germ of *The Recluse,* Wordsworth's never-to-be-completed philosophical masterwork "on Man, on Nature, and on Human Life," was sown in these conversations. Immediately after Wordsworth's departure Coleridge wrote to Cottle his twenty-year plan for the production of such an epic:

> I should not think of devoting less than 20 years to an Epic Poem. Ten to collect materials and warm my mind with universal science. I would be a tolerable Mathematician, I would thoroughly know Mechanics, Hydrostatics, Optics, and Astronomy, Botany, Metallurgy, Fossilism, Chemistry, Geology, Anatomy, Medicine—then the *mind of man*—then the *minds of men*—in all Travels, Voyages and Histories. So I would spend ten years—the next five to the composition of the poem—and the five last to the correction of it.
>
> So I would write haply not unhearing of that divine and rightly-whispering Voice, which speaks to mighty minds of predestinated Garlands, starry and unwithering.[29]

At age twenty-five, twenty years does not seem like too great an investment of time, if the reward is immortality.

They also discovered they were both writing plays, Coleridge having been urged by Richard Brinsley Sheridan to give him something for Covent Garden. Coleridge soon added his new friend's play to the project, and finishing the two works, *The Borderers* and Coleridge's *Osorio,* became their first work together.[30] The first issue of the *Monthly Magazine,* the new liberal journal for which Coleridge was reviewing, had claimed that stage tragedy seemed "beyond the grasp of modern bards," a common viewpoint that added to their incentives.

Through a small passage at the rear of Coleridge's garden, they came to the house of the prosperous local tanner, Thomas Poole. A self-educated radical of the old English type, a self-styled "Poor Man's Friend" whose charitable actions really merited the title, Poole was also one of the leading businessmen in North Somerset, and Coleridge's benefactor and friend. From Poole, Wordsworth learned that Alfoxden House, a handsome country mansion he had seen on one of his walks with Coleridge, was vacant, and he asked Poole to make some inquiries about the terms of its availability.[31]

Poole, an engaging raconteur, regaled the poets with local stories, providing Wordsworth with incidents that later led to "The Idiot Boy" (its closing words, "The cocks did crow to-whoo, to-whoo, / And the sun did shine so cold!"), "The Farmer of Tilsbury Vale," and "Poor Susan."[32]

But by far the most compelling story Wordsworth heard from Poole was the account of a murder that had occurred outside Nether Stowey when Poole was a boy, which his father helped prosecute. Wordsworth soon turned this into a manuscript of about four hundred lines, the so-called "Somersetshire Tragedy," which he subsequently abandoned, the manuscript of which was destroyed in 1931 by Gordon Wordsworth, as being "in no way calculated to add to [W's] reputation, and [of] even less poetical merit than

'The Convict,' the only one of his published poems to which it bears resemblance."[33]

Fortunately a few scraps of manuscript have been recovered, and accounts of the murder itself are fully recorded. It concerned a charcoal burner named John Walford, who was in love with the local miller's daughter, Anne Rice. But his stepmother forbade their marriage. John was "pursued" and "solicited" in the woods by a retarded woman named Jenny, and by her he soon had two children. The parish authorities, presented with an illegitimate child, gave Walford the choice of paying for its maintenance or marrying Jenny. Walford chose the latter when the second child came, to spite his stepmother, but the marriage was a disaster, soon acted out. He may have thrown Jenny out of the house; she was given to wandering around to other nearby households and had to be sent home. One night shortly after the marriage he sent her, or they went together, to the Castle of Comfort Inn (still in business on the A39 near Holford) for some cider. On the way, he murdered her, slitting her throat with a hedge stake, severing the muscles and arteries so thoroughly that the blood soaked his clothes.

Walford pleaded innocent, but was soon convicted by his own construction of the evidence: the shilling he said he had given her for cider was found in his bloody clothes when they were discovered. At his execution a month later a huge crowd gathered, because he was reputed to be good-tempered, generous, and popular. As the cart was being positioned under the gibbet, he asked whether Anne Rice was present. "Where is Anne?" ran the whisper through the crowd. She was discovered at the edge of the crowd, hiding below the brow of a hill. "Almost lifeless," she was dragged up to the gibbet, where she kneeled and Walford talked to her for ten minutes; she said nothing. He tried to kiss her, but an officer prevented him, saying, "You had better not—it can do no good." He snatched her hand, kissed it, shed tears for the first time, declared he had commited the murder "without foreintending it," asked the assembled people and God for forgiveness, and, saying, "I am now ready," was hanged. An amazing silence fell over the crowd, so much so that the sound of the birds in the woods of nearby Bin Combe was "distinctly audible." After more than ten minutes the crowd began quietly to disperse, "not a single human being present walked away without a feeling of pity"—for John Walford.[34]

Walford's body was hung in a cage, like the Sailor's at the end of "Adventures on Salisbury Plain." Walford's Gibbet is still marked on the Ordnance Survey map, though there is nothing there but a bend in the path as one comes out of the woods on the walk from Alfoxden. "Thousands came to see him . . . it was a common saying that 'Walford looked better hung than most men did alive.' " Given the sensational materials of the crime, and the fact that the clothing disappears first from exposed corpses, one wonders if the "common saying" was not a vulgar joke.

It is not hard to see why Wordsworth was fascinated with this story, and asked Poole to write it out for him. It seemed like a case of life imitating art, so close was its triangular cast of characters to "The Three Graves."[35] Now the "ruthless mother" would be Walford's stepmother, whose grounds for forbidding his marriage can hardly have been financial, since a miller's daughter would be an excellent match for a charcoal burner. The ways in which the situation appealed (if that is the word) to Wordsworth are legion. An abandoned fiancée named Anne would obviously have stimulated his interest. Here too were parental opposition to a desired marriage and a young man stuck with an illegitimate child which forces him into an undesired marriage. The wife is seduced but then rejected, while the beloved is abandoned until the end, when she is called forth for an excruciatingly public declaration of his love. Almost two years later, in Germany, Wordsworth proposed giving the name Robert Walford to the father-in-law of the Sailor in "Adventures on Salisbury Plain" when he was trying to revise it for quick publication.[36]

What is most extraordinary about all accounts of the case, throughout the nineteenth century and into modern Wordsworth criticism, is the degree of sympathy for "poor Jack Walford." Anne Rice is given some melancholy sentimental consideration, but Jenny, the idiot girl, none at all: "a bad character." According to Poole, she was "an ordinary squat person, disgustingly dirty and slovenly . . . but nevertheless she was a woman." That was enough for John Walford to exploit her sexually. And no one says anything about his astounding self-dramatizing imposition on Anne Rice at his execution, attended by hundreds of people from all over the region.

No one, that is, but Wordsworth. In the few extant lines that are obviously intended for "A Somersetshire Tragedy," his focus is squarely on Jenny:

> Ill fared it now with his poor wife I ween,
> That in her hut she could no more remain:
> Oft in the early morning she was seen
> Ere Robert to his work had cross'd the green.
> She roam'd from house to house the weary day,
> And when the housewife's evening hearth was clean
> She linger'd still, and if you chanc'd to say
> "Robert his supper needs," her colour pass'd away.

Wordsworth's attention to detail is as always keen: Jenny leaves the house not *after* Walford goes to work, but before. "She could no more remain" in her house, very likely because he was beating her, and "her colour pass'd away" when she was told to go home and cook dinner, not because she'd forgotten but because she knew the treatment that was in store for her.

A disconnected couplet adds, "Her face bespake a weak and witless soul / Which none could think worth while to teach or to controul."[37] Exactly: the couplet summarizes the whole history of Somerset commentary on the case, that "none could think [it] worth while to teach or to controul" the likes of Jenny. Wordsworth alone of all the commentators was not swayed by John Walford's good looks, popularity, "good temper," and great strength. In the extant lines of Wordsworth's manuscript, Jenny is not given a name. In her society, she has the lowest status of any of the characters, counts for least, and is Wordsworth's heroine.

One nineteenth-century commentator says the "sombre" story is better suited to Crabbe "than to the cheerful poet of Rydal Mount."[38] Our concern here is the biographical cost to Wordsworth of achieving that cheerfulness. This is precisely the kind of perspective he was increasingly drawn to: the hardest case, the toughest question, the ugliest person. But he did not publish the poem, and soon decided to give it up for an equally hard case, Margaret in "The Ruined Cottage."

With the negative catharsis of two tragedies behind him, Wordsworth turned immediately to new composition when he returned to Racedown.* The new work was first called "The Ruined Cottage," then (about 1803) "The Pedlar," and finally, as the first book of *The Excursion* (1814), "The Wanderer." He had possibly begun it before leaving for Bristol, and "A Somersetshire Tragedy" may have been begun afterwards, but the two stories and that of *The Borderers* mingled freely in his mind. He had left Mortimer wandering off across a heath not unlike the barren waste he himself had just been recrossing in his revisions of "A Night on Salisbury Plain." He emerges, five hundred years later in fictional time, but within weeks in real time, as the young man on the "bare wide Common" at the beginning of "The Ruined Cottage."

"The Ruined Cottage" is the first of Wordsworth's poems that can be called "major" without qualification. But it was never published by him in its greatest form, nor is it possible to say definitively what its best version is, for its textual status is highly problematic.[39] Yet it is one of the essential Wordsworthian texts, and his struggles with it—for seventeen years before publication, and in every republication of *The Excursion* thereafter, to 1845—

*He was considerably distracted by the formal claim finally lodged from Robinson Wordsworth in May, for payment of at least £250 of the money the Wordsworth estate owed to the Wordsworths of Whitehaven. These Wordsworths had held off as long as they could, exercising considerable restraint toward their wayward nephew. But now Robinson was about to be married, and he desperately needed the kind of nest egg that Wordsworth had in the meantime got from Raisley Calvert and the Pinney brothers.

show that, like *The Prelude,* "The Ruined Cottage" is a poem whose creation was inextricably bound up with his self-creation.

Its story is quickly told. Margaret and Robert live in a Dorset cottage where he does piecework weaving. They have been fast-forwarded, Stoppard style, from cameo roles in *The Borderers* as terrified peasants in the remote barons' wars, to helpless, unemployed small artisans of Dorsetshire, displaced by the "Minister's War" with France, ca. March 1797. They have two children and are happy. Then wartime dislocations throw him out of work, and bad harvests raise the price of bread. He works around the cottage for a while, making small repairs, but finally the sight of his hungry wife and children becomes too much for him. (Wordsworth applied the same phrase to Robert's despondency he had used for Jenny: "Ill fared it now with Robert.") He secretly enlists for the government's bounty of ten guineas and slips away one morning, leaving the money in a bag on the windowsill. Margaret waits years for his return, neglecting her house, her children, and herself. One child is taken away to an apprenticeship by the parish authorities, the other dies; finally Margaret dies too. End of story. It is another version of the story of an abandoned woman that is Wordsworth's main plot throughout the 1790s. His problem, again, is what to make of such a story. How should it be told? Even harder, How should it be heard?

In its earliest form the poem does not appear to be something very new in Wordsworth's development. It looks like yet another of the free-standing images of unexplained suffering which he produced steadily throughout 1796–97: indeed, it is the apotheosis of this form. As with many of his poems, he said he composed its conclusion first. This contains the full force of Margaret's tale without a word of explanation, forty-six forbidding lines which compress the essence of her experience into a sustained dirge. It begins, "Five tedious years / She lingered in unquiet widowhood, / A wife, and widow. Needs must it have been / A sore heart-wasting." And it ends, after detailing with remorseless pathos her waiting and watching and putting her "same sad question" about Robert to every passerby,

Meanwhile her poor hut
Sunk to decay, for he was gone whose hand,
At the first nippings of October frost,
Closed up each chink and with fresh bands of straw
Chequered the green-grown thatch. And so she sate
Through the long winter, reckless and alone,
Till this reft house by frost, and thaw, and rain
Was sapped; and when she slept the nightly damps
Did chill her breast, and in the stormy day
Her tattered clothes were ruffled by the wind

Even at the side of her own fire.—Yet still
She loved this wretched spot, nor would for worlds
Have parted hence; and still that length of road
And this rude bench one torturing hope endeared,
Fast rooted at her heart, and here, my friend,
In sickness she remained, and here she died,
Last human tenant of these ruined walls.
(MS B, 512–28)[40]

A child can read this, but what ancient wisdom is necessary to understand it? The simple repetitions and specific indications ("this rude bench," "that path," "yon gate"), relentlessly underscored by adverbs of time and place (here, here; still, still), build to a climax of almost unbearable power: she stayed here, she kept waiting and hoping, and finally she died doing it. This is "A Dorsetshire Tragedy" to match his equally unanswerable "Somersetshire Tragedy."

No one who heard these lines ever forgot them. They were the first thing Wordsworth read to Coleridge when he came for his visit in early June. Coleridge asked Dorothy to copy them out for him to send to his friend John Estlin, a Unitarian minister, and many years later he could still recall the impact of "The Ruined Cottage" on him, and express the regret that Wordsworth had not published it by itself in its original form. Mary Hutchinson, who departed the day Coleridge arrived, left with a copy of these lines in her baggage, and Lamb, Hazlitt, Southey, and others who heard versions of the poem over the next six months similarly attest to its enduring power.

These lines are the summa of the descriptions of human suffering that Wordsworth began with the female beggar of *An Evening Walk* and the Grison gypsy of *Descriptive Sketches.* Symbolic details of the beggar woman—her husband died in war and she also had two children—are made literal in Margaret's tale. In the earlier poem Wordsworth's questions are rhetorical and allusive: "For hope's deserted well why wistful look? / Chok'd is the pathway, and the pitcher broke."*[41] But the well in Margaret's overgrown garden, from which she kindly drew water for thirsty passersby, is literal and was functional: "half choaked with willow flowers and weeds," covered by spiderwebs, "And on the wet and slimy foot-stone lay / The useless fragment of a wooden bowl." In the dirge of "The Ruined Cottage" almost all the characters of Wordsworth's recent work are reprised: not only the abandoned woman but the returning soldier and sailor, "the crippled Mendicant," and the nameless wanderer who encounters them all—and must tell their tales.

*The soiled spring and the broken pitcher, favorite images of Wordsworth's, are from Ecclesiastes: "the pitcher is shattered at the spring, or the wheel broken at the well" (12:6).

The version that Wordsworth had completed by the time Coleridge arrived was no more than three hundred lines long, barely a third the length it would reach six months later, and much shorter than its nearly one thousand lines by the time of its publication in 1814. But it contained most of the essentials: hard times, Robert's departure, the Pedlar's recurring seasonal visits to Margaret's cottage, her death, and the final dirge.[42] The poem grew so long, and over so long a time, because Wordsworth had set himself a daunting double challenge: to write a full narrative of how Margaret had come to this end, and to place that narrative in a framework that would comprehend the terrible force of its ending, making it both philosophically plausible and aesthetically palatable. He wanted it to be recognized as a poem making a complete statement, and not to leave begging the ferocious questions such an ending provokes: Why do these things happen? Who is responsible? What are we to do in the face of such dying? These were challenges to the very essence of what he felt his poetic *self* to be. Margaret's tale was another of his naked accounts of suffering, but now he was determined to get beyond reportage, no matter how powerful, and achieve some kind of satisfactory conclusion. He was never wholly successful in meeting the aesthetic, philosophical, or political challenges posed by "The Ruined Cottage," but we should not underestimate the force of these challenges to his ambition and self-confidence.

The tale of Margaret is in one sense the story of human suffering under the conditions of (relatively) free individualism. To expect Wordsworth to "solve" her situation, in the sense of explaining it and pointing out preferable alternatives, is to expect too much. Marx and Freud, among others, proposed theoretical answers to situations something like this, but Wordsworth set up the situation as it is found in practice: neither social nor psychological answers will get at the whole truth. What makes the situation especially intractable is that Margaret is not simply a passive, undeserving victim, but contributes much to her own demise by fixating on her husband, thinking more about his return (he never returns) than anything else.

Political critics on both the left and the right have been driven to distraction by this poem and what they see as Wordsworth's unacceptable resolution of it. On the right are readers like Thomas De Quincey, who nearly stamped himself into the ground like Rumpelstiltskin in his annoyance with both Margaret and Wordsworth for failing to take advantage of the several agencies of help and information which existed in communities around her: the local vicar, the magistrate, the war office, the commander of the nearest army post, a store owner, or almost any responsible citizen. "To have overlooked a point of policy so broadly apparent as this vitiates and nullifies the very basis of the story."[43] De Quincey also criticized Margaret severely for "gadding about" instead of taking care of her house and children. All valid criticisms, but all inadequate to Margaret's tragedy.

On the left, critics in our own time have been very disapproving of Wordsworth's failure to develop the socioeconomic context he established at the beginning of the poem (the war with France) into a thoroughgoing critique of a political system that wages wars at the expense of its own citizens.[44] These critics, unlike De Quincey, see no meaningful help available: the whole social situation is itself so "criminal" as to make revolution almost the necessary consequence.

For both sets of critics, the issues are clear: the status quo or the revolution, which will it be? But Wordsworth's problem is, rather, what to *say* about Margaret's death, in and as a *poem*.

These are questions Wordsworth would try to answer in January 1798. In the first week of June 1797, though, his immediate problem was finding and keeping an audience. The young narrator of "The Ruined Cottage" is trapped into a heightened sense of personal guilt by the Pedlar's artful tale-telling, and Wordsworth used something of the same tactics on Coleridge. He arrived at teatime. As he came up over the hill, he saw William and Dorothy working in the garden and vaulted the fence gate, running down across the field to greet them. This famous vignette, often used to represent the birth moment of British Romanticism, perhaps did not occur where most people think it did: namely, on the road from Crewkerne where a small rise gives a first glimpse of Racedown, its front door less than a hundred diagonal yards away. But William and Dorothy were working in the gardens, which, as Racedown's present owner has pointed out to me, have always been behind the house, to the southwest. If Coleridge had come from Crewkerne, he could not have seen them from that road. But if he was coming via Chard, which lies in a straighter direct line from Nether Stowey (and he was walking the thirty miles), he would have approached the house from the west, the direction of Forde Abbey. From that smaller road he could easily have seen William and Dorothy working in the gardens at the rear, but his famous dash across the fields would have been considerably more demanding: up and down a couple of intervening hillocks, across a bushy stream at the bottom, and up a longish incline to the house, a distance of at least three hundred yards.

Whichever angle Coleridge took, the ordeal that awaited him at teatime was considerably more taxing, reminding us that Romanticism is not simply about running across summer fields to greet friends but also about hearing poems like "The Ruined Cottage" at the end of one's run—and, somehow, connecting the two experiences into one. Making that connection was the task that bound them together over the next four weeks and that finally pulled Wordsworth out of Racedown. "The Ruined Cottage" was read to Coleridge immediately; after tea he recited for them the first two and a half acts of *Osorio.* High tea indeed! The hiking endurance of these young people, so often remarked on, was nothing compared to their spiritual stamina. It must have been hard to swallow tea and biscuits after hearing "The Ruined Cottage" recited by its author, its dirge-like conclusion hammered down from the height of that craggy, melancholy face in stern Miltonic cadences, with images that came right off the roads Coleridge had just been walking.

Coleridge's visit was intended to be a brief one, but it was extended for week after week as conversations and rereadings of "The Ruined Cottage," *The Borderers,* and *Osorio* preoccupied the two young men, implicating them in each other's work and in each other's lives. All three works turned on the question of remorse for a guilt not personally incurred, but caused by sympathetic feelings of implication in unjust situations involving one's friends or loved ones. The friendship of Wordsworth and Coleridge was one of the most productive in the history of literature, and it had many levels. But in the immediate situation of their shared work, it was the aesthetic and philosophical problems of "The Ruined Cottage" that brought them together.

As June turned into July, and the time came for Coleridge to return home, neither he nor the Wordsworths could bear the thought of separation. Their acquaintance and friendship, kindling slowly over two years, had blazed into love: the kind of passion one would sacrifice almost anything to prolong. Coleridge, ever the entrepreneur, soon thought of ways to maintain it. He returned home to Nether Stowey, but for one reason only: to tell Sara that William and Dorothy Wordsworth were coming for a visit.

21 THE SPY AND THE MARINER

Nether Stowey and Alfoxden 1797

> . . . philosophic thought . . . poetic dreams
> In dell romantic . . . and perchance,
> Allfoxden's musing tenant, and the maid
> Of ardent eye, who, with fraternal love,
> Sweetens his solitude . . . .
>
> (John Thelwall, "Lines written at Bridgwater, in Somersetshire, on the 27th of July, 1797, during a long excursion, in quest of a peaceful retreat")

Coleridge went to Nether Stowey on June 28, returning next day to collect William and Dorothy for a reciprocated summer visit that he and William had already planned to last much longer. Wordsworth had prospected the Stowey neighborhood during his spring visit, found a vacant house, and made inquiries. Once it became clear at Racedown—as it did immediately—how well they all got on together, the decision to move was a foregone conclusion.

Coleridge was almost as lonely at Stowey as the Wordsworths were at Racedown. He had come there in January, seeking cheaper living quarters after Charles Lloyd, scion of the banking family and Coleridge's sometime disciple and future enemy, had left Bristol, suffering both physical and mental instability. Lloyd's father had been paying Coleridge £80 a year to maintain his son, but the young man's oddities had become impossible to support at any price. Coleridge moved out to cheaper lodgings in the country to continue his independent studies while trying to support his wife and new child by periodical writing. He was assisted by an annuity of £40 that the philanthropic Tom Poole had raised among Coleridge's remaining Bristol admirers to offset the loss of Lloyd's money. Poole found Coleridge a tiny cottage on Lime Street in Nether Stowey, two rooms down and two up, with a rear garden abutting Poole's orchard of lime and lemon trees. Coleridge made a strong emotional commitment to this cottage to bolster the image of rural poet he was building up, romanticizing what Sara later termed a "miserable cottage" and that he himself recalled as "the old hovel."[1]

Having lost half his income, Coleridge still needed more, and on most Sundays could be found walking cross-country to preach at Unitarian chapels as far away as Bridgwater and Taunton.[2] One Sunday in April an old woman on the road asked him if he knew the "vile Jacobin" who had led astray George Burnett (b. 1776), a young man of the neighborhood who like Charles Lloyd had fallen for Coleridge's charm, lost his Christian faith, and become addicted to opium.[3] Coleridge (the villain himself) replied that he did not, but commiserated—not ungenuinely—with the woman's complaints about the new "philosophic" foolishness that had drawn several young men thereabouts into idealistic schemes like Pantisocracy. Young Burnett, like young Lloyd, had been led astray by "those two extraordinary young men, Southey and Coleridge," as young Wordsworth had described them to Mathews two years earlier. Five years later, his life still sliding downhill, Burnett recalled, "The enchantment of Pantisocracy threw a gorgeous light over the objects of life; but it soon disappeared, and has left *me* in the darkness of ruin."[4] Coleridge, estranged from Southey, losing Lloyd, and with young men like Burnett now among the moral walking wounded of the intense hopes and failures of the past two years, needed a fresh draft of discipleship.[5] He found a new master instead, if not a new deity: "the Giant Wordsworth, God love him"; "I feel myself a *little man by his* side"; "T. Poole's opinion of Wordsworth is—that he is the greatest Man, he ever knew—I coincide."[6]

The visit at Racedown had been an intellectual honeymoon; the move to Stowey was more like setting up housekeeping for a lifetime together. The two poets could not get enough of each other's company, and Dorothy was the conduit through which the lively currents of their sensibilities passed. Both of them were in love with her, one way or another. Her personality was similar to Coleridge's: alert, fast thinking, attuned to slights or sympathies far beyond the moral perception of most human beings, her taste (said Coleridge) "a perfect electrometer—it bends, protrudes, and draws in, at subtlest beauties & most recondite faults." She and Coleridge were a match even in their initially critical perceptions of each other. She: "At first I thought him very plain, that is, for about three minutes: he is pale and thin, has a wide mouth, thick lips, and not very good teeth . . . . But if you hear him speak for five minutes you think no more of them."[7] He: "She is a woman indeed!—in mind, I mean, & heart—for her person is such, that if you expected to see a pretty woman, you would think her ordinary—if you expected to find an ordinary woman, you would think her pretty!"[8] Wordsworth was relaxed and open in Dorothy's presence as with no other person. Though he had known and admired Coleridge for nearly two years, he might never have embraced him so wholeheartedly had it not been for the medium of exchange provided by Dorothy's quicksilver emotions. She translated the Coleridgean fantastic into Wordsworth's more severe natural idiom.

In midsummer of 1797 the central cast of characters of the first generation of English Romantics began to assemble onstage for the first time, under the direction of Samuel Taylor Coleridge. He brought William and Dorothy Wordsworth back home with him, and he sent invitations to Charles and Mary Lamb to join them, as well as to John Thelwall and his wife, Stella.[9] Charles Lloyd would return briefly in September, his health temporarily restored, but he soon turned vicious in print. He was already writing *Edmund Oliver,* a roman à clef caricaturing Coleridge's thoughts and habits with the mean insight that only disappointed enchantment can give. Southey, in London, was kept informed of the group's activities by mail. Coleridge's creation of his Romantic generation was the first product of this miraculous year, as *Lyrical Ballads* was its last. In his retrospective on this time in *Biographia Literaria,* twenty years later, Coleridge contrived to make it appear that the production of that by then highly controversial volume had been the planned outcome of this year. But this was not true on the ground at Stowey in July 1797, where the idea was—still—the formation of a community of like-minded spirits who would sustain each other in a political climate that was becoming increasingly hostile. Just how hostile, only one of them, Thelwall, really knew.

Sara Coleridge and Tom Poole were worried about the effect of all this stimulation on Coleridge's always uncertain health, and they were right, so far as ordinary life went. But ordinary life was no longer the standard of judgment. They might better have adopted his prescription in "Kubla Khan" for the treatment of visionaries such as he felt himself becoming: "Weave a circle round him thrice, / And close your eyes with holy dread, / For he on honey-dew hath fed, / And drunk the milk of Paradise."

Sara Coleridge was kept outside this magic circle by the other three principals in it, and has remained there for posterity. But she deserves a word of defense.[10] Excluding her was mainly Dorothy's work, whose attraction to Coleridge naturally made Sara jealous. Sara was more liberal and outspoken politically than Dorothy, but she had nothing to match Dorothy's wild outbursts of passion for natural beauty. She was also much more attractive physically than any of the other three, and her pregnancy and miscarriage during this year were ample proof to Dorothy that she still held her husband's sexual attentions. To Joseph Cottle, "the pretty young Mrs. Coleridge," with her infant on her arm, "appeared like a poetic embodiment of the idea of Woman."[11] Such a sentiment, uttered aloud, would have piqued Dorothy's jealousy, for suggesting that ideal womanhood depended on external beauty and maternity. On more than one occasion, the three principals returned from a walk, "drenched with rain; in which case [Dorothy], with a laughing gaiety, and evidently unconscious of any liberty she was taking . . . would run up to Mrs Coleridge's wardrobe, array herself, without leave asked, in Mrs Coleridge's dresses, and make herself merry with her own unceremoniousness and Mrs Coleridge's gravity . . . and it barbed the arrow to [Sara's] womanly feelings, that Coleridge treated any sallies of resentment which might sometimes escape her as narrowmindedness."[12] Sara was a smart dresser as well as a considerable beauty; Dorothy's behavior looks as much like calculated bitchery as Byron's later snubbing of Southey and Coleridge for marrying the Fricker sisters, who were in trade: "two partners (milliners of Bath)."[13]

But for three precious weeks everything seemed like paradise. Dorothy gave Somerset her highest seal of approval, comparing it favorably to her idealized childhood home: the "brooks clear and pebbly as in Cumberland," the villages "so romantic," and "the woods are as fine as those at Lowther, and the country more romantic; it has the character of the less grand parts of the neighbourhood of the Lakes."[14] All of them began to throw the word "romantic" about with abandon; normally reserved for exotic scenes and fantastic love stories, it now referred to themselves, their lives, and their surroundings. Gradually the word shifted in their usage into the idea of imagination casting a shadow or light across any landscape or person or thought, making it *visible,* as if for the first time, by making it *strange.*

They certainly all seemed strange to the neighbors. Their habit of rambling about the countryside day and night was unusual in a farming region not much used to tourists, and they walked with Coleridge and sometimes with Poole, both known political extremists. In January, Coleridge had distributed a prospectus for six lectures (never delivered) comparing the English and French revolutions, and in May these Stowey liberals had disturbed customers in a tearoom with loud exclamations of joy over the news of Napoleon's success in his second Italian campaign against Austria.*[15] Wordsworth's severe silence and republican-cropped hair excited "an impression of awe and mistrust," and Dorothy's presence was especially noted by conservative country folk very sure that a woman's place was in the home and not at all sure just whose child Basil Montagu Jr. was.[16] Even Mrs. Coleridge, one of the well-known radical Fricker sisters, usually stayed home, and talked easily to the villagers about ordinary concerns of the day. It is not certain that

*The damage to their local reputations had begun three years earlier, when Coleridge and Southey visited Poole after a walking tour in Wales. The news of Robespierre's death had just been received (July 1794), and either Coleridge or Southey (it is not clear which) said, in the presence of Poole's conservative cousins, that "Robespierre was a ministering angel of mercy, sent to slay thousands that he might save millions" (Margaret E. Sandford, *Thomas Poole and His Friends,* 2 vols. [London: Macmillan, 1888], 1:103–5.

Dorothy had yet developed the pronounced "gypsy tan" which De Quincey later noted at Grasmere, but the word "dark" was applied to her and her brother, referring to their complexions or their intentions or both. Their seclusion, strange habits and topics of conversation, their unusual accent, and the fact that they received letters from France made them known as "the French people."[17] Silly people thought they might be conjurers, ordinary folk assumed they were smugglers, but the wisest heads assured everyone they must be Jacobins.[18]

They were up and about on the Quantocks from the first day, walking past John Walford's gibbet outside Stowey and up Dowsborough Hill, where the ruins of an ancient Roman fortification made them feel masters of all they surveyed. Coleridge convinced Dorothy she could see all the way to Glastonbury Tor, but this, from a maximum elevation of 1,076 feet (on Robin Upright's Hill), was only teasing.[19] The great thing about the Quantocks, they immediately discovered, was that you can stride along bare hilltops, your very brain open to the sky because of the hills' percipitous drop to the nearby sea, and then descend quickly into deeply shaded, silent combes that seem to hold secrets as mysterious as the hilltops' revelations.

Within a day or two of their arrival, perhaps on this very first excursion, William took Dorothy on a walk through Holford Combe, where they "discovered" a beautiful house in the woods. This was a nice gesture on his part, almost a lover's ploy, since the route they followed was by no means accidental. Their "wandering" led them straight from Stowey to Alfoxden House, which he knew from his conversations with Poole was empty and available. The handsome house and its magnificent setting swept Dorothy off her feet, and Poole was immediately instructed to conclude arrangements with its owner.

Alfoxden House, more than two hundred years old, was the largest house on the eastern side of the Quantocks. It was owned by Mrs. Anna St. Albyn, whose husband, Lancelot, the aristocratic rector of nearby Stringston, had died in 1791. She lived in their other house, since Alfoxden with its well-stocked deer park was much too large for her.[20] The St. Albyns had no children, and Alfoxden was to be inherited by her grandnephew, who was still a child. Invasion scares and the unsettled economy had played havoc with country house rentals, especially in the West Country (the motive for the plot of Austen's *Persuasion*). The Wordsworths were not quite as lucky as they were with Racedown, but Mrs. St. Albyn was so glad to have the house occupied, by a party recommended by the prosperous (if rather too democratical) Mr. Poole, that she agreed to rent it out at the very reasonable rate of £23 for a year—payable, in another advantageous perk, at the end of the term, with Poole meanwhile binding himself as security for payment.

Wordsworth was becoming a remarkably shrewd dealer in matters of rent and inheritance.

Compared with Racedown, which was grand enough, this was twice the house at less than half the price. Alfoxden had nine bedrooms and three parlors, "with furniture enough," Dorothy exclaimed to Mary Hutchinson, "for a dozen families like ours."[21] It was located just where the northernmost Quantocks drop down toward the sea a mile and a half away (see illustration). From its rear parlor, which soon became Dorothy's favorite, they looked across a sloping fertile landscape, over farms nestling around Kilve and East Quantoxhead to the Bristol Channel. In front of the house, to the south, "it is screened from the sun by a high hill which rises immediately from it. This hill is beautiful, scattered irregularly and abundantly with trees, and topped with fern. . . . The deer dwell here, and sheep, so that we have a living prospect." It was perfectly situated for their excursions in either direction: up into the hills or down along the sea. It is now a pleasant country hotel, and Dorothy's favorite parlor is the spacious dining room, which can seat forty or fifty guests.

A drive curves up to the house from the hamlet of Holford on the main road (A39), past an ancient pound or kennel for hunting dogs, and around a thickly wooded hill which screens the house from the village commons. Alongside this drive, down a steep bank, runs a little stream where William let Dorothy discover "a sequestered waterfall in a dell formed by steep hills covered with full-grown timber trees." This waterfall became the emblem of their year there, and a symbol of the new cultural forms they now began to create. At almost the same time that Dorothy was outlining Alfoxden's grounds for Mary Hutchinson, Coleridge was sketching in its details for Charles Lamb:

> . . . that still roaring dell, of which I told;
> The roaring dell, o'erwooded, narrow, deep,
> And only speckled by the mid-day sun;
> Where its slim trunk the ash from rock to rock
> Flings like an arching bridge;—that branchless ash,
> Unsunn'd and damp, whose few poor yellow leaves
> Ne'er tremble in the gale, yet tremble still,
> Fann'd by the waterfall!
>
> ("This Lime-Tree Bower My Prison," 9–16)

The specifically "romantic" quality they all identified in it was not simply its beauty but its *strange* beauty: it was dim at noon, its trees' leaves were almost white, not green, even in midsummer, and they were agitated not by the wind but by the air currents from the falling waters.

By July 12 Poole had concluded the arrangements for Alfoxden, and on July 13 William and Dorothy moved in—yet another significant July 13 for him to remark, to go with those of 1790 and 1793, a series to be culminated a year later in the date of "Tintern Abbey": "July 13, 1798." Charles Lamb had arrived at Stowey on July 7, partly to celebrate the volume of poetry he and Coleridge and Lloyd had published in May, but mostly for relief from a family tragedy. His sister Mary in a fit of insanity had stabbed their senile mother to death over a small domestic incident that had unhinged her delicate mind, and she was still under doctors' care. Lamb saved Mary from incarceration in a madhouse by pledging himself to care for her for the rest of her life. Lamb the ebullient, the witty, and the frequently tipsy was not much in evidence during his week's stay, but sat a quiet, recuperative spectator to the enthusiasms of Wordsworth and his sister, watching with "the silence of a grateful heart." He now met Dorothy for the first time, though he was already somewhat acquainted with Wordsworth from visits and conversations with mutual friends in the Inns of Court, where the Lambs lived until 1794. He apologized for his behavior in his thank-you letter from London: "I could not talk much, while I was with you, but my silence was not sullenness, nor I hope from any bad motive; but, in truth, disuse has made me awkward at it. I know I behaved myself, particularly at Tom Poole's and at Cruikshank's, most like a sulky child; but company and converse are strange to me. It was kind in you all to endure me as you did."[22]

William and Dorothy took Lamb out on one of their daily jaunts when Coleridge could not join them, because Sara had accidentally spilled a pan of the baby's hot milk on his foot. The day's walk was unrecorded by its participants, but it lives for posterity in Coleridge's vivid imagining of it in "This Lime-Tree Bower My Prison," written as he spent the day in Poole's orchard with his sore foot wrapped up. He imagined the uniquely Quantockian experience of coming up out of the shrouded combes to

> view again
> The many-steeply tract magnificent
> Of hill, fields and meadows, and the sea,
> With some fair bark, perhaps, whose sails light up
> The slip of smooth clear blue betwixt two Isles
> Of purple shadow!
>
> ("This Lime-Tree Bower My Prison," 21–26)[23]

Lamb departed on July 14, the day after the Wordsworths moved into Alfoxden. He just missed Thelwall, who was expected any day, and who arrived on the 17th, having walked the whole way from London. Lamb very much regretted not seeing "the Patriot," and wrote back, "I was looking out for John Thelwall all the way from Bridgwater, and had I met him, I think it would have moved me almost to tears."[24] Thelwall had become the literal embodiment of the *Peripatetic,* the name of his earlier journal. He was being "hunted from society" by a government-encouraged campaign of harassment and intimidation; he was not traveling on holiday, but to escape and hide.[25] Two or three years earlier, he had been public enemy no. 1: one of the "aquitted felons" of the 1794 treason trials and the specific target of the second gagging act, directed against large public meetings. By 1797 the Home Office's campaign against him had succeeded. He had folded his *Tribune* in March of 1796, and for the last year had been trying, with dwindling success, to rally the forces and funds of opposition in the provinces. (Coleridge's short-lived *Watchman* of early 1796 was a squib fired in the same ill-fated campaign.) As a public speaker he offered an inviting target. His lectures were broken up by hired ruffians in Norwich, and he had been hounded back and forth across the country from Yarmouth to Liverpool, denied protection by local magistrates, heckled into silence by patriotic drunks, and on one occasion "escorted" out of town by a detachment of the Inniskilling dragoons.[26]

Thelwall had few friends left in the land who were willing to receive him by the time he arrived in Nether Stowey. He and Coleridge had maintained a frank correspondence since his troubles began in April 1796. At the peak of his popularity in London, in 1795, Thelwall had been jealous of Coleridge's similar fame in Bristol, but they soon overcame their personal differences. Or rather, they realized that they differed on almost all central points of politics and religion, and as a result, Coleridge said, "we like each other uncommonly well."[27] Thelwall, like Paine, Godwin, and Holcroft, was one of the last of the pure rationalist breed: frank, honest, intelligent men, but rather one-sided personalities. "The simplifying century had set its stamp on him."[28] He was well suited to times of crisis when issues had to be presented in their starkest terms. This made him an effective open-air orator: with his personal courage and a strong set of lungs, he could have been England's Danton. But he (also like Danton) was very ill suited to times of repression and intrigue: the times that were the coming norm in England. Funding for the newly reorganized secret service reached a new high in 1797 and was maintained at these levels until the Peace of Amiens in 1802, with documentable effect on the poets' year at Alfoxden and their subsequent year in Germany.[29] Coleridge had during the past year backed off from most of his strong political opinions, especially from expressing them publicly: he had snapped his "squeaking baby-trumpet of Sedition."[30] But Thelwall's straightforwardness and Coleridge's willingness to consider almost any point of view allowed them to get on famously.

Tom Poole's native populism made him receptive to Thelwall as well, though Poole distrusted his enthusiasm for abstract natural rights as much as

Coleridge was distressed by his frank atheism. But Poole's relatives in the neighborhood, already upset by his adoption of Coleridge, were shocked when they heard Thelwall had turned up at Stowey. This, following the news that Alfoxden had been "taken by [another] one of the fraternity," made young Charlotte Poole wonder, "To what are we coming?"[31] Another cousin, asked by Poole to sing "Come, sweet Liberty" from Handel's *Judas Maccabaeus* for Wordsworth and Coleridge, demurred, explaining, "I *could* not sing it. I knew what they meant with *their* liberty."[32]

Thelwall eagerly entered into the spirit of things at Stowey. Even he began to use the fashionable word "romantic" freely, writing to his wife about "the Academus of Stowey" and "the wild, romantic dell in these grounds."[33] He was obviously enjoying himself, compared with the hazards he had undergone during the preceding year, and he and Coleridge teased each other about things that were no laughing matter to the government. To Thelwall's rationalist dictum that children should not be asked to declare belief or disbelief in a deity before they reached the age of discretion, Coleridge countered with the example of his chaotic vegetable garden, where weeds ran rampant: as they had not yet reached the age of discretion, he said, he didn't have the heart to root them out.

Their best exchange has been improved by much retelling, but it still captures perfectly this brief moment of ideological stasis, before Thelwall descended into obscurity and failure, and Coleridge and Wordsworth rose up as capitalized Romantics. Beside the strange waterfall which was their holy place, Coleridge mockingly reproached Thelwall, "Citizen John, this is a fine place to talk treason in!" "Nay, Citizen Samuel," Thelwall retorted, "it is rather a place to make a man forget that there is any necessity for treason."[34] Wordsworth's recollected version of the same exchange may be more accurate; it was certainly *safer.* He thought Coleridge had said that "it was a place to soften one's remembrances of the strife and turmoil of the world," and that Thelwall had merely replied, "Nay . . . to make one forget the world altogether."[35] No mention of treason here! But Wordsworth's version may also reflect the universalizing, *un*specifying direction his imagination was already beginning to take at the time.

Thelwall eagerly wanted to take a third share in this "literary egotistical triumvirate,"[36] but it was the unpolitical, quietistic Dorothy who remained the binding spirit of these "three persons . . . but one God," as Coleridge later conceived their union.[37] In barely another month Coleridge, who had brought him there, would warn Thelwall to move away from Stowey. Because in that month they were forcibly reminded that though they might forget the "necessity" for treason, there were others who heard them talk about it and remembered the very different duty of patriotism.

On July 23, after ten days of settling in, William and Dorothy hosted a housewarming dinner for fourteen people. The guests, besides the Coleridges, Thelwall, and Poole and his secretary, Thomas Wade, were Mr. and Mrs. John Cruikshank, of Castle Hill House in Stowey, like Wordsworth the son of an aristocrat's steward (the earl of Egmont), who had been admitted at Temple Bar the day before William Mathews in 1793.[38] The earl was not in residence at his estate near Stowey, so the young intellectuals had the run of it: Coleridge's first conversation poem, "The Nightingale," describes its overgrown gardens. Cruikshank succeeded Wordsworth as tenant of Alfoxden, a tenancy whose term was fixed by the fallout from the events of this dinner. In addition, there were the Willmotts from Woodlands, an estate across the main coaching road. He was the son of a Sherborne silk manufacturer and later became a confidential steward for the Wedgwoods. The remainder were other veterans of the Pantisocracy enthusiasm who still flitted around the captivating flame of Coleridge's genius: John Chester, a farmer's son from Dodington who followed him to Germany, and the unhappy George Burnett, "the wreck of Pantisocracy."[39] It was a gathering of liberal intelligentsia, like-minded spirits opposed to the present government.

The main course was a leg of Poole's lamb, gaily ordered by Coleridge to be sent over to "The Foxes" at all-fox-den. The main entertainment was a dramatic reading of *The Borderers* under the trees: a gloomy set of after-dinner speeches, to be sure, but one that reflected the disaffected mood of the group. (One would give a lot to know who read each role.) During dinner Thelwall, wearing his radical's white hat, "talked so loud and in such a passion" that he frightened one of the servants, Thomas Jones, so much that he feared to approach the table again. Thomas, who may have been a free-lance informer,[40] told his fellow servants about the ranting he had heard. It fit so well with the gossip that was already accumulating about the strange newcomers that the story traveled rapidly across the country, from kitchen to kitchen, picking up lurid details as it went. In less than two weeks the rumors from Alfoxden had reached the ears of justices of the peace and doctors and lawyers right along the road from Cannington to Bridgwater to Bristol to Bath. Such gossip was part of a national mania for denouncing "suspicious" individuals, events, or publications that had grown steadily since the passage of the gagging acts.[41] The Home Office had all it could do to respond to, let alone check out, the almost daily "informations" it received from around the country, especially from the southern coastal counties.

On August 8 Dr. Daniel Lysons of Bath sent a letter to the duke of Portland at the Home Office, alerting him to suspicious goings-on at Alfoxden; three days later he followed it up with more details. From his cook, a friend of a woman servant who was a friend of Charles Mogg, who was a friend of Thomas Jones, he had learned that "the Master of the house has no wife with him, but only a woman who passes for his Sister," that he and his friends went about the countryside on "nocturnal and diurnal excursions," carrying camp stools and "a Portfolio in which they enter their observations which they have been heard to say were almost finished," and that they were "very attentive to the River near them."[42]

The Home Office reacted instantly. Even before Lysons's second letter arrived, John King, the permanent undersecretary, had dispatched one of his top agents, James Walsh, to investigate. Walsh was already at Hungerford, east of Bath, interrogating Mogg when Lysons's additional information came in. He sent back new particulars (hedging them with the warning that "Mr. Mogg is by no means the most intelligent man in the world"): "some French people had got possession of the Mansion House" (Alfoxden), that they washed and mended clothes on Sundays, that they were taking plans and measures of the house and other places in the country, and that they had asked Christopher Trickie (who had been a huntsman for the St. Albyns) whether the waterfall brook was navigable to the sea, "and upon being informed . . . that it was not, they were afterwards seen examining the Brook quite down to the Sea." Trickie, who lived by the Alfoxden dog kennel, either misheard the question or served an ill turn to the new tenants of the big house, since anyone who saw that brook would know it could not be navigable anywhere. (As Coleridge later noted, it emptied out on "a tract of coast that from Clevedon to Minehead scarcely permits the approach of a fishing boat!")[43] Wordsworth made Trickie into a pathetic, poor, old, sick, and dying man in "Simon Lee," who is excessively grateful for small favors. But the vicar of Over Stowey had a firmer grasp on the real Trickie's character—not unlike his name—when he called him "as rascally faced a fellow as ever I met with."[44]

King replied immediately, on August 12, instructing Walsh to proceed to Alfoxden to confirm these reports, but to avoid arousing suspicion so that that the tenants might be arrested on the spot, if warranted. Walsh was to get their names and descriptions and follow their movements. A bank note for £20 for expenses was enclosed—almost as much as the Wordsworths' yearly rent. King's instructions clearly reflect the government's increasingly sophisticated and sensible handling of internal intelligence matters: all reports were received with initial skepticism and subjected to double-checking.[45]

Three days later Walsh reported from the Globe Inn at Stowey, "the nearest house I can get any accommodation at." He had cleared up a good deal of the mystery simply by eavesdropping on his landlord's conversation about "those Rascalls from Alfoxton." One of them is "the famous Thelwall," who had already left, and the whole "Nest of them" are protected by Mr. Poole, "a Tanner of this Town." They were not French, but the landlord assured him "they are people that will do as much harm, as all the French can do." Walsh was pretty sure "this will turn out no French affair, but a mischiefuous [*sic*] gang of disaffected Englishmen." Just before signing off, he added, "I have just procured the name of the person who took the House. His name is *Wordsworth* [Walsh's emphasis] a name I think known to Mr. Ford."

By the next day Walsh had the whole story more or less straight: the Wordsworths' removal from Racedown, Poole's standing in the community and his radical organization, the Poor Man's Club, Coleridge's reputation ("a Man of superior Ability . . . frequently publishing . . . soon to produce a new work"), that Wordsworth's woman servant, Peggy Marsh, called her master "a Phylosopher," and that "a Great Counsellor from London" and a gentleman from Bristol had just arrived (Basil Montagu and Azariah Pinney). This is the last report in the file, and it may well have been the end of the affair as far as the Home Office was concerned.

But the significance of this episode was massively forestalled for posterity by Coleridge's hilarious send-up of it in Chapter 10 of *Biographia Literaria* as the "Spy Nozy" incident. Coleridge cast it as a Shakespearean comic subplot, complete with Walsh as red-nosed Bardolph, and Sir Philip Hales, Bart., of Cannington (to whom Undersecretary King directed Walsh to apply for any additional assistance he needed) as Sir Dogberry. He says the spy tracked them for three weeks with "truly Indian perserverance" (three days was more like it), and hid behind their favorite seat at the sea bank, where he overheard them "talk of one Spy Nozy." Walsh supposedly thought this referred to him and his "remarkable feature," but was soon convinced "that it was the name of a man who made a book and lived long ago. [Spinoza]." Coleridge said that Walsh assured his superiors "that both my friend and myself were as good subjects, for aught he could discover to the contrary, as any in His Majesty's dominions." This was certainly not Walsh's testimony.

Coleridge further embroidered his tale to say that he met Walsh in the main road between Holford and Stowey and that Coleridge soon convinced him he was "no friend of jacobinism." This was true as to Coleridge's emerging state of opinion, for he would soon "deprecate the moral & intellectual habits" of both the opposition and "the *democrats*" as worse than the *aristocrats': "they wear the *filthy garments* of vice."[46] But it was manifestly false as to Walsh's estimate of him.

Finally, Coleridge fleshed out his account with a report of Sir Philip Hales's interrogation of the garrulous innkeeper of Stowey. This cross-examination at cross purposes verified only (a) that if Coleridge ever harangued local people with seditious talk "they would not have understood a word he said" and (b) that as to his observations of the landscape, "Why, folks do say, Your honour! as how that he is a *Poet,* and that he is going to put Quantock and all about here in print; and . . . I suppose that the strange gentleman [Wordsworth] has some *consarn* in the business."[47]

The long-term effect of Coleridge's joke has been to divert—in both senses—attention from the seriousness of the episode and from the idea (still potentially damaging to his career in 1817 when the *Biographia* was published) that he and "the strange gentleman" could have had anything to do with Jacobinism. It helped to establish the enduring image that they were only harmless poets, not political writers or activists, and that the government was making the kind of mistake that bureaucratic blinders and political hysteria usually produce. This is far from the truth. Whatever we think of Pitt's wartime policy, or of Portland's surveillance of domestic dissent, the government acted correctly and efficiently according to its lights. Pitt's government was very shaky in the spring and summer of 1797 because of the failure of its peace negotiations in late 1796, leading it to intensify its efforts against internal dissent, a policy it could pursue almost with impunity following the Foxite Whigs' "secession" from Parliament in March for a period of nearly three years. The Whigs did not resign; they adopted a parliamentary tactic of "non-attendance" to register their disgust at Pitt's policies. But in practical terms it meant Parliament lacked effective watchdogs over government actions. As a result, a meeting at the Crown & Anchor on May 18 urged all reformers to minimize their differences and maintain solidarity, "for the reign of Terror and Proscription has begun in England."[48] The report on "the Alfoxden gang" thus came in just at the beginning of Pitt's "reign of terror." Especially notable is the speed and accuracy of the Home Office's reaction, given the large numbers of similar reports it was getting from everywhere. It is even more noteworthy that the initial reports made no mention of Thelwall. Yet within a week of its receipt of an unsolicited piece of information from a doctor in Bath, the Home Office had dispatched and funded its top agent (Walsh was not a "spy": he used his own name, and was a salaried Home Office employee), who crossed the country and sent back all the details necessary to dispose of the case. For the case was disposed of by Walsh's information. None of the government officers ever suggested that a *mistake* has been made, still less a hilarious one, only that the suspicious persons were not French or French agents, but a gang of disaffected Englishmen, who are well known—and thus accounted for—in their disaffection.

In the summer of 1797 Pitt's concern was invasion, especially in the West Country, not internal dissent. On February 22 a small French fleet had appeared off Ilfracombe, just beyond Linton, and engaged in some small depradations as it made its way toward Bristol. Bad weather kept it out of the Bristol Channel, but it landed twelve hundred troops at Fishguard, in Wales, up around the southwest corner of the Pembrokeshire coast from Bristol. Although the local militia and an army detachment under Lord Liverpool quickly captured this force, which was made up largely of impressed French convicts, subsequent investigation and publication of their orders threw the countryside into alarm. They were called the "Black Legion," commanded by an American, Colonel William Tate, whose immediate superior was Lazare Hoche, Napoleon's leading admiral, who had commanded the abortive invasion of southwest Ireland at Bantry Bay in December 1796.[49] Tate's orders had been to stage a terrorist raid, disable as much of Bristol's shipping as possible, and then to sail up around the coast to do the same thing at Chester and Liverpool. The strategic aim was to weaken England's ability to respond to a larger Irish insurrection, which came, again unsuccessfully, the next year.[50]

By March newspapers in Bristol and Bath were crying out alarms against enemies and traitors "insulting" the coasts, and declaring "there are Englishmen so debased as to be ready to lend an assisting Hand towards enslaving their Country."[51] These were some of the "ancestral voices prophesying war" whose echoes are heard in "Kubla Khan." There was even a run on the Bank of England. John Pinney Sr., who knew about French invasions from having surrendered Nevis to them briefly during the American war, collected his stock certificates from the bank when he heard of the Fishguard landing and put them in the secret hiding place he had constructed in his house in Great George Street for precisely such emergencies.

In April and May there had been huge mutinies in the British fleets at Spithead (Isle of Wight), the Nore (Thames estuary), and Yarmouth, with many officers beaten and set ashore. These were put down with shrewd acquiescence (at Spithead) and unforgiving executions (at the Nore), a lucky combination of strategies that probably saved England from losing much of its coastal fleet to the enemy.[52] Traditionally appalling shipboard conditions had been worsened by a nearly tenfold increase in sailors during the decade: the ships were crammed full of impressed "quota-men" and hundreds of Irishmen ready to revolt against England, as many of their compatriots did the following year. These mutinies did not go unnoticed in the Stowey neighborhood: Charlotte Poole put them down in her diary as "occasioned by the black contrivances of the Democrats."[53]

The reports from Dr. Lysons played right into this scenario. But what saved the members of the "gang" at Alfoxden from further investigation and harassment was not their innocence but their being *recognized*. The government knew all about disaffected Englishmen, thank you very much, Dr. Lysons. One can almost hear the sarcasm in Walsh's reference to "the famous Thelwall." Walsh had been hounding Thelwall for nearly five years, and they knew each other very well. Walsh had personally arrested Thelwall in London on at least one occasion, and was so familiar to Thelwall that he did not dare attend his lectures, for fear of provoking him into an extemporaneous version of his crowd-pleasing performance, "On Spies and Informers."[54] Walsh and John King were well aware how Thelwall had been hounded across the country during the past year, having orchestrated some of this harassment themselves. They knew he was in full retreat to a safe hiding place; Walsh had simply uncovered him one more time.

Poole and Coleridge, though two of the most visible antigovernment figures in Somerset, were evidently new to Walsh, who worked mainly in London and Ireland. He ignored any suggestion of political danger attaching to Coleridge and laid out Poole's threat solely in terms of the number of warm bodies he could command as head of the Poor Man's Club: about 150. This information was relevant to fears of invasion because it was a constant refrain of the hawks in Paris that a sizable proportion of the English population would rise up to join a revolutionary invasion force. The poems of Wordsworth and Coleridge and others during this period show that these hopes were not entirely unfounded. Coleridge in "Fears in Solitude," written the following April in response to another invasion scare, trembles for his country because its atheism and rash policy had provoked and deserved one. Wordsworth's vaguely threatening conclusion to "Goody Blake and Harry Gill" might be said to carry the same message in code: "Now think, ye farmers all, I pray, / Of Goody Blake and Harry Gill." Think what? Kind thoughts? Or think about what might happen if the needs of the poor are not attended to? Even Joseph Gill had been moved to a nicely ambiguous piece of doggerel on the subject:

> Subjects wicked were
> Savage Murders threatening—
> Sad Tumults forbear
> Swords War and fighting.[55]

The West Country was a good place to land such an invasion, being directly across the Channel from Brest, the principal port of the French navy. The duke of Monmouth had done so with some success in 1685: he landed at Lyme Regis, was crowned king at Taunton, besieged Bristol, retreated to Bridgwater, and was finally surrounded at Sedgemoor. Three years later the Dutch prince of Orange landed at Tor Bay in Devon with far better results, proceeding unopposed to London and the English throne, as William III. The whole country is only thirty-five miles wide between Lyme Regis and Bridgewater Bay, and could easily be cut off. Accurate reports of huge landing craft being constructed at Brest were received regularly during these years, and the next spring Napoleon made what he later considered his worst decision: to confront England, his last remaining enemy in the field, not on its own ground but in Egypt.

The only name besides Thelwall's that Walsh underlined in his reports was "*Wordsworth* a name I think known to Mr. Ford." Walsh is not saying that Wordsworth is "famous" like Thelwall—that is, a known political agitator whom we no longer need worry about. Nor does he imply that his superior, John King, will recognize the name. Rather, he says he thinks it will be known to Richard Ford, the Bow Street magistrate who was one of the three or four people involved with William Wickham in the liaisons between the Home Office, the Alien Office, and the Foreign Office which were the origin of the modern British secret service. Ford had been chief magistrate in all but name since 1794, was consistently rewarded by Portland for his services, and was a particular favorite of the king's, who often invited him to court; in 1800 he was made superintendent of aliens and in 1801 knighted and named chief London magistrate.[56] The activities of his group were "modern" in that they did not simply gather information about undesirable foreigners or disaffected Englishmen but also operated clandestinely to provoke actions that aided the policies of the government in power: assassinations, disinformation, and fifth-column groups in France and Switzerland, the ultimate goal of which was to defeat and defuse the continuing force of the French Revolution by "underground war."[57] The new system was called "preventitive policing."[58]

How did Walsh know that Ford would probably recognize Wordsworth's name? Nicholas Roe, who has investigated the matter most thoroughly to date, suggests that Ford's knowledge might have come in one or more of three ways: through the government's interception of letters between Wordsworth and Annette, through its knowledge of Wordsworth's associates and activities in London in 1795, or through Richard Wordsworth, who as a lawyer might have known Ford in his capacity as a magistrate.[59] All three possibilities are likely, but especially the first two, for they most closely corroborate the important fact that *Walsh* knew that Ford knew Wordsworth. Letters from Annette had reached Racedown, and the government from 1794 had in place a regular system of interfering with the mails. Traditional scholars mildly observe that it "is not usually remarked that William's former activities had put him on the government files,"[60] but fail to explore the future implications of such activities. Walsh knew Thelwall very well and Wordsworth had come closest to Thelwall (through Godwin) in 1795, when they shared many of the same friends and opinions. It was also in 1795 that Portland's secret accounts book recorded a payment to George Dyer, whom both Wordsworth and Coleridge knew well and with whom they were frequently in company then, before Wordsworth and Tweddell and Losh and other young men suddenly left town. The third possibility, that Ford knew Wordsworth's name because Richard Wordsworth was also in the legal profession, is the weakest. For if Ford knew Richard in his professional capacity, or socially, these are not the kinds of acquaintance that would have come to James Walsh's attention, except by the merest happenstance. Although the Bow Street runners were a "higher grade" of persons than the former generation of informers (who were often recruited from known criminals), Walsh was no gentleman and would never have been in company socially with either of his superiors, for class as well as security reasons.[61]

Both Ford and King, furthermore, knew people who knew Wordsworth and Coleridge, or knew *about* them.[62] Both Ford and King were highly intelligent men, not reactionary fanatics; both were interested in the theater, and good friends of Sheridan. Ford had a large financial interest in Drury Lane; his father had been its manager when Wordsworth was attending it in 1791, the year that Ford's liaison with the actress Dora Jordan had ended (they had four children, and she was frequently called Mrs. Ford) when she advanced to better things as mistress of the duke of Clarence, the future William IV. George Canning, undersecretary in the Foreign Office and soon to be founding editor of the *Anti-Jacobin* (the government's unofficial watchdog against the liberal media), was on extremely friendly terms with John King, whom he considered "one of the worthiest and best sort of men in the world," dining with him regularly. King corresponded intimately with both Grenville and Burke, and had such a high opinion of himself that some people said he confused his surname with the prerogatives of his office.[63] Canning's good friend George Ellis, another *Anti-Jacobin* contributor, had been tutored by King's brother; Ellis later became a friend of Wordsworth as well as Coleridge. Canning, whose mother was a provincial actress, was also a good friend of Sheridan's; their relationship was so close "that some believed Canning was [Sheridan's] ward."[64] Sheridan also knew Coleridge well and had by this time already asked him to contribute a script for consideration at Drury Lane. So there are plenty of personal and literary relations, as well as public political ones, that could have made the name "*Wordsworth* . . . known to Mr. Ford." We also have to remember how small these offices were; in 1796 the entire Home Office staff, from the duke of Portland down to the housekeeper, consisted of twenty-five persons.[65] The secret service operated out of its "smallest garret," and comprised three men and a clerk; every piece of Home Office business crossed the desks of the two undersecretaries, King and Ford.

Walsh was a hardened professional, and his reports from the field were terse and accurate. Whether he construed the stakes to be a foreign invasion or simply keeping his employers happy, he had excellent motives for being as accurate as possible. His knowledge that Ford probably knew Wordsworth is a similarly firm deduction. He is not saying something on the order of, By the way, Mr. Wordsworth says hello, or, Here's a funny coincidence: this Wordsworth is somebody Mr. Ford knows! No, Walsh clearly expects King to relay the information to Ford, and he also clearly does so by way of confirmatory information, not as a basis for further *action*. Summarized officially, his comments about Thelwall and Wordsworth come to this: We know all about Thelwall in one way, and we know all we need to know about Wordsworth in another way—and that's all we need to know, or do, about this gang at this point. Wordsworth may have appeared to them not merely as a disaffected Englishman but as one of those liberal, ambitious, naive, and poor young Englishmen, often associated with journalism or the theater, who frequently proved ripe for suborning by the Home Office if and when a need arose. Whether the need had arisen earlier, in 1795, we do not know. Nothing further is said at present. But when we see in June of 1799 that Portland's secret book records a payment of nearly £100 to "Mr. Wordsworth," these nagging questions about some kind of Wordsworthian connection to the secret service will rise again. The most sinister explanation one could offer of the "Spy Nozy" incident, as a radical counterpoint to Coleridge's very successful cover-up, is that Walsh could leave and report the case closed because he had found that another operative was already in place on the ground: Our man in Somerset, Mr. Wordsworth. Wickham had instituted the modern innovation of having agents work independently of each other, and it would hardly be the first time in the shady history of espionage that one spy found himself spying on another. Nosy spy indeed!

But if the spy's report closed the government's case, local knowledge that he had been there soon had far-reaching implications for the Alfoxden gang. Mrs. St. Albyn, already made uneasy by reports of her new tenants' strange habits, now declared that she would not renew their year's lease: very early notice, since they had signed it barely a month before. Tom Poole, who had brokered the arrangement, pleaded with her in the terms he knew she would be most likely to respond to, assuring her of Wordsworth's respectable social standing by pointing out that Wordsworth's uncle Cookson was a clergyman like her dead husband, and a canon of Windsor besides, well known to Dr. Fisher, the late vicar of Stowey, who had also served in that capacity. "William Wordsworth, of all men alive, is the last who will give any one cause to complain of his opinions, his conduct, or disturbing the peace of any one."[66] If Mrs. St. Albyn had tried to corroborate this opinion by checking with the Reverend Cookson, Poole's case would have been pretty badly undercut. Few people in Somerset at the time were as generous as Thomas Poole, but even he crossed out two sentences in the draft of his appeal before sending it to Wordsworth's landlady. The first claimed that Wordsworth was "a Man of fortune sufficient to make him independent." This was changed to say he was "a man fond of retirement, fond of reading and writing"; that is, he *lived* like a man of fortune. The second sentence was cut altogether, because it was not true: "William Wordsworth never concerned himself [with] and thoroughly disapproved [of] Mr. Thelwall's proceedings."

All to no avail. Mrs. St. Albyn kept her foot down: the lease would expire at Midsummer 1798. The annus mirabilis of English Romanticism had its terminus ad quem in sight almost as soon as it started. But what could be more romantic than to know the exact date when one's paradise will be lost? Along with everything else that happened during this wonderful year, the constant knowledge that there was a point beyond which its joys could not be prolonged added energy, as well as anxiety, to Wordsworth's writing and self-knowledge. Much later he stoutly denied that the termination of the lease had any effect on his plans, or that he even knew about it, or that he had ever wanted to stay at Alfoxden longer than he did, and that Thelwall's presence had caused the "ludicrous" mistake in the first place.[67] But this is all mere persiflage to keep covered the evidence of youthful indiscretions, and unfair to Thelwall besides. Poole's letter to Mrs. St. Albyn and Coleridge's letters to Thelwall and Cottle show that the event was common neighborhood knowledge, which would hardly have been kept from Wordsworth, the tenant in question, if he was "caballed against *so long and so loudly.*"[68] So too does the fact that the most incendiary local gossip stopped after this time. The Alfoxden gang members were still scorned and ridiculed as democratical rascals, but the government had done its part, and there was nothing further to be gained by trying to alarm the authorities. Ironically, Tom Poole and poor Sara Coleridge suffered most and longest. In 1799 a new vicar opened his diary with this observation: "Saw that Democratic hoyden Mrs. Coleridge who looked so like a friskey girl or something worse that I was not surprised that a Democratic Libertine should choose her for a wife. . . . Met the patron of democrats, Mr Thos Poole who smiled and chatted a little . . . . Satan himself cannot be more false and hypocritical."[69] One might well prefer the reports of some spies to those of certain parsons.

This intense climate of opinion explains Coleridge's letters to Thelwall between August 19 and 21, responding to Thelwall's wish to become part of the "literary egotistical triumverate." Thelwall wanted a cottage near Coleridge; alternatively, the idea had been broached of his taking a few rooms in Alfoxden, where the Wordsworths were wafting about in splendor. Coleridge agreed to make some inquiries, but what he found, in addition to what he already knew, made him warn Thelwall to go away, at least as far as Bridgwater, until his quiet habits might convince people that his pockets were full of poems, not plans for "the transportation or ambush-place of a French army."[70] He might have told Thelwall all this during his visit, but the atmosphere seems to have become noticeably worse after the Home Office's visit. Now he was obliged to disabuse Thelwall of the cute notion that Alfoxden was "a fine place to talk treason in." He solemnly informed him of the "very great odium" which Poole incurred by bringing him (Coleridge) to Stowey. "My peaceable manners known attachment to Christianity had almost worn it away," but then Wordsworth arrived, and things went from bad to worse. "You cannot conceive the tumult, calumnies, apparatus of threatened persecutions which this event has occasioned round about us. If *you* too should come, I am afraid, that even riots dangerous riots might be the consequence . . . *all three* together—what can it be less than plot damned conspiracy—a school for the propagation of demagogy & atheism?" Thelwall would be the last straw.

This contemporary account by Coleridge of the situation is a lot less humorous than his "Spy Nozy" version. It also shows that Wordsworth's behavior and reputation were alarming to people. Coleridge satirically paraphrased locals' commentary on them both: he himself was "a whirl-brain that talks whatever comes uppermost; but that Wordsworth, he is the dark traitor. You never hear him say a syllable on the subject [politics]."[71] Provincial paranoia, or shrewd country realism?

Thelwall knew all too well what kinds of manifestations his appearance tended to spark off. Not that he imagined giving any more public lectures. On the contrary, his "Lines written at Bridgwater, in Somersetshire, on the 27th of July, 1797, during a long excursion, in quest of a peaceful retreat" show that "a peaceful retreat" was all he wanted. Like Wordsworth at Tintern Abbey a year later, he wanted to escape a world "that kindness pays with hatred." (Wordsworth used similar phrases: "sneers of selfish men . . . greetings where no kindness is.") Like Coleridge's conversation poems and like "Tintern Abbey," but more transparently, Thelwall's "Lines" record the final turn by which the revolutionary hopes and actions of the 1790s turned inward to the form of culture we call Romanticism. In "solitary haunts" of "hermit-like seclusion," with "some few minds congenial," he will listen in safety while "the trump of Truth . . . wakes The Ruffian Crew of Power." This directly anticipates Wordsworth's avowal that he has "learned / To look on nature, not as in the hour / Of thoughtless youth, but hearing oftentimes / The still, sad music of humanity." Thelwall hopes to dwell "in philosophic amity" with Coleridge and their wives, and he *thinks* they might be joined by a third:

> and, perchance,
> Allfoxden's musing tenant, and the maid
> Of ardent eye, who, with fraternal love,
> Sweetens his solitude.

That eye and its love will also appear in "Tintern Abbey," when Wordsworth "catch[es] from thy wild eyes these gleams / Of past existence" (that is, his "former pleasures").

Forty years later Thelwall's second wife wrote very cautiously to Wordsworth for his recollections of this period of Thelwall's life: "what he always in after time, termed 'his exile' . . . the interregnum between his political and scientific careers: from 1796 to 1801."[72] It was similarly an interregnum between Wordsworth's and Coleridge's political and poetical careers, but Mrs. Thewall knew that times had changed, and she narrowed the scope of her request accordingly: "Of course I do not wish to have any political reference to the acquaintance which then subsisted between you; but merely of that communion of kindred minds, which poetry and literature linked in the bonds of friendship." How much of the origins of English Romanticism is consistently hidden beneath that "merely"! She wanted only what Thelwall cherished in this visit: its romance, without "any political reference." Wordsworth's reply, though cordial, made no reference at all to politics or even to her mention of it; he spoke only of Thelwall's "enthusiastic attachment to Poetry" and his sensitivity "to the beauty of Rural Nature."[73]

After the flurry of scandal caused by the visits of Thelwall and Walsh, things calmed down. As summer waned, a different set of guests arrived, beginning with (as Walsh had noted without knowing their names) Montagu and Azariah Pinney. These two, and James Tobin and Tom Wedgwood, who followed in the second week of September, were, we might say, the second tier of Wordsworth's friends.[74] These young men were neither as brilliant nor as outspoken as Thelwall or Lamb. Tobin was the son of the elder Pinney's partner, a strong defender of the rights of slave traders, and the brother of John, Wordsworth's exact contemporary, who was, like Wordsworth and Coleridge at this time, trying to get a play produced in London. As "dear brother Jem," Tobin appears in the first line of the original version of Wordsworth's "We Are Seven."

These visitors were primarily lawyers and businessmen, or the well-off sons of successful entrepreneurs and industrialists. In their visits and topics of conversation we notice a shift, though not a strictly chronological one, in the interests of Wordsworth and Coleridge: further away from political action and toward projects that might return a profit while allowing time free for writing. They were not so much escaping from politics as groping toward an idea of *producing human beings* who would be worthy of the new freedoms the French Revolution held out so promisingly. As these hopes dwindled in the sordid machinations of National Directory politics and were overshadowed by the rising specter of Napoleon, Wordsworth's naive but radical researches into the nature of human nature took on increasing urgency. For every Tom Poole, there were all too many Thomas Joneses, Charles Moggs, and Christopher Trickies, or "Simon Lees" and "Harry Gills." People in general did not seem ready for political freedom, the rights it offered, and the responsibilities it entailed. Hence the idea of constructing an education for democracy began to emerge among this small circle of thinkers, as it already had elsewhere in Europe, most notably in Germany in the work of Professor Immanuel Kant at the University of Königsberg, and the circle of writers around Fichte and Schelling at the University of Jena, near Weimar.

Tom Wedgwood, heir to one of the largest industrial fortunes in England, had enthusiastic ideas about liberal social reform and extensive means at his disposal to realize them. His idea was to put Godwin's rationalism into practice by founding a school which would begin training minds at the nursery level, based on Locke's theory of association of ideas, as recently refined in David Hartley's "vibranticles," or brain waves.[75] This school would carefully monitor its pupils' sensory experiences, anticipating the colored glass beads and graduated wooden rods of Maria Montessori's schools for Italian orphans a century later, or the "Skinner box" of behaviorist psychologists in our own time. It shared the drawback of all such purely rationalistic thinking about pedagogical practice, that measurable success would require taking control of infants as early as possible, gathering them in ever-larger primary schools, which would, in their ultimate implication, weaken the nuclear family as the basic unit of society in order to reform humanity from the nursery.

Wedgwood, who had not yet met Coleridge, thought Wordsworth might be a good director for such an experimental school. Wordsworth was associated with ideas of education in the minds of these wealthy young Bristol liberals because of his and Dorothy's care for the son of their friend Montagu, and because old John Pinney had considered them as possible tutors for his youngest child. Montagu, who had tutored both of the older Pinney brothers, highly recommended Wordsworth for his success with his son. Montagu's favors were further motivated by his now assiduous courting of Wedgwood's sister Sarah, a fabulously rich heiress-in-prospect. He had lost a Chancery suit against the estate of his late father, the notorious fourth earl of Sandwich, and had renounced his law practice in a (temporary) fit of Godwinian consistency against this perversion of justice.[76]

But Wordsworth's pedagogical credentials for this scheme were almost exactly the opposite of Wedgwood's Godwinian principles. William and Dorothy had succeeded in unspoiling Basil Montagu Jr. by allowing him to run free in the country, with "no other companions, than the flowers, the grass, the cattle, the sheep," and by giving him little household duties to perform. Years later little Basil was notably ungrateful in his recollection of the Wordsworths' "plain living" program.[77]

The Wedgwood plan was proto-utilitarian, the sort of education satirized by Dickens nearly half a century later in M'Choakumchild's school in *Hard Times.* But where nineteenth-century utilitarianism sought the greatest good of the greatest number, the Wedgwood plan, like Condorcet's in Paris, aimed at the eighteenth century's much higher goal: human perfectibility. Wedgwood's board of directors was virtually a short list of the last pure philosophes in England: Godwin, Holcroft, Horne Tooke, and the Bristol physician,

Germanist, and minor poet Thomas Beddoes. Wordsworth's surprisingly sharp satire in Book V of *The Prelude* against the "dwarf man" and "monster birth" produced by modern educational theories owes much to this brush with Wedgwood's project and with the possibility, very real at the time, that he might have to accept it in order to make ends meet. Coming from the heir to the Wedgwood fortune, such an offer was hard to refuse.

But Wedgwood soon decided that Coleridge, not Wordsworth, was the man to invest in for the systematic production of genius. Abandoning the idea of a school, the Wedgwoods in January would settle an annuity of £150 on Coleridge for his own maintenance. The amount was more than twice the proceeds Wordsworth could expect from his legacy from Raisley Calvert, even if his ambitious investment plan for it had worked out, and his comments on Coleridge's good fortune are so restrained as to expose his envy: citing "the unexampled liberality of the Wedgwoods towards Coleridge," he soberly "hope[d] the fruit will be good as the seed is noble."[78]

The Wordsworths' ties with London's intellectual and political world were by no means broken, however. In September, William and Dorothy contributed five shillings to a fund for Mary Godwin, the daughter of Godwin and Mary Wollstonecraft, and future author of *Frankenstein* and future wife of Percy Bysshe Shelley.[79] Her mother had died on September 10 from puerperal fever arising from complications in giving birth. The amount of William's pledge was collected from his brother Richard by Francis Tweddell (brother of John), who had been present at the November 1792 gathering of British radicals in Paris that Wordsworth also probably attended. But a certain degree of separation from this London set is suggested by Wordsworth's comment that he looked forward to reading Godwin's distressingly frank *Memoirs* of his wife "with no tormenting curiosity."[80]

On September 22 John Wordsworth shipped out from Torbay for India, as second mate on the *Duke of Montrose*.[81] He was rising steadily in rank, and on each voyage he invested his own and his sister's money for increased profits. At this rate, when he shipped out in 1801 as captain, at last, of the family bottom, the *Earl of Abergavenny,* he would eventually have recouped the siblings' entire fortunes and put them all on a solid footing of financial independence for life.

Between rounds of well-heeled guests hatching speculative projects, both Wordsworth and Coleridge were hard at work revising their tragedies for stage production. They had a strong incentive to do so. Coleridge, with his usual entrepreneurial generosity, had piggybacked Wordsworth onto Sheridan's invitation to Coleridge to submit a script on "a popular subject" for Covent Garden. Their plan was to have Coleridge submit his play, *Osorio,* first, so as not to prejudice Wordsworth's submission; after they'd got Sheridan's reaction to *Osorio,* they would try to strike again with *The Borderers.* Coleridge sent off his manuscript on October 16, to William Bowles, who relayed it via a friend, the Covent Garden musician William Lindley, to Sheridan.[82] Becoming impatient for Sheridan's reply, Coleridge then secured Wordsworth an invitation from the Covent Garden manager to read *The Borderers,* and a promise to produce it "immediately" if he accepted it. One of Poole's nephews gave a push to the effort by chatting up the popular London actor Thomas Knight, a Dorsetshire man, on the merits of Coleridge's and Wordsworth's plays.

Coleridge was not quite sure what Sheridan meant by a "popular" subject: a well-known historical incident, or a fictitious one? His preference was clearly for the latter, which he defended by citing *King Lear, Othello, Hamlet,* and *Romeo and Juliet.* Among contemporary authors, he cited Schiller's *The Robbers* as more powerful than his *Fiesco,* based on a failed republican coup d'état in sixteenth-century Genoa and recently translated by their acquaintance John Stoddart. Published in 1796 by Joseph Johnson, Stoddart's translation sought to capitalize on *The Robbers'* "great degree of popularity" by presenting what Schiller called the "reverse" of the earlier play: not "the victim of an extravagant sensibility [but] a victim of Art and Cabal."[83] Wordsworth's version of *The Robbers, The Borderers,* partly stimulated by Stoddart's example, combined elements of both plays, but took to heart Schiller's warning that "the political hero is much less calculated for dramatic representation" unless his defect, lack of heart, be supplied by the writer's "poetical excellence."

Wordsworth's and Coleridge's plays are similar in their derivation from *The Robbers,* but also in their differences from it, for they are more like each other than like Schiller's play. They were much more concerned about guilt and redemption than Schiller, more about the consequences of crime than the crime itself, and especially about *remorse,* as Coleridge made explicit later giving this title to *Osorio.* Schiller's Karl Moor might be called proto-Byronic, whereas Wordsworth's Mortimer and Coleridge's Osorio are . . . proto-Wordsworthian. Both plays feature two male characters, one of whom is trying to traduce, or kill, the other. Wordsworth focused on an "amiable" young man who is being tempted into remorse*lessness* by another young man, who has managed to overcome his feelings of remorse. Coleridge, by contrast, shows the belated remorse but final forgiveness of his villain—as if Wordsworth's Mortimer, having learned the causes of Rivers's amorality, were to try to convert him *back* to conventional morality.

Why all this fixation on guilt? the theater professionals in London might well have asked. If they, like the Home Office, had sent a spy to Alfoxden, they might have learned something about the sources of this peculiarly unspecific guiltiness which seems to have been hanging in the moral atmosphere between Stowey and Alfoxden. Coleridge added a spy passage to his play after the visit of James Walsh: Osorio suborns a Moor to inform on his brother Albert, who is arrested by a despicable representative of officialdom in the play, a prosecutor for the Inquisition. Coleridge's note on Osorio, the evil brother, sounds very much like Wordsworth's essay on Rivers: "I wished to represent a man, who, from his childhood had mistaken constitutional abstinence from vices, for strength of character—thro' his pride duped into guilt, and then endeavoring to shield himself from the reproaches of his own mind by misanthropy."[84] In fact, this sounds more like Rivers than like Osorio, whose abstinence from vice is not notable in the action of the play. But it sounds still more like Wordsworth's misanthropic semi-self-portrait in the "Lines Left upon a Seat in a Yew-tree," which had enjoyed great esteem during the combined Racedown and Stowey visits of June and July, and had a haunting aftereffect on Lamb. Lamb asked Coleridge to send him a copy of it, because it seemed to sum up the emotional intensity of his visit: "But above all, *that Inscription!*—it will recall to me the tones of all your voices."[85] Did Coleridge's essay also represent Wordsworth, or more generally the temptation to self-sufficient individuality that they were all feeling as they began to exercise their creative powers in the company of respected equals?

Several passages in Coleridge's play echo these possibilities. One directly versifies his own note on Osorio:

> What if his very virtues
> Had pamper'd his swoln heart, and made him proud?
> And what if pride had duped him into guilt,
> Yet still he stalk'd, a self-created God?
>
> (III.92–95)

"Self-created God" is a phrase similar to the ones Coleridge used indiscriminately in other contexts to praise Wordsworth, and it echoes Rivers's flattery of Mortimer: "self-stationed" to protect the borders of his world. Another passage closely paraphrases the conclusion of Wordsworth's yew tree lines: "He was a man different from other men / And he despised them, yet revered himself" (IV.83–84). (Wordsworth: "true dignity abides with him . . . who . . . can still suspect, / And still revere himself.") At the end, Osorio, exposed by the loving brother he has sought to destroy, feels remorse and asks for forgiveness: this is the main difference between him and Rivers. But the attraction he represents in both plays is identical: "Thou blind self-worshipper!"

Wordsworth's and Coleridge's fascination with this kind of amoral, creative, and manipulative character was partly a projection of, and partly a defense against, a temptation they felt strongly themselves, and their simultaneous remorse for having given in to it. Wordsworth had abandoned Annette and withdrawn from political activism; Coleridge had withdrawn from political writing and from Pantisocracy, and the strains of his relationship with Sara were becoming evident, notably increased by the presence of Wordsworth and especially of Dorothy. This self-centered, egotistical character also represented the temptation they felt their entire intellectual generation sliding into; isolated in an utterly polarized political situation, they still felt they should *do* something: cynical detachment was not an option.

Finally, in November, with both plays sent off to meet their fate, the three romantic wanderers were left alone to their own devices (Sara had the baby and the washing to look after). They could now branch out more in their walks than they had during the busy summer. They initiated what became a habit during the rest of the year: taking the same walk twice. This had been easy to do, up and around the Quantocks, or back and forth between Stowey and Alfoxden. But it required more time and planning, and cost more money, when they had to stay overnight on longer routes.

Early in the month they struck out right along the hilltops above the coast, past Minehead and Porlock to Lynmouth and Lynton. The walk was a revelation to William and Dorothy. They felt as if they were on the hills of Cumberland, but with sea views added, as though the fells of home had been moved fifteen or twenty miles north toward Solway Firth. You can occasionally catch glimpses of the Irish Sea from Lake District peaks, but only on clear days in certain places. Whereas the Exmoor downs, though considerably lower than the Cumbrian hills, give a similar feeling of altitude because they rise sharply to over a thousand feet within less than a mile of the level sea, which at this point broadens out from the Bristol Channel into the Irish Sea.[86]

The breeze off the sea was more than exhilarating, in November. They came down, with the hills, at Porlock. Then they "kept close to the shore about four miles," where they rose up into the first excitement of this trip. "Our road lay through the wood, rising almost perpendicularly from the sea." This brought them to Culbone Church, a very strange, not to say weird church, reputed to be the smallest in England, at thirty-five by twelve feet. This uncanny place, buried almost inaccessibly between three steep hills, provoked Coleridge to write "Kubla Khan"—that, and an attack of dysentery (diarrhea).[87] An attack of dysentery on a walking tour is a common occurence, especially after a none-too-good pub lunch, if followed by a four-mile shoreline trek and a sudden uphill push. Coleridge made a quick run up the rest of the steep into the clearings at the top, to find relief at one of the farmhouses there.

A good deal of critical ink has been spilled on the question of which "lonely farm-house" it was, exactly, where Coleridge composed this orientalist fantasy of English creativity. The claims of Ash Farm and Silcombe Farm seem equally good—both tidy bed-and-breakfasts now, as well as working farms—or the vanished Withycombe Farm. But Richard Holmes is surely right to redirect our focus back down to Culbone itself as the real geographical source of "Kubla Khan." He remarks the erotic geography of the steep little valley falling down toward the church in the dell, their "flanks" curving sharply down into the thick foliage, at the bottom of which (as Coleridge knew, having just climbed up from there) a stream of water gushed out directly below the tiny church—a Coleridgean fountain to match Alfoxden's waterfall.[88]

> But oh! that deep romantic chasm which slanted
> Down the green hill athwart a cedarn cover!
> A savage place! as holy and enchanted
> As e'er beneath a waning moon was haunted
> By woman wailing for her demon-lover!
> And from this chasm, with ceaseless turmoil seething,
> As if this earth in fast thick pants were breathing,
> A mighty fountain momently was forced:
> Amid whose swift half-intermitted burst
> Huge fragments vaulted like rebounding hail . . . . (12–21)

Culbone was and is a place of mystery. It had been a place of religious retreat—or exile—for centuries: a leper colony in the seventeenth century, a hiding place for Jacobites in 1715, the refuge of a band of freed but scorned East Indian servants until 1751. Since the 1760s it had been undergoing something of a revival, thanks to the new owner of Ash Farm, in whose manor it was, who renovated the chapel to counteract the activities of local Methodists. Even today its shelter hut offers, besides icy water from that same natural fountain, a mixture of spiritual brochures: Christian, environmental, and New Age mystical. Up above, in the normal world of the high road, the bartender will nod and wink about the strange doings of various hippie groups or solitaries who occasionally visit the place, including a wealthy "American lady" who recently held forth there as resident guru.

The poem's "dome of pleasure" becomes, in this reconstruction of its physical inspiration, the tiny church itself, very odd to see in the middle of that steep woods, making one wonder what determined act of creation could erect it there, like the creative fiat of a powerful Oriental khan. And the infamous "person from Porlock" who supposedly interrupted Coleridge in the writing down of his opium-induced dream (he normally took laudanum, opium diluted in water, as an "anodyne" for his ailments) could well have been William and/or Dorothy, who probably returned to Porlock to get better medication for him. No other person, then or at any other time when he was living at Stowey, would have "called . . . on business from Porlock," since no one else would have known he was there. Dorothy had some bemused recollections of their emergency rest stop there; she took to calling the domestic water cans and chamber pots at Alfoxden "kubla" cans.[89]

Each of these November walks engendered its own wandering poem project, initially conceived as a way of defraying expenses. This was a common practice: Thelwall paid for his walk across England to Stowey by sending it in installments to the *Monthly Magazine.* By the time they reached the terminus of this first extended walk, the Valley of Stones (or Rocks) west of Lynton, they had decided on their topic: "The Wanderings of Cain," modeled after the incredibly popular translation (1761) of Salomon Gessner's *Death of Abel.* This work of "loose poetry" or metrical prose had been widely praised as "the most finished copy of primeval nature anywhere extant," a confused judgment that reminds us of the contemporary popularity of Macpherson's "translation" of Ossian's *Fingal,* and explains how both poems could frequently be ranked above *Paradise Lost.*[90]

The Valley of Stones added inspiration for this prehistoric theme. It is a desolate enclosed landscape, filled with free-standing rocks that look like ancient monuments. The topic was, again, very like the one they had been pursuing in their dramas, the remorse-racked villain. Picking up where Gessner left off, with Cain heading into the wilderness with his wife and children, the text of Wordsworth and Coleridge's incomplete prose poem is obsessively concerned with the effects on Cain's mind of remorse for having killed his brother. Gessner explained how Cain came to commit his murder: he was traduced with dream visions by "an inferior spirit of Hell," who was discontented under Satan's rule. He murders Abel when, starting up from a nightmare, he mistakes him for this "seditious" spirit. Coleridge and Wordsworth wanted to show, instead, how Cain experienced the consequences of his crime. He has lived out his whole life racked by remorse and is ready to commit suicide or even to sacrifice his son for relief, but the spirit of flame leading him on is revealed at the crucial moments to be not Abel's ghost but an evil spirit named Anamelech. Hence his remorse is shown to be a delusion. Cain is an Osorio who has killed his brother, a Rivers tricked by false spirits, a companion to Wordsworth's wandering Sailor in "Adventures on Salisbury Plain," who (like Gessner's Cain) lurks about the neighborhood of his home, unable to return to it without suffering the ultimate punishment. At the end Cain seems to achieve redemption by rushing to rescue a woman and some children from a tiger's attack in the wilderness—a group that turns out to be his own family.

The idea was for a three-part prose poem. They would each write one part, and whoever finished first would take on the third. Wordsworth's part, the first, was the easiest, since it was mainly to describe Cain being led across the wilderness by the fire spirit. Coleridge wrote his part, but he recalled with a smile thirty years later the ridiculousness of the plan, so far as Wordsworth was concerned: that "a mind so eminently original [should] compose another man's thoughts and fancies," and that "a taste so austerely pure and simple [should] imitate the Death of Abel":

> I see his grand and noble countenance as at the moment when having despatched my own portion of the task at full finger-speed, I hastened to him with my manuscript—that look of humorous despondency fixed upon his almost blank sheet of paper, and then its silent mock-piteous admission of failure struggling with the sense of the exceeding ridiculousness of the whole scheme—which broke up in a laugh: and the Ancient Mariner was written instead.[91]

This sounds almost as if they went on immediately to compose "The Rime of the Ancient Mariner," and this is almost true. They had barely returned from this first walk when, on November 12 or 13, they set out on a second one, a more carefully planned reprise of the first. Even their departure time, 4:30 P.M., was carefully chosen to get them down to Watchet, five miles from Alfoxden on the coast, in time to see the sun set across Blue Anchor Bay. They probably spent the first night at the Bell Inn at Watchet, and here their next joint project was hatched, to pay for the costs of this second trip. It was to describe, not the wanderings of Cain, but a larger Christian archetype of Cain, the wandering Jew. Many items in the landward geography of this fabulous poem can be located, item by item, along the Somerset coast, from Watchet through Minehead to Lynton: the harbor town from which the Mariner embarks and the hermit in the wood to whom he returns at the end, pleading for forgiveness—surely a denizen of the oak woods around Culbone Church.

Wordsworth's contributions to "The Ancient Mariner" were considerably greater than those to "The Wanderings of Cain," though it soon became apparent, probably on that first night at Watchet, if not the next night at the Ship Inn in Porlock, that the poem's meter, mystery, and archaism were beyond, if not his abilities, then his interest. He suggested "some crime to be committed" which, as in *The Borderers* and "Adventures on Salisbury Plain," would bring onto the protagonist "the spectral persecution, as a consequence of that crime and his own wanderings."[92] He had been browsing in George Shelvocke's *Voyage round the World by the Way of the Great South Sea* (1726) just before they left Alfoxden, and noted there the immense wingspan of the albatross, sometimes reaching twelve feet. " 'Suppose,' said I, 'you represent him as having killed one of these birds on entering the South Sea, and that the tutelary spirits of these regions take upon them to avenge the crime.' " We can recognize in these tutelary spirits the guilty but helpless consciences of Wordsworth and Coleridge, and "these regions" as not so much Somerset (still less the South Pacific) as the theater of the mind in which all their poems were now being staged. Wordsworth says he also suggested the idea of the ship's ropes and sails being worked by the dead crew (after they have paid the price of the Mariner's crime), while the idea of the specter ship on which the "Night-mare Life-in-Death" plays dice with Death for the Mariner's soul derived from a dream of their Stowey friend John Cruikshank. Having thus accounted for the crime which sets the action going, the main course of the action, and its two most dramatic ocean settings, Wordsworth would seem to merit a rather large share of credit for "The Ancient Mariner": all Coleridge had to do was write it! But Wordsworth made some more "trifling contributions" as well, in which we clearly recognize his signature: the Wedding Guest's helpless fixation on the skinny Mariner: he "listen'd like a three years' child; / The Mariner has his will"; and the Wedding Guest's terrified expression of fear at the Mariner's appearance: "thou art long, and lank, and brown, / As is the ribbed sea-sand." The little girl of "We Are Seven" begins to emerge in the first couplet, and the Discharged Veteran from near Hawkshead will shortly emerge from the second couplet: "A foot above man's common measure tall, / And lank, and upright . . . His legs were long . . . long and shapeless . . . His arms were long and lean . . . and his mouth / Shewed ghastly in the moonlight."[93]

No other poems or incidents are recorded after the beginning of this auspicious tour, though it lasted more than a week. The novelty had worn off, the second time around. They continued on to Lynton, and then circled back by an inland route, crossing Exmoor and skirting the Brendon Hills to Dulverton, returning home from the opposite (southwest) side of the Quantocks from which they had departed.

They got back on November 20, and William and Dorothy departed for London almost immediately, to shepherd *The Borderers* through its reading and revision in London. Thomas Knight, Covent Garden's principal actor, had expressed "great approbation" of it, but suggested that Wordsworth come to town to make "certain alterations."[94] Wordsworth went with alacrity. Staying again with his old family friend Samuel Nicholson in Cateaton Street, Wordsworth "curtailed" his play on the spot during the first week of December, trying to follow Knight's suggestions, most probably for the character of Rivers, whom Knight would have acted, since the best actors usually played the most villainous characters. While waiting to hear the fate of *The Borderers,* Wordsworth visited old friends, going around to Godwin's on December 13 with James Tobin, and dining three times with Southey, whom Dorothy now met for the first time, remarking his "virtuous habits."[95]

Coleridge got word on December 2 that *Osorio* was rejected because of "the obscurity of the last three acts." On the 14th Knight relayed the same negative verdict on *The Borderers* from Mr. Harris, the theater manager, who pronounced it "impossible that [the play] should succeed in the representation."[96] Sheridan's manager and actors must have thought their two aspiring Somerset playwrights were a bit too much in each other's company, for both plays were rejected for the same reason: metaphysical or philosophical obscurity.

Like many another disappointed playwright, Wordsworth attributed his rejection to the "depraved" state of the theater at the time, and he and Dorothy left town in a huff the same day. Neither he nor Harris was wrong: *The Borderers* is virtually unrepresentable, and the state of the London stage was very bad. Even a hardened city hack like Holcroft despaired of anything good getting performed, though he located the depravity in the house, not on the stage: "half filled with prostitutes and their paramours; they disturb the rest of the audience."[97]

Wordsworth pretended defensively he did not really expect his play to be performed, but this self-protective afterthought is belied by the report of his relatives, and his own behavior. The Halifax relatives who were in contact with Nicholson give clear evidence of the fond hopes of their young nephew and cousin for his new venture. "They were induced to believe he [Harris] would accept [the play] and that it would have a prodigious run." Cousin Martha Ferguson stoutly assured her brother that "from all accounts it was a Masterly performance—a Tragedy of a very uncommon Sort—beautiful language—and universally admir'd by all who read it."[98] Even after the rejection, which seemed most unfair to this family, the Rawsons and Fergusons continued to wish them well, with indulgent overtones: "they are deeper in plays and poetry than ever"; "they are happy in having very fertile imaginings, which are a continual source of entertainment to them."[99]

Before they got the bad news, William and Dorothy went to Covent Garden and Drury Lane as much as they could, since William's temporary status as playwright gave them "no difficulty in obtaining orders for Covent Garden, and . . . once for Drury Lane."[100] They saw Mrs. Siddons in *The Merchant of Venice,* Thomas Morton's opera *The Children in the Wood,* probably Garrick's adaptation of Southerne's *The Fatal Marriage,* a ballet performance of Milton's *Comus,* and Richard Cumberland's new comedy, *False Impressions.*[101]

Wordsworth was in fact combing the theater for salable ideas. Six months later, when he was in Bristol supervising *Lyrical Ballads* through the press, he made a point of going to see Matthew ("Monk") Lewis's *The Castle-Spectre,* which had opened in London on the very day *The Borderers* was rejected. Lewis, who had become a millionaire at age nineteen from the success of his salacious Gothic novel *The Monk* (1795), had struck it rich again: with Dora Jordan featured as the romantic ingenue, *The Castle-Spectre* reportedly earned £18,000 in the three months of its London run. Such figures commanded attention. Wordsworth had Coleridge buy him a copy of the text in January, and went to see the play as soon as he could. He said, "If I had no other method of employing myself Mr. Lewis's success would have thrown me into despair. The Castle Spectre is a Spectre indeed. Clothed with the flesh and blood of £400 received from the treasury of the theatre it may in the eyes of the author . . . appear very lovely."[102]

This is a mixture of sharp criticism and sour grapes. For though *The Castle-Spectre* is nothing if not transparent, especially when compared to the "obscurity" of *Osorio* and *The Borderers,* it too is heavily indebted to Schiller's *The Robbers,* as Lewis cheerfully acknowledged. In a lightweight vehicle Lewis had succeeded with the representation of a theme essentially identical to the one that mesmerized Wordsworth and Coleridge. His play also features two characters, brothers—one who has apparently murdered the other and whose life is eaten away by remorse as a result. Similarly, Lewis's purpose is "To lay th'exulting villain's bosom bare."[103] But for the existential aspect of amoral action, he created a separate character, the villain's black African bodyguard, Hassan, who directs vengeance "at large against [white] mankind" because slave traders murdered his wife and child. This strategy solves (too easily, no doubt) the problem bedeviling Wordsworth's and Coleridge's plays, by casting their motiveless malignity onto a minor, exotic character whose philosophical rantings could be disregarded by members of the audience who wanted to concentrate on the conventional Gothic revenge romance in the play's main action. Hassan is Rivers in blackface, relegated to a subordinate position in the band of outlaws. (Lewis's play also has four black bodyguards, corresponding to Wordsworth's borderers and Coleridge's Moors.)

The Castle-Spectre is a silly play, mixing Gothic exaggeration with a bawdy pseudo-Shakespearean subplot and vaguely uplifting humanitarian sentiments, hardly the kind of thing we can imagine Wordsworth or Coleridge putting their name to in public. But it is "liberal" in both its theatrical and political sophistication. Its huge success showed the Somerset playwrights not simply that the public taste was "depraved" but that it was rather sophisticated, and that if they wanted to address their modern audiences successfully—that is, with both integrity and profit—they would have to produce texts that seemed familiar even as they broke new ground.

Wordsworth thus had reason to feel chagrined as well as contemptuous of Lewis's success and was perhaps a little startled at how close this enterprising young man had come to concerns so near his heart. *The Castle-Spectre* is set in the "romantic" north, with action stretching from Northumberland to

Conway Castle in North Wales, and a hero and heroine who are self-styled "Romantic enthusiasts," addressing their love to each other in sentiments clothed with images of natural beauty from the Cheviot Hills. Like that of *The Borderers,* its action occurs during the period of the barons' league, and its hero, the Earl Percy disguised as a shepherd, cautions his fellow aristocrats to reflect "that their vassals are man as they are, and have hearts whose feelings can be grateful as their own." For such lines, and his sympathetic representation of the blacks' sarcasm about "European gratitude," Lewis was attacked for "sentiments [that] were violently democratic" and for supporting "the Cause of Equality."

But Wordsworth must have been most startled when Mrs. Jordan said in the epilogue, "My shoulder felt a Bow-Street runner's tap," accusing her of killing Count Osmond, the play's villain, "alias Barrymore"—the actor who played him. Protesting in vain against the "design" of "Townshend"—the name of an actual "larned Justice" to whose Bow Street court the runner means to deliver her—she says she has fled to the theater instead: "Just is my cause, and English is my jury!"[104] This comic confusion of an actress with her role is as much a satire on the government's bumbling as Coleridge's later "Spy Nozy" episode, showing how active such "runners" were, and how unpopular, making one wonder if rumors of the Somerset incident had reached London by this time. The possibility is not far-fetched: though Coleridge had a hard time getting word from Sheridan about *Osorio*'s fate, he later heard a scene from it declaimed at a party by a Miss DeCamp, who said she'd got it from Linley the musician, who had also passed it on to Charles Grey, Samuel Whitbread, and Sir Francis Burdett, leading Whig and radical politicians.[105]

If Coleridge's manuscript could be passed around, so could Wordsworth's. When Wordsworth heard the last words of Lewis's play, he indeed thought he was hearing something very familiar. They are delivered by the brother who turns out not to have been killed, but who has spent sixteen years in a solitary dungeon instead, yet who can now forgive the brother who wronged him: "Oh! in his stately chambers, far greater must have been his pangs than mine in this gloomy dungeon." This contrast between the moral sufferings of aristocratic villains and the physical pains of prisoners thrown unjustly into dungeons was exactly the one Wordsworth had drawn in "The Convict," which appeared over the signature "Mortimer" in the *Morning Post* on December 14, the very evening of which *The Castle-Spectre* opened at the Theatre Royal in Drury Lane. Had Wordsworth seen it that night, instead of six months later, he could be forgiven for thinking that Lewis had cribbed his conclusion from a hurried perusal of the morning papers. As it was, the prologue addressed the play to unhappy youths who "Mourn slighted talents, or desert opprest, / False friendship, hopeless love, or faith betray'd." These were states of mind largely identical with those Wordsworth had voiced in his yew tree lines the previous summer and would repeat in his Tintern Abbey lines in the coming one, and they were very much part of a common climate of disillusionment and hopelessness that was penetrating all young liberals' opinions at the time.

22 THE MARINER AND THE RECLUSE

Nether Stowey and Alfoxden 1798

Not Chaos, not
The darkest pit of lowest Erebus,
Nor aught of blinder vacancy, scooped out
By help of dreams—can breed such fear and awe
As fall upon us often when we look
Into our Minds, into the Mind of Man—
My haunt, and the main region of my song.
("Prospectus" to *The Recluse*)

William and Dorothy spent the Christmas and New Year holidays visiting their wealthy friends in Bristol, the Pinneys and Wedgwoods, though they stayed with the Nonconformist Cottle. By January 3 they were back at Alfoxden, alone, with no prospects of any kind in front of them. "The play is rejected," Dorothy glumly informed their friends. But this emptiness was a perfect limbo for writing. In terms of viable writing projects Wordsworth was back where he was when he left Racedown: with an unsatisfactory version of "The Ruined Cottage" and without Coleridge. Coleridge was in Shrewsbury, investigating a call to a Unitarian church there, at the invitation of a Reverend Hazlitt. He dazzled the minister's son, named William, and decided to accept the call, which would pay him a badly needed £120 a year. His prospects were no better than Wordsworth's, and he had a wife and child to support. He was rescued from this hard career decision by the annuity which the Wedgwoods now bestowed on him—"£150 for life, legally secured to me, *no condition whatever being annexed.*"[1]

For most of January, William and Dorothy lived their frugal life alone, William writing in the morning while Dorothy tended to household duties with Peggy Marsh. In the afternoons and evenings they walked together over the hills. And they both wrote. Over the holidays, Dorothy had got a small journal in which she began to make a record of what interested her each day. Her "Alfoxden Journal" is filled with minute descriptions of landscape and weather effects; there is hardly a single reference to public society in it. In five months the only things she noted beyond their daily routines and nature's various appearances were the receipt of Godwin's *Memoirs* of Mary Wollstonecraft and walking over to the local squire's house at Crowcombe to protest their house tax. Of the French invasion of Switzerland, which began in late January, and from which William dated his loss of hope in the French cause, she says not a word, though she does mention meeting "a razor-grinder with a soldier's knapsack upon his back, and a boy to drag his wheel," which might have reminded them of the *Anti-Jacobin*'s ferocious satire on Southey's knife-grinder poem.[2]

She was not, of course, just then starting to make observations about nature. Rather, she was beginning to write down what it had been her habit for years to notice, stimulated by the example of her brother's descriptive sketches and the widespread fashion of cultivating the Picturesque. Her skill, and her differences from William as a writer, are evident from her first entry, for January 20, 1798:

> The green paths down the hill-sides are channels for streams. The young wheat is streaked by silver lines of water running between the ridges, the sheep are gathered together on the slopes. After the wet dark days, the country seems more populous. It peoples itself in the sunbeams. The garden, mimic of spring, is gay with flowers. The purple-starred hepatica spreads itself in the sun, and the clustering snow-drops put forth their white heads, at first upright, ribbed with green, and like a rosebud when completely opened, hanging their heads downwards, but slowly lengthening their slender stems. The slanting woods of an unvarying brown, showing the light through the thin net-work of their upper boughs. Upon the highest ridge of that round hill covered with planted oaks, the shafts of the trees show in the light like the columns of a ruin.[3]

The details in this excellent description can be visualized much more easily than those in her brother's poetry; many readers respond to Wordsworth's nature poetry as though the Wordsworth they are reading were Dorothy, not William. Her description moves down the hills with the water, into their own garden, nourished by those runoffs, and then returns us to the top of the hills. Like that of Shelburne before her or Thoreau after, Dorothy's nature writing is best when it moves effortlessly from exact observation to metaphoric interpretation, as it does here, developing the adjective "populous" into the striking neologism "peoples itself," and then tapering off into a light personification of the flowers. William immediately recognized these possibilities and turned them into verse:

> these populous slopes
> With all their groves and with their murmurous woods,

Give a curious feeling to the mind
Of peopled solitude.[4]

He has not necessarily improved on Dorothy by putting her words into blank verse: we don't need to be told that the mind is given "a curious feeling"; in Dorothy's words, we feel it ourselves. If good writing means showing, not telling, Dorothy's passage is the better of the two. Wordsworth's paradoxical "peopled solitude" is fine, but so is Dorothy's eerie last phrase, "like the columns of a ruin," sharply contrasting all the fecund natural details with a sudden stark reminder of humankind.

It is true that there is "no Dorothy herself" in most of her journal entries: she almost never says "I think" or "I felt," or gives any personal opinion.[5] She was after all writing for herself. Many of her entries lack verbs, but are surprisingly active nonetheless: the activity she records is often simply that of *being.* But to conclude from this apparent lack of personality that she has "no style" is unwarranted. It was her style to project no personality in her writing: in person she was just the opposite. In this she was wholly different from her brother, whose poetic landscapes are informed by, if not actually transformed into, his own mental landscape. This difference is especially clear from his adaptation of her journal entry for January 25: "Went to Poole's after tea. The sky spread over with one continuous cloud, whitened by the light of the moon, which, though her dim shape was seen, did not throw forth so strong a light as to chequer the earth with shadows. At once the clouds seemed to cleave asunder, and left her in the centre of a black-blue vault. She sailed along, followed by multitudes of stars, small, and bright, and sharp. Their brightness seemed concentrated (half-moon)."

William turned this into "A Night-Piece":

The sky is overspread
With a close veil of one continuous cloud
All whitened by the moon, that just appears,
A dim-seen orb, yet chequers not the ground
With any shadow—plant, or tower, or tree.
At last a pleasant instantaneous light
Startles the musing man whose eyes are bent
To earth. He looks around, the clouds are split
Asunder, and above his head he views
The clear moon & the glory of the heavens.
There in the black-blue vault she sails along
Followed by multitudes of stars, that small,
And bright, & sharp along the gloomy vault
Drive as she drives. How fast they wheel away!
Yet vanish not! The wind is in the trees;

> But they are silent. Still they roll along
> Immeasurably distant, and the vault
> Built round by those white clouds, enormous clouds,
> Still deepens its interminable depth.
> At length the vision closes, & the mind
> Not undisturbed by the deep joy it feels,
> Which slowly settles into peaceful calm,
> Is left to muse upon the solemn scene.[6]

Just about everything in William's poem is also in Dorothy's journal. Of course, he was walking with her and had his own perceptions of the scene as well as her journal entry to work from. (Coleridge seems to have been present too; he recorded this observation: "Behind the thin / Grey cloud that cover'd but not hid the sky / The round full moon look'd small.")[7] Wordsworth adds a metaphysical contrast between the sound of the wind in the trees and the apparent silence of the spheres, but his largest addition is "the musing man" who is excited by the vision. In fact, insofar as "A Night-Piece" is a poem at all, its meaning is contained in the slight difference between the observer's musing before and after "the vision." Before, he was musing inattentively. Afterward, he is "not undisturbed by the deep joy" his mind feels, which gradually settles into a "peaceful calm" that allows him to return to his musings, but upon a "scene" that has now become "solemn." One can get more out of William's version than Dorothy's, but more need not be equated with better. The delicacy of his sensibility is marked by the way visual changes in the landscape rouse him, with his negative admission that he is "not undisturbed" by joy. This is already a mind whose poetry arises from "emotion recollected in tranquillity."

But, close as William and Dorothy were in their writing this winter, the next two or three months were the period of the closest literary collaboration between Wordsworth and Coleridge, as they helped each other complete "The Ruined Cottage" and "The Rime of the Ancient Mariner." Their joint work on these poems is much closer than either their collaboration on *Lyrical Ballads* (mostly composed by Wordsworth between March and May) or their work in parallel on their two dramas. Between February 11, when Coleridge came over to Alfoxden after his return from Shrewsbury, and March 23, when he showed up with a completed version of "The Rime," the two poets were in almost daily contact.[8] Their hopes for stage success dashed, they turned, in the dead of winter, to the narrative trunks of two poems, one naturalistic, the other Gothic.[9] "The Ruined Cottage" at this time consisted of approximately two hundred lines which gave the outline of the tale of Margaret: she is now dead, and her story is told by someone like a peddler ("A wanderer among the cottages") to someone else, who doesn't know her. Wordsworth now expanded his spare narrative first to over five hundred lines, then to more than nine hundred.[10] Coleridge's poem consisted of about three hundred lines, covering mainly the Mariner's voyage, the shooting of the albatross, and the ship's subsequent becalming in the South Seas. The intertwined stories of Margaret and the Mariner beautifully represent the imaginative bond between Wordsworth and Coleridge at this time, but the close connection between these two poems has been obscured by the fact that "The Ancient Mariner" appeared in *Lyrical Ballads,* while "The Ruined Cottage" did not see light until 1814, as the first book of *The Excursion.* If they had been published together, as seemed possible for a brief moment in the spring, they would have given a twist to the beginnings of English Romanticism much different from that provided by *Lyrical Ballads.**

The similarities between "The Ruined Cottage" and "The Ancient Mariner" become clear immediately if the two poems are set side by side. In both we have a narrative of intense suffering, told by an old and uneducated man to a young man, evidently better educated and of higher class, the effect of which is to fundamentally shatter the young man's immediate preoccupations and which seems likely to change his life forever after. The Wedding Guest, stunned, turns *from* the bridegroom's door and rises the morrow morn, "A sadder and a wiser man." Similarly, the young narrator of "The Ruined Cottage" "turn[s] aside in weakness" from the Pedlar, almost unmanned by grief after hearing the tale of Margaret's decline and death, and must be rescued from despair by the Pedlar's calm words of wisdom. In two early attempts at a conclusion, Wordsworth had his young narrator reflect on the story's meaning—"and to myself / I seem'd a better and a wiser man"—or thank the Pedlar for it: "And for the tale which you have told I think / I am a better and a wiser man." These phrases draw the ending of "The Ancient Mariner" directly into the picture, but we cannot be entirely sure which poet took them from which.[11] The Pedlar's wisdom about nature's "calm oblivious tendencies" parallels, in function if not in doctrine, the Mariner's moral to his tale: "He prayeth best, who loveth best / All things both great and small." Both morals are appropriate to their unlettered speakers, but seem very inadequate to the devastating effect of the tales they've told, and in both poems the wise old narrators are portrayed as notably *un*wise during the course of the main action they relate to their young auditors.

Beyond these narrative parallels, there are others: (1) a derelict structure

**Peter Bell,* begun in late April, is often taken to be Wordsworth's counterpart to the "Ancient Mariner," but it is less a full partner than a junior one. It is an interesting poem, but no match for the "Ancient Mariner," as "The Ruined Cottage" abundantly is.

(cottage or ship) set in the midst of (2) a wide, bare natural expanse (common or ocean), which becomes (3) a scene of moral instruction in which (4) ugly or grotesque natural objects (weeds or water snakes) function symbolically as signs of the narrators' agony, but also become the focus of their redemption: the Mariner blesses the water snakes "unawares" and finds that he can pray at last; the Pedlar, passing the dead Margaret's cottage with troubled thoughts, suddenly sees, in the weeds and spear grass "silver'd o'er" with mist, an "image of tranquillity" so strong that he can "walk along [his] road in happiness."

Of course the poems are also different. Coleridge's is a stylized imitation of a ballad romance, which arouses readerly expectations very different from those of Wordsworth's clear, elevated blank verse. Coleridge's archaic diction is more appropriate to its subject, in contemporary terms. Wordsworth's blank verse and chaste diction would have led contemporary audiences to expect a serious poem; they would have expected lower-class characters like a weaver's wife and a peddler to be treated balladically, if not comically. Wordsworth consistently did cast such characters into ballad form in his contributions to *Lyrical Ballads,* which he began composing immediately after bringing "The Ruined Cottage" to a close. But the challenge to readerly expectations created by his use of a modernized Miltonic blank verse for common subjects was a major part of his now emerging revolutionary program for the course of English poetry.

In expanding their poems, the two poets articulated the sufferings of their protagonists—spread them out, diversified their time and details, and developed the character of their narrators, as well as their effect on their young auditors. Margaret's sufferings are now drawn out over the course of five years, as stages in an excruciatingly painful decline, which are marked by the Pedlar's seasonal rounds. These additions increase our sense of Margaret's pain both by prolonging it and by projecting it—the poem's master touch—onto the ruination of her cottage. The Pedlar comes back, winter, summer, spring, and fall, notes signs of decay in Margaret's house and garden, then meets her and has his suspicions confirmed by similar signs of decay in her. It is a cruelly effective strategy for representing a process that would otherwise be almost too painful to read: the slow death of a human being. It depends for its effect on the obtuseness of the Pedlar, who, like the Mariner in the action of his rime, is not wise *yet.* It is also a potentially pornographic or sadomasochistic strategy, as Wordsworth recognized, for he has the Pedlar address exactly this point when he resumes Margaret's story at the urging of his young auditor.

> I begg'd of the old man that for my sake
> He would resume his story. He replied,

"It were a *wantonness,* and would demand
Severe reproof, if we were men whose hearts
Could hold vain dalliance with the misery
Even of the dead, *contented thence to draw*
A momentary pleasure never marked
By reason, *barren* of all future good."
(MS B.278–85; italics added)

The shocking idea that recounting the sufferings of a dying woman could be a kind of necrophilia is unconsciously censored by most readers of these lines, who interpret them in the perspective of the establishment Wordsworth. But Wordsworth's diction suggests it, line by line, especially his reference to the erotic literary fashion of Cavalier dalliance. The lines respond, self-censoriously, to the Pedlar's first announcement that Margaret, whom he "loved . . . as my own child," is dead. Both she and her cottage are represented as flirtatious demon lovers of the disaster which befell them:

She is dead,
The worm is on her cheek, and this poor hut,
Stripped of its outward garb of household flowers,
Of rose and jasmine, *offers to the wind*
A cold bare wall whose earthy top is tricked
With weeds and the rank spear-grass. She is dead,
And nettles rot and adders sun themselves
Where we have sat together *while she nursed*
Her infant at her bosom.
(MS B.157–65; italics added)

Immediately, the Pedlar asks forgiveness—"I feel I play the truant with my tale"—and he rights the moral balance by introducing Margaret's husband, Robert, "an industrious man, sober and steady." But it is clear that his relations with Margaret were deeply passionate (though not sexual) and that he uses this kind of quasi-erotic language to manipulate his young listener's interest in her. This is very much the sort of thing we saw Wordsworth doing in his descriptions and proposed revisions of the relations between the Sailor and the Female Vagrant on Salisbury Plain, or between the Alpine wanderer and the dancing girls in *Descriptive Sketches.*

Wordsworth further articulated Margaret's sufferings by giving them moral significance. He did this through the character of the Pedlar, who has a simple but not uneducated rural background among the "grave livers" of Scottish Presbyterianism. This boyhood biography closely resembles Wordsworth's, and many passages describing the Pedlar were taken over wholesale into the first drafts of "the poem on the growth of my own mind" which he began writing in Germany at the end of this year.

His way of writing about himself is now noticeably different from what it had been earlier in the 1790s, because he gives a new spiritual significance to his outdoor childhood adventures, a method of spiritual heightening he owed largely to the transcendental philosophy of Spirit he was imbibing almost daily in conversations with Coleridge. This was the language of "the One Life within us and abroad" that Coleridge had first tried out in 1795 on a disapproving Sara in "The Aeolian Harp." This philosophy is so often taken as the essence of English Romanticism, especially of the Wordsworthian type, that it tends to be prematurely installed as the meaning of the complicated and fragmentary texts which were being worked out experimentally in situ. What Wordsworth absorbed from Coleridge as "The Ruined Cottage" progressed was a revelation of a spiritual life in all natural things, with which human consciousness could sympathize. More familiar in its lightly catechical form ("One impulse from a vernal wood / May teach you more of man . . . Than all the sages can"), it appears everywhere in the Pedlar's new biography:

> He was a chosen son:
> To him was given an ear which deeply felt
> The voice of Nature in the obscure wind,
> The sounding mountain and the running stream.
> To every natural form, rock, fruit, and flower,
> Even the loose stones that cover the highway,
> He gave a moral life; he saw them feel
> Or linked them to some feeling.
>
> (MS B76–83)

This was not the rationalized nature of Deism, or a distillation of Unitarianism, but a philosophic transcendentalism with classical analogues from Neoplatonism, given renewed life by Spinoza, which was at this moment gaining a powerful influx of philosophical energy in Germany through the various writings of Kant, Fichte, the Schelling brothers, Schlegel, and Hegel. Their *Naturphilosophie* was an intellectual beachhead established against the morally and emotionally deadening consequences of relentless Enlightenment rationalism. The simplistic application of reason to human affairs seemed, by 1798, to have gone disastrously askew in the French Revolution. Both Wordsworth and Coleridge had lent their minds, hopes, and energies wholeheartedly to this process, and now that Godwin was being quoted in the newspapers to sound like an out-of-office Robespierre, both of them were in full retreat from the chilling religious and political implications they saw in the thought of their erstwhile London friend and mentor.

The *process* by which the Pedlar became a kind of nature philosopher who can comprehensively interpret Margaret's sufferings is still more radical. In the short form of the poem Wordsworth read to Coleridge and Lamb in June 1797, the Pedlar had much less moral authority. He was scared and superstitious about the ruin of Margaret's cottage: as a character, Wordsworth built him up from a compulsive neighbor who haunted her ruin like a morbid Peeping Tom. This is the character we see in the fragment titled "Incipient Madness," another in the series of "mad songs" that Wordsworth wrote during 1796–97.

Wordsworth's strained mental condition attracted him to the ways in which minds could be overthrown or broken down, suggesting the depth of his own mental crisis. He would never have written *The Prelude* without these preliminary negative researches. In "Incipient Madness" an unnamed narrator returns, night after night, to a ruined cottage, fascinated by "a broken pane which glitter'd in the moon / And seemed akin to life."[12] No indication is given why he does this, but it seems clear that someone associated with the cottage has died and that he assuages his grief for this death by fixating on this lively speck of light. The language also anticipates the sexual diction in "The Ruined Cottage": his "sickly heart" fastened on this speck "like a sucking babe," and "many a long month / Confirm'd *this strange incontinence.*" The speaker's compulsion appears to be a twisted kind of lover's constancy, as his vigils outlast those of a glow worm, a blackbird, and a linnet—the most steadfast of which stayed around for more than three years!

I alone
Remained: the winds of heaven remained—with them
My heart claimed fellowship and with the beams
Of dawn and of the setting sun that seemed
To live and linger on the mouldering walls.

(45–49)

This is very close to the "cold bare wall whose earthy top is tricked / With weeds and the rank spear-grass" in "The Ruined Cottage," and to the benign sunset image which finally enabled Wordsworth to bring that troubling poem to an end, once he had thoroughly steeped his Pedlar in Coleridge's pantheism:

Together casting then a farewell look
Upon those silent walls, we left the shade
And ere the stars were visible attained
A rustic inn, our evening resting-place.

(MS D.535–38)

These lines conclude the "reconciling addendum" composed in March of 1798, but Wordsworth did not represent any this-worldly solutions for the sufferings of Margaret, because they are inadequate to those sufferings as he has presented them. Margaret does not need food or money; her problem is a broken heart, and she will not give it up, though she knows full well she should: " 'I am changed, / And to myself . . . have done much wrong, / . . . I have slept / Weeping, and weeping I have waked; my tears / Have flowed as if my body were not such / As others are, and I could never die.' "[13] In her immortal grief Margaret claims kinship with the two female characters Coleridge was creating at the same time: "the Night-mare LIFE-IN-DEATH" and the demon lover of "Kubla Khan," and her ruined cottage is a Wordsworthian counterpart to the frightening landscape Coleridge imagined at Culbone Church: "A savage place! as holy and enchanted / As e'er beneath a waning moon was haunted / By woman wailing for her demon-lover!"

Not everything in the relations between these two poems was so serious, however, as we see by the similarities between Coleridge's parody of "This Is the House That Jack Built" and the final dirge of "The Ruined Cottage":

On a Ruined House in a Romantic Country

And this reft house is that the which he built,
Lamented Jack! And here his malt he pil'd,
Cautious in vain! These rats that squeak so wild,
Squeak, not unconscious of their father's guilt.
Did ye not see her gleaming thro' the glade?
Belike, 'twas she, the maiden all forlorn.
What though she milk no cow with crumpled horn,
Yet *aye* she haunts the dale where *erst* she stray'd;
And *aye* beside her stalks her amorous knight!
Still on his thighs their wonted brogues are worn,
And thro' those brogues, still tatter'd and betorn,
His hindward charms gleam an unearthly white;
As when thro' broken clouds at night's high noon
Peeps in fair fragments forth the full-orb'd harvest-moon![14]

Coleridge was that most un-Germanic creature, a philosopher with a sense of humor, and he sensed that his serious new pupil needed lightening up from time to time. The last simile is good physic for readers who come to Romantic poetry looking only for easy sentimental beauty.

Significant as the twin births of "The Ancient Mariner" and "The Ruined Cottage" were, an even larger creative event was occurring simultaneously. Wordsworth was being created as the poet of *The Recluse; or, Views of Nature, Man, and Society.* This was the title of the grand epic poem he announced to Tobin and Losh in early March, a project which stayed with him through the rest of his creative life, as the magnum opus to which that life was devoted. It title may have been suggested by Thelwall, who refers to himself as "the new Recluse" in his autobiographical preface to his *Poems* of 1801.[15] But images of recluses and hermits were becoming fashionable, as many writers opted for classical expressions of pastoral retreat to escape the oppressive climate against free expression that was settling down over England.

By a strict accounting Wordsworth completed barely half of *The Recluse. The Prelude* was its "portico," and *The Excursion* was its second, narrative section, though other parts of it can be identified in his manuscripts or in poems recycled to other contexts.[16] But the project's qualitative importance to him—first as an inspiring ideal, later as a crippling obligation—far outweighs the number of lines he wrote for it. To be the poet of *The Recluse* was the most comprehensive of Wordsworth's self-creations. The Poet of the preface to *Lyrical Ballads* and "the chosen Son" of *The Prelude* are versions of the same identity, only slightly less grand and heroic. In his description of each of these incarnations, he uses hyperbolic language to express the existential divinity of this Poet figure and his proposed accomplishments. To Tobin and Losh, he was still relatively restrained: the poem will "convey most of the knowledge of which I am possessed. . . . I know not any thing which will not come within the scope of my plan."[17]

But in the verse "Prospectus" to *The Recluse,* composed two years later, his ambition goes far beyond the "considerable utility" he claimed for his poem in early 1798: "I must tread on shadowy ground, must sink / Deep—and, aloft ascending, breathe in worlds / To which the heaven of heavens is but a veil . . . / . . . Jehovah—with his thunder, and the choir / Of shouting Angels, and the empyreal thrones— / I pass them unalarmed" (28–35). In such biblical, Miltonic language Wordsworth projects his best image of himself: a poet-prophet-philosopher, whose words will speak to all people everywhere about everything: Nature, Society, and individual consciousness. The dimensions of this figure are godlike, and if Milton's more traditional epic theme—the ways of God to man—seems left out of these expressions, it is because the divine role has been taken up by the poet himself. These dimensions are so large that they could hardly be filled out by any single human being, and Wordsworth explicitly invoked his need for "a greater Muse" than Milton's to aid him. When we recoil, as we usually do, from Wordsworth's egotism elsewhere in his work, we should keep in mind that the projected form of his ego image was much larger than anything he published in his lifetime.

Coleridge was also present at the birth of this Poet figure, partly as midwife, partly as parent; even more than the *Lyrical Ballads, The Recluse* was "half the child of my own brain." He did not have even Wordsworth's comparative hesitations when he wrote to Cottle the day after Wordsworth wrote Tobin to announce the same blessed event:

> —The Giant Wordsworth—God love him!—even when I speak in the terms of admiration due to his intellect, I fear lest those terms should keep out of sight the amiableness of his manners—he has written near 1200 lines of a blank verse, superior, I hesitate not to aver, to any thing in our language which any way resembles it. Poole . . . thinks of it as likely to benefit mankind much more than any thing, Wordsworth has yet written.[18]

For the next seven years Coleridge's references to *The Recluse* never fall below the level of these superlatives of greatness, firstness, and largeness. An example from 1804: "I prophesy immortality to his *Recluse,* as the first & finest philosophical Poem, if only it be (as it undoubtedly will be) a Faithful Transcript of his own most august & innocent Life, of his own habitual Feelings & Modes of seeing and hearing."[19]

The size of this projected image, both of poet and of poem, should be measured not only against Wordsworth's unsuccessful efforts to complete it but against other similar projects of the egotistical Romantic imagination: Goethe's *Faust,* and the incomplete epic projects of all the major English Romantic poets, *Jerusalem, Hyperion, Don Juan, Prometheus Unbound* (the only one actually finished), Whitman's unending *Leaves of Grass,* and many other chefs d'oeuvre of the nineteenth century's religion of art: Beethoven's symphonies, Turner's "impressionist" masterpieces, Wagner's *Ring* operas, and Tolstoy's *War and Peace*—this last also focused, like *The Prelude,* on a single individual's imagined contest of will with a leader of the French Revolution.

These are a mixed bag, but a very big one, and all part of the vision of total human creativity which Wordsworth at the beginning of March 1798 took over from a much closer source: Coleridge's *The Brook,* an epic of similar magnitude which he had been dreaming about for several years. In his search for its organizing metaphor, Coleridge seized upon their symbolic brook behind Alfoxden House, with results that led the government to suspect him of plotting against the nation's security:

> I sought for a subject, that should give equal room and freedom for description, incident, and impassioned *reflections on men, nature, and society. . . .* Such a subject I conceived to have found in a stream, traced from its source in the hills among the yellow-red moss and conical glass-shaped tufts of bent, to the

> first break or fall, where its drops become audible, and it begins to form a channel; thence to the peat and turf barn, itself built of the same dark squares as it sheltered; to the sheep-fold; to the first cultivated plot of ground; to the lonely cottage and its bleak garden won from the heath; to the hamlet, the villages, the market-town, the manufactories, and the sea-port. My walks therefore were almost daily on the top of the Quantocks, and among its sloping combes.[20]

After the unforeseen results of his search, when reported by Christopher Trickie to the authorities, Coleridge said he planned to dedicate *The Brook* "to our then committee of public safety as containing the charts and maps, with which I was to have supplied the French Government in aid of the plans of invasion."[21] But, joking aside, *The Recluse,* like *The Brook,* was clearly aimed at the fallout from the French Revolution. Coleridge conceived it as "a poem, in blank verse, addressed to those, who, in consequence of the complete failure of the French Revolution, have thrown up all hopes of the amelioration of mankind, and are sinking into an almost epicurean selfishness, disguising the same under the soft titles of domestic attachment and contempt for visionary *philosophes.*"[22] He was, however, concerned not with the *threat* but with the *failure* of the French Revolution to provide a model for transforming English society.

Like their twin drama projects, like "The Wanderings of Cain," like the dovetailed narratives of "The Ruined Cottage" and "The Ancient Mariner," *The Recluse* project was made up of thoroughly mixed parts of Coleridge and Wordsworth. Even its shift of titles, from *The Brook* to *The Recluse,* expresses the nature of each man's imagination: Coleridge's darting, restless brook, constantly threatening to overflow the capacious reservoir of his great mind; Wordsworth's silent, withdrawn, solitary, and awesomely self-contained recluse. Like all their other joint projects except *Lyrical Ballads,* it too was finally unsuccessful. But the fragments of the failed *Recluse* were so large, and the idea of acknowledging its failure so unthinkable, that the project kept Wordsworth going through the rest of his creative life, until the young Wordsworth had become a very old Wordsworth, well into the 1840s, when he finally admitted he would never finish it.

In March of 1798 *The Recluse* consisted of the newly expanded "Ruined Cottage," plus two or three other poems, which together add up to the thirteen hundred lines Wordsworth spoke of to Tobin and Losh. The first of these others was "The Old Cumberland Beggar," another narrative of unrelieved suffering, drafted the previous year, but now expanded with contemporary political commentary (against parish workhouses), as "The Ruined Cottage" had been expanded with philosophical commentary. The second was Wordsworth's description of his encounter with a figure very similar to Margaret and the Cumberland beggar: the Discharged Veteran he had run into near Far Sawrey in about 1788. This did not see publication until it appeared posthumously in *The Prelude* of 1850. These three narratives of suffering were originally free-standing poems of nearly unrelieved bleakness, like Wordsworth's other unpublished Racedown fragments. But now he began trying to incorporate into them lines of explanation and understanding, to achieve a larger perspective of reconciliation. This effort is what makes them parts of the now christened *Recluse:* "views of nature, man, and society," giving "authentic comment" to the sounds of "humanity in fields and groves / Pip[ing] solitary anguish" ("Prospectus," 76–77).

A fourth poem, rounding out the thirteen hundred lines, was probably "A Night-Piece," which emerged from Dorothy's notebook, not published until Wordsworth's first collected edition in 1815. It fits the others as a prologue or coda, sketching a visionary perspective on the landscapes through which the other three narratives move. On its open road—the inevitable Wordsworthian mise-en-scène—we see "the glory of the heavens" instead of an old beggar, a sick veteran, or a weaver's abandoned wife. Wordsworth's task in the other three poems was to link, somehow, that sense of natural glory to human suffering.

The first *Recluse* poems set human suffering, of a very contemporary British kind, in specific British landscapes, to suggest how, *in this context,* it might be understood or properly cared for. They try to make sense out of suffering, but are far from "the still, sad music of humanity" to which Wordsworth had attained by July at Tintern Abbey, to say nothing of "the soothing thoughts which spring from human suffering" that he was able to achieve in the transcendental mind-set he adopted by the time he completed the Intimations Ode (1804). They do not preach a doctrine of acceptance; their goal is more limited: simply to keep the observer (all Wordsworth surrogates) from being overcome by grief and despair at what he sees, and cannot help. This sense-making comfort comes in the Pedlar's "reconciling addendum," and in the Discharged Veteran's "ghastly" trust that God will always provide a Good Samaritan on any road. In "The Old Cumberland Beggar," Wordsworth's more provocative political message is that it is better to let such old beggars die "in the eye of Nature," on their usual rounds in neighborhoods that know them, than make them captives in the "HOUSE, misnamed of INDUSTRY." Whether this life and death in nature is better than the workhouse is hard to say, both as social policy and as poetic statement. "Tintern Abbey" will say that "Nature never did betray the heart that loved her," and recommend that Dorothy should "therefore . . . let the misty mountain-winds be free / To blow against thee." But the effects of such weather are a lot worse for beggars:

> let his blood
> Struggle with frosty air and winter snows;
> And let the chartered wind that sweeps the heath
> Beat his grey locks against his withered face.
>
> (173–76)

This policy-statement poem has seemed to many readers a betrayal of the poor to the doctrines of Wordsworth's new religion, even to those who agree that poems need not provide successful solutions to the social problems they raise.

But rhetorically the three *Recluse* narratives of 1798 do not come to bad conclusions; they are complete in this respect. Rather, their conclusions are unsatisfying in the sense of philosophical conviction or political persuasion. They raise as many questions as they answer. But few philosophical systems or political programs can answer the question satisfactorily, for it is the problem of undeserved or incommensurate human suffering, which is to say, the problem of evil. This is the problem that Romanticism is always accused of avoiding or slighting, and sometimes did ignore. But Wordsworth's high Romantic argument always forced him to confront this question, for it is the question that always challenged his faith in the powers of the creative human imagination. This problem surfaced daily in Wordsworth's and Coleridge's conversations at this time: human suffering and, as its simultaneous companion, the question of their own guilt or remorse for it, and their possible complicity in it. Facing these questions comprehensively was the task of *The Recluse.* Wordsworth's determination to achieve it led inexorably to repeated imaginative crises which kept the poem forever unfinished: but the challenge, faced so confidently in early 1798, always returned to haunt him, forbidding him from ever putting it aside. This paradoxical relation between inspiration and dejection explains better than almost any other set of Romantic texts the uncanny connection between the power of Romantic imagination and its tendency to produce magnificent fragments at least as often as it produces satisfying aesthetic wholes. The typical Romantic Ode to Dejection is not cynical weltschmerz but the underside of all its Odes to Joy, from Schiller's to Wordsworth's to Thoreau's.

Given the force of this double bind, clear in two hundred years of hindsight but barely emerging into the light of day in the first week of March 1798, it is not surprising to learn that Wordsworth's announcements to Tobin and Losh are the last we hear of *The Recluse* at this time. Though he said all his eloquence would be devoted to it for the next year and a half, in fact nothing more of it was written for almost exactly that period of time: until he and Dorothy were again ensconsed together in a new home, at Grasmere, at the beginning of 1800.

TRIUMPHS OF FAILURE

23

Wordsworth's *Lyrical Ballads* of 1798

> Readers accustomed to the gaudiness and inane phraseology of many modern writers . . . will perhaps frequently have to struggle with feelings of strangeness and aukwardness: they will look round for poetry, and will be induced to enquire by what species of courtesy these attempts can be permitted to assume that title.
>
> "Advertisement" to *Lyrical Ballads* (1798)

The Recluse project was shelved almost as soon as it was announced. Coleridge, who had fathered the idea, was the cause of its delayed (and ultimately aborted) birth. In January and February, still desperate for cash, he proposed one project after another to Joseph Cottle: a third edition of his *Poems,* or a new edition with a second volume to include "The Rime of the Ancient Mariner."[1] But in early March the first payment of the Wedgwood annuity arrived, and Coleridge's great aim in life began to crystallize: an *opus maximum* that would answer the mechanistic materialism of eighteenth-century rationalism.[2] In contemporary philosophical terms, this meant refuting Godwin's *Political Justice* with a view of life that recognized a spiritual dimension and embraced the value of human emotions.[3] To achieve this, he proposed acting on the dream he had been entertaining for over two years: to go to Germany to learn, in their original language, the new transcendental philosophies pouring forth from the fountainhead of Kant and the Jena circle. But this journey, which did succeed in making Coleridge a more profound philosopher, was an all-but-mortal wound to *The Recluse,* which he had conceived as the epic poem of the new philosophy.

The plan was broached at the beginning of March and discussed in earnest during a ten-day visit (March 9–18) of the Coleridges to Alfoxden, the first time Sara and little Hartley had stayed for more than a day. As they strolled about the grounds watching Hartley play with Basil, many family and financial details had to be worked out. The general idea was to export their small communal group to more congenial surroundings abroad. James Losh and his new wife, Cecilia Baldwin (a distant Cumberland cousin of William and Dorothy), were invited, and John Chester, the local farmer's son, volunteered to come along as Coleridge's factotum. Sara was at first included in the plans until the obvious impediment of two small babies was faced seriously. There was some hope of hooking up with John Tweddell, or at least getting information from him about living conditions in Germany; Tom Wedgwood's recent trip there was another source of information. They planned to spend about two years abroad; one for learning the language and a second for gaining mastery of the new philosophy. Coleridge readily accepted William's wish to go along with him and assumed he would keep on writing *The Recluse,* so high was his estimate of his friend's productive power. Wordsworth had the same expectations in mind when he told Tobin, "The work of composition is carved out for me, for at least a year and a half."[4]

Coleridge's plan, though ultimately a distraction from *The Recluse,* did provide a solution to the Wordsworths' immediate dilemma, that their lease was running out. They had known this since the "spy" scandal of the previous summer, but they mentioned it only now, as if it were news, to friends and relatives. Their other options, before the German plan was set afoot, were to return to Racedown or to take a walking tour in Wales and then proceed north via Yorkshire and the Hutchinsons to Cumberland.[5] But both these plans would again impose on the generosity of friends. A third possibility was to stay put; Tom Poole made inquiries about a house near Alfoxden. All these ideas were swept aside once the German tour was suggested. Dorothy, making a virtue of necessity, disingenuously told Aunt Rawson, "we are glad that we are not shackled with the house."[6] Their cousins recognized that "Dorothy lays it all down in a very agreeable manner," but they took it with a grain of salt, considering the plan "a curious one." Perhaps more important was the recognition that, by this decision, "they are become profess't Authors."[7] William had at last chosen his profession, in his family's eyes.

As Coleridge went, so went the Wordsworths. William needed him more than Coleridge needed Wordsworth. He was necessary to Wordsworth as a constant source of new ideas and unstinting praise, not to mention the philosophical framework of the grand new project they had just unveiled as the summa of their careers. Wordsworth had an inhibiting effect on Coleridge's poetical production, but Coleridge's conversation was terrifically stimulating to Wordsworth. Everyone recognized that William had been writing with immense power since the beginning of the year. By early March he had composed thirteen hundred lines of the four poems that then constituted *The Recluse,* and between March and May he composed the bulk of the poems that became *Lyrical Ballads.* Coleridge told Hazlitt that

Wordsworth's "soul seems to inhabit the universe like a palace, and to discover truth by intuition, rather than by deduction."[8] Dorothy reported to Mary Hutchinson, "His faculties seem to expand every day, he composes with much more facility than he did, as to the *mechanism* of poetry, and his ideas flow faster than he can express them."[9] And by the first week in April, Wordsworth himself confidently reported to Cottle, "I have gone on very rapidly adding to my stock of poetry."[10]

Such language, addressed to Cottle, was purposely commercial. For once the decision for Germany had been taken, the question of how to pay for it arose immediately—for the Wordsworths. They were still in bad financial straits. The payments of the Calvert bequest had been delayed, and the payments on Wordsworth's loans to Montagu and Douglas had been even slower. He had touched Poole, Cottle, and Tobin for loans at different times during the year, and in June, as they were leaving Alfoxden, Dorothy had to ask Richard for money to finish paying its very nominal rent.[11] Coleridge had his annuity, but he was not offering to bankroll the whole enterprise. He could not, and remain true to the Wedgwoods' conditions, especially as they had no very high opinion of Wordsworth, because of his failure to respond enthusiastically to their proposed academy of genius. (But they did come to Wordsworth's aid, allowing him to draw checks on their commercial accounts in Hamburg.) To raise funds, the poets proposed to sell some of their stock-in-trade, poetry, exactly as they had planned to pay for the expenses of their November walking tour by jointly writing "The Ancient Mariner."

They approached Cottle with two concrete proposals. One was to publish *The Borderers* and *Osorio* together, now that hopes for their stage career were at an end.[12] Another was to publish "Adventures on Salisbury Plain" and "The Ruined Cottage" together, with a few other poems in a similar vein. Both of these volumes were more or less ready to go to press, and Cottle was prepared to give twenty guineas or more for each, a nice sum to set them on their way, since the estimated cost of passage to Hamburg was twenty-five guineas.[13]

Why they did not go forward with either or both of these eminently doable plans remains a mystery, another *mirabilis* of this year which, in terms of new composition, was more of a *demi-annus.* Both these volumes were complete, and internally consistent, while a book called "Lyrical Ballads" was neither, and did not yet exist in anybody's mind as such. Why not publish them? The reason they did not proceed with these plans, which would have drastically altered their image in literary history (not necessarily for the worse), seems to have been Wordsworth's astonishing rate of production, stimulated by the distraction of the German trip. The immediate need was for salable poems. *The Recluse* might save the world, but it was barely begun, years from being finished, and of doubtful market value in any case. Perhaps the frustrated stage career of their two dramas did not augur well for their success as published texts. The combined "Salisbury Plain" and "Ruined Cottage" idea was kept alive, but Wordsworth was rightly worried about its lack of "variety," since its shorter poems had the same tone as its two long, bleak title poems. The only conditions they insisted on for a new volume were anonymity (mostly Coleridge's idea) and joint publication (mostly Wordsworth's). Wordsworth didn't want to publish his new poems without Coleridge's supporting company, and Coleridge's estimate of the market value of their names was succinct: "Wordsworth's name is nothing—to a large number of persons mine *stinks.*"[14] This "large number" included a few very powerful persons, the writers for the *Anti-Jacobin,* who throughout the year had regularly returned to their thinly veiled attacks on Southey and Coleridge as leading representatives of the Jacobin school of poetry. If Canning & Co. got wind of the fact that Coleridge was coauthor of a volume that looked, superficially, like more of Southey's knee-jerk liberal sympathy, the effect on sales could have been disastrous.

So, under strong personal pressure of his need to raise money in order to follow Coleridge, Wordsworth did a very unusual thing, whose oddity is rarely remarked on, because of the subsequent fame of the volume which resulted. He began writing short poems: ballads and lyrics that could be produced quickly to fill up a volume, of the kind familiar to readers of magazine verse at the time—pathetic narratives of the deserving poor and sentimental lyrics expressing melancholy feelings in beautiful natural settings. Between the first week of March and mid-May, Wordsworth composed about a dozen of the nineteen poems by him which finally appeared in *Lyrical Ballads:* a total of nearly fifteen hundred lines of poetry in some sixty days.[15] Once he relaxed from the hard work of *The Recluse,* he began sleeping late—till seven or eight o'clock[16]—and this phenomenal output was the result. The regular rhyme and meter of the ballad, and its ease of variation, was the "mechanism" of poetry which Dorothy noted had become so productive for him. During much of this period neither he nor Coleridge had definitely in mind the shape or title of the volume that became *Lyrical Ballads;* this open-endedness doubtless helped Wordsworth's rate of production: he just wrote, without worrying very much about the form in which all these poems would be contained. He would soon begin *The Prelude* on the same open "plan."

Wordsworth had, as of March 1798, written only one and a half ballads in his entire life: the tale of lovelorn Mary Rigge of Colthouse, in 1787, and his fragmentary start on "The Three Graves," which he turned over to Coleridge. His interest for several years had not been in short poems at all, let alone ballads. He was determined to write long poems, narrative poems in blank verse with strong meditative overtones and heavy moral implications, taking his inspiration not from the ballad revivals of Bishop Percy and Robert Burns but from the epic examples of Milton and Spenser. Furthermore, he was just now deeply interested in the idea of integrating those long poems into an even larger, quasi-epic series, *The Recluse.*

His switch to ballads and lyrics at this time is as startling as if the young Beethoven (his exact contemporary) had turned from composing his first and second symphonies to writing songs or bagatelles based on five-finger keyboard exercises. (There is a coincidental parallel between Wordsworth's pathetic ballads of 1798 and Beethoven's "Pathetique" Sonata of that year.) This is not to denigrate songs and ballads in favor of symphonies and epics, but to underscore the great difference between what Wordsworth had been doing up to the time the German trip was broached and what he now undertook to do. The poems he wrote were not all that different from other magazine verse of the time, though far better in quality—and far bleaker in their descriptions of human suffering. Ballads deal mainly in the curses of slain heroes and the tears of lovelorn maidens, not the curses of freezing old women on landlords for narrowly enforcing their property rights, or the tears of shepherds who have to sell their sheep in order to qualify for parish relief. But it was not Wordsworth's subjects so much as his handling of them that ultimately differentiated *Lyrical Ballads* from a flood of similar works in this age of "poetical inflation."[17] Regarded as an exercise in literary primitivism, the volume was rather behind than ahead of the times.[18] Eighteenth-century universalism had produced a spate of real and fictitious "primitive" or uneducated poets, such as Stephen Duck, the Thresher Poet, and "Lactilla," Ann Yearsley, a Bristol milkwoman.[19] But *Lyrical Ballads* is far more literary than primitive: Wordsworth did not use the same rhyme scheme twice in ten ballads. His psychological and sociological attitude toward his ballad subjects is even more unusual. He is not sentimental; he lets most of his characters speak directly to the reader, without introduction or condescension, and though his delineation of their suffering seems sympathetic, he rarely draws the charitable moral which his description of them seems to be leading up to. Though scarcely dispassionate, many of them read like case studies in abnormal psychology, or man-in-the-street interviews without editorial commentary.[20]

Discussion of Wordsworth's "lyrical ballads" has been conducted so much in light of the late eighteenth-century ballad revival, of Wordsworth's increasingly defensive prefaces to successive editions of the volume, and of Coleridge's account of their "experiment" in *Biographia Literaria* (twenty years later) that these familiar categories can well be ignored in favor of what Lamb called the "living circumstances" of their composition: *The Recluse* and its sudden interruption for the trip to Germany. It should be much better known than it is that the accounts offered by Wordsworth and

Coleridge as to how, when, and why the *Lyrical Ballads* of 1798 came to be written differ widely from what the poets were actually doing at the time, or said they were. Many textbooks and innumerable classrooms continue to project the image of Wordsworth and Coleridge coming together in 1797, igniting a spark of mutual creativity that led inexorably to the publication of *Lyrical Ballads* a year later. But recent scholarship has found almost no evidence of a "plan" they were developing for the volume at this time, especially not of the division of their labor between supernatural and natural poems that Coleridge suggested in *Biographia Literaria*.[21]

This is not to say that Coleridge and Wordsworth were not talking about many of the issues that appear in the preface and in *Biographia Literaria*. Above all, they were talking about "common language" poetry and about ordinary people as fit subjects for such poetry. They were also discussing the ways such subjects and speakers could reveal important truths about the nature of man, even when presented without explanatory frameworks of either traditional (religious) or contemporary (political and philosophical) interpretation, other than "Nature" itself: namely, the given world of natural forms around them. But aside from "The Ancient Mariner," a ballad raised to operatic proportions, there is little sign of any talk about ballads, or of Wordsworth's composing them, or looking for models to practice on, until the announcement of the trip to Germany. On the contrary, until then we see Wordsworth pulling out of every ballad project they broached. But once he committed himself, he did so with a vengeance.

His production of these poems, besides being amazingly rapid, was astonishingly contemporary: it seemed that all he had to do was read about, or look at, something to turn it into a poem. "The first mild day of March" was probably exactly that, sometime between the 6th and the 11th, and the "morning task" Dorothy is asked to set aside in order to go for a walk may not be housekeeping duties but her copying work on "The Ruined Cottage" ("bring no book").[22] His need was not for inspiration but simply for material, almost any material. Cottle was requested on March 7 to send Erasmus Darwin's *Zoönomia* "immediately," and within a week it was sent back, having answered its purpose: the account of superstitious autosuggestion which Wordsworth turned into "Goody Blake and Harry Gill," occasionally setting Darwin's own words to meter.*[23] The same was true of "The Complaint of a Forsaken Indian Woman," quickly adapted from Samuel Hearne's *Journey from Prince of Wales's Fort in Hudson's Bay to the Northern Ocean,* which Wordsworth received on April 14.[24]

*Darwin's old woman, "like a witch in a play," curses, "Heaven grant, that thou never mayest know again the blessing to be warm." Wordsworth's less supernatural *"canty* dame" prays, "God! who art never out of hearing, / O may he never more be warm!"

When books were not ready to hand, neighbors were pressed into service. Christopher Trickie was transformed into "Simon Lee," as Wordsworth literally enacted his advice to his reader:

> O reader! had you in your mind
> Such stores as silent thought can bring,
> O gentle reader! you would find
> A tale in every thing.
>
> (73–76)

A once prosperous farmer in Holford became the speaker of "The Last of the Flock." He had to sell off all his sheep, one by one, reducing himself to demonstrable poverty before he could qualify for parish charity under the ruinous Speenhamland system. Wordsworth had rarely seen

> . . . a man full grown
> Weep in the public roads alone.
> But such a one, on English ground,
> And in the broad high-way, I met . . . .
>
> (3–6)

These poems were vignettes not simply of poverty but of the emotions it provoked—emotions which Godwin in *Political Justice* had dismissed as uselessly sentimental: gratitude, and affection for one's own property.[25] The incidents they recounted were literally "incidental" to their emotions, accounting for Wordsworth's ability to make such rapid use of such diverse material. As he said later in the preface, "the feeling therein developed gives importance to the action and situation and not the action and situation to the feeling." But what the feeling *is,* is difficult to say, and is often left purposely vague: "Now think, ye farmers all, I pray, / Of good Blake and Harry Gill." The poems were called both Jacobin and anti-Jacobin,[26] and it is difficult to generalize the attitude toward poverty they express. On the one hand, poverty appears as a sad, dangerous, not ennobling, occasionally corrupting, unattractive condition, often unrelieved and sometimes unrelievable. But Wordsworth's speakers are also forceful, psychologically complex, fiercely loyal and stoical, and very much self-contained: most of them do not speak until spoken to.

People of Wordsworth's class widely viewed poverty as part of the nature of things, to be aided by charity, but not systematically eradicable. The poor might become less poor, but they were not expected to rise out of their condition, which was defined as a permanent social rank: the "lower orders." An attitude of sentimental concern for all forms of human weakness had been increasing throughout the eighteenth century, but this is not Wordsworth's attitude in *Lyrical Ballads,* though Dorothy did attempt to aid particular individuals. The poor rates in the parish of Alfoxden more than tripled during the 1790s.[27] Religiously liberal but socially conservative persons like Hannah More (sponsor of Ann Yearsley), whose *Village Politics* qualifies her as a Wordsworth or a Southey of the right, thought conditions in Somerset were unbearable and identified the cause clearly: "all the land in a parish is swallowed up by a few great farmers."[28] Harry Gill was one of these farmers on the way up, till Goody Blake's curse brought him low.

Even objects were transformed into poems, like a blasted thorn bush atop the Quantocks, which Wordsworth transformed from a bit of notebook doggerel into one of the longest and most difficult of all his ballads:

> A thorn that wants its thorny points,
> A toothless thorn with knotted joints,
> Not higher than a two-years' child,
> It stands upon that spot so wild.[29]

He worked up "The Thorn" from this scrap of observation into a symbol for a story that he had yet to write. The incidence of infanticide by unwed mothers was so common at the time as to require no specific sources, and it took no great leap of imagination from this to thoughts of his own illegitimate child.* Annette and Caroline also seem to have entered into "The Mad Mother." The mother's statement "Thy father cares not for my breast" resembles Annette's imaginary conversation with William, holding Caroline at her breast as his surrogate.[30]

The net effect of Wordsworth's channeling his *Recluse* power into the ballads and lyrics of spring 1798 was like directing the Alfoxden waterfall into an ordinary drinking glass. His efforts to control the resulting distortion, and minimize the discrepancy between his homely subjects and the vast range of their implied meanings, is the actual working "plan" of the 1798 *Lyrical Ballads:* to incorporate a metaphysical faith in spontaneous grace—symbolized by images of natural beauty—with an ethic of concern for all human beings. Around *The Recluse*'s "views" of Man and Society, Wordsworth had been attempting to construct a coherent philosophical framework in which they could be interpreted in the positive light of the beauty of external Nature. To justify the ways of man to Nature, as it were.

And he was failing in this effort, for the very good reason that such a connection is very difficult to establish logically, outside some system of *belief*—Christianity, for example. Wordsworth's failure to advance *The Recluse* in March was not a failure of poetic power. On the contrary, it was a triumph of poetic power unleashed but uncontained, a failure to fit his imagination into recognizable poetic form. Coleridge never forgot the impact "The Ru-

*See the postscript to this chapter for additional lines in this direction.

ined Cottage" had on him, but like the other *Recluse* poems, it tends to knock readers out of the framework of poetry, or art, altogether, making "enjoyment" seem a superfluous consideration and raising questions about the need for social action which are always potentially revolutionary, and not only in the repressive political atmosphere of England in 1798. (A third treason trial was going on exactly at this time, from March to June, against the conspirators in the United Irishmen's aborted uprising, featuring extorted confessions, suborned informers, convictions, and executions.) Wordsworth's first efforts in this direction had actually tended more to contradict than to confirm the operation of a benign grace in human existence. In short, he had arrived at a philosophical impasse, and that is exactly where one does arrive when trying to establish a self-evident, positive connection between natural processes and human, cultural ones.

We might expect the first four *Recluse* poems to have a significant relation to the other poems Wordsworth was composing at this time, and this is exactly what we do find: his lyrical ballads of 1798 are the triumphs of a failure. That is, some very successful poems—successful in achieving poetic closure through generic familiarity—emerged from his failure to get on with *The Recluse.* But they still carry, vicariously, the power of *The Recluse*'s inspiration, even as they disguise some of its troubling philosophical and political implications in more conventional forms. Finished, in the sense of being satisfactorily concluded, is precisely what the four *Recluse* poems of early 1798 were *not,* powerful though they are. But finished, in the sense of coming to "The End" in a satisfactory way, is just what Wordsworth's lyrical ballads of 1798 are: the same persons and issues are present, but their genres do not lead us to expect a "conclusion" in the sense of a comprehensive philosophical or political explanation.

Wordsworth repeatedly flirted with the difference between these two kinds of endings: "O reader! had you in your mind / Such stores as *silent thought* can bring, / O gentle reader! you would find / A tale in every thing." The narrator protests that his account of old Simon Lee's pain "is no tale; but should you *think,* / Perhaps a tale you'll make it." Throughout Wordsworth's contributions to the 1798 volume, words like "think," "thought," and "reason" are used as shorthand substitutes or stand-ins for the absent but implied philosophical system which was to inform *The Recluse,* which would account for the wide discrepancy between natural beauty and human moral ugliness.

Wordsworth transferred the vexing power of *The Recluse*'s philosophical burdens and its generic ambiguity into the smaller poetic forms of *Lyrical Ballads* by a single, simple strategy. He divided his work on *The Recluse* into two different types of poems: ballads which pose difficult questions, and lyrics which imply profound answers. These are the two different kinds of poems, clearly announced in the volume's title, which articulate its imaginative structure. Only at the very last moment, in the "Lines Written above Tintern Abbey," did he try to bring the two concerns back together in the same poem, and then only with the utmost caution.

There are five lyrics of meditative natural description, all identified with the same initial title word, "Lines," designating their conventionally informal, sketchy quality, while situating their utterance with sometimes exhaustive precision, from the "Lines Left upon a Seat in a Yew-tree, which stands near the lake of Esthwaite, on a desolate part of the shore, commanding a beautiful prospect," to the "Lines Composed a Few Miles above Tintern Abbey, on Revisiting the Banks of the Wye during a Tour. July 13, 1798."

Second, there are ten ballads or tales about suffering poor people, especially mothers and fathers and children, making up (with the addition of Coleridge's "Rime") most of the poems usually understood to be the "lyrical ballads" of the title: that is, semimysterious narratives involving ordinary people, but written in rhyme schemes much more intricate than those typical of the authentic folk ballad. (There are, in addition, four "dialogue" poems, printed together in two pairs, which act out the double thematic aspect of the volume's main division into lyrics and ballads.)

As in the four poems he wrote for *The Recluse* in January–March, the narrative element bulks much larger in Wordsworth's contributions to *Lyrical Ballads* than the lyric element. But the interpretive burden carried by his ballads of March–May is much *less* than that of the *Recluse* poems. The success or failure of Wordsworth's experiments in narrative technique in his ballads of 1798 has always been a prominent topic in critical discussion of his work, but by comparison with the narrator-auditor situation in the *Recluse* poems, his lyrical ballads are far simpler. Wordsworth achieved this simplicity by radically reducing the function of the by-standing auditor who "hears" the tale of woe and "tells" it to the reader. In the *Recluse* poems this narrator is a sensitive young man, essentially Wordsworth himself, who feels his mental stability severely threatened by the sad stories he hears. But in his ballads of 1798 there is little danger of such "contamination" from the suffering object to the narrating subject of the poems, since the narrator is very little present. In most of them, a poor, old, decrepit, or deranged person tells his or her life story to a bypassing interlocutor, whose presence is necessary only to get the story going ("I followed him, and said, 'My friend, / What ails you? wherefore weep you so?' ") and whose reactions to it are represented very minimally, if at all, in the poem. In the ten ballads the narrative situation ranges from no external narrator at all, in "The Complaint of a Forsaken Indian Woman," to the highly involved narrator of "The Convict"—whose high degree of involvement in the action is the main reason that poem is so unsuccessful.

"Old Man Travelling" is the hardest poem to place on this spectrum, and Wordsworth's treatment of it shows he was well aware of the specific difficulty he faced. The narrator says quite a lot at the beginning of this "sketch," heavily interpreting the "patience" and "perfect peace" of the slow-moving old beggar. But the original last six lines, spoken by the old man, are about his son dying in the Falmouth naval hospital, and appear to question so radically the benign interpretation of his life offered by the narrator that the poem threatens to break into two contradictory parts. Wordsworth recognized this flaw and subsequently excised the last six lines, in keeping with his overall narrative strategy in his lyrical ballads (relative to the *Recluse* poems) but in reverse: instead of reducing the role of the narrator to a minimum, he here reduced the speaking voice of the suffering object to nil.

The lines may have been cut also because of their very close similarity to Southey's "The Sailor's Mother" from *English Eclogues:* "Sir, I am going / To see my son at Plymouth, sadly hurt / In the late action, and in the hospital / Dying, I fear me, now." One can never be sure who is borrowing from whom at this time, but the relation of Wordsworth's lyrical ballads to Southey's poems composed and published both before and after *Lyrical Ballads* illustrates my point about the "plan" of the volume. Southey always connects his incident and its meaning together: his "ballad" interest clearly supports his "lyric" impulse. He always lets us know what he thinks, or what his poor subject is thinking; in either case, the result is not very impressive. "The Sailor's Mother" goes on piling up pathetic details till even sympathy turns hard-hearted. The last exchange between the woman and her interlocutor is so lame that it makes us appreciate how much more Wordsworth's reticence achieves.

TRAVELLER

Well! well! take comfort
He will be taken care of if he lives;
And should you lose your child, this is a country
Where the brave Sailor never leaves a parent
To weep for him in want.

WOMAN

Sir, I shall want
No succour long. In the common course of years
I soon must be at rest; and 'tis a comfort.
When grief is hard upon me, to reflect
It only leads me to that rest the sooner.

This relation between suffering and a moral reaction to it is transparent and simplistic. Wordsworth wanted to imitate the model, the "mechanism" that

Southey produced so much "at his ease," but to avoid the direct connection between suffering and sympathy that Southey draws. He had all the more reason, because the connection he was suggesting is not simply between human sympathy and human suffering but between the latter and a kind of metaphysical outrage on Nature's part.

The "lines" or lyrics in this division of Wordsworth's labors on *Lyrical Ballads* are half as many in number, and proportionately much shorter than the ballads. Just as Wordsworth keeps interpretive commentary to a minimum in his ballads of 1798, so in most of these "lines" he keeps to a minimum any *narrative* explanation of the speaker's situation, so they tend to become full, credal statements about "seeing into the life of things" through natural forms. However, the "lines" adhere less purely to this division of poetic kinds than the ballads: they tend to hint more at the larger political and philosophical implications behind the *Lyrical Ballads.* This is clearest in the mournful refrain which cuts across the otherwise self-indulgently playful "Lines Written in Early Spring": "Have I not reason to lament / What man has made of man?"*

The usefulness of this view of the plan of *Lyrical Ballads* can be seen in comparing Wordsworth's worst poem in the volume, "The Convict," with his best one, "Lines Composed above Tintern Abbey." "The Convict" is a companion piece to Coleridge's "The Dungeon." Significantly, they are the only two poems in the 1798 volume that approach direct social commentary, both written under the influence of Southey's "Botany Bay Eclogues" (1794). A large part of the failure of "The Convict" can be explained by reference to Wordsworth's difficulties with *The Recluse,* for it is the only one of his ten ballads or narratives of suffering in which the narrator both directly addresses the suffering person *and* offers directly to comment on the causes or meaning of his suffering. Its situation is similar to what would have obtained if the young man in "The Ruined Cottage" had come upon Margaret in the last days of her decline, without the company of the Pedlar or the benefit of his philosophical long views, and had tried to say some reassuring words to her. Thus "The Convict," which dates from 1796 at Racedown, the period of Wordsworth's immediate recoil from political activism, helps us appreciate how much he had achieved by 1798 by way of universalized human narratives—as distinct from immediate political protests—in his *Recluse* poems.

In contrast to "Tintern Abbey," "The Convict" turns very abruptly from

*Burns's "Man Was Made to Mourn" has been instanced as a source for this sentiment, common to liberal writing as the 1790s wore on: "Man's inhumanity to Man / Makes countless thousands mourn" (*Lyrical Ballads and Other Poems,* ed. James Butler and Karen Green [Ithaca: Cornell Univ. Press, 1992], 349).

its opening scene of natural beauty to a highly articulated scene of human distress, thus causing an abrupt shift in tone, which in "Tintern Abbey" is managed much more gradually, until Wordsworth can smoothly achieve the harmonic moral tonic of "the still, sad music of humanity." The narrator of "The Convict" defends his presence at the convict's cell—actually a defense of the entire poem—by insisting that he is not "idle." Not, that is, a moral prig, as Southey very often appeared in his similar poems of this time, blandly congratulating himself on the difference between his situation and the convict's. "The Convict" differs from Southey's "Botany Bay Eclogues" only in its degree of sympathy with the criminal: Southey's convicts all admit their crimes and endure the hardships of the penal colony with more or less resignation, depending on their religious faith or the steady supply of grog to help them forget their troubles.

We are left in a position of impotence at the end of "The Convict," wishfully indulging fantasies of power to no purpose, because there is no persuasive authoritative alternative, no wise old Pedlar, for example, to instruct us in "that secret spirit of humanity" which still endures despite nature's "calm oblivious tendencies." This is the kind of meditation Wordsworth had not yet learned to construct when he finished "The Convict," but which he had learned, with a degree of mastery unsurpassed in the language, by the time he wrote "Tintern Abbey." The speaker of "The Convict" is much less successful, has in fact nothing more to say, must almost literally shut up at the point at which his poem ends, because he has attempted to draw *direct* and *immediate* connections between (1) his appreciation of natural beauty, (2) his sensitivity to human suffering, and (3) his own function as commentator connecting the two, when he undertakes to respond to that portentous tear that "asks of me why I am here."

These were precisely the triangulated relationships, "on Man, on Nature, and on Human Life," that Wordsworth had been trying to integrate in his *Recluse* poems of early 1798, and had been failing to, because of his narrating subject's "contamination" by the emotional force of the poor people whose suffering he tries to present and interpret authoritatively. After early March he pursued these *comparatively* easier experiments successfully by separating the two themes—natural beauty and human morality—he had been trying unsuccessfully to integrate. His specific *act* of separation was the expedient of removing—from between the two kinds, as it were—his own narrating presence, leaving him with his lyrical ballads of 1798: five sets of "lines" in which he could expand upon his appreciation for natural beauty, but say very little by way of explaining or applying its significance; ten ballads or other narratives in which the presence of the narrating subject is minimal, especially by way of offering explanatory comment on the human suffering he describes. Instead of fully integrating these themes in a single large poem, Wordsworth could hope, by the artfully juxtaposed arrangement of his poems, that the reader would supply the necessary "thought," "thinking," or "reason" variously alluded to throughout the volume—in a word, its philosophy. The *Lyrical Ballads* are not *all* triumphant, of course, but even in the worst of them—and perhaps especially in that one—we can see the seams of Wordsworth's magnificent effort of expediency, which allowed him to snatch triumphs out of his failure.

By mid-April, Wordsworth had added so much to his "stock" of new poetry that he invited Joseph Cottle to come from Bristol to hear them. But Cottle did not come, and by the time Wordsworth renewed the invitation on May 9 he had added so many more poems to his inventory that he hinted to Cottle of "another plan which I do not wish to mention till I see you; let this be *very, very,* soon."[31] He was still promising the Salisbury Plain poem to Cottle, but clearly the new plan, which would become *Lyrical Ballads,* was beginning to gain ascendancy in his mind.

So great were Wordsworth's productive powers, however, that, beginning about April 20, he began writing another poem, *Peter Bell,* which had not figured in any of the plans dangled before Cottle, but which was ready for his consideration by the end of May, and was nearly as long in its original form (about fourteen hundred lines) as all of Wordsworth's 1798 lyrical ballads put together! Though not published until 1819, *Peter Bell* was a tour de force of willed imagination, for it was Wordsworth's attempt to respond to Coleridge's "Ancient Mariner." The relation of these two poems does match the division of labor between natural and supernatural modes that Coleridge described in the *Biographia,* which scholars have searched for with so little success in *Lyrical Ballads. Peter Bell,* moreover, combines a narrative of suffering with a redemptive plot as no other of Wordsworth's ballad contributions to the 1798 volume do. It is one of Wordsworth's most radical experiments suffusing common people and common language with imaginative power, but like "The Idiot Boy" it establishes the limits of his effectiveness by occasionally surpassing the borders of disbelief and falling into self-parody.

By mid-May, *Peter Bell* and most of Wordsworth's other 1798 lyrics and ballads were finished. He needed a rest. At the same time another work of creation came to term: Sara Coleridge was delivered of her second son on May 14, named for the philosopher Berkeley. Two days later Coleridge set off with Wordsworth and Dorothy on yet another walking tour, to visit the perpendicular rock formations at Cheddar Gorge, twenty-five miles away in the direction of Bristol. This was an easterly pair to their favorite westerly walk to the Valley of Stones. Unfortunately for those who expect Romantic poetry to arise naturally out of the landscape, no poetic record was made of this jaunt, except for a few images of Cheddar Gorge in *Peter Bell:*

> The rocks that tower on either side
> Build up a wild fantastic scene—
> Temples like those among the Hindoos,
> And mosques and spires and abbey windows
> And castles all with ivy green.
>
> (726–30)[32]

Wordsworth had publishing, not landscapes, on his mind. Instead of returning to Stowey with Coleridge and Dorothy, he continued on to Bristol.

His ostensible mission was to bring Charles Lloyd back with him so that Lloyd and Coleridge could talk out the hurt feelings and misunderstandings caused by Coleridge's publishing three sonnets (by "Nehemiah Higginbottom") in the *Monthly Magazine* the previous November that parodied the stylistic mannerisms of Lloyd, Lamb, and Coleridge himself. The three had just then published a joint volume, and Lloyd was not disposed by age or temperament to take the joke well. The incident showed some of the risks of having Coleridge as a collaborator, and it illustrates the extent to which friends and enemies alike in the literary world communicated with, or insulted, each other through barely coded insider jokes: Coleridge's sonnets could as well have appeared in the *Anti-Jacobin.* One of them was the sonnet "On a Ruined House in a Romantic Country," which glanced at Wordsworth's "Ruined Cottage."* Lloyd was trying desperately to get rid of the "Jacobin" label which his association with Coleridge had stuck on him. In the spring he had retaliated with a roman à clef called *Edmund Oliver,* which caricatured the sexual, alcoholic, and political aspects of Coleridge's dissipated undergraduate career (the title character seduces a radically inclined heiress, who dies giving birth to their child), based on information only Southey could have supplied: "The incidents relative to the Army were given me by an intimate friend, who was himself eyewitness to one of them, and can produce testimony to the truth of the other two."[33] But so rich was the mixture of motives swirling among this group of friends that *Edmund*

*In 1799 Southey extended this textual debt by publishing his own "The Ruined Cottage," a transparent rip-off of Wordsworth's manuscript poem, with Southey taking the role of the Pedlar and "Charles" (Lloyd or Lamb) playing the young man. The slackening of dramatic tension and devaluation of moral significance is so great, compared with Wordsworth's poem, that he must have wept more in frustration than in anger when he came to Southey's tepid conclusion: "I pass this ruin'd dwelling oftentimes, / And think of other days. It wakes in me / A transient sadness; but the feelings, Charles, / Which ever with these recollections rise, / I trust in God they will not pass away."

Oliver was also partly intended as an *homage* to Coleridge for "saving" Lloyd from Godwinism: it is a respectable example of the anti-Jacobin novel of Sensibility. This mixture of motives did not escape the sharp eyes of the *Anti-Jacobin Review,* which praised Lloyd for abandoning perfectibility theory, but took him to task for his pacifist and leveling tendencies.[34]

Wordsworth learned that Lloyd was no longer in Bristol before he parted from Dorothy and Coleridge, but this did not deter him, for he had errands of his own in mind: to get Cottle down to Alfoxden to hear the new poems and talk business. He had an almost physical determination to get his volume into print, a nervous, hands-on involvement far different from Coleridge's. Once in town, Wordsworth caught hold of Cottle and bore him home in triumph (in Cottle's chaise) on May 22 for a week's stay.

But before he left he took time to catch one of the last performances of Lewis's *The Castle-Spectre,* whose success and similarity to his and Coleridge's plays based on Schiller still rankled. Within two weeks, however, they were very happy that their plays based on *The Robbers* had been neither performed nor published. On June 4 and 11 the *Anti-Jacobin* ran a devastating parody of Schiller, titled *The Rovers; or, The Double Arrangement.* Though aimed at a variety of then popular turgid imitations of German tragedy, the title clearly singled out Schiller as the leader of the pack. The points of possible contact between *The Rovers* and *The Borderers* and *Osorio* must have made Wordsworth and Coleridge wonder if someone in London had slipped a copy of their rejected plays into unfriendly hands. Its heroine, like Wordsworth's, was named Matilda, and its "author" was Mr. William Higgins of St. Mary Axe, an all-purpose comic persona used by the *Anti-Jacobin* to represent sometimes Godwin, sometimes Erasmus Darwin, and, in this case, evidently, sometimes Coleridge of Ottery St. Mary, who writes "from his Study . . . the window of which looks upon the parish pump," as Coleridge's cottage in Stowey very nearly did. The hero's song at the end of the prologue is generically Germano-Gothic, but its proximity to the academic plans and travel destination of the Somerset authors was uncomfortably close:

> Whene'er with haggard eyes I view
>   This Dungeon, that I'm rotting in,
> I think of those Companions true
>   Who studied with me at the U—
>   —NIVERSITY of *Gottingen,*—
>   —NIVERSITY of *Gottingen.*
> *(Weeps, and pulls out a blue kerchief,*
> *with which he wipes his eyes;*
> *gazing tenderly at it, he proceeds—)*

There first for thee my passion grew,
Sweet! sweet! MATILDA POTTINGEN!
Thou wast the daughter of my TU—
—TOR, *Law Professor* at the U—
—NIVERSITY of *Gottingen*—
—NIVERSITY of *Gottingen.*

Sun, Moon, and thou vain World adieu,
That Kings and Priests are plotting in:
Here doom'd to starve on water-gru—
—el never shall I see the U—
—NIVERSITY of *Gottingen!*—
—NIVERSITY of *Gottingen!*—
*(During the last Stanza Roger dashes his
head repeatedly against the walls
of his Prison; and, finally, so hard
as produce a visible contusion.)*

When Wordsworth and Cottle arrived at Stowey, they found that young William Hazlitt had arrived the day before. Hazlitt, taking up Coleridge's invitation from January, had walked the entire 160 miles from Shrewsbury. For the next three weeks, we have something like life studies for events at Stowey and Alfoxden, from Hazlitt's retrospective essay "My First Acquaintance with Poets" (1823). Hazlitt's recollections, though colored by time (and his by then long-standing disputes with his former idols), retain the first impressions of an intelligent young man who was seeing for the first time in his life the great world of ideas which he believed poets inhabited.

Wordsworth burst into the Coleridges' cottage, hungry as a bear, and "instantly began to make havoc of the half of Cheshire cheese on the table," sourly commenting that "his marriage with experience" had given him a better appreciation "of the good things of this life" than the abstemious Southey could understand. He dismissed *The Castle-Spectre,* saying that " 'it fitted the taste of the audience like a glove.' " Hazlitt recognized this was no praise, for "according to the severe principles of the new school [they would rather] reject than court popular effect." Hazlitt remembered clearly how Wordsworth looked:

> I think I see him now . . . gaunt and Don Quixote-like . . . quaintly dressed (according to the *costume* of that unconstrained period) in a brown fustian jacket and striped pantaloons. There was something of a roll, a lounge in his gait, not unlike his own Peter Bell. There was a severe, worn pressure of thought about his temples, a fire in his eyes (as if he saw something in objects

> more than the outward appearance), an intense high narrow forehead, a Roman nose, cheeks furrowed by strong purpose and feeling, and a convulsive inclination to laughter about the mouth, a good deal at variance with the solemn, stately expression of the rest of the face.

But Hazlitt was as evenhanded as Wordsworth was single-minded, and when Wordsworth looked out the window to comment, " 'How beautifully the sun sets on that yellow bank!' " the young man thought, " 'With what eyes these poets see nature!' " Through Wordsworth and Coleridge, Hazlitt was enjoying the domestication of the Picturesque, seeing nature as an aesthetic object, not as an upper-class pastime but as part of the fabric of everyday life, between hungry mouthfuls of Cheshire cheese after a fast drive in an open chaise.

When Wordsworth and Cottle arrived home at Alfoxden, Dorothy set out a picnic calculated to kindle Cottle's fond memories of the bread and ale he had shared with these bohemian nature lovers the year before. But as Wordsworth climbed down from the chaise he dropped the festive bottle of brandy on the stones in front of the door. Then they discovered that the large cheese they had brought from Bristol had been stolen off the back of chaise. Next, it appeared that neither William nor Cottle knew how to unharness the horse. Peggy Marsh took charge of that, but in the excitement she forgot the salt, so the first dinner with their prospective publisher consisted of bread and lettuce on the grass. But whereas during the last summer all was *in potentia,* now Wordsworth had plenty of "stock" ready to hand, and the disastrous dinner could be treated as a joke.

In Wordsworth's absence Coleridge had been reading Wordsworth's new poems to Hazlitt at Alfoxden, with Dorothy as their "frugal" hostess, and the next morning they came back over to Alfoxden to hear Wordsworth read *Peter Bell.* They sat on the branches of an old ash that resembled a banyan tree, two of its branches growing in and out of the ground, "which gave to each the appearance of a serpent moving along by gathering itself up in folds."[35] Hazlitt was enchanted by each poet's voice, and keenly remarked their individual differences: "Coleridge's manner is more full, animated, and varied; Wordsworth's more equable, sustained, and internal. The one might be termed more *dramatic,* the other more *lyrical."* Coleridge read as he composed, "walking over uneven ground, or breaking through the straggling branches of a copse-wood; whereas Wordsworth always wrote (if he could) walking up and down a straight-gravel walk." The movements of their minds seemed to match those of their bodies and their voices.

That night, walking back to Nether Stowey, Wordsworth and Hazlitt got into "a metaphysical argument . . . in which neither of us succeeded in making ourselves perfectly clear and intelligible." As with almost everything

Wordsworth did now, this argument was soon turned into poetry: the matching pair of "Expostulation and Reply" and "The Tables Turned." In both, Wordsworth's natural metaphysics wins out over Hazlitt's earnest Dissenter's insistence on book learning. Hazlitt had already launched himself into his masterwork, *On the Principles of Human Action,* which he then called by the more accurate title of *The Natural Disinterestedness of the Human Mind.* Against Hazlitt's Godwinian insistence on the disinterestedness of the human mind, Wordsworth preferred its "wise passiveness," open to Nature's action: "One impulse from a vernal wood / May teach you more of man; / Of moral evil and of good, / Than all the sages can." Such sentiments, often taken straight as Wordsworthian gospel, were in the context of their composition deliberately reductive provocations, calculated ripostes to the brash confidence of a brilliant but callow young man.

Almost all the poems that make up *Lyrical Ballads* were read to Cottle during the next week, either in the park at Alfoxden or under "two fine elm-trees" in Tom Poole's garden, "while we quaffed our *flip,*" or on the group's de rigueur hike along the coast to the Valley of Stones. At the end of the week Cottle went back to Bristol, carrying all these poems with him, except "Tintern Abbey," which was neither planned nor dreamed of at this time. The title, *Lyrical Ballads,* seems to have been proposed at or about this time, for Hazlitt recalls Coleridge's using it on a walk to Linton, along with his claim that it was to be an "experiment . . . to see how far the public taste would endure poetry written in a more natural and simple style than had hitherto been attempted."[36]

Coleridge's contributions to the volume were finally quite small, numerically. The balance they had aimed at was upset by Wordsworth's phenomenal rate of production, and some of Coleridge's comments to Cottle give the appearance of struggling to keep his place in the volume.[37] This was just the reverse of their several previous attempts at collaboration, where Wordsworth had always been the one to drop out. But with "The Ancient Mariner" as its first, longest, and most striking poem Coleridge more than deserved his title to joint authorship. Also, given their placement of the poems (three of Coleridge's four poems coming first), a reader who went sequentially through the book would have "heard" Coleridge's "full, animated, and varied" voice for nearly a third of its length before he came to Wordsworth's "more equable, sustained, and internal" one. Coleridge's underrepresentation was not for lack of poems as he later claimed, pleading the unfinished state of "Christabel" and "The Ballad of the Dark Ladie." He had his great "conversational" poems ready to hand, which would have fit in very well, and "Kubla Khan"—which would not have. He published a small volume of his own that fall, containing "France: An Ode," "Fears in Solitude," and "Frost at Midnight." However, the first two of these were too topical for the effect the volume aimed at, and "Frost" could have been linked too easily by reviewers to such already published poems as "Reflections of Having Left a Place of Retirement," thus exposing the author's identity. As to anonymity, any reader who wanted to could pretty easily have established the fact that *Lyrical Ballads* were written in the West Country between March and July of 1798 simply by toting up the place-names and dates sprinkled through it. "The Nightingale," subtitled "A Conversational Poem," was a last-minute change, replacing "Lewti, a Circassian Love-Chant" (itself a rewriting of Wordsworth's teenage effort "Beauty and Moonlight"). The substitution was an improvement on all counts, for it matched the mood of Wordsworth's "lines," and may have been made when Coleridge learned that "Tintern Abbey" had been added. It also helped protect the volume's anonymity, since he had published "Lewti" in April under one of his well-known pseudonyms, "Nicias Erythraeus." His other two contributions, "The Foster-Mother's Tale" and "The Dungeon," were both extracted from the remains of *Osorio* and had as little to do with the overall effect of the volume as Wordsworth's "The Convict."

Wordsworth, having committed himself at last, and with the quit notice for Alfoxden soon to arrive, threw himself into the preparations for the volume. He followed Cottle to Bristol in late May and kept returning compulsively, staying two weeks at the beginning of June. He worried Cottle with small changes and matters of detail (about the number of lines per page, for example), all delivered with pompous authority. James Losh recorded the effect of Wordsworth's manner at the time: "pleasant and clear, but too earnest and emphatic in his manner of speaking in conversation."[38] Coleridge followed their conversations by mail, explaining to Cottle (who was worried about the volume's lack of unity) that they "are to a certain degree *one work,* in *kind tho' not in degree,* as an Ode is one work—& . . . our different poems are as stanzas, good relatively rather than absolutely:—Mark you, I say *in kind* tho' not in degree."[39] This was desperate reasoning, provoked by the fact that "The Ancient Mariner" is the volume's most *dis*unifying poem, a tendency exacerbated by its placement at the beginning. Coleridge was, characteristically, using the Aristotelian, scholastic distinction between kind and degree as a rhetorical smoke screen to impress the naive, nervous Cottle. Taken literally, his argument would mean that none of the poems could stand alone on its own merits. But it does point to the truth that the volume's ensemble, ballads of suffering plus lines of natural beauty, produces its unsettling but enduring master impression.

Postscript

Sometime evidently during his work on "The Thorn" Wordsworth produced a strange poem which he never published and which Moorman acutely suggests is, "perhaps, a reminiscence of his last unhappy days with Annette."[40]

> Away, away, it is the air
> That stirs among the withered leaves;
> Away, away, it is not there,
> Go, hunt among the harvest sheaves.
> There is a bed in shape as plain
> As from a hare or lion's lair
> It is the bed where we have lain
> In anguish and despair.
>
> Away, and take the eagle's eyes,
> The tiger's smell,
> Ears that can hear the agonies
> And murmurings of hell;
> And when you there have stood
> By that same bed of pain,
> The groans are gone, the tears remain.
> Then tell me if the thing be clear,
> The difference betwixt a tear
> Of water and of blood.[41]

The standard scholarly view is that this is a Gothic fragment reminiscent of Wordsworth's earlier work.[42] But it is neither a fragment nor particularly "Gothic," except as Gothic is taken to signify a melodramatic expression of painful emotions. The novelist A. S. Byatt's artistic response goes more directly to the heart of the poem's matter.

> The source of this emotion is impossible to trace—guilt over Annette, obscure fear of the nature of his feelings for Dorothy, or some more purely dramatic and fictional impetus have all been suggested—but the emotion itself is clear enough and sharply expressed. With its direct emphasis on sexual pain and guilt, its elaboration of a kind of strained and agonized universal sensuality, and its further religious guilty sense of having committed a crime which is observed by the whole of nature and judged, the poem expresses acute anxiety with an immediacy rare in Wordsworth's personal poetry.[43]

The poem is a riddle or conundrum poem, like Wordsworth's "Argument for Suicide," or Thel's hysterical questions in Blake's *The Book of Thel:* "Why a tender curb upon the youthful burning boy! / What a little curtain of flesh on the bed of our desire?" The riddle is, Can you find the bed I'm talking about? And if you can, can you appreciate the kind of pain it represents? It has relevance to the tale of infanticide in "The Thorn," and scholarly tracings to Burger's "The Lass of Fair Wone" are useful, though the parallels between the two situations are quite broad.[44] (Burger's girl delivers—and then kills—her baby in the same bower where she was seduced.) But "Away, away" asks a question both more complex and closer to Wordsworth's personal experience.

It says you will not find the bed where you are looking for it, but "among the harvest sheaves": it is a bed of autumn. Its "withered leaves" and "harvest sheaves" echo the "rustling aspins" and "the falling leaf" at the end of *Descriptive Sketches,* written in October 1793 as Wordsworth lurked outside Orléans, where Annette had been spirited to a bed, hidden from him, for her lying-in. To find this bed requires superhuman, supernatural capabilities, though its shape carries a plain meaning: namely, you can see clearly that two people have been lying there. But profound resources of understanding are evidently required to grasp the meaning of this plain evidence. The immediate pains are gone, but not the grief: "the tears remain." Its final question is, Who can adjudicate between two different kinds of pain, and of tears, those "of water and [those] of blood"? The poem's implied answer is that the answer will *not* be clear.

The poem is as good as similar puzzle poems in *Lyrical Ballads* of much lighter touch: "We Are Seven" and "Anecdote for Fathers." "The Thorn" itself is a conundrum, but its puzzles are fobbed off onto its loquacious narrator, a retired old sea captain who cannot make sense of the thorn and its nearby mound and pond, despite the rumors of the neighborhood and the impatient, nearly hysterical proddings of his frustrated auditor: "But what's the thorn? and what's the pond? / And what's the hill of moss to her?" But the voice of "Away, away" is masterful and lordly: find it if you can, it dares us, "Then tell me if the thing be clear"—in the confident expectation that it will not be.

Two kinds of beds came together in Wordsworth's mind here, those where he lay with Annette and those where he frequently lay with Dorothy. Both women, for different reasons, must be disappointed of his love, but it is impossible for him to say which loss is worse, the tear of water (Annette's) or of blood (Dorothy's).[45] Insofar as the poem has a source, it also has to do with mistresses: Herrick's "Away with silks, away with Lawn," which pleads, "Give me my Mistresse, as she is, / Drest in her nak't simplicities."[46] On February 26 Dorothy recorded, "We lay sidelong upon the turf, and gazed on the landscape till it melted into more than natural loveliness."[47] At about the same time, Wordsworth jotted down that

In many a walk
At evening or by moonlight, or reclined
At midday upon beds of forest moss,
Have we to Nature and her impulses
Of our whole being made free gift.[48]

Lying down on the ground together was a common practice with them. They would imagine they were dead, listen to their own breathing, pay minute attention to the sounds around them: clearly sensual behavior, but hard to tell "if the thing be clear, the difference" between it and sublimated sexual behavior. In "The Three Graves," Edward also lies down in a bower, not with Mary, his beloved, but with Ellen, her sisterly friend. "With shut-up senses, Edward lay," but said, "See, dearest Ellen! see! / 'Tis in the leaves, a little sun, / No bigger than your ee," and they pass the time arguing about what color the rays are. The eye/spy motif is also present here.

Other fragments related to "Away, away" ask bluntly why Nature does not immediately reflect human suffering, the kind of sentiment that comes out in *Lyrical Ballads* only in lighter, teasing questions: if Nature seems to take so much pleasure in its own beauty, "Have I not reason to lament / What man has made of man?" One of these fragments, published only in 1992, is evidently related to both "Away, away" and "The Three Graves":

Are there no groans no breeze or wind?
Does misery leave no track behind?
Why is the earth without a shape and why
Thus silent is the sky?
Is every glimmering of the sky,
Is every [?lamphole] in the world an eye?
Has every star a tongue?[49]

Here too we have the riddle form, and the idea of nature's "eyes" spying on mankind, with the question of why nature does not shape itself to the forms of human misery: because *then* its facts and meaning would be clear to everyone.

WYE WANDERING 24

O sylvan Wye! Thou wanderer through the woods,
How often has my spirit turned to thee!
("Lines Written above Tintern Abbey")

Wordsworth returned to Alfoxden in mid-June to collect Dorothy and their few furnishings. They said good-bye to their wonderful residence on June 25, after setting Peggy Marsh, pregnant and unhappy, on her way back to Racedown and her loutish blacksmith husband.[1] Pausing a week at Stowey with Sara (Coleridge was off rambling with Hazlitt), they departed for Bristol on July 2.

They spent a few days with Cottle in his lodgings above his new shop in crowded, noisy Wine Street.[2] Dorothy registered the shock of the change immediately: "You can scarcely conceive how the jarring contrast between the sounds which are now for ever ringing in my ears and the sweet sounds of Allfoxden makes me long for the country again. After three years residence in retirement a city in feeling, sound, and prospect is hateful."[3] She soon got her wish to return to the country.

They sought out James Losh in Shirehampton, a quiet suburb on the Avon near the Channel where he resided for his health (it now consists mainly of industrial fuel storage tanks), but he had gone to Bath for special treatments following a relapse.[4] They went immediately in pursuit and spent July 8 with him and Cecilia at their rooms in Bath, taking all three meals with them. At dinner that night was Losh's friend Richard Warner, whose *A Walk through Wales, in August 1797* had appeared in February, a day-by-day hiking guidebook featuring a frontispiece of Tintern Abbey and neat little woodcut maps at the head of each chapter to show the day's recommended route. The company admired the new book, which immediately prompted Wordsworth to follow in Warner's footsteps while simultaneously retracing his own from 1793. Warner, glad to meet a fellow landscape enthusiast, invited the Wordsworths to dine with him next day at his house. He and Wordsworth had several experiences in common in Wales, including the difficulty of seeing anything clearly from the top of Snowdon. Warner said, "Our great object was . . . to traverse Snowdon" (his tour went from Bristol to North Wales and back), but he had had the same bad luck there as Wordsworth had seven years earlier. On being informed by the guide at Beddgelert that the day was unfavorable, he and his companions tried another route, and after two hours of "very severe labour" made it to the top, only to find themselves surrounded by mist: "we literally could not see the distance of a dozen feet."[5]

Coleridge or Cottle may also have recommended a Wye trip to Wordsworth, recalling their expedition to Tintern Abbey in 1794 with Southey and the Fricker sisters. It had started badly because squabbles between Coleridge and Southey upset the itinerary and they got lost in the woods. When they finally arrived, they were thrilled to see the abbey by romantic moonlight and torchlight. They had intended to vary the sublime visual effects by visiting the iron foundry farther up in the hills, but only Southey and Cottle had gone on, because only they had horses. This trip started a vogue for the Wye tour among Cottle's stable of young writers.[6]

Another immediate stimulus for the Wordsworths' getaway jaunt was an essay by Thelwall entitled "The Phenomena of the Wye, during the Winter of 1797–98," which had just appeared in the *Monthly Magazine* for May. It not only showed the spirit in which most people visited the area (Thelwall was now living on the banks of the river at Llyswen) but also indicated how thoroughly he had changed his writing persona from radical to connoisseur: "an excursion on the Wye has become an essential part of the education, as it were, of all who aspire to the reputation of elegance, taste, and fashion."[7]

After dinner on July 9 the Loshes returned to Shirehampton with the Wordsworths, who spent the night with them. Next morning William and Dorothy set out on a walking tour of the Wye valley, following Warner's route. This trip resulted in the most famous poem in *Lyrical Ballads* after "The Ancient Mariner." But although "Lines Composed a Few Miles above Tintern Abbey" magnificently concludes the 1798 volume, there had been no suggestion, as of early July, that another poem was needed for the volume, still less that Wordsworth should take a trip in order to write one. As things stood, *Lyrical Ballads* would have ended with "The Convict." A feeling that the volume ended on a lame note may have been on William's mind as he and Dorothy set out on what was intended to be not a poetry-writing expedition but a therapeutic escape from the shock of their return to the noise and bustle of a large city.

They crossed over to Chepstow by the ferry and walked along the road, which sometimes follows, sometimes avoids, the looping curves of the Wye.[8] This walk can be taken only with great difficulty now, as the highway (A466) has no shoulders, and the hiking paths (Wye Valley Walk and Offa's Dyke Path) have been relocated to the tops of the hills and cliffs on both sides of the river. They reached the village of Tintern and its ruined Cistercian abbey early that day (it's only five miles from Chepstow) and had ample time to tour the abbey and its grounds.*

On the morning of the 11th, they set off upriver again, heading for Monmouth and Goodrich and their noted ruined castles. The visual contrast of picturesque ruins with dramatic cliffs and deep woods was the primary focus of all the standard guidebooks for this popular tour, especially Gilpin's *Observations on the River Wye . . . Made in the Summer of 1770* (1782; 3rd ed., 1792), which Wordsworth had with him, as well as newer ones like Warner's, though both of these took more realistic account of local economic and social conditions than Wordsworth's poem does.

Wordsworth later said he began composing his poem "upon leaving Tintern, after crossing the Wye." This suggests that he started his oral composition—his singsong humming to himself in five-beat lines—on the morning of the 11th, since the only bridges crossing the Wye were upriver to the north, nearby at Brockweir or farther up at Bigsweir. His reference to the river's "sweet inland murmur" and his footnote to this line ("The river is not affected by the tides a few miles above Tintern") support this location, because the river stops being affected by the enormous action of the ocean tides (hence "sweet," not salty) between these two bridges, one to three miles above Tintern. Up to this point the water is a muddy brown; beyond, it turns clear, dark, and deep. His opening landscape description seems to record a backward look downriver toward the abbey, moving down from the "mountain-springs" and "cliffs" where he stood, across the more cultivated "plots of cottage ground" and "orchard tufts," and ending with selective images of the village, the beggars in the abbey, and the nearby iron and char-

*The abbey is now splendidly preserved for modern tourism, with the usual gains and losses. A few years ago one of the specials on the menu of the quite good restaurant next to the parking lot was a stuffed salmon called "The William Wordsworth." Walkers wishing to approximate Wordsworth's younger, leaner experience should climb up to the ruins of St. Mary's Chapel on the hill overlooking the abbey to the west. Though technically off-limits, its moldering walls, broken floors, and lush, overgrown graveyard give a more powerful feeling of vanished sacrality than the comprehensive archaeological information supplied by the National Trust for the abbey itself. Threatening graffiti ("Beware! This is Holy Ground!") and surprised trysting lovers bring one closer to Wordsworth's experience, as hidden or revealed in his poem, than one might suspect.

coal industries: "wreathes of smoke sent up in silence" and "vagrant dwellers in the houseless woods."

They spent the night of the 11th at Goodrich, and on the 12th they walked all the way back down past Tintern to Chepstow. At the end of the day they took one of the many tour boats that plied the river back up to spend another night at Tintern. Thus Wordsworth was at or around the abbey on every day of this tour, which he said was "a ramble of four or five days," but probably four, since they could easily have returned to Bristol on the 13th, and he said he "composed the last 20 lines or so as he walked down the hill from Clifton to Bristol."[9] Returning to Cottle's house and shop that evening, he delivered the completed poem, of which he said "not any part of it was written down till I reached Bristol," to the printers the next day: July 14.

This is the bare bones of their itinerary. But in the last ten years "Tintern Abbey" has become the focus of an extraordinary controversy, which turns very much on where Wordsworth walked and what he saw on this trip. Where one stands now on "Tintern Abbey" makes a big difference in Romantic scholarship—whether one stands with Wordsworth, "a few miles above" the abbey, or with Gilpin, Warner, and many contemporary critics, down in the ruins of the abbey itself. Older critics, steeped in Wordsworthian "nature worship," praise the poem for its universality and are even puzzled (if not disappointed) to find residual traces of his concern for humanity in it.[10] But contemporary critics, having learned how the "nature poet" has been homogenized by an adulating tradition, have seized on those same traces as the last evidences of a radicalism Wordsworth was now trying, like Charles Lloyd and John Thelwall and many others, to hide.

The debate turns mainly on the "uncertain notice" that Wordsworth gives to the smoke rising from the trees, since we know that the smoke was rising from the thriving, around-the-clock iron industry of small forges in the wooded hills above the abbey, and from the kilns which burnt these trees to produce the charcoal needed for the forges. The river was thick with the traffic of this industry, as well as with boats serving the busy tourist industry. Both were by-products of the war: the iron forges, to produce cannon and other matériel; the tourists, because picturesque British locales were more in demand with so much of the Continent closed to touring. Furthermore, Wordsworth's tentative suggestion that the smoke "might seem" to come from "vagrant dwellers in the houseless woods" touches with extreme delicacy on a fact known to everybody who visited the abbey: that it was the shelter and resort for many beggars and vagabonds, who made their living by cadging from the well-to-do tourists who came to visit it, under the pretext of offering them "tours."

Warner's *Walk* gave details about both the beautiful aspects of the scene and the ugly ones that Wordsworth softens. The noise of the forges kept him awake on a hot summer's night, and he could accommodate "the dingy beings who melt the ore . . . in their horrible employment" to his cultural purpose only by alluding to Virgil: "we saw Virgil's description realized . . . Etna, the forges of the Cyclops, and their fearful employment."[11] But he was capable of viewing other human activities in a complementary relationship to nature in a way that anticipated Wordsworth: "The little cottages scattered at the feet [of the cliffs], neat residences of industrious labour, form a pleasing accompaniement; exhibiting simplicity combined with majesty." Wordsworth framed this image too: "These plots of cottage-ground, these orchard tufts . . . these pastoral farms / Green to the very door."

But though Warner's vistas were fresh in memory from their recent conversation, Wordsworth seems to have relied more on Gilpin's standard guidebook. His reference to "these steep and lofty cliffs" and the way in which *thought* "connect[s] / The landscape with the quiet of the sky" was directly indebted to Gilpin's attempt to bring the region's *smoke* into a more pleasing aesthetic perspective: "Many of the furnaces, on the banks of the river, consume charcoal, which is manufactured on the spot; and the smoke, which is frequently seen issuing from the sides of the hills; and spreading its veil over a part of them, beautifully breaks their lines, and unites them with the sky."[12]

The point is not to belabor Wordsworth's use of Gilpin: doubtless he improves on him, and being borrowed by Wordsworth is probably the best thing that ever happened to Gilpin's guidebook. It is more interesting to consider some uses Wordsworth did *not* make of Gilpin, in light of his demonstrable familiarity with this guidebook. Wordsworth's "vagrant dwellers," less pitiable than Warner's "dingy beings," are far less so than the ones Gilpin encountered in the abbey and described with a shocked candor that quite breaks through his otherwise conventional picturesque perspective. More than half the pages Gilpin devotes to Tintern are given over to these distracting beggars. His tone in general is fastidious, not to say mincing, as he recommends one viewing station or criticizes another. He facetiously proposed, for example, taking a hammer to certain corners of the abbey to make its appearance more ruinous. (In his guide to the Lakes, he complained that Grasmere lacked banditti.)[13] But when he meets the beggars, his aestheticizing manner breaks down in the shocked honesty of his human response: "The poverty and wretchedness of the inhabitants were remarkable." They lived in huts among the ruins, and "the whole hamlet" congregated at the gate, offering "tours." Gilpin and his party followed one of these, a "poor woman [who] could scarce crawl; shuffling along her palsied limbs, and meagre, contracted body." She led them to what she said was "the monks' library," but "it was her own mansion":

> all indeed she meant to us was the story of her own wretchedness; and all she had to shew us, was her own miserable habitation. We did not expect to be interested; but found we were. I never saw so loathsome a dwelling . . . a cavity between two ruined walls; which streamed with unwholesome dews . . . not the merest utensil, or furniture of any kind. We were rather surprised, that the wretched creature was still alive; than that she had only lost the use of her limbs.[14]

Such a powerfully ambiguous passage, standing out from its bland polite surroundings in Gilpin, and reinforced by his own experience, had an enormous impact on Wordsworth. Reading this passage, and seeing firsthand what it described, seemed like an image from his own recently completed ballads, which everywhere recapitulate what Gilpin heard: "all indeed she meant to tell us was the story of her own wretchedness." Compare the Female Vagrant: "She ceased, and weeping turned away, / As if because her tale was at an end." Much of Wordsworth's learning "to look on nature, not as in the hour / Of thoughtless youth" derived from following out the implications of Gilpin's reluctant expression of surprise: "we did not expect to be interested; but found we were."

In "Tintern Abbey" 's summation of his self-creation, Wordsworth tried, by oblique references to "uncertain notice[s]" and "vagrant dwellers" in the Wye's secluded landscape, to bring together the two themes he had separated in most of his compositions since early March, the ballads of suffering and the lyrics of natural celebration. This is clear in the justification he gives for the significance of his return to Nature, and to this landscape in particular:

> For I have learned
> To look on nature, not as in the hour
> Of *thoughtless* youth, but hearing oftentimes
> The still, sad music of humanity,
> Nor harsh nor grating, though of ample power
> To chasten and subdue.
>
> (89–94; italics added)

He has added *thought* to his aesthetic pleasure, of a specifically moral, humanistic kind, such as he recommended at the end of "Goody Blake": "Now *think,* ye farmers all, I pray, / Of Goody Blake and Harry Gill."

But so great is his caution, or his fear of upsetting his new creative balance, that it can be argued with equal cogency that he strove mightily to *prevent* such thoughts from intruding too forcefully into the poem. "Vagrant *dwellers"* (a cautious oxymoron) are not quite as bad off as vagrants, to say nothing of beggars, especially when they are immediately replaced by "some hermit," an almost entirely fictional character or picturesque appurtenance, wholly self-sufficient in his isolation: "where by his fire / The hermit sits alone." This anachronistic hermit was also suggested by Gilpin: "a man of warm imagination, in monkish times, might have been allured by such a scene to become an inhabitant of it."[15]

This is not to say that Wordsworth should have added some ruins, human or architectural, to his landscape a few miles above Tintern Abbey. Nor is his loco-descriptive meditative poem required to demonstrate the relation between landscape viewing and social responsibility. But the poem itself is full of language which simultaneously invites and resists such probing questions, opening up precisely those areas of concern that it seeks to contain in more manageable aesthetic terms. By posing this ostensibly personal poem of nature worship in such terms, Wordsworth forces us to consider what he is *not* doing as well as what he is doing, and to appreciate how hard-earned his sweeping affirmations in the poem are.

He and Dorothy had not gone up the Wye valley to see the iron works, still less to see beggars squatting in the abbey. They went there, as to the Valley of Stones and Cheddar Gorge, to enjoy the scenery and for a respite from the noisy city. They went for relief in nature—and they found instead more human misery, which Wordsworth almost but not quite excluded from his poem. But once again he was stimulated to compose by the strong force of contrast. Finding at Tintern something shockingly different from what he anticipated, he was forced or released into composition, literally to *compose* his thoughts. He began on that morning of July 11 when they left Tintern heading north, and he could begin to *re*flect on the thoughts he had had in the abbey the day before.

"Tintern Abbey" also resulted from another of his strongest stimulants to composition, the release of tension after a period of great concentration that had not been fully rewarding. After the intense time of composition from early March to late May, when he wrote thousands of lines of original poetry, most of it unlike anything he had ever done before, he went on a tour for relief. But instead, a vision of the meaning and shape of his entire life flowed in upon him, and flowed out in his most characteristic idiom, which is represented nowhere else in the 1798 *Lyrical Ballads:* the fluent iambic pentameter blank verse of his great model, Milton, which he transformed (as in *The Recluse* poems of January–March) into the clear, colloquial diction of modern conversation. It is addressed to Dorothy as Adam addressing Eve, reassuring her that their paradise lost could yet be a paradise regained, as hand in hand they left their Edenic but precarious lives at Racedown and Alfoxden and moved, with thoughtful steps and slow, back out into the dangerous public world.

In the only other poem in *Lyrical Ballads* that tries to bring nature and suffering mankind close together, "The Convict," Wordsworth maintains this faith by wishful thinking about social reform. The poem's reference to transportation as a more humane alternative to imprisonment possibly popped back into his head as, leaving the abbey, they learned that the hilltop settlement north of Tintern Parva (Little Tintern) was called Botany Bay, prompting Wordsworth to rethink the sentimental liberalism of what stood, until the morning of July 11, as the last poem in his forthcoming volume.

Not that "Tintern Abbey" is more liberal than "The Convict." On the contrary: it suggests no social action, only asserts the speaker's faith that nature defends him from the threats of society. It makes very small claims indeed for what nature's "forms of beauty" produce by way of moral social action: "such [feelings], *perhaps,* / As *may* have had no *trivial* influence / On that best portion of a good man's life; / His *little, nameless, unremembered* acts / Of kindness and of love." This is far from revolutionary. Only an extremely quietistic view of human morality would call such unknown actions "the best portion" of anybody's life. But this was as much as Wordsworth was now capable of saying, by way of healing the split in *The Recluse*'s intentions which the triumphant "failures" of his lyrical ballads represented.

The triumph of "Tintern Abbey" is its awareness of its own weakness and proximity to failure. Though usually read as a deeply affirmative statement of secular or existential faith, it achieves its affirmations in ways that are shot through with the signs of their own deconstruction. These are more than Wordsworth's rhetorical sincerity and skill, acknowledging honest doubts; it is a risk that at every moment threatens to end the poem. Each of its verse paragraphs after the first one begins with or turns upon language that undercuts the statement it is making: "If this be but a vain belief," "Not for this faint I, nor mourn nor murmur," "Nor perchance, / If I were not thus taught," "Nor, perchance— / If I should be where I no more can hear / Thy voice," "Nor wilt thou then forget."* It is precisely the *dubiety* of thought and belief, of education and of faith, that underscores the natural religion of "Tintern Abbey." If one reads the poem emphasizing its negatives rather than its positives (and it is moot to say which reading is more natural), it sounds like a Lord's Prayer uttered by Thomas the Doubter, urging itself along to affirmation by constantly raising objections that it must then overcome, inducing a kind of philosophical stuttering. In each paragraph, these

*These turns of argument came to Wordsworth from Milton's peroration of his introduction to his translation of Bucer's *De Regno Christi* (1557), again showing how deeply he interiorized his hero's thought patterns. Milton was challenging Parliament to rise to the the occasion and pass the laws needed for a more justly Protestant commonwealth. His concluding rhetoric is a mounting series of if-this-be-not-enough constructions, aimed at real or implied antagonists, very similar to the pivotal sentences in "Tintern Abbey": "Nor doe I forget," "Not that I have now more confidence," "Or if perhaps wee may obtain," "If this be not anough to qualifie my traducers . . . I shall not for much more disturbance . . . intermitt the prosecution of those thoughts which may render me best serviceable, either to this age, or if it so happen, to posteritie."

negatives are linked to images of human suffering or evil, usually in cities and always in groups. In the first paragraph great care is taken that any mention of human activity should not "disturb the wild green landscape." In the second "the din of towns and cities" and "hours of weariness" are generalized into "the heavy and the weary weight / Of all this *unintelligible* world." In the third it is "the fretful stir / Unprofitable, and the fever of the world." In the fourth, it is "the still, sad music of humanity" itself. And in the fifth it is "evil tongues, / Rash judgements . . . the sneers of selfish men, / . . . greetings where no kindness is, [and] all the dreary intercourse of daily life."

What one notices about these statements of social suffering, taken together, is that they do not add up to any very great sum of evil, of the kind we usually silently supply when we read the sonorous phrase "still, sad music of humanity." (For example: poverty, death, disease, war, or all the irrevocable losses of love and life, unmerited and inescapable in the human condition.) They sound, rather, much like the experiences Wordsworth had in London in 1795, which caused him to flee, experiences he was now being made sharply aware of again: the lonely feelings of rejection suffered by a sensitive person in conditions of intensely competitive work in urban markets, where gossip, hasty or ill-formed judgment, jealousy, and smooth hypocrisy all contribute to the feverish pace at which one's business fails to move along as profitably as one wishes. In this way, the "Lines Composed . . . above Tintern Abbey," the last-composed poem in the book, respond to the "Lines Left upon a Seat in a Yew-tree," one of the volume's earliest composed works, and one with equally recognizable self-references, to a youth who "to the world / Went forth, pure in his heart, against the taint / Of dissolute tongues, 'gainst jealousy, and hate, / And scorn, against all enemies prepared, / All but neglect" (14–18).

"Tintern Abbey" 's composition, on the one hand so immediate, contemporaneous, and personal, was at the same time so heavily indebted to a variety of poetical sources that it can be considered a summa of Wordsworth's literary experience to this point, as well as of his personal history.[16] Besides debts to contemporary poetry, others have noted distinct echoes of Shakespeare, Milton, and the Bible, and the influence of Coleridge's "conversational poems" is also marked (for example, "Nature never did betray the heart that loved her" echoes "Nature ne'er deserts the wise and pure" from "This Lime-Tree Bower"). Not merely the fact but the *specificity* of his echoes is important. He hears Shakespeare's, Milton's, and the Bible's heroes in their time of crisis, as they contemplate what Wordsworth himself was contemplating: the need, and the cost, of public action in the world. Hamlet: "How . . . unprofitable / Seem to me all the uses of this world" (cf. "the fretful stir / Unprofitable, and the fever of the world"). Samson: "So much I feel my genial spirits droop" (cf. "Nor . . . should I the more / Suffer my genial spirits to decay"). Milton: "though fall'n on evil dayes, / On evil dayes though fall'n, and evil tongues" (cf. "neither evil tongues . . . nor all / The dreary intercourse of daily life"). The psalmist: "He maketh me to lie down beside the still waters . . . Yea, though I walk through the valley of the shadow of death, I will fear no evil: for thou art with me" (cf. "For thou art with me, here, upon the banks / Of this fair river").[17]

Such a broad range of allusive language raises to view another register of language in the poem, which is usually excluded from critics' consideration as much as its language of social pain: namely, as noted earlier, the passionately erotic language that contains his feelings for Annette, "more like a man / Flying from something that he dreads, than one / Who sought the thing he loved." Through each of its five paragraphs, words of passion are invoked, but only (like its social terms) to be chastened by gestures simultaneously taming that passion. Some of it is physiological: "sensations sweet, / Felt in the blood, and felt along the heart." Some of it is moral: "Feelings too of unremembered pleasure . . . of kindness and of love." Some of it is human passion projected onto natural objects: "How oft, in spirit, have I turned to thee / O sylvan Wye! Thou wanderer through the woods, / How often has my spirit turned to thee!" And some of it is displaced from himself into eroticized landscape painting: "The sounding cataract / Haunted me like a *passion*," the woods and mountains "were then to me / *An appetite: a feeling and a love.*" But "that time is past, / And all its *aching joys* are now no more, / And all its *dizzy raptures.*"*

Here follows his hard lesson of learning "to look on nature, not as in the hour of thoughtless youth," with its resulting transformation: "Therefore am I still / A *lover* of the meadows and the woods" (103–5). He is still a lover, but now of Nature, not another person. And yet there is another person present in the poem, his sister, Dorothy. The final portrait of Dorothy is in fact a portrait of William's passion, as reflected in her eyes:

> [I] read
> My former pleasures in the shooting lights
> Of thy wild eyes! Oh! yet a little while
> May I behold in thee what I was once,
> My dear, dear Sister!
>
> (117–22)

This language of passion is the more noteworthy because its reference to himself five years earlier is not true in terms of his supposed attachment to

*The sense of intimacy and love associated with Tintern continues in Wordsworth's love letters to his wife fourteen years later, upon her first visit to the Wye: "of all my Poems the one [in] which I speak of it will be the most beloved by me" (*The Love Letters of William and Mary Wordsworth,* ed. Beth Darlington [Ithaca: Cornell Univ. Press, 1981], 242).

nature then, on the basis of anything we know he was writing in 1793 or just after. Instead, his language at that time was full of thoughts of Annette, insofar as we saw it deflected from his letters to her into his erotic description of the Female Vagrant of "A Night on Salisbury Plain," or in his extensive sexual heightening of *Descriptive Sketches* in his revisions of 1794. He was not such a lover of nature in 1793, and he is not so much a lover of humanity in 1798.[18] The sequence of his development had been more nearly the opposite: from love of man to love of nature, or rather, from *despair* of loving man to finding relief in nature. What he imagines happening to Dorothy is what he now recognizes has happened to him: "When these *wild ecstasies* shall be matured / Into a sober pleasure."

He was going on a walk with his sister, prior to leaving England again for the first time in five or six years. All his memories of 1793 at this place came flooding back. Now, repressing his feelings for Annette, he in effect weds himself to nature via Dorothy (or vice versa) with the invocation of "a holier love" in nature a few miles above the altar of the ruined abbey in the valley. Thoughts of divorce and marriage sprang to his mind from very deep sources in his past experience and reading. A partial source for his strange definition of the "best portion of a good man's life" as "his little, nameless, unremembered acts / Of kindness and of love" is one of Milton's divorce tracts: "whereby good men in the best portion of their lives . . . are compelled to civil indignities."[19] In Milton's text, "the best portion of their lives" refers specifically to men's sexual happiness in marriage. But Wordsworth altered this source as he did the many other sources of this most derivative, yet most original of poems. Milton's "civil indignities" refers to restrictions against divorce deriving from papist superstitions, whereas Wordsworth's "best portion of a good man's life" includes acts of love so small as to be nameless and unremembered—which would include Caroline Wordsworth, so far as public acknowledgment is concerned.

This intense mingling of public and private registers for passion was especially volatile because, at the very moment *Lyrical Ballads* was being set up in type, the whole Alfoxden gang was exploded by the *Anti-Jacobin*. In a long, impressive, scorched-earth satire called "The New Morality," published in its last number, July 9, just after Parliament rose at the end of June, it pilloried them as "ye, five other wandering bards that move, / In sweet accord of harmony and love, / C——-dge and S—th—y, L—-d and L—mbe, & Co. / Tune all your mystic harps to praise LEPAUX!" (Larevellière-Lépaux was the current president of the French Directory, and a patron of the state religion of "Theophilanthropie.")[20] "Coleridge & Co." were being mopped up as small fry under the influence of the *Anti-Jacobin*'s larger targets—Godwin, Paine, Holcroft, Thelwall, and David Williams (a Welsh radical), in a virtual Who's Who, or last call, of English radicalism in the 1790s. Their Tory antagonists knew very well whom they were aiming at. The references to "wandering" and "harmony and love" show that the satirists knew something about their targets' movements, including the Pantisocracy fiasco, and had studied the contents of their recent volumes carefully. Wordsworth is almost certainly the "Co.," since it signifies only one person (to bring the total to *"five* wandering bards") and since he had been identified by name with the other four in George Dyer's well-meaning praise of "Pantisocracy's harmonious train" in *The Poet's Fate* the year before.[21] The entire 1797–98 run of the *Anti-Jacobin* had contained shrewd assessments of the nature of the "Jacobin" poetry produced preeminently by Southey, and also by Coleridge and Erasmus Darwin among others, along with a strongly political bias against its merits. Coleridge's poem "To a Young Ass" was the direct target of these lines from "The New Morality":

> Mark her fair Votaries, prodigal of grief,
> With cureless pangs, and woes that mock relief,
> Droop in soft sorrow o'er a faded flow'r;
> O'er a dead Jack-Ass pour the pearly show'r:—
> But hear, unmov'd, of *Loire's* ensanguin'd flood,
> Choak'd up with slain;—of *Lyons* drench'd in blood;
> Of Crimes that blot the Age, the World with shame,
> Foul crimes, but sicklied o'er with Freedom's name. . . .
> (140–48)

If "The New Morality" appeared on July 9, it arrived in Bristol the day before William and Dorothy set off on their tour of the Wye valley. However, the last numbers of the *Anti-Jacobin* are misdated, so though July 9 is usually understood to be the date of its last appearance, there is a possibility that the last number, containing this apocalyptic condemnation, appeared just *after* Wordsworth returned from his tour, on July 16.[22] The effect of this attack from the very center of England's political power may well be registered in "Tintern Abbey" 's nervous language about "the sneers of selfish men."

Then, before the month was out, but after Wordsworth had turned "Tintern Abbey" over to Cottle, the *Anti-Jacobin*'s more pedestrian successor, the *Anti-Jacobin Review and Magazine; or, Monthly Political and Literary Censor,* led off the poetry section of its inaugural number with Gillray's famous print illustrating "The New Morality" (see illustration). Here, Lépaux is represented as "the holy Hunch-back" priest, holding the new religion's bible, titled *Religion de la Nature.* As a caption, "Explanation of the Satyrical Print," it printed just those lines of Canning and Frere's brilliant satire pertaining to the procession of English liberals and radicals who wanted to enshrine Jacobinism as England's state religion. In this reprint the names of the "five wandering bards" are the first proper names to appear, even before "Paine, W-ll-—ms, G-dw-n, H-lc-—ft," "Th-lw-—l, and ye that lecture as ye go." Someone had also paid close attention to the bards' names, for the implied spelling of Lamb's name has been corrected from "L-—be," as it appeared in the last issue of the *Anti-Jacobin*.

In the cartoon Wordsworth's friends appear smaller than Fox and the major political figures, but closer to the throne of revolutionary atheism. Coleridge and Southey have asses' heads, courtesy of Coleridge's "To a Young Ass," a democratical effusion on the premise that asses have rights and feelings too: the sort of poem that made the *Anti-Jacobin*'s satire very easy to produce. Lamb and Lloyd are "Toad and Frog," to associate them, by a silly alliterative transfer, with the cartoon's other witches' brew monstrosities and unnatural growths: vipers, monkeys, crocodiles, and Erasmus Darwin's *bonnets rouges* roses from *The Loves of the Plants.* They hold their *Blank Verses* in their mouths, dedicated to Southey and published in February by the Arch brothers, who would soon become the London publishers of *Lyrical Ballads.* The two raggedy boys in Liberty caps in front of them may be their human forms, or other youngsters led astray (like George Burnett and Richard Reynell), in which case, by a process of elimination, the large right hand just visible supporting the "Cornucopia of Ignorance" from below would be that of the fifth partner in their wandering "Co.": Wordsworth's. The arm and hand appear to belong to a large, strong man, which fits Wordsworth's description, if one of the editors gave it to Gillray. (Somebody always supplied Gillray with details to visualize: he would have been unlikely to know about Coleridge's dactylics, for example.) This assumes a good deal of literalism on Gillray's part, but that was precisely his genius: to take physical, personal details and exaggerate them grotesquely, often to the displeasure of Canning and Frere, who aimed for a higher level of ideological debate and were often embarrassed by Gillray's vulgar caricatures of people with whom, enemies or not, they had to work in the government.*

Such a vehement, extended, and brilliant attack made it abundantly clear (to Cottle, among others) that a volume bearing the name of Coleridge would do no good to any other name linked with his, for it would imme-

*Gillray's print for "The Knife-Grinder" displeased the editors because the "Friend of Humanity" did not resemble its ostensible target, George Tierney (MP for Southwark). In fact, he very much resembles Southey, the author of the poem being satirized. Gillray's cartoons were not printed in the *Anti-Jacobin* itself; he produced them immediately after the issue in which their subjects appeared, as separate prints. "The New Morality" is the largest and most uninhibited of these, Gillray being less under Canning's editorial control for it. His cartoon illustrates lines 318–53 of the poem and moves in exactly the sequence of the poem, from right to left, ending with the Leviathan, the Whig Duke of Bedford, and those following in his "yeasty" train (the foam of Samuel Whitbread's brewery). See Draper Hill, *Mr. Gillray the Caricaturist* (London: Phaidon, 1965), 67.

diately be made to "stink" too. This was no time to offer the reviewers a double target, especially one that could be associated with the hapless Southey and his flaccid poems sympathizing with the suffering poor, as Wordsworth's ballads assuredly would be by readers who did not bother about fine points of difference. No one was making subtle discriminations in this highly polarized climate of opinion. The religion of nature at the end of "Tintern Abbey" would not have been much differentiated from Lépaux's *Religion de la Nature.* For one thing, it was not all that different.

The July 13 date in the title of "Tintern Abbey," which the opening lines urge us to subtract back five years, to July 13, 1793, had been headlined by Southey for the same reason in a poem in the *Morning Post* which Wordsworth saw on the morning after his return to Bristol: "July Thirteenth. Charlotte Corde Executed for Putting Marat to Death." This poem reflects the thoroughly anti-Jacobin Southey, celebrating the fifth anniversary of Corday's act in a way that the *Anti-Jacobin* would have approved: "Timely thine end, and with the good on earth / Thy mem'ry dwells, and with the good in Heav'n, / CORDE, O martyr'd Maid! thy spirit lives!"[23] In terms of contemporary politics and poetics, Wordsworth's problem was to avoid both the knee-jerk liberalism of Southey's former "Jacobin" poems and the bathetic pieties of his new anti-Jacobinism, while at the same time escaping the *Anti-Jacobin*'s much more intelligent but thoroughly unforgiving satirical razor.

The "Advertisement" to *Lyrical Ballads* may have been been written by Wordsworth at this time, alone in Bristol, under fire, and separated from Coleridge. Like its successive revisions in the prefaces of 1800 and 1802, it lacks Coleridge's subtle persuasive powers. It proceeds, in its three main paragraphs, to insult its readers by assuring them that, whatever they may think of poetry in general or these poems in particular, they are most assuredly wrong, either because their taste has been improperly educated or because they have not devoted enough attention to the study of poetry. It speaks with the voice that James Losh complained of, "too earnest and emphatic." But if Wordsworth imagined himself to be answering the editors of the *Anti-Jacobin,* his assertiveness sounds more brave than pompous. A culture war in political poetics had been waging for the better part of a year, and Wordsworth's "Advertisement" may best be read as a salvo back in the direction of the "Introduction to the Poetry of *The Anti-Jacobin,*" from its very first issue. There, the *Anti-Jacobin* had spoken with its own lordly authority about the true nature of poetry, and lamented the present cultural situation, in which it seemed "that good Morals, and what We should call good Politics, are inconsistent with the spirit of true Poetry." This being the case, it elected "to go to the only market where [poetry] is to be had good and ready made, that of the *Jacobins*"—a frank admission—but to present it "with such precautions, as may conduce at once to the safety of our Readers principles, and to the improvement of our own Poetry."[24] Hence Wordsworth's reference to Sir Joshua Reynolds, who "observed [that 'an accurate taste in poetry'] is an acquired talent, which can only be produced by severe thought, and a long continued intercourse with the best models of composition," was a deliberate invocation of the kind of authority that "readers of superior judgment" would be disposed to accept. But Wordsworth also made his volume's provocation obvious by imagining the scene that would be created when these poems appeared, like lower-class intruders barging into a genteel eighteenth-century drawing room: these sneering "readers of superior judgment . . . accustomed to the gaudiness and inane phraseology of many modern writers . . . will look round for poetry, and will . . . enquire by what species of courtesy these attempts can be permitted to assume that *title.*" Who are *they?* Who invited *them?*

Wordsworth was, in effect, responding to the *Anti-Jacobin*'s invitation in "The New Morality" to some "bashful Genius, in some rural cell" to rise up in response to "thy Country's just alarms": "Wield in her cause thy long neglected arms: / Of lofty Satire pour th'indignant strain" (76–77). The main address of "The New Morality" (like Pope's *Dunciad*) is a call for a strong national poet to rise up and take on the task of moral regeneration which the editors had been preparing for by therapeutic satire. It is not wholly out of the question that they actually had Wordsworth in mind, and hence protectively did not mention his name. They certainly knew who he was, and their description of this ideal poet has many similarities to his career to date:

> . . . for who can tell
> What bashful Genius, in some rural cell, [Racedown? Alfoxden?]
> As year to year, and day succeeds to day, [1796–98?]
> In joyless leisure wastes his life away?
> In him the flame of early Fancy shone; [*An Evening Walk?*]
> His genuine worth his old Companions own; [Frere the old Cantab?]
> In childhood and in youth their Chief confess'd, [Wordsworth's reputation at Hawkshead and Cambridge?]
> His Master's pride [William Taylor?], his pattern to the rest.
> Now, far aloof retiring from the strife
> Of busy talents, and of active life, [London, 1795?]
> As, *from the loop-holes of retreat,* he views [remaining contacts with London friends?]
> Our Stage, Verse, Pamphlets, Politics, and News, [packets of books and newspapers sent to Racedown and Alfoxden?]

> He loaths the world,—or with reflection sad
> Concludes it irrecoverably mad;
> Of Taste, of Learning, Morals, all bereft,
> No hope, no prospect to redeem it left.
> (55–70; italics added)

"Tintern Abbey" may be in part Wordsworth's response to this invitation, adapting it to his only somewhat different purposes. At the very least, he would have been startled to read lines that hit so close to his own situation. Calls for a great new English poet had been echoing throughout the 1790s, and Wordsworth's poetic self-creation was, as we saw in the links between *The Recluse* and the *Lyrical Ballads* prefaces, intimately connected with an idea of his poetry *and* his life forming a model for national regeneration.

Maybe the *Anti-Jacobin* editors had somebody else in mind, or nobody in particular. But if they knew Francis Wrangham, they perhaps knew that he and Wordsworth had collaborated on a Juvenalian satire very much on the order of the one they call for, calling for renewed moral leadership from the upper classes. Such knowledge on their part is not at all unlikely. Canning and Frere, when they were not engaged in their semiclandestine production of the *Anti-Jacobin,* were regularly in contact with the wholly clandestine operations of the government's secret service, run by Wickham, King, and Ford, the latter two of whom had less than a year earlier received a full set of reports on the disaffected Alfoxden gang, naming Coleridge and *"Wordsworth"* in particular. John King's brother had tutored Canning's friend George Ellis, a major *Anti-Jacobin* contributor, and Frere had overlapped with Wordsworth for three years at Cambridge, and with Coleridge for one: the former singled out in undergraduate gossip for his dreamy poetical strolls along the Cam and for his vigorous walking tour across France in the summer of 1790; the latter, for the reputation of transcendent genius he brought with him even as freshman. Despite their differences in political persuasion, the groups of young men who produced the *Anti-Jacobin* and those who produced (or talked about producing) the *Philanthropist* were not very different in class and education, or in their desires for a moral reform of the country—although they saw different evils—or in their literary brilliance and ambition. Young men like Wrangham, Montagu, and Wordsworth had family political backgrounds very much like those of Canning and Frere—rather more conservative than theirs, in fact. Wordsworth in particular had a strong line of connections from his native relations with the Lowthers and the Howards, through his uncles Cookson and Robinson, to Wilberforce and thence right up to Pitt. Pitt himself was an occasional contributor to the *Anti-Jacobin*'s inspired high-jinks, though he kept a concerned eye on it, lest it go too far or be too closely connected with his government.

"The New Morality," a poem widely ignored and underrated in literary history, is one of the last representatives of a grand tradition of verse satire stretching back at least as far as Dryden. The largest target of this satiric tradition had always been excessive zeal or "enthusiasm" in religious and political matters, following the terrible events of the English civil war. Now these excesses were seen to be rising horribly renewed in a French Revolution which some well-intentioned but misguided young Englishmen seemed to want to bring back home. In this perspective the *Anti-Jacobin*'s final appeal to some "bashful Genius, in some rural cell" could have been to the young Wordsworth, putting in public, patriotic terms the appeal to his better, established self that William Cookson and John Robinson had put to him in personal, familial terms throughout the 1790s. It was a last invitation to come in from the cold, home again, to return to the fold. Instead, he left the country again—but, as we shall see, perhaps not before accepting that invitation on some kind of terms.

William and Dorothy spent another month at Shirehampton before starting their trip to Germany. At the beginning of August, Coleridge arrived back from a trip to London and across the southern counties on which he had tied up the loose ends of his complicated personal and business affairs. As soon as they met, they told Coleridge about their wonderful walk up the Wye and read him the poem that, he only now learned, formed the great climax of *Lyrical Ballads.* Enchanted, he immediately proposed that they repeat the trip for his benefit: "a dart into Wales." This followed the pattern of the past year, where one good walk was always the best excuse for another. As enthusiastic as ever, they set off the next morning at six o'clock, August 3 or 4.

Yet once again Wordsworth beheld the steep and lofty cliffs of the Wye valley, but this time after only a couple of weeks, not "five long winters," and no poetry was produced by anyone on this trip, so far as we know. They took at least a week for this jaunt, making a circular route of it, up the Wye and back down via the Usk valley, ten miles to the southwest—or perhaps the other way around.[25]

But on this trip their focus was specifically political, not obliquely so, as in Wordsworth's most recent set of "lines." The turning point of their route was at Llyswen, where the Wye and the Usk come closest together, and where John Thelwall had finally found a place where he thought he was safe from persecution. Thus the annus mirabilis of English Romanticism was framed by Coleridge and Wordsworth's two visits with "the famous Thelwall": prospective and hopeful at Alfoxden in 1797, retrospective and disappointed at Llyswen in 1798. Wordsworth had already set his "Anecdote for

Fathers" (usually dated April 1798) at "sweet Liswyn farm." The little boy in the poem, clearly young Basil Montagu, expresses his preference for his former home at "Kilve by the green sea" (directly below Alfoxden) because, when pressed repeatedly by his obtuse father for a reason, "At Kilve there was no weather-cock." Little Basil was an inveterate liar, though the poem suggests that "The Art of Lying May Be Taught" partly because of adults' habit of wheedling reasons out of children when none are needed.

Wordsworth's use of the name of Thelwall's hideaway seems a bit cavalier, like his use of Montagu's mother's name in "The Thorn," since he knew of Thelwall's continuing troubles. Or it may suggest that he empathized with these difficulties more than we have realized and that the preferences expressed in "Anecdote for Fathers" are more adult than childish. The little boy's desperate nonreason, that there was no weathercock at Kilve, might have an adult subtext: that is, here at Llyswen, we are too much reminded of which way the winds blow. (In fact, there was a weathercock at Racedown, but none at Alfoxden.)[26] Wordsworth had not, until this moment, ever been "here at Liswyn farm," and he may have revised his earlier composition accordingly.[27] Clearly the adult speaker in the poem regrets intensely his time at or near Kilve, though he will not say why, beyond the 1798 *Lyrical Ballads'* ubiquitous verb for hidden significances, "think":

> My *thoughts* on former pleasures ran;
> I *thought* of Kilve's delightful shore,
> My pleasant home, when spring began,
>
> A long, long year before.
> A day it was when I could bear
> *To think, and think, and think again;*
> With so much happiness to spare,
> I could not feel a pain.
>
> (9–16; italics added)

These lines are rarely attended to, given readers' normal concentration on the poem's humorous situation. But it certainly had been "a long, long year" for all of them.

Wordsworth in 1838 assured the second Mrs. Thelwall, "Your impression is correct that I, in company with my Sister and Mr. Coleridge, visited him at his pleasant abode on the banks of the Wye."[28] The spot was beautiful—"an enchanted dormitory," Thelwall called it—but his experiences there had not been. The local parson had stirred up opinion against him as soon as Thelwall arrived—on one occasion he was attacked with a pickax—and finally issued a general warning to his neighbors that he would shoot any intruder on his grounds.[29] Like those of Wordsworth and Coleridge at Alfoxden, his country ramblings at all hours and abstruse musings about Man, Nature, and Society made the superstitious locals imagine he was a conjuror. He now considered himself "the new Recluse," exiled from the busy urban scenes of his former triumphs. Was he taking the title back from Wordsworth, who, after the passage of this busy year in which they all shifted their priorities, might already have appeared to Thelwall as the *old* recluse?[30]

They had a lot to talk about, recalling the excitement Thelwall's appearance at Alfoxden had provoked almost exactly a year earlier. But there were no more jokes about "this being a fine place to talk treason in." The visit of the Home Office agent, eight months of excoriating attacks by the *Anti-Jacobin,* the recent arrest of Joseph Johnson, the subpoena served to Daniel Stuart, Coleridge's editor at the *Morning Post,* and the mounting war fever made them all too aware of the "the necessity [*not*] to talk treason," or anything remotely resembling it.*

There may have been some unspoken hurt feelings, if Thelwall felt himself abandoned by Coleridge, one of his last loyal friends, and as he observed the intimate attachments that had developed in the intervening year between these "three persons with one soul." There may have been some envy, too, as he heard their plans to leave the country altogether.

But if Wordsworth and Coleridge were retrenching their politics, Thelwall was doing so even more obviously. He was compiling a volume of poems in which he determinedly said good-bye to his political career, insisting on his role as "the Disciple of the Muses; not The Lecturer and Leader of Popular Societies now no more": "my soul is sick of public torment." The best poems in the volume had already been written, and were certainly read to Wordsworth and Coleridge. They expressed "the pangs of disappointed hope, and keen regrets" for a world "that kindness pays with hatred." These sentiments, written at Bridgwater the year before, when he began to realize he would not be able to live near Coleridge and Wordsworth, had already influenced Wordsworth's last-composed poem for *Lyrical Ballads* ("greeting where no kindness is"), as one after another of this young generation of the 1790s went into reclusive retirement.

*These were only the public signs of higher levels of government surveillance and repression. In January, William Wickham had returned from directing the "underground war" against France to join Portland and John King at the Home Office, bringing some of his crack agents with him. King and Richard Ford now began working together even more closely. Charles Fox paid the new arrangements a bitter compliment, calling them more effective than the secret police of the old and revolutionary French regimes combined. Wickham would have thought this underestimated them: in his report to Portland in 1801 of what the revamped "Alien Office" had accomplished, Wickham called it—without irony—"the most powerful means of observation and information . . . that ever was placed in the Hands of a Free Government." See Ann Hone, *For the Cause of Truth: Radicalism in London, 1796–1821* (Oxford: Clarendon Press, 1982), 74–79.

Returning to Bristol, William and Dorothy collected their few belongings and left town around midmonth, traveling across country with Coleridge and Basil by foot, wagon, coach, and post chaise to London.[31] They made a wide detour north to visit the duke of Marlborough's Blenheim Palace, at Woodstock, stopping the night at nearby Oxford, where Wordsworth got his first look at Southey's alma mater.

They stayed in London till mid-September, when they departed for Germany via Yarmouth. During their month in London, they hoped to observe *Lyrical Ballads'* reception firsthand, since after "Tintern Abbey" was handed over to Cottle, Dorothy expected the book to appear in six weeks.[32] Instead, they found themselves involved in last-minute efforts to make sure it would appear at all.

After all the protracted negotiations with Cottle to publish a book that would help defray their travel expenses, the deal suddenly appeared to be unraveling. Although a stock of books had been printed up in Bristol by late August, Cottle seemed to be getting cold feet, for either financial or political reasons or both—reasons not easily separable in the publishing business in England in 1798. He seems to have learned that Southey intended to write a negative review of the volume (which he did, in the *Critical Review* for October, the earliest notice the book received). Though such a motive for selling the impression or its copyright "seems almost too bad to believe," it is hardly out of the realm of practical morality in the publishing business then or now.[33] Cottle contacted a large London publisher (Longman) about sharing in the publication in order to spread the risk, an arrangement he had worked out with Longman earlier in the year for the second edition of Southey's *Joan of Arc.*[34] Wordsworth initially helped in this effort, but when Longman showed no interest, he on his own approached Joseph Johnson, without telling him that Cottle had already purchased the copyright for *Lyrical Ballads.*

Johnson, still the most prestigious liberal publisher in the country, apparently agreed, consistent with his loyalty to his authors, and even though he was soon to go to jail for six months for publishing Gilbert Wakefield's *Reply to Some Parts of . . . [Bishop Watson's] Address to the People of Great Britain.* This ruling, which Fox considered the final destruction of liberty of the press in England,[35] sent Wakefield into Dorchester jail for two years, whence he emerged a dying man: more evidence to Wordsworth and his friends of the present costs of careers based on battling the established order. (This incident is also referred to in "The New Morality," both poem and cartoon.) They interpreted the sentence very much as the *Monthly Magazine* would two years later on the occasion of Wakefield's death: a sign of the government's determination to pick "a victim of name and character sufficient to inspire a wide alarm."[36] Wordsworth and Coleridge were already enough "inspired" by signs of alarm to take steps ensuring that they would not be the government's next victims "of name and character."

Wordsworth asked Cottle to send his already printed books to Johnson and apply to Richard Wordsworth for whatever money he felt he had coming for his work so far. Cottle, however, refused, out of either anger or embarrassment that Wordsworth should have so little confidence in his marketing skills. (Wordsworth was right: Cottle went bankrupt eighteen months later.) Instead, Cottle worked out a different proxy arrangement with the reputable, but not notably liberal, Arch brothers in Gracechurch Street, and the famous volume finally hobbled into public view bearing their imprint on October 4, two weeks after its anonymous authors had left the country.

The controversy began as soon as the volume appeared, with the review that Southey had primed and ready from his inside knowledge of the authors and their poems—including his knowledge that they would be out of the country when it appeared. Southey excoriated "the author" for wasting his talents on an ill-conceived language experiment. He blasted almost all the ballads, infamously dismissing "The Ancient Mariner" as "a Dutch attempt at German sublimity."[37] His criticisms are all the more remarkable since Wordsworth's ballads of everyday life in the underclass were the poems most like the "Botany Bay Eclogues," which Southey himself had published in 1797, that drew him into the *Anti-Jacobin*'s main line of fire. But of course that was the very reason for Southey's venom: to get himself out of the "Jacobin" camp by any means necessary. His closing praise for "Tintern Abbey" as not inferior to anything "in the whole range of English poetry" was too little, too late. But his conclusion, that its author had wasted his talents "upon uninteresting subjects," was one that Wordsworth would soon come to agree with, in practice.

Though Wordsworth and Coleridge did not learn about this review for several months, it only confirmed what they already knew, that in England in 1798 it was becoming impossible to tell friends from enemies. This was another reason for going to Germany. In Wordsworth's case, it may be that he tried to solve the problem by deciding to be friends with his enemies and to respond to government repression by joining in its administration, even as he appeared to be escaping from it.

25

"MR. WORDSWORTH"

Hamburg, 1798

"To paid Mr. Wordsworth's Draft, £92/12/-"
(duke of Portland's secret paybook,
June 13, 1799)

With John Chester serving as their baggage handler and all-purpose trip manager, Coleridge and the Wordsworths arrived at Yarmouth on September 15. They stayed the night on shore, giving Coleridge time to look up the disappointed Pantisocrat George Burnett, now tutoring Southey's younger brother; they had a long recriminatory conversation. Burnett was politically disillusioned, a common feeling at the time, but he also felt personally betrayed in his former enthusiasm for Coleridge.[1] Wordsworth too was about to learn more regarding the cost of following this brilliant lodestar who drew disciples after him like a comet, in directions impossible to chart. In Germany, however, Coleridge was the one who followed his course, Wordsworth the apparently directionless one, with decisive results for both.

There was also in Yarmouth at this time a Home Office agent named Walsh, son of the James Walsh who had visited Somerset the year before and fingered the "gang of disaffected Englishmen."[2] He was stationed there as part of a new liaison set up between the Home Office and the Alien Office in July, to take note of departing and arriving foreigners or other suspicious persons, check their papers, and take instructions from Whitehall as to whether they should be allowed to proceed or asked to leave the country.[3] Given the continuing high level of Home Office surveillance of Thelwall (Yarmouth had been the scene of one of the worst attacks on him in 1797), and given Coleridge's notoriety wherever he went, this next stage of the Somerset group's disaffection was duly noted.[4]

At this same time another of the former Pantisocrats, Charles Lloyd, went to Cambridge to study Greek with Wordsworth's brother Christopher. The Reverend Cookson, ever on the lookout for his nephews' reputations and determined to save the youngest, having lost his elder, wrote to Christopher recommending caution, asking "whether or no intimacy with so marked a character might not be prejudicial to his academical interests." "This," said Coleridge, sardonically reporting the incident, "is his usual mild manner."[5] We can imagine what Cookson thought of William's departure for Germany. But Christopher assured Cookson that Lloyd was no longer a democrat, and for textual proof transcribed some favorable passages from *Edmund Oliver.* He was lucky to find a copy, for Lloyd's father, to recoup his son's reputation, was trying to buy up and destroy all remaining copies of the novel, which he considered insufficiently anti-Jacobincal. Families as well as governments were in hot pursuit, conducting search-and-destroy missions against any remaining vestiges of revolutionary sentiment in their heirs and scions. It was a good time to leave the country.

The party of four departed Yarmouth on September 16 at precisely 11 A.M. and spent two days crossing the North Sea, sailing almost due east from Yarmouth to Cuxhaven, at the mouth of the Elbe. They had good winds on a swelling sea. The Wordsworths retired immediately down into their cabin and were, according to Coleridge, "shockingly" sick the whole time. Coleridge was impressed by the momentous occasion of leaving his country for the first time, but his spirits were raised when a gentleman standing by pointed to the sea and said, "This, too, is a Briton's country."[6]

Coleridge had a great time crossing, his enjoyment not at all "decreased by the Sight of the Basons [*sic*] from the Cabin containing green and yellow specimens of the inner Man & brought up by the Cabin-boy every three minutes."[7] His account of it reads like the standard chauvinistic traveler's joke, featuring a Dane, a Swede, a Prussian, a Hanoverian, and a Frenchman, the humor based mainly on their poor command of English—by an Englishman who spoke no other modern tongue. The Dane, returning home from his St. Croix plantation to enjoy an income of £10,000 a year, latched onto Coleridge by way of "pioneering to his own Vanity." " 'Vat imagination! vat language! vat fast science! vat eyes!—vat a milk vite forehead!—O my Heafen! You are a God!' " Amusing as this is, we observe that the Dane picked up remarkably quickly on just those points of mind and body that Coleridge most prided himself on. Rich as he was, the Dane "declaimed like a Member of the Corresponding Society about the Rights of Man; & how . . . he thought the poorest Man alive his Equal." To prove it, he would send the Swede, "Mr. Nobility," an impoverished baron dependent on him, to fetch wine from their cabin instead of Jack, his mulatto serving boy: *"And the Swede went!"* Coleridge let himself be identified as "Un Philosophe," though he claimed it was a title for which he had "the greatest disgust." The Dane proceeded to attack Christianity like "that rude blunderer, Mr. Thomas Paine," until Coleridge professed his belief in God, whereupon he sank "50 fathoms immediately" in the Dane's graces.

The Hanoverian was the son of an army contractor living in Soho who had made a fortune from the war. The Prussian was a traveling merchant who looked suspicious and told obscene stories, "a few valuable as philosophical facts of the manners of the Countries, concerning the natives of which he related them." They were translated by another passenger, the *"English* Youth," "a genteel Youth who spoke German perfectly." By the end of the trip both the young Englishman and the dubious Prussian had got themselves adopted into the Dane's "Train of Dependents."

Coleridge hardly slept at all during the trip—Chester seems to have done the sleeping for the group as well. On the second night, "I partook of the Hanoverian's & Dane's wines, & Pine apples—told them some hundred Jokes, and passed as many of my own. Danced all together a sort of wild dance on the Deck—Wordsworth and Sister bad as ever."[8] When everybody else passed out, he turned his roving eye toward nature: "About 4 o'clock I saw a wild duck swimming on the waves—a single solitary wild duck—You cannot conceive how interesting a thing it looked in that round objectless desart of waters."

The Frenchman was sick during the crossing, down in the cabins with the Wordsworths, and by the time they got into the calmer waters of the Elbe, "Wordsworth had introduced himself to a kind of confidential acquaintance with the French Emigrant who appeared a man of sense and who was in his manners a most complete gentleman. He seemed about fifty. It was agreed that if possible we should live together." This they did, until they left Hamburg for Goslar. The Frenchman, whose name was De Leutre (Coleridge spelled it De Loutre), "talked with rapture of Paris under the monarchy—& seemed not a little enamored of London, where he had lived in style, & where his favorite Niece resided, a married woman." De Leutre was being deported by order of the duke of Portland because (he said) of the influence of some émigrés who were angry at him for refusing to lend them money.[9] "He seemed very deeply *cut* at heart—a man without hopes or wishes," though he "attached no blame either to the Alien act, or to the minister who had exerted it against him," which suggests a direct personal contact with Portland in the matter. He took it all so calmly that Coleridge asserted, "Such a man, I think, I could dare warrant guiltless of *espionage* in any service, most of all in that of the present French directory."[10] But this—setting aside the nil value of a Coleridgean warrant at the Home Office—

may have been exactly the point: not that De Leutre was a French agent but that his genteel equanimity, and his interest in Wordsworth, arose from his being an English one, or both.

At Cuxhaven, they negotiated with the ship's captain to take them up the river to Hamburg by packet boat. They were delayed by thick fog, and the ship had to be rowed with a pilot part of the way. As soon as they landed in Hamburg, Wordsworth and De Leutre set off in search of lodgings, leaving Chester to guard Dorothy and the luggage, while Coleridge hastened to deliver his letters of recommendation to the Wedgwoods' agents, the Von Axens. To their surprise, most hotels and inns were full, but they found rooms at last in Der Wilde Mann, which Coleridge thought must be named after its landlord. It was dirty and expensive, like almost everything they saw, but it had to do. Dorothy was shocked to be shown to her room by "a *man*," but they kept their complaints to themselves, for they found the Germans ready to fight if criticized. When Wordsworth complained about the price of bread, the baker knocked the loaf out of his hands and refused to refund his money.[11] Coleridge briefly considered accepting the Dane's invitation to stay at the King of England, on the comfortable Godwinian principle that he could learn something about rich Jacobin fellow travelers by observing them at luxurious close quarters. But he thought the better of it, though he accepted some hospitality from the Swede at the almost equally grand Hotel de Hamburgh.[12] Oddly, Wordsworth did not at first stay at the inn with Dorothy but, leaving her in the care of Chester and De Leutre, went to the Duke of York hotel, run by an ex-seaman. He went there to see John Baldwin, the brother of James Losh's wife, Cecilia.[13] Why he should have had to stay in the same hotel with Baldwin is not clear, unless he, like Coleridge, was arranging other local contacts.

Hamburg was a neutral city and Germany the only country outside Scandinavia open to travelers, because of the threatening presence of French armies almost everywhere else in Europe.[14] The city was teeming with agents and spies from all European governments. It was the hub of French efforts to keep the German principalities out of the war—and of English determination to draw them into it. Its atmosphere was something like that of Zurich or Casablanca in the early years of World War II. Intense political infighting had begun in October of 1797, when Napoleon forced Austria out of the war by a combination of military defeats and territorial concessions, ending the so-called First War of the Allied Coalition, ratified in the Treaty of Campo Formio (named after the village in northern Italy where it was signed). This left England alone in the field against republican France. The treaty's terms for settling the peace of Europe were still being worked out in a diplomatic convention at Rastatt, near Baden-Baden in southwest Germany. This treaty, along with the coup d'état of 18 Fructidor (September 4,

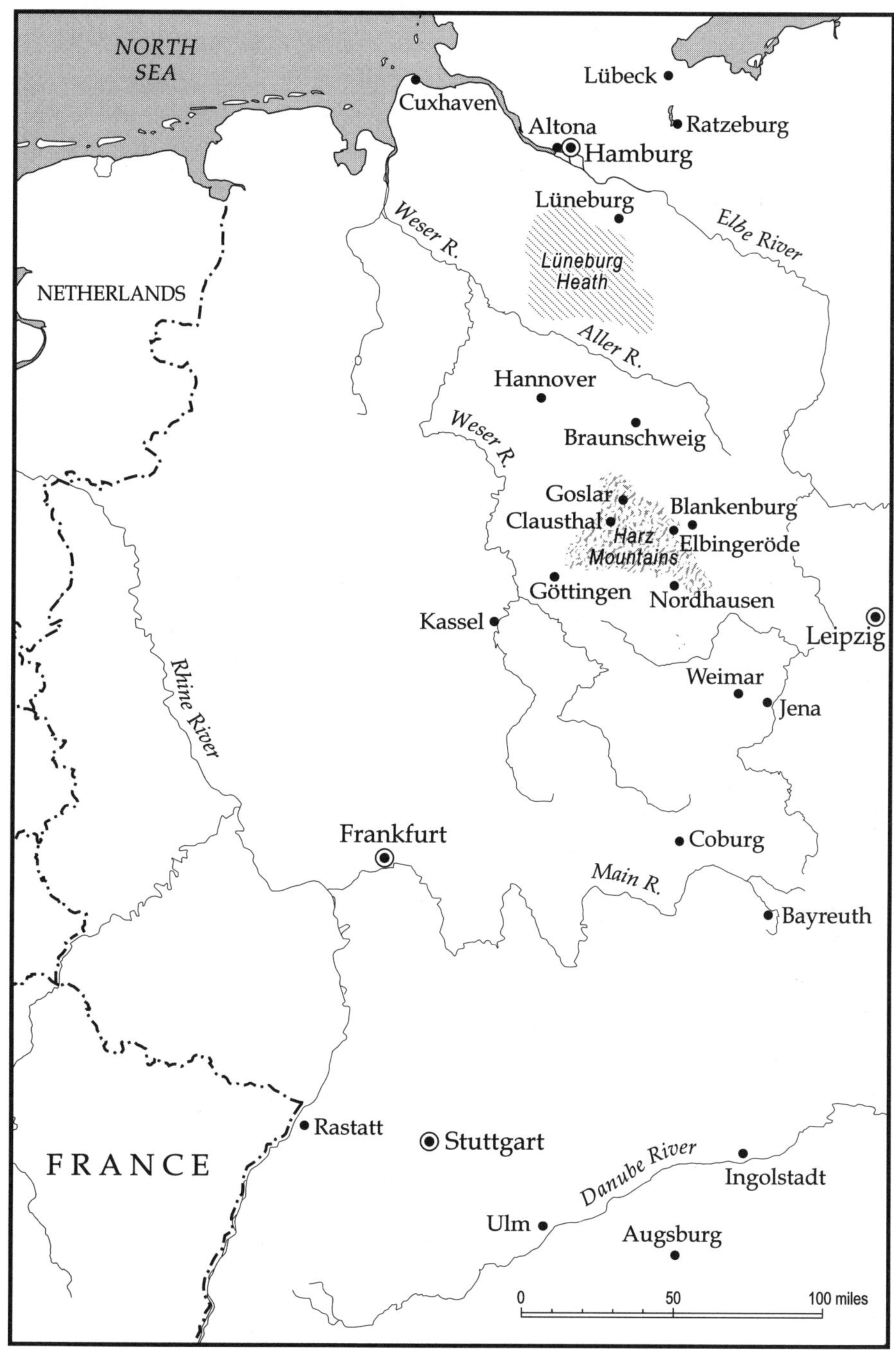

Wordsworth's and Coleridge's Germany, 1798–1799.

1797), when the principal royalist directors, deputies, and generals (including Pichegru) were arrested, had ended British hopes of influencing French politics by "electoral" means—that is, by bribing the directors and spending huge sums of money to influence key provincial elections.

These were the setbacks that had determined young George Canning to bring British public opinion solidly behind the war effort, resisting Grenville's despair "of any permanent tranquillity in the midst of all this wreck and convulsion of everything around us."[15] On top of his job as Grenville's undersecretary in the Foreign Office, Canning's zeal led him to start up the *Anti-Jacobin* to combat ideological liberalism in the press and in contemporary poetry. The political reverses of autumn 1797 also meant that continuing British clandestine efforts on the Continent came to depend increasingly on the advice and actions of desperate royalists. These efforts were directed by James Talbot (a.k.a. James Tindal), whose so-called Swabian agency operated in southern Germany, cooperating with the royalist Comité de Bayreute, with the ultimate aim—as Grenville learned with alarm in January 1799—of assassinating all five members of the new Directory.[16] In September of 1798 Talbot was authorized to spend up to £400,000 to raise and equip an army of Swiss *affidés* (recruits sworn to secrecy) that would be the tool to prize Austria out of the Campo Formio treaty. Talbot's authorization came in a letter dated September 11, carried from London by his secretary and confidential courier, his younger brother, Robert. The younger Talbot must have taken a ship for Germany close to the time of Wordsworth's departure (September 16), making us think of that unidentified *"English* Youth" on the boat who spoke German so fluently and who seemed to be a companion of the sinister Prussian.

To monitor these intensified activities in Hamburg, Grenville had set up a British chargé d'affaires in May of 1798, Sir James Craufurd (or Crawfurd), to report back to London the actions of all suspicious persons arriving from Britain.[17] Craufurd thus became the focal point for the receipt and forwarding of intelligence from what he called his "own police force" in Hamburg, though in fact the Foreign Office had many other agents on the ground that Craufurd didn't know about.[18] In practice, "suspicious persons" meant mainly Irishmen, especially after the defeat of the French expeditionary force under Humbert in August, and the demise of a short-lived "Republic of Ireland."* Irishmen were flooding into Hamburg in September, including leaders like Napper Tandy; this was why the inns and hotels were so crowded. Craufurd was a zealous worker, who considered Hamburg more a *foyer de révolution* than an *entrepôt de commerce.* At the outset of his

*Wordsworth's college contemporary Robert Stewart, Viscount Castlereagh, by now a member of both the Irish and the British Parliaments, was acting chief secretary for Ireland at the time, and played an active military role as well as a political one in suppressing the rebellion.

work, which lasted till 1800, he was suspicious of everybody. But over the course of two years he moderated his zeal as he saw how difficult it was to tell friends from enemies in this place at this time, and came to appreciate the effect his words might have on innocent people's lives.

There is no mention in Craufurd's dispatches of Wordsworth or Coleridge; their names probably appeared in supplementary lists, now lost, of "English citizens," whom Craufurd normally did not comment on. But on September 25, in the week that Wordsworth and Coleridge were getting settled in Hamburg, Craufurd wrote Grenville that he had taken an extraordinary risk (and paid an extraordinary bribe of 250 louis) in order to obtain the names of three agents of the Directory residing in London, and of "some standing in the commercial world." He had arranged to be hidden in the apartments of the French chargé d'affaires, where a council of confidential agents met by night to read over dispatches. Taking such a risk was unusual for the cautious Craufurd; if he'd been detected, it would have caused a serious international incident. But he thought the prize was worth the price: he learned that the three agents were M. Grefulke (or Grefule), a Mr. Bibbes, and one De Leutre, "who we have since heard has been sent away under the Alien Bill."[19] Hence, Coleridge's character witness notwithstanding, he and Wordsworth were traveling with a known agent of the Directory, with whom Wordsworth soon struck up a "very confidential" relationship. They themselves could have been the means by which Sir James had "since heard" of De Leutre's deportation, since he was writing to report a successful scoop, but found that he had been anticipated, sometime shortly before September 25, in revealing the names of one of his prizes.

On September 28, at the end of Wordsworth's and Coleridge's first week in Hamburg, Craufurd wrote to assure William Wickham, Grenville's chief of foreign espionage, "You may rely on the most scrupulous caution respecting *the two individuals* mentioned to me in your letter" (Craufurd's emphasis).[20] A month later, after the poets had left town, Craufurd again referred to "the person whose *name is not to be mentioned*" (his emphasis).[21] Could these two individuals have been Wordsworth and Coleridge? The shift from two unmentionable names to one is noteworthy: they evidently came to Craufurd's attention as a pair, but only one was actually involved in secret business. This circumstance fits well with everything we know about the two poets' behavior, both at Alfoxden and aboard the ship from Yarmouth: Coleridge talked a lot but was harmless, Wordsworth was silent but "dark" and had entered into a "confidential" relation with at least one suspect person, M. de Leutre.*

*There are other details in Craufurd's subsequent correspondence that suggest he may be referring to Wordsworth: for example, the person in question is clearly operating somewhere in the country away from Hamburg, and has had a prior association with Richard Ford: "our friend here,

A year later, after Wordsworth had left Germany, another query about De Leutre came to Grenville's attention from the British law officer at Hamburg. De Leutre was now identified as Baron de Leutre, "His Majesty's Electoral Minister residing at this court." This suggests that De Leutre had switched sides and revealed—or more likely invented—his title. The nature of the law officer's inquiry was technical and trivial: whether De Leutre's English secretary was obligated to pay taxes on his property in Wandsworth. But the secretary's name was "Mr. Best," and Thomas Best was the name of one of the contributors to the *Philanthropist* in 1795, who had also worked with Thelwall on the *Imperial and Biographical Magazine.*[22] The mélange of personalities and possibilities here is typical of the time and the place, and the near-impossibility of sorting out how they came to know each other is of a piece with the uncertainty with which we must regard their political allegiances and actions. But if De Leutre had his secretary with him when he left England, and if this man was Thomas Best, formerly of the published *Philanthropist,* he could well have been the means of introducing Wordsworth, formerly of the projected *Philanthropist,* into his new "confidential" relations with him. He is also another candidate for the *"English* Youth" on board their ship who spoke fluent German.

The point of all these observations becomes clearer the subsequent June, when the duke of Portland made the following entry in his payment book for secret intelligence services rendered: "To paid Mr. Wordsworth's Draft, £92/12/-." This information, published here for the first time, was not known publicly until 1993, when Portland's journal was offered for sale to the Wordsworth Library.[23] By itself, it is not conclusive evidence of Wordsworth's acting on behalf of the new "Secret Department." Wordsworth is not a rare name, though not a very common one, and if any other first name than "William" could be attached to this entry, its significance for our story would fall to the ground (though a Richard, a John, a Christopher, or a Robinson would be almost as interesting). But when we see the context in which the entry is made, its significance tilts rather sharply toward young Wordsworth:

6/4	Crawfurd	£60
6/11	Ford	£200
6/13	To paid Mr. Wordsworth's Draft, £92/12/-	
6/15	Crawfurd	£170
" "	"	£185

who is not to be named . . . has hitherto received [his monthly allowance] through Mr. Ford, if I remember well" (Hampshire PRO, Wickham 1/66/f.23; April 2, 1799). See Appendix B for a more detailed analysis of Craufurd's correspondence on this point.

That is to say, that in Portland's office, where financial accountability had done as much as espionage skills to put the British secret service on a modern footing, Wordsworth's name appears in a series of entries of payments made to the chief British agent in Hamburg, and one to the Home Office official whom James Walsh reported from Somerset in August of 1797 as likely to recognize *"Wordsworth* a name I think known to Mr. Ford." In a well-run office like Portland's, disbursements to related accounts were made so far as possible at the same time, on vouchers or receipts related to similar items of business. Nor is this proximity of Wordsworth's name to Craufurd's a random accident: a penciled note on the page opposite this column reads, "Expended to 4 June 1799, [for?] payment of 3 Bills drawn by Wordsworth and Crawfurd." This refers to additional payments made earlier. The payments to Craufurd and Ford are round lump sums, either regular allotments or bonuses, to judge from Craufurd's expressions of gratitude in May 1799 for the favor Grenville and the king had bestowed on his efforts.[24] But the payment made to Mr. Wordsworth looks more like the settling of a specific claim or expense account—for an amount that is very close to the amount Wordsworth drew upon the Wedgwoods' agents during his time in Germany.

Why payments to Craufurd, who was a Foreign Office agent, should appear in the books of Portland, the Home Secretary, is a good question. (Ford, we know, was the main liaison between the two offices that constituted the "Secret Department.") The most likely answer again points toward Germany. Wickham, the leader of Britain's underground war against France, had been forced to withdraw from Switzerland in the wake of 18 Fructidor. He retired first to Frankfurt, where he stayed with Captain Charles Craufurd (one of Sir James's brothers), a wounded military hero and translator of German books on warfare.[25] By early 1798 Wickham was back in London, where he was made undersecretary of the Home Office, the same position Canning held in the Foreign Office (he subsequently became Portland's private secretary). Thus the Englishman who knew more than anyone else about the government's intrigues on the Continent became the chief executive officer of the agency charged with domestic surveillance, while his opposite number, Canning, who led a semiclandestine, semiofficial literary war against the government's domestic ideological opponents (primarily journalists and poets), took over responsibility for correspondence with the remnants of Wickham's operation in Germany and Switzerland. Given the critical nature of England's political and military situation in 1798, when international and domestic affairs were inextricably tangled by combined fears of insurrection and invasion, these two men were in almost daily contact. Whether in all their conversations they ever put together the name *"Wordsworth* . . . known to Mr. Ford" with those of "C———-dge and S-—they, L-—-d and L-—b, & Co." known to Canning, we cannot be sure. But we do know they had a constant need for a supply of agents whose ability to report and carry messages confidentially could be guaranteed by patriotic loyalty, good pay, or threat of exposure, or any combination thereof. What we make of Wordsworth's place in this string of possibilities will depend in part on our interpretation in Chapter 27 of the gap in his chronological record between February 23 and April 20, 1799. But already a new significance emerges for his "kind of confidential acquaintance" with M. de Leutre, deported by Portland.*[26]

The city to which Wordsworth and Coleridge came to escape an England where they found free expression all but impossible, was if anything more spy-ridden than England itself. E. P. Thompson a generation ago created some excitement about the political dimension of the birth of English Romanticism when he said that Wordsworth and Coleridge "were hopping the draft" when they went to Germany, to avoid "the vortex of an unbearable political conflict."[27] This was a good image for 1968, when waves of student protest were breaking in Europe and America. But there was no draft in England at the time; indeed, Pitt specifically ruled conscription out of his war plans, recognizing what protests it would cause. Even if there had been, Wordsworth and Coleridge would not have been affected by it, for many reasons, ranging from their age and class standing to James Walsh's report, to Coleridge's inglorious record of previous service in the dragoons as "Silas Tomkyn Comberbacke." They went to Germany for the reasons they stated, and rather than hopping the draft, they may have been joining "the Firm," as "le Manufacture" was called in English. But in either case, to go from Alfoxden to Hamburg to escape from political conflict, or to avoid suspicion, was going from a small frying pan into a very large fire.

In Hamburg's shadowy world of spies and intrigue there were several people who had already touched the margins of Wordsworth's life earlier,

*For any hypothesis, there are disconfirming possibilities. The "Mr. Wordsworth" might be Wordsworth's cousin, Robinson Wordsworth, who had been installed in the Customs Office at Harwich, thanks to the influence of John Robinson. But this hypothesis faces difficulties greater than those which would read the entry as referring to William Wordsworth. First, William Wordsworth was almost certainly the only "Wordsworth" in Germany at this time. Second, why would Portland be paying Robinson Wordsworth for secret expenses? Robinson was new and young in the customs service; his attachment to John Robinson might have made him "serviceable" in the usual way (i.e., bribable), but it's hard to come up with any reason for such service. In many weeks of poring over these documents at the PRO over several years, I have come across only one reference of any kind to Robinson Wordsworth: a pro forma instruction from William Wickham on April 24, 1799, that he should release the Captain Cowen he had lately arrested "by Virtue of a warrant from the Duke of Portland" (PRO, HO 5/4/343). This was the normal routine of business at the time: the same sort of instructions James Walsh Jr. regularly received at Yarmouth; whereas the links between William Wordsworth, the Walshes Sr. and Jr., Richard Ford and John King, Craufurd, Coleridge, and Germany are more extensive, more plausible, and, frankly, more exciting.

whom he would have recognized if he saw them in the street or heard their names, and perhaps would have sought out—or more likely avoided—accordingly. Léonard Bourdon, the "Jacobin Schoolmaster" and persecutor of Paul Vallon, had been asked to leave Hamburg in May for advancing French interests too provocatively. But he was still represented by his secretary, William Duckett, whom the French delighted to call Descartes. Duckett had attended the meeting of the British Club of Paris on November 18, 1792, and signed its address to the French Convention, as had Nicholas Madgett, another Irishman from France who was also in Hamburg at this time; both were well marked by Craufurd. There is good reason to think that Wordsworth was also present at that momentous dinner.[28] Duckett and Madgett were the same age as Coleridge and Wordsworth, and had similar literary skills and interests, Duckett having written some flaming articles signed "Junius Redivivus" in 1795 in Ireland, while Madgett's specialty, as a former language teacher, was to draw up papers on English matters for the Directory and translate English newspapers.

M. de Leutre himself was well known to members of the French community in Hamburg.[29] He seems most likely to have been Joseph-Antoine Deleutre, from Avignon, who as papal delegate to the National Assembly in 1791–92 protested the atrocities of terrorists in his region. He (or his son) is described as a merchant, "fort riche et, en politique, ardent légitimiste": hardly a profile calculated to make him persona non grata to the duke of Portland.[30] He said he was "an intimate Friend of the Abbé de Lille, the famous Poet" (1743–1816), whom Wordsworth admired very much and whose verses on the gardens of La Source below Orléans he had invoked in a long footnote linking gardens, mistresses, and English exiles' secret retreats while finishing *Descriptive Sketches* and waiting for Annette's delivery in Orléans.[31] De Leutre took William and Dorothy to see a French painter's work on September 25, where Dorothy noted that "a very nice chearful looking fille de chambre seemed very glad to see Monsr. de Loutre."[32] Dorothy was alert to nuances of relations between the sexes, but it is hard to tell if she is being sophisticated or naive here, noting the effects of De Leutre's charm or his prior acquaintance in Hamburg—the latter possibility one of several undercutting the truth of De Leutre's account to Coleridge of his reasons for being there.

On September 21 Coleridge records that he "went to John Frederic Hauze to enquire about John Taylor's Carriage."[33] The first name might be all one name, or it might be an example of Coleridge's new habit of tossing any German and French words he learned into his writing: that is, John Frederic's *Haus.* (In the next sentence he writes, "Went with Mr Klopstock to the Voiturier to look at Carriages.") Could this have been John Frederick Pinney, who was supposed to be reading law in London at this time? We know he had a penchant for fooling his father about what he was doing, especially when it concerned the liberal intelligentsia he admired so much, compared with the world of slave plantations he wanted desperately to escape. Several of Craufurd's entries concern "One Penny an Englishman arrived from England in the packet of 1st of November. This man excites considerable suspicion having passed and repassed very frequently between England and the Continent for the last twelve months."[34] The name Pinney, we have seen, was commonly spelled Pinny or Penny: the more so when recorded from oral information, such as Craufurd usually received.*

John Hurford Stone, Helen Williams's consort, was also in Hamburg when Wordsworth arrived. He too had attended the November 1792 banquet at White's Hotel, and was known to Wordsworth. He was first noticed by Craufurd on September 28, just before the Wordsworths left town. On that same day Craufurd also noted the creation of a Theophilanthropic Society, in which "Cole an Englishman" was considered one of the leading members. Would Coleridge visit a meeting of the same society he had been guiltily associated with, bearing an ass's head, by Gillray two months before? This "Cole" was not an orally misreported *Cole*ridge, but he was someone Coleridge and Wordsworth could well have known, for he was the husband of Holcroft's daughter. (Holcroft himself came out to visit them the following May, just after the Wordsworths left, another radical émigré of 1798–99). There was also an active Philomathean Society, of the type Wordsworth and his friends had been associated with in London in 1795.[35]

Intrigue was so thick in Hamburg that you could cut it, or else too deep to cut through easily to any solid truth; but it certainly could not be avoided. Wordsworth and Coleridge were very well known to powerful persons in both the Foreign and the Home Offices, and their appearance in Hamburg would not have gone unremarked. Furthermore, they were highly noticeable. As Coleridge noted, "to be an Englishman in Germany is to be an angel." Everything, from sticking plasters to carriages, suburban landscaping, coffeehouses and hotels were called "English," both from long-standing affection for England's Hanoverian kings and dukes and, more immediately, for England's resistance to Napoleon.[36] England was called "The Great Nation," an honorific satire on France's officially designating itself *la grande nation.* Wordsworth and Coleridge were greeted especially warmly arriving when they did, just as the news of Nelson's victory in the Battle of the Nile reached Hamburg, along with that of Cornwallis's victory over Humbert and the Irish rebels at Ballynamuck on September 15. When Coleridge and

*If the owner of the carriage was John Taylor, former editor of the *Morning Post* and later proprietor of the *Sun* and the *True Briton,* the trail of espionage contacts is extended, for Taylor was one of the leading informers in Portland's stable of suborned London journalists. This John Taylor was one of eight recipients of presentation copies of *Lyrical Ballads* in 1801.

Chester walked into a concert, the orchestra, without any advance notice, broke into "Rule, Britannia!" to honor the two English strangers, and treated them to a dinner afterward.[37]

Dorothy's took little notice of great-power politics, but she did notice the social formations they produced. Her journal resembles Mary Wollstonecraft's *Letters Written during a Short Residence in Sweden, Norway, and Denmark,* a best-seller of 1796, when Dorothy and William were attentively involved in the lives and works of Godwin and Wollstonecraft. The resemblance is not surprising, since they cover some of the same ground (Wollstonecraft's tour ends in Hamburg), but it is noteworthy because Wordsworth's and especially Coleridge's poems of 1797–98 are shot through with verbal echoes and visual images from *A Short Residence.*[38]

Dorothy noted especially various kinds of moral contrasts: for example, between the cleanliness of persons and the filth in the streets, or between the constant cheating and price gouging they suffered from innkeepers, waiters, and shopkeepers, and the relative absence of begging and fighting in the streets of Hamburg compared with those of England. On her first morning she noted the difference between upper- and lower-class women's dress. "Ladies . . . some without handkerchiefs and their necks entirely exposed, long shawls of various colours thrown over their shoulders. The women of the lower orders dressed with great modesty."[39] "Notwithstanding the dirt of the houses, . . . the lower orders of women seemed in general much cleaner in their persons than the same rank in England." She could not get over the neatness of the insides of houses in nearby villages, compared to the "quite disgusting" stench of human sewage in the streets outside, and she was shocked to see a well-dressed little girl lift her petticoats and do her "business" in full view of the promenading crowd.[40]

Wordsworth and Coleridge also paid some attention to the condition of women. On his first night Coleridge noted that he "saw in the Streets not one Prostitute. I found out afterwards that they all live in one Street near Altona, and never appear out of their Houses, as Prostitutes." His account of how he found this out suggests that he might have gone looking. On Friday the 28th he walked "after dinner . . . with Wordsworth to Altona [a large suburb, "bearing the same relation to Hamburgh, as Islington to London"]—found the Prostitutes all in one street / had seen none before.—Child on ramparts riding on a saddled goat.—Divine sunset/rich light deeper than sand over the Woods that blackened in the blaze."[41] All parts of this entry are "Coleridgean," not just the sunset description.

Wordsworth, for his part, took over Dorothy's pen to record in her journal an altercation between, it would seem, a prostitute and a customer: "Yesterday saw a man of about fifty years of age beating a woman decently dressed and about 37 years of age. He struck her on the breast several times, and beat her also with his stick. The expressions in her face and attitude were half of anger and half of a spirit of resistance. What her offence had been we could not learn. It was in the public street. He was better dressed than she was, and evidently a stranger, and this brutal treatment did not excite the smallest indignation in the breast of the spectators. They seemed rather inclined to take the man's part."[42] In England, this might have become a poem like "Poor Susan" or "The Female Vagrant." But, except for a facetious verse about the cold winter, Wordsworth wrote not a line of poetry about anything he saw in Germany.

Almost all their first impressions were responses to the condition of the lower classes as compared to those in England. They came as liberal young intellectuals concerned about the state of European society after five years of war. In addition to special attention to women, they took frequent note of the treatment of Jews, who as Coleridge said were "horribly, unnaturally oppressed & persecuted all throughout Germany."[43] Sometimes they observed them from a dominant class perspective: "passed through a nest of Jews." Sometimes they used them as a cultural reference point to highlight by contrast the extremes dishonesty they experienced in all their dealings: shopping for a portmanteau to carry their clothes and books, Dorothy remarked that the only honest shopkeeper she found in a whole street of merchants was "a Jewess." And strolling out on a Sunday to suburban Blankenese, Dorothy witnessed an altercation that closely parallels the one Wordsworth saw between the prostitute and the "stranger":

> It was a fine morning but very windy. When we got nearly through the town we saw a surly-looking German driving a poor Jew forward with foul language, and making frequent use of a stick which he had in his hand. The countenance of the Jew expressed neither anger nor surprise nor agitation; he spoke, but with meekness, and unresisting pursued his way, followed by his inhuman driver, whose insolence we found was supported by law: the Jew had no right to *reign* in the city of Hamburgh, as a German told us in broken English. The soldiers who are stationed at the drawbridge looked very surly at him, and the countenances of the by-standers expressed cold unfeeling cruelty. We pass many gentlemen's houses on the road to Blankenese.[44]

With M. de Leutre and Coleridge, they attended a performance of Möller's *Count Waldron* (1776), translated for the French theater. This was probably the single play most responsible for Wordsworth's denunciation of "sickly and stupid German Tragedies" in his 1800 preface to *Lyrical Ballads* as one of the contemporary abuses of language and culture that he aimed to reform. Wordsworth walked out before it was over, but Coleridge's synopsis suggests that *Count Waldron* was very stupid indeed: "Bless me! why it is worse than our modern English plays!"[45]

They discussed the play, and the sad state of literature it reflected, with Friedrich Klopstock (1724–1803), the grand old man of German poetry. They had met him by chance, because his brother Victor was the business partner of the Wedgwoods' agent; Victor was almost as old as his aged brother, but Wordsworth and Coleridge delighted to call him "YOUNG Klopstock," playing on the currency of the adjective all over Europe at this time from the continuing popularity of Goethe's *The Sorrows of Young Werther* (1774).[46] Their visits with Klopstock were the high point of their stay in Hamburg—for Wordsworth, of his whole time in Germany, as far as learning about the nation's culture was concerned. Wordsworth spoke to Klopstock in French; Coleridge resorted to Latin, or used Wordsworth as an interpreter.

Although generally disappointed with the old man's opinions and ignorance of English culture, they respected him as "the father of German poetry." The subjective perspective and expressive use of language in Klopstock's *Odes,* written half a century earlier, is said to mark the break with the Spinozistic rationalism of early eighteenth-century German literature.[47] Thus Klopstock anticipated the revolution in German literature that Goethe, Schiller, and others were at that very moment bringing to fruition, roughly as the odes of the Wartons, Collins, and Gray are said to anticipate the Romantic revolution in English poetry. But Klopstock's odes seem as artificial to post-Romantic readers as those of Warton and Collins, and Klopstock was an innovator who had lived to see his new directions pursued much further than he wished. Although "he spoke favorably of Goethe," he found Schiller's *The Robbers* "so extravagant that he could not read it." The two young Englishmen agreed with him, but not without embarrassment, since their own recent dramatic projects had been firmly based on Schiller's play. In its favor, Wordsworth urged Klopstock to recall "the scene of the setting sun," where Karl Moor expresses remorse and laments his lost innocence. But Klopstock "did not know it. He said Schiller could not live."[48]

Klopstock knew Milton quite well, having read him in translation when he was only fourteen years old, but he ranked his verse lower than that of Richard Glover (1712–1785), the son of a Hanover merchant who was born and raised in London, and author of *Leonidas,* a terrible blank verse epic. Klopstock himself was the author of the equally turgid, and much longer, *The Messiah* (1749; 1773), and claimed it was not at all influenced by Milton's *Paradise Lost*. Wordsworth, the English poet most influenced by Milton, primly noted, "This is a contradiction of what he said before."

Klopstock had also welcomed innovation in the political sphere, only to recoil from it in a way very familiar to the two younger poets. When he first greeted his visitors, on September 26, he was in raptures over Nelson's victory on the Nile. After having been an early supporter of the French Revolution, he was now "a most vehement anti-Gallican," Coleridge sympathetically noted.[49] He had originally, like Coleridge, written poems in praise of it and been, like Joseph Priestley, honored by the French Assembly and invited to take a seat in it. Coleridge generalized from Klopstock's case to all "the literary Men" in Germany: "many *were* [supporters]; but like me have *published* abjurations of the French." "When French Liberty metamorphosed herself into a Fury," Klopstock wrote another ode "expressing his Recantation." Coleridge's comment recapitulates both the argument and imagery of his own "France: An Ode," published in the *Morning Post* as "The Recantation: An Ode" just before he left England. Klopstock's change of heart had not gone unrewarded: his pension was now paid by the court of Denmark, thanks to the influence of its extraordinarily adept prime minister, Count Bernstorff, "whose name smells like a sweet Odor thro' the whole North of Europe," a judgment Coleridge may have learned from Mary Wollstonecraft's popular *Letters Written during a Short Residence in Sweden, Norway, and Denmark*.

The work of literature that Wordsworth and Klopstock talked about in greatest detail was Christoph Martin Wieland's *Oberon* (1780), which had just been translated into English by the poetaster William Sotheby, and read by both Wordsworth and Coleridge. Wordsworth observed that "it was unworthy of a man of genius to make the interest of a long poem [twelve cantos in two volumes] turn entirely upon animal gratification." This was an extraordinarily forthright expression of opinion, for an unknown poet of twenty-eight speaking to the grand old poet of another country on his home ground. He fairly lectured poor old Klopstock on Wieland's sensuality, brushing aside his objection that different poets could choose different subjects, or that such kinds of poems were popular: "I answered that it was the province of a great poet to raise people up to his own level, not to descend to theirs." Klopstock, collapsing, agreed, "and confessed that on no account would he have written a work like the Oberon."[50]

It is true that *Oberon* advances through a series of melodramatic "Oriental" adventures by successive visual set pieces describing the naked charms of several women, but Wordsworth's stern disapproval must stem in part from an embarrassed overcorrection of his own former practice, such as the dancing Italian girls on Lake Como or the Sailor's fascination with the Female Vagrant's breasts in "Adventures on Salisbury Plain." Nor perhaps was his disapproval wholly literary, because the behavior of Wieland's hero, Huon, toward a foreign beauty, the Arab maiden Rezia, parallels his own toward Annette. They try to hold back from consummating their love, but finally they can't resist any longer. Rezia hears Huon groaning with unrequited passion and comes to his bed, producing the scene of "animal gratification" on which, according to Wordsworth, the "interest" of the whole poem turns:

> She sinks upon the spot, full throbs her heart,
> And while strange anguish like a stream of fire
> Gleams in her eyes that melt with warm desire,
> He sees the sympathizing languor dart—
> Frail nature yields—his love-bewilder'd brain
> Defies the god—his arms the maid—enchain—
> And while his glowing lip, embath'd in bliss,
> Sucks nectar-dew in each inebriate kiss,
> Impetuous passion streams thro' every throbbing vein.
> ....
> Desire, insensibly, more daring grows,
> And love, ere Hymen crowns, their secret union views![51]

The author of the revisions to *Descriptive Sketches* saw little here that he had not already written, as well or better, in the same vein. And the lovers' action, giving in to natural desires, is very close to the reason—that is, the rationalization—that Wordsworth would give to Vaudracour and Julia in *The Prelude,* indirectly explaining his own motives. Indeed, when Vaudracour celebrates Julia's beauties by hyperbole—"Arabian fiction never filled the world / With half the wonders that were wrought for him"—we can imagine that *Oberon* is precisely the "Arabian" fiction he has in mind. This love scene occurs in the seventh book. Wordsworth answered Klopstock's inquiry, if he "was not delighted with the poem" by saying that he "thought the story began to flag about the 7th or eighth book."[52] Quite right: the poem is set up to titillate us with the chances and near-misses of its beautiful protagonists, and once they've experienced what Wordsworth censoriously called their "animal gratification," its main point is over.

Wordsworth and Coleridge also briefly discussed with Klopstock the poetry and fame of Gottfried August Bürger (1747–1794), whose ballads had recently enjoyed a huge vogue in England. In 1796 seven different translations of *Leonore* appeared, including one by the young Walter Scott titled *William and Helen.* Wordsworth bought a German copy of Bürger's works to take with him to Goslar, but his low rate of progress in learning the language makes it doubtful he read very much, and the amount of scholarly attention paid to Wordsworth's use of Bürger at this time is often overemphasized. Most of Bürger's undeniable influence on Wordsworth had already manifested itself in the 1798 *Lyrical Ballads,* especially "The Thorn," from translations of German ballads. But the original title of "Poor Susan"

("The Reverie of Poor Susan") is a direct translation from Bürger's title (though not the incident of his poem), and "Hart-Leap Well" (1800) is based on a tale from Bürger's poems.

When Wordsworth criticized the lack of "manners" in Bürger, "not transitory manners reflecting the wearisome unintelligible obliquities of city-life, but manners connected with the permanent objects of nature," he was using the language of "Tintern Abbey" to criticize Bürger for not being Wordsworth.[53] There is very little of "manners," or realistic social detail, to be found—or looked for—in Bürger; his ballads are more traditional than that. Bürger's Poor Susan has nothing to do with a city: she laments her lover in a garden of symbolic love-token flowers. It is Wordsworth who transports her to London with its "wearisome unintelligible obliquities"—if that phrase can be said to describe accurately how country girls were drawn into prostitution. Given his strictures on Wieland, and his unremitting disapproval of Goethe based mainly on rumors about the great man's love life, one wonders how much Wordsworth knew of Bürger's complicated, pathetic pursuit of a succession of wives and mistresses. Coleridge certainly did, in no uncertain terms: Bürger's third wife "is now a Demirep & an Actress at Hamburgh!—A *Bitch!*"[54]

There is more relevance to Wordsworth's life situation in Schiller's extraordinarily damning review of Bürger's poems published in 1791, "which effectively silenced Bürger as a creative poet."[55] Schiller's review reads (from Wordsworth's perspective) like a draft toward the 1800 preface. It began by lamenting the decline of lyric poetry "in the current philosophizing age," and set forth the "awesome responsibility" of poetry under these conditions: "that it should assimilate all the manners, the characters, the entire wisdom of its time," creating, "out of the century itself, a model for the century. Such a task . . . called for mature and cultured hands." Bürger, far from being a *Volksdichter* (folk poet), as he claimed in his preface of 1789, only proved "that the true *Volksdichter* could no longer exist." What was wanted was refined simplicity: initiating readers " 'into the mysteries of the beautiful, the noble and the true, it should draw the *Volk* up to it, but Bürger descends to the level of the *Volk,* where he mingles, rather than edifies and elevates his art.' "[56]

Between talks with elderly dignitaries and walks out to the suburbs, the members of the party were busy seeking out proper luggage and transportation for their planned removal to somewhere cheaper in the country. The stories they heard about the costs and conditions of travel to the south, Weimar or Göttingen, were wildly inconsistent. Their English acquaintances exaggerated them, while their German ones downplayed them. "Young" Klopstock suggested Ratzeburg as a likely place: a fashionable aristocratic resort town on a lake near Lübeck, some thirty miles northeast. Coleridge was chosen to reconnoiter with Chester. He departed September 22 and returned, ecstatic, on the 27th. The place was perfect for him, but quite the contrary for the Wordsworths. It was clean and delightful, full of educated though not highly intellectual wealthy people—and very expensive, even for the kind of boarding arrangement they sought, which Coleridge had found in the home of a Lutheran pastor.

As they talked it over the night that Coleridge returned, the difference in their motives for coming to Germany became clearer, as well as the wide difference in their means of realizing them. They had not really thought through what they were going to do when they arrived, and they were quite unprepared for the expense. Wordsworth's main motive in coming to Germany with Coleridge was just that: to go wherever Coleridge went. Dorothy's goal was to be with William, preferably in Coleridge's company, but with William at all costs. Their plan of learning German in order to become profitable translators was real, but quite secondary.

Coleridge had much more serious reasons for being there. Not only was he fulfilling his desire to study German literature and philosophy at the source; he also carried the hopes—and the money—of several influential people who had invested in his ability to turn himself into an expert on German culture: the Wedgwood family primarily, but also Daniel Stuart of the *Morning Post,* and Tom Poole.[57] Expenses aside, it was clear that Coleridge would never learn the language to the extent required if he stayed with the Wordsworths. He needed to learn to speak with intelligent persons on abstruse subjects, whereas the Wordsworths were content to learn literary German in the same way they worked on their Italian over the years, reading and translating to each other in front of the fire at night.[58] Both aimed at university study of some sort, but that required learning the language first, and clearly they could not do that, together, on the Wordsworths' budget in Hamburg; still less so, in Ratzeburg. It was another perfect double bind for Wordsworth: he wanted to be with Coleridge but couldn't be, because it would spoil Coleridge's own wishes.

With these differences in motive painfully underlined by their difference in incomes, they decided to split up. Coleridge and Chester departed for Ratzeburg on September 30, ten days after their arrival at Hamburg. William and Dorothy began making plans to go to the south, somewhere near Göttingen. The University of Göttingen was highly popular with Englishmen, having been founded sixty years before by the Hanoverian George II.[59] Their decision to head for Goslar, 130 miles south of Hamburg, is not so mysterious as it sometimes seems, though the decision to go to such a remote spot ultimately had important consequences for Wordsworth. Old Klopstock was a native of the Harz region, and probably recommended it to them as the sort of wooded, mountainous country they liked.[60] It was only about fifty miles from Göttingen, on the route that Tom Wedgwood had followed a year or two before, and its location fits very well the prospectus Wordsworth had offered Losh in the spring: "Our plan is to settle if possible in a village near a university, in a pleasant, and, if we can a mountainous, country."[61]

They settled up their accounts at Der Wilde Mann and also with M. de Leutre, whom they had visited every day after Coleridge's departure. He had stayed at the inn with them until he learned of Coleridge's plans; then he put into effect his own plan to rent an "English" house in the suburbs along the river. Wordsworth drew £32 7s. 3d. from the Von Axens and asked Klopstock about the way into Lower Saxony. They packed the trunk they had bought from the honest Jewess, and on the morning of October 3 Wordsworth carried it himself three hundred yards in a driving rain to the diligence station, refusing to pay the 20d. a porter demanded for it (he offered him 8d., "which was more than a London porter would have expected").[62] He seems to have had a premonition that things might not work out for the best. In one of the last letters they posted before leaving Hamburg, he asked Tom Poole to keep an eye on Alfoxden for him; in case "any series of accidents should bring it again into the market we should be glad to have it, if we could manage it."[63] This was not the request of a man expecting to spend a year or two abroad—and had he forgotten why he had lost his lease?

Poole, for his part, was only too glad to hear of the two friends' separation. He wrote immediately to Coleridge at Ratzeburg, expressing relief that "there is an end to our tease about amalgamation etc, etc."[64] Poole lectured Coleridge like a father in this letter, urging him to apply himself industriously to learning German, and for once in his life, Coleridge took someone else's advice about work. Few episodes in his brilliant but often dilatory career are so marked by steady, day-in, day-out application to his task as his success in learning German over the next six months.*

Lamb and Southey and Lloyd shared some sneers when they heard that "the two noble Englishmen have parted no sooner than they set foot on German earth."[65] The whole scheme had seemed harebrained, especially to envious eyes, and it was not unpleasant to old friends in various states of disaffection and alienation to learn that all was not going well. Lamb's comment

*His method was uniquely Coleridgean. He learned "all the words, that could possibly be learnt, with the objects before [him]," let grammar follow after, and never bothered about pronunciation. His notebooks are full of vocabulary lists; he asked and memorized the name of everything, high or low, concrete or abstract. Then, born talker that he was, he immediately started repeating as many words as he could as often as he could, like a superior order of parrot. Thus he amazed his hosts and acquaintances in Ratzeburg, and soon acquired a reputation as a prodigy very similar to the one he enjoyed in England.

also makes clear that the idea of separating had not been contemplated when they left England.

The *separation* of Wordsworth and Coleridge in Germany was as crucial to their development as poets as their "amalgamation" at Alfoxden and Stowey had been. It is common to regard the German adventure as a failure for Wordsworth and a success for Coleridge. But this is true only insofar as what they did matches what they had projected to do. Wordsworth, who had planned to stay one or two years, returned home in less than eight months; Coleridge, who had planned to stay only three months, till Christmas, stayed for nine. In fact, the separation made the trip successful for both of them, but in ways that Wordsworth especially could not have foreseen. For yet another time in his young life, the disappointment of a projected goal created a shock of surprise that led to a huge reevaluation of what he was about and resulted in important new creative work. Like his "failures" on Simplon or Snowdon, his frustration in Germany provoked creative work that he did not realize he had in him, and certainly was not planning to write. Thus the German trip became for him, like the 1798 *Lyrical Ballads,* which was supposed to pay for it (but dismally failed to), another triumph snatched from failure. It is no accident that many of the proto-*Prelude* passages he composed there have this same quality of intense expectations foiled, but then compensated for in a different direction.

For this process, being without Coleridge was as essential as being with Dorothy. We can learn a great deal about Coleridge's German experiences from his letters and notebooks, but much less about his inner life. He gives more details about Goslar after passing through it for a few hours the next spring than Dorothy or William recorded—or preserved—of their five months there. But, in terms of the same creative economy, Coleridge wrote very little poetry in Germany other than metrical or translation experiments, and occasional or memorial verses written for specific persons or places. "My poor Muse is quite gone," he admitted. For all the entrepreneurial and intellectual success of Coleridge's stay, his poetical output is balanced, and overbalanced, by Wordsworth's statement "I have been obliged to write in self-defence." A glance at the table of contents in any chronological edition of their works will show the difference: after 1798 Wordsworth's production takes off; dozens of complete, publishable poems are written every year. Whereas Coleridge, who had been composing poems at the rate of a dozen or two a year up until now, falls off rapidly. Although he still wrote some great poems, Coleridge's career as a *productive* poet was over after 1799, whereas Wordsworth's had just begun. It began with his realization that self-production was his best line of work.

26

WRITING IN SELF-DEFENSE

Goslar, 1798–1799

As I have had no books I have been obliged to write in self-defence. I should have written five times as much as I have done but that I am prevented by an uneasiness at my stomach and side, with a dull pain about my heart. I have used the word pain, but uneasiness and heat are words which more accurately express my feeling. At all events it renders writing unpleasant. Reading is now become a kind of luxury to me. When I do not read I am absolutely consumed by thinking and feeling and bodily exertions of voice or of limbs, the consequence of those feelings.

(Wordsworth to Coleridge, Goslar, December 1798)

William and Dorothy climbed up into the diligence at five o'clock in the afternoon of October 3, and arrived in Goslar three days later. It was a wretched trip: they advanced at an average speed of five miles an hour. Dorothy was as sick from the pitching of the coach as she had been crossing the North Sea. The coach was luxuriously fitted inside with leather and fur, but with cracks and crevices above and below, "for the winds to blow through on every side." On the first stage they traveled all night, plunging along corrugated roads to arrive in Lüneburg in time for breakfast. Hamburg had been bad, but this was worse: "all seemed lifeless and dead." Continuing on across the great Lüneburger Heath, Dorothy noted desperately, "the country becomes occasionally rather interesting from its strangeness." They sought out "English" hotels and inns at every stop, hoping for a higher standard of comfort, for they were now technically in the realm of England's king, but "in the Hannoverian dominions . . . the inns were more strange and more miserable." Dorothy subsisted on wine and warm water to keep her stomach calm, while William drank coffee to stay awake. At Brunswick, the last stop before Goslar, the fare at the English Arms was thankfully somewhat better: "potatoes after the English fashion . . . beds . . . excellent with blankets etc. as in England."*[1]

*Curiously, the duchy of Brunswick (Braunschweig) came even closer to England and Wordsworth's ambience just before it expired as a political entity. In 1913 Ernest Augustus, duke

They arrived exhausted and thoroughly disoriented, as if they had come to the ends of the earth. Dorothy's last entry in her German journal is "It was on Saturday the 6th of October when we arrived in Goslar at between 5 and 6 in the evening."[2] Except for five letters and fragments of four others, we have no more direct indications of what they did during the rest of their stay in Germany until the last week of April. But we do have a very large amount of poetry written by Wordsworth at Goslar, which shows quite clearly what he did there: he thought and wrote about himself, in self-defense, especially about his formative boyhood experiences. Goslar was the local address for the feeling of spiritual emptiness from which Wordsworth's great affirmations of imaginative fullness would soon spring up. Wordsworth, poet of Englishness par excellence, was conceived in France and born in Germany. The beauties and excitements of France (and Switzerland) stimulated his sensual imagination in its young adulthood, but his loneliness and depression in Germany brought him to "manhood now mature," as he would say, safe home at Grasmere, a year later.

Goslar had been the seat of the Hohenstaufen emperors and was still a medieval free city with its own laws.[3] The Wordsworths found rooms in the center of town, in the substantial house of Frau Deppermann, widow of a former town senator and linen draper, at no. 107 Breitestrasse or, as Coleridge's readily delivered letters styled it, "la grande Rue de Goslar."[4] William was duly listed in the town's roll of lodgers as "William Waetsford, ein Engländer."[5] France and Germany helped make him a poet, but neither country could handle his peculiarly English surname. Wordsworth called Goslar "an old decaying city"; Coleridge called it "this ugly silent old desert of a City." From what they say of it, it sounds like the setting for a Kafka story or an especially bleak Bergman film. It boasted the oldest domed church in the land; inside, there was an altarpiece of the Apostles ("ugly but lively") by Lucas Cranach, a gigantic picture of a grimacing Saint Christopher, the patron of travelers, fording a river with the boy Jesus on his shoulders. It also contained a vestige of "the only assured antiquity of German Heathenism": the remains of an altar to Krodo, on which human sacrifices were performed.[6]

Goslar's contemporary aspect was almost as frightening. A center for the manufacture of vitriol, it was surrounded by smelting furnaces for the manufacture of wire. These furnaces gave off "white & blue flares . . . a grand & beautiful Object," Coleridge noted. But we hear no more about this from Wordsworth than we do of the beggars and furnaces at Tintern. So far as his surroundings were concerned, he assumed the position Hazlitt said was his

---

of Cumberland, grandson of King George V of Hanover, was made titular head of the German state, the Brunswick line having died out.

characteristic one, writing as if there were nothing but himself and the universe. He mentions only one local resident he liked: a beautiful kingfisher who "used to glance by me" during his daily walks on the town ramparts, keeping him company. "I consequently became much attached to it."[7] The best they could find to say about Goslar was that living there was "considerably" cheaper than living in England, and that of course had been the main reason for going there.[8]

Their house was very cold; that winter was the coldest recorded in the century. They had to put on overcoats to go from one room to another, and they wrapped themselves up in furs when they went out walking, which they indefatigably did, "at least an hour every day, often much more," cold or no cold. William, wrapped up in a dark fur gown and wearing a sort of helmet lined with black dog's fur, looked, Dorothy thought, "like any grand Signior," a kind of joke about their current class status.[9] He had to protect himself because his own room was above an uninsulated passageway; the phlegmatic natives calmly assured him he could expect to freeze to death some night. The one contemporary portrait he gives of himself is a projection of his own feelings onto a fly he observed crawling on their heating stove: "a disconsolate creature . . . a child of the field or the grove. . . . Alas! how he fumbles about the domains. . . . He cannot find out in what track he must crawl . . . there he stands like a traveller bemaz'd."[10] The first line of this jeu d'esprit applies solely to Wordsworth, not to the fly, and pretty well sums up his achievements in Goslar, so far as his assigned work was concerned: "A fig for your languages, German and Norse."

This unhappy Wordsworthian fly contrasts with the lightsome Coleridgean one described in a letter to Sara, for both were creatures of the poets' housing arrangements: "no Fly unimprisoned from a boy's hand, could more buoyantly enjoy it's [*sic*] element, than I this clear & peaceful [Lutheran pastor's] house, situated in this wholesome Air!"[11] The Wordsworths had hoped to find what Coleridge had found, a family or *pensione* arrangement such as William had had in Orléans, where they could begin learning German by participating in the life of the household. But these arrangements were not yet common in Germany, and what they got instead was a sort of boardinghouse where they met the other residents only at meals. Besides their taciturn landlady, a young apprentice of the house who came and sat with them in the evenings, and a friendly deaf man they met in town, they had "no other society except that of a French Emigrant Priest."[12] Who was he, and what was he doing in godforsaken Goslar? Converting Lutherans?

With their slow progress in German, it was quite a while before they could talk to anybody but this priest. Given the hints already dropped about the possibility of some sort of clandestine activity by Wordsworth, this priest should not go unremarked, though we cannot identify him. Emigré priests were some of the leading operatives and couriers for the British Swabian agency, particularly "the abbé Jean François André, alias de La Marre . . . *voyageur* par excellence, flitting about Europe and turning up in London, Paris, Mittau or Augsburg as required."[13] Not that the priest Wordsworth lived with was this André, but every agent and courier had his contacts and his safe houses. And the mention of Mittau, in what is now Latvia, is pertinent, since that is where Louis XVIII went, as guest of the half-mad Paul I of Russia, following the two worst years of his long exile—which were spent in Blankenburg, a "nasty little town" of Brunswick, about twenty-five miles southeast of Goslar.[14] He had left in February of 1798, but his residence there was well known. Coleridge made straight for it on his tour of the Harz region in early May, staying in an inn directly across from Louis's residence, the day before he came to Goslar. Louis XVIII—"Monsieur," duc de Provence, the late Louis XVI's brother—was the focus of all plots for and against a restoration: an event that between 1795 and the end of 1799 seemed to be always just around the corner.[15] Louis had left the Goslar region six months before Wordsworth arrived, but some of his retainers lingered on, and it was safer for them to stay in a neighboring town like Goslar, for Louis and his entourage were quite unpopular: he never rode out, for fear of assassins. Coleridge and his companions found out just how unpopular he was when, inquiring where he had lived, they were accosted as "French spies" and forced to give an account of themselves. (Once inside, they were treated to a showing of Louis's obscene pictures by a pretty village maid who, Coleridge shrewdly noted, seemed to know very well where the best ones were.)[16] It may be impossible to account for the presence of "a French Emigrant Priest" in Goslar in the winter of 1798–99, but Louis XVIII's recent proximity and Wordsworth's arrival is one way of doing so. Had his "confidential" friend M. de Leutre suggested Goslar as a good place to learn the language, and for other contacts as well?

As for making acquaintances among the gentility of the town—the method Coleridge employed to great advantage among the petty nobility at Ratzeburg—that turned out to be impossible for two reasons, or rather, two versions of the same reason: Dorothy. As a man and a woman constituting a kind of household, they were expected to receive visits as well as pay them, which they could not afford to do. Coleridge, as an unattached and prepossessing foreign gentleman, was free from this obligation, though *he* could afford it. But William and Dorothy as a result found no society at all: "It was once the residence of Emperors, and it is now the residence of Grocers and Linen-drapers . . . a wretched race."[17]

And many people, beginning with Frau Deppermann, did not believe that Dorothy was really William's sister: "sister" being here "considered as only a name for Mistress," as Coleridge told Sara. "It is next to impossible for any but married women or in the suit of married women to be introduced to any company in Germany."[18] But as he informed Poole (but not Sara), "It is here as in France—the single Women are chaste, but Marriage seems to legitimate Intrigue— . . . the married Men intrigue or whore—and the Wives have their Cicisbeos. I entreat you, suspect *me* not of any Cicisbeo affair—I am no Puritan; but yet it is not customs or manners that can extinguish in me the Sacredness of a married Woman, or quench the disgust I feel towards an Adultress."[19] To Wordsworth's complaints about their situation Coleridge gave two reasons, but no solutions: "your not loving to smoke; and your sister."[20] Dorothy's free and easy behavior, her walks and wild eyes, did little to dispel these suspicions. Nor did they did look or act very much like a brother and sister: William, tall, stern, and reserved; Dorothy, short, bright, and voluble.

The question arises, To what extent were these perceptions entirely mistaken, in a Germany which was just emerging from the fervid era of Sturm und Drang? Love between brothers and sisters was already a romantic fashion there, not merely a personal fact as it was for the Lambs and the Wordsworths; fact and fashion would mingle for the Byrons and the Shelleys, and for countless other young people who did not happen to be great artists. Schiller's mind and works ran compulsively on the theme, and Goethe said his deep feelings for Frau Charlotte von Stein arose in part because she reminded him of his sister Cornelia.[21] Indeed, as a cultural fashion, the Germans thought that in this one, as in so many others, they were following the lead of the English. Goethe had voiced this common German conception of Englishmen abroad in his journal of his Italian tour (1786), recording a visit from "ein Herr und eine Dame . . . ein Engländer mit einer sogenannten Schwester [with his so-called sister]."[22] In an era when arranged marriages were still the norm, especially among the rising middle classes trying to consolidate their capital gains, the idea of a *romantic* marriage was a threat to established order, not a promise of happiness. Passions doomed to find no satisfactory outlet in marriage often turned to those other beloved men or women, with whom marriage was out of the question, but with whom bonds of intimate knowledge and sympathy had been established from immemorial infancy. Both aspects of this attraction, the financial and the emotional, were powerfully (if differentially) present in the Wordsworths' case, as regards the impossibility of his marriage on the one hand and of hers on the other.

They had no household routine to attend to, a trying circumstance for Dorothy, who had been in charge of her brother's domestic life for three full years.[23] They were thus thrown more on each other's company, further frustrating their chances of learning German. They talked to each other about what their life had been like and what it had come to: "Was it for *this?*" All their measures of Germany had been made in terms of England, and now they began to measure themselves in those terms. Hadn't they been happy once? Their only shared passion was for each other, and for Coleridge, whose letters they awaited with something like lust. "Let me speak," Dorothy says at one point, "of the joy we felt at seeing your handwriting again; I burst open the seals and could almost have kissed them in the presence of the post-master."[24] To the degree that they could—or could not—love each other directly, they did so through their shared passion for Coleridge. Coleridge reciprocated their passion with a similar physicality, as he expressed it in an experiment in English hexameters, stimulated by Goethe's recently published *Hermann und Dorothea:*

William, my teacher, my friend! dear William and dear Dorothea!
Smooth out the folds of my letter, and place it on desk or on table;
Place it on table or desk; and your right hands loosely half-closing,
Gently sustain them in air, and extending the digit didactic,
Rest it a moment on each of the forks of the five-forkéd left hand,
Twice on the breadth of the thumb, and once on the tip of each finger;
Read with a nod of the head in a humouring recitativo.

All in fun (though his anatomy seems a bit off), but the poem is filled with the passion of absence: "many a wearisome mile are ye distant." The last lines said all he could, or need, say:

William, my head and my heart! dear William and dear Dorothea!
You have all in each other; but I am lonely, and want you![25]

But Coleridge was so busy with so many other people, both in Ratzeburg and in Somerset, that he was not nearly as preoccupied in thinking about the Wordsworths as they were about him. Wordsworth said plaintively, "I need not say how much the sentiment [your hexameters] affected me."[26]

While it is hard to conceive of a physically incestuous relation between William and Dorothy Wordsworth, it is equally hard to believe that the possibility was not often on their minds, whether as a temptation or a threat, at critical times like the Goslar months. The Lucy poems give access to more psychological details here, but we must get to them via Wordsworth's other "self-defence" poems, for it is in his sense of himself that he most clearly expresses his feelings for Dorothy and his determination to control them—against her advances.

In the absence of any English books to read, Wordsworth was "consumed" by quivering fits: "thinking and feeling and bodily exertions of voice and limbs, *the consequence of those feelings.*" He began to "write in self-defence," but the cure was almost as bad as the ailment: "an uneasiness at my stomach and side, with a dull pain about the heart. I have used the word pain, but uneasiness and heat are words which more accurately express my feeling." We can call these pains psychosomatic, but they were nonetheless real, and peculiarly self-impacting in his expression of them. As the soma of his psyche, they sound like birth or labor pains. That was certainly their result. Self-defense is a strong plea, sometimes used to justify manslaughter, but rarely invoked as a response to mere boredom. It sounds reactive; Wordsworth's Goslar poems may indeed have started out that way, but they soon became aggressively outgoing. He was compensating for apparently minor losses (lack of books and company) with mighty gains: a series of apparently disparate poems that, taken together, show the Wordsworthian self-creation machine shifting into high gear. The idea of gain snatched from loss, triumph from failure, applies to Wordsworth's entire German sojourn, but most of all to the "mass" of poems (as Dorothy described them) he wrote in five winter months at Goslar: an output nearly as great in quantity as his five months at Alfoxden at the beginning of the year, and arguably greater in quality, "Tintern Abbey" alone excepted. The Goslar poems are more serious in tone and theme than most of the lyrical ballads of early 1798, and their seriousness results from a massive turn inward, toward what we would call "psychological" perspectives and away from sociopolitical ones.

Soon after his arrival he drafted the beginning of an essay on morals, which advances the "Advertisement" of the 1798 *Lyrical Ballads* in the direction of the preface of 1800. He argues that poetry and art can do more to change men's moral behavior than "such books as Mr. Godwyn's, Mr. Paley's, & those of that whole tribe of authors."[27] These authors, unlike poets, "contain no picture of human life; they *describe* nothing." Their "bald & naked reasonings [are] impotent over our habits," unlike "a tale of distress," which can "incorporate itself with the blood & vital juices of our minds" because it really is connected with "the supposed archetype or fountain of the [moral] proposition existing in human life." Although he stands with Godwin on the side of moral reform, his argument distinguishes writers of the left in terms of the means of action they recommend, and declares poetry more socially effective than philosophy. Men will never be *reasoned* into good actions (on the contrary, they will use their reason to justify their bad ones), but they may be *moved* to them by powerful images. If we understood this process better, Wordsworth concludes, we might be enabled "to be practically useful by informing [ourselves] how men placed in such or such situations will necessarily act, & thence enabling us to apply ourselves to the means of turning them into a more beneficial course, if necessary, or of giving them new ardour & new knowledge when they are proceeding as they ought."

The idea that writing poetry could be more significant moral action than philosophy (especially in times when effective political action had been rendered all but impossible) connected in his mind to his conversations with Coleridge about Bürger. Wordsworth gave Bürger credit, whatever his limitations, for being "always the poet . . . never the mobbist, one of those dim drivellers with which our island has teemed for so many years."[28] As he tried to separate his project from that of Godwin and the philosophical radicals, his comment on Bürger further delimits it, distinguishing him from the wrong *kind* of poets, who produced the sentimental "drivel" with which well-intentioned liberal writers ("mobbists") like Southey flooded the magazines. Yet Wordsworth also criticized Bürger because he saw "everywhere the character of Bürger himself," adding, "I wish him sometimes at least to make me forget himself in his creations." This shows how deeply Wordsworth himself was caught up in the contradictions between subjectivity and objectivity which necessarily afflict—and energize—all attempts to speak authoritatively from one's own experience for other people. We rarely forget Wordsworth in any of his creations; in the *Prelude* lines he now began composing, he "found" himself as a man by remembering himself as a child.

But this style of argument, which continued the conversations of Alfoxden, soon disappeared from his mind as he confronted the necessity of writing without Coleridge. Wordsworth wrote three or four different kinds of poems at Goslar, and their similarities in tone, theme, and purpose are far more revealing than their superficial differences in subject matter. They are (1) his first drafts of "the poem on the growth of my own mind," or "the poem to Coleridge"; (2) the Matthew poems, on a village schoolmaster figure, essentially William Taylor, but incorporating features of other older men who befriended the boy Wordsworth; (3) the Lucy poems, on the death of a young woman or girl who is the speaker's love or inspiration, and who must be Dorothy in psychological terms, though not literally; and (4) some more ballads of the kind he wrote in the spring, again focusing on lost or abandoned women.

All these poems are concerned with the origins of Wordsworth's imaginative growth—and, almost as much, with a fear of losing contact with those sources. They are celebrations, finally, but we miss their point if we lose sight of the fact that, for the most part, they launch themselves into expression out of a fear of losing the very quality or person celebrated. They are celebrations under threat. They are *determindedly* joyful overcomings of strong initial feelings of depression and dejection: essentially Wordsworth's mood in Goslar. In all of them Wordsworth emerges as the poet of natural fullness and human relationship not because it is "natural" but because he feels so strongly that it may not be natural at all. It is precisely here that the orthodox interpretation of Wordsworth as the sage of "wise passiveness" in nature goes astray, not as an account of the evident meaning of most of the subsequent poems in his oeuvre, but as an account of the process of self-creation that led him to make those affirmations.[29] Joy is expressed in several of these passages, but it is hard to see any simple "happiness" in them. They do frequently hold up his Lake District childhood as a "blessed retreat," but he enters into it under something like a curse, the self-accusing "Was it for this?" They all reflect a common interest in the development of character, either his own or thinly veiled projections of himself, or sometimes of a sharply contrasting alter ego.[30]

In mid-December he and Dorothy finally wrote a long letter to Coleridge. They hadn't written at all for six weeks, a silence that filled Coleridge with "great Anxiety & inexpressible Astonishment." For this letter, their first report of work in progress, Dorothy excerpted three passages from the "mass" of early childhood vignettes Wordsworth had written. At bottom, these short passages were a therapy constructed out of desperation, Wordsworth pulling himself up by the bootstraps of memory. His life seemed to have come to its worst dead end so far, and he started taking stock of himself to see where or how it had all gone wrong. The three passages sent to Coleridge became the skating scene and the rowboat scene from *Prelude* I, plus a version of what became "Nutting."

The skating episode may have been stimulated as a *response* to Coleridge's description of "the pleasure of skaiting [*sic*]" on the lake at Ratzeburg. Coleridge's had sent a letter to Sara describing the skating parties he enjoyed: "the melancholy undulating sound from the Skate not without variety; & when very many are skating together, the sounds and the noises give an impulse to the icy Trees, & the woods all round the lake *tinkle!*"[31] Here is Wordsworth's version, from recollections of Esthwaite:

> Meanwhile, the precipices rang aloud,
> The leafless trees and every icy crag
> Tinkled like iron, while the distant hills
> Into the tumult sent an alien sound
> Of melancholy not unnoticed. . . .
>
> (*1799*, i.163–67)

Dorothy's response indicates another motive behind the beginnings of "the poem to Coleridge":

> You speak in raptures of the pleasure of skaiting—it must be a delightful exercise, and in the North of England amongst the mountains whither we wish to decoy you, you might enjoy it with every possible advantage. A race with William upon his native lakes would leave to the heart and the imagination something more Dear and valuable than the gay sight of Ladies and countesses whirling along the lake of Ratzeberg.[32]

This context also shows that Wordsworth's reasons for writing about himself, though egotistical in every sense, were not sui generis. These passages were offered to Coleridge as love tokens, part of the timeless ritual of courtship in which one displays to the beloved one's life in its entirety up to the moment the two lovers met. As love tokens, these passages are also letters of seduction, reminding Coleridge of the poet and the poetry he loved and admired, because his admiration was necessary to Wordsworth's self-creation. Finally, they were also holiday travel brochures for "that romantic country . . . whither," Dorothy frankly said, "we wish to decoy you." They were already making plans for the next summer.

But they are much more than attractive descriptions. All three of the first passages mailed to Coleridge have the same pattern of gain recovered from loss, matching the entire structure of Wordsworth's biographical experience in Germany. In each of them, it is not the part of the poem describing nature that makes them uniquely Wordsworthian but the parts he *cannot* describe, because it is not simply "nature." Each time, he starts off going with nature, but then that movement breaks, and something far greater than natural forms invades his consciousness. This "something" is what Coleridge meant when he said, of the conclusion of the Boy of Winander passage, "If I should meet these lines running wild in the deserts of Arabia, I should shriek out, 'Wordsworth!' " Not only the identification but also its locale is important: "the deserts of Arabia" were as wild, empty, and unearthly a place as Coleridge could at that moment imagine: we might say, on the moon. Only Wordsworth could have written them because they suggest that behind these ordinary Lake District scenes there was a landscape of imagination as threatening and alienating as if it were another planet.

The same pattern—infinite gain from finite loss—is repeated throughout the notebook from which Dorothy copied these excerpts, which forms the foundation of the first book of *The Prelude.*[33] William began it with a page of short, desultory "inspiration" passages where he tried to invoke Nature directly as his Muse: "a mild creative breeze / a vital breeze that passes gently on." But each effort to frame Nature as "a mild creative breeze" (several attempts of two or three lines each) is quickly frustrated, and produces instead "a redundant energy / Creating not but as it may / disturbing things created"; or "vexing its own creation," as he put it in the final version.[34] Then he broke off this normal start-up procedure and asked himself instead the famous self-accusing question "Was it for this?" that launched him into his lifework. The fragmentary invocations have no pronoun references at all, but one turns over the journal leaf and suddenly they flood out across the page: "I . . . I . . . I . . . my . . . my . . . my."

This paradoxical sense of creative power as destructive is at the heart of Wordsworth's first description of his early experience of his own imagination. It was hard to get started, and when it did, it destroyed its own productions. This was the power he had hoped to harness by linking it to Coleridge's philosophical range and depth. On his own again, without Coleridge's philosophical ballast, he was frustrated again. He *felt* everything that had gone to make him a creative force, but he could not produce a poem, because he had no story line to hang it on, no theme, no philosophy, not even a collection of anecdotes in which to invest it, as he had done with Erasmus Darwin's case histories and local Somerset lore in the spring. He was trying to attach conceptions of intellect and spirit to natural forms, but he had no vehicle for doing so. Or rather, he discovered he had nothing but himself, and frustrated, he asked himself in exasperation, "was it for this / That one, the fairest of all rivers, loved / To blend his murmurs with my nurse's song . . . ?" An initial question as to the possible uselessness of his whole life up to this point is set down on paper and repeated three times in the immediately following lines. It is then answered by a similarly repeated insistence that it *was not* in vain: "Ah, not in vain . . . Ah, not in vain . . . I may not think / A vulgar hope was yours."[35] It is almost moot whether we say this famous opening question is jubilantly affirmative, as most traditional Wordsworth scholars do, or vehemently negative (No, it was *not* in vain!). But the huge force (and eventual length) of the affirmative answer is proportionate to the depth of the negative doubt that provoked it. Wordsworth clung to the earth, to Nature, because he feared indeed that there *was* nothing but himself and the rest of the universe: such intense self-consciousness demands the earth itself as its ground—*"even as if* the earth had rolled / With visible motion her diurnal round."

But the question "Was it for this?" is also an old literary convention, a variation on the *ubi sunt* motif, with many antecedents from Virgil to Pope, most recently from Godwin's *Caleb Williams,* where Caleb asks himself whether his heroic efforts to achieve simple justice (that is, to justify his whole life) have been worth it.* Caleb's compulsive questions lead him to a conventional eighteenth-century generalization: "Great God! What is man?" Wordsworth's more radically individual, Romantic conclusion is, Who am I? God?[36] It is also an inevitable human question, arising about the direction of one's life or, more often, about that of one's offspring (Was it for this that I worked so hard to raise you?). But though it arose from Wordsworth's wide knowledge of traditional figures of speech, "in the loneliness and self-questioning of Goslar, the question was as urgent as death itself."[37] It is comforting to many readers of literature to think that writers always know where

*"Was it for this that I had broken through so many locks, and bolts, and the adamantine walls of my prison; that I had passed so many anxious days, and sleepless, spectre-haunted nights; that I had racked my invention . . . ; that my existence had been enthralled . . . ?" (*Caleb Williams,* vol. 3, chap. 12).

they are going; readers of Wordsworth, hooked on his "naturalness," have developed this habit into an addiction. Some scholars hold that these Goslar lines were written down as the conclusion of a poem Wordsworth had already conceived of mentally.[38] Wordsworth's compositions often developed in this way, but in this instance the idea that he knew where he was going is at odds with both the manuscript and the psychological evidence, and arises from formalist assumptions about poetry that are at the opposite extreme from the radical self-fashioning he here launched into, which we might call open-ended except that it is, more radically, open-beginning-ed: not a poem without a conclusion, but one without a starting place.

The answers that he gave to his "Was it for this?" question in 1798 are the repeated "spots of time" of childhood and boyhood adventures that are everyone's best memory of *The Prelude.* He jubilantly recalled the wonder of those adventures—they are the *materia mysteria* of his poem—but his jubilation arises from a determination to face down—to shout down, if necessary—the nagging fear that it could be, or could have been, otherwise: that it could have been "in vain."

His insistent repetition that it was "Ah, not in vain" recalls the self-interrupting structure of the poem he had most recently completed, "Lines Composed above Tintern Abbey," with their similar-sounding topic sentences: "If this be but a vain belief." The beginnings of *The Prelude* pick up right where "Tintern Abbey" left off, with the same rhetorical form, of temporary doubts silenced by ultimate affirmations. The main difference is that his retrospective time frame has been extended from "five years, and the length of five long winters" to as far back as he can remember: "from the dawn almost of life."[39]

This is perfectly clear when we hear the echo of Wordsworth's July lines on the Wye ("If this be but a vain belief, yet, oh! how oft— . . . in spirit, have I turned to thee, / O sylvan Wye!") in his December lines on the Derwent:

was it for this
That one, the fairest of all rivers, loved
To blend his murmurs with my nurse's song
And from his alder shades and rocky falls
And from his fords and shallows sent a voice
To intertwine my dreams, for this didst thou
O Derwent—travelling over the green plains
Near my sweet birth-place didst thou beauteous
Give ceaseless music to the night & day
Which with its steady cadence tempering
Our human waywardness composed my thought
To more than infant softness giving me

Amid the fretful tenements of man
A knowledge, a dim earnest of the calm
That Nature breathes among her woodland haunts. . . .[40]

Their conclusions are also similar: "Nor perchance, / If I were not thus taught, should I the more / Suffer my genial spirits to decay: / For thou art with me" ("TA", 111–14); "Yet, should it be / That this is but an impotent desire . . . / . . . need I dread from thee / Harsh judgements" (*1799*, i.450–60). Only the addressee has been changed, from Dorothy in July to Coleridge in December. Another echo shows why: "Nor while, though doubting yet not lost, I tread the mazes of this argument . . . may I well / Forget what might demand a loftier song" (*1799*, i.118–23). For Dorothy it was enough that she remember him: "Nor wilt thou then forget . . . with what healing thoughts / Of tender joy wilt thou remember me, / And these my exhortations!" Coleridge wanted him to be the Recluse, for the world; Dorothy wanted him only to be William, and hers.

But even as he began the "poem to Coleridge," Wordsworth was simultaneously drafting a new poem to Dorothy in the form of the Lucy poems. The Matthew poems are intermediary between the *Prelude* sketches and the Lucy group: poems to fatherly teachers, rather than poems to brotherly or sisterly teachers. The Matthew poems show Wordsworth's mind running on the death of another source of childhood inspiration: not his reckless adventures outdoors in the natural world, but the nurture he received from culture, in the form of the schoolteachers who befriended him at Hawkshead. If the "poem to Coleridge," his mentor now, displays the origins of his power biographically (in lieu of a philosophical account), the poems to "Matthew," his mentor then, display his origins genealogically, in the cross-grained quality of Matthew's character and especially in Matthew's sense of paradisal times lost and—with a difference—regained. Again Wordsworth is celebrating at the same time he is lamenting, the life as well as the loss of these inspiring voices. As he wrote the passages about his boyhood to show Coleridge—and convince himself—that he was still alive, so he wrote the Matthew poems—eight in all, though only two were published—to celebrate that early calling and, as a gift offering to the honored dead, to show William Taylor that his encouragement had not been in vain.

The two most famous of the Matthew poems, "The Fountain" and "The Two April Mornings," convey Matthew's expressions of irrevocable loss to the boy speaker (or the speaker as boy). The Matthew of the "Address to the Scholars of the Village School" lies "a prisoner of the ground," like the Lucy of "A slumber did my spirit seal."[41] Many of the other unpublished Matthew poems and fragments are, like all of the Lucy poems, epitaphs, but expressed as *searches* for the appropriate words in which to memorialize the beloved inspirer. They are uttered in Matthew's favorite haunts, but they are always inadequate. Even if he carved them on the thorn tree Matthew loved, "yet it seemed that still / I owed another verse to thee."[42] In one of them Wordsworth presents himself as a boy leading a choir of Hawkshead students in this his "last memorial song." This carries the weird but entirely Wordsworthian suggestion that he is bringing Matthew's blessing back to the "little noisy crew," as if the schoolboys of 1786 still existed somewhere as children.

Chronology is wrenched and layered in the Matthew poems as it is in the *Prelude* fragments to give a sense of lost-yet-recovered time, parallel to *The Prelude*'s faith in lost-yet-retained inspiration. This is only what we should expect, given what was happening to Wordsworth's mind in Goslar. Just as our life is said to flash before our eyes when we expect to die suddenly, so did Wordsworth's, in what seems to have been an extended, painful moment of dissolution.

Matthew is far from a perfect inspirational ideal. Rather, his whole being is an incongruous mixture of guises and modes: his "witty rhymes" were "half-mad." He too is a triumph of failure. He combined mirth with gravity, was loved by all the vale, yet felt fundamentally alone and underappreciated. "Glad no more," he now wears "a face of joy, because / We have been glad before." But he is most like the young Wordsworth at Goslar when he says, unblushingly, "many love me; but by none / Am I enough beloved."[43] On one level this means that because the persons he loved best—his wife and daughter—are dead, no one can replace them, not even the naive narrator, who cheerily offers, "I'll be a son to thee!" But on another level it means just what it says, as the actual life condition that Wordsworth was recognizing in himself in his almost solitary confinement in Goslar: no one can ever love us as much as we love ourselves. This is a shameful recognition that we usually keep to ourselves, but Wordsworth, sublime and fearless egoist that he was, had the courage to publish it broadcast.

The Lucy poems bring sharply into focus the fact that almost all the poems Wordsworth wrote in Goslar are about persons who are dead, or whose main action in their poems is to die. (The *Prelude* fragments insist that that little boy is not dead, or did not live "in vain.") But they are also about a person—the speaker—who is strangely obtuse about or surprised by death, living in a kind of trance: "a slumber did my spirit seal," "in one of those sweet dreams I slept."[44] They are not simply about the death of a small girl or beloved young woman; they are about the death of a female figure who is/was the poet's inspiration, especially in her immediate connection to nature. If the "poem to Coleridge" is about "the growth of my own mind," these poems to Dorothy are about the loss of her inspiration. Lucy is Wordsworth's Muse, and the group as a whole is a series of invocations to a

Muse feared or felt to be dead. Just as the first *Prelude* jottings invoked a "mild creative breeze" that became instead "a redundant energy vexing its own creation," so the Lucy poems are powerfully inspired poems on the theme of *loss* of inspiration. Their operative question is not "Was it for this?" but "What if?" As epitaphs, they are not sad, a very inadequate word to describe them, but breathlessly, almost wordlessly aware of what such a loss would mean to the speaker: "oh, the difference to me!"

These poems to Dorothy have a greater range than their point of origin in Wordsworth's love for Dorothy, but there can be little doubt that Dorothy is the biographical form of the spiritual Lucy. Strange as they are, they do have conventional aspects, the first of which is the name Lucy, by the end of the eighteenth century a cliché of pastoral poetry.[45] Lucy is not the only name Wordsworth used to refer to Dorothy in his poems (Ellen and Emma are others), but there are poems in which we know that "Lucy" refers directly to her. When she copied out "Strange fits of passion" for Coleridge—and this title well describes the group as a whole—she added a note, with an interesting slip of the pen: "The next poem is a favorite of mine—i.e. of me Dorothy." That is, it is both mine and *of* me. The last stanza of the version sent to Coleridge, canceled before publication, indicates that Wordsworth was indulging an adult fantasy in imagining the death of his beloved:

I told her this, her laughter light
  Is ringing in my ears;
And when I think upon that night
  My eyes are dim with tears.

The question is, which night does he have in mind? The night he rode to Lucy's cottage and watched the moon appear to "drop" behind it as he advanced up the hill, or the night he told her his fantasy? The latter possibility is transferred to the beginning of the poem in the new stanza Wordsworth wrote for its publication—

Strange fits of passion I have known:
And I will dare to tell,
But in the Lover's ear alone,
What once to me befell.

But when he dropped the last stanza, its comfortably "adult" conclusion is lost sight of, and we are no longer sure of the distance between the emotion felt and the tranquillity expressed.

Coleridge, copying out "A slumber did my spirit seal" for Poole, as part of his own complicated response to the news that his baby son Berkeley had suddenly died, made a positive identification of Lucy in the poem, but with only an oblique awareness of its significance. "Some months ago Wordsworth transmitted to me a most sublime Epitaph / whether it had any reality, I cannot say.—Most probably, in some gloomier moment he had fancied the moment in which his Sister might die."[46] Does "I cannot say" signify doubt or a prohibition? Years later, speaking to Crabb Robinson about Dorothy, Coleridge envied Wordsworth's having such a sister: "he also spoke of incest."[47]

In "Three years she grew," the little girl is taken as a bride by Nature, in the role of a prince of the realm, who raises her up to be just the woman he wants. Some of his requirements fit Dorothy ("wild with glee," "her virgin bosom"), and some don't ("rear her form to stately height"). But the point of the poem is less what she looks like than what she left the speaker as a legacy after going with Nature to her death:

> This heath, this calm, and quiet scene;
> The memory of what has been,
> And never more will be.

Her bequest is both a presence and an absence: he will *always* remember what *"never more* will be," just as Matthew "mourns less for what age takes away / Than what it leaves behind." The vast difference between Wordsworth's and Coleridge's beliefs about a realm of spirituality, and human access to it, can be measured by comparing this to Coleridge's epitaph, "On an Infant," dating from April of 1799. He sent it to England along with his copy of "A slumber did my spirit seal," to memorialize Berkeley. This child is not seduced by a calculating Prince Nature as in Wordsworth's poem, but departs in far more orthodox fashion: " 'Be, rather than be called, a child of God,' / Death whispered! With assenting nod . . . / The Baby bowed, without demur."[48]

Trying to prove that Dorothy is literally Lucy or that the Lucy poems refer directly to Dorothy is pointless, or beside the point. Most of them work like conundrums, to make us ask, Who is Lucy, what is she, that this swain so adores her? The powerful feelings which Wordsworth sublimates in these poems are not simply sexual, but sexual and fraternal feelings expressing, as in the *Prelude* and the Matthew poems, a fear of failing inspiration. Dorothy was not about to die, though Coleridge's pinpointing "the *moment* in which [she] might die" is an astute perception, and in *fancying* her dead, Wordsworth may be exploring a death wish, insofar as the double binds which kept him with her were the same ones that kept him from enjoying the good life with Coleridge.[49] But in either sense, immediate or lifelong, she must be dead *to him:* this is the "difference" that he expresses in the poems.

The possibility that the Lucy poems express a theme of psychological incest was first proposed forty years ago. The theory has often been rejected, more often ignored, but never systematically refuted, probably because it is so obviously relevant, though finally unprovable. If "Tintern Abbey" shows

Wordsworth in love with Dorothy, the Lucy poems, according to psychoanalytic theory, represent his determined effort to "refuse conscious recognition" of that fact under pressure of the new intensity in their relationship created by their isolation in Goslar.[50] But to reduce the meaning of these magical poems to a conscious or unconscious repressing of sexual feelings is an expense of theory in a work of shame. Yet equally wrongheaded is the determination, in supposedly defending our nature moralist, to deny the power of such feelings in their creation.

We know Dorothy is the Lucy in "The Glow-Worm" ("Among all lovely things my Love had been"), because Wordsworth told Coleridge derived from an incident at Racedown. Every Lucy in Wordsworth's poetry is not to be equated with Dorothy, but there are several other lines of evidence that lead to her. One is Wordsworth's reticence about these poems in his otherwise garrulous notes to his old neighbor Isabella Fenwick. "Composed in the Hartz forest," or "Written in Germany," is as much as he says about any of them. Thomas De Quincey noted that Wordsworth "always preserved a mysterious silence on the subject of that 'Lucy' repeatedly alluded to or apostrophised in his poems."[51]

For the purely psychological agenda of the poems, the reason that Lucy is dead, and curiously sexless for a lover, is obvious: she must be killed off and presented as never having been a *sexual* temptation in the first place, despite her highly sensual identification with the natural world.[52] If her naturalness is pushed hard enough, she will no longer be human: this is the shock recorded in "A slumber did my spirit seal": "No motion has she now, no force . . . Rolled round in earth's diurnal course, / With rocks, and stones, and trees." A more pragmatic psychological explanation, that Lucy's death expresses Wordsworth's frustration at not being able to be with Coleridge, is far from saying Wordsworth wished Dorothy were dead. Rather, the poems are simultaneously expressions of and defenses against the trauma of that event.[53]

Another version of "Nutting" has long been available (though ignored by critics), and recently published in still fuller form, which makes the essential identification of Dorothy with Lucy clearer and also suggests that the incest motivation being worked out in the poems was a temptation coming as much from Dorothy's direction as from William's, if not more so.[54] This version is nearly twice as long as the printed one, and shows that the "dearest maiden" suddenly addressed at the end of it is clearly Dorothy of "Tintern Abbey." In its published form the moral of "Nutting" about not violating Nature is stated bizarrely, as a little boy cutely decked out in old clothes for his nut-gathering expedition describes in astonishingly precocious sexual terms the "one dear nook" he will raid:

the hazels rose
Tall and erect, with milk-white clusters hung,
A virgin scene!—A little while I stood,
Breathing with such suppression of the heart
As joy delights in; and with wise restraint
Voluptuous, fearless of a rival, eyed
The banquet. . . .

(17–22)

He toys with the setting like a man who, frankly, has his pleasure right where he wants her and delights to prolong the anticipation: "In that sweet mood when pleasure loves to pay / Tribute to ease . . . of its joy secure." This highly sexed language makes the appearance of "dearest Maiden!" at the end of the poem far more surprising than Dorothy's emergence two-thirds of the way through "Tintern Abbey," and makes the speaker's admonition *to her* to "touch" these woods "with gentle hand" sound more than a bit hypocritical.

But in the longer form of the poem, the maiden has just broken off a branch of a tree herself: "Ah what a crash was that," it begins, and goes right into the admonition: "with gentle hand / Touch those fair hazels; my beloved Maid."[55] Thus Wordsworth mystifies a situation whose biographical reference in its original form was much clearer. He produces a better poem as a result. But in the original form the speaker proceeds to give the maiden a lesson in the proper way to express passion, very much as we saw Wordsworth doing in "Tintern Abbey," but now more explicitly. He says the woods all "shrink" from such "rude intercourse," and sets forth the kind of passion he would like to see in her face, as compared with the kind he actually does see—and fears:

While in the cave we sat thou didst o'erflow
With love even for the unsubstantial clouds
And silent incorporeal colours spread
Over the surface of the earth and sky.
But had I met thee now with that keen look
Half cruel in its eagerness, thy cheek
Thus rich with a tempestuous bloom, in truth
I might have half believed that I had pass'd
A houseless being in a human shape,
An enemy of nature, one who comes
From regions far beyond the Indian hills.

(6–15)

That is, he would have thought she was a gypsy, a category of persons always fascinating and upsetting to Wordsworth. As a "houseless being," this Lucy is as fearsomely *other* as the "vagrant dwellers in the houseless woods" around Tintern Abbey. Her coming from "far beyond the Indian hills" is like Coleridge's claiming he would have recognized the Boy of Winander in the "deserts of Arabia," but Wordsworth is incredulous to think that he could cry out "Dorothy!" on meeting such a passionate creature. So he asks her to calm down and modulate her feelings, to let her passion "o'erflow" more tranquilly, for him:

> Come rest on this light bed of purple heath
> And let me see thee sink to a dream
> Of gentle thoughts till once again thine eye
> Be like the heart of love and happiness,
> Yet still as water when the winds are gone
> And no man can tell whither.
>
> (17–22)

This hardly needs interpretation: Please be calm and don't alarm me with your passionate looks. Then he makes an awkward transition to the story of "Nutting," presented as his own lesson in learning how to control passion, but only after he has resettled her comfortably for such edification:

> And dearest maiden, thou upon whose lap
> I rest my head, oh! do not deem that these
> Are idle sympathies.
>
> (44–46)

The transition is awkward—in fact, it breaks the poem apart—because Wordsworth is trying to negotiate his "usual" passage from natural to human morality, which is very much harder, if not actually impossible, to cross than his naive admirers realize. It is also hard to recognize in his poetry because he has so well covered his tracks with the artistry of disguise. The sympathies he teaches Dorothy are far from "idle"; their force is highly sexual, as the language of the ensuing boyhood incident makes clear, language that rightly puzzles or shocks readers who come upon it with the orthodox image of Wordsworth in their minds.

In a closely related version of the poem the maiden is addressed as "Thou, Lucy, art a maiden 'inland bred.' "[56] This confirms that the "maiden" of "Nutting" is Lucy-Dorothy, and reveals much more besides. The internal quotation is from *As You Like It,* where they apply to the hero, Orlando, who must be gentled and tamed by Rosalind, the play's charming heroine, because Orlando is an intruder in the romantic Forest of Arden. Wordsworth's switch in genders shows that the boy/speaker and the Lucy/maiden are in effect *interchangeable,* a possibility typical of such loaded psychological fantasy material. It also points up that the problem being explored in all three versions of "Nutting" is one that the speaker and the maiden share.[57]

The incest thesis is greatly strengthened by this new evidence, which shows that Wordsworth was desperately determined to "repress a disruption of natural sibling relations."[58] The blunt fact is that, prurience aside, we do not much care whether Wordsworth had sexual relations with his sister or not. But we care a great deal if the knowledge increases our understanding and appreciation of his poetic development. His allusion to Shakespeare becomes especially interesting when correlated with an immediately following one to Ariosto: "the woods all shrink [from such rude intercourse], / As at the blowing of Astolpho's horn." Astolpho is the cousin of another Orlando, the hero of *Orlando Furioso.*[59] Astolpho restores the mad ("furioso") Orlando to his wits after he was driven to distraction by discovering the infidelity of another maiden, his beloved Angelica. This Angelica was deeply beloved by Wordsworth too; she was one of the damsels in distress he and Beaupuy used to imagine themselves rescuing as they discoursed about the human face of the French Revolution: "It was Angelica thundering through the woods / Upon her palfrey" (IX.454). Astolpho restores Orlando to his rightful role as the hero of his own epic,[60] and this is precisely Wordsworth's concern through all his Goslar poems: to remind himself that he is the proper poet for his own epic, *The Recluse,* both by right of Nature's nurture in his childhood and by the right course of nature he will preserve with Dorothy:

> Thou, Lucy, art a maiden "inland bred,"
> And thou hast "known some nurture"; but in truth
> If I had met thee here with that keen look
> Half cruel in its eagerness . . .
>
> (MS 15, 6–9)

. . . and so on, as we have seen. Ariosto's Orlando is saved from losing himself to a wild natural enchantress by the blowing of Astolpho's horn, which exposes her. Astolpho is just the story's alarm system, however. Both Orlandos are saved *by* their beloved woman, Angelica or Rosalind, a situation Wordsworth transposes from the enchanted male to the enchanted female in "Nutting" and, by variable implication, into the other Lucy poems.

Some twenty years later Wordsworth reflected on these "early hours" he spent with Dorothy in a pair of odes to "Lycoris," the name of the lost love of the shepherd Gallus in Virgil's tenth and last eclogue. Thinking of those times, Wordsworth muses,

We two have known such happy hours together
That, were the power granted to replace them (fetched
From out the pensive shadows where they lie)
In the first warmth of their original sunshine,
Loth should I be to use it: passing sweet
Are the domains of tender memory!
("To the Same," 47–51)

No prospect is so revealing as the retrospect, in Wordsworth, and these "domains" are precisely those of "Nutting," as four lines he inserted from its 1798 manuscript make clear. In the cave where he and "Lycoris" lie down to rest and cool themselves, he asks,

There let me see thee sink into a mood
Of gentler thought, protracted till thine eye
Be calm as water when the winds are gone,
And no one can tell whither. Dearest Friend!

Why, in Goslar, in 1798, should he think of "replacing" those hours unless the happiness they held were somehow felt to be suspect or censurable? Wordsworth's editors take pains as usual to keep him clean on his odd use of the name Lycoris: "It has no special significance for him."[61] But this is unlikely for a poet who knew Virgil as well as Wordsworth did. He would have known from his schooldays the significance of the tenth eclogue: it is Virgil's sad farewell to the pastoral mode as he continues his career's ascent toward the epic. This significance of Eclogue X had been famously kept up in English by Milton's "Lycidas," and was very apt to Wordsworth's situation in 1798–99, relative to his epic, *The Recluse,* including the question of whether the proto-*Prelude* poems were a contribution toward or a distraction from it. In Virgil's poem this valedictory gesture is contained in a negative lesson: Gallus should give up mourning his lost Lycoris, but he can't. Eighteenth-century classical scholarship may or may not have known that Lycoris was a real person, an actress named Cytheris (a.k.a. Volumnia), mistress of several Roman poets and a friend of Antony, but it certainly knew who Cornelius Gallus was: a military leader, a statesman, and a poet, one of the very few historical persons named in the *Eclogues.*[62] And the poem itself indicates whither she has fled with her soldier lover: "among the Alpine snows or over the frozen Rhine." Here is a reason for thinking of, or responding to, her name that took Wordsworth's memory in 1820 straight back to frozen Goslar of 1798–99. Gallus is trapped in the pastoral mode. He cannot stop thinking about Lycoris, nor can he adapt to the pleasant love-'em-and-lose-'em rhythms of literary pastoral; a rough soldier, he condemns himself to a life of exile in the forest, where he will roam about carving his lover's name on trees. Ovid's *Ars Amatoria* cites Lycoris as an example of a woman made famous by her poet.[63] She was not made famous by Wordsworth, but this late appearance by her in his poems is—by a series of displacements—exposed as a screen or mask of the woman he *did* make famous, his "Lucy," who by another skein of displacements must be seen as essentially identical to that other woman he made famous, but in far different contexts, his sister Dorothy.

That Dorothy was a more passionate person than her brother is everywhere a matter of record. Her eyes are called "wild" as regularly as his expression is called "calm." "The shooting lights of thy wild eyes" in "Tintern Abbey" are clearly reflected in "the keen look / Half cruel in its eagerness" of the "Nutting" manuscripts. Her dominating presence in these manuscripts confirms, by sheer force of contrast, Wordsworth's determination to elide her emotional affect in the Lucy poems.[64] Given Wordsworth's transposal of gender roles from his Renaissance and classical intertexts, it seems clear that not only the "Nutting" versions but all of the Lucy poems are, in varying degrees, evidence of his effort to deny Dorothy a love she wanted. She had turned twenty-seven in "the cold of [a] Christmas day . . . not equalled even in this climate during the last century," alone with him. She knew by now that she would never marry and that she was in a real sense wedded to her brother for life.[65] It is hard to argue that Dorothy missed out on a writing career for her devotion, but it is certainly true that she sacrificed herself *as a woman* to William's (vocational) desires.

The Lucy poems register some of the cost of this sacrifice, which we should respect and not condescend to by another kind of anachronism that presumes to know what was "normal" for young women and sisters at the end of the eighteenth century. Dorothy knew William had had mature sexual experience, that he had a "wife" and daughter with whom she herself was also intimate, and whose frustrating separation from William she also felt deeply. She was a "maiden" too, without sexual experience but with much erotic curiosity, and she trusted him wholly and completely. He had to teach her otherwise, but schooling her away from "such rude intercourse" was the same lesson he had to learn himself. This necessity is represented in one of several passages that contain versions of the same lessons as the "poem to Coleridge." When he attested that even as

> A child I held unconscious intercourse
> With the eternal beauty drinking in
> A pure organic pleasure from the lines
> *Of curling mist or from the smooth expanse*
> *Of waters coloured by the cloudless moon,*[66]

we can recognize in this landscape a sublimated lover's body, of the sort we saw Wordsworth drawing as early as his boyish metaphor of "the tufted grove" of Grasmere's cottage "peeping through . . . the veil . . . flutter[ing] . . . loosely chaste o'er all below" his lover's neck. Its last two lines chime exactly with the way William said he preferred to experience Dorothy's love:

> While in the cave we sat thou didst o'erflow
> With love even for the unsubstantial clouds
> *And silent incorporeal colours spread*
> *Over the surface of the earth and sky.*[67]

The whole effort is to render their intercourse "unconscious," "pure," and "incorporeal."[68] Wordsworth had to gain control of his passion for Dorothy in order to relay the same lesson to her. He said in "Tintern Abbey" she would be the future bearer of his "holy" love for nature, "when these [her] wild ecstasies shall be matured / Into a sober pleasure." In the longer version of "Nutting" he becomes the instructor of that maturing process; the *Prelude* fragments show it occurring in his childhood, and the other Lucy poems show the pain of his renouncing her. Their "gloomier" moment was not, as Coleridge *could not* say, his fancying the moment when she might die but his recognizing the moment when she must die *for him.*

Some devout readers of Wordsworth's poetry will insist forever that "Nutting" and its related texts are only about trees and reverence for nature. They *are* about this, but their highly charged erotic language shows that Wordsworth's reverence for natural bodies went well beyond trees, and any interpretation that insists on a literal reading of these loaded images and metaphors will find itself forced to explain a far stranger passion—for hazelnuts—than the altogether common and eternal one of a lonely brother and sister for each other, so mysteriously and powerfully confronted, and magnificently tamed, by the Lucy poems and their related intertexts.

Wordsworth wrote a few other poems in Goslar besides those about Lucy, Matthew, and himself, and they too are mostly about dead persons—abandoned women or, in "A Poet's Epitaph," a direct representation of his own death—the two closely related topics that were his constant preoccupation through his works and days at Goslar. "A Poet's Epitaph" is the autobiographical form of Wordsworth's epitaph writing in Goslar, but its self-pity serves to underscore the determined *rejection* of self-pity that started *The Prelude* there. Though influenced by his memories of similar laments from Theocritus and Burns, the poem is thoroughly Wordsworth.[69] The parade of unworthy mourners to the poet's grave is stylized and conventional, but each one has a specific identity in Wordsworth's youthful biography—in manuscript, the poem is called *"The* Poet's Epitaph"—which he here scores off: none of them are worthy to visit his grave. Not the Statesman (Lowther), the Lawyer (Robinson), the Doctor or Divine (Cookson), the Soldier (surely *not* Beaupuy), the Physician-Philosopher "that would peep and botanize / Upon his mother's grave" (Darwin),[70] and, last and least, especially not the Moralist (Godwin): "*He* has neither eyes nor ears; / Himself his world, and his own God . . . An intellectual All in All!" These are mean-spirited cheap shots, the hurtful sneers of a wounded ego which cannot recognize the similarity of that last characterization to his own egotism. As in Gray's "Elegy," the mourner and the mourned come together at the end of this poem, and the one worthy mourner is as recognizably Wordsworth as the fly on his stove or the little boy of "Nutting." He approaches "with modest looks, / And clad in homely russet brown"; his Nature Boy persona is well in train. The claims made for his insight are very modest ("some random truths he can impart"), but the similarity of his actions fits Wordsworth very well:

> But he is weak, both man and boy,
> Hath been an idler in the land; . . .
>
> —Come hither in thy hour of strength,
> Come, weak as is a breaking wave!
> Here stretch thy body at full length;
> Or build thy house upon this grave.
>
> (53–54, 57–60)

That last line can hardly be improved on, as a summary epigram for the whole range of Goslar epitaphs, and the heroic effort of writing in self-defense that Wordsworth made in Germany. He threw himself on the feared-dead body of his former imaginative self and began to build up the house of his future self, the "Wordsworth" of *The Prelude* and subsequent literary history, by taking sustenance from what seemed to be the grave of his own best hopes. The Goslar lyrics are more "refined" and apparently more "universal" than the Alfoxden ballads and lyrics, but not simply because Wordsworth has removed most of the social context or immediate emotion of the poems written that spring.[71] They are more refined (that is, tranquil) and more universal precisely because they are more personal and deeply, intimately emotional, though Wordsworth carefully excised or sublimated almost all the signs of that intimacy out of them. If the Lucy and Matthew poems make the loss of a loved one "a constant of human experience,"[72] it is because Wordsworth knew that loss so intimately and also knew that there were other ways than death of losing loved ones.

27

DESTINATION UNKNOWN

Southern Germany, February–April 1799

I travelled among unknown men,
In lands beyond the sea;
Nor, England! did I know till then
What love I bore to thee.
(ca. 1801)

Life was claustrophobic in Goslar that polar winter, and both William and Dorothy longed to be out and away. They had proposed leaving Goslar very shortly after they arrived, and were still talking of doing so in December. But they stayed on, probably because William was writing so well, and soon found themselves frozen in. William could draw comfort from Dorothy's company that was not available to his alter ego, the half-frozen fly on their stove: "No brother, no mate has he near him—while I / Can draw warmth from the cheek of my Love." But even this had begun to pall—or get too warm for comfort—by early February. Then, when it was still quite cold, they directed a series of letters to friends and family members, announcing their intention to leave Goslar and travel south, probably to Weimar, possibly as far as Switzerland. William drew on his Wedgwood account for the remainder of the total amount he expected to spend in Germany, £40, in case "we should prolong our stay beyond our expectations." It was easier to change money in Goslar, where they were at least slightly known, than it would be on the road. A tour of southern Germany at this time could easily take them through a dozen different principalities, some with "Pais [*pays*] Neutre" signs hung on trees, some without. The £40 was more than the total (£32) he had spent in four and a half months, for a tour they said would last no longer than two months, and when they got back to Hamburg at the end of April, he drew out another £25. Well over half their total expenditure in

Germany was laid out during the two months they spent somewhere in the south of Germany, primarily for transportation and perhaps for lodging on this trip, since their frugal eating habits always saved them money. Where did they go and what did they do?

On February 23 they left Goslar. They walked through the forests along the foot of the Harz Mountains for four days, passing through Clausthal and Osterode and other small towns, arriving at Nordhausen on February 27, a total distance of about fifty miles (see map). Their habits of sharp observation took in a great deal in these four days, noting tough women porters who looked like barbarians, a decayed gibbet where they were incongruously "saluted with the song of . . . a pair of larks a sweet, liquid and heavenly melody heard for the first time, after so long and severe winter," and a view of the Brocken, "the Mont Blanc of the Hartz forest" and fabled site of *Walpurgisnacht.*[1] In Osterode they were required to show their passports to some suspicious soldiers and were detained until their letters arrived in the trunk that was following them by wagon. After he had seen their letters, the burgomaster let them continue.[2] Were these the letters of introduction they had for Weimar, or just routine travel documents? In any case, they guaranteed safe conduct the rest of the way to Nordhausen.

Nordhausen was the terminus for diligences to "all the considerable towns of Saxony," especially Weimar and Jena, another fifty miles farther south. But at Nordhausen the Wordsworths' trail runs cold, and we see or hear no more of them for two months, when they pass hurriedly through Göttingen on April 20, staying only one night, appearing "melancholy & hypp'd [morbidly depressed]" to a perplexed Coleridge, before hurrying on to Hamburg and home.

There is a confused report that would place them in Göttingen in mid-March for a couple of days, but though this might account for their whereabouts from February 27 to ca. March 14 (that is, they might have traveled from Nordhausen down to Weimar and back up to Göttingen), it still leaves more than a month unaccounted for. The report is based on the 1836 memoirs of one of the young men, Clement Carlyon, who was part of Coleridge's hard-drinking set at Göttingen, expanded by a notoriously unreliable literary racounteur, William Howitt, in 1847.[3] Neither Coleridge nor the Wordsworths left any record of such a visit, though William's statement that they planned "to saunter about for a fortnight or three weeks at the end of which time you may be prepared to see us in Gottingen" does fit its time frame.[4] All it amounts to is a story of Coleridge and his friends angering some locals at an inn in Hesse-Cassel, about fifteen miles southwest of Göttingen, where they had gone to visit the "romantic Castle" of a Count Birdlipsch.[5] Carlyon heard the account at second hand, having arrived in

Göttingen after the incident occurred, and he says the two poets left Dorothy behind because they were in an "entire inter-communion of thought, thereby becoming the whole world to each other."

Another version of this tale conflates the trip to Hesse-Cassel with Coleridge's two "Harz-Reise" tours, but claims that the Wordsworths didn't go along, because the other young men didn't think it was proper to bring a young woman along.[6] It might not have been proper to travel with *them,* given their carousing habits, but that Wordsworth should leave Dorothy alone anywhere on this trip is as unlikely as that he and Coleridge would accede to the younger men's notions of feminine propriety. And his "inter-communion" with Coleridge was far more apt to include Dorothy than exclude her. But even if this unlikely incident occurred, it still leaves a good month unaccounted for, puts an out-of-the-way loop in their itinerary, and creates the puzzle as to why, after so many months of missing Coleridge, they should see him again so briefly on such unsatisfactory terms, and then go off on their own again.

So we come to the third and last set of "lost" months in young Wordsworth's life, to add to the autumn of 1793 and the six months in London in 1795. There are three possibilities for accounting for this time in Germany. The first is that they did what they said they would: toured around more southerly locales until time, the weather, expenses, boredom, or discomfort drove them home—where, as their early February letters indicate, they had decided to go anyway. But in one of these letters Wordsworth suggests alternative possibilities, saying that if they are not back in Hamburg in two months—"if we should prolong our stay beyond our expectations"—"our letters will be forwarded to us," presumably by Remnant, the wonderfully named English bookseller, who knew where to reach them.[7]

The second possibility is that they went to Weimar to see the splendid court and intellectual life that was unfolding there. Goethe was there, at the height of his powers, resuming work on *Faust,* publishing the *Propyläen* journal, staging parts of Schiller's *Wallenstein,* and seriously reintegrating himself into the official and cultural life of a place and a time that ranks among the most brilliant in the world history of arts and letters. The *Balladenjahr* had just ended, with its confident cultural reaffirmations, and Schelling, Fichte, and the elder Schlegel were visiting frequently from Jena; Steffens and Novalis were not far away.[8] Goethe's friendship with Schiller (often compared to Wordsworth's with Coleridge) was ripening through correspondence, though Schiller did not actually come over to Weimar to live until December. Dorothy said they had letters of introduction for Weimar, and if they did (from Klopstock? from Thomas Beddoes, the Bristol Germanist?), it is a wonder they did not go.

The third possibility is that they were embarked on some kind of errand or messenger service for the Foreign Office, specifically having to do with closing the "Swabian agency" run by James Talbot and his brother Robert. Talbot was informed by a letter from Grenville in early March that he was to "hand over the whole of his Mission to an Officer who would be sent out," primarily the more than £75,000 that had been forwarded to him (of £400,000 authorized) for paying his subagents, bribing French royalists, and helping to arm and outfit Swiss volunteer troops and some regular Austrian army units.[9] The policy decision to close the agency had been taken in mid-January, when Grenville discovered that the wild Lord Camelford, his own brother-in-law and Pitt's cousin (and lover of Lord Stanhope's daughter), had been detained at Dover with evidence on his person of a plot to assassinate some or all of the five French directors.[10] This was the plot, Grenville now realized with horror, that Talbot had been aiding and abetting all along, with funds that, if not recouped, would lead to a public accounting by the treasury, forcing Grenville to repay from his personal fortune, probably costing him his position in the government as well, possibly forcing a new election, and discrediting England abroad.[11]

Not a word, not an image, not a memory survives that is traceable to these two months. This fact alone, it seems safe to say, rules out the Weimar possibility. That Wordsworth should have been in Weimar and never said a word about it is even more incredible than that he should have been all set to go there, letters of introduction in hand—and then not gone! This is one of the great near-misses of literary history, that the young Wordsworth, approaching thirty, did not meet or see the mature Goethe at the height of his powers, when he was only fifty miles away from him and apparently fully intending to go there. He would have been received at some acceptably decent level: Coleridge's experience at Ratzeburg shows how favorably genteel, educated Englishmen were regarded in Germany, as Coleridge and Wordsworth already knew from the experience of their friends John Tweddell and Tom Wedgwood.

The first possibility, touring the south, is of course the most likely in default of other evidence: they did what they planned to do and then never said a word about it to anyone. Dorothy's letters provide meticulous information about their four days' walk from Goslar to Nordhausen, but what happened to the next two months?

The fact of complete silence fits the third possibility very well, for that is exactly what we would expect for an errand or mission into southern Germany to relay or deliver orders, or pick up papers or money as part of the process of closing Talbot's Swabian mission. Not that Wordsworth himself was the "Officer . . . sent out." For a mission of such political delicacy, this was probably Grenville's own brother, Tom, who arrived in Germany in March as an envoy to the German courts.[12] But the decisive tactical decisions were taken in London between March 22 and May 25, covering the period of Wordsworth's disappearance, especially the first week of this period, when Grenville was totally in charge of all foreign policy decisions, Pitt having fallen into a funk of discouragement over the war effort.[13]

There are references to a "lost" journal that William and Dorothy kept together which might shed light on this period. This may not be a separate booklet, but could refer to fourteen pages torn out of the "Hamburg journal" or to some fifty pages torn out of the "Christabel Notebook," since these notebooks were not discrete units but were used for many different purposes (language exercises, poetry drafts, partial accounts, and the like).[14] It is remarkable, though not impossible, that they should lose a whole journal, leaving a large gap in an otherwise uninterrupted sequence from January 1798, when Dorothy began her Alfoxden journal, until she started her Grasmere journal in May 1800. But ripping out pages that contained compromising information would make sense.

Coleridge seems to refer to this "lost" journal in 1800 when he explained to the publisher Thomas Longman why he hadn't delivered his promised account of Germany (he never did). But his explanation, if it is not mere temporizing, raises as many questions about the contents of this putative journal as it answers. Coleridge said Wordsworth "offered me the use of his Journal tho' not of his name," for an "account of Germany farther south than I had been" (that is, below Göttingen). Coleridge proposed to substitute chapters adapted from this journal for his own "obnoxious" account "of the Illuminati [which] would raise a violent clamour against me & my publisher."[15] The Illuminati were a secret brotherhood of freethinking intellectuals, akin to the Freemasons, who were active in southern Germany around Ingolstadt (Victor Frankenstein's university).[16] Though officially disbanded in 1785, they continued to figure prominently in some of the wildest conspiracy theories of the French Revolution, which was already well on its way to becoming the great grandmother of all modern political conspiracy theories. The influence of the Illuminati persisted especially in the universities, most particularly at Göttingen, where the English influence gave plausibility to charges of "religious infidelity," the usual code phrase for presumed revolutionary conspiracies.[17] The *voyageurs* of the royalist underground, James Talbot informed his superiors, communicated by "universally known passwords and signs, 'given as in Freemasonry,' which enabled political travellers to receive help wherever they went."[18] Hence the implied contents of Wordsworth's journal are not very reassuring for a neutral interpretation of it: it was less "obnoxious" than an account of the Illuminati, but still something that Wordsworth did not want his name associated with. Why not, if he and Dorothy were just touring? Was there something about being present in southern Germany that he knew would compromise him with some people, or blow his—or their—cover?

Their earliest plans had included a trip southward. Dorothy had been hoping to visit Switzerland when she wrote to Aunt Rawson the previous summer explaining the German trip: "If the state of Europe will permit . . . we shall travel as far as the tether of a slender income will permit."[19] William had taken his copy of Ramond de Carbonnières's translation of Coxe's *Travels* in Switzerland with him, his faithful guide in 1790. But this "translation" was much more than that. An Alsatian, Carbonnières was a disciple of Sturm and Drang, and had Germanized and romanticized the sober English Coxe, adding references to many German and Swiss persons and places that interested Wordsworth: Klopstock, Gessner, and Lavater among them.[20] Christopher Wordsworth's *Memoir* hints that his aunt and uncle went pretty far south, "to a more genial climate."[21]

By February of 1799 their travel hopes had contracted to a trip of "a couple of months," or a wish to "saunter about for a fortnight or three weeks."[22] For one thing, they had less money than they had hoped for, and all of it was borrowed. For another, "the state of Europe" did *not* permit unrestricted rambling, especially in southern Germany, since in October Austrian and Swiss troops had reoccupied some towns in Switzerland and engaged the French in skirmishes both above and below its border with the German principalities.[23] This was the beginning of General Suvorov's famous campaign, in which his first English liaison officer was Robert Craufurd, Sir James's brother. He was following in the footsteps of their other brother, Charles, who had been invalided home the previous year, via Frankfurt, where he was visited by Wickham in retreat from the debacle of 18 Fructidor, the end of the Directory—and of England's efforts to infiltrate and control it.[24] So we can assume that English communications between Hamburg and the south were well kept up, on both professional and personal grounds.

In the spate of letters William and Dorothy sent off in early February, they informed almost everybody they knew about their plans. This was just good sense, when heading in the direction of warfare in a foreign country, though their relatives, if they had had anything like modern access to news, would have been stunned at the folly of a tour in that direction. They had had reason to wonder similarly about William's trips to the Continent in 1790 and 1791—to say nothing of 1793, when they may have been manipulated precisely so as *not* to have anything to remark. One indication of what their relatives knew is especially tantalizing. On March 31 Mrs. Rawson wrote to one of the Ferguson cousins, lamenting that William was "spending his Youth in so unprofitable a way" and forwarding two of Dorothy's letters (now lost) with this introduction: "I mean to send you Dorothys two Letters from Goslar in lower Saxony they intend—but you will see what they intend."[25] Obviously, Dorothy would not have given any information about an errand for the Foreign Office, and her projection of a "little circuit from town to town" is plausible: the weather was too cold and wet for real wandering; they would have had to walk predetermined distances in order to end up in a town or village each night. That's what they started out doing, on foot from Goslar, and what they seem poised to continue doing, by diligence, from Nordhausen. But they also left themselves little escape clauses. They would tour around, "unless we should meet with so pleasant a residence in Saxony as should induce us to stay here longer than seems at present likely. If we do not, we shall go to Hamburgh at the end of two months"; their mail would be forwarded, if they prolonged their stay beyond their expectations.[26] This is just about what they did do, but they did not see anything past Nordhausen worth recording or, if recorded, worth saving.

Have we seen this kind of behavior somewhere before in the biographies of young William and Dorothy Wordsworth? Indeed we have. Their open-plan excursion into Saxony sounds like their double, and perhaps duplicitous, accounts of William's projected tour to the west of England in the summer and fall of 1793 and their proposed reunion at Halifax at the end of it—neither of which actually occurred, though both together provided a plausible cover story for William's clandestine trip back to France. The large number of letters they sent off at one time (eight in all, though only three survive)[27] could suggest a deliberate misinformation campaign with the same aim: tell everybody concerned where we're going, so each person's report would confirm others' inquiries, and then go somewhere else, that can't be traced or checked—and keep quiet about it forever after.

To state all these alternatives as cautiously as possible, we can rest on Mark Reed's considered judgment: their travels that spring, without any other alternative explanation, "must have been far different from what was originally projected if their only visit [to Göttingen] was that of late April."[28] The interesting question is, *How* "far different"?

What would Wordsworth have been doing, if he was on a mission, even if only as a subcontracted courier, for the Foreign Office? For this, we have not a clue, but only educated guesses: some kind of pickup or delivery, of a receipt or a message, to the Swabian agency's main area of operations, which was one to two hundred miles south of Nordhausen, inside an equilateral triangle formed by Augsburg and Ulm at its southernmost point, Frankfurt at its northwest angle, and Bayreuth at its northeast. Although called the Swabian agency by the British, the French royalists called themselves the Comité de Bayreute, and its agents were centered there and at Coburg, both in Franconia, closer to Nordhausen and Weimar. (Wordsworth later described Goslar, inaccurately, as the former seat of the Franconian emperors.)[29] Though Louis XVIII had gone into Russia, his agents were still in place, "all of whom had subordinate agents in the provinces," of whom the Wordsworths' "French Emigrant Priest" in Goslar could have been one.[30]

Without the entry in Portland's paybook and other evidences of the British secret service's knowledge of Wordsworth, accented by this gap in his life record, which in turn coincides with the winding up of the Swabian agency, these conjectures might seem unwarranted. But with these two kinds of evidence—one documentary, the other a conspicuous lack of documentation—some kind of hypothesis seems required. As with the 1793 trip to France, the mildest possibility seems the most plausible (he stayed in Wales then, he toured southern Germany now). But there is no evidence to support it. In both cases the only available evidence tends to support the wildest possibility.

Whatever Wordsworth thought about spies and provocateurs in Germany, he—"that *dark* one!"—wasn't—saying anything. His acquaintance with M. de Leutre was so "confidential" that neither he nor Dorothy ever said anything about it. Coleridge was well aware that there were spies everywhere in Germany. In May, when he and his party of young English friends made their first trip to the Harz Mountains, responding to William and Dorothy's enthusiastic descriptions, they headed straight for Blankenburg. "Some enquires which we had made concerning him [Louis XVIII] at Rubeland [the next town but one before Blankenburg] had occasioned a suspicion of our being Spies, [&] one fellow whom we asked answered us—'I'll die for my King & Country / & what sort of French Fellows are you?' Hence we were shy of the Subject."[31] At about the same time, Coleridge rang an early change on his "Spy Nozy" motif:

—On Mr Ross, usually cognominated *Nosy,*
I fancy whenever I spy nosy
Ross
More great than Lion is Rhynose-
ros[32]

This notebook entry follows one on the tomb of Lucas Cranach, so there is a good possibility that it was written in or near Goslar. Were Coleridge and his friends being followed? The doggerel is made up of equal parts of specific reference and sheer wordplay: "Spy Nosy Ross" is transformed by sound and sense into "Rhy-nose-ros." Any spy could be considered "nosy," and Coleridge may already have thought of James Walsh in this way, though his account of him in the *Biographia* was still two decades off. Given his interplay of linguistic pun and objective reference, we can wonder if "Lion" means "lyin'," or refers to the British Lion, and if its matching Unicorn is "cognominated" by one real animal that does resemble it, the rhinoceros. This kind of speculation is the very opposite of determinative, to be sure (though Coleridge loved it), but conflicts between "The Lion and the Unicorn" were a traditionally popular way of encoding civil unrest and dissension in the British body politic. It is clear that Ross is someone Coleridge knew, possibly a suspected spy in the large community of British students at Göttingen, some of whom (like Coleridge himself) the Foreign Office might have wanted to keep an eye on. Would some such fear have made the Wordsworths go through town in such a hurry in April, especially if this was the only time they had seen their beloved friend since October? Or was it the even worse fear of being recognized and *acknowledged* by the likes of Ross?

The Foreign Office had no trouble keeping track of Wordsworth; four of the five extant letters he and Dorothy sent to England, including three of the eight sent off detailing their travel plans in early February, were franked through the Foreign Office. And the person in that very small office who was directly in charge of controlling Talbot and communicating with Craufurd was George Canning, the undersecretary, late editor of and main contributor to the *Anti-Jacobin,* whose last long blast at Britons sympathetic to "the New Morality" of republican ideology and Theophilanthropic/Masonic mumbo jumbo had been directed against "C-—-ridge and S-—they, L-—d and L-—mbe, & Co."

Wordsworth was well aware of the insecurity of the post, for he "dare[d] not trust . . . to a letter" his final communication from Nordhausen, about "a new invention for washing" they had seen, which they hoped to patent when they returned, assuring Coleridge, "You shall be a partner, Chester likewise."[33] What modern convenience was lost to posterity when the Wordsworth washing machine failed to go into production? Wordsworth went merely so far as to explain that "only one washing bason [would be] necessary for the largest family in the kingdom." Needing money as badly as they did, and "wishing not to be in debt" when they returned, they didn't want their get-rich-quick scheme to fall into other hands, because they knew that the mails were opened. That is one explanation for their guardedness. Or is this a coded reference to something else? Something that could *guarantee* his not being "in debt when I return"? Certainly the debts of one "Mr. Wordsworth" were notably relieved by Portland's payment in June. Was he involved in some other kind of laundering operation? Of Grenville's money, for example? That use of the verb "to launder" is an anachronism, of course. But what kind of invention could this have been? It must have been a pretty big basin, to accommodate "the largest family in the kingdom." Would that be King George's family—that is, all loyal Englishmen? And would its "immense saving" be realized in basins, labor, time, or money?

How Wordsworth got himself into this position (if he did) is a matter that demands some conjecture. In a sense, he had passed from the surveillance, or control, of the Home Office to that of the Foreign Office, via the *Anti-Jacobin*. He could have been a man marked for compromise as early as 1791, and his associates and likely activities in France in 1792–93 and London in 1795 would not have removed him from suspicion; quite the contrary. If we presume that he knew far more than he let on about James Walsh's report in 1797, we can readily imagine that he was horrified to find himself suspected by the government and that he volunteered his services as a way of dispelling suspicion, or at least agreed to serve when asked.[34] Yet his name was already "well known" to Richard Ford by then: how so? If he was a government courier now, had he also been one in the late summer of 1793, when presented with another opportunity to mix business with pleasure or to cover private business with public business? Southey and Lloyd took no less self-serving steps, and far more public ones, to try to remove their "Jacobin" labels.

Perhaps William Cavendish, the duke of Portland, saw in the various reports about young Wordsworth from his operatives Walsh, Ford, and Canning an opportunity to reclaim—to *turn,* in technical espionage terms—the wandering son of the hapless lawyer who had prepared Sir James Lowther's briefs against Portland at the beginning of their long dispute over the rights to Inglewood Forest near Penrith thirty years earlier. If so, Portland's draft on "Mr. Wordsworth's" behalf returns us to the scenes of Wordsworth's childhood in a way that uncannily parallels—and materially supports—those first drafts of *The Prelude* by which Wordsworth, "writing in self-defense," sought to recover and preserve himself as a poet. Whether the offer came in friendly terms or as threatened blackmail, the shifting nature of Wordsworth's opinions on revolution and social reform would have made co-operation more palatable, especially if it was sufficiently lucrative.

For he was developing a vast sense of the entitlements of genius. In Goslar he composed several hundred lines of blank verse "argument," a series of five syllogisms about the necessary independence of the creative mind.[35] They are preoccupied with the negative effects on genius of the "law severe of penury" and the need to earn a living; they form an economic subtext to the ideology of genius presented in the grander passages of nature worship he interleaved with his boyhood "spots of time." He did not send these arguments to Coleridge, nor did he ever publish them, except for occasional lines drafted into service to shore up weak spots in the logic of both *The Prelude* and *The Excursion*. In general, they urge the need for freedom in all human minds if men are to perform good actions, since economic hardship will prevent, and prudential moralisms will not sufficiently produce, the essential spontaneity that is the hallmark of true morality. But at bottom they are efforts to construct a philosophical justification of the need for the Poet to be financially independent in order to be morally and creatively independent. He was very concerned not to be in debt when he returned to England, and he knew he had been accumulating nothing *but* debt during his months in Germany. He had received no word about the sales of *Lyrical Ballads,* and though he knew that Montagu and Douglas owed him money, he also knew about their aristocratic propensity to put off repaying any debt—as they continued to do for more than a year after he returned.

Furthermore, he and Coleridge had now seen themselves, as Englishmen, as far different from the kind of revolutionary "angels" he and Robert Jones had seemed to be to the "saucy" Frenchmen when they sailed down the Rhône in 1790. They saw that England was regarded as Europe's last best hope against a revolutionary republicanism that had turned toward imperial expansion. As Coleridge said, "being abroad makes every man a Patriot & a Loyalist—almost a Pittite!"[36] His young friends in Göttingen were impressed by Coleridge's keen appreciation of the political difficulties Pitt faced in getting England through the crises of 1798–99, despite Coleridge's opposition to the war and his continuing loyalty to Fox.[37] Wordsworth returned to England in 1799 far less "disaffected" than Walsh had reported him in 1797, or than Canning had satirized "Coleridge & Co." for being in 1798. He was still three years away from the great "Sonnets on National Liberty and Independence," but on the way to them he wrote a late Lucy poem which looked back to the "melancholy dream" of Goslar with a firm statement of its outcome:

> I travelled among unknown men,
> In lands beyond the sea;
> Nor, England! did I know till then
> What love I bore to thee.

This is a kind of *re*-conversion poem, underscored by the same deep signature of all his inspirations in Goslar, the death of Lucy: "And thine [England] too is the last green field / That Lucy's eyes surveyed." He vowed, "Nor will I quit thy shore a second time."

Something like this was already their mood when they stopped overnight with Coleridge on April 20–21, "melancholy & hypp'd." Coleridge noted "they burn with such impatience to return to their native Country, they who are all to each other."[38] He walked five miles out of town with them along the coach road toward Hanover and Hamburg. Wordsworth was "affected to tears" when Coleridge told him that Poole was the man "in whom alone I had felt an *anchor!*"[39] Poole feared for Coleridge's "amalgamation" with Wordsworth, but Coleridge saw that Wordsworth was suffering from the opposite malady: "dear Wordsworth appears to me to have hurtfully segregated & isolated his Being / Doubtless, his delights are more deep and sublime; but he has likewise more hours, that prey on his flesh & blood."[40]

They left Hamburg as soon as they got there, sometime between April 26 and 28, just as Europe began to fall apart behind them. On April 28 George Harward, Craufurd's subagent at Cuxhaven, began to think that all this surveillance had gone far enough. He hoped that an Austrian victory over the French would "perhaps allow us to despise the efforts of insignificant individuals" to travel to and from England.[41] William and Dorothy Wordsworth might have appeared as just such "insignificant individuals," but Harward's liberal hopes were misplaced, for on that very day the French deputies to the Rastatt peace conference were assassinated by some Austrian hussars. This assassination solidified French distrust of all monarchies, confirmed their worst fantasies about "perfidious Albion," and assured the reentry of Austria into the war along with the princes of southern Germany. Though not in the way James Talbot intended when he fruitlessly spent thousands of Grenville's pounds in *his* assassination plot, the Austrian hussars had achieved part of the goal the British Foreign Office had been working toward since 1793: widening the war with France. But like most political assassins, the hussars got far more and much worse than they bargained for. Wordsworth left Germany and returned home just as the die was cast that would lead, by November, to the end of the Directory and the transfer of power to a new government, headed by a "consul": the 18 Brumaire of Napoleon Bonaparte.

At this same time in April, Sir James Craufurd in Hamburg closed the net he had been carefully positioning all year, arresting the Irish republicans and their French agents: Napper Tandy, General Blackwell, George Peters (a.k.a Corbet), Hervey Mountmorres, and others.[42] Craufurd's efforts were well rewarded by his superiors, as his note of gratitude to Grenville makes clear:

> I cannot express to you my Lord my gratitude for the most gracious approbation with which His Majesty has been pleased to honour my humble endeavours in his service. Unconscious as I was of having deserved it I cannot now venture to call it unmerited since His Majesty has thought fit to confer it.[43]

Craufurd's arrests were not carried out solely at his own discretion: they were timed to coordinate with arrests of United Irishmen conspirators in London taverns in March and April under the direct supervision of Pitt, Portland, and Wickham, the precise timing of which had been their main preoccupation since late February: coincidentally, the time at which Wordsworth left Goslar and disappeared.[44]

The payments recorded in Portland's book in early June mark the wrap-up of Wickham's espionage work in London, for he now returned to the

Continent to continue his work on the ground, coordinating military strategy at Schaffhausen, in Switzerland, with Colonel Craufurd, who was now appointed British attaché to the Austrian and Russian general staffs.[45] The colonel's brother, Sir James, was paid £415 in three installments in early June. Paid, that is, by the duke of Portland, home secretary and head of the "Secret Department," not by Grenville, the foreign secretary, Craufurd's normal superior. On June 13 "Mr. Wordsworth" was paid £92 12s. from the same account. The amount is so close to the figures we have for Wordsworth's drafts upon the Wedgwood agents as to warrant further suspicion of a meaningful correlation. As we noted earlier, the payment to Wordsworth looks like the settlement of an odd-amount expense claim, for which receipts might well have had to be presented. The total Wordsworth drew on the Wedgwoods while in Germany was £97 7s. 3d., a difference from the payment to "Mr. Wordsworth" of only £4 15s. 3d. He had taken an advance of £20 from them with him, and he borrowed three guineas (£3 3s.) from Coleridge in Göttingen, which they agreed to consider an advance from the Wedgwoods, for a total of £120 10s. 3d. But he had instructed Richard to pay back the £20 to the Wedgwoods before he left for Germany, so the exact amount of Wordsworth's Wedgwood debt on his return was £100 10s. 3d. This amount agrees with the Wedgwood records, despite Wordsworth's statement on his return that his total debt to them was £110 13s.[46] If the Home Office's "Mr. Wordsworth" was indeed William Wordsworth and he was claiming expenses for services rendered, he could hardly have presented a receipt to George Canning from Coleridge, of all people. Hence, subtracting the loan from Coleridge, we are returned to the figure of £97 7s. 3d. as the total drawn on the Wedgwoods while in Germany, from which it is not difficult to imagine another £4 15s. 3d. being deducted as some nonallowable expenses by the shrewd and careful accountants who were at the base of Portland's financial arrangements with Parliament: for example, 20 marks (about 16s.) for Bürger's poems and Percy's *Reliques*.[47]

These figures in themselves do not tell us what the Wordsworths were doing in southern Germany, but the coincidences do add up. On June 10—that is, between the dates of the two payments to Mr. Wordsworth—Grenville wrote to George Hammond (after Canning and Frere, the highest-paid of Grenville's secret operatives) regarding a friend of "Baron" de Leutre's whom he recommended to Grenville's attention.[48] In the context of these administrative coincidences, it could be said that Wordsworth's books and Portland's come close to balancing each other, and that the slight but firm weight of this evidence is the straw that tips the balance toward the likelihood that the creation of the Poet in Germany involved not only his declaration of independence from Coleridge's mind ("Was it for this?"), and his declaration of independence from Dorothy's heart ("with gentle hand touch . . . beloved Maid"), but also a declaration of *de*pendence on the coffers of the nation-state that he now, after a terrible year of isolation and self-exile, said "he had learned to know the value of." He was normalizing his sexual relations with Dorothy at the same time that he was normalizing his political relations with the British government, and it is fitting that both processes were completed on the same mysterious trip. As Coleridge said, Wordsworth's words always mean *all* of their possible meanings, and the "value . . . he had learned" may have been £92 12s., a figure also very close to the £100 a year that he had been saying throughout the decade was his ideal minimum for a life of independent creativity.

If he was to avoid the penalty of the "law severe of penury" which "blocks out the forms of nature," he may have decided that his "liberty of mind" made it worthwhile to strike a deal with the "Secret Department" for an offer that might have been pretty hard to refuse anyway, if it was threatening to harass or expose him.[49] His justification for this higher liberty is expressed in language that shows that his conception of it went beyond the law. Or rather, that it put him outside the bounds of law, so that, like Rivers-Oswald in *The Borderers*—but as a member of the establishment rather than as an outlaw—he acts by "the light of circumstance," putting himself (in his own estimation) beyond conventional judgments for betraying, or in this case cooperating with, the powers that be:

we know
That *when we stand upon our native soil,*
Unelbowed by such objects [like financial obligations] as oppress
Our active powers *those powers themselves become*
Subversive of our noxious qualities:
And by the substitution of delight
And by new influxes of strength *suppress*
All evil; then the being spreads abroad
His branches to the wind; and all who see
Bless him, rejoicing in his neighborhood.
There is one only liberty; 'tis his
Who by beneficence is circumscribed;
'Tis his to whom the power of doing good
Is *law and statute, penalty, and bond,*
His prison, and his warder, his who finds
His freedom in the joy of virtuous thoughts.[50]

This is a highly unusual way of defining a "freedom of the universe" derived from the "active principle alive in all things." The whole passage uses political language—but of a police state—as a metaphor for the individual's internal regulation of his own higher morality.[51] Those to whom such freedom is granted are first made "subversives" against their own evil ("noxious") tendencies, and then locked up in the prison house of their own virtue, rather than in "the close prison-house of human laws." The "freedom of the universe" operates, internally, almost like a secret police against our own worst impulses, far more effective than "chains . . . shackles, and . . . bonds" (26–27). This recalls the antiminstrel demon-police in "The Vale of Esthwaite" and is not unlike the operation of the "Secret Department," whose chief organizational merit (as Wickham explained to Portland) was linking the Home Office to the Foreign Office in such a way that "no other office could ever know anything of what was passing there, unless instructed from the Fountain Head."[52] In both cases, the common element (for Wordsworth) was the connection between writing poetry and making money: then, to escape having "to delve in Mammon's joyless mine"; now, to avoid the "law severe of penury." A similar mode of operation characterizes Wordsworth's conception of the moral force of his imagination, flowing from its fountainhead, in language that seems purely metaphorical but that, upon closer examination, appears—as we see so often in texts deriving from the contexts of his young life—to be literally descriptive as well.

Was this rhetoric adopted by a man who had been offered the alternatives of cooperation or exposure and imprisonment? The Irish republican rebels who had been at large in Hamburg when he arrived in September 1798 were now under arrest, he learned when he returned there in April 1799. What price rebellion? Or, since it is hard to imagine what acts Wordsworth could have been threatened with arrest for committing, is it the conflicted, double-bind rhetoric of a man who has accepted money from the "warders" of the state's prisons rather than face—what he feared to face after his German sojourn, when he again stood "upon our native soil"—those other penalties, of "the law severe of penury," a crushing load of debt, which would make him "the worst of slaves, the slave / Of his own house"?[53]

He would soon find that "house," but it would be a "home": home at Grasmere. In his poem of that title Wordsworth would develop these sociopolitical images in ways that suggest his allegiance to England, demonstrated by his willingness to cooperate with the "Secret Department," was not ultimate, but the price he was willing to pay in the name of a higher allegiance, to his own imagination and a powerful, personal conception of himself as the Poet of his nation.

Postscript

If Wordsworth was working secretly for Pitt's government in the late 1790s, the fact forces some adjustment in our sense of the poetical revolution he and Coleridge promulgated, and of the costs of creating himself as the Poet of the prefaces to *Lyrical Ballads.* At a minimum, it means that he and his poetry existed much more within the confines of established social and cultural norms than the traditional romanticizing of his poetical revolution acknowledges. His later conservatism thus appears less as a betrayal of his younger self than as its continuation in more public (and more extreme) forms. This was a suspicion that his younger contemporaries always had of him and that recent scholarship has substantially confirmed.[54] It is also a tendency that this biography has documented from his earliest days, beginning with his family's close association with the archconservative house of Lowther.

But it is important to keep the fact—if it is one—in perspective. First of all, he was doing nothing illegal, and his service may have been at the lowest level of contract work for operations he knew nothing about, though he cannot have been unaware of their fundamental nature. Leftist historicist critics of Wordsworth's antiradical ideology may have a field day with this new information, because it seems to confirm their frequent thesis about the inevitable complicities of genius with the established order. There is some truth to this, obviously. Any imaginative work will have a political coloration, ultimately, in one direction or another, and none will ever be politically correct except from a perspective that shares those politics. There is always a strong desire to want great art to be on the side of human liberation, and there are few eras in which this desire was stronger—or more contested—than the Romantic period. There is little question that much of Wordsworth's work at the turn of the century was firmly based on "liberation politics"; the question is how much its political implications are compromised by his other political allegiances and actions. But before we pillory him for not remaining steadfast to the ideology of the French Revolution, we should remember that that ideology was shifting on an almost daily basis throughout the 1790s.

The historicist critique of Wordsworth's implication in the power structures of his time commonly suffers from being insufficiently historical. It is anachronistic in its tendency to see liberation politics as something clear and consistent in the 1790s. And it is unimaginatively historical when this anachronism leads it to produce very bland, inadequate interpretations of the possibilities of political action around 1800. The pressures on young men like Wordsworth and Coleridge trying to maintain their integrity, while also somehow keeping body and soul together materially, were enormous. They were not independently wealthy, such actions as they did take during the 1790s had already effectively removed them from the help of the family and friends on whom they were dependent, and they did not have to look far beyond their own circle to see a variety of unprofitable martyrdoms: those of William Frend, John Thelwall, Gilbert Wakefield, and William Godwin, just to start to list.

Finally, the direction of their politics and its effect on their writings were part of a very general trajectory for the times, reflected in the lives and works of thousands of intellectuals in all European countries, and in the new United States of America as well, no friend to Jacobin politics. That Coleridge and Wordsworth moved from left to right is not news, of course, but what we have seen in the last five or six chapters refines our understanding of the concrete details of their movement and should increase our sympathy with it as well. But by the same token, the five or so chapters preceding the last six showed that Wordsworth's involvement in the politics and poetics of the left was also deeper than we have realized. His extreme movements toward the right must thus be understood in light of his stronger-than-recognized movements toward the left. There were no "free" trips in either direction: going home to Grasmere looks like an escape, but insofar as it was paid at government expense, it was more like an early witness-protection plan, except that the witness stood in danger of being recognized by no one but himself, and had to fear the "unjust Tribunals" not of the state but "of treachery and desertion in the place / The holiest that I knew of—my own soul" (X.377–80).

PART THREE

WHAT IS A POET?

1799–1807

"WE HAVE LEARNT TO KNOW ITS VALUE" 28

Sockburn-on-Tees, May–December 1799

> It is a grazing estate, and most delightfully pleasant, washed nearly round by the Tees, (a noble river), and stocked with sheep and lambs which look very pretty, and to me give it a very interesting appearance.
>
> (Dorothy Wordsworth)[1]

Returning to Yarmouth at the end of April after seven upsetting months abroad, William and Dorothy rapidly pushed on north to the Hutchinson family estate at Sockburn-on-Tees, just south of Darlington. Directly on their route lay Norwich, where Christopher was to be ordained on May 12, sponsored by William Cookson.[2] But they did not stop to offer congratulations; the happy occasion of Christopher's next successful step up the ladder of preferment would not have been well complemented by a visit from William after yet another fruitless trip abroad. Cookson, who would soon himself advance to the dignity of doctor of divinity (Dorothy said his appearance suited it), now held William in still-lower esteem for having dragged his sister into his disreputable lifestyle.

The Hutchinsons were just about the last people left in England to take them in. Sockburn had been their only viable choice when they had to leave Alfoxden, before they grasped the straw of a sabbatical in Germany. This family of young adults, two men and three women, had been living independently for five years after coming into an inheritance of over £2,000 from their parents and uncles.[3] Mary was twenty-nine, the same age as Wordsworth, Sara twenty-four, and Joanna nineteen. George and Thomas were twenty-one and twenty-six, respectively; their eldest brother, Henry, was at sea, like John Wordsworth. Sockburn-on-Tees was a self-sufficient estate on its own isolated peninsula in the Tees, eight miles east of Scotch Corner, the gateway to Scotland and the north.[4] The house resembled Racedown, but was bigger, with large wings extending off each side of the main building. The farm, a low-maintenance grazing estate, produced about £200 year. Although of very similar background to the Wordsworths, the Hutchinsons enjoyed a more comfortable status, a difference that had long distressed Dorothy: "they are quite independent and have not a wish ungratified, very different indeed is their present situation from what it was formerly when we compared grievances and lamented the misfortune of losing our parents at an early age and being thrown upon the mercy of ill-natured and illiberal relations."[5]

In his first letter after returning, William said, "We are now at Sockburn with Mary Hutchinson."[6] Mary was the focus of their visit, as she now became the object of William's affections, which slowly intensified over the next three years. His new romantic interest was not a conscious decision, but rather a feeling acted on spontaneously, provoked by the passionate and frustrating relations that had surfaced between him and Dorothy in Goslar.[7] More than erotic relief (which was surely not explicit), Mary and her siblings represented *domesticity* to William and especially to Dorothy: feelings of home and family that had been starved abroad in a strange land. The moment was that precious though precarious one of young adults on their own, living out the last days of youth. But ideas of marriage and settling down were in the air. At Sockburn for the next seven months—months that went by as quickly as the same number had dragged interminably in Germany—William and Dorothy saw the embodiment of their oldest dream: brothers and sisters living together, unmarried, in great harmony—and substantial comfort. The feeling "Nor, England! did I know till then / What love I bore to thee" began at Sockburn, stimulated by relief at escaping from the claustrophobia felt in Goslar, compounded with a new appreciation of England's role as the opponent of tyranny, and all brought together in an idyllic country manor house, surrounded by old childhood friends.[8]

Despite sexual and political tensions lurking just beneath the surface of their life (and each in its own way unspeakable), the idyll of Sockburn-on-Tees restored William's spirits. He responded by composing most of Part Two of the 1799 *Prelude* there, inspired by feelings of joyous community precisely contrary to the feelings of alienation in Goslar that had forced him to produce the fragments that became Part One.[9]

He wrote bluffly to Cottle, "We are right glad to find ourselves in England, for we have learnt to know its value," but the new feelings between him and his country were not exactly reciprocal: "I am in want of money."[10] He owed over £100 to the Wedgwoods, and he and Dorothy wanted to contribute something to their maintenance, as their visit stretched into summer and fall. Before they could decide where to live, they had to get their finances in order.

William began by trying to discover the fate of *Lyrical Ballads.* Little had gone as he had planned. Cottle still owed him twenty of the thirty guineas promised as an advance, and had not turned over the volume's copyright to Joseph Johnson as Wordsworth had asked. The Arch brothers' sales of the book had been satisfactory, though not sensational, and Cottle was very vague as to its prospects. "Can you tell me whether the poems are likely to sell?" Wordsworth asked exasperatedly.[11] The earliest review, Southey's quick and dirty ambush, had not helped and was extremely aggravating since *Lyrical Ballads* had been a money project from the start. It was still the only property Wordsworth had for producing income, and he continued to regard it very much in that light. Even his objection to Southey's review was not to his hypocrisy or his judgment but his motive: "He knew that money was of importance to me. If he could not conscientiously have spoken differently of the volume, he ought to have declined the task of reviewing it." His own motives were unabashedly commercial: "I care little for the praise of any other professional critic, but as it may help me to pudding."[12] But Southey's attack on "The Ancient Mariner," along with some other reviewers' criticisms of it, convinced Wordsworth "that The Ancyent Mariner has upon the whole been an injury to the volume, . . . the old words and the strangeness of it have deterred readers from going on."[13]

Other professional critics, though, began to take notice of the book and helped him toward pudding more than Southey had. Most reviews of *Lyrical Ballads* (1798) appeared after the Wordsworths' return in 1799, so leisurely was the pace of reviewing, and so enormous the glut of poetry on the marketplace: the years around the turn of the century saw one of the few poetry "booms" in the history of English literature. The *Monthly Magazine* in its half-yearly roundup of "Domestic Literature" granted *Lyrical Ballads* "unusual success" in attempting "to imitate the style of our old English versifiers," though it too took exception to "The Ancient Mariner."[14] Almost all reviewers found something to admire as well as to criticize; they tended to divide most sharply on "The Idiot Boy" and "The Thorn," either loving or hating them. "Tintern Abbey" and "The Nightingale" were most frequently singled out for praise, and "The Mad Mother" ("Her eyes are wild") seemed a bizarre favorite with everyone. Dorothy Jordan, the leading actress in Sheridan's melodrama-pantomime, *Pizarro,* a big hit when it opened on May 24 at Drury Lane, appeared onstage with her own most recent baby in her arms and proposed to sing a few stanzas of "The Mad Mother" when the play was staged again.[15] The interest of London's most popular actress brought its still-anonymous author to the leading edge of London cultural gossip.

The first new review Wordsworth saw after his return was by Dr. Charles Burney (father of Fanny) in the *Monthy Review* for May 1799. Neither Burney nor the journal was reactionary, but represented conventionally liberal middle-class opinion. He complained of the general "gloom" of the volume, astutely locating its source in its "implied criticism of the social system."[16] He saw some dangerous Rousseauism in the attitudes expressed in the "Yew-tree Seat" lines, an excess of tenderness for convicted criminals in "The Dungeon" and "The Convict," and "a general stigma on all military transactions" in "The Female Vagrant." These are all accurate observations, though others might appreciate them differently. In fact, Wordsworth agreed with most of them: he dropped "The Convict" forever and excised the most strident stanzas from "The Female Vagrant" ("dog-like, wading at the heels of war . . . with the brood / That lap . . . their brother's blood"). Burney encouraged the author to treat "more elevated subjects and in a more cheerful manner," and Wordsworth by and large followed this kind of advice. Though there is nothing in the 1800 *Lyrical Ballads* quite as elevated as "Tintern Abbey," there is a good deal more cheerfulness. Instead of "The Ancient Mariner," which seemed to cause problems, Wordsworth proposed to "put in its place some little things which would be more likely to suit the common taste." Hence the pleasant "Expostulation and Reply" and "The Tables Turned" would open the new first volume instead of Coleridge's weird mariner, who was unceremoniously relegated to the back of the book, just before "Tintern Abbey."[17] Six months earlier Wordsworth had confidently lectured old Klopstock on an author's moral necessity to rise above market considerations, but when his own "pudding" was concerned he was ready to follow the opinion of professional reviewers.

The volume's greatest success was passing muster with the *Anti-Jacobin Review,* successor to Canning and Frere's media scourge. Pitt's bulldogs would have sniffed out its radicalism as readily as Dr. Burney, but their more plodding successors did not spot these nuances. Coming out very late (April 1800), this review praised *Lyrical Ballads* for "genius, taste, elegance, wit, and imagery of the most elevated kind." For an author as desperate for money as Wordsworth, any praise was gratifying, but this was very bland and almost entirely off the mark: taste, elegance, and wit were the standard contemporary aesthetic virtues, bestowed alike on polite poems, drawing-room furniture, or high-society portraits. Though Wordsworth adapted many of his new poems to the taste of the times, it is a measure of his integrity that he took strong exception to exactly these virtues in the preface of his next edition.

His high hopes of "so much better a prospect" by placing his book with Johnson were dashed not only because Cottle was dilatory but because Johnson was now in jail, serving out a six-month term for publishing Gilbert Wakefield's *Reply to Some Parts of the Bishop of Llandaff's Address to the People of Great Britain* (1798). This spelled finis to Johnson's important *Analytical Review* and marked the beginning of the end of his career as the leading publisher of liberal social criticism and avant-garde literature. The climate of opinion had been pushed steadily rightward during their months abroad, as pedestrian efforts like the *Anti-Jacobin Review* kept pace with the government's constant tightening of screws on expressions of dissent.

Perhaps more painful when it came to Wordsworth's ears was the word of mouth about *Lyrical Ballads* circulating among his family and friends. Margaret Spedding thought the poems were "really such queer odd sort of things that if everybody was of my mind, profits would not answer for a journey."[18] She wasn't wrong: Dorothy had told people they would leave for Germany with £40 from the book, but they had got only £10. Sara had written to Coleridge that they "were not well esteemed here, but the Nightingale and the River Y." To Poole she was blunter: "The Lyrical Ballads are laughed at and disliked by all with very few excepted."[19] Her opinions were motivated by jealousy, but no less discomfitting for that. By the time Coleridge returned to London, Wordsworth was so touchy about the volume's reception that when Coleridge reported having heard Godwin comment favorably on it to no less a personage than Fox, Wordsworth sulkily impugned Godwin's motives, intemperately calling him "a polite liar," "a worse philosopher," and "a puppy." "Ergo the account is smoke or something near it."[20]

But gradually, as late reviews came trickling in, and the need for money did not go away, and sales continued until the first edition was exhausted in just over a year, Wordsworth began to consider another edition, or another publication. He turned over his pile of manuscripts to see what might be serviceable.[21] He had worried in Germany about the whereabouts of *The Borderers* manuscript and was glad to learn it was safely lodged with Poole. (Another opportunity for it opened up the next summer with Sheridan, who was sent a copy by Coleridge and John Stoddart and urged to stage it, but by then Wordsworth was committed to a new edition of *Lyrical Ballads* and adopted a take-it-or-leave-it attitude, refusing to make any alterations.)[22] He began to "hew" down *Peter Bell* and think about its compatibility in a volume with either "The Ruined Cottage" or "Adventures on Salisbury Plain." But he responded to reviewers' comments on the "gloominess" of *Lyrical Ballads* by turning most of his new work in a lighter direction than these depressing narratives, so that none of these long poems saw the light of day for at least another fifteen years. He had about a dozen new poems from Germany, concerning two mysterious characters named Lucy and Matthew, but he was not, in any of his thoughts about publishing in 1799, concerned with expanding *Lyrical Ballads* except by way of increasing his profits.

His only income was a twice-yearly dividend of £7 10s. on the 3 percent consols Richard had purchased while he was in Germany.[23] He soon learned from Richard that his loans to Montagu and Douglas from the Calvert bequest were faring as badly as ever; they were not paying up; out of their sight, he had slipped their minds. The best Montagu could do was to keep up premiums on an insurance policy on his life, Wordsworth's desperate measure against losing almost everything he'd got from Calvert five years before. William made Richard take a hard line with Montagu: "I shall be under the absolute necessity of pursuing those steps which will be extremely distressing to myself and unpleasant to you unless you immediately remit me the Balance due."[24] Richard hinted that Montagu was "intimately acquainted" with "persons in affluent circumstances" who might help him, so Montagu hit up his old student John Pinney, asking his help to avoid the moral embarrassment of owing money to such a superior being as Wordsworth. But Pinney had had enough of his old tutor's combination of aristocratic disdain and Godwinian persiflage, and started paying the annuity Montagu owed him directly to Wordsworth, outraging Montagu and embarrassing Wordsworth.[25] Montagu still did not remit anything, but no action was taken against him. His friend Douglas finally paid his £100 on July 13 (that date again!), 1800, putting Wordsworth in a position to pay back the Wedgwoods at last, to whom he had been sending a string of extenuating letters about his debt, "owing to irregularities, mistakes respecting the publishing of my poems, and other causes."[26] But "there is no evidence in Richard Wordsworth's accounts with William that he repaid this [Wedgwood] debt in 1800."[27] Instead it was John, the only entrepreneur in the family, who instructed Richard to pay the debt, prompted by Dorothy's inquiry if it would be proper to invest the £100 received from Douglas in John's next voyage, which indicates that they still had the sum at their disposal.[28]

Assuming that their financial situation would eventually get better, since it could hardly get worse, William and Dorothy began thinking about where to go. Though they were now standing at the gateway to the north, they had no immediate plans to visit, let alone live in, the Lake District. Sockburn became the jumping-off point for their probes in that direction in the fall, but in the spring their only motive toward the Lakes remained that of Dorothy's flirting invitation to Coleridge from Goslar: "wherever we finally settle you must come to us at the latter end of next summer, and we will explore together every nook of that romantic country."[29]

The Hutchinsons were in transition too, for by the next spring their own idyll split up under the constant bourgeois pressure to increase the size of estates. George went to a new property at Bishop Middleham, near Durham, taking Sara as his housekeeper, and Thomas went to Gallow Hill, near Scarborough, taking Mary with him. Joanna traded visits between them.[30] The Hutchinsons' discussions about moving to their new properties gave the Wordsworths an extra push, but William's development toward poetical independence did not initially involve thoughts of going to live in Cumberland or Westmorland, regions that were still for him and Dorothy, as for most people, places for "romantic" holidays, not permanent residence.

Their Halifax relatives expected them to take a house near Sockburn in Northallerton, the closest town.[31] Coleridge expected Wordsworth to return to Alfoxden, which suggests that the row over their behavior in 1797 had subsided and that their opinions which prompted it had also changed. When he learned in September that Wordsworth "renounce[d] Alfoxden altogether," Coleridge considered taking it himself.[32] It was certainly a much better place than the Lime Street cottage, where Sara had spent a hard winter enduring the illness and death of baby Berkeley by herself, supported only by strong Tom Poole in her wandering husband's absence.

A drama was shaping up that neither of the principal actors quite foresaw. Coleridge expected that Wordsworth would follow *him,* as he had without hesitation for the past two years, "unless he should find in the North any person or persons, who can feel & understand him, can reciprocate & react on him."[33] "As I do," is the unspoken complement of the sentence. Wordsworth did not find any such persons; the Hutchinsons were great old friends but not creative soul mates. Instead, it was "the North" itself that began to draw him, in no small measure because he continued writing about it constantly in the poem to Coleridge, which now increased the usefulness that it had started to have in Germany: a means of drawing Coleridge after *him*. The proto-*Prelude* was in this sense a lever that helped shift the balance of creative power from Coleridge to Wordsworth.

Wordsworth tried other, more transparent strategies to tempt his friend, bragging up the libraries of Sir Frederick Vane-Fletcher at Hutton Hall, near Penrith, and of Sir Wilfrid Lawson at Brayton Hall, near Cockermouth, for Coleridge's use.[34] This played to their former fantasy of spending summers at Cambridge, reading voraciously to build up intellectual stock for writing at leisure the rest of the year somewhere in the country. Wordsworth said he "deemed the vicinity of a Library absolutely *necessary* to his health, nay to his existence," but Coleridge claimed he needed "old books chiefly, such as could be procured any where better than in a Gentleman's new fashionable Collection."[35] These statements of their requirements were at cross-purposes; Coleridge did need libraries for his many projects, but not Wordsworth, most of whose poetry required no book research at all, beyond the amazing catalog of former poets he carried ready in his head. Coleridge thought his friend needed company more than libraries, but like much advice this was truer for the giver than for its recipient, for Wordsworth needed other people almost as little as he needed books. He did absorb ideas from other people, but with such rapid comprehensiveness that he didn't need them *for long.* He eventually built up a very considerable library after he settled in Grasmere, but at his death, his library contained no classics of philosophy and few philosophical books, strictly speaking, of any sort except ones on political theory.[36]

Plans went back and forth during the summer to little purpose, but Coleridge was being drawn toward Wordsworth as if by magical incantation, in his role as the addressee of the expanding *Prelude,* which Wordsworth now brought to an end by incorporating Coleridge into it. At the end of Part One, Coleridge was asked to listen sympathetically to Wordsworth's "lengthen[ing] out / With fond and feeble tongue a tedious tale" (i.448–49). This alliterative joking was appropriate to their situation in Germany, where Wordsworth admitted he was indulging "the weakness of a human love for days disowned by memory" instead of writing *The Recluse.* "Yet should it be . . . / That I by such inquiry am not taught / To understand myself," he knew he need not "dread from thee / Harsh judgements" (458–59). During the summer and fall of 1799, Coleridge did not give "harsh judgements" on the poem that became *The Prelude,* but he repeatedly wished Wordsworth were writing *The Recluse* instead, neither man having yet divined that Wordsworth's "preparatory" poem for the more philosophical *Recluse* was itself "the philosophic song" he was destined to write. "I am anxiously eager to have you steadily employed on 'The Recluse' . . . for in my present mood I am wholly against the publication of any small poems." A month later he wrote, "I long to see what you have been doing. O let it be the tail-piece of 'The Recluse!' for of nothing but 'The Recluse' can I hear patiently. That it is to be addressed to me makes me more desirous that it should not be a poem of itself."[37]

In his first renewed commentary on *The Recluse,* however, Coleridge provided Wordsworth with a new rationale for it, which Wordsworth immediately co-opted into *The Prelude.* "I wish you would write a poem, in blank verse, addressed to those, who, in consequence of the complete failure of the French Revolution, have thrown up all hopes of the amelioration of mankind, and are sinking into an almost epicurean selfishness, disguising the same under the soft titles of domestic attachment and contempt for visionary *philosophes."* This charge appears, with only minimal alteration for blank verse, as the new conclusion of "the poem to Coleridge":

> . . . if in these times of fear,
> This melancholy waste of hopes o'erthrown,
> If, 'mid indifference and apathy
> And wicked exultation, when good men
> On every side fall off we know not how
> To selfishness, disguised in gentle names
> Of peace and quiet and domestic love—

> Yet mingled, not unwillingly, with sneers
> On visionary minds . . . .
>
> (ii.479–86)

He hasn't fallen off, Wordsworth concludes, because his "gift is yours / Ye mountains, thine O Nature." This is the "philosophy," or the anchoring god term, of both *The Prelude* and *The Recluse.* Suddenly, the "tedious tale" of his life has been given a point and a mission: it could save their entire generation from the dashed hopes of the French Revolution.

Most specifically, the "good men" who had become contemptuous of visionary minds refers to James Mackintosh (1765–1832), the brother-in-law of Daniel Stuart, and later of Josiah Wedgwood, who had been their close acquaintance among the wealthy liberal intelligentsia in Bristol. Mackintosh would soon be instrumental in persuading Stuart to make Coleridge his highest-paid contributor.[38] But Coleridge did not let gratitude interfere with despising this man who, as he rightly saw, was leading the tide of apostasy away from liberal reform ideas.* Mackintosh's *Vindiciae Gallicae* (1791), the most closely reasoned of all responses to Burke's *Reflections,* has been called "the ablest ideological defence of the French Revolution ever written."[39] But between February and June of 1799 he delivered a series of lectures entitled "The Laws of Nature and of Nations," attacking the course of the Revolution and refuting the arguments of his own pamphlet. They were so successful they were repeated the following spring.[40] Mackintosh was no reactionary, and remained throughout his career a liberal Whig, but these lectures became the public symbol of liberal intellectuals abandoning all hope of encouragement from the example of France. Hazlitt sourly recorded their devastating effect, bitterly rating them the best speeches Mackintosh ever gave. "The volcano of the French Revolution was seen expiring in its own flames, like a bon-fire made of straw: the principles of Reform were scattered in all directions, like chaff before the keen northern blast. . . . As to our visionary sceptics and Utopian philosophers, they stood no chance with our lecturer . . . . Poor Godwin, who had come, in the *bonhommie* and candour of his nature . . . was obliged to quit the field, and slunk away after an exulting taunt thrown out at 'such fanciful chimeras as a golden mountain or a perfect man.' "[41] Coleridge attended five lectures in the second series, but could stomach no more.

The first part of the proto-*Prelude* had reported out the health of Wordsworth's imagination in its natural environment. Now that imagination was given a cause. At this moment *The Recluse,* which was to follow directly from

*Two years later Coleridge published "The Two Round Spaces," signifying the two holes of a privy on which the devil and his grandmother sit contentedly awaiting the Last Judgment so that they may take away the soul of "This Counselor sweet! This Scotchman compleat!"

this conclusion, was the necessary poem of modernity, the work that would keep men from sliding into despair at the apparent failure of their best hopes for social and human reformation. Thelwall and Godwin were also among the "good men" falling into despair; they were not such turncoats as Mackintosh, but both shifted and trimmed their views. And "visionary minds" also included Coleridge, while the "gentle names of peace and quiet and domestic love" would seem to include Wordsworth's name as well and eventually led to his arguing, in "Home at Grasmere," that his and Dorothy's "retreat" there was anything but that.

Coleridge spent most of his time after returning from Germany making emotional repairs to his relations with his immediate family and friends. Mending two fences at one stroke, he reconciled with Southey, and the two brothers-in-law spent the late summer touring the West Country with their wives and children. To avoid provoking his brothers, the clergyman and the colonel, he joined in toasts to king and country in a new access of patriotism that was, like Wordsworth's, as genuine as it was expedient.[42] One of his friends mischievously sent a set of Paine's works to a friend of his brother's, who muttered against his continuing association with "dark-hearted Jacobins," and Coleridge readily admitted that some of them were "shallowists."[43] He was still under official surveillance, and dashed off another variation on his "Spy Nosy" theme, this one "On Naso Rubicund, Esq. a dealer in Secrets" (identified as Sir William Anderson).[44]

Back at Stowey he and Southey whipped up a satirical ballad called "The Devil's Thoughts," which they published to great acclaim in the *Morning Post* for September 6. This attacked hypocrisy and profiteering in wartime, featuring the old device of the devil paying a visit to his "snug little farm the earth," pleased to see his enterprises getting on so well. Unlike the horrific "War Eclogue" he had written a year earlier, where three hags of the Apocalypse (Fire, Famine, and Slaughter) give thanks for their feasts in the Vendée to the master whose name they riddle transparently—"Letters four do form his name" (P-I-T-T)—this satire aimed at the more traditional and safer target of sham and pretension, and was not a personal attack. His new enemy was the polarization and caricature replacing any semblance of argument in the national community.

But for most of the fall he dithered. What finally got him up north were increasingly alarming accounts of Wordsworth's health. These complaints were not wholly fictitious, but they were psychosomatic: the pains around his heart that Wordsworth reported in Germany when, as now, he was working on the poem that invoked his friend as Muse. It was typical of Coleridge's erratic behavior that he left for Sockburn very suddenly, commandeering Cottle and his chaise without bothering to tell Sara that he was leaving or where he was going, so within three months of his return she was left alone again, not knowing where her husband was.[45] This reprehensible behavior had its reasons, though no excuse: by going clandestinely to see Wordsworth, Coleridge sought to avoid opening the barely healed wounds of Sara and her staunch ally, Poole, both of whom continued to feel that close association with the Wordsworths boded no good for him.

Wordsworth, it turned out, was not so sick after all, or else his illness was part of the plan to "decoy" Coleridge to them. Coleridge arrived on October 26, and William popped out of bed the next day, ready for a month-long walking tour in harsh November weather. Of his first impressions of Sockburn and the Hutchinsons, Coleridge had time only to note, fatefully, "Few moments in life so interesting as those of an affectionate reception from those who have heard of you yet are strangers to your person."[46] The Hutchinsons had been hearing about the "wonderful" Coleridge for nearly four years, but this was their first meeting. "Interesting" was a mild word to describe the meeting that would lead to the heartbreak of his life, his passion for Mary's sister, Sara, a name whose mocking repetition of his wife's name he never tired of twisting into symbolic permutations, especially as the "Asra" of his great "Dejection: An Ode."

They set out next morning, Wordsworth and Coleridge and Cottle. But Cottle, though mounted on Sara's mare, Lily, turned aside almost immediately at Greta Bridge, barely twenty miles on the way. Perhaps the prospect of the long hike ahead daunted him. This was not the Bristol coast path, and Lily could not have gone to many of the places they were headed. Very likely Wordsworth did not resist making some further expressions of dissatisfaction with Cottle's handling of *Lyrical Ballads.* Coleridge, for his part, was less interested in *Lyrical Ballads* than in getting Wordsworth back to work on *The Recluse.* Probably Cottle sensed that the two friends wanted to be alone. Even Dorothy was left behind; she had imagined "follow[ing] at your heels and hear[ing] your dear voices again," when she teased Coleridge about exploring "every nook of that romantic country." But she had to wait her turn.

With Cottle gone, the two friends took a coach over the Stainmore wastes of the Pennines. They were headed for Penrith, but at Temple Sowerby, the last stage before Penrith, a very odd coincidence occurred. "I learned," Wordsworth reported later, "from the address of a letter lying on the table with the Cambridge post mark, the Letter from Kit to Mrs. C[rackanthrope] that he was gone to Cambridge. I learned also from the Woman that John was at New-biggin. I sent a note—he came, looks very well—."[47]

But Dorothy knew very well why John was at Temple Sowerby. It was on the main road a mile from Newbiggin, the closest thing left to an ancestral estate in which the Wordsworth siblings had a legitimate interest. Christopher Crackanthorpe had just died, on October 15, and John and Christopher were there for the funeral, along with their uncle Cookson.[48] Both

William and Dorothy had known at Sockburn of his final illness, and she was after all Uncle Christopher's favorite niece. William would not have gone to the funeral in any case, for he despised this uncle for not having given him a fair share of their maternal grandmother's estate when she died in 1792. But his brief stop at Temple Sowerby provided the essential news that led him there in the first place: "Your Uncle has left you [Dorothy] £100, nobody else is named in his Will."[49] He was not legacy hunting, exactly, but doing the quite usual thing, checking to see what they'd got from the estate. Dorothy reacted more in pity than in anger: "He did not so much as name the name of his Brother [William Cookson] or one of his nephews!" That is to say, not one of them would inherit, not even the dutiful John or Christopher. The worst had happened: all the estate that Christopher Cookson had inherited, and gratefully changed his name to Crackanthorpe to acknowledge, passed entirely out of family hands into those of his widow, née Cust, William and Dorothy's aunt Crackanthorpe, "despised by everyone for her excessive pride." Of course, everybody knew how these things happened: the "poor man" was not "a free agent in the making of his will."[50] (William Calvert had thought as much at the death of his brother Raisley.) Once again the Wordsworths had to face the blunt reality that their relatives would not help them and that they must help themselves.

Still, they had linked up with John, a much better companion than Cottle. William had not seen him for over two years, and Coleridge now met him for the first time. Coleridge wrote Dorothy, "Your Br. John is one of you; a man who hath solitary usings [*sic*] of his own Intellect, deep in feeling, with a subtle Tact, a swift instinct of Truth & Beauty."[51] John, the "silent poet," had the physique of his older brother and the quick sensibilities of his sister, strangely combined in a taciturn seafaring officer of great responsibility and growing wealth, whose hazardous profession was now made more dangerous by war.

Few people can have experienced a guided tour of the Lake District such as Wordsworth now gave Coleridge. And yet, for all its natural splendor, albeit in "forbidding . . . savage and hopeless" November weather,[52] it was a case of life imitating art: a voyage not of discovery but of confirmation and illustration. During the next three weeks Wordsworth brought Coleridge directly into most of the scenes from his childhood that he had been writing about for him over the course of the past year. The tour was a tour de force, to show Coleridge the places on which the imaginative power of *The Prelude* was based, as the necessary foundation of *The Recluse.* Coleridge had at last been decoyed into that "romantic country," and he was, on this tour with this guide, a sitting duck. Of course, it knocked him over.

They made two huge contiguous loops through the whole district, first down past Windermere to Hawkshead and up to Keswick over Dunmail

Raise (with a week's stay at Grasmere in the middle), then west around through Ennerdale and Wastdale and back up again to Keswick via Borrowdale, with side trips into Buttermere and Crummock Water, and possibly to Cockermouth.

Starting from Penrith, they made straight for Hawkshead. They stopped to inspect a small property of Richard's at Sockbridge, near Barton, where they had lunch with the Reverend Thomas Myers, father of Wordsworth's cousin and Hawkshead and St. John's schoolmate, and continued on to Bampton for the first night. They moved rapidly along the outside perimeter of the district, following a route Wordsworth had often taken in his boyhood trips back and forth to school. Between Barton and Bampton they saw Lowther Castle rising in the east, and the next day, as they passed under Walla Crag on Hawes Water, Coleridge learned a local superstition, with contemporary commentary: "On the bold rock Lord Lonsdale's Father's spirit. Walla Crag—Sir James would let them rest in Lowther Hall."[53] Robert Lowther (1681–1745), a former governor of Barbados who suppressed Jacobite sympathizers there amid charges of corruption, libel, and bigamy, died of a heart attack during the last Jacobite invasion of Westmorland, despite the brave success of his steward, Wordsworth's grandfather, in saving his gold and plate. His corpse was said to have refused to stay in its grave at Lowther, so a priest put the body under a large rock at Walla Crag.[54] Coleridge's comment (learned from Wordsworth, of course) implies that even Sir James, "the bad Earl," would not be so inhospitable. As they went along, Wordsworth's mind ran much on the injustices of his situation caused by the Lowthers, as obscurely indicated by another of Coleridge's journal entries: "Universities—Pox—Impotence—Lord Lonsdale."*

Low-hanging mists prevented them from going directly over the mountains to Ambleside, so they crossed Kentmere Common and came out of the hills at Troutbeck, into Windermere. Here too picturesque appreciation mixed with aesthetic and social criticism of Wordsworth's old antagonists. Wordsworth was "much disgusted with the New Erections and objects about Windermere," and Coleridge noted at the "Head of the Lake of Wynandermere—Mr Law's white palace [at Brathay]—a bitch!—Matthew Harrison's House where Llandaff lived [Calgarth] / these and more among the mountains!"[55] Richard Watson still lived at Calgarth, and when Coleridge

**NSTC,* 1:520. Lowther had also been at Cambridge (Peterhouse), but only for a year (1752–53), when he was sixteen. In that atmosphere at that age, he could well have contracted the pox and become impotent. He married Lady Mary Stuart (Lord Bute's daughter), but they had no children. George III was married the day after him, and some courtiers made a bet that Princess Charlotte would be brought to bed with child before Lady Mary. They won their bet: Lowther had no children, a circumstance that ultimately led to Wordsworth's regaining his inheritance from him. See Hugh Owen, *The Lowther Family* (Chichester: Phillimore, 1990), 281, 284.

came to live in the Lakes he expanded his attacks on this liberal but dangerous antagonist of their generation: "that beastly Bishop, that blustering Fool, Watson, a native of this vicinity, a pretty constant Resident here, & who has for many years kept a Rain-gage, considers it as a vulgar Error that the climate of this Country is particularly wet."[56] Wordsworth also pointed out Rayrigg, the inherited estate of his first "passionately loved" friend in poetry, John Raincock Fleming, of whom he had just recently written so strangely in the proto-*Prelude,* "at this time / We live as if those hours had never been" (ii.387–88).

At Hawkshead, Wordsworth sadly observed "great change amongst the People since we were last there."[57] He especially regretted the loss of the "grey stone of native rock" which was the "centre" of the schoolboys' games, now "split and gone to build / A smart assembly-room that perked and flared / With wash and rough-cast, elbowing the ground / Which had been ours" (ii.31–39). Happy as he was to be back, his commentaries along the way suggest a sense of resentful displacement. The saddest change "amongst the People" was the death of Ann Tyson three year before, which William and John learned of only now.

They hurried on to meet those "divine Sisters, Rydal & Grasmere," where Coleridge said he received "the deepest delight."[58] Grasmere is the natural hub at the center of the Lake District, and they spent nearly a week there (November 3–8), staying at the old inn near the church and taking day trips out in various directions. Grasmere was one of the places on the tour where Wordsworth had not spent any time as a child, except for passing through occasionally between Penrith and Hawkshead. In his letters to Dorothy, William's growing enthusiasm closely correlated with *Coleridge's* fascination with the place, and his own "mad" plan was roused by Coleridge's admiration: "C. was much struck with Grasmere and its neighbourhood and I have much to say to you, you will think my plan a mad one, but I have thought of building a house there by the Lake side."[59] John said he would give them £40 to buy the land. Coleridge's first sight of the vale—"Embraced round by Hill's arms behind—before us what ridges & on the side of that little spot of Lake What an awful mount!"[60]—was repeated in one of the most ecstatic passages of "Home at Grasmere": "Embrace me then, ye Hills, and close me in!"

John left them on November 5 to return to the business of finding investors for his next voyage. They walked with him as far as Grisedale Hause and Tarn, below Helvellyn. Something of the difference between Coleridge's and Wordsworth's landscape descriptions, and indeed of their personalities, is revealed by comparing what they said about this day. Wordsworth merely noted, "This day was a fine one and we had some grand mountain scenery—the rest of the week has been bad weather."[61] Wordsworth's descriptive powers (and interests) are much weaker than they are often assumed to be; what he saw in landscape were emotions, human figures supported or destroyed by nature, and, above all, himself. But Coleridge, who was collecting images for his notebook, gives both more details and more emotion:

> On the top of Helvellin
>
> First the Lake of Grasmere like a sullen Tarn / then the black ridge of mountain—then as upborne among the other mountains the luminous Cunneston Lake—& far away in the Distance & far to the Lake the glooming Shadow, Wynandermere with its Island—Pass on—the Tairn—& view of the gloomy Ulswater & mountains behind, one black, one blue, & the last one dun /
>
> Greisdale Halse [*sic*]—Gowdrell Crag—Tarn Crag—that smoother Eminence on the right is called Fairfield.[62]

Coleridge's description also reveals his fascination with the names in the district, its "native" language: "In the North every Brook, every Crag, almost every Field has a name—a proof of greater Independence and society more approaching in their Laws and Habits to Nature."[63] This anticipates Wordsworth's "Poems on the Naming of Places," and his claim that the "passions" of men in "low and rustic life" are "incorporated with the beautiful and permanent forms of nature." But, theory aside, the fact is that in the Lake District, as in many rural places, "names" are not proper but common nouns. "Tarn Crag" is as descriptive as it is nominative, and "Fairfield" nearly so. All over the region, place-names are essentially place descriptions: How Foot (foot of the hill), Gill Foot (end of the brook), Troutbeck (brook with fish), and so on. What appear to outsiders as names are to the people who live there merely descriptive locators. Coleridge applied this new linguistic principle to his children's names, which he now took from the landscape instead of from philosophy as he had with Hartley and Berkeley: Derwent was born in Keswick the next summer; if he'd been a girl, she would have been called Greta, after the other river that runs into Derwent Water at Keswick.

The two poets occasionally disagreed on the manners and character of country people. Wordsworth cared less for the scenery, but he stuck up for the people, while Coleridge noted, "People in the country—their vindictive feelings—."[64] For Wordsworth, the people and the landscape went together, but for Coleridge as often as not, they clashed. Admiring the sweeping curve of the northern outlet of Grasmere Vale, between Helm Crag and Stone Arthur, he suddenly dropped his view to the bottom: "all between on both sides savage & hopeless—obstinate Sansculottism."

Back down at Rydal, they again ran afoul of aristocrats' efforts to control the landscape. They entered the grounds of Rydal Hall, seat of Sir Michael le Fleming, who had erected a special house over Rydal Beck to provide a framed picturesque view of Upper Rydal Falls. It was open by permission to acceptable persons, but the two poets' appearance was evidently not acceptable: "While at Sir Fleming's a servant, red-eyed &c, came to us, to the Road before the Waterfall to reprove us for having passed before the front of the House." Coleridge responded with the authority of his new landscape appreciation: "our Trespass of Feet [was nothing to] the Trespass on the Eye by his damned White washing!"[65] But Wordsworth said nothing of the sort about the incident: "The evening before last we walked to the upper Water fall at Rydal and saw it through the gloom, and it was very magnificent."[66]

After the week at Grasmere they crossed over the "inverted Arch" of Dunmail Raise to Keswick and began the third week of their tour with a swing through the western lakes, along Bassenthwaite and then down through Ennerdale to Wastdale and back up via Borrowdale. Probably they visited the Speddings, for they spent a night at Ouse Bridge at the top of Bassenthwaite, but it is not clear if they went to Cockermouth, even though they seemed headed in that direction. Coleridge later noted, "Cockermouth—and why I never went there."[67] "Why" might be, in the context of this tour, because Wordsworth wanted to go back alone, or didn't want to go there at all, for reasons too emotional to contemplate with tranquillity. His and Dorothy's sight of their old home in 1794 had been upsetting, and he had already come across more than enough reminders of how his various inheritances in the region had been denied him, without seeking out more.

At Buttermere on November 11 they first saw Mary Robinson, daughter of the landlord at the Fish Inn, where they spent the night.[68] Mary was just a local beauty then, though a striking one, "marked by unexampled grace." But she would become a national cause célèbre three years later when she was seduced into marriage with a bigamist, John Hatfield, posing as an MP and the brother of the earl of Hopetoun. Like the gray stone of Hawkshead broken up to make a "smart" assembly room, this Mary Robinson became for Wordsworth a symbol of the many ways in which his native district was being exploited and distorted by outsiders, tourists, developers, and venal local aristocrats. She, "the artless daughter of the hills," was symbolically related to him, Nature's "chosen Son," because "we were nursed—as almost might be said— / On the same mountains," and connected, he suggests, by the umbilical cord of the River Cocker, he at its mouth and she at its source in Buttermere (VII.342–43).

Next day, over in Ennerdale, they heard the story of James Bowman and his son, both of whom fell to their deaths from crags while tending their sheep, the son apparently while sleepwalking.[69] This became one of the incidents in "The Brothers," the first poem Wordsworth began composing when he and Dorothy moved to Grasmere. It is also informed by his recent experience of having been with John for two weeks, since the brother who returns to his home vale is a seaman, while the one who stayed and died was the shepherd. True to Coleridge's perception of the region's names and Wordsworth's imaginative installation of himself in it, the shepherd is given a new name symbolizing his fatal place, James *Ew*bank.

They passed on up through Borrowdale, Coleridge frantically recording images like a high-speed movie camera on automatic pilot: "for Borrodale—Brooks in their anger—all the Gullies full & white & the Chasms now black, now half hid by the mist, & ever & anon the waterfall in them flashing thro' the mists."[70] Passing up Derwent Water, they passed another outrage on the landscape, "King Pocky's" island (Derwent Island), with its mock church, from which the new owner, Colonel John Pocklington, had removed the steeple: "Ey! Ey! turn'd my Church to a Presbyterian Meeting . . . shaved off the Branches of an Oak, Whitewashed & shaped it into an Obelisk—Art beats Nature."

Returning to Keswick, Coleridge found waiting for him a letter from Daniel Stuart, offering him a place as lead writer for the *Morning Post;* he would become its highest-paid contributor, with his mornings free.[71] It was an offer he couldn't refuse, and he determined to return to London immediately. Wordsworth felt his prey slipping from his grasp just when he thought he had netted him. A sense of déjà vu—second nature to him anyway—must have swept over him as he thought of himself almost five years earlier, rushing off to London from nearly the same spot to join William Mathews in newspaper work, though of a far less certain and lucrative nature. They also ran into William Calvert, reminding Wordsworth of Raisley and all he owed to him from that same hopeful moment, though his gift was now precariously tied up in uncertain debts. (Calvert, ever the practical money man, coolly observed of a certain Miss Dykes that he would pay two guineas for her "were she on the Town.")[72]

They headed back to Penrith for Coleridge to get the stage. Stopping at Threlkeld on the way, Coleridge recorded another superstition Wordsworth told him: "In the Civil Wars beyond [*sic*] York & Lancaster a Clifford, Earl of Cumberland, wandered about under Sattelback [*sic*] & deemed by the Shepherds an astronomic mysterious man."[73] This Henry Clifford was a spirit after Wordsworth's own heart, for he had been deprived of his estates for killing the duke of York's son, and lived for twenty-four years as a shepherd on the lands of his father-in-law, Sir Lancelot Threlkeld.[74] The "Song at the Feast of Brougham Castle" (1806) was composed on the occasion of the happy outcome of his penitence: "Upon the Restoration of Lord Clifford, The Shepherd, to the Estates and Honours of his Ancestors." This idea of the worthy son restored is the biographical leitmotif to *The Prelude*'s dominant theme, "Imagination, How Impaired and Restored."

Wordsworth himself looked heroic to Catherine Clarkson, wife of the great antislavery agitator, at whose country estate, Eusmere, at the head of Ullswater, they made their last stop on November 17. "He has a fine commanding figure is rather handsome & looks as if he was born to be a great Prince or a great General." She also noted his partiality to Coleridge: "He seems very fond of C. laughing at all his Jokes & taking all opportunities of shewing him off & to crown all he has the manners of a Gentleman."[75] She seems to have expected something worse, probably from family gossip, which she knew well from her husband's close association with Wilberforce and William Cookson.

Coleridge was greatly excited by Ullswater, running up and down the shore recording effects of light and shadow. He drew intricately numbered diagrams to establish the exact visual perspective for William's description of the "huge cliff" that seemed to stride after him, "like a living thing," in his stolen rowboat: probably either Black Crag or Stybarrow Crag.[76] Said Coleridge, "I turn my Back to the Lake / & what a Cliff!"[77] His descriptions, compared with Wordsworth's, show, for all their energy and detail, not that Wordsworth's are better, but again how different they are. Wordsworth was more concerned with "*un*known modes of being" that utterly blank out "familiar shapes / Of hourly objects, images of trees, / Or sea or sky, *no* colours of green fields" (i.124–26; italics added).

On their last morning at the Clarksons', Coleridge sat on a tree stump looking down the lake at another image of a hill, which was also quite different from anything in Wordsworth: "that round fat backside of a Hill [◠] with its image in the water made together *one* absolutely undistinguishable Form—a kite or a Paddle or keel turned to you / the road appeared a sort of suture ["opening" deleted], in many places exactly as the weiblich τετρα–γραμματον is paintd in anatomical Books! I never saw so sweet an Image!!"[78] The phrase he discreetly codes in German and Greek, "feminine four-letter word," does not register a contrast to the beauty of the scene, but, quite the contrary, its fondly accented center. He remembered it well, as did William, for the next summer when he was making his own solo tour he recalled "that round *backside* Hill that the Wordsworths & I laughed at there."[79]

Wordsworth remained in the district, but Coleridge headed for London via Sockburn—a significant detour—where he stayed nearly a week. Back at the Hutchinsons' without William, he was the undivided center of everyone's attention. He fondly quoted a question overheard in conversation on his arrival a month earlier, "Miss Mary Hutcheson & Cottle immediately after Tea on our arrival, 'Pray, what do you think of Mr Coleridge's [first] appearance?' "[80] The only "you" to whom this question could have been addressed was Sara Hutchinson, and Coleridge happily indulged himself in recalling her polite, charming, embarrassed reply. On his last night they all played like children in front of the fire, at "Conundrums & Puns & Stories

& Laughter," and again his intense recollections slipped into a foreign tongue: "et Sarae manum a tergo longum in tempus prensabam, and [*sic*] tunc temporis, tunc primum . . . ."[81] The entire Latin passage reads, in translation, "And pressed Sara's hand a long time behind her back, and then, then for the first time, love pricked me with its light arrow, poisoned alas! and hopeless." Seven more lines are heavily obliterated in the journal.[82] His recollections continued, helplessly, "I just about to take Leave of Mary—& having just before taken leave of Sara—. I did not then know Mary's & William's attachment: The lingering Bliss, / The long entrancement of a True-love Kiss."

If he was half in love with the Lakes, Coleridge was now all in love with Sara Hutchinson (and partly with Mary as well, it seems). Some part of his decision the next summer to return to live there was based, fatalistically, on the hope of seeing her more often. As Wordsworth had fallen for that "divine sister," Grasmere, under the charm of Coleridge's enthusiasm, so Coleridge had a predilection for falling in love with the sisters of his best friends, first with Sara Fricker and now with Sara Hutchinson.[83] It was not mere coincidence that Coleridge should be meeting the love of his life at the same time that Wordsworth was beginning to think about marrying; both of them had prior romantic relationships that were proving, in their different ways, untenable.

His emotions completely aroused, Coleridge began a poem later called "Love," which he soon published in the *Morning Post* as "Introduction to the Ballad of the Dark Ladie." (Sara's hair was a beautiful auburn.) It records the effect on a beautiful auditor of a minstrel reciting a doleful tale of a lady rescued "from outrage worse than death" by a knight she had earlier rejected. This story is "The Ballad" itself, which Coleridge had already composed but never published. He may have recited it to the company that fateful night, or fantasized about the effect of doing so. One stanza says all that mattered to him:

> She listened with a fitting blush,
> With downcast eyes and modest grace;
> For well she knew, I could not choose
>   But gaze upon her face.[84]

The happy denouement of the ballad is repeated in the scene of its telling, when the meaningful look goes in the other direction:

> She wept with pity and delight,
> She blushed with love, and virgin-shame;
> And like the murmur of a dream,
> I heard her breathe my name.

Her bosom heaved—she stepped aside,
As conscious of my look she stepped—
Then suddenly, with timorous eye
She fled to me and wept.

She half enclosed me in her arms,
She pressed me with a meek embrace;
And bending back her head, looked up,
And gazed upon my face.

(77–88)

The knight's heroism in the tale is transformed in the "Introduction" to the minstrel's creative power in telling it, and each one wins his dark lady.

William, back in Grasmere after leaving Coleridge at Penrith, spent a week arranging to take the house he had seen. He returned to Sockburn the day after Coleridge left, and found Mary alone, Sara and Dorothy having gone to see one of the brothers. He wrote Coleridge, "I was sadly disappointed in not finding Dorothy," but added, "Mary was a solitary housekeeper and overjoyed to see me."[85] Occasions were conspiring to make their decisions about where to settle more complicated, for both delight and disaster, than their intellectual considerations about access to libraries.

The "mad" decision to go "home" to Grasmere did not take long, once Dorothy returned to Sockburn; William returned on November 25, and they left on December 17. It was a foregone conclusion once William started talking about his tour. Their necessary preparations were minimal, as they had next to nothing in the way of household goods, only their clothes, their books, and a growing collection of William's manuscripts and Dorothy's journals.

They set off on horseback—coach fare was beyond their budget—William riding Lily, and Dorothy mounted behind George Hutchinson.[86] But this was only for about twenty miles; once past Richmond, they continued on foot, a three-day march of some sixty miles in mid-December directly across "Wensley's long Vale and Sedburgh's naked heights" to Kendal. "Bleak season was it, turbulent and bleak."[87] This was another of those arduous, definitive walks on the itinerary of the young Wordsworth and, in its way, the last of them. It was not his longest, but in the symbolic arc of his career it was a Long March of mythic proportions, through a Wilderness into their Promised Land—the sort of similes he soon began using in "Home at Grasmere," where he raised them to even higher levels, Eden and Paradise. As for Dorothy, well, to take a young woman of her class and family background out on the public road in such weather and walk from the east to the west side of the country, . . . well! Of course, she loved it. Both she and

William boasted about their rate of progress: twenty-one miles the second day, ten miles in a little over two hours through the highest pass, seven miles in an hour and a half coming down into Sedbergh—not just brisk walking, but almost respectable jogging times.[88]

They went fast for many reasons—cold, excitement, economy—but also because they interrupted their forward progress with frequent sightseeing. Wensleydale traverses a very barren part of England, providing the only road route across this part of the Pennines. They passed through the villages of Leyburn, Askrigg, and Hardale, but they marked their progress by the three waterfalls they visited, at Aysgarth, Askrigg, and Hardraw Force, which Wordsworth described in a carefully crafted letter to Coleridge, written on Christmas Day from their new home at Grasmere.[89] This letter was not merely an exercise in picturesque description but, like the November walking tour and the early *Prelude,* part of the Wordsworths' effort to keep Coleridge interested in their surroundings and draw him to them.

Like Coleridge's description of the waterfalls at Alfoxden and Culbone, these contain as much imagination as description. Wordsworth could write effective prose description when he wanted to, but here he manipulates perspective to maximize the effect of seeing one thing through another, particularly the veil or curtain of the falling water itself. His presentation of Aysgarth is delightfully Spenserian—"such a performance as you might have expected from some giant gardiner employed by one of Queen Elizabeth's Courtiers, if this same giant had consulted with Spenser and they two had finish'd the work together." By this, he concludes lamely, "you will understand that with something of vastness or grandeur it is at once formal and wild." At Askrigg the falls seemed more architectural, like "a tall arch or rather nitch which had shaped itself by insensible moulderings in the walls of an old castle," and distorted their sense of distance: "The steeple of Askrigg was . . . not a quarter of a mile distant, but oh! how far we were from it." But, oh, the difference to them.

Wordsworth's metaphors became even more exotic for their "view of a *third* waterfall" (his italics acknowledge his excess), Hardraw, where a single column of water drops nearly one hundred feet into a pool, and "the groundwork was limestone veined and dappled with colours which melted into each other in every possible variety." He tried to reproduce "the enchanted effect produced by this Arabian scene of colour as the wind blew aside the great waterfall behind which we stood and hid and revealed each of the faery cataracts in irregular succession or displayed them with various gradations of distinctness, as the intervening spray was thickened or dispersed." He knew Coleridge was fascinated by the movement of wind or water across natural objects (like trees) which move, bend, and recover without losing their essential form, though streaked by rapid passages of light and color. For example, here is Coleridge at Saddleback Tarn (Scales Tarn) the following summer: "it falls perpendicular, water-color—meets a rock, & rushes down in steep slope, all foam, till the last two feet when the rock ceases but the water preserves the same color & inclination as it were there / the pool into which it falls is almost a circle, ten yards in diameter with blue slates at the bottom."[90] The knotty intensity of both descriptions attempts to show how one thing appears *through* another, as Coleridge would generalize it in *Biographia Literaria*'s account of the origin of *Lyrical Ballads:* "the power of giving the interest of novelty by the modifying colours of imagination. The sudden charm, which accidents of light and shade, which moon-light or sun-set diffused over a known and familiar landscape, appeared to represent the practicability of combining both [truth to nature and novelty]. These are the poetry of nature."[91] Since they were not painters or watercolorists, these natural movements looked to them not like color but like the rhythm and meter of poetry as it went through or across the words in a line, giving life to the images they described.

William had felt their walk's symbolic force before they got to these three waterfalls, by a different fall, or leap—of faith and imagination. They had said their "sorrowful" farewell to George Hutchinson near Hart-Leap Well, five miles beyond Richmond. In olden times, according to local legend, a noble stag leapt to its death there, down "four roods of sheer ascent," after a thirteen-hour chase by a knight named Sir Walter. The stag breathed his last into a spring at the bottom of the hill, which was his birthplace. Sir Walter raised a pleasure dome there for his "wondering Paramour," and there was much "merriment within that pleasant bower." But now "the pleasure-house is dust:—behind, before, / This is no common waste, no common gloom"; "Something ails it now; the spot is curst."[92] Wordsworth said a peasant told them the story of the place, and there is a place called Hart-Leap Well, but like the November walking tour with Coleridge, this was a case of life confirming art rather than inspiring it. For the main incidents of the cursed hunter are present in Bürger's poems which Wordsworth had purchased in Germany, and Walter Scott had issued three versions of the poem between 1796 and 1798.[93] But Wordsworth's Sir Walter admires his "gallant" prey, unlike Scott's Earl Walter. And none of his sources treat the story as a cautionary homecoming tale in the way Wordsworth does. It is a homecoming sanctified by death, always present at Wordsworth's deepest imaginative moments, and it contains a warning to themselves not to triumph over nature by trying to arrange it to suit themselves: "Never to blend our pleasure or our pride / With sorrow of the meanest thing that feels." Wordsworth's concern is not with the knight—he lies "in his paternal vale"—but with the place, or rather with the creature that died trying to return home.

Some lines in "Home at Grasmere" make clear that the millennial "milder day" of "Hart-Leap Well" is not far off and that it is coming, paradoxically, very close to the "bleak season" of December 1799. The sign of its coming is the journey of William and Dorothy Wordsworth to their new home, cast as Paradise Regained:

> when the trance
> Came to us, as we stood by Hart-leap Well—
> The intimation of the milder day
> Which is to come, the fairer world than this—
> And raised us up, dejected as we were
> Among the records of that doleful place . . . .[94]

The "trance" was a "Vision of humanity and of God / The Mourner, God the Sufferer," in which they found a very specific message:

> A promise and an earnest that we twain,
> A pair seceding from the common world,
> Might in that hallowed spot to which our steps
> Were tending, in that individual nook,
> Might even thus early for ourselves secure,
> And in the midst of these unhappy times,
> A portion of the blessedness which love
> And knowledge will, we trust, hereafter give
> To all the Vales of earth and all mankind.
> (248–56)

It is important not to back away from the implication—indeed the clear statement—of these lines in order to appreciate the final stages of Wordsworth's self-creation as the Poet of the 1800 and 1802 prefaces and the 1805 *Prelude.* "Seceding" (an unusual but precisely chosen political word) to their own "hallowed spot," they are, like John the Baptist in the Wilderness, precursors to a worldwide regeneration. The "unhappy times" of revolutionary despair that Coleridge said *The Recluse* should address, and that Wordsworth promptly incorporated into *The Prelude,* were soon to be changed by the example of their private lives. To the extent that their "secession" was funded by payments for service in the duke of Portland's secret service, their creation of a mythic "home" at Grasmere can be regarded as their safe passage out of the world of active, dangerous politics, or as a subsidized retreat to a safe house in the provinces.

They arrived at Kendal on December 19, fairly sprinting the last seven or eight miles from Sedbergh. They spent the rest of that day buying necessary furniture and utensils, and on the 20th they proceeded to Grasmere by post chaise, creating a far different impression on their new neighbors than if they had come straggling up the road as "Wild Wanderers."

The house they entered was the first one they came to, descending the old road over from White Moss Common, precisely at the bottom of the hill. It had been readied by William's arrangement with an elderly neighbor lady, Molly Fisher, who lit the fires and who used to say later to Dorothy, "I mun never forget 't laal [little] striped gown and 't laal straw bonnet as ye stood here" (by the fire).[95] The sun set as they entered their "home within a home [and] . . . love within a love," bringing a "composing darkness" to the "little shed / Disturbed, uneasy in itself, as seemed, / And wondering at its new inhabitants."[96]

In those first nights, the longest of the year, they saw a good omen in the sky: Jupiter was visible from December 20 to 23, largest of the planets and king of the gods, William's particular emblem.[97] The next night (December 24) they associated it with another star in another sky, and Dorothy forever afterward memorialized Christmas Eve and Christmas Day with recollections of their arrival in Grasmere as much as for the Christian holiday. Nor was the Star of Bethlehem far from William's mind when, soon after, he composed the conclusion to "Home at Grasmere," with a prayer to a secularized Holy Spirit ("thou prophetic Spirit, Soul of Man") for what his poetry might become, in the same kind of rhetoric he had adopted to prophesy the coming of the "milder day" that their advent in Grasmere would bring:

> Thou human Soul of the wide earth that hast
> Thy metropolitan Temple in the hearts
> Of mighty Poets; unto me vouchsafe
> Thy guidance . . . that my verse may live and be
> Even as a Light hung up in heaven to chear
> Mankind in times to come![98]

HOME AT GRASMERE 29

"Embrace me then, ye Hills, and close me in!"
("Home at Grasmere," MS B, 129)

William had rented a cottage at the southern end of Grasmere valley, in a little collection of houses known as Town End, half a mile from the town center across open fields. Once an inn called the Dove & Olive Branch, the house itself was nameless while the Wordsworths lived there (till 1808); its modern name, Dove Cottage, was bestowed later. But Wordsworth and Coleridge played with the "peaceful" possibilities of the old name.[1] Wordsworth rang many variations on Grasmere as the "Vale of Peace" in the poem he soon began writing, "Home at Grasmere," and Coleridge extended the metaphor in his picture of their picnic on the lake's island in July: "the Image of the Bonfire, & of us that danced round it—ruddy laughing faces in the twilight—the Image of this in a Lake smooth as that sea, to whose waves the Son of God had said, PEACE!"[2]

But Wordsworth in fact found it difficult to achieve peace there, and gradually recognized that he would never find it in any *place* except in the mind and language of an idealized poet, "a man speaking to men." With this discovery he was, by the end of 1800, poised to enter the final stage of his self-creation.

"My little cabin," as Wordsworth described it, was small indeed.[3] Compared with the elegant spaces of Racedown, Alfoxden, and Sockburn—and his own grand birthplace in Cockermouth—it seemed like a doll's house, particularly for a man as tall as he. It was even smaller than Coleridge's tiny cottage in Nether Stowey, though divided into more rooms: three and a half

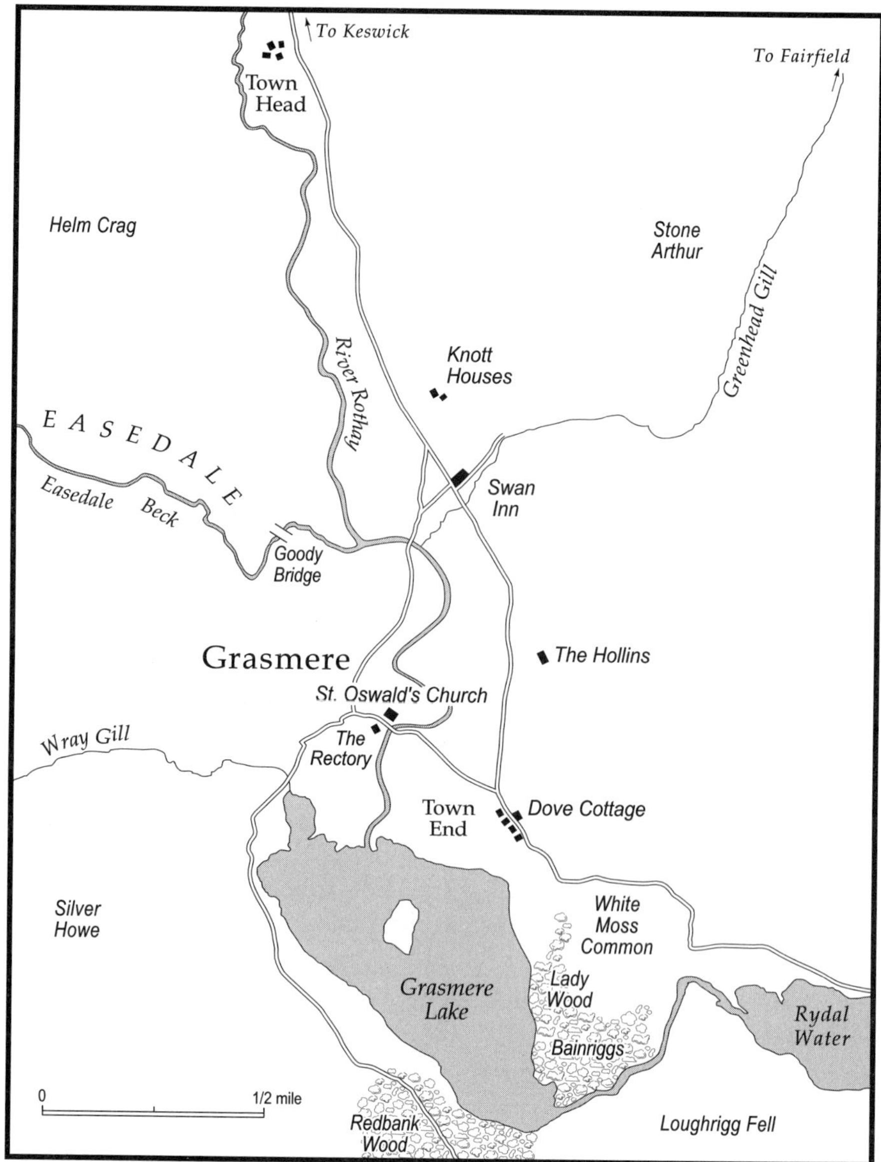

Grasmere, ca. 1800.

down, four up, though some were unfinished storage and work rooms. The entry room—wainscoted in dark oak, with leaded windows and a fireplace—had been the barroom. Dorothy made it her kitchen, next to her bedroom. William's bedroom, upstairs, adjoined the large front room which they made their living and reception area. The ceilings were all so low that William walked indoors with his head permanently bent.

Small as it was and famous as it has become, Dove Cottage was not regarded initially as a place where they would stay very long. They thought of building in the fields between their cottage and the lake, on the plot for which John had offered a loan of £40, and Dorothy had a farm all picked out on Butterlip How in Easedale, if only she "could afford to have a bad interest [i.e., risky or usurious] for [her] money."[4]

It is hard to correlate a place with poetry, though we do it to a fault with Wordsworth's outdoor poems. But the "phenomenological" dimension of Wordsworth's imagination, relative to his bodily living space, is intriguing. At Town End he was in the smallest house he had ever lived in, yet he wrote most of his greatest poetry there. His habit of composing out of doors became a necessity at Grasmere: no house could be less suited for striding about humming words at five beats to the bar. Its Lilliputian dimensions worked like a counterweight to his ambitions, concentrating his mind on giant exertions.

Though small, Dove Cottage was cheap, eight or perhaps as little as five pounds per year, far less than even their nominal rent at Alfoxden.[5] They soon arranged with John Fisher, the local cobbler, across the road in Sykeside cottage, for Mrs. Fisher's older sister, Molly, to help with the washing up and other housework, for two shillings, a sixpence more than the going rate.[6]

Expecting little of their neighbors, they were agreeably surprised. "The manners of the neighbouring cottagers have far exceeded our expectations," William wrote Coleridge five days after their arrival.[7] Dorothy had a clear sense of the local hierarchy and of their place in it: "We are very comfortably situated with respect to neighbours of the lower classes [who were attentive without being servile]" and "also upon very intimate terms with one family in the middle rank of life, a Clergyman."[8] This was the family of the eighty-five-year-old Reverend Joseph Sympson, for the past forty years vicar of Wythburn, a remote parish on the other side of Dunmail Raise. Sympson had had great prospects in his youth, moving among "high-born friends." Both his high expectations and his subsequent disappointments made him more interesting to Wordsworth than the vicar of Grasmere, who disapproved of him and Dorothy for their odd habits, particularly William's of not attending church.

Closer to them among the "middling sort" were the Oliffes at Hollens (or

Hollins) Farm just north of Town End, named after its profusion of holly trees.[9] Their good friends the Speddings, at the upper reaches of the middle class, were farther away, at Mirehouse, beyond Keswick. They improved their acquaintances with the Clarksons, at Eusmere at the top of Ullswater, till Catherine Clarkson became Dorothy's most intimate personal friend.[10] As for the aristocrats, they had nothing to do with the Le Fleming family, over the hill and through the woods at Rydal Hall. Wordsworth had already been warned about trespassing there, but in the next fall they were given temporary shelter in an anteroom there during a rainstorm, while "a grand Ball" was in progress.[11]

They soon met their other neighbors, mostly poor people of the village, and explored every nook and cranny in the valley, until its coordinates were as familiar to them as if they were extensions of their house, as in a sense they were. Like Dove Cottage, the entire Vale of Grasmere appeared "so narrow," "so small," compared with the high hopes Wordsworth brought with him, his mind chock-full of "many records of my childish years."[12] On first seeing it, "I looked, I stared, I smiled, I laughed; and all / The weight of sadness was in wonder lost." The reaction is typical of adult returns to childhood haunts, but there was a huge tension between Wordsworth's "sadness" and his "wonder," a tension soon released in his earliest Grasmere poems.

Town End, tucked away into the southeast corner of the valley, has an air of peeping out at the rest of it. Dunmail Raise and Helm Crag were the limit of their horizon to the north, with Easedale and Far Easedale fading away to the northwest—the "Black Quarter," Dorothy called it, because the mountain storms came mostly from that direction. But Easedale was their favorite place for walks and poetry composing, being the easiest way to get up quickly into the hills. To the west, Silver How loomed up across the lake, with its perfect little island in the middle. Behind them, hidden from view by the woods along the river Rothay, rose Red Bank and Loughrigg. Immediately beside them, their eastern perspective was closed off by the sharp incline of their "little orchard plot," which rose up to How Top, and above that to the whole Fairfield range, making their house the "rocky corner in the lowest stair / Of that magnificent temple which doth bound / One side of our whole vale with grandeur rare."[13] Moving north along this eastern ridge were the summits of Stone Arthur and Seat Sandal, leading toward Helvellyn, invisible in the northern distance beyond Dunmail Raise.

In the "Poems on the Naming of Places," Wordsworth started claiming these sites in the name of his own imagination, but he also encountered their resistance to being christened by strangers. It was the same with the neighbors. Their strong first impressions of the Fishers, the Sympsons, the Ashburners, the Greens, and many other families were soon strategically incorporated by William's imagination into poetry. He drafted them into "Home at Grasmere"—his new start on *The Recluse,* and later into Books V–IX of *The Excursion* (1814), the only part of his master project he ever published—as evidence that country life was more virtuous than city life. But they also showed it was equally difficult. Almost all these stories show—true to the families' actual histories—how they recovered from a full measure of life's disappointments.

The Reverend Sympson and his disappointed hopes were one case in point. Another was John and Agnes Fisher, who struggled all their life to pay off the mortgage he had been forced to take out for their marriage—necessitated by a "mishap" pregnancy. John Fisher summed up the economic situation when he said there would soon "be only two ranks of people, the very rich and the very poor."[14] Those who had land were forced to sell or mortgage it for cash, "and all the land goes into one hand," a version of the same process in which Wordsworth's father had aided James Lowther. Foreclosures and heavy encumbrances were common in the ruinous economy of the time, and Wordsworth put them at the heart of "Michael," the last poem in his new edition of *Lyrical Ballads,* the one he said carried its main message. Michael loses his son in his struggle to save his land. Similarly, Agnes Fisher lost her youth and vivacity and gained only the sense of having wasted her talents and opportunities: "Bound—by vexation, and regret, and scorn, / Constrained forgiveness, and relenting vows" (*Excursion,* VI.712–13). By contrast, it was Wordsworth who succeeded in Grasmere.

The neighbors at least had roofs over their heads, but a constant procession of even more unfortunate wayfarers passed by the cottage. Its location made it a natural stopping place for travelers resting after their climb over from Rydal, or preparing to ascend in that direction. Most who stopped were desperately poor, for the years 1799–1801 saw particularly intense poverty in the northwest of England, with food riots in Lancaster, Wigan, and Birmingham.[15] Hardly a week went by without Dorothy's recording her conversation with one of them, some of whom found their way into her brother's poems, most famously the old leech gatherer whom they encountered just outside their cottage.[16] Their number was legion: "a poor woman from Hawkshead"; "a widow of Grasmere, a merry African from Longtown" (at the Scottish border); a tall woman whose two small sons denied she was their mother; a slightly mad hatter; the Hawkshead boy who looked surprised when she asked if he had enough to eat; a soldier from Cockermouth of exactly William's age (hence probably known to him) who had lost his leg in battle and returned home, only to find "he could earn more money in travelling with his ass than at home"; the "Cockermouth traveller," a woman who dealt in thimbles and other domestic hardware, whose husband forbade her to use an ass because, he said, "it is the tramper's badge"; the little girl from Coniston whose "step-mother had turned her out of doors"; and the woman from nearby Rydal, "stout and well dressed," forced to beg because of "these hard times!"[17] They sent one little girl back to Kendal with a note to call on the mayor, a former schoolmate of William's.

The friendly reception at Dove Cottage encouraged still more wanderers to stop. Dorothy gave them what penny or scrap she could afford, in exchange for an account of themselves, for William. This was the general rule of hospitality for visitors at Town End: "if you like to have a cup of tea with us, you are very welcome; but if you want any meat;—you must pay for your board."[18]

William continued for a while to write poems about these people. He still wanted to know about the mental states their suffering drove them to, or else he imagined them for himself. He was pitilessly interested in what their life experience had done to their minds, not in their present hunger or debts or rheumatism. His focus on them was the same as on himself: "the growth of my own mind," and how their imaginations were "impaired" or "restored."

John returned to them in early January. His behavior illustrates the enormous emotional pressure surrounding their establishment, after nearly twenty years, of a home in the Lakes. He walked out to Town End from the inn near the church, but as he stood in front of the cottage he was overcome by emotion. He returned to the inn and sent word by messenger to prepare William and Dorothy—who did not know when he would arrive—for the shock of this belated homecoming. Then he walked back to Town End, and they were reunited under the first roof they could call their own since Dorothy had been sent away to Halifax in 1778.[19]

In late February, William traveled over to Sockburn to fetch Mary Hutchinson for a visit that lasted six weeks. With devoted friends and family around him, Wordsworth turned again to *The Recluse,* which now became the poetical justification of his career, recasting it in terms of his move to Grasmere. "Home at Grasmere" is set up to show that he had reached the destination his whole life had been pointing toward. He had everything he wanted, within reason, and no more excuses. It was time to realize his genius as he defined it: the poem's manuscript subtitle is "Book First, Part First of *The Recluse.*" Far from the usual image of a poet's life as simply writing and publishing poems, *The Recluse* was an epic with its poet narrator as its hero. But it took years to complete just one book of a poem that might have had thirty such books; Wordsworth did not finish it until 1806, after he had completed *The Prelude.* The challenges it presented, and his difficulty in overcoming them, brought him to the final stages of his self-creation as the Poet of the preface to *Lyrical Ballads,* the hero of *The Prelude,* and the William Wordsworth of subsequent English literary history.

He composed about six hundred lines of the poem in 1800 before its insuperable contradictions forced him to break off composition.[20] These lines constitute a Romantic Ode to Joy in one of the highest keys ever attempted. No small part of Wordsworth's achievement was avoiding the incoherence such odes often fall into, like the youthful effusions of Shelley or Keats later or the contemporaneous efforts of German Romantics like Novalis. His Ode to Joy launches itself, whether by design or by accident, over the brink of its own ecstasy into the depths of its dialectical contrary, the Ode to Dejection. Unlike the conventional pastoral poet, who writes himself into his chosen landscape as a refuge from worldly suffering and corruption, Wordsworth wrote himself out of it, as he gradually, reluctantly acknowledged the social responsibility he was shirking.

The poem opens with a "spot of time" that may be real or imaginary: these are normal alternatives in any poem, but here they become matters of life and death. He remembers himself as a boy gazing down on the valley and experiencing a visionary moment of notably unboyish thoughts:

> "What happy fortune were it here to live!
> And if a thought of dying, if a thought
> Of mortal separation could come in
> With paradise before me, here to die."
>
> (9–12)[21]

"Paradise before me" goes Milton one better, topping *Paradise Lost*'s final vision of "the earth was all before them." But Adam and Eve were leaving Paradise, while William and Dorothy are returning to it. Vaunting himself above not only Milton but even Milton's biblical sources, Wordsworth's thanksgiving hymn vies with the Song of Songs, with the striking variation that his erotic language refers not to the expectant community of believers but to the receptive landscape: "Embrace me then, ye Hills, and close me in!"

He made a vow: "here should be my home, this Valley be my World." As he advanced poetically into the landscape that he and Dorothy had just entered physically, there was no expression too extreme for his joy, as he lays claim to the land in the name of his own imagination.

> The unappropriated bliss hath found
> An owner, and that owner I am he.
> The Lord of this enjoyment is on Earth
> And in my breast.
>
> (85–88)

What Being . . . since the birth of Man
Had ever more abundant cause to speak
Thanks . . . ?
The boon is absolute . . .
. . . among the bowers
Of blissful Eden this was neither given
Nor could be given . . . .

(117–25)

This is astonishing language for an essentially non-Christian writer and one who, as Coleridge said, meant *all* of every word he wrote. Each phrase has to be considered not only as rhetorical hyperbole but as deeply felt personal testament: "The Lord . . . is on Earth." These are the most extreme expressions of joy in Wordsworth's oeuvre, his least tranquil, most emotional mood; it is an unnerving sight, this human embracing of the divine.

The segments of "Home at Grasmere" written in 1800 advance by a series of such rhetorical leaps and bounds, each exclamation more sweeping than the last. After the opening boyhood "spot of time," the poem follows the sequence of their December walk through Wensleydale and the apparent confirmation of their hopes with the coming of spring and the birds' riotous pleasure in it, reflecting their own inner satisfaction. The poem works toward identification with its very moment(s) of composition, toward saying, Here am I, writing this poem. If all its linguistic peculiarities were compressed into a single sentence, they would collapse all tenses into one: Once upon a time I am living happily ever after. It bursts into—and eventually through—its own moments of inspiration. Every aspect of it strives toward self-identification: it is full of images of reflection and circularity, tautological arguments, and redundant syntax.

It comes as no surprise to any levelheaded reader that this dizzying, surreal absurdism could not be long sustained, and that the denomination of the first wild days of March 1800 as a unique imaginative entity—new century, new career, new revolutionary agenda—should falter in the face of real time. But it came as an untoward shock to Wordsworth, and we can see the shock waves registered in the poem. At the very height of his *"O altitudo!"* Wordsworth looks down, sees poverty, death, and evil, and plunges to the ground, not to resume the poem for over five years. Just when he seems to be parsing his poem off the page of the landscape, he reads something he doesn't like:

But two are missing—two, a lonely pair
Of milk-white Swans. Ah, why are they not here?

> These above all, ah, why are they not here
> To share in this day's pleasure?
>
> (322–25)

The repetitions, the reiterated gasp, the insistent questioning—all the poem's self-reflective characteristics implode upon it. And the reason is presented as nakedly as the ecstasy: he and Dorothy have identified themselves with these two swans to an extraordinary extent: "to us / They were more dear than may be well believed." But we can believe it, when we see what their disappearance does to the poem, for William and Dorothy had drastically over-invested themselves in their symbolic identification with the swans:

> . . . their state so much resembled ours;
> They also having chosen this abode;
> They strangers, and we strangers; they a pair,
> And we a solitary pair like them.
>
> . . . .
>
> Shall we behold them yet another year
> Surviving, they for us and we for them,
> And neither pair be broken?
>
> (338–41, 348–50)

The poem's extreme symbolism rebounds onto its narrator. Wordsworth pitched his claims for the special qualities of Grasmere so high that this ridiculous literalism threatens to spoil it. He goes immediately on the defensive: the bulk of the remaining lines composed in 1800 show him backpedaling furiously to restore the damage he has done. But it was no good; he ultimately backs himself into a corner, out of the poem, and breaks off.

The extremes to which he goes to explain the swans' absence are the best guarantee of the utter sincerity of the joy which preceded his discovery of it. His first conjecture is that they may have been shot by Grasmere "dalesmen." This was a good possibility. Dorothy refers to "the swan hunt" in her journal, an organized destruction of the decorative species of swans introduced at Windermere twenty years earlier, which were very unpopular with the local residents because they were so noisy and aggressive.[22] But this commonsense explanation leads Wordsworth into an even worse crisis in his poem: lack of moral confidence in Grasmere's natives. He apologizes both to the place and to his poem for even "harbouring this thought": "Recall, my song, the ungenerous thought; forgive, / Thrice favoured Region, the conjecture harsh."[23]

Evidence of human frailty has introduced a complication into the argument which soon became insuperable. Other human beings have come on the scene, and *The Recluse*'s difficult social theme ("Human Life") disrupts the Man-Nature bonding Wordsworth celebrates. Contrary to sentimental views of Wordsworth's happy return to the Lake District—views which often make much of the phrase "home at Grasmere"—the poem of that title challenges and indeed destroys the sentimental view, showing Wordsworth's clear awareness that his greatness as a poet could never be built on Grasmere, the Lake District, or even all of Nature.*

Aldous Huxley's funny but cheap shot, in "Wordsworth in the Tropics," is only the cynical underside of this same erroneous sentimental interpretation. It may be true that it's easier to celebrate nature in Cumberland than in the tropics (easier for an Englishman, anyway), but Wordsworth, *as* Wordsworth, would have come to the same impasse if he had been born and raised in India, Canada, Australia, or any other "wild" place in Britain's expanding empire. No empire, no earthly place, was big enough for his godlike conception of imagination: what he learned in the moments of composition in Grasmere in 1800 confirmed what he had already intuited in the Simplon in 1790 and on Snowdon in 1791: the inadequacy of a literal faith in natural transcendence.

Frustrated in his composing, he goes on desperately to assert that Grasmere's dalesmen were not swearing, wrathful, selfish, envious people who shoot swans. They may have been poor, hungry, and ill clothed, but "extreme penury is here unknown . . . they who want are not too great a weight / For those who can relieve" (440–48). This special pleading contradicts the plentiful evidence in Dorothy's journal, and the poem's sequential composition breaks off at the interesting words "so here there is . . ." (457). The implied simile is intended to point a moral drawn from the geographical form of the valley: "*as* these lofty barriers break the force / Of winds—this deep vale *as*

*The film shown at Wordsworth's Cockermouth birthplace under the auspices of the National Trust (as of the mid-1990s) exemplifies this simple linking of the "essence" of his poetry to the Lake District landscape. It is understandable as a device to stimulate tourism: scene after scene is shown in glorious technicolor, sometimes with a snippet of poetry, but more often with a rich baritone voice-over driving home the lesson that "this is the place"—precisely the lesson "Home at Grasmere" is unable to teach. The film's usual effect on its audiences indicates that they rightly demand more human interest, and that Wordsworth's reputation as a poet is poorly served by such one-to-one correlations with nature. Hardly anyone stays till the end: teenage couples leave first, cursing this confirmation of their worst school memories of Wordsworth; children and babies go next, literally bored to tears by its finally pointless connection of pictures and poetry. At the end, there are only diehard foreign tourists, grimly determined to take whatever is dished out, and British couples of advanced middle age, the husbands having abandoned themselves to their wives' wishes for the afternoon, secure in the promise of a pint in the pub when the ordeal is over. By the time the last sunset fades with the last symphonic chord, almost everyone left has learned the lesson of Wordsworth's contemporary cultural packaging: bliss is it in that dark to be asleep.

it doth in part / Conceal us from the storm—*so* here there is . . . ." But nothing follows; there is no moral counterforce equivalent to nature's mighty forms that will conceal social poverty and political corruption from him or from his responsibility to combat them.

In another manuscript fragment of this time, Wordsworth charmingly described a "lyric spirit of philosophy" that came over him when, alone in a remote spot that seemed "shut out from man . . . by an inalienable right," he would see "some vestiges of human hands, some steps of human passion." These would prompt "the poetry of thoughts" to start running in his head, leading him "through moods of sadness & delight."[24] But in "Home at Grasmere" the signs of human passion break in and destroy the texture of natural beauty. When he reached this impasse, Wordsworth could write only a brief coda, which in fact becomes the moral guarantee, in a variety of forms, of all his subsequent failed efforts on *The Recluse.* Falling back into the same rhetorical habit of swerving from unstable argument to assertive personality that he had developed in "Tintern Abbey" ("If this be but a vain belief"), he projected an image of the one spiritual community he could vouch for, and one that could actually complete his interrupted simile, except for its radical diminution of his claims:

> And if this
> Were not, we have enough within ourselves,
> Enough to fill the present day with joy
> And overspread the future years with hope—
> Our beautiful and quiet home, enriched
> Already with a Stranger whom we love
> Deeply, a Stranger of our Father's house,
> A never-resting Pilgrim of the Sea,
> Who finds at last an hour to his content
> Beneath our roof; and others whom we love
> Will seek us also, Sisters of our hearts,
> And one, like them, a Brother of our hearts,
> Philosopher and Poet, in whose sight
> These mountains will rejoice with open joy.
> Such is our wealth: O Vale of Peace, we are
> And must be, with God's will, a happy band!
> (859–74)

The upsetting social dimension exposed by the pair of missing swans is finally stabilized by an image of an extended family, William and Dorothy, John, the Hutchinson sisters, and Coleridge. This was as far as Wordsworth's social vision could extend with confidence in 1800. Setting the poem aside till 1806, he then tried to generalize Grasmere's meaning in a series of tales of stoic men and clever animals intended to prove "that solitude is not where these things are" (solitude, that is, as selfish escapism). But in the 1800 portions of "Home at Grasmere," the identification of the master poem with the master's life came too quickly. Having cast himself and Dorothy as the Adam and Eve of a new Eden, the strain of saving the world *from this place* soon proved to be too much.

He could not bring his *plot* to a satisfactory denouement, but he did manage to leap to a conclusion: the great "Prospectus" of *The Recluse* that he published with *The Excursion* in 1814. These lines conclude "Home at Grasmere" by projecting a vision of what *could be* to fulfill the promises made by the poem—the same strategy Wordsworth used in the 1799 *Prelude.* All conclusions of any segment of *The Recluse* follow this same onward-looking pattern. The strategy is effective to a degree, promising "something evermore about to be." But it is also fatal, because it pays out more promissory notes to be honored, at ever-higher rates of interest, as creative desperation forces Wordsworth to claim still more for his epic.

The "Prospectus" begins, "On Man, on Nature, and on Human Life," the same phrase Wordsworth used to announce *The Recluse* to Tobin and Losh in March of 1798. It establishes a balance between individual integrity and social responsibility in the world as given ("Nature"), which constitutes at once the glory and the stumbling block of the democratic Romantic imagination. In this vision, the individual genius is the inspirer, not the leader, of the people, singing

Of virtue and of intellectual power,
Of blessed consolations in distress,
Of joy in widest commonalty spread,
Of the individual mind that keeps its own
Inviolate retirement, and consists
With being limitless the one great Life—
(966–71)

Invocations are supposed to begin, not end, poems. But Wordsworth says that his epic to come will surpass Milton's:

. . . fit audience let me find though few!
Fit audience find though few—thus prayed the Bard,
Holiest of Men. Urania, I shall need
Thy guidance, or a greater Muse, if such
Descend to earth or dwell in highest heaven!
For I must tread on shadowy ground, must sink

Deep, and, aloft ascending, breathe in worlds
To which the Heaven of heavens is but a veil.
(972–79)*

He justifies this outstripping of Milton (from the invocation to Urania in Book VII of *Paradise Lost*) on the grounds that the heaven and hell of the new epic are higher and deeper than his predecessor's:

Not Chaos, not
The darkest pit of lowest Erebus,
Nor aught of blinder vacancy, scooped out
By help of dreams—can breed such fear and awe
As fall upon us often when we look
Into our Minds, into the Mind of Man—
My haunt, and the main region of my song.
(980–90)

Wordsworth's "egotism" has been much on display in these pages, but it is a measure of his stature as a culture hero to reflect that millions of people believe this now, making their inner consciousness of themselves the psychic bedrock of their reality. In this sense, Wordsworth is not an egoist but a realist.

Having staked out his claim to his "main region," Wordsworth proceeded to elaborate its two adjacent territories, Nature and Society. Nature's Beauty is presented as a combination of the Promised Land, the Elysian Fields, and Paradise all rolled into one:

Beauty, whose living home is the green earth,

....

. . . . waits upon my steps,
Pitches her tents before me when I move,
An hourly Neighbour. Paradise and groves
Elysian, fortunate islands, fields like those of old
In the deep ocean—wherefore should they be

*Probably no sources need be sought for this language beyond the Bible, *Paradise Lost,* and the Book of Common Prayer—with the important proviso that Wordsworth took them personally. But there is another source close to hand that has been overlooked, Coleridge's translation of Schiller's dithyramb "The Visit of the Gods," composed ca. October 1799. This fragment turns on the conceit that, since its speaker could never entertain the gods adequately (because of their annoying habit of dropping by in groups), they should entertain *him:* raise him up to heaven, receive him royally, and bestow their powers on him, singing in chorus: "Quicken his eyes with celestial dew, / That Styx the detested no more he may view, / And like one of us Gods may conceit him to be!" The godlike perspective as much as the language seems to echo Wordsworth's "Prospectus," a possibility seconded by Coleridge's notebook remark on his translation: "and remember Wordsworth's remark" (*NSTC,* 494 (notes); *PSTC,* 1:310–11).

A History, or but a dream, when minds
Once wedded to this outward frame of things
In love, find these the growth of common day?
(991–1001)

But Human Life, or Society, is presented far more negatively:

. . . I oft
Must turn elsewhere, and travel near the tribes
And fellowships of men, see ill sights
Of passions ravenous from each other's rage,
Must hear humanity in fields and groves
Pipe solitary anguish, or must hang
Brooding over the fierce confederate storm
Of Sorrow, barricadoed evermore
Within the walls of cities—may these sounds
Have their authentic comment, that even these
Hearing, I be not heartless of forlorn!
(1015–25)

Wordsworth constantly tried, and constantly failed, to integrate a vision of imaginatively redeemed society into *The Recluse*'s epic mission, as he had been doing since "Tintern Abbey," which uses some of these same images. This is what halted his progress on "Home at Grasmere," and it continued to do so in each of his efforts to move *The Recluse* forward. His determination not to neglect "Human Life" spelled the doom of *The Recluse,* but it also gave it its fitful glory and guaranteed that though it could not be finished, it could never be abandoned. Almost from the beginning, it has been the criticism of Wordsworth's egotism and his "nature worship" that they lead him, in Matthew Arnold's phrase, to turn his eyes "from half of human fate."[25] But the manuscripts of his master project, largely unpublished until recent times, show that he was determined to turn his vision *toward* "the tribes and fellowships of men," determined to give it "authentic comment." He usually failed, not only because of the superhuman difficulty of the task, but also because of his tendency to represent general human experience in the heightened terms of his own painful experiences in the world. Thus the splendid egoism of his goal was undercut by the selfish egotism of his evidence.

He ended the "Prospectus" with a prayer to a Holy Spirit of poetry for inspiration, a prayer that turns finally into a fourth topic, which appears to be an afterthought: himself, William Wordsworth. This shift soon led to his replacing *The Recluse* as his epic subject with a new and better one, the story of his own self-creation, *The Prelude.*

And if with this
I blend more lowly matter—with the thing
Contemplated describe the mind and man
Contemplating, and who and what he was,
The transitory Being that beheld
This vision, when and where and how he lived,
With all his little realities of life—
Be not this labour useless.

(1034–41)

However, this was not a "labour" that in 1800 he could conceive of as useful. He had followed Coleridge's orders and got back to work on *The Recluse,* which as Stephen Gill wonderfully says was rapidly becoming "Coleridge's dream and Wordsworth's secret."[26] He had produced a mythopoeic vision of Grasmere Vale as the Garden of Eden and discovered that, like its original, it could not stand the sight of sin or evil. There was no serpent, no apple (unless natural beauty itself was the temptation), but there was evidence that men could wantonly destroy Nature's beauty.

The "Prospectus" lines leap over these difficulties by insisting that he will produce an integrated vision of Man, Nature, and Society not just in Grasmere (population 250) but throughout "the human soul of the wide earth." It is often easier to propose solutions for the world's ills than for one's own family and neighborhood, but to smile at the extravagance of Wordsworth's solutions in the "Prospectus" is to miss the point. Wordsworth's worry was whether he was being extravagant *enough,* whether his poetry would adequately reflect the goal he saw before him. As his great American disciple Thoreau said, "It is a ridiculous demand which England and America make, that you shall speak so that they can understand you. . . . I fear chiefly lest my expression may not be *extra-vagant* enough . . . . I desire to speak somewhere *without* bounds; like a man in a waking moment, to men in their waking moments; for I am convinced that I cannot exaggerate enough even to lay the foundation of a true expression."[27] Thoreau here echoes Wordsworth's claims for the poet of democracy ("a man speaking to men"), and his meditation on Walden Pond—he called it his "lake country"—is so close in spirit and imagery to "Home at Grasmere" that one might think he had read it, even though the publication of *Walden; or, Life in the Woods* (1854) preceded the posthumous publication of "Home at Grasmere" (1888) by over thirty years.

While this terrific creative struggle was working in Wordsworth's mind—in essence, the constitutive struggle of his entire career—he was living a very ordinary and happy life. The spring, summer, and fall of 1800 were like the extended house-warming party of a newly married couple. Over nine seasonable months, almost all their old and new friends visited the newly established, newly respectable couple. No longer freeloading vagabonds, they had an address and were "at home" to guests.

James Losh and his wife, Cecilia, their distant cousin, came, the near-recruits of the German tour. He was the first recipient of *The Recluse*'s birth announcement and editor of the *Œconomist,* a journal devoted to nonviolent social reform. Losh was beginning the career as lawyer and public-spirited citizen that would make him an outstanding "Northern Worthy." After John Marshall stopped by, the husband of Dorothy's oldest friend, Jane Pollard Marshall, Dorothy reopened their correspondence after a silence of over three years. She tactfully tried to smooth over broken connections: "My dear Jane, I will say nothing of my sorrow and remorse for having neglected you so long; . . . [but] Professions are idle and useless; you are disposed to love and to forgive me and I feel that I must trust to those kindly dispositions for your *entire* pardon."[28] She presumably intended to pay a compliment to Jane's housekeeping by repeatedly remarking how fat her husband was, but in the Wordsworths' plain-living regimen at Grasmere nobody ever gained weight.

In September their new friends the Clarksons came down from Eusmere to see the end result of the real estate prospecting trip of the previous November. Catherine Clarkson soon became Dorothy's intimate friend, replacing Jane Pollard Marshall.[29] Also from the November walking tour came the Reverend Thomas Myers, his son Thomas, brother of William's school and college chum, now successfully married to John Robinson's granddaughter, Lady Mary Nevill.

They began to draw some permanent visitors after them. Charles Lloyd came, less welcome but still hanging on to the vision of creative community they had started generating in Somerset. He and his new wife moved into a house in Brathay, near Ambleside, in the fall.[30] Lloyd had married a merchant's daughter in April 1799 and moved first to Penrith, then back to Cambridge, then back up north. The Wordsworths could hardly object, since, despite the trouble Lloyd inevitably caused, he would soon be related to them by marriage. Christopher, tutoring Lloyd at Cambridge while they were in Germany, had fallen in love with Lloyd's sister Priscilla during a Christmas vacation visit, partly confirming Uncle Cookson's fear that his association with Lloyd would be "prejudicial." They were soon engaged. Coleridge considered Lloyd a "rascal"; Dorothy defended him, but in admitting he was "a dangerous acquaintance" she made a distinction without much difference.[31] Lloyd's main fixation was Coleridge, so he provides a more objective view of the Wordsworths: "We have not any society except the

Wordsworths'. They are very unusual characters. Indeed Miss W. I much like. But her Brother is not a man after my own heart. I always feel myself depressed in his society."[32] Wordsworth was capable of great animation and vivacity, but only in the presence of a handful of picked people. To the rest of the world he showed a face of extreme reserve, and with Lloyd he had good reason to be cautious.

John Stoddart was a friend from the Montagu-Pinney set who showed up, once in the spring and again in the fall, returning from a tour of Scotland with his elegant friend James Moncrieff. Stoddart was a nervy young man with large ambitions and some literary ability. But unlike Lloyd, he could be cultivated to do some good. Wordsworth talked with him night and day when he was there, and arranged for him to write a review of the second edition *Lyrical Ballads* whenever it came out, an indication of his increasing professionalism. Stoddart was reading for the law, and would soon advance to the influential position of chief justice of Malta, Britain's primary Mediterranean naval base after Gibraltar. John Pinney was also eagerly awaited, as Coleridge informed Tobin: "Wordsworth builds on his [Pinney's] coming down this autumn."[33] Neither Stoddart nor Pinney was really such a good friend, but they were wealthy and influential and good to know.

Finally, there came Robert Jones, boon companion of the 1790 tour, to celebrate his friend's settling down, after a decade of further wanderings, in the valley he would never leave, except to turn around its corner into Rydal in 1813.

By far the most important visitor was Coleridge, who arrived April 6, the day after Mary left for Yorkshire.[34] He stayed for a month, and by the time he left it was decided he would return to live there. Dorothy set about making inquiries for suitable accommodation and soon found Greta Hall in Keswick, a beautifully situated mansion, renovated with an observatory, owned by William Harrison, who ran a successful cartage company and was the model for the employer of Wordsworth's "The Waggoner."[35] The rent was £42 per year: reasonable, though much more than the Wordsworths were paying. But Jackson was a kindly indulgent soul, and he waived the first six months' rent, gave Coleridge the run of his substantial reference library, and became, with his housekeeper, a sort of grandparent to little Hartley.[36]

Coleridge left for the south on May 4 to collect his family and make arrangements for the move north. On May 14 William and John left for a visit of nearly a month at Gallow Hill, where Mary Hutchinson was now keeping house for her brother. They were going a-courting, though it was not perfectly clear in everyone's mind just who was courting whom. None of the parties had any parental wishes to defer to, and as Mary was of age and in possession of her inheritance, she was free to choose any suitor she wished. John was clearly the better prospect of the two. He pointedly reminded her of this when he wrote her at the end of the year, following his appointment as captain of the *Earl of Abergavenny,* that he expected to be "a very *rich man*" from the China trade in less than ten years.[37]

The two brothers toured around extensively while in Yorkshire, venturing some fifty miles west to Knaresborough, but they did not travel the sixty miles up to Bishop Middleham (above Sockburn) to visit Sara Hutchinson. After William and Mary married in 1802, some people hoped that John might marry Sara, but this did not seem a likely option in 1800. Sara was the one member of this whole group of family and friends "on whose judgement [William] relied totally," even in matters touching revisions of his poetry.[38] Coleridge later joined in the family's hopes that John and Sara might marry: "the silent poet" would have provided an unthreatening rival to his unrequited passion for her. But one trembles to contemplate the dimensions his internal crisis would have taken had William married Sara instead of Mary—an attachment that Coleridge soon enough fantasized into reality.

In this era of arranged marriages, there are many stories of one brother (or sister) losing out to another in a competition that everyone understood to be fairly open. Jane Austen's *Persuasion* and many other novels have plots that turn on the frustration—or correction—of right or wrong choices in the marriage game. In real life too, it was by no means rare for the primary suitor's brother to end up as the bridegroom, or for a younger sister to win the bride's place. To the extent that John deferred to, or lost out to, William in the courtship of Mary Hutchinson, we can add another item to the cost of the creation of the Poet. But although William had been regarding Mary with renewed attention since his return from Germany, Mary for all her mildness had an independent mind that chose him over his quiet brother, and she clearly admired the lifestyle at Town End. Her sister Joanna told John Myers, "My Sister Mary was very much delighted indeed with Grasmere, and the Wordsworth way of life, she says she [never saw] so compleat a Cottage in her life, and [every] thing [so] very comfortable as they have."[39]

The real loser in this mating game was Dorothy. The purpose of the brothers' trip is unmistakable from the fact of her being left behind, since she would not otherwise have been an unwelcome companion, but quite the contrary. Dorothy and Mary were good friends, and she could hardly have stayed behind because the trip was too rigorous, having *walked* most of the same distance five months before, into the teeth of December winds. But the prospect of watching William pay his addresses to Mary would have been too painful to behold.

This is quite clear from her Grasmere journal, which begins precisely at the time of her two brothers' departure. Its opening passages show her feelings projected onto her landscape descriptions, just as in her brother's poetry.[40] The separation of the two Grasmere swans was the symbolic fact that spelled the doom of "Home at Grasmere," but William's absence was a real fact that provoked a new and deeper voice in her journals, giving her landscape descriptions a profoundly human weight.

> *May 14th, 1800.* Wm. and John set off into Yorkshire after dinner at ½ past 2 o'clock, cold pork in their pockets. I left them at the turning of Lowwood bay under the trees. My heart was so full that I could hardly speak to W. when I gave him a farewell kiss. I sate a long time upon a stone at the margin of the lake, and after a flood of tears my heart was easier. The lake looked to me, I knew not why, dull and melancholy, and the weltering on the shores seemed a heavy sound.[41]

This point at Lowwood is exactly where the "little unpretending rill" empties into Windermere, the very spot at which she and William, six years earlier, had stopped for lunch on their walk from Kendal to Windy Brow to start living together for the first time in their lives. Their hearts were full of the memory, but they could not say much about it in John's presence. Steeling her will, Dorothy dedicated her journal to a very specific purpose, a love offering: "I resolved to write a journal of the time till W. and J. return, and I set about keeping my resolve, because I will not quarrel with myself, and because I shall give Wm. pleasure by it when he comes home again." Turning back alone, she gave a halfpenny to a begging woman, arrived home with a headache, talked to another young woman who was begging money to help bury her husband, and ended the day's entry with a deep irrational wish: "Oh! that I had a letter from William!"[42]

Two days later she started a letter to Mary, but could not finish it. A walk to Rydal gave her the courage to do so: "Grasmere was very solemn in the last glimpse of twilight . . . . I had been very melancholy in my walk back. I had many of my saddest thoughts, and I could not keep the tears within me. But when I came to Grasmere I felt that it did me good. I finished my letter to M.H. Ate hasty pudding and went to bed."[43]

And so the entries continue, shifting from melancholy, to landscape, to restoration, to writing or receiving (or hoping for) letters, all the way through till William's return on June 7. After three weeks, the letters and the person seemed indistinguishable: "No letter, no William." These are the diary entries of a woman whose heart is breaking but who is determined not to lose her mind under the strain. She will preserve what remains to her in the relationship: to give him pleasure via the medium of her diary.

She did not receive nearly as many letters as she sent, and toward the end of the month she got one that called for still more resolve on her part. William wrote, "When you are writing to France say all that is affectionate to A. and all that is fatherly to C."[44] This is all that remains of a letter that Gordon Wordsworth destroyed.[45] It reminds us that Annette was always somewhere on their minds, even though very few letters between them ever made it through, and opens a crack into their hidden world of intense, changing relations. Dorothy had written to Gallow Hill to tell William about the letter from Annette, but "all" that was left of the affection between him and Annette was something that it fell to Dorothy to express; he would not write the letter himself from Gallow Hill, nor even wait a week till he returned. He had felt for some time that his emotions were no longer engaged to Annette, possibly when the depths of Dorothy's passions were revealed in Germany, and they both realized the need for him to attach his sexual passions elsewhere. Dorothy was used to writing to Annette, but that she should also be charged to say "all that is fatherly" to Caroline does seem a cruel imposition. Perhaps she gained inspiration from the rather unusual selection of Shakespeare's plays she read in William's absence: *A Midsummer Night's Dream, Macbeth, King John,* and *Timon of Athens.* In all of them, tragedy is precipitated (or avoided) by the hero's failure (or willingness) to follow the advice and desires of the woman closest to him.

When Dorothy's hero finally returned, at eleven o'clock at night on June 7, they stayed up till four in the morning, talking about the visit and its implications for their future together.[46] John came only the next day—possibly to give William time to break the news gently to Dorothy that he, not John, was likely to become Mary's husband.

The next three weeks were spent walking, fishing, and making minor household repairs and improvements. Coleridge, Sara, and baby Hartley arrived, on June 29.[47] One fraught set of emotions was added on top of another. Each one of the five adults cramped into the three small sleeping rooms of the cottage had thoughts or dreams troubled by desire, jealousy, hope, and frustration. Any talk about the Hutchinsons made the Wordsworths edgy in ways that only they could know of, while Coleridge was oppressed by the same topic in ways that nobody knew but himself. Relations between Dorothy and Sara Coleridge were never of the best, and to have Sara there, six months pregnant, at such a time and in such close quarters, tried Dorothy sorely. They stayed a month before moving on to Keswick. In the north–south tug-of-war over the location of their creative headquarters, Wordsworth had won.

Wordsworth was pulling Coleridge to him, away from worldly success. While Wordsworth hunkered down in the country, Coleridge had achieved a high level of prominence as what we would now call a columnist. In only five months of writing leading paragraphs and columns for Stuart's *Morning Post,* he had established a position in contemporary social debates much more central than he had enjoyed five years earlier, and effectively greater than any he achieved later, except in posthumous reputation. He published at least seventy-six paragraphs or essays in this time, a rate of about four per week,[48] an amazing rate of production for such a notorious procrastinator and misser of deadlines. As he noted with pleased surprise, "it is not unflattering to a man's Vanity to reflect that what he writes at 12 at night will before 12 hours is over have 5 or 6000 readers!"[49] He was working so hard partly because he wanted to pay the Wedgwoods for the additional expenses of his German tour: a considerably different response from Wordsworth's to the same situation.

His writings dealt with just about every question of national polity, such as "The Prosperity of the Kingdom." But he was crucially concerned with war issues, especially the question of whether Pitt should seek a negotiated settlement with Napoleon. His main target was fanaticism of every sort, on both the left and the right. In the polarized climate of 1800, this made his a noticeably independent, even lonely voice, and helps explain the sometimes scatological venom with which he attacked former allies who now "fell off on every side" (as Wordsworth paraphrased it in *The Prelude*) to one entrenched position or another.

Coleridge was ruminating a sequence of satires on satirists, in the vein of his "Nehemiah Higginbottom" sonnets of 1797, and his earlier "Sonnets on Eminent Characters." One of his lists of "Characters for the satire" lined up his principal targets in order of importance:

> Canning & the Anti-Jacobins
> Mackintosh
> Pursuits of Literature [James Mathias]
> Lloyd & his Gang
> Peter Pindar [John Woolcot][50]

He had good reason to put the *Anti-Jacobin* at the top of his list, since the most recent of its several anthologized reprints, *The Beauties of the Anti-Jacobin* (1799), had added a scathing footnote to the reference to "Coleridge & Co." in "The New Morality": "He has left his native country, commenced citizen of the world, left his poor children fatherless and his wife destitute. *Ex hic disce* [this from his] friends Lamb and Southey!"[51] Coleridge was encouraged to sue for libel, but decided against it. Among his reasons for not doing so was the fact that these writers were not wholly unspeakable enemies, but sometimes close acquaintances, or friends of friends. Later in the year—writing back to Davy with a happy vision of "Skiddaw, & Glaramára, and Eagle Crag, and you, and Wordsworth, & me on top of them!"—he contrasted his come-hither fantasy with an image of Davy-at-home: "your room, the Garden, the cold bath, the Moonlight Rocks, Barrister Moore & simple-looking Frere."[52] John Hookham Frere, Canning's main collaborator on the *Anti-Jacobin* two years earlier, was now as close to Coleridge's group as Mackintosh, who two years before had seemed a stalwart friend and ally. Even his old encourager George Dyer kept his former friends' names uncomfortably public by including them in his *Public Characters for 1799–1800,* a sort of anthology of high-level gossip with commentary. Dyer praised Southey's "pastoral and rural imagery," and asserted that both Southey and Coleridge were republicans. With friends like this in the present climate of opinion, one hardly needed enemies, as Coleridge ruefully noted: "all his [Dyer's] Friends make wry faces, peeping out of the Pillory of his advertisemental Notes."[53]

But urban literary life, for all its excitement, was a scene of intense strife and jealousy, as it always is, and now with the added pressure of dangerous political threats. So Wordsworth's northern blandishments fell on receptive ears. Coleridge like Wordsworth was concerned more about his long-term reputation than about his immediate success, and he began to feel, "I have too much trifled with my reputation."[54] He knew he had "greatly improv[ed] both in knowledge & power" as a result of writing under such pressure, but he was getting a bit sick of what he called "athanasiophagous," the devouring of immortality by anticipation, seeing them all (himself included) as "Modest Creatures!—Hurra, my dear Southey!—You [Davy] & I, & Godwin, & Shakespeare & Milton . . . shall march together!"[55] Most of Coleridge's poetical contributions to the *Morning Post* were lightweight in comparison with his prose pieces, and he was again occasionally using Wordsworth's rejected or incomplete poems to help fill out his obligations. But he also reprinted seven of Wordsworth's poems from the 1798 *Lyrical Ballads* in the *Morning Post* between April and September, keeping his name before the public in anticipation of the new edition.[56] Still, he had begun to feel that his own days as a poet were numbered.

Both of these impulses, lust for immortality and disgust with the egotistical literary life, one the dark side of the other, connected with Wordsworth's similar concerns in "Home at Grasmere" and the ongoing *Prelude.* Wordsworth's awareness and jealousy of his friend's new success is apparent in passages of "Home at Grasmere" which try to reorient his provincial hideaway into a position of national centrality, with perhaps some hidden references to his clandestine activities in Germany. Though he and Dorothy were "a pair seceding from the common world," he insisted that their choice was actually the more socially responsible one:

> Society is here:
> The true community, the noblest Frame
> Of many into one incorporate;

. . . .

. . . a multitude
Human and brute, possessors undisturbed
Of this recess, their legislative Hall,
Their Temple, and their glorious dwelling-place.
(818–20, 825–28)

This is to say that effective social writing could be done just as well in Grasmere as in London: indeed, better. The tug-of-war between the two poets was not simply between north and south but between competing notions of where best to establish a center of influence in national cultural debates, and with what kind of writing.

When he first came to Grasmere in early April, Coleridge had spent his free time finishing his translation of Schiller's *Wallenstein*. This was his most serious literary production of the period, the "money-book" on which he expended a great deal of effort in hopes of financial reward, though he gained very little. But the theme of the play as well as hopes for profit kept him engaged with it. *Wallenstein* was Schiller's effort to get beyond the Sturm und Drang of *The Robbers,* reflecting his reaction against the course of the French Revolution.[57] Coleridge and Wordsworth, having invested themselves deeply in *The Robbers* for *The Borderers* and *Osorio,* were now also being forced into fundamental reconsiderations of their hopes for the French Revolution, and of the kind of writing that should follow from, or announce, such a reorientation. They wanted to avoid pathetic public recantations like Mackintosh's. Like *The Robbers, Wallenstein* is a study in power and betrayal, asking how loyalty to the state and political necessity can be maintained when it threatens the integrity of one's principles and personal desires. The same question informs "Home at Grasmere."

At the same time Coleridge was trying to finish a play of his own on the same topic, called *The Triumph of Loyalty.*[58] The "triumph" in its title was ironic, as in Shelley's later *The Triumph of Life,* signifying the rule of loyalty-or-else. It concerns the efforts of two friends, Earl Henry and his Spanish comrade Sandoval, who have just returned victorious from campaigning abroad, to rid their capital of an evil chancellor who has corrupted it in the meantime—a clear polemical reference to Pitt, and perhaps to Wordsworth's and Coleridge's recent "campaign" in Germany. At their return a traitor has been executed for "trafficking with France against the independence of his Country," another hint at the contemporary world of spies and intrigue to which Coleridge and Wordsworth were no strangers.

The play's comic subplot reflects concerns about language that soon showed up in Wordsworth's expanded preface to *Lyrical Ballads.* Sandoval's groom, Barnard, is "A sedulous eschewer of the popular / And the colloquial—one who seeketh dignity / I' th' paths of circumlocution!" His flowery diction is constantly undercut by another servant, Ferdinand, who bluntly translates what Barnard says into the vernacular. When Barnard says, "Even Lucifer, Prince of the Air, hath claims upon our Justice," Ferdinand glosses, "Give the Devil his Due!"

In the main plot, questions of passion and sincerity are linked in ways similar to Wordsworth's linking them in the preface. Earl Henry cherishes an impossible love for his queen, doubtless reflecting some of Coleridge's passion for Sara Hutchinson. Sandoval sympathizes with him, but claims "thou [art] never great / But by the Inspiration of great Passion." Henry transfers his love to another, the daughter of the executed traitor, but their passion is more calmly diffused than sharply erotic. Instead of sexual satisfaction, they seem to achieve something more like a unity of being, reflecting Wordsworth's and Coleridge's homoerotics of nature: "Life was in us: / We were all life, each atom of our frames / A living soul."[59] Coleridge said similar things better in other texts at other times; their relevance here is their contemporaneity with Wordsworth's movement from the aestheticized, private politics of "Home at Grasmere" to the linguistically coded politics of the preface to *Lyrical Ballads.*

The emotional temperature in this little gathering of provincial gentry-professionals at Grasmere in July of 1800 rose to the degrees we usually associate with the more demonstrative Byron and Shelley circles on Lake Geneva in 1816, when creative inspiration, love, sexual attachment, and practical necessity came together in ways that would seem to have rendered productive work impossible, but that became instead the defining creative moments of their existence.

30 A.K.A. *LYRICAL BALLADS*

Lyrical Ballads of 1800

> ... the human mind is capable of excitement without the application of gross and violent stimulants; and he must have a very faint perception of its beauty and dignity who does not know this, and who does not further know that one being is elevated above another in proportion as he possess this capability. It has therefore appeared to me that to endeavor to produce or enlarge this capability is one of the best services in which, at any period, a Writer can be engaged; but this service, excellent at all times, is especially so at the present day.
>
> (Preface, 1800)

In the supercharged emotional atmosphere of Town End, summer 1800, the single most famous edition of poetry in English began to be put together. Wordsworth had been composing at a great rate since arriving in Grasmere; his production in 1800 outstrips even the annus mirabilis of 1798. By midsummer he had written roughly the first half of "Home at Grasmere" and the "Prospectus" to *The Recluse,* as well as most of the poems that would make up the second volume in the new edition of *Lyrical Ballads.* Adding to all the emotional stress in the cottage, there was the physical pain that intense composition always produced: "he writes with so much feeling and agitation that it brings on a sense of pain and internal weakness about his left side and stomach, which now often makes it impossible for him to write when he is in mind and feelings in such a state that he could do it without difficulty."[1] That is to say, he found it difficult to write even when he felt like doing it. No relief came from "emotion recollected in tranquillity," the outward calm with which Wordsworth covered his violent inner states of mind.

The first report of a new volume came from Coleridge to Southey on April 10. "Wordsworth publishes [i.e., will publish] a second Volume of Lyrical Ballads, & Pastorals. He meditates a novel—& so do I—but first I shall re-write my Tragedy" (either *Wallenstein* or *The Triumph of Loyalty*).*[2]

*What novels they were meditating is anybody's guess. Wordsworth had kept in mind since 1792 the idea of adapting Helen Maria Williams's story of the du Fosses to his own experiences;

This decision signaled the end of work on *The Recluse,* just as it had been interrupted by the first volume of *Lyrical Ballads* in 1798. It also broke Wordsworth's "solemn" promise "not to publish on his own account"; he had vowed to Coleridge during their November walking tour that only "pecuniary necessity" could lead him to publish again soon.[3] Dorothy had begun reading German again, "preparatory to translating," but she could not do that alone, and "if Wms name rises amongst the Booksellers we shall have no occasion for it."[4] By July a new financial need had began to rise in his mind. As he contemplated marrying Mary Hutchinson, he realized he would need more income to support her in a style at least approximating what she was accustomed to. She was a country heiress living in comfortable circumstances, and no matter how much she admired the Wordsworths' cottage life from afar, William felt he was honor bound to provide for her as a man in his station should.

From Coleridge's report the first title proposed for the new volume seems to have been *Lyrical Ballads and Pastorals.* This squares with Wordsworth's note to "The Brothers" that he had intended to produce "a series of pastorals, the scene of which is laid among the mountains of Cumberland and Westmorland." Many of the new poems fit that description, and five have the word "pastoral" in their subtitles or notes, suggesting that a still more accurate title for the new book could have been *Lake District Pastorals.* The title of the new edition was not planned to be *Lyrical Ballads* at all, and it became so only by default, when, despite seven months of Wordsworth's insistence to the contrary, his new publisher, Longman, finally refused his request to call the volume by the title he really preferred: "Poems in Two Volumes, by W. Wordsworth."[5] This title, not *Lyrical Ballads,* was Wordsworth's consciously intended and repeatedly specified title for the world-famous volume that finally appeared in January 1801. Wordsworth's preferred title became exactly the title of the next new volume he published, *Poems, in Two Volumes,* by W. Wordsworth, in 1807. Coleridge reported this new title as a fact to Southey, Godwin, and others throughout the summer and fall, further specifying that the *Lyrical Ballads* title was to be "dropt" entirely, "& his 'Poems' substituted."[6]

The title of the 1798 volume was to be dropped (or retained only for the first volume of the new edition) because most of Wordsworth's new poems did not fit the pattern established by his ten lyrical ballads of 1798. They had formed the majority of his nineteen poems in the earlier volume, but only twelve of his much larger number of new poems (forty-one) were ballads

---

it ultimately became "Vaudracour and Julia." The recent letter from Annette, along with his request that Dorothy—not he—answer it, might have prompted him to distance the affair still further into the realm of fiction.

at all, and only two them had that strange quality of social criticism mixed with emotional expressivism that is so marked in 1798: "Ruth" and "Poor Susan," both written earlier. The Matthew poems can be called lyrical ballads, but though the Lucy poems are mysteriously lyrical, they are not ballads, except for "Strange fits of passion." His other new ballads were merely sentimental variations on the genre: "The Waterfall and the Eglantine," "The Oak and the Broom," "The Idle Shepherd-Boys," "The Two Thieves," and "Andrew Jones." Wordsworth wanted nothing to do with the old title, which nevertheless got attached to his new volume. For him, the key word on the title page was not "Poems" but "Wordsworth."

Another reason for changing the title, Dorothy explained, is that "Mrs. Robinson has claimed the title and is about publishing a volume of *Lyrical Tales* [1800]. This is a great objection to the former title, particularly as they are both printed at the same press and Longman is the publisher of both the works."[7] But though Wordsworth kept urging the change, Longman would not budge. At his splendid book emporium in London, Thomas Longman calculated that any confusion either with the *Lyrical Ballads* of 1798 or with Robinson's *Lyrical Tales* was more likely to help than hurt sales. He also knew that the author's name, "By W. Wordsworth," added little or nothing to its market value.

As late as October, in his drafts of a preface for the new edition, Wordsworth was keeping up a clear distinction between the old volume and the new one: "The first Volume of these Poems, under the title of Lyrical Ballads, had already . . . been submitted to general perusal." But the published preface drops the reference to a former title, with the result that *both* volumes were presumed to be *Lyrical Ballads,* as they have been ever since. A great deal of confusion would have been avoided on many counts had Wordsworth got the title he wanted. But a great deal of the controversy generated by his preface would also have been diminished, with incalculable effects on his and Coleridge's long-term reputations. They certainly did not plan it this way, for much of the controversy caused them no end of annoyance, but at the same time its continuance helped immeasurably to make them famous.

If Wordsworth had obtained the title he wanted, several things would be clearer. First, he did not consider the forty-one poems now published to be lyrical ballads in any meaningful sense, even though a few of them could be linked with the experimental poems of 1798. Second, the preface he composed in September was not for a concept that he labeled "lyrical ballads" or "lyrical pastorals." The preface is not at all concerned with defending hybrid genres, except to attack arbitrary distinctions between poetry and prose. Rather, it argues the need for a thorough renovation of polite definitions of poetry as a whole. Third, because of Longman's insistence on sticking with the original title, all of the forty-one new poems have often, inappropriately, been discussed as lyrical ballads, sometimes with brilliantly ingenious results, but often with glaring inconsistencies—which are hardly surprising, considering that Wordsworth held no brief for them as lyrical ballads. Fourth, the only part of Wordsworth's request that Longman did accede to was the designation of a single author, "W. Wordsworth." This was agreed to by all parties, including Coleridge, so the loose presumption that Wordsworth forced his friend out of the picture is not quite true.

Wordsworth threw himself enthusiastically into preparations for the new volume, enlisting old and new friends and relations in the process. He began of course with Dorothy and Coleridge, but included John as his London informant and agent, John Stoddart and others as prospective reviewers, and a brilliant young scientist named Humphry Davy, as his main agent and editor with the printers in Bristol, Biggs & Cottle.[8] Wordsworth had never met Davy, but he did not scruple to load him with all kinds of responsibilities for dealing with the printers. But Davy was good friends with Coleridge, and their mutual friend James Tobin was his laboratory assistant at Dr. Thomas Beddoes's Pneumatic Institute, so he joined in readily and eagerly looked forward to meeting the enigmatic author of whom his friends spoke so highly.

Having successfully drawn Coleridge to the north after him, Wordsworth now made it clear that he, not Coleridge, was the boss of the new project. Coleridge had been the entrepreneur of the 1798 volume, but Wordsworth was the one who saw it through the press. Now he adopted both roles. From July to October he sent a constant stream of finicky, inconsistent directions, pleas, and orders to Davy, requiring attention to the smallest details of page setup, white space, and type bars, with frequent instances of that most annoying part of the printing process, revisions necessitated not by mistakes but by an author's second thoughts. Wordsworth's second thoughts often ran considerably beyond the number two.[9] His determination to take control of his life as a poet was complemented by Coleridge's unconcern.[10] This was Wordsworth's show and Coleridge knew it, stepping aside to let his friend have full sway. He was busy making money by other means, brilliant journalism and exacting translations; he still had his Wedgwood annuity, and besides he believed in the division of labor even in cultural matters: "I would leave to every man his own Trade."[11] But this was not Wordsworth's way at all; in the preface he hectors and instructs his readers almost as particularly as he did poor Humphry Davy.

Poole and Wedgwood, who had been worried about Wordsworth's and Coleridge's "amalgamation" in Germany, were horrified to hear Coleridge's new expressions of abasement before his friend's poetic genius. When Poole protested his "prostration" before Wordsworth, Coleridge answered that "since Milton no man has *manifested* himself equal to [Wordsworth]," and he told Godwin he considered himself "unworthy to unloose" the latch of Wordsworth's shoe.[12] To Wrangham he said that Grasmere and Wordsworth were equals worthy of each other: "neither to Man nor Place can higher praise be given." "He is a great, a true Poet—I am only a kind of a Metaphysician."[13] Statements like this, which Coleridge made to almost everybody he knew, go beyond admiration to masochism, making it appear that Coleridge had sunk below "amalgamation" to something bordering on a willed incorporation into the body of Wordsworth's work.

Coleridge's name appears nowhere in the volume, though five poems by the author's "Friend" are listed in a note. That Coleridge's name should be so utterly elided seems unnecessary, considering the éclat it would have added, following his journalistic successes throughout the year; but the polemical spirit of his new reputation may have been another reason not to mention it. Yet his name certainly did not "stink" as it did in 1798, and Wordsworth's keeping it off of the volume does not sort well with his telling Coleridge in 1799 not to deny "the story that the L.B. are entirely yours," because such a story was "the best thing that can befall them."[14] The fact is that Wordsworth at that time did not have a clear idea of what he was talking about, as regards the value of a *name* in London's literary marketplace.

The poems which finally appeared in January were notably different from the nineteen poems by Wordsworth from 1798. None of the new poems approached the level of "Tintern Abbey" 's artistic achievement, but it could be argued that the overall level of sheer literary excellence is higher in 1800 than in 1798. The second volume, Dorothy thought, "is much more likely to please the generality of readers."[15] Only three of the poems in 1798 had a light or humorous tone, whereas fully a quarter of the 1800 poems are amusing. There were far fewer poems containing the kind of social critique Dr. Burney had noticed; only "Poor Susan," "Ruth," and "The Old Cumberland Beggar" are comparable in this respect, and they were composed in Germany or Alfoxden or even earlier. There is also much less concern with abnormal states of mind and with the single clearest cause of this derangement in 1798: people being cast out of their homes or communities.[16]

Instead, Wordsworth's new emphasis is on how communities, or more specifically *pairs or couples* as the smallest units of community, can be preserved. This theme was the motor driving "Home at Grasmere," and it continued into "The Waterfall and the Eglantine," "The Oak and the Broom," "The Idle Shepherd-Boys," "The Pet-Lamb," "The Two Thieves," and several others. The archetypal situation of the 1798 poems was a narrator's conversation with a solitary outcast; in 1800 the basic situation is a threatened loss of *partnership,* or a delayed, tragic recognition of its value, which has heretofore been taken for granted. Not that the poems of 1800 are all happy ones; far from it. But their unhappiness arises from a suddenly perceived loss of love, in a relationship, a family, or a community, whereas in 1798 the great danger was mental breakdown, caused by apparent rejection from English society itself. The solitaries of 1798 have long since lost their mates or partners and are struggling to stay in touch with, as the Female Vagrant says, their "inner self." The 1800 poems can be called more "universal," since they depend less on specific social causes from the late 1790s, but the losses they express, though real and painful, are much less extreme.

Almost all the poems Wordsworth composed for the second edition of *Lyrical Ballads* are concerned in one way or another with the proper way to live among simple people in the country, usually explicitly identified as the Lake District. Setting aside the larger issues Wordsworth addressed in his preface, most of the poems actually composed in 1800 deal with the *content* question of country living—which is to say, with his and Dorothy's own everyday experience. They are concerned with (1) how their new surroundings should be named or identified (five are gathered together as "Poems on the Naming of Place"), (2) whether and how one should build there (four fall under the rubric of "Rural Architecture"), and (3) how one should judge the customs of village folk (five poems like "The Idle Shepherd-Boys").

Finally, there is a "control" group of four or five poems dealing with the crisis question (similar to "Home at Grasmere") of how *prior love relationships* can be maintained in this new setting—or cannot be. "The Brothers" is the first of these, and the first Wordsworth began composing after he and Dorothy settled in, while the last of this group, "Michael," is last in every way: last composed and also the thematic conclusion of the volume. "Hart-Leap Well" forms a sort of traveling prologue to this theme, while "The Waterfall and the Eglantine," "The Oak and the Broom," and the Scottish ballad of "Ellen Irwin" are lighter variations on this love theme. The remaining poems, not composed in the nervous euphoria of 1800, have significant tangential relations to these groupings: the Lucy poems to the broken-pair theme, and the Matthew poems to both that and the local-customs theme.

In biographical perspective the poems Wordsworth composed in 1800 for *Lyrical Ballads* were as much of a piece with the daily texture of his life as the two very different sorts of poems he composed for 1798's "triumphs of failure." The 1800 poems might glibly be called the "failures of triumph," insofar as their cautionary notes echo the failure of his straightforward effort in "Home at Grasmere" to identify himself with his native region.

In "The Brothers" a happily anticipated homecoming reunion is spoiled by the death of one of the brothers. This is an unlikely topic for the joyous mood that Wordsworth's return home has assumed in popular cultural mythology, but it is an altogether likely one for the dialectically contrary poet we can now recognize him to be, one who often expressed the depths of his joy by exploring its opposite. Leonard the mariner has come home after twenty years at sea "to resume / The life which he lived there." Wordsworth too had effectively left his family home in 1779, following his mother's death, and returned twenty years later. John Wordsworth, from whom William and Coleridge had parted just a few days before they came to Ennerdale, where they heard the incident on which the poem is based, had gone to sea at age fifteen. Leonard's age is given as twelve at his departure, but Wordsworth changed this to fifteen when he republished the poem in 1815. The two boys were orphans whose grandparents outlived their parents, as also happened to the Wordsworth children. Their grandfather lost the lands which had been in the family for five generations, "buffeted with bond, interest, and mortgages": a parallel to John Wordsworth Sr.'s losing his estate to the unpaid debts of Lord Lonsdale—and also to the precise number of generations through which the Wordsworths traced their family's emigration from Yorkshire to Cumberland to rebuild their gentry fortunes.

But all these parallels are given a reverse twist by Wordsworth. Leonard does not reveal his identity to the parish priest who tells him what happened to his brother James, because "now, / The vale, where he had been happy, seemed / A place in which he could not bear to live." There are just ten small words in one strong line, revealing Wordsworth's empathy with a self-created situation that holds up a tragic mirror to his own Ode to Joy. Leonard returns to sea, where he is now "a grey-headed mariner." This glances at Coleridge's "old navigator," but Leonard combines the roles of Ancient Mariner and Wedding Guest, becoming a sadder and a wiser man not from hearing fantastic tales of otherworldly deeds and spirits but from a homely account of a common accident on the fells.

The five poems on "The Naming of Places" are less about names than about the moral propriety of bestowing them on places not one's own. (Two others, not included in the group, have the same quality, describing Sara's Gate and John's Grove.)[17] Like the broken-pair poems, these Wordsworthian Just-So stories are less explanations of how certain places got their names than cautionary tales about the risk involved in presuming to *name* anything. As such, they reflect the lessons he learned from the difficulty of composing "Home at Grasmere." His textual note on the poems is commonsensical: "By persons resident in the country and attached to rural objects, many places will be found unnamed or of unknown names, where little incidents will have occurred, or feelings been experienced, which will have given to such places a private and peculiar interest." But this should be balanced against Coleridge's observation the preceding November about the large number of landscape features in the north which *do* have names, because some of the places now named by the Wordsworth circle already had names, notably the lonely "eminence" called Stone-Arthur, which they now implicitly renamed Stone-William.

William's identification with nearby Stone-Arthur is the most straightforward in this group. They passed beneath it almost daily on their walks between Town End and Town Head. It is "the loneliest place we have among the clouds," so Dorothy gave it "my name." But there was also a heavenly portent, whose significance is not revealed in the poem: "The star of Jove, so beautiful and large / In the mid heavens, is never half so fair / As when he shines above [this eminence]." Jupiter was Wordsworth's planet in the astrology of his imagination, which he linked to the Star of Bethlehem in the "Prospectus" to *The Recluse* to symbolize his hopes for his poetry. Nobody knew this but Dorothy, which gave her a title of authority to bestow the name, William's Eminence. This, and their love: "She who dwells with me, whom I have lov'd / With such communion, that no place on earth / Can ever be solitude to me." Dorothy's love removes the appearance of his solitude, and this, plus the peak's association with Jupiter, makes *it* worthy to bear *his* name, not vice versa.

"Emma's Dell" is really Emma's Waterfall, hinting that the waterfall in "The Waterfall and the Eglantine" is also female: Dorothy's wild passion runs roughshod over the mild compromises offered by William's eglantine—this replays in coded country allegory the sexual situation of the full version of "Nutting." Her waterfall wildness is stressed repeatedly: "wild nook," "wild place," and so on. The waterfall hits the traveler with a shock of surprise as he labors up the Easedale path to where Blindtarn intersects with Sow Milk Ghyll. Just when everything seems softened "down into a vernal tone . . . a deep contentment," one turns a corner and confronts a waterfall so "ardent" that all calm is fled. The shock wakes Wordsworth up to the realization that there is something *else,* beyond or different from nature's "contentment" that is uncontrollably wild, and this quality he associates with Dorothy. After the sudden revelation of such wild ardency, the speaker plods onward, "in the confusion of my heart," reflecting obscurely: "our thoughts at least are ours." Apparently this means that our thoughts can *resist* taking these outward evidences of identity too literally. There is a moment of blurred perception when his eye catches "a single mountain cottage" on a nearby hill, and this drives the name home: "Our thoughts at least are ours, and this wild vale, / My EMMA, I will dedicate to thee." The "thought" may well have been the wish that they could live together in yon mountain cottage, which was almost certainly the farmhouse on adjacent Butterlip How that Dorothy said she would buy if she could accept "bad interest" for it. Parallel to the language of tamed passion he addressed to Dorothy in "Tintern Abbey" and in "Nutting," this passion will be acknowledged only "Years after we are in our graves," by the shepherds to whom he reveals his naming fantasy.

At the other end of the sequence, Mary's Nook is as peaceful as Dorothy's dell is wild. The pool described is in Rydal Upper Park, and *"we* have named [it] for you." The name is assigned as the joint title of William and Dorothy, honoring Mary-the-Peaceful. As always in these Grasmere moments of discovery, the title of authenticity is signed by death: the man who "should plant his cottage here . . . would so love it that in his death hour / Its image would survive among his thoughts."

"To Joanna" and "Point Rash-Judgement" correct the other naming poems' attempts to make one-to-one applications of their names to Grasmere's places. Coleridge makes his only appearance in the latter, but all three walkers—he, Dorothy, and William—are faulted for thinking that the peasant they see fishing should be out helping with the harvest. They project a sturdy middle-class response to the troubles of the working class: "We all cried out, that he must be indeed / An idle man, who could thus lose a day / Of the mid harvest, when the labourer's hire / Is ample." But when they came closer, they saw that he is "too weak to labour in the harvest field." Unlike similar poems in the 1798 volume, such as "Simon Lee" and "Goody Blake," the thrust of this one is not against the social or human conditions that have worn the poor fisherman down but against their own status as outsiders and observing moralists, who should know better than to leap to such rash judgments.

Like the morals tacked on to "The Ruined Cottage" and "The Ancient Mariner," this one does not speak at all adequately to the man's condition. It permits only aesthetic closure, explaining the extravagant name they have cleverly given to a little abutment they found "on a new-discover'd coast"—that is, the southeast shore of Grasmere. The poem's more important meaning comes at its beginning, in the hammer blows it directs at the dreamy scene it establishes, which many readers would unhesitatingly label Wordsworthian:

> . . . in our vacant mood,
> Not seldom did we stop to watch some tuft
> Of dandelion seed or thistle's beard,
> Which, seeming lifeless half, and half impell'd
> By some internal feeling, skimm'd along . . . .
> (16–20)

This is "Tintern Abbey" 's mode of perception, things half perceived and half created, and Wordsworth indulges himself for twenty lines of fairy-tale identifications with Grecian naiads, Queen Osmunda, and "the Lady of the Mere / Sole-sitting by the shores of old Romance." But this easy reading of

Nature's morality is harshly corrected by human evidence to the contrary, when they see the man "using his best skill to gain / A pittance from the dead unfeeling lake / That knew not of his wants." The harsh corrective is of a piece with the charm of the fantasy: only a man who wished nature were humanly beautiful would need to remind us (and himself) that it is not: the "Lady of the Mere" is not nearly as generous to beggars as the lady at the Town End cottage.

Wordsworth linked "Joanna's Rock" to "Nutting" by saying that these two "show the greatest genius of any poems in the second volume."[18] The judgment is just for "Nutting," but a bit rash for "To Joanna." The real point of contact between the two is not their quality but their theme: two young women's initiation into the mysteries of a religion celebrating an independent life in nature. Nineteen-year-old Joanna Hutchinson at first laughed at William's "ravishment" when he stood before the "intermixture of delicious hues" on the side of a tall rock beside the river Rotha between Grasmere and Rydal. But when her laughter echoes hyperbolically through the entire Lake District, from Skiddaw in the north to Kirkstone in the south, "the fair Joanna" is drawn "to my side . . . as if she wish'd / To shelter from some object of her fear." For this involuntary recognition of something akin to the laughter of the gods, Wordsworth carved Joanna's name on the rock. This amounts to her enrollment into an illicit religion, professed by we "who look upon the hills with tenderness . . . who are transgressors in this kind, / Dwelling retired in our simplicity." His honoring of Joanna's spontaneous fear is set against the disapproval of the old religion, represented by the "gloomy" Grasmere vicar who chides Wordsworth for apparently "reviving obsolete Idolatry . . . like a Runic Priest." Though not a druid, Wordsworth was becoming in effect the priest of a new dispensation, which finds and worships spirit in places and ways different from those of Christianity: this is the only poem besides the rechristening of Stone-Arthur in which his view of place-names is presented unqualifiedly as the correct one.

The four poems on "rural architecture" represent the negative corollary to the positive lessons of the "Poems on the Naming of Places." Though he was self-indulgent toward his group's naming of places (since they were, after all, private and temporary), he was very hard on improper building in paradise. His main complaint was against newcomer's whitewashing their houses, making them stand out too starkly from the surrounding landscape. A close second was cutting down stands of native trees to replace them with more "picturesque" varieties or, worse, plantations of fast-growing, profitable larches for the lumber industry. The latter was a practice of his old nemesis

Bishop Richard Watson at Calgarth, whose landscape politics were thus diametrically opposed to Wordsworth's, though their public politics were now much closer than they had been in 1793.

The tonic note of this group is struck by the "Lines Written with a Slate-pencil upon a Stone, the Largest of a Heap Lying near a Deserted Quarry, upon One of the Islands at Rydale." It explains how Sir William Fleming, ancestor of Michael le Fleming of Rydal Hall, finally did *not* build his "pleasure-house" on the tiny island just off the shore of Rydal Water. He desisted when he discovered that "a full-grown man might wade" from the shore to the island "and make himself a freeman of this spot." The place itself prevented him from commiting an outrage upon it, and so his remaining heap of building stones is a monument to his educability. The poem refuses to blame him, calling him "a gentle Knight." Instead, it cautions those who, like William and Dorothy, come "on fire with . . . impatience to become / An Inmate of these mountains . . . disturb'd / By beautiful conceptions." But the stones of Sir William's *un*built "trim mansion" provide a symbolic context for the right kind of local builders: "the linnet and the thrush, / And other little builders who dwell here."

Against this negative example, Wordsworth sets three examples of architecture that are appropriate to the region—that is, to his unique sense of it. The "outhouse" or small barn on Grasmere island (a later version of which is still there) makes the obvious connections for modern, post-Romantic readers, though they were more novel in 1800. Though it is "rude," and though other buildings "have maintained / Proportions more harmonious," still "the poor / Vitruvius of our village" has here created "a homely pile" whose form follows its function, of sheltering lambs and heifers. But it also has another, more special function, combining the ordinary and the fantastic in a new measure: it provides a place where "one Poet" can make "his summer couch" and look out through its door to see "Creations lovely as the work of sleep, / Fair sights, and visions of romantic joy."

This "poor Vitruvius" "had no help / From the great city," and Wordsworth in the poem titled "Rural Architecture" explicitly distances himself from the kinds of work he had seen going forward in cities in the 1790s. He joins some neighbor boys, "George Fisher, Charles Fleming, and Reginald Stone," in building a stone man on the top of Great How, at the north end of Wythburn (now Thirlmere); they name him "Ralph Jones, the Magog of Legberthwaite dale." This stone construction is perfectly attuned to the interaction of man and nature: when the winds blow it down, "the very next day / They went and they built up another." In 1800 (but canceled thereafter until 1820) Wordsworth included a final stanza that made the application of this simple lesson considerably more pointed:

—Some little I've seen of blind boisterous works
In Paris and London, 'mong Christians or Turks,
Spirits busy to do and undo:
At remembrance whereof my spirits will flag.
—Then, light-hearted Boys, to the top of the Crag!
And I'll build up a Giant with you.

(19–24)

With these lines, Wordsworth joins in the boys' sport as therapy for his traumatic years in Paris and London. The "spirits busy" there were not building houses but a "giant" New Man, actively in the French Revolution or abstractly in the perfectibilian extremes of Godwin's *Political Justice,* both of which Wordsworth now regards as "blind boisterous works." Christians and Turks enter into the picture as code words for theists (like Robespierre) or infidels (like Godwin and Thelwall). Running lightheartedly with the neighbor boys to the top of Great How, "to build up a Giant with" them, Wordsworth also has his own hidden agenda, for an architecture not built with stones but with spirit: *he* is that Giant, but in a new dispensation ("the Giant Wordsworth, God love him"). A poem that looks like a moment of country comic relief was also, in the mind of the very "busy spirit" of its author, a poem of vindication against the public agendas of the world.

The deep message of his "Inscription" for the site of St. Herbert's Hermitage on the island in the middle of Derwent Water is the same: there is now a spirit in these Lake District places that recognizes and can build upon the spirit of the place. According to Bede's *Ecclesiastical History,* Saint Herbert prayed every night that he might die at the same moment as his former helpmate Saint Cuthbert, who had moved to a similar solitary confinement on Windermere. And his prayer was answered: "Those holy men both died in the same hour." One hopes that Cuthbert was let in on the arrangement. The question is not impertinent, for Wordsworth, weird as ever, has altered Bede's account to make the two hermits separate forever, whereas in Bede they paid each other annual visits. The inscription is thus not really for the building but for the kinds of spirits that inhabit it, and about isolated spots where one stays true to one's beloved. It is thus addressed to a person who is a version of Wordsworth himself and his own present love situation, whether the reference is to Dorothy or Coleridge, or both:

If thou in the dear love of some one friend
Hast been so happy, that thou know'st what thoughts
Will sometimes, in the happiness of love
Make the heart sink, then wilt thou reverence
This quiet spot.

(1–5)

This is the state of mind he called "Strange fits of passion," and it illustrates his dire need for "emotion recollected in tranquillity." But though Herbert on Derwent Water and Cuthbert on Windermere are close enough stand-ins for Coleridge in Keswick and Wordsworth in Grasmere, this was not the kind of emotion Wordsworth harbored for his friend. Rather, it is emotion sanctified by death, a state mystically induced over and over again by William and Dorothy during the past five years to sublimate and subdue their passion for each other.

The poems in *Lyrical Ballads* of 1800 about local people and customs are milder. Among them only "The Childless Father" tries to be serious, and it merely wonders if, "perhaps," old Timothy the huntsman thought of his dead daughter when he took the house keys with him as he left to join the fox hunt on "Hamilton's grounds." She had died just six months earlier. The spectator-narrator cannot say anything directly about the state of Timothy's moral refinement, for "in my ears not a word did he speak." But he is pretty sure on the basis of other evidence: "he went to the hunt with a tear on his cheek." In an era when orphans were less common than dead children, the peculiar force of Wordsworth's simple title might have seemed less strange, but it is surprising how often modern readers treat the title of this poem as if it were the more expectable "Fatherless Child," rather than the other way around.

The other local-color poems also treat real or potential moral dilemmas with a lighter touch. The idle shepherd boys don't attend to their business, daring each other to cross a deep crevice on a narrow outcropping, and very nearly lost a valuable lamb as a result. They fetch a conveniently nearby "poet" to rescue it, who "gently" upbraids them, "And bade them better mind their trade." This is brave, when a poetical newcomer instructs the locals in their moral duty, but Wordsworth actually did try out his views on some real shepherds in Grasmere. In a fragment drafted for "Michael," he notes that a shepherd "would have [?stared] at you . . . if you in terms direct / Had asked," if he loved the place. He more likely would have said it was "a frightful pl[?ace]."[19] But if you talked with them "of common things / In an unusual way, and give to them / Unusual aspects . . . [then] this untaught shepherd stood / Before the man with whom he so convers'd / And look'd at him *as with a Poet's eye.*"[20] The man who would "so converse" with the shepherds was of course Wordsworth, but the trite moral of "The Idle Shepherd-Boys" is not its point. Instead, it is a redaction of the *Et in Arcadia ego* theme with a happy ending, thanks to a savior who is "A Poet . . . who loves the brooks / Far better than the sages' books." There is no reason in the world that he should, except for the fact of his identity: William Wordsworth.

Wordsworth took great satisfaction in a "little monitory anecdote" that exploded Southey's complaint that he should not have had the boys trim their hats with a "green Coronal" of "Stag-horn, or Fox's Tail": "Just as the words passed his [Southey's] lips two boys appeared with the very plant entwined round their hats."[21] So much for realism. The symbolic consequence of one of the boys' leap across the crevice is to make him appreciate what he has only when he seems about to lose it all, halfway across the arch: "he hears a piteous moan— . . . his heart within him dies— / His pulse is stopp'd, his breath is lost . . . / And, looking down, he spies / A Lamb, that in the pool is pent / Within that black and frightful rent" (60–66). In this, its moment of truth, "The Idle Shepherd-Boys" anticipates the two crucial visionary self-recognition scenes of *The Prelude.* They are also on mountains, but their lost sheep is William Wordsworth, and their "frightful rent" is "the mind's abyss" in the Simplon Pass and "the deep and gloomy breathing-place" on Snowdon.

"Andrew Jones" is about a hateful man who steals pennies from crippled beggars and teaches his children to do the same. Hence Wordsworth's opening line, "I hate that Andrew Jones," only seems like comic hyperbole. He really does hate him and wants to deport him from paradise in the worst possible way, in contemporary terms: "[I] wish'd the press-gang, or the drum / With its tantara sound, would come / And sweep him from the village!" The press-gang and the recruiting officers were villains to Wordsworth's earlier victims, like the Sailor and Soldier in the Salisbury Plain poems. But here they have become subsidiary demons policing paradise, called out to rid it of unworthy spirits.

"The Two Thieves" is the comic antidote to "Andrew Jones." The "thieves" were real people, old Daniel MacKeith and his grandson, aged ninety and three, respectively, who went about Hawkshead stealing wood chips, peat, and other small things lying about. But everyone on the village knew that Daniel's daughter would "gladly repair all the damage that's done." In just letting him be, Wordsworth treats him the same as the Old Cumberland Beggar, and a surprising last line drives this moral home harder than we expect: "Long yet may'st thou live, for a teacher we see / That lifts up the veil of our nature in thee." What? Wordsworth's note to the poem pretends that its moral is the recognition that we may all come to such pitiable senility. But the repeated action of the poem strongly suggests that behind "the veil of our nature" is a fundamental larceny in our souls, and this, rather that the sheer fact of aging, is the problem of evil that "Home at Grasmere" confronted and that the *Lyrical Ballads* of 1800 tries to defuse.

Finally, little Barbara Lewthwaite, the Wordsworths' next-door neighbor, cannot understand why her "Pet-Lamb" will not eat or drink: "Drink, pretty Creature, drink!" she urges. Wordsworth identifies with her to such an extent "that I almost received her heart into my own," and the rest of the poem is a kind of poetical transmigration into Barbara's mind and heart, as Wordsworth imagines what she would say if she could write a poem. The apparent subject of the poem is thus the programmatic one for the volume: the poetry implicit in the souls of ordinary people. But the deeper subject, unstated but strongly implied, is again the troubling one of "Home at Grasmere," the question whether *either* of its characters, little girl or adult narrator, can penetrate to the sense of loss that makes the *lamb* unhappy:

> —poor Creature can it be
> That 'tis thy Mother's heart which is working so in thee?
> Things that I know not of belike to thee are dear,
> And dreams of things which thou canst neither see nor hear.
>
> (49–52)

The poet tries to interpret the girl trying to interpret the lamb, but it is one thing to receive a little girl's heart into one's own, quite another to inhabit the soul of another species. Although the poet pretends to wonder how much of the song is his and how much Barbara's, neither of them directly addresses the more basic question, that there are relations to the natural world that are better and more appropriate than even the best of human arrangements.

There is one poem that fits no category in the volume, either those from Germany in 1799 or those from Grasmere in 1800, and like many exceptions, it has rule-proving properties. Nothing is known about the genesis of the "Song for the Wandering Jew," except that it may refer to the Jews William and Dorothy saw being ill treated in Hamburg.[22] It reminds us of Wordsworth's ability to say something completely different from what he seems to be saying or from what he usually says—his ability, marked in the preface, to admit to doubts and qualifications that, if taken seriously, would upset his entire train of thought: "If this be but a vain belief, yet oh!" The Jew's song is an adaptation of the famous passage of Matthew 8:20 ("foxes have holes, and birds of the air have nests; but the Son of man has nowhere to lay his head") to the Lake District. The torrents, eagles, and ravens all have their resting places, but not the speaker:

> Day and night my toils redouble!
> Never nearer to the goal,
> Night and day, I feel the trouble,
> Of the Wanderer in my soul.
>
> (17–20)

The poem deserves to be better known, "if only for the last two lines."[23] One reason it is not better known may be that paying honest attention to these last lines confirms what is implicit in almost all of Wordsworth's other *Lyrical Ballads* written at Grasmere: namely, that his homecoming was fraught with doubt and disappointment, which he could celebrate only with difficulty, or ratify by allying it to the final homecoming, of death.

The Great Preface

All these poems were finished by the beginning of July. During July and August, Wordsworth sent them off in batches to Biggs & Cottle. With this work in train, and letters going off to Bristol almost daily, Wordsworth turned in early September to composing a preface he thought the new edition needed. But in the immediate circumstances of his life, the famous preface to *Lyrical Ballads* arose from issues having as much to do with *The Recluse* as with the poems in the 1800 edition. Just as the new volume's title was in a real sense inaccurate, or unintended, so the preface is frequently concerned with issues quite different from those of the poems in the volumes, especially when considered as lyrical ballads. Like his preferred title (which was still "*Poems,* by W. Wordsworth" at this point, so far as he knew), the preface was an introduction more of himself and his views on poetry than of the individual poems in either volume. It announced his reappearance in public for the first time in seven years, terrifically eventful years in England, to readers who had long since forgotten the young collegiate author of *An Evening Walk* and *Descriptive Sketches.*

Coleridge promised to help compose the preface, but he didn't, though he later claimed that it was "half the child of my own brain"; indeed, though its ideas arose out of mutual conversations, "it was at first intended, that the Preface should be written by me [Coleridge]."[24] This would have been a sensible arrangement: one man writing a preface to a new edition of his friend's work, deferring to the other's greater productive energy. Coleridge was far better qualified to write such a preface, and he would come to wish very much that he *had* written it, for he spent much time over the next fifteen years explaining which ideas in it were his and which were not, trying to extricate himself from what soon became a permanent English cultural tradition: attacking or defending the literary and linguistic claims of the preface to *Lyrical Ballads.* Defending himself against the excesses of Wordsworth's preface was Coleridge's most important motive for writing his *Biographia Literaria* (1817), which explained his entire literary life in terms of its relations, pro and con, to Wordsworth's theory and practice. For Coleridge clearly recognized what is only now becoming apparent, that much of Wordsworth's preface was itself a literary biography, displaced into another literary genre from Wordsworth's other contemporaneous efforts to write himself large, *The Recluse* and *The Prelude*.

Coleridge had had ideas similar to those expressed in the preface about the philosophical tendency of poetical expressions at least since 1796, when he told Thelwall, "My philosophical opinions are blended with, or deduced from, my feelings."[25] In his preface to *Sonnets by Various Authors* that same year, he spoke of his poems' generating "a habit of thought" which tends to "create a sweet and indissoluble union between the intellectual and the material world." In a brief prefatory note attached to his "Introduction to the Ballad of the Dark Ladie," he coyly apologized for publishing "a simple story, wholly uninspired with politics or personality" in these days when, "amid the hubbub of Revolutions," one novelty followed after another "so rapidly." This directly anticipates Wordsworth's statement about the debilitating effects of mass media in modern urban life: "The most effective of these causes [that 'blunt the discriminating powers of the mind, and . . . reduce it to a state of almost savage torpor'] are the great national events which are daily taking place, and the encreasing accumulation of men in cities, where the uniformity of their occupations produces a craving for extraordinary incident." The two men shared the same conviction, that poetry—their kind of poetry—was more important than these great events and that it might even provide a way toward solving the dilemmas they create. Typically, however, Wordsworth took Coleridge's tongue-in-cheek apology straight and recast it, without irony, into a blunt, provocative statement.

In his notebook entries in late August, Coleridge spoke of the "recalling of passion in tranquility" and of "poetry [as] past passion with pleasure," phrases that clearly anticipate Wordsworth's "emotion recollected in tranquillity." But they may, as well, reflect Wordsworth's contributions to the conversation, since this particular need, to distance himself from the force of immediate emotion, was much more Wordsworth's than Coleridge's.

In Coleridge's idealist mind-set, any topic was immediately generalized to metaphysical dimensions. While Wordsworth was composing the preface, Coleridge told Davy he was meditating an essay on poetry that "would in reality be a *disguised* System of Morals & Politics."[26] This too is an aspect of Wordsworth's preface, for many of the poems in the volumes were still, in the two authors' minds, part of a covert program of cultural warfare against established moral and political powers as well as literary ones. This purpose was implicit—though heavily disguised—in the motto on the title page of the new second volume, a Renaissance Latin phrase that translates as "How utterly unsuited to your taste, Papinianus!" Papinianus was a Roman lawyer, and the allusion was a slap at James Mackintosh for his embarrassingly public recantation of his former sympathies for the ideals of the French Revolution.[27]

So, like *The Recluse,* the preface was a text of philosophical social reform that Coleridge first wanted to write himself, but then urged Wordsworth to write instead.[28] It covers many of the same topics as *The Recluse,* obscurely transposed into issues of rhyme, meter, and diction. The motive of the preface is thus vastly incommensurate with its matter. Many of its issues are displaced versions of the questions of imaginative authority and poetic identity Wordsworth and Coleridge had been writing and talking about for three years. But they had been doing this in relation to *The Recluse* (or to its "tail-piece" on the development of Wordsworth's mind, *The Prelude*), not in relation to *either* volume of *Lyrical Ballads.* Not only is "the intention behind the *Lyrical Ballads* pastorals quite as large as that which had conceived *The Recluse,*" it is in essence the *same* intention.[29] The key terms of *The Recluse*—"On Man, on Nature, and on Human Life"—are clearly present in the preface's central formulations, when Wordsworth refers to "the most valuable object of all writing, whether in prose or in verse, the great and universal passions of men [Man], the most general and interesting of their occupations [Society], and the entire world of nature [Nature]." But the scope of *The Recluse*'s ambition, which was nothing less than the secular redemption of society, was much too big for a preface, especially one that appears to introduce poems that, whatever their merits, are much slighter productions than we would expect for an epic of human secular redemption. Lamb, who knew something of his two friends' larger projects, put his finger on this aspect of the preface: "[it associates] a *diminishing* idea with the Poems which follow, as having been written for Experiments on the public taste, more than having sprung (as they must have) from living and daily circumstances."[30] Nonetheless, enough of the heroic epic impulse imbedded in the preface does shine through it to help explain how it achieved its hold on English-speaking audiences everywhere. Of all the creative confusions and cross-purposes which helped make the preface to *Lyrical Ballads* such a controversial document in English literature and culture—guaranteeing the centrality of Wordsworth's reputation both as a target of attack and as a rock of defense—none has been more overlooked than this one: that the preface is motivated by the Poet's duty to renew his entire culture, English in the first instance, but implicitly universal. A theory of the creative imagination's role in improving human society is presented mainly in terms of a theory of poetics: metrics, diction, and style. The connections between the two can be worked out, but it takes a lot of time and hard work, far beyond what readers normally expect to give to a preface, and many loose ends are still left hanging. If Wordsworth worried that the "old words" in "The Ancient Mariner" had made it hard for readers to "go on" into the rest of the 1798 volume, it is hard to imagine how he thought they would advance more easily through the forbidding logical and rhetorical thickets of the 1800 preface.

At some point toward the end of the summer, Coleridge shifted the burden of responsibility for the preface onto Wordsworth by provoking him into prose: "I trust . . . that I have invoked the sleeping Bard with a spell so potent, that he will awake & deliver up that Sword of Argantyr, which is to rive the Enchanter GAUDY-VERSE from his Crown to his Fork."[31] Wordsworth marked the spot where they made the decision: the deserted quarry on the southerly shore of Rydal Water, where Sir Walter Fleming had quarried the stones for his pleasure house.[32] This is not to suggest that the preface, like the pleasure house, might better have gone unfinished, but it does indicate that when it lost its architect, Coleridge, the builder's energy and enthusiasm soon made him lose sight of the original proportions they had in mind. Instead of writing or even helping to revise the preface, Coleridge spent much of August and September rambling about, writing wonderful descriptive passages about the Lakeland fells, where it seemed like "heaven and earth [were] greeting each other." He was avoiding being at home, where Sara was approaching the term of her third pregnancy. But he was also avoiding the hard labor of creativity which Wordsworth now undertook at Grasmere. Coleridge's presence at the scene of either birth would have done, as he said to Wordsworth about the projects he proposed to him, "great good."

Once it was clear that Coleridge was not going to help, Wordsworth completed the entire preface, arguably the most influential document of literary theory in English, in the last two weeks of September.[33] He was so full of energy for his self-defining project that he began and nearly finished yet another preface, which would have introduced the second volume. But he decided not to print it, because it grew too long from the many quotations that "must unavoidably be spun into it."[34] If we take the first preface as a measure of Wordsworth's ideas of length, this second one must have been very long indeed. From his mention of the many quotations in it, it sounds like an early version of the "Essay, Supplementary to the Preface" that he published with his first collected edition in 1815. That essay is essentially a polemical history of English literature as a spiritual progression toward the works of William Wordsworth.

Wordsworth's 1800 preface is at once frighteningly aggressive and terribly defensive. It is the speech of a man convinced of the purity of his goals and motives, but unsure of the arguments he is using to defend them, and of the audience to which he is speaking. In fact he assumes his audience will for the most part disagree with his premises. Coleridge's Spenserian image of Wordsworth as "the sword of Agantyr," roused to slay the enchanter

Gaudy-verse, is apt for the intention of the preface, but many readers have had the uneasy feeling that the sword was somehow directed at them. Repeatedly, Wordsworth goes further than he needs to in urging his claims, particularly in his long, turgid insistence on the essential identity between the language of poetry and that of prose. He was trying to say everything he most deeply believed all at once, on the first real occasion he had to do so in his life. He strains to unify everything, to assert the kind of moral authority he felt he must have as the bard of *The Recluse:* high seriousness and low subjects, poetry and prose, the great literature of the past and his own poems in the present. He often starts much further down, at the foundations of his subjects, than he needs to or than most readers would expect him to in a mere preface. But this foundational or metaphysical aspect of the preface is what forces its claims upon our permanent attention: it delves into the nature of the human mind, and the mind's relations to language and the external world.

Wordsworth did not write the preface so quickly because he was expert in matters of style and diction. He wasn't, which helps to account for the vehemence of his tone and the unnecessary extremes to which he forced his arguments. At the very outset, he set aside the "full account" which his theoretical principles would require, as having insufficient space to "point out" how language and mind "act and react" on each other. This is still a lively linguistic controversy, as to whether thinking precedes language, or can only be done *in terms of* language—that is, *in terms.* But Wordsworth says he would have provided this fuller "account" for a purpose, not as an abstract scientific project, because his real concern is with the "present state of taste in this country, and whether it is healthy or depraved." This in turn would require "retracing the revolutions not of literature alone but of society itself." In short, the preface is a revolutionary document in two senses, both in what it sets forth and in its being *about* revolutions—and even more, about the interaction, or interdependence, of cultural and political revolutions.

Wordsworth was implying a full field theory of the way in which language-in-culture affects and even constitutes human nature in social forms. The *presumption* that language and mind do interact in this way to produce culture and society is very largely accepted, two hundreds years later, in societies worried about cultural products far more pernicious than "frantic novels, sickly and stupid German Tragedies, and deluges of idle and extravagant stories in verse." His interest was partisan, not abstract, because he wished to *change* the present unhappy situation: he clearly believed that "the present taste" of the country *was* "depraved." He even set up a standard of value according to which progress could be measured. In a time when talk of "the rights of man" had begun to sound a bit hollow, if not seditious, Wordsworth proposed a theory not of human equality but of a hierarchy based on the value of the healthy human mind in a depraved society. Far from being a "leveller" as Hazlitt later described him, Wordsworth at this point was a democratic elitist. "One being is *elevated above another* in proportion as he possesses the quality" of *not* requiring "gross and violent stimulants" for the excitement or healthy exercise of his mind. This sets up a hierarchy of sensibility, or imagination, apart from the civil rights of birth or citizenship. Stimulating this higher type of imagination is "the best service" that a writer "can be engaged in at the present time," because there are so many more forces working to support and extend these degrading forces than there are counteracting them. They are pervasive and interconnected: the "great national events which are daily occurring," the growth of cities (as poor country people sought employment in the war economy), the boring, uniform tasks of the emerging industrial system, which produce in turn a craving for "extraordinary incident," "gratified" by "hourly intelligence" (newspapers), bringing full circle the system of language/mind stimulation and degradation to which Wordsworth alluded at the outset.

The preface thus aims at a whole system of cultural production, setting up a literary oppositional cottage industry to counter "great national events." Wordsworth's confidence is not, however, based on his poems alone; he is not so unguarded. Rather, it was his faith in "certain inherent and indestructible qualities of the human *mind*" and in "the great and permanent objects that act upon it" (that is, natural forms) that gave him confidence to await "the approach of a *time* when the evil will be systematically opposed by men of greater powers and with far more distinguished success." No one has ever suggested who these "men" might be, but from their position at the end of a long sequence of arguments promising a vast vindication in the future, we immediately recognize Wordsworth's rhetorical strategy from "Tintern Abbey" in 1798, the 1799 *Prelude,* and the 1800 "Prospectus" to *The Recluse.* As at those moments, his point of reference is himself and Coleridge, and he is referring to their major projects, to which *Lyrical Ballads* was, in 1800 as in 1798, connected primarily as a prospectus, fund-raiser, and advertising flier.

While Wordsworth was pushing the preface to a conclusion, riding roughshod through logical impasses, guided by the light of his emerging conception of the Poet, Coleridge, instead of helping or even checking Wordsworth's argument, was trying to finish a great work of his own. For about two months, between August and October, the plan was that "a Poem of Mr Coleridge's was to have concluded the Volumes." This poem was "Christabel."[35] Wordsworth thought that the second preface he drafted was justified by the bulk of a volume that would contain a "new long poem" by his friend. As late as the first week in October, "Christabel" was still scheduled with the printers for inclusion, although in a letter of September 15 Wordsworth expressed annoyance when he learned that it had already been set up in type and inserted in the second volume.[36] He immediately directed that it be replaced by "The Pet-Lamb," "The Fly" (his working title for the Goslar poem about the fly on their stove), and "The Childless Father," with instructions that nothing more be done with "Christabel" "till you received further intelligence from Mr. Coleridge."

On October 4 Coleridge read to William and Dorothy at Grasmere all of "Christabel" that he had completed—largely the poem as we know it today, ending with its action ominously suspended between the protagonists. Sir Leoline berates his daughter Christabel for her apparently inhospitable looks at Geraldine, the witch who unbeknownst to him has seduced Christabel the night before, after Christabel has rescued Geraldine from what she represents to Christabel as a gang rape by "five warriors." William and Dorothy were "exceedingly delighted" with it the night they heard it, and they heard it again the next day with "increasing pleasure." But Wordsworth soon began to have doubts about it, and three days later it was out of the project. Wordsworth's unilateral decision against "Christabel" severely damaged Coleridge's self-confidence as a poet. He had crucially recognized Wordsworth as Milton's successor when nobody else in the world would have done so, but the brutal commitment of Wordsworth to his own poetic program did not permit him a similar generosity toward Coleridge. On the contrary, even when "Christabel" was still slated for the volume, Wordsworth revised his prefatory phrase about it, "the long and beautiful Poem of Christabel," by crossing out the words "long and beautiful."[37]

Wordsworth's treatment of "Christabel" reflected his new attitude toward "The Ancient Mariner," because it was in the same suspicious supernatural vein. Its apparent lack of conclusion did not bother him: he didn't think it was *meant* to have more of a conclusion. This is an astute literary insight. The psychological aspect of the poem's Gothic tragedy has already occurred in its present form: we see clearly that Sir Leoline is about to lose his beloved daughter, not simply through Geraldine's sexo-magical machinations, but also because of his foolish male pride as a rescuer of women in distress, and his fantasy of generously reconciling with Geraldine's supposed father, the estranged friend of his youth, Sir Roland de Vaux of Tyremaine.

Instead, Wordsworth gave as his reason for dropping it his sense that there was too abrupt a change between Parts I and II, as the poem's setting shifted from Somerset to Grasmere. More justifiable was his feeling that the poem, slightly longer in its final form than "The Ancient Mariner," was ill suited to the contents of the rest of the volumes.[38] He told Longman that "the Style of this Poem was so discordant from my own" that it was better to drop it.[39] In fact, its difference in style, otherwise unexceptionable (it was, after all, announced as being by another author), amounted to a contradiction in terms, once the high argument of the preface had been set forth at such length. The same could be said of "The Ancient Mariner," but its place was assured, and "Christabel" 's similarity to it was no good argument with Wordsworth for including it.

Coleridge morosely conceded to Davy that Wordsworth "thought it indelicate to print two Volumes with *his name* in which so much of another man's work was included—& which was of more consequence—the poem was in direct opposition to the very purpose for which the Lyrical Ballads were published."[40] However, though Coleridge was crushed by the decision, there is no evidence that he expected, had "Christabel" been included, to gain any more profit from the new edition, or even that the title page would have credited any author other than "W. Wordsworth." What Coleridge wanted, more than credit or profit, was support and encouragement, and this is just what he did not get from Wordsworth. True, he had let Wordsworth down on the preface, he had written none of the poems he promised for the naming-of-places group, and he remained painfully prone to denigrating his own abilities before Wordsworth, even though he struggled manfully to argue himself out of such pathetic dependency. "I would rather have written Ruth, and Nature's Lady ['Three years she grew'] than a million such poems [like 'Christabel'] / but why do I calumniate my own spirit by saying, *I* would rather—God knows—it is as delightful to me that they *are* written . . . my mind has disciplined itself into a willing exertion of it's powers, without any reference to their *comparative* value."[41] Nonetheless, such discouragement at such a time was a nearly mortal wound to his poetic spirit.

By rejecting "Christabel," Wordsworth not only lost the justification for his long second preface but also effectively cut off the last quarter of the second volume as it then stood, presenting himself with the necessity of coming up with a poem or poems of similar length to replace it. This poem was "Michael."[42] Publication was delayed for a full three months until Wordsworth could finish it, beginning from October 12. First he rummaged about in his stock of manuscript poems but rejected what he found there because, "being connected with political subjects I judged that they would be injurious to the sale of the Work," whereas "there can be no doubt that ['Michael'] will be highly serviceable to the Sale."[43] The rejected poems were most probably "The Ruined Cottage" and "Adventures on Salisbury Plain," which in their extant versions of ca. 1800 could still be characterized as political—markedly so when compared with Wordsworth's new productions for the second volume.[44]

"Michael" is the conclusive poem of the 1800 *Lyrical Ballads* in every sense. Aside from the unpleasant circumstances of its composition, and the moot question of whether it would have been composed without them, Wordsworth's production of it over the next two months was a remarkable indication of his fully developed powers as a professional poet. He could, virtually on demand, write a powerful poem to order, both appropriate to the contents of the volume in question and, even more impressive, fully congruent to the theoretical requirements laid down in its preface. "Michael" is, in this respect, the only poem in the entire collection to have been written to the specification of a previously enunciated model, since it alone follows rather than precedes the preface in time of composition. It does this particularly with regard to Wordsworth's dictum that, in these poems, unlike most narrative poems, the feeling was to give importance to the action rather than vice versa.

Its story is quickly told: Michael's son Luke leaves home to earn money to save the family's lands, but falls into dissipation and flees the country. But the *feeling* of the story is almost unspeakable, either in Michael's last charge to Luke or in his thoughts after Luke's fall, which are entirely contained in the vignette of his repeated returns to the sheepfold the two of them started on the day Luke left: he "never lifted up a single stone." Wordsworth confirmed the poem's theoretical importance by claiming that "Michael" contained his most important "views." "Michael" at the end of the second volume forms a natural complement to "The Brothers" near its beginning, in that both are sad stories of the ultimate *failure* of efforts to preserve the integrity of home and family in the harsh economy of this district.

It was not easy. Dorothy recorded ten days of discouragement for one day of good work. But Wordsworth occasionally reached his hard-earned conclusions by easier, more lighthearted routes. His first effort to get started, now known as the "Ballad Michael," is very good-humored about Coleridge, even though Wordsworth had just rejected his poem in favor of this one: "Two shepherds we have, two wits of the dale / Renown'd for song, satire, epistle and tale—."[45] The "doggerel strain" they produce sounds—at first—far different from "Michael":

> . . . all their suggestions and taunts to repeat,
> And all that sly malice so bitter and Sweet,
> My pen it would sadly distress;
> When I say that our maidens are larks in their glee
> And fair as the moon hanging over the sea
> The drift of those rhymes you will guess.[46]

This "pastoral ballad is sung far and near," but the speaker considers it a "thoughtless . . . falsehood." Being thus invited to "guess" at the meaning of a tale that the "Ballad Michael" sets out to correct, we could guess, on the basis of this hint, either that it is a story of a young man seducing and abandoning a local girl, or of a young man abandoned *by* one of those local beauties, or that the poem itself is a seductive love compliment to the ladies—all versions of local stories that Wordsworth had already written.

Though "Michael" in its published form seems far from scandal of this sort, there are more than a few similarities—which can hardly be coincidental—in its situation and that of the poem it replaced, "Christabel," despite their superficial differences. Both are Lake District family tragedies caused by an excess of fatherly pride: Sir Leoline's, for his reputation, and Michael's, for what amounts to much the same thing, his financial independence and land ownership. In both, a beloved only child is lost to "dissipation," though Christabel is overtly seduced by Geraldine whereas Luke gives in to "evil courses" in the "dissolute city." Both poems are set roughly along the western edge of the Helvellyn-Fairfield range of hills. Michael's sheepfold is located in Greenhead Ghyll just below Stone-Arthur, and though Sir Leoline's castle is in Langdale, Geraldine's father's house is modeled on Castle Rock of Triermaine, at the north end of Thirlmere. It was also known as "The Enchanted Castle of St. John's."[47] If Sir Leoline's bard, Bracy, had been allowed by Leoline to carry out his dream-inspired rescue mission, he would have traveled up from Langdale through Grasmere to Castle Rock, along the most common route for both poets' comings and goings, virtually the High Street of the district. Bracy was a name Coleridge considered giving his new son (born September 14), before—as in so many other matters now—he acceded to a more Wordsworthian vision of things and called him Derwent, after the river.

At its very beginning, "Michael" was called simply "The Sheepfold." Dorothy records that she and William set out on October 11 to find it, which they did: "built nearly in the form of a heart unequally divided."[48] This means they went looking for a landmark that someone had told them about, perhaps in response to a direct request for some information on which Wordsworth could base a tale, the same method he had used so efficiently in Somerset in writing his poems for the first *Lyrical Ballads.* Tales of losing land by foreclosure were so common in the hard times of 1799–1800 that Wordsworth's jottings in "Ballad Michael" suggest it had become almost the standard story of the region:

> it is the first
> Which in this vale our children hear, perhaps
> A hundred and a hundred years again
> 'Twill be retold among us . . . .[49]

As a place-bonding story "Michael" does have the archetypal quality of telling how someone who left a tightly knit community suffered bad consequences, and left his family to mourn. This is strongly reinforced by

Wordsworth's allusions to tales of the Patriarchs of Genesis and their sons, and (in reverse) to the story of the Prodigal Son. Since the impulse of young people in provincial places is often to escape, especially when times are hard, such a tale serves as a cautionary threat. Several of the local versions of the story available to Wordsworth were about young men running away from home to seek fame and fortune in the city, sometimes finding it, sometimes not. But all these stories put the onus for blame (or praise) on the young man, whereas in "Michael" Luke is sent away *by* his father to save the family: he fails, but the responsibility falls back on the father for the course of action he chose for his son.

There were several aspects of this situation that Wordsworth found easy to develop because they applied to his own life in the region, allowing him to get into this material quickly by self-identification, almost a necessity for every poem he wrote. He too had been a promising local boy of suddenly reduced expectations who was sent out into the world to help recoup his family's fallen fortunes. And he, like Luke, had failed in that effort, both in the world's eyes and in the eyes of most of the members of his extended family. To them, and perhaps to himself, it might well have appeared that "in the dissolute city [he] gave himself / To evil courses." This could as easily have been radical political activism as the fleshly pleasures we more usually supply for such a reference, though they too played their part in Wordsworth's youthful experience.

The perfunctory quality of Luke's decline and fall at the end of "Michael" makes it clear that his story is only the catalyst, not the primary focus of the poem's meaning. A "shame" so great as to drive him into exile "beyond the seas" could only, given the story's circumstances, have something to do with money. He does not send home the money that the whole arrangement depends on; he lets his father down. But the language that Wordsworth used to describe this "shame" ("dissolute city," "evil courses," "ignominy and shame") is so close to that of "Tintern Abbey" and the yew tree lines that we must feel Luke's experience is very close to Wordsworth's own, in terms of temptations and possibilities, if not in literal fact.

Furthermore, Michael's problems arose from the failure of yet another son, "his brother's son," to whom Michael had pledged some of his own lands "in surety." This is what Richard Wordsworth of Whitehaven had done for the three younger sons of his dead brother, John Wordsworth Sr. He had not pledged land in bond to their fiscal responsibility, but he was liable for the bills they contracted, especially those of the eldest of the three, William, who not only contracted many more debts than his brothers, John and Christopher, but also had much less prospect of ever paying him back for his outlays. In addition, Richard Wordsworth's own son, Robinson, had been cruelly inconvenienced at the time of entering adult life (college and marriage) by the refusal and inability of that other Prodigal Son, William, to pay off the debts he had accumulated, in the process of becoming what he called "a chosen Son."

Brother John also entered into the composition of "Michael." Isabella, Michael's wife, has hopeful thoughts for Luke's departure based on the real story of Richard Bateman of Ings (near Windermere), who "Beyond the seas . . . grew wondrous rich." This was the exact form of the Wordsworths' hopes for John's success, which John himself expressed bluntly to Mary Hutchinson when he told her, "I shall be a *very rich* man." It was fitting that John should enter into the last poem composed for the 1800 volume, since he had already entered its first composed one, "The Brothers," and because both together are at the very heart of the volume's defining group of poems dealing with broken pairs and failed homecomings.

The poem's blame for this falls hardest on Michael. If we pay attention to the poem, rather than to the sentimental images often conjured up from it, we can see that more goes through the old man's mind than the simple thought that Luke will never return, or even that he may lose half his land and that things will never be the same again. Michael's decision that Luke should be sent to *earn* the needed bond money sets the tragedy in motion. This decision is what goes through Michael's mind as he contemplates the unfinished sheepfold, not Luke's weakness and errors. Michael is something like the shepherd in "The Last of the Flock," but his possessiveness is brought out not by poverty but by pride of ownership. The lands had been "burdened" (under lien) when they came to Michael, and not till he was forty was even half of his inheritance really his. Now, by his nephew's failure, exactly half is put under threat of loss again. "His mind was keen, / Intense and frugal," like that of Agnes Fisher, and for the same reason. He was a workaholic, and it occurs to him only late in life that he might want an heir to receive all that he has built up: he is sixty-six when Luke is born. He "lov'd his Helpmate; but to Michael's heart / The Son of his old age was yet more dear," and he starts taking the boy out to work with him at a very early age. Even his "female service" to the infant Luke can be construed as an effort to protect his investment, to bring the boy along quickly so that he can enter into his father's male service. By age five Luke was "to his office *prematurely* called," and by age ten he "could stand against the mountain blasts." Wordsworth mentions his age because he wants us to remark it. Things in nature "were dearer now" to Michael than they had been before because of the promise represented by his son, but Wordsworth rejects this observation impatiently, as something trite and irrelevant: "why should I relate / That . . . ?" (208–9). All the emphasis is on the father's feelings for his son *in relation to* his land.

The pathetic scene of Michael's last conversation with Luke at the sheepfold uses language that comes close to revealing the selfish tendency of Michael's reasoning. He lays a heavy burden of paternal guilt, or psychological debt, on Luke, telling him how much he has loved him since his birth. He takes the boy on a narrative tour of all the events of his life, and though "Luke had a manly heart" he soon starts sobbing aloud with gratitude. This finally forces Michael to realize, "Nay . . . I see / That these are things of which I need not speak." As an alternative, he converts the same story of family indebtedness back through his own parents, but his gratitude to them is finally expressed as yet another duty for Luke: "I wish that thou should'st live the life they liv'd." He points to the sheepfold as the "covenant" between them: another bond to be kept, but not by money. His language begins to stutter as his deepest fears start to emerge: "I knew that thou could'st never have a wish / To leave me, Luke,—thou hast been bound to me / Only by the links of love." But these, as Wordsworth knows, are the strongest indentures of all, and Michael here sounds nearly as much like "The Mad Mother" as like the father of "The Last of the Flock"—or like Wordsworth himself at the end of "Tintern Abbey," pleading with Dorothy to keep his life in her mind forever.

"Michael" rounds off the defining pattern of broken pairs and broken homes that strike the dominant note of the new poems Wordsworth wrote in 1800. In it the pair poems, the place poems, and the local-customs poems of the new volume all come together, in the up-gathering conclusion of the entire volume. The unfinished structure of the sheepfold stands for human disappointment amid nature's beauty. It represents the tragic disappointment of the very hopes that its central symbol was supposed to represent. The unfinished sheepfold is the broken bond of love, as perhaps it seemed to William and Dorothy from the first moment they saw it, looking like "a heart unequally divided." In relation to Wordsworth's hopes for Grasmere almost exactly twelve months earlier, this poem, completed on December 9, 1800, represented a strong corrective to what he now recognized as very naive hopes. Everything is gone: "the ploughshare has been through the ground / On which it stood." "Michael" shows his recognition that the assumption of an easily enduring link between land, man, and language could not stand the test of reality. In "Home at Grasmere" another bonding symbol of the human significance of the natural landscape, the paired swans, was all too easily broken, throwing both poet and his poem into disarray. But "Michael," rather than explaining why this ideal is not tenable, conveys instead the devastating realization that it cannot be so.

Just as the concerns of *The Recluse* are buried beneath the alternately turgid and splendid arguments of the preface, so are they evident in "Michael." Wordsworth defended his reference to "the earliest of those Tales that spake to me / Of Shepherds" because they spoke to him "On man, the heart of man, and human life" (33), words virtually identical to those with which he announced the birth of the *Recluse* project two and a half years earlier. But where "Home at Grasmere" finally achieved a satisfactory conclusion by Wordsworth's attaching the forward-looking vision of the "Prospectus" onto its tales of tragedy, Michael gets no such satisfaction: he knows his lands are lost and his dreams destroyed. By telling Michael's story, Wordsworth hoped to achieve what was denied Michael, not in his landholdings but in his own stock-in-trade, poetry:

> *Therefore,* although it be a history
> Homely and rude, I will relate the same
> For the delight of a few natural hearts,
> And with yet fonder feeling, for the sake
> Of youthful Poets, who among these Hills
> Will be my second Self when I am gone.
> (34–39)

This bequeathing of himself to his successors parallels his pledging himself to Dorothy in "Tintern Abbey" and to Coleridge in *The Prelude.* Wordsworth will perpetuate himself through his poetical heirs, precisely as Michael could not. But like Michael's desire to propagate himself, Wordsworth's legacy is expressed in language that suggests his heirs may get more than they bargained for, or that the gift may entail the assumption of an identity not their own: *"be my second Self* when I am gone."

This is to read the poem at its deepest autbiographical level, which is concerned preeminently with the creation of the Poet. Wordsworth's immediately contemporary readers saw it in terms much more of its object than of its narrowly defined subject. Humphry Davy said it was full of just pictures of what human life ought to be like. At the biographical level, however, Wordsworth's sympathy for the composite character of Michael, great as it is, was not just for the difficulties of poor country life in 1800, or even for his private cautionary lesson about the danger of naive identification with the place. It was also a symbol of his own disappointment at his failure to push forward on *The Recluse.* He had piled up "stones" for it and worked on it "many a day." But there were also many days, as there were in the composition of "Michael," when he went either to his study or out to Easedale and other favorite composing haunts, "and never lifted up a single stone." Michael's sheepfold, begun but never finished, becomes a permanent record of failure. So too did Wordsworth's *Recluse* manuscripts, as they mounted up through the years.

Rapidly, between December 9 and January 25, right through the Christmas holidays, Dorothy's birthday, and their anniversary "homecoming" celebration on December 25, everything in the volume was brought to a conclusion. *Lyrical Ballads* (1800) acutally appeared on January 25, 1801. Also in January, Coleridge's health suddenly collapsed, and for the next three months he confined himself to the upper rooms of Greta Hall.[50] He was suffering a very acute reaction to the effects of trying to be someone else's "second Self."

SELLING THE BOOK, CREATING THE POET 31

Lyrical Ballads, 1801–1802

> . . . what is meant by the word Poet? What is a Poet? To whom does he address himself? And what language is to be expected from him? He is a man speaking to men . . . the rock of defense of human nature . . . carrying everywhere with him relationship and love . . . in spite of things silently gone out of mind and things violently destroyed, the Poet binds together by passion and knowledge the vast empire of human society.
>
> (Preface to *Lyrical Ballads,* 1802)

Well before the actual publication date of the two-volume second edition of *Lyrical Ballads* (January 25, 1801), Wordsworth had been moving decisively to control its reception, to avoid the lame mistakes and petty disasters that had afflicted the first, single-volume edition. The book was almost completely in his charge, with Coleridge ill and sulking over Wordsworth's rough treatment of "Christabel." Coleridge was always more concerned about what Wordsworth thought of him than about public opinion; Wordsworth had once felt the same way about Coleridge's esteem—now he wanted similar approval from the public at large.

John Stoddart duly delivered his flattering review, which appeared in the moderately liberal *British Critic* in February; the first review in print, it helped ensure that other reviewers, less committed or lazier, would follow suit.[1] The strategy worked—aided, of course, by the poems themselves—and by summer it was clear that the volume would be a success. Throughout the year Daniel Stuart plugged the new volume in the *Morning Post,* reprinting nine of Wordsworth's poems between January and August, starting with three in a row in the first three days after the volume appeared: "Lucy Gray," "To a Sexton," and "The Childless Father."[2]

Two weeks before the book appeared, the poets arranged for presentation copies to be sent to eight important public figures.[3] This was a small number by prevailing public-relations standards, but the eight were carefully chosen to represent a wide spectrum of cultural opinion: "persons of eminence *either in Letters or in the state.*"[4] There were three women and five men, roughly divided between "Letters" and "state." The women and man of letters were Dorothy Jordan, the famous actress and mistress of the duke of Clarence, whose admiration of "The Mad Mother" was well known to the poets; Anna Letitia [Aikin] Barbauld, the popular Dissenting author of children's poetry, supporter of the antislavery movement and the French Revolution (who had recently published a poem "To Mr. S. T. Coleridge," urging him to leave "the maze of metaphysic lore"); and Matthew ("Monk") Lewis.

The political men were Sir James Bland Burges (1752–1824), possibly because of Wordsworth's admiration for his poem *Richard Coeur de Lion,* but (since this had only just appeared) more probably because of Burges's influential position as a friend of Pitt, Wilberforce, and George III, which included many years of highly paid confidential work in the Foreign Office;[5] William Wilberforce, antislavery leader and bosom friend of William Cookson, who had been hearing for years about the vagaries of Cookson's nephew; Charles James Fox, the country's forlorn last hope for reform, still isolated in his self-exile from Parliament, though soon to return; and John Taylor, former editor of the *Morning Post* and later publisher of the *True Briton* and the *Sun* (in which Burges also had an interest). Many years later Taylor disingenuously said he was surprised that he was "known at all to a poet of such original merit," but in 1801 his cultural status was much higher than Wordsworth's. Finally, they sent a copy to the duchess of Devonshire, Georgiana Cavendish (1757–1806), arguably the most powerful political woman in the land, at least in opposition, from her long friendship and daring efforts on behalf of her dear friend Fox, especially in the Westminster election of 1784, when she traded kisses for votes with some of Fox's dirtiest urban constituents.[6]

Five of these eight letters survive, in copies or replies or other references that allow us to deduce their contents. Their rhetorical flexibility—to put it mildly—shows how determined the two poets were to make their book succeed, and their willingness to adapt their pitches to a wide variety of audiences in order to achieve that goal. If these letters alone existed, but not the volume they refer to, they would read like a literary instance of the parable of the blind men feeling the elephant, so different are the inferences that can be drawn from them about the *Lyrical Ballads* of 1800. Except that, in this instance, the poets took on the role of an actively self-reporting elephant, giving to each of their "blind" correspondents the version of their book that would strike them most favorably.

Coleridge, more used to the protocols of literary politics, drafted all the letters except the one to Fox, but all were signed by Wordsworth alone. Only from Fox did they receive anything more than a polite reply.[7] That half the chosen recipients were key political figures, of both left and right, shows how political Wordsworth's sense of his volume's significance still was, despite its avoidance of overt political reference. All of the letters emphasize that the poems in *Lyrical Ballads* are "written on a theory professedly new, and on principles which many persons will be unwilling to admit," so each of the recipients became, willy-nilly, a specific auditor to some version of the preface's scolding lecture.

The letter to Wilberforce is in the handwriting of Dorothy—of her who had once been teased about him as a beau. It associates *Lyrical Ballads* with Wilberforce's recent *Practical View of the Prevailing Religious System of Instruction* (1797), suggesting, "In the composition of them I had been a Fellow-labourer with you in the same Vineyard."[8] This was stretching a slim resemblance, but Coleridge's metaphor connecting the humility of religious workers to the simplicity of the poems' language, which, like a nun, "walk[s] 'in silence and in a veil,' " is completely over the top: hardly a poem in the lot can be associated with that cliché. As in the preface, the poets supported their logic with impressive-sounding analogies that are not logically watertight. As actions are to affections—Coleridge proposes and Wordsworth endorses—so is the linguistic sign to its real referent: a plausible-sounding formulation (the former "expresses" the latter), but almost equally plausible the other way around, as regards actions or affections. Nevertheless, it served the purpose of connecting these poetical actions with Wilberforce's religious ones on the basis of their mutually chaste avoidance of "gaudy ornaments." Wordsworth's assertion that the feelings in his poems were more important than the actions they describe was also slipped in here, though it is surely more of a Romantic idea than a Christian one.

If to Wilberforce the letter writer sounds like a Sunday school teacher, to Burges he sounds like a linguistic scholar. This letter is almost as conservative as Wordsworth's letter to Fox (below) was liberal. This is not real duplicity, but actually represents a possibility in any full interpretation of the volumes' range of political emphasis. The letter takes pains to make sure that their "revolutionary" quality, explicitly referred to at the beginning of the preface, will be understood in the old but fast-disappearing sense of the word, as a *return* to good old traditional standards, not abstract innovation for its own sake. It asserts that poems are, or should be, written in the diction of "the community," not of the individual, an assertion based on the philosophically quite new suggestion that language is as much our master as our servant. It further asserts blithely that most English writers since the time of Dryden—that is, for the whole last century—have ignored this truth (overlooking the strong emphasis in all Neoclassical writing on *decorum*), with the result that "the simplicity of our national character" has been injured and "reverence for our ancient institutions and religious offices" weakened.[9]

Such a letter could have been sent to Burke, had he still been alive, though Burke would probably have noticed what Burges presumably didn't: that, such protestations aside, the quality and effectiveness of British institutions is ferociously criticized by implication in many poems in both volumes, especially in the first. The letter argues, in short, from the corruption of language to the corruption of the state, in a way that anticipates Orwell's essay "Politics and the English Language," and reflects the views of reformers as various as Luther, Muhammad, and Jesus Christ.

Monk Lewis is addressed as a language *performer:* "a mind . . . acute . . . in the detection of the ludicrous and the faulty." Given the hilarity some of the balder *Lyrical Ballads* provoked in many readers, this might look like asking for trouble from the author of *The Castle-Spectre.* But Wordsworth had swallowed his former contempt for Lewis's success and now sought his help to emulate it. His linguistic argument is here twisted around so that printed literature becomes part of the problem to which the accompanying book of printed poems is part of the solution. "Our written language has been receding from the real language of life" with "alarming rapidity," and "the increasing circulation of books" thus works to "adulter[ate] our moral feelings," and hence "the language of real life itself," thus "poisoning our future literature at its best and most sacred source."[10] Without saying so directly, the letter leaves it to Lewis to draw the only conclusion by which the presentation volume can break this viciously circular chain of bad causes: *it* must be written in "the real language of life." Their ploy worked: John Wordsworth soon relayed to Grasmere a fan letter and complimentary poem he received from Lewis. Both are lost, but from John's comments we can see that Lewis, whose moderate liberalism was clearly displayed in *The Castle-Spectre,* had leapt to the book's social challenge in a way that even Fox would refuse to. John called his poem "quite a caricature of its kind . . . 'The Convict' is nothing compared to [it]." "The Convict" had by now become a family in-joke; it was the most overtly political poem of Wordsworth's in the whole collection, and the only one he had cut from the new edition. "They ought to have made a parson of him instead of a M.P.," John concluded, reminding us that Lewis, as well as Wilberforce and Fox, was a member of the House of Commons.

Wordsworth's letter to Fox is much longer and more political than the other seven. Like the letter to Wilberforce, it tries to connect the program of *Lyrical Ballads,* "however feebly," with its recipient's public work.[11] It sets forth Wordsworth's position much more clearly (hence more vulnerably) than the preface; one wishes he had dared to address the public in this vein. Starting out defensively, he acknowledges that these poems might give Fox "an unfavorable idea of my intellectual powers." The letter is thus dedicated to removing this presumed negative, and on the same rhetorical excuse offered in the preface: "My letter should be short; but I have feelings within me which I hope will . . . excuse the trespass."[12] He has another principle as well, which Fox would only see as a compliment, but which we can recognize as the further emergence of the Poet of *The Recluse* in his role as friend of mankind. Wordsworth praised Fox's political flexibility, his ability to deal with men as individuals as well as "in bodies" (what his enemies called his corruptibility), saying it has "made you dear to Poets; and . . . if . . . there has been a single true poet living in England, he must have loved you." As it happened, there *was* one such true Poet, and he here expresses his love for Fox by co-opting Fox's politics to his own poetics. "But were I assured that I myself had a just claim to the title of a Poet," he continues, coming ever closer to the heart of his matter, he still wouldn't have presumed to send Fox these volumes had it not been for "The Brothers" and "Michael," the two poems which in Wordsworth's view carried the spirit and the letter, respectively, of the whole project.

He then launched into a social critique that went far beyond Fox's immediate political stand against the war, though the war was the immediate cause of the "calamitous effect[s]" which Wordsworth presciently if haphazardly intuited as evils inherent in the new industrial state. He identifies it as the "rapid decay of the domestic affections among the lower orders of society," an observation that liberals and conservatives alike could applaud, though they would draw very different conclusions from it. He identifies its causes in the spread of manufacturing, heavy postal taxes (a constant concern to Wordsworth as bourgeois literary entrepreneur), workhouses and soup shops, and—wrapping all up into one—the disproportion between wages and prices. Wordsworth, like almost everyone else in 1801, was only dimly becoming aware of the larger revolution that we call industrial, looming behind the French one, stimulated in no small degree by England's need to develop the military machinery to counter Napoleon's threat. Wordsworth did see clearly, however, that people were being displaced from working at home to "*manu*factories," where people became "hands." Even Thelwall, in his contemporaneous poem on child factory workers he had observed en route to Llyswen in "the Bottoms of Gloucestershire," had not gone much beyond this perception.

> Towers from each peaceful dell the unwieldy pride
> Of Factory over-grown; where Opulence,
> Dispeopling the neat cottage, crowds his walls
> (Made pestilent by congregated lungs,
> And lewd association) with a race
> Of infant slaves, brok'n timely to the yoke
> Of unremitting Drudgery . . . .[13]

Blake's "Chimney Sweeper" of the *Songs of Experience* (1794) had plumbed the psychological depths of the coming industrial disasters, but Wordsworth saw that this movement of people from their home places would have an inevitably dehumanizing effect, which he expressed in terms of their ability to "read" and express their emotions. People "read" their homes like a *text:* "a tablet upon which they [their domestic feelings] are written which makes them objects of memory in a thousand instances." It is this domestic attachment which renders them fit subjects for poetry. He quoted an eighty-year-old Grasmere neighbor who had cared for her invalid husband for months, but had now become lame herself: "it would burst my heart," she said, if they were "boarded out among some other Poor of the parish . . . having kept house together so long."[14] Wordsworth interprets her language as arising directly from her domestic emotions: "These people could not express themselves in this way without an almost sublime conviction of the blessings of independent domestic life." A profoundly human language arises, not simply from our sense of place, but from the words wrenched out of us when we fear to *lose* that place. This is what made his old neighbor poetical, what "The Brothers" and "Michael" show by their negative examples, and what Wordsworth himself had learned on his pulses when he tried to connect himself to his home region without a full appreciation of its complicating human dimensions.

Summing up for Fox, Wordsworth claimed that *Lyrical Ballads* would "in some small degree enlarge our feelings of reverence for our species . . . by shewing that our best qualities are possessed by men whom we are too apt to consider, not with reference to the points in which they resemble us, but to those in which they manifestly differ from us." Or, more simply, in a ringing peroration that Fox the great political speaker could appreciate, "to shew that men who do not wear fine cloaths can feel deeply." Little more than that need be said to substantiate Wordsworth's claim to have revolutionized the course of English poetry. Hence it is interesting that he should follow up these provocative words with a quotation from Quintillian in the original Latin, addressed to Fox as a fellow member of the educated elite of England. Quintillian's dictum could easily have been included in the preface, though it would have revealed that some of the preface's most revolutionary-sounding claims were actually nearly two thousand years old: "For it is feeling and force of imagination that make us eloquent. It is for this reason that even the uneducated have no difficulty in finding words to express their meaning, if only they are stirred by some strong emotion."[15]

Fox's reply, when it finally came in late May, was both gratifying and frustrating. Fox wrote carefully and at some length, but did not take the smallest nibble at the political-linguistic bait Wordsworth offered. Instead, for all his advanced political views (though none as advanced as these), he showed himself to be a member of the old school when it came to poetry. Or rather, of the most acceptable version of the "new" school, since he declared himself an enthusiastic lover of Cowper.[16] Rather than penetrating to the social implications of "The Brothers" and "Michael," he stopped at their surface, protesting that he was "no great friend to blank verse for subjects which are to be treated of with simplicity."[17] Fox frankly said he expressed this reservation only because he admired so many of the other poems, even some of those written in blank verse, surely referring to "Tintern Abbey." To his credit as a reader, he chose as his favorites "Goody Blake," "The Mad Mother," "The Idiot Boy," and "We are Seven," all from the 1798 volume, and among the most extreme of Wordsworth's sociolinguistic experiments. To his credit as a politician, he also took the trouble to pay a compliment to Wordsworth's nearly hidden coauthor, having read Wordsworth's grudging footnote in the preface carefully enough to recognize that "Love" and "The Nightingale" were by another hand, and Fox certainly knew who Coleridge was. But his final words show his interest flagging, and *Lyrical Ballads'* brief purchase on the pinnacles of power slipping away. "The Nightingale" would, he said, be of use in combating the prejudice against them!

The letter to John Taylor was almost the reverse of the one to Fox politically, judging by Wordsworth's answer to Taylor's reply. He asserted that he and Coleridge had the same views on what Taylor "with great propriety call[ed] jacobinical pathos."[18] Whether Taylor had said *Lyrical Ballads* had it or avoided it is unclear, but Wordsworth goes to great lengths to give *Coleridge* a clean bill of health for having recognized his error in using such unfortunate expressions: "he deeply regretted that he had ever written a single word of that character." "Those writers who seem to estimate their power of exciting sorrow for suffering humanity, by the quantity of hatred and revenge which they are able to pour into the hearts of their Readers . . . are bad poets, and misguided men." From a literature of activism—published, by Coleridge, unpublished, by Wordsworth—he claims, quite otherwise than to Fox, that they have shifted to a literature of emotional universalism: "Pity, we agreed, is a sacred thing, that cannot, and will not be prophaned."[19]

That he should make this apologia to John Taylor is as interesting as the poets' choosing Taylor to receive a presentation volume in the first place. The *True Briton* was only one newspaper among many, and not the most important. But it was a violently conservative paper, especially compared with the *Morning Post,* their liberal mainstay and support. That was perhaps reason enough to send a copy to Taylor: to balance their overtures to journalists between left and right as they did their political ones. But Taylor, known mainly for his comic journalism and what we would call gossip columns, had other qualifications that may have drawn the poets to him and made them willing to confess their former political errors to him. Like his father and grandfather before him, Taylor has been the oculist to George III, but he soon became the "eyes" of the government in another way. He was one of the main journalists providing clandestine information to the government in the mid-1790s, along with "his good friend" William Jackson, whom he succeeded in 1787 as editor of the *Morning Post,* and who spectacularly commited suicide in court when convicted as part of the United Irishmen's plot in 1798.[20] It is unlikely that the young Wordsworth and Coleridge would have known of Taylor's secret activities in the mid-1790s. But it is equally unlikely that they would *not* have known about the gossip and innuendo regarding Taylor's domestic espionage by 1801, given their close association with Stuart, who took over the *Morning Post* from him. If one were trying to cover over traces of youthful Jacobinism, what better way than to send a book of reformed poems to a potentially virulent enemy, and then follow it up with a fawning reply agreeing with his strictures against "jacobinical pathos"?

Wordsworth followed up his letter to Taylor with one to Taylor's sister, Anne, who had also written to him, wondering about the range of his life experiences, since "Tintern Abbey" and other poems hinted at a considerable personal history behind the events they alluded to.[21] This letter is usually treated in Wordsworthian biography as one of his typically pompous replies to a naive young admirer. But Anne Taylor was neither young nor naive; she was a partner in her brother's many enterprises. Receiving a very particular inquiry about his life from the sister of a man he knew to be a government informer, Wordsworth provided her a carefully laundered version of his autobiography. In one concise paragraph, he gave her the outline of his entire youthful life, as though it simply ran across the twenty-five miles from Cockermouth to Grasmere, pointedly concluding that in it "there will be little which will throw any light on my writings . . . in truth my life has been unusually barren of events, and my opinions have grown slowly and, I may say, insensibly."

To the sister of a man who passed confidential information about revolutionary sympathizers to government officials, Wordsworth cautiously said nothing about his own experiences specifically *in France,* only that he had spent the last of his university summer vacations "in a pedestrian tour in the Alps," and that since he left Cambridge his time "has been spent in travelling *upon the Continent,* and in England: and in occasional residences in London, and in different parts of England and Wales." He added, "At present I am permanently fixed in my native country."[22] Miss Taylor was told that she must be aware of "how very widely different my former opinions must have been from those which I hold at present." This was a very unspecific indication of change, since he doesn't say what opinions he's talking about, and leaves it open to her (and her brother) to connect it with his earlier comments about avoiding "jacobinical pathos." His main point is that the meaning of his life, as of his style, lay in its degree of *change,* despite his claim that it was a life "barren" of events and that his was a mind "insensible" to its own growth. Many lives are barren of dramatic events, but Wordsworth's was certainly not one of them. Similarly, many minds may be insensible of their own growth, but again Wordsworth's was very much the contrary: few minds can have been as extremely sensible of their own growth and change as his. Nevertheless—and for precisely that reason—he presents it as "slow" and "insensible" because this kind of consciousness is the least *self*-conscious and therefore (according to his logic) the most natural. *The Prelude* will labor strenuously to suggest that his mind grew "insensibly," but Wordsworth's little qualifying cough to Miss Taylor—"and, I may say, insensibly"—shows his awareness of the paradox here: how can the growth of consciousness be presented as if it was unconscious? As he would shortly write, it was the "ministry" of Nature

> To interpose the covert of your shades,
> Even as a sleep, betwixt the heart of man
> And the uneasy world—'twixt man himself,
> Not seldom, and his own unquiet heart . . . .
> (XI.16–19)

The man who longs so much for this natural quiet is one whose own mind and heart must often have been very "uneasy" and "unquiet."

While these public communiqués were being sent out, private communications were not immediately encouraging. John reported from London that he heard very little mention of the new edition, except that people didn't seem to *get* the poems on first reading.[23] This troubled Wordsworth, who had blamed "The Ancient Mariner" for just that problem in the reception of the first edition. But that he could have expected any other reaction to poems apparently so familiar yet purposely so unusual is an instance of his peculiar mixture of immense self-confidence with an inability to recognize that others might not automatically see him as he saw himself. Nevertheless, by the end of the year a young marquis of the Lowther clan, John Lowther Johnstone, saw the queen herself give a copy of *Lyrical Ballads* to a friend; by then the quantity as well as the quality of the book's readership had been assured.[24]

To unknown correspondents whom he now began to hear from for the first time in his life, Wordsworth was as patiently (or maddeningly) tutorial as he was to all readers of the preface, or to the national leader of the opposition. From friends they naturally got praise, but not always enough of it. Charles Lamb's enthusiastic letter of appreciation was similar to Charles

Fox's, honestly saying that none of the new poems had affected him as forcibly as "The Ancient Mariner," "Tintern Abbey," and "The Mad Mother," though he singled out the "Song of Lucy" and "The Old Cumberland Beggar" among the new ones as especially good. He unfortunately added the quite true observation that the latter was "too like a lecture." Fox might say whatever he liked, but from his friends Wordsworth expected nothing but full marks, and Lamb was soon the bemused recipient of letters from both Wordsworth and Coleridge taking issue with his literary judgments.[25] As Lamb wrote to his friend Thomas Manning,

> I had need be cautious henceforward what opinion I give of the "Lyrical Ballads." All the North of England are in a turmoil. Cumberland and Westmorland have already declared a state of war. . . . I received almost instantaneously a long letter of four sweating pages from my Reluctant Letter-Writer [Wordsworth] . . . with a deal of stuff about a certain Union of Tenderness and Imagination, which in the sense he used Imagination was not the characteristic of Shakespeare, but which Milton possessed in a degree far exceeding other Poets: which Union, as the highest species of Poetry . . . "He was most proud to aspire to"; then illustrating the said Union by two quotations from his own 2d vol. (which I had been so unfortunate as to miss) . . . . [A]fter one has been reading Shakespeare twenty of the best years of one's life, [it is hard] to have a fellow start up, and prate about some unknown quality, which Shakespeare possessed in a degree inferior to Milton and *somebody else!!*[26]

Lamb had never said that "he did not *like*" any of the poems, but so much was riding on the volume's reception (for Wordsworth) that any omission was taken as a slight, and Lamb had fatally neglected to say a word about "Michael."[27]

The humorous discrepancy between Lamb's reaction to the poems and Wordsworth's counterreaction shows how much the ideals of the *Recluse* project suffused the new volumes. But though Lamb was as usual funny, Wordsworth was, as more often than not, right. Yet his "unknown quality," linking sublime imaginativeness with humane tenderness, was so new that even Lamb could not adequately recognize it. (John Keats, almost a generation later, would assert that Wordsworth had it to an even greater extent than Milton.) Wordsworth, his head full of massively expanding notions of the role of the Poet and of himself filling that role, had as usual assumed too much about even his sympathetic readers' intuitions of his meaning. With his mind literally *pre*occupied by the forming shapes of *The Recluse* and *The Prelude,* he could not see how the apparently simple *Lyrical Ballads,* with their hectoring preface, could fail to reveal it. Even less could he see that the apparent discrepancy between the "low" ballads and the "high" preface actually worked to obfuscate, not clarify, their relation to his new conception of the Poet. The "four sweating pages" Lamb received were, like those to Fox,

Wordsworth's intensely personal glosses on the preface, and neither the Lamb of letters nor the Fox of politics, though among the most brilliant minds of the era, could quite grasp what he was being offered.

A letter of Thomas Wilkinson's (whose garden spade Wordsworth would later memorialize) shows how pervasive the self-creation project had become by this time. Wilkinson, writing not to but about Wordsworth, described meeting him in February, and gave a thumbnail sketch of what, since Wilkinson must have got it from the source, we can recognize as the first full, if miniature, version of the creation of the Poet, that soon began expanding massively for posterity. He "sprung originally from the next village" (Wilkinson is writing from Yanwath, a hamlet just south of Penrith), "turned his back on all Preferment, and settled down contentedly with his sister and his Muse. He is very sober and amiable," and writes in simple language that anyone can understand. "His name is William Wordsworth."[28]

Along with famous, friendly, and unknown correspondents, the little household now began to receive a trickle of unknown or unannounced visitors, which in the latter years of Wordsworth's life would swell to a procession of holiday makers who, then as now, liked to season their mountain walks and lake excursions with a visit to the poet who seemed to lift the moral dimensions of these activities to a transcendental plane. Some visitors gave clear signs of his new cultural importance. Richard ("Conversation") Sharp and Samuel Rogers came in the spring with a letter of introduction from Josiah Wedgwood.[29] Rogers (1763–1855) was the leading poet of mainstream high culture during most of Wordsworth's lifetime, somewhat the successor of Samuel Johnson in upholding conventional poetic decorum, though his gracefully descriptive verse seems soporific now. Independently wealthy and personally generous, Rogers presided over London literary culture from a beautiful mansion in Westminster. Wordsworth was careful not to bore him by insisting on his poetical theories. The friendly disposition of culture brokers like Rogers would help make his poetic revolution look respectable; it led eventually to the friendship and patronage of other influential persons, notably Sir George Beaumont, one of the founders of the National Gallery. Conversation Sharp was, as his name implies, an almost equally important acquaintance, for he was the kind of drawing-room wit who was invited to all the best parties, and whose clever repartee could make or break a poet's reputation in high society.

The steady stream of visitors made 1801 a fallow year so far as new compositions went.[30] Wordsworth rested on his laurels and enjoyed the visits, having produced so much under difficult pressures in 1800. In a kind of delayed reaction, he sometimes felt so exhausted and unwell that he thought he might have to give up poetry altogether,[31] though this was a usual symptom of his psychosomatic relation to his own poetry. But when he and

Dorothy went to visit Coleridge in April, when Coleridge had supposedly recovered from his physical illness, they found that his mental health was much worse, especially in his unhappy relations with Sara Coleridge. Dorothy saw the "radical fault" as Sara's "want of sensibility."[32] This, though true, was not Sara's fault, and coming from Dorothy, whose radical sensibility even Coleridge stood in awe of, it sounds like the observation of a superior being on an inferior species.

They gave some desultory thought to moving closer together again. William Calvert, whom Coleridge called Wordsworth's "intimate friend," proposed fixing up Windy Brow for them to live in, and adding a little laboratory to attract Humphry Davy.[33] It was a nice idea, but never very seriously pursued. It shows, though, that the idea of a small band of like-minded intellectuals was the furthest extent of their social vision in the repressive climate of England. They may or may not have known that Thelwall was still being harassed, in Manchester in July, but in July Coleridge wrote Southey an astonishing letter about taking up sinecure positions as "Negro-drivers" on the Pinney estate in the Caribbean. "Now mark my scheme!—St. Nevis is the most lovely as well as the most healthy Island in the W. Indies—Pinny's Estate is there . . . . Now between you & me I have reason to believe that not only this House is at my service, but . . . perhaps, Pinny would appoint us sine-cure Negro-drivers at a hundred a year each, or some other snug & reputable office. . . . I & my family, & you & Edith, & Wordsworth & his Sister might all go there—& make the Island more illustrious than Cos or Lesbos. . . . Wordsworth would certainly go, if I went."[34] Was he serious? Certainly he was not wholly facetious, even granting Coleridge's very long suit in that department, and it makes one wonder with what degree of moral penetration any of these astute young men regarded the base on which their cultural productions partly rested.

After their return from Keswick in late April, William invited Mary Hutchinson to come out and fix her "cypher"—her code name—on some part of what they now clearly considered their imaginative property, as her sister had already done for "Sara's Gate." This "curious but unmistakeable love letter"[35] is all the more curious because William and Dorothy had already affixed Mary's cypher on the Lake District for all England to see, on the grove above Town End, as published in the "Poems on the Naming of Places."

In May, John Wordsworth sailed on his next China voyage, his first as captain of the *Earl of Abergavenny,* having been solemnly sworn in by the East India Company's chairman with a stern official warning against engaging in illegal trade.[36] It was in anticipation of this voyage that John, pressing his own marriage suit, had assured Mary the previous December that he would be "a very *rich man.*"[37] (His friends were more emphatic: *"a rich dog."*)[38] He turned down an offer of £5,000 to buy his command, believing he'd make a profit of at least £6,000 on this trip, a 66 percent return on his investment. But the bottom had dropped out of the woolen market in China, and he lost several thousand pounds instead. He would face losses of another sort on his return in September of 1802, when he found that William had won Mary's hand in the meantime. But the family financial plan was still that he would make them all rich, and John's £9,000 investment in the voyage included over £350 from William and Dorothy.

In June, Longman reported that all but 130 copies of the second volume of the new *Lyrical Ballads* had been sold (the two volumes could be purchased separately) and called for the preparation of a third edition. In less than six months the second edition was almost sold out; this was great success. Wordsworth had bargained for the copyright to revert to him for the following (fourth) edition, which appeared in 1805. So after a trip to Scotland in September—his first—to attend the wedding of Basil Montagu,[39] he settled down in the autumn and winter of 1801–2 with renewed deliberation to extend his imaginative control over his most valuable literary property.[40] A side trip they made in Scotland, to visit James Mackintosh, the revolutionary apostate, helped prompt further changes in Wordsworth's views on the difficulties of maintaining political consistency, and played an important part in the imaginative consistency he now began to attribute to the character of the true Poet. Seeing James Losh at Newcastle on the way home also sharpened his personal memories of the "changes" that the "opinions" of all his generation had undergone in the last decade.[41]

"What Is a Poet?"

Wordsworth's changes in the texts of the poems and his reordering of their position for the new edition of 1802 do not amount to much, but his additions to the preface are of the first importance as indications of his increasingly self-conscious movement toward self-creation as "the main region" of his song. These are nine long paragraphs on the nature of the Poet which he inserted in the midst of his labored discussion of "the strict affinity of metrical language with that of prose." These additions answer his self-posed question "What is a Poet?" by, in effect, pushing the shaky literary theory of 1800 aside in favor of unarguable personal testimony, thus preparing the way—along with several significant life events—for the resumption of *The Prelude* in 1803, not as a distraction from *The Recluse* but effectively as its replacement.

Theoretically, the additions to the preface published in 1802 shift Wordsworth's poetics from a mimetic to an expressive theory of art to defend his "natural language" poetry.[42] In strictly logical terms, he substituted *himself* for the "class" of human beings on which his linguistic observations and claims are based, instead of the class of rural workers on which his arguments were founded in 1800. In short, "Wordsworth's new ideas imply that he will, in some sense, write poetry by expressing himself rather than by imitating the utterance of others."[43] At the same time he widened his metaphysical criteria for the validity of his argument, from "permanence" and "naturalness" to "general truth," thus facilitating his "replacement of the rustic by the poet as the norm of human behavior," leading to his new emphasis "on the poet as his own subject, as representative man."[44] This new emphasis had even less connection with actual poems of 1798 and 1800 than with the preface of 1800, and though its connection to the *Prelude-Recluse* project is much stronger, it remained largely speculative and invisible, given the incomplete state of those poems at this time, not to mention their nonpublic status throughout Wordsworth's life.

This is not to say, exactly, that Wordsworth had consciously changed his theory of poetry: the claims of the 1800 preface remain intact, taking up roughly the first third and the last third of the preface in its newly expanded form. The logic of his argument in 1800 was shaky enough, though rhetorically splendid, but it is not particularly strengthened by his addition of an expressive theory of poetry. It would have been, if Wordsworth had (a) given any indication that he recognized his own shift in logical ground and (b) expressed his preference for one poetic logic over the other. But he doesn't, even though such a radical shift in medias res is one of his most characteristic rhetorical habits. In fact, his expressive theory is stronger logically than his mimetic one: we can argue a good deal about the behavior and language of rural workers, but not very much about one man's self-report. However, the *appearance* that his mimetic theory was somehow founded on a body of social evidence remains desirable, for, by the same token, we can easily reject or ignore any one person's claims for himself, but it is harder to ignore the claims on our attention of an entire large class of human beings. It was not hard for most readers of poetry in 1800 to do this, however, since most of them would have considered poetry primarily as a "polite" accomplishment, and most of them would simply not have accepted Wordsworth's claim to Fox that "men who do not wear fine cloaths can feel deeply."

Hence it was to Wordsworth's advantage to keep both theories in play, whether or not he recognized their inconsistency, though his additions complicate the logical tangle of the preface immensely. Coleridge sorted out many of these inconsistencies in his chapters on *Lyrical Ballads* in *Biographia Literaria* (1817), but that book has been read even less attentively by most people than the various prefaces of *Lyrical Ballads.* The brief "Advertisement" of the first edition had avoided almost all these problems by presenting the volume as a language "experiment." What had been hypothesized in

1798 was theorized in 1800, and now retheorized for 1802. This logical tangle continued to serve in an unintended but highly effective way to keep the issues of Wordsworth's poetry and poetics alive in the public eye, since much of what he said was humanly and democratically so impressive, even though other things he said were obviously nonsense, and sometimes arrogant nonsense to boot. Wordsworth could hardly have devised a more effective strategy to keep his poems alive by "word of mouth" (a concept he would have loved) than the accumulating and contrasting logical-rhetorical levels of his various prefaces.

He was not really writing a theory of poetics as such. Rather, he was extending the logic of his own self-creation, as the hero of *The Prelude* and the bard of *The Recluse,* into the language of theory, which just happened to be a theory of language. In this respect, the additions of 1802, like the 1800 preface itself, are more metaphors than arguments, expressive of the concept of the Poet Wordsworth felt himself becoming. The additions of 1802 are much more clearly related than the 1800 preface to his rapid development in self-consciousness since 1797: the best glosses on his question "What is a Poet?" are the "Prospectus" to *The Recluse,* composed about two years earlier, or the "Conclusion" of *The Prelude,* composed about three years later.

These additions, simply as expressions of intention, are the most moving of Wordsworth's statements about himself: "a Poet . . . is a man speaking to men . . . bringing everywhere with him relationship and love." They articulate what he felt he was doing in the 1798 ballads, even as they soften the considerable extent to which his poems often bring with them alienation and despair, *not* relationship and love. And yet, considering how literal we almost always find Wordsworth to be, when we are in a position to examine the circumstances of his utterances closely, the phrase "relationship and love," for all its fine generality, can also be seen as the simple, concrete fact of his most powerful narratives. He is out on the road, and he speaks to men—and to women too, even more than to men. He talks to them about their life, about what brought them to the pass in which he now finds them.[45] He could not offer them much—Dorothy was more likely to give a penny than William—but he offered them "relationship" and, for what it is worth, "love." Not to them directly: Wordsworth was not the man to say, "I love you" or "God bless you," or "Have a nice day." But he loved them enough to make a poem of them, to empathize with their situation enough that their story is immortalized. His poems often continue on from the point where his speakers leave off, as in the case of the Female Vagrant, who "ceased, and weeping turned away, / As if because her tale was at an end / She wept;—because she had no more to say / Of that perpetual weight which on her spirit lay."

Wordsworth did not continue his man-in-the-street role very long after he settled in Grasmere; for one thing, people began to recognize him, and he was more effective in accosting strangers—as Coleridge recognized, calling him *Spectator ab extra.* Not that he was unfeeling. Rather, he was personally so strong in himself that he did not let his own reactions get in the way of attending very closely to what these people had to say. To the despair of his merely political critics, he paid less attention to the causes of their suffering than to its effects, for the effect is what they *feel:* "what afflicts my peace with keenest ruth / Is, that I have my inner self abused" ("The Female Vagrant"). As for causes, let those who can think on them: "Statesmen! ye / Who are so restless in your wisdom" ("The Old Cumberland Beggar").

Wordsworth's argumentative tone continues in the 1802 additions to the preface because he was not very clear himself about the nature and the validity of his claims. The lack of fit between his mimetic and expressive theories of the Poet shows up most glaringly when he follows his apparently friendly claim, that a poet is only a man speaking to men, with a series of qualifications that indicate, if we attend to them seriously, that this is not exactly—or even remotely—so. He says he is using the language we might expect from the Poet as "a man speaking to men," but with—"it is true"—the following list of differences: (1) a more lively sensibility, (2) more enthusiasm, (3) more tenderness, (4) greater knowledge of human nature, (5) a more comprehensive soul ("than [is] supposed to be common"), (6) more pleased with "his own passions and volitions," (7) more rejoicing "in the spirit of life that is in him," (8) who sees the same spirit "in the goings-on of the Universe," (9) or creates them "where he does not find them," (10) more affected by absent things as if they were present, (11) with greater ability to conjure up apparently real passions "than anything which, from the motions of their own minds merely, other men are accustomed to feel in themselves," (12) a "greater readiness and power in expressing what he thinks and feels," and (13) especially such thoughts and feelings as "by his own choice, or from the structure of his own mind, arise within him without immediate external excitement." By the end we are so far from the nature of rural occupations on which this purified language is supposedly based that we could say Wordsworth has reproduced a version of the philosophical conundrum known as "the ship of Theseus," wherein the constant repair and replacement of the ship's parts at some point produce a ship that is materially different from the one Theseus originally built. Wordsworth has added so much to his "man speaking to men" that he is more like a superman speaking to men. His last casual qualification—"or from the structure of his own mind"—even suggests that poets are actually born different, that genius is largely a matter of heredity.

The 1802 additions are Wordsworth's "glorious affirmation" of his "sublime and comprehensive credo" of the role of the Poet.[46] The social role of the Poet in the eighteenth century—didactic, moral, and sentimental in various combinations—was being threatened, petering out in anti-Jacobin satire and Sunday school religious sentiment, as social problems began to mount up far beyond what poets as gentleman clerics, or London attorneys, or Grub Street hacks, or Oxbridge scholars could offer their educated readers. Wordsworth went deeper, though with no very clear program of action, to insist that all these people were human beings before they were the parish poor, or God's children, or the working class. "Bringing everywhere with him relationship and love," he could bring with him only the relationship of one human being to another: "The rock of defense of human nature." That is why these additions sound so much like Scripture.

Reviewers, who are trained by profession to look for points of weakness, did not have any trouble finding them in the third edition of *Lyrical Ballads,* with its ever-larger red flag of a preface waving in their faces. This, plus the thoroughly politicized nature of magazine reviewing at the time, guaranteed that the book would be set up as a free-standing target. The *Anti-Jacobin* had specifically singled out "Coleridge . . . & Co." in 1798, and written a series of prefaces of its own on the true nature of poetry. Knowing full well that Coleridge was the "Friend" referred to in the *Lyrical Ballads* preface and that Wordsworth was his "Co.," William Gifford, who in 1802 moved on from the *Anti-Jacobin* to become the first editor of the phenomenally successful *Edinburgh Review,* charged his new bulldog, Francis Jeffrey, to keep up the attack on them. Jeffrey used the same phrase, only now recasting it as "Wirdsworth [*sic*] & Co." and associating it directly with "the laudable exertions of Mr. Thomas Paine to bring disaffection and infidelity within the comprehension of the common people."[47] Besides confirming that Wordsworth's political identity was well known to London's reviewing coteries in 1797–98, the shift in the phrase from Coleridge to Wordsworth also reflected the literary world's knowledge as to who was now "in company" with whom.

It was lucky, in this respect, that the poets had moved to the Lake District, for otherwise they would surely have continued to be belittled as "Jacobin" poets rather than as "Lake Poets," and would have been considered, and perhaps totally humiliated, like the "Jacobin" novelists of the era, who have until very recently been effectively erased from the cultural map of the times—names like Godwin, Bage, Thelwall, and Hays. Wordsworth and Coleridge would as surely have been cast as the founders of the "Jacobin school" of poets as Shelley and Byron became the "Satanic school" and Keats and Leigh Hunt the "Cockney school." Calling them the "Lake school" or "Lakers" was in its day a provincial put-down. But its pejorative quality gradually wore off—in no small part because Wordsworth *was* able to create the taste by which he was to be appreciated—so that today the phrase has become not only honorific but even inaccurate and misleading, by identifying the spirit of Wordsworth's poetry with its apparent place of origin.

32 PEACE, MARRIAGE, INHERITANCE

> There was a time when meadow, grove, and stream,
> The earth, and every common sight,
> To me did seem
> Apparelled in celestial light,
> The glory and the freshness of a dream.
> It is not now as it hath been of yore;—
> Turn wheresoe'er I may,
> By night or day,
> The things which I have seen I now can see no more.
> ("Ode: Intimations of Immortality," Spring 1802)

In the early fall of 1801 came news that transformed Wordsworth's life, so much that a year later he looked like a different man. The two major obstacles that lay between him and his full adult regeneration—ability to provide for a mate and freedom from previous emotional commitments—were removed within months of each other. Shortly after October 1 newspapers reported that preliminary agreement for a truce had been reached at Amiens, concluding an effort that the British government had secretly been pursuing for five years. The process had been dangerously interrupted by the assassinations at Rastatt in 1799, and was now concluded on terms far less advantageous to England, because of Napoleon's successes in the meantime. Although the terms were so undesirable that the Peace of Amiens ended in less than a year, it was time enough for Wordsworth to set his life in order.

The peace was not officially signed until March 27, 1802, but its terms were clear in October, and they included reopening France to travel by private persons. William could see Annette again. In February, Dorothy began to refer in her journal to letters to and from a mysterious "Frenchman in London," probably an agent for their trip, and another indication of Wordsworth's confidential contacts with France.[1] It is not altogether clear why they would need an agent, but it may have been because Annette, alias "the Widow Williams," was under surveillance by Napoleon's secret police. The depth and importance of Wordsworth's attachment to Annette for every aspect of his life between 1793 and 1801, no matter how invisible it seems at times, is evident from the alacrity with which he moved to resolve it now. Letters now crossed freely between Grasmere and Blois—letters subsequently destroyed, not lost or confiscated—and four months after the peace was signed, William and Dorothy were in Calais, where they spent the entire month of August with Annette and Caroline.

A sense of deep personal relief suffuses Wordsworth's writing in the winter of 1801–2, bolstering his confidence in the ideal of the Poet he celebrated in his additions to the preface of *Lyrical Ballads.* In December he began three new activities, all crucial steps toward the final creation of the Poet—or rather, crucial missteps. He reread "The Ruined Cottage" with a view toward finishing it; he began a rapid course of reading and "translating" Chaucer; and, on the day after Christmas, he made a brief stab at extending *The Prelude.*[2] Each of these actions, in the context of his additions to the preface, show his growing consciousness that *he* was the Poet he was talking about and that his creation of that Poet was as important and as difficult as stating what his poems could do for mankind.

His brief start on *The Prelude* was the least important of these three actions, for it still seemed like a distraction from his main work at hand. In lines that correspond roughly to the first two hundred lines of the present Book III ("Residence at Cambridge"), he started describing his university experience. But only half of them say anything about Cambridge. Instead, he soon fell back into defending the relevance of his subject, repeating a sequence he had been through three times in the last two years: at the conclusion of the 1799 *Prelude,* in the "Prospectus" lines of *The Recluse* (1800), and, most recently, in his additions to the preface. Once again, he felt he had to reassure Coleridge that he was speaking "of genius, power, / Creation, and divinity itself . . . *for* my theme has been / What passed within me" (III.171–74; italics added). The explanatory weight on the little conjunction "for" is as great as that carried by his casual admission in the preface that, "it is true," the Poet was a bit different from other men. There it entailed a dozen qualifications that removed his "man speaking to men" far beyond other men; here, in just four words, he accelerates from genius to divinity. Once we grant his explanation, the rest of his defense carries the field: "This is in truth heroic argument." But what exactly *was* the argument? Here his brief restart on *The Prelude* faltered: "I wished to touch [this argument], / With hand however weak—but in the main / It lies far hidden from the reach of words."

Reading and translating Chaucer was intended as therapy for the mighty poetic issues he was grappling with. Yet Wordsworth did nothing lightly, and when it came to poetry, every issue was an ultimate one. His modernizations of Chaucer's *Canterbury Tales* are quite good; some were published in the

1820s and 1840s. In the economy of Wordsworth's creative development, Chaucer was the only one remaining of the big four in English literature whom he had not confronted, challenged, and tried to make his own. He had thoroughly assimilated the languages of Shakespeare and Spenser (that is, he had mastered them without being overmastered by them), and Milton's language, mythos, and career were the pattern of his own. Chaucer seemed an easier challenge because he was still regarded as a coarse comic author writing in a "primitive" or underdeveloped form of English. The result was not very important in terms of poetic product, but in terms of Wordsworth's poetic process of creating the Poet, this winter fireside pastime was very much of a piece with his reviving efforts to make good on the self-advertisements he had just added to the preface to *Lyrical Ballads,* his one effective public venue. Chaucer had already been drafted into Wordsworth's project in the 1800 preface: "the affecting parts of Chaucer are almost always in language pure and universally intelligible even to this day." This is an overstatement, though not without some truth, and Wordsworth's "translations" can be seen as his effort to bring this "morning star" of English literature into line with his own revaluations of it.

The effort was not purely literary, however: the first tales he and Dorothy chose to read were those associated with the "Marriage Group," reflecting their current preoccupations: by the end of February their closest friends knew that marriage was impending between him and Mary Hutchinson.[3] William and Dorothy started with the perennial first choice of first-time readers of any age, the bawdy "Miller's Tale," a version of which had been de rigueur in Wordsworth's informal Cambridge education. None of these marriage tales were, however, among the ones he eventually published.

By far the most difficult of his three writing efforts this winter was his attempt to bring "The Ruined Cottage" to a satisfactory conclusion, and it was by far the least successful. Beginning in late December and for the next two months, Dorothy's journal records one painful episode after another of William's attempt to make progress on the poem, the same poem that had been the catalyst, in the winter of 1797–98, of his emergence into poetic manhood. Now it gave him headaches, upset stomachs, and bad nights of sleep, all of which she, faithful companion and copyist, fully participated in. Several times they were both reduced to tears, once from reading Book XI of *Paradise Lost* (Adam and Eve's realization that they must leave Paradise) after a particularly unproductive day. Their tears flowed not simply for Milton's grandeur, or for the discrepancy between Milton's achievement and his own (though such comparisons were never far from Wordsworth's mind), but because Milton had succeeded so powerfully in writing the definitive religious version of the story Wordsworth was trying to retell in modern, secular terms.

Almost all the signs of Margaret's decline in "The Ruined Cottage" are presented in terms of her garden: if Wordsworth had called his poem "The Ruined Garden," its intention as a humanistic tale of fall and redemption would stand starkly revealed. Now the hopeless tragedy of Margaret's abandonment resonated again with his renewed consciousness of Annette's long "unquiet widowhood" as both "Wife and Widow," as it had in the poem's first creation five years earlier. Sometimes his revisions seemed good, especially of the first part (mainly Margaret's story), but on a second reading they would appear uninteresting: the ratio of bad days to good on this project was about ten to one. On February 28 Dorothy recorded, "Disaster Pedlar," and within a week all further work on it came to a halt.[4] Finally, William instructed her to hide all the manuscripts and to keep them from him even if he asked for them, like an addict determined to break his habit.[5] His need to create *The Recluse* was a powerful stimulant, but at the same time it was a dangerous substance that threatened to destroy him. A large measure of Wordsworth's extreme toughness is revealed in this gesture of self-denial.

Turning to "The Ruined Cottage" was exactly the right thing for him to do at this juncture in his development: having reaffirmed the quasi-divine stature of the Poet in his additions to the preface, it was time to produce the Poem. The problem was that he still could not create a narrator of healing power commensurate with the terrible tale of Margaret's suffering. Not the facts of Margaret's life, but they way they were framed, presented, *and received* was his new concern, if the Poet was indeed to be "a man speaking to men . . . bringing everywhere with him relationship and love." The change in his focus is clearly signaled by his change of title to "The Pedlar": the Pedlar brought those qualities with him, but they did no good to Margaret; hence they must be transferred to whoever *heard* the tale of Margaret, in this case, the young wandering narrator of the whole poem, whose name (or title) would be "The Poet," when the much revised poem was finally published as Book I of *The Excursion.* Like *The Prelude,* "The Pedlar" is the story of the creation of a Poet, by an initiating figure whose authority comes not from education (Nurture) but from Nature. The Pedlar is a shepherd boy who has made good, a Luke who left home but became a prodigal of wisdom, not of shame.

But Wordsworth could not bring it off, though his manuscripts show clearly enough the kind of figure he intended. They also show, by their incorporation of whole sections of the 1799 *Prelude,* that this figure is not an old Scots peddler but someone else from the north of England with a wider education and a wider range of traveling experience: the Poet, himself.

Instructing Dorothy to hide the manuscripts, Wordsworth soon rebounded from his impasse. Within a few days of the Pedlar "disaster," he began composing a long series of short poems, over thirty in all, that kept him active through the end of July.[6] The story of Wordsworth's renascence in the spring of 1802, as amazing in its way as that of spring 1798, is intimately bound up with his latest failure on *The Recluse,* in combination with his decision to get married. This is usually the man's decision, and certainly was so in the early 1800s, and once again in Wordsworth's romantic history it had been influenced by the decisions of two other men whose actions often crossed and marked his self-creation, William Pitt and Napoleon Bonaparte.

Two days after "The Pedlar" was put to rest for its long sleep, Wordsworth began composing "The Sailor's Mother"; he finished it the next day. This became the new pattern in Dorothy's journal for the next four months: start a poem one day, finish it the next, or very shortly thereafter. The difference from her painful series of "Pedlar" entries could not be more pronounced. Pushing aside *The Recluse* and starting to plan for his marriage, Wordsworth's poetic confidence was reinforced by strong feelings from every level of his life: personal, financial, and national. A forthcoming settlement of the Lowther estate intensified what was already a time of very good feeling by adding the prospect of a second settlement to that of the first—for of course Mary's dowry would include her own substantial inheritance.

This happiness is clearly reflected in the lyrics he composed this spring, some of which are among his most popular, though not his best or most characteristic work. They are Wordsworth's easy pieces, poems about butterflies and robins, daisies and celandines. If not quite as simple as they seem—their author being, after all, Wordsworth—they are certainly much easier than the poems of either of the two earlier springs (1800 and 1798) when he had also trained his large imagination on small subjects. They have little burden of trouble: neither the social problems, *Recluse* burdens and money-raising pressures of 1798, nor the unhappy recognitions of 1800 that his accommodation to Grasmere was not going to be as easy as he had expected. If the lyrics of 1800 move the human tragedies of 1798 onto the smaller stage of Grasmere, those of 1802 transpose the human problems of 1800 into moralistic symbolisms of plants and animals—a direction already apparent in "The Waterfall and the Eglantine" and "The Oak and the Broom," and now pursued further.

At least this is how they appear when read separately. In the thick texture of Wordsworth's life and other writings of the time, their simple optimism is considerably qualified. He began with a few more ballads in his original vein of 1798, like "The Sailor's Mother" and "Beggars," but these are almost the last we see of such characters in his poetry, except for brief cameo appearances in *The Prelude.* Some of them are only nominally lyrical ballads. "Alice Fell; or, Poverty" is a sentimental Good Samaritan story, written to order at the request of a Scotch friend of the humanitarian Thomas Clarkson, about a little orphan girl who wept inconsolably for the loss of her cloak when it got caught in a coach wheel. The narrator gives money to the innkeeper at the next stop for a new cloak " 'of duffil [*sic*] grey, / As warm a cloak as any man can sell!' " In our last sight of little Alice, all her troubles are apparently over: "Proud creature was she the next day, / The little orphan, Alice Fell!" What the poem tells us about the subject of its subtitle is that the woes of poverty are pretty easily overcome. In 1798 the little girl would not have been so easily placated, but might, like her soul sister of "We Are Seven," have insisted that no cloak could ever replace the one she had lost, the last of her family possessions, literally the last remnant of her family. "The Tinker" is another ruddy celebration of the dirty but hardworking underclass: "Who leads a happy life / If it's not the happy Tinker?" The tinker is fortunately fully employed, yet the poem ends by suggesting that he is strong beyond all material circumstance: "Laughing, laughing, laughing, / As if he would laugh himself dead. / And thus, with work or none, / The Tinker lives in fun." Any irony lurking in the second line has to be supplied by the reader—a reader of the 1798 *Lyrical Ballads,* for example.

Wordsworth soon turned from this small cast of poor people to a large number of natural objects—birds and butterflies, flowers and trees—from which many readers of many anthologies have formed their idea of a comfortable Wordsworth. There are nearly two dozen poems like "To a Cuckoo," "To a Butterfly," and "To the Daisy," in which the connection between external nature and human nature is presented in the most uncomplicated manner imaginable. But complications appear when we look more closely and compare them with Wordsworth's other contemporaneous work. Not that there's anything fundamentally wrong with such simple equations between natural beauty and human happiness, which we may all feel at any time.

For Wordsworth these simple equations were very hard to maintain, because his mind was evidently filled with feelings of a quite opposite nature. In all of them, he says, more or less, Yes, daisy [robin, linnet, cuckoo, etc.], there you are in your simple beauty, and I will be like you. Or, in his own words, "We meet thee [daisy], like a pleasant thought, / When such are wanted." But even a throwaway like that last one opens up a crack like those in W. H. Auden's teacups, "that lead to the land of the dead."[7] Pleasant thoughts are sometimes very badly wanted, and may be very hard to come by. Some of these poems give lyric expression to the sense of wonder Wordsworth had put in a much higher key in "Home at Grasmere" and the "Prospectus" to *The Recluse.*[8] At least they try to: the celandine is called the "Herald of a mighty band, / Of a joyous train ensuing." But even this

"Prophet of delight and mirth" is "Ill-requited upon earth." In "To the Cuckoo" the note of an insistent yet unspoken need sounds a bit more loudly: "Even yet thou are to me . . . The same whom in my schoolboy days / I listened to . . . And I can listen to thee yet . . . till I do beget / That golden time again." The poems as a group might be called conversational transcendentalism, a mode that Wordsworth soon began to elaborate into the full-blown philosophical Idealism of his next stage of development.

Despite the happy surface of these poems, his specifically poetic problem of 1802 was actually far worse than that of 1798 and 1800. It concerned not his attitude toward the suffering poor but the status of his own imagination. In 1798 and 1800 he could turn almost anything into a strong poem, but in 1802 his capacity for invention, no stronger than ever, fell mainly on flowers, birds, and insects, and the results were not nearly as impressive. This is evident less in individual poems than in the gap between two very different kinds of poetry he was writing. For the happy lyrics of 1802 are counterbalanced—indeed almost negated—by two poems, both of which were begun, but neither of which could be finished, at this time: "Resolution and Independence" (known first as "The Leech-Gatherer") and the first four stanzas of what became the Intimations Ode. In them we hear indeed the voice of the *Recluse* bard, a bard very much worried about his staying power.

In "The Leech-Gatherer" the problem is specifically Wordsworth's lack of confidence in himself as a poet, his deep awareness of the difficulty he faced in maintaining the role of the Poet which he had now fully articulated publicly. The creatures of the other spring lyrics are there in plenty: the stock dove, the magpie, and the blue jay. But though "all things that love the sun are out of doors," and he tries to be with them, he cannot do it:

> But, as it sometimes chanceth, from the might
> Of joy in minds that can no further go,
> As high as we have mounted in delight
> In our dejection do we sink as low;
> To me that morning did it happen so . . . .
>
> (22–26)

These mood swings are soon generalized as a vocational crisis: "We Poets in our youth begin in gladness; / But thereof come in the end despondency and madness." "Madness" is a hard word here, but even harder is the mild-looking conjunction "thereof": his gifts are the very source of his present despondency.

William and Dorothy had met the leech gatherer in Town End in October of 1800. His actual story was considerably worse than that in the poem, for he no longer gathered leeches at all but lived by begging, "and was making his way to Carlisle, where he should buy a few godly books to sell." His wife and ten children were all dead, except "one, of whom he had not heard for many years, a sailor." Of this hopeless character Wordsworth makes a stronger one, who still goes about on his "employment hazardous and wearisome," but "with God's good help, by choice or chance . . . in this way he gained an honest maintenance." However, Wordsworth made him strong not, as in "The Tinker" or "Alice Fell," in order to present a more hopeful picture of poverty in England but in order that *he* could take sustenance from the old man's perseverance:

I could have laughed myself to scorn to find
In that decrepit Man so firm a mind.
"God," said I, "be my help and stay secure;
I'll think of the Leech-gatherer on the lonely moor!"
(137–40)

"Resolution and Independence" is a poem about the mental qualities named in its title as necessary ingredients in the character of a major poet, one who would avoid not only the excesses of a Chatterton or a Burns but also the irresponsibility of a Coleridge: "how can He expect that others should / Build for him, sow for him, and at his call / Love him, who for himself will take no heed at all?" These lines reflect the attitude toward Coleridge's behavior that was beginning to form, and harden, in the new household at Grasmere. "The Leech-Gatherer" faces up to the problem of imaginative loss in a stronger way than Coleridge's contemporaneous "Dejection: An Ode,"[9] but Wordsworth's poem was written in the knowledge of his impending marriage and the resolution of his failed past romantic history, whereas Coleridge's was written in the certainty of his marriage's disaster and the heartbreaking knowledge that his desired independence from it would never come. As they moved from young manhood into mature adulthood and assumed the responsibilities of marriage, household, and livelihood, the first phase of their Romanticism came to an end.

The same desperate search for assurance is evident in the first four stanzas of the other major poem Wordsworth began that spring, where it is totally undercut by his certain *lack* of assurance.

There was a time when meadow, grove, and stream,
The earth, and every common sight,
    To me did seem
    Apparelled in celestial light,
The glory and the freshness of a dream.

So far, so good. But there is no begetting such "golden times" again, as he had insisted to the cuckoo:

Town End, by T.M. Richardson

Dove Cottage is on the right.

Georgiana Cavendish, the Duchess of Devonshire, engraving by Bartolozzi after the portrait by Downman (published 1788)

Mary [Robinson] of Buttermere, by James Gillray (published July, 1800)

Samuel Taylor Coleridge, by James Northcote (1804)

Thomas De Quincey, by John Watson Gordon

Walter Scott, from portrait by Henry Raeburn

Mr. John Wordsworth

Sara Hutchinson

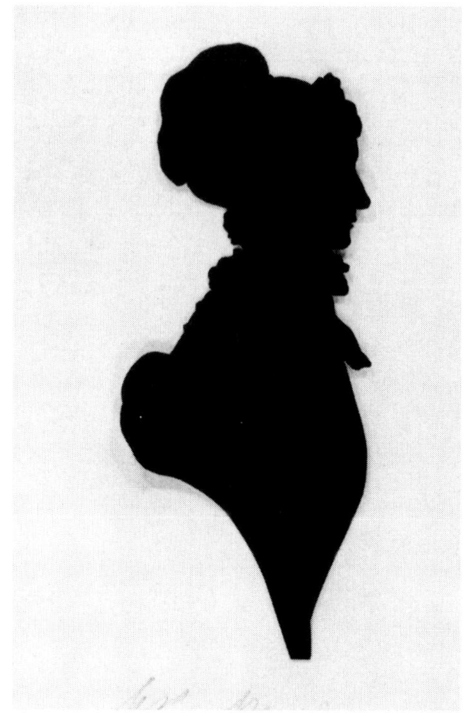

Mary Hutchinson Wordsworth

It is not now as it hath been of yore;—
Turn wheresoe'er I may,
By night or day,
The things which I have seen I now can see no more.

These are of course the opening lines of the great ode "Intimations of Immortality from Recollections of Early Childhood." But in 1802 it was Wordsworth's ode to mortality, not immortality, like Coleridge's companion crisis poem, "Dejection," and it arose from the same source: recollections of early childhood which Wordsworth realized he had irrevocably lost. Try as he will, through four desperate stanzas, he cannot keep his faith. The last of them begins, "Ye blessèd Creatures, I have heard the call / Ye to each other make; . . . The fulness of your bliss, I feel—I feel it all." But it ends, "Whither is fled the visionary gleam? / Where is it now, the glory and the dream?" He did not know, what we always already know from literary history when we sit down to read this poem (which by his order is supposed to stand last in every collection of his verse), that he would finish the poem two years later with seven somber stanzas, based on the ancient myth of the preexistence of the soul, that manage to take comfort from the sheer fact of loss. That is, he did not lay the first four stanzas aside saying to himself, I'll finish this later with a more upbeat ending. No, he abandoned them in despair. Nor are these four stanzas fragmentary; they make a complete statement that begins very much like the other lyrics of this spring. But they end where none of the rest dared tread, with the sense of imaginative death, brought on by the joys of impending marriage and full adult establishment, yet darkly shadowed by his continuing sense of failure on *The Recluse,* his own challenge to his achieving full poetical maturity.

Compared with the smaller, finished lyrics of that spring, the first version of "Resolution and Independence" and the stanzas of the ode constitute a terrible self-critique: the same person could not hold both views simultaneously. But in an unpublished manuscript Wordsworth tried to do just that. Composed before April 22, this fragment is as important to his imaginative character as "Away, away" and "Nutting" are to understanding his sexual nature. Both turn on the image of being buried alive, and in both the possibility is as much a tempting release as a threatened horror.

These Chairs they have no words to utter,
No fire is in the grate to stir or flutter,
The ceiling and the floor are mute as stone,
My chamber is hushed and still,
And I am alone,
Happy and alone.

Oh who would be afraid of life,
The passion the sorrow and the strife,
    When he may be
    Sheltered so easily?
May lie in peace on his bed
Happy as they who are dead.

At this point Wordsworth drew a line across his paper, and began again with the notation "Half an hour afterwards." But though the next two stanzas seem, like the last seven of the Intimations Ode, to answer the problem of the first two stanzas, these two states coexist, or codepend, in Wordsworth's soul, and the conditions of the solution he described are not all that different from those of his problem:

I have thoughts that are fed by the sun.
    The things which I see
    Are welcome to me,
    Welcome to every one:
I do not wish to lie
    Dead, dead,
Dead without any company;
    Here alone on my bed,
With thoughts that are fed by the Sun,
And hopes that are welcome every one,
    Happy am I.

O Life, there is about thee
A deep delicious peace,
I would not be without thee,
    Stay, oh stay!
Yet be thou ever as now,
Sweetness and breath with the quiet of death,
Be but thou ever as now,
    Peace, peace, peace.[10]

If people left notes saying why they had decided *not* to commit suicide lying next to the suicide note of their original impulse, we could say that Wordsworth's fragment combines both macabre genres. Nor is this a fragment in the sense of being an incomplete utterance; it is as complete and well rounded as the four stanzas of the ode or his "Argument for Suicide" six years earlier. The genre of the suicide note is a constant leitmotif in his movement toward becoming the master Poet of life and natural affirmation, the ultimate dejection beneath his various odes to immortality.

A week later he and Dorothy re-created the mise-en-scène of this poem.

They climbed up into John's Grove and lay down next to each other in adjoining trenches, imagining they were lying in their graves. The singularity of this behavior is not lessened by our knowledge that they had often done it before. It seems to have been a form of therapy for subduing their strong erotic attraction to each other. In January, the day after Mary left following her Christmas visit—no time for lying outdoors in trenches—a similar complex of feelings had come over them. They read *Descriptive Sketches,* talked of Lake Como, and thought of Mary.[11] That Wordsworth's youthful erotic experiences on his walking tour should come back to mind—nay, be purposely brought back by reading that part of the poem—shows not only their train of thought but also their frank honesty with each other about their feelings. The coming joys of 1802 were all the more intense for the deep emotions of a quite different sort that had to be kept down.

These contradictory emotions are apparent in poems and letters concerned with the coming happy event itself. On April 25, 1802, two days after his thirty-second birthday, he began "A Farewell," which Dorothy referred to in her journal as "On Going for Mary"; he worked on it for the next two months before getting it right (it was not published until 1815).[12] His difficulties with the poem are significant, for it is apparently a simple piece, merely telling their garden to look after itself while they are gone. As a farewell, it is addressed more to Dorothy than to Annette: the renunciation of the sister had, after ten years, become harder than renouncing the lover. It marks the departure from *their* Grasmere as decisively as "Home at Grasmere" had marked their arrival two springs before.[13] Their garden "nook" is addressed as a child—"Nature's child indeed"—who is being prepared for the new mother coming to take care of her, as if she were the offspring of an earlier marriage. This new mother will not replace her old mother, but will rather be added to the two parents the little garden/child has known so far, who are designated by the poem's consistently first-person plural voice: "*We* go for One to whom ye will be dear." Wordsworth makes only one slip from this plural form of address, and it is a revealing one: "And in this bush our sparrow built her nest, / Of which *I* sang one song that will not die" (55–56). His high valuation of "The Sparrow's Nest" is noteworthy because that poem is less about a sparrow than about Dorothy, and it is not about their Grasmere garden at all but about their Cockermouth one, and about Dorothy's tenderly calming William's passionate nature:

> She gave me eyes, she gave me ears;
> And humble cares, and delicate fears;
> A heart, the fountain of sweet tears;
> And love, and thought, and joy.
> ("The Sparrow's Nest," 17–20)

This was a deeply buried personal allusion that Dorothy knew all about, but Mary would have to learn: "Help us to tell Her tales of years gone by."

The garden would also have to help them with another task, odder yet as an expression of the emotions of a couple returning from their honeymoon: "Joy will be flown in its mortality; / Something must stay to tell us of the rest." If Mary was reassured that he was giving up Annette, whom she had long known about, she was also being clearly given to understand that he was *not* giving up Dorothy. Twice during the spring Dorothy emphatically put down any suggestion that they might leave Grasmere, no matter how cramped, for Gallow Hill, no matter how spacious.[14] On June 17 Dorothy came home and "found William at work attempting to alter a stanza [the first or the fifth] in the poem on our going for Mary, which I convinced him did not need altering." William ruefully acknowledged that there were several parts of the poem that "neither D. nor C. [Coleridge] understand."[15] The little poem's ostensible subject, their garden, is heavily overdetermined by its real one, the realignment of erotic allegiances. When it at last seemed finished, Dorothy wrote the following carefully indented list on the blotter page of her journal:

Dorothy Wordsworth
William Wordsworth
    Mary Wordsworth
        May 29th 6 O clock
Sitting at small table by window
    Grasmere 1802[16]

The day after William began writing "A Farewell," Dorothy read Shakespeare's "The Lover's Complaint" to him in bed. This was no accidental choice. It is the lament of an abandoned woman, heard from "the concave womb" of "a sist'ring vale" by "a reverend man" who has known the "bluster" of the city and retired to the country. The woman tried to keep her honor safe from a young man who was the magnet of all maidens' eyes and vows, but she fell prey to his special talent with words and arguments: "He had the dialect and different skill, / Catching all passions in his craft of will."[17] His especially fiendish talent was to use the language of virtue in order to pervert it: "He preach'd pure maid, and prais'd cold chastity." This might well have been Dorothy's reaction to "Nutting." The young man's special ploy, which finally overthrows the young woman's scruples, is his claim that he has received pledges of love from "a sacred nun, or sister sanctified," and that he says his resistance to these extreme pleas is the mirror-image of the woman's power over him: "I strong o'er them, and you o'er me being strong." She could not "scape the hail of his all-hurting aim," and so she fell, knowing miserably that she'd do it all over again, though he "Would yet again betray the fore-betray'd, / And new pervert a reconciled maid!" The sisterly diction throughout the poem, the references to a nun's broken vows, and the emphasis on the lover's verbal skills—all of these resonate powerfully with Dorothy's and William's feelings as they contemplated the breakup of their intense domestic relations. It is remarkable that Dorothy should seek out this little-known Shakespeare poem to read at this painful juncture in their lives. Like their rereading of the Lake Como sections of *Descriptive Sketches,* it was a searing antidote to their deeply shared pains.

The unpublished poem called "Travelling" was composed at about this same time. Its complicated connections with the full form of "Nutting" written in Germany three years earlier (Chapter 26) show how much the memory of their former intimacy now rose up to test their resolve for the coming new departures in their life. On the night of May 4 Dorothy repeated its opening words, "This is the spot," "over and over again" to William "while he was in bed."[18]

The whole time was fraught with powerful, tender emotions passing between the two households. Dorothy thanked Mary for a "sweet letter" addressed to a vague but debilitating illness she was suffering: "a kind of stupefaction and headache . . . a feeling of something that has been amiss."[19] She also informed Mary, "You must know that we have changed rooms, my regular sleeping bed is [now] William's, I make John's my sick bed." She averts to still-deeper emotions: "I *could* write far, *far,* more, but William says it does me no good."[20]

In the midst of all this emotional turmoil, on May 24, another seemingly intractable life problem suddenly loosened and fell into the solutions column. Sir James Lowther died, widely unlamented, of "a mortification of the bowels," and his creditors, the Wordsworths among them, began lining up to present their claims on his estate. They had some anticipation of the event, which entered into their wedding plans, for it was widely known that Sir James had "for many years . . . been in a precarious state of health."[21] His successor was a very distant cousin (he had no children), William Lowther, a much more decent man, who soon advertised his wish to honor all just claims on the estate.

In October, Brother Richard presented the new viscount (the earldom was discontinued) his family's claim for £10,388 6s. 8d., an enormous amount in terms of the economy that William and Dorothy had been maintaining for seven years.[22] Richard, true to the bookkeeping exactitude of the whole Wordsworth clan, had included in his claim the interest for twenty years of nonpayment on an original debt of £4,660 4s. 10d.[23] But William insisted that they drop the claim for interest and take a less legalistic, more conciliatory tack. This fit better William Lowther's clear statement of intentions, advertised in the *Cumberland Pacquet* and other regional newspapers, that he would not pay the interest on his predecessor's debts unless "compelled thereto by *Law.*" William recommended that they appeal "to Lord Lowther's Honour and Conscientiousness," adding, "It would be proper to state the utter destitution of my Sister on account of the affair."[24] He did not scruple to suggest that they appeal for help and influence to "some of my Uncle Wm's [Cookson's] Friends," such as Wilberforce, or Christopher's new connections in the Church of England hierarchy, such as the bishop of Norwich, though most of these people cared little for—as they saw it—his self-created problems.[25]

Wordsworth's behavior resembles his eagerness when Raisley Calvert's estate fell in his way, on the slim proceeds of which he and Dorothy had been living for seven years.* He would rather be sure of some of the money than press for more and risk losing it all. He had dared to press Calvert for more, but this was over ten times as much, and besides Lowther was an aristocrat, not the sickly younger son of an aristocrat's steward, and William had learned his lesson when it came to dealing with aristocrats' justice: "What success was a poor man ever known to have against a very rich one in a Law suit?" A very similar statement had been part of his unpublished protest to the bishop of Llandaff ten years earlier, but he was no longer in a position to protest the social order: he needed its benefits to support his wife and family. Richard's claim to the interest was just, but William's preferred approach won out, very likely because he and Dorothy, taken as a unit, needed their shares much more badly than Richard, John, or Christopher needed his. A compromise amount of about £8,000 was duly paid in early 1803. William's greater need was further pointed up in family terms by the will of John Robinson, who also died in 1802. Robinson, long the Wordsworth boys' protector, provided something for Christopher and John, but he left not a penny to William, who had ten years earlier so boldly and foolishly rejected Robinson's offers and advice about Cambridge and the church.

Wordsworth's nervous anxieties about his upcoming separation, marriage, and inheritance intensified his agitation about his soon-to-appear additions to the *Lyrical Ballads* preface; the last batch of copy—very likely final drafts of the "What is a Poet?" additions—had been sent off by early April.[26] Longman advertised the new edition sparingly: only two advertisements have been found between January and June 1802. But Wordsworth again got

*He probably composed his sonnet "To the Memory of Raisley Calvert" at about this time, as if belatedly recalling to whom he "owed many years of early liberty." Though the sonnet begins, "Calvert!," more than half of it is devoted to the "name" of the speaker, and "the lays / Of higher mood, which I now meditate" (*PW,* 3:20). Hayden gives May 21, 1802, as the earliest possible date of this sonnet, which suggests that Wordsworth wrote it when he learned that Lowther's end was near.

a steady stream of free publicity in Stuart's *Morning Post,* which printed nine poems from the second edition between January and August, almost all including statements about the volume's title or the author's name. (From the beginning of February he had begun for the first time to make contributions to the *Morning Post* in his own name, no longer passing off unwanted poems to Coleridge for his use.) Many of the poems printed by Stuart were subsequently picked up for reprinting by the influential *Lady's Magazine,* which had a circulation of almost 10,000.[27] The printed volumes duly arrived at Dove Cottage in mid-June.[28]

On July 9 they departed for what could be conceived of as the opposite of a wedding trip, a trip of divorcement.[29] They went via Gallow Hill and spent ten days at the end of the month with Mary before proceeding to France, discussing what they should say to Annette. They arrived in London on July 29; three days later they were in France. Their only pause was a memorable one, looking back at the city as they crossed Westminster Bridge at six o'clock in the morning en route to Dover. Dorothy's journal entry on it contains almost all the details of William's famous sonnet on it, completed after their return. "All that mighty heart [was] lying still!"—quite in contrast to their own hearts' condition, but the force of contrast was again for Wordsworth the impulse to creative composition. They arrived on August 1 at Calais, where by previous arrangement they met Annette and Caroline at the lodging house of Mme Avril in the rue de la Tête d'Or, where they stayed for the next month.[30]

Of their visit to Calais, we know almost nothing. The sum total of Dorothy's journal for the whole trip is two pages, almost wholly concerned with the beautiful sunsets they saw as they walked on the beach. There is not a word describing either Annette or Caroline (though both are named), except for Caroline's reaction ("delighted") to seeing "the fiery track" of boats' wakes on calm hot nights. But description was hardly necessary; three of the four principals in the affair were together, walking the beach day after day, saying and resaying what had to be said. The Wordsworths presented a rather shabby appearance to Annette, coming out of rural retirement in their mended country attire, while she was more vibrant than ever, an active counterrevolutionary with a lengthening police record for harboring priests and other royalists.[31] They met in Calais and stayed in Calais; this was not a vacation trip, and nobody stays in Calais in August, not even Calaisians if they can help it. Thousands of English travelers, Charles Fox foremost among them, were flocking through the town en route to Paris, to see the city that had effectively been cut off from London for almost ten years, revolutionized and republicanized in the interim, and soon to be imperialized.

Wordsworth's sense of déjà vu was pounding in his head as he compared coming to Calais in August 1802 with his arrival there twelve years earlier, on July 13, 1790. In a sonnet written on the road to Ardres (ten miles inland) on August 7, he recalled the joy that he and Jones had seen on that "too-credulous day," the first Fête de la Fédération, when "from hour to hour the antiquated Earth / Beat like the heart of Man." But now, "sole register that these things were," he heard two solitary greetings: " *'Good morrow, Citizen!'* a hollow word, / As if a dead man spake it!" He says he did not "despair," but the sonnet ends with an image that exposes a strong sense of vulnerability: it was a warm August, but he felt "pensive as a bird / Whose vernal coverts winter hath laid bare." Was he thinking of that image of a pair of birds weathering the autumns storms on the Channel that provides one of our metaphoric scraps of evidence for his 1793 trip to France?

Instead of biographical revelation, his Calais sonnets manifest another form of Wordsworthian displacement, which is only a fancy term for his profound need to recollect his emotions in tranquillity. Now, instead of displacing the political into the personal as he usually did, he reversed the process and pushed the personal into the political. This was just the opposite of what Annette had done with her life, accepting her status as "Widow Williams" and throwing herself into underground resistance on behalf of God, king, and country. But what could William say about Annette that he could publish? Caroline was another matter, as he saw her running, "surprised by Joy, impatient as the wind." Little girls running on beaches need no explanation; thousands of readers of this sonnet have silently assumed Wordsworth is talking about his legitimate English daughter (Dora, born 1804), not realizing it is his illegitimate French one. Wordsworth was a great ventriloquist: he had to throw his voice through other persons; he could not ventriloquize himself—could not, in this case, create a character and a story that would make sense out of the life situation he had created for himself ten years earlier. Instead, he ventriloquized Annette as La Belle France, secure in the knowledge that his critical comments about the sad decline of Liberty in France would not be taken personally by Annette if she should ever chance to read them.

Published together as "Sonnets on National Independence and Liberty" in 1807, though many appeared in the *Morning Post* during 1802–3, their dates of composition show that Wordsworth's mastery of the sonnet form rose to greatness in the space of just a few months. Dorothy had begun reading Milton's sonnets to him in late May.[32] Two months later, under the intense pressure of one of the most difficult trips of his life, gathering up the raveled threads of his young manhood, he began writing sonnets at a level that had not been achieved in England since Milton, though Wordsworth had written no more than half a dozen of them to this point in his life. In fact he wrote both more and better than Milton. *The Prelude* does not match

Paradise Lost as a finished work of art, but Wordsworth's sonnets, especially his political ones, do surpass Milton's, and on virtually the same theme: the disappointment of revolutionary hopes for human redemption. Much of his success, it is true, comes from the fact that he had Milton not only as a precursor and a model but also as a subject: "Milton! thou shouldst be living at this hour." And not only Milton but the other republicans of the English civil war with whose lost revolutionary cause Wordsworth could now identify himself, as he returned to the scenes of his revolutionary youth. The tension that pervades the sonnets he wrote in Calais is of the same kind that runs between his sweet lyrics and terribles odes of the spring. But now the tension was between his low estimate of England, his even lower estimate of France, and his unhappy acceptance of the need to hang on, if to nothing else, at least to England's past reputation for liberty and manliness: "Oh grief that Earth's best hopes rest all with Thee!"[33] The friends of his youth rise fresh in his mind, and his hailing of "Milton!" and "Toussaint!" (the Haitian leader treacherously jailed by Napoleon) is echoed by similar calls to "Calvert!" and "Jones!" "Great men have been among us [Sidney, Marvell, Harrington, and Vane] . . . they knew how the genuine glory was put on." But their knowledge has been lost: "Lords, lawyers, statesmen, squires of low degree" all post forward to Paris (he saw them going by) in unseemly haste "to bend the knee . . . before the new-born Majesty" of Napoleon.[34]

We look in vain for a glimpse of Annette or Dorothy in these sonnets, but we can find Wordsworth in them, not as himself, but in his imaginative projection—not Milton, but as the man of the hour himself: "I grieved for Buonaparte, with a vain / And an unthinking grief! The tenderest mood / Of that Man's mind—what can it be?"[35] He grieved because he imagined that he knew what Bonaparte's moods were like: he supposes that they were much like his own, in their wayward violence and destructiveness. But Bonaparte has not learned Wordsworth's lesson: "The Governor who must be wise and good" must temper "the sternness of the brain" with "thoughts motherly . . . and the talk / Man holds with week-day man in the hourly walk / Of the mind's business." Proposing village small talk as corrective therapy for Napoleon Bonaparte was like trying to calm intimations of mortality with reassurances from daisies and cuckoos. Throughout these sonnets the desideratum is a man of Napoleon's power and Wordsworth's peace: a "master spirit," like "the invincible Knights of old," and a nation "risen, *like one man,* to combat . . . for liberty and right." This is the source of his new patriotic feelings: "What wonder if a Poet now and then, / Among the many movements of his mind, / Felt for thee [England] as a lover or a child!"[36] His particular "wonder" is stimulated biographically by the fact that, at just this time, his feelings for *his* lover and *his* child were being revived and reengaged, along with his conviction that he was the necessary Poet for these unruly times.

Leaving Annette and Caroline to make their way back to Blois alone, William and Dorothy returned to Dover on September 1, Dorothy gazing back toward France with "many a melancholy and tender thought." But William's joy looked the other way, happily recognizing that of everything he saw "all, all are English." He pushed his personal situation into statements that seem to be solely political and patriotic—"Thou art free, / My Country!" But they apply equally to him: he too was "free." It was "enough . . . for one hour's perfect bliss, to tread the grass / Of England once again . . . with such a dear Companion at my side." Having left his former dear companion in France, he is now ready to accept an hour's perfect bliss instead of those earlier emotions that he will shortly recall as much wider reaching, though far less stable: "Bliss was it in that dawn to be alive, / But to be young was very heaven!"

They spent three weeks in London with Basil Montagu and enjoyed an unexpected family reunion when John landed with the *Earl of Abergavenny* on September 11. Christopher came up to town to be with them.[37] Reconciliations with other relatives were in order, so Dorothy and William went out to Windsor Castle with Christopher as intermediary to visit Canon Cookson and family, then in residence as the king's chaplain. This was the first time either of them had seen the Cooksons since Dorothy's clandestine escape from Forncett eight years earlier.[38] Formally if coolly forgiven, they went back to London to hold a family council to discuss the new arrangements, domestic and financial, that would result from the coming marriage that would expand their family for the first time. William and Dorothy were now understood to constitute one unit in the group, and Dorothy consistently reduced the amounts she had coming to her to what she considered her bare minimum of necessity, ceding the rest to William's greater need. Together, they were a union of the neediest, since unlike Richard and John and Christopher they had no dependable separate income, and *they* now had a wife to support.

John's latest voyage had not been successful. Besides losing several thousand pounds on his investment, he faced a fine of £300 from "those vile and abominable Monsters at the India House" for encroaching on the company's monopoly in "camlets," a fabric made of silk and wool, in his private trade allowance.[39] Officers' private trading was not smuggling, for the goods were duly registered, but this particular practice represented an attempt by the ships' officers to profit from their own company's monopoly. The practice was widely condoned; in 1801 nearly half of all ships' cargoes in camlets were part of the officers' trade allowances.[40] John had merely been caught in one of the East India Company's periodic fits of enforcing its own rules. As he told Dorothy, "we began to think we had a *right* to smuggle them—We are the first that they have fined and of course we think it very hard and very unjust."[41] But he had to pay the fine—reduced to £200 through negotiation—before being allowed to sail again. These reverses increased his desperation to realize the profits that would make him a rich man and permit his brother the poet "to do something for the world"—which meant, in the family plan, completing *The Recluse.* For John it would mean getting into the even more illegal and dangerous, but vastly more profitable, trade in the commodity that could make a man "a rich dog" in a single voyage—opium.

There was also some other private settling and adjusting of emotional relations. John sent a letter to Mary Hutchinson from London on September 12, the day after he landed, having rushed from port to Richard's lodgings at Staple Inn:

> My dearest Mary,
>
> I have been reading your Letter over & over again My dearest Mary till tears have come into my eyes & I know not how to express myself thou ar't kind & dear creature But what ever fate Befal me I shall love thee to the last and bear thy memory with me to the grave.
>
> Thine aff'ly
> John Wordsworth[42]

The letter from Mary that he was answering must have been waiting for him at Portsmouth. It was her explanation to him of her reasons for marrying William. But John was plighting his troth, too: like Dorothy, he was vowing never to marry anyone else. Each of them would remain faithful in his or her own way to the two partners in this marriage, which John and Dorothy now formally accepted as the emotional center of their lives. William and John had taken their turns, and their chances, wooing Mary over the past two years. William had won out, but John used his brother's words to help deliver a powerfully loaded farewell to his beloved: the last sentence of his letter is a verbatim quotation of Michael's last words to Luke as he bids him good-bye at the sheepfold in Green-head Ghyll, never to see him again. Nor did John ever see any of them again: between this time and his death in February 1805, he was in England for a total of nine months, but he never traveled north to visit them.[43]

On September 22 they headed north for the wedding, which took place in Brompton Church near Gallow Hill on October 4,[44] almost a year to the day after the preliminary Treaty of Amiens had been announced. Appropriately for the formal quality of a major family alliance, all three Hutchinson sisters came down to meet the stagecoach at Scarborough.[45] The arrival, the preparations, the marriage, and the departure of William and Mary and Dorothy for Grasmere all took place within the next ten days. The strange story of the night before the wedding is well known, though Dorothy's symbolic—or symptomatic—behavior was not so strange in that era of Sensibility as it seems today. She put the wedding ring on her forefinger when she went to bed. Next morning she dressed herself all in bridal white and returned the ring to William for the ceremony. But he first slipped it back on her third finger and "blessed [her] fervently." Dorothy succumbed to a fit of hysteria and threw herself down as if dead until the small party returned from the church at eight o'clock in the morning.[46] She went out to meet them as they returned, but again was overcome and had to be led back to the house.[47]

Like the letters exchanged at the time of "A Farewell" in May, and the July talks with Mary and the August talks with Annette, the occasion was overloaded with emotions. But they all moved with great deliberation and fortitude to get through it. This was not a wedding to be celebrated with large parties of friends: these would take place gradually over time, at Grasmere. The only known wedding presents were a new gown for Mary—from John Wordsworth—and a set of silver spoons for Dorothy from one of the Ferguson cousins in America.[48] Nor was there any honeymoon: William, Mary, and Dorothy set off for Grasmere immediately after breakfast, along the same route that William and Dorothy had followed in their long march three years earlier. William and Dorothy kept their thoughts to themselves, of their walk through Wensleydale in 1799, or read them silently in each other's eyes. Never was Mary's natural reticence more of a blessing than on this trip, though it ripened and bore fruit as years went by, as she and William accomplished that most unromantic of lifeworks, falling more in love after marriage than before. But Mary also had thoughts of her own to nurse, musing on John's letter.

In less than three months Wordsworth had definitively reorganized his relations with all three of the women in his life. In the strictly clinical terms of psychosexual development, he was at this point young no longer.

If Dorothy's behavior was strange, Coleridge's was even stranger, though perhaps both were normal for rejected lovers. On October 9 the following announcement appeared in the *Morning Post,* a deadpan imitation of a conventional society-news wedding announcement:

> Monday last, W. Wordsworth, Esq. was married to Miss Hutchinson, of Wykeham, near Scarborough, and proceeded immediately, with his wife and his sister, for his charming cottage in the little Paradise Vale of Grasmere. His neighbour, Mr. Coleridge, resides in the Vale of Keswick, 13 miles from Grasmere. His house, (situated on a low hill at the foot of Skiddaw, with the Der-

went Lake in front, and the romantic River Greta winding round the hill) commands, perhaps, the most various and interesting prospects of any house in the island. It is a perfect *panorama* of that wonderful vale, with its two lakes, and its complete circle, or rather ellipse, of mountains.[49]

This seems to have been a droll joke concocted by Coleridge, Lamb, and Daniel Stuart, pushing Wordsworth's wedding announcement aside for a gratuitous advertisement of Coleridge's house. But on October 4, the wedding day itself, Coleridge had published—and this was no coincidence, still less a joke—a version of "Dejection: An Ode." This was not a nice wedding greeting, though not altogether out of keeping with the strained emotional atmosphere at Gallow Hill on that day. With the name William changed to Edmund, and Sara Hutchinson made into an anonymous "Lady," Coleridge here bade a bitter farewell both to his love life and, as it seemed, to his imaginative powers, on the occasion of Wordsworth's seemingly triumphant union of them both.

> There was a time when, though my path was rough,
> This joy within me dallied with distress . . .
>
> But now afflictions bow me down to earth:
> . . . each visitation
> Suspends what nature gave me at my birth,
> My shaping spirit of Imagination.
>
> (82–86)

Very possibly it was Coleridge's publishing of "Dejection" at this cruel juncture that determined Wordsworth eventually to answer it, in an extended version of his Intimations Ode.

Far less impressive than "Dejection" and much less funny than the *Post*'s wedding announcement was a sly, mean dig that Coleridge published on October 11, at the end of a series of twenty-one epigrams he had been publishing since the end of September, some translated or imitated from an obscure German satirist named Wernicke, but some, like this one, original compositions.[50] Called "Spots in the Sun," it is sardonically addressed to a father confessor who has been looking at the sins of others so long that, like someone looking at the sun, he is blinded to his own. Though the confessor reprimands the poem's speaker, he has failed to see the beam in his own eye, for the speaker has often found him "At Annette's door, the lovely courtesan!"[51] This line could no more be a coincidence than the appearance of "Dejection" on Wordsworth's wedding day. "Spots in the Sun" makes a personal comment on the great debate about imagination versus nature that connects "Dejection" and the Intimations Ode. The subtext, which perhaps only six people in England could understand, was, Let him who has been lecturing me about my unhappy, doomed feelings toward Sara Hutchinson look to his own feelings, compromised between her sister, Mary Hutchinson, and Annette, his quondam "lovely courtesan." The poem's ostensibly "good man" does not win Annette's "charms": no, "he comes to hear her sins!" Coleridge was sniping at the same vein of pretentious moralizing in Wordsworth that led Dorothy to read Shakespeare's "Lover's Complaint" to him in May, even using the same image of a father confessor violating his trust to become a seducer.* We do not know when Coleridge penned in the margin of his *Poems* (1797) the Latin phrase "atque utinam opera ejus tantum noveram," next to his note acknowledging his having borrowed the phrase "green radiance" from Wordsworth's *An Evening Walk*. Its bluntness—"and would that I had known only his works"—seems to belong to the time of their open quarrel eight years later.[52] But such thoughts were surely beginning to occur to Coleridge, as he contemplated the latest accounting of the cost, to him, of Wordsworth's creation of the Poet.

The fall of 1802 was a quiet, tense time of adjustment to complex new living arrangements. Dorothy moved upstairs, giving her old bedroom up to William and Mary, but the "smallness [of the cottage] and the manner in which it is built [let] noises pass from one part of the house to the other."[53] Such evidences of the physical part of her brother's marriage that came to her attention troubled Dorothy considerably, and William had to use care in his oral and written expressions—both of which were very frank and intense—of sexual passion for Mary, because he feared Dorothy found them "obnoxious."[54] Nonetheless, it was Dorothy, as always, who wrote the necessary delicate letters to Annette about their new life.[55]

What he did do was start translating again, this time from the Italian of Ariosto and Metastasio, advancing as rapidly and fluently as he had through Chaucer's works a year earlier.[56] Any work like this was undertaken somewhat guiltily because it distracted him from the masterwork which he was to compose, now that he was fully established in its title role as the Recluse. He was hardly a literal recluse, but from the perspective of London literary

*This instance of the poets' resort to the common practice of publishing privately coded messages makes one wonder, in turn, about the possible real identities of "William and Annetta" in Mary Robinson's poem "The Granny Grey, A Love Tale," published in her *Lyrical Tales* (1800). These two young lovers are kept apart by Annetta's censorious, envious granny, until William exposes her as a "witch." Thus ridiculed, she relents and approves the lovers' match. The situation is virtually identical to that in "The Three Graves," which Wordsworth had turned over to Coleridge to finish, and Mary Robinson was very good friends with Coleridge in 1799–1800 after his return from Germany. He may have gossiped with her, woman of the world par excellence, though now pathetically ill, about William's hidden affair, and this possible reference to it—along with her co-optation of Wordsworth's preferred title for the second edition of *Lyrical Ballads*—may not be entirely coincidental.

life Wordsworth's isolation in Grasmere looked reclusive enough to match the outlines of his poetic fiction. But though he could not yet bring himself to accept the epic challenge of his self-created role as Recluse-Poet, as a plain poet he was strong as ever: the translations of Ariosto and Metastasio (plus Milton's Italian poems) are excellent, and were published a year later in the *Morning Post*.[57] Much of his energy and fluency in this task came from the subject matter he selected, for all the poems, including those by Milton, are about taking leave of one's beloved, or recalling loves lost long ago and far away. Ariosto's Orlando laments "his fair Lady lost"—Angelica, Wordsworth's constant fantasy image of his perfect lover—and Metastasio laments his Laura in words that could only recall Annette to Wordsworth's mind: "Though far off, still in union, / I will be thy companion; / And thou, who knowst if ever / Thou wilt remember me!"[58]

Peace had been achieved, marriage consummated, and inheritances assured. But each of them at costs—political, financial, and emotional—that remained to be accounted for in the capitalization of the Poet.

33

DISCIPLES AND PARTNERS

The National Poets of Scotland and the Grasmere Volunteer

Breathes there a man, with soul so dead,
Who never to himself hath said,
This is my own, my native land!
Whose heart hath ne'er within him burned,
As home his footsteps he hath turned,
From wandering on a foreign strand!
(Scott, *The Lay of the Last Minstrel,* VI.i)

At the beginning of 1803 Wordsworth expanded his new role as public poet: eight of his political sonnets appeared in the *Morning Post* between January and September, all signed "W.L.D." This was a signature he had last used in late 1795, from the depths of his retreat at Racedown, for a proper little poem, "On Classick Learning," in the *Weekly Entertainer.* Then the code name seems to have signified "Wordsworth Libertati Dedicavit" (Wordsworth dedicated to liberty), although in that particular poem it conveys the sense of still-dedicated-to-liberty-despite-appearances-to-the-contrary.[1] Now, eight years later, his dedication to liberty was both more forthright and less dangerous: more patriotic, less reformist. But his growing reputation—Stuart puffed him as "one of the first poets of the age"—and increasingly well-known position as a poet in rural retreat made it equally possible for readers to understand the initials as Wordsworth Lake District. These "little political essays" are not activist interventions on current events; they view the bustle of political contest from the brooding perspective of a reclusive sage removed from the world of action.[2]

The previous fall Coleridge had addressed two open letters to Fox in the *Morning Post,* arguing brilliantly against the cultural bind into which he and Wordsworth and their ex-radical friends had been cast. Taking as his title the very phrase being used to tar them, "Once a Jacobin Always a Jacobin," Coleridge had complained bitterly against the government's relentless pursuit of men like Thelwall and himself who had at first admired the ideals of the French Revolution.[3] The letters were part of a larger attack on Fox for leading the peace party in its deluded belief that Bonaparte represented a chance for peace in Europe. Wordsworth's sonnets extended this critique. These attacks hurt Fox deeply.[4] Whatever cultural profit Coleridge and Wordsworth had hoped to gain from sending him a copy of *Lyrical Ballads* two years earlier, proposing an alliance between his politics and their poetry, was now apparently expended.

Instead, the spring and summer of 1803 were marked by financial transactions far more profitable than book sales. On the first of March, William and Dorothy received their share of the first payment on the Lowther debt, over £1,300, followed by another £700 in July.[5] It came in good time, for Basil Montagu's account with them was still nearly £500 in the red, over half the total amount of the Calvert bequest on which William had made his ill-considered loan seven years earlier.[6] Their new investments were much larger and safer: in July they purchased 2,500 consols at 3 percent for £1,315, plowing two-thirds of their revenue from the Lowther payment back into low-risk bonds.[7]

Still larger profits lay tantalizingly in view. The total Wordsworth family investment in John's next voyage (from May 1803 to August 1804) came to nearly £8,000. John had large losses to cover from his last voyage, but if this one was successful they would soon all be independently wealthy. No one dreamed it was to be his last complete trip. Nor was its profit at all what they had hoped for: on his return he reported he sold his woolen goods "neither ill nor well . . . Opium and Quicksilver were the only things in the China market that sold to any profit," and he had carried little of either.[8] As a result, he stepped up his insistence to the major owners of the *Earl of Abergavenny* "of the *necessity* of my having a better than a China direct voyage."[9] A "China direct" voyage meant a nonstop trip out, except for supplies and repairs. But a scheduled stop on the way, usually in India, meant that a ship could nearly double its profits by selling a load of English goods in India and taking on local goods there for China. The most valuable of these local goods was opium, which was most easily taken on in Bengal, where the East India Company enjoyed a monopoly on its culture and distribution.[10]

Though officially forbidden and occasionally regulated, the opium trade had been going on since at least the 1730s, and led eventually to the Opium War of 1839–42. The trade was England's strategy, thinly disguised as private enterprise, to reverse the huge imbalance of payments resulting from the immense increase in tea imports to England. The East India Company was the primary agency by which opium was introduced into China, developing a market of consumers there to offset all the tea drinkers in England. The imp of opium cut a demonic figure in the leaves at the bottom of every cup of English breakfast tea. The rulers of China protested frequently but weakly against this corruption of their people, and there was of course widespread condoning and aiding of the smuggling operations by agents in the ports and coastal areas who profited from it. To his great delight but ultimate destruction, John Wordsworth by a fluke would get the Bengal route for his next voyage.

Growing fame brought still more profit to his brother, the prospering recluse, in the summer, when he met Sir George Beaumont, who was renting part of Greta Hall. Beaumont, an aristocratic connoisseur and painter, was a regular visitor to Keswick, having spent his honeymoon there in 1778 (the year of Wordsworth's mother's death). He exhibited his rendition of the famous view from Greta Hall for his first appearance in the Royal Academy in 1779.[11] Meeting Wordsworth through the offices of his fellow tenant Coleridge (whom Beaumont thought slightly disreputable), he was so taken with the personal presence of the author of *Lyrical Ballads*—which he greatly admired—that he arranged for two small pieces of land at Applethwaite, adjacent to the Calverts' Ormathwaite property, to be purchased in Wordsworth's name as a token of his esteem.[12] This grand gesture of implied patronage made Wordsworth wary at first, but Beaumont charmingly (if somewhat cloyingly) assured him that he expected nothing in return, and only wanted "to live & die with the idea that the sweet place with its rocks, banks, & mountain stream are in the possession of such a mind as yours."[13] Thus began a friendship with another upper-class patron that was to be the most personally affectionate one in Wordsworth's life, though his political loyalties were always, like his father's before him, committed to the Lowther interest. Both marked his growing conservatism, but Beaumont's friendship showed Wordsworth how his nature mythology could disguise aspects of his early work that might trouble the established artistic and political classes.

The summer also brought other kinds of discipleship, less grand but more intense. Among the growing number of letters from unknown admirers was one from the young (seventeen) Thomas De Quincey, who had just returned to his mother's house after running away from school and spending the winter in poverty among prostitutes and beggars in London. De Quincey was in a sense Wordsworth's first literary son, his letter of homage arriving within a month of the birth of the poet's first biological son, John ("Johnny"), on June 18.[14] (The baby was named for his seafaring uncle, thus satisfying both parents' powerful feelings of emotional debt to their brother.) De Quincey was one of the first conscious disciples of the new English brand of Romanticism. He was attracted to the new dispensations announced in *Lyrical Ballads,* just as young men like Charles Lloyd, George Burnett, and Robert Lovell had been the last disciples of Wordsworth's and Coleridge's old school of utopian radicalism. De Quincey listed his ten favorite English poets in his diary, beginning with Spenser, Shakespeare, and Milton, and ending with "William Wordsworth!!!"

De Quincey spent over two weeks drafting and revising his letter, deeply absorbing Wordsworth's own language; it reads like a prose digest of "Tintern Abbey." He touched all the major keys: "the Dignity of your moral character," "the transcendency of your genius," "your name is with me forever linked to the lovely scenes of nature." He hinted at the possibility of a visit, with the total abasement—and cheeky self-confidence—of the new convert: "to no man on earth except yourself and *one* other (a friend of your's [Coleridge]), would I thus lowly and suppliantly prostrate myself."[15] Wordsworth's reply to De Quincey's youthful romantic excess shows good sense and tact. He appreciated De Quincey's praise and admiration, but warned him against overvaluing his poetry: "You are young and ingenuous and I wrote with a hope of pleasing the young and the ingenuous and the unwordly above all others, but sorry indeed should I be to stand in the way of the proper influence of other writers."[16] He ended by assuring his young admirer, "It will give me great pleasure to see you at Grasmere if you should ever come this way."

Over the next four years De Quincey flirted with the idea of visiting his idol, twice making excursions to the Lakes but losing his nerve both times. Finally in 1807, having cultivated Coleridge and his family during a sojourn in Somerset, he returned to the Lakes as the escort of Sara and the children and imposed himself on the Wordsworths, replacing them as tenant of Dove Cottage after they left in 1808. Eventually De Quincey's habits, from opium addiction to all-too-romantic liberties with the truth, severely strained Wordsworth's relations with him. But De Quincey was not always a liar: like many another disillusioned devotee, such as Charles Lloyd, he could be cruelly incisive in describing—and reporting in print—the personal habits and failings of his onetime heroes.

In this same July of 1803 Wordsworth also paid the price of another necessary ingredient to a growing reputation: three guineas for a portrait by one of the hundreds of painters who toured about the land, recording the prosperous features and estates of the expanding, rising middle class. This painter was also a disciple of sorts, William Hazlitt, he of the enchanted visit to Nether Stowey in 1798. Hazlitt had come north at Coleridge's invitation, fresh from three months in Paris spent copying portraits by Titian and other Italian masters at the Louvre.[17] He painted portraits of both his heroes, but both pictures were universally condemned. Lady Beaumont said he made Wordsworth look more like a philosopher than a poet: this was a criticism. Though this portrait seems to have been destroyed, the chance that it was not, and that it gives us a picture of Wordsworth exactly at the time he was realizing himself as the Poet of his polemics, makes it an appropriate symbolic frontispiece for a biography of the young poet who in so many other ways hid himself from the gaze of posterity. That it looks older than a thirty-three-year-old man was part of everyone's reaction at the time, as Coleridge reported: "Mrs. Wilkinson *swears,* that your Portrait is 20 years too old for you—& mine equally too old." Mrs. Wilkinson also said they looked "too lank." Both featured long faces, less appropriate for Coleridge than for Wordsworth, but Coleridge defended them on imaginative grounds: "the Likeness with him is a secondary Consideration—he wants it to be a fine Picture."[18]

Hazlitt, "that roving God Pan," wore out his welcome in 1803 even more disgracefully than De Quincey did, but not because of bad painting. Now twenty-five, he was already giving rein to his irascible, independent personality and slovenly disregard for his physical appearance, coupled with an unattractive man's angry lust toward the opposite sex.* Coleridge lamented "how easily roused to Rage & Hatred, self-projected" his young friend was, and how deeply buried in the depths of his anger was any "expression of Kindness . . . one Gleam of the Light of Love on his countenance."[19] Wordsworth supported Hazlitt in disputing with Coleridge the existence and nature "of the Divine Wisdom," but he was solidly behind Coleridge in disapproving their mercurial disciple's sexual behavior.

The incident is clouded by contemporary efforts to hush it up and distorted by Wordsworth's and Coleridge's later efforts to put Hazlitt in the worst possible light. What apparently happened is that a girl in Keswick called him "a black-faced rascal," whereupon he pushed her down and attempted to rape her. Finding himself thwarted, he "lifted up her petticoats & *smote* her on the *bottom.*"[20] A gang of the girl's friends soon came looking for the "out-comer" (outlander), proposing to give him a ducking in the lake. Coleridge and Southey barely got him out of town, leaving his clothes and painting materials behind him. He ran through the countryside, a randy, shoeless Ichabod Crane, arriving at Grasmere about midnight. The Wordsworths took him in and sent him on his way in the morning, supplied with some clothing and a few pounds to get him home to Shropshire. Coleridge's and Wordsworth's credit with their neighbors was damaged for a time by their association with this outrageous young man, who behaved all too much like the immoral city dwellers who were the stuff of rural rumor.

At the time, neither Coleridge nor Wordsworth took the defamatory attitude toward the incident that they adopted in later years, after Hazlitt's blast

*A couple of years later Lamb took him to visit some pretty girls in London, and reported that Hazlitt "sat and frowned blacker and blacker, indignant that there should be such a thing as Youth and Beauty, till he tore me away . . . in perfect misery and owned he could not bear young girls. They drove him mad" (E. V. Lucas, *The Life of Charles Lamb* [London: Methuen, 1905], 1:273).

against country life in his review of Wordsworth's *The Excursion* in 1814. Taking as its thesis the proposition that "all country people hate each other," Hazlitt's diatribe contains several details which echo the scandal of 1803: "They hate all strangers, and have generally a nick-name for the inhabitants of the next village"; "Having no circulating libraries to exhaust their love of the marvellous, they amuse themselves with fancying the disasters and disgraces of their particular acquaintance. Having no hump-backed *Richard* to excite their wonder and abhorrence, they make themselves a bug-bear of their own, out of the first obnoxious person they can lay their hands on"; "They get up a little pastoral drama at home, with fancied events, but real characters."[21] This was a long way from the pastoral ideology of *Lyrical Ballads,* but in 1803 both Coleridge and Wordsworth were soon writing to Hazlitt in all amicability, especially Wordsworth, who wished he would come back and paint some of the marvelous brook scenery he had discovered at Upper Rydal Falls, "some of the finest old stumpified staring trees I ever saw . . . infinitely finer in winter than summer time."[22] He signed himself "very affectionately yours" and made no reference to the "abominable and devilish propensities" he attributed to Hazlitt fifteen years later.

In what would look like the new couple's postponed honeymoon—except that the bride was not included—William and Dorothy traveled in Scotland from mid-August to mid-September, leaving Mary at home with two-month-old Johnny. They picked up Coleridge along the way, who of course left Sara in Keswick with their three children. Romanticism did much to bring the ideal of romantic love into general currency, but no one has ever said it was easy being married to a Romantic poet. The old ménage à trois was on the road again. All authorities agree that this was a strange trip for any of them to be taking at this time. Coleridge was always ready to seize any excuse for leaving home, but he was dreaming of a warm climate, which he certainly did not find in Scotland. Dorothy was devoted to her new nephew, yet was leaving him at a time when Mary had barely recovered her strength from a strenuous first delivery. The best explanation seems to be that William and Dorothy were trying to help Coleridge by attempting to revive the spirit of Stowey from six years earlier.

The whole trip had self-consciously romantic overtones. They drove by themselves, in what Dorothy gaily called their "outlandish Hibernian vehicle," a small open Irish touring carriage.[23] Their first stop was Carlisle, where Coleridge, "impelled by Miss Wordsworth," paid a visit to the cell of John Hatfield, who had just been condemned to death for impersonating an MP in his bigamous seduction of Mary Robinson, "the Beauty of Buttermere."[24] Coleridge had had a big success the previous winter with a series of five articles in the *Morning Post* on the topics "The Romantic Marriage" and "The

Keswick Impostor." He had romantically exaggerated Mary's naive passion, while at the same time intensifying Hatfield's mysteriously malignant motives.[25] Prison visits to the condemned were far more common then than now, like deathbed farewells, but still it is hard to imagine what Coleridge had to say to Hatfield, whom he did not know. He came to the same conclusion: "*vain,* a hypocrite / It is not by mere Thought, I can understand this man."[26]

The poets' solicitude for their idealized Beauty of Buttermere, relative to their altogether conventional treatment of their wives, suggests a conscious search for emotional data that is properly called Romantic, especially in light of their recent difficult severing of their youthful romantic attachments, Annette Vallon and Sara Hutchinson. Wordsworth did not accompany Coleridge on his visit to Hatfield's cell. Perhaps it seemed to him a too literal reprise of his own poem "The Convict," whose "Jacobincal pathos" he had come to scorn. But it is fitting, though apparently entirely coincidental, that Wordsworth was the one to stop and look at Hatfield's execution site, in Longtown at the Scottish border, on their return trip. The desperation of hardened criminals and ravings of abandoned lovers were subject matter congenial to Coleridge, while Wordsworth's imagination was more stimulated by reflecting on dead ones.

Romantic subjectivity continued unabated once they crossed the border. Scotland had been a land of faraway romance to Wordsworth since childhood, though it lay only twenty-five miles north of his family's traditional center at Penrith. But he had never visited it except for the brief trip to Basil Montagu's wedding two years earlier. Their first impressions were of Robert Burns, at Dumfries. William and Dorothy, but not Coleridge, visited Burns's grave with "melancholy and painful reflections" on the fate of another self-created national poet, whose native-language poetry experiment was even more radical than Wordsworth's, and who had paid the price in ruined reputation for not managing his career according to prevailing standards of what poetry should be like and how poets should live.[27] Burns had died in 1796, but after a splendid military funeral, his reputation began declining immediately, under politically motivated attacks on his drunkenness and debts.[28]

Wordsworth admired Burns greatly as a poet and innovator, but the three poems he composed about him from this trip were cautionary lessons about joining the life of the poet and the life of the man too closely. The poems are not very good; what is remarkable about them is how long Wordsworth took to finish them. He wrote one poem full of conventional moral advice (addressed to Burns's sons) after he finished *The Prelude* in 1805; but the two poems on Burns himself were started later and finished much later, not appearing in print until 1842, in his valedictory lifetime edition, *Poems, Chiefly of Early and Late Years.*

He could not approve of Burns's lifestyle, but neither could he deny his poetry, and most of all he could not avoid identifying with him in an intensely personal, physical way as he meditated on his grave.

> I shiver, Spirit fierce and bold,
> At thought of what I now behold:
> As vapours breathed from dungeons cold
> Strike pleasure dead,
> So sadness comes from out the mould
> Where Burns is laid.
>
> And have I then thy bones so near,
> And thou forbidden to appear?
> As if it were thyself that's here
> I shrink with pain;
> And both my wishes and my fear
> Alike are vain.
> ("At the Grave of Burns," 1–12)

Where, exactly, is the "here" of line 9? Does it point to Burns's corpse under the sod or to Wordsworth's identification with it; or is he imagining that he himself is Burns, standing on his own grave? This weird little Gothic lyric presses on to several more degrees of identification. Wordsworth suggests that he and Burns were neighbors ("Criffel's hoary top" is "by Skiddaw seen"), "and loving friends we might have been . . . True friends though diversely inclined." He claims he grieved more deeply than other "thousands" when Burns died, because he had hailed Burns's light "when first it shone," because it "showed my youth / How Verse may build a princely throne / On humble truth." This was more true in retrospect than in the actual chronology of Wordsworth's poetical development. And the poem, written by a no longer young Wordsworth, can do no more than pray for God's forgiveness on a sinner, a statement not only smugly conventional but much beside the point.

To his credit, Wordsworth had second thoughts—almost always his best ones—and he wrote another poem, "Thoughts," commenting on the first. This one pushes aside Burns's "sorrow, wreck, and blight," and rises to two stanzas that are by far the best of the more than two hundred lines in Wordsworth's works devoted to Burns. In them Wordsworth's identification with Burns becomes complete—or rather, Burns is completely assimilated to the role of Poet Wordsworth had now conceived for himself.

> Through busiest street and loneliest glen
> Are felt the flashes of his pen;
> He rules 'mid winter snows, and when
> Bees fill their hives;

Deep in the general heart of men
His power survives.

What need of fields in some far clime
Where Heroes, Sages, Bards sublime,
And all that fetched the flowing rhyme
From genuine springs,
Shall dwell together till old Time
Folds up his wings?
("Thoughts," 43–54)

"Deep in the general heart of men" is where Wordsworth sought—successfully—to lodge himself, and the second stanza is a direct recasting of the *Recluse* "Prospectus" lines in Burns's honor ("Paradise, and groves Elysian . . . why should they be / A history only of departed things?"). To commemorate this important visit, he and Dorothy bought a one-volume edition of Burns's poetry in Stirling the next day, to put on their shelf next to the Kilmarnock edition that William had bought for Dorothy when he left for Cambridge in 1787.

The weather soon turned terrible, and after two weeks Coleridge left them to go ahead faster on foot, and to escape the exposure to the elements he suffered in their open touring car. They were making the standard "short tour," but Coleridge lacked William's and Dorothy's willingness to sit and shiver in the rain as they took one detour after another in search of picturesque vistas. Some of their digressions lodged in William's memory and produced such favorite poems as "To a Highland Girl" and "Stepping Westward."* Tensions with Coleridge had started almost immediately, and the trip, which had been intended to restore their old camaraderie, showed instead that they were no longer "one spirit in three persons." They squabbled over housing and scheduling arrangements and argued about details of Scottish landscape and history that none of them in fact knew very well. Coleridge did not lack stamina: on his own, he walked another 263 miles through the Highlands in eight days![29] But his mental state was awful. He began the terrible "Pains of Sleep" at this time, with its remorseless, Dantean exploration of "the unfathomable hell" within him, as he confronted all his worst demons: "Thirst of revenge . . . Desire with loathing strangely

*Dorothy's memory was still more prodigious, for though she did not keep a journal, on her return she began composing her *Recollections of a Tour Made in Scotland, A.D.* 1803, the most self-consciously crafted of all her journals. Her careful polishing of it over the next two years suggests she may have intended it for publication. It stands up well in comparison with hundreds of other Scottish "tours" published in England between 1750 and 1850, providing a sympathetic Romantic complement to Samuel Johnson's curmudgeonly *Journey to the Western Islands of Scotland,* published twenty-eight years earlier. But like Johnson she used England—Cumberland especially—as a yardstick to measure Scotland's beauties, and found them wanting.

mixed / On wild or hateful objects fixed. / Fantastic passions! maddening brawl! / And shame and terror over all!"

But their separation was beneficial to Wordsworth, for it meant that his first meeting with Walter Scott came when he was alone with Dorothy, on September 17, and did not have to share his host's attention with his dazzling, voluble friend. The meeting, at Melrose, was arranged by John Stoddart through his legal connections with Scott.[30] From it Wordsworth got more valuable lessons on how to set about becoming the Poet of one's nation.

Scott, affable and affluent, was already a laird of the manor in the Borders, in a way that Wordsworth could conceive of only in imaginary terms in Cumberland. He was sheriff of Selkirkshire, a quasi-political legal office that he executed with a combination of fairness and panache that earned him respect and admiration throughout the Borders. Wordsworth's father had been a sheriff too, if only of the bleak stretch of coast between Millom and Whitehaven. And when financial necessity forced Wordsworth to petition the new Lord Lowther for a similar post ten years later, the office he got—distributor of stamps for Cumberland—was, though lucrative, very far from Scott's in popularity, being roughly equivalent to that of a tax collector.

Scott had just published his *Minstrelsy of the Scottish Border,* a three-volume collection of authentic and imitated "Historical" and "Romantic" ballads, refined for middle-class tastes, that started his rise to fame. Though close to Wordsworth's common-language project in some ways, its allegiance to the lore of the folk was fundamentally different from Wordsworth's need to transform his materials by the force of his own imagination. Where Scott's language normalizes the ancient peasant vernacular, while Burns retained it, Wordsworth can more accurately be said to *ab*normalize it. Scott was just then working on *The Lay of the Last Minstrel,* and recited parts of the first four cantos to William and Dorothy. It was a creative extension of his antiquarian work on the *Minstrelsy,* and when it was published, in January 1805, it made him instantly famous, the kind of success Wordsworth always longed for but never got.

It was a pivotal moment in the literary history of the two men and their two countries. If Coleridge had come along, it would have been even more interesting, since the *Lay* is very much built up from Scott's adaptation of the fantastic supernaturalism of "The Rime of the Ancient Mariner" and the Gothic medievalism of "Christabel." Stoddart had recently recited part of "Christabel" for Scott, and Scott immediately appropriated its fast-paced, irregular four-beat meter, as well as many details of setting and mood. Indeed, the *Lay* starts out as a virtual plagiarism of "Christabel":

> The feast was over in Branksome tower,
> And the Layde had gone to her secret bower;

Her bower, that was guarded by word and by spell,
Deadly to hear, and deadly to tell—
Jesu Maria, shield us well!
No living wight, save the Ladye alone,
Had dared to cross the threshold stone.

(I.i.1–7)

There were plenty of other precedents for Scott's poem in the ballad revival and in Gothic fiction, but *The Lay of the Last Minstrel* has good claim to be the original of one of the most popular aspects of British Romanticism: the revival of romance in a fashionably sophisticated mode. The poem can be read at a single sitting, its feuds and battles and magicians entertaining all the way through. Scott's voluminous notes (a third of the book) give historical—or at least antiquarian—weight to its legendary incidents. This particularized localism is far removed from almost every significant example of Wordsworth's poetry we have seen, though he would soon try his hand at gaining this kind of success with *The White Doe of Rylstone* (begun 1807, published 1815). *The Borderers* had been set on the English side of the same landscape that Scott invokes in the *Lay* with loving exactitude (as in "Kendale's archers, all in green"). But *The Borderers'* imaginative sources were only nominally local: they really arose from "the haunt and main region of [Wordsworth's] song . . . the impulses of [his] own mind."

Scott was just then organizing a volunteer cavalry troop of young gentlemen from Edinburgh because of renewed fears of a French invasion following the breakdown of the Peace of Amiens that summer. After training in arms and dealing with logistics every day (he was the quartermaster), Scott in the evenings recited to the Wordsworths a "lay" of reunification: the convoluted plot of the *Lay* ends with a marriage that stops the family feud between the Cranstouns and the Buccleuchs, which is celebrated in the context of a still-larger truce between the English, led by Lord Howard, the earl of Carlisle, and the Scottish border lords. In short, it deals intimately with the mutual neighbors and neighborhoods, historically magnified, of both young men, thoroughly romanticizing the English-Scottish border wars, a three-century-long horror story of "reiving" (raiding) and feuding of the most unspeakable kind.[31] Scott's *Lay* furthers the continuing cultural work of peaceable assimilation between England and Scotland since the Act of Union of 1715, motivated in part by the threat of invasion from a more radically disruptive foreign power and ideology; its lesson is that England and Scotland have more in common than not.

Beyond this, and probably more important to both men personally, was the self-reflexive aspect of Scott's *Lay.* Like *The Prelude,* which Wordsworth would take up again on his return home, dealing with his personal experience of that same foreign power which now threatened them, the *Lay* attempts to deal with postrevolutionary disappointment and despair. The present tense of Scott's poem is the late 1680s; the last minstrel is "the last of the race, who, as he is supposed to have survived the Revolution, might have caught somewhat of the refinement of modern poetry, without losing the simplicity of his original model." Change the reference of "Revolution" from English to French, and the same supposition fits the poetic programs of both Scott and Wordsworth, in their different ways.

Politics is to a large extent replaced by poetry in *The Lay of the Last Minstrel:* the bad old days are gone, but poetry lives on, chastened, humble, and humane. Both he and Wordsworth, young men aged thirty-three and thirty-two, respectively, were already casting themselves as "last" minstrels, poets of older cultural orders destroyed by present politics. Scott's revolutionary disappointment was 150 years old, but Wordsworth's was still active. Scott took refuge in poeticized history; Wordsworth constructed his refuge, for public consumption, in a poeticized nature. But his private retreat in *The Prelude* was more like a personalized history. In 1803, however, both myths were enlisted under the banner of the *Lay*'s most famous words, "Breathes there the man, with soul so dead, / Who never to himself hath said, / This is my own, my native land!" Possibly the most stirring lines ever written in English in support of nationalism, they express a sentiment to which both poets were, not without reluctance, bending their imaginations under the twin pressures of foreign invasion and revolutionary disillusionment. The next three lines, however, spoke far more personally to Wordsworth's life situations than to Scott's: "Whose heart hath ne'er within him burned, / As home his footsteps he hath turned, / From wandering on a foreign strand!"

This was not all evident at the time, but both men immediately recognized that they shared many interests, and similar social standing, and the friendship which began in 1803 ripened steadily, carefully cultivated by Wordsworth, through the rest of their lives until Scott's death in 1832. Like his visit to Burns's tomb, Wordsworth's visit to Scott stimulated several new poems, but they notably lack the stress his Burns poems caused him. The most successful of them, "Yarrow Unvisited," succeeds partly because it is an oblique statement by Wordsworth that he will not be diverted by another man's myth. On their way home William and Dorothy stopped at the little inn at the crossroads of Clovenford. They had only to walk over a hill to see the picturesque river Yarrow, celebrated by Scott, and they had endured far worse discomforts for lesser sights in the earlier part of their tour. Dorothy, recast in dialect as Wordsworth's local "winsome Marrow" (companion), longs to go, but he bluntly refused: "Strange words they seemed of slight and scorn." His reason for this "strange fit of passion" was to keep Yarrow as an imaginative resource, not to cash it in and be disappointed, as he had been by Mont Blanc, the Simplon Pass, and Snowdon. "We have a vision of our own; / Ah! why should we undo it?" No matter what happens to us in life, he concluded, " 'Twill soothe us in our sorrow, / That earth hath something yet to show, / The bonny holms of Yarrow!" He was right: the unseen vista was always a more powerful stimulant to his creative imagination than the one seen. "Yarrow Visited," written in 1814, when they finally did visit it, tries to say that the "genuine image" is a fair exchange for the one of "fond imagination," but it is a tepid tribute of scene painting.

The real rival to "Yarrow Unvisited" is the third poem in this triptych, "Yarrow Revisited," composed in 1831, but published only in 1834. And it gains its power from another loss: not of Yarrow but of the "Great Minstrel of the Border" himself. For it was written on the occasion of their melancholy last visit to Scott, before he departed for Italy in a vain attempt to restore his health. It is a tribute to the power of poetry itself: "what were mighty Nature's self . . . Unhelped by the poetic voice / That hourly speaks within us?" Wordsworth recalled through the layers of his memory both his 1814 visit and his 1803 nonvisit to Yarrow, collapsing them into a combined image of Scott *and* his last minstrel, standing beneath "proud Newark's" ruined towers with its "winding stair that once / Too timidly was mounted / By the 'last Minstrel,' (not the last!) / Ere he his tale recounted." His parenthetical aside was both prayer and prophecy, for by the time Wordsworth published the volume, "this wondrous Potentate" was dead. Like not visiting Yarrow, imagining Scott dead released for Wordsworth the flow of inspiration that opened during his visit of September 1803, when he first heard the lay of the "Great Minstrel of the Border," before he crossed back over the border to begin his own work on his own side.

On their way home Wordsworth's new sense of otherness, always a strong catalyst to his poetry of identity, was further stimulated when a passerby in Peebles questioned him about his nationality "in a mysterious manner."[32] But there as elsewhere in the southern Borders, he found that the mere mention of Scott's name smoothed the way before them. Wordsworth wanted to be the poet of the people, but, in Scotland as in France and Germany, being a stranger in a strange land is what helped him become the most English of poets. In a larger sense his otherness was otherworldly: he is in some ways the most *human* of poets because of his deep attraction to states that are not national but extraterrestrial, the sublime of imagination and the abject of death.

When they returned home, Wordsworth, fired by Scott's example, threw himself into the activities of the Grasmere Volunteers, which had been formed in response to panic fears of a French invasion that were sweeping the country. Napoleon was rumored to be building a tunnel under the Channel, which was not true, or a special fleet of landing craft at dockyards all along the coast from Dunkerque to Brest, which was. The volunteers were under the general command of Lord Lowther, as lord lieutenant of Cumberland and Westmorland, and they took their training seriously, soon becoming regarded as the best county unit in the north. Wordsworth's participation was not an aberration, or simply a piece of poetical grandstanding to show solidarity with the local yeomanry à la Scott. Dorothy drily estimated that if the invading French ever reached Grasmere it would be too late for fighting, but she was correct to say that "surely there never was a more determined hater of the French [than William] nor one more willing to do his utmost to destroy them if they really do come."[33] William was one of the tallest and strongest of the recruits, and one of the fittest of those over thirty. His fantasy image of himself as a general and leader of men came close to reality here, a fact he later signaled in his private mythology by using the name Oswald in *The Excursion* for George Dawson, a young volunteer who died in 1807 of a chill caught swimming in the lake.[34]

Giving the name Oswald to a patriotic militiaman, "the finest young man in the vale" (whose father was clerk to the distributor of stamps), was both a literary and a literal case of turncoatism, since another Oswald in Wordsworth's life oeuvre was the anarchic revolutionary of *The Borderers,* based on the radical Colonel John Oswald from Wordsworth's experience in France, would-be assassin of George III and actual commander of republican troops. We have to look very hard for textual evidence of Wordsworth's migration from radical activist to government agent—whether intelligence courier or stamp distributor—but this seems to be one. Wordsworth's creation of Oswald-Dawson is not just a piece of gratuitous praise for a nice young man. It is George Dawson infused with the imaginative spirit of William Wordsworth, world conqueror and redeemer. Wordsworth picks up on the fact that the Dawson boys, because of their father's position, "took more delight in scholarship, and . . . a wider view of social interests than was usual among their associates."[35] The "wider view" that he gives Dawson is a close approximation of his own experiences on the Continent, projected onto a scene of the young Oswald teaching the local yokels how to read the map of contemporary Europe: " 'Here flows,' / Thus would he say, 'the Rhine, that famous stream!' "

> *Thence, along a tract*
> *Of livelier interest to his hopes and fears,*
> His finger moved, distinguishing the spots
> Where wide-spread conflicts then most fiercely raged;

Nor left unstigmatized those fatal fields
On which the sons of mighty Germany
Were taught a base submission.
(*Excursion,* VII.794–800; italics added)

In context, this refers to Napoleon's victories at Austerlitz (1805) and Jena (1806), but we can be quite sure that young Oswald's "livelier . . . hopes and fears" were positioned close to the "tracts" young Wordsworth moved across in Germany in 1799, a likelihood confirmed when his map description goes on into Switzerland and touches the bases of Wordsworth's 1790 tour and its subsequent recapitulations in *Descriptive Sketches* and *The Prelude.* If there was any doubt that this "favourite son" (*Excursion,* VII.853) is coterminous with the "chosen Son" of *The Prelude,* it is removed by Wordsworth's peroration, which would be ridiculous hyperbole if applied to George Dawson of Grasmere, but is nothing at all beyond the mark in comparison to the kind of rhetoric Wordsworth applies to the Bard of *The Recluse:*

No braver Youth
Descended from Judean heights, to march
With righteous Joshua; nor appeared in arms
When grove was felled, and altar was cast down,
And Gideon blew the trumpet, soul-inflamed
And strong in hatred of idolatry.
(VII.811–16)

The more difficult question, for Wordsworth, was whether the Poet of *The Prelude* also merited these high titles. By the end, he had convinced himself that he did, for he and Coleridge, as "Poets of Nature," will also succeed in combating *idolatry* like the composite Joshua-Oswald-Dawson, though idolatry of a more contemporary, reactionary political cast: "too weak to tread the ways of truth, / This age fall[s] back to old *idolatry* . . . return[s] to servitude as fast / As the tide ebbs" (XIII.431–34).

Wordsworth's enthusiasm for the Grasmere Volunteers was more patriotic than political: during his conversations with Hazlitt that summer he had repeated his striking comment from their first meeting in 1798, that he wished George Tierney had shot out Pitt's tongue in their duel that year.[36] Pitt's insidiously effective speeches had first provoked and then prolonged the war, which was now being resumed with England very much on the defensive, but Wordsworth the volunteer was determined to fight to save his country, even from the consequences of a politics he abominated.

He soon withdrew from active participation in the drills, but he wrote two poems out of the experience which show a delicious enthusiasm for combat, victory, and, especially, glorious death. His "Lines on the Expected Invasion" are a come-one, come-all invitation to British monarchists and republicans, urging them to join forces and, if need be, "perish to a man," to "save this honoured land from every Lord / But British reason and the British sword."

The sonnet "Anticipation" strikes the same note, but in triumph, after a French invasion was repulsed. The invasion never came, but Wordsworth had his poem ready for the occasion, his imagination as usual not needing the actual event to stimulate it. (Beaumont published it without his consent in the *Courier.*) By now he had a long mental history of imagining himself in mortal but ultimately victorious conflict with the villainous leaders not of France, exactly, but of its Revolution, to which he had declared his youthful fealty but which he felt had betrayed him, thus (as he saw it) betraying his imagination. The sonnet is addressed to the nation as a symbolic family, from old men to "merry wives," to children and even to babies, who seem to toddle out from the first stanzas of the Immortality Ode to join in the victory parade: "Clap, infants, clap your hands!" Like almost all other Wordsworthian expressions of the Sublime, this paean to military glory ends with the final blessing of death:

> Divine must be
> That triumph, when the very worst, the pain,
> *And even the prospect of our brethren slain,*
> *Hath something in it which the heart enjoys:—*
> In glory will they sleep and endless sanctity.
> (10–14; italics added)

The last line, following the interruption of the dash, has the quality of a pious, tacked-on moral, badly out of step with the steady escalation of the poem's rhetoric, which dashes pell-mell from its very first line: "Shout, for a mighty Victory is won!" The emotional climax is reached in the penultimate line, with another one of those unspoken "somethings" that are a regular feature of the Wordsworthian Sublime: "something evermore about to be," "something far more deeply interfused." The emotional "something" of glorious death in combat can be a quite widespread emotion, but finding it in "the *prospect* of our brethren slain" is a perspective with special resonance in Wordsworth's heart, not because he was a sadistic voyeur but because he so often projected his imagination into the realms of death.

In November, Thelwall showed up, of all people, starting out on the endless trek that was to continue for the remainder of his life. He was trying to eke out a living as another kind of language professional, an elocutionist, but sooner or later he always suffered the consequences of his early identification with the cause of revolutionary reform, as local authorities or vigilantes discovered his past and ran him out of town. This fate had begun for him—and very nearly so for Wordsworth and Coleridge—during a similar time of invasion hysteria in Somerset five years earlier. But he was welcomed to dine at the Wordsworth's cottage and stayed on an extra day to talk over old times, and their present career costs.

He was about to pay these costs at an even higher rate. His elocution lectures at Edinburgh in December were disrupted by an audience provoked by Francis Jeffrey and Scott's friend William Erskine, to whom Thelwall was nothing more than "once a Jacobin always a Jacobin," the phrase that kept hitting close to Wordsworth and Coleridge.[37] Thelwall published pamphlets in Edinburgh and Glasgow in 1804 to expose the plot against him, but they were honest words thrown into the teeth of a reactionary whirlwind. He also tried to answer Jeffrey's political smears from a review of April 1803, against his *Poems Written Chiefly in Retirement* (1802), and wrote in January 1804 seeking Wordsworth's advice in his pamphlet wars. Thelwall was being tarred with two brushes, one for his actual radicalism, the other for his poems supposed similarity to the "Lake School" that Jeffrey had first labeled in his explosive attack in the first number of the *Edinburgh Review.* This review was really aimed at Wordsworth, particularly the revolutionary potential Jeffrey accurately saw in the preface to *Lyrical Ballads:* "a kind of manifesto that . . . very ingenuously set forth . . . that it was their [i.e., these 'followers of simplicity'] capital object 'to adapt to the uses of poetry, the ordinary language of conversation among the middling and lower orders of the people.' "[38] That object was enough for Jeffrey to call them Jacobins: they were attacking the roots of society by perverting its hierarchies of language usage. But this plain style of language was not at all poor Thelwall's style: for all his liberal sympathies, his language was for the most part conventional poetic diction.

Thelwall did not get much help from Wordsworth, who pleaded other poetical commitments as his excuse: "As to the criticisms which you request of me, . . . I cannot at present find time to make them. I am now after a long sleep busily engaged in writing a Poem of considerable labour [*The Prelude*]."[39] Instead, Wordsworth offered Thelwall some tame improvements in style, and recommended he answer the *Edinburgh* on moral rather than personal grounds, attacking "their wicked and detestable abstract opinions." He distanced himself as much as possible from any kind of "school" of poetry, professing to know nothing about these reviews, while at the same time showing a considerable familiarity with their main outlines. His oblique reference to *The Prelude* at this juncture and the fact that this is the last extant letter from Wordsworth to Thelwall suggest that an important corner in the origins of British Romanticism had been turned. But lest we think Wordsworth turned too far or too early away from his radical youth, we should note that at this same time he received from William Frend, the charismatic liberal Cambridge professor of the early 1790s, Frend's latest book, *Patriotism; or, The Love of Our Country.* Dedicated to the "Volunteers of the United Kingdom," it is "such a vehemently pro-English utterance that it is impossible to imagine that its author had ever suffered persecution from Church and State."[40] Finding a position of poetical integrity between reaction on the one hand and ruin on the other was an extremely difficult undertaking in these years, and Wordsworth's attempt to carve one out for himself deserves more respect than scorn.

Coleridge too longed to escape from his present existence, but for personal domestic reasons, not public political ones. His continuing poor health fed his growing conviction that the damp climate of the Lakes region was bad for him, though the terrible state of his marriage, exacerbated by his jealousy of Wordsworth's domestic situation, "living wholly among *Devotees,*" contributed more than the climate to his unease.[41] He was investigating the possibility of being somebody's secretary abroad, but he mostly wanted to get away to a warmer climate. He raised with John Wordsworth the possibility of accompanying him on his next voyage, a crazy idea for which all lovers of English literature owe John a vote of thanks, for dissuading Coleridge from an ill-fated voyage on which two-thirds of the passengers drowned. Coleridge's latest idea, as of December 1803, was to go to Madeira or Sicily, but at the last minute Humphry Davy's enthusiastic account of Malta, coupled with John Stoddart's new appointment as king's advocate there, sent him to Valletta, England's strategic Mediterranean port. He spent fifteen months there, his immense charm and talents—always at their best when no strings were attached—soon raising him to the post of acting public secretary for Sir Alexander Ball, the British governor.[42] Wordsworth did not want Coleridge to leave, not only because he disapproved of what was clearly yet another abandonment of his wife and children, but because he felt Coleridge was abandoning *him.* One concrete way of expressing his disapproval was to refuse to help Coleridge pay for his projected trip; instead, he arranged a loan from the wealthy poetaster and dilettante William Sotheby in London.[43]

34 THE END OF *THE PRELUDE*

Oh, yet a few short years of useful life,
And all will be complete—thy race be run,
Thy monument of glory will be raised.
(XIII.428–30)

Coleridge's impending departure gave Wordsworth a new excuse to return to *The Prelude:* it became simultaneously a bon voyage gift and a powerful magnet to pull Coleridge back to him. Coleridge passed through Grasmere just before Christmas on his way to London, and suddenly broke down under the weight of his many ailments: physical, psychological, and psychosomatic. He spent three weeks in bed, screaming from opium nightmares, soothed and nursed back to sleep by Dorothy and Mary. As he recovered, he tried to get Wordsworth back on track for *The Recluse,* rather than wasting his energies on smaller tasks, or even diverting them to "the poem to Coleridge." He wrote to Poole predicting success in this effort, using metaphors from his own coming sea voyage: "I rejoice . . . that he has at length yielded to my urgent & repeated—almost unremitting—requests & remonstrances—& will go on with the Recluse exclusively.—A Great Work, in which he will sail; on an open Ocean, & a steady wind; unfretted by short tacks, reefing, & hawling & disentangling the ropes . . . this is his natural Element."[1]

Wordsworth's devoted women were set to copying out the existing parts of the poem, and on January 4 Wordsworth read to him "the second Part of his divine Self-biography [i.e., Part Two of *1799*] . . . in the highest & outermost of Grasmere"—most likely Far Easedale.[2] What neither man fully realized was that the "divine Self-biography" would shortly become the "Great Work" itself, in which Wordsworth would indeed sail on, unfretted not only by "short tacks" (which for Coleridge meant Wordsworth's short poems) but also by "reefing & hauling & disentangling the ropes" (which for Wordsworth signified Coleridge's complex philosophical ideas for *The Recluse*).

Two years earlier Wordsworth had hesitantly extended the biographical line of the "poem to Coleridge" beyond his seventeenth year, the point at which the 1799 text ended. There was no strong reason to do this in the structure of the text as it then stood, nor was there now. That its author was now thirty-three instead of twenty-nine did not make it necessary to extend the poem. What *1799* needed to make it a finished poem was more at the beginning—an antecedent to its abrupt opening question "Was it for this?"—not more at the end. It certainly did not need a run-up of over seven thousand additional lines, narrating eleven more years of the author's life, to make his leap into *The Recluse*'s themes of "Man, Nature, and Human Life" any surer.

In one sense, Wordsworth returned to *The Prelude* by the path of least resistance. In another sense, his return to *The Prelude* was a heroic decision, which effectively turned him away from the older didactic, metaphysical model of *The Recluse* to the new existential, performative model of *The Prelude.* The significance of this shift was not recognized immediately, and not admitted even when recognized. The poem he now resumed was an answer, the only one he knew for sure, to the question he had posed in his expanded preface to *Lyrical Ballads:* "What is a Poet?" He had listed the essential ingredients and given the basic outline there, but now he had to show—at least to himself—that *he* contained those elements and that his own life could fill in the outlines of that ideal Poet figure. The question "Was it for this?" would be answered by another, "What is a Poet?"

Even without the pressing claims of *The Recluse,* the decision to resume *The Prelude* was not easy. Deciding to write one's autobiography is, *in strictly autobiographical terms,* almost the most important of one's life actions: without it, no autobiography.[3] It appears that anyone can write an autobiography: we are the foremost authority and presumably have all the facts at our disposal. But where will we start and when will we stop? Will we tell the whole truth—and what would that be? Who will read it? Is the story of our life interesting to anybody but ourself? Inherent interest may not even be a relevant consideration, for many people have had interesting lives but few have written interesting autobiographies about them: the exceptions are wonderful, not usual. The possibility that it is all an absurd self-indulgence rises up quickly after one takes the apparently easy decision to *write* one's life. Thus Wordsworth's decision in early 1804 to cross his Rubicon, stepping from the end of the 1799 *Prelude* to a fresh page of "the poem on his own life," was as decisive in his imaginative life as crossing the Simplon Pass or climbing Mount Snowdon.

The theme of the poem did not change, but he now gave it a much different plot, not just a longer story. Its crisis was now not the loss of his mother or his boyhood fears and ecstasies in the hills of Hawkshead; instead, it was the crisis of his age and his participation in it, including—but not quite revealing—his love affair with Annette Vallon. In a way, this extension was necessary, for the conclusion of the two-part *Prelude* had spoken of the political disillusionment of his generation, but failed to give any evidence of the speaker's participation in it. Wordsworth's readiness to write about the subject he knew best, himself, was thus massively complicated by what he recognized it would entail: the need to write about the one contemporary subject on which everybody in his world had an opinion, the French Revolution. Many of these opinions were more informed than his, but if he stated the grounds of his own authority—direct participation (both secret and subversive) in many of the Revolution's most exciting events—he would immediately render himself an unreliable narrator, either a Jacobin sympathizer or a renegade informer.

Nevertheless, he persevered and, once he was committed to his task, the basic composition of *The Prelude* followed rapidly, in another of his amazing biennial bursts of poetic productivity: 1798, 1800, 1802, and now 1804, when most of the new poem was written, especially in the spring, his favorite season for composing.[4] He composed the books that became III–V largely between January and March of 1804; these were followed in order of composition by VI, IX, and the first half of X between April and July. He added Books VII–VIII and the remainder of X in October–December. There were of course countless additions, deletions, switches, and revisions in this process, to say nothing of the forty-year process of revision that followed, and almost all original composition came to a halt when the tragic news of John's drowning reached Grasmere on February 11, 1805. The completion of the poem, between March and May 1805, was a hurried affair; it no longer followed the chronology of his life, and used summary material, much of it composed earlier, to create the final books, XI–XIII.[5] But by a rough estimate he was, between January 1804 and May 1805, often composing at the rate of one hundred lines of powerful blank verse a day.

His decision to resume was certainly liberating. He worked straight through most of 1804, with only a brief summer vacation, completing the entire chronological narrative of the poem as we now have it. Its narrative line might have developed differently had John's tragedy not intervened. At first Wordsworth simply pursued the chronological record of his education through his Cambridge years and summer vacations, apparently intending a five-book bildungsroman of the kind familiar to the eighteenth century from such works as Johnson's *Rasselas* or Beattie's *The Minstrel*.[6] But by early March he abandoned this plan and dismantled his manuscript, making the so-called five-book *Prelude* of 1804 a largely conjectural version of the poem.

Neither the two-part version of 1799 nor this hypothetical five-book version is an autobiographical poem in the sense that the thirteen- and fourteen-book versions are. They are preparatory poems or *epyllions,* introductory works to a larger one to follow. For nearly five years *The Prelude* had assumed this relation to *The Recluse,* but now it took on a life of its own. Despite this large change in direction, Wordsworth pushed on chronologically, though he knew that by describing his 1790 walking tour and his subsequent experiences in France he was forcing his poem beyond any received idea of poetical (or personal) development possible before 1789. By going into the French Revolution, Wordsworth's poem on the growth of his mind went, like all of European civilization, beyond existing models not only of society but also of human identity and self-definition. Yet he began composing his French Revolution passages at a time when his own reactions to the present form of that cataclysmic event were almost the opposite of what they had been ten years earlier. Now he was a member of the Grasmere Volunteers, the published author of several patriotic sonnets on national liberty and independence, and sick with worry over his best friend's departure into one of the war's most dangerous theaters.

There is no telling where Wordsworth's narrative might have stopped had John not drowned. When that occurred, he stopped telling a story. He finished off *The Prelude* when he was thirty-four going on thirty-five, but by February of 1805 he had extended his chronological line only five or six years beyond where *1799* had ended: namely, from 1787 to ca. 1792–93. The poem's *narrative* ends with its hero at age twenty-three, with some bits and pieces referring as far forward as age twenty-five. The years 1793–98 are not significantly represented in *The Prelude* at all, those traumatic "five long years" for which he had given thanks for his recovery in "Tintern Abbey." These are the hidden years of his life, and they are also hidden in his autobiographical poem. They are the years of the probable clandestine return to France, the first hideaway with Dorothy, the London misadventures with the *Philanthropist,* the second hideaway at Racedown, the spy scare in Somerset, and the escape (or mission?) to Germany. In all of these he was very much more involved in political activism and danger (personal danger then, career danger now) than anything in the poem we have, for though Books IX–X are about revolution, they are mainly about French, not English, politics. Wordsworth seemed set on a course that leads into these years, and there are traces suggesting that he was ready to go further: for example, the crisis that breaks up Book X, when he "yielded up moral questions in despair," is best dated as late summer 1795, when he hurriedly left London for Racedown. But that is just about where the story, as narrative, ends.

John's death changed all this. The grief was too intense, the poem already too long, and the conclusion it was driving toward had already been composed several times. Filling in the years 1793–98 would have embroiled him in hopeless tangles and unexplainable embarrassments which would not aid his narrative but frustrate it, as they had his life. Better to summarize how his "Imagination" had been "Impaired and Restored" (the running title of the last three books) in Nature (XI), in Society (XII), and in the Mind of Man (XIII): a triad of *Recluse* terms with which to end *The Prelude.* He did not *complete* the biography of his youth and young manhood: rather, he decided to regard what he had written thus far *as* complete. The end of *The Prelude* thus also marks finis to the composition of "Wordsworth"; the story of young Wordsworth comes to a close at the point where it disappears into Wordsworth's reappropriation of it as the basic poetic material of his writing life.

John's death was The End in another sense as well, for it meant that Wordsworth's financial circumstances would never advance much beyond what they already were. Fate, which had smiled so broadly on him in 1802–3, now turned its face the other way. John had expected "a very good voyage . . . if not a *very great* one."[7] William and Dorothy were heavily invested in it, taking advances on their share of their Lowther payment to invest even more.[8]

John was confident of a "very great" return because he had at last prevailed on his ship's main owners to give him one of the routes that stopped in India. He expected it would be the Bombay stop, but when an in-house favorite who had been given the ultimate prize, the Bengal stop, declined it as being too risky, it fell into John's lap. Though officially outlawed by China in 1799, the traffic in opium more than doubled in that very year and doubled again in 1800–1804, with 60 percent of it going to China.[9] In the words of John's biographer, it is "obvious . . . that John and his associates felt no compunction about relying on Bengal's opium as a major asset to private trade on a 'better voyage.' "[10] It was "private trade" because the opium was taken on board as part of the officers' private cargo allowance, like the "camlets" for which John's wrists had been slapped in 1802. But the officers' trade in camlets only interfered with the company's legitimate trade profits; opium was forbidden by company rules and the laws of both governments, though in fact the trade went on very lucratively, condoned by the company and encouraged by the British government. John needed the opium trade to recoup his recent losses and to realize the great profit that had always fired "his schemes for making a quick fortune at sea," which were motivated in turn by his desire to give his brother the independence to do something for the world: "I will work for you," he said.[11] His hope and desperation are evident in the size of his total investment in this trip, nearly £20,000, more than double that of his last voyage, and much of it borrowed. He expected a profit of £10,000 on the first leg alone, even more from his cargo of rice and forbidden opium taken from Bengal to China, and still more from the teas he would carry on his voyage home.[12]

When his ship left Portsmouth with its fleet and escorts, John was determined "to arrive in Bengal with the first ship," and this eagerness contributed to his disaster. For when the fleet turned back to Portland harbor to wait out some heavy weather it encountered, the *Earl of Abergavenny* was the last to put about because it was leading the pack out of the Channel. As a result, it was the last to pick up a pilot to negotiate the tricky turn around Portland Bill into the harbor, and it ran up against the Shambles, a bank of rocks just below water level off the east tip of the bill. John's first words to the pilot as they foundered show how much the purpose of the voyage weighed upon his mind: "O Pilot, you have ruined me!"[13] John's behavior as captain was unimpeachably heroic throughout the seven agonizing hours it took for the ship to sink. One hundred fifty-five of the 387 persons aboard were taken off the ship or pulled from the water, but John refused to leave his command and went down with the *Earl.* His body washed up on shore months later, not far from where William had seen hundreds of bodies from another wrecked convoy of Indiamen, when at Racedown ten years earlier.

With the loss of the family bottom, the family fortunes were also in shambles. The few hundred pounds William and Dorothy had invested were safely insured, but the huge profits which would have given William Wordsworth full leisure to become the poet of *The Recluse* would now never be realized. It is hardly a total explanation, but it is a material fact worth noting that both of Wordsworth's masterworks came to grief—*The Prelude* prematurely ended, *The Recluse* permanently delayed—in part because of reverses in England's imperial trade operations, particularly in the riskiest, most illegal, and morally reprehensible part of it, the opium "war" on China. We can resist the temptation to make moral preachments on the fact, but it cannot be set aside as irrelevant to the cost of the creation of the Poet.

John's death not only initiated *The Prelude*'s endgame; it began the transition of the young Wordsworth into the Wordsworth of public memory and literary history. Three strands of life activity bound these poetical events together over the next two years. First, there was the family's wish to leave Dove Cottage, perhaps to leave Grasmere or the north altogether, as a growing family and painful memories there became hard to bear. Second, a subtle competition opened up between Wordsworth's intended major poems, *The Prelude* and *The Recluse,* and his other, more salable poems, in which the latter finally won out, with the fourth edition of *Lyrical Ballads* in 1805 and *Poems, in Two Volumes* in 1807. Third, the public sphere continued to shape his career, as Napoleon's successes on the Continent dashed England's hopes of victory and Wordsworth found himself increasingly a man without any heroes but himself.

The possibility of leaving Town End was raised within a month of the news of John's death and pursued sporadically until late 1807, when the family decided to move to Allan Bank, on the north shore of Grasmere. William and Dorothy thought of moving back down south to coincide with Coleridge's return, and for seven months, from late October 1806 to June 1807, the entire Wordsworth entourage—including Coleridge—were guests of the Beaumonts at their estate at Coleorton, between Derby and Leicester. Alternatively, they contemplated other residences in the Lake District, particularly Belmount near Hawkshead, the large stone house with a grand view of Esthwaite where Wordsworth as a poor orphan schoolboy had been entertained by the Reverend Brathwaite and his family. Land deals were also proposed with a view toward building their own house. While at Coleorton, Wordsworth suddenly learned he had become the owner of a small "Broad How" farm in Patterdale that he thought he had lost to a higher bidder, the local rector. Lord Lowther had made up the £200 difference in price when he was approached, much to Wordsworth's embarrassment, by the well-meaning Thomas Wilkinson. How, Wordsworth asked in exasperation, could Wilkinson think that if the price was too high for his own money, he would be willing to pay it by using another man's?[14]

Practical needs motivated these plans and inquiries. Thomas Wordsworth was born in June 1806, joining his brother, John, and sister, Dorothy ("Dora"); every bed in the house was now sleeping two persons. But there were strong emotional needs as well, produced by John's death. "The set is broken!" Coleridge cried out on hearing the tragic news, and some of the old associations of place were very hard to bear, though Wordsworth stoically overcame them, one by one. In the June after John's death he went fishing at Grisedale Tarn with a neighbor but had to leave almost immediately, overcome with grief at the memories of his separations from John at just that spot, in company with Coleridge in 1799 and with Dorothy in 1800. But within days he returned, alone, determined to engage in John's favorite sport, fishing, and his own, composing poems, to recollect his overpowering emotions in an enforced tranquillity. The result, "Elegiac Verses in Memory of My Brother, John Wordsworth," is poetically and doctrinally routine: Wordsworth's recognition that he must "with calmness suffer and believe." But it conveys the instant horror of the first shocking news:

> Sea—Ship—drowned—Shipwreck—so it came,
> The meek, the brave, the good, was gone;
> He who had been our living John
> Was nothing but a name.

But this fierce attempt to cauterize his emotions by his own poetry could not change the fact that the days of their youth had ended, and the imminent departure from Dove Cottage was the physical sign that the days of young Wordsworth were numbered.

At several points in these two years, the domestic drama spilled over into the creative struggle between the projected great works of Wordsworth's heroic poetic career and those of his ordinary public career. In the first week of April 1805, after the immediate, uncontrollable grief which shook the house had subsided, he composed some lines about John for inclusion in *The Recluse.* These were more than occasional elegiac verses, Dorothy insisted to Lady Beaumont: "I should not say a *poem* for it is a *part* of the Recluse."[15] That Wordsworth's first return to major composition following John's death was to *The Recluse,* not *The Prelude,* shows how much he regarded the former as the work for which John had been risking his life. Dorothy concurred: "I trust he will perform something that may mend many hearts, and that his beloved Brother would have approved." But these lines disappeared into thin air. He "composed much" by his usual method of outdoor striding and humming, but the lines "came from [him] in such a torrent" that they evaporated. He was "overpowered" by his subject. "I could not hold the pen myself, and the subject was such, that I could not employ Mrs Wordsworth or my Sister as my amanuensis."[16]

Immediately following this failure he turned instead to completing *The Prelude,* which he did extremely quickly, assembling Books XI–XIII in the space of a month between late April and late May 1805, mostly by rearranging already composed materials. Here again Wordsworth's mountainous strength is evident. He brought the poem on his life to a close with three books titled "Imagination, How Impaired and Restored" at the very time his imagination had been *un*restorably impaired by his brother's death. He finished it not in steady repose but in deep grief, a train of associations that continued into the great "Elegiac Stanzas Suggested by a Picture of Peele Castle in a Storm, Painted by Sir George Beaumont," of 1806, with its chilling submission to "a new control:" "A power is gone, which nothing can restore; / A deep distress hath humanized my soul."

Completing *The Prelude* was a major step, but with John dead, Wordsworth no longer had the stomach to keep on writing about his own life. His dissatisfaction with *The Prelude,* now widely considered the greatest long poem in English of the nineteenth century, is registered in his letter to Beaumont in June 1805, immediately after he finished writing it. "It was not a happy day for me I was dejected on many accounts; when I looked back upon the performance it seemed to have a dead weight about it, the reality so far short of the expectation; . . . and the doubt whether I should ever live to write the Recluse and the sense which I had of this Poem being so far below what I seem'd capable of executing, depressed me much."[17] But it gave him a new idea: "This work may be considered as a sort of portico to the

Recluse, part of the same building, which . . . if I am permitted to bring it to a conclusion, and to write, further, a narrative Poem of the Epic kind, I shall consider the *task* of my life as over."

Once *The Prelude* was completed, preparing a clean copy was the next step, a large and arduous task that naturally fell to Dorothy, who took three months through the winter of 1805–6 to produce manuscript A; a second copy, manuscript B, was produced by Mary later in 1806. These two manuscripts were the first parts of an astonishing corpus for which there is no exact parallel in English literature: the more than ten major manuscripts of full copies of *The Prelude,* and at least that many partial ones, that Wordsworth's female copyists produced between 1805 and 1839 (aided by a secretary, John Carter, after 1813).[18] If printed as published works, they would constitute a body of poetry longer than all the rest of Wordsworth's poetical works put together. The differences between some of these versions are very small, but that does not lessen the extraordinariness of their extent—rather the reverse, as it relates to Wordsworth's sense of his mission as the Poet. It was thought worthwhile, and everyone concerned pitched in energetically, to spend countless hours copying and recopying hundreds and thousands of lines for which in most instances perfectly usable clean copies already existed. A unique creative economy was at work when, say, five hundred lines were recopied for five words to be changed. The discrepancy reveals not only the extent of Wordsworth's egotism—that is the easy reaction—but the height of his epic conception of the Poet. Such compulsive rewriting also reveals on the practical level that this was a poem that *lived* in manuscript, for which cold print was feared to be fatal to any inspiration that might yet be found in the strong, beautiful young body which it constantly rearranged.

With the work of copying in train, Wordsworth again set himself to meet his implied contract with both John and Coleridge by pushing *The Recluse* forward. Until Coleridge returned and Wordsworth saw him, he kept his creative eye steadily on *The Recluse,* even as he continued to mark time with smaller pieces. But another sea disaster damaged his hopes in the month before the bad news about John, when Coleridge reported that Major Ralph Adye (1764–1804), to whom he had entrusted his notes for *The Recluse,* had en route back to England died of plague at Gilbraltar, where all his personal belongings and baggage were burned as a quarantine measure. This report may be regarded with a certain amount of skepticism. On the one hand, Wordsworth's hopes for Coleridge's notes were inordinate. Even before Coleridge left England, Wordsworth pleaded for them with premonitions of disaster: "I am very anxious to have your notes for the Recluse. I cannot say how much importance I attach to this, if it should please God that I survive you, I should reproach myself for ever in writing the work if I had neglected to procure this help."[19] This sounds like a desperate student asking for the notes of an important class lecture he has missed—and worried more about his performance than the possible death of his professor.

There really was a Major Adye who did die, despite the suspiciously ironic nature of his name. (That the name was likely pronounced "aid" only increases the irony.) Coleridge probably *had* given him some notes, during Adye's visit to Malta, since producing voluminous notes for other people's poems was one of his most fertile modes of writing. But there are some inconsistencies in Coleridge's account that raise the suspicion he may have used Adye's death as a pretext to explain to all who were expecting notes, letters, poems, travel journals, newspaper stories, or anything else from him why they had not got them. Daniel Stuart, the Beaumonts, Sara Coleridge, and others all received letters lamenting that the death of "that good Man Major Adye!" had resulted in the destruction of all Coleridge's writings to them. In one notebook entry Coleridge's standard formula for the event—"And Major Adye is dead! There died a good man!"—is a later insertion, "as if to retract the preceding sentences" wherein he had intimated his own feelings of failure: "yet I felt that in telling the Truth I was conveying falsehood."[20] But with this wholly Coleridgean alibi solidly in place, he could allow himself some self-pity: "One large, and (forgive my vanity!) rather important, set of Letters to you on Sicily and Egypt, were destroyed at Gibraltar among the papers of the most excellent man, Major Adye, to whom I had entrusted them on his departure from Sicily."[21] For good measure, he referred to other sets of letters thrown overboard from the *Arrow,* the *Acheron,* and an unspecified—and thus unspecifiable—"merchant Vessel."

But even if we give Coleridge the benefit of the doubt, it remains uncertain whether these notes would have helped much to produce *The Recluse.* After the publication of *The Excursion* ten years later, Coleridge sent Wordsworth a long letter full of regretful suggestions about what *The Recluse* should have been—another favorite Coleridgean perspective. But his observations do not differ fundamentally from what he had been saying about *The Recluse* all along, even before a word of it was written.[22] It was to show how a certain conception of an independent, creative imagination, fostered by "Nature," could work to transform and redeem secular society. That is, it was the lesson of *The Prelude* writ large, with "Wordsworth" rewritten as "Everyman." But with the death of Adye and the ruination of Coleridge, it became clear to Wordsworth that no recipe for *The Recluse* was forthcoming.

His own inventive powers remained woefully inadequate to the task, but he nevertheless tried: in the summer of 1806 he returned to the portions of "Home at Grasmere" that he had composed in 1800 and completed it, bravely penning, "Book First, Part First of *The Recluse,*" across the top of the first page of the finished manuscript. He did this by employing materials he had ready to hand: Grasmere neighborhood stories of human fortitude and moral sensitivity in harsh rural surroundings without benefit of culture and education. For example, there was the local farmer who commited adultery with the family's maid, then let his farm run to ruin from remorse, and finally died broken in spirit. Wordsworth moved these oddly unsettling moral tales from the literal to the symbolic level. Instead of identifying himself with a natural and human inspiration he believed to be resident in Grasmere, as he had done disastrously in 1800, he now extended this spirit by a kind of ersatz generalization: he wrote about *other people,* and more of them, to suggest a plausibly larger range for *The Recluse.* He tried to increase this plausibility by adding a conclusion which stitched his folksy Grasmere narratives onto the epic, mythic, apocalyptic claims of the "Prospectus": "Is there not / An art, a music, and a stream of words / That shall be life, the acknowledged voice of life?"[23] This rhetorical question about a possible transparency between ordinary and artistic language states the intention of *The Recluse* at its best, an intention frequently realized in many of Wordsworth's smaller poems, when freed of the weighty responsibility of *proving* it. But beyond this he could not go.

And just as he tacked the "Prospectus" onto the end of "Home at Grasmere" to give it—more than a sense of an ending, a sense of something evermore about to be—so when he came to *The Excursion,* he relocated the "Prospectus" to its beginning, to point the direction where this poem was intended to go. Naturally, unfriendly contemporary reviewers and pundits had a great deal of fun with the very large "Watch This Space" advertisements for his always-under-construction self that Wordsworth incautiously offered to public view. His habit of attaching concluding or prefatory notes that enormously increased the implied scope of the work at hand was the same one he had relied on throughout the last years of his youth, in the ever-expanding prefaces of *Lyrical Ballads.* Like the many manuscripts and conclusions of *The Prelude,* they are repetitions with variations in the same Romantic fugue of self-creation.

35
PRESENTING THE POET

> . . . that Lay
> More than historic, that prophetic Lay
> Wherein (high theme by thee first sung aright)
> Of the foundations and the building up
> Of thy own Spirit thou hast dared to tell
> What may be told . . . .
>
> (Coleridge, "To William Wordsworth: Composed on the Night after His Recitation of a Poem on the Growth of an Individual Mind," January 1807)

All this stopgap ended abruptly late in October of 1806, when the Wordsworths finally reestablished contact with Coleridge. As late as September, Wordsworth was still composing fresh work that he regarded as part of *The Recluse.*[1] But when the family headed south on their trip to the Beaumonts, they learned at their first stop, Kendal, that Coleridge had returned to the north. Not to Keswick, however. Instead, he had gone to Penrith, where he hoped to find Sara Hutchinson. He just missed her; she had left a few hours before his arrival, to join the Wordsworths. Overlooking the bad omen that Coleridge had gone first to see Sara his beloved, not Sara his wife, the Wordsworths immediately sent a message—to Keswick—for him to join them. He came dashing into Kendal almost as soon as the messenger departed, and not from Keswick but from Penrith, for he had set off immediately in pursuit of Sara. They were all shocked by his appearance, and saddened when they learned that he intended to separate from his wife. But they were scandalized when they realized he was trying to act out his fantasy of establishing a connection with Sara Hutchinson. Postponing their trip for two days, they huddled together in strained conversations in the hotel rooms and streets of Kendal, trying to talk him out of his desires while still hoping to reestablish their old relationships. But Coleridge was adamant, preoccupied with his own dreams and disasters.

Wordsworth, for his part, remained as preoccupied with himself as with his friend. He wrote a poem on the occasion, "A Complaint," a petulant lover's lament that his friend's love for him was no longer what it had been: "A fountain at my fond heart's door . . . Blest was I then all bliss above!" The poem fixates on the speaker's loss; there is not a word about what might have caused the lover's change of heart. Seeing the depths of Coleridge's unbalanced passion for Sara, Wordsworth jealously realized that the "well of love" he thought Coleridge poured out only for him was, if not dried up, no longer flowing: "the waters sleep in silence and obscurity." His jealousy was soon returned with interest.

Reuniting with Coleridge had been the focus of their hopes for the two years since his departure, both in terms of living (would they go south to join him?) and of writing (*The Recluse* would emerge when Coleridge returned). But his appearance and his defeated willpower made it clear that all was changed forever. Coleridge soon did arrange a separation from his wife. But his desperate wish that he might establish a relationship of some sort with Sara Hutchinson involved almost the only woman in the world with whom the Wordsworths could not countenance his having an intimate association. To make matters worse, Coleridge began to form the notion that Wordsworth had supplanted him in Sara's affections and was having an affair with his sister-in-law. This fear did not burst out immediately, but the seed was planted at Kendal. On the morning of October 28 Mary and Dorothy and the children climbed into a chaise and departed southward. Sara and William and Coleridge saw them off, and then Coleridge climbed resignedly into the coach heading back toward Keswick. But he knew the rest of the travel plan: that Sara and William would follow the next morning, after staying one more night together in Kendal. The two southward traveling parties rejoined at Derby at noon on the 30th, William and Sara having traversed in thirty-six hours the same distance that the slower-moving chaise with the children took two and a half days to cross.[2] The train of morbid thoughts laid down in Coleridge's fervid imagination when he thought about Wordsworth's last night in Kendal was the fuse leading to his explosion at Coleorton two months later.

During the long comfortable winter at Coleorton, as guests of the rich and generous Beaumonts, they had no trouble adapting themselves to this higher style of life (the palatial residence was until recently the headquarters of the National Coal Board). Wordsworth made himself useful by meticulously planning an elaborate winter garden on the grounds. His family also adopted the habit of regular churchgoing, and continued it—even William —after their return to Grasmere. Wordsworth had plenty of lesiure time to devote to *The Recluse* if he had wanted to. Instead, he turned from it to more expedient work on his forthcoming *Poems in Two Volumes,* which appeared in April 1807, arguably the single greatest collection of his works. A canceled "Advertisement" in the first of these volumes made clear their relation to *The Recluse:*

> The short poems, of which these Volumes consist, were chiefly composed to refresh my mind during the progress of a work of length and labour, in which I have for some time been engaged; and to furnish me with employment when I had not resolution to apply myself to that work, or hope that I should proceed with it successfully. Having already, in the Volumes entitled Lyrical Ballads, offered to the World a considerable collection of short poems, I did not wish to add these to the number, till after the completion and publication of my larger work; but, as I cannot even guess when this will be, and as several of these Poems have been circulated in manuscript, I thought it better to send them forth at once.[3]

This was certainly honest, but much too exposed, and Wordsworth or his editors did well to cancel it. But such a statement was wholly in keeping with his compulsive notion that any work he produced should be introduced, or defended, by referring to still-larger works and intentions that lay behind it. He did not mind exposing the therapeutic nature of his other poetry ("when I had not resolution to apply myself"), or his doubts about his staying power ("or hope that I should proceed with it successfully"), or even about completing the project as a whole ("I cannot even guess when this will be"), so long as his poems appeared in some kind of relation to his ideal self-creation as the Poet of *The Recluse.*

This was not his only motive for publication. Longmans had brought out a fourth edition of *Lyrical Ballads* in the fall of 1805, the first edition from which Wordsworth enjoyed the increased profits that came with owning the copyright. Its appearance underscored, for peers and critics who paid attention to this sort of thing, that he had been recycling essentially the same version of his poetry, and of himself, to the reading public for seven years, from 1798 to 1805. What *else* could Wordsworth write? was a question implied in several unsympathetic reviews. Furthermore, the extent to which he was identified solely with *Lyrical Ballads* did his reputation little good in the conservative cultural consensus that was emerging, for *Lyrical Ballads* had by now, through its regular biennial reappearances, become the flagship—and the target—of the "Lake school" of poetry, that newly dominant reviews like the *Edinburgh* continued to bombard as unreconstructed Jacobinism. The lively reputation that it preserved for Wordsworth among a growing circle of admirers gave him little comfort in terms of its ideological fallout, even less so as his own opinions about both poetry and politics were now moving to a more centrist position.

It was not only the shock of Coleridge's appearance that led Wordsworth to redirect his poetic activities in late 1806 but also his perceptions of a changing world that a long visit to London the previous spring had brought home to him. At the time, Mary was expecting her third child (in June), and William was not much help around the crowded little house, so he was packed off to London in March for a visit of two months. This visit brought him personally closer to the centers of British cultural and political power than he had ever been before, and what he saw and heard forced him to recognize that the world of his youth no longer existed, and convinced him of the need to change with the times.

Pitt had died suddenly in January, heartbroken over the continued failure of his policies against Napoleon, and Grenville was called on to form a new ministry, the hugely promising "Ministry of All Talents." Its great promise was not borne out, but for the moment it looked as though the Whig heroes of the 1790s were back in the saddle. Grenville, object of Wordsworth's scorn in his Juvenal imitation of 1795, was prime minister, with the aging Fox as foreign minister, brought in over the king's objections. Charles Grey's son entered the Cabinet (he was prime minister when the Reform Bill finally passed in 1832), as was Thomas Erskine, redoubtable champion of the 1794 treason trials.

Wordsworth's uncle Cookson was also closely involved in these changes, informally, but in ways that only underscored for Wordsworth how near his life, yet how far his works, were from official favor. Cookson had continued to rise in George III's esteem as canon at Windsor, following his tutorship of the king's sons, and was now almost as close to the king as John Robinson had been twenty years earlier. That January, Cookson bragged to the painter Joseph Farington that he had got another lucrative sinecure, called a "gown living" of more than 120 guineas a year, at "the King's especial and immediate application" to the lord chancellor on his behalf.[4] Farington noted that "Cookson has now got the best of the Canons' houses at Windsor," and remembered that the preceding year the bishop of Exeter had assured him that Cookson "will not stop where he is now," because the king agreed that "he did not know a person to whom he would sooner attend for advice and discretion."[5] Cookson advised George not to make any concessions to the incoming Whigs, and though his views did not prevail, he certainly had no extra good words to give the king on behalf of a nephew whose public reputation was several degrees to the left of Whiggism.

After visiting with Christopher in Lambeth, Wordsworth moved across the river to Grosvenor Square to be near the Beaumonts and spent much of his time at their spacious town residence. He also spent some time with Basil Montagu, who was rising successfully in the law, and on May 19, near the end of his visit, he attended a "rout" hosted by Fox's wife. Samuel Rogers, his patron in literature as Beaumont was in art, introduced Wordsworth to Fox. They had a very satisfactory exchange, which Wordsworth improved over years of retelling it. Fox clearly knew who Wordsworth was, rising from his beloved gaming table with the greeting "I am very glad to see you, Mr. Wordsworth, though I am not of your faction."[6] This is all Rogers recorded in his diary, except for the explanation that Fox meant "he admired a school of poetry different from that to which Wordsworth belonged." The thrust startled Wordsworth, but he was equal to it, elegantly capping it by replying, "But in poetry you must admit that I am the Whig and you the Tory." This is very good, almost the wittiest thing Wordsworth ever said, but it developed over years of rethinking the moment and recollecting his emotions about it into tranquillity, for it derives from a manuscript of 1843 prepared by Humphry Davy's sister-in-law for her children. She said Wordsworth mentioned it, "the only such mention I ever heard from him," as "a *bon-mot* of my own."[7]

Wordsworth still dined with his old radical friends in London, making several calls on Godwin, once in company with Horne Tooke, now seventy. Both were much subdued, older, and radical no more, discredited not only by constant governmental harassment and amateur vigilantism but also by geopolitics far beyond their control. Godwin was even quieter than Thelwall had become, forced to make a living writing children's books for "The City French and English Juvenile Library," hiding behind the cover of his second wife's bookshop (a pioneer in high-quality children's literature), publishing pseudonymously, and borrowing heavily (but repaying lightly) from all his acquaintances. Like Wordsworth's, his works fared well with the *Anti-Jacobin Review* and other neoconservative watchdogs only because the real identity of their author was not known.[8]

Wordsworth's meetings and reflections on times past were not merely coincidental. He also dined with John Taylor, part-owner of the *True Briton* and the *Sun,* who had been sent a copy of the 1800 *Lyrical Ballads.* Taylor, true to his informer's habits, gossiped with Farington that he found Wordsworth "strongly disposed to Republicanism." This meant, according to Taylor, that Wordsworth's "notions are that it is the duty of every Administration to do as much as possible to give consideration to the people at large, and to have *equality* always in view; which though not perfectly attainable, yet much has been gained towards it & more may be."[9] Taylor preferred Wordsworth's poetry to Coleridge's or Southey's, but thought "that all of them affecting to be simple & natural . . . frequently reduce their expressions to what may almost be called *Clownish.*" For good measure, he passed along the bishop of London's opinion that "whatever merit there might be in them it was not *legitimate Poetry.*" We don't know what Wordsworth and Taylor said face to face, but John Taylor was not the man to politely mask his opinions, and Wordsworth was no more subtle when it came to answering a direct question.

Nonetheless, a sharp inquiry about the legitimacy of his poetry and his politics, and the realization that such gossip was being repeated about town, chimed ominously in his memory with Walter Scott's amused report the previous August (1805) that John Southey, Lord Somerville, on hearing that Wordsworth had got into Scott's "good company," told Scott he still had doubts about the loyalty of Wordsworth and Coleridge, feeling they were still republican sympathizers; he proudly claimed responsibility for setting the spy on them in 1797 in Somerset.[10] Somerville's comment showed that, ten years later, memories were still sharp and that clever drawing-room repartee could be based on claiming to have sniffed out Wordsworth's radicalism before it was reformulated as literature. Wordsworth had joined in the laughter at Scott's report, but had not bothered to tell Scott how plausible the government's actions were, given his and Coleridge's and Thelwall's reputations in 1797.

Scott was brought back to his mind during the 1806 London visit by the runaway success of *The Lay of the Last Minstrel,* which had been published late in 1805. Wordsworth jealously admitted, "I did not expect it would make much sensation: but I was mistaken; for it went up like a balloon."[11] He had been present at the creation of the *Lay,* a "political" poem so distanced in time and overlaid with legend that any application to England's or Scotland's present moment was moot. When Wordsworth compared the success of Scott's apparently "timeless" tale with the prospects of the 8,000-line poem on his own life that Dorothy and Mary were at that moment fair-copying in Grasmere, his heart failed within him. What the mass of casual readers would have seen, had *The Prelude* been published then, was simply—despite its disclaimer about "youthful errors"—that this young man had been very heavily involved indeed with the Revolution's leaders and with their English sympathizers.*

Fox's death in September of 1806 touched a still-deeper chord in Wordsworth's memory. He composed three poems in response to it, the "Lines Composed at Grasmere . . . after a stormy day, the Author having just read

*This was still the reaction of most readers when *The Prelude* was finally published in 1850, but by then it had become a tiresome matter of "that old business of the French Revolution," no longer a matter of active concern. This was not because fears of revolution had subsided—hardly, two years after 1848, the "Year of Revolutions," which saw publication of *The Communist Manifesto*—but because any ideas of revolutionary change in England had been thoroughly relegated to the dustheap of crackpot ideas by the great majority of middle-class readers, thanks to government domestic policy and constant conservative overreaction to events in Europe.

in a Newspaper that the dissolution of Mr. Fox was hourly expected," and the fragmentary lines "The rains at length have ceased" and "To the Evening Star over Grasmere Water." His grief for the loss of Fox was so great because, as at the grave of Burns, he felt the general loss personally. "Many thousands now are sad" was a cliché truism. But when he goes on to say, "A Power is passing from the earth / To breathless Nature's dark abyss," the lines thrill because we can feel in them Wordsworth's similar lines about himself in the Simplon Pass or on Mount Snowdon. Similarly, "To the Evening Star over Grasmere Water" remains a twelve-line fragment rather than a finished sonnet because Wordsworth could not bring himself to add the necessary two lines that would complete his identification with Fox, such as he had made in his dedicatory letter of 1801. But we can recognize their connection from the fragment's similarity to the imagery of "Hesperus":

> The lake is thine,
> The mountains too are thine, some clouds there are,
> Some little feeble stars, but all is thine,
> Thou, thou art king, and sole proprietor.

Jupiter was his planet, and Hesperus was his star. To say that these lines are egotistical is to miss—or make—the essential point: Wordsworth aspired to a self-definition that transcended historical egotism or personal success. But at these moments and in these places, he began to realize that the epic story of his own imaginative development could never hope for a sympathetic reading in a world dominated by the likes of John Taylor, John Somerville, and Francis Jeffrey. With the passing of heroes like Fox, politicians—and readers—who could sympathize even when they disagreed, Wordsworth knew the "fit audience" he sought was gone, at least for the time being.

Hence he was extremely upset when, within weeks of comfortably settling in at Coleorton in the fall, he received a letter from his old friend Francis Wrangham cheerily proposing that they resurrect their Juvenal satire of 1795–97. Possibly Wrangham felt that, with both Pitt and Fox dead, its political bite was now tame enough for safety. Or maybe he thought it gained in timeliness with the installation of the Ministry of All Talents, and that its whacks on "Grenville's onion head" would be great fun now that Grenville was prime minister.

This was not at all the light in which Wordsworth regarded the idea; he was horrified. Not only were many of the persons named in it still living, and just then returned to power; his own personal and political relations to them had changed markedly. A line like "Must honour still to Lonsdale's tail be bound?" would simply not do, when "Lonsdale" now signified William, not James, Lowther, a neighbor and benefactor whom Wordsworth was assiduously cultivating, not the tyrant of his youthful life. Individual lines could have been changed, of course, but he wanted to bury the whole ethos of this part of his past, and he was nearly frantic in his determination to quash the project. He was highly successful in doing so, because the full version of this satire has only just appeared.[12]

He fired back at Wrangham a volley of reasons why they should drop the idea, including explicit directions that any verses by him in Wrangham's possession should be immediately destroyed (they weren't). He began with a high-minded literary rationale for declining to participate, "I have long since come to a fixed resolution to steer clear of personal satire; . . . with respect to public delinquents or offenders . . . I should be slow to meddle even with these."[13] But he ended with a set of practical reasons that arose immediately from the present stage of his self-creation as the Poet.

> I would most willingly give them up to you, fame, profit, and everything, if I thought either true fame or profit could arise out of them: I should even with great pleasure leave you to be the judge in the case if it were unknown to everybody that I ever had a concern in a thing of this kind; but I know several persons are acquainted with the fact and it would be buzzed about; and my name would be mentioned in connection with the work, which I would on no account should be.

As in his letters to William Calvert in 1795, or to his brother Richard on the occasion of James Lowther's death, Wordsworth's emotions blur his syntax. And with good reason. With *Lyrical Ballads* a sitting target for charges of "Jacobinical pathos," with *Poems in Two Volumes* in the last stages of preparation, and with *The Prelude* finished and awaiting Coleridge's arrival for its first performance, such an exposure of his "youthful errors" was the last thing he needed. It would have confirmed the still-lively suspicions of people like John Taylor and Lord Somerville that Wordsworth was steeped in republicanism, a confirmed opponent of monarchy, aristocracy, and the established order. That he was no longer, actively, any of those things mattered less to him than that he would be *perceived* as such, and he well knew that no amount of explanation would satisfy such implacable opponents. His phrase about a "judge in the case" hints at thoughts about the government's increasingly successful prosecutions for treason and sedition, and his fear that his "name would be mentioned" by "several persons . . . acquainted with the fact" could refer equally well to the kind of gossip he had heard about town in the spring or to crown witnesses in a trial. The Juvenal verses were a clear exposure of the young Wordsworth in all his edgy strength; like *The Prelude* and other evidences of this young man's existence (most of which he retained in unpublished manuscripts), they had to be hidden or destroyed if the creation of the Poet was to succeed.

Hence Wordsworth's thoughts about his career were particularly sharp and sensitive when Coleridge arrived on December 21, having arranged his separation from Sara Coleridge in an emotional debacle at Keswick in November. He had undertaken to provide for the education of his two surviving sons, and he brought little Hartley with him, for a visit that lasted until April.[14] In some respects these months together did knit up and restore the old relationships. The Wordsworths had Coleridge to themselves, and could modulate the upsetting effect of Sara Hutchinson's presence on him by daily routines of an ordinary domesticity more in tune with reality. But not before Coleridge tormented himself to the last degree of agony in his amazing fantasy life.

Fate could not have decreed a crueler twist in the creation of the Poet than that Coleridge, in his state, should at this time have had to listen to Wordsworth's first full presentation of *The Prelude.* But he contrived to make matters worse for himself by convincing himself that William was now pursuing an affair with Sara Hutchinson. His fantasy of their sexual encounter was so detailed and graphic that it took up three sheets in his notebook—which, in a gesture of caution highly uncharacteristic in such a vast and unbuttoned account of his private thoughts, he (or a nervous heir) carefully cut out. All that remains is a very precise notation of the time and the place: **"THE EPOCH.** Saturday, 27th December, 1806—Queen's Head, Stringston [Thringstone], 1/2 a mile from **Coleorton Church,** 50 minutes after 10."[15] The words "The Epoch" are written in larger, bolder letters than any other words in Coleridge's huge collection of notebooks. There is no further indication of what might have happened at that time to excite his suspicions, except in the emotional debris from it which haunted him for the rest of his life, especially over the next two years.

Coleridge's next notebook entry shows one avenue he took to escape from the self-torture of the "Hell of Thought" into which he now fell: "were it not for riotous Dancing . . . feasting, dancing, wine, which drown and hang in you every honest Thought," and keeps you equally from raising your eyes to heaven and from feeling "the Hell that is already round you, upon you, in you."[16] The following September, after quoting a bitter misogynist couplet from Propertius ("What profits it for maids to found temples in honour of Chastity, if every bride is permitted to be whate'er she will?"), he wrote a long, tortured, and extremely subtle analysis of his desire to make himself worthy of Sara's love, "even to make her already loving me love me to that unutterableness, that impatience at the not enoughness of dependence, with which I love her!"[17] But even this excruciating meditation on the exquisite reciprocities of love ("to make her Love of me delightful to her own mind") is crossed by Wordsworth's shadow, at once censorious and lascivious:

> O! what mad nonsense all this would sound to all but myself—and perhaps even She would despise me for it—no! not despise—but be alarmed—and learn from *W*—to pity & withdraw herself from my affections. Whither?—O agony! O the vision of that Saturday Morning—of the Bed / —O cruel! is he not beloved, adored by two—& two such Beings— / and must I not be beloved *near* him except as a Satellite?—But O mercy mercy! is he not better, greater, more *manly,* & altogether more attractive to any [*sic*] the purest Woman? . . . W. is greater, better, manlier, more dear, by nature, to Woman, than I—I—miserable I!—but does he—O No! no! no! no! he does not—he does not pretend, he does not wish, to love you as I love you, Sara! . . . No! he is to be beloved—but yet, tho' you may feel that if he loved you, . . . even *partly* as *I* love you, you should inevitably love him . . . yet still he does not *so* love you— . . . I alone love you so devotedly, & therefore, therefore, love me, Sara!—Sara! love me![18]

And in 1808 the "thunder-cloud" of "that miserable Saturday morning!" could still break fresh upon him, when he recollected "the anxious fears, <of which> I scarcely dare be conscious. But *then* was the first Thunder-Peal! But a minute and a half with ME—and all that time evidently *restless & going*—An hour and more with κκ.θχκκ.θυ [Wordsworth] *in bed*—O agony!"[19]

That all this is Coleridge's fantasy, not fact, is the more likely possibility. But that it is fact cannot be ruled out, given Wordsworth's commanding sexual presence and the reality that Sara was much the liveliest and most attractive of the three rather plain women of the household—and the one whose critical opinions about his poetry Wordsworth paid most attention to. "A Complaint" showed that Wordsworth was jealous of Coleridge's love for Sara because he felt it diminished Coleridge's love for him. That he might have seduced Sara in revenge seems a motive too sinister for even the most glacial interpretation of his character. But that Coleridge could have fantasized such a motive is not at all out of character for his mercurial imagination. Later in life Coleridge was still exorcising the demon of this thought, analyzing the "Strange Self-power in the Imagination, when painful sensations have made it their Interpreter."[20] His vivid imagination gave a living, breathing sense of reality to something he knew—or should have known—not to be true: "That dreadful Saturday Morning, at [Coleorton], did I *believe* it? Did I not even *know,* that it *was* not so, *could* not be so? Would not it have been the sin against the Holy Ghost . . . if I had dared to believe it conscientiously, & intellectually! Yes! Yes! I *knew* the horrid phantasm to be a mere phantasm . . . even to this day the undying worm of distempered

Sleep or morbid Day-dreams—."[21] One would almost have to *be* Coleridge to imagine how sexual jealousy of Wordsworth could be construed as a sin against the Holy Ghost, but whatever facts he based his fantasy on, their disposition required an unreliable witness and unscrupulous prosecutor, roles which Coleridge was all too ready to assume, in his mind, especially against himself.

Whether something really happened that Saturday morning or not, it is in the highest degree amazing that Coleridge could sit still to listen to *The Prelude* delivered in its master's voice later the same week. His ability to hear the poem in a properly receptive frame of mind was beaten down to a nadir of hatred, anger, shame, and humiliation. It is a vast and terrible tribute to the power of both men's mind and character that Wordsworth finished *The Prelude* and delivered it to its intended auditor at this time, and that Coleridge rose to the occasion with almost the last significant poem of his life. If the composition of *The Prelude* was brought to an end by John Wordsworth's death, its presentation to Coleridge produced the epitaph for Coleridge's poetical career, written by himself, and titled "To William Wordsworth: Composed on the Night after His Recitation of a Poem on the Growth of an Individual Mind." In Malta he had written a relatively untroubled response to the parts of *The Prelude* he had taken with him. Titled "Ad Vilmum Axiologum," it paid homage to the literary reincarnation of the young Wordsworth with an in-joke, since Coleridge knew that Wordsworth had first appeared in print as Axiologus in 1787, with his sonnet on Helen Maria Williams's tears. The effect of *The Prelude* registered in these lines is benign and general: "All have welcomed thy Voice," which resounds in "the Hearts of the Pure, like caves in the ancient mountains." If his praise went as high as praise could go—"This is the word of the Lord!"—it was no further than Coleridge was always ready to go in his admiration of "the Giant Wordsworth, God love him!"[22]

But the verses written on the night of January 7, 1807, "To William Wordsworth," are both greater poetry and much more painful in their revelation of *The Prelude*'s effect on their intended auditor. In drafts written within hours of his first hearing it, Coleridge praised it in terms that magnificently sum up Wordsworth's career achievement:

> that Lay
> More than historic, that prophetic Lay
> Wherein (high theme by thee first sung aright)
> Of the foundations and the building up
> Of thy own Spirit thou hast dared to tell
> What may be told, to the understanding mind
> Revealable . . . .

The lines also give full emphasis to the importance of the French Revolution in the creation of Wordsworth the Poet, in images recalling the triumphal celebrations of a Roman emperor: "Where France in all her towns lay vibrating . . . beneath the burst / Of Heaven's immediate thunder . . . thou wert there, *thine own brows garlanded, / Amid the tremor of a realm aglow, /* Amid a mighty nation jubilant."

The poem is indeed an *homage* to much of Wordsworth's entire oeuvre, from direct allusions to the Intimations Ode ("thoughts all too deep for tears") to the fact that its overall structure is an amalgam of "Tintern Abbey" and Coleridge's "Dejection: An Ode." Like the ode's admission of the imaginative crisis caused by his hopeless love for Sara Hutchinson, "To William Wordsworth" becomes a farewell to Coleridge's hopes for a poetical career, in humble prostration before Wordsworth's. Even before the reading ended, Coleridge could see his friend "in the choir of ever-enduring men," unaffected by Time, "among the archives of mankind." As he listened, "with a heart forlorn," his spirits revived only to the extent that he knew *he* was lost, "even as Life returns upon the drowned." The sense of his life that flooded over him was a terribly unfair indictment of all his failures, both real and imaginary:

> [of] fears self-willed, that shunned the eye of Hope;
> And Hope that scarce would know itself from Fear;
> Sense of past Youth, and Manhood come in vain,
> And Genius given, and Knowledge won in vain;
> . . . [all] but flowers
> Strewed on my corse [*sic*], and borne upon my bier,
> In the same coffin, for the self-same grave!
>
> (66–70, 73–75)

This is the same kind of death imagery he used in "Dejection," prompted now not simply by a recognition of Wordsworth's greater poetic powers but also by his excruciatingly painful conviction of his friend's greater sexual attraction to his beloved Sara Hutchinson. Wordsworth was "better, greater, more *manly,* & altogether more attractive to any the purest Woman," both in poetics and in erotics. The semi-apocryphal story of an argument between Hemingway and Fitzgerald in a Paris bathroom in the 1920s over the relative size and virtues of their sexual organs is Modernism's farcical return upon the thoroughly Romantic tragedy of defeat which Coleridge now felt he had suffered at the hands of Wordsworth, in poetry as well as love. But he did not let such unmanning thoughts destroy his poem: "That way no more! . . . ill beseems it me . . . To wander back on such unhealthful road, / Plucking the poisons of self-harm!"

Instead, begging Wordsworth's pardon, he returned to a conclusion of praise that summons up Coleorton's prescribed domestic antidote for his violent passion: the scene of all of them listening together, he and Dorothy and Mary and Sara, "eve following eve, / Dear tranquil time, when the sweet sense of Home / Is sweetest!" A sudden thought drew him back to their trip to Germany, the three of them alone together. His soul lay passive beneath the power of Wordsworth, "driven as in surges now beneath the stars, / With momentary stars of my own birth, / Fair constellated foam," an image he clearly recalled from his night alone on deck during their passage to Hamburg eight years earlier, when "cloud-like foam dashed off from the vessel's side, each with its own small constellation."[23] And when Wordsworth had finished, and Coleridge saw "round us both / That happy vision of beloved faces"—a vision that had been horribly and permanently disfigured for him ten days before—he forgave all, though he never forgot it, in a profound gesture of religious submission: "And when I rose, I found myself in prayer."

EPILOGUE

Hiding the Man; or, Emotion Recollected in Tranquillity

> Poetry is the spontaneous overflow of powerful feelings: it takes its origin from emotion recollected in tranquillity: the emotion is contemplated till by a species of reaction the tranquillity disappears, and an emotion, kindred to that which was before the subject of contemplation, is gradually produced, and does itself actually exist in the mind.
>
> (Preface to *Lyrical Ballads,* 1800)

After reading *The Prelude* to Coleridge with devastating effect in early 1807, Wordsworth did something unusual, the significance of which was not immediately clear to either man, and which has been almost wholly lost sight of since. But it was consistent with many other actions he took in regard to his youth: he hid the poem from public knowledge, keeping it by him during the remaining forty-three years of his life.

The choice not to publish "the poem on the growth of my own mind" inevitably produced the compulsion to *keep on* writing it. Not by extending it parallel to his ongoing life but by perfecting its youthful epiphanies through endless revision. At the time Wordsworth's assumption was that *The Prelude*'s publication would depend on his finishing *The Recluse.* But this deferral gradually hardened into a *retroactive* decision against publishing *The Prelude,* as first years, then decades, passed and no *Recluse* appeared, though the existence of both poems was announced in the preface of *The Excursion,* published in 1814 and identified as Part Two of *The Recluse.*

Instead, Wordsworth's story of self-creation was self-canceled, and the nonappearance of *The Prelude* thus matches other acts defining the young Wordsworth. It became yet another hidden aspect of his youthful self, similar to gaps within *The Prelude* itself, such as his affair with Annette Vallon, his political actions on both the left and the right, the aborted business of the *Philanthropist,* the absence of any particulars from the "five long years," 1793–98, and the omission of almost all references to the fact that he was writing thousands of lines of poetry while the other life actions of *The Prelude* were going on.

If he had published *The Prelude* in 1807, even with these omissions—but scandalously more so had he included them—he would have been not only England's first clearly Romantic poet but also its greatest republican poet since Milton. This would of course have massively complicated Lord Byron's appearance in that role with the publication of *Childe Harold's Pilgrimage* five years later, which produced perhaps the definitive literary celebrity-creating event in English literature: "I awoke and found myself famous." This was the kind of fame Wordsworth had courted all along, but he was not prepared, as Byron was, to accept—nor could he afford to—its consequences, neither the ecstasy of adulation nor the fury of reaction. But *The Prelude*—"Childe William's Pilgrimage"—was far riskier than almost anything in Byron's lightly veiled autobiography, not excluding strong hints of sexual impropriety involving his sister. Had it appeared in 1807, Wordsworth would have awakened to find himself *in*famous.

The Prelude brought Wordsworth's youth to an end both chronologically and compositionally. A question that the present book provokes, "*Was* Wordsworth ever young?," is not, then, facetious but serious, because Wordsworth went to such lengths to bury his youthful self. The young Wordsworth is the hidden Wordsworth, hidden first by omissions and elisions in his autobiographical poem and then buried deeper by its being kept out of sight until he was dead—allowing the public to view his younger self in his coffin (as it were), as he had imagined himself in 1803 viewing the buried body of Robert Burns. Paradoxically, the public appearance of Wordsworth's youth was postponed until after his death. *The Prelude* was the story he could not tell his nation, only his family and friends. Telling it aloud (so to speak) would have confirmed the suspicions of many readers in 1807 that he was indeed a kind of conspirator and—as unsympathetic reviewers were already saying of *Lyrical Ballads*—that his poetry reflected his revolutionary ideals and experience.

Anyone who teaches Wordsworth's poetry for very long will occasionally toy with the idea of what his image in literary history would be had he died young—at age thirty-six, for example, Byron's age when he died at Missolonghi, and Wordsworth's age when he read *The Prelude* to Coleridge. In essence, he did die: the story of his youth ends there and, so far as public reputation was concerned, publishing *The Prelude* then or dying then would have amounted to much the same thing. I do not propose to kill Wordsworth off, ca. 1807: more than half his life and much of his best poetry remained ahead of him. But it's not the story I wanted to tell. Neither did he; and how to preserve the story of his youth became the obsession of the rest of his life.

His name for this process was "recollecting emotion in tranquillity." We have long thought the phrase applied only to Wordsworth's method of composing, to his ability to draw images up out of "hiding places ten years deep," as he said of the twenty-years-delayed *Peter Bell.* Typically, he generalized this process to apply to all poetry, but of course it does not describe the compositional or emotional habits of all poets—as we have only to think of his alter ego Byron to realize. But it does apply to Wordsworth's composition of his whole life, both in *The Prelude* and in its posthumous appearance from hiding places not ten but fifty years deep. The very phrase "hiding places" for wherever he kept his memories and images of his life is at once a kind of Freudian slip and another of those literal metaphors I referred to in this book's Prologue. "Hiding places" are not lapses of memory, things forgotten and gone out of mind; they are secret caches of desire, emotion, excitement, and shame: Wordsworth's young life is full of them, and they are more numerous, and deeper, than we thought.

The Wordsworth we know and honor is above all the poet of *full presence:* of effort, expectation, and desire, and "something evermore about to be." Hence it is not surprising but expectable that his absences—his gaps, his lacunae—should be, when we can find them or when we stumble into them accidentally, not shallow but as deep as his heights are high. He said as much many times, especially when talking about himself as a poet:

> Not Chaos, not
> The darkest pit of lowest Erebus,
> Nor aught of blinder vacancy, scooped out
> By help of dreams—can breed such fear and awe
> As fall upon us often when we look
> Into our Minds, into the Mind of Man—
> My haunt, and the main region of my song.

Or, again: "By our own spirits are we deified; / We Poets in our youth begin in gladness; / But thereof comes in the end despondency and madness." If the present book has accomplished its mission, it should now be clear that such statements are not only relevant to Wordsworth's philosophical and psychological themes but true to his biography as well.

The hidden and unpublished Wordsworth of *The Prelude* is not an anomaly; on the contrary, he follows a pattern consistent with many of his other works' appearance, or nonappearance. The Salisbury Plain poems and *The Borderers* were not published until 1842, "The Ruined Cottage" did not appear until 1814 (buried in the turgid *Excursion*), and *Peter Bell* and its companion, *The Waggoner,* radical experiments of 1798, did not appear until 1819. Furthermore, all these and his other published "juvenilia" are themselves disguised versions of their young author, since they were first carefully doctored by an older man's revisions. The "Letter to the Bishop of Llandaff" did not appear at all, but it was carefully preserved, and the Imitation of Juvenal, which Wordsworth thought safely destroyed, appeared in full only two hundred years after its first composition. All of these texts were work of the hidden years, those "five long years," 1793–98, and each, in its early form, betrays a far more politically engaged author than even the radical language experimenter of the 1798 *Lyrical Ballads.* Wordsworth suffered more than his fair share of political abuse for *Lyrical Ballads,* and if *The Prelude* had appeared anytime during the war with Napoleon, or during the immediate postwar years of renewed agitation for reform (and redoubled suppression of it), it would have identified its author far too closely—for *his* success—with the decade of the 1790s. Moreover, if it had included even the breath of a hint that he, a.k.a. Mr. Wordsworth, also "had business on the other [Tory] side of the road," as he sneeringly said of the bishop of Llandaff, the consequences would have been even worse, as they always are for turncoats and double agents.

Wordsworth might have suffered the fate of Thelwall and Holcroft, or Robert Bage and Mary Hays, or any of the long-forgotten names of England's first "Lost Generation." Instead, by cutting, pasting, altering, delaying, or simply denying the appearance of his radical youth, he created and projected a substantially different image of himself as the Poet. First announced heroically in the 1802 additions to the preface, it was first personified in the eponymous character of that name in *The Excursion,* whose only "action" is to observe and comment on a long argument between a nonpolitical Pedlar and a too political Solitary (both aspects of Wordsworth himself, as Hazlitt immediately recognized) about the meaning of the French Revolution for England. Wordsworth slaved over the poem from 1808 until 1814, for he meant it to be his first fully realized address to the cultural reform of his nation. But as the *observer* of the great ideological debate of his era—which *The Excursion* leaves still unresolved—Wordsworth became his audience, or the part of it he had by then identified with: the Poet of *un*reformed England.

Although he published a dozen new volumes of poetry after 1807, the number is misleading. Some, as noted, had been written as much as twenty years earlier, while others were very occasional in nature, versified travelogues from his tours, such as the *Memorials of a Tour on the Continent, 1820* (1822), though often containing many good poems. Within the poetic economy of the Wordsworth household, moreover, many of these publications were viewed as stopgaps or deck clearings to allow—or force—William to get on with *The Recluse,* the avowed goal of his self-defined career as Poet. But the temptation to shorter forms that Coleridge had warned against always reasserted itself, especially in sonnet sequences, even though some of these, like *The River Duddon* (1820), are among the best of their kind in English.

The Prelude too continued to prevent *The Recluse,* as it always had, in Wordsworth's cross-grained refusal to accept—or his inability to deny?—that he himself was his own best story. In 1819 and in 1832 valuable time was expended in preparing new fair copies of "the poem on the growth of my own mind," while virtually countless partial manuscripts and smaller revisions of it continued throughout his life. And he found another way to expand the image of his life, not by extending the chronological range of *The Prelude* but, from 1815 on, by arranging the poems in his editions of his collected works—seven in all, between 1815 and 1849—according to the life stages and emotions of an individual human being: "Poems Written in Youth," "Poems Referring to the Period of Childhood," "Poems Referring to the Period of Old Age," and "Poems of the Fancy," "Poems of the Imagination," "Poems of Sentiment and Reflection," interspersed with the tours and memorials and reflections of that same very comprehensive figure. Thus did Wordsworth's works appear to define his life, an impression that many decades of publishing practice reinforced, before readers and critics began finally to complain about this way of having their perception of the poet managed from beyond the grave.

Yet, to a surprising extent, Wordsworth's actual life from 1807 to 1850 recapitulates the history of constant textual self-(re)-creation that we see in his sequestering *The Prelude* for posterity and publishing his juvenilia in old age. It is an overstatement, but not an untrue one, to say that much of what he did during the last forty-four years of his life was a repetition of what he had already done in his first thirty-six years.

This is especially true of his travels. He went to Scotland two more times, in 1814 and 1831, to visit Scott and places in Scott's poetry (Yarrow in particular) he had missed in 1803. In 1820 he and Dorothy and Mary took the "re-tour" of the Continent that consciously repeated his 1790 walking tour, and in 1828 he traveled on the Rhine with Coleridge, and in 1837 in France and Italy with Henry Crabb Robinson, both trips covering some of the same ground again. And he returned twice to Wales: once in 1824 to visit Robert Jones, his 1790 companion, and once in 1841—his last extended trip out of the Lake District—to revisit the most important site of all his signature *re*-visitations, Tintern Abbey, the Wye valley and the Quantock Hills around Alfoxden.[1]

But now it was not "Five years have past," but forty-eight years past. That his past would have weighed heavily on his mind in these trips hardly needs arguing, but one detail illuminates how that mind worked upon its past. Coming to Goodrich Castle, Wordsworth sought out the little girl who had assured him in 1793, "O Master! we are seven." The enormous retentive power of Wordsworth's early imagination—as well as its egocentrism—is indicated by both his expectation and its frustration: he could not locate the girl, because he had forgotten to ask her name. "It would have given me greater pleasure to have found in the neighbouring hamlet traces of one who had interested me so much; but that was impossible, as, unfortunately, I did not even know her name."[2] To expect Wordsworth to have asked her name, or to think him egocentric for not doing so, is to wish for a different author, and to assume a very different attitude toward memory and creativity than Wordsworth's. Many of us might have said, What's your name, little girl? But Wordsworth, even at age twenty-three, wondered instead, "a simple child . . . That lightly draws its breath . . . What should it know of death?" She knew more than he did—in his role of the obtuse adult narrator—and what she knew was more important than her name. It was the continuity of life over death that "interested [him] so much," and the same interest made his own later life a continuation of his early years.

By 1841 he knew more about death than to have to ask, because it had by then frequently interrupted his lifelong task of self-preservation. *The Prelude* itself was "finished" by a death—John's drowning—and three of Wordsworth's five children preceded him in death, Catherine and Thomas dying within six agonizing months of each other in 1812 (aged four and six), and his beloved Dora, named for her aunt Dorothy, in 1847, a month before her forty-fourth birthday. By then Dorothy herself had effectively left Wordsworth's life, her mind having collapsed completely in 1835—very shortly after the death of Sara Hutchinson—though Dorothy did not die until 1855.

Eighteen thirty-five was the year after Wordsworth had written his last great poem, inspired, like so many of his greatest ones, again by death: "Extempore Effusion upon the Death of James Hogg." More than a tribute to "The Ettrick Shepherd," it was Wordsworth's conscious tribute to the passing of his entire generation: Hogg, Scott, Lamb, Coleridge, Crabbe, and Hemans. And his consciousness of his youth remained strong even in their deaths:

> Yet I, whose lids from infant slumbers
> Were earlier raised, remain to hear
> A timid voice, that asks in whispers,
> "Who next will drop and disappear?"

The timid voice was not his. Like the little girl at Goodrich Castle, he could hear the conventional question, but reply with the unconventional answer, invigorating even in its relentless impermanence:

> Like clouds that rake the mountain-summits,
> Or waves that own no curbing hand,
> How fast has brother followed brother,
> From sunshine to the sunless land!

With his politics as with his travels, Wordsworth repeated himself. The clichéd image of him shows radical youth being replaced by reactionary old age. But his youth was radical because he turned against his conservative world, and then returned to it. Not the label but the process was the essence of his self-creation, in his life, as in poems from *The Borderers* to "Tintern Abbey." Continuing his family's generations-long allegiance to the Lowther interest, Wordsworth in 1812 appealed to Lord Lonsdale for a public office to help support a family that poetry was clearly not going to be able to. In 1813 he was named stamp distributor for Westmorland, part of the government's tax collection service, and six years later he was made a justice of the peace for Westmorland, exactly as his father had been. This was largely a reward for his strenuous efforts on Lowther's behalf in the decisive postwar election of 1818, canvassing as tirelessly his father had done and publishing *Two Addresses to the Freeholders of Westmorland,* which helped seal the fate of reform for half a generation more.

Wordsworth worked hard for the conservative Lowther interest in the election of 1818 and vehemently opposed the Reform Bill of 1832 and Catholic Emancipation not only because his political ideas had changed. These actions also reflect his career-oriented realization that reform did not fit the image of the Poet that he had decided to present to the public. Though it survived the whirlwind of revolution, his self-image was eventually wrecked on the rocks of reform. In the new era after 1832 Wordsworth was indeed a Lost Leader. As both Tennyson and Browning learned to their sorrow when they published their quintessentially Romantic first volumes in 1830 and 1833, most English readers did not want that kind of poetry any more. Self-consciousness, Carlyle declared in his definitive essay "Characteristics," in that same watershed year of 1832, was the disease of the new age, not its cure. His prescription, "Close thy Byron, open thy Goethe," meant, Close the book of enthusiastic individualism and open the book of pessimistic social earnestness.

Wordsworth, presciently, had already closed his Romantic book on himself, finished it and hidden it away. His public reputation grew accordingly, as De Quincey aptly noted, "Up to 1820 the name of Wordsworth was trampled underfoot; from 1820 to 1830 it was militant; from 1830 to 1835 it has been triumphant." And the triumph continued: in 1838 Wordsworth was awarded the D.C.L. at the University of Durham, and in 1839 Oxford followed suit. And so on into the 1840s, when (in 1843) he became poet laureate following Southey's death after thirty dull years in the post, and in 1846 he was elected an honorary member of the Royal Irish Academy, and would have been named lord rector of Glasgow University but for university political infighting.

Wordsworth's career succeeded as much as Scott's in honors or as Byron's in fame, but nowhere near as successfully as theirs in the area that mattered greatly to him—money. Wordsworth wanted to succeed financially out of immediate and pressing personal necessity. Without the independent fortune that John's voyages promised, he needed all the help he could get. When he became stamp distributor for Westmorland in 1813, he moved to Rydal Mount on the Le Flemings' estate, the grandest house in Cumberland he had lived in since his birth. He had completed the circle his father and grandfather had started for him in the Lowthers' service. The circle now circumscribed the little boy behind the Cockermouth mansion—who had imagined himself a naked savage bronzed by the sun—turning him into a poetic figure, a figure of speech.

Wordsworth was successful in his gamble with posterity for his reputation. Inexorably, he became *the* poet of his era. But the costs he paid in compromise were commensurate with his gains. Byron and Shelley were effectively exiled from England and died romantically abroad; defiling their memory became a lively cultural cottage industry in Victorian England, but they have survived with their integrity intact. Blake took an even harder road to artistic integrity, at the terrific cost of almost complete obscurity during his lifetime. Coleridge stayed more in the mainstream of society by making a profession of worrying at its margins, religious, political, psychological, and educational. Keats alone had a career whose trajectory looks like Wordsworth's, but he died young, thus preserving his Romanticism intact. Had he lived, he might be remembered as Dr. John Keats, a pioneer in, say, the prevention of infectious diseases in industrial slums, who had dabbled in poetry before he too accepted the wisdom of Carlyle's dictum (they were born the same year, 1795), closing his Byron and opening his Wordsworth. The Wordsworth he admired most was the poet of *The Excursion,* which Keats, seeing the gold beneath its dross, hailed as "one of the three greatest things to rejoice at in this age." If Wordsworth convinced only this one member of his "fit audience, though few," it was enough.

Other poets of the era who compromised with their revolutionary and reactionary times gained their profits immediately, Southey and Rogers and Crabbe among them. Several women writers who enjoyed phenomenal success then are only belatedly being remembered now: Charlotte Smith, Mary Robinson, Anna Barbauld, Felicia Hemans, and others. For the most part, these contemporaries lost out with posterity. Only Wordsworth hit the perfect balance between revelation and secrecy. But it cost him his soul, or rather the best image of his soul, for relatively few readers know the Wordsworth of *The Prelude,* let alone its many different versions, to say nothing of the facts it cuts and tailors. Fewer still have ever glimpsed the Bard of *The Recluse,* a shadowy figure as large and threatening as any of Blake's Giant Emanations. Instead, they know and love (or hate), the poet of the English

Lake District, eminently adaptable to tourism, gardening, calendar art, and mournful private reflections on the difficulties of modern public life.

There is a view, more English than American, that Wordsworth went wrong when he fell for Coleridge's line that he should write "the first great philosophic poem" in English. Stephen Gill expresses this succinctly: "Coleridge was quite wrong. Lyrical utterance was for Wordsworth a natural mode."[3] Scholars holding this view disapprove of the "twentieth-century preoccupation" with "The Ruined Cottage," *The Prelude,* and "Home at Grasmere"—that is, with the failed *Recluse* project in all its dimensions. Yet it will be clear that I share that preoccupation to a considerable extent. Because it was never, for Wordsworth, simply a matter of deciding to carry on writing one kind of poetry instead of another. If it had been, where are his lyrics of 1795–98? Can the long poems of those years simply be discounted as mistakes? Or, if adherents of the simple, lyrical Wordsworth say that he was, in 1798 or in 1800 or in 1802, finding his "natural" lyrical voice, how would they account for the marked differences between the *Lyrical Ballads* of 1798 and those of 1800, or the still greater differences between both of them and the embarrassing simplicities of the lyrics of spring 1802? In which do we hear his "natural" voice?

In all of them, of course. And what we hear, what makes all of these sets of lyric, dramatic, and narrative poems indubitably "Wordsworthian," are the deep echoes of *The Recluse* project, mounting "like an unfathered vapour" from "the deep, abyssmal breathing place" of Wordsworth's imagination, to resonate powerfully in simple lyrics about little girls or old beggars, and apparently transparent narratives about shepherd boys and idiot boys.

These resonances are not, it is true, easy to identify or appreciate, but they are impossible to account for if one is not aware of their deep substructure. Only in "Tintern Abbey" does this buried presence come close to the surface of the *Lyrical Ballads.* But without *The Recluse* there would be no Margaret, no Lucy, no Matthew, no Michael, no Ruth *as they exist in Wordsworth's poetry.* There never was much of a *Recluse,* though parts of it exist and can be studied with profit. What we have instead, partway between the characters of Wordsworth's narratives (the "real men" of his preface) and the godlike Bard of *The Recluse,* is the character of the Poet himself, as first announced in the 1802 additions to the preface of *Lyrical Ballads* and then developed further in his return to the poem "on the growth of my own mind" between 1803 and 1805. He is never named in *The Prelude,* but we fully recognize the man of whom it speaks: William Wordsworth.

This is easy to say with the benefit of two hundred years' hindsight, but these relationships began to emerge only in the last hundred years, starting with A. C. Bradley's lectures at the University of Edinburgh in the 1890s, published in 1909. It took a good deal of twentieth-century "preoccupation" with them to bring them to light, since most serious philosophical interpretation of Wordsworth remained stuck with the Idealist metaphysical presumptions he shared with Coleridge, even as both of them were moving beyond them, in practice, to more modern notions of truth based on the contextual consciousness and practices of any truth-claiming subject. But it was not easy for Wordsworth to articulate his self-recognition, not in 1802, nor in the subsequent composition of *The Prelude,* to say nothing of its publication, an event he deferred all the rest of his life because he said that "it was a thing unprecedented in literary history that a man should talk so much about himself." It was not quite so unprecedented even then, if we think of Augustine, Petrarch, and Rousseau, but it is a thing with many precedents now, and *The Prelude* itself is one of the most important of them all.

Although the final fair-copy state of *The Prelude* indicates that Wordsworth expected it to be published posthumously, no specific set of written instructions indicating his intentions exists. Even the title was not clearly agreed on, except perhaps by verbal understanding with Mary. *The Prelude,* like *The Excursion* and *The Recluse,* is hardly a striking title for a major poem. All his life, it had been "the poem to Coleridge" or "the poem on the growth of my own mind." There is no "-iad" suffix in English to indicate topicality, like *Iliad* or *Aeneid,* the story or the "matter" of Troy and Achilles, of Aeneas and Rome. Like them, *The Prelude* is a foundational epic, but it declares the independence of the human imagination: The Imagination-iad or Imagiad. To avoid such a barbarism we would have to call it, lamely, Of Imagination. But the real subject of the poem is more specific, and can be roughly adapted to the old form of epic titles. It could be called *The Words worthiad,* or perhaps *The Axiologiad,* referring to the *materia* of the semirevolutionary Wordsworth and demirevolutionary England. More specifically, given its narrow range, it is not a general treatise on imagination but a long-withheld story of obscure self-creation: *The Hidden Wordsworth.* That young man's exciting life—as poet, lover, rebel, spy—was the source of the emotions that Wordsworth needed the rest of his life to recollect in tranquillity.

APPENDIX A:

Genealogical Chart Showing Intermarriages between Robinson, Wordsworth, Cookson/Crackanthorpe, amd Monkhouse Families

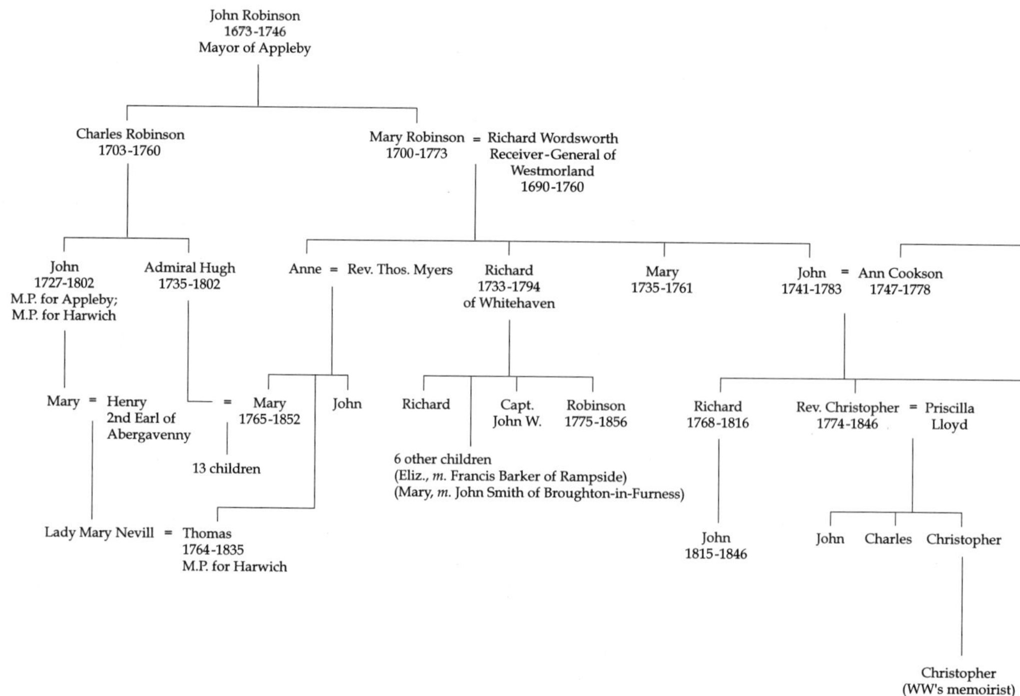

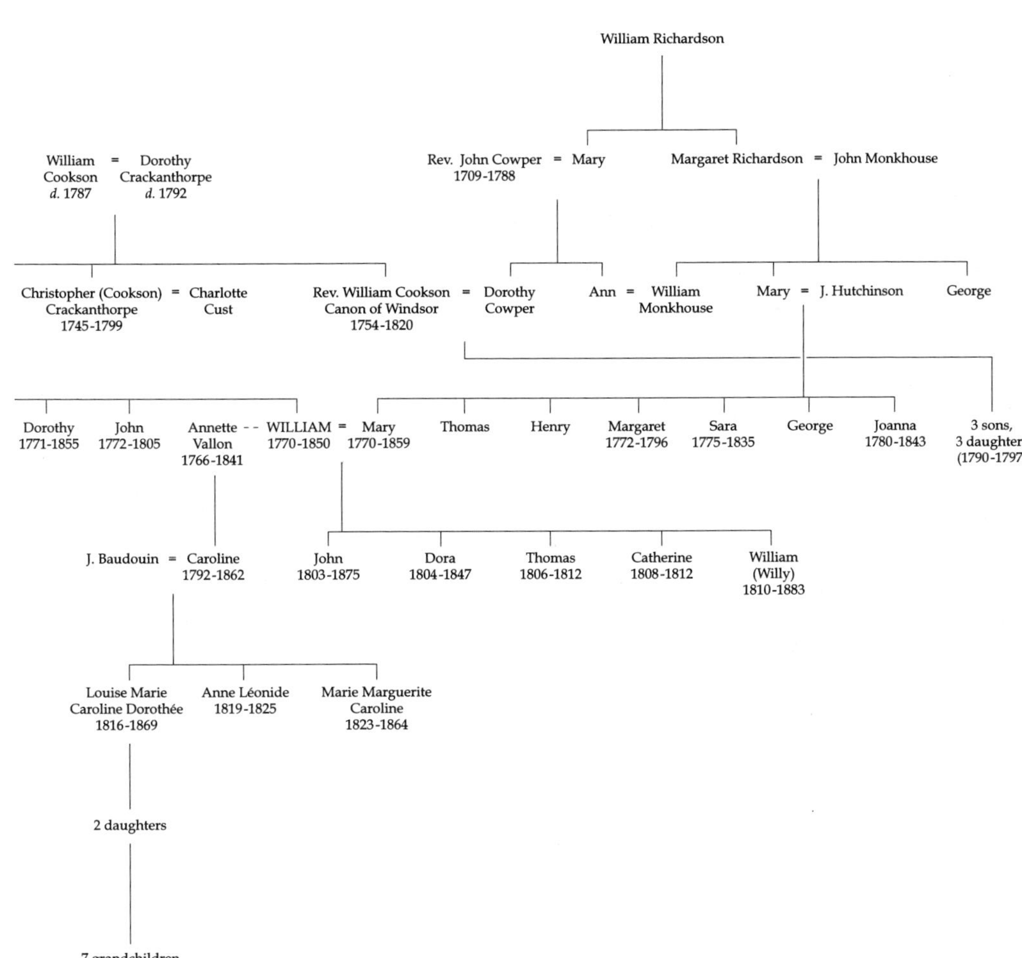
William Richardson
William Cookson d. 1787 = Dorothy Crackanthorpe d. 1792
Rev. John Cowper 1709-1788 = Mary
Margaret Richardson = John Monkhouse
Christopher (Cookson) Crackanthorpe 1745-1799 = Charlotte Cust
Rev. William Cookson Canon of Windsor 1754-1820 = Dorothy Cowper
Ann = William Monkhouse
Mary = J. Hutchinson
George
Dorothy 1771-1855
John 1772-1805
Annette Vallon 1766-1841
WILLIAM 1770-1850 = Mary 1770-1859
Thomas
Henry
Margaret 1772-1796
Sara 1775-1835
George
Joanna 1780-1843
3 sons, 3 daughters (1790-1797)
J. Baudouin = Caroline 1792-1862
John 1803-1875
Dora 1804-1847
Thomas 1806-1812
Catherine 1808-1812
William (Willy) 1810-1883
Louise Marie Caroline Dorothée 1816-1869
Anne Léonide 1819-1825
Marie Marguerite Caroline 1823-1864
2 daughters
7 grandchildren

APPENDIX B:

Was "Wordsworth" the "Name Not to Be Mentioned"?

On September 28, 1798, Sir James Craufurd assured William Wickham, "You may rely on the most scrupulous caution respecting *the two individuals* mentioned to me in your letter" (Craufurd's emphasis).[1] Early in November, after Wordsworth and Coleridge had left Hamburg, Craufurd again referred to "the person whose *name is not be mentioned*" (also his emphasis).[2] The timing of Craufurd's report and Wordsworth's "confidential" association with Baron de Leutre, a deported agent of the Directory, in conjunction with the duke of Portland's payment to "Mr. Wordsworth," raises the possibility of a significant relationship between Craufurd's unmentioned name(s) and those of Wordsworth and Coleridge.

To say that the case is difficult to document is to understate the obvious: the whole point was to make these activities difficult to document then (even to other parts of the British government), to say nothing of two hundred years later. As Craufurd himself protested, "you must be very sensible of the imperfectibility of attaining even a slight knowledge of one tenth of the people who go from hence to England in all kinds of vessels."[3] Even when reports were made, key documents were routinely destroyed. In particularly sensitive or embarrassing cases, such as this one evidently was, names were not mentioned, and of course many names were false ones. Wickham himself, on whose meticulous record keeping and collecting so much of our knowledge of this secret service depends, destroyed some of his entry books and registers, with the tantalizing notation that they contained "curious information respecting the ill-intentioned of our own countrymen."[4] Since he did not destroy many which (like Craufurd's) do mention the names of known spies, we may hazard the guess that those that *were* destroyed protect the future reputations of others who were either (a) not professional spies but occasional employees or (b) not permanent enemies of the state but temporary enthusiasts of the French Revolution. The latter category would include both Wordsworth and Coleridge; a slight but persistent trail of names, innuendos, and coincidences throughout the 1790s suggests that the former may include Wordsworth.

Craufurd was familiar with the protocols for dealing with the names of respectable persons of upper-class or higher cultural reputation who passed through his purview. We can see this in his defense of Herbert Croft, author of *Love and Madness,* the sensational account of the murder of Martha Ray, Basil Montagu's mother, whose name Wordsworth adopted for "The Thorn." "Attempts have also been made I believe to calumniate Sir Herbert Croft, who is at Altona, on the score of his political principles, for which there never was the smallest foundation whatever. He is the person who wrote the life of Young in Johnson's lives of the Poets as you will recollect, and is I have every reason to think a perfectly respectable man."[5]

Three of Wickham's most important operatives were in Hamburg when Wordsworth and Coleridge arrived, but none of them seem to fit in the time frame of Craufurd's comment about the name not to be mentioned.[6] Samuel Turner, whose information had led to the arrest of the Irish conspirators in February 1798, kept his cover by "fleeing" to Hamburg with some of those who escaped arrest, and promptly continued his deep infiltration of the United Irishmen there. Craufurd had already written to Wickham about him, by name, by early September. George Orr came in a similar fashion, arriving with Napper Tandy and the other survivors of the ill-fated Irish uprising in August. In his case, the time frame is better for associating him with Craufurd's unmentionable names, but the public circumstances of his arrival make such hush-hush measures as reflected by Craufurd unlikely. James Powell, possibly the most effective field agent of all, had sailed from Yarmouth in April and was already burrowed deep in the councils of the United Irishmen when Turner and Orr arrived and would not have been newly mentioned by Craufurd in September.

Powell and Orr knew nothing of each other's role. This was standard operating procedure, as Craufurd understood, though several of his letters request pathetically that he not be kept quite so rigorously out of the various loops that Grenville and Portland (and Canning and Wickham as their immediate subordinates) were casting overseas. "I find my dear Sir that you have several correspondents here. If there are no weighty reasons against the communication may I ask you who they are. You will I hope believe that I do not feel one particle of jealousy on the subject but they might as they seem to know something of what passes here be of much use to me in this great populous town where one can never have agents enough & where so many are the opportunities of carrying on all kinds of secret practices that one never can hope to learn everything."[7]

Craufurd had already referred to Powell by name a month earlier, along with an Irishman named Richardson, so he is not likely to have been the individual referred to. (Craufurd apparently did not know that "Richardson" was but another alias of Samuel Turner.) He does not mention *Powell* again in these papers, though he does refer at least once more to Richardson, who was Powell's partner.

A better possibility is that Craufurd is referring to James Talbot himself, the on-ground head of the "Swabian agency." Talbot was aided by his brother Robert as secretary and courier, and the two together would fit the pattern of Craufurd's reference, first to *two* unmentionable persons, which shortly shifts to just one, as James was clearly the important figure, his younger brother a mere functionary. Nor does Craufurd mention the Talbots anywhere that I have looked. Craufurd knew of Talbot's operation, especially since his own brother Robert was recovering from battle wounds in Frankfurt, and Craufurd was trying desperately throughout the winter of 1798–99 to get him a passport for travel through the many principalities that lay between Frankfurt and Hamburg.

Talbot's own communications with Wickham show him stressing the difficulties of his situation ("You will agree with me this mode of life is not gay") and engaging in a good deal of special pleading, evidently aimed at getting more money. This behavior fits *one* of the unnamed individuals Craufurd refers to, but not both. Craufurd regularly refers to two different individuals in this context. One is characterized by being "unmentionable"; the other, by his constant demand for more money. Generally the context of Craufurd's dispatches suggests they are different persons, but there are two instances in which there seems to be a slight overlap, both of which fit with Wordsworth's circumstances in Goslar.

On February 12, 1799, just before Wordsworth disappeared from view into southern Germany, Craufurd offered a belated explanation for two bills drawn on Wickham, one for £100 and the other for £90. "The £100 was for Richardson; the £90 for the other who begged I would let him have it on account of the allowance made to him which he finds a difficulty in drawing."[8] Wordsworth did have difficulty drawing money in Germany, and though he had no "allowance" that we know of, he might well have represented his line of credit with the Wedgwoods in that way. Or, if he had an allowance from Wickham's operation, he could have had difficulty drawing on it from Goslar. A second reference of Craufurd's to this problem also points plausibly toward Wordsworth's situation. "Our friend here, who is not to be named, finding a difficulty in getting money for his Bills in the obscure situation in which he is here, has earnestly requested that I would draw on you for the monthly allowance which is made to him, and which hitherto he has received through Mr. Ford, if I remember well. I have therefore drawn upon you Bills at two months dated yesterday, for £60, which I paid to him a month ago, but I have hitherto neglected drawing for it. I shall have to draw again the same amount in a month, as I shall have the like payment to make to him then."[9] This was written on April 2, shortly before Wordsworth resurfaces to view in Göttingen. At Goslar, Wordsworth was certainly in an "obscure situation," as he was at any time after he left there until he turned up at Göttingen. Still more important, this communiqué includes the additional information that this particular operative has "hitherto" been funded by Richard Ford, one of the two direct links between the Foreign Office and the Home Office, and the man James Walsh thought—with about the same degree of certainty implied by Craufurd's "if I remember well"—would recognize "the name *Wordsworth.*" Ford received a payment of £100 from Portland at the same time "Mr. Wordsworth" was paid his £92 and James Craufurd received his reward for special services rendered in the spring of 1799.

Talbot was also in an "obscure" situation, in a monastery near Ulm, and probably communicated with Craufurd by mail at times. But I have found no record that Talbot was ever in Ford's pay, and the biggest disqualification of Talbot for being one of the unnameable agents is the trifling sums involved, relative to the staggering amounts Talbot was receiving from Grenville. Hence at this level (that is, payments of £90–100) James Powell would seem a more likely candidate, and the mention of Richardson (his partner) in the same context supports it. But Powell, like Talbot, was always grasping for money, the main motivation for seeking this kind of work, whereas "our friend" who is "earnestly . . . begging" for some help sounds like a more refined, gentlemanly type, like Wordsworth. And, as we have seen, Craufurd *does* name Powell, so he is somewhat disqualified on that count, unless we accept the awkward proviso that Craufurd *stopped* mentioning him after a certain point, having been reprimanded by his superiors.

That Craufurd was occasionally reprimanded is clear from his reply to an order not to interfere with Wickham's and Grenville's couriers: "I understood perfectly the spirit of the order respecting couriers. *None but French* have ever yet come in question. I am infinitely obliged to you at all times of any explanation."[10] Powell would not have been used as a courier, but Robert Talbot definitely was, and William Wordsworth, as an apparent gentleman of leisure traveling on other business (poetry and philosophy was his line), had the plausible outward appearance that would have made him a good candidate for this position as well.

Many other persons were involved in Craufurd's dealings, several of whom are clearly not Wordsworth. But Craufurd specifically excludes Wickham's "unmentionable" operative from this grasping type: "not that I mean to include in this number either our friend to whom I have alluded above or *another* [Craufurd's emphasis], by any means but [crossed out] I know that they are obliged to great expence."[11]

From Cuxhaven on April 25, 1799—that is, at almost exactly the time the Wordsworths must have been there—Craufurd wrote expressing his satisfaction that Portland was "satisfied with the Information relative to certain persons, which I had the honor to transmit to you."[12] This reference is so studiedly vague (since he was always transmitting information about many persons) that the identities of these "certain persons" must have been well understood between them.

On this same date, Craufurd wrote about a young lady, a Miss Preble, who said she was English but who he thought was American, and whom he suspected of conveying letters to people in France, though possibly innocent herself. By April 28, the Wordsworths' presumed date of departure, Craufurd had learned that Miss Preble had actually been sent to England by the Directory. But again, he insists, the whole thing may be false, "for I am very little inclined to credit any of these gentry, having been so frequently deceived." "Any of these gentry" would also include the Wordsworths, and it could be that their departure, "melancholy and hypp'd" as they were, reflected their unhappiness with their mission in Germany, an unhappiness Craufurd might here be reflecting, following his high hopes some months earlier for what this unnameable agent might accomplish, despite the "obscure situation" in which he was placed in the country.

Abbreviations

BL *Biographia Literaria,* ed. James Engell and W. Jackson Bate, vol. 7, pt. 2 of *The Collected Works of Samuel Taylor Coleridge,* gen. ed. Kathleen Coburn, (Princeton: Princeton Univ. Press, 1983)

BRS Ben Ross Schneider, *Wordsworth's Cambridge Education* (Cambridge: Cambridge Univ. Press, 1957)

CEY Mark L. Reed, *Wordsworth: The Chronology of the Early Years, 1770–1799* (Cambridge: Harvard Univ. Press, 1967)

CLSTC *Collected Letters of Samuel Taylor Coleridge,* ed. Earl Leslie Griggs, 2 vols. (Oxford: Clarendon Press, 1956)

CMY Mark L. Reed, *Wordsworth: The Chronology of the Middle Years, 1800–1815* (Cambridge: Harvard Univ. Press, 1975)

CPWSTC *The Complete Poetical Works of Samuel Taylor Coleridge,* ed. Ernest Hartley Coleridge, 2 vols. (1912; reprint, Oxford: Clarendon Press, 1957)

DC Dove Cottage

DHRF Albert Soboul, ed., *Dictionnaire historique de la Révolution Française* (Paris: Presses universitaires de France, 1989)

DNB *Dictionary of National Biography*

DS William Wordsworth, *Descriptive Sketches,* ed. Eric Birdsall (Ithaca: Cornell Univ. Press, 1984)

DVE David V. Erdman, *Commerce des Lumières: John Oswald and the British in Paris, 1790–1793* (Columbia: Univ. of Missouri Press, 1986)

EL Emile Legouis, *The Early Life of William Wordsworth, 1770–1798: A Study of "The Prelude,"* ed. Nicholas Roe (London: Libris, 1988)

DWJ *Journals of Dorothy Wordsworth,* ed. Ernest de Selincourt, 2 vols. (New York: Macmillan, 1941)

EPF William Wordsworth, *Early Poems and Fragments, 1784–Mid 1797,* ed. Jared Curtis and Carol Landon (Ithaca: Cornell Univ. Press, 1998)

EW William Wordsworth, *An Evening Walk,* ed. James Averill (Ithaca: Cornell Univ. Press, 1984)

FO Foreign Office

GMH1 George McLean Harper, *William Wordsworth: His Life, Works, and Influence,* vol. 1 (London: John Murray, 1916)

Hayden John O. Hayden, ed., *William Wordsworth: The Poems,* vol. 1 (New Haven: Yale Univ. Press, 1981)

HCR Henry Crabb Robinson, *Diary, Reminiscences, and Correspondence,* ed. Thomas Sadler, 3 vols. (London: Macmillan, 1869)

HO Home Office
HRCU Historical Register of Cambridge University
IF Isabella Fenwick Notes
LB William Wordsworth, *Lyrical Ballads and Other Poems, 1797–1800,* ed. James Butler and Karen Green (Ithaca: Cornell Univ. Press, 1992)
LCML *The Letters of Charles and Mary Lamb,* ed. Edwin W. Marrs, 2 vols. (Ithaca: Cornell Univ. Press, 1975–76)
LEY *The Letters of William and Dorothy Wordsworth: The Early Years, 1787–1805,* ed. Ernest de Selincourt, 2d ed., rev. Chester L. Shaver (Oxford: Clarendon Press, 1967)
LJW *The Letters of John Wordsworth,* ed. Carl H. Ketcham (Ithaca: Cornell Univ. Press, 1969)
LLY *The Letters of William and Dorothy Wordsworth: The Later Years,* 2d ed., ed. by Alan G. Hill, 5 vols. (Oxford: Clarendon Press, 1978–93)
LMY *The Letters of William and Dorothy Wordsworth: The Middle Years,* 2d ed., rev. Mary Moorman (Oxford: Clarendon Press, 1969–70)
Memoirs Christopher Wordsworth, *Memoirs of William Wordsworth,* 2 vols. (London: Edward Moxon, 1851)
MM1 Mary Moorman, *William Wordsworth: The Early Years, 1770–1803* (Oxford: Clarendon Press, 1957)
NR Nicholas Roe, *Wordsworth and Coleridge: The Radical Years* (Oxford: Clarendon Press, 1988)
NSTC *The Notebooks of Samuel Taylor Coleridge,* notes and text, ed. Kathleen Coburn, 4 vols. (New York: Pantheon Books, 1957–)
PP Pinney Papers
PRO Public Records Office
Prose *The Prose Works of William Wordsworth,* ed. W. J. B. Owen and Jane Worthington Smyser, 3 vols. (Oxford: Clarendon Press, 1974)
P2V William Wordsworth, *Poems, in Two Volumes and Other Poems, 1800–1807,* ed. Jared Curtis (Ithaca: Cornell Univ. Press, 1983)
PW William Wordsworth, *The Poetical Works,* ed. Ernest de Selincourt and Helen Darbishire, 5 vols. (1940–49; reprint, Oxford: Clarendon Press, 1967–72)
RH Richard Holmes, *Coleridge: Early Visions* (New York: Viking, 1993)
SG Stephen Gill, *William Wordsworth: A Life* (Oxford: Clarendon Press, 1989)
Thirteen William Wordsworth, *The Thirteen-Book Prelude,* ed. Mark Reed, 2 vols. (Ithaca: Cornell Univ. Press, 1991)
TWT T. W. Thompson, *Wordsworth's Hawkshead,* ed. Robert Woof (London: Oxford Univ. Press, 1970)
WAG William Wordsworth, *The Prelude 1799, 1805, 1855,* ed. Jonathan Wordsworth, M. H. Abrams, and Stephen Gill, Norton Critical Edition (New York: W. W. Norton, 1979)
WAV Emile Legouis, *William Wordsworth and Annette Vallon* (1922), expanded by Pierre Legouis (Hamden, Conn.: Archon Books, 1967)
WFD George McLean Harper, *Wordsworth's French Daughter: The Story of Her Birth, with the Certificates of Her Baptism and Marriage* (1921; reprint, New York: Russell & Russell, 1967)
WL Wordsworth Library

NOTES

Prologue

1. Alan Liu, *Wordsworth: The Sense of History* (Stanford: Stanford Univ. Press, 1989), 36.
2. *Wordsworth at Cambridge: A Record of the Commemoration Held at St. John's College, Cambridge, in April 1950* (Cambridge: Cambridge Univ. Press, n.d.), 70.
3. BRS, 70.
4. *CMY,* 215; Frances Blanshard, *Portraits of Wordsworth* (Ithaca: Cornell Univ. Press, 1959), 142; William Carew Hazlitt, *Memoirs of William Hazlitt,* vol. 1 (London: R. Bentley, 1867), 103n; dating by the National Gallery of Scotland, per request of the portrait's present owner, 1993.
5. This skin condition is seen most clearly in the painting by Margaret Gillies from 1840, and in the drawing by Leonard Wyon, done in 1847 (Blanshard, *Portraits,* plates 20 and 30a). Wordsworth was then over seventy and the condition more noticeable.
6. "My First Acquaintance with Poets" (1823).
7. Reeve Parker, " 'In Some Sort Seeing with My Proper Eyes': Wordsworth and the Spectacles of Paris," *Studies in Romanticism* 27 (1988): 389–90.
8. *LLY,* 8:161–62.
9. J. K. Stephen, "A Sonnet" ("Two voices are there"), in George Kitchin, *A Survey of Burlesque and Parody in English* (Edinburgh: Oliver & Boyd, 1931), 237.
10. George W. Meyer, *Wordsworth's Formative Years* (Ann Arbor: Univ. of Michigan Press, 1943); MM1; Herbert Read, *Wordsworth* (London: Jonathan Cape, 1930); Hugh Fausset, *The Lost Leader: A Study of Wordsworth* (New York: Harcourt, Brace, 1933); Malcolm Elwin, *The First Romantics* (London: Macdonald, 1947); Wallace Douglas, *Wordsworth: The Construction of a Personality* (Kent, Ohio: Kent State Univ. Press, 1968).
11. GMH1; SG.
12. Frederick W. Bateson, *Wordsworth: A Re-interpretation* (London: Longmans, Green, 1954); Richard Onorato, *The Character of the Poet: Wordsworth in "The Prelude"* (Princeton: Princeton Univ. Press, 1971).
13. *La Jeunesse de William Wordsworth* (Paris: Masson, 1896); 1st English ed. tr. J. W. Matthews (London: Dent, 1897). It has recently been reprinted with a valuable introduction by Nicholas Roe (London: Libris, 1988), cited as EL.
14. Stephen Greenblatt, *Renaissance Self-Fashioning: From More to Shakespeare* (Chicago: Univ. of Chicago Press, 1980).
15. *The Prelude, or Growth of a Poet's Mind,* ed. Ernest de Selincourt (Oxford: Clarendon Press, 1926); *"The Prelude," 1798–1799,* ed. Stephen Parrish (Ithaca: Cornell Univ. Press, 1977).

16. Jonathan Wordsworth and Stephen Gill, "The Five-Book *Prelude* of Early Spring 1804," *Journal of English and Germanic Philology* 76 (1977): 1–25.
17. *The Fourteen-Book "Prelude,"* ed. W. J. B. Owen (Ithaca: Cornell Univ. Press, 1985); *Thirteen.*

Chapter 1: The Ministries of Fear and Beauty

1. Alexander Carlyle, *Anecdotes and Characters,* ed. James Kinsley (London: Oxford Univ. Press, 1973), 213.
2. Lonsdale letters (March 16, 1742), cited in J. V. Beckett, *Coal and Tobacco: The Lowthers and the Economic Development of West Cumberland, 1660–1760* (Cambridge: Cambridge Univ. Press, 1981), 15–16.
3. Eric Robertson, *Wordsworthshire* (London: Chatto and Windus, 1911), 24.
4. Richard Ferguson, *Cumberland and Westmorland M.P.'s from the Restoration to the Reform Bill of 1867* (London: Bell and Daldy, 1871), 410.
5. Hugh Owen, *The Lowther Family* (Chichester: Phillimore, 1990), 292–95.
6. George III to Lord North, March 9, 1779, quoted ibid., 287.
7. Brian Bonsall, *Sir James Lowther and Cumberland and Westmorland Elections, 1754–1775* (Manchester: Manchester Univ. Press, 1960), 67.
8. Ibid., 152.
9. Beckett, *Coal and Tobacco,* 16–17.
10. Ibid., passim; see also Neil McKendrick, John Brewer, and J. H. Plumb, eds., *The Birth of a Consumer Society: The Commercialization of Eighteenth Century England* (Bloomington: Indiana Univ. Press, 1982).
11. GMH1, 15–16.
12. M. Dorothy George, *Hogarth to Cruikshank: Social Change in Graphic Satire* (London: Allen Lane, 1967), 87.
13. Bonsall, *Lowther,* 50.
14. J. V. Beckett, "The Making of a Pocket Borough: Cockermouth 1722–1756," *Journal of British Studies* 20 (1980): 140–57 (citing P. Habbakkuk).
15. John Wordsworth Sr. to James Lowther, July 3, 1778, Lowther Papers, Kendal PRO.
16. John Cannon, *Parliamentary Reform, 1640–1832* (Cambridge: Cambridge Univ. Press, 1973), 50–51.
17. *LEY,* 65; *LMY,* 2:410.
18. Appleby lost its representatives to Kendal as soon as the Reform Bill of 1832 was passed (Bonsall, *Lowther,* 152).
19. Robertson, *Wordsworthshire,* 23.
20. Owen, *Lowther Family,* 283.
21. To Captain Hugh Robinson, Oct. 1764. A copy of this letter is on display in the Cockermouth house.
22. Robertson, *Wordsworthshire,* 25.
23. WL, MS 1/2; Woof (TWT), 32, n. 1, 35, n. 1.
24. WL, MS 1/2/ff., 19–32, 36–42, 64–65.
25. *CEY,* 42.
26. Robertson, *Wordsworthshire,* 25.
27. John Beckett, "Estate Management in Eighteenth-Century England: The Lowther-Spedding Relationship in Cumberland," in *English Rural Society,* ed. J. Chartrer and D. Hey (Cambridge: Cambridge Univ. Press, 1990), 69.
28. Ibid., 72.

29. WL, MS 8/157.
30. SG, 14; GMH1, 19.
31. Joanne Dann, "Some Notes on the Relationship between the Wordsworth and the Lowther Families," *Wordsworth Circle* 11 (1980): 81.
32. Robertson, *Wordsworthshire,* 12.
33. WL, MS 1, box 1 (Wordsworth Family Contemporary Relations), category 2, item 3.
34. MM1, 8.
35. MM1, 13.
36. Owen, *Lowther Family,* 298; MM1, 13.
37. Bonsall, *Lowther,* 61.
38. Owen, *Lowther Family,* 287.
39. *DNB;* Stephen Ayling, *Fox* (London: John Murray, 1991), 74n.
40. Letter of May 21, 1751, quoted in Beckett, "Estate Management," 66, n. 29.
41. Bonsall, *Lowther,* 70.
42. Mark Kishlansky, *Parliamentary Selection: Social and Political Choice in Early Modern England* (Cambridge: Cambridge Univ. Press, 1986), 141.
43. Ibid., 146–47.
44. Bonsall, *Lowther,* 104.
45. Wilson Pearson to James Lowther, Sept. 15, 1772, Lowther Papers, Kendal PRO.
46. Ferguson, *Cumberland,* 125.
47. April 24, 1757, in *The Manuscripts of the Earl of Lonsdale* (London: Historical Manuscripts Commission, 1893), 129.
48. Ferguson, *Cumberland,* 126.
49. Dann, "Notes," 81.
50. Bonsall, *Lowther,* 89–105.
51. Dann, "Notes," 81.
52. Bonsall, *Lowther,* 70.
53. Carlyle, *Anecdotes,* 213.
54. Ferguson, *Cumberland,* 153.
55. *LEY,* 7.
56. *LEY,* 4.
57. Robertson, *Wordsworthshire,* 16.
58. *CEY,* 41, n. 2.
59. MM1, 15–16.
60. *PW,* 4:409.
61. MM1, 4.
62. MM1, 16.
63. Frederick W. Bateson, *Wordsworth: A Re-interpretation* (London: Longmans, Green, 1954), 49.
64. "Catechizing," *Ecclesiastical Sonnets,* III.xxii, in *PW,* 3:395.
65. "Autobiographical Memoranda," in *Prose,* 3:372. All the following prose recollections are from this source unless otherwise indicated.
66. *PW,* 3:397. The long-lasting impact of the public penance is further indicated by Wordsworth's sonnet defending the fierce denunciatory rite of "Commination," read out against sinners on Ash Wednesday: though "this delicate age / Look only on the Gospel's brighter page: / Let light and dark duly our thoughts employ" (*PW,* 4:398).
67. GMH1, 21.
68. "Autobiographical Memoranda," in Christopher Wordsworth, *Memoirs of William Wordsworth* (London: Edward Moxon, 1851), 1:9.

69. "Home at Grasmere," lines 706–14 (italics added).
70. *PW,* 4:2, and IF.
71. IF, in "Composed by the Sea-Shore" (*PW,* 4:397).
72. Robertson, *Wordsworthshire,* 36–37.
73. Cited in WAG, 470, n. 3.
74. EL, 233.
75. "To a Butterfly" (1802), lines 6, 9–10, 13–18.
76. "Address from the Spirit of Cockermouth Castle," in *PW,* 4:23.
77. "The Sparrow's Nest," lines 3–4, 11–12, 18.
78. "To the Daisy" (1802), lines 1–4, in *PW,* 2:135.
79. WAG, 9, n. 8.
80. The simile "like a grave" is from the earliest version: *1799,* I.312–13.
81. WAG, 9, n. 9.
82. Robertson, *Wordsworthshire,* 12.
83. George Pryme, *Autobiographic Recollections* (Cambridge: Deighton, Bell, 1870), 76–77, 105.
84. WAG, 9, n. 8; MM1, 11.
85. *CEY,* 45.
86. TWT, 33.

Chapter 2: The Vale of Esthwaite

Any account of Wordsworth's Hawkshead must be heavily indebted to the man who wrote the book on it, T. W. Thompson, *Wordsworth's Hawkshead* (London: Oxford Univ. Press, 1970), cited as TWT, and to Robert Woof, who organized and edited its veritable thickets of information for publication. In citing my debts to Thompson, I have tried as much as possible to distinguish between his researches and Woof's.

1. Eric Robertson, Wordsworthshire (London: Chatto and Windus, 1911).
2. *CEY,* 47; Woof, TWT, 34, n. 1.
3. GMH1, 35.
4. *CEY,* 55, 64.
5. Woof, TWT, 373.
6. These time divisions are simplified for clarity. *CEY* (49, n. 4) cautions that it is not always possible to tell which home the boys departed to for vacations, or which one they returned from, or whether they all went back and forth together. *CEY,* TWT (3), and Woof (373) have differing interpretations of the evidence about where the boys spent their summers. Some time spent in Hawkshead seems plausible on the basis of the many summertime activities Wordsworth describes there.
7. Eileen Jay, *Wordsworth at Colthouse* (Kendal: Westmorland Gazette, 1981), 7. The name is no longer in use.
8. MM1, 28.
9. TWT, 12.
10. TWT, 71.
11. TWT, 104.
12. TWT, 222, quoting Wordsworth's *Guide to the Lakes* (1926 ed.), 122.
13. TWT, 211–14.
14. TWT, 56.
15. SG, 23.

16. Jay, *Wordsworth,* 7, 18.
17. *CEY,* 296.
18. Jay, *Wordsworth,* 7.
19. TWT, 71–72; Jay, *Wordsworth,* 20.
20. TWT, 43, paraphrasing Thompson's conversations with Mary Hodgson in 1905.
21. MM1, 27.
22. *LLY,* 4:210.
23. TWT, 306–7.
24. Woof, TWT, 209n.
25. Woof, citing Liverpool sources, TWT, 209n.
26. Woof, TWT, 209n.
27. *The Prelude,* II.174; TWT, 78–79, 147.
28. *LEY,* 56–57.
29. *European Magazine, and London Review* (Cornhill: J. Sewell), 9 (March 1787): 204–5. I deduce Greenwood's authorship from the eight poems in the March issue (of a total of seventeen) which are signed with pseudonyms and are not translations. Three slightly more impressive pieces signed "Rusticus" might be coded from "Greenwood," but they are written as if from Dover. Neither Greenwood's contribution nor that of Axiologus is in any marked way above or below the standard of quality in the magazine's small poetry section.
30. TWT, 74–76.
31. *Correspondence of Thomas Gray,* ed. Paget Toynbee and Leonard Whibley, 3 vols. (Oxford: Clarendon Press, 1935), 3:1098.
32. MM1, 24.
33. TWT, 21.
34. TWT, 246–47.
35. TWT, 248.
36. TWT, 49.
37. Woof, TWT, 131, n. 1, 375.
38. TWT, 53.
39. TWT, 207.
40. TWT, 243.
41. IF, *PW,* 5:373.
42. TWT, 154.
43. TWT, 239–41.
44. TWT, 229, citing "W.S." from Kendal.
45. TWT, 230.
46. TWT, 225.
47. TWT, 234.
48. *The Prose Works of William Wordsworth,* ed. Alexander Grosart, 3 vols. (London: Edward Moxon, 1876), 3:205.
49. TWT, 152.
50. TWT, 165.
51. TWT, 158.
52. TWT, 175.
53. TWT, 183.
54. "Autobiographical Memoranda," *Memoirs,* 1:12.
55. Quoted in TWT, 188–89.
56. Budworth, quoted in TWT, 189–90.

57. TWT, 263; italics added.
58. TWT, 54.
59. TWT, 53, n. 1.
60. TWT, 53.
61. TWT, 50, John West, personal communication.
62. William Hutchinson, *An Excursion to the Lakes: In Westmoreland and Cumberland, August 1773* (London, 1774), 68–70, quoted in SG, 19n.
63. TWT, 129, quoting Wordsworth, *PW,* 1:319.
64. Woof, TWT, 117, n. 1.
65. Woof, TWT, 129, n. 3.
66. Woof, TWT, p. xix.
67. TWT, 130.
68. Woof, TWT, 92–93, quoting one of Mingay's newspaper advertisements.
69. TWT, 94.
70. Woof, TWT, 131, n. 2.
71. J. V. Beckett, "The Making of a Pocket Borough: Cockermouth, 1722–1756," *Journal of British Studies* 20 (1980): 145.
72. Years later, Wordsworth's own son John would marry the granddaughter, also Isabella, of John Christian and Isabella Curwen (TWT, 21, 127–31; Woof notes, xviii, 374–75).

Chapter 3: "While We Were Schoolboys"

1. EL, 31, 55–57.
2. John Burnett, *A History of the Cost of Living* (Harmondsworth: Penguin, 1969), 147.
3. TWT, 151.
4. MM1, 25n.
5. Burnett, *Cost of Living,* 158; TWT, 115, 104.
6. MM1, 26.
7. TWT, 85.
8. Eileen Jay, *Wordsworth at Colthouse* (Kendal: Westmorland Gazette, 1981), 28. Some scholars have found mathematical principles deeply functional in Wordsworth's oeuvre: Geoffrey H. Durrant, *Wordsworth and the Great System: A Study of Wordsworth's Poetic Universe* (Cambridge: Cambridge Univ. Press, 1970); Lee M. Johnson, *Wordsworth's Metaphysical Verse: Geometry, Nature, and Form* (Toronto: Univ. of Toronto Press, 1982).
9. *Prose,* 3:372.
10. IF, *PW,* 4:422. Ovid was a general Hawkshead favorite, not just Wordsworth's special taste, since his *Metamorphoses* had been famously translated by George Sandys (1579–1644), son of the school's founder (I am grateful to John West, present curator of the school, for this and other information).
11. Bruce Graver, "Wordsworth's Translations from Latin Poetry" (Ph.D. diss., Univ. of North Carolina, 1983), ii, 65–68.
12. Annabel Patterson, *Pastoral and Ideology: Virgil to Valéry* (Berkeley: Univ. of California Press, 1987), 193–262.
13. Jay, *Wordsworth,* 28–29; TWT, 344–45.
14. WAG, 384, n. 3, citing *Paradise Lost, Paradise Regained,* and *At a Solemn Music.*
15. *LEY,* 56.
16. Scholarly research on Wordsworth's *reading,* as distinct from the literary influences that can be traced in his writing, has in a sense only just begun. Duncan Wu, *Wordsworth's*

Reading, 1770–1799 (Cambridge: Cambridge Univ. Press, 1993); idem, *Wordsworth's Reading, 1800–1915* (Cambridge: Cambridge Univ. Press, 1995); Robert Paul Kelley, "The Literary Sources of William Wordsworth's Works, 10 July 1793 to 10 June 1797" (Ph.D. diss., Univ. of Hull, 1987).

17. *Memoirs,* 34.
18. *Memoirs,* 10.
19. *CEY,* 54, n. 5.
20. *Gil Blas,* vol. 1, bk. 1, chap. 2.
21. Marilyn Gaull, *English Romanticism: The Human Context* (New York: Norton, 1988), 259.
22. E. H. King, "James Beattie's Literary Essay: 1776, 1783," *Aberdeen University Review* 45 (1974): 389–401.
23. MM1, 54.
24. The full story of male Romantic writers' debt to their female contemporaries is just now being written. It frequently presents the unsavory spectacle not only of unacknowledged debts but also of nonpayments accompanied (or disguised) by critical denunciations of precisely the qualities that the male poet loved most. Among many others that might be cited are Marlon Ross, *The Contours of Masculine Desire: Romanticism and the Rise of Women's Poetry* (New York: Oxford Univ. Press, 1989); Stuart Curran, ed., *The Cambridge Companion to British Romanticism* (Cambridge: Cambridge Univ. Press, 1993); Anne K. Mellor, ed., *Romanticism and Feminism* (Bloomington: Indiana Univ. Press, 1988); and Anne K. Mellor, *Romanticism and Gender* (New York: Routledge, 1993).
25. Bishop Hunt, "Wordsworth's Marginalia on *Paradise Lost," Bulletin of the New York Public Library* 73 (1969): 85–103; Kelley, "Literary Sources," 220; Mary Jacobus, *Tradition and Experience in Wordsworth's "Lyrical Ballads" (1798)* (Oxford: Oxford Univ. Press, 1976), 244n, 258n.
26. In WL, DC.
27. *PW,* 4:403.
28. Kelley, "Literary Sources," 220.
29. Jacobus, *Tradition,* 39–44, 105–9, gives excellent accounts of Thomson's philosophical influence on Wordsworth's verse, and of such compositional devices as the "topographical episode" (which anticipates the "spots of time") and the placement of another figure, or companion, in the scene to give plausible human scale to the rhapsodic praises of nature.
30. WAG, 286, n. 6.
31. "How sweet the walk along the woody steep" (Isle of Wight, 1793), Hayden, 116.
32. *PW,* 5:410.
33. Edward Walford, "Life of Bishop Percy," in his edition of the *Reliques.*
34. *Reliques* (1765), 1:xxi.
35. Hayden, 945–46.
36. See Everard King, *James Beattie* (New York: Twayne, 1977). King may overstate Beattie's influence at times, but most early influences on Wordsworth have been so understated that one can hardly blame him. See Abrams, "Wordsworth and Coleridge on Diction and Figures," *English Institute Essays* (New York: Columbia Univ. Press, 1954), 171–201, and Oliver Elton, *A Survey of English Literature, 1730–1780* (London: Arnold, 1928), viii, which notes that in *The Minstrel* " 'the growth of a poet's soul' [is] mildly anticipated."
37. *LEY,* 100–101.
38. MM1, 73–74.
39. SG, 29, n. 73.

40. George Crabbe, *The Complete Poetical Works,* ed. Norma Dalrymple-Champneys and Pollard, 3 vols. (Oxford: Clarendon Press, 1988), 1:668.
41. *LLY,* 3:348.
42. MM1, 101–2.
43. *The Poetical Works of John Langhorne, D.D.,* ed. J. T. Langhorne [his son] (London: Mawman, 1804), 13. All quotations of Langhorne's work are from this edition.
44. To William Mathews, Nov. 7, 1794, *LEY,* 135.
45. Jacobus, *Tradition,* 44–51 and passim; also Jonathan Wordsworth, *William Wordsworth: The Borders of Vision* (Oxford: Clarendon Press, 1982), 231–32, 248–49, 295–98, 333–59.
46. *Memoirs,* 11–12.

Chapter 4: "Verses from the Impulse of My Own Mind"

1. *CEY,* 58–59n.
2. "The Vale of Esthwaite," lines 469–70.
3. *CEY,* 60.
4. *CEY,* 60.
5. *CEY,* 61.
6. *LEY,* 616n; Richard Ferguson, *Cumberland and Westmorland M.P.'s from the Restoration to the Reform Bill of 1867* (London: Bell and Daldy, 1871), 433.
7. *CEY,* appendix 3, "Wordsworth's Earliest Poetic Composition," 298–301.
8. *Memoirs,* 1:10.
9. The most thorough critical account of Wordsworth's earliest poetry is Paul Sheats, *The Making of Wordsworth's Poetry, 1785–1798* (Cambridge: Harvard Univ. Press, 1973). It treats the juvenilia primarily in terms of contemporary materialist versus idealist theories of perception.
10. *CEY,* 298, quoting Justice Coleridge.
11. James Butler, "The Muse at Hawkshead: Early Criticism of Wordsworth's Poetry," *Wordsworth Circle* 20 (1989): 140.
12. Sheats, *Making,* 5. The only exceptions are "The Vale of Esthwaite" and a fragment of an imitation of Ossian.
13. Edmonds translation, 43.
14. Bruce Graver, "Wordsworth's Translations from Latin Poetry" (Ph.D. diss., Univ. of North Carolina, 1983), 19–28, comments on Wordsworth's accuracy and stylistic felicities.
15. Cornish translation, 53, 55.
16. Hayden, 922; Owen, xvii.
17. *CEY,* 70.
18. TWT, 60.
19. TWT, 66.
20. *CEY,* 67.
21. TWT, 66.
22. Averill notes that the *European Magazine* had published favorable reviews of William's poetry, as well as other poetic tributes to her (*EW,* 33).
23. *Memoirs,* 1:13.
24. *CEY,* 74–76.
25. *PW,* 1:318.
26. *CEY,* 72.

27. Zera Fink, ed., *The Early Wordsworthian Milieu* (Oxford: Clarendon Press, 1958), 104.
28. Hayden, 50–66; *PW,* 1:270–83; *EPF,* 401–525. All my citations are to the Hayden text.
29. "Pale spectres! are ye what ye seem? / . . . / Fix'd are their eyes, on me they bend— / Their glaring look is cold!" ("Irregular Fragments, Found in a Dark Passage of the Tower," cited by Sheats, *Making,* 8.)

Chapter 5: Stranger, Lounger, Lover

Ben Ross Schneider's *Wordsworth's Cambridge Education* (cited as BRS) is the indispensable book here. Its only weakness arises from its basic strength: having identified the hegemony of Newtonian scientific thought at Cambridge, Schneider proceeds to interpret all practices and behaviors there as direct or indirect reflections of it. This is plausible for intellectual history but too abstract to capture the randomness of everyday college life. Hence Schneider's account must be fleshed out with anecdotal evidence, much of which he himself cites: principally the memoirs of Henry Gunning and George Pryme. These must be supplemented, in turn, by the many official registers, archives, and histories of the university.

This leads to Wordsworth's grandnephew Christopher Wordsworth's *Social Life at the English Universities in the Eighteenth Century* (1874), a compilation without much thesis, complementary to his *Scholae Academicae: Studies at the English Universities in the Eighteenth Century* (1877). This grandnephew (1848–1938) could still talk to his father (d. 1885) and others who were there, though not many of Wordsworth's own generation: his grandfather, the poet's brother, died in 1846. So he drew, as I have, on more ephemeral texts which constitute much of the record of "social life," principally the anecdote books and "lounging" books which Wordsworth also enjoyed. The most useful of these are a series published anonymously by Richard Gooch (d. 1849) between 1823 and 1835: *The Cambridge Tart* (1823), *Facetiae Cantabrigienses* (1825), and *Nuts to Crack* (1835)—the latter including Oxford as well. Each book includes material from its predecessors, but in essence these are tales of the unreformed, eighteenth-century university, not to be taken as reliable facts, except where they are corroborated, as they mostly are, by serious memoirists like Gunning and Pryme, and by official university documents.

One of the most interesting of these books is J. M. F. Wright's anonymous ("by a Trinity-Man") *Alma Mater; or, Seven Years at the University of Cambridge.* Wright entered college about 1815, a generation after Wordsworth, but his account, like Gooch's collections, bears testimony to the marked consistency of university life between 1760 and 1820: the reign of George III. Wright is an interested party, not a historian, but his two-volume work matches well with other such sources. It is part exposé, part university novel, part college guide for students and parents, and part self-advertisement—not unlike Book III of *The Prelude.*

Schneider makes an interesting methodological point, with reference to Gunning, that has applicability to Wordsworth. Many nineteenth-century biographers "were careful to suppress the youthful errors of their subjects," especially of the Jacobin variety, so that "it is now difficult to find out who the *undergraduate* republicans were and what they did *as republicans"* (BRS, 143–44; italics added). Schneider "knows that Gunning could have revealed far more than he did of the politics of friends whose republican aberrations were quiet and unnoticed, however sincere," but he did not, because he wanted to preserve or restore "the good reputations of his radical friends and acquaintances."

1. SG, 429, n. 17.
2. GMH1, 67.
3. GMH1, 56; *London Magazine,* April 1, 1827, 445.

4. J. M. F. Wright, *Alma Mater; or, Seven Years at the University of Cambridge,* 2 vols. (London: Black, Young and Tavistock, 1827), 2:167.
5. If a student did not want to take orders, he could also use a Cambridge fellowship to read for the law at the Inns of Court (BRS, 8).
6. WL, Cookson-Cowper correspondence, April 12, 1788.
7. Percy H. Fitzgerald, *The Royal Dukes and Princesses of the Family of George III: A View of Court Life and Manners for Seventy Years, 1760–1830* (London: Tinsley Brothers, 1882), 2:248.
8. Bute's wife was Mary Wortley, only daughter of Lady Mary Wortley Montagu, hence James Lowther's wife was the granddaughter this important woman of letters (James Lee McKelvey, *George III and Lord Bute: The Leicester House Years* [Durham: Duke Univ. Press, 1973], 4); John Brooke, *King George III* (New York: McGraw-Hill, 1972), 87, 102–3.
9. WL, Cookson-Cowper correspondence, April 24, 1782: "I am told by high authority viz. the King that I look thin."
10. GMH1, 62.
11. John Pollock, *Wilberforce* (London: Constable, 1977), 43.
12. Ibid., 20.
13. Ian Christie, "John Robinson, M.P., 1727–1802," in *Myth and Reality in Late-Eighteenth-Century Politics* (Los Angeles: Univ. of California Press, 1970), 177.
14. Ibid., 145–82.
15. *LEY,* 18, n. 4. The letter is dated April 6, 1788, shortly after Robinson received news of Wordsworth's first-class ranking in his first college examination.
16. *LEY,* 694.
17. *LEY,* 11, n. 2.
18. MM1, 90; Henry Gunning, *Reminiscences of the University, Town and Country of Cambridge, from the Year 1780,* 2d ed., 2 vols. (London, 1855), 1:211–20.
19. Arthur B. Gray, *Cambridge Revisited* (1921; reprint, Cambridge: Par Stephens, 1974), 43.
20. George Pryme, *Autobiographic Recollections* (Cambridge: Deighton, Bell, 1870), 44.
21. E. A. Benians, "St. John's College in Wordsworth's Time," in *Wordsworth at Cambridge* (Cambridge: Cambridge Univ. Press, 1950), 2; Heather E. Peek and Catherine P. Hall, *The Archives of the University of Cambridge: An Historical Introduction* (Cambridge: Cambridge Univ. Press, 1962), 53.
22. Gunning, *Reminiscences,* 1:129.
23. Benians, "St. John's," 3; *Prelude,* III.49–50.
24. Wright, *Alma Mater,* 1:83–84.
25. MM1, 92.
26. Benians, "St. John's," 1.
27. Alec C. Crook, *From the Foundation to Gilbert Scott: A History of the Buildings of St. John's College Cambridge, 1511–1885* (Cambridge: Cambridge Univ. Press, 1980), 16.
28. Ibid., 165–68.
29. "After so splendid a start . . . there must be college reasons [for the decline]" (ibid., 144–46).
30. *Eagle,* 28.
31. MM1, 90, which cites only nine names.
32. TWT, 74.
33. *Eagle,* 33–34; SG, 429, n. 9.
34. TWT, 52; Woof, TWT, 357–58; Robert Forsyth Scott, ed., *Admissions to the College of*

St. John the Evangelist in the University of Cambridge (Cambridge: Cambridge Univ. Press, 1903), 62.

35. Benians, "St. John's," 4–5; BRS, 66; Pryme, *Recollections,* 155–58; *DNB.*
36. MM1, 90.
37. Crook, *Foundation,* 70.
38. Benians, "St. John's," 3; Wright, *Alma Mater,* 2:176–77.
39. MM1, 124.
40. *Memoirs,* 1:14; John West informs me that reading the first six books of Euclid was standard pedagogic practice at Hawkshead and therefore not evidence of special mathematical precocity on Wordsworth's part.
41. MM1, 154; GMH1, 247.
42. BRS, 45.
43. BRS, 43–44; Christopher Wordsworth, *Social Life,* 98ff.
44. MM1, 103.
45. Benians, "St. John's, 4–5.
46. *LEY,* 19; *Nuts,* 150.
47. BRS, 3.
48. MM1, 86.
49. Gunning, *Reminiscences,* 1:128.
50. Benians, "St. John's," 3; Pryme, *Recollections,* 44.
51. Wordsworth's quotation from Thomson's *Castle of Indolence* (WAG, 196, n. 1).
52. *Gradus ad Cantabrigiam,* 85, cited in Christopher Wordsworth, *Social Life,* 378, which also cites *Facetiae Cantabrigienses,* itself often called "the complete Lounging Book."
53. Pryme, *Recollections,* 51.
54. WAG, 94, n. 7.
55. *Facetiae,* 123.
56. Bishop Hunt, "Wordsworth's Marginalia on *Paradise Lost,*" *Bulletin of the New York Public Library* 73 (1969): 167–83.
57. BRS, 46.
58. Christopher Wordsworth, *Social Life,* 142.
59. Gunning, *Reminiscences,* 1:24, 50; Charles H. Cooper, *Annals of Cambridge,* vol. 4, *1688–1849* (Cambridge: Metcalfe and Palmer, 1852), 409.
60. Gunning, *Reminiscences,* 2:147.
61. Wright, *Alma Mater,* 1:98; Christopher Wordsworth, *Social Life,* 397–98, suggests that each of the "beauties" had her favorite church of resort.
62. Wright, *Alma Mater,* 1:143.
63. Ibid., 175.
64. Gunning, *Reminiscences,* 2:170.
65. Christopher Wordsworth, *Social Life,* 369–71, 398.
66. Wright, *Alma Mater,* 2:119–20.
67. Ibid., 1:124.
68. Gunning, *Reminiscences,* 2:113; Christopher Wordsworth, *Social Life,* 353.
69. Christopher Wordsworth, *Social Life,* 353, citing Cooper, *Annals,* 409; the date of this letter is 1766.
70. Gunning, *Reminiscences,* 2:117.
71. Ibid., 1:204.
72. Ibid., 25–26.
73. A less symbolic etymology for "maidens" derives it as a euphemism for "middens"

(sewage outfall), across which a causeway would be quite useful. I am grateful to John Kerrigan of St. John's for this suggestion.

74. Christopher Wordsworth, *Social Life,* 362–63; the language is from Charles I's injunction of 1629, but it was still in force in the eighteenth century.
75. Wright, *Alma Mater,* 2:142–44, 1:40n.
76. William Knight, *Coleridge and Wordsworth in the West Country: Their Friendship, Work, and Surroundings* (London: Elkin Matthews, 1913), 65.
77. Wright, *Alma Mater,* 1:167.
78. Pollock, *Wilberforce,* 15.
79. Beth Darlington, ed., *The Love Letters of William and Mary Wordsworth* (Ithaca: Cornell Univ. Press, 1981).
80. MM1, 88.
81. *Facetiae,* 163.
82. Quoted by NR, 109, which adds Godwin's observation on Coleridge's condition: "loose in sexual morality—spends a night in a house of ill fame, ruminating in a chair: next morning meditates suicide."
83. Wright, *Alma Mater,* 1:223–24, 2:108–10.

Chapter 6: Young Love-Liking

1. WL, MS 2. The passage may contain some words reported verbatim from another bystander, since Wordsworth would not have known personally that one of the hills "about 6 years ago was clothed with wood."
2. Alan Liu, *Wordsworth: The Sense of History* (Stanford: Stanford Univ. Press, 1989), 63–64.
3. *CEY,* 82–83n.
4. John Pollock, *Wilberforce* (London: Constable, 1977), 81–83.
5. WAG, 132, n. 8.
6. James Reiger, "Wordsworth Unalarm'd," in *Milton and the Line of Vision,* ed. J. Wittreich (Madison: Univ. of Wisconsin Press, 1975), 186.
7. WAG, 142, nn. 4 and 5.
8. I am indebted to Skip Willman for pointing out the implication of some of these connections.
9. "Elegy XIX," 25–27; I am indebted to Skip Willman for uncovering this parallel.
10. WAG, 148, n. 8.
11. Beth Darlington, "Two Early Texts: *A Night-Piece* and *The Discharged Soldier,*" in *Bicentenary Wordsworth Studies in Memory of John Alban Finch,* ed. Jonathan Wordsworth (Ithaca: Cornell Univ. Press, 1970), 434.
12. WAG, 150–51.
13. By 1789 Dorothy was living with the Cooksons in Norfolk; Mary left Penrith sometime early in the summer of 1789 to live with her brother Tom in Durham (*CEY,* 87–88, 93–94).
14. Liu, *Wordsworth,* 63–64, cites language from guidebooks of the Picturesque which clearly suggests the erotic associations of "intricate" landscape beauty, and the concomitant associations of sadism with its corollary, "roughness."
15. *LEY,* 10.
16. MM1, 75.
17. *CEY,* 80–84.
18. *CEY,* 90n.

19. All line references are to the Reading Text of the 1793 edition established by James Averill, *An Evening Walk* [*EW*], to which I am also indebted for information about the chronology of its composition.
20. MM1, 117.
21. *EW,* 5.
22. MM1, 115, n. 1. Moorman also remarks echoes of the countess of Winchilsea's "Nocturnal Reverie" and Collins's "Ode to Evening" (100–101). Emile Legouis's study of parallel locutions lists still more verbal echoes.
23. Cited in *EW,* 54.

Chapter 7: Weighing the Man in the Balance

1. [Richard Gooch], *Facetiae Cantabrigienses* (1825), 71–72.
2. GMH1, 56, quoting J. B. Mullinger, *History of the University of Cambridge.*
3. BRS, 95.
4. *LEY,* 18.
5. HRCU, 303, 463–65.
6. Alec C. Crook, *From the Foundation to Gilbert Scott: A History of the Buildings of St. John's College Cambridge, 1511–1885* (Cambridge: Cambridge Univ. Press, 1980), 71.
7. *Memoirs,* 1:14.
8. Ibid.
9. Henry Gunning, *Reminiscences of the University, Town and Country of Cambridge, from the Year 1780,* 2d ed., 2 vols. (London, 1855), 1:202–4, 206–7.
10. BRS, 105.
11. *Prelude* I.169–238, esp. 185–219; cf. Kenneth R. Johnston, *Wordsworth and "The Recluse"* (New Haven: Yale Univ. Press, 1984), 127–31.
12. Alan Liu, *Wordsworth: The Sense of History* (Stanford: Stanford Univ. Press, 1989), 23–31.
13. J. M. F. Wright, *Alma Mater; or, Seven Years at the University of Cambridge,* 2 vols. (London: Black, Young and Tavistock, 1827), 1:250–51.
14. BRS, 113–63, and passim.
15. BRS, 106–7.
16. Wright, *Alma Mater,* 2:12–13.
17. Hayden, 114.
18. MM1, 122–23; *CEY,* 94n.
19. MM1, 122, n. 2.
20. *LEY,* 666–67.
21. BRS, 156–63.
22. BRS, 156–57.
23. Christopher Wordsworth, *Social Life at the English Universities in the Eighteenth Century* (Cambridge: Deighton, Bell, 1874), 238; Gunning, *Reminiscences,* 2:8; though this applies to the period after the 1794 treason trials, it was always Tweddell's manner.
24. C. V. Le Grice, *A General Theorem for a College Declamation* (1796), quoted in BRS, 162–63.
25. *DNB.* It is not improbable that Wordsworth knew Le Grice's satire, since Le Grice, besides being an old schoolfellow of Coleridge and Lamb, was a classmate and keen competitor with Christopher Wordsworth at Trinity from 1792 to 1796, when they belonged to the same literary set; Le Grice won the declamation prize—with a serious poem—and Christopher finished second.

26. BRS, 172–73.
27. BRS, 84.
28. BRS, 165.
29. BRS, 31.
30. BRS, 19, citing D. A. Winstanley, *Unreformed Cambridge* (Cambridge, 1935), 50–52.
31. "Thoughts Suggested by a College Examination," line 72 (first published in *Hours of Idleness,* 1807).
32. George Pryme, *Autobiographic Reminiscences* (Cambridge: Deighton, Bell, 1870), 92. This was the standard ca. 1800.
33. The lower two classes were ranked, but this ranking, unlike the printed tripos lists, has not been preserved for Wordsworth's year.
34. Gunning, *Reminiscences,* 1:226–27.
35. BRS, 35.
36. BRS, 14; HRCU, 464.
37. *London Magazine,* April 1, 1827, 445–46.
38. HRCU, 462–67.
39. BRS, 38.
40. Charles H. Cooper, *Annals of Cambridge,* vol. 4, *1688–1849* (Cambridge: Metcalfe and Palmer, 1852), 425.
41. *Wordsworth at Cambridge* (Cambridge: Cambridge Univ. Press, 1950), 33–34.
42. Henry Gunning, quoted in Graham Chainey, *A Literary History of Cambridge* (Cambridge: Pevensey, 1985), 93.
43. Wright, *Alma Mater,* 1:122.
44. "A man ambitious of a good place in a Tripos found he could not dispense with a private tutor" (T. G. Bonney, *Memories of a Long Life* [Cambridge: Metcalfe, 1921], 28); Bonney is speaking of "former times"—that is, before mid-nineteenth-century reforms.
45. Christopher Wordsworth, *Social Life,* 112; *Gradus ad Cantabrigiam,* 62.
46. Dr. Littleton, "A Letter from Cambridge to a Young Gentleman at Eton," in [Richard Gooch], *The Cambridge Tart* (1823), 99–101.
47. E. A. Benians, "St. John's College in Wordsworth's Time," in *The Eagle: Wordsworth at Cambridge* (Cambridge: Cambridge Univ. Press, 1950), 10.
48. "Poetical Effusion," by Mr. Ayloffe of Trinity College, in *Cambridge Tart,* 20–21.
49. "Happy the youth in Euclid's axioms tried, / Though little skilled in any art beside; / Who, scarcely skill'd an English line to pen, / Scans Attic metres with a critic's ken. / . . . / Such is the youth whose scientific pate / Class-honours, medals, fellowships, await" ("Thoughts Suggested by a College Examination," lines 9–12, 23–24).
50. BRS, 84.
51. HRCU, 465; there were twenty-two senior optimes and sixteen junior optimes, a total of fifty-nine honors degrees.
52. Benians, "St. John's," 34.
53. Bonney, *Memories,* 29.
54. Wright, *Alma Mater,* 2:15.
55. Ibid., 1:57n; Benians, "St. John's," 7.
56. Benians, "St. John's," 9.
57. Wordsworth uses the same dwarf/world disproportion to express his contempt for the students formed by such contemporary education: the "dwarf man," who "can string you names of districts, cities, towns, / The whole world over" (*Prelude,* V.295, 335–36).

58. MM1, 98–99, rightly queries his "curious" decision not to follow his own course of study, in open defiance of college rules and "parental" expectations.
59. MM1, 99–100.
60. Chainey, *Literary History,* 91.
61. MM1, 1:99–100; see also Dorothy Wordsworth, *LEY,* 62, on the tour's pretensions.
62. III.340–41; WAG, 108, n. 9, citing Wordsworth's *Guide to the Lakes* (*Prose,* 2:184).

Chapter 8: Something of a Republic

1. BRS, 143.
2. Frida Knight, *University Rebel: The Life of William Frend (1757–1841)* (London: Victor Gollancz, 1991), 80–84.
3. BRS, 7, 118.
4. BRS, 126.
5. Laurence Fowler and Helen Fowler, eds., *Cambridge Commemorated: An Anthology of University Life* (Cambridge: Cambridge Univ. Press, 1984), 132 citing E. H. Barker, *Literary Anecdotes and Contemporary Reminiscences* (1852).
6. Knight, *Rebel,* 85–88.
7. Quoted in BRS, 115.
8. BRS, 59ff., for Frend's career.
9. BRS, 138–40; Knight, *Rebel,* 86.
10. BRS, 150.
11. NR, 89; BRS, 98, citing Dyer's *Memoirs,* 194.
12. Henry Gunning, *Reminiscences of the University, Town and Country of Cambridge, from the Year 1780,* 2d ed., 2 vols. (London, 1855), 1:302.
13. Ibid., 309.
14. BRS, 116–17.
15. Charles H. Cooper, *Annals of Cambridge,* vol. 4, *1688–1849* (Cambridge: Metcalfe and Palmer, 1852), 362–63.
16. Knight, *Rebel,* 88.
17. Ibid., citing R. B. Barlow, *Citizenship and Conscience* (Philadelphia, 1963), 267.
18. March 22, 1789, *LEY,* 666.
19. *CEY,* 91–92, 96; *LEY,* 25, n. 2.
20. MM1, 125, citing IF.
21. Donald Reiman goes far to correct Coleridge's exaggerations with common sense and critical acumen in his facsimile edition of Bowles's early poems (New York: Garland, 1978), v–xiii.
22. Marlon Ross, *The Contours of Masculine Desire: Romanticism and the Rise of Women's Poetry* (New York: Oxford Univ. Press, 1989).
23. To Pollard, Jan. 25, 1790, *LEY,* 27. All quotations in this paragraph are from this letter or that of April 30, 1790 (*LEY,* 24–32).
24. GMH1, 83.
25. WAG, 112, n. 7.
26. Translated and quoted in BRS, 70–71. Parr's long Ciceronian catalog of university benefits include many that Wordsworth also cites—friendships, equality, competition, amusements—but Parr presents them as realities, not ideals to be regretted, as Wordsworth does.

27. *DNB.*
28. Neil McKendrick, John Brewer, and J. H. Plumb, *The Birth of a Consumer Society: The Commercialization of Eighteenth-Century England* (Bloomington: Indiana Univ. Press, 1982).
29. E. A. Benians, "St. John's College in Wordsworth's Time," in *Wordsworth at Cambridge* (Cambridge: Cambridge Univ. Press, 1950), 2.
30. Gunning, *Reminiscences,* 2:282, 1:186.
31. Pitt and his running mate, the future duke of Grafton, polled 351 and 299 votes, respectively; their opponents, the old Whigs, got 278 and 181.
32. IF, in *PW,* 4:409 (italics added).
33. Cooper, *Annals,* 419, 437, 445–47.
34. Gunning, *Reminiscences,* 1:189.
35. Byron, "Thoughts Suggested by a College Examination," lines 63–64, 67–68. Petty was another MP.
36. For this synopsis of very complex political events and maneuvers, I have drawn principally on Eric J. Evans, *Political Parties in Britain, 1783–1867* (London: Methuen, 1985), 2–15.
37. George Pryme, *Autobiographic Recollections* (Cambridge: Deighton, Bell, 1870), 175.
38. C. R. Benstead, *Portrait of Cambridge* (London: Robert Hale, 1968), 118.

Chapter 9: Golden Hours

1. June 26, 1791, *LEY,* 52.
2. *LEY,* 37.
3. MM1, 135.
4. Letter 29, describing Mount Grimsel.
5. TWT, 361. The Moore volume was given in 1786; the Coxe was dedicated in 1787 and 1790, when Fletcher's two younger brothers left, though not actually presented until 1792. Probably they had it with them in Cambridge, or bought it there.
6. *LEY,* 37.
7. *LLY,* 3:297, 448.
8. Cited by Donald E. Hayden, *Wordsworth's Walking Tour of 1790* (Tulsa: Univ. of Tulsa, 1983), 2.
9. *PW,* 4:58–59.
10. *CEY,* 97.
11. Helen Maria Williams, *Letters from France,* ed. Janet Todd, vol. 1 (Delmar, N.Y.: Scholar's Facsimiles, 1975), 14.
12. HCR, I.372.
13. Racedown notebook, cited in *CEY,* 101, n. 6.
14. GMH1, 100.
15. Alan Liu, *Wordsworth: The Sense of History* (Stanford: Stanford Univ. Press, 1989), 15–17, following Mona Ozouf.
16. Chroniclers of the trip have had difficulty reconciling various accounts of how the two travelers proceeded after Lyons. Without restating all the evidence, I am following Harper's hypothesis, entertained but not confirmed by Reed, and supported implicitly by Hayden's evidence, that they continued south on the Rhône by boat for a day and a half, disembarking at St.-Vallier. See GMH1, 90; *CEY,* 102, n. 10; Hayden, *Tour of 1790,* 17–21, 123.

17. EL, 110.
18. *Correspondence of Thomas Gray,* ed. Paget Toynbee and Leonard Whibley, corr. H. W. Starr, 3 vols. (Oxford: Clarendon Press, 1971), 1:128.
19. Unfortunately, his very first response, a letter written to Dorothy during his stay at the Grande Chartreuse, has never been found, nor does Dorothy seem to have received it (*LEY,* 32). It would probably have contained his immediate responses to his river trip with the *fédérés.*
20. *Prelude,* II.122.
21. GMH1, 90.
22. *LLY,* 4:176; Raymond Havens, *The Mind of a Poet: A Study of Wordsworth's Thought with Particular Reference to "The Prelude"* (Baltimore: Johns Hopkins Univ. Press, 1941), 423.
23. WAG, 208, n. 8.
24. MM1, 135–36. The "gleam of arms" Wordsworth saw in 1790 was probably only a contingent of troops on a domiciliary visit, if not simply part of the small detachment of guards that the government had long provided for the protection of the place. In later versions this "gleam" becomes "the military glare of riotous men," prompting readers of *The Prelude* to recall still later stages of revolutionary excess and disillusionment.
25. *LEY,* 33.
26. "The Tuft of Primroses" (1808), *PW,* 5:360–61.
27. EL, 113.
28. *LEY,* 33.
29. Saussure published his *Voyages dans les Alpes* in four volumes between 1779 and 1796. His account of his ascent of Mont Blanc was translated into English by the Reverend Mr. Martyn, professor of botany at Cambridge, in 1788. An Englishman named Beaufoy made the ascent a few days after Saussure and reported his findings in a paper delivered to the Royal Society on December 13, 1787 (William Coxe, *Sketches on the Natural, Civil and Political State of Swisserland* [1776; reprint, London: J. Dodsley, 1799], 787–88).
30. Coxe, *Sketches,* 778.
31. Coxe cites modern calculations to debunk ancient accounts of higher mountains, concluding "that there are no mountains, except those in America . . . which are equal to the altitude of Mt. Blanc" (*Sketches,* 780). He is cautiously dismissive of natural philosophers who thought there might be higher points in Asia or Africa: "conjectures are now banished from natural philosophy; and, until it be proved from undoubted calculations . . . Mt. Blanc may be fairly considered as more elevated" (781).
32. Coxe, *Sketches,* 778.
33. Paul D. Sheats, *The Making of Wordsworth's Poetry, 1785–1798* (Cambridge: Harvard Univ. Press, 1973), 69.
34. Coxe, *Sketches,* 778.

Chapter 10: Golden Days and Giddy Prospects

1. *LEY,* 33 (italics added). For the facts of Wordsworth's Simplon crossing I am indebted to Donald Hayden's account, which summarizes the various findings of Moorman, Reed, Wildi, and Bernhardt-Kabisch. All these scholars make their own deductions and interpretations as well.
2. VI.565. This might be taken for Beristal, a tiny village about three hours above Brig,

but Wordsworth does speak of noon, of lunch, and of "the board" that he says the hasty muleteers left them lingering over after lunch.

3. Dorothy, referring in 1820 to the "immense" new building erected by Napoleon at the top of the pass, says it is "to be used as an Inn instead of the Old Spittal" (*DWJ,* 2:260).
4. Max Wildi, "Wordsworth and the Simplon Pass," *English Studies* 40 (1959): 228.
5. *1850,* VI.566–67.
6. Alan Liu, *Wordsworth: The Sense of History* (Stanford: Stanford Univ. Press, 1989), 23–31, 519–20.
7. Again the 1850 version tries to make the place more to blame for their error: its "track . . . held forth / Conspicuous invitation to ascend a lofty mountain" (570–73).
8. For Freerberg, see Wildi, "Simplon Pass," 224–32. For an unnamed hamlet, see Ernest Bernhardt-Kabisch, "Wordsworth and the Simplon Revisited," *Wordsworth Circle* 10 (1979): 381–84. Wildi's interpretation implies that they had lunch in the inn at Simplon Village; Bernhardt-Kabisch's, that they lunched in the Stockalper spital back nearer to the summit. Since Wildi's account of their itinerary has them taking the wrong turn near the little hamlet of Gabi (Gstein), another 800 feet lower than Simplon Village, I tend to accept Bernhardt-Kabisch's view of the matter, even though the missed *direction* is easiest to imagine on Wildi's route.
9. The 1850 version, continuing Wordsworth's pattern of intensifications in revision, italicizes the entire phrase, making it the longest statement so rendered in the poem.
10. Only VIII.711–27 are strictly speaking manuscript alternatives for VI.525–48 (WAG, 304, n. 7). But VIII.728–41 clearly show Wordsworth's determination to get his imagination working again after external disappointment.
11. *DWJ,* 2:260–61.
12. *LEY,* 34.
13. *DS,* line 179 (Wordsworth's note). Technically speaking, the stream is called the Doveria until it joins the Tusa at Gondo Village.
14. WAG, 218, n. 6.
15. Johannes von Müller, cited in Pfarrer Arnold's *Der Simplon* (1947), cited by Wildi, "Simplon Pass," 230. (The Toggia is another name for the Doveria.)
16. *DWJ,* 2:258 (italics added), cited in MM1, 142.
17. MM1, 142, Wildi, "Simplon Pass," 232, *CEY,* 106, and Donald E. Hayden, *Wordsworth's Walking Tour of 1790* (Tulsa: Univ. of Tulsa, 1983), all refuse to hazard a guess, though Wildi does say it must have been "some kind of traumatic experience."
18. Cf. "The Boy of Winander" episode in *Prelude* IV, or De Quincey's account of Wordsworth and Coleridge listening for the mail coach (for news of the Peninsular campaign) with their ears to the ground.
19. The formulation is Geoffrey Hartman's, in his revised preface (1971) to his seminal study of Wordsworth's "apocalyptic" imagination, *Wordsworth's Poetry, 1787–1814* (New Haven: Yale Univ. Press, 1964).
20. *LEY,* 33.
21. I am indebted to my late friend Louis Hawes for firsthand information about the Borromean Islands.
22. Wordsworth's itinerary entry: *CEY,* 106; Hayden, *Tour of 1790,* 56–57. Scholars dispute the most likely route.
23. *PW,* 4:387–88, 479.
24. *DS,* line 90 (Wordsworth's note).
25. Coxe, *Sketches,* 891.
26. *LEY,* 34.

27. Moorman allows that "the girls were not above a little flirtation" (MM1, 143); this is doubtless true, but a notably one-sided perspective. Harper sees them smiling "from their arbored gardens at the swift-striding English boys" (GMH1, 96), but does not pause to inquire if the girls were smiling *back*. Legouis and F. W. Bateson, being French and psychoanalytic, respectively, take a more generous view of the sexual possibilities here, but do not pursue them. Harper is closer to what I think should be remarked when he notes that the "iron restraint of his later years" caused Wordsworth "to erase or blur" the hints dropped in *Descriptive Sketches* about these girls.
28. Birdsall, in *DS,* 12–14.
29. *DS,* 143–45 (Huntington Quarto transcriptions).
30. Coxe, *Sketches,* 893.
31. *DS,* 149 (Huntington Quarto transcriptions).
32. Hayden, *Tour of 1790,* 64.
33. Ibid., 67.
34. Raymond Havens, *The Mind of a Poet: A Study of Wordsworth's Thought with Particular Reference to "The Prelude"* (Baltimore: Johns Hopkins Univ. Press, 1941), 429, wisely notes that "most of the memorable experiences recorded in *The Prelude" are* unpleasant.
35. *DWJ,* 2:219–20.
36. *DWJ,* 2:243.
37. *DWJ,* 2:244.
38. In 1820 the family touring party broke apart for several days because of Dorothy's determination to see exactly where her brother had been on Como in 1790. They first spent two days there and then went to Milan. But Dorothy wanted to see more of Como, "for the sake of Gravedona," and so she returned with William, while Crabb Robinson and the others remained in Milan. *DWJ,* 2:239.
39. Hayden, *Tour of 1790,* 64.
40. Lane Cooper, *A Concordance to the Poems of William Wordsworth* (New York: E. P. Dutton, 1911), 1002.
41. The scene is similar to one he described to Dorothy to illustrate the "softness and elegance" of the Italians compared to the "severity and austereness" of the Swiss. "It was with pleasure I observed at a small Inn on the lake of Como, the master of it playing upon his harpsicord, with a large collection of Italian music about him. The outside of the instrument was such that it would not have much graced an English drawingroom, but the tones that he drew from it were by no means contemptible" (*LEY,* 36).
42. Wordsworth notes that these two lines are free translations from Petrarch.
43. This is compatible with one of Hayden's options: "did he backtrack and actually return to the western shore of Lake Como just north of Gravedona?" (Hayden, *Tour of 1790,* 65).
44. *DWJ,* 2:221.
45. *PW,* 3:186–88.
46. *PW,* 3:482–83.
47. *DWJ,* 2:223.
48. GMH1, 92.
49. *DWJ,* 2:190.
50. *BL,* chap. 4.
51. *DS,* 187.
52. *DS,* line 475n.
53. *LEY,* 34.
54. *LEY,* 35.

55. MM1, 146.
56. *DS,* line 564n.
57. *DWJ,* 2:147 (italics added).
58. Cited in Hayden, *Tour of 1790,* 83. Dorothy agreed: "in fact, the middle part of this day's journey reminded us more of the Lakes of England than any Lake country we saw during the whole tour" (*DWJ,* 2:135–36).
59. *DWJ,* 2:134.
60. *LEY,* 36.
61. *Prose,* 1:9.
62. GMH1, 92. The fifth "reverie," or promenade, is most concerned with this area.
63. *The Confession of Jean-Jacques Rousseau,* anonymous English translation of 1783 and 1790, ed. A. S. B. Glover (New York: Heritage Press, 1955), 624.
64. "They Approach the Rapids under the Castle of Heidelberg" and "Author's Voyage down the Rhine (Thirty Years Ago)," in *PW,* 3:169.
65. Gunther Rothenberg, in *Encyclopedia Americana* (1989), 17:242.

Chapter 11: The Mighty City

1. *LEY,* 37.
2. *CEY,* 115, n. 29.
3. *CEY,* 115, n. 29.
4. *LEY,* 46–47; MM1, 150. All references to Dorothy's correspondence in this section are from *LEY,* 38–47, 50–54 (Oct. 20, 1790, and May 23 and June 26, 1791).
5. *DWJ,* 2:86.
6. *PW,* 1:296–98. Reed says, "There appears no reason why the poem should not be . . . dated" in late 1790 or early 1791, after the walking trip, thus avoiding the confusion created by the traditional 1794 dating, which would imply Wordsworth's neglecting Annette Vallon to address an extremely prescient love poem to Mary Hutchinson (*CEY,* 302–3).
7. Horace, *Odes and Epodes,* tr. Joseph Clancy (Chicago: Univ. of Chicago Press, 1960), 80.
8. *LEY,* 45.
9. *LEY,* 52.
10. HRCU, 464–65.
11. Another route from Cambridge came into Shoreditch and Bishopsgate via Tottenham and Stoke Newington.
12. Of the fifteen principal coaching inns in London in the early 1790s, over half were in Cheapside.
13. DC, MS 52 (*Thirteen,* 2:693).
14. *LEY,* 44. Dorothy asked Jane Pollard for all the details in this "subject which you rightly judged to be more interesting to me than any other . . . how she was dressed &c &c &c. You will know how to interpret these etcs." Dorothy wanted to know how her aunt could enter into physical intimacy with a man who had already been married, as she contemplated a different kind of intimacy with her brother.
15. MM1, 161.
16. James Boulton, *The Language of Politics* (Toronto: Univ. of Toronto Press, 1963), 265–71.
17. Arthur Beatty, *William Wordsworth: His Doctrine and Art in Their Historical Relations* (1922; reprint, Madison: Univ. of Wisconsin Press, 1960), 231, citing *DNB.*
18. *Excursion* II.219–21, *app. crit.* There is no warrant in Fawcett's biography, however, for

Wordsworth's representation of the Solitary's downfall: "His sacred function . . . at length renounced; / . . . every day and every place enjoyed / The unshackled layman's natural liberty; / Speech, manners, morals, all without disguise / . . . the course / Of private life licentiously displayed / Unhallowed actions" (II.263–69). This is not a case of mistaken information on Wordsworth's part, but, as M. Ray Adams suggests, artistic manipulation of his materials, on the basis of his own experience. See Adams, "Joseph Fawcett and Wordsworth's Solitary," in *Studies of the Literary Backgrounds of English Radicalism* (Lancaster, Pa.: Franklin and Marshall College Studies, 1947), 190–226.

19. Tantalizingly, a Henry Wordsworth lived in Jewin Street off Aldersgate, one block away from where Wood Street gives into Fore Street near Cripplegate Churchyard. He signed himself "Citizen Wordsworth" in a list of contributors to the defense of the leaders of the London Corresponding Society who were arrested in May 1794, leading up to the Treason Trials. See Roe, "Citizen Wordsworth," *Wordsworth Circle* 14 (1983): 21–30.
20. M. Dorothy George, *Hogarth to Cruikshank: Social Change in Graphic Satire* (London: Allen Lane, 1967), 50–52; idem, *London Life in the 18th Century* (London: Kegan Paul, Trench, Trubner, 1925), 113.
21. *PW,* 2:217, 507.
22. Peter Manning, "Placing Poor Susan: Wordsworth and the New Historicism," *Studies in Romanticism* 25 (1986): 351–69; David Simpson, "What Bothered Charles Lamb about Poor Susan?" *Studies in English Literature* 26 (1986): 589–612.
23. *A Treatise on the Police of the Metropolis,* new ed. (London, 1797). Colquhoun estimated 115,000 persons, or one in nine, was engaged in criminal activity, which for him included both "illegal" and "immoral" behavior.
24. Mary Cathcart Borer, *An Illustrated Guide to London, 1800* (New York: St. Martin's Press, 1988), 207.
25. "Thy turtles [? Wilston] and thy Venison, Wright," *PW,* 1:306; Walter Thornbury, *Old and New London: A Narrative of Its History, Its People, and Its Places* (London: Cassell, Petter and Galpin, 1873–78), 418. Carol Landon and Jared Curtis, in *EPF,* 813, correct De Selincourt's conjecture of Wilston to Wilchere, owner of the King's Head Tavern; Stephen Wright was a meat provisioner in Charing Cross.
26. In DC, MS 47, 29v, an additional line has been inserted between 640 and 641, and then crossed out, which Reed transcribes as "From [?door] or [?] or [?] [?breathed]" (*Thirteen,* 2:349, 1:486).
27. Thornbury, *London,* 1:230–31.
28. Pat Rogers, intro. to Boswell's *Life of Johnson,* ed. R. W. Chapman (Oxford: Oxford Univ. Press, 1980), xv–xxviii.
29. George, *Hogarth,* 126.
30. André Parreaux, *Daily Life in England in the Reign of George III,* trans. Carola Congreve (London: Allen & Unwin, 1969), 138–39. The name gained its currency from the character played by Garrick in Benjamin Hoadley's *The Suspicious Husband* (1779), a rake who seduces women but cheerfully lets them go if they love another, thus gaining the sobriquet of "Honest Ranger."
31. *LEY,* 49.
32. EL, 170–76. Laurence Goldstein sees some of this achievement, but when he says that Wordsworth, "perceiving no essential vitality in London . . . participates in no magical attraction," he has fallen under the sway of the Wordsworthian ideology (*Ruins and Empire: The Evolution of a Theme in Augustan and Romantic Literature* [Pittsburgh: Univ. of Pittsburgh Press, 1997], 140), as has Mary Moorman when she feels "something is missing" in Book VII (MM1, 155). Nature is missing, of course, but not Imagination.

33. Neil McKendrick, John Brewer, and J. H. Plumb, *The Birth of a Consumer Society: The Commercialization of Eighteenth-Century England* (Bloomington: Indiana Univ. Press, 1982).
34. Borer, *Illustrated Guide,* 188.
35. IX.32, MS variant (*Thirteen,* 2:783).
36. George, *Hogarth,* 129, citing a turn-of-the-century German visitor's account.
37. IX.179; George, *Hogarth,* 33–34.
38. Marjorie and C. H. B. Quennell, *A History of Everyday Things in England,* vol. 3, *The Rise of Industrialism, 1733–1851,* 5th ed. (London: B. T. Batsford, 1950), 91. There was no central sewer system until 1865.
39. Borer, *Illustrated Guide,* 111.
40. "Newspapers Thirty-five Years Ago," in *The Last Essays of Elia.* Lamb noted, "Already one paragraph, and another, as we learned afterwards from a gentleman at the Treasury, had begun to be marked at that office, with a view to its being submitted at least to the attention of the proper Law Officers." Such attention helps account for the early presence of Lamb and Southey in Gillray's cartoon of 1795 "Copenhagen House," anticipating their more famous appearance in Gillray's "The New Morality" of 1798 (see prints).
41. VI.686; Thornbury, *London,* 1:44–45; WAG, 264, n. 7.
42. Richard Altick, *The Shows of London* (Cambridge, Mass.: Belknap Press, 1978), 184.
43. Ibid., 128–40, 184. Thomas Girtin's later, more ambitious Eidometropolis had a similar view, 9 feet high and 216 feet in circumference; it may have been visited by William and Dorothy in 1802, when Lamb showed them around the city after their trip to France to see Annette Vallon (WAG, 240, n. 5).
44. George, *Hogarth,* 110.
45. Claire Tomalin, *Mrs. Jordan's Profession: The Actress and the Prince* (New York: Alfred A. Knopf, 1995), 72–75, 124–27.
46. MS var. (DC, MS 52; *Thirteen,* 2:708).
47. Borer, *Illustrated Guide,* 65, 143; Parreaux, *Daily Life,* 136.
48. Parreaux, *Daily Life,* 136.
49. The MS makes clear that the quack is Graham, by referring to "some Scotch Doctor" (*Thirteen,* 2:97).
50. Altick, *Shows,* 82.
51. Richard Schwartz, *Daily Life in Johnson's England* (Madison: Univ. of Wisconsin Press, 1985), 88.
52. George, *Hogarth,* 96. Graham's sister-in-law was Catherine Macauley, the "romantic republican," whose history of England was published in seven volumes, 1763–83.
53. *PW,* 1:306; Juvenal, lines 168–73; *EPF,* 11–12.
54. GMH1, 114.
55. Female fashions followed suit, with "nudités gauzeuses," high-waisted dresses flowing freely beneath the bodice, which exposed much more of the breast. The extreme décolletage shown in Rowlandson's, Cruikshank's, and Gillray's cartoons does not much exaggerate the fashion (George, *Hogarth,* 136).
56. *Parliamentary History,* vol. 29, col. 421.
57. Boulton, *Language,* 265–71. Mackintosh later recruited Coleridge to the *Morning Post.*
58. *PW,* 4:409.
59. Ernest de Selincourt, ed., *The Prelude,* rev. Helen Darbishire (Oxford: Clarendon Press, 1959), 565, citing Haydon's *Autobiography* for 1815. Pitt was consolidating his position

for the coming struggle with France; in April he made his cousin William Wyndham foreign secretary, with the title of Lord Grenville.

60. *Thirteen,* 2:719, 721.
61. *1850,* VII.535.
62. All references to the May 6 debate are from *Parliamentary History,* vol. 29, cols. 365–98.
63. *Parliamentary History,* vol. 29, cols. 418–22. These comments were made on May 11, the day on which the constitutional debate was resumed—which, given the uproar on the 6th, drew even more spectators to the gallery.
64. *1850,* VII.540–43.
65. Cf. Mary Jacobus, " 'That Great Stage Where Senators Perform,' " *Studies in Romanticism* 22 (1983): 353–87; James K. Chandler, *Wordsworth's Second Nature: A Study of the Poetry and Politics* (Chicago: Univ. of Chicago Press, 1984), 235–38.
66. Borer, *Illustrated Guide,* 154, citing Horace Walpole.
67. Schwartz, *Daily Life,* 80; George, *Hogarth,* 77, quoting John Hookham Frere, "Loves of the Triangle," *Anti-Jacobin,* May 7, 1798.
68. Borer, *Daily Life,* 152, quoting Sophia von La Roche.
69. De Selincourt, ed., *The Prelude,* 563.
70. WAG, 238, n. 5, citing James Maxwell's Penguin edition (London, 1971).
71. Wordsworth returned to London for a few weeks at the end of the summer to consult with John Robinson on the delicate matter of his future, and he probably returned to his haunts in the City prior to his brief visit to Cambridge in October. His other London sojourns in the 1790s do not coincide with the fair's dates, except possibly 1798, when he was busy with last-minute preparations for the trip to Germany.

Chapter 12: The Mighty Mind

1. For most of the geographical details in this section, I am indebted to Donald E. Hayden, *Wordsworth's Travels in Wales and Ireland* (Tulsa: Univ. of Tulsa, 1985), 3–16.
2. *LEY,* 109.
3. *LEY,* 51.
4. I am grateful to Mark Reed for this suggestion.
5. *CEY,* 317; Hayden, *Travels in Wales,* 4.
6. *PW,* 1:43.
7. The present Snowdon Ranger Path is another possible route, running roughly parallel to Rhyd-Ddu about three miles farther north, but it is longer and easier—neither of which would have recommended it to Wordsworth and Jones.
8. Thomas Pennant, *A Tour of Wales, 1773* (London: Henry Hughes, 1778–84), 163.
9. Ibid., 160.
10. Ibid., 165.
11. Jonathan Wordsworth, "The Climbing of Snowdon," *Bicentenary Wordsworth Studies in Memory of John Alban Finch* (Ithaca: Cornell Univ. Press, 1970), 453.
12. *1850:* "a midnight hour."
13. XIII.45–56; cf. "the mountains huge appear . . . and their broad backs upheave / Into the clouds" (*PL,* VII.285–87).
14. Pennant, *Tour,* 164.
15. WAG, 460, n. 5; also cited as a source is James Clarke's *Survey of the Lakes* (1787), which recounts a walk up Skiddaw at 4 A.M., and the pleasant effect of hearing the domestic

sounds of the valley rising through the mist that lies thick in the valley, but which, halfway up the mountain, "appears so strong that you might walk upon it; I can compare it to nothing so much as to a vast sheet of ice covered with snow" (73), cited in Zera Fink, *The Early Wordsworthian Milieu* (Oxford: Clarendon Press, 1958), 46–47.

16. *Collections Historical and Archaeological relating to Montgomeryshire* (London: Richards, 1879), 53–84.
17. May 14, 1829, *LLY,* 2:78–79; Wordsworth places the episode "five and thirty years ago," which would put it in 1794, but all authorities agree that his phrase is an approximation and that 1791 is the actual date.
18. Alan Liu, "Wordsworth and Subversion, 1793–1804: Trying Cultural Criticism," *Yale Journal of Criticism,* no. 2 (Spring 1989), 75–76.
19. Ibid., 77, 91, n. 16; Liu pushes these and other possibilities to their interpretive limit, to suggest Wordsworth's implication in a kind of "silent" radicalism in the 1790s.
20. M. Dorothy George, *Hogarth to Cruikshank: Social Change in Graphic Satire* (London: Allen Lane, 1967), 87.
21. I thank my colleague Donald Gray for help on the meaning and connotations of "Taffy." It derives from the supposed Welsh pronunciation of David (that is, Dafydd), which is to say, from the English *representation* of the Welsh pronunciation.
22. MM1, 166, n. 2.
23. MM1, 186, n. 1, citing N. Sykes, *Church and State in the XVIIIth Century.*
24. George Aungier, *The History and Antiquities of Syon Monastery, the Parish of Isleworth, and the Chapelry of Hounslow* (London: Nichols, 1840), 212.
25. The other two were Northumberland House and Alnwick Castle. Hugh Smithson had become Hugh Percy in 1750 upon the death without male issue of his father-in-law, Algernon Seymour (ibid., 124–25).
26. *LEY,* 60, n. 2.
27. *LEY,* 694; Frank Rand, *Wordsworth's Mariner Brother* (Amherst, Mass.: Newell Press, 1966), 14.
28. Aungier, *History,* 179.
29. *LEY,* 57–58.
30. *LEY,* 54.
31. *CEY,* 118; MM1, 169; EL, 191. John Robinson, otherwise so helpful to his nephews, was circumspect about testifying against Lowther (*LEY,* 57, n. 2), knowing full well the temper of his former employer.
32. *LEY,* 62.
33. *LEY,* 61.
34. Richard Wordsworth to Richard Wordsworth of Whitehaven, Nov. 7, 1791, *LEY,* 61, n. 1.
35. *LEY,* 63, n. 1.
36. *CEY,* 123, citing *LEY,* 66.

Chapter 13: Revolution and Romance

1. *CEY,* 123–25.
2. GMH1, 137; Michael L. Kennedy, *The Jacobin Clubs in the French Revolution: The First Years* (Princeton: Princeton Univ. Press, 1982), 114, n. 4.
3. *LEY,* 68. He was fortunate in exchange rates throughout his visit: the value of French

currency fell by 25 percent between Nov. of 1791 and June of 1792. See Donald M. Sutherland, *France, 1789–1815: Revolution and Counterrevolution* (New York: Oxford Univ. Press, 1986), 139.

4. DVE, 104.
5. James Billington, *Fire in the Minds of Men: Origins of the Revolutionary Faith* (New York: Basic Books, 1980), 29–30; the following details about the Palais Royal are also from this work.
6. Mercier, *Tableau de Paris,* trans. and abridged as *The Waiting City,* ed. Helen Simpson (Philadelphia: Lippincott, 1933), 273, 276.
7. Raoul Hesdin, *The Journal of a Spy in Paris during the Reign of Terror, January–July 1794* (New York: Harper, 1895), 64–65. A tourist guide to prostitutes in the Palais Royal neighborhood (addresses, prices, specialities) had been prepared for the Fête de la Fédération in 1790, ostensibly with a view to protecting young men from the provinces. By the time Wordsworth arrived in late 1791, it had gone through five editions. See Jean Robiquet, *Daily Life in the French Revolution,* tr. James Kirkup (New York: Macmillan, 1965), 68.
8. *LEY,* 62.
9. *Paradise Lost,* II.951–52: "a universal hubbub wild / Of stunning sound and voices" (WAG, 314, n. 1).
10. *CEY,* 125–26. Brissot's first name was Jacques, though in later published attacks on him, his enemies frequently gave his name as Jean-Pierre. See Eloise Ellery, *Brissot de Warville* (Boston: Houghton Mifflin, 1915), 4.
11. Gary Kates, *The Cercle Social, the Girondins, and the French Revolution* (Princeton: Princeton Univ. Press, 1985), 199. Louis asked Brissot to form a ministry on March 15, 1792, and dismissed this "Brissotin" ministry on June 12. Much of the political jockeying before the putsch of Aug. 10 involved trying to get these "patriot" ministers reinstated.
12. Ellery, *Brissot,* 223–25.
13. Brissot lived in the rue Grétry, five or six streets north of the Palais Royal. James MacGillivray, "Wordsworth and Brissot," *Times Literary Supplement,* Jan. 29, 1931, 79, makes a plausible case for locating Wordsworth there, but Wordsworth denied a similar statement in Barron Field's unpublished *Memoirs of Wordsworth,* ed. Geoffrey Little (Sydney: Australian Academy of the Humanities, 1975), 26, n. 12.
14. J. G. Alger, *Englishmen in the French Revolution* (London: S. Low, 1889), 19–21.
15. There is a possibility that Wordsworth attended the Sunday, Dec. 4, meeting instead, or as well. Items of business that day that he could have remembered were a letter from the Orléans club in favor of opening meetings to the public, and a subscription raised by Léonard Bourdon for a young soldier who had been thrown out of his regiment for expressing opinions favoring the new constitution. See François-Alphonse Aulard, *La Société des Jacobins: Recueil de documents pour l'histoire du club des Jacobins de Paris,* 6 vols. (Paris: Librairie Jouaust, 1889–97), 3:271–72.
16. *LEY,* 71.
17. Sutherland, *France,* 129–30.
18. GMH1, 156.
19. Speech of late Nov. 1791, cited in Sutherland, *France,* 136. Louvet was a Girondin delegate from the beginning; however, as this speech and many of his writings before Sept. 1792 indicate, he was far from moderate.
20. Kates, *Cercle Social,* 228.
21. *LEY,* 70.

22. Eric Robinson, "An English Jacobin: James Watt, Jr.," *Cambridge Historical Journal* 11 (1953–55): 349–55. Many English visitors were there on business, since the climate for opening up new markets seemed very promising.
23. *CEY,* 126, n. 15. Watt left Paris hurriedly on Oct. 7, 1792, for Nantes. His route lay through Orléans, and it is possible that he saw Wordsworth there, given the small number of Englishmen remaining. Since Wordsworth left shortly after this to return to Paris, it would make sense to interpret his statement as meaning he found Watt to *have been* there before him.
24. Helen Maria Williams, *Letters from France,* ed. Janet Todd, 8 vols. in 2 (Delmar, N.Y.: Scholar's Facsimiles, 1975), vol. 1, letter 9.
25. DVE, 139, 144.
26. Kates, *Cercle Social,* 199.
27. Aulard, *Jacobins,* 3:267; DVE, 122–27.
28. Philip A. Brown, *The French Revolution in English History* (1918; reprint, London: George Allen & Unwin, 1923), 92.
29. Except where noted otherwise, all details about these Paris journals are from Kates, *Cercle social,* 177–217, passim.
30. Marcel Reinhard, *Chute de la royauté* (Paris, 1969), 190, cited in DVE, 129, n. 62.
31. "Master pamphlets" refers not only to English tracts like Burke's *Reflections* and Paine's *Rights of Man* but also to their French counterparts. A bundle of papers identified as "French Pamphlets and Ephemera" was listed in the sale catalog of Wordsworth's library after his death (GMH1, 151).
32. DVE, 131 (my translation).
33. Billington, *Fire,* 44; its offices were near the Théâtre Français (the present Théâtre Odéon).
34. Kates, *Cercle Social,* 190, n. 27; DVE, 130.
35. *LEY,* 118.
36. Kates, *Cercle Social,* 186.
37. Simon Schama, *Citizens: A Chronicle of the French Revolution* (New York: Alfred A. Knopf, 1989), 582–83.
38. Le Brun's model was supposed to have been Louise de la Vallière, a mistress of Louis XIV, who like Annette Vallon was from Blois and who like Wordsworth's Julia retired to a convent to spend the last years of her life repenting her sins. See Alan Liu, *Wordsworth: The Sense of History* (Stanford: Stanford Univ. Press, 1989), 371.
39. *The Despatches of Earl Gower, English Ambassador at Paris from June 1790 to August 1792,* ed. Oscar Browning (Cambridge: Cambridge Univ. Press, 1885), xxxi; *The Diary and Letters of Gouverneur Morris,* ed. Anne Carey Morris (New York: Scribner's Sons, 1888), 457, n. 1; Jean-Eugène Bimbenet, *Histoire de la ville d'Orléans,* 5 vols. (Orléans: H. Herluison, 1884–88), 5:1046.
40. Bimbenet, *Histoire,* 5:1072.
41. MM1, 174.
42. NR, 42.
43. *The Correspondence of Mr. Joseph Jekyll* (London: Algernon Bourke, 1894).
44. Ibid., 38.
45. *LEY,* 63, n. 1.
46. *LEY,* 69.
47. *LEY,* 69, n. 3.
48. The year before, Foxlow had ridden, Paul Revere-style, from Versailles to Paris with news that the king was coming to the Maison de Ville. He was greeted with acclama-

tion by the tumultuous crowd, but his horse was "borrowed" for "service to the state" and returned some days later considerably the worse for wear. See *LEY,* 69, n. 3; MM1, 174, n. 2, 206, n. 4; Williams, *Letters,* vol. 2.

49. *LEY,* 70; Williams, *Letters,* 2:33–34. Williams also used the archaic Latinate construction for the names of political classes.
50. Except as noted, all details about Annette Vallon, her family, and their connections in Orléans and Blois are based on Emile Legouis's pioneering work, *William Wordsworth and Annette Vallon* (1922), expanded by his son Pierre (cited as *WAV*).
51. The words are those of, respectively, the police prefect of Blois in 1804, a scholar of the French Resistance (Régis Bouis) in 1944, Guillemin de Savigny, the mayor of Blois in 1818, cited in *WAV,* 90, 156–58, and in Frederick W. Bateson, *Wordsworth: A Reinterpretation* (London: Longmans, Green, 1954), 92. Bouis's comments are intended as compliments, since he associates Annette with the spirit of the French Resistance in World War II, but the Napoleonic prefect used similar language. Savigny's comments were made as part of a dossier compiled to get Annette a pension after the Restoration for heroic action in the service of the king.
52. *WAV,* 27.
53. *WAV,* 100.
54. *LEY,* 87; Bateson, *Wordsworth,* 85. Dorothy continues, "[It] demonstrates itself every moment of the Day when the Objects of his affection are present with him . . . in a sort of restless watchfulness which I know not how to describe, a Tenderness that never sleeps, and at the same Time such a Delicacy of Manners as I have observed in few Men."
55. After the facts of Wordsworth's affair became public in the 1920s (the family—except his young children—knew all about it from the beginning), some biographers, in a state of Freudian shock, made Annette the key to all Wordsworthian mysteries. Others, determined to defend him from any untoward passion, have stressed his youthful naïveté and condescended to Annette as a creature of sentimental excess, "all sensibility," "devoid of intellectual curiosity," an "over-generous disposition," whose "pathetic strain never relaxes" (*WAV,* 32; *WFD,* 7).
56. *WAV,* 55.
57. *Correspondence of Jekyll,* 8–9; Alger, *Englishmen,* 164.
58. *WAV,* 13.
59. Deborah Kennedy, "Revolutionary Tales: Helen Maria Williams's *Letters from France* and Wordsworth's 'Vaudracour and Julia,' " *Wordsworth Circle* 21 (1990): 109–14. SG, 66, opines that Wordsworth's shifting to third-person narration for the story of Vaudracour and Julia in *The Prelude* suggests "that [Wordsworth] did not regard the relationship as a personal crisis or as having contributed in any significant way to his development as a poet"—while cautioning that this interpretation says "something" about 1804 but "nothing" about 1792. I am convinced that the affair contributed greatly (if ambivalently) to his development, that Wordsworth knew it, and that telling the story in a disguised, third-person form is one of the many indexes of its importance to him.
60. *WAV,* 127 (italics added).
61. Sutherland, *France,* 132–34.
62. Reed favorably cites James R. MacGillivray's suggestion about the identifications of time and place in this passage (*CEY,* 129, n. 1).
63. *LEY,* 75–76.
64. *LEY,* 62, 76.

65. The other Englishman was likely Edmund Dayrell, aged twenty-eight, the brother-in-law of the widow of an English officer living in La Chaussée suburb, northeast of the city. She had remarried a M. de Clenard, who in that same Feb. 1792 sold his estate to Dayrell. Dayrell may have been hedging his bets by attending the "Amis," and with good reason, since his property was confiscated as a "collusive" purchase the next year, after Clenard emigrated (Alger, *Englishmen,* 237–38).
66. George McLean Harper, "Wordsworth at Blois," in *John Morley and Other Essays* (Princeton: Princeton Univ. Press, 1920), 121.
67. GMH1, 168.
68. Ruth Necheles-Jansyn, *The Abbé Grégoire, 1781–1831: The Odyssey of an Egalitarian* (Westport, Conn.: Greenwood, 1971), 114.
69. *WAV,* x.
70. *WAV,* 48–49, 89, 149. This police report is from 1804, but the Vallons were already being watched when Wordsworth arrived in 1792.
71. Harper, "Wordsworth at Blois," 117.
72. He also had ties with the brother parish of Hôtel Dieu in the main part of town, near the Jacobin Club (*WAV,* 9, 156; MM1, 179).
73. *Correspondence of Jekyll,* 51.
74. *WAV,* 47–48.
75. *WAV,* 19.
76. The classical allusion from the *Moniteur* is quoted in Nicholas Roe, "Wordsworth's Account of Beaupuy's Death," *Notes and Queries* 32 (1985): 337; the story of the monument is given in Donald E. Hayden, *Wordsworth's Travels in Europe* (Tulsa: Univ. of Tulsa, 1988), 14–16.
77. Facts in this paragraph are from MM1, 192; NR, 55; GMH1, 162; DVE, 140.
78. DVE, 178.
79. GMH1, 168.
80. NR, 56.
81. NR, 53, citing *Procès Verbal.*
82. NR, 55.
83. MM1, 196.
84. "Discours prononcé dans l'Eglise Cathédrale" (March 3, 1792), in *Oeuvres de l'Abbé Grégoire,* vol. 4, *Grégoire Evèque Constitutionnel* (Paris: Editions d'histoire sociale, 1977), 203; "Discours sur la Fédération du 14 juillet 1792," ibid., 215.
85. "The girls who herd the cows are always at work with their distaffs, and the cap is always clean and perhaps laced, while the feet are without shoes and stockings." *Correspondence of Jekyll,* 32 (1775).
86. NR, 59.
87. NR, 66–69; Grégoire, *Oeuvres,* 3:233; *Prose,* 1:32.
88. Grégoire, *Oeuvres,* 3:207.
89. NR, 66.
90. MM1, 187–88.
91. Ellis Yarnall, quoted in *Memoirs,* 2:491.
92. *LEY,* 77 (italics added).
93. DVE, 214, n. 5, citing Kennedy, *The Jacobin Clubs,* 66, 365. Not surprisingly, Gorsas had a bad rap sheet with the police of the ancien régime: "Gorsas: proper for all kinds of vile jobs. . . . put in [jail] by personal order of the king for having corrupted children whom he had taken in as lodgers, he has withdrawn to a fifth floor on the rue Tictone

. . . produces *libelles* . . . is suspected of having printed obscene works." See Robert Darnton, *Literary Underground of the Old Regime* (Cambridge: Harvard Univ. Press, 1982), 26. Darnton seems to accept the police verdict, calling him the "excrement of literature" (10).

94. *DHRF,* 193.
95. Danton, to the duc de Chartres (the future Louis-Philippe): "It was I myself" who organized the massacres; Marat, in *L'Ami du peuple:* "the people have made themselves dictators by killing traitors." See Peter Vansittart, *Voices of the Revolution* (London: Collins, 1968), 183–85.
96. Wordsworth, "Letter to Llandaff" (*Prose,* 1:38); Wollstonecraft to William Roscoe, quoted in Vansittart, *Voices,* 185.
97. Joseph Jekyll, fifteen years earlier, insouciantly indicated his need for more funds by telling his father he wished to be more in the "company" of Sir Robert, as if he were a real person.
98. *LEY,* 81.
99. *CEY,* 134–35.
100. MM1, 201.
101. MM1, 197.
102. *Memoirs,* 2:491.
103. "Remember also your Creator in the days of your youth . . . before the silver cord is snapped, or the golden bowl is broken, or the pitcher is broken at the fountain, or the wheel at the cistern. . . . Vanity of vanities, says the Preacher" (Ecclesiastes 12:1, 6, 8).
104. Later editions try to minimize the geographical strain at this point by beginning the conclusion with the words "And oh, fair France!" The poem does contain a brief reference to "Gallia's wastes of corn" at the outset (line 47) before moving on to the Grande Chartreuse.
105. NR, 71.
106. Bimbenet, *Histoire,* 5:1228.
107. GMH1, 170; NR, 70–71; SG, 437, n. 124; Georges Lefebvre, *Etudes Orléanaises,* 2 vols. (Paris: Commission d'histoire économique et sociale de la Révolution, 1962–63), 2:78–86.
108. SG, 437, n. 124.
109. NR, 70–71.
110. The passage as a whole is devoted to showing how "all nature smiles," in the "milder light" of the clouds, the "power" of "the watchful bird," "the charm'd thought" stimulated by the sound of the water-mill, "the sweeter cadence" of "the distant flail," and the "richer gold" of "the sun-gilt groves" (756–73).
111. MM1, 201.
112. *WFD,* 26; the following details are from the same source (15–16). Things could get very confused when the old religious ideologies and the new political ones confronted each other. Helen Williams records the oddity of speaking to an enthusiastic French Catholic supporter of the Revolution who doubted its efficacy for England, "because you are all heretics there."
113. All details in this paragraph are from Kates, *Cercle Social,* 235–41.
114. Schama, *Citizens,* 579, 649.
115. Vansittart, *Voices,* 167–69, 200, citing Chateaubriand's *Mémoires.* Chateaubriand is not a neutral witness, but no one was, and his impressions are similar to those of Buzot and Blanc-Grilli, a deputy from Marseilles.

116. Kates, *Cercle Social,* 241.
117. Quoted ibid., 177.
118. *Quatre-vingt treize,* pt. 2, bk. 3, chap. 10.
119. J. M. Thompson, *Leaders of the French Revolution* (New York: Barnes & Noble, 1962), 93–95.
120. Favret, 286.
121. On Nov. 8, 16, 25, 29, and Dec. 2 and 16. Reeve Parker, " 'In Some Sort Seeing with My Proper Eyes': Wordsworth and the Spectacles of Paris," *Studies in Romanticism* 27 (1988): 380–83. I am indebted to Parker's brilliant article for all points of detail, and several of interpretation, in this paragraph.
122. Kates, *Cercle Social,* 239.
123. Parker, "In Some Sort Seeing," 376–77.
124. *Mémoires de Madame Roland* (Paris: Boudouin, 1820), 1:188–89.
125. Charles Nodier's term for the coterie of young men around Bonneville under the Directory (*Oeuvres,* 3:331, cited in Kates, *Cercle Social,* 275).
126. In the margin of his copy of Burke's collected works (London, 1803–27), vol. 7 (1815), 305; now in the collection of the Wordsworth Library.
127. GMH1, 177. Bateson, *Wordsworth,* 96, suggests a minor political post, but this is hard to credit, for either France or England.
128. DVE, 211, 225.
129. Alger, *Englishmen,* 50–51; Albert Goodwin, *The Friends of Liberty: The English Democratic Movement in the Age of the French Revolution* (Cambridge: Harvard Univ. Press, 1979), 510–12.
130. Alger, *Englishmen,* 346. Cowper berated Hayley for the Revolution's extremes after Louis's execution: "the French have made me weep for a king of France, which I never thought to do, and they have made me sick of the very name of liberty, which I never thought to be" (letter of Jan. 29, 1793, quoted in Brown, *French Revolution,* 89).
131. Alger, *Englishmen,* 326.
132. GMH1, 149–50.
133. These characteristics are based on the description of the signatories in Alger, *Englishmen,* 337–42.
134. *WAV,* 125.
135. DVE, 233.
136. Robert Hughes, *The Fatal Shore* (New York: Alfred A. Knopf, 1986).
137. "Quelle est cette ombre épouvantée [appalling] / Louis! qui frappe ton regard? / —Malheureux! reconnais Stuart / —A ma couronne ensanglantée. / —Viens, viens, il dit, et dans l'abîme / Stuart le plonge en l'embrassant." *Recueil des actes du Comité de salut public,* vol. 1, ed. F.-A. Aulard (Paris, 1889), 303–4.
138. GMH1, 137.
139. DVE, 239.
140. *WFD,* 29–30.
141. *Despatches of Earl Gower,* 262.
142. DVE, 241.
143. Henry Blackwood, a future admiral, provides a case parallel to what might have happened to Wordsworth. He too had gone to France in Dec. 1791, aged twenty-one, to learn French. He too returned via Paris the following Dec., with a bag of domestic articles for an émigré at Brussels. The bag was searched and found to contain letters; he was arrested and called before the Committee of Public Safety on Jan. 13, 1793. The

letters were not political, but he was accused of having dealings with enemies of the Revolution. By the merest of whims, the committee recommended that the Convention release him, to give Europe "an example of the virtue of [the Revolution's] hospitality." See Alger, *Englishmen,* 113–14.

144. *Despatches of Earl Gower,* 268.

Chapter 14: Castaway

1. DVE, 237.
2. Phillip A. Brown, *The French Revolution in English History* (1918; reprint, London: George Allen & Unwin, 1923), 85.
3. Lucyle T. Werkmeister, *A Newspaper History of England, 1792–1793* (Lincoln: Univ. of Nebraska Press, 1967), 92–93.
4. Brown, *French Revolution,* 85–87.
5. Werkmeister, *Newspaper History,* 92–93.
6. *Morning Post,* Jan. 3, 1793.
7. "Constructive treason," though dating from the fourteenth century, came back into its own again in 1794–95, after the treason trials and the gagging acts. It asked of a text whether its meaning could be "construed" as "tending toward" treason. When enough pressure was applied, the number of texts that could be found to be doing so was remarkable. It was a highly literate tool of espionage, worthy of men trained in the linguistic and logical niceties of the Cambridge examination system.
8. DVE, 238–40, citing Werkmeister's *Newspaper History of England,* 134–51.
9. Thomas De Quincey, in *Tait's Magazine,* April 1839, 248, quoted in *Recollections of the Lake Poets,* ed. Edward Sackville-West (London: Lehman, 1948), 170.
10. MM1, 219.
11. "Autobiographical Memoranda," in *Prose,* 3:374.
12. H. W. Piper, *The Active Universe: Pantheism and the Concept of the Imagination in the English Romantic Poets* (London: Athlone Press, 1962), 66–67.
13. Excerpts are reprinted in *EW,* 303–6, and *DS,* 299–301.
14. Werkmeister, *Newspaper History,* 311; GMH1, 237.
15. *Monthly Review,* Oct. 1793, 216–18, quoted in *DS,* 300–301.
16. *Gentleman's Magazine,* March 1794, 252–53, quoted in *EW,* 305–6.
17. GMH1, 186n, citing Christopher Wordsworth's journal for Nov. 5, 1793.
18. GMH1, 186, citing *LEY.*
19. *LEY,* 120.
20. MM1, 213.
21. *CEY,* 140, citing *Farington Diary,* 2:230.
22. James Boulton, *The Language of Politics* (Toronto: Univ. of Toronto Press, 1963), 265–71, lists over fifty published responses to Burke between 1791 and 1793.
23. EL, 226.
24. *Anecdotes of the Life of Richard Watson* (London: Cadell & Davis, 1817), 257, 266.
25. GMH1, 215.
26. *Anecdotes of Watson,* 268.
27. Werkmeister, *Newspaper History,* 92–93, 180; *Morning Post,* Feb. 20, 1793. Beaconsfield was the name of Burke's elaborate country estate.
28. *LEY,* 87; GMH1, 217.

29. MM1, 226.
30. *Prose,* 1:31. The bridge metaphor is from Addison's "The Vision of Mirza," which Wordsworth knew was "well known to your lordship" since Watson had referred to it in his appendix. All citations to the "Letter" are from this edition, 31–49.
31. So personal is the nature of Wordsworth's attack that it has been suggested that he sent a copy of the letter to Watson himself (EL, 227). This seems doubtful to me, though not impossible.
32. The portions of *Prelude* X which allude broadly to events of 1793 include several pointed epithets about apostasy or renegadism which apply better to Watson than to almost any other public figure: "apostacy from ancient faith" (284); "scoffers in their pride, / Saying, 'Behold the harvest which we reap / From popular government and equality' " (430–32); "the shame of a false prophet" (798); "Enough, no doubt, the advocates . . . / Of ancient institutions had performed / To bring disgrace upon their very names" (849–51); "sorrow for the man / Who either had not eyes wherewith to see, / Or seeing hath forgotten" (857–59).
33. Brown, *French Revolution,* 94–97.
34. SG, 77.
35. *The Works of Mary Wollstonecraft,* ed. Janet Todd and Marilyn Butler (London: Pickering, 1989), 122.
36. Ibid., 123.
37. July 10, 1793, *LEY,* 97.
38. *LEY,* 81, n. 2.
39. *LEY,* 103n.
40. *Morning Post,* July 1, 1793.
41. Richard J. Hutchings, *Isle of Wight Literary Haunts* (Newport: Isle of Wight County Press, 1989), 18–19.
42. *CEY,* 142.
43. Preface to *Guilt and Sorrow* (1842).
44. For example, the secretary to Walsingham, the postmaster general, opined in summer 1793 that "perhaps the commissary to the French prisoners might be rendered serviceable in all such cases where the circumstances are suspicious" (Postmaster General's Reports [The Freeling Papers], PO Archive, vol. 63, 149–50). This was in response to a Winchester MP's report of suspicious correspondence between French émigrés there and French prisoners near Gosport, directly across the harbor from Portsmouth. Such people were "rendered serviceable" by bribes.
45. MM1, 230, n. 3.
46. Paul D. Sheats anticipates several of my observations, in his excellent study of Wordsworth's early stylistic development, *The Making of Wordsworth's Poetry, 1785–1798* (Cambridge: Harvard Univ. Press, 1973), 79–83.
47. *EPF,* 738.
48. "Tintern Abbey," lines 89–92.
49. Dorothy Wordsworth to Jane Pollard, Aug. 30, 1793, *LEY,* 109.
50. Dorothy told Jane Pollard in Aug. that Wordsworth had informed the Griffiths in Halifax of his intention to go to Chester, the coach terminus for North Wales, "at the latter End of the summer" (*LEY,* 108).
51. The definitive scholarly text of both poems is *The Salisbury Plain Poems of William Wordsworth,* ed. Stephen Gill (Ithaca: Cornell Univ. Press, 1975). I refer to the first version as *NSP* and to the second as *ASP.*

52. Gill cites the various sources of the poem which do *not* come from Wordsworth's own experience: Rousseau, Chatterton, Spenser, antiquarian writers on Stonehenge, and Lake District memories (438, n. 27).
53. *LLY,* 3:616.
54. Gill, *Salisbury Plain Poems,* 74, citing *Gentleman's Magazine* 63 (856–57).
55. Cited in Anne Janowitz, *England's Ruins: Poetic Purpose and the National Landscape* (Oxford: Blackwell, 1990), 96.
56. Wordsworth in old age firmly placed the poem's composition in 1793–94, with the exception that "much of the Female Vagrant's story was composed at least two years before," perhaps as early as 1791. This is a big exception, since her story in the first version is nearly half the poem. It is not impossible that he heard such a story in 1791, though it is hard to imagine where and when: on his tour of Wales that year?
57. Zera Fink, *The Early Wordsworthian Milieu* (Oxford: Clarendon Press, 1958), 88–89, 134–35.
58. *LEY,* 136.
59. Compare the countess of Pembroke's *Arcadia,* a poem known to Wordsworth: "The lovely clusters of her brests, / Of *Venus'* babe the wanton nests: / Like pommels round of Marble cleere: / Where azurde veines well mixt appeere. / With dearest tops of porphyrie."
60. For example: "The herculean Commonwealth had put forth her arms, / And throttled with an infant godhead's might / The snakes about her cradle" (*Prelude,* X.362–64).
61. *PW,* 1:330.
62. *CEY,* 146, n. 12, cites Reed's and Carol Landon's reasons for supposing these poems to be about Chepstow Castle, though there are several other candidates in the Wye valley (Goodrich, for example).
63. DC, MS 11, used by permission of Dove Cottage Trustees. I am grateful to Jared Curtis for help in deciphering some words in the manuscript and for the conjecture of "Hymettus" in 1.12. A printed version of the fragmentary text appears in *EPF,* 743. The reconstruction of the missing phrases is entirely my own, and not based on manuscript evidence, the page being torn away at these points. Queried words in brackets not in italics are conjectures based on illegible handwriting.
64. *EPF,* 740.
65. This conjectural reading is from Hayden, 117.
66. *Morning Post,* July 29, 1793, 3.
67. *PW,* 2:530 (italics added).
68. IF, in *PW,* 2:527.
69. Gilpin also compared the plain to the ocean (quoted in Janowitz, *England's Ruins,* 104).
70. The dead man's daughter is named Rachel, the name Wordsworth proposed for the Female Vagrant in some revisions of the Salisbury Plain poems. And the widow's thoughts of her orphaned children seem like an adult echo of the stout little girl Wordsworth had just met at Goodrich Castle: " 'Seven are they, and all fatherless!' " (*Peter Bell,* 1120). Given these possibilities, one may wonder how much the narrator of the poem speaks for Wordsworth when he describes his return home from his French travels: "I was lost / Where I have been, but on this coast / I feel I am a man."
71. *CEY,* 316.
72. Donald E. Hayden, *Wordsworth's Travels in Wales and Ireland* (Tulsa: Univ. of Tulsa, 1985), 22.

Chapter 15: A Return to France?

1. MM1, 231, 239–42; SG, 77–78; *CEY,* 147–49.
2. *LEY,* 109.
3. *LEY,* 97.
4. *LEY,* 100–101.
5. MM1, 211.
6. *LEY,* 96.
7. *LEY,* 108.
8. SG, 74; Gill adds Wordsworth's moodiness as another reason for the tour's sudden breakup.
9. *Reminiscences,* ed. J. A. Froude (New York: Harper, 1881), 333. All references are to this edition, 331–37.
10. Ibid., 334.
11. GMH1, 209.
12. *The Writings and Speeches of Edmund Burke,* vol. 9, ed. R. B. McDowell (Oxford: Clarendon Press, 1991), 184–85.
13. Thomas De Quincey, *The Collected Writings,* ed. David Masson. 11 vols. (Edinburgh: Adam and Charles Black, 1890), 3:106.
14. *Alaric Watts: A Narrative of His Life,* 2 vols. (1884; reprint, New York: AMS Press, 1974), 2:286–87.
15. *DHRF,* 193.
16. *Alaric Watts,* 2:280.
17. De Quincey, *Collected Writings,* 3:95. This sounds similar to Carlyle's "austere candour" and is worth emphasizing, since Alaric Watts, who was only fifteen to seventeen years old at the time of his visits to Stewart's house, was probably reporting Stewart's account of Bailey's account, rather than Bailey's verbatim.
18. *WAV,* 125–26, translation by Ilinca Zarifopol-Johnston.
19. *WAV,* 26, 31.
20. *WAV,* 128–30 (italics added). Annette's letter contains much more in the same vein.
21. *WAV,* 29. HO, 31/1, contains orders for allowing mail packets to continue going back and forth, along with detailed instructions on how to stop and search them and all other French vessels. In late 1795 Wordsworth received a letter from Annette in which she mentions "having despatched half a dozen," of which he apparently received none (*LEY,* 161).
22. The *Times* was the paper most likely to come to Wordsworth's attention in his wanderings of mid-1793. Its account of events in France were of course partisan by modern standards. But it was not thoroughly a government organ, though not as liberal as the *Morning Post,* which would probably have been Wordsworth's choice had he been in London.
23. I draw on Donald M. Sutherland, *France, 1789–1815: Revolution and Counterrevolution* (New York: Oxford Univ. Press, 1986), 166–200, for most historical details in what follows, except where otherwise noted.
24. HMW, 2:125.
25. Simon Schama, *Citizens: A Chronicle of the French Revolution* (New York: Alfred A. Knopf, 1989), 714; Eloise Ellery, *Brissot de Warville* (Boston: Houghton Mifflin, 1915), 330, suggests that Brissot's presses, though threatened, were spared at this time.

26. Details are from *WAV,* 40–44, based on records in the Archives Nationales.
27. Louis Jacob, *Les Suspects pendant la Révolution, 1789–94* (Paris: Hachette, 1952), 100, 102.
28. *Quatre-vingt treize,* pt. 2, bk. 2, chap. 2. Historians agree that "the position of the rebels still looked formidable" at this time (Schama, *Citizens,* 704), and speculate that if they had struck east along the Loire following the fall of Saumur on June 9, instead of moving west toward Nantes, they could well have reached Paris, overrunning Blois en route.
29. HMW, 2:91; *DHRF,* 511; Schama, *Citizens,* 728.
30. Charles A. Dauban, *La Démagogie en 1793 à Paris* (Paris: Henri Plon, 1868), 257.
31. Schama, *Citizens,* 730, 735.
32. One such accusation ran thus: "Il avait fait des radiations [erasures] de mots dans les jugements rendus dans les procès des assassins de L. Bourdon et dans celui de Charlotte Corday" (Dauban, *Démagogie,* 300).
33. Dauban, *Démagogie,* 269–70, reporting the words of Harmand de la Meuse.
34. Harvey Mitchell, *The Underground War against Revolutionary France: The Missions of William Wickham, 1794–1800* (Oxford: Clarendon Press, 1965); Olivier Blanc, *Les Hommes de Londres: Histoire secrète de la Terreur* (Paris: Albin Michel, 1989). Blanc's thesis is that much responsibility for the Terror can be laid to Pitt's agents for destabilizing France. If this were true—which I doubt—it would constitute one of the greatest triumphs of the British or any other secret service. Hugo's judgment, based on the war policy alone, is harsher but more accurate: "Pitt was in truth a state malefactor. Policy has treasons sure as an assassin's dagger. Pitt stabbed our country and betrayed his own" (*Quatre-vingt treize,* pt. 3, bk. 1, chap. 16). This was substantially Wordsworth's view (X.275–89, 635–56), in language no less harsh: "in their weapons and their warfare base / As vermin working out of reach . . . [to] make an end of liberty."
35. Alfred Cobban, *Aspects of the French Revolution* (New York: G. Braziller, 1968), 230–31; Maurice Hutt, *Chouannerie and Counter-Revolution: Puisaye, the Princes, and the British Government in the 1790s,* 2 vols. (Cambridge: Cambridge Univ. Press, 1983), 1:103–5.
36. Cobban, *Aspects,* 229–31.
37. HO, 98/4.
38. Sutherland, *France,* 200; Richard Bienvenu, ed., *The Ninth of Thermidor: The Fall of Robespierre* (New York: Oxford Univ. Press, 1968), 21–24.
39. Wilfred Kerr, *The Reign of Terror, 1793–94: The Experiment of the Democratic Republic and the Rise of the Bourgeoisie* (Toronto: Univ. of Toronto Press, 1927), 188–89.
40. Bienvenu, *Ninth of Thermidor,* 62.
41. Kerr, *Reign of Terror,* 191–93.

Chapter 16: A Return to France: The Evidence of Speculation

1. Reed establishes the outside parameters for Wordsworth's departure from Wales as somewhere between late Aug. and perhaps after Sept. 15, though not ruling out a date as late as early Oct. (*CEY,* 145).
2. Donald M. Sutherland, *France, 1789–1815: Revolution and Counterrevolution* (New York: Oxford Univ. Press, 1986), 226; Charles A. Dauban, *La Démagogie en 1793 à Paris* (Paris: Henri Plon, 1868), 388; Simon Schama, *Citizens: A Chronicle of the French Revolution* (New York: Alfred A. Knopf, 1989), 766.
3. HMW, 2:5.
4. William Kerr, *The Reign of Terror, 1793–94: The Experiment of the Democratic Republic and

the Rise of the Bourgeoisie (Toronto: Univ. of Toronto Press, 1927), 203–4. Well into Oct. there were jurisdictional disputes between the Convention and the Committee of Public Safety over who should enforce the law, and by what means. See Louis Jacob, *Les Suspects pendant la Révolution, 1789–94* (Paris: Hachette, 1952), 95–118, passim.

5. Sutherland, *France,* 226; Kerr, *Reign of Terror,* 204.
6. Pt. 3, bk. 1, chap. 1; pt. 2, bk. 2, chap. 2. Hugo's republican general has the same view of the situation: "The ocean no longer belonged to [France]. In this ocean was England. . . . a man would fling her a bridge . . . a man would go to Pitt, to Craig, to Cornwallis, to Dundas, to the pirates, and say, 'Come!' " (pt. 3, bk. 5, chap. 2).
7. George McLean Harper, "Did Wordsworth Defy the Guillotine?," in *Spirit of Delight* (New York: Henry Holt, 1928), 53.
8. Schama, *Citizens,* 693.
9. Gorsas may have first visited his daughter in Rennes after quitting Caen and before going to Paris, so the similarity of his route with Wordsworth's must remain conjectural (*DHRF,* 511).
10. They were Sir Robert Smith, James Hartley, Edward Slater, and Thomas Marshall (Harper, "Did?," 63). Smith can be pretty firmly identified with the group of English spies in France. See Olivier Blanc, *Les Hommes de Londres: Histoire secrète de la Terreur* (Paris: Albin Michel, 1989), 64.
11. Dauban, *Démagogie,* 454.
12. Details in this paragraph are drawn mainly from Kerr, *Reign of Terror,* 208–20.
13. J. G. Alger, *Paris in 1789–1794: Farewell Letters of Victims of the Guillotine* (London: G. Allen, 1902), 143–44.
14. Ibid., 144.
15. François-Alphonse Aulard, *La Société des Jacobins: Recueil de documents pour l'histoire du club des Jacobins de Paris,* 6 vols. (Paris: Librairie Jouaust, 1889–97), 6:384–85; Kerr, *Reign of Terror,* 212; Jacob, *Suspects,* 64–66.
16. *Ninety-three* (London: T. Nelson and Sons, n.d.), pt. 3, bk. 1, chap. 1.
17. DVE, 275–81.
18. Quoted in Michael Ross, *Banners of the King: The War of the Vendée, 1793–4* (New York; Hippocrene, 1975), 320. Details of Beaupuy's movements in the post-Cholet campaign are drawn from this work, except where noted.
19. Le Mercier considered him "nothing more than a crook from the Palais-Royal," but he was as brave as he was vicious (Ross, *Banners,* 195).
20. The rumors of the Beaupuy's death were evidently quite widespread, since so recent an authority as Ross reports him dead, in his detailed account of the action.
21. Compare an account of the effect of the loss of two Vendean leaders at the battle of Cholet: "the sight of their two leaders, mortally wounded, prostrated our soldiers; they lost all the fire which had hitherto inspired them. The mainspring which had motivated their courage had been snapped . . . and they abandoned the field." (Poirier de Beauvais, reporting the loss of d'Elbée and Bonchamp, quoted in Ross, *Banners,* 226.)
22. *Moniteur,* Dec. 27, 1793, cited by Nicholas Roe, "Wordsworth's Account of Beaupuy's Death," *Notes and Queries* 32 (1985): 337. Beaupuy's brother Pierre actually was killed in the Vendée (MM1, 197), another source of confusion.
23. George Bussière and Emile Legouis, *Le Général Michel Beaupuy (1755–1796)* (Paris: F. Alcan, 1891), 118.
24. J. M. Thompson, *English Witnesses of the French Revolution* (Oxford: Blackwell, 1958), 245–46.
25. "To William Wordsworth" (line 11).

26. Strictly speaking, X.278–89 is a passage more obscurantist than obscure, as Wordsworth tries to criticize Pitt's policy without revealing his own, for he himself also had a "policy" at the time, expressed in the unpublished "Letter to the Bishop of Llandaff." WAG, 374, n. 1, explicates these "four remarkably cryptic points."
27. These lines were cut from *1850,* following Wordsworth's general policy of revision over forty-five years, of making all historical references less specifically applicable to him.
28. Richard Bienvenu, ed., *The Ninth of Thermidor: The Fall of Robespierre* (New York: Oxford Univ. Press, 1968), calculates 22 executions in Aug., 72 in Sept., 179 in Oct., and 491 in Nov. In Dec. and later the numbers began to reach "industrial levels," in Schama's chillingly precise phrase.
29. Schama, *Citizens,* 783, quoting Achard; cf. Laparra, president of the Society of Friends of Liberty and Equality in the Vendée: "Strike, strike great blows against these infamous heads!" (643).
30. *The Prelude,* ed. Ernest de Selincourt (Oxford: Clarendon Press, 1926), 580 (italics added).
31. Pt. 2, bk. 4, chap. 1; pt. 3, bk. 3, chap. 15.
32. Dauban, *Démagogie,* 115–16.
33. James MacGillivray, "Wordsworth in France," *Times Literary Supplement,* June 12, 1930, 496.
34. MM1, 215.
35. The entire process could of course be interpreted as running in the opposite direction: namely, that we see in Wordsworth's representation of Vaudracour's passion a covert form of his own passion for Dorothy, rather than for Annette. In fact, the two possibilities cannot be mutually exclusive.
36. Dickens, preface to *A Tale of Two Cities* (italics added). Dickens ends by deferring to Carlyle's expertise, much as Carlyle deferred to Wordsworth's experience: "It has been one of my hopes to add something to the popular and picturesque means of understanding that terrible time, though no one can hope to add anything to the philosophy of Mr. Carlyle's wonderful book."

Chapter 17: Legacy Hunting

1. *LEY,* 103.
2. *LEY,* 94–95.
3. Phillip A. Brown, *The French Revolution in English History* (1918; reprint, London: George Allen & Unwin, 1923), 95–107.
4. BRS, 216.
5. *LEY,* 94.
6. *LEY,* 113.
7. MM1, 243. Dorothy's language is retrospective, from 1802; it is significant that much of our evidence for their first impressions of their return to the Lake District comes from that year, when Dorothy was accompanying William and Mary on their wedding trip.
8. MM1, 243; *PW,* 3:4–5.
9. MM1, 244.
10. *LEY,* 113–16. These and the following quotations are from these two letters, both from late April.
11. *The Prose Works of William Wordsworth,* ed. Alexander Grosart, 3 vols. (London: Edward Moxon, 1876), 2:327.

12. MM1, 27.
13. Dorothy to Jane Pollard, *LEY,* 115.
14. *LEY,* 116–18.
15. Hayden, 511. The poem was composed in Jan. 1802 and first published in the *Morning Post* on Feb. 12.
16. *CEY,* 155.
17. *LEY,* 120.
18. Most of these revisions were never published; on the contrary, when Wordsworth reissued the two poems in 1836, he substantially cut them both.
19. *EW,* 136. All citations of Wordsworth's revisions are from this edition.
20. Lines 358–60, 366–67.
21. Lines 686–88; *EW,* 153n.
22. *LEY,* 120, n. 4.
23. *LEY,* 121.
24. *LEY,* 123–24.
25. Letter to Lady Beaumont, Aug. 1805 (MM1, 248–49).
26. *PW,* 5:340. De Selincourt dates this fragment (which I have quoted in its entirety) from 1795; Moorman estimates 1796 (MM1, 249). The specific anticipations of "Tintern Abbey" are many and obivous. The anticipations of *The Prelude* are closest to the beginning of the 1799 version: "O Derwent, travelling over the green plains, / Near my "sweet birthplace," didst thou, beauteous stream, / Make ceaseless music through the night and day" (lines 7–9; cf. *1805* I.277–79).
27. *LEY,* 118.
28. *LEY,* 126–27.
29. MM1, 250.
30. *LEY,* 121, n. 2.
31. *CEY,* 151; River Duddon sonnets, XXI.
32. WAG, 386, n. 9.
33. SG, 88.
34. Wordsworth returned on a Sunday, which Reed works out to be either Sept. 21 or 28 (*CEY,* 158, n. 14); *LEY,* 129–30 (all quotations in this paragraph are from the letter to William Calvert, Oct. 1, 1794).
35. The date of his baptism was Sept. 16, 1773 (*LEY,* 126, n. 1).
36. *LEY,* 129–30.
37. This is far different from the way most of Wordsworth's biographers have presented the matter. They follow Wordsworth's lead in *The Prelude,* taking a view of it based on spiritual insights removed as far as possible from material circumstances. Moorman, in MM1, 251, says that Raisley was "moved by something in Wordsworth's manner and person . . . [to make] that gallant bet with the future"; Robert Gittings and Jo Manton, in *Dorothy Wordsworth* (Oxford: Oxford Univ. Press, 1988), 49, honor his "selfless devotion in the face of imminent death."
38. Feb. 23, 1805, *LEY,* 546.
39. Wordsworth published a similar tribute to Calvert during his lifetime, in the *Poems, in Two Volumes* of 1807 (*PW,* 3:20), which uses similar language: "That I, if frugal and severe, might stray / Where'er I liked" (lines 6–7).
40. *LEY,* 131 (italics added).
41. *LEY,* 130, n. 1. The total cash mentioned in Raisley Calvert Sr.'s will is £840, but a codicil increased Raisley Jr.'s cash benefit.
42. *LEY,* 131.

43. *LEY,* 132, n. 1.
44. Oct. 13, 1794, *LEY,* 132, n. 1.
45. *LEY,* 133–34.
46. Letters of May and June 1797, *LEY,* 184–88.
47. Letters of Nov. 7, Dec. 24, and Jan. 7, *LEY,* 134–36.
48. MM1, 251.

Chapter 18: Philanthropy or Treason?

1. "Ought I explicitly to declare the sentiments I entertain?" (*Political Justice,* 1:272, cited in NR, 176–77.
2. *LEY,* 119.
3. *LEY,* 123.
4. *Conciones ad Populum* ("The Plot Discovered"), 1795.
5. *LEY,* 124.
6. Nov. 17, 1794, *LEY,* 135. In about 1809, drafting a biography for one of his alter egos, the Solitary of *The Excursion,* Wordsworth recalled his image of the city as a "mighty gulph" of talents, but gave it a more positive spin: "London, then a fountain of great hopes" *(PW,* 5:48, *app. crit.).*
7. Dec. 24, 1794, and Jan. 7, 1795, *LEY,* 138.
8. *LEY,* 139, n. 2.
9. Mary Moorman says this magazine was of "extreme radical opinion [and] ran for six months, when Pitt's 'Gagging Acts' must have killed it. It was scurrilous in style and contained nothing which could have issued from the pen of Wordsworth" (MM1, 256n). Moorman was the first Wordsworth scholar to examine this journal, but virtually everything she says about it is inaccurate. It ran for eleven months, not six, was not extremely radical in opinion, only intermittently scurrilous in style or content, and contained many things which could have issued from the pen and mind of Wordsworth.
10. May 19, 1792, *LEY,* 76.
11. May 23, 1794, *LEY,* 118.
12. *LEY,* 126.
13. Lewis Patton, ed., *The Watchman,* in *The Collected Works of Samuel Taylor Coleridge,* gen. ed. Kathleen Coburn, 16 vols. (Princeton: Princeton Univ. Press, 1983–), 2:xxxix.
14. *LEY,* 125.
15. *LEY,* 125.
16. E. P. Thompson, "Wordsworth's Crisis," *London Review of Books,* Dec. 8, 1988, 3–6, reviewing Roe, *Wordsworth and Coleridge: The Radical Years.*
17. *Recollections of the Life of John Binns* (Philadelphia: Parry & M'Millan, 1854), 43.
18. Publication dates from H. T. Dickinson, *British Radicalism and the French Revolution, 1789–1815* (Oxford: Blackwell, 1985), 19–20. On the basis of their similar formats, Michael Scrivener, *Poetry and Reform: Periodical Verse from the English Democratic Press, 1792–1824* (Detroit: Wayne State Univ. Press, 1992), 91–92, calls the *Philanthropist* "really a continuation" of *Politics for the People.*
19. RH, 83.
20. Phillip A. Brown, *The French Revolution in English History* (1918; reprint, London: George Allen & Unwin, 1923), 139; Scrivener, *Poetry and Reform,* 96; BRS, 221. Best published a popular book on angling in 1787 (11th ed., 1822) and a long poem, *Matilda,* in 1789. If his dates are 1753–1815, he was briefly at Wordsworth's college, St. John's (1772–73),

but this man was an officer in the Kent militia (1782–98), and hence an unlikely hack from Eaton's stable. The other identifiable *Philanthropist* writer was William Green, possibly the author of *The Art of Living in London* (1785), which recommends virtue in the face of temptation. A third contributor, George Peopleton, may be a name or a pun. Six other contributors used initials (J.B., B.W., R.F., H.E., A.M.L., and W.); on the last of these, see below. All other contributions (other than extracts) are unsigned or use code names: Junius, Common Sense, Liberty Pig, Aristides, Pax, etc. All of these except "Liberty Pig" point to a classically educated group of contributors.

21. GMH1, 267–68.
22. *CEY,* 164, citing Godwin's diary.
23. *Twixt Tyne and Tweed,* 3:84.
24. Thus MacGillivray interprets Wordsworth's comment to Losh in 1798, that "I have not forgotten your apprehensions from Sea-sickness" (*LEY,* 213), cited by *CEY,* 139.
25. Hazlitt, *The Spirit of the Age* (1825), 31; Godwin is quoted from MM1, 263.
26. GMH1, 265. The novel was called *Alwyn; or, The Gentleman Comedian.*
27. *Memoirs of the late Thomas Holcroft, Written by Himself, and Continuing to the Time of His Death, from His Diary, Notes, and Other Papers,* ed. William Hazlitt (London: Longman, Hurst, Rees, Orme & Brown, 1816), 85–88. Holcroft's son shot himself in 1789, as he was being approached by his father on board the *Fame,* on which he was trying to flee the country after stealing some money from Holcroft. The incident created a sensation, and invidious connections were drawn between the boy's death and his father's well-known irascibility. Hazlitt's account is more sympathetic, maintaining that the boy had, if anything, been spoiled by his father's indulgence and high hopes. "The shock which Holcroft received was almost mortal . . . and the impression was never completely effaced from his mind" (142).
28. BRS, 150.
29. Binns, *Recollections,* 45; Peter H. Marshall, *William Godwin,* (New Haven: Yale Univ. Press, 1984), 87. John Binns was also a member of the Philomatheans.
30. Marshall, *Godwin,* 172.
31. *LEY,* 126, 128.
32. *LEY,* 169.
33. Nicholas Roe, "Wordsworth, Samuel Nicholson, and the Society for Constitutional Information," *Wordsworth Circle* 13 (1982): 197.
34. GMH1, 265–66n.
35. E. P. Thompson, *The Making of the English Working Class* (New York: Vintage Books, 1966), 145.
36. "Godwin's theory and Wordsworth's scheme for [the *Philanthropist*] coincide exactly" (Roe, *Radical Years,* 180–83).
37. *CLSTC,* 1:156, cited in Nicholas Roe, "Radical George: Dyer in the 1790's," *Charles Lamb Bulletin,* n.s. 49 (Jan. 1985): 22.
38. Hazlitt, "My First Acquaintance with Poets," in *The Complete Works,* ed. P. P. Howe, 21 vols. (London: J. M. Dent, 1932), 17:112.
39. *LEY,* 170–71.
40. *A Man of Ten Thousand* (London: Robinson, 1796). The hero, played by Kemble, is ruined when a tornado destroys his Caribbean plantation, but is restored to fortune by winning £20,000 in the lottery. But he is shown to be worthy of the heroine, because they alone are concerned about "the Negroes and the Poor . . . whom the afflicting heavens have left shelterless," when everybody else is concerned only with loans, creditors, collateral, and social appearances.

41. SG, 105, also makes this point, noting that Godwin's preface is "perfectly well written."
42. Thompson, "Crisis," 4.
43. Ibid.
44. GMH1, 251.
45. *LEY,* 140, n. 2. Wordsworth's address is written on the cover of a letter from Coleridge (but not in Coleridge's hand) to Dyer, dated March 10, 1795.
46. NR, 195.
47. Parallels between the two journals are presented in more detail in my "Philanthropy or Treason? Wordsworth as 'Active Partisan,' " *Studies in Romanticism* 25 (1986): 371–409. My conclusions in that essay are here extended by subsequent work by Roe, Thompson, Scrivener, and myself.
48. NR, 278 (italics added by Roe).
49. *CEY,* 159.
50. MS B, lines 193–96.
51. Wordsworth's later compulsive revisions of the first two lines might be construed equally as efforts to revive, or to remove, the tic of an old memory: "If this belief from heaven is sent, / If such be Nature's holy plan" (1820); "From Heaven if this belief be sent" (1827–32); "If this belief from heaven be sent" (1837).
52. MM1, 261.
53. MM1, 261.
54. Croft wove the stories of Hackman and Chatterton together to fit his title.
55. Quoted in MM1, 261.
56. *LEY,* 147, n. 4.
57. *LEY,* 183–84.
58. For the details of these transactions, see MM1, 269–70, 297.
59. He was also a four-time winner of the Seatonian Prize (1794, 1800, 1811, 1812), a competition open to university alumni.
60. *LEY,* 156n–157n.
61. Stephen Gill, ed., *The Salisbury Plain Poems of William Wordsworth* (Ithaca: Cornell Univ. Press, 1975), 37n.
62. Nov. 20, 1795, *LEY,* 159: "I recollect reading the first draft of it to you in London." Wordsworth was in the process of drastically changing the "first draft" to, as he said, "almost another work," the "Adventures on Salisbury Plain."
63. *LEY,* 156, n. 3.
64. *EPF,* 781–821. I am very grateful to the editors, Carol Landon and Jared Curtis, for allowing me to see a prepublication typescript of their brilliant reconstruction of this work.
65. Percy, raised to the peerage in a new creation of the dukedom, also fits the type of the "upstart" country knight that Juvenal satirizes, though Howard does not. Una Tuckerman, "Wordsworth's Plan for His Imitation of Juvenal," *Modern Language Notes* 40 (1930): 211, notes that the poem's references to Drake, Marvell, and Captain Cook also fit this pattern, of virtuous commoners rising from humble origins to save or bring glory to their country.
66. *PW,* 1:302, 2:13–14; *EPF,* 808. All citations will be to the latter text.
67. In a letter of Nov. 1795, Wordsworth proposed to Wrangham that they incorporate a reference, suggested by Southey, to one of their contemporaries, Lord Courtenay (1768–1815), by the same means, translating his family's motto ("Whence have I fallen? What have I done?") into their text (*LEY,* 158, n. 10).
68. *CEY,* 166.

69. G. G. Ramsay's literal translation, in the Loeb Classical Library edition.
70. "To Cash paid Geo: Dyer Esq. on account of Luttrell Tempest. 200." Duke of Portland's Secret Service Account Book, 4 verso. Cited courtesy of WL. I have not been able to identify "Luttrell Tempest."
71. Bernard Porter, *Plots and Paranoia: A History of Political Espionage in Britain, 1790–1988* (London: Unwin Hyman, 1989), 32–33. Two other such agents were the minor dramatists Charles Stuart *(The Distress'd Baronet)* and Leonard McNally (active between 1794 and 1803). Spies who dealt in Irish matters were paid nearly twice as much as those who limited their activities to England, because of the greater danger and urgency of an Irish rebellion.
72. *EPF,* 821, from the inside back cover of DC, MS 2. There are seven more brief entries on this cover, almost all in different inks or different handwriting, suggesting different times of entry. Six of these others are on obviously different subjects as well: bits of natural description. But the one immediately following this one has an eerie resonance with it, if we think of Mathews dead in the West Indies in 1801, "a disappointed man." It reads, "And the dead friend is present / in his shade."
73. Nov. 20, 1795, *LEY,* 158.
74. Binns, *Recollections,* 54–56.
75. Bergan Evans and Hester Pinney, "Racedown and the Wordsworths," *Review of English Studies* 8 (1932): 8.
76. SG, 92.
77. MM1, 268, citing Ernest de Selincourt, *Dorothy Wordsworth* (Oxford, 1933), 58–59.
78. Binns, *Recollections,* 47.
79. PRO, HO, 65/1. These orders went out on the 26th, three days before the meeting.
80. MM1, 268.
81. *Memoirs of Charles Mathews, Comedian,* ed. Anne Mathews (London: Richard Bentley, 1838), 314.
82. Between lines 622 and 624; MS 52, 271v, 272r; *Thirteen,* 2:876.
83. Godwin picked it up from Jeremy Bentham's more broadly utilitarian *Principles of Morals and Legislation,* 1789 (BRS, 226n). Wordsworth also uses it in X.615.
84. WAG, 406, n. 5.
85. These striking parallels to Wordsworth's 1795 London experience are all the more pointed when we consider that this history of disillusionment was *not* very much like Fawcett's, as Wordsworth surely knew. In his old-age note to Isabella Fenwick, Wordsworth said, "Poor Fawcett, I have been told, became pretty much such a person as I have described; and early disappeared from the stage, having fallen into habit of intemperance, which I have heard (though I will not answer for the fact) hastened his death." His fudging language casts considerable doubt on the accuracy of his statement. Hazlitt recalled that the failure of the French Revolution "preyed upon [Fawcett's] mind and hastened his death" (Holcroft, *Memoirs,* 192n), but also remembered passing "some of the pleasantest days of my life" with Fawcett in his retirement in Hertfordshire; he was, "of all the persons I have ever known, . . . the most perfectly free from every taint of jealousy or narrowness." Fawcett remained a thorough Godwinian all his life. He was remembered in his obituary in the conservative *Gentleman's Magazine* as "an eccentric character" whose works were full of the "spirit of invention and bombast" (GMH1, 261–64).
86. For the nervous breakdown, see *Diaries and Correspondence of James Losh,* Publications of the Surtees Society, vol. 171 (London, 1962), 1:xiii; for tuberculosis, *LEY,* 185, n. 2.
87. BRS, 229.

88. BRS, 227, citing *Remains of John Tweddell* (1815).
89. *Memoirs of Mathews,* 315.
90. *LEY,* 154–55.
91. The poem's author is Vicomte de Ségur; it appeared in *Almanach des Muses, ou Choix Poesies fugitives de 1792, Année 1793* (*CEY,* 24, n. 12; Hayden, 114–16); the *Morning Chronicle* version is printed in *EPF,* 723.

Chapter 19: Of Cabbages and Radicals

1. Richard Pares, *A West-India Fortune* (Hamden, Conn.: Archon Books, 1950) 159. Pinney's trading house was not the biggest in Bristol, but it was one of the most successful, surviving when hard times drove others under, thanks to Pinney's cautious lending policies.
2. Ibid., 121.
3. All information on Pinney is from Pares, *Fortune,* unless otherwise noted.
4. In 1782 Pinney was one of the two planters who arranged the island's peaceful surrender to a French fleet, and who cooperated with the occupiers until they left shortly thereafter. See Bergen Evans and Hester Pinney, "Racedown and the Wordsworths," *Review of English Studies* 8 (1932): 3.
5. The records are not clear, but it appears that the younger Pinneys were paying their father for the house (ibid.)
6. Pares, *Fortune,* 63.
7. Evans and Pinney, "Racedown," 2–3.
8. Pares, *Fortune,* 155.
9. Ibid., 149.
10. Quoted by Winifred F. Courtney, "Nevis, West Indies, and the English Romantic Writers," *Charles Lamb Bulletin,* n.s. 71 (July 1990): 250.
11. Oct. 20–24, 1795, *LEY,* 153.
12. Robert Woof, Wordsworth and Coleridge: Some Early Matters," *Bicentenary Wordsworth Studies in Memory of John Alban Finch,* ed. Jonathan Wordsworth (Ithaca: Cornell Univ. Press, 1970), 83–90. "Lines on an Autumnal Evening" quote lines 31–32 of *EW;* they were published in the Sherborne *Weekly Entertainer* of Oct. 28, 1793.
13. William Knight, *Coleridge and Wordsworth in the West Country: Their Friendship, Work, and Surroundings* (London: Elkin Matthews, 1913), 8.
14. GMH1, 282.
15. Thelwall was keenly aware of Coleridge's success in Bristol. See NR, 145–56.
16. *The Poet's Fate,* ed. Donald Reiman (New York: Garland, 1979), 26–28.
17. Gill lived at Harlescombe Farm, a few hundred yards away from the main house (Evans and Pinney, "Racedown," 9, 14).
18. PP, MSS XVIII.
19. Nov. 30, 1795, *LEY,* 160.
20. *CLSTC,* 1:325.
21. MM1, 285.
22. Tom Mayberry, *Coleridge and Wordsworth in the West Country* (Phoenix Mill: Alan Sutton, 1992), 77; *Persuasion,* chap. 11.
23. Evans and Pinney, "Racedown," 5.
24. Mayberry, *West Country,* 76.
25. Crowe's book, though not a "pure" landscape poem, is imbued with the "Old" or

"Country" Whig principles that John Pinney also represented. The poem projects a vision of free-enterprise liberalism that on other occasions got Crowe into hot water. The poem he read at a 1793 reception for the duke of Portland at Oxford was suppressed for its antiwar sentiments. See John Williams, *Wordsworth: Romantic Poetry and Revolution Politics* (Manchester: Manchester Univ. Press, 1989), 10–18.

26. William Crowe, *Lewesdon Hill* (Oxford: Woodstock Books, 1989), 4, 28.
27. *LEY,* 162.
28. *LEY,* 162.
29. *LEY,* 141, 146.
30. MM1, 269.
31. *LEY,* 180.
32. *LEY,* 180.
33. *LEY,* 163.
34. March 7, 1796, *LEY,* 166.
35. Wordsworth cut these lines from the poem after 1815 *(PW,* 4:173, *app. crit.).*
36. Hermann J. Wuscher, *Liberty, Equality, and Fraternity in Wordsworth, 1791–1800* (Stockholm: Almqvist & Wiksell International, 1980), 97.
37. *LEY,* 178.
38. Gill's diary, Sept. 29, 1795, cited in Evans and Pinney, "Racedown," 10–11.
39. Information about Gill is from Pares, *Fortune,* 142; Evans and Pinney, "Racedown," 14; MM1, 276, 308.
40. Mrs. Cecil Thelwall, *The Life of John Thelwall* (London: J. Macrone, 1837), 1:319.
41. May 7, 1797, *LEY,* 184.
42. "The Ruined Cottage," MS B.193–95.
43. *LEY,* 154.
44. *LEY,* 162.
45. XII.163–64.
46. MM1, 314, n. 2.
47. *The Ruined Cottage and The Pedlar,* ed. James Butler (Ithaca: Cornell Univ. Press, 1979), 463.
48. "Will his heart become much either softened or expanded, who breathes the atmosphere of a dungeon? Surely it would be better in this respect to imitate the system of nature, and, if we would teach justice and humanity, transplant those we would teach into a natural and reasonable state of society" (*Political Justice,* 2:754–55, quoted in *EPF,* 768).
49. *PW,* 1:316.
50. SG, 95.
51. *LEY,* 159.
52. Frederick W. Bateson, *Wordsworth: A Re-interpretation* (London: Longmans, Green, 1954), 119; MM1, 295.
53. SG, 91.
54. MM1, 262.
55. Paul D. Sheats, *The Making of Wordsworth's Poetry, 1785–1798* (Cambridge: Harvard Univ. Press, 1973), 129.
56. Ibid., 112–13.
57. Feb. 27, 1799, *LEY,* 256.
58. *LEY,* 159.
59. Carol Landon, "Wordsworth's Racedown Period: Some Uncertainties Resolved," *Bulletin of the New York Public Library* 68 (1964): 106–7.

60. Leslie Chard, *Dissenting Republican: Wordsworth's Early Life and Thought in Their Political Context* (The Hague: Mouton, 1972).
61. I am indebted to Michele Thomas for this analysis of the *Monthly Magazine*. The *Monthly*'s success contrasts with the reverses suffered by radical writers who fanned out into the provinces in early 1796 in search of subscribers. Thelwall was prevented from speaking in Norfolk, and his colleagues John Gale Jones and John Binns were arrested in March during a joint expedition to Oxford (Phillip A. Brown, *The French Revolution in English History* [London: George Allen & Unwin, 1923], 153). In this context, Coleridge's efforts for the *Watchman* were more successful than most.
62. DVE, 110.
63. SG, 108.
64. March 21, 1796, *LEY,* 169.
65. Evans and Pinney, "Racedown," 12.
66. Pares, *Fortune,* 166.
67. Woof, "Some Early Matters," 90–91.
68. *LEY,* 165.
69. Pares, *Fortune,* 166.
70. Evans and Pinney, "Racedown," 4–7.
71. Woof, "Some Early Matters," 90.
72. *LEY,* 167–68.
73. *LEY,* 167–68, 178. The latter letter is from 1797, but Wordsworth's financial condition was the same both years.
74. March 25, 1796, PP; SG, 116–17.
75. *LEY,* 169.
76. MM1, 299.
77. *LEY,* 169–71.
78. *CEY,* 186.
79. Landon, "Racedown Period," 100.
80. Ellen was a common literary name, but it is one that Wordsworth regularly used to refer to Dorothy, particularly in poems dealing with the emotional undercurrents of their domestic situation.

Chapter 20: An Independent Intellect

1. EL, 270.
2. *Miscellanies* (London, 1886), 118, quoted ibid., 269.
3. Richard Matlak, *The Poetry of Relationship* (New York: St. Martin's Press, 1997), pt. 1, passim.
4. Ibid., 7; Alan Liu, *Wordsworth: The Sense of History* (Stanford: Stanford Univ. Press, 1989), 308 (italics added).
5. All quotations from *The Borderers* are from the early version (1797–99) in the edition by Robert Osborn (Ithaca: Cornell Univ. Press, 1982).
6. WAG, 402, n. 8.
7. Reeve Parker, " 'In Some Sort Seeing with My Proper Eyes': Wordsworth and the Spectacles of Paris," *Studies in Romanticism* 27 (1988). When Wordsworth was in Paris, on Nov. 26, 1792, an adaptation of *Othello* opened in which Iago's villainy was not revealed until the very end of the play, as in *The Borderers.* In this production, Desdemona is being forced to marry the Duke's son because of her father's opposition to her suitor,

the military hero Othello. This twist on the father-daughter-suitor triangle is not found in any other of Wordsworth's likely sources (ibid., 300). The adaptation was by Jean-François Ducis, the leading French presenter of Shakespeare, and the title role was taken by François-Joseph Talma, the most histrionic of the revolutionary actors. This version of the play was published in late Sept. 1793, when Wordsworth may have been in Paris, and performed again on Oct. 31, 1793, the day of the Girondins' mass execution. Ducis was a Girondin supporter.

8. "Desultory Observations on *The Robbers,*" *Cabinet* 1 (1795): 84–91, 153–64.
9. Quoted by RH, 79.
10. William and Dorothy also read Henry Brooke's *Gustavus Vasa* "with pleasure" in Racedown's library, a play of 1739 that was still banned from performance in England: its depiction of an evil minister leading his royal master astray was deemed seditious by the lord chancellor. It had special appeal to Wordsworth as the story of a young northern prince who, incognito among the miners in Sweden, leads a plot that frees his country from corrupt domination. It stayed in Wordsworth's memory as the kind of epic story he would have written had he not decided his own life story was a better example of such heroism: "how Gustavus found / Help at his need in Dalecarlia's mine" (I.211–12).
11. SG, 109, 445, n. 102.
12. *Regicide Peace,* 249.
13. Ibid., 247.
14. Marijane Osborn, "Wordsworth's *Borderers* and the Landscape of Penrith," *Transactions of the Cumberland and Westmorland Antiquarian and Archaeological Society,* n.s. 76 (1976): 144–58. Wordsworth also referred to guides and surveys of the Lake District by Gilpin, Clarke, West, and Hutchinson to refresh his memory (Osborn edition, 18–19), and read Redpath's *History of the Borderers,* "but found nothing there to my purpose" (*PW,* 342).
15. M. Osborn, *"Borderers,"* 148–50.
16. Gerald N. Izenberg, *Impossible Individuality: Romanticism, Revolution, and the Origins of Modern Selfhood, 1787–1802* (Princeton: Princeton Univ. Press, 1992), 166–67.
17. In Wordsworth's early drafts the captain's daughter entrusts her father's safety to her beloved, Rivers. She goes mad when she learns what has happened; similarly, Matilda in the play's final scenes calls down heaven's vengeance on *her* father's murderer, unaware that it is her beloved Mortimer.
18. These double strands of Matilda's origins in the persons of Annette and Dorothy are worked out in greater psychobiographical detail by Matlak, in *Poetry of Relationship.* I am grateful to Professor Matlak for allowing me to read his book in manuscript.
19. Izenberg, *Impossible Individuality,* 196.
20. Ibid., 198, 207.
21. Ibid., 200. Izenberg shows that this principle of individualism is self-contradictory: the self that declares such radically unique authority is inevitably nihilistic; since there is no ground of moral obligation it can point to, it must strive to eliminate all rival claimants.
22. Paul D. Sheats, *The Making of Wordsworth's Poetry, 1785–1798* (Cambridge: Harvard Univ. Press, 1973), 133.
23. *LEY,* 177.
24. *LEY,* 181.
25. *LEY,* 179, n. 1. He returned from this voyage two years later, in Aug. 1799, shortly after William and Dorothy returned from Germany.
26. *CEY,* 194–95.
27. MM1, 309.

28. *CLSTC,* 1:320.
29. *CLSTC,* 1:320–21.
30. SG, 120.
31. *LEY,* 190, n. 3.
32. Hayden, 942.
33. Jonathan Wordsworth, "A Wordsworth Tragedy," *Times Literary Supplement,* July 21, 1966, 642. Gordon Wordsworth's action was extraordinary, for the man who more than any other is responsible for preserving the collection that forms the basis of the libraries, museums, bookshops, conference centers, and related buildings and activities that now make up the Wordsworth Trust in Grasmere. How bad can "The Somersetshire Tragedy" have been to merit destruction, considering the many pages of ephemeral materials that are (appropriately) preserved in such a collection? It seems more likely that it was not the quality of the verse but the nature of the tale that influenced Gordon Wordsworth's bad decision, yet the story is homologous with *The Borderers* and other works of the Racedown period.
34. Factual details are from Jonathan Wordsworth, "Tragedy"; Frederick W. Bateson, *Wordsworth: A Re-interpretation* (London: Longmans, Green, 1954), 130–32; and *LB,* 459–63.
35. The ballad was probably already partly composed, but Wordsworth's completion of his poems was never exactly sequential, so Poole's story may also be reflected in the ballad.
36. *LEY,* 256, n. 4.
37. Quoted by Jonathan Wordsworth, "Tragedy."
38. W. L. Nichols, *The Quantocks and Their Associations* (2d ed., 1891), quoted ibid.
39. The definitive account of the early versions of the poem is James Butler's: *The Ruined Cottage and The Pedlar* (Ithaca: Cornell Univ. Press, 1979).
40. All textual citations are to the Butler edition, MS B, the earliest extant complete version (March 1798), which is more than twice the length of the version Wordsworth composed in the spring of 1797.
41. *EW,* 255–56; Butler edition, 7.
42. Butler edition, 14; Jonathan Wordsworth, *The Music of Humanity* (London: Thos. Nelson, 1969), 9–16, proposes a slightly longer first version, about 370–400 lines.
43. Thomas De Quincey, *The Collected Writings,* ed. David Masson, 11 vols. (Edinburgh: Adam and Charles Black, 1890): 6:306.
44. Jerome McGann, *The Romantic Ideology* (Chicago: Univ. of Chicago Press, 1983); Marjorie Levinson, *Wordsworth's Great Period Poems* (Cambridge: Cambridge Univ. Press, 1986); James K. Chandler, *Wordsworth's Second Nature: A Study of the Poetry and Politics* (Chicago: Univ. of Chicago Press, 1984).

Chapter 21: The Spy and the Mariner

1. Margaret E. Sandford, *Thomas Poole and His Friends,* 2 vols. (London: Macmillan, 1888), 1:200.
2. GMH1, 307.
3. Tom Mayberry, *Coleridge and Wordsworth in the West Country* (Phoenix Mill: Alan Sutton, 1992), 74; EL, 359.
4. Sandford, *Poole,* 2:132–37. Burnett's friends continued to try to help him: the next year, he was a Unitarian minister at Yarmouth, where he tutored Southey's younger brother, and in 1802 he replaced George Dyer as a secretary in Lord Stanhope's house.

5. Richard Reynell was the name of another of these forgotten hangers-on in the circle of friends that became the first generation of English Romantics.
6. *CLSTC,* 325–27.
7. *LEY,* 189.
8. *CLSTC,* 1:330.
9. RH, 152–53.
10. Sara's full defense has been magnificently delivered by Molly Lefebure in *The Bondage of Love* (New York: Norton, 1986), esp. 91–94.
11. Quoted in Sandford, *Poole,* 1:202.
12. De Quincey, *Works,* 3:198–99, cited by Lefebure, *Bondage,* 93.
13. *Don Juan,* III.xciii.
14. *LEY,* 189.
15. Sandford, *Poole,* 1:211, 219.
16. Ibid., 238–39.
17. MM1, 338.
18. Mayberry, *West Country,* 96.
19. Robert Gittings and Jo Manton, *Dorothy Wordsworth* (Oxford: Oxford Univ. Press, 1988), 72.
20. MM1, 324.
21. Aug. 14, 1797, *LEY,* 190.
22. *LCML,* 1:117–18.
23. The "two isles" are lighthouse sand spits, Steep Holm and Flat Holm.
24. *LCML,* 1:118.
25. Prefatory memoir, *Poems, Written Chiefly in Retirement* (Hereford, 1801). The full story of Thelwall's harassment is told in E. P. Thompson, "Hunting the Jacobin Fox," *Past and Present,* no. 142 (1994): 94–140.
26. GMH1, 319.
27. RH, 156.
28. EL, 363.
29. Ann Hone, *For the Cause of Truth: Radicalism in London, 1796–1821* (Oxford: Clarendon Press, 1982), 80.
30. *CLSTC,* 1:397.
31. GMH1, 320–21.
32. Sandford, *Poole,* 1:244.
33. Quoted by RH, 156.
34. *Specimens of the Table Talk of the Late Samuel Taylor Coleridge* (London: John Murray, 1835), 103.
35. To Mrs. John Thelwall, Nov. 16, 1838, *LLY,* 3:640.
36. EL, 370.
37. To Godwin, Nov. 19, 1801, *CLSTC,* 2:775.
38. *LEY,* 211, n. 2.
39. Sandford, *Poole,* 1:207.
40. NR, 262.
41. EL, 373.
42. PRO, HO, 42/41; the entire extant correspondence is printed by A. J. Eagleston, "Wordsworth, Coleridge, and the Spy," *The Nineteenth Century and After* 54 (1908): 300–310.
43. *BL,* 1:197.
44. Mayberry, *West Country,* 97.

45. Hone, *Cause of Truth,* 60ff.
46. March 10, 1798, *CLSTC,* 1:396.
47. *BL,* 1:194–95.
48. Hone, *Cause of Truth,* 29–30, 53.
49. Ian Gilmour, *Riots, Risings, and Revolutions: Government and Violence in Eighteenth-Century England* (London: Pimlico, 1993), 416, 441.
50. NR, 257.
51. *Felix Farley's Bristol Journal,* March 4, 1797, cited ibid., 248.
52. Gilmour, *Riots,* 444.
53. Sandford, *Poole,* 1:222.
54. NR, 258–59.
55. From Gill's diary, cited in NR, 239.
56. Hone, *Cause of Truth,* 69–70; R. R. Nelson, *The Home Office, 1792–1801* (Durham: Duke Univ. Press, 1969), 116; Claire Tomalin, *Mrs. Jordan's Profession: The Actress and the Prince* (New York: Alfred A. Knopf, 1995), 132.
57. Elizabeth Sparrow, "The Alien Office, 1792–1806," *Historical Journal* 33 (1990): 366–67; cf. Harvey Mitchell, *The Underground War against Revolutionary France: The Missions of William Wickham, 1794–1800* (Oxford: Clarendon Press, 1965).
58. Roger Wells, *Insurrection: The British Experience, 1795–1803* (Gloucester: Alan Sutton, 1983), 37–38.
59. Nicholas Roe, "Who Was Spy Nozy?" *Wordsworth Circle* 15 (1984): 49.
60. Gittings and Manton, *Dorothy Wordsworth,* 71.
61. George Pryme, *Autobiographic Recollections* (Cambridge: Deighton, Bell, 1870), 27.
62. Information in this paragraph is from Hone, *Cause of Truth,* 69–70; Nelson, *Home Office,* 33–36, 115–16; Tomalin, *Mrs. Jordan's Profession,* 85, 119; and *Canning's London Journal,* 33, 36, 282.
63. Dropmore Papers, British Library, Add. MSS 69038; Nelson, *Home Office,* 35.
64. Wendy Hinde, *Castlereagh* (London: Collins, 1981), 22.
65. Nelson, *Home Office,* 176.
66. Sept. 20, 1798, quoted in Sandford, *Poole,* 1:242.
67. MM1, 339; GMH1, 327–28; *PW,* 1:363.
68. April 1798, *CLSTC,* 1:403.
69. *Paupers and Pig Killers: The Diary of William Holland, a Somerset Parson, 1799–1818* (Gloucester: Alan Sutton, 1984), 15.
70. *CLSTC,* 1:343–44.
71. *BL,* chap. 10.
72. WL, MS 17–20.
73. *LLY,* 3:641.
74. *CEY,* 205.
75. For this account of Wedgwood's experiment, I am indebted to MM1, 333–37, and SG, 130–31.
76. MM1, 350.
77. "Autobiographical Memoranda" in WL, MS 17–20.
78. *LEY,* 211, 213.
79. *CEY,* 206.
80. *LEY,* 212.
81. *LEY,* 216, n. 1.
82. *LEY,* 192, n. 1.
83. *Fiesco,* tr. G.H.N. and J.S. [John Stoddart] (London: Joseph Johnson, 1796).

84. *CPWSTC,* 519; all quotations from *Osorio* are from *CPWSTC.*
85. *LCML,* 117.
86. Mayberry, *West Country,* 101.
87. Most biographers, following Coleridge's always dubious lead, put its composition in Oct., but I agree with Reed and Margoliouth in assigning its inspiration and much of its composition to the first of their two Nov. tours. Coleridge would hardly have "retired to a lonely farm-house between Porlock and Linton" if he had been suffering from dysentery, or for any reason: Culbone is twenty-five miles as the crow flies from Nether Stowey, a good day's walk. Nor was Coleridge lugging along the four-pound weight of *Purchas his Pilgrimmage.* His memory could easily recall it for his famous lead-in lines: "In Xanadu did Kubla Khan / A stately pleasure dome decree."
88. RH, 164n.
89. Gittings and Manton, *Dorothy Wordsworth,* 73.
90. John Livingston Lowes, *The Road to Xanadu: A Study in the Ways of the Imagination* (Boston: Houghton Mifflin, 1927), 257–58.
91. *CPWSTC,* 1:286–87.
92. IF, in *The Prose Works of William Wordsworth,* ed. Alexander Grosart, 3 vols. (London: Edward Moxon, 1876), 3:16–17.
93. From the earliest MS of these lines (ca. Jan. 1798), established by Beth Darlington, *BWS,* 434.
94. *LEY,* 197.
95. MM1, 351.
96. *LEY,* 196.
97. Raymond Postgate, *Story of a Year: 1798,* (New York: Harcourt, Brace, 1969), 38–39.
98. *LEY,* 197, n. 1.
99. Martha Ferguson and Elizabeth Threlkeld Rawson, respectively, quoted in Gittings and Manton, *Dorothy Wordsworth,* 81, 76.
100. *LEY,* 196.
101. *LEY,* 196, n. 1.
102. *LEY,* 210–11.
103. *The Castle-Spectre* (1798; reprint, Oxford: Woodstock Books, 1990).
104. There were actually three Townshends connected with the secret service during the 1790s, so the name had good topical currency: a police officer, an undersecretary, and Thomas Townshend, Lord Sydney, the second home secretary after its reorganization in 1782 (Nelson, *Home Office,* 199).
105. Clement Carlyon, *Early Years and Late Reflections* (London: Whittaker, 1836), 1:180. This incident occurred in 1799, but similar ones could have occurred at other times as well.

Chapter 22: The Mariner and the Recluse

1. RH, 178.
2. Entries for April 14–15 and Feb. 22, *DWJ,* 15, 9.
3. *DWJ,* 1:3.
4. *PW,* 5:341.
5. Robert Gittings and Jo Manton, *Dorothy Wordsworth* (Oxford: Oxford Univ. Press, 1988), 77.
6. Earliest MS text of the poem, established by Beth Darlington, "Two Early Texts," *Bi-*

centenary Wordsworth Studies in Memory of John Alban Finch, ed. Jonathan Wordsworth (Ithaca: Cornell Univ. Press, 1970), 431.

7. *NSTC,* vol. 1, entry no. 216.
8. *CEY,* 218–28.
9. RH, 172.
10. All facts about the poem's composition are from *The Ruined Cottage and The Pedlar,* ed. James Butler (Ithaca: Cornell Univ. Press, 1979).
11. Paul Magnuson, *Coleridge and Wordsworth: A Lyrical Dialogue* (Princeton: Princeton Univ. Press, 1988), 112–13.
12. Butler edition, 468–69.
13. MS B.399–410.
14. "Sonnets Attempted in the Manner of Contemporary Writers" (III), by "Nehemiah Higginbottom," *Monthly Magazine,* Nov. 1797.
15. NR, 235.
16. Cf. Kenneth R. Johnston, *Wordsworth and "The Recluse"* (New Haven: Yale Univ. Press, 1984).
17. *LEY,* 212, 214.
18. *CLSTC,* 1:391.
19. *CLSTC,* 2:1034.
20. *BL,* 1:195–96 (italics added).
21. *BL,* 1:196–97.
22. Ca. Sept. 10, 1799, *CLSTC,* 527.

Chapter 23: Triumphs of Failure

1. *LB,* 6.
2. An edition of the extant portions of the *opus maximum,* edited by Thomas McFarland, is scheduled as vol. 15 of Coleridge's *Collected Works,* published by Princeton Univ. Press.
3. SG, 143.
4. March 6, 1798, *LEY,* 212.
5. *LEY,* 199; MM1, 370.
6. *LEY,* 220.
7. Edward Ferguson to Samuel Ferguson, Aug. 8, 1798, *LEY,* 226 n. 1.
8. Hazlitt, "My First Acquaintance," in *The Complete Works,* ed. P. P. Howe, 21 vols. (London: J. M. Dent, 1932), 17:117.
9. *LEY,* 200.
10. *LEY,* 215.
11. SG, 144.
12. *CEY,* 226.
13. *LEY,* 216.
14. May 28, 1798, *CLSTC,* 1:412. Anna Seward, the old "Swan of Lichfield," an important figure among the older generation of "bluestockings," had never heard of Wordsworth, though she knew and admired the work of Coleridge, Southey, and Lloyd, and considered them a "school" (*Letters* [Edinburgh, 1811], cited in Wallace Douglas, *Wordsworth: The Construction of a Personality* [Kent, Ohio: Kent State Univ. Press, 1968], 25).
15. *LB,* 10.
16. MM1, 368–69.
17. John E. Jordan, *Why the "Lyrical Ballads"?: The Background, Writing, and Character of*

Wordsworth's 1798 "Lyrical Ballads" (Berkeley: Univ. of California Press, 1976), 118, citing Robert Mayo, "The Contemporaneity of the *Lyrical Ballads," PMLA* 69 (1954): 486–522; Jordan lists fifty volumes of poetry that appeared in 1798, several with titles or subjects similar to *Lyrical Ballads* (187–89).

18. Marilyn Butler, *Romantics, Rebels and Reactionaries* (Oxford: Oxford Univ. Press, 1981), 58–64.
19. Jordan, *Background,* 90–93.
20. MM1, 377; Alan Bewell, *Wordsworth and the Enlightenment* (New Haven: Yale Univ. Press, 1989), demonstrates Wordsworth's considerable debt to the fledgling discipline of eighteenth-century anthropology.
21. In Mark Reed's estimation, the only literary plan which can be demonstrated as occupying much of the two poets' attention in late 1797 and early 1798 is that of *The Recluse.* See his "Wordsworth, Coleridge, and the 'Plan' of the *Lyrical Ballads," University of Toronto Quarterly* 34 (1964–65): 238–53.
22. *LB,* 8.
23. *LEY,* 198, 214; *CEY,* 224, 226.
24. *LB,* 6.
25. MM1, 382–83; *LB,* 346.
26. RH, 190.
27. *LB,* 353.
28. MM1, 383, n. 1.
29. *LB,* 283 (lines 5–8 of 13-line fragment).
30. MM1, 385, n. 2.
31. *LEY,* 218.
32. As with their first trip to Linton, they may have followed up this trip to Cheddar with another within a week. But this seems unlikely, given their range of worries and responsibilities at the time, and Reed deduces only one (*CEY,* 236–37).
33. *Edmund Oliver* (Bristol: Bulgin & Rosser, 1798; reprint, Oxford: Woodstock Books, 1990), xii.
34. *Anti-Jacobin Review and Magazine,* Aug. 1798, 178–80. The *Review* was the immediate successor to Canning and Frere's *Anti-Jacobin, or Weekly Examiner.* Lloyd's reputation, demonized by generations of Coleridge's biographers, has been fairly rehabilitated by Graeme Stones, "Charles Lloyd and *Edmund Oliver:* A Demonology," *Charles Lamb Bulletin* 95 (July 1996): 110–21, and Richard C. Allen, "Charles Lloyd, Coleridge, and *Edmund Oliver," Studies in Romanticism* 35 (1996): 245–94.
35. IF, in *LB,* 345.
36. Hazlitt, "First Acquaintance," 120.
37. RH, 189; SG, 149–50.
38. Losh's *Diary,* cited in *LEY,* 225.
39. *CLSTC,* 1:412.
40. MM1, 358n.
41. Hayden, 354; *LB,* 285.
42. De Selincourt calls it "a curious survival of Wordsworth's earlier and more crudely 'romantic' taste" (*PW,* 4:471).
43. A. S. Byatt, *Unruly Times: Wordsworth and Coleridge in Their Time* (London: Nelson, 1970), 21.
44. Fritz Schulze, "Wordsworthian and Coleridgean Texts (1784–1822)," in *Strena Anglica,* ed. Gerhard Dietrich and F. Schulze (Halle, 1956), 225–58, cited in *LB,* 455: "The lair was a bed of pain wherefrom groans and tears arose. It can only have been a place of

childbirth. The haunted speaker is the mother who has borne there her babe and murdered him immediately after" (241).

45. The tears might be identified the other way around, if "tears of blood" and the reference to "the agonies of hell" are taken to refer to the Terror, and the painful separation it wrought between William and Annette.
46. Herrick, *Hesperides,* no. 402: "Clothes do but cheat and cousen us," in *The Complete Poetry,* ed. J. Max Patrick (New York: New York Univ. Press, 1963), 208. Herrick's poem is not a riddle, however. There is no record of Wordsworth's having read Herrick, but he might have been led to do so out of curiosity for certain experiences they shared. Herrick had also been a Johnian at Cambridge, and his reputation was best known in the West Country, where he had been for nearly fifty years vicar of Dean Prior in Devonshire, except for twenty years of exile in London during the civil war. He died in 1674.
47. *DWJ,* 1:10.
48. *PW,* 5:343–44.
49. *LB,* 284.

Chapter 24: Wye Wandering

1. MM1, 399–400.
2. Basil Cottle, *Joseph Cottle of Bristol* (Bristol: Bristol Historical Association, 1983), 9.
3. July 3, 1798, *LEY,* 223.
4. *LEY,* 222, n. 1, for details of Wordsworth's visit with Losh and Warner.
5. Richard Warner, *A Walk through Wales, in August 1797* (Bath: Cruttwell, 1798), 121–25.
6. Cottle, *Joseph Cottle,* 5.
7. Mary Jacobus, " 'Tintern Abbey' and Topographical Prose," *Notes and Queries,* n.s. 18 (1971): 366–69.
8. Detailed accounts of Wordsworth's likely itinerary and timetable by John B. McNulty, Geoffrey Little, and Kenneth R. Johnston are summarized in Donald E. Hayden, *Wordsworth's Travels in Wales and Ireland* (Tulsa: Univ. of Tulsa, 1985), 27–37.
9. *PW,* 2:517.
10. EL, 285; John E. Jordan, *Why the "Lyrical Ballads"?: The Background, Writing, and Character of Wordsworth's 1798 "Lyrical Ballads"* (Berkeley: Univ. of California Press, 1976), 1–8; MM1, 380, takes this view also, but does ask, "Did he not claim too much for the all-sufficiency of 'Nature'?" This view is continued for posterity in the definitive scholarly edition of *Lyrical Ballads,* which observes that Wordsworth affirms his faith in nature *"in spite of* his 'hearing oftentimes / The still, sad music of humanity' " (italics added). It may seem a small difference, but I would say Wordsworth's affirmations arise *because* he could still hear that sad music.
11. Warner, *Walk,* 230, citing *Aeneid,* VIII.431.
12. Jacobus, " 'Tintern Abbey,' " 367; William Gilpin, *Observations on the River Wye and Several Parts of South Wales, Related Chiefly to Picturesque Beauty, Made in the Summer of 1770* (London: R. Blamire, 1782), 12.
13. I am grateful to Pamela Woof of the Wordsworth Museum for this information.
14. Gilpin, *Observations,* 35–37.
15. Jacobus, " 'Tintern Abbey,' " 368; Gilpin, *Observations,* 32.
16. Mary Jacobus, the leading authority, concludes that, "more than any other, *Tintern Abbey* is the poem for which Wordsworth's predecessors had smoothed the way"

(" 'Tintern Abbey,' " 103–4). She cites particularly Thomson, Akenside, Bowles, and Cowper in the loco-descriptive tradition.

17. *LB,* 357, citing parallels adduced by W. J. B. Owen and Jonathan Wordsworth.
18. SG, 155.
19. *PW,* 2:518.
20. For details about the poem and Gillray's cartoon, see Dorothy M. George, *Catalog of Political and Personal Satires Preserved in the Department of Prints and Drawings in the British Museum,* vol. 7, *(1793–1800)* (London: Trustees of the British Museum, 1942), 468–72.
21. SG, 118.
22. In their original newspaper form, nos. 34 and 35 are both dated Monday, July 2; no. 36 (the final number) is dated July 9. No. 35 carries the following notice under the title: "The Concluding Number Will Be Published on Saturday next, July 7." In the collected editions which began to appear immediately, the date of no. 35 is corrected to July 9, but no. 36 keeps that same date as well. It is possible that the last two numbers came out on or near the same date, as special issues. Each of the last three numbers opens on a valedictory note: "Before we take our leave of the Public" (no. 34), "The Session of Parliament being now closed" (no. 35), and "We have now completed our Engagement with the Public" (no. 36).
23. *The Contributions of Robert Southey to the "Morning Post,"* ed. Kenneth Curry (University: Univ. of Alabama Press, 1984), 74–75.
24. *Anti-Jacobin,* Nov. 20, 1797, 31–32.
25. Hayden, *Travels in Wales,* 34–37.
26. SG, 300. Llyswen is usually understood to be a stand-in for Racedown, which might be true so far as Wordsworth's conversations with Basil about their former residence are concerned.
27. Geoffrey Little has argued for the presence of Kilve and Llyswen in the poem, against the usual view that they stand for Racedown and Alfoxden, respectively. He also thinks that some of the landscape of "Tintern Abbey" comes from Thelwall's part of the Wye, noting similarities between Wordsworth's description and Thelwall's account of "the wild and picturesque scenery of the neighbourhood" in his Prefatory Memoir. See his " 'Tintern Abbey' and Llyswen Farm," *Wordsworth Circle* 8 (1977): 80–82.
28. *LLY,* 3:640.
29. Thelwall, Prefatory Memoir, *Poems, Chiefly Written in Retirement,* i–xlviii.
30. NR, 235, also speculates that the title of Wordsworth's master project may have come from Thelwall.
31. *CEY,* 245.
32. *LEY,* 226.
33. GMH1, 356–57.
34. Details of these transactions follow the account in Jordan, *Background,* 41–52.
35. Ann Hone, *For the Cause of Truth: Radicalism in London, 1796–1821* (Oxford: Clarendon Press, 1982), 48.
36. *Monthly Magazine,* Oct. 1, 1801, quoted ibid., 49.
37. *Critical Review,* 2d ser., 24 (Oct. 1798): 197–204.

Chapter 25: "Mr. Wordsworth"

1. *CLSTC,* 1:420.
2. PRO, HO 5/3.

3. PRO, HO 5/4.
4. Home Office surveillance of Thelwall in 1798–99 is recorded in PRO, HO 42/43/f.37 and 42/46/fs. 235, 240. See P. J. Corfield and Chris Evans, "John Thelwall in Wales: New Documentary Evidence," *Bulletin of the Institute of Historical Research* 59 (1986): 231–39. A survey of HO correspondence preserved from 1798 does not produce any mention of Wordsworth or Coleridge (PRO, HO 42/43 and 44). But the records are very incomplete: for example, there is only a single item of a ship captain from Yarmouth registering the foreigners who sailed with him, on Sept. 28, twelve days after the Wordsworths and Coleridge sailed. There are more of these from Dover and Liverpool, but in 1798 there would have been hundreds of such reports from every port.
5. GMH1, 375.
6. *BL,* 2:160. These and other recollections by Coleridge are from "Satyrane's Letters," three chapters added to *Biographia Literaria* (1817) to fill up its second volume. They are based on his letters and notebook entries of 1798, fleshed out with later reflections.
7. *CLSTC,* 1:421. All references to the crossing are from this letter to Sara, written Oct. 3 from Ratzeburg, and one to Tom Poole of Oct. 26, unless otherwise noted.
8. *CLSTC,* 1:425–26.
9. On Aug. 18 Wickham acknowledged his receipt on Aug. 9 of a "letter in favour of M. De Leutre" from the Messrs. Le Chevalier (PRO, HO 5/4/89). This could have been either a defense or a denunciation of his character; "in favour of" often meant nothing more than "in regard to" in official correspondence.
10. *BL,* 2:179–81.
11. *DWJ,* 1:27.
12. *CLSTC,* 1:433; RH, 209. Godwin used this excuse for sponging off "that scoundrelly money-lender" King, the proprietor of "that execrable vehicle of Jacobinism" the *Telegraph.*
13. *LEY,* 229, n. 1.
14. MM1, 409.
15. Grenville to Pitt, Oct. 8, 1797, quoted in Harvey Mitchell, *The Underground War against Revolutionary France: The Missions of William Wickham, 1794–1800* (Oxford: Clarendon Press, 1965), 218. Grenville continued, "If this country could but be brought to think so, it would be ten thousand times safer . . . to face the storm, than to shrink from it."
16. Information about the general political situation is from Georges Lefebvre, *The French Revolution,* trans. Elizabeth Moss Evanson, 2 vols. (New York: Columbia Univ. Press, 1962), 2:192–212; that about the Foreign Office and the Swabian agency from Elizabeth Sparrow, "The Swiss and Swabian Agencies, 1795–1801," *Historical Journal* 35 (1992): 873–74.
17. PRO, FO 158/3 and 4.
18. Ann Hone, *For the Cause of Truth: Radicalism in London, 1796–1821* (Oxford: Clarendon Press, 1982), 51, 67; Hampshire PRO, (38M49) Wickham 1/66/fs. 1–40, passim.
19. PRO, FO 33/15/f.81.
20. Sept. 28, 1798, Hampshire PRO, Wickham 1/66/f.9.
21. Nov. 2, 1798, Hampshire PRO, Wickham 1/66/f.10.
22. Nov. 8, 1799, PRO, FO 83/2288/f.3.
23. It has since been purchased by the Wordsworth Trust, Reference No. 1994.125.
24. PRO, FO 158/4.
25. *DNB,* 5:38–39.
26. Coleridge crossed out a reference to De Loutre in his notebook. In the entry "Wordsworth went with the agreeable French Em. to seek a Hotel," the words "with

the agreeable French" are crossed out; presumably "Em." should have been too. Why Coleridge should censor his own notebook is hard to say, unless his fear of surveillance was very great; more likely it was just a correction of fact. See *NSTC,* 1:336; *CEY,* 249–50, n. 46.

27. E. P. Thompson, "Disenchantment or Default? A Lay Sermon," in *Power and Consciousness,* ed. Conor Cruise O'Brien and William Vanech (New York: New York Univ. Press, 1969), 168.
28. J. G. Alger, *Paris in 1793–1794: Farewell Letters of Victims of the Guillotine* (London: G. Allen, 1902), 339–40, 343–44.
29. *CLSTC,* 1:459–60.
30. *Dictionnaire de biographie française,* 10:815. None of the four De Leutres from this period who are listed in biographical dictionaries were titled aristocrats; but none of their English associates could have proved or disproved that.
31. One source for Wordsworth's use of "the springs of Dove" in "She dwelt among the untrodden ways" has been proposed as De Lille's *Les Jardins* (1780), though it seems more likely that he had one of the three English rivers of this name in mind (*LB,* 384, citing Beatty, 32–33, 318–319).
32. *DWJ,* 1:24.
33. *NSTC,* 1:339/f8.
34. PRO, FO 158/4.
35. PRO, FO 158/3.
36. *CLSTC,* 1:429.
37. RH, 209.
38. Richard Holmes notes many of the similarities, in the introduction to his edition of *A Short Residence* (Harmondsworth: Penguin, 1987), 26–43.
39. *DWJ,* 1:22.
40. *DWJ,* 1:31.
41. *NSTC,* 1:346/f14v.
42. *DWJ,* 1:27.
43. *CLSTC,* 1:473.
44. *DWJ,* 1:29.
45. *BL,* 2:183–84.
46. *LEY,* 229, n. 1; *CLSTC,* 1:436; *Prose,* 1:93.
47. *New Encyclopaedia Britannica,* 15th ed. (1993), 6:911.
48. *Prose,* 1:93.
49. *CLSTC,* 1:442.
50. *Prose,* 1:94.
51. Canto VII.xiv–xvi, *Oberon, a Poem, from the German of Wieland,* ed. Donald Reiman (New York: Garland, 1978), 2:8–9.
52. *Prose,* 1:93–94.
53. SG, 160, citing *LEY,* 255.
54. *CLSTC,* 1:438.
55. William Little, *Gottfried August Bürger* (New York: Twayne, 1974), 53.
56. Ibid., 53–54; the last quotation is from Schiller. It is not certain that Wordsworth read this review at this time, but Coleridge had, and he could easily have directed Wordsworth to it, or summarized its main points to him in conversation. See *NSTC,* 1:787 (notes); L. A. Willoughby, "Wordsworth and Germany," in *German Studies Presented to Professor H. G. Fiedler* (Oxford: Clarendon Press, 1938), 445.
57. RH, 217.

58. GMH1, 364.
59. Donald E. Hayden, *Wordsworth's Travels in Europe* (Tulsa: Univ. of Tulsa, 1988), 39.
60. Willoughby, "Germany," 437.
61. *LEY,* 213.
62. *DWJ,* 1:28.
63. *LEY,* 231.
64. *CLSTC,* 1:419, n. 1.
65. *LCML,* 1:141.

Chapter 26: Writing in Self-Defense

1. *DWJ,* 32–34.
2. *DWJ,* 34.
3. Robert Gittings and Jo Manton, *Dorothy Wordsworth* (Oxford: Oxford Univ. Press, 1988), 89.
4. The house is now no. 86, a movie theater (Donald E. Hayden, *Wordsworth's Travels in Europe* [Tulsa: Univ. of Tulsa, 1988], 39; Ernest Bernhardt-Kabisch, personal communication).
5. L. A. Willoughby, "Wordsworth and Germany," in *German Studies: Presented to Professor H. G. Fiedler* (Oxford: Clarendon Press, 1938), 432.
6. *CLSTC,* 1:513–14. The picture of Saint Christopher was "universal in all the churches I have seen," wrote Dorothy, who recorded another one at the cathedral of St. Michael in Hamburg (*DWJ,* 28).
7. *PW,* 4:414.
8. *CLSTC,* 1:454.
9. *LEY,* 245, 242.
10. "Written in Germany, on One of the Coldest Days of the Century," lines 11–12, 16, 18, 21 (*LB,* 225–26).
11. *CLSTC,* 1:420.
12. *LEY,* 246.
13. Elizabeth Sparrow, "The Swiss and Swabian Agencies, 1795–1801," *Historical Journal* 35 (1992): 873.
14. Philip Mansel, *Louis XVI* (London: Blond and Briggs, 1981), 79.
15. Ibid., 110
16. *CLSTC,* 1:508–9.
17. *LEY,* 249.
18. *CLSTC,* 1:459–60.
19. *CLSTC,* 1:458. Still, he won admirers: he singled out Countess Kielmansegge, "a very beautiful little Woman," whose husband was Lord Howe's cousin, and whose heart he won by translating his sonnet on seeing his firstborn child (ibid., 429).
20. *CLSTC,* 1:440.
21. Peter Boerner, *Johann Wolfgang von Goethe, 1832–1982,* trans. Timothy Nevil and Nancy Boerner (Bonn: Inter Nationes, 1981), 44–45.
22. Cited in Willoughby, "Germany," 433, n. 4.
23. SG, 158.
24. *LEY,* 253–54.
25. *CLSTC,* 1:451–52.
26. *LEY,* 236.

27. The fragmentary essay is printed in *Prose,* 1:103–4.
28. *LEY,* 234.
29. Mary Moorman's account may be taken to stand for many: she says Wordsworth in Goslar begins his "blessed retreat into the past," joyfully recording his "early happiness" in childhood (MM1, 419).
30. *LB,* 20.
31. RH, 212.
32. *LEY,* 238–39.
33. WL, MS JJ.
34. *1799,* 123.
35. *1799,* 124–25.
36. A series of contributions to the *Times Literary Supplement* in 1975 produced examples of uses of the "Was it for this?" rhetorical formula from Thomson to Pope, Milton, Ariosto, and Virgil (WAG, 1, n. 2).
37. Alastair Conran, "On the Goslar Lyrics," in *Wordsworth's Mind and Art,* ed. Alastair Thomson (Edinburgh: Liver & Boyd, 1969), 158.
38. MM1, 419.
39. XI.334–35.
40. WL, MS JJ (22–36).
41. GMH1, 390.
42. *LB,* 300.
43. "The Fountain," lines 55–56.
44. A textual source of this trance state or reverie has been traced by Kent Beyette to Erasmus Darwin's *Zoonomia,* cited in *LB,* 383–84.
45. Herbert Hartman, cited in *LB,* 383–84.
46. *CLSTC,* 1:479.
47. Willoughby, "Germany," 434n, citing Robinson's diaries (ed. Morley, 1922), 38.
48. *CPWSTC,* 1:312.
49. Richard Matlak, "Wordsworth's Lucy Poems in Psychobiographical Context," *PMLA* 93 (1978): 46–65.
50. Frederick W. Bateson, *Wordsworth: A Re-interpretation* (London: Longmans, Green, 1954), 151.
51. Cited ibid.
52. Ibid., 153.
53. Matlak, "Lucy Poems," 50–60.
54. The history of critical neglect of "Nutting" is set forth in Gregory Jones, " 'Rude Intercourse': Uncensoring Wordsworth's 'Nutting,' " *Studies in Romanticism* 36 (1996): 213–43. Jones develops a psychosexual interpretation of the poem that fits well the context of William's and Dorothy's life in Goslar.
55. *LB,* 302–7, prints the versions from both DC MSS 15 and 16.
56. DC, MS 16, printed in *LB,* 305–7.
57. Bateson, *Wordsworth,* 153; Jones, " 'Rude Intercourse,' " 228–43.
58. Douglas Thomson, "Wordsworth's Lucy of Nutting," *Studies in Romanticism* 18 (1979): 287–98.
59. Ibid., 298, n. 17. Wordsworth was working on an imitation of a passage from Ariosto in the MS containing one of the longer versions of "Nutting."
60. Thomson, "Lucy," 289.
61. *PW,* 4:423. Carl Ketcham says Wordsworth used it "only because it was well established

as a pseudonym" (*Shorter Poems, 1807–1820,* ed. Ketcham [Ithaca: Cornell Univ. Press, 1989], 545).

62. Information about the Eclogue X is from the editions by C. Day Lewis (1963) and Robert Coleman (1977).
63. Ketcham edition, 545.
64. Thomson, "Lucy," 288–95.
65. *LEY,* 243.
66. WL, MS JJ (147–51) (italics added).
67. DC, MS 15, lines 6–9 (italics added).
68. "Is it not nature's capacity to deaden an 'unquiet heart' that is at the center of Wordsworth's desire to simulate its soothing 'music and voice'?" (Thomson, "Lucy," 297).
69. T. E. Casson and Russell Noyes have traced these allusions, cited in *LB,* 396.
70. Suggested by James Averill, cited in *LB,* 396.
71. Bateson, *Wordsworth,* 150; SG, 160–61.
72. SG, 161.

Chapter 27: Destination Unknown

1. *LEY,* 251.
2. *LEY,* 252.
3. Clement Carlyon, *Early Years and Late Reflections* (London: Whittaker, 1836), 1:186–97; William Howitt, *Homes and Haunts of the Most Eminent British Poets* (London: R. Bentley, 1847), 2:257–58.
4. *LEY,* 254.
5. Edith J. Morley, "Coleridge in Germany (1799)," in *Wordsworth and Coleridge,* ed. E. L. Griggs (Princeton: Princeton Univ. Press, 1939), 222–24. It is hard to take the count's name seriously; perhaps Coleridge made it up or mangled it in the act of writing it down.
6. Morley, "Coleridge in Germany," 221.
7. *LEY,* 248.
8. Peter Boerner, *Johann Wolfgang von Goethe, 1832–1982,* trans. Timothy Nevil and Nancy Boerner (Bonn: Inter Nationes, 1981), 64, 98; L. A. Willoughby, "Wordsworth and Germany," in *German Studies: Presented to Professor H. G. Fiedler* (Oxford: Clarendon Press, 1938), 451.
9. Bodleian Talbot MSS, b.27, fols. 54–57 (no. 3), and précis copy in PRO, FO 74/23, cited by Elizabeth Sparrow, "The Swiss and Swabian Agencies, 1795–1801," *Historical Journal* 35 (1992): 880, n. 101.
10. Ann Hone, *For the Cause of Truth: Radicalism in London, 1796–1821* (Oxford: Clarendon Press, 1982), 129.
11. Sparrow, "Swabian Agencies," 880. Grenville's official accounting speaks in the cool language of an experienced statescraftsman: for bills "originally drawn by that Gentleman [Talbot] for secret service but it not having been judged advisable to apply the Produce of them to that Service the money was repaid by him to the Billholders who gave him bills in London" (British Library, Add. MSS 69077).
12. Peter Jupp, *Lord Grenville, 1759–1834* (Oxford: Clarendon Press, 1985), 214.
13. ibid., 224.

14. MM1, 430; Stephen Parrish, ed., *The Prelude, 1798–1799* (Ithaca: Cornell Univ. Press, 1977), 3 (for MS 19); *LB,* 717 (for MS 15).
15. Dec. 15, 1800, *CLSTC,* 1:654–55.
16. *New Columbia Encyclopedia* (1975), 1315.
17. Carlyon, *Early Years,* 3:46.
18. Sparrow, "Swabian Agencies," 871, n. 51, citing Bodleian Talbot MSS.
19. *LEY,* 221.
20. Willoughby, "Germany," 438–39; *LEY,* 235.
21. GMH1, 369. Christopher is inaccurate about other details of their departure from Goslar, and so not completely trustworthy.
22. *LEY,* 244, 254.
23. Sparrow, "Swabian Agencies," 877.
24. Ibid., 868.
25. *LEY,* 254, n. 2.
26. *LEY,* 245–46.
27. *CEY,* 262.
28. *CEY,* 264–65, n. 4.
29. IF, for "Written in Germany" (*LB,* 393).
30. Philip Mansel, *Louis XVI* (London: Blond and Briggs, 1981), 94.
31. *CLSTC,* 1:508.
32. *NSTC,* 1:432/f50. Coleridge's comment on his pun: "bad in itself—& . . . it looks damn'd ugly upon paper."
33. *LEY,* 257.
34. I am grateful to Elizabeth Sparrow for this suggestion.
35. They are printed together in *LB,* 307–16.
36. *CLSTC,* 1:510.
37. RH, 233.
38. *CLSTC,* 1:484.
39. *CLSTC,* 1:490–91.
40. *CLSTC,* 1:491.
41. Hone, *Cause of Truth,* 93 (Hampshire PRO, Wickham 1/66).
42. Elizabeth Sparrow, "The Alien Office," *Historical Journal* 33 (1990): 374.
43. PRO, FO 153/4.
44. Hone, *Cause of Truth,* 90–91.
45. Jupp, *Lord Grenville,* 223.
46. *CEY,* 266, n. 6. All figures are from *CEY,* 236–82, passim. Possibly the discrepancy between the Wedgwood figure and Wordsworth's comes from an oral transcription error, as the two amounts, spoken aloud, sound quite similar. Reed accounts for the discrepancy by estimating that Wordsworth drew £10 2s. 9d. on the Wedgwoods sometime between early Feb. and late April, but that figure is simply the difference between the Wedgwood accounts and the amount Wordsworth claimed he owed them.
47. *DWJ,* 1:31.
48. HO 33/10/199; British Library, Add. MSS 69076.
49. These quotations are also from the discursive blank verse fragments (i and ii) written at Goslar (*LB,* 307–9).
50. From the fragment beginning, "There is an active principle in all things" (*LB,* 309, lines 29–44; italics added).
51. The paradoxial way in which the concept of the modern political subject, the "free" individual, developed in tandem with the emergence of the modern state, potentially

responsible for everything in the lives of its citizens, has been explored provocatively by Michel Foucault *(Discipline and Punish)* and Louis Althusser (*Lenin and Philosophy,* esp. the essay "Ideological State Apparatuses").

52. Wickham to Portland, Jan. 3, 1801, British Library, Add. MSS 33107 (Pelham Papers), fol. 1, cited in Hone, *Cause of Truth,* 73.
53. Fragment iii ("For let the impediment be what it may"), *LB,* 311 (lines 17–18).
54. See esp. James Chandler, *Wordsworth's Second Nature: A Study of the Poetry and Politics* (Chicago: Univ. of Chicago Press, 1984). Chandler's thesis is based on parallels between Burke's writings and Wordsworth's poetry after 1796.

Chapter 28: "We Have Learnt to Know Its Value"

1. Mid-April 1795, *LEY,* 142.
2. *LEY,* 270.
3. There were seven children in all: Margaret had died in 1796, age twenty-four.
4. MM1, 436–37.
5. Mid-April 1795, *LEY,* 141–42.
6. *LEY,* 257.
7. Frederick W. Bateson, *Wordsworth: A Re-interpretation* (London: Longmans, Green, 1954), 155, says Mary "was the real object of their visit."
8. "I travelled among unknown men" (April 1801).
9. Stephen Parrish, ed., *The Prelude, 1798–1799* (Ithaca: Cornell Univ. Press, 1977), 27.
10. *LEY,* 259, 264.
11. *LEY,* 263.
12. *LEY,* 267–68.
13. *LEY,* 264.
14. *Monthly Magazine* 6 (1799): 514.
15. *CLSTC,* 1:653–54; Claire Tomalin, *Mrs. Jordan's Profession: The Actress and the Prince* (New York: Alfred A. Knopf, 1995), 179.
16. *LEY,* 267, n. 1.
17. *LEY,* 264.
18. Quoted by SG, 163n.
19. *CLSTC,* 1:489, n. 1.
20. *LEY,* 276–77.
21. SG, 164–65.
22. *CMY,* 72; MM1, 485
23. *CMY,* 75.
24. *LEY,* 678.
25. MM1, 439.
26. *LEY,* 262.
27. *LEY,* 285, n. 1.
28. *CMY,* 99,n. 62. The final discrepancy, between £100 and the £110 13s. actually owed Wedgwood, "remains unexplained."
29. *LEY,* 241.
30. MM1, 476.
31. *LEY,* 265, n. 1.
32. *CLSTC,* 1:527.
33. *CLSTC,* 1:491.

34. MM1, 435.
35. *CLSTC,* 1:491.
36. Bateson, *Wordsworth,* 121; Chester L. Shaver, *Wordsworth's Library: A Catalogue* (New York: Garland, 1979).
37. *CLSTC,* 1:527, 538, 575. Curiously these three important statements about Wordsworth's masterpiece are preserved only in Christopher Wordsworth's *Memoirs,* 1:159, from letters that were destroyed (MM1, 443, n. 1). Why they should have been destroyed, after excerpting comments that are not wholly flattering to Wordsworth, is puzzling, since most letters were being saved by this time. Only the most incriminating ones, like those referring to Annette, were systematically destroyed. This leads one to wonder what information they might have contained about the French Revolution (for whose failure Coleridge proposed *The Recluse* as remedy) or their German sojourn (their most recent point of reference regarding Wordsworth's work on the *The Prelude*).
38. *LEY,* 276 n. 2.
39. Melvin Lasky, cited in *Biographical Dictionary of Modern British Radicals,* 1:306.
40. *NSTC,* 1:634 (notes).
41. "Sir James Mackintosh," in *The Spirit of the Age; or, Contemporary Portraits* (1825), in *The Complete Works of William Hazlitt,* ed. P. P. Howe, 21 vols. (London: J. M. Dent, 1932), 11:98.
42. RH, 241–42.
43. *CLSTC,* 1:528–30.
44. *CLSTC,* 1:536, published in *Morning Post,* Dec. 7, 1799 (*PSTC,* 2:958).
45. *CLSTC,* 1:542, n. 1.
46. *NSTC,* 1:493 (text).
47. *LEY,* 271. William's letter is an extract from a lost manuscript, with some parts missing or not transcribed.
48. *LEY,* 297.
49. *LEY,* 271.
50. *LEY,* 297.
51. *CLSTC,* 1:543.
52. MM1, 1:447–51.
53. *NSTC,* 1:510 (text).
54. *NSTC,* 1:510 (notes); Hugh Owen, *The Lowther Family* (Chichester: Phillimore, 1990), 273–76.
55. *LEY,* 271; *NSTC,* 1:511 (text).
56. *CLSTC,* 2:740.
57. *LEY,* 271.
58. *CLSTC,* 1:543–54.
59. *LEY,* 272.
60. *NSTC,* 1:515 (text).
61. *LEY,* 272.
62. *NSTC,* 1:515 (text).
63. *NSTC,* 1:519 (text).
64. *NSTC,* 1:521 (text).
65. *NSTC,* 1:514 (text).
66. *LEY,* 272.
67. Notebook 15, cited in *NSTC,* 1:535 (notes).
68. *CEY,* 279.

69. *CEY,* 279.
70. *NSTC,* 1:541 (text).
71. MM1, 452.
72. *NSTC,* 1:564 (text).
73. *NSTC,* 1:559 (text).
74. *PW,* 2:516.
75. *CEY,* 280, n. 24, quoting a letter in the possession of Jonathan Wordsworth.
76. WAG, 4, n. 2.
77. *NSTC,* 1:549 (text).
78. *NSTC,* 1:555 (text).
79. *NSTC,* 1:798 (text).
80. *NSTC,* 1:571 (text).
81. *NSTC,* 1:1575 (text); the entry is a recollection from three years later.
82. *NSTC,* 1:1575 (notes).
83. RH, 251.
84. *CPWSTC,* 1:332.
85. *LEY,* 274.
86. MM1, 1:453.
87. "Home at Grasmere," MS B, lines 223, 218.
88. SG, 169.
89. *LEY,* 273–81, and appendix 6.
90. Aug. 17, 1800, *NSTC,* 1:793 (text).
91. *BL,* chap. 14, paragraph 1.
92. "Hart-Leap Well," lines 169–70, 124.
93. *LB,* 378.
94. MS B, lines 236–41.
95. Dec. 25, 1805, *LEY,* 661, quoted by MM1, 458.
96. MS B, lines 261–67.
97. *CEY,* 284.
98. MS B, lines 1027–34.

Chapter 29: Home at Grasmere

1. MM1, 459–71, for most details of the house and neighborhood.
2. *CLSTC,* 1:612.
3. *LEY,* 290.
4. *DWJ,* 1:42.
5. £8 is the figure usually given, but Reed records the smaller amount, on the authority of James Losh's *Diary* (*CMY,* 84, n. 44).
6. MM1, 465.
7. Dec, 24 and 27, 1799, *LEY,* 275.
8. *LEY,* 298–99.
9. MM1, 468.
10. *DWJ,* 1:60, n. 1.
11. *DWJ,* 1:65.
12. "Miscellaneous Sonnets," I.iii (*PW,* 2:2).
13. "A Farewell," lines 2–4 (*PW,* 2:23).

14. *DWJ,* 1:40.
15. Ian Gilmour, *Riots, Risings, and Revolutions: Government and Violence in Eighteenth-Century England* (London: Pimlico, 1993), 428–30.
16. David McCracken, *Wordsworth and the Lake District: A Guide to the Poems and Their Places* (Oxford: Oxford Univ. Press, 1985), 32.
17. *DWJ,* 1:49, 51, 65, 37, and passim.
18. *CMY,* 59, n. 10 (Wordsworth's advice to Harriet Martineau when she moved to Ambleside).
19. MM1, 471.
20. Kenneth R. Johnston, *Wordsworth and "The Recluse"* (New Haven: Yale Univ. Press, 1984), 370, n. 10. The two textual authorities on the composition of the manuscript, Beth Darlington and Jonathan Wordsworth, differ in the amount of composition they assign to 1800 or to 1806, though they agree that most significant work on the poem is assignable to these two years. I follow Darlington in accepting that the poem's final form was not achieved until the latter date; however, it may well be, as Jonathan Wordsworth argues, that most of its *composition* dates from 1800, albeit in fragmentary, unsequential order.
21. All line references are to MS B, unless otherwise indicated, in Darlington's edition. This is an earlier version than MS D, which is printed in *PW,* 5:313–39.
22. Oct. 17, 1800, *DWJ,* 67.
23. These two lines are from MS D, lines 269–70.
24. *LB,* 615 (DC, MS 30, *Michael* MS 1, 4^{r}).
25. "Stanzas in Memory of the Author of 'Obermann,' " lines 53–54.
26. SG, 190.
27. "Conclusion," *Walden; or, Life in the Woods.*
28. *LEY,* 293.
29. MM1, 475; *DWJ,* 60, n. 1.
30. MM1, 474.
31. *CMY,* 87; *LEY,* 296.
32. *CMY,* 107, n. 70.
33. *CLSTC,* 1:613.
34. *CMY,* 61.
35. RH, 278.
36. RH, 278.
37. *CMY,* 103, n. 64. MM1, 472, says that "one might take [John's letters to Mary] for love letters" except that their main subject was William's forthcoming volume of poetry. But this subject hardly disqualifies them: it might have provided a comfortable pretext.
38. SG, 204.
39. *CMY,* 61, n. 15; bracketed words are conjectures for gaps caused by the seal.
40. I am indebted to Anca Vlasopoulos for pointing out this connection between the Grasmere journal and its initiating occasion, in a paper delivered at the Interdisciplinary Nineteenth-Century Studies conference at the College of William and Mary, Williamsburg, Va., in April 1994.
41. *DWJ,* 1:37.
42. *DWJ,* 1:38.
43. *DWJ,* 1:39.
44. *LEY,* 282.
45. *CMY,* 61; it is probably the one Richard received and paid a shilling postage due on on April 2.

46. *CMY,* 67.
47. *CMY,* 69.
48. RH, 254.
49. *CLSTC,* 1:569.
50. *NSTC,* 1:567.
51. *CLSTC,* 1:552, n. 6.
52. *CLSTC,* 1:630.
53. *CLSTC,* 1:549.
54. *CLSTC,* 1:651.
55. *CLSTC,* 1:651, 557.
56. Butler and Green, in *LB,* 24.
57. RH, 267–68.
58. *CPWSTC,* 2:1060–73; *CLSTC,* 1:650, n. 1.
59. Coleridge published these lines in 1817 in *Sibylline Leaves,* as "The Night Scene."

Chapter 30: A.k.a. Lyrical Ballads

1. *LEY,* 298.
2. *CLSTC,* 1:585.
3. *CLSTC,* 1:543; *LEY,* 267.
4. *LEY,* 300.
5. Butler and Green, in *LB,* 28; *LEY,* 297, 303–4.
6. *CMY,* 85; *CLSTC,* 1:621.
7. *LEY,* 297.
8. *LEY,* 283, n. 6.
9. *LEY,* 285–311, passim.
10. MM1, 442–43.
11. *CLSTC,* 1:635.
12. *CLSTC,* 1:582, 620.
13. *CLSTC,* 1:658.
14. *LEY,* 281.
15. *LEY,* 298.
16. To say as Moorman does that "the same normality characterizes all the poetry of this year" (MM1, 480) is to state a half-truth for *Lyrical Ballads* only by ignoring "Home at Grasmere," which might be read as the work of a man gone mad with joy.
17. The poem on John's Grove, finished in 1802, "When, to the attractions of the busy world," was added to the group in the 1815 edition.
18. John Wordsworth to Mary Hutchinson, Feb. 25, 1801, cited in MM1, 506.
19. *LB,* 623.
20. MM1, 500 (italics added).
21. IF, in *LB,* 385.
22. Michael Mason, ed., *Lyrical Ballads* (London: Longman, 1992) 340; *LB,* 388–89.
23. MM1, 480.
24. *CLSTC,* 2:811.
25. *CLSTC,* 1:279.
26. *CLSTC,* 1:632.
27. MM1, 501; *LB,* 377.
28. MM1, 492.

29. SG, 189.
30. *LCML,* 1:266–67.
31. *CLSTC,* 1:611–12.
32. *CMY,* 70.
33. *DWJ,* 1:61–62.
34. *LB,* 740.
35. *LEY,* 309.
36. *LEY,* 302.
37. *CLSTC,* 1:631n.
38. MM1, 489–90.
39. *LEY,* 309.
40. *CLSTC,* 1:631.
41. *CLSTC,* 1:632.
42. Butler and Green, in *LB,* 28.
43. *LEY,* 309.
44. Butler and Green, in *LB,* 30.
45. *LB,* 319.
46. *LB,* 319.
47. *NSTC,* 1:802.
48. *DWJ,* 1:65–66.
49. *LB,* 320.
50. RH, 297.

Chapter 31: Selling the Book, Creating the Poet

1. *CMY,* 107; MM1, 505, n. 4.
2. Robert Woof, "Wordsworth's Poetry and Stuart's Newspapers, 1797–1803," *Studies in Bibliography* (Charlottesville: Univ. of Virginia, 1962), 151.
3. *CMY,* 108.
4. *LEY,* 310 (italics added).
5. Burges was the fourth highest-paid of Grenville's secret service operatives during the 1790s, after Canning, Frere, and George Hammond, receiving a total of £64,541 16s. 5d. (Dropmore Papers, British Library, Add. MSS 69076).
6. *LEY,* 325, n. 1.
7. Alexander Grosart, ed., *The Prose Works of William Wordsworth,* 3 vols. (London: Edward Moxon, 1876), 3:205–6; MM1, 502.
8. *LEY,* 684–85.
9. *LEY,* 683.
10. *LLY,* 5:2–3; Reed conjectures that the letter was addressed to Lewis (*CMY,* 108–9).
11. Moorman characteristically downplays the letter's political aspect (MM1, 503), though she is anticipated by Wordsworth himself, who complained in embarrassment when it was published without his permission in 1838, by which time he was wholly given over to burying all evidence of his youthful Jacobinism (*LLY,* 2:957).
12. *LEY,* 312–15.
13. "On Leaving the Bottoms of Gloucestershire . . . Aug. 12, 1797," in *Poems Chiefly Written in Retirement* (Herford, 1801), 137. Wordsworth knew these lines and remembered them in his picture of the factory boy as a "mean Being" in *The Excursion,* especially Thelwall's idea of "lewd association": "These structures rose, commingling old and young, / And unripe sex with sex, for mutual taint" (VIII.339–40).

14. *LEY*, 314.
15. *Institutio Oratoria*, X.vii.15, trans. H. E. Butler in Loeb Classical Library edition.
16. Stephen Ayling, *Fox* (London: John Murray, 1991), 201.
17. Grosart, ed., *Prose*, 2:205–6.
18. *LEY*, 325.
19. *LEY*, 326.
20. John Taylor, *Records of My Own Life* (London: E. Bull, 1832), 1:176.
21. *LEY*, 326–28.
22. *LEY*, 327 (italics added).
23. MM1, 507.
24. *CMY*, 138.
25. MM1, 506–7.
26. *LCML*, 1:245–47.
27. *LEY*, 316.
28. Quoted in *CMY*, 110, n. 3.
29. *CMY*, 119.
30. SG, 192.
31. MM1, 508.
32. Quoted in MM1, 509.
33. *CLSTC*, 2:670; *CMY*, 109.
34. July 25, 1801, *CLSTC*, 2:747–48.
35. SG, 204.
36. *CMY*, 120; *LJW*, 29.
37. *LJW*, 76–77.
38. *LJW*, 31.
39. *CMY*, 122–23.
40. *Prose*, 1:112; SG, 190.
41. *CMY*, 123.
42. My account of the difference between the 1800 and 1802 prefaces derives largely from W. J. B. Owen's brilliant, dispassionate analysis in *Wordsworth as Critic* (Toronto: Univ. of Toronto Press, 1969), 57–114. Owen's account deserves to be better known than it is; a digest of it ought to be reprinted with every edition of *Lyrical Ballads* that includes or refers to either preface.
43. Ibid., 65.
44. Ibid., 113, 106.
45. Cf. Frederick Garber, *Wordsworth and the Poetry of Encounter* (Urbana: Univ. of Illinois Press, 1971).
46. SG, 196.
47. *Edinburgh Review* 4 (1804): 329–30, cited in Marilyn Butler, *Romantics, Rebels and Reactionaries* (Oxford: Oxford Univ. Press, 1981), 62. Francis Horner recognized Jeffrey's allusion to "Coleridge & Co." from "The New Morality," and objected that the hit was "too low" (John West, personal communication, citing the *Life of Francis Horner*).

Chapter 32: Peace, Marriage, Inheritance

1. *CMY*, 147.
2. *CMY*, 138.
3. *CMY*, 149.

4. *CMY,* 150–52.
5. *CMY,* 120.
6. *CMY,* 150.
7. "As I Walked Out One Evening," lines 43–44.
8. SG, 194.
9. SG, 200–201.
10. Hayden, 541–42 (DC, MS 44).
11. *CMY,* 141.
12. *PW,* 2:468.
13. SG, 205.
14. *CMY,* 155, 176.
15. *DWJ,* 1:159; *LEY,* 365.
16. *CMY,* 174, n. 44.
17. All line references are to *The Riverside Shakespeare,* vol. 2 (Boston: Houghton Mifflin, 1971), 1782–86.
18. Hayden, 988, citing *DWJ,* 1:143.
19. *LEY,* 361–62.
20. *LEY,* 364.
21. W. J. B. Owen, *Wordsworth as Critic* (Toronto: Univ. of Toronto Press, 1969), 302–4, quoting *Times* of May 24 and 28, 1802.
22. *LEY,* 370; MM1, 558–60; SG, 207.
23. *LEY,* 371 n. 2.
24. *LEY,* 361.
25. *LEY,* 360.
26. *CMY,* 159n, 179.
27. *CMY,* 179, n. 55; Robert Woof, "Wordsworth's Poetry and Stuart's Newspapers, 1797–1803," *Studies in Bibliography* (Charlottesville: Univ. of Virginia Press, 1962), 151.
28. *CMY,* 157.
29. *CMY,* 180.
30. *CMY,* 189.
31. Robert Gittings and Jo Manton, *Dorothy Wordsworth* (Oxford: Oxford Univ. Press, 1988), 135.
32. SG, 209.
33. "England! the time is come," line 14.
34. "Great men have been among us," lines 1, 6; "Calais, August, 1802," lines 3–7.
35. "1801," lines 1–3.
36. "When I have borne in memory what has tamed," lines 12–14.
37. *CMY,* 191–92.
38. Gittings and Manton, *Dorothy Wordsworth,* 137.
39. *LJW,* 126, n. 3.
40. *LJW,* 215–16.
41. *LJW,* 126.
42. *LJW,* 125–26.
43. Frank Rand, *Wordsworth's Mariner Brother* (Amherst, Mass.: Newell Press, 1966), 86.
44. SG, 211.
45. *CMY,* 194.
46. SG, 211.
47. *CMY,* 195–96.
48. Gittings and Manton, *Dorothy Wordsworth,* 139.

49. *LJW,* 218; MM1, 574–75.
50. *CPWSTC,* 2:963–70.
51. *CPWSTC,* 2:969.
52. Robert Woof, "Wordsworth and Coleridge: Some Early Matters," *Bicentary Wordsworth Studies in Memory of John Alban Finch,* ed. Jonathan Wordsworth (Ithaca: Cornell Univ. Press, 1970), 83.
53. *LEY,* 295.
54. *The Love Letters of William and Mary Wordsworth,* ed. Beth Darlington (Ithaca: Cornell Univ. Press, 1982), 157.
55. *CMY,* 198. The letters do not survive, only Dorothy's journal entries about writing "to France." William may have written too, but there is less evidence for it.
56. *CMY,* 201.
57. Between Oct. and Dec. 1803 (Woof, "Newspapers," 184–85).
58. Hayden, 582, 585.

Chapter 33: Disciples and Partners

1. Robert Woof, "Wordsworth's Poetry and Stuart's Newspapers, 1797–1803," *Studies in Bibliography* (Charlottesville: Univ. of Virginia, 1962), 159, n. 13, citing Thomas Hutchinson's conjectural translation.
2. Ibid., 155.
3. *Essays,* 1:373, cited in RH, 338.
4. *CMY,* 202.
5. *CMY,* 211, 218.
6. *CMY,* 210.
7. *CMY,* 218.
8. *LJW,* 37–38, 143.
9. *LJW,* 143; John had 1/16 share in the ship's ownership.
10. Frank Rand, *Wordsworth's Mariner Brother* (Amherst, Mass: Newell Press, 1966), 46.
11. SG, 218.
12. *CMY,* 217–18; SG, 218.
13. Cited in SG, 219.
14. *CMY,* 213, 218.
15. Quoted in Grevel Lindop, *The Opium-Eater: A Life of Thomas De Quincey* (New York: Taplinger, 1981), 102–4; I am indebted to this fine study for other information about De Quincey.
16. *LEY,* 400.
17. Ralph M. Wardle, *Hazlitt* (Lincoln: Univ. of Nebraska Press, 1971), 70–80, for details of Hazlitt's visit to the Lakes.
18. *CLSTC,* 2:957–58.
19. *NSTC,* 1:1616–19, quoted in Wardle, *Hazlitt,* 79.
20. *Diary of Benjamin Robert Haydon,* ed. Willard Pope, 5 vols. (Cambridge: Harvard Univ. Press, 1960–63), 2:470.
21. *The Complete Works of William Hazlitt,* ed. P. P. Howe, 21 vols. (London: J. M. Dent, 1932), 19:21–24.
22. *LLY,* 3:1349–50.
23. *DWJ,* 1:255.
24. *CMY,* 221.

25. RH, 339.
26. *NSTC,* 1:1432.
27. *DWJ,* 1:198.
28. James A. Mackay, *RB: A Biography of Robert Burns* (Edinburgh: Mainstream Publishing, 1992), 627–50.
29. Robert Gittings and Jo Manton, *Dorothy Wordsworth* (Oxford: Oxford Univ. Press, 1988), 145.
30. *CMY,* 234.
31. George Macdonald Fraser, *The Steel Bonnets: The Story of the Anglo-Scottish Border Reivers* (London: Barrie & Jenkins, 1971).
32. *DWJ,* 1:389.
33. *LEY,* 403.
34. *PW,* 5:467.
35. *PW,* 5:467.
36. *CMY,* 216, n. 15.
37. *CMY,* 244, 249.
38. *Edinburgh Review,* Oct. 1802, quoted in *LEY,* 432, n. 1.
39. *LEY,* 432.
40. SG, 234.
41. *CLSTC,* 2:1013.
42. Walter J. Bate, *Coleridge* (New York: Macmillan, 1968), 118.
43. RH, 359.

Chapter 34: The End of The Prelude

1. *CLSTC,* 2:1013.
2. *NSTC,* 1:1801.
3. Paul John Eakin, *Fictions in Autobiography: Studies in the Art of Self-Invention* (Princeton: Princeton Univ. Press, 1985), 181–278; *Touching the World: Reference in Autobiography* (Princeton: Princeton Univ. Press, 1992), 54–70.
4. *CMY,* 247–48. The complicated story of the composition of the text of *The Prelude* can be read profitably in Mark Reed's introduction to his definitive text of the thirteen-book version (cited as *Thirteen*) and in the briefer accounts by Jonathan Wordsworth, M. H. Abrams, and Stephen Gill in their composite edition of all three major versions (cited as WAG).
5. *Thirteen,* 3–58 (esp. 3–5); WAG, 515–20.
6. Jonathan Wordsworth and Stephen Gill, "The Five-Book *Prelude* of Early Spring 1804," *Journal of English and Germanic Philology* 76 (1977): 1–25.
7. *LJW,* 41.
8. SG, 213–14.
9. Frank Rand, *Wordsworth's Mariner Brother* (Amherst, Mass.: Newell Press, 1966), 46–47, citing C. N. Parkinson, *Trade in the Eastern Seas* (1937), 78, 350.
10. Rand, *Mariner Brother,* 47.
11. *LJW,* 57. "William's welfare was his life's work" (54).
12. *LJW,* 41.
13. *LJW,* 44; I am indebted to Carl Ketcham's moving account of the ship's end.
14. *LMY,* 77.
15. *LEY,* 576.

16. *LEY,* 586.
17. *LEY,* 594.
18. *The Fourteen-Book "Prelude,"* ed. W. J. B. Owen (Ithaca: Cornell Univ. Press, 1985), 9–10.
19. *LEY,* 452.
20. *NSTC,* 2:2397 (text and notes).
21. *CLSTC,* 2:1165.
22. Cf. Kenneth R. Johnston, *Wordsworth and "The Recluse"* (New Haven: Yale Univ. Press, 1984), 341–48, for discussion of Coleridge's letter and its bearing on the project.
23. "Home at Grasmere," lines 620–22.

Chapter 35: Presenting the Poet

1. *CMY,* 335.
2. *CMY,* 336–37.
3. *P2V,* 527.
4. *The Farington Diary,* ed. Joseph Greig, 8 vols. (London: Hutchinson, 1922–28), 3:139.
5. Ibid., 79.
6. *Recollections of the Table-Talk of Samuel Rogers* (London: Edward Moxon, 1856), 88.
7. George McLean Harper, *William Wordsworth: His Life, Work, and Influence,* vol. 2 (London: John Murray, 1916), 113; *CMY,* 323; SG, 249.
8. Peter H. Marshall, *William Godwin* (New Haven: Yale Univ. Press, 1984), 268; William St. Clair, *The Godwins and the Shelleys* (New York: W. W. Norton, 1989), 284–85.
9. *Farington Diary,* 3:249.
10. Kenneth Curry, ed., *New Letters of Robert Southey,* 2 vols. (New York: Columbia Univ. Press, 1965), 1:392, 401.
11. *Table-Talk of Samuel Rogers,* 206n.
12. *EPF.*
13. Nov. 1, 1806, *LMY,* 89.
14. Walter J. Bate, *Coleridge* (New York: Macmillan, 1968), 119–20.
15. *NSTC,* 2:2975.
16. *NSTC,* 2:2976.
17. *NSTC,* 2:3148.
18. *NSTC,* 2:3148.
19. *NSTC,* 2:2975 (notes).
20. *NSTC,* 2:2975 (notes); no date given (from Notebook L, ff22^{v}–23).
21. Ibid.
22. *CPWSTC,* 391–92.
23. When Coleridge printed the poem in *The Friend,* he footnoted these lines with the description from his German notebooks.

Epilogue

1. The only really new trip he took was a visit to Ireland in 1829, with John Marshall, Jane Pollard's husband and MP for Leeds.
2. *PW,* 1:362.
3. SG, 202.

Appendix B

1. Sept. 28, 1798, Hampshire PRO, Wickham 1/66/f.9.
2. Nov. 2, 1798, Hampshire PRO, Wickham 1/66/f.10.
3. Jan. 22, 1798 (clearly a mistake for 1799), Hampshire PRO, Wickham 1/66/f.18.
4. Ann Hone, *For the Cause of Truth: Radicalism in London, 1796–1821* (Oxford: Clarendon Press, 1982), 74–75.
5. July 12, 1798, Hampshire PRO, Wickham, 1/66/f.2.
6. All information about these three is from Hone, *Cause of Truth,* 61.
7. Aug. 31, 1798, Hampshire PRO, Wickham, 1/66/f.6.
8. Feb. 12, 1799, Hampshire PRO, Wickham, 1/66/f.20.
9. April 2, 1799, Hampshire PRO, Wickham, 1/66/f.23.
10. Jan. 22, 1799, Hampshire PRO, Wickham, 1/66/f.18. (The year is given as 1798 but is clearly a slip for 1799.)
11. Nov. 9, 1798, Hampshire PRO, Wickham, 1/66/f.12.
12. April 25, 1799, Hampshire PRO, Wickham, 1/66/f.23.

Bibliography

Alger, J. G. *Englishmen in the French Revolution*. London: S. Low, 1889.

———. *Paris in 1789–1794: Farewell Letters of Victims of the Guillotine*. London: G. Allen, 1902.

Altick, Richard. *The Shows of London*. Cambridge, Mass.: Belknap Press, 1978.

Aulard, François-Alphonse. *La Société des Jacobins: Recueil de documents pour l'histoire du club des Jacobins de Paris*. 6 vols. Paris: Librairie Jouaust, 1889–97.

Ayling, Stephen. *Fox*. London: John Murray, 1991.

Bate, Walter J. *Coleridge*. New York: Macmillan, 1968.

Bateson, Frederick W. *Wordsworth: A Re-interpretation*. London: Longmans, Green, 1954.

Beatty, Arthur. *William Wordsworth: His Doctrine and Art in Their Historical Relations*. 1922. Reprint, Madison: Univ. of Wisconsin Press, 1960.

Benians, E. A. "St. John's College in Wordsworth's Time." In *Wordsworth at Cambridge*, 2–11, 30–36. Cambridge: Cambridge Univ. Press, 1950.

Benstead, C. R. *Portrait of Cambridge*. London: Robert Hale, 1968.

Bienvenu, Richard, ed. *The Ninth of Thermidor: The Fall of Robespierre*. New York: Oxford Univ. Press, 1968.

Billington, James. *Fire in the Minds of Men: Origins of the Revolutionary Faith*. New York: Basic Books, 1980.

Bimbenet, Jean-Eugène. *Histoire de la ville d'Orléans*. 5 vols. Orléans: H. Herluison, 1884–88.

Binns, John. *Recollections of the Life of John Binns*. Philadelphia: Parry & M'Millan, 1854.

Bonsall, Brian. *Sir James Lowther and Cumberland and Westmorland Elections, 1754–1775*. Manchester: Manchester Univ. Press, 1960.

Borer, Mary Cathcart. *An Illustrated Guide to London, 1800*. New York: St. Martin's Press, 1988.

Brown, Phillip A. *The French Revolution in English History*. 1918. Reprint, London: George Allen & Unwin, 1923.

Browning, Oscar, ed. *Despatches of Earl Gower, English Ambassador at Paris from June 1790 to August 1792*. Cambridge: Cambridge Univ. Press, 1885.

Burnett, John. *A History of the Cost of Living*. Harmondsworth: Penguin, 1969.

Bussière, George, and Emile Legouis. *Le Général Michel Beaupuy (1755–1796)*. Paris: F. Alcan, 1891.

Butler, James. "The Muse at Hawkshead: Early Criticism of Wordsworth's Poetry." *Wordsworth Circle* 20 (Summer 1989): 140.

Butler, Marilyn. *Romantics, Rebels and Reactionaries*. Oxford: Oxford Univ. Press, 1981.

Carlyle, Alexander. *Anecdotes and Characters*. Edited by James Kinsley. London: Oxford Univ. Press, 1973.

Chainey, Graham. *A Literary History of Cambridge.* Cambridge: Pevensey, 1985.

Cobban, Alfred. *Aspects of the French Revolution.* New York: G. Braziller, 1968.

Coleridge, Samuel Taylor. *Biographia Literaria.* Edited by James Engell and W. Jackson Bate. Vol. 7, pt. 2 of *The Collected Works of Samuel Taylor Coleridge.* General editor Kathleen Coburn. Bollingen Series 75. Princeton: Princeton Univ. Press, 1983.

———. *The Collected Works of Samuel Taylor Coleridge.* General editor Kathleen Coburn. 16 vols. Bollingen Series 75. Princeton: Princeton Univ. Press, 1983–.

———. *The Collected Letters of Samuel Taylor Coleridge.* Edited by Earl Leslie Griggs. 2 vols. Oxford: Clarendon Press, 1956.

———. *The Complete Poetical Works of Samuel Taylor Coleridge.* Edited by Ernest Hartley Coleridge. 2 vols. 1912. Reprint, Oxford: Clarendon Press, 1957.

———. *The Notebooks of Samuel Taylor Coleridge.* Notes and text. Edited by Kathleen Coburn. 4 vols. Bollingen Series 50. New York: Pantheon Books, 1957–.

———. *Specimens of the Table Talk of the Late Samuel Taylor Coleridge.* Edited by H. N. Coleridge. 2 vols. London: J. Murray, 1834.

Conran, Alastair. "On the Goslar Lyrics." In *Wordsworth's Mind and Art.* Edited by Alastair Thomson, 157–80. Edinburgh: Liver & Boyd, 1969.

Cooper, Charles H. *Annals of Cambridge.* Vol. 4, *1688–1849.* Cambridge: Metcalfe and Palmer, 1852.

Cooper, Lane. *A Concordance to the Poems of William Wordsworth.* New York: E. P. Dutton, 1911.

Coxe, William. *Sketches on the Natural, Civil and Political State of Swisserland.* 1776. Reprinted with additions, London: J. Dodsley, 1779.

Crabbe, George. *The Complete Poetical Works of George Crabbe.* 3 vols. Edited by Norma Dalrymple-Champneys and Arthur Pollard. Oxford: Clarendon Press, 1988.

Crook, Alec C. *From the Foundation to Gilbert Scott: A History of the Buildings of St. John's College Cambridge, 1511–1885.* Cambridge: Cambridge Univ. Press, 1980.

Dann, Joanne. "Some Notes on the Relationship between the Wordsworth and the Lowther Families." *Wordsworth Circle* 11 (1980): 80–82.

Dauban, Charles A. *La Démagogie en 1793 à Paris.* Paris: Henri Plon, 1868.

De Quincey, Thomas. *The Collected Writings.* Edited by David Masson. 11 vols. Edinburgh: Adam and Charles Black, 1890.

Erdman, David V. *Commerce des Lumières: John Oswald and the British in Paris, 1790–1793.* Columbia: Univ. of Missouri Press, 1986.

Evans, Bergen, and Hester Pinney. "Racedown and the Wordsworths." *Review of English Studies* 8 (1932): 1–18.

Farington, Joseph. *The Farington Diary.* Edited by Joseph Greig. 8 vols. London: Hutchinson, 1922–28.

Ferguson, Richard. *Cumberland and Westmorland M.P.'s from the Restoration to the Reform Bill of 1867.* London: Bell and Daldy, 1871.

Fink, Zera, ed. *The Early Wordsworthian Milieu.* Oxford: Clarendon Press, 1958.

Fitzgerald, Percy H. *The Royal Dukes and Princesses of the Family of George III: A View of Court Life and Manners for Seventy Years, 1760–1830.* London: Tinsley Brothers, 1882.

Fowler, Laurence, and Helen Fowler, eds. *Cambridge Commemorated: An Anthology of University Life.* Cambridge: Cambridge Univ. Press, 1984.

George, M. Dorothy, ed. *Catalog of Political and Personal Satires Preserved in the Department of Prints and Drawings in the British Museum.* Vols. 6–7, *1784–1800.* London: Trustees of the British Museum, 1938–42.

———. *Hogarth to Cruikshank: Social Change in Graphic Satire.* London: Allen Lane, 1967.

———. *London Life in the 18th Century.* London: Kegan Paul, Trench, Trubner, 1925.

Gill, Stephen. *William Wordsworth: A Life.* Oxford: Clarendon Press, 1989.

Gilmour, Ian. *Riots, Risings, and Revolutions: Government and Violence in Eighteenth-Century England.* London: Pimlico, 1993.

Gilpin, William. *Observations on the River Wye and Several Parts of South Wales, Related Chiefly to Picturesque Beauty, Made in the Summer of 1770.* London: R. Blamire, 1782.

Gittings, Robert, and Jo Manton. *Dorothy Wordsworth.* Oxford: Oxford Univ. Press, 1988.

Goodwin, Albert. *The Friends of Liberty: The English Democratic Movement in the Age of the French Revolution.* Cambridge: Harvard Univ. Press, 1979.

Graver, Bruce. "Wordsworth's Translations from Latin Poetry." Ph.D. diss., Univ. of North Carolina, 1983.

Gray, Arthur B. *Cambridge Revisited.* 1921. Reprint, Cambridge: Par Stephens, 1974.

Harper, George McLean. "Did Wordsworth Defy the Guillotine?" In *Spirit of Delight.* New York: Henry Holt, 1928.

———. *William Wordsworth: His Life, Works, and Influence.* Vol. 1. London: John Murray, 1916.

———. *Wordsworth's French Daughter: The Story of Her Birth, with the Certificates of Her Baptism and Marriage.* 1921. Reprint, New York: Russell & Russell, 1967.

———. "Wordsworth at Blois." In *John Morley and Other Essays,* 111–24. Princeton: Princeton Univ. Press, 1920.

Havens, Raymond. *The Mind of a Poet: A Study of Wordsworth's Thought with Particular Reference to "The Prelude."* Baltimore: Johns Hopkins Univ. Press, 1941.

Hayden, Donald E. *Wordsworth's Travels in Europe.* Tulsa: Univ. of Tulsa, 1988.

———. *Wordsworth's Travels in Wales and Ireland.* Tulsa: Univ. of Tulsa, 1985.

———. *Wordsworth's Walking Tour of 1790.* Tulsa: Univ. of Tulsa, 1983.

Hazlitt, William. *The Complete Works of William Hazlitt.* 21 vols. Edited by P. P. Howe. London: J. M. Dent, 1932.

Hesdin, Raoul. *The Journal of a Spy in Paris during the Reign of Terror, January–July 1794.* New York: Harper, 1895.

Hinde, Wendy. *Castlereagh.* London: Collins, 1981.

———. *George Canning.* 1973. Reprint, Oxford: Basil Blackwell, 1989.

Holcroft, Thomas. *Memoirs of the late Thomas Holcroft, Written by Himself, and Continuing to the Time of His Death, from His Diary, Notes, and Other Papers.* London: Longman, Hurst, Rees, Orme & Brown, 1816.

Holmes, Richard. *Coleridge: Early Visions.* New York: Viking, 1993.

Hone, Ann. *For the Cause of Truth: Radicalism in London, 1796–1821.* Oxford: Clarendon Press, 1982.

Hughes, Robert. *The Fatal Shore.* New York: Alfred A. Knopf, 1986.

Hunt, Bishop. "Wordsworth's Marginalia on *Paradise Lost,*" *Bulletin of the New York Public Library* 73 (1969): 167–83.

Izenberg, Gerald N. *Impossible Individuality: Romanticism, Revolution, and the Origins of Modern Selfhood, 1787–1802.* Princeton: Princeton Univ. Press, 1992.

Jacob, Louis. *Les Suspects pendant la Révolution, 1789–94.* Paris: Hachette, 1952.

Jacobus, Mary. *Tradition and Experience in Wordsworth's "Lyrical Ballads" (1798).* Oxford: Oxford Univ. Press, 1976.

Johnston, Kenneth R. *Wordsworth and "The Recluse."* New Haven: Yale Univ. Press, 1984.

Jordan, John E. *Why the "Lyrical Ballads"?: The Background, Writing, and Character of Wordsworth's 1798 "Lyrical Ballads."* Berkeley: Univ. of California Press, 1976.

Jupp, Peter. *Lord Grenville, 1759–1834.* Oxford: Clarendon Press, 1985.

Kates, Gary. *The Cercle Social, the Girondins, and the French Revolutions.* Princeton: Princeton Univ. Press, 1985.

Kelley, Paul. "The Literary Sources of William Wordsworth's Works, 10 July 1793 to 10 July 1797." Ph.D. diss., Univ. of Hull, 1987.

Kennedy, Michael L. *The Jacobin Clubs in the French Revolution: The First Years.* Princeton: Princeton Univ. Press, 1982.

———. *The Jacobin Clubs in the French Revolution: The Middle Years.* Princeton: Princeton Univ. Press, 1988.

Kerr, Wilfred. *The Reign of Terror, 1793–94: The Experiment of the Democratic Republic and the Rise of the Bourgeoisie.* Toronto: Univ. of Toronto Press, 1927.

Knight, William. *Coleridge and Wordsworth in the West Country: Their Friendship, Work, and Surroundings.* London: Elkin Matthews, 1913.

Lamb, Charles, and Mary Lamb. *The Letters of Charles and Mary Lamb.* Edited by Edwin W. Marrs. 2 vols. Ithaca: Cornell Univ. Press, 1975–76.

Lefebvre, Georges. *Etudes Orléanaises.* 2 vols. Paris: Commission d'histoire economique et sociale de la Révolution, 1962–63.

———. *The French Revolution.* 2 vols. Translated by Elizabeth Moss Evanson. New York: Columbia Univ. Press, 1962.

Legouis, Emile. *The Early Life of William Wordsworth, 1770–1798: A Study of "The Prelude."* Edited by Nicholas Roe. London: Libris, 1988. [Originally published as *La Jeunesse de William Wordsworth.* Paris: G. Masson, 1896.]

———. *William Wordsworth and Annette Vallon.* 1922. Expanded by Pierre Legouis. Hamden, Conn.: Archon Books, 1967.

Lindop, Grevel. *The Opium-Eater: A Life of Thomas De Quincey.* New York: Taplinger, 1981.

Liu, Alan. *Wordsworth: The Sense of History.* Stanford: Stanford Univ. Press, 1989.

Lowes, J. L. *The Road to Xanadu: A Study in the Ways of the Imagination.* Boston: Houghton Mifflin, 1927.

Mackay, James A. *RB: A Biography of Robert Burns.* Edinburgh: Mainstream Publishing, 1992.

Magnuson, Paul. *Coleridge and Wordsworth: A Lyrical Dialogue.* Princeton: Princeton Univ. Press, 1988.

Manning, Peter. "Placing Poor Susan: Wordsworth and the New Historicism." *Studies in Romanticism* 25 (Fall 1986): 351–69.

Mansel, Philip. *Louis XVI.* London: Blond and Briggs, 1981.

Marshall, Peter H. *William Godwin.* New Haven: Yale Univ. Press, 1984.

Mathews, Charles. *Memoirs of Charles Mathews, Comedian.* Edited by Anne Mathews. 4 vols. London: Richard Bentley, 1838.

Matlak, Richard. *The Poetry of Relationship.* New York: St. Martin's Press, 1997.

———. "Wordsworth's Lucy Poems in Psychobiographical Context." *PMLA* 93 (1978): 46–65.

Mayberry, Tom. *Coleridge and Wordsworth in the West Country.* Phoenix Mill: Alan Sutton, 1992.

McCracken, David. *Wordsworth and the Lake District: A Guide to the Poems and Their Places.* Oxford: Oxford Univ. Press, 1985.

McKendrick, Neil, John Brewer, and J. H. Plumb. *The Birth of a Consumer Society: The Commercialization of Eighteenth-Century England.* Bloomington: Indiana Univ. Press, 1982.

Moorman, Mary. *William Wordsworth: A Biography.* Vol. 1, *The Early Years, 1770–1803.* Oxford: Clarendon Press, 1957.

Nelson, R. R. *The Home Office, 1792–1801.* Duke Historical Publications. Durham: Duke Univ. Press, 1969.

Owen, Hugh. *The Lowther Family.* Chichester: Phillimore, 1990.

Pares, Richard. *A West-India Fortune.* Hamden, Conn.: Archon Books, 1950.

Parreaux, André. *Daily Life in England in the Reign of George III.* Translated by Carola Congreve. London: Allen & Unwin, 1969.

Pennant, Thomas. *A Tour in Wales, 1773.* London: Henry Hughes, 1778–84.

Piper, H. W. *The Active Universe: Pantheism and the Concept of the Imagination in the English Romantic Poets.* London: Athlone Press, 1962.

Pollock, John. *Wilberforce.* London: Constable, 1977.

Porter, Bernard. *Plots and Paranoia: A History of Political Espionage in Britain, 1790–1988.* London: Unwin Hyman, 1989.

Postgate, Raymond. *Story of a Year: 1798.* New York: Harcourt, Brace & World, 1969.

Pryme, George. *Autobiographic Recollections.* Cambridge: Deighton, Bell, 1870.

Quenell, Peter. *Romantic England: Writing and Painting 1717–1851.* London: Weidenfeld & Nicholson, 1970.

Rand, Frank. *Wordsworth's Mariner Brother.* Amherst, Mass.: Newell Press, 1966.

Reed, Mark L. *Wordsworth: The Chronology of the Early Years, 1770–1799.* Cambridge: Harvard Univ. Press, 1967.

———. *Wordsworth: The Chonology of the Middle Years, 1800–1815.* Cambridge: Harvard Univ. Press, 1975.

Robertson, Eric. *Wordsworthshire.* London: Chatto and Windus, 1911.

Robinson, Henry Crabb. *Diary, Reminiscences, and Correspondence.* Edited by Thomas Sadler. 3 vols. London: Macmillan, 1869.

Roe, Nicholas. "Citizen Wordsworth." *Wordsworth Circle* 14 (Winter 1983): 21–30.

———. "Imagining Robespierre." In *Coleridge's Imagination: Essays in Memory of Peter Laver,* ed. R. Gravil, L. Newlyn, and N. Roe, 161–78. Cambridge: Cambridge Univ. Press, 1985.

———. *The Politics of Nature: Wordsworth and Some Contemporaries.* London: Macmillan Academic and Professional, 1992.

———. "Radical George: Dyer in the 1790's." *Charles Lamb Bulletin,* n.s. 49 (Jan. 1985): 17–26.

———. *Wordsworth and Coleridge: The Radical Years.* Oxford: Clarendon Press, 1988.

———. "Wordsworth, Samuel Nicholson, and the Society for Constitutional Information." *Wordsworth Circle* 13 (1982): 197–201.

———. "Wordsworth's Account of Beaupuy's Death." *Notes and Queries* 32 (Sept. 1985): 337.

Rogers, Samuel. *Recollections of the Table Talk of Samuel Rogers, to Which Is Added "Porsoniana."* London: Edward Moxon, 1856.

Ross, Marlon. *The Contours of Masculine Desire: Romanticism and the Rise of Women's Poetry.* New York: Oxford Univ. Press, 1989.

Sandford, Margaret E. *Thomas Poole and His Friends.* 2 vols. London: Macmillan, 1888.

Schama, Simon. *Citizens: A Chronicle of the French Revolution.* New York: Alfred A. Knopf, 1989.

Schneider, Ben Ross. *Wordsworth's Cambridge Education.* Cambridge: Cambridge Univ. Press, 1957.

Schwartz, Richard. *Daily Life in Johnson's London.* Madison: Univ. of Wisconsin Press, 1985.

Scrivener, Michael, ed. *Poetry and Reform: Periodical Verse from the English Democratic Press.* Detroit: Wayne State Univ. Press, 1992.

Sheats, Paul D. *The Making of Wordsworth's Poetry, 1785–1798.* Cambridge: Harvard Univ. Press, 1973.

Simpson, David. "What Bothered Charles Lamb about Poor Susan?" *Studies in English Literature, 1500–1800* 26 (Autumn 1986): 589–612.

St. Clair, William. *The Godwins and the Shelleys: A Biography of a Family.* New York: W. W. Norton, 1989.

Soboul, Albert, ed. *Dictionnaire historique de la Révolution Française.* Paris: Presses universitaires de France, 1989.

Sparrow, Elizabeth. "The Swiss and Swabian Agencies, 1795–1801." *Historical Journal* 35 (1992): 861–84.

Sutherland, Donald M. *France, 1789–1815: Revolution and Counterrevolution.* New York: Oxford Univ. Press, 1986.

Taylor, John. *Records of My Own Life; by the Late John Taylor, Esquire.* London: E. Bull, 1832.

Thompson, E. P. "Disenchantment or Default? A Lay Sermon." In *Power and Consciousness,* ed. Conor Cruise O'Brien and William Vanech. New York: New York Univ. Press, 1969.

———. *The Making of the English Working Class.* New York: Vintage Books, 1966.

Thompson, J. M. *English Witnesses of the French Revolution.* Oxford: Blackwell, 1958.

Thompson. T. W. *Wordsworth's Hawkshead.* Edited by Robert Woof. London: Oxford Univ. Press, 1970.

Thornbury, Walter. *Old and New London: A Narrative of Its History, Its People, and Its Places.* 6 vols. London: Cassell, Petter and Galpin, 1873–78.

Tomalin, Claire. *The Life and Death of Mary Wollstonecraft.* London: Weidenfeld & Nicolson, 1974.

———. *Mrs. Jordan's Profession: The Actress and the Prince.* New York: Alfred A. Knopf, 1995.

Tuckerman, Una. "Wordsworth's Plan for His Imitation of Juvenal." *Modern Language Notes* 40 (1930): 209–15.

Welford, Richard. *Men of Mark Twixt Tyne and Tweed.* 3 vols. London: W. Scott, 1895.

Vansittart, Peter. *Voices of the Revolution.* London: Collins, 1968.

Wardle, Ralph M. *Hazlitt.* Lincoln: Univ. of Nebraska Press, 1971.

Watts, Alaric. *Alaric Watts: A Narrative of His Life.* 2 vols. London: R. Bentley, 1884. Reprint, New York: AMS Press, 1974.

Wells, Roger. *Insurrection: The British Experience, 1795–1803.* Gloucester: Alan Sutton, 1983.

Wildi, Max. "Wordsworth and the Simplon Pass." *English Studies* 40 (1959): 224–32.

Williams, Helen Maria. *Letters from France.* 8 vols. in 2. Edited by Janet Todd. Delmar, N.Y.: Scholar's Facsimiles, 1975.

Willoughby, L. A. "Wordsworth and Germany." In *German Studies Presented to Professor H. G. Fiedler,* 432–58. Oxford: Clarendon Press, 1938.

Wollstonecraft, Mary. *The Works of Mary Wollstonecraft.* Edited by Janet Todd and Marilyn Butler. London: Pickering, 1989.

Wordsworth, Christopher. *Social Life at the English Universities in the Eighteenth Century.* Cambridge: Deighton, Bell, 1874.

Wordsworth, Dorothy. *Journals of Dorothy Wordsworth.* Edited by Ernest de Selincourt. 2 vols. New York: Macmillan, 1941.

Wordsworth, John. *The Letters of John Wordsworth.* Edited by Carl H. Ketcham. Ithaca: Cornell Univ. Press, 1969.

Wordsworth, Jonathan. "The Five-Book Prelude of Early Spring 1804." *Journal of English and Germanic Philology* 76 (1977): 1–25.

———. *Music of Humanity.* London: Thomas Nelson, 1969.

———, ed. *Bicentenary Wordsworth Studies in Memory of John Alban Finch.* Ithaca: Cornell Univ. Press, 1970.

Wordsworth, William. *Descriptive Sketches.* Edited by Eric Birdsall. The Cornell Wordsworth. General editor Stephen Parrish. Ithaca: Cornell Univ. Press, 1984.

———. *Early Poems and Fragments 1784–Mid 1797.* Edited by Jared Curtis and Carol Landon. The Cornell Wordsworth. General editor Stephen Parrish. Ithaca: Cornell Univ. Press, 1998.

———. *An Evening Walk.* Edited by James Averill. The Cornell Wordsworth. General editor Stephen Parrish. Ithaca: Cornell Univ. Press, 1984.

———. *Lyrical Ballads and Other Poems, 1797–1800.* Edited by James Butler and Karen Green. The Cornell Wordsworth. General editor Stephen Parrish. Ithaca: Cornell Univ. Press, 1992.

———. *Poems, in Two Volumes and Other Poems, 1800–1807.* Edited by Jared Curtis. Ithaca: Cornell Univ. Press, 1983.

———. *The Poetical Works.* Edited by Ernest de Selincourt and Helen Darbishire. 5 vols. 1940–49. Reprint, Oxford: Clarendon Press, 1967–72.

———. *The Prelude, 1798–1799.* Edited by Stephen Parrish. The Cornell Wordsworth. General editor Stephen Parrish. Ithaca: Cornell Univ. Press, 1977.

———. *The Prelude 1799, 1805, 1855.* Edited by Jonathan Wordsworth, M. H. Abrams, and Stephen Gill. Norton Critical Edition. New York: W. W. Norton, 1979.

———. *The Prose Works of William Wordsworth.* Edited by Alexander Grosart. 3 vols. London: Edward Moxon, 1876.

———. *The Prose Works of William Wordsworth.* Edited by W. J. B. Owen and Jane Worthington Smyser. 3 vols. Oxford: Clarendon Press, 1974.

———. *The Ruined Cottage and The Pedlar.* Edited by James Butler. The Cornell Wordsworth. General editor Stephen Parrish. Ithaca: Cornell Univ. Press, 1979.

———. *The Salisbury Plain Poems.* Edited by Stephen Gill. The Cornell Wordsworth. General editor Stephen Parrish. Ithaca: Cornell Univ. Press, 1975.

———. *Shorter Poems, 1807–1820.* Edited by Carl Ketcham. The Cornell Wordsworth. General editor Stephen Parrish. Ithaca: Cornell Univ. Press, 1989.

———. *The Thirteen-Book Prelude.* Edited by Mark Reed. 2 vols. The Cornell Wordsworth. General editor Stephen Parrish. Ithaca: Cornell Univ. Press, 1991.

———. *William Wordsworth: The Poems.* Vol. 1. Edited by John O. Hayden. New Haven: Yale Univ. Press, 1981.

Wordsworth, William, and Dorothy Wordsworth. *The Letters of William and Dorothy Wordsworth: The Early Years 1787–1805.* Edited by Ernest de Selincourt. 2d ed. Revised by Chester L. Shaver. Oxford: Clarendon Press, 1967.

———. *The Letters of William and Dorothy Wordsworth: The Later Years.* Edited by Ernest de Selincourt. 2d ed. Edited by Alan G. Hill. 5 vols. Oxford: Clarendon Press, 1978–93.

———. *The Letters of William and Dorothy Wordsworth: The Middle Years.* Edited by Ernest de Selincourt. 2d ed. Revised by Mary Moorman. 2 vols. Oxford: Clarendon Press, 1969–70.

Wordsworth, William, and Samuel Taylor Coleridge. *Lyrical Ballads.* Edited by Michael Mason. London: Longman, 1992.

Wright, J. M. F. *Alma Mater; or, Seven Years at the University of Cambridge.* 2 vols. London: Black, Young and Tavistock, 1827.

Wuscher, Hermann J. *Liberty, Equality, and Fraternity in Wordsworth, 1791–1800.* Stockholm: Almqvist & Wiksell International, 1980.

INDEX

Account of London (Pennant), 275
Act of Union of 1715, 802
Adam, Robert, 27
Addison, Joseph, 244, 261*n*
"Address to Liberty" (Tweddell), 163
"Address to Poverty," 446, 481
"Address to Silence" (Wordsworth), 446
Address to the Inhabitants of Cambridge (Frend), 177
Address to the Members of the Church of England (Frend), 178
"Address to the Ocean" (Wordsworth), 446, 490
"Address to the Public" (London Corresponding Society), 438, 441
"Address to the Scholars of the Village School" (Wordsworth), 642
"Adventures on Salisbury Plain" (Wordsworth), 345–46, 483, 489, 501, 508, 509, 544, 567, 568, 624, 677, 743
  analysis of, 483–85
  Coleridge's praise of, 488–89
"Ad Vilmum Axiologum" (Coleridge), 831
Adye, Ralph, 818–19
Aeneid (Virgil), 72, 843
"Aeolian Harp, The" (Coleridge), 557
Aikin, Lucy, *see* Barbauld, Anna
Akenside, Mark, 74, 96
Albion, 249
Alfoxden House, 507, 520, 550–51, 605, 628, 636, 637
  Coleridge's description of, 521
  Hazlitt's visit to, 581–83
  Home Office investigation of, 525–34, 606
  "Spy Nozy" incident and, 527–28, 533, 535, 548
  visitors to, 522–23, 536–38
  WW's departure from, 588–89
  WW's renting of, 520–21
  see also Nether Stowey
"Alfoxden Journal" (Dorothy Wordsworth), 550–51
"Alice Fell; or, Poverty" (Wordsworth), 773–74, 776
Alien Office, British, 433*n,* 531, 606*n,* 609
Almanach du Père Gérard, L' (Collot d'Herbois), 289
Almanack of Goodman Gerard, The (Oswald), 290
American Revolution, 186, 343, 350
Amiens, Peace of, 11, 296, 523, 769, 787, 802
Amis de la Constitution, 300–301, 303, 309
  see also Jacobin Clubs
Amis des Noirs, Les, 287, 291
Anabasis (Xenophon), 118
Anacreon, 71, 98–99
Analogy of Religion, Natural and Revealed, to the Constitution and Course of Nature (Butler), 162, 166
Analytical Review, 486, 676
"Ancient English Minstrels, The" (Percy), 83–84
"Ancient Mariner," *see* "Rime of the Ancient Mariner"
Anderson, William, 682
André, Jean François, 633
"Andrew Jones" (Wordsworth), 723, 734
"Anecdote for Fathers" (Wordsworth), 586, 604–5
Annales Patriotiques et Littéraires (Carra), 309
Anna St. Yves (Holcroft), 494
Annual Register, 87
"Anticipation" (Wordsworth), 807
Anti-Jacobin, 117, 352*n,* 532, 568, 579–81, 606, 608, 614, 662, 663, 718, 767
  "New Morality" satire by, 598–603, 604, 607, 717
  Pitt and, 603–4
Anti-Jacobin Review and Magazine; or, Monthly Political and Literary Censor, 580, 599, 676, 677, 825

Arabian Nights, 48, 75
Arcadia (Sidney), 148
Arch brothers, 600, 608, 675
"Argument for Suicide" (Wordsworth), 481–82, 585, 778–79
Ariosto, Ludovico, 306, 408, 649, 790–91
Armfield, Thomas, 311*n*
Army of the Coasts of Cherbourg, 372
Arnold, Matthew, 6, 710
Ars Amatoria (Ovid), 651
Art of War, The (Fawcett), 242
Ash Farm, 542
Association for the Protection of Liberty and Property against Republicans and Levellers, 185, 254
As You Like It (Shakespeare), 648–49
Aubrey, John, 487
Auden, W. H., 774
Augustine, Saint, 843
Austen, Jane, 110*n,* 281, 423, 472–73, 520, 714
Austerlitz, battle of, 806
Austria, 612, 614, 665
"Autobiographical Memoranda" (Wordsworth), 74
"Autumn" (Thomson), 83
"Away, away" (Wordsworth), 585–87, 777
Axiologus (pseudonym), 831

Bage, Robert, 494, 767, 837
Bailey, Thomas, 366, 383
"Baker's Cart, The" (Wordsworth), 479–80
Baldwin, John, 612
Ball, Alexander, 809
"Ballad Michael" (Wordsworth), 744–45
"Ballad of the Dark Ladie, The" (Coleridge), 583, 691–92, 737
Ballynamuck, battle of, 620
"Bamborough Castle" (Bowles), 352
Bank of England, 529
Barbauld, Anna (Lucy Aikin), 74, 79, 80, 325, 752, 841
"Bard, The" (Gray), 266
"Bard's Epitaph, A" (Burns), 86
Barère, Bertrand, 382
Barker, Elizabeth, 417
Barker, Francis, 417
Barker, Robert, 251
Bartholomew Fair, 261–63, 279
Bastille, fall of, 162, 254
Bateman, Richard, 747
Bateson, F. W., 10
Beattie, James, 74, 87, 360, 466, 812
  WW influenced by, 78, 83, 84–86, 88–89, 272–73, 277
Beaumarchais, Pierre-Augustin de, 437
Beaumont, George, 418, 422, 761, 807, 816, 817–18, 819, 825
  WW's first meeting with, 794
Beaumont, Lady, 795, 817
Beaupuy, Michel-Arnaud Bacharetie de, 302–7, 308, 310, 311*n,* 321, 323, 338, 370, 379, 384, 435, 442, 649, 653
  death of, 307, 385–86
  in *Prelude,* 305, 307
Beaupuy, Nicholas de, 311*n*
Beauties of the Anti-Jacobin, The, 717
Beautiful, 19, 35, 36, 38–39
"Beauty and Moonlight" (Wordsworth), 100, 104, 584
Beauty of Buttermere, The (play), 252
Beckett, John, 23*n*
Beddoes, Thomas, 537–38, 656, 724
Bede, Venerable, 732
Bedford, Duke of, 365
Beethoven, Ludwig van, 561, 569
"Beggars" (Wordsworth), 773
Behn, Aphra, 123
Belgium, 231–32, 376
Bell, John, 466
Bellenden, William, 182
Belmore, Lord, 342
"Benevolus" (pseudonym), 431
Benoni, David, 101, 102, 356
Benson, John, 45, 53, 54, 58
Bernstorff, Count, 624
Best, Thomas, 434, 616
Bibbes, Mr., 615
Bible, 596–97, 709*n*
Biggs & Cottle, 736
Biographia Literaria (Coleridge), 180, 518, 569, 570, 578, 661, 694, 736
  Lyrical Ballads in, 764
  "Spy Nozy" incident in, 527–28
Birdlipsch, Count, 655
Birkett, Edward, 125, 127, 190
Birkett, Ted, 58
"Birth of Love, The" (Wordsworth, transl.), 467
Blackbarrow Foundry Company, 55
Blackburn (student), 166
Blackburne, Francis, 176
"Black Legion," 529
Blackmore, Richard, 487
Blackwell, General, 665
Blackwood's Magazine, 366*n*
Blair, Hugh, 78
Blake, William, 162, 224, 243, 248, 324, 585–86, 756, 841

Bligh, William, 68, 496*n*
Bloss, General, 385
Boccaccio, Giovanni, 486
Bonneville, Nicolas de, 322
Bonney, T. G., 170
Bonnycastle, John, 164
Book of Common Prayer, 34, 709*n*
Book of Martyrs (Foxe), 72
Book of Thel, The (Blake), 224, 585–86
Borderers, The (Wordsworth), 286, 322, 444, 479, 480, 485, 486, 488, 494–505, 510, 511, 515, 544, 547, 548, 567, 580, 677, 719, 802, 836, 840
  Annette Vallon and, 501, 502
  biographical connections in, 502–4
  Coleridge and, 507
  Covent Garden's rejection of, 545–46
  dramatic reading of, 525
  Godwinism rejected in, 491, 495–96
  guilt theme in, 539–40
  literary sources of, 497–99
  moral dilemma in, 494–95
  Paradise Lost as source of, 499
  plot of, 496–97, 500
  preface to, 468, 497, 501–2
  as *Prelude*'s forerunner, 497–99, 504
  Rivers character in, 499–500, 501, 540, 545, 667
  Schiller's *Robbers* and, 539
  setting of, 500–501
  themes of, 494–95
  WW's identification with, 501–3
  WW's personal history and, 495
Borromeo, Count, 212
Boswell, James, 31*n,* 130, 245–46, 329–30, 449
"Botany Bay Eclogues" (Southey), 576, 577, 608
Bounty, 68, 496*n*
Bourdon, Léonard, 290, 314, 371, 373, 376, 382–83, 392, 619
Bowles, William, 180–81, 332, 343, 352, 539
Bowman, James, 688
Bowman, Thomas, 72
"Boy of Winander" (Wordsworth), 48
Brabançonne (Brabant) revolution, 232
Bradley, A. C., 842–43
Braithwaite, Philip, 50–51, 76
Braithwaite, William, 53, 63–64, 67
Brathwaite, Reginald, 64, 116, 152, 231, 816
Brathwaite family, 64–65
Braxfield, Judge, 402
Brissot, Jacques-Pierre, 282, 287, 289, 291–92, 301, 317–18, 320, 321, 323, 326, 329, 365, 366, 371, 382–83, 435
Bristol West Indies Trading Company, 468
British Club, 324, 326, 328, 619
British Critic, 751
British Museum (London), 247
Brook, The (Coleridge), 561–62
Brothers, Richard, 459
"Brothers, The" (Wordsworth), 297*n,* 688, 722, 744, 747, 755, 756, 757
  assessment of, 726–27
Browning, Robert, 6, 840
Brunswick, Duke of, 310
Bucer, Martin, 595*n*
Buckingham, Duke of, 258
Bucks of the First Head (Rowlandson), 120
Budworth, Joseph, 62–63
Bulletin des amis de la vérité, 318
Bunyan, John, 172
Burdett, Francis, 548
Bureau de l'Esprit Public, 318
Bürger, Gottfried August, 637, 666, 694
  Lyrical Ballads influenced by, 625–26
Burges, James Bland, 752, 753
Burke, Edmund, 30*n,* 177, 182, 185, 242, 254, 275, 305, 324, 334, 336, 339, 340, 364–65, 433, 486, 494, 499, 532, 681, 754
  "dagger" speech of, 330
  Fox's debates with, 254–57
  in *Prelude,* 255, 256
  as target of liberals, 447
Burleigh, Henry, 435, 444
Burnet, Thomas, 487
Burnett, George, 517, 525, 600, 609, 794
Burney, Charles, 675–76, 725
Burns, Robert, 72, 74, 324, 339, 569, 576*n,* 652, 776, 803, 827, 835
  WW influenced by, 78, 81, 83, 85–87
  WW's poems on, 798–800
Bute, John Stuart, Lord, 20–21, 30*n,* 112, 120
Butler, Joseph, 162, 166, 169
Butler, Samuel, 172
Butler, Tom, 158
Buzot, François, 319
Byatt, A. S., 585
Byron, George Gordon, Lord, 5, 6, 9, 122, 131, 165, 169, 185, 199, 203, 519, 720, 767, 835, 836, 840–41

Cabinet, 441, 498
Caleb Williams, see Things as They are; or, Caleb Williams
Calvert, Ann, 423

Calvert, Raisley, 341, 342, 401, 405, 428, 452, 510*n*, 538, 677, 684, 689
death of, 401, 426
in *Prelude*, 422
WW's financial arrangements with, 401, 417, 418, 420–25, 429–30, 450, 782
Calvert, William, 340–41, 342, 343, 345, 347–48, 360–61, 362, 401, 405, 416, 420, 424, 425–26, 452, 684, 689, 762
WW's correspondence with, 421–22, 423, 828
Calvert Charitable Trust, 405*n*
Cambridge University, 111–34
described, 114–15
dress of, 120–21
educational process of, 111–12, 118–19
examination system of, 156, 164–67, 173
French Revolution and, 175–76
freshman curriculum of, 118–20
leisure reading at, 123–24
mock debates at, 164–65
nonacademic pursuits at, 121–24
as Pitt's power base, 184–86
political life of, 176–80
in *Prelude*, 171–74, 770
St. John's College of, 115–17, 119–20, 156, 157, 159, 184
sexual licentiousness at, 120, 127–30
social life of, 124–27
student categories at, 119–20
Unitarianism and, 176–77
WW's arrival at, 113–14
WW's academic career at, 122–23, 155–58, 165–66, 168–74, 186–87, 240
WW's final exam at, 239–40
WW's friendships at, 116–19, 170–71
WW's sexual experience at, 130–32
Camelford, Lord, 657
Campbell, Thomas, 96
Campo Formio, Treaty of, 612–13
Canning, George, 117, 532, 599, 600, 603, 614, 617, 662, 663, 664, 666, 676, 848
Cannonian club, 438
Canterbury Tales (Chaucer), 770–71
Carbonnières, Ramond de, 659
Carlisle, Lord Howard, Earl of, 802
Carlyle, Thomas, 19, 362–64, 366, 382, 383, 387, 840, 841
Carlyon, Clement, 655–56
Carnot, Lazare, 303
Carra, Jean-Louis, 287, 292, 309–10, 365
Carter, Elizabeth, 74, 79–80
Carter, John, 818
"Castaway, The" (Cowper), 92
Castlehow, Frank, 53, 58, 59, 76
Castlehow, Jonathan, 58
Castlehow, Ruth, 58
Castlehow, Tom, 53, 58, 59, 76
Castlereagh, Robert Stewart, Viscount, 117, 614*n*
Castle-Spectre, The (Lewis), 546–49, 580, 581, 754
"Castle to the Author" (Wordsworth), 38
Castley (student), 125
"Catechizing" (Wordsworth), 34–35
Cato's Letters, 466–67
Catullus, 98–99
Causes and Consequences of the Present War, The (Erskine), 486
Cavendish, Georgiana, 752
Cercle Social, Le, 291, 323
Cervantes, Miguel de, 76
Chantonnay, battle of, 375
"Character, A" (Wordsworth), 191
"Characteristics" (Carlyle), 840
Charles I, King of England, 326, 342
Chatterton, Thomas, 74, 78, 776
Chaucer, Geoffrey, 132, 169, 790
WW's modernizations of, 770–71
Chaumette, Pierre "Anaxagoras," 389
Chepstow Castle, 352*n*, 353–54
Chester, John, 525, 566, 609, 611, 612, 620–21, 627, 662
Chesterfield, Lord, 77
Chevallier, William, 128, 158
Cheverny, Comte de, 302
Childe Harold's Pilgrimage (Byron), 835
"Childless Father, The" (Wordsworth), 742, 751
Children in the Wood, The (Morton), 546
"Chimney Sweeper" (Blake), 756
China, 793–94
Cholet, battle of, 384, 385
"Christabel" (Coleridge), 583, 745, 751
"Lay of the Last Minstrel" and, 801–2
WW's rejection of, 741–43
"Christabel Notebook," 658
Christian, Edward, 68, 72, 114, 278, 414, 496*n*
Christian, Fletcher, 68, 496*n*, 499
Christian, John, *see* Curwen, John Christian
Christie, Thomas, 314
Chronique du mois, 290–91, 317, 322
Churchill, Charles, 84
Church of England, 58
Citizen, 439
"City French and English Juvenile Library," 825
Civil Constitution of the Clergy, French, 197, 292
Clare, John, 78
Clarence, Duke of, 133*n*, 251, 532, 752
Clarissa Harlowe (Richardson), 239–40

Clarke, James, 153
Clarkson, Catherine, 689–90, 712
Clarkson, Thomas, 179, 261, 774
Classical Arrangement of Fugitive Poetry (Bell), 466
"Clericus" (pseudonym), 450–51, 454–55
Clifford, Henry, 689
Cloots, Jean-Baptiste "Anarchasis," 381
Coburg, Prince of, 376
Coleridge, Berkeley, 578, 644, 645, 679, 687
Coleridge, Derwent, 687, 745
Coleridge, Hartley, 565, 687, 713, 716, 829
Coleridge, Samuel Taylor, 4, 5, 11, 13–14, 50, 52, 74, 80, 100, 117, 119, 133, 157, 160, 163, 169, 178, 179, 180, 249, 252, 260, 285*n*, 332, 387, 391, 428, 429, 433*n*-34*n*, 436, 437, 438, 439, 444, 451–52, 457, 463, 471, 473, 486, 490, 492, 498, 504, 532, 536, 547, 550, 555, 576, 581, 588, 589, 603, 604, 607, 608, 615, 626, 637, 642, 644–45, 652, 663, 664, 669, 677, 679, 709*n*, 711, 714, 727, 733, 741, 744, 749, 751, 760, 770, 780, 783, 794, 795, 796, 806, 808, 816, 837, 838, 839, 841, 842, 843
  Alfoxden House described by, 521
  Borderers and, 507
  "Cain" collaboration and, 543–44
  in Cheddar Gorge walking tour, 578–79
  and creation of Romanticism, 514, 518–19
  Dorothy's relationship with, 517–18, 541, 684
  in German tour, 565–66, 609–11, 618, 619–22, 627, 629, 631–33, 635, 655–56, 657, 661–62, 847, 848
  Grasmere visited by, 686, 713, 716, 719
  guilt and remorse in poetry of, 539–41, 543
  health of, 518, 750, 762, 809, 810
  Home Office's spy investigation and, 526, 527–28, 530, 531
  at Jesus College, Cambridge, 279
  Klopstock visit and, 623–24
  "Kubla Khan" composed by, 541–43
  in Lake Country tour, 683–90
  Lloyd and, 516, 517–18, 579–80, 712–13
  on *Lyrical Ballads* of 1800, 721–22, 724–25
  Malta sojourn of, 809
  Morning Post position and, 689–90, 716–18, 725
  Nether Stowey and, 516–18, 543–44
  "New Morality" satire on, 599, 600–601
  open letter to Fox by, 792–93
  opium used by, 542
  Osorio revised by, 538–39, 540
  pantheism of, 558–59
  poetry-reciting manner of, 582
  politics and, 483–84
  preface of *Lyrical Ballads* and, 736–40
  Prelude and, 810–11
  presentation copies of *Lyrical Ballads* and, 752, 753
  pseudonyms of, 584
  Racedown visit of, 514–15
  Recluse and, 465–66, 506–7, 561, 564–66, 680–82, 810–11, 818–19
  Recluse notes lost by, 818–19
  rejection of *Osorio* and, 546
  "Ruined Cottage" and, 512–15, 553, 572–73, 579
  Salisbury Plain poems and, 488–89
  Sara Hutchinson and, 683, 690–92, 720, 762, 789, 790, 821–22, 829–31, 832
  satires by, 717
  in Scotland tour of 1803, 797–98, 800
  sense of humor of, 559–60, 579
  at Sockburn-on-Tees, 682–83
  "Spy Nozy" incident and, 527–28, 533, 535, 548
  Thelwall's exchanges with, 523–24
  Wedgwood and, 538, 565, 567
  on WW, 566–67
  WW-Mary Hutchinson wedding and, 788–90
  WW's correspondence with, 630, 631, 638, 692, 693–94
  WW's poetry and presence of, 637–40
  WW's poetry as perceived by, 227–28
  WW's recital of *Prelude* to, 831–33
  see also Wordsworth-Coleridge relationship
Coleridge, Sara Fricker, 471, 506, 515, 522, 541, 557, 565, 578, 588, 677, 678, 682–83, 691, 716, 739, 762, 795, 797, 798, 819
  Coleridge's separation from, 821–22, 829
  described, 519
  Romantic circle and, 518–19
  "Spy Nozy" incident and, 534
Collier, Mary, 78
Collins, William, 74, 79, 169, 446, 623
Collot d'Herbois, Jean-Marie, 289, 290, 291
Colman, George, 253
Comité de Bayreute, 614, 660–61
Committee of Public Safety, French, 326, 382
Committee of Surveillance, 322
Communist Manifesto, The (Marx), 826*n*
"Complaint, A" (Wordsworth), 822, 830
"Complaint of a Forsaken Indian Woman, The" (Wordsworth), 570, 574
"Complaint of Ninathoma" (Coleridge), 490
Comus (Milton), 546
Condorcet, Marquis de, 291, 537
Confessions (Rousseau), 231

Congreve, William, 123
Conservative party, British, 184
Constitutional Society, 183
"constructive treason," 330, 428
"Convict, The" (Wordsworth), 446*n,* 508, 548, 574, 584, 589, 676, 754, 798
human suffering as subject of, 480–81
social reform in, 594–95
"Tintern Abbey" and, 576–77, 594–95
Cookson, Ann, *see* Wordsworth, Ann Cookson
Cookson, Christopher, *see* Crackanthorpe, Christopher Cookson
Cookson, Dorothy Cowper, 150
Cookson, Dorothy Crackanthorpe, 33, 44–45, 65, 150, 161
Cookson, William (grandfather), 33, 40, 149, 150
Cookson, William (uncle), 66, 110, 112, 114, 116, 118, 119, 120, 132, 149, 157, 158, 160, 173, 178, 182, 235, 236, 240, 276, 330, 316, 319, 323, 337, 359, 368, 403, 496*n,* 502, 533, 603, 604, 610, 653, 673, 683, 684, 690, 712, 752, 781
George III and, 824
marriage of, 149, 150
Wilberforce's friendship with, 112–13, 333
WW's break with, 333–34
WW's reconciliation with, 786
Cookson family, 31–33, 34, 46
Cooper, Anthony Ashley, 78
Cooper, Thomas, 289, 327
Corday, Charlotte, 306, 373–74, 390, 601
Cordeliers Club, 288
Corneille, Pierre, 373
Corn Laws, 256, 436
Cornwallis, Charles, Lord, 620
Corporation Act, 242
Cottle, Joseph, 483, 488, 507, 518, 534, 550, 561, 565, 567, 570, 578, 580, 581, 582, 583, 584, 588, 589, 591, 600, 607–8, 675, 676, 682, 683, 684, 686
Country Election, The (Hogarth), 22
"Country Justice, The" (Crabbe), 88
Count Waldron (Möller), 622–23
coup d'état of 18 Brumaire, 665
coup d'état of 18 Fructidor, 612–17, 659
Courier, 807
Courrier des LXXXIII départements (Gorsas), 309
Cowen, Captain, 618*n*
Cowley, Abraham, 169
Cowper, William (cousin), 276
Cowper, William (poet), 72, 74, 81, 96, 277, 324, 757
WW influenced by, 91–92
Cowperthwaite, Thomas, 59, 61, 62
Coxe, William, 190, 200, 201, 205, 213, 214*n,* 216, 226, 659
Crabbe, George, 74, 84, 277, 510, 839, 841
WW influenced by, 87–88
Crackanthorpe, Charlotte Cust, 149–50, 683, 684
letter of reproach to Dorothy by, 407–8
Crackanthorpe, Christopher Cookson, 31, 33, 53, 68, 94, 105, 118, 135, 161, 180, 402, 407, 409, 414, 469, 502
death of, 683–84
marriage of, 149–50
Wordsworth family as treated by, 109–10
Crackenthorp, Gilbert, 65
Cranach, Lucas, 631, 661
Crashaw, Richard, 169
Craufurd, Charles, 617, 659
Craufurd, James, 614–15, 616*n,* 617, 619, 620, 659, 662, 665, 666, 847–51
Craufurd, Robert, 659, 666, 849
Critical Dissertation on the Poems of Ossian (Blair), 78
Critical Review, 331, 607
Croft, Herbert, 449, 848
Cromwell, Oliver, 116
Crowe, William, 473, 475
Cruikshank, John, 522, 525, 545
Cumberland, Ernest Augustus, Duke of, 112, 630*n*–31*n*
Cumberland, Richard, 546
Cumberland Pacquet, 782
Cursory Strictures (Godwin), 437
Curtis, Jared, 457
Curwen, Henry, 29, 68
Curwen, Isabella, 68
Curwen, John Christian, 65, 67, 68, 341
Custine, Adam Philippe de, 303

Danton, Georges-Jacques, 288, 310
Darwin, Charles, 332, 484
Darwin, Erasmus, 332, 570, 580, 599, 600, 640, 653
Davenant, William, 342–43
Davy, Humphry, 717, 724, 737, 743, 749, 762, 809, 825
Dawson, George, 805–6
"Day with Wordsworth, A," 366*n*
Death of Abel (Gessner), 543
"Decay of Beggars in the Metropolis, The" (Lamb), 259–60
"Dejection: An Ode" (Coleridge), 683, 776, 789, 832
Intimation Ode and, 777, 831

De Leutre, Joseph-Antoine, Baron, 611–12, 615, 616, 618, 619, 622, 628, 633, 661, 666, 847
De Lille, Jacques, 619
democracy, 22, 162
De Moribus Germanorum (Tacitus), 119
Demosthenes, 159, 162, 163
Denunciation of the Crimes of Maximilien Robespierre (Louvet), 317
Deppermann, Frau, 631, 633
De Quincey, Thomas, 365, 366–67, 646, 796
  Grasmere visited by, 795
  "Ruined Cottage" criticized by, 513–14
  WW admired by, 794–95
  on WW's growing reputation, 840
de Saussure, Horace-Bénédict, 199, 248
Descriptive Sketches (Wordsworth), 163, 189, 198, 200, 201–2, 236, 324, 333, 336, 340, 437, 471, 512, 556, 586, 619, 624, 736, 779, 781, 806
  allusion to Caroline's birth in, 312–13
  closing scenes of, 312–14
  dedication of, 266
  erotic imagery in, 409, 598
  French Revolution and, 315–16
  genre figures in, 348
  Grégoire's influence on, 307
  Minstrel's influence on, 272–73
  publishing of, 329–32, 334
  reviews of, 331–32
  revisions to, 408–9
  1790 walking tour in, 205, 209, 213, 214–15, 220–21, 222, 224–25, 226
Desmond (Smith), 282
De Statu (Bellenden), 182
"Devil's Thoughts, The" (Coleridge), 682
Dialogues on the Rights of Britons, 290
Diary, The; or, Woodfall's Register, 327
Dickens, Charles, 7, 247, 400, 495, 537
Dickinson, Emily, 131
Dictionary (Johnson), 77
Diderot, Denis, 303
Dillon, Theobald, 303, 309
Directory, French, 295, 299, 325, 598, 614, 615, 619, 657, 659, 665, 851
Discourse on Inequality (Rousseau), 183, 350
Diversions of Purley, The (Horne Tooke), 183
Don Juan (Byron), 561
Donne, John, 145, 169
Douglas, Charles, 450, 470, 475, 567, 664, 678
Douglas, Wallace, 10
Dove Cottage, 697–99, 795, 815, 817
Dovedale, description of, 135–36
Dryden, John, 71, 72, 74, 169, 343, 487, 604, 753
Duck, Stephen, 78, 569
Duckett, William, 619
du Fosse, Monique, 284, 311, 317
du Fosse, Thomas, 284, 311, 317, 330, 394
Dufour, André-Augustin, 298, 312, 316, 327, 372
Duke of Montrose, 506, 538
Dumouriez, Charles-François, 303, 325
Dunciad (Pope), 602
"Dungeon, The" (Coleridge), 576, 584, 676
Dyer, George, 177–78, 436, 437, 438, 439, 456, 470–71, 531, 599, 718
Dykes, Miss, 689

Earl of Abergavenny, 180, 277, 343, 478, 506, 538, 714, 762, 786, 793
  sunk, 475, 815
Early Life of William Wordsworth, The (Legouis), 10
East India Company, 37, 71, 186, 762, 787
Eaton, Daniel Isaac, 434, 446*n,* 456
Eaton, Henry, 434
Ecclesiastes, Book of, 512*n*
Ecclesiastical History (Bede), 732
Economy of Charity (Trimmer), 181
Edict of Fraternity, 325
Edinburgh Review, 767, 808, 823
Edmund Oliver (Lloyd), 518, 579–80, 610
"Education de l'amour, L' " (Wordsworth, transl.), 467
Edwards, Thomas, 179, 436
"Edwin and Eltruda: A Legendary Tale" (Williams), 80
"Effects of War, The" ("Philanthropos"), 446*n*
Egmont, Earl of, 525
Egremont, Lord, 28, 38
Eldred, Thomas, 386
elections, British:
  of 1757, 28
  of 1768, 24, 27, 29–30, 32, 68
  of 1780, 29, 94–95, 184
  of 1784, 24, 184–85, 752
  of 1790, 185
  of 1818, 840
Elegiac Sonnets (Smith), 80, 181, 282
"Elegiac Stanzas, Suggested by a Picture of Peele Castle, in a Storm, Painted by Sir George Beaumont" (Wordsworth), 418, 817
"Elegiac Verses in Memory of My Brother, John Wordsworth" (Wordsworth), 816–17
"Elegy Written in a Country Church Yard" (Gray), 72–73, 87, 94, 653
Elements (Euclid), 118–19, 157, 166
Elgin, Lord, 465
Eliot, T. S., 6, 74
Elizabeth I, Queen of England, 78

"Ellen Irwin" (Wordsworth), 726
Ellis, George, 532, 603
"Emma" (Wordsworth's use of), 404
"Emma's Dell" (Wordsworth), 727
Emmendingen, battle of, 302, 307
Encyclopédie (Diderot), 303
England, 7, 8, 96, 162, 163, 334, 403
  Act of Union and, 802
  electoral politics in, 21–22
  "heresy hunt" of 1792 in, 329
  importance of college associates in, 117
  invasion fears in, 528–29
  middle class of, 71, 76
  naval mutinies in, 529
  Opium War and, 793–94, 814
  poetry "boom" in, 675
  secret service of, 523, 530–33, 603
English Eclogues (Southey), 575
Enquiry concerning Political Justice (Godwin), 179, 408, 428, 436–37, 438, 440, 463, 484, 491, 495, 497, 565, 732
Epictetus, 79
Erdman, David, 311*n,* 327
Erikson, Erik, 172
Erskine, Thomas, 437, 486, 824
Erskine, William, 808
Essay on Human Understanding (Locke), 158, 159
"Essay on Morals" (Wordsworth), 157
Essay on Population (Malthus), 117
Estlin, John, 486, 512
Ethelinde; or, The Recluse of the Lake (Smith), 282
Euclid, 118, 119, 157, 166, 167
European Magazine, 54, 102
Evelyn, John, 72
Evening Walk, An (Wordsworth), 51, 150–54, 155, 161, 181, 313–14, 324, 340, 437, 471, 736, 790
  beggar woman theme in, 153, 512
  as biographical, 150–51
  Dorothy Wordsworth in, 150–51, 152
  genre figures in, 348
  literary borrowings in, 153–54
  Milton in, 411
  publishing of, 329–32, 334
  reviews of, 331–32
  revisions to, 408–13, 483
Excursion, The (Wordsworth), 242, 397*n,* 464, 663, 701, 796–97, 819, 834, 836, 837, 841, 843
  George Dawson in, 805–6
  "Prospectus" in, 820
  Recluse and, 560
  "Ruined Cottage" and, 510, 554, 772
Excursion to the Lakes, An, 66
Exeter, Bishop of, 824
"Expostulation and Reply" (Wordsworth), 583, 676
"Extempore Effusion upon the Death of James Hogg" (Wordsworth), 839
"Extract from the Conclusion of a Poem, Composed in Anticipation of Leaving School" (Wordsworth), 103

Fabre d'Eglantine, Philippe-François-Nazaire, 374
False Impression (Richard Cumberland), 546
"Farewell, A" (Wordsworth), 779, 788
"Farewell" sonnets, 102–4
Farington, Joseph, 824, 825
Farish, Charles, 53, 84, 85, 97, 116, 120, 170, 187
Farish, John, 84, 97
Farish, William, 53, 97, 116
Farmer, Richard, 186
"Farmer of Tilsbury Vale, The" (Wordsworth), 507
Fatal Marriage, The (Southerne), 546
Faust (Goethe), 561, 656
Fawcett, Joseph, 242, 437, 441, 464
"Fears in Solitude" (Coleridge), 530, 583–84
"Female Vagrant, The" (Wordsworth), 676, 766
Fénelon, François de, 463
Fenwick, Isabella, 8, 153–54, 191, 646
Ferguson, Martha, 546
Festival of Reason, 389
Fête de la Fédération, 288, 784
  1790 walking tour and, 191–92, 194–95
Feuillants Club, 288
Fichte, Johann Gottlieb, 537, 557, 656
Fielding, Henry, 22, 74, 76
Fiesco (Schiller), 491, 539
Fingal (Ossian), 543
First War of the Allied Coalition, 612
Fisher, Agnes, 701, 747
Fisher, George, 731
Fisher, John, 699
Fisher, Molly, 696
Fishguard, French landings at, 528–29
Fitzgerald, F. Scott, 832
Fitzroy, George Henry, 185
Fitzwilliam, Earl, 435*n*
Fleming, Charles, 731
Fleming, Fletcher, 53
Fleming, Jane Taylor, 53
Fleming, John Raincock, 50, 51–53, 63, 64, 66, 68, 107, 109, 113, 116, 137, 170, 187, 686
Fleming, Michael le, 66, 687–88, 731

Fleming, Walter, 739
Fleming, William, 731
Fletcher, Henry, 29
"Fly, The" (Wordsworth), 742
Ford, Richard, 251, 285*n,* 527, 531–32, 603, 606*n,* 615*n,* 617, 618*n,* 663, 850
Foreign Office, British, 10, 379, 531, 532, 614, 617, 620, 656, 660, 662–63, 665, 668, 752, 850
Forest Trees (Evelyn), 72
Fortnight's Ramble to the Lakes (Budworth), 62
"Foster-Mother's Tale, The" (Coleridge), 584
"Fountain, The" (Wordsworth), 59, 642
Fouquier-Tinville, Antoine-Quentin, 314
Fourteen Sonnets, Elegiac and Descriptive (Bowles), 180
Fox, Charles James, 95, 179, 182, 184, 185, 435, 600, 606*n,* 607, 664, 677, 759–61, 764, 783, 824
  Burke's debates with, 254–57
  Coleridge's open letters to, 792–93
  death of, 826–27
  and presentation copy of *Lyrical Ballads,* 752, 754–77, 793
  WW's first meeting with, 825
Foxe, John, 72
Foxlow, Francis, 294
Foxlow, Thomas, 294, 323
Fragments of Ancient Poetry Collected in the Highlands of Scotland (Macpherson), 78
France, 7, 9–10, 21, 162, 174, 175, 179, 183, 185, 531, 631
  constitutional debate in, 257
  coup of 18 Brumaire in, 665
  coup of 18 Fructidor in, 612–14, 617, 659
  England's declaration of war against, 334, 387–88
  Fête de la Fédération in, 191–92, 288, 784
  first republic of, 308
  see also French Revolution
France, WW's sojourn of 1791–92 in, 284–328
  Blois segment of, 300–311
  Orleans segments of, 292–300, 311–16
  Paris segments of, 285–92, 316–28
  Prelude and, 287, 291
  preparations for, 281–83
  WW's emotional debt to, 313
France, WW's sojourn of 1793 in, 358–400, 783, 784
  Annette's correspondence and, 367–69
  Carlyle's remembrance of, 362–64, 366
  French Revolution and, 370–75
  Gorsas's execution and, 362, 363–65, 381–82, 383, 389–90, 391
  Halifax plot and, 359–62
  in *Prelude,* 387–95
  Recluse on failure of, 562
  Vendean revolt and, 370–73, 375, 379, 383, 384, 385–87
  "Walking" Stewart and, 365–67
"France: An Ode" (Coleridge), 583–84, 624
Frankenstein (Shelley), 538
Franklin, Benjamin, 469
"Frantic Lady, The" (Percy), 84
French, William, 436
French Revolution, 7, 9, 22, 162, 163, 175–76, 177, 183, 184, 186, 189, 196, 230, 242, 279, 282, 284–85, 296, 334, 343, 397*n,* 420, 494, 495, 502, 531, 604, 649, 658, 669, 719, 792–93, 807, 837
  arrests of Englishmen in, 378, 381–83
  Bourdon and affair of notables of Orleans in, 371–74
  Burke-Fox debates and, 254, 255, 256–57
  Cambridge and, 175–76
  in *Descriptive Sketches,* 315–16
  Dicken's identification with, 400
  Edict of Fraternity and, 325
  émigré issue and, 299, 310
  English secret agents and, 374–75, 382
  English sympathizers with, 285–86, 289, 294, 311, 323–26, 328, 366
  execution of Louis XVI and, 331, 335–36, 370
  "Federalist" revolt in, 372
  Girondins in, 287–88, 317–18, 326, 342, 358, 362, 363, 366, 371, 372, 375, 379, 382, 389–90
  Gorsas's execution in, 353, 362, 363–65, 381–82, 383, 389–90, 391
  journées of 1793 and, 372, 374
  Law of Suspects and, 378–79, 381
  Lyons revolt and, 383
  Mackintosh's criticism of, 681–82
  massacres of 1792 and, 287, 288, 310–11, 312, 313, 314, 317–19, 322, 336
  party politics and, 287–88
  in *Prelude,* 318, 319–21, 390–92, 812–13, 826*n*
  priests and, 299, 301–2, 310, 383
  publications of, 289–92, 309–10
  salons and, 321–22
  Vendean revolt and, 370–73, 375, 379, 383, 384, 385–87
  wars of, 334, 806
    Fishguard landings in, 528–29
    Hondschoote debacle in, 376–77
    Rastatt assassinations in, 665, 769
  WW at service of, 322–23
  see also Reign of Terror

French Revolution (Carlyle), 363
Frend, William, 117, 175–77, 178, 189, 236, 436, 439, 440, 450, 456, 670, 809
Frere, John Hookham, 117, 599, 600, 603, 666, 676, 717–18
Freud, Sigmund, 513
Frewen, Edward, 118, 496*n*
Fricker, Edith, 471, 519–20, 589
Fricker, Sara, *see* Coleridge, Sara Fricker
"Friend of Humanity" (Gillray), 600*n*
"Friend of the People" (Marat), 318
Friends of the Liberty of the Press, 341
Friends of the Rights of Man Associated at Paris, 324, 327
Frost, Robert, 74
"Frost at Midnight" (Coleridge), 583–84
Froude, J. A., 364*n*
Fry, Elizabeth, 249, 481

Gagging Acts, 458, 465, 523, 525
Gallus, Cornelius, 650–51
Gamble, James, 311*n*
Garforth, John, 29, 65
Garrick, David, 546
Gawthorp, Thomas, 55, 116, 120, 124, 163, 167, 187
Gellet-Duvivier, Jean, 294, 314, 372, 373
"General Theorem for a College Declamation, A" (Le Grice), 163
Genius of Nonsense, The (Colman), 253
Gentleman's Magazine, 395
George, Prince of Wales, 112
George II, King of England, 627
George III, King of England, 24, 112, 113, 115, 163, 246, 251, 258, 276, 319, 323, 326, 330, 333, 440, 454, 752, 758, 805, 824
Georgics (Virgil), 72
Gérard, Michel, 289–90
Germany, 9, 10, 175, 536–37, 557, 565, 566
Germany, WW's tour of, 604, 833
  British secret service and, 614–18
  Coleridge in, 565–66, 609–11, 618, 619–22, 627, 629, 631–33, 635, 655–56, 657, 661–62, 847, 848
  crossing to, 610–11
  De Leutre and, 611–12, 615, 616, 618, 619, 622, 628, 633, 661, 666, 847
  departure from, 607, 609–10
  émigré priests and, 632–33, 661
  finances and, 654–55
  Goslar segment of, 630–34, 654–55
  Hamburg segment of, 618–23
  Klopstock visit in, 623–25
  "lost" months of, 656–58, 666–69
  Lucy poems and, 635, 637, 642, 643–53, 664, 677
  Lyrical Ballads and, 567–69
  Matthew poems and, 642–43, 645, 653
  motives for, 627
  Pinney, Jr., and, 619–20
  poetic development and, 629
  as possible spy mission, 657–58, 660–63
  proposal for, 565–67
  southern Germany segment of, 654–57, 659–60
  WW-Dorothy relationship and, 633–34, 645–50
  WW's and Coleridge's separation in, 627–29
  WW's poetic production in, 631, 637–46, 649–53, 663–64
Gerrald, Joseph, 402, 432, 441, 465
Gerusalemme Liberata (Tasso), 173, 408
Gessner, Salomon, 543, 659
Gibson, John, 59, 61–63, 76
Gifford, William, 767
Gilbanks, Mr., 32
Gil Blas of Santillane (Lesage), 75–76
Gill, Joseph, 472, 476, 477–78, 490, 530
Gill, Stephen, 10, 711, 842
Gillray, James, 599–600, 620
Gilpin, William, 153, 342, 347, 590, 591, 592, 593, 594
Girondin, 287–88, 317–18, 326, 342, 358, 362, 363, 366, 371, 372, 375, 379, 382, 389–90
Glorious Revolution, 22, 178, 325, 435
Glover, Richard, 487, 623
"Glow-Worm, The" (Wordsworth), 646
Godwin, William, 9, 179, 248, 331, 340, 434, 436–37, 448, 462, 465, 468, 470–71, 481, 484, 490, 494, 499, 523, 537, 538, 545, 550, 557, 565, 580, 598, 621, 637, 640, 653, 670, 677, 681, 682, 722, 724–25, 732, 767, 825
  Borderers's rejection of, 491, 495–96
  as model for *Philanthropist,* 427, 428, 431, 438, 440, 441–43, 447, 461, 462, 463
  WW influenced by, 408
  WW's criticism of, 439–40
  WW's visits with, 441–42, 449
Goethe, Johann Wolfgang von, 11, 162, 203, 561, 623, 626, 634, 635, 657
  Schiller's friendship with, 656
Goldsmith, Oliver, 74, 88
"Goody Blake and Harry Gill" (Wordsworth), 477, 530, 570, 593, 729, 757
Gordon Riots of 1780, 249, 260
Gorsas, Antoine-Joseph, 287–88, 291, 292, 309–10, 318, 323, 342, 366, 371, 372, 379, 387, 435

execution of, 353, 362, 363–65, 381–82, 383, 389–90, 391
Gouges, Olympe de, 295
Gower, Lord, 292, 320
Gradus ad Cantabrigiam, 120, 121, 122, 123, 126, 128, 129, 167
Graham, James, 252–53, 254
Graham of Claverhouse, 228
Grande Armée Catholique et Royale, 370, 387
"Granny Grey, A Love Tale, The" (Robinson), 790*n*
Grasmere, 692, 748
Coleridge at, 686, 713, 716, 719
decision to depart from, 815
De Quincey's visit to, 795
described, 693–94, 697–99, 700
Dove Cottage of, 697–99, 795, 815, 817
John Wordsworth's visit to, 702
Mary Hutchinson's visit to, 702
neighbors of, 699–701
poetry written at, 699, 700–701, 702
post-wedding living arrangements at, 790
Thelwall's visit to, 807–8
travelers and, 701–2
visitors to, 702, 712–13, 716, 719
WW's move to, 693–95, 696
see also "Home at Grasmere"
Grasmere Volunteers, 804–5, 806, 813
Gray, Thomas, 55, 72, 73, 74, 87, 90, 94, 114, 117*n,* 169, 173, 187, 189–90, 192, 194, 196–97, 198, 209, 225, 266, 332, 446, 623, 653
Great Britain, *see* England
Great Expectations (Dickens), 358, 400
Great Fire of London of 1666, 241
Greenwood, Robert Hodgson, 53–54, 76, 84, 85, 116, 120, 170, 187, 240
Grefulke, M., 615
Grégoire, Henri, 296, 301, 306, 307–9, 315, 323, 326, 327, 338, 379, 389, 435, 442
Grenville, William Wyndham, Lord, 289, 327, 330, 386, 458, 532, 614, 615, 616, 617, 657, 658, 662, 665, 666, 824, 827, 848, 850
Grey, Charles, 185, 548, 824
Griffith, Robert, 402
Grimshaw, Mary, 238
Guides to the Lakes (West and Gilpin), 153
Guilt and Sorrow (Wordsworth), 346, 485
Gunning, Henry, 178, 184

Habeas Corpus Acts, 411
Hackman, James, 449
Hague, Peace of the, 232
Hales, Philip, 527
Halfwell, 475
Hamer, Ezekiel, 275–76
Hamilton, Emma, 253
Hamlet (Shakespeare), 539
Hammond, George, 666
Handel, George Frideric, 524
Hard Times (Dickens), 537
Hardwicke, Lord, 249
Hardy, Thomas (political organizer), 433–34
Harlot's Progress (Hogarth), 243
Harper, George McLean, 10, 21, 369*n*
Harrington, James, 785
Harrison, Benson, 61*n*
Harrison, John, 59–61, 62, 96
Harrison, Matthew, 61*n,* 685
Harrison, Tony, 74
Harrison, William, 713
"Hart-Leap Well" (Wordsworth), 626, 695, 726
Harward, George, 665
Hatfield, John, 688, 797–98
Haute Cour Nationale, La, 293
Hauze, John Frederic, 619
Hawkins, John, 246
Hawkshead:
Cambridge students produced by, 113–14
curriculum of, 70–71
death theme and, 47–49
described, 55–56, 69–70, 90–91
drowned man incident at, 47–48
educational philosophy of, 69–70
educational system of, 43–44, 58–59
excursions and adventures at, 45–46
in *Prelude,* 46–47
Tysons and, 44–45, 47
WW's perception of beautiful moment at, 47–48
WW's poetry and, 57–64, 97–104
WW's second childhood at, 42–44
Hayden, Donald E., 782*n*
Haydon, Benjamin, 4
Hayley, William, 324
Hays, Mary, 767, 837
Hazlitt, William, 3–4, 5, 7, 8, 439, 459, 469, 491, 512, 550, 566–67, 588, 631–32, 681, 806, 837
Alfoxden House visited by, 581–83
scandal of 1803 and, 796–97
WW described by, 581–82
WW's metaphysical argument with, 582–83
WW's portrait by, 3–5, 795–96
Heaney, Seamus Justin, 74
Hearne, Samuel, 570
Hébert, Jacques-René, 310, 389
Hegel, G.W.F., 557

Heisenberg, Werner, 13
Hemans, Felicia, 839, 841
Hemingway, Ernest, 832
Henry III, King of England, 500
Henry VIII, King of England, 352
Herbert, George, 169
"heresy hunt" of 1792, 329
Hermann und Dorothea (Goethe), 635
Herrick, Robert, 586
Herries, Robert, 293, 312
Higgins, Godfrey, 436
History of Rome (Livy), 158
History of Standing Armies in England (Trenchard), 432, 441
Hitchcock, Alfred, 497
Hitchcock, John (gardener at Racedown), 476, 477
Hoche, Louis-Lazare, 303, 529
Hogarth, William, 22, 243, 246, 252
Hogg, James, 131, 839
Holcroft, Thomas, 332, 403, 434, 436–40, 462, 463, 494, 523, 537, 546, 598, 620, 837
Holmes, Richard, 542
"Home at Grasmere" (Wordsworth), 38, 153, 682, 686, 692, 694–95, 696, 703–6, 710, 720, 721, 726, 727, 735, 749, 774, 779
  absent swans motif of, 704–5, 707, 715, 748
  assessment of, 704–7
  coda of, 707
  communities theme of, 725
  completion of, 819–20
  divine inspiration and, 703–4
  erotic language in, 703
  Milton and, 703
  nature vs. beauty and, 706–7
  opening of, 703–4
  problem of evil and, 734
  Recluse and, 702–3, 706, 707–8, 819–20
  Walden's similarity to, 711
  WW-Coleridge relationship and, 718–19
Home Office, British, 285*n*, 374, 433*n*-34*n*, 456–57, 458, 459, 609, 617, 620, 663, 666, 668, 850
  Alfoxden House investigated by, 525–34, 606
  harrassment of Thelwall by, 522–25
Homer, 71, 74
Hondschoote, battle of, 376–77, 388
Hood, Lord, 343, 375, 388
Hopetoun, Earl of, 688
Horace, 237
Horne Tooke, John, 183, 291, 403, 434, 437, 537, 825
Horsey, Samuel (King of the Beggars), 259–60
House of Commons, British, 71, 255, 330, 754
House of Lords, British, 415
Howard, Charles, 20, 452
Howard, Henry, 341, 405
Howard, John, 248, 481
Howard family, 27
Howitt, William, 655
Hudibras (Butler), 172
Hughes, Ted, 74
Hugh Trevor (Holcroft), 494
Hugo, Victor, 321, 358, 359, 370, 372, 379, 381, 383, 384, 385, 386, 389, 392, 400
Hume, David, 291
Hunt, Leigh, 767
Hutchinson, George, 673, 678, 692, 694
Hutchinson, Henry, 491, 673
Hutchinson, Joanna, 408, 678, 714, 730
Hutchinson, Margaret, 491
Hutchinson, Mary, *see* Wordsworth, Mary Hutchinson
Hutchinson, Sara, 678, 714, 839
  Coleridge's passion for, 683, 690–92, 720, 789, 790, 821–22, 829–31, 832
Hutchinson, Thomas, 673, 678
Hutchinson family, 673–74, 678–79, 683, 690, 716
Huxley, Aldous, 484, 706
Hyperion (Keats), 561

Ianson family, 406, 415
"Idiot Boy, The" (Wordsworth), 62, 507, 578, 675, 757
"Idle Shepherd-Boys, The" (Wordsworth), 723, 725, 726, 733–34
Iliad (Homer), 843
Illuminati, 658
Imlay, Gilbert, 381–82
Imperial and Biographical Magazine, 434, 616
"Incipient Madness" (Wordsworth), 558
Inquiry into the Nature of Subscription to the Thirty-nine Articles (Dyer), 177
"Inscription" (Wordsworth), 732
"Inscription for the Apartment in Chepstow Castle where Henry Marten, the Regicide, was imprisoned thirty years" (Southey), 352*n*
Institutes of Natural Law (Rutherford), 157
Interior Ministry, French, 318
Intimations Ode, *see* "Ode: Intimations of Immortality from Recollections of Childhood"
Introduction to Astronomy (Bonnycastle), 164
"Introduction to the Ballad of the Dark Ladie" (Coleridge), 691–92, 737
"In Vain" sonnets, 353

Irton, Martha, 67, 143
Isle of Wight, 342–45, 351, 360, 362
  WW's recollections of, 388
Isola, Agostino, 173

Jackson, William, 758
Jacobin Clubs, 285, 287–88, 290, 292–93, 300–301, 309, 318, 324, 382
Jacobinism, 8, 40, 73, 176, 178, 275, 276, 290, 297, 317, 322, 372, 373, 758, 823
James I, King of England, 500
James II, King of England, 296, 297
Jebb, John, 176, 177, 179
Jeffrey, Francis, 767, 808, 827
Jekyll, Joseph, 293, 302, 316
Jena, battle of, 806
Jena circle, 565
Jerusalem (Blake), 561
Jews, 622, 735–36
"Joanna's Rock" (Wordsworth), 730
Joan of Arc (Southey), 488, 607
Joe Miller's Jest Book (The Wit's Vade-Mecum), 123
Johnson, Joseph, 248, 329, 331, 334, 339–40, 408, 434, 539, 607, 608, 675
  arrest of, 606, 676–77
Johnson, Samuel, 77, 78, 79, 81, 86, 164, 245–46, 255, 452, 761, 800*n*, 812
Johnson's Questiones Philosophicae, 165
Johnstone, John Lowther, 759
Jones, Anne, 264
Jones, Edward, 265
Jones, John, 264, 266
Jones, John Paul, 37
Jones, Mary, 265
Jones, Robert, 7, 119, 124, 158, 159, 162, 163, 167, 169, 171, 235, 236, 345, 356, 358, 361, 362, 388, 397, 402, 664, 713, 784, 838
  in *Lyrical Ballads,* 191
  in Wales walking tour, 265–66, 268, 274, 276
  in walking tour of 1790, 188–89, 191, 192, 194–96, 198, 199, 200, 203, 205, 206–7, 211, 213, 214–15, 218, 220, 222, 223, 226, 227, 230–31, 232, 285
Jones, Thomas, 525, 536
Jonson, Ben, 169, 280, 343
Jordan, Dorothea "Dora," 133, 251, 285*n,* 532, 547, 548, 675
  and presentation copy of *Lyrical Ballads,* 752
Joseph II, Holy Roman Emperor, 232
Journal of a Tour of the Lakes (Gray), 189
Journey from Prince of Wales's Fort in Hudson Bay to the Northern Ocean (Hearne), 570
"Journey to Snowdon" (Pennant), 268
Journey to the Western Islands of Scotland (Johnson), 800*n*
Joyce, James, 97, 174
Judas Maccabaeus (Handel), 524
"July Thirteenth. Charlotte Cordé Executed for Putting Marat to Death" (Southey), 601
"Junius" letters, 30*n*
"Junius Redivivus" (pseudonym), 619
Juvenal, 159, 163, 244, 253, 433
  WW's and Wrangham's satire on, 451–58, 461, 490, 505, 603, 824, 827–29, 837

Kant, Immanuel, 210, 441, 536, 557, 565
Keats, John, 184, 703, 760, 767, 841
Kemble, Fanny, 54
Kemble, John, 242, 251
"Keswick Impostor, The" (Coleridge), 797–98
King, John, 433*n,* 526, 527, 529, 531–32, 603, 606*n,* 618*n*
King John (Shakespeare), 716
King Lear (Shakespeare), 498, 539
King of the Beggars, *see* Horsey, Samuel
Kirkby, Agatha Sawrey, 101, 102
Kirkby, David, 101, 102, 492
Kirkby, William, 101–2
Klopstock, Friedrich, 623–25, 627–28, 656, 659, 676
Klopstock, Victor, 623, 626
"Knife-Grinder, The" (Gillray), 600*n*
Knight, Thomas, 539, 545–46
Knott, Michael, 65
"Kubla Khan" (Coleridge), 518, 529, 559, 583
  geographic source of, 541–43

Laclos, Choderlos de, 286
"Lady Bothwell's Lament" (Percy), 84
Lady's Magazine, 783
Lafayette, Marquis de, 288, 310, 337, 366*n*
Lake Country tour of 1799, 683, 684–90
Lake District Pastorals, see Lyrical Ballads (1800)
Lamartelière, Jean-Henri, 322
Lamb, Charles, 5, 117, 163, 243, 249, 259–60, 261, 434, 438, 471, 512, 518, 536, 540, 558, 579, 600, 628–29, 717, 789, 796*n,* 839
  Lyrical Ballads reaction of, 759–61
  on preface to *Lyrical Ballads* of 1800, 738
  Stowey visit by, 522–23
  WW's friendship with, 491
Lamb, Mary, 261, 518
Lamballe, Marie-Thérèse-Louise de, 310–11
Lancaster, Thomas, 41
Landon, Carol, 457
Langhorne, John, 74, 84
  WW influenced by, 87, 88–90

Laplanche, M., 383
Larevellière-Lépaux, Louis-Marie de, 598, 599, 601
Larkin, Philip, 74
La Rochejaquelein, Henri, 385, 386–87
"Lass of Fair Wone, The" (Bürger), 586
"Last of the Flock, The" (Wordsworth), 571, 747, 748
Laval, battle of, 385, 386
Lavater, Johann Kaspar, 659
Law, Edward, 176
Law of Suspects, 378–79, 381
"Laws of Nature and of Nations, The" (Mackintosh), 681
Lawson, Giles, 29, 31
Lawson, Wilfrid, 679
Lay of the Last Minstrel, The (Scott), 792, 801–3
  "Christabel" and, 801–2
  success of, 826–27
Leader, Nicholas Philpot, 484
Leaves of Grass (Whitman), 561
le Brun, Charles, 292
Lebrun-Pindare, Ponce-Denis-Écouchard, 326
Lectures on Rhetoric and Belles Lettres (Blair), 78
"Leech-Gatherer, The" (Wordsworth), 775–76
Légion du Nord, 384
Legislative Assembly, French, 285, 287, 289, 303, 304, 309, 310
Legouis, Emile, 10, 369*n*
Le Grice, Charles, 163
Leonidas (Glover), 623
Leonore (Bürger), 625
Leopold II, Holy Roman Emperor, 232
Lesage, Alain-René, 75–76
"Letter on the Present Character of the French Nation" (Wollstonecraft), 339
Letters from France (Williams), 284, 314, 330, 339, 486, 487, 498
Letters on a Regicide Peace (Burke), 499
Letters Written during a Short Residence in Sweden, Norway, and Denmark (Wollstonecraft), 621, 624
Letter to a Noble Lord (Burke), 365
"Letter to the Bishop of Llandaff" (Wordsworth), 64, 307, 324, 328, 343, 346, 350, 351, 352, 333–40, 430, 441, 448, 782, 836–37
  and decision not to publish, 334, 339–40, 371
  as defense of republicanism, 337
  Gérard in, 290
  Philanthropist's essays compared with, 446
  as seditious, 339
  Watson's published sermon and, 334–36
Levine, Philip, 74
Lewes, Betsey, 20
Lewis, Matthew "Monk," 469–70, 485, 546–49, 580, 752, 754
Lewthwaite, Barbara, 734–35
"Lewti, a Circassian Love-Chant" (Coleridge), 100, 584
Liaisons dangereuses, Les (Laclos), 286, 437
Life of Johnson (Boswell), 245–46
Lindley, William, 539
Lindsey, Theophilus, 177
"Lines, Addressed to the Editor of the *Philanthropist,* on contrasting it with the general History of this Country, and the Writers of the present Day in particular" ("Clericus"), 450–51
"Lines Composed a Few Miles above Tintern Abbey" (Wordsworth), 91, 140, 159, 162, 222, 329, 352, 353–54, 373, 397, 410, 413, 485, 522, 535, 563, 574, 583, 584, 588, 590–98, 599, 601–2, 607, 626, 636, 645, 651, 675, 676, 710, 725, 741, 746, 757, 758, 760, 795, 813, 832, 840, 842
  "Advertisement" to, 601
  assessment of, 595–96
  ballad-lyric union in, 593
  composition of, 590–91, 594
  "Convict" and, 576–77, 594–95
  Dorothy in, 399–400, 597–98, 748, 749
  erotic language of, 597–98, 646–48, 652
  erotic passion underlying, 397–99
  human suffering in, 595–96
  in *Lyrical Ballads* of 1798, 589–90
  Lyrical Ballads of 1800 and, 728, 729–30
  Milton as model for, 594, 596–97, 598
  poetical sources of, 596–97
  Prelude and, 641
  Southey's praise of, 608
  WW-Dorothy relationship and, 646–68, 652
  WW's self-creation and, 593
"Lines Composed at Grasmere . . . after a stormy day, the Author having just read in a Newspaper that the dissolution of Mr. Fox was hourly expected" (Wordsworth), 826–27
"Lines Left upon a Seat in a Yew-tree" (Wordsworth), 540, 574, 596, 676
"Lines on the Expected Invasion" (Wordsworth), 806–7
"Lines Written as a School Exercise" (Wordsworth), 96, 98

"Lines written at Bridgwater, in Somersetshire, on the 27th of July, 1797, during a long excursion, in quest of a peaceful retreat" (Thelwall), 535
"Lines Written in Early Spring" (Wordsworth), 576
"Lines Written with a Slate-pencil upon a Stone, the Largest of a Heap Lying near a Deserted Quarry, upon One of the Islands at Rydale" (Wordsworth), 731
Littledale, Henry, 415
Liverpool, Lord, 528
Lives (Plutarch), 373
Livy, 158–59
Lloyd, Charles, 471, 522, 591, 600, 610, 628, 663, 794, 795
  Coleridge and, 516, 517–18, 579–80, 712–13
Lloyd, Priscilla, 712
Locke, John, 158, 159, 160, 537
London, Bishop of, 825
"London" (Blake), 243
London Chronicle, 291
London Corresponding Society, 314, 341, 434, 459
  "Address to the Public" of, 438, 441
London Hermit, The; or, Rambles in Dorsetshire (O'Keefe), 342
London, WW's sojourn of 1791, 240–63
  Bartholomew Fair of, 261–63, 279
  Burke-Fox debates and, 254–57
  in *Prelude,* 240–41, 244, 246–47, 250, 251–52, 255, 258, 260, 261, 262
  prostitution and, 243–45, 247–48, 251–52, 338
  WW's associates in, 330–31
  WW's residence in, 240, 241, 242
  WW's walks in, 246–52, 258–59
London visit of 1806, 824–26
Longman, Thomas, 658, 722, 723–24, 742, 763, 782
Longmans-Owen-Rees (publishers), 248, 823
Losh, Cecilia Baldwin, 566, 588, 589, 612, 712
Losh, James, 116, 170, 187, 289, 341, 436, 465, 506, 531, 560, 562, 564, 566, 584, 588, 589, 601, 612, 628, 708, 712, 763
Losh, William, 116
"Louisa, After Accompanying Her on a Mountain Excursion" (Wordsworth), 408
Louis XVI, King of France, 163, 192, 257, 281, 288, 299, 301, 322, 324, 326–27, 350, 502, 633
  execution of, 331, 335–36, 370
Louis XVII, King of France, 370
Louis XVIII, King of France, 633, 661
Loutherbourg, Philippe de, 251
Louvet, Jean-Baptiste, 288, 291, 317–18, 321, 323, 329, 342, 372, 379, 487
Louvet, Lodoiska, 321
"Love" (Coleridge), 691, 757
Love and Madness (Croft), 449, 848
Lovell, Robert, 471, 794
"Lover's Complaint, The" (Shakespeare), 780–81, 790
Loves of the Plants, The (E. Darwin), 600
Lowell, Robert, 74
Lowther, James (Lord Lonsdale), 10, 19–21, 27, 28, 31, 34, 55, 68, 73*n,* 117*n,* 182, 184–85, 245*n,* 277, 323, 348, 405, 411, 469, 497, 502, 653, 663, 727, 827–28
  background and personality of, 20–21, 27
  death of, 781–82
  in debt to Wordsworth family, 31, 94, 105, 150, 236, 278, 316, 414, 415, 417, 773, 781–82, 793
  in election of 1768, 29–30
  in Juvenal satire, 452–53
  Lord Portland's rivalry with, 29–30
  political ambition of, 22–24
  royal honors bestowed on, 94–95
Lowther, Robert, 685
Lowther, William, 781–82, 801, 805, 816, 827–28, 840
Lowther family, 53, 68
"Lucy Gray" (Wordsworth), 751
Lucy poems, 136, 635, 637, 642, 643–53, 664, 677, 726
  as ballads, 723
  incest theme of, 645–49
"Lycidas" (Milton), 650
"Lycoris" odes, 649–50
Lyrical Ballads (1798) (Wordsworth and Coleridge), xxiii, 59, 74, 76, 77, 84, 100, 183, 290, 322, 340, 518, 546, 553, 554, 555, 562, 565–87, 594, 604, 605, 606, 620*n,* 622, 629, 664, 669, 683, 694, 713, 719, 774, 837, 842
  "Advertisement" of, 565, 636, 764–65
  "Ancient Mariner" in, 738–39, 742–43
  assessment of, 569
  ballad elements vs. lyric elements of, 573–74, 576
  Bürger's influence on, 625–26
  Coleridge's contribution to, 583–84
  critical reviews of, 675–77
  Germany tour and, 567–69
  Holcroft's criticism and preface of, 332
  human suffering in, 576, 578
  Jones caricatured in, 191

Lyrical Ballads (*continued*)
in *Morning Post,* 718
narrative technique of, 574–76
outcast theme of, 725
"poetical inflation" and, 569
poverty theme of, 571–72
production rate of, 566, 568–69, 570
publication of, 598, 600, 607–8
puzzle poems in, 586, 587
Recluse and, 573–74
sales of, 675
sources of material for, 570–72
Southey's critical review of, 607–8, 675
Southey's poetry compared to, 575–76
"Tintern Abbey" as final poem in, 589–90
title of, 583
WW-Coleridge relationship and, 569–70
Lyrical Ballads (1800) (Wordsworth), 721–68, 790*n,* 794, 797, 820, 825, 828
"Ancient Mariner" in, 742–43
in *Biographia Literaria,* 764
"Brothers" in, 726–27
"Christabel" rejection and, 741–43
Coleridge and preface to, 736–40
Coleridge on, 721–22, 724–25
communities theme of, 725
later editions of, 763, 765–66, 767, 815, 823
letters on, 752–53
local-color poems in, 733–35, 748
loss of partnership as theme of, 725–26
love theme of, 726, 732–33
"Michael" in, 743–49
in *Morning Post,* 718, 751, 782
"Poems on the Naming of Places" in, 727–28, 730–31
poetic theory in preface of, 738–41, 760–61, 763–67
preface of, 721, 723, 736–41, 743, 751, 760–61, 763–67, 770–71, 782, 808, 811, 834, 837, 842
presentation copies of, 751–57
proposed titles for, 722–24, 736
public reception of, 751, 759–60
publishing of, 749–50
religion and, 730
reviews of, 751, 823–24, 835
rural architecture poems in, 726, 730–32
sales of, 763
"Tintern Abbey" and, 728, 729–30
"What is a Poet?" question of, 763–67, 782, 811
WW-Coleridge relationship and, 724–25, 750–51
WW-Dorothy relationship and, 727–28, 733
Lyrical Tales (Robinson), 723, 790*n*
Lysons, Daniel, 525–26, 529

Macbeth (Shakespeare), 211–12, 256, 498, 716
McDonnell, James Joseph, 435*n*
Machiavelli, Niccolò, 432, 486
MacKeith, Daniel, 734
Mackintosh, James, 255, 291, 324, 340, 681–82, 718, 719, 737–38, 763
French Revolution criticized by, 681–82
MacNeice, Louis, 74
Macpherson, James (Ossian), 78, 543
Madgett, Nicholas, 619
"Mad Mother, The" (Wordsworth), 84, 572, 748, 752, 757, 760
Malthus, Thomas, 117, 118, 484
Man As He Is (Bage), 494
Manchester Constitutional Assembly, 289
Manners, Catherine, 331–32
Manning, Thomas, 760
Man of Ten Thousand (Holcroft), 440
Manuel, Pierre, 290
"Man was Made to Mourn" (Burns), 576*n*
Marat, Jean-Paul, 306, 310, 318, 319, 342, 372, 436
assassination of, 373–74
Margarot, Maurice, 351, 402
Marie Antoinette, empress of France, 232, 374, 375
trial and execution of, 382, 383
Markham, Penny, 477–78
Marlowe, Christopher, 169
Marriage of Figaro, The (Beaumarchais), 437
"Marseillaise, La" (Rouget de Lisle), 196, 325
Marsh, Peggy, 527, 550, 582, 588
Marshall, Jane Pollard, *see* Pollard, Jane
Marshall, John, 712
Marten, Henry, 352*n*
Martial, 123
Martin, John, 57
Marvell, Andrew, 169, 343, 785
Marx, Karl, 513
Mason, William, 332
Mathews, William, 50, 119, 157, 254, 266*n,* 408, 420, 425, 444, 446*n,* 457, 467, 470, 484, 488–89, 525, 689
death of, 466
Philanthropist project and, 427–30, 431, 434–35, 438, 439, 442, 448
WW's correspondence with, 54, 74, 265, 278, 279, 286, 300, 309, 332, 348, 412, 426, 427, 433–34, 471, 478, 490
WW's failing relationship with, 449, 466, 471

Mathey, Brigitte, 381–82
Mathias, James, 717
Matthew poems, 637, 642–43, 645, 653, 677, 723, 726
Maude, Thomas, 49, 116
Memoir (Christopher Wordsworth), 659
Memoirs (Godwin), 538, 550
Memorials of a Tour on the Continent (Wordsworth), 205, 837
Merchant of Venice, The (Shakespeare), 546
Mercier, Louis-Sebastien, 286, 309–10, 323
Méricourt, Théroigne de, 295
Merry, Robert, 324
Messiah, The (Klopstock), 623
Metamorphoses (Ovid), 72
Metastasio, Pietro, 790–91
"Michael" (Wordsworth), 701, 726, 733, 755, 756, 757, 760
  as autobiographical, 746–77, 749
  in *Lyrical Ballads* of 1800, 743–49
Middleton, Thomas, 119
Midsummer Night's Dream, A (Shakespeare), 716
Millar, John, 116, 120
"Miller's Tale" (Chaucer), 132, 771
Milner, Isaac, 178
Milton, John, 37, 73, 74, 100, 106, 121, 125, 126, 127, 148, 154, 164, 169, 198, 254, 271, 286, 287, 343, 432, 445, 451, 487, 499, 546, 560, 595*n*, 623, 650, 703, 760, 791, 795, 835
  disinterment of, 245
  in *An Evening Walk,* 411
  "Home at Grasmere" and, 703
  as model for "Tintern Abbey," 594, 596–97, 598
  Recluse and, 708–9
  WW influenced by, 141–43, 144, 214, 219, 221, 393, 395–97, 771, 784–85
Mingay, Mr., 67, 173
"Minister's War," 352, 511
"Ministry of All Talents," 824, 827
Minstrel, The (Beattie), 78, 272–73, 360, 466, 812
Minstrels of Winandermere, The (Farish), 53, 85
Minstrelsy of the Scottish Border (Scott), 801
Mirabeau, Comte de, 337
Miranda, Francisco, 303, 314
Mogg, Charles, 525–26, 536
Moira, Lord, 386
Moncrieff, Henry, 491
Moncrieff, James, 713
Moniteur, 385, 386, 429
Monk, The (Lewis), 546–47
Monmouth, Duke of, 530
"Monody" (Bowles), 181
Montagu, Basil, 158, 170, 458, 459, 460, 470, 475, 476, 488, 490–91, 506, 527, 536, 603, 664, 763, 786, 798, 824–25, 848
  WW's friendship with, 449–50, 469
  WW's loan to, 450, 567, 678, 793
Montagu, Basil Caroline, 449, 469, 475–76, 519, 537, 565, 605, 607
Montesquieu, Baron de la Bréde et de, 232, 291, 432
Montessori, Maria, 537
Monthly Magazine, 486–87, 507, 543, 579, 589, 607, 675
Monthly Review, 89, 675–76
Moor, John, 57
Moore, David, 57
Moore, John, 190
Moorman, Mary, 10, 52, 140*n,* 360, 399, 460, 585
Moral Philosophy (Paley), 157, 166, 185
More, Hannah, 572
Moreau, General, 302
Morning Advertiser, 249
Morning Post, 100, 249, 285*n,* 341, 354, 457, 486, 601, 606, 624, 627, 682, 691, 716, 752, 757–58, 782–83, 784, 788, 789, 792
  Coleridge's position with, 689–90, 716–18
  Lyrical Ballads selections in, 718, 751, 782
"Mortimer" (pseudonym), 486, 501, 548
Morton, Thomas, 546
Mountmorres, Hervey, 665
Mozart, Wolfgang Amadeus, 75, 292
Muir, Thomas, 339, 351, 402
Muldoon, Paul, 74
Munro, Captain, 320, 324, 327, 328, 366
Myers, John, 111, 113, 116, 119, 120, 124, 132, 157, 158, 162, 163, 169, 171, 251, 277, 714
Myers, Mary, 278
Myers, Thomas, 180, 277, 475, 685, 712
Myers, Thomas, Jr., 712
"My First Acquaintance with Poets" (Hazlitt), 581

"Nancy of the Vale" (Shenstone), 91
Napoleon I, Emperor of France, 117, 159, 207, 295, 299, 303, 325, 343, 444, 487, 519, 530, 536, 612, 620, 665, 717, 755, 769, 773, 785, 793, 806, 815, 824
  Campo Formio Treaty and, 612–13
  fall of Toulon and, 375, 388
  Italian campaigns of, 487, 519
Narrative of the Disinterment of Milton's Coffin, 245
National Assembly, French, 183, 197, 289–90, 318, 335, 619, 624

National Convention, French, 257, 310, 314, 317, 318, 319, 321, 322, 323, 324, 325, 326–27, 371, 372, 373, 381, 382, 383, 384, 389, 619
Natural Disinterestedness of the Human Mind (Hazlitt), 583
Nature, 6, 19, 39, 48, 55, 90, 96, 104, 131, 343–44, 354, 398, 400, 484, 570, 575, 587, 708, 759, 772
Naturphilosophie, 557
Needham, Mother, 243
Nelson, Horatio, 620, 624
Nemerov, Howard, 74
Neoplatonism, 557
Nepean, Evan, 374
Netherlands, 461
Nether Stowey:
  creation of Romantic community at, 518–20
  Fishguard landings and, 528–29
  Home Office spy investigation and, 525–34
  housewarming dinner at, 524–25
  Lamb's visit to, 522–23
  neighbors' perception of Coleridge at, 519–20
  November walks at, 541–55
  Thelwall's visit to, 522–25, 526, 528, 529–30
  WW-Coleridge joint project at, 543–44
  WW's move to, 516–17
  see also Alfoxden House
"Netley Abbey" (Bowles), 352
Nevill, Henry, 180, 277
Nevill, Mary Robinson, 277, 475*n,* 712
Nevill, William, 277
Newbery, John, 248
Newland Mills Company, 55
"New Morality, The" (*Anti-Jacobin* satire), 598–603, 604, 607, 717
"New Morality, The" (Gillray cartoon), 599
Newton, Isaac, 71, 115, 120, 122, 159, 160, 162, 164, 167, 249
Nicholson, John "Maps," 123, 124
Nicholson, Samuel, 241–42, 245, 437, 438, 545, 546
Nicholson, Thomas, 41
Nicholson, William, 438
"Nicias Erythraeus" (pseudonym), 584
"Nightingale, The" (Coleridge), 525, 584, 675, 757
"Night on Salisbury Plain, A" (Wordsworth), 345, 408, 451, 598
  revised, 482–85
"Night-Piece, A" (Wordsworth), 551–52, 563
Nile, Battle of the, 620, 624
Ninety-three (Hugo), 358
Norfolk, Duke of, 31, 277, 340, 342, 405
  see also Howard, Charles; Howard, Henry
North, Lord, 27, 30*n,* 95, 113, 182
"Northern Enlightenment," 70
Northumberland, Hugh Percy, Duke of, 83, 277, 452
Norton, C. E., 364*n*
Norwich, Bishop of, 782
Nouvelle Héloïse, La (Rousseau), 199
Novalis (pseudonym), 656, 703
"Nut-Brown Maid, The" (ballad), 84
"Nutting" (Wordsworth), 638, 646, 648–53, 727, 730, 777, 780–81

"Oak and the Broom, The" (Wordsworth), 723, 725, 726, 773
Oberon (Wieland), 624–25
Observations of Western England (Gilpin), 347
Observations on the River Wye . . . Made in the Summer of 1770 (Gilpin), 590
"Ode: Intimations of Immortality from Recollections of Early Childhood" (Wordsworth), 417, 563, 769, 775, 777–78, 789, 832
"Ode on the Poetical Character" (Collins), 79
Odes (Klopstock), 623
Odes on Various Subjects (Warton), 79
"Ode to Melancholy" (Carter), 80
"Ode to Spring" (Aikin), 79
"Ode to the Genius of Westmorland" (Langhorne), 89
"Ode to the River Eden" (Langhorne), 89
Oeconomist, 436, 712
Oedipus at Colonus (Sophocles), 157
"Old Cumberland Beggar" (Wordsworth), 62, 87–88, 562, 563, 725, 760, 766
  in *Recluse,* 562–63
"Old Man Travelling" (Wordsworth), 575
Old Slaty (merchant), 55–56
Oliffe family, 699–700
Olynthiacs (Demosthenes), 162
"On an Infant" (Coleridge), 645
"On a Ruined House in a Romantic Country" (Coleridge), 559, 579
"Once a Jacobin Always a Jacobin" (Coleridge), 792
"On Classick Learning" (Wordsworth), 792
"On Going for Mary," *see* "Farewell, A"
"On Liberty" (Montesquieu), 432
"On Naso Rubicund, Esq. a dealer in Secrets" (Coleridge), 682
Onorato, Richard, 10
"On Seeing Miss Helen Maria Williams Weep at a Tale of Distress" (Wordsworth), 102

"On Spies and Informers" (Thelwall), 529
"On the Influence of Some Human Institutions on Human Happiness" (Rigby), 441
"On the Lord Gen. Fairfax at the Siege of Colchester" (Milton), 451
On the Principles of Human Action (Hazlitt), 583
"On This Day I Complete My Thirty-sixth Year" (Byron), 11
Opium War, 793–94, 814
Opticks (Newton), 71, 162
Oracle, 446*n*
Orlando Furioso (Ariosto), 408, 649
Orléans, Duc d', 286, 294, 314
Orr, George, 848
Orwell, George, 754
Osorio (Coleridge), 507, 515, 538–39, 547, 548, 567, 580, 584, 719
  Covent Garden's Rejection of, 545–46
  revised, 538–39, 540
  Robbers and, 539
  spy passage in, 540
Ossian, *see* Macpherson, James
Osterly (ship), 506
Oswald, John, 286, 290, 291, 322, 324, 365, 381, 805, 806
  Borderers and, 501
  death of, 384
Othello (Shakespeare), 498, 539
Otway, Thomas, 169
Ovid, 71, 72, 74, 651
Owen, Robert, 366

Paccard, Michel, 199
Paine, Tom, 9, 179, 185, 248, 255, 287, 291, 305, 323, 324, 327, 331, 338, 339, 340, 350, 381, 483, 523, 598, 611, 682
"Pains of Sleep" (Coleridge), 800–801
Paley, William, 120, 156, 157, 164, 166, 186
Palmer, Thomas Fyshe, 177, 339, 351, 402
"pamphlet wars" of 1791–95, 242, 334
Pantisocracy, 471, 517, 541, 599
Papinianus, 737
Paradise Lost (Milton), 37, 73, 124, 126, 138, 221, 251, 256, 411, 543, 623, 703, 709, 771
  Dawn Dedication in, 141, 148
  Prelude compared with, 784–85
  Prelude influenced by, 141–44, 146–47
  as source for *Borderers,* 499
Paris Commune, 320
Parker, Thomas, 41
Parkin, Anthony, 282
Parliament, British, 21, 27, 29, 94, 113, 179, 246, 264, 330, 402, 435, 458, 470, 595*n,* 598, 614*n,* 752
  Burke-Fox debates in, 254–57
  Whigs' "secession" from, 528
Parr, Samuel, 182–83, 465
"Pathetique" Sonata (Beethoven), 569
Patriote français, 291–92, 320
"Patriotic Ode" (Lebrun-Pindare), 326
Patriotism; or the Love of Our Country (Frend), 809
Paul I, Emperor of Russia, 633
Peace and Union Recommended to the Associated Bodies of Republicans and Anti-Republicans (Frend), 178
Peake, James, 65, 72
Pearce, William, 118
"Pedlar, The" (Wordsworth), 510, 772–73
Peigne, Marie-Victoire-Adelaide, 327
Pembroke, countess of, 148
Pennant, Thomas, 266, 268, 270, 271, 273, 274
Penny, William, 116
Penrith Beacon, 40, 110, 149, 410
Percy, Bishop, 569
Percy, Thomas, 74, 666
  WW influenced by, 78, 83–84
Peripatetic, 448, 523
Perrin, Father, 327
Persuasion (Austen), 472–73, 520, 714
Peter Bell (Wordsworth), 101, 578, 582, 677, 836
  Cheddar Gorge in, 579
  composition of, 578
  as counterpart of "Ancient Mariner," 554*n*
  Salisbury Plain poems and, 355–57
  West England tour and, 355–57
Peters, George, 665
"Pet-Lamb, The" (Wordsworth), 725, 742
Petrarch, 843
"Phenomena of the Wye, during the Winter of 1797–98, The" (Thelwall), 589
Philanthropist, 291, 328, 427–67, 481, 484, 498, 502, 603, 616, 813, 834
  Eaton and, 434–35, 440
  essays in, 432, 435, 442–47, 453
  February 1795 tea party and, 435–38, 456
  Godwinian model for, 427, 428, 431, 438, 404, 441–43, 447, 461, 462, 463
  Juvenal project and, 451–52
  "Letter to Bishop of Llandaff" compared with, 446
  Mathews and, 427–30, 431, 434–35, 438, 439, 442, 448
  name of, 431–32
  poverty theme of, 445–46
  Prelude and, 461, 462–64
  proposed aims of, 430–32
  Racedown scheme and, 459–60

Philanthropist (*continued*)
radical phase of, 441
reprints in, 440–41
Salisbury Plain poems and, 451
satire on clergymen in, 453–54
talent theme in, 443–44
topics in, 447–49
unstable editorial policy of, 440–41
verse in, 433
WW's authorship in, 445–47, 450–51
WW's departure from London and, 449–51, 459–62
WW's moral crisis and, 462–64
"Philanthropos" (pseudonym), 446*n*
Philippic (Demosthenes), 162
Philip II, King of Macedon, 162, 163
Philipson family, 348
Philomathean Society, 442, 462, 620
Philosophical Journal, 438
Pichegru, Jean-Charles, 366, 447, 461, 614
Pig's Meat, 434
Pilgrim's Progress (Bunyan), 172
Pinney, Azariah, 458–59, 470, 473, 487–88, 491, 510*n*, 527, 536
Pinney, Charles, 475
Pinney, John Frederick, 458–59, 470, 486, 487–88, 491, 510*n*, 619–20, 677, 713
Pinney, John Pretor, 459, 468–70, 471, 472, 473, 475, 477, 478–80, 489–90, 529, 537
Piozzi, Hester Thrale, 246
Pitt, William (the Elder), 112
Pitt, William (the Younger), 24, 68, 110, 112, 113, 117, 173, 178, 179–80, 182, 252, 254, 255, 256, 289, 311, 323, 326, 334, 350, 376, 379, 388, 402, 430, 432, 433, 441, 451, 458, 487, 528, 603, 618, 657, 664, 665, 668, 717, 719, 752, 773, 806, 827
Anti-Jacobin and, 603–4
Cambridge power base of, 184–86
death of, 824
1780 election and, 94–95
Pizarro (Sheridan), 675
Place, Francis, 324
"Pleasures of Change, The" (Wordsworth), 95–96
"Pleasures of Hope" (Campbell), 96
"Pleasures of Imagination" (Akenside), 96
"Pleasures of Memory" (Rogers), 96
Pliny the Younger, 216
Plutarch, 373
Pneumatic Institute, 724
Pocklington, John, 689
Poems (Coleridge), 565, 790
Poems (Cowper), 91
Poems (Thelwall), 560
Poems (Wordsworth), 215
Poems, Chiefly in the Scottish Dialect (Burns), 86
Poems, Chiefly of Early and Late Years (Wordsworth), 798
Poems, in Two Volumes (Wordsworth), 722, 815, 822–23, 828
"Poems in the Stanza of Spenser," 466
Poems on Several Occasions (Carter), 79–80
"Poems on the Naming of Places" (Wordsworth), 687, 726, 727–28, 730–31, 762
Poems Written Chiefly in Retirement (Thelwall), 808
"Poet, The" (Hogarth), 246
poetry, 737, 756
"Cockney" school of, 767
"common language," 570
concept of Poet and, 760–61
"Jacobin" school of, 767
"Lake" school of, 823
Lyrical Ballads preface and theory of, 738–41, 760–61, 763–67
as moral act, 636–37
"Satanic" school of, 767
science and, 13
of Sensibility, 54, 74, 75, 77–78, 81, 85–86, 87, 90, 92, 96, 102, 180, 237, 266*n*
"What is a Poet?" question and, 763–67, 782, 811
WW's dedication to, 137–38, 146–47
see also Romanticism; Wordsworth, William, poetry of
"Poet's Epitaph, A" (Wordsworth), 86, 652–53
Poet's Fate, The (Dyer), 471, 599
"Point Rash-Judgement" (Wordsworth), 729
Poitiers, Diane de, 306
Political Catechism (Robinson), 437
Political Justice, see Enquiry concerning Political Justice
Politician, 434
"Politics and the English Language" (Orwell), 754
Politics for the People, 434, 440, 446*n*
Pollard, James, 85
Pollard, Jane, 109, 181, 182, 229, 238–39, 265, 359, 360–61, 402, 403–4, 406, 472, 475, 712
Poole, Charlotte, 524
Poole, Thomas, 507, 509, 516, 517, 518, 519, 520, 522, 523–24, 525, 526, 530, 533, 534, 536, 539, 566, 567, 583, 627, 628, 634, 677, 679, 683, 810
on WW-Coleridge relationship, 664–65, 724–25
Poor Man's Club, 527, 530

"Poor Susan" (Wordsworth), 242–43, 507, 625–26, 723, 725
Pope, Alexander, 71, 74, 83, 96, 455, 602, 640
Porson, Richard, 176, 183
Portland, Duke of, 29–30, 433*n,* 454, 458, 525, 528, 531, 532, 533, 606*n,* 609, 611, 619, 665, 668, 695, 848, 850, 851
  WW in paybook of, 616–17, 661, 662, 666, 847
Portrait of the Artist as a Young Man (Joyce), 97
Poulett, Earl, 475
Pound, Ezra, 6, 74
Powell, James, 457, 848, 849, 850
Powell, Samuel, 116
Practical Treatise on Regeneration, A, 181
Practical View of the Prevailing Religious System of Instruction (Wilberforce), 753
Preble, Miss, 851
Prelude, The (Wordsworth), xxiii, 4, 6, 7, 9, 10–13, 19, 35, 43, 46–47, 50, 52, 55, 69, 75, 85, 105, 139, 147–48, 151, 157, 159, 161, 168, 195–96, 245*n,* 287, 292, 316, 332, 342, 343, 374, 387, 397, 410, 413, 443, 461, 479, 511, 558, 568, 624, 637, 639, 645, 653, 663, 684, 686, 693, 695, 710, 718, 737, 738, 741, 749, 759, 760, 763, 764, 770, 773, 802, 803, 806, 808, 819, 820, 828, 838, 841, 842, 843
  ascent of Snowdon in, 270–73
  Beaupuy's death in, 385–86
  Borderers as forerunner of, 497–99, 504
  Burke-Fox debates and, 255–56
  Cambridge days in, 116, 121–23, 131
  Cambridge University in, 171–74, 770
  composition of, 674, 812–13
  compulsive rewriting of, 818
  "Conclusion" of, 765
  Cowper's influence on, 91–92
  and decision not to publish, 834–36, 837, 843
  end of, 813–15
  end of WW's youth and, 835–36
  fair copies of, 818
  France as described in, 365
  French Revolution in, 318, 319–21, 390–91, 812–13, 826*n*
  French sojourn of 1791–92 in, 287, 291
  French sojourn of 1793 in, 387–95
  Hawkshead in, 46–47
  "Home at Grasmere" and, 702–3, 706, 707–8, 819–20
  Hondschoote battle in, 376–77
  John Wordsworth's death and, 93–94, 96, 812, 813–15, 817, 839
  London sojourn in, 240–41, 244, 246–47, 250, 251–52, 255, 258, 260, 261, 262
  Milton and, 708–9
  moral crisis of, 462–64
  Paradise Lost's influence on, 141–44, 147, 784–85
  Philanthropist and, 461, 462–64
  plot of, 811–12
  as "poem to Coleridge," 642, 643, 651–52, 680–81, 811
  Recluse and, 560, 563
  resumption and completion of, 810–11, 817–18
  rowboat scene of, 638
  Salisbury Plain in, 346, 350
  sexuality in, 131–33
  skating scene of, 638
  summer vacation of 1788 in, 136–37
  Taylor in, 72–73
  "Tintern Abbey" and, 641
  versions of, 12
  Wales walking tour in, 266, 270–73
  walking tour of 1790 in, 197, 200–202, 203, 205, 208, 209, 214, 215–16, 219, 220, 221, 224–25, 226, 228, 231–32
  Wedgwood project satirized in, 538
  Wilberforce in, 362–63
  worthy son theme of, 689
  WW-Coleridge relationship and, 677–81
  WW's recital to Coleridge of, 831–33
Pretor, Michael, 469
"preventitive policing," 531
Price, Richard, 177, 242, 275
Priestley, Joseph, 175, 287, 324, 471, 624
Priestley, William, 175, 177
Principia (Newton), 159, 164
Prior, Matthew, 169
Progress of Famine, The (Churchill), 84
Prolusiones Juveniles (Tweddell), 436
Prometheus Unbound (Shelley), 561
Propyläen, 656
"Prosperity of the Kingdom, The" (Coleridge), 717
Provence, Duc de, 633
Provisional Executive Council, French, 326
Public Characters for 1799–1800 (Dyer), 718
Purcel, Bartholomew, 64
Pye, Henry, 330

Quatre-vingt treize (Hugo), 359, 370*n,* 385, 392
Quebec, constitution of, 257
Quintillian, 756

Rabelais, François, 123
Racedown Lodge, 459–60, 468–93, 516, 563
  and Austen's *Persuasion,* 472–73
  Coleridge's visit to, 514–15

Racedown Lodge (*continued*)
described, 468–69, 472
domestic life at, 475–77, 478
Gill and, 476, 477–78
landscape surrounding, 473–75
London visit during WW's stay at, 490–91
Mary Hutchinson's visit to, 491–92, 493
Montagu Jr.'s education at, 475–76
non-rental arrangement and, 468–69, 480, 489–90
poetry produced and revised at, 476–77, 479–86, 491–92
WW's readings at, 486–87
Rackstraw's Museum, 249
Raincock, Fletcher, 53–54, 58, 116, 170, 187, 190
Raincock, John, *see* Fleming, John Raincock
Raincock, William, 48
Raine, Jonathan, 436
Rake's Progress (Hogarth), 252
Ranger (magazine), 37
Rape of the Lock, The (Pope), 265, 455
Rasselas (Johnson), 812
Rastatt assassinations, 665, 769
Rawson, Mrs., 403, 566, 659
Ray, Martha, 449, 848
Rayment, Robert, 311*n*
"REASONS Why the People Are the Best Keepers of Their Own LIBERTIES" (anonymous), 441
Recluse, The (Wordsworth), 13, 464, 568, 569, 572, 594, 595, 602, 649, 650, 683, 684, 685, 760, 763, 764, 772, 773, 775, 787, 821, 822, 834, 837, 838, 841, 843
assessment of, 842
Brook and, 561–62
Coleridge's encouragement and, 465–66, 506–7, 561, 562, 564–66, 680–82, 810–11, 818–19
Excursion and, 560
as failure, 710–11, 722, 748–49, 777
and failure of French Revolution, 562
"Home at Grasmere" and, 702–3, 706, 707–8, 819–20
human suffering in, 563–64, 576–77
invocation in, 708–10
loss of Coleridge's notes for, 818–19
Lyrical Ballads and, 573–74
Lyrical Ballads preface and, 736–38, 740
nature vs. society in, 709–10
poems constituting, 562–64
Poems in Two Volumes and, 823
Prelude and, 560, 563
"Prospectus" to, 550, 709–10, 721, 727, 741, 748, 765, 770, 774, 800, 820
"Ruined Cottage" in, 562–63
unfinished state of, 562, 564, 565, 567, 573–74
WW's self-creation and, 560
Recollections of a Tour Made in Scotland (Dorothy Wordsworth), 800*n*
Reed, Mark, 10, 660
Reeves, John, 185, 254
"Reeve's Tale" (Chaucer), 132
"Reflections of Having Left a Place of Retirement" (Coleridge), 584
Reflections on the Revolution in France (Burke), 177, 242, 254, 255, 275, 334, 336, 494, 681
Reform Bill of 1832, 824, 840
"Regency Crisis of 1788–89," 112
Regno Christi, De (Bucer), 595*n*
Reign of Terror, 295, 297, 310, 374, 375–76, 378, 387, 392
execution of Gorsas in, 353, 362, 363–65, 381–82, 383, 389–90, 391
Law of Suspects and, 378–79, 381
Religion de la Nature (Larevellière-Lépaux), 601
"Religious Musings" (Coleridge), 489
Reliques of Ancient English Poetry (Percy), 78, 83–84, 666
Reminiscences (Carlyle), 364*n*
Remnant (bookseller), 656
Repentant Magdalene, The (le Brun), 292
Reply to Some Parts of the Bishop of Llandaff's Address to the People of Great Britain (Wakefield), 607, 676
republicanism, 176–77, 182–83, 195, 307–8, 337, 411, 825
"Llandaff letter" as defense of, 337
"Resolution and Independence" (Wordsworth), 775, 776
as self-critique, 777–78
Reveries of a Solitary Walker, The (Rousseau), 231
Revolutionary Tribunal, French, 371, 375, 376, 391, 393
"Revolution Debate" of 1790–95, 340
Reynell, Richard, 600
Reynolds, Joshua, 98, 602
Rice, Anne, 508, 509
Rich, Adrienne, 74
Richard Coeur de Lion (Burges), 752
Richardson, Samuel, 239
Rigby, Dr., 441
Rigge, Mary, 101, 104, 132, 356, 492, 568
Rigge, William, 101–2
Rights of Man (Paine), 255, 257, 350
"Rime of the Ancient Mariner, The" (Coleridge), 544–45, 553, 562, 565, 567, 570, 574, 578, 583, 584, 608, 675, 676, 729, 738–39, 801

human suffering in, 555–56
in *Lyrical Ballads,* 738–39, 742–43
Peter Bell as counterpart to, 554*n*
Ruined Cottage's similarity to, 554–55
Ring des Nibelungen, Der (Wagner), 561
River Duddon, The (Wordsworth), 837
Road to Ruin, The (Holcroft), 332, 437
Robbers, The (Schiller), 4, 322, 497–98, 499, 539, 547, 580, 623, 719
(also known as *Die Raüber and Les Voleurs*)
Robert, chef de brigands (Lamartelière), 322, 497–98
Robespierre, Maximilien, 72, 73, 162, 288, 290, 294, 310, 311, 317, 318, 319, 320, 321, 329, 372, 382, 384, 388, 389, 461, 732
death of, 418–20, 519*n*
Robinson, Henry Crabb, 224, 645, 838
Robinson, Hugh, 25, 113, 277–78
Robinson, John "Jack," 27, 28–29, 31, 67, 80, 94, 95, 113, 150, 180, 182, 241, 277, 282, 323, 416, 452, 453, 502, 603, 604, 618*n,* 653, 712, 824
death of, 782
Harwich curacy offer of, 276, 278–81, 333, 495*n*
Robinson, Mary (Beauty of Buttermere), 133, 252, 688, 797–98
Robinson, Mary Myers, 113
Robinson, Mary "Perdita," 331–32, 723, 790*n,* 841
Robinson, Robert, 177–78, 437
Rochester, John Wilmot, Lord, 123
Roe, Nicholas, 531
Rogers, Samuel, 96, 761, 825, 841
Roland, Manon, 319*n,* 321, 323, 487
execution of, 390
Roland de La Platière, Jean-Marie, 310, 318
Romanticism, 206, 208, 212, 228, 277, 280, 323, 708, 776, 794, 808
Alfoxden House and, 521–22
Coleridge and creation of, 514, 518–19
Coleridge-Thelwall exchanges and, 523–24
composition of "Tintern Abbey" and, 591
philosophy of Spirit in, 557–58
problem of evil in, 564
Robbers and, 498
Scotland tour of 1803 and, 797–98
1790 walking tour as archetype of, 190–91
"Spy Nozy" incident and, 525–34
Thelwall's "Lives" and, 535–36
WW-Coleridge Germany sojourn and, 618
see also poetry
"Romantic Marriage, The" (Coleridge), 797
Romeo and Juliet (Shakespeare), 539
Romilly, Samuel, 319*n*
Romp, The (play), 133*n*
Roubillac, Louis-François, 122
Rouget de Lisle, Claude-Joseph, 196
Rousseau, Jean-Jacques, 69, 117, 183, 190, 198–99, 231, 291, 299, 318, 350, 476, 483, 843
republican ideology of, 315
Rowlandson, Thomas, 120, 262
"Rowley Poems" (Chatterton), 78
Royal Irish Academy, 840
"Ruined Cottage, The" (Southey), 579*n*
"Ruined Cottage, The" (Wordsworth), 57, 83, 86, 314, 446*n,* 448, 479, 501, 510–15, 550, 553–59, 567–68, 570, 576, 579, 677, 729, 743, 770, 771, 772, 836, 842
alternate titles of, 510
"Ancient Mariner" compared to, 554–55
Coleridge and, 512–15, 553, 572–73, 579
composition of, 511–13
criticism of, 513–14
Excursion and, 510, 554, 772
final dirge of, 559
human suffering in, 512–13, 555–57
as major work, 510–11
philosophy of Spirit and, 597–99
plot of, 511
in *Recluse,* 562–63
sexual diction in, 598
Southey's imitation of, 579
subjects of, 479
WW-Coleridge relationship and, 514–15, 553
WW's self-creation and, 510–11
"Rural Architecture" (Wordsworth), 726, 730–32
Russia, Imperial, 256
"Ruth" (Wordsworth), 723, 725
Ruth, Book of, 238
Rutherford, Thomas, 157
Rutland, Duke of, 87
Rutledge, James, 287, 324

"Sailor's Mother, The" (Southey), 575
"Sailor's Mother, The" (Wordsworth), 773
St. Albyn, Anna, 520, 533–34
St. Albyn, Lancelot, 520
St. James Chronicle, 245
St. John's College, Cambridge, 115–17, 119–20, 156, 157, 159, 184
Saint-Just, Louis de, 322, 382, 389
Salisbury Plain poems, 163, 345–50, 353, 446, 734, 836
empathy for poor in, 346
Female Vagrant in, 347–50
genre figures in, 348
Peter Bell and, 355–57

Salisbury Plain poems (*continued*)
Philanthropist and, 451
WW as character in, 348–49
see also "Adventures on Salisbury Plain"; "Night on Salisbury Plain, A"
Samson Agonistes (Milton), 395
Sandwich, Earl of, 449, 537
Sandys, Edwin, 70, 91
Sandys, George, 72, 487
"Satire on Modern Clergymen," 453–54
Satterthwaite, Michael, 94–95
Savenay, battle of, 387
Schelling, Friedrich von, 537, 557, 656
Schiller, Johann von, 4, 322, 491, 497–98, 503, 539, 547, 564, 580, 623, 626, 634, 709*n*, 719
Goethe's friendship with, 656
Schlegel, August Wilhelm von, 656
Schlegel, Friedrich von, 557
"Schoolmistress" (Shenstone), 90
"Scots Wha Hae" (Burns), 339
Scott, Walter, 625, 694, 792, 801–4, 826
WW's friendship with, 801, 803
Yarrow poems inspired by, 803–4
Seasons, The (Thomson), 51, 81–82
Seditious Meetings Bill, 458
Seditious Practices Act, 339
Seduction (Holcroft), 437
Selincourt, Ernest de, 12
Sense and Sensibility (Austen), 281, 423, 473
Sensibility, poets and poetry of, 54, 74, 75, 77–78, 81, 85–86, 87, 90, 92, 96, 102, 180, 237, 266*n*
Sentinelle, 318
Seward, Anna, 332
Sexton, Anne, 74
Shakespeare, William, 74, 280, 445, 498, 596, 649, 716, 771, 790, 795
as source for *Borderers,* 498–99
Sharp, Richard "Conversation," 761
Shaw, Mr., 71
"Sheepfold, The" (Wordsworth), 745
see also "Michael"
Shelley, Mary Godwin, 538
Shelley, Percy Bysshe, 6, 7–8, 9, 131, 203, 435*n*, 703, 719, 720, 767, 841
Shelvocke, George, 544
Shenstone, William, 74, 87, 88
WW influenced by, 90–91
Sherborne *Weekly Entertainer,* 490, 496*n*, 499
Sheridan, Richard Brinsley, 27*n*, 185, 245, 251, 285*n*, 507, 532, 538–39, 546, 548, 675, 677
Shone, Hugh (Snowdon guide), 268, 270
Shuter, William, 3, 4
Siddons, Sarah, 133, 242, 251, 546
Sidney, Sir Philip, 148, 785
Silcombe Farm, 542
Simeon, Charles, 130
"Simon Lee" (Wordsworth), 525, 571, 729
Sketches on the Natural, Civil, and Political State of Switzerland (Coxe), 190, 200
Skirving, William, 339, 351, 402
"Slumber did my spirit seal, A" (Wordsworth), 644, 646
Smart, Christopher, 169, 187, 189
Smith, Charlotte, 74, 180, 181, 287, 288, 324, 325, 332, 490, 841
WW influenced by, 80–81
WW's visit with, 282
Smith, John, 417
Smith, Mary Wordsworth, 161, 417
Smollett, Tobias, 22, 75–76
Society for Constitutional Information, 178, 242, 438, 441
Society for the Prevention of Cruelty to Undergraduates, 168*n*
Society for the Promotion of Christian Knowledge, 178
Society of the Friends of the Constitution, *see* Jacobin Clubs
Society of the Rights of Man and of the Citizen, 287
Sockburn-on-Tees, 673–74
Somerset, Duke of, 68
"Somersetshire Tragedy, A" (Wordsworth), 507–10, 512
Somerville, John Southey, Lord, 826, 827, 828
"Song for the Wandering Jew" (Wordsworth), 735–36
"Song of the Feast of Brougham Castle" (Wordsworth), 689
Songs of Experience (Blake), 756
"Sonnet on Seeing Miss Helen Maria Williams Weep at a Tale of Distress" (Wordsworth), 80
"Sonnet on the River Wye" ("M."), 354
Sonnets by Various Authors (Coleridge), 737
"Sonnets on Eminent Characters" (Coleridge), 717
"Sonnets on National Independence and Liberty" (Wordsworth), 664, 784
Sorrows of Young Werther, The (Goethe), 623
Sotheby, William, 624, 809
Southerne, Thomas, 546
Southey, Robert, 4–5, 117, 249, 352*n*, 364*n*, 420, 429, 471, 488–89, 490, 498, 506, 512, 517, 518, 519, 545, 568, 575–77, 581, 589, 628, 637, 663, 682, 717, 718, 722, 734, 762, 796, 825, 840, 841

critical review of *Lyrical Ballads* by, 607–8, 675
"New Morality" satire of, 599–601
"Ruined Cottage" imitated by, 579
"Tintern Abbey" praised by, 608
"Sparrow's Nest, The" (Wordsworth), 37, 38, 779–80
Spectator, 74, 261*n,* 265*n*
Spedding, John, 23*n,* 26, 27, 143, 406
Spedding, Margaret, 406, 677
Spedding, Maria, 67, 143
Spedding, Mary, 406
Spence, Thomas, 434
Spenser, Edmund, 74, 100, 169, 693, 771, 795
Spinoza, Baruch, 527, 557
Spirit, philosophy of, 597–99
"Spots in the Sun" (Coleridge), 789–90
"Spy Nozy" incident, 10, 527–28, 533, 535, 548
Stanhope, Philip, Earl of, 289, 335, 657
"Stanzas Suggested in a Steamboat off St. Bees' Head" (Wordsworth), 80–81
Steele, Richard, 244
Stein, Charlotte von, 634
Stendhal, 495
"Stepping Westward" (Wordsworth), 800
Sterne, Laurence, 54, 75, 123
Stevens, Wallace, 74, 321
Stewart, John "Walking," 365–67
Stockalper, Kaspar, 206, 210
Stoddart, John, 491, 539, 677, 713, 724, 751, 801, 809
Stone, John Hurford, 294, 314, 324, 325, 374, 382, 487, 620
Stone, Reginald, 731
"Strange fits of passion" (Wordsworth), 644, 723
Stuart, Daniel, 249, 606, 627, 681, 689, 716, 751, 758, 783, 789, 792, 819
Stuart, Mary, 20–21
Sublime, 36, 38–39, 66, 210, 218, 807
Sun, 329, 620*n,* 752, 825
Survey of the Lakes (Clarke), 153
Suvorov, Aleksandr V., 659
Swabian agency, 614, 657, 660–61, 849
Swaine, Edward, 239
Swift, Jonathan, 74, 76, 487
Swinburne, Algernon Charles, 6, 495
Switzerland, 531, 631
Sydney, Algernon, 432, 486
"Sylvanus Amicus," 448
"Sylvanus Theophrastus," 448
Sympson, Joseph, 699

"Tables Turned, The" (Wordsworth), 583, 676
Tacitus, 119, 159
Talbot, James, 614, 657, 658, 662, 665, 849, 850–51
Talbot, Robert, 614, 849, 850
Tale of Two Cities, A (Dickens), 400
Talleyrand-Périgord, Charles-Maurice de, 335
Tandy, Napper, 665, 848
Task, The (Cowper), 91–92
Tasso, Torquato, 173, 306, 408
Tate, William, 529
Taylor, Anne, 758–59
Taylor, Jane, *see* Fleming, Jane Taylor
Taylor, John, 457, 619, 620, 752, 825–26, 827
and presentation copy of *Lyrical Ballads,* 757–58
Taylor, "Turk," 126
Taylor, William, 58–59, 72–74, 75, 80, 87, 92, 94, 97, 98, 101, 102, 158, 169–70, 177, 419, 420, 637, 642
Telegraph, 429, 435*n,* 446*n*
Tell, William, 228
Ten Minutes Advice to Freshmen, 123
Tennyson, Alfred, Lord, 169, 840
Terrot, William, 119, 124, 156, 158, 162–63, 169, 187, 240
Test Acts, 128, 176, 177, 179, 186, 242, 437
"Thanksgiving after Childbirth" (Wordsworth), 35
Thelwall, John, 252, 340, 403, 433–34, 436, 448, 471, 489, 516, 518, 543, 589, 591, 598, 616, 670, 682, 732, 737, 767, 792–93, 825, 826, 837
Coleridge's exchanges with, 523, 524
government campaign against, 523–25, 609, 762, 807–8
Grasmere visited by, 807–8
"Lives" of, 535–36
at Llyswen, 604–6
Stowey visit of, 522–25, 526, 528, 529–30
Thelwall, Stella, 518
Theocritus, 652
Theophilanthropic Society, 620
Theophilanthropie, 598
Theseus, 766
Things as They Are; or, Caleb Williams (Godwin), 358, 437, 448–49, 463, 484, 494, 495, 640
Thirty-second Bassigny regiment, French, 303, 304
"This Is the House That Jack Built," 559
"This Lime-Tree Bower My Prison" (Coleridge), 522, 596
Thomas, Thomas, 273–74, 276
Thompson, E. P., 8, 618
Thomson, James, 51–52, 74, 76, 87, 106, 108, 164
WW influenced by, 76, 81–83, 85–86

Thoreau, Henry David, 13, 551, 564, 711
"Thorn, The" (Wordsworth), 449, 572, 585, 586, 605, 625, 675, 848
"Thoughts" (Wordsworth), 799
Thoughts on Subscription (Frend), 177
"Thoughts Suggested by a College Examination" (Byron), 122
"Three Cottage Girls, The" (Wordsworth), 223
"Three Graves, The" (Wordsworth), 492–93, 509, 568, 587, 790*n*
"Three years she grew" (Wordsworth), 645
Threlkeld, Elizabeth, 110, 241–42
Threlkeld, Lancelot, 689
Thucydides, 159
Tierney, George, 600*n,* 806
Times (London), 249, 374, 376
Timon of Athens (Shakespeare), 716
"Tinker, The" (Wordsworth), 774, 776
"Tintern Abbey," *see* "Lines Composed a Few Miles above Tintern Abbey"
"Tirocinium; or, A Review of the Schools" (Cowper), 91, 96
"To a Butterfly" (Wordsworth), 37–38, 774
"To a Cuckoo" (Wordsworth), 774–75
"To a Daisy" (Wordsworth), 37, 774
"To a Highland Girl" (Wordsworth), 223, 800
"To a Lady Who Hates the Country" (Warton), 79
"To a Sexton" (Wordsworth), 751
"To a Young Ass" (Coleridge), 599, 600
"To a Young Lady Who Had Been Reproached for Taking Long Walks in the Country" (Wordsworth), 407–8
Tobin, James, 468, 491, 536, 545, 560, 561, 562, 564, 566, 567, 708, 713, 724
Tobin, John, 468, 478
Tobin, John, Jr., 468, 491, 536
"To Joanna" (Wordsworth), 729
Toleration Acts, 177
Tolstoy, Leo, 495, 561
"To Mr. S. T. Coleridge" (Barbauld), 752
"To the Evening Star over Grasmere Water" (Wordsworth), 827
"To the Memory of Raisley Calvert" (Wordsworth), 782*n*
Tour in Wales, A (Pennant), 266, 268
Tour . . . of the Wye (Gilpin), 342
tous les républicains de France sur la Société des Jacobins de Paris, A (Brissot), 317, 318
Toussaint L'Ouverture, François-Dominique, 261, 785
"To William Wordsworth: Composed on the Night after His Recitation of a Poem on the Growth of an Individual Mind" (Coleridge), 11, 821, 831–32
Traitorous Correspondence Bill, 339
"Travelling" (Wordsworth), 781
Travels in Switzerland (Coxe), 659
Travels in the East (Sandys), 72
Treasonable Practices Bill, 458
treason trials, 427, 433, 436, 437, 506, 523, 573
Trenchard, John, 432, 441, 467
"Tria Lumina Anglorum," 182
Tribunal redoutable, Le (Lamartelière), 322
Tribune, 434, *523*
Trickie, Christopher, 526, 536, 562, 571
Trimmer, Sarah, 181
Trinity College, Cambridge, 115, 156
Tristram Shandy (Sterne), 54, 74, 123, 265*n*
Triumph of Life, The (Shelley), 719
Triumph of Loyalty, The (Coleridge), 719–20, 721*n*
True-Briton, 329, 620*n,* 752, 757, 825
Turkey, 256
Turner, J.M.W., 561
Turner, Samuel, 848, 849
Tussaud, Mme., 250
Twain, Mark, 57
Tweddell, Francis, 289, 323, 325, 538
Tweddell, John, 117, 158, 163, 166, 170, 240, 251, 436, 465, 538, 566, 657
Two Addresses to the Freeholders of Westmorland (Wordsworth), 840
"Two April Mornings, The" (Wordsworth), 59, 642
"Two Round Spaces, The" (Coleridge), 681*n*
"Two Thieves, The" (Wordsworth), 723, 725, 734
Tyrwhitt, William, 179
Tyson, Ann, 44–45, 47, 50, 53, 63, 90, 94, 101, 110, 116, 134, 137, 138, 146, 152, 161, 356
  death of, 686
Tyson, Hugh, 44, 57, 70, 94, 101
Tyson, "Tailor," 54

Unitarianism, 176–77, 557
United Irishmen, 457, 573, 665, 758, 848

"Vale of Meditation" (Wordsworth), 265
"Vale of the Esthwaite, The" (Wordsworth), 98, 103, 104–9, 150–51, 668
  demons in, 107–8
  Gothicism of, 104–7
Vallière, Madame de la, 293
Vallon, Annette, 7, 12, 149, 290, 302, 304, 305, 306, 307, 311, 312, 314, 315, 325, 326, 330, 335, 337, 338, 339, 349–50, 353, 354, 357, 358, 359, 364, 370, 373, 374, 378–79, 384–85, 386, 388, 391, 401, 408, 419, 430,

460, 467, 485, 490, 493, 503, 597, 619, 624, 772, 780, 790, 798
Borderers and, 501, 502
in Calais visit, 769–70, 783–86
described, 295
Dorothy's correspondence with, 360, 367, 369, 371–72, 396, 399
Dorothy's relationship with, 368–69
family background of, 296–97
and intention to marry WW, 316–17, 368–69
"Mad Mother" and, 572
Revolution and, 308–9
"Tintern Abbey" and, 598
Williams as family name of, 327
WW-Dorothy relationship and, 399–400, 486, 502
WW's correspondence with, 333, 360, 367–68, 371–72, 398, 492, 502, 531
WW's love affair with, 285, 295–99, 300, 313
in WW's poetry, 585–86
and WW's sense of betrayal, 396, 398
Vallon, Caroline, *see* Wordsworth, Caroline
Vallon, Paul, 295, 300, 302, 314, 316, 327, 371–72, 373, 376, 619
Vane-Fletcher, Frederick, 679
"Vanity of Human Wishes" (Johnson), 164
"Vaudracour and Julia" (Wordsworth), 393–94, 397, 722*n*
Vaughan, Felix, 251, 289, 293
Vendean revolt, 370–73, 375, 379, 383, 384, 385–87
Vergniaud, Pierre-Victurnien, 322
Victoria, Queen of England, 112
Victory, 343
View of Society and Manners in France, Switzerland, and Germany, A (Moore), 190
Village, The (Crabbe), 87
Village Politics (More), 290, 572
Vindication of the Rights of Man (Wollstonecraft), 255
Vindiciae Gallicae (Mackintosh), 255, 681
Virgil, 71–72, 74, 592, 640
tenth eclogue of, 649–50
"Visit of the Gods, The" (Schiller), 709*n*
Voyage Around the World by the Way of the Great South Sea (Shelvocke), 544

Wade, Thomas, 525
"Waggoner, The," 62, 713, 836
Wagner, Richard, 561
Wakefield, Gilbert, 117, 170, 183, 607, 670, 676
Walden; or, Life in the Woods (Thoreau), 711
Wales, Prince of, 332
Wales, walking tour of, 264–76
ascent of Snowdon in, 266–73
Jones in, 264–66, 268, 274, 276
Mathews and, 265, 279
in *Prelude,* 266, 270–73
Reverend Taffy incident in, 274–76
Walford, Jenny, 508, 509–10, 511
Walford, John, 508, 509–10, 520
Walker, Thomas, 327
walking tour of 1790, 188–232, 397, 813
as act of rebellion, 188–89
as archetype of Romanticism, 190–91
Belgian Revolution and, 231–32
Chartreuse segment of, 196–98, 210, 226
crossing of Alps in, 203, 205–12
dangerous waterfall incident in, 230–31
in *Descriptive Sketches,* 205, 209, 213, 214–15, 220–21, 222, 224–25, 226
disappointments in, 202, 211–12, 227, 229
Dorothy-WW correspondence on, 190, 199, 205, 208, 209, 213, 214, 218, 229
1820 reprise of, 197, 210–11, 219–20, 223–24, 227, 229–30, 231, 838
Einsiedeln segment of, 228–29
erotic episode in, 214–26
Fête de la Fédération episode in, 191–92, 194–95
Gondo Gorge segment of, 208–12
Gravedona incident in, 218–21
Gray's precedent for, 189–90, 196–97, 198
itinerary of, 189, 190, 226
Jones in, 188–89, 191, 192, 194–96, 198, 199, 200, 203, 205, 206–7, 211, 213, 214–15, 218, 220, 222, 223, 226, 227, 230–31, 232, 285
Lake Como segment of, 213–26
Lake Lucerne segment of, 226–27
Mont Blanc segment of, 198, 199–201, 210, 214
pace of, 192–94
in *Prelude,* 197, 200–202, 203, 205, 208, 209, 214, 215–16, 219, 220, 221, 224–25, 226, 228, 231–32
Walk through Wales in August 1797, A (Warner), 588–89, 591–92
Wallenstein (Schiller), 656, 719, 721*n*
Walpole, Horace, 189, 192, 194, 197*n*
Walsh, James, 526–31, 536, 537, 540, 609, 617, 618, 661, 663, 664, 850
Walsh, James, Jr., 609, 618*n*
"Wanderer, The" (Wordsworth), 510
"Wanderings of Cain, The" (Coleridge and Wordsworth), 543–44, 562
War and Peace (Tolstoy), 561
"War Eclogue" (Coleridge), 682

Warner, Richard, 588–89, 591, 592, 593
Warton, Joseph, 74, 76, 79, 80, 180, 623
Warton, Thomas, 74, 78, 180, 623
Watchman, 179, 436, 488, 523
"Waterfall and the Eglantine, The" (Wordsworth), 723, 725, 726, 727, 773
Watson, Jemima, 129
Watson, Richard, 64, 67, 115, 120, 126, 129, 338, 339, 340, 348, 453–54, 685–86, 731, 782
  Grégoire contrasted with, 307
  published sermon of, 334–37
  see also "Letter to the Bishop of Llandaff"
Watt, James, Jr., 289, 311, 323, 324, 327
Watts, Alaric, 365–66
"We Are Seven" (Wordsworth), 355, 536, 545, 586, 757, 774
Wedgwood, Josiah, 681, 724, 761
Wedgwood, Sarah, 537
Wedgwood, Tom, 289, 470, 566, 628, 657
  education scheme of, 536–38
Weekly Entertainer, 792
"Weldonious" (pseudonym), 431
Wernicke, Christian, 789
West England, tour of, 341–62
  carriage accident in, 345, 361
  Isle of Wight segment of, 342–45, 351, 360, 362, 388
  Peter Bell and, 355–57
  Salisbury Plain segment of, 345–50, 351, 356
  sonnet fragments of, 351–54
Westermann, François-Joseph, 385
Weston (highwayman), 59
"What is a Poet?," 763–67, 732, 811
Whitbread, Samuel, 245, 548, 600*n*
White Doe of Rylstone, The (Wordsworth), 802
Wickham, William, 374, 433*n,* 531, 533, 603, 606*n,* 615, 618, 659, 665–66, 668, 847, 848, 849, 851
Wieland, Christoph Martin, 624–25, 626
Wilberforce, Barbara Ann Spooner, 181–82
Wilberforce, William, 10, 66–67, 110, 117, 126, 130, 137, 143, 173, 178, 179, 185, 241, 256, 261, 287, 316, 337, 387, 470, 603, 690, 782
  Cookson's friendship with, 112–13, 333
  Dorothy Wordsworth's relationship with, 181–82
  in *Prelude,* 362–63
  and presentation copy of *Lyrical Ballads,* 752–53
Wilkinson, Joshua, 330, 341
Wilkinson, Thomas, 761, 816
William and Helen (Scott), 625
William III, King of England, 177, 325, 530
William IV, King of England, 133*n,* 251, 532, 752
Williams, David, 598–99
Williams, Helen Maria, 54, 74, 76, 80, 102, 108, 180, 192, 282, 285, 289, 291, 293, 294, 311, 317, 321, 323, 324, 325–26, 331, 371, 374, 378, 379, 381, 394, 498, 505, 620, 721*n,* 831
  Letters of, 284, 314, 330, 339, 486, 487, 498
Willmott family, 525
Wilson, Thomas, 324
Wimpfen, General, 372–73
"Winter" (Thomson), 81
"Wisdom and Spirit of the Universe" (Wordsworth), 49
Wishert, Thomas, 57–58
Wollstonecraft, Mary, 9, 131, 248, 255, 311, 331, 381–82, 488, 538, 550, 621, 624
  "Letter" of, 339–40
Wood, James, 126
Woodfall, William, Jr., 327, 328
Woof, Robert, 61*n*
Woolcot, John, 717
Wordsworth, Ann Cookson (mother), 19, 35, 36, 44, 79
  death of, 33, 41
  family background of, 31–32
  WW's recollection of, 33–34
Wordsworth, Caroline (illegitimate daughter), 12, 298, 327, 330, 335, 349, 356, 357, 359, 368, 370, 372, 384, 388, 401, 572, 598, 716, 770
  birth of, 312
  in Calais visit, 783–84
Wordsworth, Catherine (daughter), 839
Wordsworth, Christopher (brother), 32, 44, 49, 71, 75, 94, 105–6, 120, 137, 161, 168, 171, 238, 239, 282, 332, 471, 610, 659, 673, 683, 712, 746, 782, 786, 824
Wordsworth, Dorothy "Dora" (daughter), 784, 816, 839
Wordsworth, Dorothy (niece), 61*n*
Wordsworth, Dorothy (sister), 23–24, 31, 32, 41, 44, 67, 86, 91, 94, 107, 109, 110, 121, 130, 135, 157, 171, 185, 188, 232, 235, 241, 261, 265, 276, 278, 281, 298, 314, 319, 327, 337, 341, 343, 345, 358, 397, 401–2, 409, 411–12, 413, 416, 425, 426, 460, 463, 489, 490, 493, 505–6, 512, 514, 524–25, 537, 546, 563, 564, 568, 570, 580, 588, 594, 636, 677, 678, 679, 682, 683, 688, 722, 723, 724, 726, 731, 742, 744, 761–62, 765, 782, 787, 810, 816, 817, 818, 826
  at Alfoxden House, 516–17, 521–22
  in *An Evening Walk,* 150–52
  Annette Vallon and WW's relationship with, 399–400, 403–4

Annette Vallon's correspondence with, 360, 367, 369, 371–72, 396, 398, 399, 722*n*, 790
Annette Vallon's relationship with, 368–69
on Beattie's influence, 85
in Calais visit, 769–70, 783–86
Charlotte Crackanthorpe's letter of reproach to, 407–8
in Cheddar Gorge walking tour, 578–79
churchgoing habit acquired by, 838
Clarkson and, 712
Coleridge's correspondence with, 638–39, 684
Coleridge's relationship with, 517–18, 520, 541, 684
death of, 839
described, 519–20, 634, 651
in 1820 rewalk of 1790 tour, 197, 210–11, 219–20, 223–24, 227, 229–30, 231
financial tensions and, 414–15, 423
in German tour, 604, 607, 612, 619, 621–22, 627, 629, 654, 656, 658–60, 661
German tour and WW's relationship with, 633–34, 645–50
at Goslar, 630–31, 632–35
at Grasmere, 692–93, 695, 696, 713, 718
Halifax plot and, 359–62, 368, 386, 660
on Hutchinson family, 674
investments with John Wordsworth of, 343, 506, 538, 762–63, 814–15
journal of, 550–53, 621–22, 630–31, 658, 673, 692, 714–15
Lamb's first meeting with, 522
landscape descriptions by, 715
Lowther debt settlement and, 793
Lyrical Ballads and WW's relationship with, 727–28, 733
on *Lyrical Ballads* of 1800, 725
Matilda character and, 502
personality of, 517, 651
Pinney brothers and, 487–88, 491
post-wedding living arrangements and, 790
at Racedown, 471–72, 473, 475–78, 482, 486, 487–88
Romantic circle and, 518–19
sacrifices by, 651
Sara Coleridge and, 518–19
in Scotland tour of 1803, 797, 800, 803, 805
in Somerset walks, 541, 542–43
in "Tintern Abbey," 399–400, 748, 749
"Tintern Abbey" and WW's relationship with, 646–48, 652
Wilberforce's relationship with, 181–82, 753
at Windy Brow, 405–8, 459
as writer, 551–52
WW-Mary Hutchinson wedding and, 788
WW's childhood recalled by, 37–38
WW's correspondence with, 190, 199, 205, 208, 209, 213, 214, 218, 229, 686, 715–16
WW's impending marriage and, 714–16, 771–72, 773, 778–81
on WW's poetic production, 567
in WW's poetry, 642, 644, 645–49, 651
WW's poetry and descriptive writing of, 551–53
WW's poetry as criticized by, 332
WW's relationship with, 36, 147–51, 152, 160–61, 236, 237–39, 295–96, 349–50, 359–62, 485–86, 517, 585, 586, 634–35, 637, 651–52, 666–67, 674, 715–16, 727–28, 733, 778–79, 786, 788
in Wye tour, 589–90, 599
Wordsworth, Elizabeth (aunt), 118, 413, 415–16
Wordsworth, Favel (cousin), 415
Wordsworth, Gordon (modern descendant), 507–8, 716
Wordsworth, John (brother), 32, 44, 50, 70–71, 93, 137, 180, 238, 277, 282, 415, 478, 673, 683, 715, 724, 727, 746, 754, 759, 782, 786, 809, 839, 841
death of, 418, 787, 812–15, 831
Dorothy's investments with, 343, 506, 538, 762–63
Grasmere visited by, 702
in Lake Country tour, 684, 686, 688–89
Mary Hutchinson and, 713–14, 716, 747, 762, 763, 787, 788
in opium trade, 787, 793–94, 814–15
Prelude affected by death of, 93–94, 96, 812, 813–15, 817, 839
Wedgwood debt and, 678
WW's elegy to, 816–17
Wordsworth, John (cousin), 403, 415, 496*n*
Wordsworth, John (father), 20, 28, 33, 60, 61–62, 65, 70–71, 95, 102, 150, 278, 348, 415, 417, 502, 727, 746
career of, 19, 22–23, 24, 31, 34
death of, 39, 41, 44, 48, 93–94, 96
estate of, 94
financial interests of, 25–26
Lowther-Portland rivalry and, 29–30
Wordsworth, John (son), 794, 797, 816
Wordsworth, Mary Hutchinson (wife), 32, 66, 101, 110, 147, 149, 161, 181, 205, 223–24, 295, 312, 399, 408, 502, 521, 567, 673, 674, 678, 683, 690–91, 692, 771, 773, 779, 781, 790, 810, 818, 822, 824, 826, 833, 838
Grasmere visited by, 702

Wordsworth, Mary Hutchinson (wife) (*continued*)
John Wordsworth and, 713–14, 716, 747, 762, 763, 787, 788
at Racedown, 491–92, 493
wedding of, 787–88
WW's courtship of, 714–15, 722, 762
WW's love of, 787–88, 790
Wordsworth, Richard (brother), 5, 32, 35, 41, 42, 44, 50, 60, 70, 93, 137, 147, 180, 189, 191, 234, 238, 241, 279, 282, 287, 288, 293, 294–95, 297, 312, 330, 347–48, 403, 408, 411, 414, 416, 417, 422, 424–25, 426, 450, 460, 531, 538, 567, 608, 666, 677–78, 685, 781, 782, 786, 828
Wordsworth, Richard (grandfather), 26, 40
Wordsworth, Richard (uncle), 26–27, 44, 94, 105, 150, 359, 387, 413, 417, 423, 424, 469, 746
death of, 414, 422
Wordsworth, Robinson (cousin), 416, 426, 510*n,* 618*n,* 746–47
Wordsworth, Thomas (son), 816, 839
Wordsworth, William:
in abandoned quarry incident, 39–40
biographers of, 10
birth of, 20
boyhood friendships of, 49–55, 56
at Cambridge, *see* Cambridge University
childhood of, 17, 19, 31, 32, 36, 38–40, 41, 42–43, 46–47
churchgoing habit acquired by, 822
code name of, 311*n*
conservatism of, 669–70, 794
and cover-up of "juvenile errors," 6–7, 9
in crisis of self-confidence, 503
criticism disliked by, 332
cultural racism of, 261
as dedicated to poetry, 137–38, 146–47
described, 3–4, 49, 147, 191, 519, 581–82, 584
discharged veteran encounter of, 137, 144–47
earliest known nonpoetic writings of, 135–36
earliest pictures of, 17–19
early education of, 32, 43–44, 58–60, 67, 69–75
early readings of, 74–76
egotism of, 560–61, 709–10, 818
first published poem of, 80
growing reputation of, 761, 794–96, 823–24, 840
Hawkshead character types and, 57–64
Hawkshead notebooks of, 97–98
Hazlitt's portrait of, 3–5, 795–96
languages ability of, 72, 98–99, 173, 279–80, 323
later travels of, 838
library of, 679–80
literalistic metaphors used by, 7–8
London visit of 1806 by, 824–26
named Westmorland stamp distributor, 840–41
National Trust film on, 706*n*
as noble savage, 17–19, 20, 34
personality of, 35, 49–50, 150, 439, 502
as poet laureate, 840
poetry as recited by, 582
political education of, 304–5
politics rejected by, 483–84, 487
psychosomatic pains of, 635–36, 682–83, 721, 761–62, 771
Rampside sojourn of, 417–19
reading habits of, 97–98
religion and, 198, 229
republicanism and, 182–84
Robespierre's death and, 418–20
secret service connection of, 530–33
self-creation of, 8, 10–12, 13–14, 43, 77, 94, 154, 345, 403, 483, 498, 560, 593, 636, 638, 695, 760–61, 763, 770, 771, 772
sexual experience of, 130–34, 136–44, 145, 147, 492
success and, 840–41
violent temperament of, 35–36, 38, 41, 45
as wine connoisseur, 125–26
Wordsworth, William, poetry of:
Annette Vallon in, 585–86
beggar's theme of, 260, 355–56
bigamy theme of, 260, 355–56
Bishop of London on, 825
Bowles's poetry vs., 180–81
boyhood in, 46–47, 49
Bürger and, 636–37
Burns's legacy and, 798
Calais sonnets and, 784–86
Coleridge's perception of, 227–28
Coleridge's presence and, 637–40
contemporary poets' influence on, 76–92
diction of, 297–98, 555–56
discharged veteran encounter and, 137, 144–47
Dorothy in, 642, 644, 645–49, 651
Dorothy on production of, 567
Dorothy's criticism of, 332
Dorothy's descriptive writing and, 551–53
drowned man and, 39–40, 93*n*
earliest surviving lines of, 96, 98
early influences on, 71–73
eroticism and sexuality of, 98–100, 131–34, 138–44, 145, 147, 254, 298, 409, 485, 586–87, 645–48, 652, 777

"farewell" sonnets and, 102–4
father's death and, 94–97, 109
feminine influence on, 79–81
first collected works of, 103
first published volume of, 51
flawed communication in, 50–51
on Fox's death, 826–27
Germany trip and, 629
Goslar stay and, 631, 636, 637–42
Hawkshead "character" types in, 57–64
Hawkshead days in, 97–104
hermit theme of, 222
hidden and unpublished works of, 836–37
human suffering in, 408, 479, 480–81, 483, 486, 563, 574
ideology of Genius and, 663–64
literary borrowings in, 153–54
loss of inspiration theme of, 644–45
love relations in, 485–86
on Mary Rigge, 100–102, 133–34
and mastery of sonnet form, 784–85
"Matthew" character of, 59–62, 96
minstrel as prototype in, 84–85
"new" gentry and, 65–66
"oriental" diction of, 297–98
picaresque novel and, 75–76
poetry of Sensibility and, 77–78, 81, 85–86, 87, 90, 92
posterity and, 841–43
Racedown production of, 476–77, 479–82, 491–92
Racedown revisions of, 482–86
and renascence of 1802, 772–78
Scott's influence on, 803–4
social thought in, 408, 410–12
strolling method in composing of, 51–52, 137–38
and switch to ballads, 568–69
"Was It for This?" motif of, 640–41, 644, 666, 811
wayfaring encounters as theme of, 56–57
WW-Dorothy relationship and, 645–50
WW's dedication to, 137–38, 146–47
WW's egotism and, 560–61
WW's imaginative growth and, 637–38
see also specific works
Wordsworth-Coleridge relationship, 506–7, 635, 645, 648, 666, 716, 776, 809, 810
"Adventures on Salisbury Plain" and, 488–89
"Christabel" rejection and, 741–43
Coleridge-Sara Hutchinson relationship and, 821–22, 829–31, 832
collaboration and imaginative bond in, 553–59, 583–84
first meeting and, 471–72
"Home at Grasmere" and, 718–19
Lyrical Ballads (1798) and, 569–70
Lyrical Ballads (1800) and, 724–25, 750–51
onset of, 514–15
philosophy of spirit in, 557–58
Poole on, 664–65, 724–25
Prelude and, 677–81
Prelude recital and, 831–33
Racedown visits and, 472, 506–7, 512–15
"Ruined Cottage" and, 514–15, 553
Scotland tour of 1803 and, 800–802
WW's poetic production and, 566–67, 637–40
WW's self-creation and, 637–40
"Wordsworth in the Tropics" (Huxley), 706
Wrangham, Francis, 117, 158, 170, 240, 450, 459, 467, 469, 475, 477, 486, 489, 603, 725
Juvenal project and, 451–56, 458, 490, 505, 603, 827–28
Wren, Christopher, 115, 241, 247
Wright, J. M., 127–28
Wycherley, William, 123
Wye walking tours of 1798, 588–94, 599, 604
composition of "Tintern Abbey" and, 590–98

Xenophon, 118, 159

Yarnell, Ellis, 313
"Yarrow Revisited" (Wordsworth), 804
"Yarrow Unvisited" (Wordsworth), 803–4
"Yarrow Visited" (Wordsworth), 804
"Year of Revolutions," 826*n*
Yearsley, Ann, 78, 569, 572
Yeats, William Butler, 74
York, Duke of, 376, 453, 689
Young, Edward, 160, 162, 164
Young Man Luther (Erikson), 172
Young Philosopher, The (Smith), 282

Zoönomia (Erasmus Darwin), 570

211-12 [209-12]
346ff – Salisbury plains
445 lit & social criticism
525f – Mogg!
543 "Kubla Cans"
711 – poet & democracy –
(& Thoreau too)
738ff Prelude L.B.
835 – title of book!

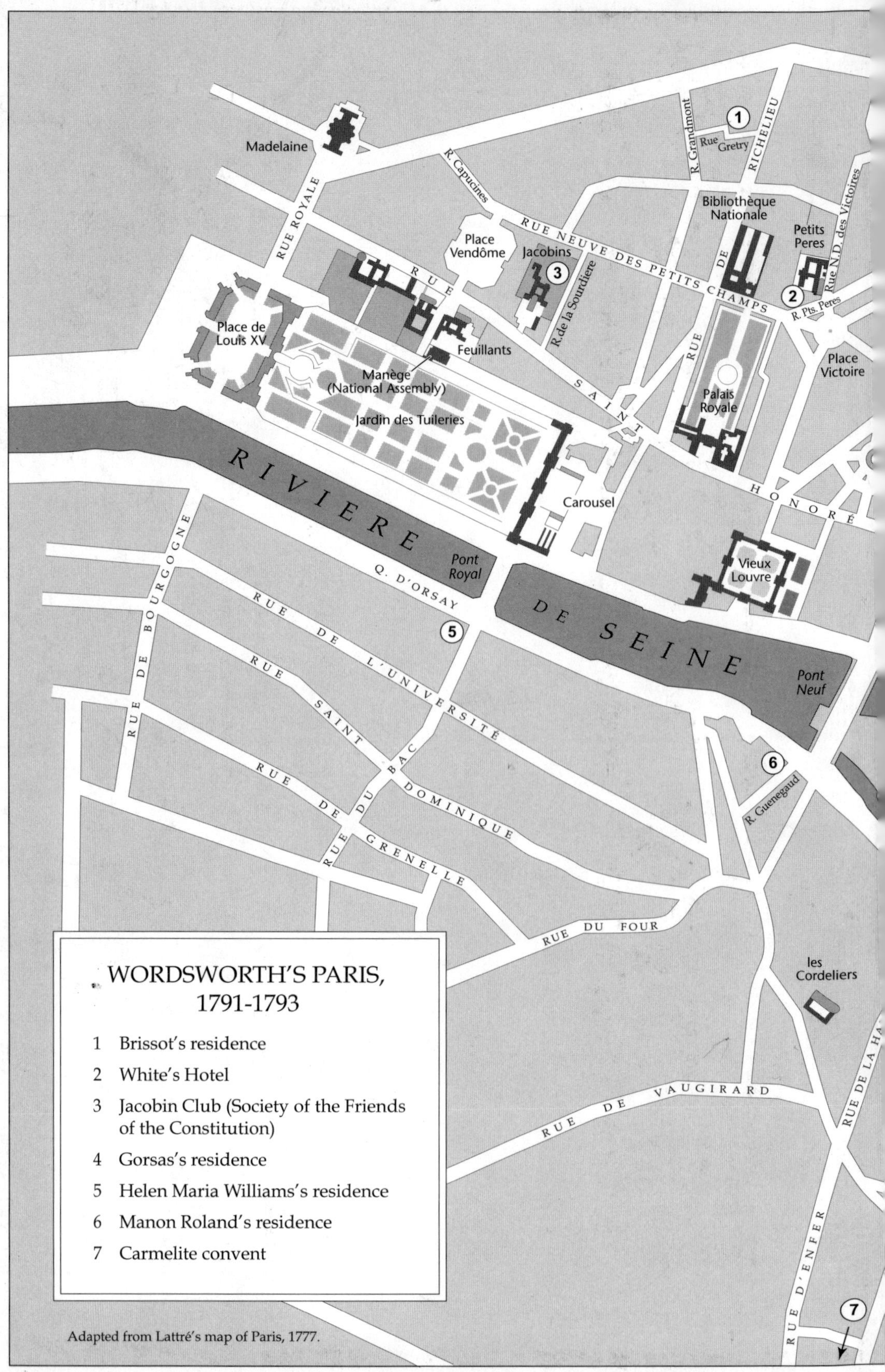
Madelaine
RUE ROYALE
R. Capucines
R. Grandmont
Rue Gretry
RICHELIEU
Bibliothèque Nationale
Petits Peres
Rue N.D. des Victoires
RUE NEUVE DES PETITS CHAMPS
R. Pts. Peres
Place Victoire
Place Vendôme
Jacobins
R. de la Sourdiere
RUE
DE
Place de Louis XV
Feuillants
Manège (National Assembly)
SAINT
HONORÉ
Palais Royale
Jardin des Tuileries
Carousel
RIVIERE DE SEINE
Pont Royal
Vieux Louvre
Pont Neuf
Q. D'ORSAY
RUE DE BOURGOGNE
RUE DE L'UNIVERSITÉ
RUE SAINT DOMINIQUE
RUE DU BAC
RUE DE GRENELLE
R. Guenegaud
RUE DU FOUR
les Cordeliers
RUE DE VAUGIRARD
RUE DE LA HA
RUE D'ENFER
1
2
3
5
6
7
WORDSWORTH'S PARIS, 1791-1793
1 Brissot's residence
2 White's Hotel
3 Jacobin Club (Society of the Friends of the Constitution)
4 Gorsas's residence
5 Helen Maria Williams's residence
6 Manon Roland's residence
7 Carmelite convent
Adapted from Lattré's map of Paris, 1777.